The Collins Press

Published in 2000 by
The Collins Press
West Link Park
Doughcloyne
Wilton
Cork
Ireland

British Library Cataloguing in Publication data.

Design and typesetting by Paradigm Publishing Services

Printed by Zure, Spain

This publication has received support from
the Heritage Council under the
2000 Publications Grant Scheme

ISBN: 1-898256-80-2 (Hardback)
ISBN: 1-898256-15-2 (Paperback)

Front cover picture of Inishmurray, Co. Sligo courtesy of Klaus D. Francke/Bilderberg

Note to Readers
The material in this book was, of necessity, prepared for publication over an extended period of time.
While every effort has been made to keep the contents up to date, legislative, administrative and other
changes continuously affect the subject matter.

Currencies
Monetary values are in Irish pounds for topics involving the Republic of Ireland and in pounds sterling
for Northern Ireland and the remainder of the United Kingdom.

CONTENTS

PART 1 NATURAL, MAN-MADE AND CULTURAL HERITAGE

Section 1 Natural and Man-Made Heritage

Section 2 Cultural Heritage

Section 3 Heritage and the Arts

PART II CONSERVATION AND INTERPRETATION

Section 1 Heritage of the Written Word

Section 2 Conservation

Section 3 Interpretation and Museology

PART III THE ADMINISTRATION AND BUSINESS OF HERITAGE

Section 1 Administration

Section 2 Business Development

ACKNOWLEDGEMENTS

The Introduction to follow describes how this work originated and will accordingly clarify why certain agencies and their personnel are thanked here. We express appreciation to those present and former secretarial, administrative, library and academic staff of University College, Cork, whose contribution to the implementation and instruction of UCC's heritage studies courses facilitated the creation of the book. Interest in the venture on the part of the University's Board of Heritage Studies was a continuing source of support. We thank the many state, semi-state and private-sector organizations which assisted UCC's heritage programmes since their inception, notably by securing work-experience placements throughout Ireland for heritage *Diploma* class members. The part played by Bord Fáilte and the Regional Tourism Organizations, CERT, FÁS and Shannon Development deserves particular mention in this regard. Encouragement received from personnel at FÁS South West Region was of major significance from the outset. The European Community/European Union must be thanked for financial support from the Advanced Technical Skills programme of the European Social Fund, from its ERASMUS scheme and from its COMETT and LEONARDO exchange programmes, the latter two administered in Ireland by Hibernia-UETP, which enabled many students to gain post-qualification experience in United Kingdom and continental European centres and institutions. We are most obliged to our fellow authors for committing time and energy to the writing of their chapters. Their cooperation during all stages of the project was indispensable. The patience of friends and family who have lived with this enterprise in recent years must also be gratefully recorded. *Táimid faoi chomaoin mhór acu san go léir a thug lámh chúnta dúinn d'fhonn an saothar a thabhairt chun críche.*

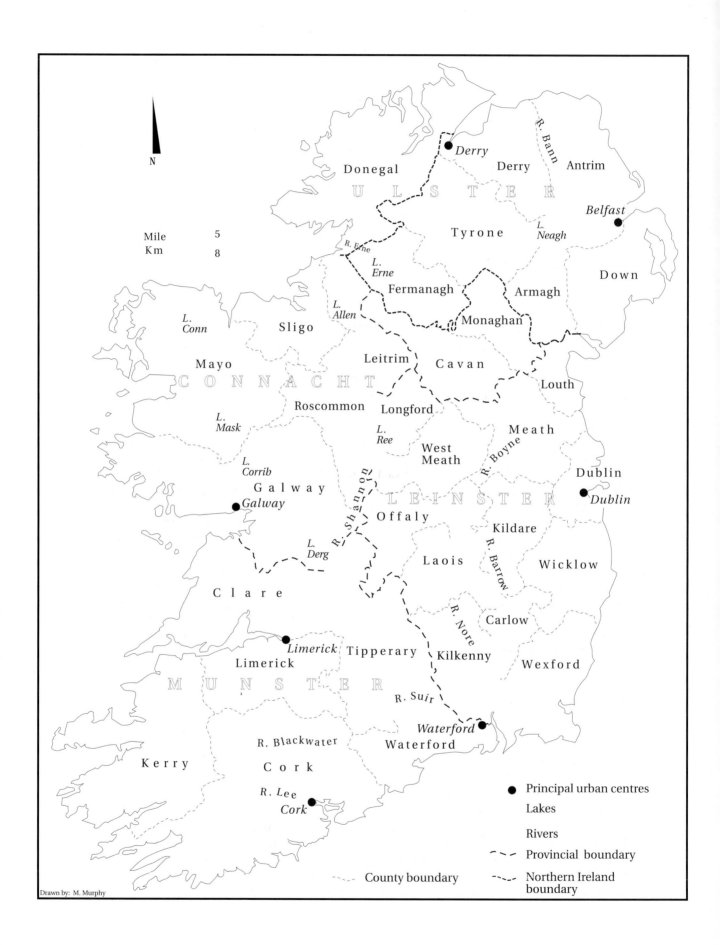

N

Mile 5
Km 8

U L S T E R

Donegal
Derry
Derry
Antrim
R. Bann
Tyrone
Belfast
L. Neagh
Down
R. Erne
L. Erne
Fermanagh
Armagh
L. Allen
Monaghan
L. Conn
Sligo
Leitrim
Cavan
Mayo
C O N N A C H T
Louth
Roscommon
Longford
Meath
L. Mask
L. Ree
West Meath
R. Boyne
L. Corrib
Dublin
Galway
Galway
L E I N S T E R
Dublin
L. Derg
R. Shannon
Offaly
Kildare
R. Barrow
Clare
Laois
Wicklow
R. Nore
Carlow
Limerick
Tipperary
Kilkenny
Wexford
Limerick
M U N S T E R
R. Suir
Kerry
R. Blackwater
Cork
Waterford
Waterford
R. Lee
Cork

● Principal urban centres
Lakes
Rivers
– – – Provincial boundary
- - - County boundary
- - - Northern Ireland boundary

Drawn by: M. Murphy

INTRODUCTION

This book presents a broadly based overview of Irish heritage. It also examines the way in which the country's inheritance is administered and promoted. The introduction outlines how the publication evolved and took shape. It then indicates where the volume stands in relation to other titles in the same general area. We trust that the work may help bring about a greater understanding of a key aspect of Irish life and secure its long-term welfare. The interests of Ireland's heritage are perhaps best served in two ways. The first is to increase awareness of its diversity and complexity. The second is to entrust its advancement to people suitably equipped to discharge this responsibility. The story of how the publication came about begins with an effort to make opportunities available to the latter category of person in particular.

BACKGROUND

The text owes its origins to a one-year, full-time postgraduate course entitled the *Diploma in Irish Heritage Management* which was developed at University College, Cork, in the late 1980s (Buttimer 1992). The programme was initiated to train Irish studies graduates in the provision of products and services for the heritage segment of the Irish tourist industry. A principal objective was to obtain meaningful employment for students who encountered the depressed economic conditions of that decade as they emerged from university humanities departments or from colleges of education. Few could find work in the fields for which they were qualified, in teaching, for example. Many faced involuntary emigration. Their formation had provided such graduates with valuable but underutilized skills. Among their attainments were familiarity with different aspects of Irish tradition, the capacity to conduct research and to communicate knowledge about Ireland. It was not evident that Irish tourism was availing of those strengths in order to make our culture better known to visitors, whether domestic or from overseas.

The Irish government was conscious of the necessity to improve the country's economic conditions and to prepare it for the advent, by 1992, of the highly competitive Single Market in Europe. Towards this end, it identified key sectors of the economy and sought to enhance them in order to contribute to national regeneration. Tourism was one such area. In the Republic's *Ireland National Development Plan 1989–93* (1989), the administration of the day noted that 'Ireland has considerable assets which can be effectively marketed to international tourists: a rich cultural heritage, a tradition for friendliness and hospitality, a relatively unspoilt environment and a folk tradition which is still reflected in a vibrant performing arts sector' (p. 18). The government proposed to commit exchequer and European Community funding towards the strengthening of tourism, and encouraged private-sector investment. It seemed reasonable to assume that appropriately trained personnel would be required to develop heritage projects of the kind envisaged in the Irish administration's blueprint. In light of these promising external circumstances, the UCC authorities formally endorsed the proposal to establish the *Diploma*. Drafting a curriculum then followed.

It was assumed students would have had no business background prior to taking the course, but would need training to equip them for the commercial aspect of their careers and in making their learning accessible to others. Departments in the Faculty of Commerce drew up, and later taught, a core business syllabus consisting of units of management, marketing, economics (particularly relating to tourism), basic accounting and financial management. Arts Faculty representatives concentrated on heritage-related requirements. Members of the Departments of Archaeology, Folklore, Geography and Modern Irish created, and afterwards offered, a syllabus consisting of three inter-linked components. The first section dealt with the academic, institutional and legislative aspects of heritage. A second module focussed on the running of museums, heritage centres and other agencies, with an emphasis on collecting, preserving and presenting heritage data. Thirdly, those taking the *Diploma* were required to complete a heritage research project. This element was intended to underline the fact that fresh insights into the tradition must derive from sound scholarship. In the absence of such scholarship, it is difficult to imagine that material presented to a discriminating public can be continually enriched or renewed. When on-campus instruction was completed, it was envisaged that students would spend an extended period working in an environment where heritage was an essential element. They would also be assigned administrative or managerial tasks while at work. Representatives of various agencies involved in tourism and training, Bord Fáilte and the Regional Tourism Organizations, CERT, FÁS and Shannon Development, identified and supported suitable placements. They offered advice on the contents of the curriculum as well.

The course received financial assistance from the Advanced Technical Skills (ATS) programme of the European Social Fund, administered in Ireland by the state's Department of Education and the Higher Education Authority. This enabled staff, equipment and library costs to be met and student fees to be subvented. Support was made available during a five-year start-up period, with decreasing financial aid in each successive year. The heritage *Diploma* was apparently the first postgraduate programme with a substantial humanities component awarded such competitive funding in Ireland. Following initial preparations, the course began in 1990-91 and has continued since that time. Students admitted had degrees in a range of Irish studies subjects, archaeology, English, folklore, geography, history, Irish language and literature and music. Modifications to admissions regulations enabled those with qualifications in cognate disciplines like anthropology or art history to be accepted. A further expansion of the range of suitable prerequisites is anticipated. To date, graduates from all parts of Ireland, in addition to Britain, continental Europe and the United States, have taken the programme. They have gone on to secure employment in enterprises connected with heritage in this country and elsewhere.

With this groundwork in place, it became possible to develop various other features which would have a bearing on the formation of the present publication (Buttimer 1998). Firstly, external linkages were consolidated. In 1991–92, the *Diploma* became a member of a network of European institutions offering tourism-related courses under the EC's ERASMUS programme (Commission of the European Communities 1992, p. 763). Educational centres in the United Kingdom, France, Spain and Portugal, among others, were participants in the scheme, which facilitated staff and student exchange. Our exchanges were with Canterbury College, Kent, and the University of Lille. Shortly afterwards, connections were made with the EC's COMETT programme. This enabled post-qualification technical training to be obtained throughout the Community and in EFTA countries. Under it and its successor, LEONARDO, *Diploma* graduates have been placed in cultural centres and institutions in Iceland, Norway, Scotland, England and France, as well as other destinations. By means of these associations and through its own resources, a guest lecturer series was established during each year. It came to form an essential component of our teaching. Specialist visiting Irish and international speakers have included experts in conservation, museology, library and information technology, business consultants, researchers, marketers and senior administrators. The establishment of a biennial conference on a topic of general relevance to heritage, beginning in 1993, further strengthened extra-mural ties. The 1995 theme was on information technology and heritage, the colloquium being held under the auspices of the COMETT programme (Stevens and James 1995). At the 1997 UCC conference, the focus was on heritage and funding, with heritage and the environment discussed during the 1999 event.

A second innovation occurred as students completed the *Diploma* and wished to further their studies. This led to the creation of a master's degree in 1993–94, consisting of research work in thesis form on a heritage-related subject. Topics investigated have included women and cultural tourism, public administration, explorations of the heritage factors in the choice of Ireland as a study-abroad destination and a range of other issues.

Our colleague, John Sheehan, of the Department of Archaeology played a major part in the consolidation and furthering of many of these developments when he took over as Course Director for the period 1993–96. In his time, the original *Diploma* syllabus was revised and upgraded. He was succeeded in this capacity during the years 1996–99 by Dr Kevin Hourihan of the University's Department of Geography. Dr Hourihan augmented the master's programme and coped with the demands of securing funding in the post-ATS situation. Colin Rynne has since become the first full-time Director of Heritage

Studies at UCC. Further modifications to the syllabus are now envisaged in response to changing internal and external circumstances (for details, see *http://www.heritagediploma.com*). Coordinators working with the Director at earlier stages (listed here with their departmental affiliation at the time of appointment) included Rhoda Cronin (Archaeology), Helen Guerin (Management and Marketing) and Ita Harris (Folklore). An administrative framework first established on an *ad hoc* temporary basis supervised course management, reviewing matters like processing examination results and approving budgets. From this, there evolved a formally constituted Board of Irish Heritage Studies. Membership comprises all staff and external representatives directly involved with the subject or with placement support. The chairperson holds office for three years, and the position rotates among participating departments. Previous incumbents have included geographer Professor W. J. Smyth (1993–96) and folklorist Gearóid Ó Crualaoich (1996–99).

STRUCTURE AND CONTENT

A considerable amount of teaching, research and practical experience in matters related to heritage had accumulated as a result of the measures outlined above. In 1997, Neil Buttimer, who established the original heritage *Diploma*, proposed to the Board of Heritage Studies that it consider producing a publication to give expression to this experience. Interdisciplinary programmes often go unrecorded as participants tend separately to present research findings in their own subject-specific journals or monographs. The Board approved, and on its instruction, calls for proposals were sent out. When the project was first suggested, Colin Rynne drew the Board's attention to a title issued under the auspices of the Association of Independent Museums in the United Kingdom, namely a *Manual of heritage management* (Harrison 1994). This consisted of an extensive number of short chapters on various topics like Vision, Strategy and Corporate Planning, Funding and Operations Management as these affected British heritage. Chapters were interspersed with an equally sizeable complement of case studies dealing with specific projects like mill restoration, the organization of festivals, enterprise-specific business plans and the like. The *Manual of heritage management's* format influenced the shape our book assumed. Its all-embracing approach, particularly the large number of short presentations it contained, suggested that our title might become correspondingly inclusive in a variety of ways. Authors could comprise both heritage *Diploma* teaching staff and colleagues, such as librarians and archivists, who had made their specialist skills available to the course. Approaches might be made to visitors who lectured on the programme since it began or graduates employed in heritage enterprises regarding which they had formed a valuable impression. Contributors from each of these categories are represented in the completed work.

The prototype highlighted a second opportunity. This was to expand the range of subject-matter treated. As stated earlier, the initial heritage *Diploma* and later masters degree had their origins in certain humanities departments. However, heritage embraces other topics besides cultural subjects. The creation of this title enabled us to bring in studies on Ireland's environment. These are offered here from the outset and are present in many other sections and chapters. In so doing, it has not been our purpose to replicate work on the natural world already published elsewhere. Thus readers are referred to existing studies of the Irish landscape, for example (Aalen *et al.* 1997; Heritage Council 1999), or to the British heritage manual for an examination of how landscape has been interpreted in the United Kingdom (Harrison 1994, pp. 68–9, 72–8). The humanities aspect itself has been enlarged to comprise topics on which formal instruction was not offered as part of UCC's taught heritage courses, hence the presence of subjects like toponomy and family history. Science and sport are included. The text's administration and business horizons have also been widened. Here, papers on trusts and law-related issues will be found which hitherto were not part of our formal instruction, although their importance is clear.

The *Manual of heritage management* partially influenced directions given to contributors regrading matters of style of presentation. Our authors were asked to submit concise statements on their subjects so that, overall, the book could become as broadly based as was intended. Material was to be authoritative in the opinion of an expert but accessible to a reader who had no previous contact with any of the fields under investigation. This matches our teaching experience of introducing students to areas unfamiliar to them but with which they are likely to have to interact in future. Any given paper would offer a definition of its topic and outline its evolution and infrastructure. The latter could encompass the administrative, financial, legislative, staffing or other circumstances associated with it, together with trends and tendencies in policy development. In brief, chapters would look at how each field operates and is managed, mentioning its advantages or drawbacks as the situation warranted. An up-to-date statement of the essentials of the activities covered would therefore be conveyed.

The space allocated would have to comprise all text as well as any illustrative material (figures, tables or other) contributors proposed to provide. From the beginning, we decided not to employ footnotes or endnotes, and to select the more economical author-date referencing system, so that attention would not be deflected from the main points being put forward. The available space would also include a bibliography of essential reading if the author wished to incorporate such material. Practice has varied in this regard. Some writers opted to include extensive reading lists. Others have concentrated on the actual subject-matter. We have not sought to influence their decision in this connection. The frequent mention of website addresses, either within the main narratives or accompanying bibliographies, reflects the current widespread use of information technology. All our fellow authors may have wished to amplify certain themes or arguments. The only impediments to this were constraints imposed by the book's structure and objectives. Some contributions are obviously lengthier than average. We hope that the significance of the topics treated in them, together with the fact that they have not been set out comprehensively in this way in previous publications, will justify occasional departures from the norm.

Although chapters investigate widely different topics, we nonetheless hope that a uniformity of presentation is evident throughout the finished product. This should aid readers as they advance from section to section and into areas which may be new to them. Those who explore the volume in greater depth are likely to discover other interconnections. Chapters echo each other or enlarge on the themes in question, even if the subjects dealt with might seem radically distinct at first glance.

The model for this publication (Harrison 1994) contained an extensive set of case studies. They explored quite precise issues, their background, problems and solutions to the challenges faced. We have included similar items here, as follows. Some or our case studies appear as free-standing entities. Others occur either within the body of chapters or as adjuncts at the end. Certain short chapters are themselves virtual case histories by nature. The same bibliographic and referencing conventions spoken of above apply to this strand of the book. The case study material, while plentiful, it is not as abundant as in our exemplar for two reasons. The first is to allow as much room as possible for major topics to be addressed, particularly those which were relatively neglected. The second is the underlying difference between conditions in the United Kingdom and those of Ireland. Britain has a larger network of museums and heritage centres, for instance. Many have been established for longer than any of their counterparts here. There is a greater tradition of analysing and writing about them. We hope that the present publication will encourage the production of further case histories involving Ireland. UCC's heritage masters degree should contribute to this process.

Apart from adhering to the foregoing instructions, authors determined how their subject was presented. The editors, on the other hand, were responsible for eliciting submissions as well as the layout of the book's sections and chapters. The sequencing is fairly transparent. Part One is largely definitional. It provides perspectives on what constitutes Ireland's heritage. We commence with the fundamental setting of the natural environment. The story of the country's built inheritance then follows, from the earliest period to the present, including town and countryside. Cultural heritage is not necessarily as amenable to the same chronological approach. Treatment of it is therefore largely thematic. Language and the historical sciences chapters, among other disciplines, explore issues like identity and self-expression. The relevant sub-section includes an article by our historian colleague, the late Dr John O'Brien (*ob*. 1999), who unexpectedly passed away as work on the volume was in preparation. The attempt to build bridges between the academic world and an interested public was a feature of his career and is the theme of his paper. The representational and performance elements of Ireland's cultural patrimony bring Part One to a close. Their presence here counters the tendency to view heritage and art as mutually exclusive.

Part Two is concerned with the maintenance and presentation of Ireland's environmental and cultural inheritance. This section of the book comprises a spectrum of interests spanning technical matters but also wider considerations. Objects, structures and documents, already examined under another guise in Part One, are primarily at issue. A number of chapters outline the specialist professional requirements of acquiring, accessioning and storing material or taking steps to ensure its preservation. Institutions discharging these roles, whether libraries, archives or museums, have their own history and heritage, and this side of their affairs is not overlooked. Much of Part Two is taken up with the question of how Ireland's patrimony is revealed to the wider community, a central concern of our work. Chapters consider the choice of material or subjects presented for viewing, the media used for this purpose and the effectiveness of the results.

Part Three examines the broader organizational setting in which heritage operates. This incorporates a spread of agencies from executive and legislative bodies to smaller-scale groupings. Their structures, resources and functions are looked at in the first sub-section. The European Union is among the most significant supra-national entities to which Ireland is affiliated. Accordingly, both its evolution and workings, particularly as they relate to places and people in this country, have been outlined at length. Government itself and quasi-governmental agencies throughout the island of Ireland come next. Their framework and *modus operandi* are set out as well, with specific reference to our subject area. Voluntary interest groups have a lengthy history of involvement with heritage. One of their more notable roles has been to offer a critique of public and private initiatives. Similar commentary is offered here as a constructive contribution to the debate on the effectiveness of policy and its implementation.

Part Three's final sub-section includes the four main elements of the Commerce Faculty's initial input into UCC's heritage programmes, management, marketing, economics and the accountancy and regulatory environment. Certain of these are introductory chapters setting out their subjects' evolution and general principles. A different approach has been taken in the case of others. Because a large number of recent studies have discussed, in broad terms, both economics and the part heritage plays in it (Peacock 1995), as well as the nature of the Irish economy itself (Turley and Maloney 1997; Leddin and Walsh 1998), we have not sought to repeat the exercise. General overviews of Irish tourism have been published (Cronin and O'Connor 1993; Deegan and Dineen 1997) to which the reader is directed for further enlightenment. We focus instead on specific issues of wider import. These are the demonstrable monetary and employment value of heritage for certain regions of Ireland, the basis on which finance can be allocated to support heritage projects, the structure of heritage-based industries and the distinctive requirements of those who work in them, the impact transportation policy may have on the nature of visitors to Ireland, among other matters. One strand unites all chapters in this section. This is the drawing together of worked examples reflecting the management, business and administration of Ireland's natural and cultural heritage. We trust that the contents of Part Three will fill in existing gaps in industry- or sector-specific coverage of these areas.

Not all aspects of Irish heritage or its development are represented here. This would have been impossible to achieve. Instances of topics which have been deliberately omitted have already been mentioned. Others are now highlighted both to signal our awareness of their importance and state why they are absent. Our treatment of language does not encompass Greek and Latin, nor their significant contribution to the artistic and cultural life of this country. However, there is a well-established introduction to these subjects in Ireland (Stanford 1984), while work on Latin authorship in these islands is flourishing (Sharpe 1997). There is no explicit examination of religion as such. Despite this, the investigation of individual denominations, church-state relations or inter-faith conflict is more than adequately handled in individual monographs and general histories. A recent position paper looks at how to take account of the country's built ecclesiastical inheritance, as well as religious objects and artefacts (Heritage Council 1998). Also absent are education, abundantly covered in particular and general studies, and emigration and its impact, the subject of ongoing enquiry (Bielenberg 2000).

While there are omissions, conversely, we would point to compensatory strengths. One of these deserves particular mention. Our publication originated in the south of Ireland. We have nevertheless attempted to include material from all parts of the island of Ireland. Separate chapters deal with the northern or the southern manifestations of many specific topics. Some articles encompass the two territories within their coverage. Each region is often unacquainted with the institutions or agencies charged with heritage promotion in the other. This work can hopefully contribute to the overcoming of such unfamiliarity.

The book may prove of interest to different categories of reader. Because it originated in an educational context, it can serve as a textbook for courses in heritage studies, arts administration, museology and other disciplines. As stated earlier, administrators, directors, managers and planners are numbered among the authors. Other members of these professions might find its contents to be of relevance to their work. It should be of use to individuals or groups undertaking projects with a heritage dimension who seek to learn how to structure and give expression to their activities. Many communities have made such attempts over the past decade or more. We hope that the work attracts readers from outside Ireland as well as from the country itself. Given the spectrum of issues dealt with, the volume may function as a handbook on Irish studies courses for those coming into contact with Ireland for the first time. Another constituency are readers wishing, for comparative purposes, to see what Ireland's recent experience of the heritage domain has been. Here we are thinking of representatives of other European states of equivalent size, possibly with similar upheavals in their cultural and other traditions. They may be contemplating management of their heritage, perhaps in the context of admission to the European Union.

THE WORK IN CONTEXT

Our study forms part of a steadily increasing literature on heritage in general and on Ireland in particular. It may be opportune to clarify the book's relationship to other publications in these areas. The net effect of much of this writing is to add to the store of knowledge about and awareness of this country and its traditions. Our general objectives are similar. Accordingly, we see our volume as complementary to other titles. We nonetheless argue that it also makes its own distinctive contribution, particularly because it has been developed for its own purposes from the background described earlier. Complementarity and difference will be apparent when this volume is compared with the recently issued *The Irish heritage and environment directory 1999* (Deevy 1998). The latter summarizes legislation covering both the Republic of Ireland and Northern Ireland, together with some international measures (pp. 1–30). At its core are an inventory of state, semi-state, local and private organizations involved in heritage (pp. 31–155), a listing of heritage attractions and visitor centres, by county (pp. 156–282), with mention of specialist education courses at undergraduate and postgraduate level (pp. 283–314), archival and library resources and funding agencies (pp. 315–47). Its usefulness in this regard has already helped establish the *Directory* as an indispensable *vade-mecum* for all who come into contact with heritage in Ireland.

The information it contains is, by its nature, of short-term validity and subject to alteration, as details such as addresses, telephone numbers or indeed personnel change. It is likely that the *Directory's* sponsors, The Heritage Council, will seek to update presentation from year to year. Readers seeking data of this kind are referred to subsequent volumes as they appear, especially as such data impact on the contents of our title. In contrast, we focus on medium- to longer-term structural issues. Thus, to take examples where overlap occurs, our writers look at the setting in which legislation was formulated and explore the realities of attempting to interpret and implement it in specific situations. The practical, day-to-day workings of individual institutions and centres are examined in depth here too. Heritage also comprises other elements besides the environment. Subjects like folklore and ethnology are consequently treated in this book, with their guiding principles and actual operations being investigated. We therefore stress the analytic and discursive aspect to our title as opposed to the compilatory character of a directory.

We share this analytic approach with *From maestro to manager: critical issues in arts & culture management* (Fitzgibbon and Kelly 1997). This volume contains dimensions, certain of which, like strategic planning, are not explicitly developed in the present work. They are nonetheless fully implicit in it, as we shall see, particularly as far as planning for heritage at a national level is concerned. A series of interviews with directors and managers of cultural centres is also included. The reader may wish to consult *From maestro to manager* for accounts of these issues, which are of undoubted importance to heritage. Given its origins in University College, Dublin's postgraduate programmes in arts administration, the book's emphasis is consequently more on theatre, opera and music institutions. Alternative strands of natural and cultural activities are to be found in the sections and chapters below, as well as different operational parameters. The discursive mode of treatment sets the present text apart from compendia like the *Oxford companion to Irish literature* (Welch 1996) and the *Oxford companion to Irish history* (Connolly 1998). Each of these constitutes a rich assemblage of specific points of information. Our book also stresses the importance of presenting the salient facts of a given subject. Its central emphasis is, however, on uncovering in a systematic manner the dynamic infrastructural characteristics of the fields investigated. We bring together in the same volume a range of interlinked heritage disciplines in a manner which the Oxford companions may not have done, being focussed instead on distinct, individual subjects.

Ireland is not the only country on whose traditions much recent writing has appeared. We spoke earlier of the influence the United Kingdom-based *Manual of heritage management* has had on the formation of this book. Many other works also analyse heritage development in Britain and elsewhere (Hewison 1985; Lowenthal 1985, 1997; Samuel 1995). Instructive insights into the Irish situation can come from them. These publications investigate the extent to which recourse to the past in the UK, as seen in heritage centres and other institutions, reflects introspective national self-analysis viewed against the demanding backdrop of industrial decline and other transformations in British society. In Ireland, by way of contrast, it would appear that interest in our inheritance highlights at least in part a different process. This is one of self-discovery, as the country re-establishes contact with its traditions, an experience which can be both challenging and celebratory. Credit for much of the rediscovery must go to a considerable growth in research relating to this country from the middle of the twentieth century onwards. The expansion of Irish third-level institutions in recent decades, the increase in work on Ireland conducted by overseas scholars and the number of agencies now involved with various aspects of its patrimony have all contributed to this enlargement. Our publication is a direct beneficiary of these developments in being able to draw for its expertise from the work of personnel associated with many such institutions.

Studies of the United Kingdom point to other more negative dimensions to heritage promotion. These comprise its questionable employment as a psychological support, the seeking of solace in a temporal zone, the past, with which we thought we were familiar and avoiding the uncertainty of the future. Exploitation is also visible in making use of the tradition for purely commercial or utilitiarian purposes. Heritage development in Ireland may not have been entirely free of either of these dimensions (Brett 1996), and we conclude with some comments on the commercilization aspect. It was mentioned at the outset that the Irish administration made public-sector finance available for heritage projects in the context of tourism development in the period 1989–93. Tourism was accorded equal prominence in the successor to the first plan, covering the years 1994–99 (Government of Ireland 1993, pp. 63–8), with a specific section heading on 'Culture and heritage' (p. 65). The government recently issued its intentions for the planning period 2000–06 (Government of Ireland 1999). In contrast to its predecessors, tourism is not an autonomous entry as such. The emphasis instead is on issues like regional and infrastructural development. Because heritage was so closely linked with tourism in the earlier planning documents, the fact that it is not accorded prominence on this occasion is noteworthy. This is not to say that heritage is absent. There are statements about the training of museum staff and information technology, for instance. However, they are not present in the same overt manner as before, but have to be searched for as one reads through the narrative. The plan proposes to spend considerable amounts of money on capital projects like road construction. While it is confirmed that there will be environmental impact assessments, recent commentary has questioned the adequacy of these steps to guard against the loss of landscapes, for example (Mathews 2000).

The danger therefore exists that heritage will be looked on as being of value for its immediate benefits mainly. Contributors to the present publication are likely to see its worth in a different light. Many have had an extended involvement with their subjects and are deeply committed to them. We submit that their underlying motivation is to understand their topic on its own terms and to the highest possible standards, while developing and promoting it with care and with its present and future well-being in mind. Similar principles are at the core of UCC's heritage courses. There are unquestionably many demands on government's attention when it comes to the setting of national priorities. However, as the state has a particular duty on behalf of the community at large with respect to what is one of the world's great cultures, it is to be hoped that the heritage of Ireland will continue to feature highly in the list of the administration's major interests.

Bibliography

Aalen, F., Whelan, K. and Stout, M. 1997 *Atlas of the Irish rural landscape*. Cork.

Bielenberg, A. (ed) 2000 *The Irish diaspora*. London.

Brett, D. 1996 *The construction of heritage*. Cork.

Buttimer, N. 1992 'Diploma in Irish Heritage Management' in S. Browne (ed) *Heritage and tourism*, the Second Conference on the Development of Heritage Attractions in Ireland, 28–29 January (Dublin), Session 6, pp. 1–6.

Buttimer, N. 1998 'Ár n-oidhreacht agus ár n-arán laethúil', *The Irish Review* **22** (Summer), pp. 81–8.

Commission of the European Communities 1992 *ERASMUS and LINGUA Action II directory 1991/92*. Brussels and Luxembourg.

Connolly, S. J. (ed) 1998 *The Oxford companion to Irish history*. Oxford.

Cronin, M. and O'Connor, B. (eds) 1993 *Tourism in Ireland: a critical analysis*. Cork.

Deegan, J. and Dineen, D. A. 1997 *Tourism policy and performance: the Irish experience*. London.

Deevy, M. (compiler) 1998 *The Irish heritage & environment directory 1999*. Bray.

Fitzgibbon, M. and Kelly, A. (eds) 1997 *From maestro to manager: critical issues in arts & culture management*. Dublin.

Government of Ireland 1989 *Ireland National Development Plan 1989–93*. Dublin.

Government of Ireland 1993 *Ireland National Development Plan 1994–99*. Dublin.

Government of Ireland 1999 *Ireland National Development Plan 2000–06*. Dublin.

Harrison, R. (ed) 1994 *Manual of heritage management*. Oxford.

Heritage Council 1998 *Taking stock of our ecclesiastical heritage*. Kilkenny.

Heritage Council 1999 *Policies and priorities for Ireland's landscape*. Kilkenny.

Hewison, R. 1987 *The heritage industry: Britain in a climate of decline*. London.

Leddin, A. J. and Walsh, B. M. 1998 *The macro-economy of Ireland*, fourth edition. Dublin.

Lowenthal, D. 1985 *The past is a foreign country*. Cambridge.

Lowenthal, D. 1997 *The heritage crusade and the spoils of history*. London and New York.

Mathews, P. 2000 'National Development Plan', *Heritage Outlook* (The Heritage Council/An Chomhairle Oidhreachta) **1** (Summer), p. 8.

Peacock, A. 1995 'A future for the past: the political economy of heritage', Keynes Lecture in Economics, *Proceedings of the British Academy* **30**, pp. 189–243.

Samuel, R. 1995 *Theatres of memory — vol. 1: past and present in contemporary culture*. London.

Sharpe, R. 1997 *A handlist of the Latin writers of Great Britain and Ireland before 1540*. Turnhout.

Stanford, W. B. 1984 *Ireland and the classical tradition*, second ed. Dublin.

Stevens, T. and James, V. (eds) 1995 *The future for Europe's past*, Proceedings of COMETT Workshops, Port Talbot (15–17 February), Centre d'Estudisi Recursos Culturals, Barcelona (13–15 March), University College, Cork (23–25 May). [Swansea.]

Turley, G. and Maloney, M. 1997 *Principles of economics: an Irish textbook*. Dublin.

Welch, R. (ed) 1996 *The Oxford companion to Irish literature*. Oxford.

The Natural Heritage

GRACE O'DONOVAN

Heritage, by definition, means inherited property, inherited characteristics and anything transmitted by past ages and ancestors (Chambers 1992, s.v.). We are all born into the world in a particular place and what we find there is fully our own heritage, that which we have inherited from those who have gone before. It covers everything, from objects and buildings to the environment. The environment affects us directly — it is the air we breathe, the water we drink, the food we eat. These are the fundamental requirements of our physical life, the thin skin of organic matter between the soil and the air which provides us with our outward needs.

Our natural heritage is what has survived of the natural world through the millennia up to man's occupation of the earth, and that is constantly changing. Humans have come to use nature as a resource in terms of fuel consumption, building space and food production, with the result that less and less of the natural world is left. Natural biodiversity world-wide is in sharp decline as a result, and along with that is the inevitable breakdown of the earth's buffering capacity to absorb the damage inflicted. Ozone depletion and global warming (Sweeny 1997; Feehan 1994) are only two of the repercussions of the misuse of natural resources. The current accelerating destruction of the rainforests, by accident or by design, is a critical barometer of the loss of biodiversity, the function of much of which we scarcely know anything about. We are currently facing an episode of mass extinction the like of which has never been experienced heretofore in the history of the earth (Wilson 1992). Other great extinctions have occurred throughout time and these come and go in almost predictable cycles. However, with the intervention of man, we face imminent destruction of the plant life of the planet, a new departure from which we may never recover (Quammen 1996). Not only is this mass destruction depriving us of the countless species which may be of some use to us in the future, it is also depriving

us of the aesthetic appreciation of this glorious diversity for its own sake. Somehow, in a very short time, we have become so separated from our natural heritage that we no longer notice when something is lost. In the space of a single generation, we have become disconnected from the land, and some of us may never know the joy of watching a flower unfold or a bird of prey swoop.

Putting our natural heritage in perspective, Ireland's flora and fauna are depauperate compared to our European counterparts with only *ca.* 850 native plant species, for instance, compared to Britain's 1,172 and France's 3,500. This is due to our island status, being smaller than other mainland European countries, and also because we were cut off for longer from Europe after the last Ice Age 13,000 years ago. When the sea level rose 7,000 years ago and obliterated the land bridge between what is now Britain and Ireland, any further migrations were severely hindered. However, due to our less industrialized landscape, we still have otters and red squirrels and choughs in abundance when they are in serious decline in Europe. Our westerly position and mild climate have also allowed several Mediterranean species to settle here which are not found in Britain, namely the strawberry tree (*Arbutus unedo*), the Kerry slug (*Geomalachus maculosus*), a magnificent black slug with distinctive white spots, the dense-flowered orchid (*Neotinia intacta*), the greater butterwort (*Pinguicula grandiflora*), a beautiful insectivorous plant found on blanket bog and two species of St Patrick's Cabbage (*Saxifraga spathularis* and *S. hirsuta*). These last two species form hybrids throughout their distribution in Ireland, unlike the plant's European counterparts where it barely mixes at all (Waldren and Scally 1993). These rarities set Ireland apart and hint at the complicated ecology underlying their occurrence and distribution.

In the following chapter, therefore, an outline of the natural heritage found in Ireland will be given, with special emphasis on habitats of international importance. This is followed by a resumé of the state of habitat and species conservation in Ireland, finishing with a description of our National Parks.

IRISH HABITATS

Ireland, as an island located on the north-western fringe of Europe, has an abundance of what may be termed natural heritage. Its island status and current low population have contributed to the continued existence of many natural and semi-natural habitats. However, there is little handed down in terms of ecological care or awareness from our history books. In times when our population was double or more what it is today, we know that the human hand had touched every corner of this land in terms of agricultural activity. Remnants of ridge and furrow are everywhere to be found along with *fulachta fiadha* (ancient cooking places), ringforts, burial mounds, ranging from the Stone Age to Famine times (O'Kelly 1989). What follows here are the categories of habitat that have remained semi-natural despite, and indeed sometimes because of, human intervention.

WETLANDS AND MIRES

Lakes and turloughs

Ireland is blessed with many lakes, 4,000 at least, covering 2% of the land surface (Murray 1996). They range from highly acidic, unproductive lakes in the Wicklow hills to limestone lakes such as Ennell and Sheelin in the midlands which are renowned for their fishing resource and bird communities. Lakes have not escaped pollution from farming activities and in the 1970s Lough Neagh was classed as one of the most polluted lakes in Europe (Wood and Gibson 1973). However, by controlling nutrient input to these lakes, a general improvement has been achieved since then (Clabby *et al.* 1992). Our groundwater, which is one of our major renewable resources, provides 20–25% of our drinking water in Ireland (Daly 1992). At present only 3% of groundwater is extracted for this purpose and, as such, is thought to be underutilized. Threats are more insidious to this resource as it is hidden for the most part, but general anthropogenic pollutants such as faecal bacteria and ammonia are a continuing worry, and point source pollution is a problem with the increased use of slurry spreading, landfill, fertilizers and pesticides (Thorn 1986).

A type of lake found nowhere else in the world except Ireland is the *turlough*. Due to high rainfall levels over the porous, bare carboniferous limestone in the west of Ireland, the limestone has been steadily eroded by the slightly acidic rain. Eventually, underground caverns are formed by the percolating rainwater and a whole network of sponge-like connections is formed below ground which fill up or drain away again depending on the season. In winter, the water table rises in these caverns and fills up all the available spaces. The water then appears above ground in depressions to form shallow, transient lakes. As summer approaches, the procedure is slowly reversed and the water retreats into the fissured, porous caverns once more. These lakes are not only famous for their ephemeral nature but have a unique flora and fauna associated with them too. As the water escapes from the turloughs only slowly through what are known as swallow holes in the limestone, the vegetation on the sides and floor of these lakes has evolved to survive according to the level of water cover at different times of the year, in a somewhat similar fashion to a tidal zonation. The very rare fen violet (*Viola persicifolia*) is to be found in abundance here, its next (very depauperate) station being the Norfolk broads in East Anglia, UK. The rare fairy shrimp (*Tanymastix stagnalis*) has also been found recently and is confined to this habitat (Young 1976). The lime-rich turlough grasslands are highly sought after as fodder in the summer months in an otherwise inhospitable landscape for grazing animals, and have been traditionally grazed for centuries (Feehan and O'Donovan 1993). Fewer than 60 turloughs of >10 ha have survived to the present day due to drainage and improvement.

Rivers

There are approximately 75 river catchments in Ireland of which the Shannon is the largest, draining 10,400 km^2. They represent a variety of different ecological types from fast-flowing acid streams which flow off mountains to the sluggish, more productive waters of the midlands. River quality throughout the country has been surveyed, and from 1987–90 there has been an increase in moderately and slightly polluted lengths and a decrease in very polluted lengths, with 76% classed as unpolluted. The control of eutrophication is now seen as the major challenge in river quality (EPA 1995; McGarrigle, Lucey and Clabby 1996).

Fish communities in these rivers are much less diverse than they were due to human impact over the last two centuries. The recorded fish fauna are 42 native and 13 introduced species and, according to Maitland (1996), eight of these are under threat and two are believed to be extinct. Six of the threatened species occur in Ireland (whereas only two occur in Britain): sturgeon, allis shad, twaite shad, arctic char, smelt and pollan. Pollan is very unusual in being in Ireland at all as its distribution elsewhere is much further north in arctic rivers.

Rare and unusual stocks of fish species also occurring in Ireland are the river, sea and brook lampreys. Stock individuality has evolved over thousands of years and, for instance, three distinct genotypes of brown trout (*Salmo trutta*) have been recognized in Lough Melvin, Ireland. While living together, they spawn separately in different parts of the lake and hence retain reproductive isolation (Ferguson and Mason 1981). The current answer to protecting and rejuvenating these rare species is habitat restoration and stock transfer to new sites.

Other notable species of water bodies at risk are the otter, the freshwater mussel and the natterjack toad. The otter has declined severely in Europe in recent times but is still relatively common in Ireland. The main causes of its decline in Europe are habitat loss and water pollution. Studies in Cork have shown that high levels of organochlorines and PCBs are responsible for some deaths. Pollution resulting from agricultural intensification causes deaths of invertebrates and fish, and this in turn reduces the prey resource of the otter. Drainage schemes can also cause major disruption to otter habitats. There is no conservation legislation for river courses covering their whole length or even for provision of river corridors between conserved areas, and this is considered essential for future viable otter conservation (O'Sullivan 1996). The freshwater mussel (*Margaratifera margaratifera*) is in serious decline throughout Europe due to deterioration in habitat and fishing for its pearls. It is still relatively common in Ireland although it is in decline in the north and east, reflecting a general deterioration in water quality. An ecophenotype of this species, *durrovensis*, a hard-water form occurring in the Nore catchment, is seriously under threat however, being now the only hard-water form extant in Europe (Chesney 1996). The natterjack toad is the only toad species in Ireland. Its distribution is limited to some sand-dunes in Kerry (EPA 1996) and the main threats to its survival are recreation and tourism developments. An ecological study is currently being carried at NUI Cork and a translocation programme by Dúchas, the government Heritage Service, is underway in two sand-dune systems in Wexford.

Bogs

Weather has been a major influencing factor in the formation and continued interest of our natural heritage. Given our location on the Atlantic fringe, our mild weather, high rainfall and high winds have been the instigators for the formation of many of our internationally renowned habitats and unusual species assemblages along the western seaboard. For instance, our bogland formations owe everything to 'inclement' weather and the rearrangement of our geological landscape by the last glaciation. Movement of soil and rock by ice disrupted many of the existing drainage patterns in the midlands, leaving a waterlogged landscape behind. These lakes and marshes eventually developed into the raised bogs we have today. These have spawned much interest, firstly in terms of their economic value and latterly their conservation value, being unique in European terms, not only for their flora and fauna but for the fact that they have survived intact

as long as they have. On the western seaboard, heavy rainfall (some of the highest levels in Europe) saw to inevitable waterlogging of the soil and the formation of what is called blanket peat over many hectares from Donegal to Kerry. One can only guess at the misery and despair this degradation in the weather must have caused as farmers watched their land being slowly transformed into useless bog.

Ironically, it is only now we are unearthing the whole story as our bogs are being systematically removed for fuel. What that has shown us is that the bogs became an integral part of Irish life, albeit begrudgingly, as people adapted to the creeping black peat, and for many centuries it was used and abused according to character. Many human bodies have been preserved in almost perfect condition and bear witness to a more ruthless age when the bog was used as a convenient concealment area and dumping ground. Due to the lack of biological activity in its increasingly acidic matrix, its unique preservation qualities were exploited for preserving food such as butter, and for hiding everything from bodies to books to hoards of gold artefacts. The bog held all sorts of other secrets too. Because nothing decayed there, pollen from all the plants that ever grew around the bog and were mobile enough to be carried by the wind were deposited in the acid mire. They have survived to the present day and have left an impeccable record of vegetation history of our landscape back to the retreat of the last ice age and before. The study of vegetation history using pollen found in the layers of the peat is known as palynology, and only began relatively recently in Ireland (Mitchell 1986; Mitchell and Ryan 1997). It also charts the impact of man with the reduction in tree cover and the appearance of pollen of grains used in agriculture. One of the most remarkable finds under the peat has been the bones of the giant Irish deer, *Megaloceras giganteus*. This deer dominated our landscapes when grassland was abundant before the spread of tree cover. Many of their skeletons have been unearthed and one can only speculate why large numbers were found in bogs and why only the males were preserved.

In conservation terms our bogs are unique, not only for their large coverage of our landscape (17% land area) but for their formation: our raised bogs are the deepest in Europe (up to 13 m; Feehan and O'Donovan 1996). On top of that, Ireland was the most tardy of the European countries in reclaiming the peat for energy on a large scale. It is only some fifty years since the semi-state body set up to exploit the bogs, Bord na Móna, was established. In the light of this relative sluggishness, awareness of the uniqueness of this habitat on an international scale has just caught up with its wholesale destruction in this country, and there is just still time to preserve the best examples before it is all gone. Much of this awareness, it has to be said, has been forced upon us

3

by our European counterparts who, seeing too late the devastation of their own bogs, are anxious to preserve ours for European posterity. Professor Mathijs Schouten of the Dutch Wildlife Service was instrumental both in raising our awareness of our bogland heritage through his post-doctoral studies here (Schouten 1984) and in raising funds for their preservation through the Dutch Foundation for the Conservation of Irish Bogs, a charity which he initiated in Holland. Money from that fund was used to buy several of our threatened bog types and these were then returned to the Irish government for future generations to enjoy. The struggle to secure other examples of intact bog is continued by the Irish Peatlands Conservation Council, a non-governmental organization, which sees its role now, as well as purchase, mainly in education through raising public awareness.

Callows and fens

Other wetlands of importance are the Shannon callows, traditionally cut for reeds to make thatch and almost the last outpost for the corncrake in Ireland. This bird has suffered a severe decline in recent years due to agricultural improvement and more severe cutting regimes, as they tend to nest in grassland. These extensive floodplains have so far escaped attempts at drainage due to their size (Heery 1993). Fens, though once extensive in Ireland as the precursor of our bogs, are few and far between today. They also form a fringing ring around the circumference of raised bogs, known as laggs, but are now much fragmented and reduced due to drainage and turf cutting. Some notable examples of large fens are Pollardstown fen in county Kildare and Kilcolman Nature Reserve in north Cork.

TERRESTRIAL HABITATS

Woodlands

Our woodlands have suffered an even greater demise than our bogs with less that 0.5% native deciduous woodland left by 1700 (McCracken 1971). Much of the destruction occurred in the sixteenth century when Irish woodland was removed wholesale for shipbuilding, charcoal, foundries and the like by the English planters and not managed in a sustainable manner. However, there is evidence that our forested landscape was much depleted before then, to 6% of land cover (Rackham 1995). This observation is backed up by a long history of dense population, judging by the vast number of ringforts (4,000) and raths present from the Iron Age. There is little incentive to plant broad-leaved woodland today although some grants are available, but long-term investment is required. Coillte, the semi-state forestry body, currently has an aggressive planting regime targeted at 30,000 hectares per annum (O'Carroll 1995), mostly Sitka spruce, until 17% land cover is achieved (the

European average). Such planting of non-native trees can be a problem in terms of habitat destruction, as much planting to date has occurred on upland and lowland blanket peat throughout the country. Both private and state planting was occurring piecemeal as planning permission was not needed for areas less than 200 ha. This has since been reduced to 50 ha. This has left us with a legacy of uncoordinated patches with no regard for landscape aesthetics (An Taisce 1996). Surveys of the remnants of woodlands are scant, with some records for woodlands over limestone (Kelly and Kirby 1982) and ancient Killarney woodlands (Kelly 1981). Our swamp woodlands have recently been inventoried by Kelly and Iremonger (1997) and we have still a remnant of one of the best alluvial forests in the British Isles, namely the Gearagh in county Cork (O'Reilly 1955). The latter was only surveyed because it was imminently to be chopped down to make a reservoir for the Electricity Supply Board (ESB) in the early 1950s. Luckily, a representative strip of this woodland about one mile in length remains and is in the custody of the ESB, designated as a National Nature Reserve.

Grasslands

Our natural and semi-natural grasslands are another less obvious natural heritage which have been rapidly declining since the 1960s. This is mainly due to improved agricultural techniques and a sharp rise in the use of artificial fertilizers. Seventy percent of our island is covered in grass and, due to our mild climate and high rainfall, we have some of the most productive grasslands in Europe, with almost year-round growth in certain of our most southerly counties. This has led to the success of a large beef and dairy industry for which Ireland is renowned. However, our semi-natural grasslands are some of the most interesting habitats we have in conservation terms. The Burren limestone grasslands, which flourish on the bare limestone karst dominating parts of Clare and Galway, are unique in global terms due to the almost unseemly combination of arctic, alpine and Mediterranean plants which quite happily cohabit the same piece of soil (Webb and Scannell 1983). There is now a significant threat to these grasslands in the form of reclamation (Drew and Magee 1994), where stones in fields are removed by bulldozers, the existing limestone grassland ploughed up, topsoil added from somewhere else and reseeded with more productive grasses. Another type of limestone grassland found in Ireland occurs on eskers, a post-glacial landscape formation whereby rivers, formed under the melting glaciers, deposited silts and gravels. Once the ice retreated altogether, raised banks several kilometres long were left behind which have since been used for grazing, road building and gravel extraction. Grasslands formed on these eskers are species-rich (**Fig. 1.1**) and form unique assemblages in

Fig. 1.1 The green-winged orchid (Orchis morio), *a rare and threatened plant found on eskers. Small populations survive in patches of esker grassland threatened by fertilization, gravel extraction and erosion.*

some cases. These grasslands are now extremely fragmentary and susceptible to improvements. They are also important for butterflies which are indicators of grassland diversity (Duggan 1998). Even though most of these limestone grasslands are now designated for conservation, it has not stopped this kind of piecemeal destruction for, as yet, there is no legal status attached to these designations.

Most of our hay meadows have succumbed to more productive silage making which provides a double insult in that the increased fertilizer applications required severely reduces biodiversity, and the early cutting dates precede the flowering times of most grasslands, thus losing one of the most evocative images of grasslands at the height of summer. A generation of children may never have seen a hay meadow in flower. In a recent study of Leinster grasslands (Byrne 1996), neutral hay meadows are almost non-existent in the east of Ireland today and can only be found where the plough cannot easily reach. Some hay meadows still exist on old estates or stud farms where the old hay-making traditions are

still maintained. Our acid grasslands, found mostly in upland areas or coastal regions, are rapidly being eaten up by forestry plantation or general improvement. A thorough grassland survey of Ireland has not been carried out since the 1960s when Austin O'Sullivan completed his doctorate (1965). As most of the major agricultural changes have occurred since then, a resurvey is long overdue.

COASTAL AND MARINE
Salt marshes and sand-dunes
Our salt marshes and sand-dunes are at present being inventoried (Curtis 1991; Curtis and Sheehy-Skeffington 1998), and their ecology studied (AFF 1977; Fay and Jeffrey 1995). In recent times, another coastal grassland type was defined, that of machair (Basset and Curtis 1985). There are sixteen such recognized machair sites found along the north-west coast of Ireland from Galway to Donegal (**Fig. 1.2**). They are formed when sand is blown some distance inland by gale-force winds over extensive areas. They are also of cultural importance as they often coincide with Irish-speaking (*Gaeltacht*) areas. They are aligned with similar grassland types in western Scotland and are derived from their classification there.

Marine
Despite having one of the longest coastlines relative to our island size in the world, the marine habitats have received the least attention from Irish ecologists/biologists until relatively recently (Kelly and Costello 1995; Wilson and Lawlor 1996). Ireland is at the northern limit for warm-water Lusitanean species and at the southern limit for arctic species. The former effect is due mainly to the Gulf Stream, simultaneously allowing Mediterranean species to get a foothold and limiting the extent of the arctic component. There is also the rare feature of where limestone pavement meets the sea, which supports the Mediterranean species of sea urchin *Paracentrotus lividus*. This species has black spines and is very striking in its habitat, boring pockets for itself into the limestone. It is considered a delicacy in France for its roe and has become rare as a result.

Recognition of the importance of our marine resources is reflected in the setting up of Roinn na Mara (the Department of the Marine) in 1987 and the establishment of the Marine Institute in 1992. Heightened public awareness has been created by the Blue Flag campaign backed by the enforcement of EU Directives and voluntary participation in such surveys as Coastwatch (Carroll and Dubsky 1995). Detailed inventory of littoral communities has been carried out in Northern Ireland (Erwin *et al.* 1990), for Ireland in general (ISSG 1990) and for marine algae (Norton 1985). Recently, a classification of benthic marine biotopes has been completed around Britain and Ireland which was funded

Fig. 1.2 An aerial view of machair grasslands at Dooaghtry, county Mayo. This habitat occurs at only 16 sites in restricted parts of the north-west of Ireland. Traditional grazing maintains this formation and current threats to its continued existence are enclosure and tourism.

by the EU programme LIFE (Costello 1995) with a view to identifying sites for conservation. In conservation terms there are only two Irish marine reserves, one at Lough Ine in county Cork, a very species-rich sea lough (Myers *et al.* 1991), and, more recently, Strangford Lough in Northern Ireland. Other marine sites are protected by default for other factors such as bird protection, but no inventory has been made to discover how much overlap there is between these two. Marine mammals have received some attention in the literature, particularly whales (Fairley 1981) and dolphins (Rogan and Berrow 1995). Strandings are often the only way of studying the occurrence of these marine mammals in our waters and the causes of their death. These are published regularly in the *Irish Naturalists' Journal* as 'Cetacean Notes'. A dolphin survey in the Shannon estuary is currently underway, carried out by staff of the Zoology and Animal Ecology Department in University College, Cork. Seals have also received some attention, being a relatively common mammal around Ireland (Summers *et al.* 1980), and are also currently being researched in UCC (Kiely and Myers 1998) and UCD. At the landscape level, a Coastal Zone Institute has been set up in Cork to address the management problems associated with all areas influenced in the coastal zone, both inland and seaward (Mulcahy *et al.* 1992)

HABITAT CREATION

Some wildlife areas have been created as a result of man's intervention and two of these are worthy of note. The first is Bull Island in Dublin Bay formed when the Bull wall was erected over one hundred years ago. The wall

disturbed the flow of sediment in the Bay and gradually a sand bar built up at right angles to the wall. This bar is nearly two miles long now and displays a range of interesting habitats including fore-dune, grey dune and dune slack with many orchid species present and extensive saltmarsh and mudflats on the side facing the city. The mudflats are renowned for winter visitors such as Brent Geese and many other wildfowl. It is a Ramsar site and our first designated World Biosphere Reserve in 1974 (Jeffrey 1977). The second is another famous area of reclaimed land known as the Wexford Slobs, when, between 1847 and 1898, an extensive sand bar was created. This is now an internationally important site for many bird species, including the Greenland white-fronted goose, and the slobs represent 10% of its breeding ground in the world.

Since the removal of much of our raised bogs by Bord na Móna, vast tracts of bare peat have been created and a problem is now arising as to what to do with them. Returning the areas to agriculture was the main plan but with the advent of set-aside and Common Agricultural Policy (CAP) reform, grassland production was already being targeted for reduction, and other forms of use had to be explored. Vegetable growing was considered at Lullymore but did not do well. Afforestation is a major endeavour, but peat soils have often proved to be a disaster for tree growth. More recent novel ideas such as growing cranberries on reclaimed peat are currently being carried out. Another serious consideration is allowing many sites to return to wildlife, encouraging natural succession to occur. Some sites have been deliberately flooded to provide wetland sites for birds and these have been successful so far, for example Turraun bog, county Offaly.

CONSERVATION OF OUR NATURAL HERITAGE

'Natural' heritage is a somewhat loose term in Ireland where almost all our habitats and landscapes are moulded by human activities. Even today, however, Ireland has a rich natural heritage due to our currently low population levels, and this has allowed areas of natural and semi-natural habitats to survive within the overall matrix of land use. Our hedgerows are still numerous and we have many surviving wetlands despite an aggressive drainage programme in the 1960s and 1970s by the Office of Public Works (OPW) (Cabot 1985). On the other hand, also due to our low population, inventories of our habitats and species are slow to be carried out. This is also true of our conservation record, which is poor compared to other European countries.

SPECIES

At the species level, most of the work for plant and animal species, until very recently, has been carried out by amateurs. Naturalists' Field Clubs have been in operation since the early 1900s, particularly in Belfast and Dublin (DNFC 1986), and individuals have carried out extensive national surveys for species such as woodlice (Doogue and Harding 1982), mollusca (Ross 1984; Nunn 1994) and microlepidoptera (Bond 1995). The Botanical Society of the British Isles (BSBI) has been responsible for the systematic recording of the flora throughout Britain and Ireland on a 10 x 10 km^2 basis within vice-counties along the National Grid. The distribution maps are rather crude, however, and not very useful for conservation purposes as they are not recorded by habitat primarily. An atlas of the flora of these isles was produced (Perring and Walters 1976). It is currently being updated and a new atlas is scheduled for this year, 2000. A map of this sort is a reflection of the people available to complete it. As there are few professional botanists in Ireland, many species may go unrecorded or are under-recorded. Heroic work on a national scale was carried out by the naturalist Robert Lloyd Praeger, and his many books and publications are a testimony to this (Praeger 1934, 1939 and 1950). On a professional level, the first Irish flora was compiled in 1943 by David Allardice Webb, a professor of Botany in Trinity College, Dublin. The tradition has been carried on right up to the present day with a flora of inner Dublin by Wyse Jackson and Sheehy-Skeffington (1984), the flora of Connemara and the Burren (Webb and Scannell 1983), the flora of Sherkin Island (Akeroyd *et al.* 1997) and several county and regional floras also (Colgan 1904; Brunker 1950; Booth 1979; Hackney 1997 and Doogue *et al.* 1998). A full list of the occurrence of our vascular plant flora by vice-county is to be found in Scannell and Synnott (1987).

A serious attempt at discovering the status of our flora and fauna has been carried out under the Red Data scheme whereby scarce and threatened species have been identified at the national level with a view to conserving the most vulnerable. The Red Data books, initiated by the International Union for the Conservation of Nature (IUCN) in 1978, were set up to identify plants and animals under threat world-wide. For Irish plants, this was completed in 1987 (Curtis and McGough 1988) in response to the *Wildlife Act* which was passed in 1976. Here, 52 species of wildflowers were given legal protection and classified according to the level of threat: endangered, vulnerable, rare, extinct and indeterminate. Similar books have been completed for mammals (Whilde 1993). Bryophytes are to follow shortly (Stewart and Church, in preparation) and the plant book is currently being revised. These books bring into sharp focus the vulnerability of our species and reflect their rate of extinction due to the many factors that impinge on biodiversity today. Bird and butterfly identification books have also proliferated in recent times (for instance D'Arcy 1981; Hickin 1992).

Rare plant species conservation has been carried out at TCD Botanic Gardens by maintaining a collection of native Irish plants in cultivation. Collections were undertaken from known vulnerable sites and propagated after noting their ecological requirements in the field (Wyse-Jackson 1984). Artificial environments were also created using peat beds and limestone rockeries for rare native calcifuges and calcicoles, and a seed bank facility was initiated using domestic freezers. This important work is being enlarged and extended with grants from OPW and the Irish Genetics Resources Conservation Trust (Waldren 1998).

An official Irish biological records centre does not exist at present in southern Ireland, although one did reside with An Foras Forbartha, the planning agency, before it was dissolved. Those records are now deposited with Dúchas, the Parks and Wildlife Service, and there are contracts currently running for the continuation and integration of all extant biological records. There is a recently formed centre in operation in NI, the Centre for Environmental Data and Recording (CEDAR), based in the Ulster Museum.

HABITATS

At the habitat scale, much research has been carried out in the universities and by the Wildlife Service over the years, but little of this has reached the general public. Postgraduate research on bogs has been particularly well served in recent years, for instance by Schouten (1984), Doyle (1990), Madden and Doyle (1990), O'Connell and Doyle (1990), Doyle and Dowding (1990), Kelly (1994). A general survey of all bog types and their exploitation was carried out by Hammond (1979) and on raised bogs in particular by Cross (1990). A blanket bog inventory is underway also. These surveys take many years to complete and are often somewhat obsolete by the time they are published due to the rapid exploitation of bogs by Bord na Móna and an increasing number of private enterprises. Owing to increased headage payments for sheep in recent times, large tracts of blanket bog may have been irretrievably damaged and eroded due to overgrazing. Several studies have been conducted on this problem (Bleasdale and Sheehy-Skeffington 1997; MacGowan and Doyle 1996). Fortunately, a recent review of headage payments should help to alleviate this situation. Upland blanket bog is also seriously under threat (An Taisce 1996). Most of the problems here relate to the rapid increase in forestry planting by Coillte, as mentioned earlier.

An argument has been put forward that these bogs were created as a result of man's interference and deteriorating climate. Therefore, this reversal of landscape to forestry is not necessarily a bad thing. However, the changes wrought today are very rapid, not allowing vegetation to recover or adapt to this change. Also, although some of these bog habitats are not very species-rich, due to Ireland being the last outpost in Europe with examples of these unique formations, we are duty-bound to conserve at least some examples of all our bog types, for biodiversity to be conserved at the landscape scale.

National Nature Reserves (NNRs) have been in existence for many years in Ireland as a way of preserving sites for wildlife. Most of these are state-owned or leased but some are in private ownership also (for instance Kilcolman Fen, Cork). There are currently *ca.* 76 in Ireland (Wildlife Service 1990). They are one of the few designations that have legal status under the *Wildlife Act* 1976.

An inventory of all habitats (Areas of Scientific Interest, ASIs) in Ireland was carried out in the early 1980s by An Foras Forbartha (AFF 1983). This identified *ca.* 1,800 sites at the time and was by no means an exhaustive list by this organization's own admission. Each site was classified as international, national, regional or local importance. These categories were somewhat subjective and often incorrect. With the advent of EU legislation regarding habitats in the Habitats Directive, funds were made available to reappraise the original ASIs for future designation. This survey relocated the original sites and was mainly involved in mapping boundaries, renaming them as Natural Heritage Areas (NHAs) and entering them into a Geographical Information System (GIS) (Lockhart *et al.* 1993). According to a recent estimate calculated by An Taisce (1996), the National Trust for Ireland, a staggering 30% of the original ASIs have been damaged or lost. A subset of these sites is currently being designated for Special Areas of Conservation (SAC) status which will be legally binding and will require management plans to be carried out by the landowners (Ó Críodáin 1994). Government grants will become available for implementing these plans and provide the necessary compensation for loss of potential earnings on the land.

Northern Ireland has a similar network of sites called ASSIs or Areas of Special Scientific Interest which are managed by local Wildlife Trusts. The National Trust (UK) also has many properties in the province (*ca.* 35 sites), some of which contain substantial areas of wildlife (The National Trust 1996), particularly along the coast, for example the Murlough reserve in county Down. The National Trust had long experience in wildlife management, particularly in the use of different grazing practices for enhancing sites for flora, butterflies, bats and birds (Bullock and Harvey 1995).

More recently, a spate of books on distinctly Irish habitats has been written for the interested lay person, namely a general book on the habitats of Ireland (Mills 1988), the Shannon callows by Heery (1995), Bull Island (Jeffrey 1977), bogs (Feehan and O'Donovan 1996) and regional accounts such as several on the Burren (Nelson 1991; O'Connell and Korff 1991; D'Arcy and Hayward 1992), Connemara (Whilde 1997), Clonmacnoise (Tubridy 1984), Wicklow (Nairn and Crowley 1998) and Kerry (Carruthers 1998). A very distinctive type of publication which deserves mention are the maps created by Tim Robinson of the Burren (1977) and the Aran Islands (1990). These handy maps are drawn with such loving care and with much research and show not only features of the landscape and the natural heritage but also contain a wealth of knowledge of the archaeological sites in the area, of which we have many.

Classification of habitats using phytosociological methods has been carried out extensively by a small but dedicated suite of botanists. Many scientists have been engaged in this worthy task in Ireland, starting with Braun-Blanquet and Tüxen (1952). Disciples of this endeavour have pieced together our unique classifications over the years, writing on bogs (Moore 1968; Doyle 1990), grasslands (O'Sullivan 1965), woodlands (Kelly 1981; Kelly and Kirby 1982; Iremonger 1986; Kelly and Iremonger 1998), wetlands (O'Connell, Ryan and MacGowran 1980; Mooney and O'Connell 1990), several of which are brought together in one volume by White (1982). A preliminary classification of all Irish plant communities has also been presented in the latter volume.

A relatively recent initiative, also funded by the EU, is the Rural Environment Protection Scheme (REPS). Set up about seven years ago with a very large budget underpinning it (*ca.* £280 million per annum), this scheme was initiated to encourage the farming community across the board to reduce farm pollutants, reduce stocking and fertilizer levels and retain/maintain areas of wildlife interest (DAFF 1996). This included reparation of walls and gates to improve the visual appearance of the landscape. The scheme, up to recently, was voluntary and funded only up to 100 acres at £50 an acre. On larger farms, the scheme had to be implemented on the whole farm for the same compensation. This has served to discourage larger farmers from getting involved in it. There are extra payments (25%) in REPS for those who:

(i) have an NHA;

(ii) are organic;

(iii) have rare breeds;

(iv) have degraded land (overgrazed/eroded);

(v) have long-term set-aside strips (riparian), and

(vi) support leisure/tourist activities.

These supplements are not cumulative. Those farmers who have SACs on their land are now obliged to be in REPS and, very recently, payments have been added for farms larger than 100 acres up to a maximum grant of £9,000 per year for the next fifteen years. Take-up of the scheme was slow initially but now up to 30,000 farmers have signed up. To date, there has been little or no monitoring of the scheme by the Department of Agriculture except for spot checks. It will be a challenge to see if the scheme has resulted in a marked improvement in wildlife enhancement, and research projects, funded by Teagasc, the agricultural advisory authority, are currently in train to assess the effect of the scheme in biodiversity terms.

LAND USE

In terms of land use, both historical and present-day, several publications and reports are relevant. Two of the earliest books of their kind were published by John Feehan, one on his native Sliabh Blooms, county Offaly, the subject of his doctorate at Trinity College, Dublin (1979), the other being an environmental history of Laois (1984). These books represented a new departure at the time in that they were aimed at the general public and are no less scholarly for that. The late Professor Frank Mitchell has provided us with a wealth of erudite books on the history and development of the Irish landscape since prehistoric times; there is little to match the panoramic view he has painted for us all in his *The Shell guide to reading the Irish landscape* (1986) and its later edition (Mitchell and Ryan 1997). A notable atlas of rural Ireland has been published recently, edited by Aalen,

Whelan and Stout (1997), which is as handsome as it is informative.

The EU has funded many conservation initiatives of late; one of the most important has been the interpretation of the whole of Ireland's land cover with the use of satellite imagery called the CORINE (Co-ordination of Information on the Environment) database (CORINE 1994). This database contains 44 land-cover classes for the whole country and can be abstracted to obtain information on a county basis, including the percentage area of each land-cover class. It is available free of charge in disk or CD format and maps are available with land-cover classification interpreted for a reasonable cost from ERA MAPTEC, Dame Street, Dublin 2. This database has filled an otherwise large gap in our knowledge of the country as a whole as there was no up-to-date land-cover inventory for the whole of Ireland prior to this. It will also be useful for future map creation and comparison, and already a land-cover change map has been created for the coastal region (EU-funded LACOAST) in a 6 km band around the whole country, comparing changes over a ten-year period. This type of map will inform us of current changes in land-use unthinkable before now, but at present its potential is very under-utilized. Coillte, the semi-state body for forestry development, has recently compiled a GIS inventory of all Ireland's woodlands, both state-owned and private, dividing them into 16 categories of both deciduous and coniferous stands. Another type of national land-use inventory was created in relation to the badger population in Ireland. This was done on a 1 km square basis, each one located at the south-west corner of every 10 km square in the country. Habitat and environmental date were recorded in each square (Smal 1995). This will also be useful for land-use change should the badger survey be repeated in the future.

LANDSCAPE

Relatively little research has been carried out at the landscape scale in Ireland compared to our European counterparts. One of the earliest studies to integrate several landscape elements successfully is the Clonmacnoise Heritage Zone report (Tubridy 1984) where habitat conservation, archaeology and cultural heritage were elegantly woven into a rich tapestry. This showed us for the first time that all these elements were important and worthy of integration instead of dealing with each facet separately, an approach which may inevitably lead to conflict. With the advent of GIS and remote sensing, studies of this nature will become increasingly important in the near future. Studies on hydrology in the west of Ireland on the Clare/Galway karst have successfully employed GIS recently (Coxon *et al.* 1993). Many of our county councils have recently installed GIS systems which will ultimately aid in the planning process.

Some landscape studies have been carried out, mainly in universities: catchment studies related to mining activity in Avoca, county Wicklow (Gray 1996), habitat creation and restoration in the Anne valley, county Waterford (Harrington and Phillips 1996) and landscape classification of the Lee valley, county Cork, in terms of land use, conservation and economics (Cassidy 1999). A handsome book on landscape management using regions as a theme is by Moore *et al.* (1997), where coastal management of the south-west of Ireland is dealt with. In an effort to gather all the disparate themes of landscape together, including the aesthetic as well as the scientific, a landscape forum has been set up which holds a symposium every year (O'Regan 1995). This has been very successful and provides a useful outlet for those who now study at the landscape scale, in all its guises, from art to local government. It also has been a useful lobbying vehicle to put pressure on government to pass a *Landscape Act*.

There are few designations which protect landscapes in southern Ireland. The Environmentally Sensitive Areas (ESAs) scheme, which has taken off in the UK and Northern Ireland, never established itself properly in southern Ireland, although two areas were mooted for designation: Sliabh Blooms in Offaly and Slyne Head in Connemara. In the north, five ESAs have been established in areas of exceptional scenic beauty, comprising 20% of the land cover (Sperrins, Slieve Gullion, Mournes, Antrim coast/Rathlin and West Fermanagh/Erne lakeland; DANI 1993). The scheme is voluntary but has been well funded, and has resulted in these landscapes being protected from certain damaging developments. Monitoring is currently being carried out to discover their efficacy since their inception (Cambell, Cameron and McAdam 1998, 1999) and significant differences have been found after six years. SACs by default have superseded the ESA scheme in southern Ireland and, by linking up as many sites as possible within an SAC (including buffer zones), a measure of control can be exercised at the landscape scale. This is particularly obvious in the Burren, for example, where many habitats converge on a single landscape ecotope such as the karst limestone. The linking factor is the unique hydrology which connects the sites in an underground network of anastomozing channels, a system which could very easily be contaminated by groundwater pollution and drainage. A case in point is the study contracted by the government in 1996 to see whether it was feasible to drain the Gort area in county Galway to prevent seasonal flooding. After an exhaustive and expensive analysis, it was deemed to be an unacceptable course of action as the hydrology was too sensitive (and indeed too difficult!) to change.

Because of their beauty, our landscapes have become a tourism resource, and 'scenery' is top of the list of tourist surveys conducted by Bord Fáilte, the Irish Tourist Board. In this context, 25 landscapes 'of outstanding scenic quality' have been identified and a mechanism is sought whereby landscapes may be protected at the same time as being developed sustainably for tourism. Such a plan would help to prevent further planning conflicts in sensitive areas (Meldon and Skehan 1996).

NATIONAL PARKS

In 1971, IUCN defined the criteria and international standards for National Parks (NPs). They fall under four headings:

• legal status;

• a budget to provide protection;

• 1,000 ha with no damaging development therein;

• prohibition of exploitation of natural resources.

Dúchas, the National Heritage Service, has overall responsibility for National Parks in Ireland. Dr Alan Craig of Dúchas stated 'a National Park exists to conserve interesting plant and animal communities and associated landscapes in their natural state and, under conditions compatible with that purpose, to provide appreciation of them by the visiting public. National Parks are usually the largest protected areas in a country, protecting the most significant features' (Craig, in Jeffrey 1984). The Parks and Wildlife Service, as it was known then, from the start had a policy of land purchase in terms of its National Parks. Of necessity they are small compared to other NPs in the UK and Europe which are based on the management agreements of existing landowners. Therefore Park property is governed by the *State Property Act* of 1954, but there are no bylaws for Parks as such. A bill is in preparation for Parks legislation at present (Paul Kelly, Parks and Wildlife, pers. comm.). Research is considered to be essential for management purposes within the Parks but is not a primary objective in itself. Park staff are confined to inventory compilation, mapping and monitoring rather than pure research. There are six National Parks to date in Ireland: Killarney (county Kerry), Connemara, Wicklow, the Burren (county Clare), Glenveigh (county Donegal) and another, recently designated, for Mayo.

KILLARNEY NATIONAL PARK

The Killarney National Park was bequeathed to the state in 1932 by the Bourn Vincent family and had its own parliamentary act (the *Bourn Vincent Memorial Trust Act* 1932). It consisted of Muckross House and gardens and a large estate of lakes, mountains and native oak woodland, some 4,300 ha in area. It has since been expanded to 10,289 ha and designated as a Biosphere Reserve in 1982, a European designation. The geology is principally sandstone and limestone, and the oak woods and yew woods are representative of some of the last vestiges of native woodland in Ireland. There are extensive bogs in the uplands and the Park contains the only population of native red deer in the country. The strawberry tree (*Arbutus unedo*), normally a shrub of the Mediterranean, is found within the Park, developing into a tree on the edges of the native oak woodland here — another indication of the effects of the Gulf Stream. It has a management plan in place (Killarney National Park Management Plan 1990) and many associated attractive publications on landscape, butterflies and Muckross Park and Gardens. Apart from being the oldest and largest of the NPs, it also seems to be the best funded at present, with a large park staff of rangers and much research undertaken within it (Kelly 1981; Iremonger 1986; Kelly and Iremonger 1997). Current experiments involve using native cattle breeds on the more mountainous parts to reduce purple moor grass and re-establish a more diverse vegetation (Dunne and Doyle 1998; Harrington, Dúchas, pers. comm.).

WICKLOW NATIONAL PARK

This Park was established officially in 1991 and currently encompasses 15,930 ha, spreading over parts of counties Wicklow and Dublin. It contains blanket bog, heath, woodland, freshwater lakes and rivers. There are rare arctic-alpine species in the uplands and hybrid deer of red and sika. It is traditionally sheep-grazed with turf-cutting rights still in place, and also contains a monastic settlement at Glendalough.

Regarding the history of the site, after the last ice age, the natural vegetation would have been Scots pine. These were removed by early pastoralists around 4000 BC and the area was sheep and cattle-grazed up to the eighteenth century. Woodland removal by the English settlers prior to 1600 for ship-building, tanning, iron smelting and charcoal removed a substantial amount of native woodland. Some of this was replanted and coppiced and estates were managed for deer hunting. Sika deer were introduced in 1860 and inter-bred with the native red deer. Sheep numbers have doubled in recent years due to increased ewe headage premia, and upland commonage was shared on a townland basis. In this century, much afforestation of exotic conifers has taken place, both privately and by the state. Concurrent with this was turf cutting which accelerated during the Second World War due to importation restrictions on coal. Up to 25,000 tons of peat were exported to Dublin per annum during this period. These combined threats were responsible for the establishment of a National Park in the region. Two nature reserves were already present (Glendalough woods and Glenealo valley) and these were

to form the nucleus of the Park. The then Forest Service was persuaded to relinquish other lands that were no longer required for planting, and yet other lands were acquired from the Powerscourt estate. On establishment of the Park, the government promised to extend it in size to 30,000 ha and provide a visitor centre (Wicklow Mountains National Park Study 1997).

THE BURREN NATIONAL PARK

The Burren region consists of 100 square miles of bare karst limestone in county Clare. It is famous for its unique flora, with representations of arctic-alpine and Mediterranean flora co-existing together (Webb and Scannell 1983). The climate is exceptionally mild (average annual temperature 10°C) with few frosts, and it has high rainfall (1,800 mm per annum). In 1973, an area of land owned by Trinity College, Dublin, was to become the starting point for a Burren National Park. Purchase has continued to the present day, resulting in 1,673 ha being officially designated as a National Park in 1991. The Park contains turloughs, limestone hills (**Fig. 1.3**) and grassland, native woodland and the only part of the Burren that has experienced tectonic movement as shown in the unusual folding at Mullaghmore. Pre-glaciation, the whole area would have been covered in shale. This has been stripped off by the actions of the ice, leaving a dramatic landscape of bare karst limestone with areas of drift-derived soils or till. There is a wealth of soil types present within the Park, ranging from peats to brown earths, to gleys and rendzinas (O'Donovan 1987), which undoubtedly contributes to the high floristic value of the area. Several important habitats are to be found here, namely:

(i) limestone pavement which provides niches for shade-loving plants in its grykes or cracks;

(ii) limestone grassland which is species-rich and unusual in character;

(iii) heath where peat occurs;

(iv) hazel scrub in abundance, and

(v) fens and turloughs.

The only part of the Burren not represented in the Park is the distinctive coastal flora found to the north at Black Head. Thus, this area is a recognized hot-spot for nearly every branch of wildlife, from flora to butterflies, birds to mosses and lichens. Feral goats and pine martins occur here and hares are very common. The area is cattle grazed extensively. As the Park is not fenced in any way, concern was expressed about the effect of the goat population on the native trees present. As a result a cull

Fig. 1.3 A view of the Burren National Park from the top of Mullaghmore, showing the extensive areas of karst interspersed with our unique limestone grasslands.

was undertaken in 1994 to reduce goat numbers in the Park. Despite being infiltrated with animals from local domestic herds, this feral goat population is the largest in Europe (Bullock and O'Donovan 1995) and as such is an important feature of this landscape. They have been used in the UK on National Trust land to help reduce shrub encroachment in similar areas, for example Cheddar Gorge, with success. A more positive approach to our goat population should be encouraged and more research is being conducted to discover the role of goat grazing within the Park (Byrne 1996).

In relation to the Wicklow NP and the Burren NP, a major controversy ensued when European Structural Funds were made available to build interpretative centres (ICs) within the Park confines. Local objection, particularly from the Burren Action Group, to such developments within the Parks forced a revision of the planning laws in 1993 with regard to state-owned property. The right of state bodies to erect developments on their own land without planning permission was revoked. Unfortunately, due to time restrictions for the spending of EU Structural Funds, construction on both interpretative centres had begun. Planning permission was then sought and Environmental Impact Studies were conducted on both sites. However, permission was not given, with the result that the Luggala (Wicklow) site had to be completely dismantled and returned to its former

condition and the Burren site has also been turned down.

This situation arose mainly because the state located the ICs within the boundaries of their own property on sites which were considered inappropriate in terms of existing infrastructure, access and sensitive landscapes and without due consultation with outside interested parties. The result was deep division within the local communities between those who saw the ICs as a means of employment against those who were outraged by the inappropriate sitings. This did nothing to promote good relations between the local communities and the Park authorities — one of the main tenets of a National Park. Another difficulty was that there was no management plan in existence for the Park at the time, but that has since been rectified (Burren National Park Study 1996a, b and c).

GLENVEIGH NATIONAL PARK

The Glenveigh National Park is centred around a 10,000 ha estate formerly owned by an American art collector called Henry McIlhenny. The estate had a turbulent and troubled history in the early 1900s as the then landlord, George Adair, had all his tenants evicted because his agent had been murdered in the hills. The introduction of blackfaced sheep onto the mountains at that time was more profitable than the tenants' cattle, so it suited the landlord to get rid of them anyway. Adair built the castle seen in the grounds today and introduced red deer onto the estate for hunting purposes. It had been variously occupied by a war veteran, an archaeologist and two art collectors up to the time the lands were bequeathed to the state in 1975 by McIlhenny. Eight years later, he also bequeathed the castle and gardens and in 1986 the Park was open to the public for the first time (O'Keeffe 1986). Since then, the Park has been extended to 16,548 ha and includes two nature reserves — Lough Barra Bog and Meenachullion Bog. The former estate consists of a castle with formal gardens nestling beside a deep lake with mountains rising on either side. The lake has a sandy beach juxtaposed with a bog in the valley, and there is native oak woodland on the steep slopes and mountain blanket bog in abundance. The main area of conservation work here has been the removal of the invasive shrub *Rhododendron ponticum*, a veritable weed in the woodland understory (Cross 1982). This attractive shrub was introduced as cover for game on the estate but has since become rampant, not only in this Park but also in Wicklow and Killarney. Volunteer work camps called Groundwork struggled for years with the plant, trying to remove and kill it. By hiring professionals, removal has been particularly successful in Donegal, having removed up to 75% of it. This has left the woodland temporarily scarred and shaken but will be beneficial in the long term, encouraging the native ground flora to recover. Research on the vegetation history of the Park has been carried out by Telford (1977).

CONNEMARA NATIONAL PARK
Situated in the heart of the west of Ireland, this Park covers 2,000 ha of mountains, bogs, heaths and grass-lands. It enjoys a mild climate and heavy rainfall, over 1,600 mm per year, which means in reality that it rains for 250 days out of 365! The geology is mainly metamorphic rock, mostly resistant quartzite with schists and marbles. Glaciation over 10,000 years ago finally shaped the area with deposits of sands and gravels, boulder clay and erratics, and these have formed the basis for the vegetation of the Park.

Much of the present Park was formed by part of the Kylemore Abbey estate and the Letterfrack Industrial School. The rest was in private ownership. There is a visitor centre and this was converted from farm buildings erected around 1890. In the past, the lands were grazed by cattle and vegetables were grown in the lowlands, shown by the existence of ridge and furrow, a reminder of our more populous past. There are many other clues to the past including megalithic court tombs over 4,000 years old, an old well still in use and the remnants of the old Galway road abandoned some one hundred years ago.

The main floristic interests in the Park are in the blanket bog. The peat formed a blanket over the landscape since the last glaciation and is up to 5 m deep in places. Not only are there the common bog species present such as bog asphodel, bog myrtle, bog cotton and purple moor grass, several insectivorous species are also found here such as sundews and butterworts. Here also are elements of arctic-alpine vegetation in the form of roseroot, starry saxifrage and mountain sorrel, but there is also a Mediterranean element in the presence of pale butterwort, St Dabaoc's Heath and St Patrick's Cabbage. The most important animal present in the Park is the Connemara pony which is highly prized. This animal is now fully domesticated, but a pure-bred herd is being reared within the Park to conserve this unique equine breed. Native red deer were wiped out in this area over 150 years ago, but a nucleus of a new herd is being established at present.

MAYO NATIONAL PARK
Mayo NP is the latest addition to our National Park heritage. Most of the Park is intact blanket bog and was previously under threat from drainage, turf cutting and overgrazing. It is centred around the Owenduff-Nephin SAC with a core area of 24,000 ha. There is also a visitor centre proposed at Croaghan. The Park area may be extended to include marine areas such as Achill and Mullet to the west and Glenamoy bog towards the north.

CONCLUSION
As a nation, we have been sluggish to recognize and cherish our natural heritage. It has taken prompting from abroad and learning lessons from other countries' mistakes to make us realize that we have many unique habitats for which we should be proud to be responsible. We still have an abundance of natural heritage due to our slow economic development compared to other European countries, but all that is rapidly changing. Since becoming a member of the EU, much structural development has taken place and its acceleration has caused destruction of habitat in recent years. Government is aware that one of our best assets is our unspoilt countryside and, as tourism is one of our biggest sources of revenue, then action must be taken to maintain it. European legislation has been timely in this respect and has forced us to designate areas of natural heritage. However, unless we learn how to manage that heritage in a responsible way, then much may still be lost through ignorance and mishandling. Not enough funding is being given to heritage management, with the result that the existing professional expertise is overloaded, and wildlife protection often falls on the shoulders of the non-governmental organizations. This results in a fractured, piecemeal approach to conser-vation, with no overall strategy evident outside of imposed legislation. We have come a long way in the last

thirty years in terms of inventory; now we need to go further and learn how to manage our natural heritage intelligently and co-operatively.

We have a unique opportunity here to integrate our natural heritage into the overall weave of the human and industrial landscape, so that it becomes an integral part of our lives and minds and not just fragments of a lost era to be gaped at by visitors, like animals in a cage. This requires education of the guardians of the countryside, be they farmers or wildlife rangers, so that progress can be made. In the global scheme of things, biodiversity is severely threatened and we have little inkling of what the knock-on effect will be on critical factors such as productivity and other ecosystem services. We owe it to ourselves, to our children and the planet to preserve as much of our own diversity as we can as an insurance against future global disaster.

Bibliography

Aalen, F. H. A., Whelan, K. and Stout, M. 1997 *Atlas of the Irish rural landscape*. Cork.

Akeroyd, J. and Murphy, M. (eds) 1997 *Flora of Sherkin Island*. Dublin.

AFF (An Foras Forbartha) 1977 *Sand dunes. Formation, erosion and management*. Dublin.

AFF (An Foras Forbartha) 1983 *Areas of scientific interest in Ireland*. Dublin.

An Taisce 1996 *Evaluation of environmental designations in Ireland*. Dublin.

Bassett, J. A. and Curtis, T. G. F. 1985 'The nature and occurrence of sand-dune machair in Ireland', *Proceedings of the Royal Irish Academy* **85 B**, pp. 1-20.

Bleasdale, A. and Sheehy-Skeffington, M. 1991 'Influence of agricultural practices on plant communities in the Connemara' in Feehan 1992, pp. 331-6.

Bond, K. G. M. 1995 'Irish microlepidoptera checklist', *Bulletin of the Irish Biogeographical Society* **18**, pp. 176–262.

Booth, E. 1979 *The flora of county Carlow*. Dublin.

Braun-Blanquet, J. and Tüxen, R. 1952 'Irische Pflanzengesellschaften', *Veroff. Geobot. Inst. Zurich* **25**, pp. 224–15.

Brunker, J. P. 1950 *Flora of county Wicklow*. Dundalk.

Bullock, D. J. and Harvey, H. J. 1995 *The National Trust and nature conservation*. London.

Bullock, D. J. B. and O'Donovan, G. 1995 *Observations on the ecology of large herbivores in the Burren National Park, with particular reference to the feral goat (*Capra hircus*)*, unpublished report (Forbairt/British Council). Dublin.

Burren National Park Study 1996a *Draft conservation guidelines for proposed natural heritage areas*. Dublin.

Burren National Park Study 1996b *Draft management plan*. Dublin.

Burren National Park Study 1996c *Draft strategy for north Clare area*. Dublin.

Byrne, C. 1996 'Semi-natural grassland communities in eastern Ireland: classification, conservation and management', doctoral dissertation, TCD.

Byrne, D. 1996 *The effects of grazing by cattle and goats on the karstic vegetation of the Burren, Co. Clare*. Proceedings of the Irish Botanist's Meeting, UCD. Dublin.

Cabot, D. 1985 *The state of the environment*. Dublin.

Cambell, J., Cameron, A. and MacAdam, J. H. 1998 'Re-monitoring of heather and woodland within Northern Ireland's environmentally sensitive areas' in *Proceedings of the Irish Botanists' Meeting* (Dublin).

Cambell, J., Cameron, A. and MacAdam, J. H. 1999 'Monitoring of environmentally sensitive areas in Northern Ireland — an overview' in *Proceedings of the Irish Botanists' Meeting* (Belfast).

Carroll, M. and Dubsky, K. 1995 *Coastal zone management: from needs to action*. Dublin.

Carruthers, T. 1998 *Kerry: a natural history*. Cork.

Cassidy, A. 1999 'An examination of the functions of nature of the river Lee catchment, co. Cork, Ireland with socio-economic implications using GIS techniques', M.Sc. thesis, UCC.

Chambers 1992 *Maxi paperback dictionary*. Edinburgh.

Chesney, H. 1996 'Irish pearl mussels: going, going, gone?' in Reynolds 1996, pp. 142-50.

Clabby, K. J., Lucey, J., McGarrigle, M. L., Bowman, J. J. and Toner, P. 1992 *Water quality in Ireland, 1987–90. Part 1. General assessment*. Dublin.

Colgan, N. 1904 *Flora of county Dublin*. Dublin.

CORINE (Cordination of Information on the Environment) 1994 *CORINE land-cover project* (Ireland), unpublished report. Dublin.

Costello, M. J. 1995 'The BioMar (Life) project: developing a system for the collection, storage and dissemination of marine data for coastal management' in K. Hiscock (ed) *Classification of benthic marine biotopes of the north-east Atlantic*, Proceedings of the BioMar-Life workshop held in Cambridge 16–18 November 1994 (Peterborough), pp. 9–17.

Coxon, C. E., Mills, P., Pipes, S. and Rybaczuk, K. 1993 'Demonstration of the role of GIS in utilising the role of Quaternary geological data in groundwater protection studies' in P. Coxon (ed) *Glacial events*, IQUA annual symposium (Dublin) pp. 8–10.

Cross, J. R. 1982 'The invasion and impact of

Rhododendron ponticum in native Irish vegetation' in J. White (ed) *Studies on Irish vegetation* (Dublin).

Cross, J. R. 1990 *The raised bogs of Ireland: their ecology, status and conservation*. Dublin.

Curtis, T. G. F. 1991 'A site inventory of the sandy coasts of Ireland' in M. B. Quigley (ed) *A guide to the sand dunes of Ireland* (Galway).

Curtis, T. G. F. and Sheehy-Skeffington, M. J. 1998 'The salt marshes of Ireland: an inventory and account of their geographical variation', *Biology and Environment* **98 B**, pp. 87–104.

Curtis, T. G. F. and McGough, H. N. 1988 *The Irish Red Data book 1: vascular plants*. Dublin.

DAFF (Department of Agriculture, Food and Forestry) 1996 *Rural Environment Protection Scheme*. Dublin.

Daly, D. 1992 'Groundwater resources, a review of development, quality and pollution issues' in Feehan 1992, pp. 476–82.

DANI (Department of Agriculture, Northern Ireland) 1993 *Environmentally sensitive areas in Northern Ireland: guidelines for farmers*. Belfast.

D'Arcy, G. 1981 *The guide to the birds of Ireland*. Dublin.

D'Arcy, G. 1988 *Pocket guide to the animals of Ireland*. Belfast.

D'Arcy, G. and Hayward, J. 1992 *The natural history of the Burren*. London.

DNFC (Dublin Naturalist's Field Club) 1986 *Reflections and recollections: 100 years of the Dublin Naturalists' Field Club*. Dublin.

Doogue, D. and Harding, P. T. 1982 *Distribution atlas of woodlice in Ireland*. Dublin.

Doogue, D., Nash, D., Parnell, J. A. N., Reynolds, S. and Wyse-Jackson, P. (eds) 1998 *Flora of county Dublin*. Dublin.

Doyle, G. 1990 (ed) *The ecology and conservation of Irish peatlands*. Dublin.

Doyle, G. 1990 'Phytosociology of Atlantic blanket bog complexes' in Doyle 1990, pp. 75-90.

Doyle, T. and Dowding, P. 1990 'Decomposition and aspects of the physical environment in the surface layers of Mongan bog' in Doyle 1990, pp. 163–172.

Drew, D. and Magee, E. 1994 'Environmental implications of land reclamation in the Burren, co. Clare: a preliminary analysis', *Irish Geography* **27**, pp. 81–96.

Duggan, S. N. 1998 'A landscape management study of esker grasslands at Clonmacnoise, co. Offaly using multivariate analysis and GIS', M.Sc. thesis, UCD.

Dunne, F, and Doyle, G. 1998 'Changes in *Molinia*-dominated vegetation due to cattle grazing in Killarney, co. Kerry', *Proceedings of the Irish Botanists' Meeting*, UCD (Dublin).

EPA (Environmental Protection Agency) 1995 *The biological survey of river quality*. Wexford.

EPA (Environmental Protection Agency) 1996 *State of the environment*. Wexford.

Erwin, D. G., Picton, B. E., Connor, D. W., Howson, E. M., Gileece, P. and Bogues, M. J. 1990 *Inshore marine life of Northern Ireland. Survey report to Conservation Branch DoE (NI)*. Belfast.

Fairley, J. 1981 *Irish whales and whaling*. Belfast.

Fay, P. J. and Jeffrey, D. J. 1995 'The nitrogen cycle in sand-dunes' in D. W. Jeffrey, M. B. Jones and McAdam J. H. (eds) *Irish grasslands: their biology and management* (Dublin).

Feehan, J. 1979 *The landscape of Sliabh Bloom: a study of its natural and human heritage*. Dublin.

Feehan, J. 1984 *Laois: an environmental history*. Ballykilcavan.

Feehan, J. 1992 (ed) *Environment and development in Ireland*. Dublin

Feehan, J. (ed) 1994 *Climate variation and climate change in Ireland*. Roscrea.

Feehan, J. and O'Donovan, G. 1993 *The magic of Coole*. Dublin.

Feehan, J. and O'Donovan, G. 1996 *The bogs of Ireland: their natural, cultural and industrial heritage*. Dublin.

Ferguson, A. and Mason, F. M. 1981 'Allozyme evidence for reproductively isolated sympatric populations of brown trout *Salmo trutta* L. in Lough Melvin, Ireland', *Journal of Fish Biology* **18**, pp. 628–42.

Gray, N. F. 1996 'Field assessment of acid mine drainage contamination in surface and ground waters', *Environmental Geology* **27**, pp. 358–61.

Hackney, P. (ed) 1997 *Stewart and Corry's flora of the north-east of Ireland*. Belfast.

Harrington, R. and Phillips, A. 1996 *A GIS study of the Anne Valley, co. Waterford*, unpublished report, Geography Department, TCD.

Hammond, R. F. 1979 *The peatlands of Ireland*. Dublin.

Heery, S. 1995 *The Shannon floodlands*. Galway.

Hicken, N. 1992 *The butterflies of Ireland: a field guide*. Cork.

Iremonger, S. F. 1986 'An ecological account of Irish wetland woods; with particular reference to the principle tree species', doctoral dissertation, TCD.

ISSG (Irish Sea Study Group) 1990 *Irish Sea Study Group reports*. Liverpool.

Jeffrey, D. W. (ed) 1977 *North Bull island, Dublin Bay: a modern coastal natural history*. Dublin.

Jeffrey, D. W. (ed) 1984 *Nature conservation in Ireland: progress and problems*. Dublin.

Kelly, D. L. 1981 'The native forest vegetation of Killarney, south-west Ireland. An ecological account',

Journal of Ecology **69**, pp. 437–72.

Kelly, D. L. and Kirby, E. N. 1982 'Irish native woodlands over limestone' in White 1982, pp. 181–98.

Kelly, D. L. and Iremonger, S. F. 1997 'Irish wetland woods: the plant communities and their ecology', *Biology and Environment* **97 B**, pp. 1–32.

Kelly, K. S. and Costello, M. J. 1995 'Marine-related papers published in the Irish Naturalists' Journal, 1925-1994', *Irish Naturalists' Journal* **25**, pp. 85-120.

Kelly, M. L. 1994 'A study of the vegetation of Clara and Raheenmore bogs, co. Offaly', doctoral dissertation, TCD.

Kiely, O. and Myers, A. A. 1998 'Grey seal (*Halichoerus grypus*) pup production at the Iniskea Island group, co. Mayo, and Blasket Islands, co. Kerry', *Biology and Environment* **98 B** 2, pp. 87–104.

Killarney National Park Management Plan 1990. Dublin.

Lockhart, N., Madden, B., Wolfe-Murphy, S., Wymer, E. and Wyse-Jackson, M. 1993 *National ASI survey: guidelines for ecologists*, unpublished report, Dublin.

MacGowan, F. and Doyle, G. J. 1996 'The effects of sheep grazing and trampling by tourists on lowland blanket bog in the west of Ireland' in P. S. Giller and A. A. Myers (eds) *Disturbance and recovery in ecological systems* (Dublin), pp. 20–32.

Madden, B. and Doyle, G. 1990 'Primary production on Mongan bog' in Doyle 1990, pp. 147–61.

Maitland, P. S. 1996 'Threatened fishes of the British Isles, with special reference to Ireland' in Reynolds 1996.

McCracken, E. 1971 *The Irish woods since Tudor times: their distribution and exploitation*. Belfast.

McGarrigle, M. L., Lucey, J. and Clabby, K. C. 1996 'River-water quality in Ireland 1987–90' in Reynolds 1996, pp. 31–7.

McGee, E. and Bradshaw, R. 1990 'Erosion of high level blanket peat' in Doyle 1990, pp. 109–20.

Meldon, J. and Skeehan, C. 1996 *Tourism and the landscape. Landscape management by consensus*. Dublin.

Mills, S. 1988 *Nature in its place: the habitats of Ireland*. London.

Mitchell, F. 1986 *The Shell guide to reading the Irish landscape*. Dublin.

Mitchell, F. and Ryan, M. 1997 *Reading the Irish landscape*. Dublin.

Mooney, E. P. and O'Connell, M. 1990 'The phytosociology and ecology of the aquatic and wetland plant communities of the lower Corrib basin, co. Galway', *Proceedings of the Royal Irish Academy* **90 B**, pp. 5–97.

Moore, J., Hobbs, G., Elliot, R., Nairn, R. and Partridge, K. 1997 *The south-west coast of Ireland*.

Moore, J. J. 1968 'A classification of the moors and wet heaths of Northern Europe' in R. Tüxen (ed) *Pflanzensoziologische systematik* (Den Haag), pp. 306–20.

Mulcahy, M. *et al.* 1992 'Coastal zone management' in Feehan 1992, pp. 409–13.

Murray, D. 1996 'Freshwater resources, systems and habitats in Ireland' in Reynolds 1996, pp. 3–19.

Myers, A. A., Little, C., Costello, M. J. and Partridge, J. C. 1991 *The ecology of Lough Ine*. Dublin.

National Botanic Gardens Management Plan. Dublin.

Nairn, R. and Crowley, M. 1998 *Wild Wicklow: nature in the garden of Ireland*. Dublin.

Nelson, E. C. 1991 *The Burren*. Anglesea.

Nelson, E.C. 1999 *Wild plants of the Burren and Aran Islands*. Cork.

Norton, T. A. (ed) 1985 *Provisional atlas for the marine algae of Britain and Ireland*. Huntingdon.

Nunn, J. 1994 'The marine mollusca of Ireland 1. Strangford Lough, co. Down', *Bulletin of the Irish Biogeographical Society* **17**, pp. 23–214.

O'Carroll, N. 1995 'Forestry in the Republic of Ireland — an industry in transition' in Pilcher and Mac an tSaoir 1995, pp. 51–8.

O'Connell, J. W. and Korff, A. 1991 *The book of the Burren*. Galway.

O'Connell, M. 1994 *Connemara: vegetation and land use since the last Ice Age*. Dublin.

O'Connell, C. A. and Doyle, G. J. 1990 'Local vegetation history of a pine woodland on Clonfinnane bog, co. Tipperary' in Doyle 1990, pp. 23–40.

O'Connell, M., Ryan, J. B. and MacGowran, B. A. 1980 'Wetland communities in Ireland: a phytosociological review' in P. D. Moore (ed) *European mires* (London).

Ó Críodáin, C. 1994 'Combining the Habitats Directive with EU agri-environmental objectives in Ireland' in M. Maloney (ed) *Agriculture and the environment* (Dublin), pp. 43–52.

O'Donovan, G. 1987 'An ecosystem study of grasslands in the Burren National Park, co. Clare', doctoral dissertation, TCD.

Keeffe, C. 1986 *The history of Glenveigh*. Dublin.

O'Kelly, M. J. 1989 *Early Ireland: an introduction to Irish prehistory*. Cambridge.

O'Regan, T. (ed) 1995 *Irish landscape forum*. Cork.

O'Reilly, H. 1955 'Survey of the Gearagh, an area of wet woodland on the River Lee, near Macroom co. Cork', *Irish Naturalists' Journal* **11**, pp. 279–86.

O'Sullivan, A. M. 1965 'A phytosociological survey of Irish lowland meadows and pastures', doctoral dissertation, UCD.

O'Sullivan, W. M. 1996 'Otter conservation: factors affecting survival, with particular reference to drainage and pollution within an Irish river system' in Reynolds 1996, pp. 117-33.

Perring, F. H. and Walters, S. M. 1976 *Atlas of the British flora*. Wakefield.

Pilcher, J. R. and Mac an tSaoir, S. S. (eds) 1995 *Woods, trees and forests in Ireland*. Dublin.

Praeger, R. L. L. 1934 *The botanist in Ireland*. Dublin.

Praeger, R. L. L. 1939 *The way that I went*. Dublin.

Praeger, R. L. L. 1950 *The natural history of Ireland*. London.

Quammen, D. 1996 *The song of the Dodo*. Pimlico.

Quinn, A. 1977 *Sand dunes: formation, erosion and management*. Dublin.

Quirke, B. (ed) *A place to treasure: Killarney National Park*. Cork.

Rackham, O. 1995 'Looking for ancient woodland in Ireland' in Pilcher and Mac an tSaoir 1995.

Reynolds, J. D. 1996 *The conservation of aquatic systems*. Dublin.

Robinson, T. 1977 *The map of the Burren*. Galway.

Robinson, T. 1990 *Connemara Part 1: Introduction and gazetteer; Part 2: a one-inch map*. Roundstone.

Rogan, E. and Berrow, S. 1995 'Aspects of the biology of common dolphins *Delphinus delphis* from Irish waters', *Biology and Environment* **95 B**, pp. 123–68.

Ross, H. C. G. 1984 *Catalogue of the land and freshwater mollusca of the British Isles in the Ulster Museum*. Belfast.

Scannell, M. J. P. and Synnott, D. M. 1987 *Census catalogue of the flora of Ireland*. Dublin.

Schouten, M. G. C. 1984 *Some aspects of the ecogeographical gradient in the Irish ombrotrophic bogs*, Proceedings of the 7th International Peat Congress, Irish National Peat Committee (Dublin), pp. 414–32.

Sheehy-Skeffington, M. and Wyse-Jackson, P. 1984 *The flora of inner Dublin*. Dublin.

Smal, C. 1995 *The badger and habitat survey of Ireland*. Dublin.

Summers, C. F., Warner, P. J., Nairn, R. G. W., Curry, M. G. and Flynn, J. 1980 'An assessment of the status of the common seal *Phoca vitulina vitulina* in Ireland', *Biological Conservation* **1**, pp. 115–23.

Stewart, N. F. and Church, J. M. (in preparation) *Red Data books of Britain and Ireland. Bryophytes*. Peterborough.

Sweeney, J. (ed) 1997 *Global change and the Irish environment*. Dublin.

Telford, M. B. 1977 'Glenveigh National Park: the past and present vegetation', doctoral dissertation, TCD.

The National Trust 1996 *Visitor's handbook*. London.

Thorn, R. H. 1986 'Factors affecting the leaching of nitrate to groundwater in the Republic of Ireland' *Irish Geography*, **19**, pp. 23–32.

Tubridy, M. (ed) 1984 *Creation and management of a heritage zone at Clonmacnoise, co. Offaly, Ireland*. Dublin.

Waddell, J., O'Connell J. W. and Korff, A. 1994 *The book of Aran*. Galway.

Waldren, S., Martin, J., Curtis T. G. F. and O'Sullivan, A. (in press) 'Genebanks and biodiversity conservation: the Irish threatened plant genebank project' in B. S. Rushton (ed) *Biodiversity: the Irish dimension* (Dublin).

Waldren, S. and Scally L. 1993 'Ecological factors controlling the distribution of *Saxifraga spathularis* and *S. hirsuta* in Ireland' in M. J. Costello and K. S. Kelly (eds) *Biogeography of Ireland: past present and future* (Dublin), pp. 45–56.

Webb, D. A. 1943 *A new Irish flora*. Dundalk.

Webb, D. A. and Scannell, M. J. P. 1983 *Flora of Connemara and the Burren*. Cambridge.

Whilde, A. 1993 *Threatened mammals, birds, amphibians and fish in Ireland. Irish Red Data book 2: vertebrates*. Belfast.

Whilde, A. 1994 *The natural history of Connemara*. London.

White, J. (ed) 1982 *Studies in Irish vegetation*. Dublin.

Wicklow Mountains National Park Study 1997, Dublin.

Wildlife Service 1990 *Report for 1990*. Dublin.

Wilson, E. O. 1992 *The diversity of life*. Harmondsworth.

Wilson, J. and Lawlor, I. 1996 'Irish marine habitats' in Reynolds 1996, pp. 47–55.

Wood, D. B. and Gibson, C. E. 1973 'Eutrophication and Lough Neagh', *Water Research* **7**, pp. 173–87.

Wyse Jackson, P. 1984 'Irish rare plant conservation in the Trinity College Botanic Gardens, Dublin' in D. W. Jeffrey (ed) *Nature conservation in Ireland, progress and problems* (Dublin), pp. 95–7.

Young, R. 1976 '*Tanymastix stagnalis* (L.) in co. Galway, new to Britain and Ireland', *Proceedings of the Royal Irish Academy* **76 B**, pp. 369–78.

The Archaeological Landscape

GABRIEL COONEY, TOM CONDIT AND EMMET BYRNES

Economic success and development in Ireland in recent years have added significantly to the pressure on the archaeological resource. Unchecked, this pressure often can result in the destruction of archaeological sites and a consequent loss of important historical and cultural information (Cooney 1991, 1995; Woodman 1992). Changing patterns of land use and the growth and redistribution of population and settlement, coupled with the growing efficiency and altered methods of agriculture and forestry, encouraged by both European Union and state policy and finance, have considerably influenced the nature of landscape transformation (Aalen *et al.* 1997). At the same time there has been a major shift in the philosophy underlying archaeological legislation and heritage management, nationally and internationally, towards a recognition of the necessity of adopting a landscape approach rather than a concentration on individual sites as the basis for protecting and managing the archaeological resource. This forms part of a wider awareness and concern about landscape generally (Aalen 1996). In this regard one can compare the original European Convention on the Protection of the Archaeological Heritage (1969), with its emphasis on sites and excavations, with the revised 1992 Valetta Convention, which the Irish government ratified in 1996, where the stress is now placed on the archaeological heritage in its broadest context.

Since the 1970s the archaeological infrastructure of the state, both the public service and regulatory bodies (the National Monuments and Historic Properties Service of Dúchas, the Heritage Service and the National Museum of Ireland, each within the Department of Arts, Heritage, Gaeltacht and the Islands), and private consultancy firms, have had to move very quickly to keep up with the pace of development. The richness of the archaeological resource, the completion of a basic national archaeological inventory and its incorporation into the planning process have meant that developers and development agencies are involved with archaeological matters on a regular basis. One illustration of this is the growth in the number of excavation licences issued per year, from fewer than 150 in the early 1990s to over 400 in 1996 (Bennett 1997) and to over 500 in 1997. On the one hand this has led to an unprecedented growth in the archaeological consulting or contract industry, but on the other to equally unprecedented pressure on the under-staffed state authorities. It is the reaction to and mitigation of the impact on archaeological remains that are at the core of the practice of archaeological heritage management at present. There are of course other, perhaps less obvious, pressures on the archaeological resource, such as the presentation of archaeological sites and monuments to the public as part of our tourist infrastructure. The latter can raise their own problems which have to be overcome to avoid permanent damage to archaeological remains and to ensure a degree of sustainability in their use as a heritage attraction (see discussion in McManus 1997).

Knowledge of archaeological landscapes and their conservation, protection and presentation should be among the principal concerns of the cultural heritage manager (Aalen *et al.* 1997). If we really want to grapple with the scale and pace of change which is taking place across the Irish landscape, then, by definition, it is necessary to adopt and utilize a landscape perspective. Accordingly in this chapter an outline of the nature and significance of the archaeological resource is provided. The range and types of impact taking place throughout the country are discussed. Attention is drawn to some of the procedures, problems and features of cultural heritage management with respect to Ireland's archaeological landscapes. A summary background to the legislation and the statutory bodies involved is provided. Finally we suggest how a better approach to the recording, management and preservation of these landscapes may be achieved to enhance the welfare of this general area.

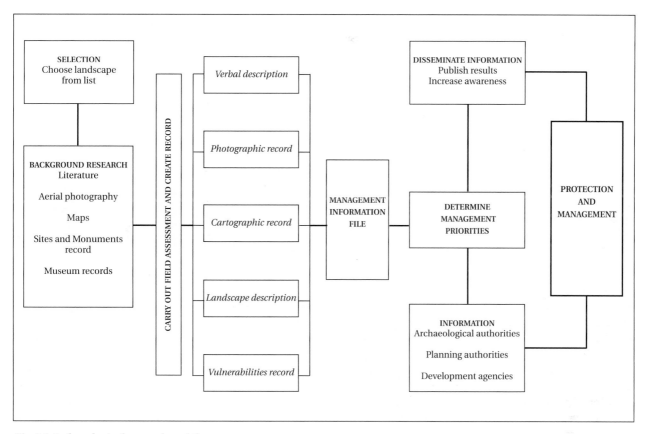

Fig. 2.1 Archaeological research and the management process.

THE SIGNIFICANCE OF THE ARCHAEOLOGICAL RESOURCE

Recognition of the range and variability of the archaeological resource is important to any appreciation of the significance of this resource (**Fig. 2.1**). Archaeology is a significant component of our cultural heritage and is inter-linked with other topics which fall under the term 'heritage', such as history, folklore, mythology and place-name studies. Archaeology is becoming an increasingly valuable resource through growing public interest, its educational value and the recognition that it is a major element in the attractiveness of Ireland as a tourist destination, since many visitors are drawn here having read or seen information on Ireland's archaeological riches. Furthermore, this archaeological resource can be utilized to spread tourism more evenly throughout the country. The archaeological aspect of heritage is a vital ingredient in the combined characteristics which give our landscape its distinctive appearance and flavour.

The results of the study of Ireland's archaeological heritage have much to offer our educational system. There is a great deal to be learned about the past through research into the physical evidence of archaeological remains, reading the past from the landscape. We have perhaps tended to underplay this evidence in favour of exploring our culture in historical, text-based terms. It is of fundamental importance to remember that archaeology offers a range of insights into daily life in the historic

period itself, from AD 500 on (see for example Hurley *et al.* 1997). It is our only source of evidence for human settlement for the seven thousand years of Irish pre-history, beginning before 7000 BC (Cooney and Grogan 1994; Waddell 1998). There is also a dynamic quality to the archaeological record. New sites and information are constantly coming to light, new methodologies and theoretical perspectives are regularly challenging traditional interpretations of the past (for example O'Conor 1998; O'Sullivan 1998).

However, in an environment where commercial and infrastructural projects are rapidly on the increase, the archaeological resource, the sites and monuments themselves, are under sustained development pressure, both directly from the threat of destruction and also from encroachment on their environs. While work is still ongoing to calculate accurately the nature and quantity of recent destruction of monuments throughout the Irish landscape, regional and local statistics suggest it has been very substantial (Aalen 1985; O'Sullivan *et al.* 1999). It has been estimated that between 30–60% of monuments have been removed since the mid-nineteenth century and particularly in the last thirty years (Barry 1979; Cooney 1983; Cabot 1985). The irreplaceable nature of sites and their vulnerability to partial or total levelling make the recording and preservation of the archaeological inheritance a serious

Fig 2.2 Prehistoric court cairn at Creevykeel, county Sligo.

management issue.

Many problems which arise in the management of this resource are related to the range of perceptions of what constitutes the archaeological patrimony. Often the parties involved in development projects are unfamiliar with the legislation and practices which are at issue in the conservation and protection of archaeological heritage. Private developers often fear the involvement of archaeologists because they see archaeology as a prohibitive and conservation-based discipline. This perception is further compounded by the view that archaeological considerations introduce significant time delays and costs. There is often very little appreciation of the non-renewable nature of the archaeological heritage or the public relations and economic benefit to be gained from treating it with respect. Many have also formed the opinion that archaeology is purely about excavation of subsurface remains. In this regard the archaeological profession has not helped in changing attitudes towards the resource, with our emphasis on startling new finds from excavations rather than on trying to inform the public of the value of archaeology as a means of understanding processes and patterns in the past in a holistic way. The sustainability of our archaeological heritage demands that we pay greater attention to the benefits of preservation of sites and monuments *in situ* in the landscape.

THE NATURE OF THE IRISH ARCHAEOLOGICAL RESOURCE

To appreciate more fully the range of views outlined above it is necessary to outline the essential features of the archaeological heritage of Ireland. The emphasis in this chapter is on the rural landscape, although of course there is also a very rich urban archaeological record (see for example Bradley 1995; Thomas 1992). The focus is chiefly on sites in the landscape. The wealth of the portable archaeological record in the collections of the National Museum of Ireland and other centres is already well documented (Ryan 1991).

The whole island of Ireland can be treated as an archaeological landscape, one that has been lived in for more than nine thousand years, containing the remains of the activities and lives of previous generations (Aalen *et al.* 1997; Mitchell and Ryan 1997). It is the differential visibility of these remains that makes the Irish landscape such a rich and historical 'document'. It is recognized internationally that because the character of landscape change in Ireland has until recently been gradual and piecemeal, there has been a higher rate of survival of visible archaeological sites than in other west-European countries. There is a wide variety of types of archaeological remains in the landscape, which in turn require various approaches for their effective management. As many as 150,000 archaeological sites are listed on the Sites and Monuments Record in the Irish Republic alone

(Condit 1991). These range from the temporary camps of mesolithic foragers (the first Irish settlers, from around 7000 BC) indicated by scatters of stone tools, to the industrial archaeological complexes of buildings and structures of the nineteenth century.

Archaeological sites occur in almost every type of terrain: upland, lowland, lacustrine, estuarine or coastal areas, agricultural land, marginal land, raised bogs and blanket bogs. Where archaeological remains do survive above ground and are easily visible in the landscape, their condition and nature can vary quite significantly. Some were deliberately constructed in antiquity as monuments with ceremonial or religious significance, while others may be the ancient remains of settlement or domestic activity (see NMHPS 1991; Stout and Keane 1996).

CONDITIONS OF SURVIVAL OF ARCHAEOLOGICAL SITES

In terms of the state of preservation of archaeological sites Darvill (1987, 6; Darvill *et al.* 1987) has defined three categories of condition: upstanding buildings or structures, earthworks and subsurface or buried remains. These important categories will now be described in some detail.

Upstanding structures

Upstanding remains are the most obvious in the public eye because of their high visibility and distinctive characteristics. Among the most impressive structures of this type are the megalithic monuments of the Neolithic period and the beginning of the Bronze Age (4000–2000 BC), such as Newgrange in the Brú na Bóinne complex,

county Meath, or the range of early Christian and medieval ecclesiastical sites (AD 500–1600), like the Rock of Cashel ecclesiastical complex, county Tipperary. A third broad category consists of the wealth of stone fortifications from the early Christian period onwards, including medieval castles (**Figs 2.2** & **2.3**). Because of their obvious significance, many such monuments are deemed to be of national and international stature. However, only a relatively small percentage of them are actually in state ownership or guardianship (Cooney 1991), and not all of these are currently presented to the public.

Earthwork monuments

There are many types of earthwork monuments throughout the Irish countryside (**Fig 2.4**). They have a very wide chronological span, from the prehistoric round burial barrows, which can date from the Neolithic to the Iron Age (4000 BC to AD 500), to the ubiquitous ringforts of the early Christian period (AD 500–1200) to the remains of later medieval settlements (AD 1200–1600). There is also a distinction to be made between those originally constructed as earthwork monuments and sites where the earthworks may be all that are left of the foundations of what were once more impressive stone-built structures, for example in the case of degraded small medieval castles or tower houses.

Subsurface remains

Some archaeological sites may have no surface traces, for example the underground refuges of the early Christian period (AD 500–1200) known as souterrains. Other sites

Fig. 2.3 Early Christian monastic enclosure on Inismurray island, county Sligo.

Fig. 2.4 Mound enclosed by crop marks of four concentric ditches: part of a larger complex of crop marks at Fenniscourt, county Carlow.

have been degraded over the centuries, either naturally or by the human hand (through ploughing or other agricultural activity for example), and may lie beneath the present ground surface. In other instances it is change in environmental conditions that has both buried and preserved the archaeological record. For instance, in the anaerobic conditions of peat bogs significant amounts of organic archaeological remains and artefacts can survive intact, as the case of wooden trackways illustrates, as at the large Iron Age trackway at Corlea, county Longford (Raftery 1997). Other prehistoric landscapes which existed before the growth of blanket bog peat can be preserved in their entirety, a notable example being the Neolithic field system, stretching over 12 square kilometres, at Céide Fields, county Mayo (Caulfield *et al*. 1998).

Furthermore, concentrations of archaeological finds, such as stone tools and weapons, in the ploughsoil or in riverine, lacustrine, estuarine or coastal locations can indicate the likelihood that subsurface archaeological remains are present (Cooney 1990; Green and Zvelebil 1990; Zvelebil *et al*. 1996). Sites like battlefields (de Buitléar 1998), hunting camps or gathering sites may have associated archaeological remains which will have little or no surface expression.

It follows from the above discrimination between sites with different degrees of visibility that the nature of surviving archaeological structures is quite diverse. Most planning authorities would be familiar with upstanding archaeological remains, whether earthen or stone-built. Indeed, some may be listed for preservation in county Development Plans. However, many others, particularly

the low-relief earthworks and subsurface remains, may not be as obvious or indeed visible at all. The recent compilation of the county Sites and Monuments Records on a national basis has brought to light many hitherto unknown sites, previously unrecognized even by local interest groups. Ongoing field survey is identifying further archaeological structures, for instance castles or tower houses, which may have been incorporated into more recent structures. Other sites may be obscured by vegetation or trees, while some earthwork sites may have been levelled in antiquity, to be identified today as cropmarks on aerial photographs. The urban archaeological heritage is a good example of the way in which archaeological sites have different degrees of visibility; the standing medieval structures have to be seen in the context of both the medieval topography, which may be preserved in the streetscape, and the archaeological deposits covered by later foundations, which can only be made accessible through archaeological survey and excavation.

In dealing with the appreciation and conservation of archaeological sites it is important not only to consider the site itself but also to understand the landscape context of a monument. For example, a Bronze Age (2500 –600 BC) burial monument located on the summit of a small knoll or hillock would have its context destroyed if the hill were to be substantially levelled or quarried as part of a development, even if the fabric of the monument itself were to be protected.

ARCHAEOLOGICAL LANDSCAPES AND RESEARCH METHODS

In Ireland there are locations which can be categorized as wilderness landscapes, natural landscapes or landscapes of scenic amenity, but there are also areas which can be distinguished as discrete because of the character of the archaeological remains. Here the combination of monuments and their settings or the occurrence of complexes of monuments serve as the basis of a definition of an archaeological landscape, that is an area where the scale and integrity of the archaeological features reflect significantly on the human history and land use of that locality (Darvill *et al*. 1993; Fairclough 1991; Fairclough *et al*. 1996 for contrasting approaches to the definition of archaeological landscapes in England). In defining such landscapes, the important issue of the visibility of the archaeological resource has also to be considered. Very often what may appear as 'blank' spaces between visible monuments will in fact contain archaeological sites which have been degraded to such an extent that they are no longer easily discernible.

The significance of an archaeological landscape is much more than just the location of a concentration of features and sites. It is the inter-connections between the components, whether those connections are chronological, spatial, social or functional, that provide additional information. Protecting such landscapes must involve not only their individual components but also the space between the monuments as both are fundamental to an understanding of their import and integrity. As stated above, no monument can be divorced from its setting. Once the significance of an archaeological landscape is recognized, then each such landscape has its own intrinsic value, not comparable with another even if both appear superficially similar. All archaeological landscapes should be valued and their distinctiveness and uniqueness recognized as part of the overall character of historic landscapes (Cooney *et al.* 1998). The contrast between them can highlight both the previous dynamism and the present diversity of the landscape.

Accepting that much of the archaeological heritage and some of the components of archaeological landscapes consist of low visibility or subsurface features, how do we identify such sites? There are many methods available. Traditional means of investigation include excavation, which may be used as a form of archaeological research or as mitigation when a site would otherwise be removed by a particular development. Test excavation is another method by which the suspected presence of subsurface archaeological remains may be confirmed. Such excavations may be useful in determining the original extent of an upstanding or partially surviving archaeological site.

Field survey and observation can help trace the survival of subsurface walls and ditches which may have a slight surface signature. When mapped, the surface evidence could present a recognizable pattern. Advances in survey techniques allow the detection of very slight surface features (Doody 1996). Fieldwalking can help to identify archaeological objects in the ploughsoil (Cooney 1990), examination of drainage sections in raised bogs may reveal structures within bogs (McDermott 1997), while probing in peat bogs can also assist in the location and mapping of archaeological remains deep within the bog or on the pre-bog ground level (Caulfield 1978; 1983). Archaeological aerial photography has proved to be an efficient and economical way of identifying earthworks and subsurface features which would otherwise elude identification on the ground (Condit 1997). A range of geophysical and geochemical methods are also used now in a dedicated way to identify subsurface archaeological features. The most popular geophysical techniques are resistivity and magetometry, whilst phosphate analysis has proved to be an effective geochemical technique (Clark 1996; Hamond 1983; for application at Tara, county Meath, see Newman 1997; at Rathcroghan, county Roscommon, see Waddell and Barton 1995; Fenwick *et al.* 1996). These methods may be employed for a variety of reasons. They can be used to establish the exact nature of a possible archaeological feature in a development area. They may also help establish the true extent of an already identified monument, or determine whether or not likely associated remains are present.

THE VULNERABILITY OF THE ARCHAEOLOGICAL RESOURCE

We wish here to discuss the impact of modern human activity on this non-renewable cultural resource. The most direct pressure is disturbance of the ground surface, resulting from forestry, construction, landscaping, road construction, pipeline laying or earthmoving. Indirect impacts can take a variety of forms. The erection of structures may have a visual impact on archaeological sites and landscapes. As a simple example, the siting of an electricity pylon close to a megalithic tomb can detract from an appreciation of the monument. Other archaeological sites such as Bronze Age stone circles and stone alignments can have sightlines to topographical or celestial features, and care should be taken to avoid any obstacles to such sightlines. A number of major impacts are now outlined, and it is important to remember that the significance of the impact also depends on the nature of the archaeological site or landscape involved.

AGRICULTURAL LAND USE

Given that agricultural land use impacts in a variety of ways on the archaeological resource, it may be useful to try to identify the major elements within this broad category. It should be noted that the Rural Environment Protection Scheme offers an important mechanism that actively encourages conservation of archaeological features within planned agricultural land use (O'Sullivan 1996).

In areas of agricultural land where tillage is undertaken many sites are subjected to gradual erosion because of ploughing. Field fence removal threatens not only the historic pattern of field boundaries but also monuments close to or incorporated in such boundaries. It also creates the potential for further damage due to more intensive farming. When fields are in pasture some sites and monuments can be vulnerable to erosion from livestock, especially in wet conditions and with high stocking rates. Reclamation or drainage schemes have the potential to impact directly on certain types of archaeological sites or features, in particular wetland sites. Interference with the qualities of the soil matrix, such as soil hydrology or the presence of peat, conducive to the preservation of organic archaeological features, may lead to the dessication of the organic remains.

IMPACTS FROM FORESTRY

Because of the rapid expansion of forestry in recent years, the figure for land with forest cover is currently 8%, and it is government policy to raise this to 17% by 2035 AD. The expansion has been due both to private investment in a favourable EU grant-aided environment and the activities of Coillte, the Irish Forestry Board, now a private limited company run on a commercial basis. While guidelines on forestry and archaeology have been issued by the Forest Service, Department of the Marine and Natural Resources, and there is co-operation between Dúchas, Coillte and the Forest Service with a monitoring scheme in place to check the impact of new afforestation projects, this system is office-based and appears to be inadequate (Cooney 1995; Johnson 1998). In reality the forestry industry is largely self-regulated. To compound the problem, most forestry activities are exempt from the planning control process. Numerous visible archaeological sites and monuments have had trees planted on or near them. Such sites may suffer an impact either from the felling of these trees when they reach maturity or from replanting in the next forestry cycle. Furthermore it is probable that significant numbers of previously unrecognized archaeological remains exist in mature plantations. These could be disturbed or destroyed during any future tree felling.

ROAD CONSTRUCTION
The actual and potential effects of roadway developments are significant because of the nature of their construction, particularly the length and scale of the linear transect of the landscape which they traverse. This leads to multiple archaeological impacts and furthermore increases the likelihood of encountering previously unidentifiable remains.

PEAT EXTRACTION
Bog development and peat production pose an especially serious problem in terms of the protection and management of the wetland archaeological heritage. This is dominated by trackways but also includes a range of other site types. It has been calculated that the original extent of raised bogs in Ireland was approximately 310,000 ha, and that under 20,000 ha remains intact. The bulk of the remainder has been lost to peat extraction. There is increasing co-operation between Bord na Móna, The Irish Peat Board, and Dúchas to mitigate these impacts, and the Irish Archaeological Wetland Unit (IAWU) has been established to undertake a systematic survey of the archaeology of the midland raised bogs (see Moloney 1994; McDermott 1997). It has been suggested that there is an overall total of 10,000 sites in the midland raised bogs.

IDENTIFICATION AND MITIGATION OF IMPACTS
Recognizing then that there is a range of land uses which can damage the resource and which have to be examined on a case by case basis, how does the archaeologist engaged in assessing the impact of a development on an archaeological site or landscape (Condit 1994) actually go about identifying that impact?

PRE-DEVELOPMENT
It is recommended that in any proposed development or planning application the chosen development area should be checked against the relevant Sites and Monuments Records (SMRs) constraint documents issued by the Office of Public Works. These constraint maps have been re-issued in recent times as the Record of Monuments and Places in order to fulfil the terms of Section 12 of the 1994 Amendment to the *National Monuments Acts*. The constraint maps of the SMRs are best understood as baseline documents which catalogue readily identifiable archaeological sites. While the list which accompanies the constraint documents provides a basic classification term for each site, it does not evaluate the site's significance. Different types of archaeological site require individually designed mitigation proposals. In the case of any developments in a historic town or village, the Urban Archaeological Surveys should also be consulted. Other valuable sources of information are the archive of information on finds and findspots in the National Museum of Ireland and local museums, and the available aerial photographic coverage (both vertical and oblique) of the area.

If the development is subject to an Environmental Impact Statement, the scoping process will, in most cases, identify whether or not there is likely to be an archaeological impact arising from any proposed development. In the event of a potential impact, the developer has to be made aware of the likely constraints and mitigation measures which may be required or enforced should the planning application proceed. The onus should be seen to be on the archaeologist to state explicitly what mitigation is necessary. While Dúchas will enforce and revise mitigation proposals, the ideal Environmental Impact Assessment process should in the first instance make developers self-regulating.

For development proposals where archaeological sites are not indicated on SMRs, careful scrutiny of the following points will assist in predicting likely significant impacts:

• Findspots of objects of archaeological interest can be a strong indication of the presence of subsurface archaeological remains nearby. Such findspots are not necessarily shown on existing archaeological constraint documents.

• The proximity of archaeological sites and monuments to a proposed development can have implications for the archaeological potential of the chosen development site.

• The larger the scale of the development (areal or linear) the greater the likelihood that previously unrecognized sites or sites with no surface indications could be encountered. For example, in recent gas pipeline and motorway developments numerous archaeological sites were identified and dealt with during construction phases (Cleary *et al.* 1987; Gowen 1988).

• The location of a particular development can also be an indication that an archaeological response may be required. For example, hilltop or upland locations are likely situations for the survival of previously unrecognized archaeological remains. Interference with fording points on rivers could disturb archaeological artefacts which may have been deposited deliberately or accidentally at such places, as happened with material in the River Boyne related to the Battle of the Boyne in 1690 (Gregory 1995).

• Tradition or place-name evidence at a chosen development can also indicate the possibility of encountering subsurface archaeological material in the course of development.

PHASES OF DEVELOPMENT
Archaeological sites can be affected at all stages of a development: at pre-construction testing on sites, during construction and during post-construction phases involving landscaping. Any ancillary works connected with the development which may occur off-site could also have an additional impact. Such ancillary or related developments should be scrutinized closely. Care must also be taken to watch out for indirect or secondary impacts. For example, dewatering associated with drainage could have a significant effect on the preservation of wetland archaeological sites, far beyond the boundaries of the actual development. The draining of lakes, for instance, could expose lacustrine archaeological sites, like *crannógs*, causing them to decompose and thus be destroyed.

What are the options available to the archaeologist in seeking to mitigate the impacts of a development on the archaeological resource?

AVOIDANCE/PRESERVATION
The most simple method of mitigation is to avoid the archaeological site or sites in question and to exclude them from development. If this is the recommended course of action care should be taken to ensure that the site is physically protected, principally to avoid accidental damage. This can be accomplished by the erection of light fencing around the designated area, including a significant buffer zone surrounding the monument itself, and the protection of the area of the monument's setting, if appropriate.

If avoidance of the site or monument is not practical, the status of the monument, its national, regional or local significance, should be assessed. It is possible that even at a late stage of the planning application process some monuments may be adjudged by the archaeological authorities to be so significant that a preservation order can be appropriate. This would mean that the monument would be protected and excluded from development under the *National Monuments Act*. Thus the plans for the development would have to be adjusted.

EXCAVATION
If it is planned that a site is to be removed or levelled, wholly or partially, as part of a development, an archaeological excavation should be the stated method of mitigation. Such archaeological excavation requires a licence from Dúchas and the National Museum of Ireland. It is a requirement that excavations be carried out by suitably qualified professional archaeologists. In many ways archaeological excavation can be a considerable logistical exercise, and both the developer and the planning authorities should be aware of the necessary timescales, the likely number of personnel involved, the extent of finance needed to cover the excavation itself, the conservation of artefacts recovered and the production of the excavation report. The developer should be fully informed that, depending on the nature of the archaeological remains uncovered during excavations, further advice from the regulatory archaeological authorities may result in additional work being recommended.

MONITORING
In the case of large-scale developments or areas which are judged to have a high archaeological potential, monitoring of construction work by suitably qualified personnel may be the appropriate method of mitigation. Again, the planning authority and the developer should be notified that archaeological excavation may be necessary in case any unpredicted remains are identified in the course of construction. The developer should be prepared to carry out such work and must ensure that sufficient time and funds are available to effect any appropriate mitigation.

LEGISLATION AND POLICY BACKGROUND
We have outlined above the nature of the archaeological resource, its vulnerability and how we can identify the scale and extent of potential impact on individual sites and landscapes. This is the process by which the basic data needed to inform decisions about the management of the archaeological heritage are gathered. The core legislation which protects the archaeological heritage and informs the management process may be found in the *National Monuments Acts* 1930–94, the principal act

was enacted in 1930 with amendments in 1954, 1987 and 1994. The legislation effecting Northern Ireland has been discussed by Hamlin (Hamlin 1997). In summary, the acts empower the Minister for Arts, Heritage, Gaeltacht and the Islands to protect both archaeological sites in the landscape and also portable archaeological objects. With regard to archaeological sites the 1994 (*Amendment*) *Act* provides for the maintenance of the Record of Monuments and Places which forms the foundation of the list of all historic monuments, namely all built structures which predate AD 1700. It restricts the activities of landowners and their agents in relation to archaeological monuments (see Sweetman this volume). There is a provision in the 1987 act to register 'archaeological areas', but the wording suggests that such an archaeological area is subject to less protection than that afforded to historic monuments. Under Section 1 archaeological areas are defined as 'areas which the Minister considers to be of archaeological importance but not including the area of an historic monument entered in the Register' of Historic Monuments (Clark 1987). Where there are complexes of related monuments, the concept of an archaeological area which was put forward by the Carrowmore Supreme Court judgement of 1989 should be taken into account. This judgement not only allowed for the protection of the megalithic tombs in the Carrowmore cemetery, near Sligo town, but also stipulated that there should be a 'fallow' area around the tombs.

, The *Planning Acts* 1963–93 also make reference to the protection of archaeological sites and monuments in the planning and development process in local authority areas. Further legislation which makes reference to the protection of archaeological heritage is the European Directive on Environmental Impact Assessment which has since become part of the *Planning Acts*. Under this Directive, Environmental Impact Statements are required to assess the effects of certain types of development and those which are over specified thresholds.

More recently under the *Heritage Act* 1995 the Heritage Council was established to advise the Minister for Arts, Heritage, Gaeltacht and the Islands on matters affecting the nation's heritage. The Council has a wide brief for statutory involvement in the identification, protection and preservation of the national heritage. Included in the definition of archaeology in the *Heritage Act* 1995 is the term 'landscape', defined as including 'areas, sites, vistas and features of significant scenic, archaeological, geological, historical, ecological, or other scientific interest'.

There are also a number of European conventions which bind signatories to the care of archaeological heritage. A general feature of the international legislation, both binding and non-binding, is a recognition of the importance of the identification and protection of archaeological areas or landscapes. The convention presented in Valetta, Malta in 1992 (The European Convention on the Protection of the Archaeological Heritage) and subsequently ratified in Ireland in 1996, specifically refers to the value of 'archaeological reserves' or protected archaeological landscapes. It further reinforces the European concept that the archaeological heritage of any given state is of concern to all European countries and not just the state involved. The convention highlights the importance of the participation of archaeologists in the planning process to ensure well-balanced strategies for the protection, conservation and enhancement of sites and landscapes.

In the management of the archaeological heritage by the regulatory bodies, Dúchas and the National Museum of Ireland, action is taken with due regard to legal constraints, principally those enshrined in the *National Monuments Acts* and the planning regulations outlined above. Given the known threats to archaeological remains and their fragility, steps to ensure that they are preserved are at the core of the management strategy. This strategy insists that those sites which, for whatever reason, cannot be preserved should be removed scientifically by means of archaeological excavation. There should, of course, be a recognition that certain sites, particularly those of national and international significance, should be preserved *in situ*, undisturbed, in their entirety. Integral to this approach is a recognition of the need to protect the setting, context or surroundings of both individual sites and monuments and complexes of such structures. The reconciliation of the preservation of the diversity of sites and archaeological landscapes and the development of the country's infrastructure is a difficult exercise, but management decisions should only be made following a detailed assessment and evaluation of the development impact.

CONCLUSION

The management of the archaeological resource is a complex issue. We have tried to illustrate this point with reference to a major element of that resource, namely the rich array of sites and monuments in the Irish rural landscape. For a variety of reasons, including the unprecedented pace of development but crucially because of an under-resourcing of the state service in terms of personnel and facilities, the current management of the archaeological resource is largely reactive. On the other hand, we should acknowledge the dramatic improvements that have taken place since the early 1980s, both from the point of view of the system of regulation and the growing professionalism of the archaeological consulting community (see Ferris 1998 for an interesting comparable scenario in Ontario, Canada). What is needed now is a long-term management strategy. We would suggest that one vital area in which a proactive policy can be realistically formulated is in relation to archaeological landscapes.

Acknowledging the need to promote a management strategy which treats the whole country as an archaeological landscape, we would argue that there is value in specifically identifying complexes of sites and monuments which can be designated as 'archaeological landscapes'. The central rationale for taking this approach is that it gives us a better and more realistic perception of how the landscape was created by people in the past. It should also provide identifiable local and regional *foci* for creating a greater awareness of the importance of archaeology as part of the character of the landscape. The basis for such an approach will be the compilation of a national inventory of archaeological landscapes with defined criteria and a framework for their management (Cooney *et al.* 1998).

While the legislative framework of the *National Monuments Acts* is important, it has to be recognised that the majority of archaeological landscapes are and will continue to be in private ownership (Meldon and Skehan 1996). Once defined, maintaining the character of and protecting such landscapes will pose important issues of partnership, co-operation and management between all the parties in the planning process, the land owners and the local communities. But in reality what better challenge can there be than to ensure the continuity of the past in the present, lived landscape of today and to sustain it for future generations?

Bibliography

Aalen, F. H. A. 1985 'The rural landscape: change, conservation and planning' in F. H. A. Aalen (ed) *The future of the Irish rural landscape* (Dublin), pp. 1–25.

Aalen, F. H. A. 1996 'Approaches to the study and management of the landscape' in F. H. A. Aalen (ed) *Landscape study and management* (Dublin), pp. 1–12.

Aalen, F. H. A., Whelan, K. and Stout, M. (eds) 1997 *Atlas of the Irish rural landscape*. Cork.

Barry, T. B. 1979 'The destruction of Irish archaeological monuments', *Irish Geography* **12**, pp. 111–3.

Bennett, I. (ed) 1997 *Excavations 1996*. Dublin.

Bradley, J. 1995 *Walled towns in Ireland*. Dublin.

Cabot, D. (ed) 1985 *The state of the environment*. Dublin.

Caulfield, S. 1978 'Neolithic fields: the Irish evidence' in H. C. Bowen and P. J. Fowler (eds) *Early land allotment* (Oxford), pp. 137–44.

Caulfield, S. 1983 'The Neolithic settlement of north Connaught' in T. Reeves-Smith and F. Hamond (eds) *Landscape archaeology in Ireland* (Oxford), pp. 195–215.

Caulfield, S., O'Donnell, R. G. and Mitchell, P. I. 1998 'Radiocarbon dating of a Neolithic field system at Céide Fields, county Mayo', *Radiocarbon* **40**, pp. 629–40.

Clark, A. 1996 *Seeing beneath the soil: prospecting methods in archaeology*. London.

Clark, R. 1987 'Annotations on the National Monuments (Amendment) Act 1987', *Irish Current Law Statutes Annotated* 11–5–x–87, 17, pp. 1–27.

Cleary, R. M., Hurley, M. F. and Twohig, E. A. (eds) 1987 *Archaeological excavations on the Cork-Dublin gas pipeline (1981–82)*. Cork.

Condit, T. 1991 'Archaeology' in K. Bradley, C. Skehan and G. Walsh (eds) *Environmental impact assessment: a technical approach* (Dublin), pp. 110–6.

Condit, T. 1994 'Cultural heritage' in *EIS evaluation handbook for local authorities* (Dublin), pp. 70–5.

Condit, T. 1997 *Ireland's archaeology from the air*. Dublin.

Cooney, G. 1983 'Archaeology as a resource' in F. Convery and J. Blackwell (eds) *Promise and performance: Irish environmental policies analysed* (Dublin), pp. 203–17.

Cooney, G. 1990 'Mount Oriel project: an introduction', *County Louth Archaeological and Historical Journal* **22**, pp. 125–33.

Cooney, G. 1991 'The archaeological endowment' in J. Feehan (ed) *Environment and development in Ireland* (Dublin), pp. 70–80.

Cooney, G. 1993 'Forestry and the cultural landscape: understanding the past in the present', *Irish Forestry* **50**, 1, pp. 13–20.

Cooney, G. 1995 'Towards a sustainable policy for the management and interpretation of the archaeological endowment' in F. Convery and J. Feehan (eds) *Assessing sustainability in Ireland* (Dublin), pp. 162–7.

Cooney, G. and Grogan, E. 1994 *Irish prehistory: a social perspective*. Dublin.

Cooney, G., Condit, T. and Byrnes, E. 1998 *Archaeological landscapes in Ireland: a pilot study*, prepared for the Heritage Council. Kilkenny.

Darvill, T. C. 1987 *Ancient monuments in the countryside: an archaeological management review*. London.

Darvill, T., Gerrard, C. and Startin, B. 1993 'Identifying and protecting historic landscapes', *Antiquity* **67**, pp. 563–74.

Darvill, T. C., Saunders, A. and Startin, B. 1987 'A question of national importance: approaches to the evaluation of ancient monuments for the Monuments Protection Programme in England', *Antiquity* **61**, pp. 393–408.

de Buitléar, M. 1998 'The archaeology of Irish battlefields', *Archaeology Ireland* **43**, pp. 18–22.

Doody, M. 1996 'Ballyhoura Hills project', *Discovery*

Programme Reports **4**, pp. 15–25.

Fairclough, G. 1991 *Historic landscapes*. London.

Fairclough, G., Lambrick, G. and McNab, A. (eds) 1996 *Yesterday's landscape, tomorrow's world: The English Heritage Historic Landscape Project* (Draft Document). London.

Fenwick, J., Brennan, Y. and Delaney, F. 1996 'The anatomy of a mound: geophysical images of Rathcroghan', *Archaeology Ireland* **37**, pp. 20–23.

Ferris, N. 1998 '"I don't think we are in Kansas anymore": the rise of the archaeological consulting industry in Ontario' in P. J. Smith and D. Mitchell (eds) *Bringing back the past: historical perspectives on Canadian archaeology* (Hull, Quebec), pp. 225–47.

Gowen, M. 1988 *Three Irish gas pipelines: new archaeological evidence from Munster*. Dublin.

Gregory, N. 1995 'River Boyne, Stalleen townland, county Meath: excavation report', *Co. Louth Archaeological and Historical Journal* **23**, 3, pp. 329–35.

Green, S. W. and Zvelebil, M. 1990 'The mesolithic colonisation and agricultural transition of south-east Ireland', *Proceedings of the Prehistoric Society* **56**, pp. 57–88.

Hamlin, A. 1997 'Legislation in Northern Ireland' in J. Hunter and I. Ralston (eds) *Archaeological resource managment in the UK: an introduction* (Gloucestershire), pp. 134–5.

Hamond, F. 1983 'Phosphate analysis of archaeological sediments' in T. Reeves-Smith and F. Hamond (eds) *Landscape archaeology in Ireland* (Oxford), pp. 47–80.

Hurley, M., Scully, O. M. B. and McCutcheon, S. W. J. 1997 *Late viking age and medieval Waterford, excavations* 1986–92. Waterford.

Johnson, G. 1998 *Archaeology and forestry in Ireland*. Kilkenny.

McDermott, C. 1997 'Filling in the blanks: an archaeological survey of the Lemanaghan Bogs, Co. Offaly', *Archaeology Ireland* **40**, pp. 22–5.

McIntosh, J. 1986 *The archaeologist's handbook*. London.

McManus, R. 1997 'Heritage and tourism in Ireland — an unholy alliance', *Irish Geography* **30**, pp. 90–8.

Meldon, J. and Skehan, C. 1996 *Tourism and the landscape: landscape management by consensus*. Dublin.

Mitchell, G. F. and Ryan, M., 1997 *Reading the Irish landscape*. Dublin.

Moloney, A., 1994 'The Irish Archaeological Wetland Unit: four years on', *Archaeology Ireland* **30**, pp. 18–19.

Newman, C. 1997 *Tara: an archaeological survey*. Dublin.

NMHPS 1991 *Monuments in the past*. Dublin.

O'Conor, K. D. 1998 *The archaeology of medieval rural settlement in Ireland*. Dublin.

O'Sullivan, A. 1998 *The archaeology of lake settlement in Ireland*. Dublin

O'Sullivan, M. 1996 'REPS, farming and archaeology', *Archaeology Ireland* **38**, 8.

Raftery, B. 1996 *Trackway excavations in the Mountdillon Bogs, Co. Longford 1985–91*. Dublin.

Ryan, M. (ed) 1991 *The illustrated archaeology of Ireland*. Dublin.

Stout, G. and Keane, M., 1996 *Farming and the ancient countryside*. Dublin.

Thomas, A. 1992 *The walled towns of Ireland*. Blackrock.

Waddell, J. 1998 *The prehistoric archaeology of Ireland*. Galway.

Waddell, J. and Barton, K. 1995 'Seeing beneath Rathcroghan', *Archaeology Ireland* **31**, pp. 38–41.

Woodman, P. C. 1992 'Filling in the spaces in Irish prehistory', *Antiquity* **66**, pp. 295–314.

Zvelebil, M., Macklin, M. G., Passmore, D. G. and Ramsden, P. 1996 'Alluvial archaeology in the Barrow Valley, south-east Ireland: the "Riverford" revisited', *Journal of Irish Archaeology* **7**, pp. 13–40.

Marine Archaeology

COLIN BREEN

Maritime archaeology is viewed from a landscape perspective in archaeology. It is a perspective which recognizes our island status and the importance of the sea in shaping our national, social and cultural identities. However, it is a viewpoint which is new to Irish archaeology and one which remains on the periphery of mainstream research. For many years the tendency among the historical and archaeological community has been to look inwards, both in theoretical and practical terms. The perception has been that past societies were essentially agriculture-based. Research has concentrated on inland low-lying dryland site types. Our understanding of past peoples is consequently heavily biased by established research agendas. Recent studies have shown that the maritime environment was culturally dynamic and differed both economically and socially from that of inland peoples. The sea was central to this difference. While some would argue that the sea itself is a barrier and by implication a border, this is not accepted here. The sea should be viewed rather as a facilitator, a provider of abundant resources central to survival and, more importantly, as enabling communication in the past. It is hoped that an increased awareness of the potential of the maritime cultural resource through research and management programmes over the coming years will help overturn the bias of conventional research agendas and correct existing prejudices.

However, maritime monuments pose their own management and conservation problems which cannot be dealt with by existing land management strategies, but require independent solutions. The primary challenge is the physical environment of the sites, which can be hugely dynamic but also very beautiful. It is important to realize that these monuments are an integral part of their environment and should not be divorced from it. You can not, for example, address the conservation of a shipwreck site without understanding the site's inter-reaction with the underwater biological ecosystem that its submergence has created, as well as its overall landscape context in its underwater setting. The oceanographic factors of the site need to be addressed as do the geomorphological processes which are active in its vicinity. These issues can only be resolved in an integrated multi-disciplinary manner with the participation of as many interests as possible.

NATURE OF THE RESOURCE

One of the primary considerations for heritage managers when approaching the management of our archaeological heritage is that it is seamless in nature. The resource does not stop at the coast but extends and is visible out through the inter-tidal zone and onto the seabed. Archaeological remains are present in every environment past communities were active in, and this wide spectrum of human activity has left its mark in the maritime zone. It is visible in the remains of settlement, defensive sites and communication networks as well as sites associated with the exploitation of the sea for food and fuel resources. The monuments which represent these activities, when placed in their proper setting, can be used to define and interpret 'maritime cultural landscapes'. Many settlements around the coast have a specific maritime function, whether they be small fishing villages or communities which have grown up around port or ferry sites. These settlements have developed their own unique identity because of the nature of the activity that the people are involved in. Quay-side warehouses and buildings, fishermen's cottages and the material remains of these people all reflect this identity. Monuments associated with marine communications are immediately identifiable, whether they include the remains of lighthouses, navigational aids, boats and ships as evidenced through wrecks, hulks and floating remains, or the waterfront structures that serviced them. Sites such as harbours, quays, jetties and landing places may have been in use for hundreds of years and have

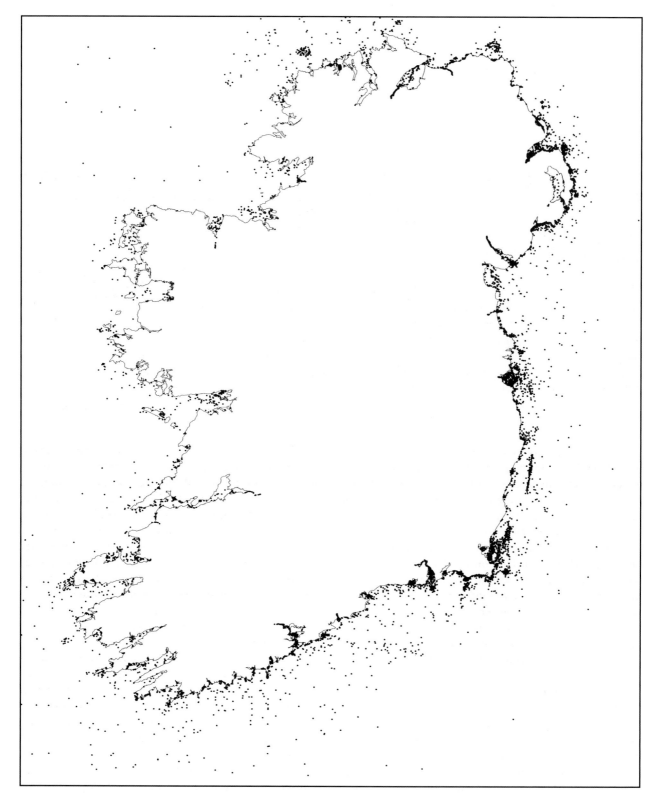

Fig. 3.1 A GIS-generated distribution map of historic wreck sites in Ireland.

evolved and developed in many different ways over that time. However, while their physical appearance might have altered, their actual position rarely does. The sea and coastline of any given region govern where craft can land, and this does not change too often.

Defence of the coast has always been a priority. Throughout the ages various forces or groups of people have posed a threat to the security of coastal peoples.

30

Fig. 3.2 An early photograph dating to ca. *1885 of the wreck of a coal schooner undergoing salvage off the port of Strangford, county Down.*

Monuments such as signal and Martello towers, coast-guard establishments, promontory forts, booms and breakwaters testify to the efforts taken to counter these threats. Sea-walls and reclamation banks point to coastal defences built against the natural erosive processes which constantly threaten our coastline.

The sea has always been an abundant provider of resources, whether for food or fuel. Fish traps and weirs occur in estuaries and the inter-tidal zone while shell middens are found right around our coastline. Kelp kilns and grids are now all that remain of the once extensive kelp industry which was an important enterprise in the eighteenth and nineteenth centuries. There is also extensive evidence around the coast for past environmental and coastal change. Palaeo-environmental deposits have been found in many estuaries around the coast. Submerged peats have been found in 10 m of water off west Cork and Kerry while the stumps of trees from old woodlands may be seen in many inter-tidal zones. These deposits can contain valuable environmental and indeed cultural material fundamental to our understanding of environmental history.

THE DEVELOPMENT OF RESEARCH IN IRELAND

The underwater world became widely accessible to the scientist and sports-person for the first time with the development of SCUBA (Self-Contained Underwater Breathing Apparatus) during World War II. The late 1950s and 1960s saw a huge upsurge in the popularity of diving and the subsequent development of archaeology under-water. Not surprisingly, it was the warm clear waters of the Mediterranean and the Caribbean which saw the most activity, and it was in these regions that the techniques of underwater work evolved. The first under-water investigations in Ireland took place on three 1588 Spanish Armada wrecks off the north and west coast in the late 1960s and early 1970s. The investigation and subsequent salvage of a number of these wrecks highlighted the wealth of artefactual remains these sites contained. However, while the public were captivated by the results of these projects, the archaeological community were slower to respond. Maritime archae-ology was perceived as being an expensive activity that should not take resources away from land archaeology. There was also a feeling among a number of Irish archae-ologists that these sites were not really part of this island's heritage. They were perceived as accidental exotic curiosities that did not really warrant attention. This should now be recognized as a fundamentally flawed argument resulting from a narrow perspective. Maritime archaeology is by its very nature an interna-tional discipline. Maritime activities and traditions vary little from country to country. A medieval ship wrecked on our shores is likely to be carrying goods and commodities familiar throughout north-west Europe, while the vessel itself would have been of a type used

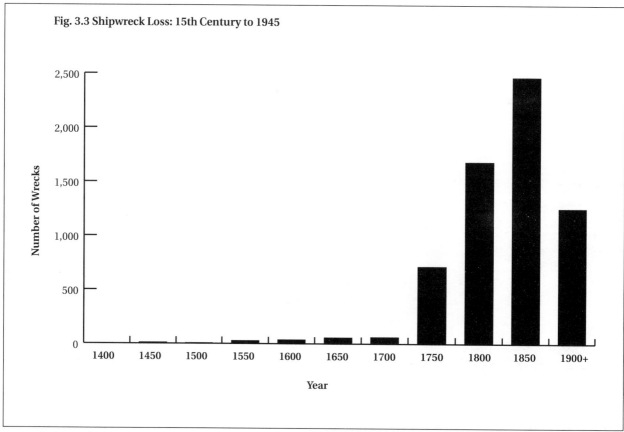

Fig. 3.3 Shipwreck Loss: 15th Century to 1945

around these shores by Irish mariners. The interpretation of such sites consequently requires a global rather than an insular perspective.

It was not until the mid-1980s that archaeologists north and south began to become actively involved in research in the underwater environment. Much of this was concentrated on the survey of *crannóg* sites on the inland lakes. Victor Buckley from the Archaeological Survey of Ireland (ASI) and Eamonn Kelly from the National Museum of Ireland (NMI) became heavily involved in survey work on these underwater sites with some outstanding results and finds, including the Lough Kinale book shrine. These archaeologists also collaborated on the Crannog Archaeology Project (CAP), a research project carried out between the state institutions in the Republic and Cornell University in the US. Eamon Kelly was later to carry out a number of underwater excavations at fording points in advance of OPW dredging operations on a number of midland rivers. The NMI also participated in and offered advice to a number of marine projects. Nessa O'Connor, a trained diver on the Museum staff, assisted in surveys of a number of wrecks off the coast. By the late 1980s a much greater awareness of archaeology underwater was apparent, especially among the diving community. Comhairle Faoi Thoinn (CFT), the Irish Underwater Council, the governing body for sports diving in the Republic, established a sub-committee on underwater archaeology. This

came at a time when green and environmental issues were coming to the fore and when the need for the conservation and protection of the environment was being realized. Archaeological remains were viewed as an integral part of the underwater environment and the protection of these cultural remains was the primary focus of the sub-committee. The establishment of Irish Underwater Archaeology Research Team (IUART) developed out of the amalgamation of this sub-committee and the underwater heritage sub-committee of the Maritime Institute, a voluntary body which runs the National Maritime Museum in Dún Laoghaire, county Dublin, and which is dedicated to the advancement of marine heritage research in Ireland. The new organization was initially led by a group of divers and archaeologists who were interested in taking the subject further. IUART's primary aim is to promote awareness of the underwater archaeological resource through a comprehensive training programme, conferences and research projects. It is an all-Ireland organization with representatives from the state institutions with responsibility for archaeology sitting on its committee. The organization is purely voluntary and membership is almost exclusively drawn from sports divers and remains constant at *ca.* 100. The Department of the Environment (Northern Ireland) (DOE NI) initially gave an annual grant to the body to aid its development while Dúchas continues to part-fund small projects the

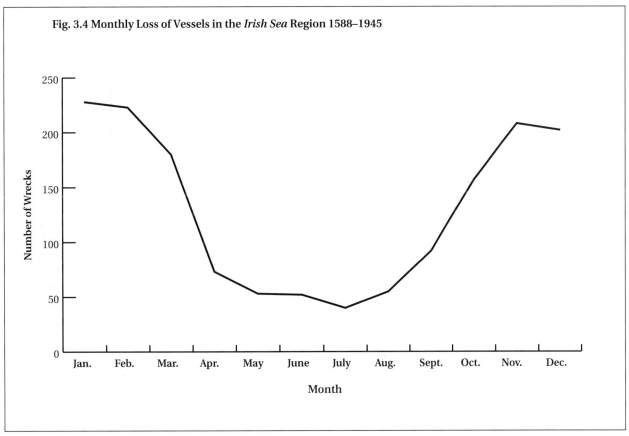

Fig. 3.4 Monthly Loss of Vessels in the *Irish Sea* Region 1588–1945

group undertakes. Its primary source of funding is membership and course fees.

Fundamental to the successful management of the archaeological resource is an understanding of the nature and extent of that resource. Central to this has been the establishment, both north and south, of Maritime Sites and Monuments Records (SMRs). County SMRs of dryland sites have been in progress on this island since the 1960s. The range of these surveys was defined by the research interests of archaeologists at that time. While they slowly evolved to take account of all archaeological sites, they failed to record inter-tidal or sub-tidal sites. This was not a deliberate policy of exclusion but reflected the lack of awareness of the potential extent of the submerged resource. It is only in recent years through the work of individual researchers that the richness of the marine environment has been highlighted. The state bodies have in turn recognized this potential, and have initiated survey programmes.

With the increased involvement of so-called amateurs, the professional community began to address the management of the submerged cultural resource. In 1990 the UK government published *This common inheritance*, a white paper dealing with archaeology and the environment. As a result of proposals for dealing with historic wrecks an Agency Agreement was signed with the Department of National Heritage in 1992, under which DOE NI accepted responsibility for wrecks in

Northern Ireland's waters under the *Protection of Wrecks Act* 1973. The wreck site *La Girona*, a 1588 Armada galleas, was subsequently designated under this act in 1993 and remains the only such site in the North. DOE NI also recognized the need for a detailed maritime survey to be undertaken. Since 1991 the Royal Commission for Historic Monuments in England have been developing a maritime sites index as part of the National Monuments Record (NMR). This work is undertaken by a dedicated team of marine researchers based at NMR headquarters in Swindon. The work of the NMR runs in tandem with that of the UK Archaeological Diving Unit based at the University of St Andrews in Scotland. This unit works on contract to the Department of Culture in London. It inspects, on an annual basis, protected wreck sites in UK waters as well as acting as an advisor to the government on archaeology underwater.

In September 1993 a similar initiative entitled Maritime Archaeology Project (MAP) was adopted by Environment Service: Historic Monuments and Buildings (ES:HMB), now Environment and Heritage Service (EHS), the archaeology body within DOE NI, and was based at the Institute of Irish Studies at Queen's University, Belfast (Breen 1996, 55). MAP's primary brief was to create a computerized database and paper archive of all maritime sites in Northern Ireland's coastal waters. This was essentially a desk-based exercise to assess and to quantify the nature of the submerged cultural resource in those waters. Information on sites such as wrecks, old harbours and landing places was taken from a number of documentary and cartographic sources including eighteenth- and nineteenth-century government reports and British Admiralty survey data. To date, in excess of 4,000 wreck records have been found and archived. MAP was also involved in a number of field-based research projects including the survey and excavation of a number of wreck sites and early landing places. An inter-tidal archaeological survey was also run in tandem with MAP and was concentrated initially in Strangford Lough, county Down. This survey involved the systematic walking, by a team of four archaeologists, of the mudflats and rocky foreshore that make up the Lough. The team uncovered a large number of site types, and its discoveries have changed the way researchers look at the coast of Down. MAP in the north has now moved into its second phase with a full-time maritime unit undertaking the coastal survey. A programme of marine remote sensing is also underway in co-operation with the Centre for Maritime Archaeology at the University of Ulster at Coleraine.

Inter-tidal surveys have also been undertaken on the Shannon and Fergus estuaries in the Republic. Research, directed by Aidan O'Sullivan, under the auspices of the Discovery Programme, has been ongoing in this area since 1993 (O'Sullivan 1993, 61). This research uncovered one of the most exciting archaeological landscapes yet found in Ireland with material reflecting mesolithic through to post-medieval activity. In February 1997 the National Monuments Service, within the then Department of Arts, Culture and the Gaeltacht, established a National Maritime Survey. This survey is essentially an extension of the existing land SMR. It extends the survey into the extensive inter-tidal and sub-tidal environments which surround this island. The survey is set up along the same lines as the ongoing one in the north. The first stage of the work involves an extensive desk-based exercise assessing the potential resource. A comprehensive computerized and paper-based record is being assembled which will eventually be incorporated into the National SMR Archive. All the personnel employed on the survey are archaeologists with commercial diving qualifications, and are fully equipped to carry out underwater surveys and operations.

RESOURCE THREATS

One of the major management questions relating to archaeology underwater is how stable is the resource. This is complicated by the fact that we are only now beginning research into the nature of the underwater environment as a whole and starting to analyze the natural dynamics of the sea and its geological and biological make-up. Attempting to reach an understanding of what happens to archaeology underwater is

therefore very difficult. We can begin with the premise that all sites underwater are different, that they undergo different site formation processes in radically different environments. A ship wrecked in a rocky gully on the Atlantic seaboard will obviously experience significantly different processes to a fishtrap erected upriver in a sheltered estuary on the east coast. What does seem apparent however is that sites eventually reach a state of natural equilibrium. This stabilization may range from the gradual destruction of a ship until all that remains are a number of cannon concreted to the bed-rock, as with the unidentified 1790s wreck in Derrynane harbour, county Kerry, to the submergence and environmental sealing of an early logboat in estuarine muds. However, this equilibrium is subject to an increasing number of negative impacts from both natural and human dynamics. There has been a common misconception that sites underwater are safe, unaffected by the many threats that dryland sites face from development, agricultural practices and industrial activity. It is increasingly obvious that this is not the case and that the underwater environment is also subject to a variety of similar marine-specific threats. The lack of awareness about the nature and extent of these threats is all the more serious when one considers that the archaeological resource is non-renewable and extremely fragile. Other marine resources such as fish stocks and benthic communities can be regenerated with careful management. The destruction of monuments is irreversible.

It has been the view in the past that the greatest threat faced by underwater sites is that of the treasure hunter. Treasure hunters are normally well-organized groups of divers who systematically strip sites of their valuable artefacts or, more commonly, sports divers removing objects from the seabed without realizing the damaging consequences of destroying the archaeological integrity of sites and removing objects without facilities for conservation. The perceived threat from these groups is reflected in the provisions of the various pieces of legislation including the *National Monuments (Amendment) Act* 1994 in the Republic and the *Protection of Wrecks Act* 1973 in the north. Many of the provisions deal specifically with divers and the licensing of diver activity. While it is true that treasure hunters have caused serious damage, especially on inland lacustrine sites, the true extent of which will probably never be known, there are even greater threats active in the marine environment itself.

It is recognized that fishermen can be an invaluable source of information relating to underwater sites. Most modern fishing vessels are equipped with up-to-date sonar and locational equipment which they use to chart fishing grounds. Obstructions on the seabed that could potentially snag nets and fishing gear, such as rock pinnacles, foul ground and potential wreck sites, are plotted to ensure they are avoided. This goes some way towards preserving sites on the seabed and is a good source for locating unknown sites. There are, however, a number of problems for archaeology associated with the fishing industry. Fish groups and other benthic communities are attracted by the ecosystem that a wreck provides, and colonies will thrive at these locations. This fact is well known to fishermen who will fish as close as possible to the sites. Accidents invariably happen when nets are caught in a wreck. Attempts to free the net can result in damage to the site. The practice of trawling, rather than drift-line fishing, can have a far more negative impact. Archaeological sites lying on the seabed tend to be low-lying and partially or wholly buried. It would be rare indeed to find a wreck of significant age sitting upright on the seabed. The dynamics of the marine environment surrounding this island mitigate against such an occurrence. Similarly, submerged landscapes and palaeo-deposits survive in a comparable form. Trawling can then have the effect of interfering with and dispersing sites over a large area. The impact of trawling has been likened to deep ploughing on land. Indeed parts of the Irish Sea and North Channel undergo far more trawling than most of our land.

Our cities and countryside have witnessed a huge increase in commercial development over the last few decades. The marine environment is no different. European funding has seen the erection of numerous piers and berthing facilities around the coastline. Sea defences are a common sight around fragile sections of our coast, protecting them against erosion. Many pipelines have been dug connecting Ireland to Britain and to a number of offshore installations. The electricity interconnector which was recently laid between Scotland and Antrim encountered twenty-two wrecks in its vicinity. With the concerns expressed about the effects of quarrying on land, more developers are turning to the extraction of sand and gravel from the seabed. This is already a large-scale commercial enterprise in England and is predicted to be increasingly common in Ireland. Between October 1994 and January 1995 a total of 276,788 m³ of sand was removed by a suction dredger from Long Bank off the south-east Wexford coast to replenish sand at Rosslare strand (ECOPRO 1996, 100). Long Bank is an area of high archaeological potential with 32 shipwreck losses recorded on it between the years 1600–1945, yet the impact on potential cultural remains appears to have been neglected in the initial environmental appraisal.

Dredging of our ports and harbours has been ongoing for many years. This is necessary to keep the shipping and navigation channels open, a fundamental requirement for the successful operation of any port. Most of our contemporary ports have long histories, many of which can trace their origins back to the Vikings in the ninth to eleventh centuries AD. This implies that channels, quays and wharves at these ports have been in operation for over one thousand years. This long period of usage has inevitably resulted in the deposition of a significant amount of artefactual material. Areas of known anchorage in particular attract much dumped material. This long period of historical usage has rarely been taken into account when it comes to dredging or reclamation work at these sites, and any mitigation that has taken place in recent years must be viewed as inadequate. It is argued here that a desk-top analysis through the examination of documentary and cartographic sources alone is not in itself a sufficient approach for investigating the effect a development will have underwater. These sources by their very nature are heavily biased towards the industrial era. They must be used in tandem with field survey techniques properly to investigate any possible impacts.

Dredging necessitates the dumping of large amounts of spoil at sea. While this could have the positive effect of covering sites, it may also have the opposite result. The dump spoil could potentially be made up of rock and other hard aggregates that could do damage when dropped on a site. Dump sites must be carefully chosen to mitigate against this, and what happens to spoil after it is dumped should also be carefully monitored. One must consider whether sediment mobility and current patterns in a certain area will result in dumped spoil being carried onto an archaeological site, even if not originally dumped on it.

Natural dynamics are also having an unquantifiable effect on our maritime heritage. The island of Ireland has a coastline of 6,331 kms. 3,164 kms of this are classified as being soft and susceptible to 'short-term' erosive processes, while 1,583 kms are deemed at risk (ECOPRO 1996, 109). Much of this 'soft' coastline is more likely to contain near-shore archaeological remains because of the nature of the environment. Monuments associated with inshore industries, such as tidal fisheries and kelp and salt extraction, are by their very nature located on or near tidal mudflats and in shallow water depths. These monuments, as a consequence of their location, can be more susceptible to the effects of erosion than monument types located on a 'hard' and more stable coastline. Away from the inshore area processes like current and wave action and seabed mobility can all inadvertently impact on archaeological remains. The continual re-exposure and burial of organic deposits on the seabed may encourage deterioration. Seabed faunal communities such as crustaceans can also further the destruction of a site. The burrowing of certain species of crabs and lobsters can break down a site and greatly disturb its stratigraphic make-up in much the same way as rabbits and other land burrowers destabilize an earthen mound or similar monument. Micro-organisms such as toredo and gribble are able to bore into and densely colonize timbers, undermining the structural integrity of a hull.

MANAGEMENT AND FUTURE DEVELOPMENT OF THE RESOURCE

The primary tool used by the state to protect the archaeological resource has been protective legislative measures. Two very different sets of legislation exist north and south of the border; these have been drawn up from different philosophical viewpoints and implemented on a different theoretical basis. The Republic on the one hand has opted for *blanket protection* of sites, a system which attempts to afford protection to all sites and indeed objects which lie underwater. The north, on the other, in line with UK legislation, has chosen the protection of individual sites on their own merits.

The relevant pieces of legislation in the Republic are the *National Monuments' Amendments' Acts* 1987 and 1994 and the *Merchant Shipping Salvage and Wreck Act* 1933. It should be noted that the High Court judgement in the Streedagh Strand Armada Case, where a group of English divers were attempting to lay a salvage claim on a number of wreck sites at Streedagh in county Sligo, recognized that wreck sites should be treated under the *National Monuments Acts* as opposed to the *Merchant Shipping Act* (Moore 1995, 41). The provisions of these acts make them some of the most comprehensive pieces of heritage legislation anywhere in Europe. The acts aim to provide full protection for all sites underwater and limit all activities carried out on them. This comprehensive system of protection has been mistakenly interpreted in the past by diving organizations and other marine users as being draconian in nature. This view shows a fundamental lack of understanding of the acts and a failure to recognize their purpose, the protection of a fragile and diminishing resource. The provisions of the acts can be summarised as follows:

• All archaeological sites and archaeological objects over 100 years old are protected. *The National Monuments Acts* also provide for the protection of wreck sites which are of major historical importance under 100 years of age. To date the *Lusitania* has been designated in this way and the *Aud*, a German ship involved in gun-running for the 1916 Rising and scuttled off Cork Harbour, is also being considered for designation.

• All activities on underwater sites are subject to a licensing system. Any person wishing to dive on an archaeological site 'lying on, in or under the seabed or on or in land covered by water' or who interferes with a site in any way must apply for a licence. This is a straightforward procedure and it is only in very rare cases that a licence to dive is refused.

• Any archaeological site or object which is found underwater must be reported to the authorities. *The National Monuments Amendment Act* of 1994 notes that the finding of archaeological objects must be reported to the Director of the National Museum, while wreck sites and other such monuments must be reported to the Commissioners of Public Works. This reporting policy ensures that sites are entered into the SMR and protective and management measures can be implemented.

The *Merchant Shipping Act* requires that all objects removed from the seabed, regardless of age, must be reported to the Receiver of Wreck. There is a network of Receivers based around the coast. The acts also provide for the involvement of the Director of the National Museum in the disposal of wrecks which come under salvage law (Kirwan 1995, 33). In the event of a salvage claim on a wreck, where no claim of ownership is present, the Director of the National Museum can decide whether the wreck is of importance, in which case the Director may take delivery of the wreck and compensate the Receiver for any expenses incurred.

The Protection of Wrecks Act 1973 has been the primary piece of protective shipwreck legislation in the UK and NI. This act provides for the designation of wrecks of special historical or archaeological importance, or for the further designation of the artistic importance of the vessel or of the objects that are directly associated with it. The primary objective of the act is to protect the wrecks from unauthorised interference and to ensure that only competent and properly equipped people survey and excavate such sites. In 1992 ES:HMB (now EHS) entered into an Agency Agreement with the Department of National Heritage to take responsibility for the act in Northern Ireland's waters. The wreck site of the *Girona*, a Neapolitan galleass which was part of the ill-fated Spanish Armada expedition of 1588, was subsequently designated as a protected site in 1993 and remains the only such site in Northern Irish waters (Designation Order 1993 No. 1; 1993/976). The designation covers an area of 300 m around Lacada Point where Robert Stenuit undertook a salvage operation on the site in 1967 and 1968. A licence has been recently granted to a local diver under the terms of the 1973 act to continue survey work under professional archaeological supervision. This licence contained a special clause allowing the diver to recover any artefacts considered to be under threat. It is envisaged that the 1973 act will be somewhat superseded by the Historic Monuments and Archaeological Objects (Northern Ireland) Order 1995 (HMAO). This Order provides for the scheduling of monuments and the protection of these monuments through management agreements with the site owner and the licensing of any work that may be carried out on

Fig. 3.5 Artefacts recovered from the nineteenth-century wreck of the Taymouth Castle.

the site. It also allows for the protection and scheduling of historic monuments in territorial waters. This will as a consequence allow for the scheduling of sites in the inter-tidal area and on the seabed. While the *Protection of Wrecks Act* will remain the primary legislative tool for wrecks, it is conceivable that if a wreck is not deemed suitable for designation, it could still be scheduled under the HMAO order.

The Merchant Shipping Act 1894, or more specifically Part IV of the act, is used to much greater effect in the area of the reporting of heritage objects recovered from the seabed. This act requires that any object brought to the surface from the seabed must be reported to the Receiver of Wreck in the Coastguard Agency in Portsmouth, who must then decide ownership of the object. If no owner is found then the Receiver can return the object or purchase it from the finder. This act has been used to good effect recently by the NI authorities. A cannon was removed by sports divers from the wreck of *L'Amité*, a French frigate wrecked in 1798 off the county Down coast near Ardglass. The cannon was never reported to the Receiver and was subsequently recovered by the RUC and handed over to EHS who initiated a conservation programme for it. While this exemplifies the primary benefit of the act, namely the compulsory reporting of finds, it still remains an out-dated and problematic piece of legislation. The problem lies with the fact that the act effectively encourages the removal of artefacts from sites. Divers or salvors can legally remove objects without any supervision or indeed advice. In reality few objects are reported. The remains of military aircraft or vessels are also protected under the *Protection of Military Remains Act* 1986.

Aside from the various pieces of national legislation there is an increasing number of European Union Directives which take account of environmental protection. European Community Directive 85/337, and more recently Council Directive 97/11/EC, require that environmental assessments are undertaken for many coastal developments. The Directives require that

archaeology and architectural heritage be recognized as an integral part of the environment and that they should be treated as such.

A fundamental problem with all heritage legislation is the actual policing of the relevant acts. The problem lies with the 'visibility' and accessibility of sites in that many of them will lie far off shore and underwater. While this could be regarded as a positive protective feature, it also works in reverse, allowing unsupervised and illegal access to sites. It would obviously be impractical to employ a large number of archaeologists to 'patrol' sections of the coast in order to enforce the legislation, but neither should the sole responsibility for the safeguarding of maritime sites rest with the police forces. It should be possible to introduce other indirect means of protection. The fundamental basis for any protective framework lies in education. User groups like divers and fishermen must be made more aware of the nature and fragility of the underwater resource. It should be possible to enact a policy of informal guardianship on any number of sites with the help of local dive operators or recognized clubs. This policy could be governed by a code of practice and would ensure that not only were sites visited and enjoyed but also protected. Coastal communities should also be made aware of the maritime heritage of their areas. An education scheme accompanied by an information booklet, similar to the variety of educational schemes adopted to inform farmers about the terrestrial resource, could also be enacted.

Much work has been done on the protection of underwater sites on paper through legislative means. However, little research work has taken place into the physical preservation of the sites on the seabed. *In situ* preservation of sites recognizes that many sites underwater are not stable and are actively undergoing erosion from a number of sources. While the only way of dealing with this active erosion in the past has been either to ignore the problem or excavate the site, new more informed methods of on-site management are being introduced. The introduction of protective membranes onto a site is one such solution. A number of different types of membrane have been used. Colin Martin has experimented with the placement of sandbags on the site of the Armada wreck *Trinidad de la Valencera* off the north coast. This method has been employed on a number of sites around the world but has to be approached with caution. The placement of such a 'hard' membrane could result in further erosion scouring under the protective 'hard' or could introduce a whole new set of erosive activities in the area directly surrounding the site. Softer membranes such as nets can be pinned to the seabed, which take account of the fluid and mobile nature of underwater sediments. The introduction of sacrificial anodes onto iron and metal wrecks and artefacts has been experimented with in the US and

Australia. This process attempts to stabilize archaeological material on the seabed without this material having to undergo the expensive process of bringing material through the traumatic air/water interface to the surface.

Other options for the protection of sites include marking them with buoys in order to prevent accidental damage from passing ships and boats. Activity exclusion areas around certain wrecks so as to ensure their preservation can be drawn up. The establishment of marine conservation parks which include sites of archaeological importance should also be envisaged. These parks would have associated educational and visitor facilities to allow access to sites in controlled and supervised conditions. Divers might follow underwater heritage trails marked out by boards and lines while non-divers could monitor work and sites through video linkups as well as visiting inter-tidal and coastal sites.

A much greater emphasis needs to be placed on researching the extensive maritime resource of this island in the future. It is a major step forward that the state bodies are now realizing their responsibility towards archaeology underwater and are initiating survey assessment programmes and associated management strategies. However, these programmes need long-term commitment and must be sufficiently financed. The state bodies must also devise a system of policing the strong existing legislation. Legislation can only work if it is implemented as thoroughly and comprehensively as possible.

Greater recognition of the importance of marine archaeological work among other marine workers is important. The whole field of marine research within Ireland is rapidly expanding in the areas of biology, geology and oceanography, but archaeology remains very much the poor relation to these disciplines. It is recognized that a multi-disciplinary approach is the only way to tackle marine research effectively, yet the other disciplines seem either uninterested or unprepared to include archaeology within their overall brief. It may be that archaeologists need to liaise systematically with marine users and researchers and begin a programme of work aimed at increasing awareness about the cultural resource. This could in turn lead to greater protection and to the inclusion of archaeology in Coastal Zone Management plans and other marine initiatives. Even within the archaeological community, maritime archaeology has yet to be acknowledged as part of the mainstream of the discipline. This is particularly obvious within the universities where not a single module was taught in the subject. Indeed most departments fail to offer a single lecture on the subject.

In short, while maritime archaeology is relatively new to Ireland, it is fundamental to our understanding of our past and to the development of an appreciation of our national identity as an island nation. It is now up to heritage managers and researchers to enhance our knowledge of our maritime heritage and to conserve and manage it effectively for the future.

CASE STUDIES
(1) TAYMOUTH CASTLE
In January 1867 the *Taymouth Castle* was wrecked in a severe storm off the north-east Antrim coast. The vessel was a composite ship, with iron framing and wooden planking, built by Charles Connell at Glasgow in 1865. The ship was on her second voyage to Singapore carrying a valuable general cargo valued then at £50,000, which included wine, spirits, pottery and iron materials. All of the crew lost their lives and little contemporary salvage took place at the wreck. In the early 1970s local sports divers located the wreck and proceeded to extensively plunder the site, a process that was to continue over the following twenty years. In June 1995 MAP was invited to visit the site by local divers who were concerned at the amount of damage being done. This initial visit confirmed the extent of the damage and the advanced state of deterioration that the wreck is in. The remains of the vessel lie at the base of steep boulder cliffs in 14 m of water. Little of the hull structure survives, but there is extensive artefactual material lying about which required some form of protective action. Unfortunately, because of the date and condition of the wreck, it was not a suitable candidate for designation under the 1973 *Protection of Wrecks Act*. Recognizing that plundering was set to continue and there was little that could be done to prevent this DOE NI funded a short survey and excavation on the site. This enabled a detailed investigation of the site to take place and allowed for a representative sample of artefacts to be recovered under controlled conditions. Everything recovered underwent professional conservation, and this material is to form the basis of a museum exhibition on the wreck. This work highlighted the fact that a successful and inexpensive response to threatened underwater sites can be undertaken, and can be used to inform and educate divers as to the benefits of archaeological practice and principles.

(2) LA SURVEILLANTE
In late 1796 the French assembled a large naval force to go to Ireland with Wolfe Tone to attempt an invasion in support of a rising. However due to poor planning and terrible weather the force was split and a large-scale landing was never achieved. One of the French frigates, *La Surveillante*, arrived in Bantry Bay in late December, but was in such bad condition after her voyage from Brest that she was scuttled. During the clearance operations after the disastrous explosion at the Whiddy Island oil terminal at Bantry Bay in 1981, the wreck of the ship

was found by Side Scan Sonar. Divers led by Tony Balfe visited the site in 1982 and confirmed her identity, as well as the fact that she was well preserved. The wreck lies off Whiddy Island at a depth of 34 m and is mostly covered with fine muds. The wreck was declared a national monument and some preliminary photographic survey work was carried out. In June 1987 a number of artefacts were lifted from the site, including two cannon. These artefacts were lifted under licence from the state. Unfortunately inadequate conservation measures were undertaken at that time and the objects have recently undergone further conservation, with various degrees of success. In 1990 a team of divers came from the UK-based Mary Rose Trust and carried out the first scientific archaeological survey of the wreck. Subsequently an Exhibition Centre was opened in 1991 with a view to the eventual excavation and raising of the wreck. Over the following years it was realized that this was probably not feasible and would be prohibitively expensive, but the Centre was still left with a dilemma. If it is to continue to prosper and develop more research on the vessel is also needed. Options now being looked at include building a replica of the vessel and more detailed video and archaeological survey work, which will in turn update the exhibition.

Bibliography

Breen, C. 1996 'Maritime archaeology in Northern Ireland: an interim statement', *The International Journal of Nautical Archaeology* **25**, 1, pp. 55–65.

ECOPRO 1997 *Environmentally friendly coastal protection: code of practice.* Dublin.

Kelly, E. P. 1993 'Investigation of ancient fords on the River Suck', *Inland Waterways News* **20**, 1, pp. 4–5.

Kirwan, S. 1995 'The Department of Arts, Culture and the Gaeltacht and underwater archaeology' in *The future of underwater archaeology in Ireland*, IUART (unpublished conference proceedings), pp. 32–36.

Moore, F. 1995 'The role of the Office of Public Works in underwater archaeology with reference to past activities, current policies and the law' in *The future of underwater archaeology in Ireland*, IUART (unpublished conference proceedings), pp. 39–43.

O'Sullivan, A. 1993 'Inter-tidal survey on the Fergus estuary and the Shannon estuary', *Discovery Programme Reports* **1**, pp. 61–8.

O'Sullivan, A. 1994 'Harvesting the waters', *Archaeology Ireland* **27**, pp. 10–12.

Urban Archaeology

Maurice F. Hurley

Ireland's rich urban archaeological heritage is comparable to the best examples in Europe. Although lacking in remains from the Roman period — urbanization in Ireland effectively began in the tenth century (Wallace 1985, 1992; Clarke 1998) — most of the major Irish cities have developed continuously for almost a millennium. Remains from the Hiberno-Norse period have been found in Dublin, Cork, Limerick, Waterford and Wexford. The latter era, characterized by the 'marked fusion of native Irish and Viking elements' (Simms 1990, 42), dates from the eleventh century onwards, and is sometimes referred to as the late-Viking Age, but is more correctly termed the 'Hiberno-Norse' period.

The extensive excavations of the Hiberno-Norse levels in Dublin (Wallace 1992) and Waterford (Hurley and Scully 1997) have unearthed spectacular remains. Due to the remarkable quality of organic preservation in the ground, we are fortunate to find a substantially intact record of ancient daily life almost every time excavations are undertaken in the historic cores of our cities. Excavations have facilitated the understanding of the layout, form and character of our late Hiberno-Norse and medieval towns. With the exception of Dublin, the relatively slow pace of urban growth, coupled with a continuity of tradition and the absence of the devastating effects of modern warfare, have ensured that our city centres contain rich concentrations of built heritage. Galway and Kilkenny retain many fine examples of late-medieval buildings, while the historic core of Cork city displays a high degree of authenticity and integrity in the layout of streets and laneways, plot size and building scale. In Waterford, where late twentieth-century developments have had a more dramatic effect on the historic streetscape, the restoration of medieval walls and castles provides the city with a visually dramatic and sustainable cultural heritage.

With the exception of city fortifications, castles and some notable historic buildings such as Christ Church Cathedral, Dublin, still in use as a place of worship, the historic character and archaeological resource of our cities remain vulnerable. Despite increasingly restrictive legislation, together with widespread public interest and concern, current building techniques continue to have an unacceptable level of impact on the buried archaeological heritage. Archaeologists' response is increasingly ambiguous, with some advocating extensive excavation in advance of construction and others preferring the minimization of impact by the design of building foundations. The latter approach is currently favoured by Dúchas, the Irish government's Heritage Service, and the present emphasis is placed on a 'presumption in favour of preservation', that is the non-disturbance of archaeological and historic architectural remains. In terms of the retention of significant buildings of historic merit, the policy is clear and unambiguous. In the context of the general preservation of the 'ordinary' streetscape architecture, much of which is dilapidated, the policy of preservation is less easily enforced even if the ideal is of unquestionable merit. Furthermore, the requisite skills and finance to restore old buildings are not generally within the grasp of the average urban householder. In cities such as Cork, where many of the buildings in the historic core continue to have a high level of upper-floor vacancy, the ground-floor businesses generate insufficient surplus to justify the outlay on restoration and modernization. The additional investment in restoration, compared with newly built accommodation, is not justifiable for most developers in the light of current demand.

Regarding the correct approach to buried archaeology, where new buildings are intended, 'the era of large, full-scale urban excavations ... has passed' (Wallace 1998, 67). New buildings are generally allowed to go ahead provided there is minimal intrusion by piles and other structural components into archaeological strata. Apart from Temple Bar in Dublin, where extensive excavation took place in advance of redevelopment, the policy of mitigation by structural modification is now generally established in Ireland. In this context, excavations like Temple Bar are viewed by some as 'useful exercises in public relations and education' (*ibid*.).

The origin of the current dilemma for archaeologists can be understood in the light of the evolution of the subject in Ireland over the past forty years. A solution leading to a consistent and widely endorsed approach must lie in archaeologists' clarification of their own aspirations. Is not societal benefit the only justification for all archaeological excavation? In this realization lies the key to a consistent policy for Irish archaeology whereby the conflicting demands of development, preservation of undisturbed strata for future research and demonstrable benefits to contemporary society can be reconciled.

THE DEVELOPMENT OF IRISH URBAN ARCHAEOLOGY
In the historic cores of most Irish cities, many once elegant eighteenth-century houses had become tenement dwellings in the nineteenth century. Following the re-housing of inner-city populations in new suburban estates in the 1950s and '60s, the old dilapidated houses were abandoned and demolished. The former residential areas became urban wasteland or were given over to surface car parks. These areas frequently coincided with the most ancient parts of our cities. In Dublin, the National Museum of Ireland selected areas for excavation where development was thought to be imminent.

The first scientific urban excavation in Ireland was undertaken in 1961 at Dublin Castle by M. Ó hEochaidhe. Between 1962 and 1981 the National Museum carried out eight major excavations in the capital, namely High Street I (1962–63), High Street II (1967–72) and Winetavern Street (1968–72), all by A. B. Ó Ríordáin. The custom was for the Museum to undertake the excavation directly with labour recruited specifically for the job in hand. At that time, there was a general gap in our knowledge of Irish cities and few could visualize the quantity, quality and complexity of the buried stratigraphy. The Dublin excavations of the 1960s and early '70s revealed a heretofore unimagined wealth of evidence for houses, artefacts, trade and environment of tenth- to thirteenth-century date.

The growing interest in urban archaeology in Ireland coincided with an increase in urban redevelopment, resulting in the substantial destruction of archaeological structures and layers. Apart from Dublin, urban excavations were not undertaken and sites were frequently destroyed or at best some salvage work was done. This amounted to nothing more than grabbing a few artefacts from the teeth of a mechanical excavator, or noting the disappearance of some ancient architectural feature.

In 1973, the Department of Archaeology, UCC, prepared a report on the archaeological potential of the vacant sites in Cork city. Fired by the spectacular success of the Dublin excavations, Professor M. J. O'Kelly organized a series of excavations concentrating on urban sites of documented historical importance. Excavation commenced in 1974 at the site of Skiddy's Castle, North Main Street, and a year later at Christ Church College, South Main Street, excavated by D. C. Twohig. As with Dublin, the extent of the surviving remains, the depth and complexity of stratigraphy, as well as the remarkable preservation of organic material, took everybody by surprise. The excavations are a classic example of what Professor Verhaeghe, in a recent lecture, terms 'archaeology in the city', that is the examination of known monuments rather than the general urban fabric.

The discoveries in Cork, especially at Christ Church College, document a general European evolution that was taking place in urban archaeology in the 1970s — a move towards excavating the 'archaeology of the city'. Christ Church College itself was only represented by the poorly preserved foundations of a late fifteenth-century building; however, while excavating these, the scope of the work expanded to concentrate on the adjacent stratigraphy. By 1977, the discovery of several levels of wattle-walled houses, wooden pathways, wells, pits and general urban refuse overshadowed the original aims of the project — in short, the excavation of the city had become a reality.

It was in Dublin that Irish urban archaeology came of age. While a small proportion of a four-acre (1.8 ha) urban block (bounded by Wood Quay, Fishamble Street, John's Lane and Winetavern Street, Wood Quay during 1974–76 and Fishamble Street during 1975–81; see Wallace 1992b), was under excavation by the National Museum, the threatened destruction of some of the richest archaeological deposits in Europe lay in the balance. Dublin Corporation intended to construct new civic offices on the site, and while this necessitated the excavation of all the endangered archaeological layers, the Corporation and the National Museum failed to agree a programme for the excavation of the entire area. On a number of occasions parts of the unexcavated site were mechanically removed (Bradley 1984; Heffernan 1988). Controversy erupted and the impasse received widespread media attention resulting in an unprecedented public outcry, protracted legal battles, political wrangles and, above all else, a rallying point for conservationists opposed to the concept of unbridled modern development in historic cities. The arguments frequently became clouded or entangled in other issues, such as the demolition of Georgian terraced houses, the relocation of inner-city communities and the erosion of traditional values, all giving vent to grievances that had finally erupted because of the destruction of part of an archaeological site.

The 'Wood Quay crisis' which for over three and a half years 'figured constantly in the headlines' (Bradley 1984, 8), raised the profile of urban archaeology to such an extent that in the eyes of local authorities, private developers and the newspapers, 'digs' had become synonymous with controversy. Archaeology was perceived as an obstacle to development. The standards and expectations of urban excavation were also raised to unprecedented levels.

Ironically, the Wood Quay issue also heralded a seemingly intractable problem for Irish archaeologists, albeit a problem that did not fully manifest itself until more than a decade later. The excavation of Wood Quay and 'saving' the site were mutually exclusive ideals. Perhaps even now some archaeologists are reluctant to accept that they did not deliver a coherent message in the late 1970s — 'Save Wood Quay' evidently meant different things to different people. Archaeologists' failure to articulate clearly their thinking on the Wood Quay issue was based on a deeply rooted paradox. All archaeological excavation is destruction insofar as the procedures can never be repeated. This was never so acutely felt until the issue became the excavation of organic stratigraphy — the so-called cultural layers of a city — whereby everything is removed by the excavation process. By contrast, when the excavation of a stone-built monument takes place, the stone structure may remain intact after the surrounding soil has yielded up its information, and the unaltered appearance of the monument belies the fact that it is of little use for future archaeological research.

The term 'preservation by record' was subsequently coined by archaeologists. It found its most significant expression to date in the UK's 'Planning Policy Guidance', *Archaeology and Planning No. 16:* 'If physical preservation *in situ* is not feasible, an archaeological excavation for the purposes of "preservation by record" may be an acceptable alternative'. In my opinion 'presentation by record' has always been a fallacy. The misnomer was evidently coined to salve the conscience of archaeologists who were unable to confront the reality that they too destroy sites in the quest for knowledge. The only distinction between good and bad excavation lies in the level and accuracy of the information obtained from the process. When the organic layers of a city are removed, an empty space is created — in effect, archaeologists have made a 'hole in the ground' (Prof. M. J. O'Kelly, quoted in Martin 1984). Following excavation, the only decision is whether or not to retain the empty space as a piece of waste ground or erect a new building. Empty spaces are the antithesis of our concept of urban regeneration. One obvious alternative is to retain as many existing buildings as possible within the archaeological zones, and by so doing preserve the underlying

strata undisturbed. Then the site is truly saved, but if archaeology is defined in terms of discovery and scholarship, contemporary society is none the wiser.

All over Ireland numerous controversies flared in the wake of the Wood Quay crisis. The most noteworthy concerned Saint Martin's Gate, Waterford, excavated by M. Moore of the Office of Public Works (1982–83). The site was fully excavated in advance of redevelopment. The foundations of the medieval gate towers were consolidated by Waterford Corporation and remain visible to the public. Similarly, the controversy surrounding Hopewell Castle, Cork, excavated in 1984 (Hurley 1985), was extensively covered in Cork newspapers. Cork Corporation intended to reveal a length of medieval city wall as part of its plan to develop a municipal park. While arrangements were being made to archaeologically excavate the layers abutting the wall, the trench was mechanically excavated and the possible foundations of the castle (one of the mural towers on the city wall) were destroyed. In the 1980s, the pace of urban redevelopment escalated. The National Museum of Ireland largely withdrew from active participation in urban excavation, but the Office of Public Works (now Dúchas, the Heritage Service) undertook some significant projects. The most notable of these were at Charlotte's Quay, Limerick, excavated by A. Lynch in 1981 (see Lynch 1984), and extensive excavations at Dublin Castle in advance of modifications to the building. Many of the features uncovered in the Dublin Castle excavations were effectively and dramatically incorporated into the sensitively adapted building. Elsewhere in Ireland, 'salvage' or at best 'rescue' excavation predominated. Thankfully the era of salvage was short-lived. The concept of rescue excavation developed and came to embrace everything from poorly funded, hastily undertaken jobs, to well-planned, well-organized and efficient projects where developer funding was the common denominator.

The concept of developer funding for the requisite amount of archaeological excavation in accordance with the level of impact likely to be caused to archaeological layers by a new building became nationally established in the 1980s. Gradually, developers began to realize that the financial outlay on archaeology was acceptable in terms of a contribution made to societal benefit. Developer-funded excavations were generally undertaken in advance of new building construction, and local authorities gradually began to include this requirement when planning permissions were issued. The process was standardized through the nationally produced Urban Archaeological Survey, whereby all of the major cities, and subsequently most historic towns, were studied. The Urban Archaeological Survey of Ireland was established in 1982 under the auspices of the Office of Public Works to prepare reports on the archaeological potential of Irish towns. The surveys included lists of the known monuments, and a general history of the urban development, as well as providing maps defining zones of archaeological potential and guidelines on policy and procedures. These zones referred to the known or suspected extent of the urban area in 1700 AD or prior to that. Under the *National Monuments Act* 1930 and *Amendments* (1954, 1987), the policy of the Archaeological Survey of Ireland was to record everything up to 1700 AD and selectively thereafter.

The mid-1980s also saw the emergence of a system of designation for areas of urban renewal, whereby tax incentives were provided by central government for new developments in specified areas. Urban Renewal Schemes were provided in the years 1986–1994, 1994–1997 and again recently. Their purpose was to foster urban renewal through the application of tax incentives for residential, commercial or industrial development. Frequently, the most decayed and derelict urban areas were the historic city centres. In Dublin, Limerick and Waterford the local authorities had, over the years, acquired considerable amounts of property through their acquisition of derelict sites. These were mostly used as surface car parks. Limerick Corporation, as part of a proposal to dispose of their sites to private developers, took the initiative by appointing a City Archaeologist in 1986. A programme of archaeological excavation followed. Several important sites were excavated, in particular King John's Castle, which was dug prior to restoration and the development of an on-site urban museum (Wiggins 1991a, b). In 1987, similar appointments were made in Waterford and Galway in order to co-ordinate excavation projects in advance of major inner-city redevelopments.

It was intended to develop a city-centre shopping complex in the heart of Galway on a site that contained part of the late-medieval urban defences (Walsh 1988). Much of this site lay outside the city walls, but the remains of the walls, turrets and bastions survived to a height of 2–3 m and were effectively incorporated within the shopping centre. Over the following years, further excavation work was done on several sections of the Galway city walls, most notably at Spanish Arch (Casey 1989), Merchant's Road/Townparks (Delaney 1990; 1991), Quay Street (Casey 1991) and St Augustine's Street (Clyne 1991).

In 1984, Waterford Corporation commenced excavation of five sites, namely High Street/Exchange Street (Stephens 1986), Deanery Garden (O'Rahilly 1986), the 'Crypt' (O'Brien 1986), Grady's Yard John Street (Murtagh 1986a) and the Watchtower, at Manor Street/Railway Square (Murtagh 1986b and 1991), as part of their programme for the enhancement and promotion of the historic character of the city. The discovery of St Martin's Gate the previous year had prompted the

Fig. 4.1 Imported thirteenth-century pottery from Saintonge region of France, from medieval Waterford excavations.

Corporation to develop the touristic potential of the historic town. The full benefits of the project were not completely realized in the short term, but it laid the foundation for a more ambitious, on-going programme of restoration of the medieval city defences.

A far more extensive excavation project commenced in Waterford, in 1986, in an area designated for the European Union Urban Renewal Scheme. It was intended to construct a city-centre shopping complex on a site where the Corporation had acquired a large amount of derelict and under-utilized property. The complex was to have basement car parks so as to maintain the unity of the streetscape and urban skyline. The site represented about 20% of the total area of what was believed to be the Viking Age town; consequently, an archaeologist was employed to co-ordinate the excavation project. Between 1986 and 1992, more than 6,000 square metres were archaeologically excavated in eleven separate sites (Hurley and Scully 1997). The project is a good example of partnership between local government, a private developer and state agencies. Waterford Corporation financed the excavation of property in their ownership prior to sale to the developer. In areas not owned by Corporation, the developer, Sisk Properties Ltd, funded the work directly. The post-excavation analysis and publication of the results were largely supported by the National Heritage Council (now the Heritage Council), by the Office of Public Works (now Dúchas) and Waterford Corporation. Many of the artefacts and information derived from the excavations were put on display in a specially developed Heritage Centre at Grey Friars Street, Waterford. The completion of the excavations without acrimonious dispute and the subsequent publication of the results in a single volume covering all aspects of the excavation and research (*ibid.*) reflect the maturity of urban archaeology and the national acceptance of the importance of our urban heritage.

By the late 1980s/early 1990s, owing to the catalyst

Fig. 4.2 Excavations of St Peter's Church, Waterford (twelfth to thirteenth centuries) in 1988.

deposit-modelling, mitigation strategies, site resolution, project management, liaison with the authorities and timetabling have all become the current parlance of contemporary urban archaeology.

Cork Corporation appointed a City Archaeologist in 1991, and shortly afterwards a similar appointment was made in Dublin. Both posts are jointly funded by Dúchas. The positions differed from earlier appointments by Limerick, Galway and Waterford Corporations insofar as the brief was not merely to resolve the archaeology of specific sites but rather to develop and secure the implementation of policy for the overall approach to the archaeological heritage of the city.

In Dublin, only a limited amount of excavation was undertaken directly by the Corporation, at Winetavern Street/Wood Quay (Halpin 1994 and 1995; Wallace 1995; Wallace and Ó Ríordáin 1994), and the emphasis was placed on the management of archaeology through the planning process with excavations, testings and so forth being undertaken by consultant/contract archaeologists. A number of extensive excavations have been conducted on foot of requirements of planning permission, such as St Audeon's Chapel (McMahon 1990 and 1993), Castle Street/Lord Edward Street (Byrne 1994), Christchurch Place (Walsh and Hayden 1994) and Francis Street (Murtagh 1995). Of note was a series of excavations undertaken in the Temple Bar area, where Temple Bar Properties, 'were charged by the government with the task of "renewing" the ... area as Dublin's cultural quarter'. The process resulted in a series of good-quality publications (Simpson 1994, 1995; Gowen and Scally 1996).

The early 1990s saw a major contribution to archaeological investigation by Cork Corporation. Three large urban sites were excavated and published (Hurley 1995, 1996; Hurley and Sheehan 1995; Hurley 1997), while an *Historic Centre Action Plan* was produced, whereby an integrated strategy for conservation was devised and subsequently implemented through the Urban Pilot Projects (O'Donnell 1998). The Cork Urban Pilot Project was undertaken between 1994 and 1998 with assistance from the European Union Regional Development Fund. A series of initiatives identified in the *Historic Centre Action Plan* was implemented with the intention of promoting the process of sustainable physical and economic regeneration of the historic core of the city. Significant heritage projects included the restoration of St Peter's Church, an historic landmark building, to house the city's Vision Centre, the restoration of a terrace of early eighteenth-century houses at Fenn's Quay; 'Living over the business', whereby existing buildings were refurbished, thereby 'sealing' the undisturbed archaeological layers from the risks of modern foundations as well as maintaining the current streetscape character; the archaeological excavation of North Gate,

provided by the Designated Area Scheme, the pace of urban re-development escalated dramatically. Ironically, the increase in urban renewal coincided with continuing restrictions on public service recruitment and the reluctance of central government to involve its personnel in excavation projects necessitated by private development. As a consequence, a new breed of archaeological practitioner began to emerge — namely the contractor/consultant. Amongst these archaeologists, a wide range of experience and a variety of expertise could be found, but a common denominator prevailed — all were keenly aware that a good excavation was one done on time and within budget. Archaeologists now had to compete against one another for contracts. In this climate, the state's archaeological services increasingly took on the role of regulators of private practice. A small number of large project companies came to dominate the new 'market economy' of archaeology, while numerous individuals operated a wide spectrum of private practices, ranging from Environmental Impact Assessment to specialist analysis and conservation of artefacts. Site evaluations, desk-based assessments,

Fig. 4.3 Excavation of the medieval wall of Cork at Kyrl's Quay, Cork, in 1992.

with associated promotion and publicity for residents and visitors and a study of the impact of modern construction techniques on excavated and unexcavated archaeological materials. Several smaller excavations were also carried out by contract archaeologists on foot of the requirements of planning permissions, while the Corporation was also responsible for bringing the report on Christ Church and Skiddy's Castle to publication (Cleary *et al*. 1997).

Currently, urban renewal has been accompanied by major infrastructural development, much of it financed through European Union Regional Development Funds. Renewal of drainage has been a feature of many historic city and town centres, such as Wexford (Wrenn 1996), Drogheda (Murphy 1995, 1996) and New Ross (McCutcheon 1996). The first modern scheme of this type undertaken in an area of rich archaeological potential was the placement of a 700 m length of sewer from Dean Street to Wood Quay in Dublin in 1989. The archaeological implications were dealt with effectively, and the excavations and subsequent publications (Walsh 1997) are a model of good practice.

While attention has largely been focused on the urban archaeology of the major cities, due to the scale of their redevelopment, excavations have also taken place in many of the smaller cities and historic towns. The rebuilding of a single-unit property in Wexford in 1988 — the area available for excavation was only 7 m by 8 m —

resulted in the excavation of ten levels of Hiberno-Norse houses at Bride Street/South Main Street (Bourke 1990, 1995). Several excavations have been carried out in Kilkenny, Drogheda, Youghal, Carrigfergus and Armagh. Archaeological trial trenching, testing and monitoring in association with re-development now take place as a matter of course in more than 120 designated historic Irish towns. Despite this, however, it is salutary to realize that there remain some misunderstanding and inconsistency in the application by local authorities of archaeological policies and requirements in urban areas.

Large amounts of money have been spent on archaeology in Irish cities and towns over the past twenty years. The situation has created the 'dilemma ... of whether commercial criteria alone are appropriate in archaeology given the nature of the subject' (Monk and Sheehan 1998, 3). Furthermore, in a discipline based on the principles of contribution to the public good, the only justifiable end for the expenditure is the retention of the information in a logical form and its ultimate dissemination for the benefit of society. Failure to do this, or excessive emphasis on one aspect at the expense of the other, can only result in compromising our aspirations, leading to cynicism and hostility.

THE FUTURE OF URBAN ARCHAEOLOGY IN IRELAND
Significant variations currently exist from one urban area to the next in the approach taken to archaeology and the

built heritage. Circumstances of survival, scales of re-development and perspectives on heritage vary. Although the *National Monuments Acts* apply as law throughout the state, different perspectives and variable resources inevitably result in a range of standards and application. Above all else, there appears to be a lack of a well-founded rationale on which to base decisions. This stems, in part, from archaeologists' failure to confront some fundamental issues. At present Irish urban archaeology is undergoing rigorous reappraisal. The Heritage Council commissioned a *Review of urban archaeology* in 1997. A Draft Final Report has been prepared by the Oxford Archaeology Unit (Heritage Council forthcoming); this was discussed at a two-day conference in Kilkenny (14-15 October 1998), and the report is to be published. A National Heritage Plan is currently being devised by the Department of Arts, Heritage, Gaeltacht and the Islands. To date, many of the suggestions have been unimaginative, largely due to the uncritical acceptance of current policies on mitigation, direct site-specific developer funding and failure to formulate a coherent research agenda or national agency for urban archaeology. In formulating such a, policy it may be useful for archaeologists to ask themselves the following questions, and, in answering them, to be honest about their values and aspirations in the light of what can reasonably be achieved.

WHO CARES WHETHER WE EXCAVATE OR NOT?

Archaeologists clearly understood what was required when it was considered inevitable that urban development equated to destruction of archaeology. When archaeologists campaigned to 'save Wood Quay' in the 1970s, few could have imagined that a short number of years later, excavation would be regarded as a 'second best option' (Halpin 1997). Has this notion got anything to do with the perception of archaeology by most Irish citizens? How are we, as archaeologists, defining what is valid, valuable and worthwhile? Is it any wonder that archaeologists currently have difficulty explaining their thinking to the world outside?

For such people, and they are most of our fellow citizens, archaeology is about discovery. It is not about our own professional insecurity and our growing refusal even to want to know what happened, if this means facing the challenges and risks of trying to do so. (Biddle 1994, 7)

IF WE CHOOSE TO EXCAVATE, WHAT ARE WE LOOKING FOR?

Now that urban archaeologists can choose to excavate or not, there must be a justification for the choice. A well-founded national research agenda is clearly required.

HAVE WE ALREADY DUG ENOUGH OF OUR CITIES?

There is a genuinely held view amongst many archaeolo-gists that urban excavation can, at present, add nothing further to the sum total of human knowledge. They would argue that we are merely piling up data and finds, thereby stretching already scarce infrastructural resources to their limit. This, of course, is a chicken-and-egg argument, for there never were enough resources anywhere, and resources tend to be made available only when pressure is greatest. Nonetheless, the proper conservation of artefacts and their long-term curation, the analysis and storage of samples from an excavation, the curation of written and photographic archives, all present a very real challenge to an already overstretched museum infrastructure. The resources allocated to this critical requirement have not expanded to keep pace with that of excavation.

Other than these, there are compelling arguments for *in situ* preservation and a moratorium on all excavation. In the absence of a well-founded research agenda, the argument for *in situ* preservation is contingent on a number of assumptions, namely, that we are satisfied that what we wish to preserve is *really* preserved, that we know of and can enforce the best structural methods and, most importantly, that we can convince the developers and public in Ireland that the investment in elaborate structural modifications is worthwhile. At present, it is obvious that many developers prefer this option only because the cost of structural modifications can be more accurately quantified and may be less than the cost of an excavation; however, in many cases, it may be as much or more. Indeed, a far greater engineering and construction cost may be involved in preservation *in situ*, and the resultant structural modifications cause loss of space and inappropriate internal configuration of buildings. In this context, the presumption in favour of preservation can amount to a daunting prospect for a developer.

Furthermore, the vagaries of public opinion likely to be attracted by a dig can be avoided. It is noteworthy that there has not been a single public outcry in Ireland about piles being inserted through an unexcavated site. By contrast, when a site has been excavated and everything in it removed by archaeologists, people tend to be horrified by the idea of covering it up. Following excavation in Dublin in the 1960s and 1970s, more than twenty years passed before new buildings went up on many of the sites. The reluctance to develop the area was in part due to the awe inspired by the material uncovered and consequent misgivings on the part of potential investors. Similarly, in Cork at Skiddy's Castle, fifteen years elapsed between the excavation and development of the site. Even then, the new building was set back from the street frontage, with a large forecourt constructed above the castle foundations. At present, there is a general lack of information amongst archaeologists and local authority planners regarding the merits and risks of piling systems and construction methods. Many engineers and developers, already aware of archaeologists' predisposition to non-excavation, are skilled at presenting site plans in the most acceptable form. Archaeologists need information in order to ask the pertinent questions. The enforcement of agreements is even more problematic. Any transgressions on a construction site can be quickly covered up. Extensive damage to archaeological layers is usually not the result of a single flagrant disregard for the agreed conditions and a method statement, but the cumulative effect of many minor incidents.

HOW CAN WE ENSURE THAT FUTURE GENERATIONS WILL CONTINUE TO CARE AS MUCH AS PEOPLE CURRENTLY DO, AND HAVE WE ANY RESPONSIBILITIES FOR THIS?

This brings us back to the issues of values, aspirations and honesty. Any *modus operandi* based on false premises will sooner or later be subject to critical scrutiny. People are always surprised and impressed to see an archaeological excavation revealing hitherto unknown discoveries. The establishment of constraint areas and restrictions on development in archaeological zones may work if public opinion supports the concept, but it requires the excavation of sites to focus people's attention on these issues. An excavation confers the status of 'monument', if not by definition, at least by the public interest shown in it. Where excavation does not take place, the public tend to believe that the reason excavation was not undertaken was that archaeologists did not care, or were not interested — in short, that there was nothing there anyway. Will an absence of excavation foster this view? Can Irish archaeology survive and outgrow its current unwillingness to discover? Can we muster the will to communicate our findings and remain in touch with public opinion? In short, archaeologists need to take the lead in identifying priorities so that we can maximize whatever research opportunities arise in the future.

Bibliography

Barry, T. B. 1987 *The archaeology of medieval Ireland.* London.

Bennett, I. (ed) 1988 *Excavations 1987: summary accounts of archaeological excavations in Ireland.* Wicklow.

Bennett, I. (ed) 1989 *Excavations 1988: summary accounts of archaeological excavations in Ireland.* Wicklow.

Bennett, I. (ed) 1990 *Excavations 1989: summary accounts of archaeological excavations in Ireland.* Wicklow.

Bennett, I. (ed) 1991 *Excavations 1990: summary accounts of archaeological excavations in Ireland.* Wicklow.

Bennett, I. (ed) 1994 *Excavations 1993: summary accounts of archaeological excavations in Ireland.* Wicklow.

Bennett, I. (ed) 1995 *Excavations 1994: summary accounts of archaeological excavations in Ireland.* Wicklow.

Bennett, I. (ed) 1996 *Excavations 1995: summary accounts of archaeological excavations in Ireland.* Wicklow.

Biddle, M. 1994 *What future for British archaeology?* Oxford.

Bourke, E. 1990 'Two 11th-century Viking houses from Bride Street, Wexford and the layout of properties on the site', *Journal of the Wexford Archaeological Society* 12, pp. 50–61.

Bourke, E. 1995 'Life in the sunny south-east', *Archaeology Ireland* 9, p. 3.

Bradley, J. (ed) 1984 *Viking Dublin exposed: the Wood Quay saga.* Dublin.

Byrne, E. M. 1994 '26–29 Castle Street/20 Lord Edward Street' in Nenk, Margeson and Hurley 1994, pp. 270–1.

Casey, M. 1989 '"Spanish Arch", Townparks' in Bennett 1989, pp. 19–20.

Casey, M. 1991 'Quay Street, Townparks, Galway' in Bennett 1990, p. 36.

Clarke, H. B. (ed) 1995 *Irish cities.* Cork.

Clarke, H. B. 1998 'Proto-towns and towns in Ireland and Britain in the ninth and tenth centuries' in H. B. Clarke, M. Ní Mhaonaigh and R. Ó Floinn (eds) *Ireland and Scandinavia in the early Viking age* (Dublin), pp. 331–80.

Cleary, R. M., Hurley, M. F. and Shee Twohig, E. 1997 *Skiddy's Castle and Christ Church, Cork: excavations 1974–77 by D. C. Twohig.* Cork.

Clyne, M. 1991 'St Augustine Street/Merchants Road, Townparks, Galway' in Bennett 1990, pp. 36–7.

Cotter, C. (ed) 1986 *Excavations 1985: summary accounts of archaeological excavations in Ireland.* Dublin.

Delany, D. 1990 'Merchants Road II, Townparks' in Bennett 1989, pp. 28–9.

Delany, D. 1991 'Merchants Road IV, Townparks, Galway' in Bennett 1990, pp. 35–6.

Gowen, M. 1991 'Rescue archaeology' in M. Ryan (ed) *The illustrated archaeology of Ireland* (Dublin), pp. 21–23.

Gowen, M. 1996 'Kilkenny, Kytler's Inn, 25–26 St Kieran's Street' in Nenk, Margeson and Hurley 1996, p. 299.

Gowen, M. and Scally, G. 1996 *Exchange Street Upper/Parliament Street, Dublin.* Dublin.

Halpin, A. 1994 'Wine Tavern Street/Wood Quay' in Nenk, Margeson and Hurley 1994, p. 275.

Halpin, A. 1995 'Wine Tavern Street/Wood Quay' in

Nenk, Margeson and Hurley 1995, pp. 267–8.

Halpin, E. 1997 'Archaeology in the planning process', *IAPA Newsletter, Bulletin of the Irish Association of Professional Archaeologists* (Spring) **24**, p. 9.

Heffernan, T. F. 1988 *Wood Quay: the clash over Dublin's Viking past.* Austin, Texas.

Heritage Council (forthcoming) *Archaeological practice in Ireland: a review of urban archaeology*, compiled by Lambrick, G. and Spandel, K. (Oxford Archaeology Unit).

Hurley, M. F. 1985 'Excavations of part of the medieval city wall at Grand Parade, Cork', *Journal of the Cork Historical and Archaeological Society* **90**, pp. 65–90.

Hurley, M. F. 1995 'Excavations in Cork city: Kyrl's Quay/North Main Street and at Grand Parade', *Journal of the Cork Historical and Archaeological Society* **100**, pp. 47–90.

Hurley, M. F. 1996 'Excavations in Cork city: Kyrl's Quay/North Main Street (Part 2)', *Journal of the Cork Historical and Archaeological Society* **101**, pp. 26–63.

Hurley, M. F. 1997a *Archaeological excavations at the North Gate, Cork, 1994.* Cork.

Hurley, M. F. 1997b 'Tasks and outlook for archaeology in Irish towns especially Cork' in *Lübecker Kolloquium zur Stadtarchäologie im Hanseraum I: Stand, Aufgaben und Perspektiven* (Lübeck), pp. 13–18.

Hurley, M. F. 1998 'Viking age towns: archaeological evidence from Waterford and Cork' in Monk and Sheehan 1998, pp. 164–177.

Hurley, M. F. and Scully, O. M. B. 1997 *Late Viking Age and medieval Waterford: excavations 1986–1992.* Waterford.

Hurley, M. F. and Sheehan, C. M. 1995 *Excavations at the Dominican Priory: St Mary's of the Isle, Cork.* Cork.

Hyde, D. 1993 *Building on the past: urban change and archaeology.* Dublin.

King, H. A. 1991 'Pennyfeather Lane/Pudding Lane' in Nenk, Margeson and Hurley 1991, pp. 210–11.

Lynch, A. 1984 'Excavations of the medieval town defences at Charlotte's Quay, Limerick', *Proceedings of the Royal Irish Academy* **84 C** pp. 300–50.

Lynn, C. J. 1991 'English St./Market Sq., Armagh' in Bennett 1991, pp. 12–13.

Martin, F. X. 1984 'Politics, public interest and the law' in Bradley 1984, pp. 38-67.

Maxwell, N. (ed) 1980 *Digging up Dublin: a future for our past?* Dublin.

McCutcheon, S. 1996 'New Ross' in Bennett 1996, p. 88.

McMahon, M. 1990 'St Audeon's Church' in Bennett 1989.

McMahon, M. 1993 'St Audeon's Church' in Nenk, Margeson and Hurley 1993, pp. 292–3.

Moran, J. 1997 'Kilkenny, William Street' in Nenk, Margeson and Hurley 1997, p. 307.

Monk, M. A. and Sheehan, J. 1998 'Research and early medieval Munster: agenda or vacuum' in Monk and Sheehan 1998, pp. 1–8.

Monk, M. A. and Sheehan, J (eds) *Early medieval Munster: archaeology, history and society.* Cork.

Murphy, D. 1995 'Magdalene Tower, Drogheda' in Bennett 1995, pp. 62–3.

Murphy, D. 1996 'Calendar Building, Bachelor's Lane, Drogheda' in Bennett 1996, p. 58–9.

Murtagh, B. 1986a 'Grady's Yard, John Street' in Cotter 1986, p. 39.

Murtagh, B. 1986b 'Watch Tower, Manor Street/Railway Square' in Cotter 1986, p. 40.

Murtagh, B. 1992 'Kilkenny Castle' in Nenk, Margeson and Hurley 1992, pp. 286–7.

Murtagh, D. 1995 '33–38 Francis Street, Dublin' in Nenk, Margeson and Hurley 1995, p. 267.

Nenk, B. S., Margeson, S. and Hurley, M. (compilers) 1991 'Medieval Britain and Ireland in 1990', *Medieval Archaeology* **35**, pp. 126–238.

Nenk, B. S., Margeson, S. and Hurley, M. (compilers) 1992 'Medieval Britain and Ireland in 1991', *Medieval Archaeology* **36**, pp. 184–308.

Nenk, B. S., Margeson, S. and Hurley, M. (compilers) 1993 'Medieval Britain and Ireland in 1992', *Medieval Archaeology* **37**, pp. 240–313.

Nenk, B. S., Margeson, S. and Hurley, M. (compilers) 1994 'Medieval Britain and Ireland in 1993', *Medieval Archaeology* **38**, pp. 184–293.

Nenk, B. S., Margeson, S. and Hurley, M. (compilers) 1995 'Medieval Britain and Ireland in 1994', *Medieval Archaeology* **39**, pp. 180–293.

Nenk, B. S., Margeson, S. and Hurley, M. (compilers) 1996 'Medieval Britain and Ireland in 1995', *Medieval Archaeology* **40**, pp. 234–318.

Nenk, B. S., Margeson, S. and Hurley, M. (compilers) 1997 'Medieval Britain and Ireland in 1996', *Medieval Archaeology* **41**, pp. 241–328.

Nolan, W. and Simms, A. (eds) 1998 *Irish towns: a guide to sources.* Dublin.

Ó Baoill, R. 1994 'Carrickfergus' in Bennett 1994, pp. 2–3.

O'Brien, M. 1986 'The Crypt' in Cotter 1986, p. 39.

O'Donnell, J. 1998 'The Cork Historic Centre Action Plan' in B. Brunt and K. Hourihan (eds) *Perspectives on Cork* (Cork), pp. 121–37.

O Rahilly, C. 1986 'Deanery garden' in Cotter 1986, pp. 38–9.

O'Rourke, D. (forthcoming) 'The effects of new buildings and services on Dublin's subterranean and built heritage', *Energy, transport and telematics in historic cities.*

Power, C. 1996 'The College Grounds, Emmet Place, Youghal' in Bennett 1996, p. 9.

Reid, M. 1997 Kilkenny, Albany Street' in Nenk, Margeson

and Hurley 1997, p. 307.

Simms, A. 1990 'Medieval Dublin in a European context: from proto-town to chartered town' in H. Clarke (ed) *Medieval Dublin: the making of a metropolis*, (Dublin) pp. 37–51.

Simpson, L. 1994 *Excavations at Isolde's Tower, Dublin*. Dublin.

Simpson, L. 1995 *Excavations at Essex Street West, Dublin*. Dublin.

Stevens, S. 1986 'High Street/Exchange Street' in Cotter 1986, p. 38.

Thomas, A. 1992 *The walled towns of Ireland*. Dublin.

Wallace, P. F. 1985 'The archaeology of Viking Dublin' in H. B. Clarke and A. Simms (eds) *The comparative history of urban origins in non-Roman Europe* (Oxford), pp. 103–45.

Wallace, P. F. 1992a 'The archaeological identity of the Hiberno-Norse town', *Journal of the Royal Society of Antiquarians* **122**, pp. 35–66.

Wallace, P. F. 1992b *The Viking Age buildings of Dublin*. Dublin.

Wallace, P. F. 1998 'Archaeology' in Nolan and Simms 1998, pp. 61–8.

Walsh, C. 1997 *Archaeological excavations at Patrick, Nicholas and Winetavern Streets, Dublin*. Tralee.

Walsh, C. and Hayden, A. 1994 'Christchurch Place, Dublin' in Nenk, Margeson and Hurley 1994, pp. 271–2.

Walsh, G. 1988 'Merchants Road, Townparks, Galway' in Bennett 1988, pp. 15–6.

Wiggins, K. 1991a 'King John's Castle, St Mary's Parish' in Bennett 1991, p. 43–4.

Wiggins, K. 1991b in Nenk, Margeson and Hurley 1991, pp. 211–12.

Wren, J. 1994 'Ashe St./Chapel Lane, Youghal' in Bennett 1994, p. 10.

Wren, J. 1996 'Wexford main drainage' in Bennett 1996, pp. 84–5.

Industrial Archaeology

COLIN RYNNE

Despite its immediate proximity to the cradle of European industrialization, most of Ireland never became industrialized in either an English or a European sense. The precise reasons for this are beyond the scope of this chapter. Suffice it to say that in English industrial archaeology explanation begins with why industrialization took place. In Ireland the issue is why it did not and, more to the point, who was to blame. 'Failure' is the key word in the economic history of Ireland, but while its resonances have been all-pervasive, it has all too often hidden the successes. Nonetheless, industrialization did take place here, although it was extremely localized, yet the island's *potential* to industrialize in the eighteenth and nineteenth centuries remains a moot point, a hypothetical possibility. Clearly Ireland never experienced the changes which industrialization brought about in countries like England, Germany and France. Yet industries of both national and international significance became established here.

The progress of truly large-scale industrialization in Ireland during the same period exhibits a pronounced regional bias. The area around the Lagan Valley in Ulster is the only Irish region to experience it. By the beginning of the twentieth century Ulster had the largest shipbuilding yards in the world and the most extensive linen industry of any industrialized region in Europe. All this is clear. The precise reasons for the 'failure' of other Irish regions to experience large-scale industrialization, however, are not. But, as will be seen below, the general lack of concentration of industry in Ireland is offset by the extent and quality of the preservation of its industrial heritage. Its predominantly agrarian society also presents rather different challenges to Irish industrial archaeologists in regard to defining the relationships between the pre-industrial elements of the eighteenth- and nineteenth-century Irish landscape and those associated with Irish industry, especially as industry was not the dominant activity in many parts of Ireland well

into the twentieth century. In real terms, Belfast was the only Victorian industrial city in Ireland; the economic fabric of both Dublin and Cork was essentially commercial rather than industrial. Small pockets of dispersed industrial activity became established near the ports and larger country towns such as Limerick, Dundalk, Waterford and Galway with varying degrees of success, but overall this patchwork of industry can in no way be compared to developments in Europe.

The question of what constitutes industrial heritage is a thorny one, and no less so in Ireland than elsewhere. Traditionally, the methodologies used by its practitioners have only notionally been 'archaeological', and this continues to trouble conventional archaeologists, particularly those who have come to the discipline from traditional archaeological backgrounds. The term 'industrial archaeology', indeed, was only coined in 1955. Moreover, even though, as Dr W. A. McCutcheon suggested, 'much of the initial unacceptability of the phrase was due to the unnecessarily narrow interpretation of the word "archaeology" then current' (1980, 372, n.1), the adoption of normal archaeological methodologies in industrial archaeological fieldwork has not been widespread. We must thus be prepared to acknowledge that industrial archaeology, in many of its current forms, does not meet archaeological needs and wants. As one recent commentator has noted, the origins of industrial archaeology 'grew from the need to record and preserve standing structures threatened with demolition rather than an inherent desire to understand about the historical period of the monument' (Palmer 1990, 275).

The diversity of interests and agendas in industrial archaeology has made it a difficult entity to define. This has as much to do with the wide range of interests found within the discipline as with the inability of its practitioners to agree on a single definition or, indeed, on the very nature of the discipline itself. The rapid growth in interest in industrial archaeology in the last three decades, particularly in the United Kingdom, has brought together an amazing collection of interest groups for whom industrial archaeology has become a 'meeting ground where older established disciplines overlap' (McCutcheon 1980, xxxix). Interest in and enthusiasm for the material remains of industrialization have been the glue which has held such interest groups together, but alone they are not, perhaps, the best building blocks for a professional and academically detached discipline. The academic credentials of industrial archaeology have thus been questioned, and not without due cause. This perceived lack of scholarly intent initially spurred its detractors, but it remains one of its greatest strengths. For the sheer diversity and increasing complexity of industrial monuments between 1750 and 1930 have always encouraged an interdisciplinary approach amongst its practitioners and, while industrial archaeologists have recently been urged to consider exactly how more 'conventional archaeological concepts and techniques apply to their own particular field' (Palmer 1990, 276), conventional archaeologists can also learn from the flexibility inherent in industrial archaeology since the 1950s.

Definitions of industrial archaeology abound, but rarely concur, and curiously much of the debate has centred on the historical period forming the basis for study for industrial archaeologists rather than on how the methodologies employed by them square with those used by archaeologists working in other periods. Industrial archaeology has recently been defined as 'a period study embracing the tangible evidence of social, economic and technological development in the period since industrialization' (Palmer 1990, 281). But, if industrial archaeology is a period study, does it simply update the physical development of the landscape since the post-medieval period (and thus include agriculture), or is it concerned exclusively with the archaeology of the cultural phenomenon called industrialization?

Agriculture and rural crafts, especially those which involved power-assisted machinery, are also considered to be of industrial archaeological interest, as are what are commonly termed service or tertiary activities such as banks, cinemas and hospitals. Other areas of interest directly associated with industrialization, such as educational establishments and housing, are as much a part of the industrial infrastructure as of the culture associated with it, and their study has increasingly been drawn into the ambit of industrial archaeology. In Ireland, however, the academic study of such structures has largely been conducted by ethnologists and architectural historians.

THE DEVELOPMENT OF INDUSTRIAL ARCHAEOLOGY IN IRELAND

In the late 1950s and early 1960s some of the earliest government-financed industrial archaeological surveys in the world were to be undertaken in county Down by the late Professor Rodney Green. Under the auspices of the Ancient Monuments Council of Northern Ireland, Green surveyed textile-processing sites of the linen industry, along with complexes associated with food-processing industries (brewing, distilling, grain milling and so forth) and aspects of the transport and communications of the area. The publication of the results of county Down survey in 1963 was the first of its type for any region of the UK or the Republic of Ireland (Green 1963; Hamond 1998, 1). Elsewhere in the UK only in Scotland, where nineteenth-century industrial buildings began to feature in the Royal Commission of Ancient and Historic Monuments' county inventories, compiled in the 1950s, had any comparable effort been made to focus attention on aspects of industrial heritage. Indeed, the Industrial Monuments Survey in England was only established by the Council for British Archaeology and the English Ministry of Public Buildings and Works in 1963, the year Rodney Green's survey was published. Unfortunately, even the most recent account of the origins of industrial archaeological survey has failed to recognize the truly pioneering work by Green and, later, by McCutcheon in Ulster (Palmer and Neaverson 1998, 2).

In 1962 the Ancient Monuments Council appointed Dr Alan McCutcheon to carry out a more detailed survey of the industrial archaeology of the province. McCutcheon embarked upon a systematic industrial archaeological study of the six counties funded by the Northern Ireland Department of Finance, and the results of his fieldwork, undertaken between 1962 and 1968, complemented by an extensive documentary survey, were published in *The industrial archaeology of Northern Ireland* (1980). This was the first comprehensive, large-scale survey of its type in either Britain or Ireland. McCutcheon's survey of the industrial archaeology of the province was also a timely one. During the 1960s, when his work was underway, many of the north's traditional industries were closing down, whilst key linen mills in the Falls and Crumlin Road areas were later to be destroyed during the 'Troubles'. Documentary sources also played a key role in the description and analysis of the industrial sites featured in his inventory, and McCutcheon must be credited as the first fieldworker to demonstrate their effectiveness in large-scale survey (McCutcheon 1966, 1983; Cunningham 1995). In 1982 a research fellowship funded by the Historic Monuments and Buildings Branch (HMBB) of the Department of the Environment, Northern Ireland (DOE NI), enabled Cormac Scally to transform the McCutcheon archive — more than 20,000 photographs, slides and glass plate negatives, business records and architectural and engineering drawings — into an Industrial Archaeological Record (IAR) for the province (Scally and Yates 1985). McCutcheon had

Fig. 5.1 The twenty-sixth lock on the Grand Canal, near Tullamore, county Offaly, with restored late eighteenth-century lock-keeper's house in foreground.

begun, but was unable to complete, a photographic survey of Belfast, and since the late 1960s, when he had completed his work, an anomalous situation had arisen whereby Belfast and its environs had not been surveyed. Clearly such an inventory was required for planning purposes and the HMBB, now the Environment and Heritage: Built Heritage (EHS:BH) agency of the DOE NI, commissioned Dr Fred Hamond and Cormac Scally to produce an industrial archaeological record of the Greater Belfast Area. Some 1,160 sites, dating from 1830 to 1930, were identified in a 180 sq km area during the course of fieldwork of the Greater Belfast Industrial Archaeology Survey (GBIAS), completed in 1988, and this has since been integrated into the province's IAR, now called the Industrial Heritage Record (IHR) (Hamond 1998, 1). During the 1980s further extensive survey work has been carried out by EHS:BH throughout the province. These include a detailed survey of Rathlin Island, off the north coast of Ulster, along with a series of thematic surveys of sites such as gasworks and canals. Other activities included a resurvey of around 500 or so sites which were singled out by McCutcheon, in his original fieldwork, as being among the most important in the six counties. In 1991 the Natural Heritage agency of the EHS also commissioned Dr Fred Hamond to undertake an industrial archeological survey within the Areas of Outstanding Natural Beauty (AONBs) in northern and eastern county Antrim (Hamond 1993).

Inevitably, perhaps, given the AD 1700 cut-off date for the inclusion of archaeological sites deemed to be worthy of study and preservation in the early *National Monuments Acts* (see below), the specific study of industrial monuments in the Republic of Ireland did not really get underway until the late 1960s and early 1970s. In reality, though, it was already flourishing, albeit under other names. The Irish Railway Record Society (IRRS), established in 1946, with active branches in the larger Irish cities and in London, has long been involved in the conservation and preservation of Ireland's railway heritage, and the establishment of an all-Ireland Steam Preservation Society has resulted in a series of ambitious restoration schemes. An abiding enthusiasm for Irish canals, coupled with a realization of their enormous potential for amenity use and tourism, led to the establishment of the Inland Waterways Association of Ireland (IWAI), co-founded by Colonel Harry Rice and Vincent Delany in 1954 (Delany 1988, 134, 177). The IWAI has been actively involved in canal conservation projects and scored a notable success in its campaign to save the Dublin section of the Royal Canal. In addition, studies of individual Irish canals — the Grand Canal (Delany 1973) and the Ballinamore and Ballyconnell Canal (Flanagan 1972) — along with general surveys of canals in Ulster (McCutcheon 1965) and in the Republic (Delany and Delany 1966), have also been published in the David and Charles series (see also Delany 1988). Studies of the Royal

Canal have also been published by Peter Clarke (1992) and Ruth Delany (1992).

Unfortunately, the enthusiasm shown for railways and inland waterways in Ireland was slow to spread to other areas. In the early 1970s the Irish Society for Industrial Archaeology was established, whose members (notably William Dick, Gavan Bowie and Ken Mawhinney) published a wide variety of short pieces on the more notable Irish sites in the periodical *Technology Ireland*. The latter were aimed at a general readership, and their expert insight, when wedded to an attractive magazine design, did much to focus attention on the country's industrial heritage. Yet by the end of the 1970s this society was defunct. A new organization, The Society for Industrial Archaeology in Munster — a predominantly Cork-based society — was established in 1986. The latter also sprang from promising origins but eventually met with the same fate. However, in June 1996 a new society, the Industrial Heritage Association of Ireland (IHAI), with a thirty-two county membership concerned with the preservation and recording of the industrial heritage of Ireland, was established. Since its foundation the membership of this society has been actively involved in survey, conservation and in influencing government policy on related matters.

Successive governments in the Irish Republic have been slow to realize that industrial archaeology forms an important part of Ireland's historic landscape, a fact all too clearly illustrated by the exclusion of such sites from previous national monuments legislation. Under the earlier acts archaeology officially ended in the year 1700, but under the 1987 Amendment to the *National Monuments Acts*, the Office of Public Works (latterly Dúchas, the state Heritage Service) became empowered to use its discretion where post-1700 sites of national importance were involved. Under this new provision the proprietors of industrial archaeological sites, deemed to be important, now required planning permission in order either to alter or demolish such sites. In 1994 a further amendment to the *National Monuments Acts* enabled industrial archaeological sites to be added to the national record of monuments, and thus be afforded a measure of statutory protection.

On the face of it, the 1994 amendment would appear to have come a little too late. Fortunately the former inadequacies of the *National Monuments* legislation were in no small part countered by local government legislation which, since the early 1960s, had been working in favour of Ireland's important historic industrial sites. Under the 1963 *Local Government (Planning and Development) Act* local authorities in Ireland were required to draft Development Plans. Furthermore, any buildings which were deemed to be of artistic, architectural or historic interest by an authority could feature on a list of sites to be included in a Development Plan which were considered to be worthy of preservation. By 'listing' a building in this way a local authority had the right to refuse planning permission for any alterations to it that were deemed to be unsuitable or which might interfere with its long-term survival. In the 1970s An Foras Forbartha (AFF) commissioned a series of county-based surveys of industrial monuments and sites in the Irish Republic, which were undertaken by Gavan Bowie on its behalf. As early as 1971 a Conservation and Amenity Service (CAAS) was established by AFF. In the years 1973 to 1975 Gavan Bowie completed survey work (mostly of water-powered mill and bridges) in eight southern counties (Cavan, Clare, Donegal, Kerry, Kildare, Louth, Monaghan and north Tipperary) and was later followed by John Courlander who undertook fieldwork in a further ten over a three-year period. These included counties Carlow, north Cork, south Dublin, Longford, Mayo, Meath, Sligo, Waterford, Wexford and Wicklow. A further, more comprehensive survey was conducted in county Kilkenny in 1986 by Dr Fred Hamond for Kilkenny County Council. This latter was also initiated by CAAS, and involved the examination of 650 sites, some 165 of which were to feature in the county development plan (Hamond 1998, 1–3).

It was not until the 1980s, however, with the initiation of the Office of Public Works-sponsored Archaeological Survey of County Cork, that the Irish government became officially involved in the systematic recording of industrial sites and monuments. The recent publication of the first volumes of the Cork Archaeological Survey (Power *et al.* 1992 [vol. 1], 1994 [vol. 2] and 1997 [vol. 3]) by the Office of Public Works, which include inventories of a selection of industrial archeological sites in county Cork compiled by Mary Sleeman, is an important development. The inclusion of selected industrial monuments (mostly windmills) in *The archaeological inventory of county Wexford* (Moore 1996) is also to be welcomed. Further survey work has been undertaken in county Dublin (Scally 1998), in Dublin's Docklands (McMahon 1998) and in the city of Cork and its immediate environs (Rynne 1998, 1999). In 1985 Ireland signed the Grenada Convention on the Protection of Europe's Architectural Heritage, but until such time as a comprehensive inventory of the many thousands of post-1700 AD sites had been prepared, little could be done to protect them. Thus, in 1991, a pilot project was initiated in Carlow town by the then Office of Public Works, and so began the survey of an estimated one million buildings in the Irish Republic. To date upwards of 30,000 buildings have been recorded in large parts of some 24 towns.

Recent legislation regularizing maintenance of local authority archives, many of which are repositories of important business archives, will also further research and survey work by facilitating access to, and by preserving, important documentary materials relating to our industrial heritage. The establishment of the Centre for Civil Engineering Heritage, Trinity College, Dublin, and the Technological Heritage Archive in University College, Galway, are further welcome developments, as is the publication of an excellent guide to the archives of the Irish Board of Works (Lohan 1994). The Mining History Society of Ireland has also been recently established to cater for a growing interest in the development of Irish mines and their history, and has reprinted Grenville Cole's important monograph on mineral resources in Ireland (Cole 1998).

The conservation of the island's industrial heritage has proceeded apace in more recent years. The National Trust in Northern Ireland has been active in restoring industrial archaeological sites such as Wellbrook Beetling Mill, Florence Court Sawmill, Castleward Corn Mill and Patterson's Spade Mill. Local interest groups and local authorities have also made important contributions to preserving the industrial heritage of Northern Ireland, as in the case of Annalong Corn Mill in county Down and Moneypenny's Lock in county Armagh. The Department of the Environment (Northern Ireland) has played an important role in listing and scheduling industrial archaeological sites within its jurisdiction. Indeed, in both jurisdictions important industrial archaeological sites, such as Ballycopeland Windmill in Northern Ireland and the Newmills complex in county Donegal, have been taken into state care, whilst the Irish and British governments have co-operated in the development of the Erne-Shannon waterway. The large-scale development of heritage tourism in the Irish Republic, fuelled by European Regional Development Funds during the 1980s, enabled a number of important sites to be restored and made accessible to the public. Again, the implementation of many such schemes, such as the Blennerville Windmill in county Kerry and Ballincollig Gunpowder Mills in county Cork, could not have come about without the active involvement of local authorities, private interest groups and state-sponsored bodies like FÁS.

PAST PROBLEMS AND CURRENT PERCEPTIONS
Industrial archaeological sites have presented very special problems to planning authorities and to state agencies entrusted with the care and maintenance of historic buildings and landscapes. At a very basic level this may involve the sheer size of some industrial enterprises, or the perceived degree of 'redundancy' of a particular building type with regard to adapting it for modern use. Yet there is also a marked bias towards buildings which, for whatever reason, are considered to be more aesthetically pleasing and thus more worthy of retention than others which are deemed not to be. If an industrial building meets this rather basic and clearly superficial criterion of value then it may well be considered worthy of retention. At best a limited number of sites will survive under this notion, but at worst this rather superficial register of value will not be applied to the original machinery. Most industrial structures dating to the early decades of the present century, indeed, are not buildings in a strict architectural sense. It is therefore well nigh impossible to apply values and criteria taken from art/architectural history to certain industrial structures. The basic policy options in regard to preservation, it is clear, should involve more than superficial visual qualities (Alfry and Putnam 1992).

The application of the term 'derelict' to describe industrial buildings and landscapes by planning authorities will often be as good as a green light to a developer to demolish and redevelop. That other historic landscapes may be equally so in the sense that, while they are of undisputed historical value they are unlikely to be 'used' for anything else, appears to matter little. Dereliction denotes fundamental untidyness, ugliness and, of course, ultimate worthlessness while in the 'derelict' state. The common response is to tidy up the 'mess' (Sharpe 1995). In recent years the tendency to 'clean up' historic industrial areas through either well-intentioned but over-designed re-adaptation or complete redevelopment has been all too evident. Buildings which have survived as ruins, for example, are a case in point. A roofless, floorless warehouse on an urban riverfront, for instance, will only in the most exceptional circumstances be allowed to escape redevelopment, whereas interference with the remains of a medieval building in a similar location will generally not be tolerated. The medieval building may have no great architectural merit nor be able to lay claims to association with an important historic personage or event. Its age, however, will almost certainly guarantee its protection. Thus as a building's value is often seen as being proportionate to its age (regardless of the frequency with which such building types occur elsewhere or even within a particular locality), 'derelict' industrial buildings dating to the last two hundred years have traditionally been unprotected. The perception that a building's historical value is directly related to its age is a deep-rooted one. Thus while surviving eighteenth - century cotton mills in the Republic of Ireland are extremely rare, it is much more likely that a preservation order would be placed on a nondescript tower house than on a cotton mill.

The idea of 'dereliction' as commonly applied to industrial buildings and landscapes definitely requires reappraisal. Apart from the connotations outlined above, dereliction has also been viewed as a component of the 'nuisance value' of redundant industrial buildings. Buildings which have been abandoned after fire or cumulative neglect, particularly in run-down urban areas, can present a danger to the public, either through

Fig. 5.2 Original valve house built in the 1860s at Dublin Corporation's Vartry Water Works in county Wicklow.

imminency of collapse, as a health hazard or simply because they attract the homeless or vandals. In these and in similar circumstances a requirement that these buildings be retained would be viewed as a severe development constraint. Regardless of the historic or technological importance of the buildings concerned, it is unlikely that either the buildings would be conserved *in situ* or that at the very least an alternative use for them would be sought.

The sites of former extractive industries such as quarries and mines can prove to be particularly troublesome. The most common problems are pollution, erosion, underground structural collapse and subsidence and general health and safety hazards resulting from the use of many extractive sites as unofficial rubbish tips and landfill sites (Briggs 1992). Moreover, the recording and conservation of these sites is extremely problematical. They can often cover several acres, whilst features such as mineshafts and adits may not be accessible to surveyors. Indeed, even if a mine or quarry is considered worthy of conservation, how does one go about it? Surface features such as engine houses, dressing floors and workers' accommodation may be an obvious focus of attention, but how does one define the extent of the underground features? Even when industrial archaeological sites and landscapes are readily acknowledged as important in themselves, or at least on a par with archaeological sites of earlier periods, basic considerations such as recording and conservation can present huge financial burdens. Cork County Council has already directed considerable resources towards the development of Ballincollig Gunpowder Mills, the largest industrial archaeological site in Ireland. The resources involved, while considerable have, nonetheless, been expended largely over the years 1986–93. If, for example, a similar complex, spatially extensive and diverse site were to require immediate recording prior to demolition or adaptation for modern use, the resources necessary for such an investigation to proceed within a short

period of time would be difficult to come by. In the first instance a prospective developer would view a requirement that such an investigation was necessary as a negative constraint, as indeed he would a stipulation that certain features of existing buildings (or indeed that the buildings themselves) be retained.

Adaptive re-use of industrial buildings is more likely to occur to them than to archaeological sites of earlier periods. This should be, and often is, a welcome development in that it allows many industrial buildings a new lease of life. Adaptive re-use can often ensure their survival by justifying their continued existence, to the extent that a building or complex of buildings can, as it were, earn their keep by accommodating alternative uses. There are, however, no general guidelines governing such developments with regard to certain key areas. The decommissioning of public utilities and components of the public transport system, for example, can present special problems. To begin with, many of the decommissioned elements, such as waterworks, electricity generating stations, railway stations and so forth, will in themselves be of industrial archaeological interest. Water distribution networks will generally be controlled by either municipal or county authorities, but there are no policy guidelines on their recording, conservation or re-adaptation. Similarly, the ESB, Iarnród Éireann and the Defence Forces are not statutorily obliged to heritage manage the sites of industrial archaeological interest either in their ownership or under their control.

As with archaeological sites of most periods, historic industrial buildings and landscapes have survived through basic inertia. Even buildings in a ruinous state have continued to survive simply because of the expense involved in demolishing them. Others, however, have lasted because their original use is still valid, as in the case of many railway stations, or because an alternative use has been found for them. Some buildings, indeed, can have been re-used several times for different industrial purposes. At any stage during a building's history accretive adaptations are likely to have occurred, and it is these adaptations which define the building's function over certain periods of time. These adaptations can vary greatly. They may be purely structural, as in the case of the addition of an extra storey, an annexe or fireproof flooring. Motive power and plant can also change through time, either through modernization or through a complete changeover to another manufacturing process. In the latter case internal changes to the building may be much more in evidence, but in all cases changes to a building's form and function will determine the extent to which it will survive the next period of technological modernization or economic change. A building or complex whose form has become too specialized is unlikely to be re-used when its original purpose has

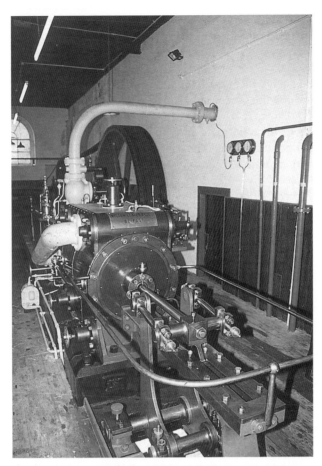

Fig. 5.3 Nineteenth-century textile mill engine in former linen weaving mill near Belturbet, county Tyrone.

become obsolete, and in consequence its chances of survival would, in normal circumstances, be considerably reduced. But in Ireland de-industrialization in many areas during the nineteenth century and subsequent economic underdevelopment have created a relatively high survival rate for many different varieties of archaeological site. Many important Irish industrial archaeological sites have also benefited from this circumstance, and have survived in recent times without protective legislation.

In the absence of statutory protection for industrial archaeological sites, and with the 1987 and 1994 amendments to the *National Monuments Acts* yet to prove their efficacy in this regard, a building must still demonstrate that it can be adapted for modern use to ensure its continued survival. In normal circumstances this will have an important bearing on planning decisions. However, the extent to which the planning authorities will be prepared to force developers to re-adapt existing buildings rather than to demolish and build anew is another matter. Regardless of its state of preservation prospective developers may be reluctant to re-adapt an historic building when the option to demolish is available, if they can demonstrate that the building is

manifestly unsuitable for their future purposes. A stipulation to have an 'archaeological record' (generally unspecified) made of the building before demolition is often the only avenue open to the planning authorities, unless a government agency such as Dúchas takes firm action.

The conservation problem is further compounded by the fact that certain types of industrial archaeological site can be impossible to adapt satisfactorily to new uses. Indeed, the most common options availed of — modern light industry, offices and domestic dwellings — are themselves quite limited. In the main these options tend to favour small industrial buildings, although in Ireland larger complexes such as defunct nineteenth-century textile mills and distilleries tend to be re-used as industrial estates. Coercion in regard to the re-use of old buildings is necessary to a certain degree, but encouragement should also be given to developers, home buyers and the like to make re-use an economically attractive option.

Regardless of the state of preservation in which an historic building's fabric has survived, original machinery surviving *in situ* can cause serious problems for its re-use. In the case of traditional water-powered flour mills, for example, where a simple two- or three-storey mill is considered for re-use as a domestic dwelling, the retention of the machinery would practically rule out any such conversion. From a conservation viewpoint, the retention of the machinery would be critical to enable the building to maintain its historic integrity; indeed the argument should be made that with the removal of the machinery the building loses its context. In other words it effectively ceases to be a mill. If the machinery has been removed long ago and the building re-used for another purpose, then the removal of the machinery can be legitimately considered to be an accretive adaptation of the site. However, if the machinery survives it should be retained, as it would be in every way as much a fixture of the site as the buildings housing it. Up until very recently the contents of buildings, owing to a legal loophole, were not protected by a listing order, but new legislation is set to remedy this.

Like all historic buildings, those associated with industrial archaeological sites also require extensive research to provide a detailed outline of their development through time, as well as extensive recording of the surviving fabric, in order to facilitate conservation and repair work. Rarely, however, is such research undertaken for industrial archaeological structures, as traditionally they have not been seen as being as important as sites of other periods. For conservation and repair work on most historic buildings before AD 1700 the consent of Dúchas is necessary. There are, however, no firm statutory guidelines on how such works should be undertaken, and at the present showing the Republic of Ireland has no equivalent of the UK's Planning Policy Guideline Note 15 (PPG 15).

CONCLUSION

Ireland occupies a unique position in Europe in terms of the extent of the preservation of its industrial sites and monuments, north and south, and in terms of the pioneering work conducted by Rodney Green and Alan McCutcheon in the recording of its industrial heritage. Around 100,000 sites of industrial archaeological interest are now believed to survive on the island, but only a very small number of these have been recorded to date, even at a basic level. Inevitably further survey work will follow, but will it keep pace with building development? As is the case with archaeological sites of all periods, thematic surveys of specific sites are urgently needed to enable important sites to be identified and to prioritize conservation needs. There is also a requirement for a national museum of industrial technology to establish, preserve and curate a national collection of industrial machinery.

Bibliography

Alfry, J. and Putnam, T. 1992 *The industrial heritage: managing resources and uses*. London.

Briggs, C. Stephen 1995 'The conservation of non-ferrous mines' in C. Stephen Briggs (ed) *Welsh industrial heritage: review* (London), pp. 32–41.

Clarke, P. 1992 *The Royal Canal: the complete story*. Dublin.

Coles, G. A. J. 1998 *Memoir of localities of minerals of economic importance and metalliferous mines in Ireland*. Dublin.

Cunningham, N. 1995 'The McCutcheon archive — a survey of industrial archaeology', *Ulster Local Studies* 15, 1, pp. 62–71.

Delany, R. 1973 *The Grand Canal of Ireland*. Newton Abbot.

Delany, R. 1988 *Ireland's inland waterways*. Belfast.

Delany, R. 1992 *Ireland's Royal Canal 1789–1992*. Dublin.

Green, E. R. R. 1963 *The industrial archaeology of county Down*. Belfast.

Hamond, F. 1993 *Antrim coast and glens industrial heritage*. Belfast.

Hamond, F. 1998 'Introduction' in IHAI 1998, pp. 1–3.

IHAI 1998 *Taking stock of Ireland's industrial heritage*. Dublin.

Lohan, R. 1994 *Guide to the archives of the Office of Public Works*. Dublin.

McCutcheon, W. A. 1965 *The canals of the north of Ireland*. Newton Abbot.

McCutcheon, W. A. 1966 'The use of documentary source material in the Northern Ireland Survey of Industrial Archaeology', *Economic History Review* 19, 2, pp. 401–12.

McCutcheon, W. A. 1980 *The industrial archaeology of Northern Ireland*. Belfast.

McCutcheon, W. A. 1983 'Industrial archaeology: a case study in Northern Ireland', *World Archaeology* 15, 2, pp. 161–71.

McMahon, M. 1998 'Recording the industrial heritage of Dublin's docklands' in IHAI 1998, 8–11.

Moore, M. 1996 *Archaeological inventory of county Wexford*. Dublin.

Palmer, M. 1990 'Industrial archaeology a thematic or period discipline?', *Antiquity* 64, 243, pp. 275–85.

Palmer, M. and Neaverson, P. 1998 *Industrial archaeology: principles and practice*. London.

Power, D. *et al.* 1992 *Archaeological inventory of county Cork. Vol. 1 – west Cork*. Dublin.

Power, D. *et al.* 1994 *Archaeological inventory of county Cork. Vol. 2 – east and south Cork*. Dublin.

Power, D. *et al.* 1997 *Archaeological inventory of county Cork. Vol. 3 – mid Cork*. Dublin.

Rynne, C. 1998 'The industrial archaeology of Cork city and its environs' in IHAI 1998, 16–9.

Rynne, C. 1999 *The industrial archaeology of Cork city and its environs*. Dublin.

Scally, G. 1998 'Industrial archaeology survey of county Dublin' in IHAI 1998, pp. 4–7.

Scally, C. and Yates, M. 1985 'The Industrial Archaeology Record for Northern Ireland', *Ulster Local Studies* 9, 21, pp. 178–80.

Sharpe, A. 1995 'Development under derelict land grants' in M. Palmer and P. Neaverson (eds) *Managing the industrial heritage: its identification, recording and management* (Leicester), pp. 133–36.

Civil Engineering Heritage

RON COX

Civil engineering heritage may be defined as the surviving works of past generations of civil engineers. Until the creation of the separate discipline of mechanical engineering in the mid-nineteenth century, civil, as distinct from military, engineering, encompassed all engineering work. Thus historically, civil engineering may be interpreted in the broadest sense to include structures built in support of industrial development and extractive industries, including power generation, as well as transportation systems and public health works. Civil engineering heritage should not be confused with industrial heritage (also referred to as industrial archaeology) which deals with all aspects of the history of technology and surviving evidence of industrial activity. Nor should it be equated with architectural heritage, an area where different assessment criteria apply and much emphasis is placed on the artistic and aesthetic qualities of a structure.

In order for local authorities and similar bodies to manage elements of civil engineering heritage, it was first of all necessary to understand their local and national significance. This could not be achieved without a nation-wide survey and the establishment of a database within which comparisons could be made regarding the relative importance and landmark value of individual heritage sites or groupings of them. Landmark value has always been regarded by civil engineering historians as of great importance in any studies of the historical development of civil engineering design and construction methods. Ireland, although never industrialized to anything like the same extent as Britain, has, nevertheless, played a part in such development. For instance, there are a number of examples of structures that may be deemed to have been at the leading edge of the technology of the day at the time of their completion. In a number of cases, Irish engineers took calculated risks in adopting and applying new design concepts and construction methods.

The approach to the recording of civil engineering heritage has developed in a somewhat different way to that adopted by industrial archaeologists. This has, to a large extent, been influenced by the resources available and the manner in which the now wider interest in civil engineering heritage has grown only slowly over the years. From being the province of a very few enthusiasts, there is currently a greatly increased awareness of the value of understanding and conserving the best of the built environment. The long struggle to gain acceptance of the importance of our inland waterways as a tourism and recreational amenity is a case in point. Had it not been for the monumental voluntary efforts of a few dedicated persons, the inland waterway network in Ireland would have long since crumbled away and have been forgotten, except by a few transport historians, and a part of civil engineering heritage would have been lost for ever.

Inland waterways are now accepted as part of our national heritage, but they also contain within themselves individual heritage items which fall into other heritage areas such as architecture, industrial archaeology and civil engineering. Thus, the policy for the future of the inland waterways is that they and their corridors should be developed in an integrated, broad-based way, conserving where possible their built and archaeological heritage features as well as protecting the unique ecological systems present in or around them. It is clear that conserving heritage enhances people's enjoyment of it, and that conservation need not be at odds with economic growth, but rather protects the very asset that such growth is seeking to exploit.

And this leads on to another aspect of the recording of civil engineering heritage in Ireland as well as in Britain. Efforts have been concentrated on recording the extant heritage, and less on what existed in the past. Timber bridges provide a good example. There were many fine instances of such bridges, like those built by the

Fig. 6.1 Fastnet Rock Lighthouse, off the coast of county Cork.

American, Lemuel Cox, at Waterford, New Ross and Derry, but timber is not as durable a material as stone, and no Irish timber bridges have survived, due mainly to the dampness of the climate. The history of such bridges is interesting, but it is difficult for the general public to relate to something which is no longer extant. Industrial heritage surveys, on the other hand, like architectural heritage inventories, tend to be all-embracing, albeit concentrating, in the first case, on the extant remains of industrial sites and, on the other, on the exterior and interior of buildings, including vernacular architecture.

Major transportation routes, such as canals, railways and roads, are, by their nature, linear features and may extend for many miles. The recording of such features cannot be regarded as solely the listing of a number of individual elements, such as locks, station buildings or bridges. In order to understand the historical or landmark value of such a civil engineering project, it is necessary to consider the concept, survey, design, construction and maintenance of the project in its entirety. It is, of course, possible, and in fact desirable, to single out particular elements in the transportation route for special attention, for instance a major bridge of some landmark value, such as largest span, first use of a

particular material, only example in the area and the like. This is vital for the assessment of the importance of items deemed worthy of conservation. Realistically, only a few structures will attract public (or private) funding for their conservation and/or restoration. Thus it is even more important that the assessment is founded on sound historical facts and on expert opinion.

THE NATIONAL ENGINEERING HERITAGE DATABASE

The recording of civil engineering heritage in Ireland has until now been carried out in a subjective way and has not been all-embracing. Nevertheless, map studies have been conducted for the whole country and each county has been visited at least once during the field recording work associated with the project. All significant transportation routes and associated infrastructure have been surveyed and their elements recorded. This subjective approach was necessitated by the limited resources available for fieldwork, but this was offset by access to expert knowledge backed up by local information in the engineering departments of local authorities.

The National Engineering Heritage Database has been in existence for a number of years and results from a project inaugurated in 1988. The project was supported by the Heritage Society of the Institution of Engineers of Ireland (IEI). A chartered civil engineer, Dr Ron Cox, was appointed project director, the principal aim of the project being to identify any items of engineering heritage in this country. Although the IEI represents all branches of the engineering profession in Ireland, the project was restricted, in the first instance, to civil engineering heritage as defined above.

The first phase involved the preparation of a draft national listing of possible sites based on a map study and literature search. In order to check the validity of this, it was necessary to visit each local authority to discuss the completeness of the listing, to draw up a priority inventory of items for recording and to carry out a visual and photographic survey of as many sites as time and resources permitted. This phase, which was supported by a small grant from the National Heritage Council (the forerunner of the present Heritage Council), was substantially completed by the end of 1989. At that stage, a photographic exhibition was mounted at the IEI to provide a visual indication of the range of engineering heritage to be recorded and to assist with the procurement of further financial support.

The recording methodology adopted was that employed by the Institution of Civil Engineers Panel for Historical Engineering Works (PHEW), which began work in 1971 and which covers the United Kingdom and Northern Ireland. However, as was noted earlier, the criteria used needed to be modified somewhat before applying them to the Irish situation. The setting of such criteria is always the subject of great debate amongst

Fig. 6.2 Mizen Head Bridge, county Cork.

engineering historians and the wisdom of selecting a particular item or site for further study was of necessity bound to be somewhat subjective at the outset of the project. Nevertheless, it was possible to lay down a number of criteria which were deemed to be appropriate to local conditions, for example the fact that the topography and the development of the economy of the country limited the extent of the engineering heritage and the lack of adequate protection provided by the then method of the protective listing of structures. The criteria adopted included:

(a) *Heritage under threat:* Items which were considered for various reasons to be under threat of removal or significant alteration (such as public utilities, waterworks, upgraded railway bridges and so forth) were surveyed and recorded first as a matter of urgency and a close watch was maintained on their well-being.

(b) *Rarity:* Ireland being, until recently, a largely non-industrial nation, examples representing the development of engineering design and construction are far fewer than is the case, for instance, in Britain. Thus, items which may be commonplace elsewhere take on a rarity value in the Irish context; 'first examples' are often of a later date then elsewhere.

(c) *Type:* It appeared that, in the early stages of the project, it was desirable to record in detail at least one or two examples of each of the main types of civil

engineering heritage, for instance railways, canals, harbours and so forth, in order to present an overview of the heritage stock.

(d) *Age:* This is a good, but not infallible, guide to the selection of an item for further investigation. It is still necessary to consider whether or not an item is a worthy example of the state of the art at the time of construction. (It was subsequently found that Ireland does in fact possess a number of examples where design and construction were pushed to new limits, as in the case of lighthouses and early railway viaducts.)

(e) *State of preservation:* In terms of its importance in the visual environment, an item generally needs to be in a reasonable state of preservation, although there are always exceptions. The Irish economy can only support preservation and maintenance of its inherited infrastructure to a limited extent. Work is normally only carried out on items of engineering heritage if public safety is being compromised (such as increased axle loadings on bridges) or the existing infrastructure is to be developed for other purposes, such as recreational pursuits and tourism, as for example in the case of the waterways.

(f) *Location:* It was considered that recording should initially be spread as widely as possible throughout the country in order to stimulate national interest in its work and generate an awareness of our engineering heritage.

Having set the criteria for selection, fieldwork associated with the second phase of the project (also funded by the National Heritage Council) commenced in 1991. In addition to completion of the standard recording forms, a computerized database was set up using Microsoft ACCESS. To date some 270 items have been recorded and entered into the database and the work is ongoing. The records may be consulted in the Centre for Civil Engineering Heritage and the Library of the Institution of Engineers of Ireland in Dublin. Copies of the records are also held in the Library of the Institution of Civil Engineering (ICE) in London.

The method of assessing civil engineering heritage sites has until now been somewhat subjective and based on general knowledge. In the future, such appraisal is likely to be more objective and based on the current work of a number of sub-panels reporting to the ICE Panel for Historical Engineering Works. These sub-panels are currently developing appraisal formulae for a number of areas including masonry and iron bridges, inland waterways, water towers and windmills. It will probably still be necessary to modify the assessment criteria used in Britain to reflect the situation in Ireland, otherwise there would be few, if any, structures worthy of top grading in this country. This is where local factors need to be considered. A good example of the application of local significance factors comes from Australia, where one fairly ordinary masonry arch bridge, dating from the 1820s, turns out to be the oldest bridge in the country and is thus accorded maximum heritage status. In a similar way, the Liffey Bridge in Dublin, a very modest span cast-iron bridge dating from 1816, would rate highly in a local context, even though there are many better examples across the water in Britain.

Arising from the database project, a publication entitled *Civil engineering heritage: Ireland*, co-authored by Dr Ron Cox and Dr Michael Gould, was issued by Thomas Telford Publications, London, in February 1998 and covers the whole of the island of Ireland. Each chapter relates to a defined geographical area. A location map, a list of described sites and a brief introduction are provided for all chapters. References for individual items are included, where appropriate, and there is appended a select bibliography relating to civil engineering heritage in this country. Each site is numbered and grid referenced. The items were selected in order to illustrate some aspect of the historic development of civil engineering skills or the scope of activity undertaken by the civil engineering profession in Ireland.

Architecture

RACHEL MOSS

The built environment provides a significant record of Ireland's history. The constant development of different types and forms of man-made structures reflects responses to changing social and economic circumstances, and can provide an insight into technological and stylistic advances. While such development is fundamental to modern requirements, increasingly the importance of maintaining older building stock is being recognized, not least for the contribution it makes to the identity of both the urban and rural landscape.

Management of the built heritage in Ireland has, until recent decades, been characterized by an imbalance in the types of building targeted for protection. Systems to ensure the protection of ancient monuments have been in place for over a century, but it is only in the last decades that official mechanisms have been initiated to embrace the broader spectrum of historic buildings. Until recent years, the lack of a centralized system of identifying more modern buildings worthy of protection, and deficiencies in supportive legislation, administration and financial assistance, have hindered efforts to maintain some of the country's more important and characteristic structures, resulting in certain significant losses. Traditionally the highlighting of such deficiencies has been initiated by the public and in particular by the voluntary sector. The manner in which architectural heritage management in Ireland has developed, therefore, has tended to be determined by broadly held attitudes toward different types of architecture and an awareness of its value, based ultimately on the understanding of Irish architectural history.

THE STUDY OF IRISH ARCHITECTURE

The formal appreciation of Irish architecture can be said to have emerged from antiquarianism. This entailed the study of buildings for the buildings' sake, and was thus conceptually separate from the numerous scattered descriptions of architecture found in the pages of social inquiries and travellers' accounts of Ireland which used buildings to reflect contemporary social conditions, or depictions of buildings on maps, the purpose of which were generally administrative or strategic. Initially, Irish antiquarianism was dominated by the Englishman. It was viewed as an extension of local English antiquarian studies into a comfortably adjacent, but uncharted colony (de Paor 1993, 123). The study of ancient material remains in England had gained a respectability with the appointment of a King's Antiquary during the reign of Henry VIII, and developed increased popularity with the publication of antiquarian anthologies such as William Camden's *Britannia* (1586). By the end of the seventeenth century the practice of travelling to ancient Greece and Rome to immortalize the architecture of the most noble of ancients in prose or sketch had become an essential element of the young English gentleman's education. For those who could not afford such a tour, the *Roma* of the Renaissance maxim *Roma quanta fuit ipsa ruina docet* ('from the ruin we learn the greatness that was Rome') was substituted by *Britannia* and *Hibernia*. The examination of the ruins of antique Greece and Rome gave rise to a classical language of architecture that permeated every corner of Europe, and outlasted the transition of architectural styles. A first-hand knowledge of the 'raw materials' was therefore essential for any self-respecting architect or patron, and accuracy of detail was crucial. Irish antiquarianism, on the other hand, concerned itself more with the etymological background of monuments. Scientific accuracy in its scholarship was not so crucial, and was rarely forthcoming. Instead, viewed through eighteenth-century eyes, the architecture of ancient Ireland revealed 'its learning, its valour, and fame ... recorded in the more durable monuments of true history' (Ledwich 1804, ii).

Throughout the eighteenth century the growth of the Romantic movement fuelled an interest in 'gothick' and 'druidic' ruins. The local gentry, of both English and

Fig. 7.1 Arcadian representation of early Irish architecture from Francis Grose's Antiquities of Ireland *(1791–5).*

more established Gaelic descent, developed a taste for antiquarian pursuits, complimented by researches into other aspects of ancient 'Celtic' culture. Examples of this include the publication in 1760 of James McPherson's *Fragments of ancient poetry*, purporting to be the work of the Celtic poet Ossian. Charles O'Conor of Belanagare established a collection of ancient manuscripts, studies of which he published in *Dissertations on the ancient history of Ireland* (1766), further inspiring the popularity for all things 'Celtic'. These developments ultimately led to the establishment of the earliest Irish antiquarian societies; amongst the foremost was the Royal Irish Academy (RIA), founded in 1785.

The socialization of antiquarian studies instituted a shift from individual studies, often carried out in isolation, to more open scholarship. The publication of transactions provided a forum for the researches of members to reach a wider audience. Surveys of monuments were also instigated. In 1779 a founder member of the RIA, William Burton Cunningham, commissioned artists Gabriel Beranger and Angelo Bigari to compile a collection of sketches of the antiquities of

Ireland (Harbison 1991, 7). A number of these were subsequently engraved, and published in Francis Grose's *Antiquities of Ireland* (1791–5), one of the earlier books comprising collections of antiquarian engravings and 'historical' notes, produced for an ever-increasing market of armchair antiquarians (**Fig. 7.1**). Grose's work (posthumously completed by Edward Ledwich) is exemplary of the sometimes bizarre theories and Arcadian representation of monuments associated with Irish antiquarian studies of the period. However, romanticisation aside, the publication and active encouragement of research into particular aspects of Irish architecture by societies like the RIA marked a significant progression in this field of studies. Into the nineteenth century these were to be further augmented by a significant number of societies which appeared at both local and national levels.

A more modern, historical approach to antiquarian studies began to emerge towards the mid-nineteenth century, largely through the influence of the Ordnance Survey of Ireland. The topographical department of the Survey, headed by George Petrie with his principal assistants Eugene O'Curry and John O'Donovan, was to revolutionize the approach to the study of Irish antiquities, combining historical scholarship with extensive field surveys. In order to establish the correct spelling of place-names, antiquarian research was carried out on topography and history, both in the field and from manuscripts. Initially it was intended to publish this information in the form of parish memoirs; however, due to financial difficulties only one memoir, for Templemore in county Derry, was completed. The comprehensive surveying of monuments, and the emergent historicism which accompanied their study, led to a more enlightened understanding of ancient Irish buildings which was prove crucial for their preservation. The aspirations expressed in the preface to Petrie's book *The ecclesiastical architecture of Ireland* (1845),

by making the age and historical interest of these memorials of our early Christianity more generally known to, and appreciated by my countrymen, some stop might be put to the wanton destruction of these remains, which is now, unhappily, a daily occurrence, and which, if not checked, may lead to their total annihilation (Petrie 1845, v-vi),

began to be reflected in the publications and activities of various individuals and antiquarian societies.

EARLY ARCHITECTURAL PRESERVATION

A concentration on the more ethereal qualities of ancient architecture through the previous century had encouraged a passive contemplation of the decay of old buildings. Active destruction was commonplace too, as large stone-built structures provided convenient quarries for local building and lime burning activities; more 'educated' acts of vandalism were conducted in the quest to obtain romantic follies for the homes and gardens of local gentry. By the beginning of the nineteenth century the revival in Anglican church building initiated by the availability of public funds had begun to take an increasingly ecclesiological turn. The importance of establishing a tangible continuity with the ancient Christian church, in what was considered to be its greatest period, saw the unsympathetic 'restoration' of several medieval ecclesiastical buildings. Medieval buildings 'restored' during this period include St Patrick's Trim (1802-3), the Augustinian Abbey at Adare (1807, 1814, 1831, 1852), Ferns Cathedral (1816-7), Armagh Cathedral (1834-40) and St Patrick's Cathedral, Dublin (1821-6, 1832-4). In a few cases one witnessed their complete replacement. Early medieval churches at Emly and Roscrea were almost completely destroyed; the fabric of the latter's twelfth-century nave being utilized to construct a new parish church in 1812.

Responsibility for curbing these alarming developments lay initially with antiquarian societies. The Kilkenny and South-East Archaeological Society (later the Royal Society of Antiquaries of Ireland) was particularly active in this respect. Together with constant lobbying for government intervention through the pages of its journal, positive action was taken by the society at a number of sites to stabilize and consolidate historic structures at risk. These included works at Jerpoint Abbey, county Kilkenny, the Franciscan Abbey, Kilkenny, Monasterboice and Clonmacnoise. Work carried out by the society at Clonmacnoise, under the supervision of Rev. James Graves, demonstrates an extraordinarily enlightened approach for the period. Monies collected by subscription were used to clear and consolidate architectural debris, in order to halt theft and further decay. Clearance in the vicinity of the Nun's Church allowed the almost complete reconstruction of two elaborately carved arches, with the insertion of plain blocks of stone where original blocks were lost. This approach, together with the publication of a comprehensive account of the project (*JRSAI* **5,** 1865, 364–71) set an important precedent for future conservation projects.

Professional architects, many influenced by the contemporary ideals of theorists such as Ruskin and Pugin, also began to nurture an interest in native architecture, examining Irish medieval buildings as models for their own designs (O'Dwyer 1997, 41–56; Sheehy 1980, 58-69). This approach was advocated through organizations such as the Irish Ecclesiological Society (founded in 1848), and is demonstrated through the writings and designs of one of its key members, architect J. J. McCarthy. The pages of the professional journals such as the *Dublin Builder* became vehicles through which an increased sensitivity towards sound restoration policies was expressed. In 1871, for example, criticism from this quarter was levelled at architect George Edmund Street for his replacement of the structurally sound sixteenth-century choir at Christchurch Cathedral with a building of his own creation. Although this did not alter the fate of the choir, it appears to have influenced the architect's preservation of over one thousand medieval moulded stones in the crypt of the building, retained and displayed in an unprecedented manner, as a demonstration of the faithfulness of his 'restoration'.

IRISH CHURCH ACT 1869

It was against this background that the earliest government responses to architectural preservation were introduced. Moves to disestablish the Church of Ireland in 1869 brought the matter to a head. A large proportion of medieval churches remained the property of the Church of Ireland, and with the withdrawal of state support, concerns were expressed as to the Church's ability to maintain large numbers of old buildings, many of which had fallen out of use. Section 25 of the *Irish Church Act* 1869, therefore, authorized the Church

Temporalities Board (the body responsible for the management of the Church's properties) to place any church or ecclesiastical ruin deemed to be of historical or antiquarian interest, and in need of conservation, but no longer used for public worship, under the protection of the Board of Works (Lohan 1994, 85). By 1877 over one hundred monuments and groups of monuments, termed 'National Monuments', were vested to the protection of the Board of Works. The first part-time Inspector of National Monuments, architect Thomas Newenham Deane, was appointed in 1875, and minimum works necessary for the security and preservation of the monuments were initiated.

The initial preservation of national monuments came about indirectly, as a response to the particular circumstances surrounding the disestablishment of the Irish Church, and was, therefore, limited to Ireland and also to ecclesiastical buildings and sites. In 1882, separate legislation for the protection of ancient monuments was introduced throughout the United Kingdom. *The Ancient Monuments Protection Act* 1882 specified in a schedule a number of non-ecclesiastical monuments of which the owner could, if desired, appoint the Commissioners as owners or guardians. *The Ancient Monuments Protection Act (Ireland)* 1892 extended provision to ecclesiastical buildings excluded under the *Irish Church Act* 1869. Although protected by separate pieces of legislation, responsibility for the care for ancient monuments was merged with that of national monuments, so that before long the only real distinction between the two was that national monuments, under the 1869 act, were maintained through a lump sum provided by the Church Temporalities Board, and ancient monuments, under the 1882 act, were funded through parliamentary vote. In 1930 the *National Monuments Act* abolished this distinction entirely, adopting the uniform term 'National Monument' and setting forth more comprehensive legislation than previous acts, which continues to form the basis of current national monuments legislation.

Following partition, responsibility for the care of ancient monuments in the north of Ireland passed from the Commissioners of Public Works to the Ministry of Finance for Northern Ireland whose statutory functions in the field were formally established by the *Ancient Monuments Act (Northern Ireland)* 1926.

POST-MEDIEVAL ARCHITECTURE

Legislative concern for the protection of ancient and medieval structures reflected the established attitude that the value of a building lay, first and foremost, in its antiquity. In the latter part of the nineteenth century, nascent nationalism further strengthened the perception of old buildings in the national psyche, as round towers and high crosses were elevated to the position of national emblems, and patrons, both ecclesiastical and secular, encouraged the emulation of Irish medieval styles in contemporary architecture (Sheehy 1980, 56–69).

The perception of post-medieval architecture during this period was less glorious. The Famine years had ironically witnessed some of the most fervent activity in the field of medieval architectural studies. The years 1845 and 1850 saw the publication of Petrie's *Ecclesiastical architecture of Ireland* (1845) and Wakeman's *Handbook of Irish antiquities* (1848), the foundation of the Celtic Society (1845), the Irish Ecclesiological Society (1848) and the Kilkenny and South-East Archaeological Society (1848) as well as the introduction of the *Act for the Better Protection of Works of Art* 1845, allowing up to six months imprisonment or public whipping for the destruction of or damage to 'Any picture, statue, monument, or painted glass in a chapel or other place of worship; or any statue or monument exposed to public view'. The same Famine period instigated a process which was irrevocably to change the face of rural, and to a lesser extent urban, domestic architecture. It marked an abrupt end to the boom in large country house building, and financial difficulties suffered by many landlords led to the sale or gradual decay of country estates.

Rural depopulation led to the destruction of large quantities of vernacular housing. This was further accelerated through the improved housing policies of the Congested Districts Board, the Land Commission and the *Labourers Acts*. In spite of the efforts of some Gaelic revivalists to maintain elements of the traditional 'cottage' form in standardized designs, as representative of native Irish culture (Fraser 1996, 46–7), associations with the 'cold, filthy and miserably small' cabins of the Famine and pre-Famine era meant that most labourers were more than happy to trade the 'Irishness' of their dwelling for increased comfort of a more 'English' home (Kennedy 1993, 176).

Post-medieval architecture acquired a symbolism of its own. Formal, architect-designed buildings were viewed as representative of colonial oppression, an attitude clearly reflected in contemporary literature. For example, for Seán Ó Faoláin, 'The heyday of this Anglo-Irish enclave was the eighteenth century; their nearest-to-hand monument is Dublin's grace, roominess magnificence and unique atmosphere; but all about the country they built gracious houses (each to be known to the tenantry as the "Big House") and pleasant seats ... which are the epitome of the classical spirit of that cultured and callous century' (Ó Faoláin 1947, 87).

The 'Big House' became almost an obsession of hatred, unequivocally demonstrated by the burning of many during the 1922 Troubles. Less explicit, but equally destructive, was the ensuing attitude of indifference to the fate of this architecturally and socially unique aspect of our cultural heritage. The Big House could no longer operate as a sustainable unit. Its function as the administrative hub of a rural economy was invalidated as the lands which it had been built to administer were redistributed through the *Encumbered Estates Acts* and the Land Commission. Mounting maintenance costs and the changing fortunes of owners meant that, in the total absence of government assistance or charitable funding mechanisms, many houses were demolished or simply left to decay.

It is estimated that within the space of one hundred years, at least 574 Big Houses in the Republic were lost, while many more have been drastically altered in order to ensure survival (Cornforth 1989, 95). Where sustainable functions were found for such buildings, such as conversion into hotels or nursing homes, the preservation of the house as an entire unit, consisting of its actual fabric and component interior decor, furnishings, outbuildings and demesne, was seldom viable.

The destruction wrought on many public buildings during the Troubles was to prove less devastating. Unlike the Big House, the function of buildings such as the Four Courts and Custom House in Dublin remained valid with the administrative transition. Increased scholarly interest in Georgian architecture demonstrated by contemporary architects contributed to the restoration, as opposed to the rebuilding, of the structures following the 1922 burnings. Such professional scholarly interest can be traced through the writings of architects such as R. M. Butler, editor of the *Irish Builder and Engineer* from 1901 to 1935, and designer of the Gandon-influenced University College, Dublin (*ca.* 1912) (McParland 1989, 163). An early call was made by the Georgian Society in 1909 to 'induce those who live in houses still containing good and interesting work both to take care of it, and to have sketches and photos taken for the Society's collection'; the pages of its five volumes of *Records* document aspects of Dublin and rural architecture, declared in the preface to the first volume to be 'monuments of brilliant society ... doomed to decay and disappearance' (*Georgian Society Record* 1909, i).

By the 1950s, doom, decay and disappearance had indeed begun to characterize the state of a significant proportion of Irish historic architecture as professional and amateur interest in post-medieval historic architecture had waned. Large areas of Dublin were redeveloped with scant regard for the older structures which stood in the way. In some cases new developments cleared areas where buildings had already decayed beyond sustainable repair; in others, sound Georgian buildings were replaced with more modern and efficient office accommodation. The shift from a residential to a commercial function of many urban structures also led to the unsympathetic conversion, and in many cases the complete destruction, of important interiors.

Although the *National Monuments Acts* in the south and *Ancient* (later *Historic*) *Monuments Acts* in the north did not explicitly exclude post-medieval structures, the traditionally established concepts of architectural heritage, and the fact that many important structures were occupied and functional, meant that virtually no statutory measures existed to protect more modern structures. A notable exception was the Casino at Marino, taken into state care as early as 1930. Initial moves to reverse the trend of destruction and development of post-medieval historic fabric once more lay with voluntary societies.

ARCHITECTURAL SOCIETIES

In 1958 the Irish Georgian Society was founded to formalize approaches to the preservation of Georgian and Victorian buildings in particular. Since then, through the efforts of the Society, financial assistance has been provided towards the preservation of important historic buildings such as Castletown House, Damer House, Roscrea, and Donerail House, county Cork, and broader public support for sensitive conservation practices has been encouraged. A general awareness of Georgian art, architecture and social history continues to be promoted through the provision of educational grants and publications including the *Bulletin of the Irish Georgian Society* (now the *Journal of Irish Architectural and Decorative Studies*), which has remained the sole periodical to deal specifically with Irish architectural history.

The Ulster Architectural Heritage Society has also made a significant contribution to academic output and policy relating to architectural preservation in Northern Ireland. Since its instigation in 1967 the Society has produced a prodigious variety of published town and area surveys, lists of buildings of merit and thematic monographs, covering all nine counties of the province. In more recent years the Society has worked in collaboration with the statutory authorities in the compilation of catalogues of historic buildings at risk, and in the provision of practical guides and directories to buildings preservation.

A number of other non-government organizations have made significant contributions to the recording, protection and management of architectural heritage. An Taisce in the south and the National Trust in the north are concerned with the sustainable conservation of both the natural and built environments. The Landmark Trust acquires and restores unusual vernacular properties which are subsequently managed and marketed as tourism accommodation. Various civic trusts and local historical societies have further contributed to heightening public awareness, the preservation of individual buildings and areas of architectural interest at a more localized level.

66

ARCHIVES

The importance of preserving sources and records of Irish architectural history was acknowledged by the foundation of the Irish Architectural Archive in 1976 as a repository for documentation relating to Irish architectural heritage of Ireland. The archive operated initially on a voluntary basis, but since 1985 has been in receipt of some state funding. The collection now contains roughly 300,000 photographs of Irish buildings of all types and ages; approximately 50,000 original architectural designs and copy drawings mainly from the eighteenth to the twentieth centuries; records from architects and surveyors and an extensive bibliographic index of eighteenth-, nineteenth- and twentieth-century architects. Following recognition of the need for a similar repository in the north of Ireland, the Monuments and Buildings Record (MBR) was established in 1992. This differs from the Architectural Archive in that it is fully state-run, and embraces publicly available state records relating to the built environment, as well as privately donated collections of relevant material.

CENTRAL GOVERNMENT

The constant growth in the number of non-governmental organizations concerned with architectural heritage, and their contributions to its protection, has not been matched by government responses. In 1985 the Irish government committed to protect its architectural heritage as part of the common heritage of Europe through its signature of the European Convention for the Protection of Architectural Heritage (Granada 1985), a commitment ratified in 1997. In spite of this, there has been a clear dichotomy between policies for development, most notably those introduced by the *Urban Renewal Act* 1986, and the somewhat disparate administration of statutory provisions for architectural heritage preservation.

Areas designated for urban renewal under the 1986 act were by and large run down, and often lay in the oldest parts of towns. Tax incentives and remissions for private-sector development in designated areas have, with few exceptions, favoured the replacement, rather than renewal, of old buildings, and set a trend for the demolition of historic fabric, often before a proper assessment of its importance has been made, a situation further exasperated by the limited time-frame in which developments have had to be built, and fully operational, in order to avail of incentives (Dowling and Keegan 1991, 63).

On the other hand, financial incentives to encourage the maintenance and preservation of the built environment have, to date, been of little real significance. Tax relief on repairs and maintenance of privately owned historic properties, on condition that the properties are opened to the public for a minimum of sixty days a year, have been available since 1982 (O'Connor-Nash 1991, 114–19). However, tax relief is only effective when owners have the available capital, and will, to maintain their property in a sensitive manner. Grant aid for the preservation of historic architecture administered through the Heritage Council continues to fall far short of demand (*Irish Times* 25 October 1997).

LEGISLATION FOR THE PRESERVATION OF ARCHITECTURAL HERITAGE:

THE REPUBLIC

Legislation relating specifically to the protection and management of the architectural heritage in the Republic of Ireland comes principally under two sets of acts, the *National Monuments Acts* 1930–94 and the *Local Government (Planning and Development) Acts* 1963–93, administered respectively by the Department of Arts, Heritage, Gaeltacht and the Islands and the Department of the Environment and Local Government (Scannell 1994, 260–71). The *Heritage Act* 1995 placed the Heritage Council's role in architectural preservation on a statutory footing.

The *National Monuments Acts* 1930–94 afford statutory protection to monuments or 'archaeological areas' in the ownership or guardianship of the Commissioners of Public Works, or a local authority, on the Register of Monuments and Places, and monuments or archaeological areas with a preservation order (see chapter 51). Although, technically, monuments of any age can be protected under the provisions of the acts, traditionally there has been a prevalence toward structures of antiquity. This bias is perhaps most explicit in the use of the phrase 'all monuments in existence before 1700 AD' in the definition of an 'historic monument' featured in the (*Amendment*) *Act* 1987 which, although not exclusive of later structures, does nothing to encourage increased value perceptions of more recent buildings. Thus, while a growing number of post-medieval structures are, in fact, being afforded protection by the *National Monuments Acts*, the key role in monitoring threats to, and providing protection for, the post-medieval architectural heritage comes under planning legislation. Responsibility for national planning policy and legislation lies with the Department of the Environment and Local Government; implementation of planning legislation and, within it, responsibility for architectural heritage at local level, lie with the local authorities.

The *Local Government (Planning and Development) Acts* 1963–93 allow for the inclusion of objectives for the preservation of 'buildings of artistic, architectural or historical interest' as well as 'the preservation of plasterwork, staircases, woodwork and other fixtures or features of artistic, historic or architectural interest and forming part of the interior of structures' in development plans. Objectives for the preservation of designated 'conservation areas', encompassing groups of buildings, street furnishings and paving, have also been included in some individual Development Plans. Although provision is made for such objectives, the inclusion of 'listed buildings' in Development Plans is not obligatory. Where a local authority does choose to include lists of buildings for preservation, no statutory guidance is given for the identification of such structures, and, in practice, the criteria under which they are drawn up often vary widely according to respective local authorities.

At present the legal standing of 'listed buildings' is weak. There is no statutory obligation on the owner of a building listed for preservation in a Development Plan to maintain it, and prosecution for breach of planning permissions on listed buildings is rarely sought by the planning authorities. Financially, no compensation is payable to owners of listed buildings refused permission for structural alterations, and little financial incentive is offered for sensitive maintenance works. In recent years the ineffective nature of this legislation has become increasingly evident, and has witnessed the unchecked destruction of important historic structures. Proposals to amend some of the major architectural preservation shortcomings of current planning legislation were therefore published in May 1998 as a joint Department of Environment and Local Government and Department of Arts, Heritage, Gaeltacht and the Islands initiative.

Under the terms of the proposed *Local Government (Planning and Development) Bill* 1998 the protection of structures of artistic, architectural or historical interest will be made a mandatory function of local authorities. They will be obliged to compile a record of structures for preservation within their areas; will be empowered to require owners to carry out maintenance work on a listed building; if necessary they may carry out maintenance work themselves, or, in extreme cases, be empowered to make a compulsory purchase order on the structure in order to ensure its preservation. Now enacted, legislation will also enable local authorities to designate 'areas of architectural importance', thus ending the non-statutory nature of conservation areas. Resources toward the employment of local authority conservation officers to administer the new legislation will be made available. A programme of grant assistance for owners of protected properties will also be established. This will be operated according to criteria laid down by an advisory group consisting of representatives from the Heritage Council and the Departments of Arts, Heritage, Gaeltacht and Islands and Environment and Local Government.

THE NATIONAL INVENTORY OF ARCHITECTURAL HERITAGE
The *Architectural Heritage (National Inventory) Act* 1999 will place the task of identifying, recording and evaluating the heritage contribution of the built environment

with the National Inventory of Architectural Heritage (NIAH), administered within the Department of Arts, Heritage, Gaeltacht and the Islands by Dúchas, the Heritage Service. A database of buildings deemed worthy of protection compiled by the NIAH will be used by local authorities as a guide to which structures within their jurisdictions should be listed for preservation in development plans.

The NIAH was initiated in 1991, and complements the work of the Archaeological Survey of Ireland through the identification and recording of the post-medieval architectural heritage of Ireland. Its recording function is carried out nationwide. To date it has focussed principally on the extensive surveying of urban areas designated for development. Inventories for Carlow (1994), Ennis, Letterkenny, Tullamore, Wicklow, Portlaoise (1997), Clonmel, Ballina, Galway, Kilkenny and Longford (1998) have been already been published, although a number of less intensive interim surveys of architectural heritage have been initiated on a county-by-county basis. The NIAH also undertakes thematic surveys, generally in co-operation with other bodies such as the Heritage Council, and a survey of Irish courthouses has been completed. Survey information is compiled on a computer database, and comprises a text description, photographic image and computer mapping information (GIS). Each individual record has a value rating attached to it which relates to the perceived architectural heritage value of the structure, group of structures or area surveyed.

LEGISLATION FOR THE PRESERVATION OF ARCHITECTURAL HERITAGE:
NORTHERN IRELAND
In Northern Ireland statutory protection for monuments comes under the provision of the *Historic Monuments and Archaeological Objects (Northern Ireland) Order* 1995. It takes two forms, the taking of monuments into state care and the scheduling of monuments. Since 1976, these have been administered by the Department of the Environment (Northern Ireland) (DOE NI) Environment and Heritage Service. Monuments in state care are either owned or leased by the DOE NI or can be entrusted to the Department's care by a Deed of Guardianship. As in the Republic, the majority of sites in state care are early. Notable exceptions include the wrought-iron screen and gates from Richill, county Armagh, now at Hillsborough (1745), and the Moira Station House and Signal Box on the main Dublin-Belfast railway line (1841). The aim is to include 'typical' types as well as the more outstanding. The scheduling process (first introduced with the *Ancient Monuments Act [Northern Ireland]* 1926) obliges the owner of a monument included in the schedule to give notice of any intended action which would affect the site. Historic monuments are included on the schedule on the

basis of period, type, condition and locality, with rarity, group value and potential for excavation also considered as important criteria.

Provision for the protection of more modern structures, still capable of modern use, and for designated Conservation Areas was introduced by the *Planning (Northern Ireland) Order* 1972, and was superseded by the *Planning (Northern Ireland) Order* 1991. This provided for a Historic Buildings Council (HBC) to advise the DOE NI Town and County Planning Service on the listing of buildings of special architectural or historic interest. Initial buildings surveys commenced in 1969, targeting buildings from the 1700s to the 1960s on an electoral ward and district basis. Structures from the post-1914 period were examined on a thematic basis with the most important examples being singled out for protection.

The 'listing' of a structure obliges its owner to apply for Listed Building Consent prior to the initiation of repairs, alterations or demolition which would affect the character of the listed building. The Environment Service can provide some grant aid for approved maintenance to listed buildings, and give free technical advice on restoration. Further financial assistance for some restoration and redevelopment in Conservation Areas and Community Regeneration and Improvement Special Programme (CRISP) towns are administered by the Planning Service.

CASE STUDY: CHRIST CHURCH CATHEDRAL

A church has stood on the site of Christ Church Cathedral, Dublin, since the eleventh century. Although the medieval cathedral was substantially rebuilt during the 1870s, substantial portions of the original medieval fabric were maintained, including most of the crypt and quantities of carved stone incorporated into the later fabric. The continuity of the building's function since the medieval period has also led to the preservation of an assortment of interior fittings of historical importance.

The cathedral is a good example of the difficulties presented by a functional building of historic and architectural importance. Administered by the Church of Ireland, congregational support is insufficient to maintain a building of Christ Church's size and complexity. The building's location in the centre of the city, and its prominent role in civic history, make it a significant tourist attraction. However, its primary function as a church presents a conflict, not only in the problem of large tourist groups disturbing religious service, but also in the provision of non-obtrusive tourist facilities. The result at present is that although tourism provides a lucrative and much-needed source of income, its full potential has not been reached.

Although in a state of 'near ruin' during the 1860s, as a functional ecclesiastical building it was excluded from the protective measures provided for by section 25 of the *Irish Churches Act* and subsequent national monuments legislation. Protection of the fabric of the church and corollary structures, including the adjacent ruined medieval chapter house, is currently provided for under the lists of buildings for preservation in Dublin Corporation's Development Plan. This requires the cathedral administration to seek permission prior to any alterations to exterior or interior, and qualifies them to apply for grant aid towards maintenance costs.

As an important historic structure, the cathedral is also eligible for discretionary financial support from the Heritage Council's architectural heritage grants system. Provision for a record to be made of the church fabric and objects within comes under the remit of the Heritage Council Churches Inventory, while a specialized inventory of loose medieval stone has recently been funded by the Council's archaeological grant.

CONCLUSION

The increased activity in architectural heritage recording and advances in more supportive legislative frameworks indicate a brighter future for the Ireland's built environment. Coupled with this, public perceptions of what constitutes architectural heritage are changing. This is demonstrated by the growing number of publications dealing with Irish architectural history which reflects a shift in concentration from the work of specific architects, or 'great' styles, to include studies of important 'everyday' buildings and structures (Shaffrey and Shaffrey 1983, 1986; Rowan 1979; Rowan and Casey 1993; Simmington and O'Keeffe 1991). The importance of maintaining more than just what is considered to be the brightest and the best at any given time is clearly demonstrated by the lessons of the past. Towns and Big Houses, once considered as representative of '800 years of oppression', are now marketed as 'Heritage Towns' and 'Historic Houses' and seen as valuable resources for the increasingly cultured tourism market. Thus, all aspects of the built environment, modern and ancient, are finally coming to be appreciated, not only for the utilitarian purpose that they might serve but also for the contribution that they make to our cultural heritage.

Bibliography

Cornforth, J. 1989 'Must Irish houses vanish?', *Country Life* **183**, 6 (9 Feb.), pp. 94–5.
Dalsimer, A. M. (ed) 1993 *Visualizing Ireland: national identity and the pictorial tradition*. Cambridge, Mass.
de Paor, M. 1993 'Irish antiquarian artists' in Dalsimer 1993, pp. 119–132.
Dowling, B. and Keegan, O. 1991 'Fiscal policies and the

built environment' in J. Feehan (ed) *Environment and development in Ireland* (Dublin), pp. 58–63.

Fraser, M. 1996 *John Bull's other homes: state housing and British policy in Ireland, 1883–1922*. Liverpool.

Gailey, A. 1984 *Rural houses of the north of Ireland*. Edinburgh.

Grose, F. 1791–95 *The antiquities of Ireland*. London.

Guinness, D. (ed) 1967 *Georgian Society Records*. Dublin.

Harbison, P. 1991 *Beranger's views of Ireland*. Dublin.

Kennedy, B. 1993 'The traditional thatched house; image and reality' in Dalsimer 1993, pp. 165–180.

Ledwich, E. 1804 *The antiquities of Ireland*. Dublin.

Lohan, R. 1994 *Guide to the archives of the Office of Public Works*. Dublin.

McParland, E. 1988 'A bibliography of Irish architecture', *Irish Historical Studies* **26**, 2, pp. 161–212.

O'Conor-Nash, P. 1991 'The Great Houses; how to breastfeed a dinosaur in the late 20th century' in J. Feehan, *Environment and development in Ireland* (Dublin), pp. 114–19.

O'Dwyer, F. 1997 *The architecture of Deane and Woodward*. Cork.

Ó Faoláin, S. 1947 *The Irish*. London.

O'Keeffe, P. and Simmington, T. 1991 *Irish stone bridges: history and heritage*. Dublin.

Petrie, G. 1845 *The ecclesiastical architecture of Ireland anterior to the Norman invasion*. Dublin.

Rowan, A. and Casey, C. 1993 *The buildings of Ireland: north Leinster*. London.

Rowan, A. 1979 *The buildings of Ireland: north-west Ulster*. London.

Scallan, Y. 1995 *Environmental and planning law*. Dublin.

Shaffrey, P. and Shaffrey, M. 1983 *Buildings of Irish towns: treasures of everyday architecture*. Dublin.

Shaffrey, P. and Shaffrey, M. 1985 *Irish countryside buildings: everyday architecture in the rural landscape*. Dublin.

Sheehy, J. 1980 *Rediscovery of Ireland's past*. London.

Vernacular Architecture

FIDELMA MULLANE

Vernacular architecture accounts for the greater part of the built environment in Ireland. The Irish cultural landscape displays a variety of forms and materials which can still be defined as traditional or vernacular. The dwelling-house, a potent symbol, provides the most obvious example. It stands as testimony to an ancient system of values, a world-view which has filtered through the millennia from the Neolithic Age to the twenty-first century, retaining many of the same essential characteristics of height, shape and width for thousands of years. These constant features remain, and are seen today in ever-decreasing numbers, as single-storey dwellings constructed on rectangular ground plans where rooms occupy the full width of the house.

There is a considerable wealth of published material pertaining to various aspects of this country's architectural history. However, there is no major volume dedicated to the subject of traditional building dealing with Ireland as a physical and cultural unit. Some research which investigates the origin and development of this architecture as an expression of society is available, but the publications which do exist deal, in general, with descriptions and distributions of materials and forms. They are found as a significant number of dispersed articles and short books now largely inaccessible to the general public. The inclusion of a comprehensive, but by no means complete, bibliography in this chapter represents an attempt to highlight national and local studies completed recently on the subject. The paper itself offers some reflections on the nature of this scholarship as well as thoughts on the role of architecture in the context of contemporary design and building.

DEFINITIONS AND RESEARCH DEVELOPMENTS

There are many definitions of vernacular architecture which range from technical ones for survey and statutory listing purposes through the versions proposed by related disciplines such as geography, ethnography, history, archaeology, sociology, architecture and anthropology. The word 'vernacular' is familiar in the context of language in Ireland. To speak in the vernacular can mean to express oneself in Irish. Traditional architecture as a cultural manifestation could be described as a less widely spoken language, an expression which is rarely heard, is seldom uttered and least understood by those who communicate in the majority language of building — the jargon of the construction industry in our so-called post-modern society.

When the term 'vernacular' is employed in the context of architecture, the word is generally used as an academic label or synonym for 'traditional'. Traditional conjures up instant mental pictures of thatched, white-washed and picturesque dwellings. In the context of conservation, thatch and most often the thatched house have been the defining element of what is vernacular. Indeed thatch is considered the most important aspect, and sometimes the only one, which receives financial support for conservation. There are instances throughout the countryside where houses have been re-thatched, sometimes using thatching styles and materials which are not local, while many of their older features such as form, windows, doors and walling are changed beyond recognition in both design and substance. In most cases thatching grants are limited to the roofs of dwellings only, to the exclusion of the roofs of other farmyard buildings. Unfortunately, where there has been a general lack of awareness of what vernacular implies, nostalgia and sentimentality define vernacular architecture. This phenomenon manifests itself in the landscape as chocolate-box architecture, the Hansel and Gretel fairytale in the woods extravaganzas and the 'lumpy wall' syndrome which pass themselves off as Irish traditional building styles.

The study of vernacular architecture in Ireland has been undertaken, for the most part, by ethnologists or folklorists and geographers, who have greatly influenced our understanding of it. Geographers hover on the edges of many disciplines and have created approaches such as the anthropo-geographical, of which E. Estyn Evans was the most important exponent. The investigation of vernacular architecture in Northern Ireland has been conducted almost entirely by geographers including Buchanan, Evans, McCourt and Gailey. This architecture's intrepretation in folk museum and folk village is also largely influenced by the ethnographers' and geographers' views. But the field of study has also by now a reasonably extended history. The first formal exploration of Irish traditional architecture was initiated in 1935 by Åke Campbell, a Swedish ethnologist, with his proposed classification of Irish house types. His two principal typologies were

(i) the house with the fire-place located somewhere near the centre, or at least not just at the gable wall, such that there are bed spaces behind the fire-place in the upper end of the house (often thatched gables), and

(ii) the house with stone-built gables and the fire-place close to the gable wall.

He called the first type the central chimney house, the second the gable chimney house (Campbell 1937, 207–8). In fact, the early twentieth-century Swedish ethnographic method remains the defining influence to the present day. This influence came mainly through Dr Seán Ó Súilleabháin to the Irish Folklore Commission and is confirmed in his *Handbook of Irish folklore* (1942). Interestingly, the literature of Irish ethnology has not yet assessed the Swedish ethnographic method or its application to the Irish situation. It is certain that Ó Súilleabháin adapted the Swedish mode of collecting and classifying to an existing Irish system which he himself had created. An acknowledgement of his success in interpreting this approach is provided by ethnologists from Sweden who now quote the *Handbook* as an excellent example of their own method. Ó Súilleabháin himself described the latter *modus operandi* thus: 'It was a subject-index, and every item of traditional information which could be construed as folklore came within its ample scope'.

Decades later the folklorist Kevin Danaher (Caoimhín Ó Danachair) re-affirmed the significance of Ó Súilleabháin's contribution when he maintained that the *Handbook* is:

still by far the most significant and useful book on Irish folk [tradition]. [It]established definitively what for us is folk tradition and what is not. Here the criterion is that of mode of transmission, not subject matter. Any item handed on by word of mouth or by example from the older to the younger people is

folk tradition. Anything learned through formal education or the printed word, or more recently through the cinema, the radio and the television, is not. [Folk tradition] reflects a complete way of life, no aspect of which can be neglected without detriment to the remainder; it possesses a creative evolution which makes the whole greater than the sum of its parts. (Ó Danachair 1982, 9)

Danaher gives an account of this definition as used in the Department of Irish Folklore which reinforces his emphasis on mode of transmission:

For us the definition is simple. Folk tradition is the totality of the information which has been transmitted from the past to the present in the traditional manner by word and by example without the intervention of formal education or the printed word. Thus the material is defined by the manner of its transmission, not by subject matter or locality or social status.

The focus on transmission is fundamental when applied to the description of our subject. It is within this context that the study of vernacular architecture has taken place in Ireland, Danaher himself being a major exponent of the approach. His characterization of folk tradition provides the basis for a working definition:

Ordinary people down through the ages and into recent and more modern times have continued to build their own houses, barns, stables and workshops and to develop them in their own way within their own resources to meet their own needs unaffected in the main by trained architects, formal styles or fashionable trends. Thus emerged and evolved the vernacular architecture, the forms and methods of which over the ages have become part of the living tradition of the ordinary people. In vernacular architecture a three-fold division is possible into domestic, agricultural and industrial buildings. Of these the first is by far the most numerous group, since everybody, no matter what his calling, must have some shelter in which to eat or sleep. Thus it includes all dwellings from the smallest hut to the largest farmhouse, as well as shops, inns and houses in villages and towns insofar as all of these belong to the vernacular tradition and were not designed by professional architects. Agricultural buildings include all those of the farmstead outside of the dwelling-house, the byres, barns, stores, fowl-runs, pigsties, cart sheds and so on, as well isolated buildings in the fields and lime-kilns, well-houses and gateways on the farm. Industrial vernacular building includes craftsmen's shops, forges, boatyards, corn-kilns, windmills and water-mills for grinding, pumping and the working of iron and textiles, and all such installations and workshops which in age or in style antedate the industrial revolution.

The foregoing definition is broad in scope and inclusive. It is based on Danaher's deep understanding of Irish cultural expression and his vast experience in the field.

Fig. 8.1 The interior of a traditional farmhouse near Castletownroche, county Cork. In the 1990s, such interiors were maintained by elderly occupants but were either completely modified or abandoned after their demise.

His framework has fundamentally influenced all researchers in Ireland as most vernacular architecture studies use it or a variation of it.

Ó Súilleabháin's and Danaher's collecting of information regarding aspects of vernacular architecture has yielded an extraordinarily rich archive, now housed in the Department of Irish Folklore, University College, Dublin. Apart from the data assembled by these authors themselves, the archive has a wealth of information relating to aspects of vernacular architecture gathered by other folklore collectors throughout Ireland using the *Handbook of Irish folklore*. The Schools' Manuscripts from the 1930s contain a vast quantity of references to almost every aspect of the subject. While there has been some criticism regarding emphasis in the material collected and of the limited publication emanating from these sources, it is certain that these data constitute one of the most important folk tradition holdings in the world.

Danaher's most significant achievement lies in the quantity of material relating to vernacular architecture obtained both through his own fieldwork and especially the postal questionnaires which he devised. Questionnaires were sent to the thirty-two counties during the 1940s in particular. The most important topics investigated were: *The Dwelling House, Roofs and Thatching, Walling Material, House Luck and Furniture*. The questionnaire on the *Bed Outshot* was not sent to all counties, only to those where the feature was expected to be found. Danaher's analysis of information from the postal questionnaires remained for the most part descriptive. Indeed, in his published work in general, the emphasis is on description of structural details such as hearth and chimney, walling materials, roofing and thatching as well as distribution patterns. This should not be taken as a criticism. If anything, his contribution to the discipline in Ireland is testimony to the amount of work that one individual could achieve.

Alan Gailey, Northern Ireland's most prolific researcher on the subject, places the study of traditional architecture within the science of ethnology:

Vernacular architecture stems from a 'little tradition' within which ideas have been transmitted mainly informally and orally, where the possibilities for individual innovation have been closely circumscribed by the attitudes of the community at large, transmitted over generations. ... Vernacular architecture does not belong within the fine arts as architecture does; rather its practice has close affinities with disciplines like ethnology and archaeology. (Gailey 1984, 7)

Gailey remains descriptive, though he offers a modified classification of house types. He emphasized the relationship between the front entrance and the hearth.

He proposed two house types, namely the direct-entry house, where the hearth is located at some distance from the front entrance and where the house is entered directly without the presence of a jamb wall or internal porch. The second house category he named the 'hearth-lobby' house whereby the main hearth is adjacent to the front entrance, the hearth and entrance being separated by a jamb wall. His interpretation of what is rural has been confined to an analysis of technical structures and form details, giving accounts of developments and distribution of types. He sums up his own work in *Rural houses in the north of Ireland*:

A significant portion of this book deals, then, with the traditional types of house found in Northern Ireland; with the internal relationships between the elements comprising them, enshrined in plan forms and visibly expressed in their elevations; with their regional variations and distributions; with explanation of their historical development; and briefly, with speculation on their possible origins. (Gailey 1984, 7-8)

The latter publication is an important baseline study in vernacular architecture in the north. It provides comprehensive documentation, and in particular technical accounts, of the main features of rural houses in the region. Gailey's research has been greatly influenced by archaeology and geography and by the writings of E. Estyn Evans, McCourt and Danaher. Gailey's work at the Ulster Folk and Transport Museum, and later the contribution of Philip Robinson, was significant in the matter of recording vernacular structures, in contributing to archival holdings and publication together with the representation of vernacular buildings at the museum.

While Irish ethnologists reject material outside the scope of a certain mode of transmission, it is interesting to note that their method and research emphasis were considerably influenced by architects' and archaeologists' approach to building where technique and function are the predominant underlying elements. The values of twentieth-century architecture, and functionalist values in particular, have greatly influenced our current understanding of traditional architecture. The functionalist philosophy presumes that an essentially functional rationale underlines traditional forms of building. While the latter was certainly an important consideration in devising form and plan, it may not have been the critical factor in the resulting shapes.

Henry Glassie represents a departure from the technical emphasis which had existed in vernacular architecture studies up to 1982. His research constitutes a transition from the study of 'the outside to the inside, from form to use, from house to home' (Glassie 1982, 760). Glassie, an anthropologist, includes an important chapter on our discipline which he significantly titles 'Home' *in Passing the time: folklore and history of an Ulster community* (1982). He evinces a desire to go beyond description and to place his research firmly within the historical continuum. He acknowledges the influence of Evans' work which he describes as superb geographic ethnography, referring in particular to *Mourne Country* (Evans 1988). The most recent significant publication in the field of vernacular studies relates to country furniture in Ireland from 1700 to 1950 (Kinmonth 1993).

Information collecting concerning aspects of vernacular architecture has been reasonably thoroughgoing through the use of the aforementioned Irish Folklore Commission Postal Questionnaire, but largely unsystematic with regard to survey on the ground. Research in Ireland has been conducted by individuals rather than by survey teams. Despite the enormous influence of Campbell's work, his plea for the systematic investigation of vernacular architecture went unnoticed. Ireland has only recently seen the establishment of a National Folk Museum, and we have no state institution which deals comprehensively with vernacular architecture. There is no policy with regard to the future of traditional buildings, there are no plans for maintenance and, as yet, financial commitment is very limited. Research to date has over-emphasized building techniques, structural details and form description. The descriptive approaches to the study of our subject are important in the light of what is currently happening to this architecture. The information collected provides the basic groundwork for typologies — a classification of form for paper landscapes, a copy of form for the silent landscapes of reconstruction and replica in folk parks, a confusion of form for the living landscapes of copy, camouflage and pastiche. However, the details of vernacular architecture as gathered by various disciplines have remained largely in the academic realm. This information has not been used as a basis for a sympathetic or deeper appreciation of Ireland's vernacular architectural heritage, a point to which we shall return again below.

Definitions of vernacular architecture can be quite technical when a specific aim such as listing is required. The working understanding devised by the Historic Building Council, and used for example in the Townlands Survey 1996–97 in Northern Ireland, is useful in that it provides a list of characteristics as well as a definition, but it views what is vernacular mainly in the context of dwellings only:

Rural vernacular or traditional architecture is the construction of small plain buildings in the countryside (particularly before 1925) where the dominant influence is siting, materials, form and design in the local folk tradition. Such vernacular buildings will have been typical of a common type in any given locality and will lack the individualistic and educated design features that characterised international fashions in formal architecture during the same period. Rural vernacular houses may be recognised as such by meeting most of the primary characteristics listed ...

Eight primary characteristics are outlined such as the absence of a formal plan, drawing or written specification; the presence of a linear, elongated rectangular plan; a typical depth of six metres; mass load-bearing walls; hearths and chimneys located along the axis of the linear plan; door openings in long walls into kitchen; doors and windows on long walls, and a linear house form which is extended along its length or by the addition of a second storey. Secondary characteristics include transverse load-bearing walls to the roof internally; the lack of longitudinal load-bearing walls internally; the lack of symmetry with regard to doors and windows especially on back walls; a defined relationship between height and width of the house. This account is quite technically specific but it does assist in the selection of houses to be considered for survey and statutory listing purposes.

In summary, the study of traditional architecture in Ireland has been confined, for the most part, to one area, the dwelling house; to one type of economy, farming, and to one kind of farm dwelling, the one-storied, one room-wide structure. It is generally agreed that the typical traditional house in Ireland is rectangular, one room wide, single storey, whitewashed and thatched, and that this architectural expression is local in form, materials and craftsmanship. The research emphasis on vernacular rural dwellings has excluded, with some notable exceptions, other vernacular building types in town and countryside. Certain aspects even of vernacular dwellings have been omitted like local slate roofs, the industrial vernacular and buildings of professions other than the farming community. Little or no work has been done on the survival of vernacular features in modern building practices. Even the much maligned bungalow retains some elements of the Irish traditional dwelling such as the large kitchen-cum-living room, the importance of the open hearth and the social significance of both of these features. The retention of elements from the vernacular tradition should not be a reason to consider the bungalow as a neo-vernacular form. Neo-vernacular can be defined as those buildings which are constructed in the style and scale of the traditional Irish house and are often referred to as 'cottages', which are most often found along the coast, individually or in groups as holiday homes.

ARCHITECTURE AND IDENTITY IN CONTEMPORARY IRELAND

Our vernacular landscapes have been referred to in travel books by almost every 'traveller', mostly English, who journeyed throughout Ireland, particularly in the eighteenth and nineteenth centuries. Their accounts, in general, did not dwell to any great extent on technical description or sympathetic observation of cultural practices but relied, for the most part, on judgmental observations regarding moral and social depredation, together with an obsessive interest in hygiene conditions. Ireland was the land of filthy hovels, pigs in the parlour, dunghills heaped at every front door. According to these observers, conditions could be improved by using the recommended English model, a model which was often implemented by 'improving landlords'. Hygiene improvements have continued unabated to the present day, the dunghill forgotten, the *en suite* is now *de rigeur*. There is no suggestion in this chapter that we return to nineteenth-century values or sanitary conditions. However, it is essential and urgent that we establish or at least re-identify the cultural references, the local model, which created a type of architecture which endured for thousands of years and which is disappearing rapidly without proper testimony. Its disappearance is not necessarily a tragedy; the loss lies in the fact that we have not tried to understand it as an important aspect of cultural expression and have failed to use it as a source of inspiration for a new architecture.

Our attitudes to culture and to our colonial legacy are probably the single most important influence on the management of vernacular landscapes. These landscapes in Ireland having long been the subject of bad press from the earliest travel writers to present-day journalists; this has shaped the way we value traditional building as a manifestation of the past. Our attitudes towards the care of our vernacular landscapes range from benign neglect to active hostility. Estyn Evans had noted this phenomenon, but remained optimistic:

... so long as there are hills and fields and settlements variously shaped by nature and by man, the regions will persist and there are significant signs that ... future generations may come to place a higher value than we do on their various homelands and cherish regional traditions that are now despised. (Evans 1988)

There are few if any studies which address the way in which societies in Ireland, past and present, appreciated their local architecture. Cultural notions change over time and in this context a dramatic shift in emphasis with regard to the built environment has taken place in the last fifty years. Where the house was once a small-scale symbol in the countryside and often constructed from perishable materials, it is now almost always built in 'permanent' materials, often in monumental proportions, a scale previously reserved to declare certain aspects of societies' power through, for example, funerary and ecclesiastical structures. Contemporary society places emphasis on such concerns as light, view, security and individualistic expression (status), and so we have large picture windows and securely locked doors. Individual statements determine scale and design where once cultural communal models were used.

Culture is a dynamic process and change in value systems is not a problem in itself. The difficulty arises when we seek to give physical expression to our new-found values in the absence of knowledge of, and confidence in, our cultural inheritance from the past, in this case traditional building values. This situation can be contrasted with the success with which Irish music, which is still vibrant in its traditional realization, incorporated contemporary instruments and successful contemporary composition, thereby creating the dynamic indigenous musical heritage of recent decades.

As we begin another millennium, the main indicator of the value placed on traditional architecture is not to be found in the folk park or in the various worthy articles and aspirations which abound in learned journals and policy documents, but rather in the quality of our contemporary landscape. Here we can see examples of traditional buildings as ruins or as they have been adapted to accommodate contemporary needs, side by side with new buildings. A preliminary survey reveals that neither traditional nor contemporary landscapes are successful and where they exist side by side, they are completely unconnected. Contemporary Irish society, with some few exceptional examples, is culturally detached from its building traditions. We are not linked to the past in the matter of using our cultural coordinates as they exist in the built environment. Such references might include, for example, orientation, siting, forms, materials and scale. Unconnectedness springs from the interpenetration of two very different sets of cultural norms. Traditional local references are now ignored, most likely forgotten in our post-colonial collective amnesia. In the context of our difficult history, this phenomenon is as regrettable as it is predictable.

Vernacular implies locality and process. It is the combination of process and locality, in this case construction and materials in their cultural context and continuity of use over time, which defines tradition. It includes language, objects and buildings as well as landscape. Cultures in general use the existing local references to replicate models or to create new ones. The most obvious local reference is material, but other fundamentals include topography, vegetation, orientation and the variety of shapes and forms assembled by masons, carpenters, thatchers and slaters within the parameters of the material and non-material needs of individual traditions.

In the past thirty years, there has been a dramatic move away from the use of local references in Irish building. The prompts, clues and hints provided by the past and evident in everyday speech and landscape are manipulated in a haze of social and cultural nostalgia or,

more conveniently, they are completely ignored. Our building standards are taken from the English tradition, from the nineteenth century back to Tudor times, but we also find evidence of North American and Continental European influences. The result can be seen throughout the countryside as our late twentieth-century neo-Irish landscape. The multiplicity of variations and interpretations of any one style which can be witnessed at present forms a plethora of pastiches, fake 'replicas' and manipulations of original features and materials. The original architectural style has become almost irrelevant as a source of inspiration and as architectural heritage. The Irish rural landscape is being overwhelmed by every kind of reference other than local ones — the suburb, the semi-detached house, brick, neo-Tudor, neo-Victorian and neo-Georgian styles. Contemporary design is virtually non-existent and where contemporary materials are employed, they are neatly camouflaged with a veneer of the aforementioned 'lumpy stone' look. Brick and Tudor beams hide the cavity blocks; synthetic lead or Georgian plastic strips decorate double-glazed picture windows; the Big House is the dream and reality of farmer and commuter alike; the demesne wall and gates surround the suburban housing estate; Victorian fire-places disguise late twentieth-century building regulation chimney flues; place-names such as 'Manor Close' and 'Tudor Lawns' remind us of more exotic landscapes and uncertain periods in our history. Is this the new Irish International Movement? Some would call it neo-vernacular. Such new building styles make the truest statement regarding the management of vernacular landscapes. Traditional architecture looks incongruous in this context and any proposal concerning its preservation and conservation is a lost cause until we grasp the nettle — contemporary building catering for the contemporary needs of Irish society in a cultural context. It is hoped that we shall find the confidence to look to our past as one source of imagination and inspiration in resolving this difficult issue.

Ireland's vernacular architecture is disappearing from the landscape. This is a type of architecture we have chosen to make redundant, practically. The culture and economy that created and supported, and ultimately justified, an Irish vernacular architecture no longer exist. In general our 'non-modernized' traditional buildings cannot serve the needs, other than those based on nostalgia, of contemporary society. Certainly we can conserve or preserve exceptional examples that will show our future generations 'the way it was and the way we were'. The maintenance of our vernacular landscapes as expressions of a redundant vernacular culture is not feasible. We can only re-inhabit the walls of traditional buildings to live in the culture of the twenty-first century. The re-adaption, rejuvenation and restoration of vernacular buildings to accommodate the requirements of a contemporary society are viable ways of maintaining a traditional building stock, but we must provide future generations with the spaces of the imagination from a heritage of ruins. Beyond the rehabilitation of some traditional buildings, our creative energies should be directed towards the achievement of an understanding of the process of creation, inhabitation and demise of a complex architecture rather than investing efforts in halting its demise. At the beginning of the twenty-first century, we are witnessing a process of abandonment of a cultural expression — vernacular dwellings — that is similar to the abandonment of ringforts as places of habitation. We should be asking not how we can 'save' traditional buildings, rather how we can bear witness to the departure of this extraordinary architecture and how we can be inspired by it to build a new and equally enduring rural architecture in the new Ireland. Our vernacular buildings will become, like the ringforts, the resting places of memory.

Bibliography

Aalen, F. H. A. 1964 'Clochans as transhumance dwellings in the Dingle Peninsula, county Kerry', *Journal of the Royal Society of Antiquaries of Ireland* **94**, pp. 39–45.

Aalen, F. H. A. 1966 'The evolution of the traditional house in western Ireland', *Journal of the Royal Society of Antiquaries of Ireland* **96**, pp. 47–58.

Aalen, F. H. A. 1967 'Furnishings of traditional houses in the Wicklow Hills', *Ulster Folklife* **13**, pp. 61–8.

Aalen, F. H. A. 1970 'The house types of Gola Island, county Donegal', *Folk Life* **8**, pp. 32–45.

Baillie, M. G. L., 1976 'Dendrochronology as a tool for the dating of vernacular buildings in the north of Ireland', *Vernacular Architecture* **7**, pp. 3–10.

Brannon, N. F. 1983 'Three bed-outshot houses in Castletown Townland, county Tyrone', *Ulster Folklife* **29**, pp. 29–32.

Buchanan, R. H. 1956 'Corbelled structures in Lecale, county Down', *Ulster Journal of Archaeology* **19**, pp. 92–112.

Buchanan, R. H. 1957a 'Stapple thatch', *Ulster Folklife* **3**, pp. 19–28.

Buchanan, R. H. 1957b 'Thatch and thatching in North-East Ireland', *Gwerin* **1**, pp. 123–42.

Buchanan, R. H. 1963 'Geography and folklife', *Folk Life* **1**, pp. 5-15.

Campbell, Å. 1935 'Irish fields and houses, a study of rural culture', *Béaloideas* **5**, pp. 57–74.

Campbell, Å. 1937 'Notes on the Irish house', *Folk Liv* **1**, pp. 207–34.

Campbell, Å. 1938 'Notes on the Irish house', *Folk Liv* **2**, pp. 173–96.

Danaher, K. 1955 'Semi-underground habitations', *Journal of the Galway Archaeological and Historical Society* **26**, pp. 75–80.

Danaher, K. 1975 *Ireland's vernacular architecture*. Cork.

Danaher, K. 1985 *The hearth and stool and all! Irish rural households*. Cork.

Danaher, K. 1992 *Ireland's traditional houses*. Dublin.

Department of the Environment (Northern Ireland) 1987 *Location, siting and design in rural areas*. Belfast.

Department of the Environment (Northern Ireland) 1994 *A design guide for rural Northern Ireland*. Belfast.

Department of the Environment (Northern Ireland: Countryside and Wildlife Branch) n.d. *Dwellings of the Mournes: a design guide*. Belfast.

Department of the Environment (Northern Ireland) Environment and Heritage Service 1988 *A sense of loss: the survival of rural traditional buildings in Northern Ireland, report of findings of townland survey 1996–1997*. Belfast.

Dublin Heritage Group 1993 *Vernacular buildings of East Fingal*. Dublin.

Estyn Evans, E. 1939 'Donegal survivals', *Antiquity* **13**, pp. 207–22.

Estyn Evans, E. 1940 'The Irish peasant house', *Ulster Journal of Archaeology* **3**, pp. 165–69.

Estyn Evans, E. 1942 'The fireside', *Louth Archaeological Journal* **6**, pp. 106–07.

Estyn Evans, E. 1954 'The rural house', *The Landmark* **2**, pp. 5–6.

Estyn Evans, E. 1955 'The Ulster farmhouse', *Ulster Folklife* **1**, pp. 27–31.

Estyn Evans, E. 1957 'The Ulster farmhouse; a comparative study', *Ulster Folklife* **3**, pp. 14–8.

Estyn Evans, E. 1966 'Some cruck trusses in Ulster', *Ulster Folklife* **12**, pp. 35–40.

Estyn Evans, E. 1969 'Sod and turf houses in Ireland' in J. G. Jenkins (ed) *Studies in folk life* (London), pp. 79-90.

Estyn Evans, E. 1973 'Traditional houses of Rathlin Island', *Ulster Folklife* **19**, pp. 13–9.

Estyn Evans, E. and McCourt D. 1968–71 'A late seventeenth-century farmhouse at Shantallow, near Londonderry', *Ulster Folklife* **14**, pp. 14–23, **17**, pp. 37–42.

Fitzsimons, J. 1990 *Thatched houses in county Meath*. Kells.

Gailey, A. 1961 'The thatched houses of Ulster', *Ulster Folklife* **7**, pp. 9–18.

Gailey, A. 1966 'Kitchen furniture', *Ulster Folklife* **12**, pp. 18–34.

Gailey, A. 1969 'Horse skulls under a county Down farmhouse floor', *Ulster Folk and Transport Museum Year Book* (Cultra), pp. 18–20.

Gailey, A. 1976a 'The housing of the rural poor in nineteenth-century Ulster', *Ulster Folklife* **22**, pp. 34–58.

Gailey, A. 1976b 'Vernacular dwellings in Ireland', *Revue Roumaine d'Histoire de l'Art, Série Beaux Arts* **13**, pp. 137–56.

Gailey, A. 1984 *Rural houses in the North of Ireland.* Edinburgh.

Geoghegan, P. n.d. *Building sensitively in Ireland's landscapes.* Dublin.

Geoghegan, P. and Culligan, D. 1988 *Building sensitively in the landscapes of Wexford.* Dublin.

Glassie, H. 1982 *Passing the time: folklore and history of an Ulster community.* Dublin.

Hughes, G. Bernard 1971 'Irish bog-wood furniture', *Country Life* **140**, 3859, pp. 1318–21.

Harrison, J. 1981 'A note on two houses in north county Dublin', *Sinsear* 3, pp. 108–11.

Kingston, B. 1990 *Achill Island. The deserted village at Slievemore: a study.* Achill Island.

Kinmonth, C. 1993 *Irish country furniture, 1750–1950.* New Haven and London.

Loughnan, N. 1984 *Irish country furniture.* Dublin.

Lucas, A. T. 1956 'Wattle and straw mat doors in Ireland', *Studia Ethnographica Upsaliensia* 11, pp. 16–35.

Lucas, A. T. 1970 'Contributions to the history of the Irish house: a possible ancestry of the bed-outshot', *Folk Life* **8**, pp. 81–98.

Lucas, A. T. 1982a 'Contributions to the history of the Irish house: smokehole and chimney' in A. Gailey and D. Ó hÓgáin (eds) *Gold under the furze, studies in folk tradition presented to Caoimhín Ó Danachair* (Dublin), pp. 50–66.

Lucas, T. 1982b 'Houses with decorative roof linings at Dunabrattin and Ballynakill, county Wexford', *North Munster Antiq. J.* **24**, pp. 81–91.

Lynn, C. J. 1978 'Early Christian period domestic structures: a change from round to rectangular plans?', *Irish Archaeological Research Forum* 5, pp. 36–7.

Maguire, 1998 *The changing vernacular landscape: a report prepared for the Community Relations council and the Ulster Architectural Heritage Society.* Belfast.

Mac Aodha, B. 1962 'Meath na dtithe ceann tuí', *Studia Hibernica* 2, pp. 209–11.

Mac Aodha, B. 1969 *An tsuirbhéireacht ar Ghaeltacht na Gaillimhe.* Galway.

Mac Giolla Meidhre, S. 1938 'Some notes on Irish farm-houses', *Béaloideas* 8, pp. 196–199.

MacSweeney, A. and Connif, R. 1998 *Ireland: stone walls and fabled landscapes.* Dublin.

McAfee, P. 1997 *Irish stone walls — history, building, conservation.* Dublin.

McAfee, P. 1998 *Stone buildings: conservation, repair, building.* Dublin.

McCourt, D. 1955 'Infield and outfield in Ireland', *Economic History Review* **7**, pp. 369–76.

McCourt, D. 1956 'The outshot house-type and its distribution in county Londonderry', *Ulster Folklife* 2, pp. 27–34.

McCourt, D. 1961 'Cruck trusses in north-west Ireland', *Gwerin* 3, **4**, pp. 165–85.

McCourt, D., Gailey, A. and Thompson, G. 1964 'The first Ulster Folk Museum outdoor exhibit: the Magilligan cottier house', *Ulster Folklife* **10**, pp. 23–34.

McCourt, D. 1964–65 'The cruck truss in Ireland and its west European connections', *Folk liv* 26, pp. 64-78.

McCourt, D. 1970 'The house with bedroom over byre: a long-house derivative', *Ulster Folklife* **15/16**, pp. 3–19.

McCourt, D. 1972 'Roof timbering techniques in Ulster: a classification', *Folk Life* 10, pp. 118–30.

McCourt, D. 1973 'Innovation diffusion in Ireland: an historical case study', *Proceedings of the Royal Irish Academy* **73** C, pp. 1–19.

McCullough, N. and Mulvin, V. 1987 *A lost tradition: the nature of architecture in Ireland.* Dublin.

McDonald, F. and Doyle, P. 1997 *Ireland's earthen houses.* Dublin.

Mülhausen, L. 1933 'Contributions to the study of the tangible material culture of the Gaeltacht', *Journal of the Cork Archaeological and Historical Society* 38, pp. 67–70.

Mülhausen, L. 1934 'Contributions to the study of the tangible material culture of the Gaeltacht', *Journal of the Cork Archaeological and Historical Society* 39, pp. 41–51.

Mülhausen, L. 1941 'Haus und Hausbau in Teileann, county Donegal', *Zeitschrift für Keltische Philologie* 12, pp. 239–261, 330–348.

Mullane, F. 1988 'The study of vernacular architecture in Ireland — an approach to some problems', *Sinsear* 5, pp. 104–40.

Mullane, F. 1994 'Traditional buildings and reconstruction' in B. Ní Fhloinn and G. Dennison (eds) *Traditional architecture in Ireland and its role in rural development and tourism* (Dublin), pp. 48–53.

Mullane, F. 1996 'The Irish house' in S. Kimura and S. Nakamura (eds) *The European house vol. 2* (Tokyo), pp. 76–97.

Mullane, F. 1997 'The management of vernacular architecture as an aspect of heritage' in T. O'Regan (ed) *Irish Landscape Forum: second landfall* (Cork), pp. 68–70.

Mullane, F. 1998 'Buildings within the spirit of the time' in T. O'Regan (ed) *Irish Landscape Forum: through the eye of the artist* (Cork), pp. 45–8.

Murray, H. 1979 'Documentary evidence for domestic buildings in Ireland c. 400–1200 in the light of archaeology', *Medieval Archaeology* **23**, pp. 81–97.

Ní Fhloinn, B. 1989 'A future for Irish vernacular architecture?' *Archaeology Ireland* **3**, 4 (Winter), pp. 147–151.

Ó Conaola, D. 1988 *An teachín ceanntuí: thatched homes of the Aran Islands*. Inis Oírr.

Ó Conghaile, M. 1988 'Bochtanas agus tithíocht' in M. Ó Conghaile (ed) *Conamara agus Árainn 1880–1980: gnéithe den stair shóisialta* (Conamara), pp. 87–101.

Ó Danachair, C. 1935 'Old houses at Rathnew, county Wicklow', *Béaloideas* **5**, pp. 211–12.

Ó Danachair, C. 1938 'Old house types in Oighreacht Uí Chonchubhair', *Jn. Royal Soc. Antiq. Ireland* **68**, pp. 226-40.

Ó Danachair, C. 1945 'The questionnaire system: roofs and thatching', *Béaloideas* **15**, pp. 203–17.

Ó Danachair, C. 1946 'Hearth and chimney in the Irish house', *Béaloideas* **16**, pp. 91–104.

Ó Danachair, C. 1955–56 'The bed-outshot in Ireland', *Folk Liv* **19**, 20, pp. 26–31.

Ó Danachair, C. 1956a 'Irish farmyard types', *Studia Ethnographia Upsaliensa* **11**, pp. 6–15.

Ó Danachair, C. 1956b 'Three house types', *Ulster Folklife* **2**, pp. 22–26.

Ó Danachair, C. 1957 'Materials and methods in Irish traditional building', *Jn. Royal Soc. Antiq. Ireland* **87**, pp. 61–74.

Ó Danachair, C. 1959 'Some distribution patterns in Irish folklife', *Béaloideas* **25**, pp. 108–23.

Ó Danachair, C. 1964 'The combined-byre-and-dwelling in Ireland', *Folk Life* **2**, pp. 58–75.

Ó Danachair, C. 1965 'Farm and field gates', *Ulster Folklife* **11**, pp. 76–79.

Ó Danachair, C. 1966–67 'Some notes on traditional house types in county Kildare', *Journal of the Kildare Archaeological Society* **14**, pp. 234–246.

Ó Danachair, C. 1967 'The botháin scóir' in E. Rynne (ed) *North Munster Studies* (Limerick), pp. 489–98.

Ó Danachair, C. 1969 'Representations of houses on some Irish maps of 1600' in J. G. Jenkins (ed) *Studies in folk life* (London), pp. 91–104.

Ó Danachair, C. 1972 'Traditional forms of the dwelling house in Ireland', *Jn. Royal Soc. Antiq. Ireland* **102**, pp. 77–96.

Ó Danachair, C. 1977 'Irish tower houses and their regional distribution', *Béaloideas* **45–47**, pp. 158–63.

Ó Danachair, C. 1981 'Farmyard types and their distribution in Ireland', *Ulster Folklife* **27**, pp. 63–75.

O'Farrell, F. 1987 *Farm buildings in the environment*. Dublin.

Ó Maitiú, S. and O'Reilly, B. 1997 *Ballyknockan: a Wicklow stonecutters' village*. Dublin.

O'Neill, T. P. 1977 *Life and tradition in rural Ireland*. London.

Oram, R. 1984 *Taken for granted*. Belfast.

O'Reilly, B. 1991 'The vernacular architecture of north county Dublin', *Archaeology Ireland* **5**, 2 (Summer), pp. 24–6.

Ó Riordáin, S. P. and O'Kelly, M. J. 1940 'Old houses near Lough Gur, county Limerick' in J. Ryan (ed) *Féil-scríbhinn Eoin Mhic Néill* (Dublin), pp. 227–36.

Ó Riordáin, S. P. and Ó Danachair, C. 1947 'Lough Gur excavations: Site J. Knockadoon', *Jn. Royal Soc. Antiq. Ireland* **77**, pp. 39–52.

Ó Riordáin, S. P. and Hunt, J. 1942 'Medieval dwellings at Caherguillamore, county Limerick', *Jn. Royal Soc. Antiq. Ireland* **72**, pp. 37–63.

Ó Siadhail, M. 1978 *Téarmaí tógála agus tís as Inis Meáin*. Dublin.

Ó Súilleabháin, S. n.d. 'House and home' *in Irish folk custom and belief* (Dublin) pp. 16–18.

Ó Súilleabháin, S. 1942 *A handbook of Irish folklore*. Dublin.

Ó Súilleabháin, S. 1976 'Beneath the Poulaphouca Resevoir' in C. Ó Danachair (ed) *Folk and farm. Essays in honour of A. T. Lucas* (Dublin), pp. 200–07.

Paterson, T. G. F. 1960 'Housing and house types in county Armagh', *Ulster Folklife* **6**, pp. 8–17.

Paterson, T. G. F. 1961 'Housing and house types in county Armagh', *Ulster Folklife* **7**, pp. 19–22.

Pfeiffer, W. and Shaffrey, M. 1990 *Irish cottages*. London.

Robinson, P. 1979a 'Vernacular housing in Ulster in the seventeenth century', *Ulster Folklife* **25**, pp. 1–28.

Robinson, P. 1979b 'Urban vernacular housing in Newtownards, county Down', *Folk Life* **17**, pp. 20–38.

Rothery, S. 1975 *Everyday buildings of Ireland*. Dublin.

Rowan, A. 1979 *The buildings of Ireland: north-west Ulster*. Harmondsworth.

Shaffrey, M. and P. 1983 *Buildings of Irish towns — treasures of everyday architecture*. Dublin.

Shaffrey, M. and P. 1985 *Buildings of the Irish countryside*. Dublin.

Shaw-Smith, D. 1986 *Ireland's traditional crafts*. London.

Ulster Architectural Heritage Society 1994 *Directory of traditional skills*. Belfast.

Ulster Architectural Heritage Society 1993–98 *Buildings at risk, catalogues 1–5 of historic buildings at risk in Northern Ireland*, **1** (1993); **2** (1995); **3** (1996); **4** (1997); **5** (1998). Belfast.

Walker, B. 1990 'A re-appraisal of the byre-dwellings at Machaire Gathlan, Bunbeg, county Donegal', *Ulster Folklife* **36**, pp. 74–9.

Weir, H. L. 1986 *Houses of Clare*. Whitegate.

Urban Heritage

KEVIN HOURIHAN

This chapter is concerned with the quality and management of urban heritage in Ireland. For the most part, this aspect of heritage has not figured prominently in images of the country (which have been dominated by rural scenes) or in tourist promotions. Yet a majority of the population now lives in cities and towns (58 percent of the population of the Republic in 1996, and an even higher percentage in Northern Ireland), and most settlements are of historic and heritage interest. Until recently, though, their management and promotion for tourism purposes have been quite poor.

This is not the case internationally, and in Europe especially, old towns and cities are seen as both important tourist attractions and highly valued elements of national heritage. An examination of tourist guides (especially the culturally oriented ones like the Blue, Baedeker or Phaidon series) will clearly identify many of them. Granted, many contain artistic treasures or individual architectural features which draw visitors, but, in addition, the ensembles of buildings, streets and open spaces which constitute the built environment of these towns are major attractions in their own right.

They are recognized as such on the most exclusive global listing of cultural heritage, the UNESCO World Heritage Sites. These emerged from the World Heritage Convention which was adopted by UNESCO in 1972 and came into force in 1976. As of December 1999 the list includes 630 properties in some 117 states, covering both sites of natural heritage (like the Giant's Causeway in county Antrim) and cultural importance (like the Boyne Valley archaeological complex in county Meath), but excluding art like music and painting. Designation as a World Heritage Site is an international recognition of value, but also carries responsibilities for the signatory states to protect and conserve them. The UNESCO listing currently includes capital cities like Prague and Budapest, artistic centres like Venice and Florence, medieval towns like Bamberg and Avila, and Renaissance

ones from Bath to St Petersburg. Many of these cities have played a pivotal role in the civilization of the continent, but the list also includes a number of small and unimportant places which have a World Heritage status, such as Telç in the Czech Republic and the wooden town of Rauma in Finland, both of which are excellent examples of historic towns in their regions. The sites in counties Antrim, Meath and Sceilg Mhichíl in county Kerry are the only designated sites in Ireland, and, realistically, no Irish town or city can aspire to World Heritage status like those mentioned above.

Another useful indication of the importance of heritage towns in Europe is the list drawn up by Bord Fáilte in association with the consulting firm Brady Shipman Martin in 1988 (Commission of the European Communities 1988). This was based on tourist guides, and so avoids the problem of commitments for funding and preservation which governments must make for the sites on the UNESCO listing. In their assessment of cultural attractions in the then ten member states of the EC, they identified dozens of cities and towns which qualified in their entirety, as well as individual cathedrals, palaces, museums and the like. As with the UNESCO centres, these are living, ongoing settlements, and in many cases are not even especially dependent on tourism.

Ireland, north or south, did not have a single town on the EC list. In part, this fairly reflects the quality of our built heritage. When compared to mainland European countries, Ireland's urban heritage is relatively new and incomplete. It excludes the classical phases of Greece and Rome, and even the medieval period is not well represented when compared to cities like Bruges in Belgium or Siena in Italy. The 'Grand Design' of the Renaissance is represented by Georgian structures, but the influence of the Industrial Revolution is present only in parts of Ulster. For the most part, developments during the twentieth century have not been particularly innovative or noteworthy.

Nevertheless, the fact remains that a majority of the population on the island of Ireland lives in cities or towns at present. In the Republic this comprises 129 places of 1,500 population or over and there are almost 200 more with populations of 500 to 1,500 (Central Statistics Office 1997). Many of these are quite old, have been the site of historic events, and together with their cultures and traditions should be an important heritage resource. There are many lessons for Ireland in the European experience, and certain of these have been introduced recently, although some important deficiencies remain. This chapter will now examine the salient features of heritage towns and the problems they have experienced during the twentieth century. It will then consider the policy measures which have developed towards them, and the outstanding difficulties which require attention.

URBAN HERITAGE QUALITIES

The single essential characteristic of a heritage town or city is obviously age; by definition, these places have existed for a considerable period of time. At the very least, this produces a sense of continuity with the past. If, as Midleton (1987) has suggested, a town without old buildings is like a person without a memory, it could be argued that the same applies to a country without old towns. Urban morphology is the academic discipline which is most concerned with the form and evolution of historic towns. It argues that there are three interrelated elements which are important: the town plan, building fabric and land use. Land uses are clearly subject to continuous change which may not necessarily cause any harm. The other two elements are regarded as the 'morphological frame', and interference with these can seriously affect the character of the built environment. This character, or sense of place, or *genius loci* as it has been called, is an integral part of the concept of heritage towns, and essentially involves an emotional experience or response to these places. Some have argued that it grows over time amongst actual residents of the place, but others suggest that tourists deliberately searching for a place-related experience are the people best attuned to the *genius loci*.

In addition to this, historic settlements are very attractive to look at. This quality of 'townscape' as it is termed, exists in the eye of the beholder, and is entirely subjective, but many believe that medieval towns with their narrow, winding streets and half-timbered houses are among the most picturesque that have ever been constructed. Many of these were also beautifully adapted to the natural terrain with locations on hilltops or river banks for defensive or trading purposes. They often appear nowadays to be not so much built on the ground as growing organically from it. The eminent Finnish architect Eliel Saarinen (1943) has described the medieval town as 'an ornamental pattern of man's art fitted into the majestic environment of nature's art ... a precious stone of the medieval time, in the precious setting of all time'. The Renaissance ideal was completely different, with its formality and grandeur, and produced another contrasting type of beauty. Beginning in Italy in the fifteenth century, new streets, squares and spatial relationships were introduced to cities (Bacon 1967; Morris 1972). Later developments further advanced these, particularly in seventeenth-century Paris, and by the eighteenth century, urban design based on Renaissance principles was being used across the entire continent (Braunfels 1988).

In the best historic townscapes, the entire built environment dates from the same time period and has very few extraneous or unsuitable elements which might detract from the overall scene. Although it can be very difficult to identify the reasons why particular townscapes are attractive, their quality can be severely affected by the demolition of a single building or the addition of a new one which is out of character with the rest of the street. Even townscapes which may not seem visually attractive, like the cities of the Industrial Revolution, are still valuable examples of city building in their particular era. At their very best, entire towns can 'represent a unique artistic or aesthetic achievement, a masterpiece of creative genius', as do those which satisfy this criterion for inclusion on the World Heritage List (like those mentioned in the introduction to this paper). In 1986, this approach was adopted by the late Donald Olsen, the eminent urban historian, in his work on nineteenth-century London, Paris and Vienna, which he titled *The city as a work of art*. (There was also a later book on *Dublin as a work of art* by Colum Lincoln [1992], although it was, probably inevitably, less convincing.)

Another inherent quality of heritage towns is a certain atmosphere or ambience which, like townscape, can be difficult to define. It is something which has developed over time and cannot be artificially created. In a memorable phrase, the American urbanist Lewis Mumford argued that 'through its complex orchestration of time and space ... life in the city takes on the character of a symphony'. Every city has its own particular rhythm, tempo and pace, but the human scale of historic places and the cultures which evolve over time are better adapted to an attractive ambience than are most of the purpose-built planned settlements of the twentieth century.

In addition to the accretions of time, many heritage cities were the sites of important events or the homes of historical figures, both of which are typically commemorated by blue plaques and incorporated into town trails. The past status or role of towns may also manifest itself in important museums, galleries or art holdings. Bruges in Belgium is an excellent example, where its medieval importance has almost become frozen in time after its harbour silted up and it lost its economic function, but the art treasures created during its heyday survive and its built environment is extremely well preserved.

Cultural events are often another reminder of the past. The famous horse race around the Piazza del Campo in Siena, the Palio, has been held every year since 1656, and is an integral event in Sienese life, although it has also been recognized as a spectacle for television and tourists. The Race of the Ceri at Gubbio in Umbria is not as well known, but is even older than the Palio. It commemorates the town's victory in a war of 1151. What sets these events apart from tourist-oriented promotions is their longevity and tradition; even today, they are as fiercely contested by local people as they were centuries ago. Their relationship with modern events is akin to the Irish pub and its thousand clones all over the world. The *craic*, like the Palio or Ceri, is not amenable to instant assembly and packaging for export to foreign cultures.

THE PROBLEMS OF HERITAGE TOWNS IN THE TWENTIETH CENTURY

For the first three-quarters of the last century, the treatment of heritage towns was very poor. For a variety of reasons ranging from ideology to neglect, almost all were affected adversely and many of them suffered irreparable harm. The most catastrophic damage was inflicted during wartime. The Great War brought the destruction of many towns in Flanders, like Ypres with its famous Cloth Hall which may have been the most impressive guild hall to have survived intact from the Middle Ages. The Second World War caused more systematic and widespread damage. The infamous Baedeker Raids of 1942 were a deliberate attempt by the Nazis to devastate five of the most attractive and historic towns in Britain in retaliation for the British bombing of the old Baltic port cities of Lubeck and Rostock in Germany. Destruction of historic places became deliberate policy on both sides later in the war, as distinct from what has become euphemistically known as 'collateral damage'. Amongst the most infamous examples were the razing of central Warsaw by the Germans in 1944 and the Allied destruction of Dresden in 1945. The latter especially has almost become synonymous with cultural barbarism. Dresden, the 'Florence of the Elbe', may well have been the most beautiful Baroque city in existence at that time, and was undefended and of no strategic importance. Fortunately, Hitler's orders to destroy Paris in 1944 were disobeyed by the German commander in the city (Collins and Lapierre 1965).

The reconstruction of European towns after the war has taken a variety of forms, some sympathetic to the pre-war fabric and others using the opportunity to 'modernize' buildings and streets which were seen as unsuited to new requirements (Diefendorf 1990, 1993). In many cases, including Dresden, this involved even more vandalism and harm. In the 1990s, the ongoing restoration of Dresden has been much more sensitive than it was immediately after the end of the conflict when the city was adapted to the new *Zeitgeist* of the Soviet zone of occupation.

Deliberate destruction of the cultural heritage did not finish with the Second World War. In 1992 there was international outrage at the Serb shelling of Dubrovnik, the 'Jewel of the Adriatic', and a protected city on the World Heritage List. Many other heritage towns were severely damaged during the war in Bosnia-Herzegovina, and some famous features like the bridge at Mostar were totally destroyed. In Italy, the Mafia has been blamed for cultural terrorism like the bombing of the Uffizi in Florence and the fire at La Fenice in Venice. Ireland also has not been spared this destruction. The bombing of Nelson's Pillar in Dublin in 1966 removed an attractive townscape feature from the city centre, and the 'Troubles' in Northern Ireland have caused massive damage to many old towns and cities.

Changes in urban transport have also brought adverse effects, with huge increases in private car ownership and declining use of public transport being world-wide phenomena. The narrow, winding streets of historic towns are particularly unsuited to large numbers of motor vehicles and have suffered accordingly, with road widenings, motorways and car parks all causing serious damage to the built environment. Facilitating the motorist was the prevailing philosophy throughout Europe until the 1970s. It is only during the past twenty years or so that most countries have been promoting the advantages of public transport over the car, and the legacy of the earlier period is evident today in many historic towns. Even now, a large number of road widenings are still planned for Dublin, despite widespread concern at the destruction which they will entail.

Another result of private transport has been increased suburbanization in most cities. This has affected historic centres in many ways. It has changed the scale of cities, leaving the historic centres as small cores in a mass of suburban development, and has caused increased traffic congestion in them. The city centres have become less attractive commercially, with suburban shopping and business centres becoming much more important. In Ireland especially, national construction policy has greatly favoured new buildings over the rehabilitation of older ones, and has implicitly allowed the older centres to fall into disrepair. This attitude culminated in the Eastern Region Development Organisation plan of 1985 when a population increase up to 560,000 was forecast for the period 1981–2011. The centre of Dublin was not considered suitable for housing even 10,000 of them, and the planners proposed that all would be accommodated in suburban developments and new towns. Even small Irish cities and towns have the same characteristic, with most new housing in suburban estates at best, and more often in ribbon development or so-called urban-generated rural housing (bungalow bliss or bungalow blight, depending on one's perspective).

The corollary of suburban growth has been the problems of the city centres, which are usually the oldest areas, and which still have a strong symbolic role to play. For most of the last century, the inner cities lost population through slum clearances and the move to the suburbs (Hourihan 1982). By the late 1980s, the centres of the largest Irish cities had lost almost all of their residential populations (Hourihan 1992). Those people who remained were often elderly and poor, and had many social problems and high rates of unemployment. The city centres were increasingly associated with drugs and crime, and became less attractive as heritage features and tourist destinations. These problems were not as acute in smaller cities and towns, although the decline of their centres was a feature common to most of them.

Neither architecture nor planning were effective in protecting heritage towns for much of the twentieth century; on the contrary, both professions were active in destroying parts of the built heritage in the name of progress. The emergence of modern architecture involved a deliberate break with the past and the discarding of much of the European architectural tradition and the kinds of styles and embellishment which had evolved over the centuries. Axioms like 'less is more' and 'form follows function' produced buildings and areas which many people found unattractive, and which made no effort to relate to existing buildings or streets. The internationalization of styles and materials made local traditions and crafts irrelevant, and threatened the distinctiveness which was an essential feature of historic cities and towns.

Architecture and planning came together through the Congrès Internationeaux d'Architecture Moderne (CIAM) which was founded in 1928. The influence of the 'Athens Charter' which emerged from the fourth congress in 1933 on the theme of 'The Functional City' was especially important. It was dominated by Le Corbusier, the eminent Swiss-born French architect, and reflected his commitment to a rigid functional zoning of cities combined with a widespread use of high-rise apartment blocks, widely spaced in open areas. Together, these became the basis of much of the post-war planning of European cities and did severe damage to the mixed land uses and human scale which were essential features of older cities especially.

When combined with the new transport planning which catered for private motor car owners, and the changes taking place in the geography of cities, the prospects for heritage towns were not very promising by the 1970s. At best, they might survive as curiosities, isolated remnants from an increasingly irrelevant past, or they might quite possibly disappear totally under a tidal wave of 'progress'.

MANAGEMENT OF HERITAGE TOWNS

Over the past quarter-century, the attitude to heritage towns has changed markedly. In part this has been motivated by economic considerations, with the role these towns play in cultural tourism, but there has also been a greater appreciation of their quality and a recognition of the need to protect them for their own sake. There is no single ideal approach to the management of these towns. Even in Europe, there are many different groups and administrative structures, ranging from the nationally centralized, like France, to those where local councils can draft their own rules and regulations, like Austria. Between these extremes are the federal states like Germany, and those where local councils have been delegated power to implement national policy, like Britain. Despite these differences, a number of models have emerged which have important advantages.

The protection of individual buildings and monuments is one of the most frequently used ways of preserving the built heritage. It became widely accepted during the nineteenth century after the edict published by Victor Hugo in France in 1832 calling for protection against demolition or excessive restoration, although the French also pioneered scientific restoration through the work of Viollet-le-Duc. The French government was also the first to provide public funds for protected buildings. The foundation of the Society for the Protection of Ancient Buildings by William Morris in Britain in 1877 was another landmark.

Curiously, the first instance of city-wide preservation occurred not in Europe, with its wealth of historic cities, but in the United States, when Charleston, South Carolina, adopted ordinances to protect its historic centre in 1931. Here again, though, the French were to advance this concept in 1962 when André Malraux, the writer and then government minister, legislated for some sixty 'Secteurs Sauvgardés' in the historic cities of France. These areas have been managed very carefully ever since, although the procedure involved has been criticized for being cumbersome and bureaucratic. There have also been unintended consequences of the process. The Marais on the east side of central Paris was one of the first Secteurs to be redeveloped, and became so successful that it was entirely gentrified by young professionals and lost its indigenous population because of increased costs. In 1967, the British government introduced a similar idea to Malraux's, that of the conser-

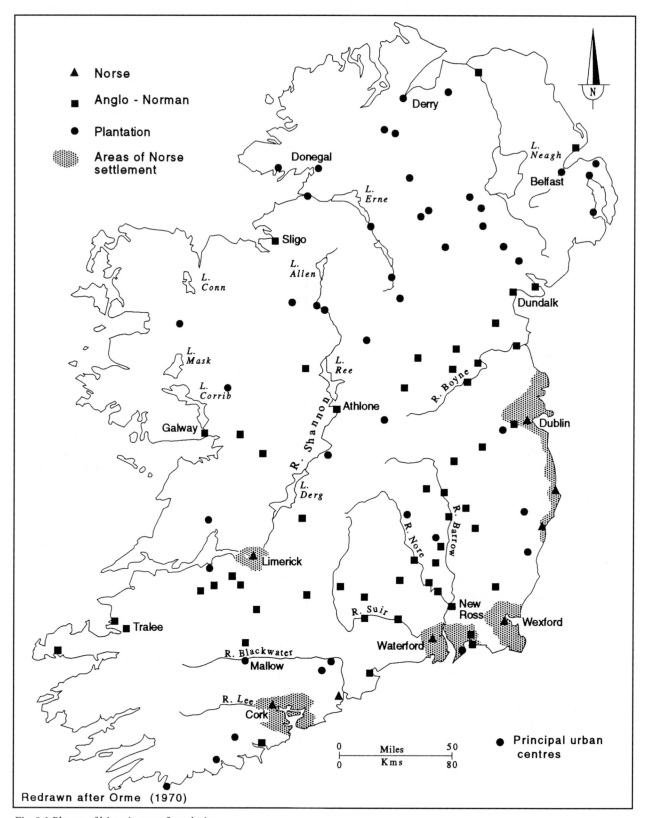

Fig. 9.1 Phases of historic town foundation.

vation area. By 1994, there were some 9,400 areas designated in the United Kingdom (Larkham 1996). They were much less selective than the French scheme, and despite considerable legislation, they have been less successful than might be expected, especially for a planned society like Britain.

Protecting the past is only one aspect of managing heritage towns; they cannot be treated as museums, but must be allowed the developments necessary for modern life. In this respect also the French have probably been the most adventurous and dynamic in Europe. The redevelopment of Les Halles in Paris, the Pyramid in the courtyard of the Louvre and the Grand Projets initiated by President Mitterand (especially the Grand Arche at La Défense) are unashamedly modern but deriving directly from the built heritage of the city. Many other cities in France have benefitted from this progressive approach. In Spain, Barcelona deserves special mention for its commitment to new squares in the 1980s and '90s (Webb 1990). Open spaces in the form of city squares deteriorated greatly all over the world during the twentieth century. Few cities created any worthwhile ones until the 1980s, but Barcelona is unique in terms of the number and variety of squares and their varying functions which it developed before the Olympics in 1992.

Contemporary planning has other initiatives which should benefit old cities. The 'Twenty-four Hour City' idea, for example, aims to create an active, lively atmosphere in a mixed-use environment which seems well suited to the humane scale and social traditions of heritage towns (Heath 1997). Overall, the CIAM-inspired movements of the post-war period which had such adverse effects on historic cities are not popular anywhere at present.

URBAN HERITAGE IN IRELAND

It is now widely accepted that there were no indigenous cities or towns in Ireland. The first wave of development came with the Norse incursions of the ninth and tenth centuries. Later these settlements became the most important cities of today (**Fig. 9.1**). Successive phases of town foundation came with the Anglo-Normans, the plantations of the sixteenth and seventeenth centuries, and the improvements of the eighteenth century. In effect, almost all of the urban system across the entire island was complete by 1800. Although relatively few old buildings survive in Irish towns by continental standards, the morphological frame of streets and open spaces is reasonably intact and does reflect the time-period and purpose for which the towns were established.

The first attempts at managing this urban heritage began in the late 1950s. The 'Tidy Towns Competition' established by Bord Fáilte had rather modest aims: tidiness is much less ambitious than the kind of aesthetics that other European countries aspired to.

Despite this, its continued existence after forty years is proof of its continuing relevance. The competition has succeeded in improving many towns and generating a kind of spirit and confidence among the more successful that has produced many spin-offs in tourism and economic development. **Fig. 9.2** shows the national winners of the competition over the period 1958–99. They include several important tourist centres like Adare (1976), Kinsale (1986) and Sneem (1987), but also many remote (and previously unrecognized) small towns which deserve great credit for the efforts involved in their success.

The running of the competition was taken over by the Department of the Environment in 1995 and has been broadened considerably. The original criterion of tidiness is now only one of nine in which competitors are judged and it accounts for less than seven percent of the total marks. The overall developmental approach is now the most important factor and towns are encouraged to prepare plans for future change. One of the limitations of the competition in the past was the failure to include the cities, but the Department is now encouraging their participation also. Another welcome innovation in 1997 was the Heritage Council prize of £2,000 for the best heritage initiative in the competition. This is awarded to that town which has 'most effectively built on and facilitated increased understanding, appreciation, enjoyment and conservation' of its heritage. The winner in 1998 was St Patrick's Church in Glenbrohane, county Limerick.

The national competition is augmented by many local ones. The town of Killarney, for example, has been running one called 'Killarney Looking Good' since 1991. This has created intense rivalry between shop and pub owners, streets and even individual householders. Similarly, Cork Corporation has sponsored a competition for attractive shopfronts which has helped generate a greater consciousness of this aspect of heritage.

An all-Ireland competition has also begun involving the top centres in the Tidy Towns from the Republic and their equivalents from the Best Kept Towns competition in Northern Ireland which is run by the Amenity Council. The competitors are judged on the basis of presentation of buildings; appearance of approach roads, streets and public facilities; presentation of open spaces, village greens, gardens and private frontages, and tidiness. In 1998, the overall winner was Loughgall in county Armagh, while Adare won the prize of Best Kept Small Town and Enniskillen was adjudged the Best Kept Large Town.

The 1960s also brought the beginning of physical planning on a nationwide, statutory basis. Unfortunately, it did not incorporate measures for the protection of the architectural heritage. The decision on whether or not to list buildings for preservation was left to each local authority, and even in 1999, there were counties which

Fig. 9.2 Tidy Towns Competition: national winners 1958–99.

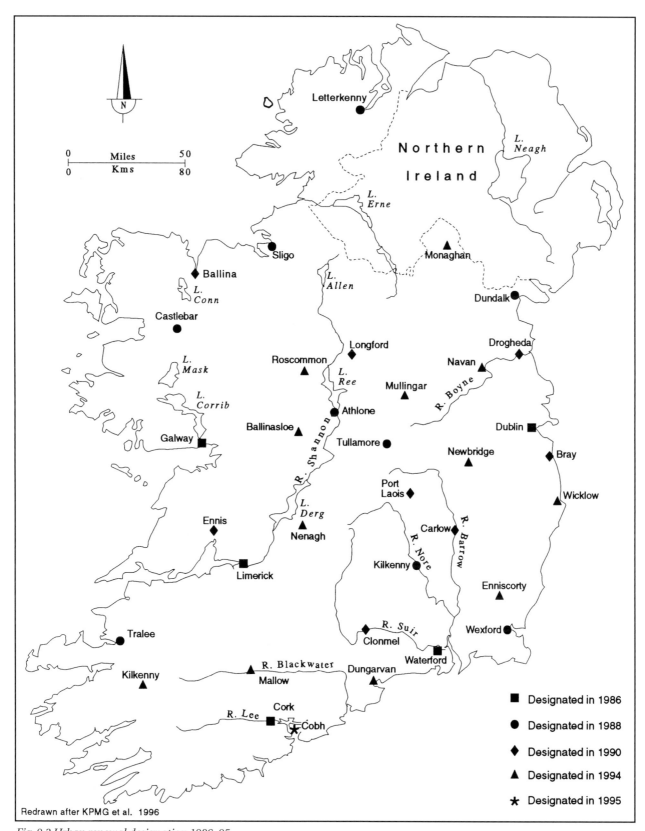

Fig. 9.3 Urban renewal designation 1986–95.

had no list of protected buildings. The report drawn up by the then Department of Arts, Culture and the Gaeltacht (1996) on a national policy for architecture argued for a reform of the system, with 'the utmost practicable obligations' on the owners of listed properties to protect them. In contrast to the recent position, future listing should also extend to interiors, fixtures and fittings which are an integral part of a building's character. On a positive note, the proposed reform would also provide financial support to the owners to discharge their responsibilities, thereby resolving another major deficiency in the present system. The report also championed the need to consider heritage buildings in their wider context, raising the possibility of area-wide conservation like that in France or Britain, and the need for new structures to relate properly to the existing built fabric. This kind of 'contextualism' is now widely accepted as essential for sensitive development.

As against these constructive proposals, the harsh reality in the late 1990s was that the European Commission was reportedly investigating formal complaints that the Irish government had failed to protect its architectural heritage and even omitted architectural heritage in implementing the EU's Directive on Environmental Impact Assessments (EIAs). The British experience of comprehensive listing and conservation areas has shown that legislation alone will not preserve historic buildings or townscapes. In Ireland, a much greater awareness and sensitivity will be necessary to appreciate and protect our built heritage, irrespective of whatever legislation will emerge from the present debate.

Despite this criticism, there have been several other constructive developments since the mid-1980s. One of the best was the Metropolitan Streets Commission established in 1985 by John Boland, then Minister for the Environment. This was charged with making proposals for the main street axis of Dublin from O'Connell Street through Grafton Street, to improve its appearance and aesthetic quality. Boland argued that the group was an equivalent of the eighteenth-century Wide Street Commissioners who had embellished the city two hundred years before. The Commission was abolished after the general election in February 1986, when C. J. Haughey was elected Taoiseach, but it succeeded in publishing its proposals which attracted considerable interest and debate. It also had more tangible results through business interests commissioning several pieces of public art in Dublin.

Urban renewal schemes have been operating in the United States and Britain since the 1930s, and were introduced to Ireland in 1986 in response to the problems of the inner cities. Initially, large areas were designated in Dublin, Cork, Limerick, Waterford and Galway for a period of three years. Private enterprise was encouraged to undertake development within them through a mixture of tax incentives. Later legislation extended the time period until 1994, and provided for renewal areas in many smaller provincial towns (**Fig. 9.3**). These incentives encouraged considerable redevelopment in the designated areas, but had two serious drawbacks, especially for heritage towns. They favoured new development over conservation and rehabilitation, and commercial enterprises over residential housing. Short-term investment was also favoured through the ten-year time span of the incentives, raising fears about the long-term viability of much of the new development.

An assessment of urban renewal from 1986 to 1996 has been made by the consultants KPMG *et al.* (1996). This shows the huge scale of investment over the period, over £1.75 billion, but also confirms many of the reservations raised about its balance. Residential development accounted for only 28 percent of the total investment, while offices accounted for 32 percent and commercial developments for 26 percent. New constructions heavily outnumbered refurbishments, with the latter accounting for only 12 percent of residential and commercial investment and just five percent of the investment in offices. Although these might renew the designated areas in the cities and towns, they would also change their character irrevocably.

A new urban renewal scheme was introduced in 1994 for a three-year period, with a much stronger bias towards conservation of existing buildings and the repopulation of declining inner-city areas. Incentives like those for 'living over the shop' have helped both the tradition of shop fronts (which were one of the finest achievements of vernacular architecture) and the problems of dereliction at upper levels which have been very widespread over the past twenty years especially. More recent innovations in urban renewal emphasise the need for local involvement and for partnership amongst the different interests involved.

In February 1999 the Department of the Environment announced a new scheme of renewal incentives to apply to Dublin, Cork, Limerick, Galway and Waterford, and thirty-eight provincial towns. This will be based on integrated area plans prepared by the relevant local authorities. In addition, another scheme will be targetted on townscape renewal in other centres which do not qualify for the main renewal programme. Incentives are also available for towns which have not been designated under the urban renewal acts. The European Union has provided support under the Structural Funds for 'Urban and Village Renewal' schemes which have been operated by county councils throughout the country. For a nationwide scheme the money available has been relatively small. Very often though it has been used for showpiece developments which have had a dispropor-

Fig. 9.4 Bord Fáilte Heritage Towns

tionate impact. For example, one of the finest town squares in the country, Wolfe Tone Square in Bantry, county Cork, has been transformed from a rundown, unsightly car park to an elaborate Italian-style piazza which provides a much-needed pedestrian area in the centre of the town.

In 1995, fifteen coastal towns were designated for a three-year period under the Seaside Resorts Renewal Scheme. This has encouraged many millions of pounds of investment and the creation of considerable employment, but much of the development has been ill-conceived and inappropriate, and rather than protecting the character of the resorts has seriously altered them. Large estates of holiday homes, commercially driven developments and inappropriate projects have reportedly caused many resorts to question the continuation of the scheme as it operates at present.

Reservations can also be expressed about the Heritage Towns scheme which was launched by Bord Fáilte in 1990. Ostensibly, this should be a showpiece programme for heritage towns in Ireland, involving 28 settlements which represent different phases of town growth and are amongst the most attractive in the country (**Fig. 9.4**). EU Structural Funds have been used to support this development, which requires the participating towns to open a heritage centre and develop a heritage trail and appropriate brochures and booklets. Suitable signage throughout the towns was also necessary. The impact of the programme has been very variable. In the most successful, some towns have developed far beyond what might have been expected by using the heritage elements as a starting point for dynamic and far-ranging growth, but others seem only to be going through the motions of the programme by opening their centres for three months during the summer and investing minimum effort in the Heritage Town status. Ideally, the scheme should optimize the uniqueness and identity of each town involved, but it often seems that they become blurred and indistinct through the replication of the same elements and motifs (signs, black and yellow bollards and the like). There is often a risk that nationwide programmes can impose a conformity which threatens the very features they are designed to enhance.

This danger also applies to public art which has been funded under the 'One Percent for Art' scheme, whereby all public projects have to devote that share of their budget (up to a maximum of £20,000) for commissioned sculpture on public view. There is a long tradition of public art in European cities, in many cases providing symbols for them, such as Mannekin Pis in Brussels or the Little Mermaid in Copenhagen. Maybe as a result of our colonial history, Irish towns are relatively poor in this respect. The 'One Percent for Art' programme provides an opportunity to subsidize modern sculpture and redress this. In theory, it seems an excellent idea, but in practice its results have varied widely. At their best, attractive art has been produced which has been quickly identified with by local people, but in other cases the reaction of residents to public art has ranged from apathy to outright hostility. Ongoing maintenance of art also requires more attention.

The development of Temple Bar in Dublin has been unique in Ireland. The cultural tradition in the area, its location and relatively good state of preservation, combined with its lack of development in the 1960s and '70s while the public transport company CIÉ was planning its conversion into a transport interchange, provided a unique opportunity for conserving and developing a historic inner city area. Many of the achievements in Temple Bar have been very positive, but there have also been accusations of insensitive and excessive development and the increasing involvement of commercial considerations. In some respects, Temple Bar has been the victim of its own success, just as was the Marais in Paris or Greenwich Village in New York.

The Historic Centre Action Plan in Cork city is another important opportunity for a heritage area (O'Donnell 1998). The initial study for this project was funded by the EU, and after the adoption of the plan in 1994, there was further EU funding as an Urban Pilot Project. Cork Corporation planners have been developing the scheme as a partnership with business and residents' interests. Rather than confining itself to narrow sectoral concerns, the plan involves a holistic approach to the historic city centre. It incorporates a number of conservation projects, but also deals with the old outdoor market, a flexible approach to traffic management and encouraging more people to live in the area. In this respect it coincided with the 1994 revision of the urban renewal scheme, and was able to exploit those incentives.

The general approach of the Cork action plan should serve as a model for other heritage cities and towns in Ireland. It pays due respect to the architectural and cultural heritage of the area, but does not attempt to fossilize it or treat the area as a museum. Rather, it treats it sensitively while attempting to promote repopulation and social and economic progress. Most of the recurrent difficulties of heritage towns, like traffic congestion, are addressed. If successful, Cork's centre should again become a living, humane environment, which is the proper role for historic urban centres and one of the most appealing features of heritage towns on the continent.

CONCLUSION

Hopefully, the prospects for historic towns and cities in Ireland are better. We have avoided the worst excesses of twentieth-century 'improvements' through our neutrality and stage of economic development, and as regards public policy, heritage towns are now seen as a resource rather than a liability. The professions involved in their management are more sensitive to their qualities and needs than was the case in the past, and the Celtic Tiger economy can afford the costs involved. However, Irish identity is still not fully an urban one, despite the fact that a majority of the population lives in cities and towns, and the greatest threat to old places probably comes from public apathy and carelessness. More education and involvement in conservation issues by the community at large would help to redress this

Bibliography

Bacon, E. N. 1967 *Design of cities*. London.
Braunfels, W. 1988 *Urban design in western Europe: regime and architecture, 1900–1900*. Chicago.
Collins, L. and Lapierre, D. 1995 *Is Paris burning?* London.
Commission of the European Communities, 1988. *Inventory of cultural tourism resources in the member states and assessment of the methods used to promote them*. Dublin, Irish Tourist Board.
Department of Arts, Culture and the Gaeltacht 1996 *Developing a government policy on architecture: a proposed framework and discussion of ideas*. Dublin.
Diefendorf, J. M. 1990 *Rebuilding Europe's bombed cities*. London.
Diefendorf, J. M. 1993 *In the wake of war: the reconstruction of German cities after World War II*. Oxford.
Eastern Regional Development Organisation 1985 *Eastern Region Settlement Strategy 2011*. Dublin, Eastern Regional Development Organisation.
Heath, T. 1997 'The twenty-four hour city concept — a review of initiatives in British cities', *Journal of Urban Design* 2, pp. 193–204.
Hourihan, K. 1982 'Urban population density patterns and change in Ireland, 1901–1979', *Economic and Social Review* 13, pp. 125–47.
Hourihan, K. 1992 'Population change in Irish cities, 1981–86: county boroughs, suburbs and daily urban systems', *Irish Geography* 25, pp. 160–68.
Kain, R. (ed.) 1981 *Planning for conservation*. London.
KPMG in association with Murray O'Laoire Associates and Northern Ireland Economic Research Centre 1996 *Study on the Urban Renewal Schemes*. Dublin.
Larkham, P. J. 1996 *Conservation and the city*. London.
Lincoln, C. 1992 *Dublin as a work of art*. Dublin.
Midleton, M. 1987 *Man made the town*. London.
Morris, A. E. J. 1972 *History of urban form: prehistory to the Renaissance*. London.
O'Donnell, J. 1998 'The Cork Historic Centre Action Plan'
in B. Brunt and K. Hourihan (eds) *Perspectives on Cork* (Cork), pp. 121–37.
Olsen, D. J. 1986 *The city as a work of art*. New Haven.
Orme, A.R. 1970 *Ireland*. London.
Saarinen, E. 1943 *The city: its growth, its decay, its future*. New York.
Webb, M. 1990 *The city square*. London.

The Irish Language

NEIL BUTTIMER

This chapter first presents a brief overview of Gaelic civilization. It summarizes the main phases into which the culture is conventionally divided. It sketches the principal trends within each, with reference to recent scholarship on the specific topics treated. The reader is directed to periodicals mentioned at the close of the paper for further studies of individual issues, as well as to standard bibliographies in the field (Best 1913; Best 1942; Baumgarten 1986). The article concentrates on the twentieth century in particular, while also bringing the narrative down to the present. This is the immediate setting in which those involved with the subject operate, either as researchers or at other levels of interaction. The paper is written in the belief that Irish is an essential key to the understanding of the traditions of this island, whether in their everyday manifestations or their more imaginative forms.

BACKGROUND

Irish has one of the oldest spoken and written histories of any European vernacular, spanning the greater part of two thousand years (Caerwyn Williams agus Ní Mhuiríosa 1979; Mac Cana 1980; Ó Murchú 1985; Caerwyn Williams and Ford 1992; McCone et al. 1994). It first emerges during what has since been termed the Old Irish period (600–900 AD) and the slightly earlier Archaic Old Irish phase. The distinctive writing system known as Ogham, mainly comprising names on monuments, largely belongs to the first of these (McManus 1991). The second sees the annotation in Irish of scriptural works like the Psalms or the Epistles of St Paul, together with Latin grammars (Stokes and Strachan 1901–03; Hofman 1996), indicating the advent of Christianity. Early poetry with both secular and ecclesiastical themes occurs among the latter sources (Murphy 1956), leading to recent debate about its nature and the balance between the external and the indigenous dimensions to Gaelic literature (Ó Corráin 1989; McCone 1990). The first large-scale flowering of the culture is now available in manuscripts of the eleventh and twelfth centuries, reflecting the era of the language known as Middle Irish (900–1200 AD). They are primarily from the midlands and Leinster (Bergin and Best 1929; Meyer 1909; Best, Bergin, O'Brien and O'Sullivan 1954–83), and some are noted for their distinctive penmanship (O'Neill 1984). These works include examples of the major branches into which the literature is divided, religious material, mythology, the Ulster Cycle (Mallory and Stockman 1994), *Fianaíocht* or mercenary works (Nagy 1985) and stories from the early Christian King Cycle, often in prose and verse combinations. Other types of composition like secular and saints genealogies (O'Brien 1962; Ó Riain 1985) are also present. Such documentation and alternative categories of work occurring slightly later enable descriptions to be made of the economy (Kelly 1997), political and social organization (Byrne 1973; Charles-Edwards 1993; Ó Cróinín 1995) and church administrative structures (Kenney 1929 etc.; Etchingham 1999) of early Ireland.

Irish remained the language of an integral culture after the arrival of the Normans in the latter part of the twelfth century. The linguistic phase in question is known as Early Modern or Classical Irish (1200–1650 AD, approximately). Its robustness is evident in the survival of a considerable number of documents from just west of the Shannon and onwards into north Connacht (Atkinson 1887; Mulchrone 1937; Macalister 1942). Their scribal background is now the subject of much active inquiry (Ó Concheanainn 2000). Their contents suggest a renaissance in Gaelic learning as writers become reacquainted with pre-Norman kingship and poetic traditions. Conversely, Munster manuscripts of the same period (Macalister 1950), containing accounts of northern Italy and copies of Marco Polo's travels in the east, exhibit ongoing contact with a wider contemporary world. This is seen also in the courtly love traditions introduced into Irish writing ultimately from French literature by the

Normans (Ó Tuama 1960 and 1988). To this period belongs the recording of poem books for aristocratic families, whether native or newcomer (for instance Mac Airt 1944, McKenna 1947; Ó Cuív 1973); the writing of one of Europe's most extensive non-classical bodies of legal material (Binchy 1978; Kelly 1988), possibly encouraged by the canon law teachings of the international universities of the day (Simms 1998); the compilation of medical manuscripts, the largest single category of extant medieval Gaelic documentation (Ní Dhonnchadha 1990), and the completion of early and later medieval historical records known as annals (Mac Niocaill 1975). All the writings in question originate in locations widely dispersed throughout the country. These works enable the social and political complexity of this phase of the Irish past to be accounted for (Nicholls 1972; Simms 1985).

Gaelic culture began to become endangered from the early 1500s onwards. Spain developed as an international power, spreading its influence not only in the Americas but into northern Europe. It was in England's strategic interest to ensure that Ireland would not come under Spanish control. This resulted in a series of measures to reassert its authority in this country, comprising colonization and warfare, lasting until the end of the seventeenth century, at which point Ireland's indigenous civilization faced imminent decline. Writings in the Irish language describe and embody reaction to some of the more important of these incidents (Caball 1998). They include the poet Geoffrey Keating's troubled response to the aftermath of the Battle of Kinsale and the decline in the power of native rulers during the early 1600s (Ó Tuama and Kinsella 1981, 84–7), Friar Ó Mealláin's verse account of the impact of the Cromwellian campaign in mid-century (*ibid.* 104–09), Dáibhí Ó Bruadair's description of the outcome of the Williamite wars in the 1690s as a form of shipwreck for his society, sentiments echoed in the next century by the composer Aogán Ó Rathaille (*ibid.* 164–67). Prose works give a more extensive insight into many of the occurrences in question, like Tadhg Ó Cianáin's diary of the voyage over sea and land of the northern O'Donnell and O'Neill chieftains to France and Italy, the event now know as the 'Flight of the Earls' (de Barra agus Ó Fiaich 1972). Contemporaries' attitudes towards the aforementioned developments were complex in many respects. Embittered followers of the Gaelic aristocracy satirized upstart commoners who were winning greater privilege just as they themselves were losing patronage and status (Williams 1981). The emergence of the ordinary people would henceforth become a dominant feature of the Irish-speaking world (McLysaght 1939 etc.). The happenings of the time brought about a great deal of speculation on the precise identity of the Irish population, particularly how to ensure reconciliation

Fig. 10.1 Title-page of the printed early seventeenth-century devotional work entitled Emanuel *or* Desiderius, *adapted into Irish by Flaithrí Ó Maolchonaire and published in Louvain in 1616.*

between its Gaelic and Anglo-Norman components in the face of adversity, determining what constituted legitimate authority and the most appropriate forms of political and spiritual allegiance (Ó Buachalla 1996). Events of the day impeded the course Gaelic civilization might have taken in one other final respect. Various European languages developed vigorous print cultures after the introduction of this medium in the fifteenth century. It was employed to produce both Protestant and counter-Reformation Catholic devotional works in Irish in the late sixteenth and early seventeenth centuries (Williams 1986; Ó Maonaigh 1962; McGuinne 1992). However, Irish writing would be deprived of this and other forms of support systems under the new dispensation after 1700.

The marginalization of Gaelic culture from the early eighteenth century onwards was not a simple process. Even if the numbers of speakers of the language declined from an estimated two-thirds of the population in the 1730s to some half about 1800, they still formed a sizeable proportion of an expanding society. There were growing levels of literacy among different classes of people. Those capable of writing Irish now included shopkeepers, tradesmen like shipwrights, carpenters, masons and tailors, as well as an extensive number of schoolteachers (Ní Shéaghdha 1990), all of whom required basic ability in reading and writing for their livelihood. The broad spread of literacy contrasts with the Middle Ages, when this competency was confined to clerics or those patronized by the aristocracy. Paradoxically, therefore, just as Gaelic culture was undermined, we have the greatest number of written sources for all of Irish before 1900. Numbers are estimates only. It appears that some 5,000 traditional Gaelic manuscripts survive, with one-third remaining to be catalogued (de Brún 1987 and 1988). It is likely that well over two-thirds of the total come from the period 1700–1850. One of the major scholarly achievements of the past eighty years has been the inventorying of the contents of these documents, held in libraries and other institutions in Ireland and overseas. The full collection of the Royal Irish Academy, totalling some 1,400 items, has been described (O'Rahilly *et al.* 1926–70), as has that of Maynooth (Ó Fiannachta *et al.* 1965–80). Well over half the National Library's material has been listed in detail (Ní Shéaghdha *et al.* 1961–), and so forth. Many of these sources are microfilmed and available in university and research libraries. All of this enables a more accurate account of the outlines of the Postclassical tradition to be presented than was possible when Daniel Corkery's *The Hidden Ireland* (1924) first drew the attention of the public at large to the topic.

Global trends such as the geographical distribution of Gaelic writing reveal its enduring strength. Over 230 scribes are known of for the Cork region in the years 1700–1850, of whom over 160 worked after 1780 (Ó Conchúir 1982). There were some 75 scribes in Limerick during 1700–1900, of whom over 50 were active after 1780 also (Ó Madagáin 1974). Waterford had some 46 copyists in the same years, with 38 of them flourishing at the end of the eighteenth century and later (Ó Súilleabáin 1992). Kilkenny had 24 scribes (Ó hÓgáin 1990). Writers from the aforementioned regions worked in cities, towns and villages as well as the countryside, a fact which helps counteract the impression that their culture was exclusively rural in nature. In fact, one of the most vigorous centres of its cultivation was Belfast. Here, the relatively liberal political environment of the 1780s and 1790s encouraged the collection of native music and song (Ó Buachalla 1968). To this time as well dates the burgeoning Ascendancy interest in Gaelic tradition evident in a growing output of translation from Irish. Dublin, with upwards of 50 scribes in the first half of the eighteenth century (Ní Shéaghdha 1989), witnessed from the 1780s onwards the establishment of institutions like the aforementioned Royal Irish Academy which, from its

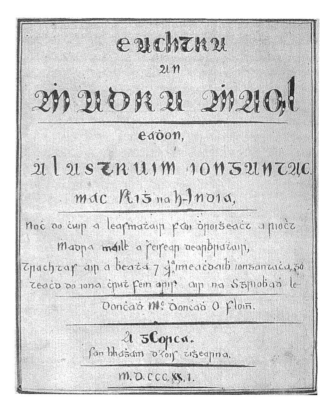

Fig. 10.2 Manuscript title-page (dated 1821) of the Arthurian saga Eachtra an Mhadra Mhaoil *copied by early nineteenth-century Cork scribe Donnchadh Ó Floinn (UCC MS T:i).*

inception, did much to foster the study of the culture. Apart from these centres of major manuscript attestation (and others, like Clare, a full study of which is awaited), one finds examples of Gaelic writing in National Library of Ireland manuscripts, for example, for areas such as Roscommon (MS G 351), Leitrim (G 436), Sligo (G 292), Mayo (G 550), Donegal (G 355), Derry (G 195), Longford (G 15), Cavan (G 687), while compositions from Carlow and Wexford are known of from other collections.

Work produced in these regions constitutes a valuable window on the civilization in terms of both language, presentation and content. Many of the manuscript materials are medieval. Some are completed in the writing style and spelling conventions of later Classical Irish. Writing exhibits the use of space-saving manuscript contractions characteristic of the early Middle Ages, even though the influence of print is evident in the use of title-pages and indexes, to name but two features. Much attention has been paid to pre-1600 palaeography and manuscript illumination in Ireland, but the distinctive later evidence is now attracting notice in collaborative scholarly ventures like the 'Irish Script on Screen' project (*http://www.isos.dcu.ie*). Changes from the medieval practice apart from those just mentioned are apparent. One sees non-Classical spelling in the source of the period, as well as the employment of new vocabulary items, reflecting the use of language at regional spoken level. In other cases, scribes would have had no training in Gaelic script or spelling. These often write in the English style and render sounds phonetically. Many valuable collections of oral verse (for instance the works of the poet Antaine Raiftearaí) have come to light in this way, particularly in the Galway area (Mahon 1996). This is also the case as regards religious texts like sermons, showing the clergy's need to communicate with an Irish-speaking population in its own vernacular. Such evidence is very useful when reconstructing Irish dialects in areas where the language has not now survived, for instance county Louth (Maynooth MS MF 4).

The quantities of manuscripts, the numbers of scribes, the country-wide distribution of material and its shape and form indicate we are dealing with yet another complex, hybrid period after 1700. There has been comparatively little investigation of actual compositions or literary genres to amplify the impressions one can form from general overviews. Pioneering work was done in the early part of the twentieth century on poetry by the likes of Tadhg Ó Donnchadha, Pádraig Ua Duinnín and the indefatigable Fiachra Éilgeach. Researchers like Pádraig de Brún, Ciarán Ó Coigligh, Liam Ó Murchú and others have continued this trend in more recent times. Editions of prose are comparatively rarer with the exception of religious material and the publication of the diary of Humphrey O'Sullivan, describing life in Callan, county Kilkenny, in the years 1827–35 (McGrath 1936–37). Gaelic reaction to important contemporary events serves to indicate the overall richness of the material. A south Kilkenny scribe Seosamh Ó Díomusaigh described battles in the opening half of the American Revolution (RIA MS 24 C 57: 174). Revolutionary teaching spread from the United States and particularly France. The Roscommon scribe Micheál O Braonáin transcribed an Irish-language version of a sermon preached by the Bishop of the Diocese of Elphin against the spread of seditious teaching in 1798 (RIA MS 23 B 27: 162). The Cork-based copyist Donnchadh Ó Floinn exchanged correspondence in Irish with his friend Micheál Óg O Longáin, who had to flee to Limerick because of his United Irish activities, relating to the career of Napoleon, for instance his success at the Battle of Jena in 1806 (RIA MS 23 G 24: 212) or his later exile to St Helena (Maynooth MS B 11: i). When parliamentary replaced revolutionary politics, Gaelic speakers took an intense interest in the career of Daniel O'Connell. Scribes recorded Irish-language versions of speeches made at his monster meetings, or prayers said on his behalf during his imprisonment in the early 1840s (RIA MS 23 M 5: 2).

O'Connell's attempts to secure self-governance for Ireland were not successful in his own lifetime. He died in the midst of what was set to become a particularly traumatic incident in Irish life, the Great Famine. Contemporary Gaelic commentators noted this event which more than any other imperilled their civilization, just as they had recorded the many outbreaks of disease or food shortages which characterized the decades after the Battle of Waterloo. Famine texts include poems from the midlands on the arrival and impact of the potato blight (NLI MS G 199: 331) or prose accounts regarding how to ventilate the crop to save it from destruction (RIA MS 3 C 7: 364). Following the failure of such measures, there are Irish-language descriptions of mortality in various districts, like the notice of over 1,000 deaths in the north-Clare parish of Kilmanaheen during the first three months of 1847 (Maynooth MS R 70: 490). Prayers were recorded for persons particularly affected by hardship, for instance mothers in childbirth. Reflections on what caused the Famine are available. For some, it occurred on account of the sinfulness of the Irish themselves (NLI MS G 199: 335). For others, it was the maladministration of the country by the English authorities and their Irish representatives which brought about the disaster (MS NLI G 545). Such poems employ metres and styles reminiscent of compositions detailing the despoliation of Ireland in Cromwellian times. They are an indicator of the cataclysmic terms in which the Famine was viewed from within the still surviving literary tradition (Póirtéir 1995), complementing the record of it in later Gaelic folklore sources (Póirtéir 1996). Famine hit hardest in regions where the language was most widely spoken, and subsequent emigration was highest from the same areas. Its demographic impact is easy to quantify but the psychological less so. One wonders to what extent the institutionalization of large numbers of people from the mid-nineteenth century onwards reflects a loss of identity resulting from the impairment of the culture brought about by the Great Hunger.

The Famine occasioned language shift on a major scale. Contemporaries like William Wilde were aware of the devastation being caused in this regard, and a later scholar, Seán de Fréine, has used the terms 'The Great Silence' as the title of a work describing the consequences of linguistic change. Detailed studies of the decline of Irish are now available for areas as far apart as the south-west (Ní Mhóráin 1997) and the north-east (Devine 1997). These are largely based on the investigation of replies to questions about respondents' command of Irish posed in censuses from 1851 onwards. Another aspect to the story of the language in the latter half of the nineteenth century is the effort made to arrest or if possible reverse the downturn in its fortunes. These attempts began in a small-scale way but ultimately grew to have an impact beyond the cultural domain only. The first organization formed to confront the unfolding situation was entitled The Society for the Preservation of the Irish Language (SPIL), founded in Dublin in 1876.

Persons associated with it had conducted research to ascertain the status of Irish in various parts of the country (RIA MS 12 Q 13). While its name explains the group's objectives, it operated by establishing a branch network in different counties, encouraging teaching of the subject in schools and supplying textbooks. Some members felt SPIL was not being active enough and broke away to establish a new entity, the Gaelic Union (GU), in 1880. This body has to its credit the creation of the first successful printed periodical devoted to the modern language, the *Gaelic Journal/Irisleabhar na Gaedhilge* (1882). In time, a younger generation of enthusiasts, particularly Eoin Mac Néill (1867–1945) and Douglas Hyde (1860–1949), felt the need to set up yet another organization, the Gaelic League, in 1893, which still exists and became the most influential of all.

Much research needs to be done on exactly how this grouping was more successful than others, but there are some general indicators as to why. Where previous bodies had been somewhat scholarly in their orientation and centralized in the capital, the League became broadly based in all senses, and embraced modernity. A recent study of its operations in county Cork (Ó Ríordáin 2000) reveals patterns of behaviour which are possibly valid for the country at large. It built on the existing work of SPIL, GU and other organizations but established more elaborate branch networks in the city and throughout the county. It managed to link the experience of older language supporters with the creativity and energy of younger enthusiasts like Donnchadh Pléimionn and Osborn Bergin. It adapted innovative action-centred teaching methods from contemporary European language instruction practice. While teaching the language was a major focus, it also provided a wider social aspect to its learning activities. Some of these were at internal branch level, like *scoraíochtaí*, cultural evenings of song, dance and storytelling in which conditions obtaining in Irish-speaking rural districts were replicated in urban settings. Others involved the interaction of a number of branches in summer outdoor cultural events entitled *aeraíochtaí*. The latter were noncompetitive, but the League soon evolved competitive events in the same domains of music, literature, folk tradition and crafts. The term for these was *feis*, with the Munster *Feis* being particularly significant. The national gathering became known as the *Oireachtas*. The adaptive reuse of terms from early Irish would in turn provide a model for the creation of adminstrative terminology when the Irish Free State was established in 1922. Many politicians and civil servants active in the early years of the southern administration had been members of the League (Breathnach agus Ní Mhurchú 1986–97).

A study of its cultural events and other publications reveals the Gaelic League's attempts at cultivating writing in Irish, from completing basic essays to composing short stories or longer novels. Certain models were conservative, for instance those based on folk narrative, but others were more adventurous, particularly when it was suggested that translations from European literature be used as exemplars. Some writers associated with the League like the Galway composer Pádraic Ó Conaire (Riggs 1994) have material of considerable originality to their credit, for instance Ó Conaire's exploration of uprootedness among the London Irish in the early nineteen hundreds. His artistic independence and creativity would show the way for others later in the twentieth century. There was a relatively traditional element to revival poetry, but even here composers like Patrick Pearse introduced new sentimentalist notes. The League invested much time and effort in drama, as this medium facilitated the participation of large numbers of people in a proactive use of the language. Plays were based on incidents in country life as well as on texts from the older literature and history, often in collaboration with personalities from the contemporary Anglo-Irish dramatic movement. The Gaelic League's cultural events made a noteworthy contribution to publicizing folk tradition in competitions for storytelling and singing. Members like Hyde involved themselves with manuscript work and edition when cooperating with newly founded organizations such as the Irish Texts Society which sought to make older and indeed contemporary Gaelic literature accessible to a wider readership (Ó Riain 1998).

The League was a voluntary body with broad interdenominational appeal at its commencement. It would continue to exhibit many of these features even down to the present, but other facets of its activities shortly became apparent. It soon evolved into a large-scale operation, with complex adminstrative structures. Increasingly professionalized cadres emerged to serve the demands of branches and classes. Among these were paid travelling teachers (*múinteoirí taistil*) and district or regional organizers (*timirí*), often trained in colleges set up for the purpose, such as Coláiste na Mumhan in Ballingeary, county Cork. Many of these became involved in efforts to obtain a more secure place for Irish in the educational system in the opening decade of the last century. Their most important undertaking was the campaign to make Irish a required subject for matriculation in the newly established National University of Ireland. This became a divisive issue within the League itself. Some members thought it would alienate nonnationalist opinion, while others fet that such a university could not properly claim to be national without a place being found within it for a subject critical to the representation of Irish experience and identity. The subject was eventually accorded compulsory status from 1910 onwards. In a sense, therefore, Irish had become part of the establishment, as the long-term impact of this move would be the necessity to consolidate its position at pre-university level. The full working out of this position took about a decade to be realized, as the years from 1910 onwards proved to be among the more turbulent in recent Irish history as well as internationally. The change in the fortunes of the Irish language which the League in particular had thus brought about would have been difficult to predict some fifty years earlier in the difficult circumstances obtaining in the immediate aftermath of the Great Famine.

THE TWENTIETH CENTURY

The story of the Irish language in the twentieth century involves two jurisdictions, the Free State and later Republic of Ireland and Northern Ireland. They are dealt with separately here, beginning with language in the south of Ireland. Its account may be divided into three main phases. The first of these is from 1922 to the aftermath of the Second World War. This is characterized by a bout of intense innovation and experimentation throught a broad range of activities, certain of which are sketched in what follows. The second phase is from the late 1940s or so to 1973. This is marked by a partial redirection away from pre-war activities, a questioning of their validity, but also some continuation of what had been put in place. 1973 was the year of Ireland's accession to the then European Economic Community, arguably the single most influential event in this country since independence, and one which had an appreciable impact on matters involving Irish. The third phase is from 1973 to the present. As this is closest in time to the point of writing, it is difficult to obtain a detached perspective on it necessary to describe it in full. However, some indicators of general tendencies are outlined.

THE SOUTH

Southern Ireland became largely independent in 1922. Various language-related measures were immediately set in train, ranging from the symbolic to the practical. Irish was recognized as an official language under Article 4 of the 1922 Constitution. The same article enabled the state to take steps on behalf of regions where it was the vernacular. The 1922 Constitution was in Irish as well as English. This made it relatively unique among contemporary western constitutions in the prominence accorded to linguistic diversity. The later 1937 Constitution further consolidated the position of the language in its Article 8. Various elements flowing from the state system established by the 1922 act incorporated the language in their proceedings. The parliament was proclaimed and assembled in Irish. A parliamentary Translation Service was inaugurated. One of its chief activities was to render all legislation into Irish, as well as a host of statutory and other instruments. Irish had not

operated in this way for centuries past, if ever. Irish-language versions of all statutes are available down to the 1980s, following which the output of dual-language versions of legal measures is less in evidence. These acts cover all areas of life, many of which had no previous representation in the language. The Oireachtas Translation Service was thus at the forefront of deciding on terminology and usage appropriate to modern requirements. Arising from this are the issues of its considerable influence on and contribution to areas like standard-setting, dictionary formation and other considerations. There is no full authoritative study of the service, despite the fact that from time to time it has numbered among its staff scholars and creative writers of the greatest distinction in modern Irish letters

The new southern state pursued a language policy in three principal areas. These were the Gaeltacht, the education system and public administration (broadly conceived). The Gaeltacht is the term used to designate those parts of Ireland where Irish has been spoken as a community language in an unbroken continuum over the generations. Much of Ireland could be so described in the nineteenth century, but the Famine, emigration and population decline meant that only certain districts, principally on the western seaboard, could be properly termed Gaeltacht regions by the beginning of the twentieth century. Irish-speaking districts had assumed a quasi-administrative identity from the 1890s with the establishment of the Congested Districts Board. This agency was set up to facilitate the economic advancement of densely populated, less-well-off parts of the country. Its activities, such as harbour improvement and pier construction, concentrated on the west. These regions also acquired special importance in the days of the Gaelic League as the remaining repositories of indigenous cultural tradition. Following independence, the government in 1925 established a Gaeltacht Commission to review policy in this area. Richard Mulcahy, an experienced member of the administration who had recently resigned as Minister for Defence over difficulties which had arisen in the army, headed the Commission. It visited Gaeltacht counties, spoke to community representatives and other interested parties and issued its report. The latter made some one hundred recommendations. The first was to designate as *Fíor-Ghaeltacht* areas where more than 80% of the population were habitual speakers of Irish and as *Breac-Ghaeltacht* regions with between 25% and 79% of the population using the language. Greater support would be directed towards *Fíor-Ghaeltacht* areas. Proposals for the improvement of social and economic conditions as well as education were recommended. It will be interesting to see how a second Gaeltacht Commission, established in April 2000 to make similar determinations (see press statements at *http://www.irlgov.ie/ealga*), will fare in contrast to its predecessor.

Housing was among the more important areas in which amelioration was attempted, both in the Gaeltacht and throughout Ireland. The southern government began a major drive in the 1920s to clear slum and derelict urban quarters, certain of which were among the most impoverished in western Europe in their day. The result was the establishment of public-sector housing projects now a feature of virtually all contemporary Irish urban areas, large and small. Gaeltacht housing initiatives from the late 1920s onwards are to be seen as part of this more broadly based undertaking. Acts were passed in each decade of the twentieth century, almost, detailing grants payable in Irish-speaking districts in respect of either the construction of new dwellings or the refurbishment of older ones. Many legislative measures also offered assistance in the erection or enhancement of farm buildings.

The Gaeltacht Commission recommended the strengthening of industry in the Gaeltacht. It counted fisheries among its objectives, suggesting the setting up of a school for young trainees in this livelihood, for instance. Fishing declined in the aftermath of the First World War, when food supplies from alternative sources became more readily available. Loans were advanced to Gaeltacht fishermen in the 1920s and 1930s for the improvement of boats and equipment. These loans proved unrepayable in the absence of proper markets. The sector has scarcely ever fully recovered from these initial setbacks. The impact on the fortunes of the Gaeltacht and its population of the failure to develop such a characteristic aspect of life in the area is probably not negligible. Manufacturing industry also attracted the attention of the Gaeltacht Commission. In the 1920s, this principally consisted of the production of clothing, with some elements of marine product processing like kelp and carrigeen moss (ingredients in foodstuffs and chemicals). Throughout the 1930s, the state made an appreciable effort in the improvement of methods of production, stock control and marketing. It established a centralized distribution service in Dublin for the sale of materials produced in the Gaeltacht which were promoted under the 'Gaeltarra' brand name. Agriculture was probably the most important economic sector in the Gaeltacht in pre-Second World War times. Steps taken to enhance this activity included land reclamation and improvement schemes carried out by the Land Commission, grants for the enhancement of breeds of cattle, sheep and other livestock and the training of Irish-speaking agricultural advisors to interact more meaningfully with Gaeltacht communities. This broad general category of land usage also witnessed the creation of the only new Gaeltacht region in the first half of the last century. The Land Commission acquired some 800 acres in Rathcarran and Gibstown, county Meath, where Irish-speaking families from Galway primarily (but also Mayo and Kerry) settled in the 1930s. It was intended that the holdings they vacated in their native districts would be redistributed among those who stayed behind to enhance the economic viability of the latters' farms.

Education was the second domain in which the state sought the advancement of Irish from 1922 onwards (Ó Riain 1994, 47–58). Government was involved in two major activities here, strengthening the sector itself and introducing the language to it. Many facets of education were comparatively underdeveloped in the 1920s. School attendance at primary level was not absolutely compulsory until 1926. Secondary schooling was available to some 10% only of the eligible segment of the population, and the proportion participating in it remained low until the mid-1960s. University was for the social and, to some extent, the intellectual elite until approximately the same time. Irish education today is in all respects unrecognizable when compared with its situation eighty years or so ago. The interplay between structural realities and language planning must accordingly be borne in mind in any consideration of this aspect of language policy. Irish was made a compulsory subject in southern primary schools from St Patrick's Day 1923 onwards. Because there had been limited provision in teacher training colleges for the instruction of primary teachers of Irish prior to 1922, short in–service courses in the language for existing teachers were provided. Subsequently, the government established a special category of Irish-speaking secondary school known as Preparatory College, pupils from which would have automatic right of entry to teacher training colleges. The objective here was to ensure a supply of instructors at primary level who would have an appreciable proficiency in the language. These institutions lasted until the 1960s. Some of them, like Coláiste Iosagán in Ballyvourney, county Cork, for males, or Coláiste Íde in Dingle, county Kerry, for females, won national recognition. Attention was paid to secondary schools other than Preparatory Colleges. They were divided into those whose subjects were taught throught Irish, partially in Irish or principally English, with special aid directed at the first of these categories. There was a lack of teachers at this level as well. In the 1920s, universities offered short in–service courses to supplement immediate deficiencies.

The introduction of Irish at primary and secondary levels necessitated the creation of teaching materials. In the mid-1920s, the state's Department of Education inaugurated a scheme whereby textbooks in all subject areas, in addition to items of general literature, would be generated. This publication service, known as An Gúm, is still in existence, and has some remarkable achievements to its credit, not least of which is the considerable volume of material it has produced and continues to issue in a wide variety of areas, business studies, the sciences and so forth (de hAe agus Ní Dhonnchadha 1938–40; Mag Shamhráin 1997). In 1929, it published *An tOileánach*, the biography of Blasket island native Tomás Ó Criomthain. This composition, one of the earliest descriptions from within of life in an Irish-speaking community, encouraged the creation of a new type of writing and won international recognition when translated. There were some negative aspects to the work of An Gúm, however. The Department of Education reserved to itself the right to refuse to accept a manuscript or to amend it as it saw fit. This effectively gave the state an early large-scale experience in the exercise of control over publications, coinciding with the passage of censorship legislation in the late 1920s. Many of the most creative writers in the Irish language from the 1930s onwards did not issue their output under the auspices of this agency but with independent publishing houses, notably the firm of Sáirséal agus Dill. These were the main publishers of Máirtín Ó Cadhain, former schoolteacher and socialist from the Connemara Gaeltacht. Many of his writings deal with the desolation of impoverished and marginalized rural communities (while also featuring the theme of uprootedness in the urban environment). His image of life in such societies as consisting, in part at least, of virtual incarceration in a timeless, cellular sameness, as seen in works like *Cré na Cille*, may have been shaped by his personal experience of imprisonment for republican activism in the Curragh during the Second World War. Sáirséal agus Dill published the works of the Cork poet Seán Ó Ríordáin who struggled with tuberculosis and imminent mortality (Ó Coileáin 1982). This lead to his questioning of all value systems, for instance those advocated by organized religion. The writings of Flann O'Brien (alias Myles na gCopaleen) took a correspondingly iconoclastic view.

The state intervened at tertiary and research levels of education also. It assigned University College, Galway, duties in respect of the teaching of subjects other than Irish through Irish, as this was the university closest to a large Irish-speaking district. It subvented initiatives in areas like manuscript cataloguing and the completion of a dictionary of early and medieval Irish (Quin 1976) undertaken by the Royal Irish Academy, and inaugurated the Irish Manuscripts Commission. The latter initially began the reproduction in facsimile format of medieval Gaelic documentation, although it subsequently focussed on a broader range of historical sources. The government formally endorsed the promotion of the study of Irish folklore through the setting up of the Irish Folklore Commission in the 1930s. A priority for this organization was the recording of elements of traditional culture from the older generations of Irish speakers for whom such lore was a living reality. The enterprise resulted in the creation of an archive of oral narrative and history of international stature. A School of Celtic Studies was established at the Dublin Institute for Advanced Studies in 1940 (Ó Murchú 1990). Among its tasks were the production of scholarly editions of texts, the description of Irish dialects, work on place-names with an Irish-language dimension and the writing of general accounts of aspects of the tradition. The publications it has issued since its foundation reveal the extent to which it revolutionized the study of many areas of the Irish past during the last sixty years (*http://www.dias.ie*).

The third large area in which initiatives were taken prior to the Second World War was administration (Ó Riain 1994, 33–46, 59–62). Here the sectors at issue were civil service and local government, the army, the police, legal and to a lesser extent health and other professions. The Gaeltact Commission, among others, had advocated the introduction of Irish to these domains in order to facilitate Irish speakers in their interaction with services from which use of the language had been excluded hitherto. A principal strand linking these disparate areas was the introduction of requirements to demonstrate a knowledge of the Irish language in order to secure admission to or qualification in these domains. The requirements were often expressed in legislative form. Many such conditions are still in force, like those obliging solicitors and barristers to show or attain proficiency in the language for the purposes of professional registration. Introduction of these steps required the creation of procedures, protocols, training manuals and other steps for which there was little precedent.

The measures outlined above would appear to have met with partial success in some respects. The Irish-speaking component of the population had been decimated from the mid-nineteenth century to the opening decade of the twentieth, down from some four million to a quarter of a million in the period, approximately. While decline certainly continued in the early twentieth century, with upwards of one hundred thousand native speakers in the south by the 1950s, it is likely that there had been some positive impact on the rate of downturn. Furthermore, increasing numbers of non-native speakers in the decades from the 1930s onwards reported a competence in the language when replying to census questions. This probably reflects the growing presence of the subject in the educational system and public affairs generally (Hindley 1990). However, regaelicization of Ireland, which can be claimed to have been public policy at the foundation of the state, was clearly not achieved. It would have been difficult to do so to begin with, given the inauspicious demographic circumstances just mentioned. Other factors also came into play. Gaelicization may have implied a reorientation towards the past, but the state simultaneously embraced modernity in many forms. This development would have tended to direct Irish life away from a traditional ethos, although this is not to argue that modernity and tradition are necessarily irreconcilable.

The impact of the contemporary world is already evident from the 1920s onwards. The Irish Free State began to finance a public telephone network as and from 1924, even if it only became a more widespread reality in the final quarter of the last century. It established a radio service in 1926 and an electricity service in 1927. Tourism came on stream in the 1930s. While traditional images of Ireland were conjured up to satisfy this overseas market, conversely, overseas visitors are likely to have awoken a consciousness of international criteria and desiderata in the host country. An international airline dates from the 1930s. By the same decade, this state's involvement in diplomacy via the League of Nations was already fully consolidated. There was lingering contact with the British Empire and what is now termed the diaspora, expatriate Irish in Britain, North America and the southern hemisphere. Missionaries, mostly Catholic but some Protestant, would have helped create a greater awareness of Africa and Asia in the inter-war years and immediately after World War II among the public at large than exists at present, arguably.

These developments gathered pace after 1945. When it set up an Arts Council, the first in either Britain or Ireland, in the early 1950s, the state began its first opening out towards forms of expression in sculpture, painting, music and other media which would not have to derive their impetus from Gaelic civilization alone. International initiatives proliferated in the post-war era. These included United States-sponsored measures for European reconstruction of which Ireland was a beneficiary, the establishment of the Council of Europe, the Organisation for Economic Cooperation and Development and the United Nations. As mentioned above, the state acceded to the EEC in 1973, having sought admission throughout the 1960s. In preparation for same, greater emphasis than before was placed on the teaching of French and German in the secondary school system. This was often at the expense of Latin, whose pedagogical materials had furnished models for how Irish itself was to be imparted. Classical and modern languages now occupy positions in the curriculum which are the reverse of those obtaining fifty or more years ago, when Latin and Greek easily outranked contemporary European vernaculars. Other forms of linguistic redirection took place as well in the 1960s. The organization known as the Language Freedom Movement provided a forum for the indication of disquiet at the hegemony of Irish in the educational system and the public sector generally. Debate between its members and supporters of Irish became quite acrimonious during that decade (Ó Canainn 2000, 19–20).

Many of these factors may have had a bearing on a highly significant decision taken in relation to Irish when Ireland formally joined the EEC. Although it was the state's first official language under the 1937 Constitution, this country did not seek to have Irish recognized as both an official and a working language of the Community (Ó Ruairc 1994, 95–7). It could have been felt that embroiling Europe in our domestic linguistic conflicts in return for its expected largesse in areas like agriculture might not have been an appropriate exchange. The irony is that one of the genuinely valuable contributions Ireland might have made was in the domain of language planning. In this, it had half a century of experience in issues like regional development, multilingual legal and constitutional drafting (Ó Cearúil 1999) and the exploration (still ongoing) of law and language rights (Ó Máille 1990; Ó Tuathail 1999) prior to joining and before many other continental states like Spain tackled the problems of their linguistic diversity internally or at a broader European level. Cultural topics have since come to enjoy far greater prominence under more recent EU treaties. Having expended much effort on the Irish language since between 1922 and mid-century, the second phase extending from the aftermath of the Second World War to the early 1970s thus witnessed the gradual dismantling of many aspects of earlier policy. The requirement to have a knowledge of Irish to be employed as a civil servant was terminated in the 1970s. The need to obtain a pass in the subject in order for a student to be awarded the state's principal secondary school qualification, the Leaving Certificate, normally the basis for entry to third-level education, was removed as well.

The third phase in the southern state's involvement with Irish extends roughly from the beginning of the 1970s to the present. While certain aspects of its approach to the language had changed, it maintained a number of others and continued to innovate in yet more. As we were about to enter the EEC, the government established Institiúid Teangeolaíochta Éireann, the Linguistics Institute of Ireland (*http://www.ite.ie*), in 1972 as a centre for research into and advice on state language policy (Ó Huallacháin 1994, 163–91). The Irish language itself is one of its primary areas of enquiry. The Institute has published numerous studies of its place in the school curriculum and more broadly based socolinguistic enquiry on the condition of the language in more localized areas as well as the country at large (Ó Riagáin 1996 and 1997). It now has an extensive remit in relation to modern continental languages and language use in applied areas like teleservices.

The state has continued its commitment to the Gaeltacht. A department of state was established in 1956 to coordinate policy towards this region; it is the ultimate forerunner of the present Department of Arts, Heritage, Gaeltacht and the Islands. However, when a commission established in 1958 to consider the revival of the Irish language finally reported in 1963, its conclusions were that policy needed more constructive augmentation. An advisory body entitled Comhairle na Gaeilge, set up in 1969 to give focus to the Commission's recommendations, suggested that a local government and development agency for the Gaeltacht be instituted. This body was formally constituted in *An tAcht um Údarás na Gaeltachta* 1979. This is a unique administrative entity in the Republic of Ireland in that its board comprises members directly elected from constituencies representing the main extant Gaeltacht regions of the north, west and south. This is to overcome the tendency towards centralization which had been evident in language planning to date and allow more discretion to Gaeltacht communities themselves. The election of thirteen members was stipulated under the 1979 act and this has now risen to 17. The current main business activities Údarás engages in are in electronics, engineering, information technology, film, television and video production, clothing, food processing and so forth. It also seeks to promote the use of Irish in businesses, establishes heritage projects, offers translation and terminological services and takes part in European partnerships. Its funding from the Irish exchequer in 1999 was just under £30 million, with other sums obtained from various forms of EU financing (*http:// www.udaras.ie*).

A third innovation on the government's part in this most recent policy period was the creation in 1978 of the state's Bord na Gaeilge. This statutory body was given a wide general remit of promoting the language among the public at large in recognition of the fundamentally bilingual nature of Irish society, an account of which is forthcoming in one of the most perceptive commentaries on language in Ireland produced in the last century (Ó Murchú 1970). Under this broad heading it has functioned in a manner reminiscent of the Arts Council. It provides funding for theatre, festivals with an Irish-language dimension and other creative activities such as publishing. Writing in Irish, involving scores of individuals, is taking place across all domains from poetry to prose and drama (Ó Cearnaigh 1995). The Bord was instrumental in supporting pre-school education in Irish when this sector of education (largely outside the formal state system) grew substantially from the late 1980s onwards from its embryonic beginnings in the early 1970s. This was an interesting innovation in that demand for the service was parent-led, as was the subsequent creation of an all-Irish primary school movement (*Gaelscoileanna*). By the 1990s, its activities had begun to extend across the border into Northern Ireland, a precursor of more recent developments to be described further below. Bord na Gaeilge supported such entities as the Belfast-based Irish-language secondary school MeánScoil Feirste in the 1990s. The Bord's grant-in-aid

from government in 1998 was approximately £3 million, during which year it had 30 staff members. Bord na Gaeilge has now been subsumed into the cross-border agency known as An Foras Teanga, which under Article 2 of the British-Irish Agreement (1999) will have a primary overall responsibility for language planning involving Irish throughout Ireland (*http:www. bnag.ie*). This brings if not full circle, at least a measure of common ground between two jurisdictions whose approach to language differed substantially for most of the twentieth century, as we shall now briefly see.

THE NORTH

The Gaelic revival was a feature of the north of Ireland as well as other parts of the country. The second branch of the Gaelic League was established in Derry. Belfast had a lively Irish-language theatre and the periodical *Shan Van Vocht* in the opening decade of the last century. Persons active in Irish circles, scholarly and other, from different denominational backgrounds included the likes of Eoin Mac Néill and Ernest Blythe, while the 1911 census (the last containing a language question to be taken in the north until 1991) revealed the existence of a small Gaelic-speaking pockets in various northern counties. Circumstances were less favourable after partition. Restrictions on the use of Irish in education were introduced, confining it to its own area and not sanctioning the teaching of other subjects through Irish. Limited time was made available to it during the school day, and funding for Irish-language colleges was curtailed. A decline in the numbers of schools offering instruction in it was reported in the late 1920s (Mac Póilín 1997). However, many schools which taught it were staffed by Catholic teaching orders which had an all-Ireland membership. Foremost among these were the Christian Brothers, for whom the whole island of Ireland was a single administrative province until the mid 1950s, enabling southern members to be sent north and vice versa, thus ensuring a certain continuity in the teaching of the subject. The order made a very significant contribution to the development of instructional materials in the language itself and in other disciplines, such as mathematics, imparted through Irish. The most comprehensive standard prescriptive grammar of contemporary Irish is the work of a native of Derry, Br Liam (Ambrós) Ó hAnluain (1910–92), whose Irish-speaking father came from Donegal (Ó Catháin 1996). Irish retained an academic presence in Queen's University, Belfast, where lecturers at various times included Seán Mac Airt and Heinrich Wagner, compiler of a famous linguistic atlas of the usage of Irish throughout the island of Ireland in the years 1949–56.

Greater access to education and a renewed sense of identity in nationalist sections of the population advanced the fortunes of the language from the 1960s onwards. Innovative programmes in the subject were developed at the New University of Ulster at Coleraine. Irish has strengthened as a community language in locations like west Belfast. Interest in the subject among unionists, while limited, is nonetheless present. There is often recourse on their part to stories from the Ulster Cycle, for example, to illustrate of the resilience of the people of Ulster in early times. According greater recognition to the language and cultural rights of all of Northern Ireland's communities was a significant component of the Belfast Agreement (1998; Mac Giolla Chríost 2000), a new departure in governmental and administrative arrangements in these islands.

TOWARDS THE PRESENT

If an enhanced role is found for Irish throughout Ireland, this may come through greater interaction between the two parts of the country in areas like the media, for example. Here the south has been innovative in latter years, with the media themselves forming part of a continuum of effort in publicizing the language stretching back to the end of the nineteenth century. The most recent effort was the establishment of an Irish-language television service, Teilifís na Gaeilge (TnaG) in 1996 (Watson 1997) following campaigns by interest groups like Comhdháil Náisiúnta na Gaeilge. The national broadcaster, Radio Telefís Éireann, was given the task setting up of the station and commission programming. Its headquarters is at Baile na hAbhann, county Galway. Its output comprises a news service, items relating to traditional music, the environment, connections with the Celtic countries and so forth. It has since changed its name to TG4 to position itself better in the emerging competitive digital and existing multi-channel environment (*http://www.TG4.ie*). The headquarters of Raidió na Gaeltacht in Casla, Connemara, is reasonably close to the television station. This has been established for almost thirty years. It began as a pirate radio, when Gaeltacht residents and Irish-language activists set up their own broadcasting unit as the state itself had not provided an exclusively Irish-language service. The radio was formally and legally instituted in 1970. It has had branch stations in Donegal and Kerry since the beginning. It commenced with a restricted broadcasting period in the afternoon, but over the years has extended its schedule to about 18 hours per day. It is now available on the Internet and through satellite broadcasting in Britain and Europe (*http://www.rnag.ie*). Programmes deal with every aspect of community life in Irish-speaking districts, linking these up in a way which had effectively not occurred for many generations previously. It has provided the best representation of rural and west-coast Irish affairs in the last quarter of the twentieth century. It recently issued a publication arising from a series of broadcasts beginning in late 1999 in which Gaeltacht people and scholars who research it described the region and its sense of identity at the commencement of the new millennium (Ó Tuathaigh, Ó Laoire agus Ua Súilleabháin 2000). Raidió na Gaeltachta's archive is now being put on CD-ROM in a collaborative venture with University College, Galway, and should become available to researchers in other institutions. This will be as significant a repository of the language in its own right as the Irish Folklore Commission collection of earlier decades.

Television and radio form part of a wider spectrum of outlets which have also comprised from time to time weekly newspapers like *Foinse*, its predecessor *Anois* and an earlier *Inniu*. Two monthly periodicals have enjoyed a particular place in this regard. One is the journal *Comhar* (de Grás 1992), which began in 1942 in university circles. Always relatively avant garde, its output comprises a mixture of opinion pieces, creative writing, book reviews and news items. All the great composers of modern literature are represented in it, and it has featured interviews with politicians of various persuasions over the years. *Feasta* is the organ of the Gaelic League (Ruiséal 1988). It has produced similar material, but is perhaps more closely identified with mainstream revivalism. Each of these titles is in its own way a successor to the heritage of publication which began in the latter part of the nineteenth century with the creation of *Irisleabhar na Gaedhilge* and *An Claidheamh Soluis*. Television, radio and these published media give the best immediate access to the mentality and preoccupations of those involved with the Irish language movement at community and other levels.

Journals and periodicals are also among the main fora for the promotion of formal study of Irish language, literature and cultural traditions. They date from the latter part of the nineteenth century as well, and reflect an international as well as a domestic aspect to the research effort. Among the earliest was *Revue Celtique* (1870–1934). It accommodated textual edition and language commentary relevant to all the Celtic languages, particularly from the medieval period. *Études Celtiques* (1936–), now issued by the Paris-based Centre National de Recherche Scientifique, continues its traditions. The longest continuous publication of its kind is *Zeitschrift für Celtische Philologie* (1899–). Commentary and edition featured here too, but in latter years more discursive items on literary or cultural material are also in evidence. The establishment in Dublin at the School of Irish Learning of the journal *Ériu* (1904–) narrowed the focus to Irish as opposed to Celtic studies. Its concern has been the elucidation of the language and literature of early and late medieval Ireland. The Royal Irish Academy took over its publication in 1926. The RIA's earlier *Transactions* and a series still in existence, its *Proceedings* (Section C), also covered or still handle

Gaelic items. *Celtica* (19[46/]50–), the in-house journal of the School of Celtic Studies in the Dublin Institute for Advanced Studies, performed a similar service, although public sector cutbacks in the late 1980s had an impact on the regularity of its appearance. *Éigse* (1939–) is supported by the National University of Ireland, and its editorship is the responsibility of the holder of the chair of Classical Irish in UCD. While it deals with all areas of Irish, it has made a specific contribution to Classical and Postclassical language and literature. The 1960s witnessed the advent of interdisciplinary studies, leading to the establishment of periodicals seeking to bring various research fields into closer contact with each other, both in Ireland and overseas. Foremost among them is *Studia Hibernica* (1961–), where many survey papers of relevance to all periods of Irish have appeared. Journals such as *Studia Celtica* (1966–), *Cambridge* (now *Cambrian*) *Medieval Celtic Studies* (1981–) and *Proceedings of the Harvard Celtic Colloquium* (1981–) perform a similar task. Interdisciplinarity is evident within titles from different time horizons like the medieval studies journal *Peritia* (1982–) and *Eighteenth-Century Ireland/Iris an Dá Chultúr* (1986–), the latter being the publication of the Eighteenth-Century Ireland Society which has broad international linkages (Voltaire Foundation 1999). Various local studies periodicals like the *Journal of the Cork Historical and Archaeological Society* (1892–) have long been collaborative. Journals published by the RIA are now availing of electronic networking for making their research findings more readily accessible (*http://www.journals.eecs.qub.ac.uk*). Others are bound to follow suit. One final type of enterprise deserves particular mention. This is the research series entitled 'Leabhair Thaighde', published by An Clóchomhar Tta. Upwards of ninety volumes have appeared under its imprint since the early 1960s on a vast range of issues in modern language and literature. An early volume, Seán Ó Tuama's study of popular love poetry (1960), also heralded the arrival of professional critical discourse in modern Irish. The recent 'Lúb ar Phár' series from the publisher Cois Life is beginning to provide a similar research outlet.

Festschrift-type volumes (with dates of publication of these given here), honouring the life's work of language and literature scholars like Tadhg Ó Donnchadha (1944), R. A Breatnach (1982), Tomás de Bhaldraithe (1986), James Carney (1989 and *Celtica* 23 [1999]), Brian Ó Cuív (*Celtica* 21 [1990]) and Conn Ó Cléirigh (1997), or historians such as Eoin Mac Néill (1940) and Francis John Byrne (2000), help identify research groupings and areas of interest at various points in time. So also do occasional state-of-the-art type overviews (McCone and Simms 1996). Colloquia serve a similar function. The more active include the School of Celtic Studies' annual Tionól, the annual Merriman Summer and Winter Schools, the Irish Conference of Medievalists and Léachtaí Cholm Cille which take place at NUI Maynooth. The quadrennial International Congress of Celtic Studies was established in 1959 and has been held to date in venues throughout Ireland, the United Kingdom and Europe. Proceedings were issued following nearly all Celtic congresses. The *Celtic Cultures Newsletter* (1983–90) of the UNESCO-sponsored Project for the Study and Promotion of Celtic Cultures kept readers aware of societies, conferences and publications involving Irish. The *Newsletter of the School of Celtic Studies* (1987–) has helped researchers to be informed of theses in progress or recently completed, among other initiatives. The home-pages of bodies like the Celtic Studies Association of North America (CSANA; *http://www.cis.upenn.edu/~csana*) now fulfil a similar information–gathering and disseminating role.

CONCLUSION

Irish experienced significant adversity since the 1600s, if not before then. For some, it came to be identified with inferiority and seemed to lack value. Conversely, during the early part of the twentieth century, it was often promoted with undue vigour in a manner which alienated many. Hopefully, the foregoing account will have suggested that it can be viewed in different terms. It is a unique and distinctive speech, closely interwoven with the affairs of this country throughout history. Material in Irish is often either the only or the principal record for this story. One challenge facing those concerned with the subject is to how to communicate its potential in a more organized manner, as part of the process of enrichment which is the special contribution of the humanities, however contentious this concept may be (Ellis 1997; Nussbaum 1997). Now that the end of a planning period covering the years 1997 to 2000 (Department of Arts, Culture and the Gaeltacht 1997) has been reached, further constructive thinking seems desirable. Greater use of information technology could help make Gaelic culture more accessible. However, delivery of educational materials via this means requires careful coordination (McCormack and Jones 1998). Modern technology may assist its development in the context of lifelong learning (Smith and Spurling 1999) as opposed to its confinement to school time. Other strategies have not been exploited hitherto as they might. It is not easy to obtain translations of Gaelic literature into English or other languages. The works of Frank O'Connor, Thomas Kinsella, Michael Hartnett, Seamus Heany and others reveal how fruitful a source of enlightenment translation can prove to be. The culture reaches a wider public in yet further ways. The Blasket Island Interpretative Centre in Dunquin, opened during 1994 and founded on sound scholarship, has drawn added attention to this unique corpus of insular Gaelic writing.

It also makes an economic contribution to the area in which it is located. The latter consideration points to a second major challenge to be met by those involved with our topic. This is how to ensure that Irish will remain a living vernacular, anticipating what shape the language itself will assume if changes to its circumstances continue to occur in time to come at the same rapid rate as they have done in the recent past (Ó Ruairc 1996; Ó Murchú agus Ó Murchú 1999).

Bibliography

Atkinson, R. 1887 *The Book of Ballymote*. Dublin.

Baumgarten, R. 1986 *Bibliography of Irish linguistics and literature: 1942–71*. Dublin.

Bergin, O. J. and Best, R. I. (eds) 1929 *Lebor na hUidre: Book of the Dun Cow*. Dublin.

Best, R. I. 1913 *Bibliography of Irish philology and printed Irish literature*. Dublin.

Best, R. I. 1942 *Bibliography of Irish philology and manuscript literature: publications 1913–41*. Dublin.

Best, R. I., Bergin, O. J., O'Brien, M. A. and O'Sullivan, A. 1954–83 *The Book of Leinster, formerly Lebar na Núachongbála*, 1–6. Dublin.

Binchy, D. A. 1978 *Corpus iuris Hibernici*, 1–6. Dublin.

Breathnach, D. agus Ní Mhurchú, M. 1986–97 *Beathaisnéis*, 1–5. Baile Átha Cliath.

Byrne, F. J. 1973 *Irish kings and high-kings*. London.

Caball, M. 1998 *Poets and politics: continuity and reaction in Irish poetry, 1558–1625*. Cork.

Caerwyn Williams, J. E. agus Ní Mhuiríosa, M. 1979 *Traidisiún liteartha na nGael*. Baile Átha Cliath.

Caerwyn Williams, J. E. and Ford, P. K. 1992 *The Irish literary tradition*. Cardiff.

Charles-Edwards, T. 1993 *Early Irish and Welsh kinship*. Oxford.

de Barra, P. agus Ó Fiaich, T. 1972 *Imeachta na nIarlaí*. Baile Átha Cliath.

de Brún, P. 1987 'The cataloguing of Irish manuscripts', *Newsletter of the School of Celtic Studies* 1, pp. 33–4.

de Brún, P. 1988 *Lámhscríbhinní Gaeilge: treoirliosta*. Baile Átha Cliath.

de Grás, M. 1992 *Comhar: innéacs 50 bliain*. Baile Átha Cliath.

de hAe, R. agus Ní Dhonnchadha, B. 1938–40 *Clár litridheachta na Nua-Ghaedhilge 1850–1936*, 1–3. Baile Átha Cliath.

Department of Arts, Culture and the Gaeltacht 1997 *Treo 2000: Commission to examine the role of the Irish language voluntary organisations*. Dublin.

Devine, C. 1997 'The Irish language in county Down' in L. Proudfoot (ed) *Down: history and society — interdisciplinary essays in the history of an Irish county* (Dublin), pp. 445–53.

Ellis, J. M. 1997 *Literature lost: social agendas and the corruption of the humanities*. New Haven and London.

Etchingham, C. 1999 *Church organisation in Ireland AD 600 to 1000*. Maynooth.

Hindley, R. 1990 *The death of the Irish language: a qualified obituary*. London.

Hofman, R. 1996 *The Sankt Gall Priscian commentary*. Münster.

Kelly, F. 1988 *A guide to early Irish law*. Dublin.

Kelly, F. 1997 *Early Irish farming: a study based mainly on the law-texts of the 7th and 8th centuries AD*. Dublin.

Kenney, J. F. 1929 *The sources for the early history of Ireland: ecclesiastical — an introduction and guide* (reprinted Dublin, 1979). New York.

Mac Airt, S. (ed) 1944 *Leabhar Branach. The Book of the O'Byrnes*. Dublin.

Macalister, R. A. S. (ed) 1942 *The Book of Uí Maine, otherwise called 'The Book of the O'Kelly's'*. Dublin.

Macalister, R. A. S. (ed) 1950 *The Book of Mac Carthaigh Riabhach, otherwise the Book of Lismore*. Dublin.

Mac Cana, P. 1980 *Literature in Irish*. Dublin.

Mac Giolla Chríost, D. 2000 'The Irish language and current policy in Northern Ireland', *Irish Studies Review* 8, 1 (April), pp. 45–55.

Mac Niocaill, G. 1975 *The medieval Irish annals*. Dublin.

Mac Póilín, A. (ed) 1997 *The Irish language in Northern Ireland*. Belfast.

Mag Shamhráin, A. (eag.) 1997 *Foilseacháin An Ghúim: liosta de na leabhair a d'fhoilsigh An Gúm ó 1926 i leith*. Baile Átha Cliath.

Mahon, W. 1996 'Scríobhaithe lámhscríbhinní Gaeilge i nGaillimhí' in Moran and Gillespie 1996, 623–50.

Mallory, J. P. and Stockman, G (eds) 1994 *Ulidia*, Proceedings of the First International Conference on the Ulster Cycle of tales, Belfast and Emain Macha 8–12 April. Belfast.

McCone, K. 1990 *Pagan past and Christian present in early Irish literature*. Maynooth.

McCone, K. *et al.* (eds) 1994 *Stair na Gaeilge in ómós do Pádraig Ó Fiannachta*. Má Nuad.

McCone, K. and Simms, K. 1996 *Progress in medieval Irish studies*. Maynooth.

McCormack, C. and Jones, D. 1998 *Building a web-based education system*. New York.

McGrath, M. 1936–37 *Cinnlae Amhlaoibh Uí Shúileabháin: the diary of Humphrey O'Sullivan*, 1–4. Dublin.

McGuinne, D. 1992 *Irish type design: a history of printing types in the Irish character*. Dublin.

McKenna, L. (ed) 1947 *The Book of Magauran*. Dublin.

McLysaght, E. 1939 *Irish life in the seventeenth century: after Cromwell* (second revised edition, Cork,

1950). Dublin.

McManus, D. 1991 *A guide to Ogham*. Maynooth.

Meyer, K. (ed) 1909 *Rawlinson B. 502*. Oxford.

Moran, G. and Gillespie, R (eds) 1996 *Galway: history and society — interdisciplinary essays in the history of an Irish county*. Dublin.

Mulchrone, K. (ed) 1937 *Book of Lecan*. Dublin.

Murphy, G. 1956 *Early Irish lyrics*. Oxford.

Nagy, J. F. 1985 *The wisdom of the outlaw*. Berkeley.

Nicholls, K. W. 1972 *Gaelic and gaelicised Ireland in the Middle Ages*. Dublin.

Ní Dhonnchadha, A. 1990 'Early modern Irish medical writings', *Newsletter of the School of Celtic Studies* 4, pp. 35–9.

Ní Mhóráin, B. 1997 *Thiar sa Mhainistir atá an Ghaolainn bhreá: meath na Gaeilge in Uíbh Ráthach*. An Daingean.

Ní Shéaghdha, N. *et al.* 1961– *Catalogue of Irish manuscripts in the National Library of Ireland*. Dublin.

Ní Shéaghdha, N. 1989 'Irish scholars and scribes in eighteenth-century Dublin', *Eighteenth-Century Ireland/Iris an Dá Chultúr* 4, pp. 41–54.

Ní Shéaghdha, N. 1990 'Gairmeacha beatha roinnt scríobhaithe ón 18ú agus ón 19ú céad', *Celtica* 21, pp. 567–75.

Nussbaum, M. C. 1997 *Cultivating humanity: a classical defense of reform in liberal education*. Cambridge, Massachusetts.

O'Brien, M. A. 1962 *Corpus genealogiarum Hiberniae* 1 (reprinted 1976, with introduction by J. V. Kelleher). Dublin.

Ó Buachalla, B. 1968 *I mBéal Feirste cois cuain*. Baile Átha Cliath.

Ó Buachalla, B. 1996 *Aisling ghéar: na Stíobhartaigh agus an t-aos léinn*. Baile Átha Cliath.

Ó Canainn, A. 2000 'Gleann na nDeor II', *Comhar* (Meitheamh), pp. 17–20.

Ó Catháin, S. 1996 'An Br. Liam Ambrós Ó hAnluain, 1910–92' in M. Ó Cearúil (eag.), *Gníomhartha na mBráithre: aistí comórtha ar Ghaelachas na mBráithre Críostaí* (Baile Átha Cliath), pp. 256–64.

Ó Cearnaigh, S. 1995 *Scríbhneoirí na Gaeilge 1945–95*. Baile Átha Cliath.

Ó Cearúil, M. 1999 *Bunreacht na hÉireann: a study of the Irish text (with original contributions by Professor Máirtín Ó Murchú)*. Dublin.

Ó Coileáin, S. 1982 *Seán Ó Ríordáin: beatha agus saothar*. Baile Átha Cliath.

Ó Concheanainn, T. 2000 'A medieval Irish historiographer: Giolla Íosa Mac Fhir Bhisigh' in A. P. Smyth (ed) *Seanchas: studies in early and medieval Irish archaeology, history and literature in honour of Francis J. Byrne* (Dublin), pp. 387–95.

Ó Conchúir, B. 1982 *Scríobhaithe Chorcaí 1700–1850*.

Baile Átha Cliath.

Ó Corráin, D. 1989 'Irish hermit poetry?' in D. Ó Corráin *et al.* (eds) *Sages, saints and storytellers: Celtic studies in honour of Professor James Carney* (Maynooth), pp. 251–67.

Ó Cróinín, D. 1995 *Early medieval Ireland, 400–1200*. London and New York.

Ó Cuív, B. 1973 *The Irish bardic duanaire or 'poem book'*. Dublin.

Ó Fiannachta, P. *et al.* 1965–80 *Clár lámhscríbhinní Gaeilge Choláiste Phádraig Má Nuad*. Má Nuad.

Ó Huallacháin, C. 1994 *The Irish and Irish: a sociolinguistic analysis of the relationship between a people and their language*. Dublin.

Ó Madagáin, B. 1974 *An Ghaeilge i Luimneach 1700–1900*. Baile Átha Cliath.

Ó Máille, T. 1990 *The status of the Irish language: a legal perspective*, Bord na Gaeilge Occasional Paper, No. 1. Dublin.

Ó Maonaigh, C. 1962 'Scríbhneoirí Gaeilge an seachtú haois déag', *Studia Hibernica* 2, pp. 182–208.

Ó Murchú, H. agus Ó Murchú, M. 1999 *An Ghaeilge: a haghaidh roimpi*. Baile Átha Cliath.

Ó Murchú, M. 1970 *Language and community*. Dublin.

Ó Murchú, M. 1985 *The Irish language*. Dublin.

Ó Murchú, M. (ed) 1990 *School of Celtic Studies fiftieth anniversary report 1940–1990*. Dublin.

O'Neill, T. 1984 *The Irish hand: scribes and their manuscripts from the earliest times to the seventeenth century: with an exemplar of Irish scripts*. Portlaoise.

O'Rahilly, T. F. *et al.* 1926–70 *Catalogue of Irish manuscripts in the Royal Irish Academy*. Dublin.

Ó Riagáin, P. 1996 'The Galway Gaeltacht 1926–1981: a sociolinguistic study of continuity and change' in Moran and Gillespie 1996, pp. 651–80.

Ó Riagáin, P. 1997 *Language policy and social reproduction: Ireland 1893–1993*. Oxford.

Ó Riain, P. (ed) 1985 *Corpus genealogiarum sanctorum Hiberniae*. Dublin.

Ó Riain, P. (ed) 1998 *The Irish Texts Society: the first hundred years*. Dublin.

Ó Riain, S. 1994 *Pleanáil teanga in Éirinn*. Baile Átha Cliath.

Ó Ríordáin, T. 2000 *Conradh na Gaeilge i gCorcaigh 1894–1910*. Baile Átha Cliath.

Ó Ruairc, M. 1994 *Ó Chomhargadh go Comhaontas*. Baile Átha Cliath.

Ó Ruairc, M. 1996 *Dúchas na Gaeilge*. Baile Átha Cliath.

Ó Tuama, S. 1960 *An grá in amhráin na ndaoine: léiriú téamáil*. Baile Átha Cliath.

Ó Tuama, S. 1988 *An grá i bhfilíocht na n–uaisle*. Baile Átha Cliath.

Ó Tuama, S. and Kinsella, T. 1981 *An Duanaire: poems of the dispossessed 1600–1900*. Portlaoise.

Ó Tuathaigh, G., Ó Laoire, L. L. agus Ua Súilleabháin, S. (eds) 2000 *Pobal na Gaeltachta: a shaol agus a dhán*. Indreabhán.

Ó Tuathail, S. (ed) 1999 *Tuairiscí Éireann, the Irish reports: tuairiscí speisialta, special reports 1980–98*. Dublin.

Póirtéir, C. 1995 *Gnéithe den Ghorta*. Baile Átha Cliath.

Póirtéir, C. 1996 *Glórtha ón Ghorta: béaloideas na Gaeilge agus an Gorta Mór*. Baile Átha Cliath.

Quin, E. G. 1976 '*Dictionary of the Irish language*, based mainly on Old and Middle Irish materials, Royal Irish Academy 1913–76: historical note'. [Dublin].

Riggs, P. 1994 *Pádraic Ó Conaire: deoraí*. Baile Átha Cliath.

Ruiséal, S. (ed) 1998 *Feasta* (mór–eagrán 1948–88) **41**, 10. Baile Átha Cliath agus Corcaigh.

Simms, K. 1985 *From kings to warlords: the changing political situation of Gaelic Ireland in the later middle ages*. Woodbridge.

Simms, K. 1998 'The contents of later commentaries on the Brehon Law tracts', *Ériu* **49**, pp. 23–40.

Smith, J. and Spurling, A. 1999 *Lifelong learning: riding the tiger*. London and New York.

Stokes, W. and Strachan, J. 1901–03 *Thesaurus palaeohibernicus: a selection of Old Irish glosses, scholia, prose and verse* (reprinted Dublin, 1975 and 1987) 1–2. Cambridge.

Voltaire Foundation 1999 *International directory of eighteenth-century studies 2000*. Oxford.

Watson, I. 1997 'A history of Irish language broadcasting: national ideology, commercial interest and minority rights' in M. J. Kelly and B. O'Connor (eds) *Media audiences in Ireland: power and cultural identity* (Dublin), pp. 212–30.

Williams, N. (ed) 1981 *Pairlement Chloinne Tomáis*. Dublin.

Williams, N. 1986 *I bprionta i leabhar: na Protastúin agus prós na Gaeilge 1567–1724*. Baile Átha Cliath.

English in Ireland

COLBERT KEARNEY

The objective of this chapter is to present a broad outline of the origins and development of Irish literature in English. It is not a literary history and so no attempt has been made to include all 'great' or 'important' writers: those included have been chosen primarily because they illustrate a significant point in the story. Because the most striking characteristic of Irish writing in English is that it is in English, there is a brief reference to Hiberno-Irish, the English spoken in Ireland, which has long been exploited by Irish writers but which is only in our time receiving the critical attention it deserves (Filppula 1999). The final part of the chapter is concerned with the status of Irish literature in English, with the central part it plays in university departments of literature and with its increasing importance in the tourism and heritage economies.

INTERSECTIONAL

In 1986 Seamus Deane, then Professor of Modern English and American Literature at University College, Dublin, published an account of the development of the writing of English in Ireland which he called *A short history of Irish literature*. Having dedicated his first chapter to 'The Gaelic Background', Deane knew that the choice of title would offend some people who believed that the primary meaning of the term 'Irish literature' was literature in the Irish language, but he defended his choice:

> By now it is neither Gaelic nor Anglo-Irish writing which is central. The conciliation between the two, although by no means complete, is sufficiently advanced to allow the use of the phrase 'Irish writing' without fear of its being misunderstood or recruited to any particular group or sect. That, at least, is one symptom of a fundamental and hopeful change. (Deane 1986, 248)

The references to 'conciliation' and to 'hopeful change' underline the political context which inevitably attends on any discussion of Irish writing, whether in English or Irish. The development of writing in English in this country is related to the fact that over the past three centuries English has continued to replace Irish as the vernacular, a transformation directly attributable to the English colonization of Ireland. To an extent that is rare, if not unique, in western Europe, the act of literary composition in Ireland since, say, 1600 has been a political act. Though circumstances may change significantly in the future, the heritage of the contemporary Irish writer — and consequently of the Irish reader — is inextricable from politics and specifically from a history of colonial oppression, change of language and assertion of national independence and national identity in a world of ever-accelerating communication.

As his life drew to a close in the early part of the eighteenth century, the Kerry poet Aogán Ó Rathaille (1675–1729) realized that he was doomed to die in poverty. In his earlier years he had enjoyed the kind of prestige and status that had been the traditional due of the poet in Gaelic culture, but latterly he had had to take to the roads, painfully conscious of the disparity between his spiritual pride and his physical degradation. Those who had patronized him had themselves been dispossessed, victims of defeated loyalties. The Battle of the Boyne in 1690 had established an Anglican Ascendancy and condemned Catholics to a life of legal slavery and economic misery. Initially Ó Rathaille had imagined that a hero from across the sea, the Stuart pretender, would free Ireland from Saxon tyranny; now he sees the futility of expecting any kind of help from any quarter. The power of *Cabhair ní ghoirfead* derives, at least in part, from the implied identity between the poet, a proud old man on the verge of death, and the country/polity in which he once had a privileged place but which is itself now mortally wounded:

Stadfadsa feasta, is gar dom éag gan mhoill

Ó treascradh dragain Leamhain, Léin is Laoi
Rachadhsa a haithle searc na laoch don chill
Na flatha fa raibh my shean roimh éag do Chríost.

Ó Rathaille's contemporary, Jonathan Swift, was born in 1667 to English parents who had recently moved to Dublin. Swift, like any ambitious young colonial, looked to London as the cultural centre of his universe; it was only when he had apparently failed to make his mark in England that he returned to Ireland to be ordained an Anglican priest and settle down to pastoral duties on the cultural frontier. But Swift's writings on controversial religious matters were noticed in London and he returned to become the foremost political pamphleteer (and one of the literary lions) of the day. He confidently expected that the Tories would repay him by appointing him to a high ecclesiastical position in England, but he had not anticipated being sent back to Dublin as Dean of St Patrick's. He was furious, perceiving his enforced return to his native land as a form of cultural exile from London and comparing his eminent position in Dublin to that of 'a poisoned rat in a hole'. Gradually, despite his distaste for Ireland and the Irish — both colonial and 'savage old Irish' — Swift came to see his own humiliation by the London establishment as typical of London's insolent and illegal treatment of Ireland. He adapted his personal resentment and literary skill to a series of causes in which he called on the Irish to stand up for themselves against English misrule. In his campaign against Wood's ha'pence he found himself appealing to 'the whole people of Ireland' to assert their freedom. Whatever about the complexities of Swift's thinking, it is undeniable that he instigated modern Irish nationality and, to quote Seamus Deane, that though 'Anglo-Irish writing does not begin with Swift ... Anglo-Irish literature does' (Deane 1986, 37). Others had written in English in Ireland but Swift was a major imaginative talent and a prolific writer who had, initially for his own Anglican class, created a sense of what it was to be Irish in the eighteenth century and produced a body of writing that succeeding generations would look back to as a model of Irish writing in English. There is a remarkable irony in the coincidence of two great writers on the same small island, neither known to the other because moving in different worlds, one consciously lamenting the inevitable decline of the Gaelic literary tradition, the other unconsciously inaugurating the Anglo-Irish tradition that would replace it when English became the vernacular of the vast majority of the people of Ireland.

HIBERNO-ENGLISH

The dominance of English is probably the most obvious mark of Ireland's colonial past. Languages surrender on economic rather than on linguistic grounds, and it was the series of plantations between the Battle of Kinsale (1601) and the Battle of the Boyne (1690) that ensured the emergence of English as the language of political and commercial power. Other colonizers, such as the Vikings and the Normans, had quickly adapted to the local culture but, animated by the Reformation, the Tudors and their successors sought to maintain an apartheid between the Protestant conquerors and their Romish subordinates:

The Cromwellian Settlement marks a crucial turning-point in the history of the English language in Ireland. It completed the work begun by the Ulster Plantations under James I: in three of the four provinces the landowners were now Protestant and English-speaking ... Everywhere except in Connacht the great houses formed centres where the English language was spoken: tenants and servants alike had to learn some English in order to communicate with their masters. The masters themselves, isolated as they were from frequent converse with their own kind, were soon affected by the gaelicized English of the native Irish with whom they spoke every day ... The English spoken in most parts of Ireland today is descended from the English of Cromwell's planters, and since the early part of the eighteenth century no other type of English has been spoken in any part of Ireland except in Ulster. (Bliss 1979, 199 ff.)

The English language spread throughout Ireland, more from the Irish desire to learn it than any English wish to impart it. Education was denied Catholics for as long as the Penal Laws were rigidly enforced and so the vast majority of Irish speakers learned English informally, picking it up from social contact and frequently from those whose knowledge was limited. This ensured that the English they spoke was heavily influenced by the sounds and structures of the Irish language. Initially Hiberno-English would have been a crudely direct translation from Irish into English; gradually, education and literacy tended to modify the more extreme variations from Standard English, but even today, despite the levelling powers of the mass media, educated Irish people preserve many non-Standard forms, especially in their speech. (Ironically, Hiberno-English, initially a mark of cultural inferiority to those who spoke Standard English, was to become one of the richest resources of Irish writers.)

It is intriguing to imagine how Irish history would have differed had, say, the vast majority of the Irish people clung to their language as tenaciously as they remained faithful to their Catholic religion. By abandoning the Irish language, the people deprived themselves of direct access to a cultural tradition of some splendour without any obvious cultural compensation. Yet, despite the appalling conditions in which the change of language occurred, Ireland has produced, as well as a host of lesser talents, some of the major figures of modern literature in English — Yeats, Joyce, Synge and Beckett. Irish writers continue to enjoy enormous prestige, most recently marked by the award of the 1995 Nobel Prize to Seamus Heaney; Irish writing is taught and researched in the English departments of all reputable universities, and those associations and summer schools that concern themselves with the work of Irish writers attract students from all over the world.

THE NINETEENTH CENTURY

Swift highlights that moment in the history of the colony when the colonizer is forced to see that he in some ways shares the fate of the colonized whom he has been taught to despise: they are both victims of metropolitan misrule. By the end of the eighteenth century, many years after Swift's death, members of the Ascendancy established an independent parliament in Dublin and swore to defend it by force of arms if necessary. Others were more advanced. The United Irishmen, inspired by the French Revolution, sought to submerge sectarian differences in the common name of Irishman and the common objective of an independent republic. The conservative majority of the Ascendancy took fright and reaffirmed their ties with England in the Act of Union; but, with hindsight, we can see that this was a futile gesture, a closing of the stable door after the horses of nationalism had bolted into the countryside.

Nineteenth-century nationalism is sometimes called 'romantic' because of its origins in a cultural shift which swept Europe around the turn of the nineteenth century, and was enormously significant in the development of modern Ireland. It involved, for example, a revival of interest in pre-Renaissance cultures, including that of the Celts. With the new vogue for all things natural and spontaneous, for imagination rather than reason, for feeling rather than thought, for wild landscape rather than landscaped gardens, Ireland and the Irish acquired a new fascination. When James Macpherson published *Fragments of ancient poetry* (1760), the first of his series of best-selling if bogus translations of Scots Gaelic poetry, all Europe was excited. Irish scholars were anxious to prove that this country had a prior claim to Ossianic material and the ensuing controversy probably led to modern Celtic Studies. In her *Reliques of Irish poetry* (1789), Charlotte Brooke made Gaelic verse available in popular form for the first time. To many people in Ireland, most of them members of the Anglican Ascendancy, this kind of antiquarianism unearthed a heritage which, predating the Reformation and colonialism, seemed to offer a possible basis for a common national identity. While Beethoven was arranging Irish tunes for a European market, educated Irish people were showing a new interest in Ireland's traditional literature, music, archaeology and folklore, and writers were beginning to lay the foundations of modern Irish literature.

In 1800, the year of the Act of Union, Maria Edgeworth's *Castle Rackrent* was published in London. A highly intelligent and motivated young woman, Edgeworth (1767–1849) was concerned with the political prospects of Ireland in the aftermath of the Union, and most of her fiction had a social objective: to castigate Ascendancy landlords who neglected their duties and thus fomented sectarian division in Ireland. Part of the enduring fascination of *Castle Rackrent* is due to the complexity of the narrative. The novel purports to be the oral report of Thady, an old retainer of the Rackrent family who seems initially to epitomise loyalty to his feckless masters, but the more attention we pay to the twists and turns of his dialect the more we suspect irony if not downright lies. In her exploitation of Irish peasant speech in this, the first Big House novel, Edgeworth revealed a major resource for later writers.

The other founding mother of the Irish novel was Lady Morgan (1776–1859), born Sydney Owenson, the daughter of an Irish-speaking Mayo actor, Robert MacOwen, and an English mother. She too had clear political objectives in her novels or 'national tales': to achieve adequate recognition for Irish Catholics and their ancient Gaelic heritage and to create a new Ireland based on the union of Catholics and Protestants. If Maria Edgeworth's work was characterized by Enlightenment philosophy, Lady Morgan's was flamboyantly Romantic. Her most interesting novel is, for all its obvious faults, *The Wild Irish Girl*, in which the bored son of an absentee landlord comes from England to the west of Ireland and falls in love with Glorvina (from the Irish for sweet-voiced), harpist daughter of the dispossessed Irish chief. The love affair is conducted mainly through the education of the young man in the incomparable achievements of the native tradition; the novel closes not with the lovers' nuptial embrace but with a vision of Ireland and England united in happy-ever-after matrimony. The novel is designed and presented in a way which sets out to explain Ireland to the English, an objective many of her successors would set themselves in these early appeals for parity of esteem.

In some ways the most interesting of the early writers of fiction was William Carleton (1794–1869). Born into a Gaelic-speaking oral tradition, he had first-hand knowledge of the Irish peasantry about whom he wrote. He was, perhaps, a little too anxious to advertise his mastery of literary English, too keen to satisfy the Protestant audience on which he depended but, for all that, he produced wonderful fictions, some wildly comic, some frighteningly brutal, and one catches in Carleton the first authentic expression of the Irish peasant experience in English.

Throughout history, from Giraldus Cambrensis on, many of those who vilified the native Irish culture as belonging to uncivilized barbarians made an exception in the case of Irish music. As part of the Romantic revival of interest in Irish traditional music, a festival was organized in Belfast in 1792 to which all the prominent harpers were invited so that their music might be recorded. (Wolfe Tone attended, not for the music but to seek support for the United Irishmen.) The consequence was Edward Bunting's *General Collection of Ancient Irish Music* (1796) which, instrumental music being free from any linguistic or religious allegiance, was generally held to be the purest expression of the Irish soul or spirit. When Thomas Moore began to write words to fit the tunes, he was not only reversing the usual order whereby musicians put poetry to music, he was also using the resources of English verse to express what he believed to be the soul of Ireland and inaugurating a century of Irish poetry that sought to translate, literally or figuratively, the older Gaelic tradition into modern English.

Moore's Irish melodies were an enormous success, so much so that Stephen Dedalus in Joyce's *A Portrait of the Artist as a Young Man* could refer to Moore, however disdainfully, as 'the national poet of Ireland'. Though it is popular today to dismiss him as a purveyor of senti-mental drawing room songs that cheapened Irish music and Irish history, it should be remembered that he was the first to find a lyric form that presented the Irish tradition in a manner acceptable to the Irish and the English. Though songs like 'The Harp That Once' may strike the modern ear as merely pretty, if we imagine them being sung in the aftermath of Robert Emmet's 1803 rebellion, we may come to enjoy Moore's diplomati-cally coded form of subversion as much as his lyric facility. Many of his songs look back to the glorious past that preceded the subjugation of Ireland and invite the audience to make contact with that past and keep faith with those who died heroically for Ireland.

Throughout the nineteenth century poets would continue to try to make that contact with the past in one way or another. J. J. Callanan (1795–1829) wrote conven-tional poetry of little merit, but he was also caught up in the popular craze for collecting folklore and literary remains of the Irish tradition, and this gave him his place in history. Callanan knew Irish and was known to be planning a collection of translations to be called *Munster Melodies*. All he produced was a handful of translations, the most interesting of which are those for which there are no known originals. The translations sound as if there is an Irish form behind them, but it may well be that Callanan had so mastered the art of translation that he could dispense with a specific original and write a kind of 'pure' Anglo-Irish verse.

In many of his translations from Irish — see, for example, his version of *Caiseal Mumhan* — Sir Samuel Ferguson (1810–86) demonstrated a rare ability to echo the tone of the original. This ability derived from a disci-plined study of the native literature and folklore and was impelled by his unusual political objective. Ferguson, a Protestant unionist and a cultural nationalist who despised Irish Catholicism and political nationalism, believed that literature could resolve the problems of Irish political culture. His original poetry, largely based on Old Irish sagas, was hugely regarded in his own time and constituted an important contribution to the devel-opment of Irish verse, but it strikes the modern ear as unrewardingly solemn.

The one poet from the first half of the century whose reputation has continued to grow is James Clarence Mangan (1803–49); increasingly we see what Joyce saw almost a century ago, that in his life and work Mangan expressed the cultural crisis of the Ireland of his time. An epitome of the Romantic artist — impoverished, addicted to alcohol and opium, haunted by some dark secret — Mangan's lack of stability made him the perfect mouthpiece for his people. And mouthpiece is unusually apt in the case of a poet who not only specialized in translation — from Irish, French and German as well as from an unlikely range of Asian languages — but also passed off his own original work as translation, as if lacking even the confidence to acknowledge his own voice. What his translations from the Irish lack in detailed replication they gain in tonal suggestion: Mangan uses an extravagant rhetorical bravura to conjure up dramatic equivalents of the originals. Best known for his apocalyptic version of *Róisín Dubh*, modern readers are more likely to esteem his dreams of an earlier, more coherent age — see, for example, 'A Vision of Connaught in the Thirteenth Century', or works, such as 'Twenty Golden Years Ago', that intimate the man behind the mouthpiece, a nineteenth-century Ó Rathaille with a Dublin accent and a stoned sardonic smile:

Wifeless, friendless, flagonless, alone,
Not quite bookless, though, unless I chuse,
Left with nought to do, except to groan,
Not a soul to woo, except the Muse —
O! this, this is hard for me to bear,
Me, who whilome lived so much en haut,
Me, who broke all hearts like chinaware
Twenty golden years ago! (Deane 1986, 82)

There is still no adequate account of the crisis of linguistic culture into which the Irish people were plunged, no convincingly detailed diagnosis of what it was like to lose contact with one literature without a compensatory introduction to another, to abandon, for example, Aogán Ó Rathaille but still to be deprived of Shakespeare. Thomas Davis (1814–45) devoted his short life to creating a national consciousness and coherent culture for all the people of Ireland. In 1842 he helped found *The Nation*, arguably the most influential newspaper in Irish history, which achieved a weekly circulation of 11,000 copies despite its relatively high price, sixpence, and despite the limited reading ability of the majority. *The Nation* had an ambitiously broad programme for national education and renewal but exerted its greatest influence through the political ballads that transmitted a version of Irish history through succeeding generations. Few of these ballads bear silent reading but, when sung to martial airs, they stirred the hearts of the Irish people with thoughts of past oppressions and future freedoms. The most famous was 'A Nation Once Again', which has acquired through the intervening years sufficient revolutionary charge to have it excluded from national broadcasting as politically incorrect.

The hopes of Davis and others were dashed in the cataclysm of famine, death and emigration of the late 1840s. The national disaster fuelled a desire for independence that expressed itself in revolutionary Fenianism in the 1860s and Parnellite agitation in the 1880s. When both these campaigns were judged to have failed they were supplanted by a new wave of cultural nationalism, a new crusade for Celtic revival.

INTO THE TWENTIETH CENTURY

When Yeats declared himself as a nationalist poet, he identified his predecessors, making Moore a notable omission:

Nor may I less be counted one
With Davis, Mangan, Ferguson,
Who sang to sweeten Ireland's wrong,
Ballad and story, rann and song. (Kinsella 1986, 309)

Yeats was at pains to make a qualification: his interest in spiritualism, far from disqualifying him as a nationalist poet, actually made his nationalist poetry more profound. As a child, Yeats had listened enthralled to stories of fairies and legendary heroes; as an adult member of various spiritualist societies, he came to believe that there was still available in Ireland a system of belief that had escaped the so-called European Enlightenment and maintained a direct line of contact back to the Druids and beyond into the Great Memory. Though such faith tends to be ridiculed today, Yeats insisted that it was at the heart of everything he set out to achieve, from his early collections of folklore to his later concern with esoteric history.

In his efforts to inspire an Irish renaissance, and especially in the work that led to the opening of the Abbey Theatre in 1904, Yeats was supported by Lady Augusta Gregory, who was also a collector of folktales and legends — including stories of the poet Raftery — still current in the area of her home, Coole Park in southeast Galway, which Yeats immortalized as the Irish equiv-

alent of an Italian Renaissance court.

Through sheer talent and force of personality Yeats established Irish poetry in English as a force in the modern world. In his long creative life he managed to integrate a wide range of interests and find poetical forms to express a range of themes, from the Celtic Twilight to his love for Maud Gonne, from his involvement in Irish revolutionary politics to an increasingly apocalyptic view of world history. He was the first recipient of the Nobel Prize in 1923.

What Yeats did for Irish poetry, Joyce did for prose fiction. The nineteenth-century novel had been dominated by writers from the Catholic middle class, some of whom were anxious to disabuse English readers of their stereotypical views of Irish people, some of whom produced whimsical caricatures that were really euphemistic versions of Punch cartoons. Joyce (1882–1941) was born into a middle-class Catholic family that had prospered and become genteel in the course of the nineteenth century but collapsed into dysfunctional squalor during his own teenage years. Joyce's rejection of his own family pretensions developed into a rejection of all the major forces of Irish life — nationalism, Catholicism, ruralism, Gaelic and literary revivalisms — in favour of a modern, cosmopolitan individualism. He made great play of his self-imposed exile from Ireland, but Ireland — or, more accurately, Dublin — dominated his thought and art to the end. (His companion in exile was Nora Barnacle from Galway who may have been a distant relation of Joyce's counterpart in the Irish-language novel, Máirtín Ó Cadhain, *anglice* Martin Barnacle.) In his collection of short stories, *Dubliners*, Joyce set out to expose the cultural paralysis that he had escaped: many of the stories are pointedly satirical but in some, such as 'Ivy Day in the Committee Room' and 'Grace', the condemnatory force is considerably weakened by the obvious delight in the characters' conversations. The autobiographical novel, *A Portrait of the Artist as a Young Man*, is an incomparable account of a Catholic upbringing; it remains to be seen how the novel will survive the passing of a faith involving such a vivid sense of sin and divine punishment. Both *Ulysses* and *Finnegans Wake* are comic masterpieces that celebrate the ordinary universe; ironically, both are written with such studious dexterity as to make them very difficult for the ordinary reader, a problem which thousands of academic critics have kindly sought to solve.

Before the foundation of the Abbey Theatre, the Dublin stage was where Irish plays, players and playwrights went before they went to or after they had been to London. No dramatist had ever made the Dublin stage a locus of Irish intellectual life, which was unfortunate because between George Farquhar (1677–1707) and Bernard Shaw (1856–1950) Irish dramatists have contributed disproportionately to the history of drama in English. It is possible that, apart altogether from their own innate gifts, being Irish and, to some extent, outsiders, these dramatists were at an advantage in a London theatre dominated by comic analyses of manners. This is obvious in the case of Wilde and Shaw, both of whom played versions of the outsider/jester — scandalous dandy and stage-Irish socialist — while exposing on the English stage the silliness they saw at the heart of English common sense.

When Shaw was asked to write a play for the Abbey, he offered *John Bull's Other Island* in which he reversed the stereotypes of the English and Irishman. Here he was developing a trend initiated by Dion Boucicault (1820–90). Born in Dublin, Boucicault had already established himself as the leading melodramatist of his day in Britain and the United States (where his work later had a profound influence on the early cinema) when he wrote a series of 'Irish' plays — *The Colleen Bawn, Arrah-na-Pogue* and *The Shaughraun* — in which he altered the characteristics of the stage-Irish to make them charming, witty and ingeniously subversive of their English superiors. They continued to be hugely successful in Ireland for more than half a century.

Though Yeats, with his heroic tragedies, and Lady Gregory, with her folk comedies, made important contributions to the Abbey Theatre, the major dramatist to emerge in the first phase was John Millington Synge (1871–1909). Synge's study of Irish at Trinity College and of comparative folklore at the Sorbonne enabled him to derive enormous benefit from his visits to Irish-speaking areas in Kerry, Galway and Mayo, and he was the first to see the potential of Hiberno-English as the basis for a dramatic poetry. The language of his plays is not a transcription of current Hiberno-English or a translation of current Irish, but a careful edition of Hiberno-English in which the Gaelic elements — syntactic and stylistic — are heightened. His depictions of life in rural Ireland were violently comic and gave offence to those nationalists whose idealism prevented them from seeing Irish life with Synge's clarity. One of the great moments in Irish cultural history was in January 1907 when the Abbey audience rioted at Synge's *The Playboy of the Western World*: in hindsight it is obvious that what enraged the rioters was not the falseness of Synge's vision but its discomforting accuracy. One of the great disasters of Irish cultural history was Synge's death at the age of thirty-seven.

The next Abbey dramatist whose efforts were crowned with a riot was Sean O'Casey (1880–1964). Born into a Dublin Protestant family that was sinking towards working-class poverty, the key moment of O'Casey's life was his encounter with 'Big Jim' Larkin, the labour leader who organized the workers so effectively as to produce the 1913 Lock-Out. O'Casey believed that what was popularly accepted as the heroic phase of modern Irish life, the movement from the 1916 Rising to the achievement of the Irish Free State in 1922, had been a disaster for the working class, that bourgeois nationalists had deluded the workers into fighting for a cause that brought them nothing but suffering and death. His first two Abbey plays, *The Shadow of a Gunman* (1923) and *Juno and the Paycock* (1924), were comi-tragedies at which the audiences were tricked into laughing at the antics and language of the characters and then made to feel uncomfortable when the apparently farcical action gave way to violence and death. His next play, *The Plough and the Stars* (1926), dealt with the 1916 Rising and infuriated the Abbey audiences by presenting martial heroism as pretentious fantasy and celebrating the true courage of those who were more concerned with community values than with Irish nationalism. Yeats came on stage to chastize the rioters and recalled the arrival of another dramatist of genius, Synge. Within a couple of years Yeats had rejected O'Casey's play dealing with the Great War, *The Silver Tassie*, which led to O'Casey breaking with the Abbey and spending the remainder of his life in England.

INDEPENDENCE

O'Casey's situation was not untypical of the writer's lot in post-independence Ireland. The Irish Free State, born into Civil War and economic frugality, expressed its gratitude for what it saw as the Catholic Church's support for Irish nationalism against Protestant colonialism by espousing anti-liberalism and anti-modernism. If the Free State made the Abbey the first state-subsidised theatre in the English-speaking world, it also introduced the *Censorship Act* of 1929 which led to the banning of almost every Irish writer of substance and also proscribed many non-Irish writers as likely to undermine the spiritual superiority of the Irish mind. The Irish Free State did not encourage criticism, and it is to the credit of many writers that they dedicated so much of their time to opening up Irish society to modern criticism.

Some poets were less oppressed by legislation than by the shadow of Yeats in which it was difficult to write an Irish poetry that was not obviously derivative. Catholicism was one means of escape and many of the leading poets of the Free State were obviously, if not always comfortably, Catholic. Austin Clarke (1896–1974) was a student of Irish poetry and sought to introduce its structures and sound-schemes into his own verse; he admired the Irish monastic tradition, contrasting its generous accommodation of flesh and spirit with the mean puritanism of contemporary Catholicism. The Catholicism of Denis Devlin (1908–59) owes more to the European tradition — he was a professional diplomat — than to the Irish parish church, enabling him to write a species of metaphysical poems in which human and divine love are identified. Patrick Kavanagh (1904–67) was to prove the most influential poet of his generation. The son of a Monaghan farmer, he was initially frustrated by rural philistinism and went to Dublin in order to forge a literary career. The vicissitudes of his life there, much of it spent eking out an existence by writing for popular journals, often led him to regret his move, but some of his explorations in verse and fiction of the Irish rural experience were very fine and he was later acknowledged as a trail-blazer by such poets as Seamus Heaney. Kavanagh epitomized the situation of the Irish writer in the forties and fifties. Apart from the problems of earning a living by his writings, he was publicly humiliated in the course of a libel action he took against *The Leader*, and it is widely believed that he was threatened by the police for what was judged to be the indecency of his work. In fact Kavanagh's verse is that of a deeply spiritual man in a Romantic Catholic tradition, celebrating the beauties of the rural landscape and finding redemption in such unsung situations as the banks of the Royal Canal.

The life of Daniel Corkery (1878–1964) had been changed by his discovery of the Gaelic League at the turn of the century, and he dedicated himself and his literary abilities to the War of Independence and the dream of an Ireland based on Gaelic Catholic traditions of rural Ireland. Though his critical works are rigidly propagandist, his short stories, some of them very fine, reflect his gradual disenchantment with the evolution of the Free State. Two of his protégés, Seán Ó Faoláin (1900–91) and Frank O'Connor (1903–66), changed much more rapidly: both had been involved on the Republican side during the Civil War and both went on to become fiercely critical of the parochial puritanism of the new state. Ó Faoláin made excellent use of *The Bell* — the most famous of those literary magazines that were the main centres of intellectual debate — to lacerate the political and religious establishments. Both he and O'Connor were gifted short story writers. Ó Faoláin's stories were the more intellectual, dramatizing the issues of conscience and freedom that inspired his criticism. O'Connor was more obviously in the oral tradition of storytelling and some of his best work — 'The Majesty of the Law' and 'The Long Road to Ummera', for example — explores the problems of rural people perplexed by the new rules of 'modern' Ireland.

Not all Irish writers flung themselves into the struggle for a more open society. The last of the great Irish modernists, Samuel Beckett (1906–89), spent most of his adult life in France, choosing to stay there during the German occupation and being decorated for his work with the Resistance. He wrote his mature work in French, translating it back into English himself so thoroughly that the English reader is never aware of the process. Beckett's writing, both fiction and drama, is a meditation on the meaningless pain of life and the absurdity of conventional morality and consequently his later works strive for a minimalism that seeks disembodied silence. Typical Beckett characters resent ever being born and long for death. Paradoxically, his grimly ironic dissection of the survival instinct makes Beckett one of the great black humorists of all time.

Brian O'Nolan (1911–66), a.k.a Flann O'Brien, a.k.a. Myles na gCopaleen, offers an interesting contrast with Beckett. Born into an Irish-speaking family, he studied Irish at University College, Dublin, where he wrote satirical articles and an MA on early Irish poetry. His two finest works were written at the outset of his literary career. *At Swim-Two-Birds* (1939) is a comic masterpiece in which several plots — from the Old Irish saga of Mad Sweeny to the contemporary Hollywood Western — are allowed to infiltrate each other with exuberance of a page from the Book of Kells. *An Béal Bocht* (1941), later translated into English as *The Poor Mouth*, is a parody of those many Gaeltacht autobiographies that formed the basis of modern Irish prose and that O'Brien had absorbed thoroughly; it is written with scholarly precision and the fury of a man who found the national culture asphyxiating. Unfortunately, O'Nolan's literary career was blighted by the fact that his masterpiece was lost in the confusion of the World War and did not emerge publicly again until 1960. In the meantime, as Myles na gCopaleen in the *Irish Times*, he became the most famous commentator on Irish affairs, enthralling his readers with an encyclopaedic campaign against the social and mental dullness of his environment. Several other novels were published in the 1960s, but while they contain many brilliant expressions of O'Nolan's obsessive fantasies, none achieved the coherence of *At Swim-Two-Birds*.

Anthony Cronin's memoir of Irish literary life in the fifties, *Dead as Doornails*, describes a philistine culture in which writers such as O'Brien, Kavanagh and Brendan Behan found it so difficult to make a living from their writings that they were forced to waste their talents in ways that drove them to dissolution. Popular resentment of writers is seen in the refusal of Irish people to echo the acclaim that Brendan Behan achieved in Britain and the United States. Behan's masterpiece, *Borstal Boy*, a literary transcription of an oral account of his confinement in England for IRA activities, was banned and Behan's media antics disdained as a national disgrace.

IN THE SIXTIES AND AFTER

Despite his suicidal inability to manage it, Behan's international success could be seen as a portent of improvements in the general situation of Irish writers, improvements that began with an economic resurgence in the sixties that led in turn to a raising of national confidence. Although most writers would still find it very difficult to achieve economic self-sufficiency and could only dream of best-selling success, within twenty years of Behan's death the standing of the Irish writer was to be changed beyond recognition.

The canonization of Irish writing in English owed a great deal to the critical writings of the American scholar, Richard Ellmann. Ellmann had already published influential works on Yeats when his monumental biography of James Joyce appeared in 1964. More than any other single book, this established Irish writing as an important and independent part of the university discipline of English Literature which had by then (in the English-speaking world) replaced Ancient Classics as the basis of a Humanities education. Before the sixties it was quite normal for writers such as Swift and Goldsmith, Shaw and Wilde to be presented as English writers rather than as writers of English; those who insisted on setting them in an Irish context were dismissed as narrow-minded nationalists. The sheer weight and detail of Irish reference in the works of Yeats and Joyce made it difficult not to see them as Irish writers who wrote in English; hence the influence of Ellmann. The universities of the United States were ahead of all others, including the Irish, in promoting research into Irish writing. Initially scholars concentrated on the major figures from the turn of the century, but gradually the scope of activity widened to include living writers, even those who were younger than the professors who analysed their work.

The English Department of University College, Dublin, was the first Irish institution to establish a separate Chair of Anglo-Irish Literature and Drama in 1964. Before the sixties Irish students read English courses that were overwhelmingly dominated by English writers — a student might read more Irish poetry at primary school than at university — but as the academic status of Irish writing rose, inevitably the Irish components in English Department courses increased. At least half of all Irish postgraduates choose to research the work of Irish writers and this has resulted in a considerable library of theses, that add to our knowledge of Irish cultural life over the past three centuries.

In 1969 the strength of the international network of academics dealing with Irish literature in English was underlined by the foundation of the International Association for the Study of Anglo-Irish Literature which continues to expand and flourish. (A sign of the times: the name was officially changed to the International Association for the Study of Irish Literatures [IASIL] in 1997.) Though there is a substantial Irish membership, the association is thoroughly international with members from all over the world, and conferences have been held in Sweden, Hungary, Holland, Italy, Egypt, Japan and the United States. There are individual associations in several countries, notably the American Committee for Irish Studies and the Canadian Associ-

ation for Irish Studies. Irish Studies, particularly strong in Japan, are growing in the Far East: an IASIL conference has been held in Japan and one is planned for Korea.

Another prestigious conference is the annual James Joyce Symposium which has been held in such cities as Rome, Venice, Copenhagen and Zurich. To mark the centenary of Joyce's birth in 1882, the delegates assembled in Dublin to discuss his works, pay homage to his birthplace and unveil a bust of Joyce in St Stephen's Green. The opening was sponsored by American Express. Few could fail to remark on the extraordinary reversal of fortune: the writer once reviled in his native city was feted as a favourite son, and the man who had believed that he was entitled to other peoples' money was honoured by what is probably the most famous credit card in the world.

But by 1982 Joyce's literary immortality had guaranteed the remission of his mortal sins. In 1954 on June 16, the date on which the action of *Ulysses* takes place, a small group including Patrick Kavanagh, Brian O'Nolan and Anthony Cronin attracted little attention when they assembled at the Martello Tower in Sandycove, setting for the opening chapter of the novel. Had they known what they were starting it is not at all certain that they would have assembled there in the first place. Nothing exemplifies more colourfully the annexation of Irish writing by tourism and other commercial interests than the cult of Bloomsday. Every year on June 16 Dublin is thronged by natives and tourists, by Joyce enthusiasts and by those who have never read a word of Joyce, by suppliers and demanders of every possible commodity that can be linked to Joyce, including reproductions of the author's face and of his central character's breakfast ('Most of all he liked grilled mutton kidneys which gave to his palate a fine tang of faintly scented urine.'). The faithful dress up in turn of the century costume, visit places associated with the novel and, inevitably, there is a series of guided pub crawls where the lack of textual authority hardly takes from the pleasure of the pint.

Looked at in one way, the Bloomsday cavortings are a harmless frolic, an excuse for kidney breakfasts, champagne cocktails, Guinness and oysters, a social gathering which a lot of people seem to find entertaining. Looked at in another, they are an insult to the depth and complexity, the greatness and compassion of our country's greatest book. (Anthony Cronin in the *Sunday Independent*, 21 June 1998)

In 1960 a mixed group of academics and local burghers established the Yeats Summer School in Sligo. They can have had little idea how successful their concept would prove: not only did the Yeats International School flourish, attracting large numbers of scholars and students from all over the world, but it would be adopted as a model by many others who exploited/created the popularity of celebrating the achievements of Irish writers in social circumstances that were at variance with the students' own experience of 'school'. The best-known of the successors is the James Joyce Summer School, founded in 1987 by the late Professor Augustine Martin, himself a former director of the Yeats Summer School; others focus on the works of Shaw, Wilde, Synge, John Hewitt and an ever-increasing number of others. Such is the reputation of Irish writing abroad that its economic possibilities have been identified by those involved in tourism; every chamber of commerce instinctively looks for a local writer around whom to organize an annual school or festival that will attract visitors to the area.

It must be almost impossible for anybody under the age of, say, fifty to appreciate the change between the social status of the living Irish writer between 1960 and 1980. Before 1960 those Irish writers who succeeded in achieving a reputation and a reasonable living did so despite the prevailing culture of hostility to any criticism to the perceived national ethos, a hostility which found its most effective expression in state censorship. By 1980 the people of Ireland had had modernism thrust upon them. The irrepressibility of television signals made British programmes available and Irish censorship of books and films seem, at least, futile. The spread of higher education and foreign travel, membership of the European Community and the diminishing influence of the Catholic Church, these were some of the factors that subverted the older sense of a national morality and allowed a more tolerant atmosphere to develop.

In 1981, in an extraordinary shift of policy, the state-sponsored Arts Council established an academy of Irish artists to be called Aosdána. Foremost among those who made this possible were Anthony Cronin, a writer who had experienced the sordid reality of pre-sixties Irish bohemianism, and Charles Haughey, a Taoiseach whose Medici flair was matched by a Napoleonic disdain for conservative bureaucracy:

It was originally envisaged as attempting to address the neglect of many Irish artists including writers, painters, sculptors and composers who were contributing enormously to artistic and cultural life in Ireland but who did not have their contributions properly recognised. (Hogan 1996, I 107)

The decisions to subsidise artists and to grant them tax-free status on their artistic earnings were acts of imaginative generosity that contrasted with half a century of state censorship and disregard. Today both central and local government accept the importance of the arts in the life of the community. The Arts Council plays a central role in Irish cultural life, supporting not only individual artists but also an increasing number of groups of artists of all kinds who could not exist without

subsidy. Apart from their contribution to the life of the community, the arts — and especially, perhaps, literature and theatre — are recognized for their economic value in terms of tourism, and so it was perhaps inevitable that the Big Two, Yeats and Joyce, would achieve the closest capitalism can come to canonization, their images being used on currency notes. Many others must for the moment settle for beatification on the usual range of souvenirs: tea-towels, posters, ash-trays, plaques and so on.

Less spectacular but much more profoundly influential was the formal admission of Irish writers, including living writers, into the English syllabus of the Leaving Certificate. For the last thirty years it has been extremely difficult for any young person to reach the age of eighteen without studying poems by Yeats, Clarke, Kavanagh and Kinsella. (Indeed, it could be argued that things have gone too far in this direction: for as long as there is a more or less guaranteed question on the Irish poetry section, there is no absolute need for the student to look at the English and American poets on the course.) There have been similar developments in fiction and drama: where once there was only Shakespeare, now there is a choice to include, for example, O'Casey and Friel.

The effects of such changes are incalculable in terms of national self-consciousness. Poetry, fiction and drama are no longer something that happens somewhere else. Students study documents of an experience close to their own rather than that of those who grew up in an entirely different culture in, say, the London of Shakespeare or Keats or Dickens. Students hear in literature the voices of their own families, friends and relations. They take for granted the possibility of achieving fame and fortune in writing themselves. It is hardly surprising that there has been in the last decade or so an explosion in young Irish writing and that there has been a consequent development in Irish publishing to accommodate the mass of new material. It may be that Irish writers have a position in Irish culture and conversation that is above the international average. It is unlikely that there is any Irish adult who has not heard of Joyce and Yeats or who would not know something about the work of Seamus Heaney or Roddy Doyle. It may have nothing to do with the intrinsic values of literature, but the general rejoicing which attended Heaney's winning of the Nobel Prize was not unreasonably compared to the pride which the nation felt in the achievements of the Irish soccer team under Jack Charlton.

When Heaney began writing poetry as a teenager he was painfully conscious of standings on the margins of the great tradition of English verse he studied at school, of speaking with an accent that was generally judged to be inferior to Received English Pronunciation, of being a Derry country boy trespassing on the hallowed turf of

English poetry:

I tried to write about the sycamores
And innovated a South Derry rhyme
With hushed and lulled full chimes for pushed and pulled.
Those hobnailed boots from beyond the mountain
Were walking, by God, all over the fine
Lawns of elocution.
Have our accents
Changed? 'Catholics, in general, don't speak
As well as students from the Protestant schools.'
Remember that stuff? Inferiority
Complexes, stuff that dreams were made on ...
Ulster was British, but with no rights on
The English lyric: all around us, though
We hadn't named it, the ministry of fear. (Heaney 1975, 63 ff.)

Today's young Irish writers probably find it hard even to imagine such intimations of inferiority. And yet one of the most striking gaps in Irish scholarship is Hiberno-English. The work of Alan Bliss in the eighties did not generate an academic passion for the language of Irish literature, partly because there were few students with the required mastery of English and linguistics. The appearance of Terence Dolan's *Dictionary of Hiberno-English* in 1998 — and the promise of an IASIL dictionary to follow — probably mark the beginning of a modern scientific study of a linguistic resource which so many Irish writers have so consciously and successfully exploited (see also Filpulla 1999).

A related aspect of Irish culture that also needs to be explored more thoroughly is the oral tradition. Just as many of the characteristics of the Irish language survived in Hiberno-English, so too ancient forms of narrative survived the translation from Irish into Hiberno-English, not least in Dublin, the epicentre of English influence, where one only has to think of the work of Joyce and O'Casey and Behan and Roddy Doyle to realize how tenaciously a peculiar delight in speech can accommodate and absorb anything that an alien culture can throw at it — from British colonialism to American television to the Internet.

When, during her inaugural address, President Mary Robinson wished to suggest her vision of a nation proud of its culture, she quoted Heaney, knowing that nobody would consider her reference obscure. When President Robinson precipitated another election by stepping down, Heaney's name was mentioned as a potential candidate. Heaney did not stand but, had he decided to let his name go forward, it is hard to imagine that any person or party would have stood against him. And had he been elected, no doubt many would have commented that he was continuing a long tradition of the Irish writer's involvement in politics.

Bibliography

Bliss, A. 1979 *Spoken English in Ireland*. Dublin.
Deane, S. 1986 *A short history of Irish literature*. London.
Filppula, M. 1999 *The grammar of Irish English: language in Hibernian style*. London and New York.
Heaney, S. 1975 *North*. London.
Hogan, R. (ed) 1996 *Dictionary of Irish literature*, 2 vols. Connecticut.
Kinsella, T. and Ó Tuama, S. 1981 *An Duanaire 1600–1900: poems of the dispossessed*. Portlaoise.
Kinsella, T. 1986 *The new Oxford book of Irish verse*. Oxford.

Irish History

J. J. Lee

WHAT IS IRISH HISTORY?

Definitions can be endlessly debated. Definitions, even uncontested ones, are always in danger of coming loaded with ideological baggage, for consensus, no less than conflict, can reflect ideological assumptions. Definition is far from uncontested among historians of Ireland, or rather would be if only they had not generally avoided, perhaps fortunately for civility, embroilment in so potentially divisive an issue.

It is no coincidence that the most sustained attempts to define the subject have been made by scholars of Irish/Ulster unionist ideological conviction. This is not to imply that their perspective on Irish history, to whose understanding they have contributed much, is any more ideologically determined than that of historians committed to other traditions, only that circumstances have conspired to make it more necessary for them to be rather more explicit about their purpose.

The first sustained systematic attempt, J. C. Beckett's Inaugural Lecture, 'The study of Irish history', in Queen's University, Belfast, in 1963, concluded that Irish history was primarily the history of the place, Ireland. For the seeker after the essence of Irish history, 'It is in Ireland itself, the physical conditions imposed by life in this country, and their effect on those who have lived here,' that 'one will find the distinct and continuing character of Irish history' (Beckett 1972, 23). In principle, this might have no ideological implications, counting as a purely technical criterion of causation. But Beckett proceeded to inject a particular perspective, for it transpired immediately that not all 'those who lived here' were equal in the face of place. On the contrary, 'It is by studying the way in which the settlers were influenced by the conditions of Irish life, and the way in which they themselves modified the influence of those conditions on the earlier population, that we may be able to identify the distinctive characteristics of Irish history, and build up a framework round which that history may be written'

(*ibid.* 25).

The logic of this was that a 'distinctive' Irish history was largely made by the 'settlers', while it largely happened to 'the earlier population'. Regular reference to the 'earlier' population, even while they continued to survive into the age of the 'settlers', or in some cases even beyond it, could also carry, for those sensitive to such terms, a connotation of their timeless primitiveness compared with the 'settlers'. While the emphasis on the impact of the 'settlers' went a certain, if unspecified, distance, in modifying the initial impression of geographical determinism, it remains unclear whether the 'earlier' population could have laid claim to a 'distinctive' history at all but for the coming of the 'settlers'.

Another intrepid Queen's man, the renowned Professor of Geography, Estyn Evans, felt himself to be heartily endorsing Beckett's emphasis on the role of 'the physical conditions imposed by life in this country' in determining its history. In choosing, however, to encapsulate the primacy of place in the succinct formulation, that 'in the long run ... geography counts for more than genes' (Evans 1996, 32), he fashioned a potentially double-edged sword, which could be wielded by propagandists on both sides for their conflicting purposes. Beckett's formulation, while obviously debatable, was also a potentially fruitful one for debate. But the primacy of the 'settlers' as the real makers of Irish history, however congenial to a unionist audience in 1963 — although, of course, the validity of any definition does not depend on the response of any particular audience — came to sound less appropriate once the Northern Ireland conflict broke out in 1968, stimulating a search for a definition, genuine or tactical, real or euphemistic, more in tune with the emerging rhetoric of 'pluralism', 'multiculturalism', 'parity of esteem' and the like.

Beckett's successor, David Harkness, duly paid deserved tribute to his predecessor in his own inaugural in 1976. While reasserting the importance of place, however, he made a valiant attempt to treat all the inhabitants of the island equally, privileging no category within Ireland as more inherently the makers of its history than any other, while simultaneously stressing the general role of external influences, rather than the special role of 'settlers', on Irish history. Another leading Irish historian — incidentally a Beckett student — George Boyce in Swansea, advocated a broadly comparable approach, if anything stressing external influences even more emphatically in the formulation that 'Irish history is the study of the way in which political and cultural influences made their way to Ireland and were modified and altered by the special conditions found in that country' (Boyce 1987, 235).

Although the Boyce model permits alternative readings of the precise mechanisms of influence, his belief that Irish history must be seen from the perspective of 'that cultural plurality which is such a marked feature of Irish and other "British Isles" history ... since ... the peoples of the British Isles destroyed as well as created each other and each other's culture' (*ibid.* 234–5) corresponds nicely to both the 'archipelago' and the 'cultural relations' models of Irish history. In the first of these, Ireland could be seen as part of an 'archipelago' of 'these islands', or even of the 'Atlantic'. Some insights can be gleaned from the archipelago approach by scholars, like Hugh Kearney, able to draw for *The British Isles: history of four nations* (1989) on decades of research stretching back to his seminal study, *Strafford in Ireland, 1633–1641* (1959), combined with the unique vantage point of writing from the USA after having taught in Ireland, England and Scotland.

The archipelago model could, however, be employed, by those unburdened by Kearney's range of disciplined historical reference, for more functional purposes. Although nominally a geographical model, the real attraction of the archipelago approach, in historically less sensitive hands than Kearney's, is that it fosters the illusion that there is no dominant power centre. The parts may be bigger or smaller, but they are all suffused with a warm archipelagic glow, all regularly interacting with one another as equals, with nothing so vulgar as power operating predominantly in one direction. 'Archipelago' has a nice subliminal ring to it, blurring and smoothing the rough realities of expansion, conquest and control.

This in turn blended nicely with the 'cultural relations' model, which provided an obvious opportunity for those desperate to drape the realities of power in the fashionable garments of culture, where all cultures could be, at least formally, equally cherished, thus air-brushing out of Irish history the crucial issue of power, of who ruled whom, even fostering the comforting illusion that cultural history itself was somehow immune from conta-mination by power considerations. The attractions of the tactic for those committed to reconciling essential existing power relations with a comforting self-image of 'democratic', 'progressive', 'liberal', 'enlightened', 'pluralist' righteousness were too alluring to be subjected to critical self-scrutiny.

Historians of a broadly Irish nationalist disposition, on the other hand, thought they confronted a less awkward challenge in formulating their idea of Irish history. Confident that a large majority of 'the Irish people' broadly supported a demand for greater political independence, they could proceed as if the issues of Anglo-Irish relations, or of power relations within Ireland, were uncomplicated, right residing with the majority in Ireland in accordance with the dominant modern ideology of 'democracy', often projected conveniently far backwards. They tended to equate Irish history, when they pondered its meaning at all, more with the history of people than of place — however evocatively they might conjure the sense of particular places.

While Beckett avoided explicit engagement with any alternative definition by an academic historian, he can hardly have been unaware that he was directly challenging this Irish nationalist approach, as formulated by Edmund Curtis, then Erasmus Smith Professor of History at Trinity College, Dublin, who had identified as his main task in the preface to his *History of Ireland*, published in 1936, and long the standard scholarly study, 'to trace the story of the majority who have finally achieved nationhood, and who in the struggle always found among the Protestant minority leaders and heroes, and a constant body of sympathy and aid. The natural ties among Irish men are, indeed, stronger than their political and religious divisions; strong enough indeed, if encouraged by our leaders, to effect that true union of all Ireland which, in spite of many great victories, remains unachieved'. This robust assertion of the centrality of the story of 'the majority who have finally achieved nationhood' was as congenial to Irish nationalist opinion of the time as was Beckett's to Ulster unionist opinion. It was precisely this orientation of Curtis's that ensured that, 'to the shame of the College', he was never elected to a Fellowship in a Trinity still saturated in Ascendancy assumptions (Lyons 1980, 8).

The dominant ethos of Irish nationalist opinion always had its internal critics. One of the most prominent, Seán Ó Faoláin, sought to confront the challenge of definition in his iconoclastic study, *The Irish*, in 1949, by protesting passionately against the psychological consequences of what he saw as 'the nationalist concept, almost wholly a political concept, of Ireland always on the defensive against foreign enemies' (vii) — though ironically explicitly excluding Curtis from his strictures! Citing Collingwood's celebrated dictum that 'History proper is the history of thought. There are no mere events in history', he described his study as 'the interpretation of the Irish mind in labour' (vii). But this formulation would provide only brief respite from an even more vigorous assault on nationalist, or rather Irish nationalist, orthodoxy. When Richard Kearney chose *The Irish mind* (1985) as the title of a volume of essays on thought in Ireland, he would rouse the ire of Conor Cruise O'Brien, who would denounce the very title as a front for IRA ideology, although the alarmed reader could be left in two minds as to whether this was because the incorrigible Irish had too many minds or no mind at all — if not at all at all, God help us.

Harkness rightly observed that Irish history had to be seen not only in a comparative context but in the context of the history of the Irish abroad, as the editors of the Royal Irish Academy's multi-volume *A new history of Ireland* (1976–) also recognized by including several valuable chapters on the topic. While much has been accomplished in the last three decades on the largely neglected history of the Irish overseas, the scope remains inexhaustible. Apart from the fact that many emigrants remained in close contact with Ireland, directly influencing the fortunes of many who remained, the experience of the emigrants themselves and their descendants can provide illuminating comparative perspective on the experience of the Irish in Ireland. This applies in principle to the history of all peoples, however defined, but given the particularly high proportion of the population which left Ireland over the past three centuries, it has exceptional relevance in the Irish case, with enormous potential for illuminating otherwise dark recesses of Irish history at home. In particular, we have often more direct access via emigrant records to those who went unrecorded in Ireland, especially poorer men and women.

The most effective manner in which the history of those who left, and of their descendants, given the diversity of their backgrounds, aspirations, destinations and experience, can be incorporated in a rigorously scholarly manner into the study of Irish history naturally poses interesting questions, with conflicting views over the definition of the Irish abroad guarding against the threat of premature harmony descending on diaspora studies (Akenson 1988; McCaffrey 1997). The history of those Irish who went as missionaries, soldiers, officials, refugees or any other guise, in the service of whatever cause, and under whatever flag, if any, obliges us to ponder the implications of the definitions we may adopt. Whatever the complications, the history of the Irish diaspora helps remind us that Irish history is broader than the history of the 'place' Ireland, and cannot, on that score alone as well as many others, be reduced to a type of geographical determinism. Recent work by Andy Bielenberg and others is supplementing this picture.

WHO DOES IT?

Important though it be for historians to formulate clear definitions of what they think they are doing, if only in the hope of making them more alert to potential internal contradictions in their interpretations, the stark reality is that, until a generation or so ago, there were very few historians indeed to ponder such matters. History was not, for the most part, an academic subject at all until the early twentieth century, at least to the extent of being organized in specialist history departments. Most writing of Irish history was undertaken either by individuals with private means, or by clergymen, or by journalists, whether turning to history out of genuine intellectual curiosity or as a source of ammunition for current conflict. It was not until the late nineteenth century, at least half a century later than in continental Europe, that the assumption became widespread in England, and therefore in Ireland, that history would be written mainly by academics, and that research would be combined with teaching.

Once the change occurred, it did so with a vengeance. 'Academic' soon came to be equated with 'professional', and 'non-academic' with 'amateur'. This was nonsense then, and it is even more nonsense now. The only valid criterion of authentic historical writing is whether evidence is used professionally or not. History is professional where evidence is used professionally, amateur where evidence is used amateurishly, however elusive conceptually and empirically the meaning of evidence may be. By no means all non-academics are amateurs and, perish the thought, not all academics may be professionals. The nonsense goes even further. Those historians whose self-image appears to depend on their status as 'professionals' have even been known to confine the designation not only to academics but to academics who happen to be members of university history departments. 'Professionals' may even be relegated to amateur status the moment they cross boundary lines from history departments to other departments. The logic is not much of an advertisement for the intellectual rigour of historical thought. This narcissistic type of self-image is not, of course, confined to historians. But historians, who pride themselves above all on the 'scientific' use of evidence, might be expected to pronounce on the basis of the use of evidence rather than occupational status. Irish historiography would be immeasurably impoverished if it were defined solely as the work of members of university history departments, although it will perforce be on these that the bulk of this survey will concentrate.

However defined, historians remained remarkably thin on the ground for a country which purported to pride itself on its history. At first sight, the creation of the National University of Ireland in 1908 might have seemed to herald a new era for the study of Irish history.

It was still in that spirit that in 1913 the Professor of Modern Languages and Registrar of UCC, W. F. T. Butler, 'one of the few scholars of his generation who tried to understand the complexities of Gaelic society in the sixteenth and seventeenth centuries' (Edwards and O'Dowd 1985, 197–8), confidently anticipated that now 'With the establishment of the National University, provision has been made for the first time for the foundation in this country of a School of Historical Science, we may look at last for the adequate treatment of our own land', which should be soon reflected in 'works corresponding to the German Handbuch, the Methodik and Grundiss of Irish History' (Lee 1968, 438).

It was not to be, for at least half a century. In some respects, it still is not. The resources simply were not provided. Staff numbers remained derisory. True, chairs of Irish history, or of history filled by historians of Ireland, were established in UCD, UCC and UCG, soon to be followed by the Lecky Chair in TCD, thanks to an endowment by Lecky's widow. But staff numbers then virtually stagnated for a generation or more. James Hogan, Professor in UCC from 1920 until 1963, had no teaching colleague at all for much of that time, and no more than two at most. Mary D. O'Sullivan, Professor in UCG from 1913 to 1957, again had no colleague for several years, and then only one for the rest. Magee College in Derry long boasted only one historian, and if Queen's Belfast had six staff in History by 1954, only Beckett was an Irish specialist. Maynooth had a small, if distinguished, succession of ecclesiastical historians, usually one at a time, in Pius Walsh, J. F. O'Doherty, P. J. Corish and Donal Kerr. Trinity had no more than five or six historians into the 1950s.

UCD had five by 1949, before embarking on rapid growth in the 1950s, a decade of successful political manoeuvring, especially by the young Desmond Williams, who adapted readily to the minefield of academic politics, which largely determined the distribution of university resources, when he returned from Cambridge in 1949. Having garnered what would prove useful experience of decision-making at a high but inchoate institutional level through his interrogation of surviving senior stalwarts of the Third Reich, Williams achieved within a decade, with the staunch support of the older Dudley Edwards, the dizzy breakthrough into the promised land of double-digit staff numbers. But it was a constant struggle. The subterfuges to which Edwards had to resort throughout the decade to keep even modest teaching opportunities open for Maureen Wall, who 'more than any other single individual ... broke through the veil of the hidden Ireland' (O'Brien 1989, Introduction, second page), provide bleak testimony to the struggle to find jobs for gifted scholars in the Ireland of the time (Dunne 1989, Memoir, third page).

In the past forty years, departments have grown out of all recognition within existing universities, now reinforced by the absorption of teacher training colleges, the ranks further augmented by the creation of the Universities of Ulster, Limerick and Dublin City, the Institute of Irish Studies at Queen's — virtually a new university for Irish affairs in its own right — the new lay university in Maynooth, significant contributions from the library, archival, museum and gallery worlds, from members of other departments and from authorities on Irish history abroad. The devoted but often unsung contribution of clergy outside the university — like Franciscans Canice Mooney, Brendan Jennings and Benignus Millet — has put all students in their debt. And citizens of independent incomes continue to contribute vigorously. The most internationally celebrated must be Conor Cruise O'Brien, who alone constitutes, in his multiple reincarnations, a virtual one-man armoured squadron, careering into battle on behalf of varieties of unionism against the hydra-headed monster of Irish nationalism in a manner which makes a fascinating case study of the relationship between ideological and scholarly values.

Growth in the number of regular publishers has been a feature of the field of Irish history for a generation or more. The change has probably been most conspicuous outside Dublin, where easier access to sources had not restricted research opportunities to quite the same extent. Certainly, to take but one example, Irish history in the past twenty-five years would look very odd indeed without the names — to mention only the long-established scholars who have published the bulk of their work while based in Galway — of Canny, Ellis, Mac Niocaill, Ó Cróinín and Ó Tuathaigh. Only a totally false modesty precludes me from listing Cork names, while a plethora of scholars now grace the study of Irish history in Northern Ireland, where once only a tiny handful preached the message. Indeed Seán Connolly was able to call on a virtual brigade of northern-based scholars to contribute to the *Oxford companion to Irish history* (1998).

Numbers are not necessarily everything, of course. It might prove an instructive, not to say purgative, exercise to compare the research and teaching performance of history staff according to size of department, whether within the same department over time or across departments at the same time. Numbers obviously did count at research student level, with the number of theses registering the expansion of the subject. The total recorded as completed in the *Irish Historical Studies* register of research rose from four in 1941 to thirty-seven in 1997. The real, as distinct from reported, increase is probably far greater, given inadequacies in the returns and the huge amount of research now conducted under the guise of taught MAs, as well as by scholars and research students in other fields and abroad.

Where staff numbers were, and in some cases still are, so small, the quality of appointments, above all of professorial appointments, becomes of course crucial. That was even more the case in a culture where, despite its alleged, and sometimes real, conservatism, high-risk appointments could be made at a young age. Given total security of tenure, mistakes could not be rectified for perhaps thirty or forty years. Many professors served strikingly long tenures. Not only did O'Sullivan hold Galway from 1913 until 1957, but Hogan held Cork from 1920 to 1963, Eoin MacNeill UCD 1909–45, Mary Hayden UCD 1911–41, J. M. O'Sullivan UCD 1909–48, A. W. Phillips Trinity 1914–39, Curtis Trinity 1914–43, Edwards UCD 1944–79, Williams UCD 1949–88, Corish Maynooth 1947–88, John A. Murphy Cork 1970–91.

The crucial issue of appointment remains to be investigated for all subjects in all Irish universities. There are few more illuminating routes to the aortic core of institutional and national cultures than their appointments systems. We need to know who the unsuccessful candidates were and how they acquitted themselves subsequently in comparison with the successful ones. Even that does not provide a decisive answer on the quality of appointment. For what we really need to know is how the unsuccessful candidates would have acquitted themselves, as teachers, researchers and colleagues, had they been successful, with access to comparable resources and opportunities — and exposure to comparable problems.

It is fashionable to assert that academic politics are so bitter because the stakes are so small. But the stakes were often very high indeed in earlier generations. One's whole life chances could revolve around appointment to a particular post, for jobs were so scarce that the alternative to senior appointment was often no appointment at all. One might move from outside the university world to senior academic positions — like G. A. Hayes McCoy from the National Museum of Ireland to succeed M. D. O'Sullivan in Galway, or later T. P. O'Neill from the National Library to Galway also, or alternatively never have the opportunity of moving at all. One could jump from being a mere 'assistant', in the hierarchical terminology of the time, to being a professor overnight — or, alternatively, remain an 'assistant' for many years to come. When one's whole life chances could depend on a single throw of the dice, the stakes were undoubtedly often very high in earlier generations. As appointment in the National University depended for long on the canvassing of electors, unimpeded by the obstacle of any formal assessment procedure until the 1970s, the throw of the dice could be arbitrary in the extreme. And yet, for all the obvious scope for abuse, it is by no means clear that the best appointments were not made as frequently as under more structured systems, if not always for more structured reasons.

Despite the criticisms that can rightly be levelled at the canvassing system, party politics played a much more limited role in Ireland, certainly in the south, than in most continental European countries, where the role of the state in appointment systems often allowed academic criteria to be subordinated to party political criteria. As the state had no role in the appointment systems of Irish universities, party political influence had to be exercised, if it were to be exercised at all, in circuitous, and often ineffective, ways. Politics did, of course, play a part in appointments, but it was much more academic politics than party politics, although the Northern Ireland situation created peculiar appointment problems there. All that said, it would be interesting to know if appointment systems injected systematic biases, whether on grounds of ideology, nationality, race, religion, gender or age, into the decisions taken, and, if so, when, and why, and how, the biases may have changed over time, north and south.

WORKING CONDITIONS: TEACHING, RESEARCH, ADMINISTRATION, PUBLIC SERVICE

Teaching was long considered more important than research in the ethos of the institutions, and in the allocation of staff time. One consequence of the lack of resources was that undergraduate teaching generally absorbed a far higher proportion of time in earlier generations than today. This was probably the case in all institutions, although more so in the smaller departments. It was not only a question of the number of lecturing hours. It was also the range that had to be covered in small departments, virtually unknown nowadays. As early as 1949, T. W. Moody in TCD recounted with disbelief the teaching load and range of his Professor in Queen's twenty years before, J. E. Todd, who 'cheerfully continued to shoulder such a burden of teaching as few Professors would have contemplated ...' (Cronne *et al.* 1949, xiv). It is not to detract from Todd's obviously prodigious performance to observe that it is probable that nothing claimed for him could not have been said about Hogan in Cork, O'Sullivan in Galway, O'Doherty in Maynooth, perhaps Hayden/Edwards in UCD, even if their degree of cheerfulness remains unrecorded. In the biggest department, UCD, it was still a pedagogic principle into the early 1960s that lecturers could, and perhaps should, teach anything. When Desmond Williams introduced the tutorial system, it was for long taken as self-evident that not only staff, but research students, could tutor on any place in any period. I recall myself being tutored on nineteenth-century Ireland and Europe in UCD in 1959, and very well tutored indeed, by John Morrall, then in between his books, *Political thought in medieval times* (1958) and *Gerson and the Great Schism* (1960). While the disadvantages for scholars intent on concentrating on their own research seem clear, it is by no means as obvious that the result of greater specialization has been better teaching.

Despite the occasional exceptions that spring to mind, it is my strong impression that a high proportion of Irish historians provided remarkably good teaching in all the circumstances. I myself have not come across a higher average level of teaching than that which my cohort had the good fortune to enjoy as undergraduates in UCD between 1959 and 1962, however much of human life was to be found in that department. The respect in which his students held James Hogan was clear at the symposium held in Cork to mark his centenary in 1998. For Jim Lydon, M. D. O'Sullivan 'had a very strong influence on all her students, and produced a quite extraordinary number of good historians' (Lydon 1995, 11). It is to O'Sullivan's colleague, Síle Ní Chinnéide, that Louis Cullen, another of Trinity's brightest luminaries but also another graduate of Galway, expresses his sense of obligation, as does Gearóid Ó Tuathaigh. For Paddy Corish, J. F. O'Doherty was 'by far the best lecturer' in Maynooth (Corish 1996, 17).

When one recollects that many of those committed to teaching Irish history had to teach not just some Irish history but all Irish history, as well as provide some outline of general European history, the challenge confronting them can be imagined. That challenge became even more intense at postgraduate supervision level, given the demands of specialist advice over so wide a range. Supervision loads could vary even more widely than undergraduate teaching loads. Although undergraduate teaching loads have declined sharply, the increase in graduate teaching has kept teaching loads relatively high by international standards, much though they appear to vary among individuals and between institutions. As with undergraduate teaching, the quality of supervision seems to have been generally high, though it would be astonishing if there were no oversights, given the range many supervisors were expected to cover.

Even had there been greater investment in historical research, however, in the earlier period, the harvest would have perforce remained limited as long as access to source material was so constrained. Far and away the biggest single obstacle to research and publication has been the under-resourcing of libraries and archives, even more of an impediment before the days of photocopier and Inter-Library Loan. Nicholas Canny's strictures on the resourcing of the Library in UCG could be echoed for several other institutions (Canny 1998, 53). Except for Trinity College, thanks to its copyright access to British published work, Maynooth with respect to aspects of ecclesiastical history, and perhaps for Queen's more generally, no university library reached western European standards. Dublin-based scholars could, however, avail of 'national' libraries and archives, while

the Linen Hall Library and the PRONI provided yeoman service in Belfast.

Even the presence of repositories did not guarantee access to material. One might have thought that the destruction of so much documentation in the Public Record Office during the burning of the Four Courts in the Civil War in 1922 would have made the new Irish Free State especially solicitous for the proper stewardship of the surviving sources. It did not. The state disgracefully neglected the Public Record and State Paper Offices until the creation of the National Archives in 1988, which, although itself suffering from under-funding, began to enhance research possibilities. It was not only the situation with regard to the PRO and the State Paper Office that caused great frustration in the south. The difficulties in securing access to the Quit Rent Office, or to genealogical material, were already a further cause for complaint in the 1930s (Gleeson 1941, 126). Cabinet papers did not become available, under a thirty-year rule, until the mid-1970s, nor papers of government departments more generally until the 1990s (O'Grady 1998). Military history archives are still in the process of being fully opened. The initiative of Dudley Edwards in establishing an Archive School in UCD after 1970, and in building up the UCD archives, has made a major contribution to historical studies, whose fruits will long continue to be reaped. The founding of archives on labour history, on business history and on women's history, since about 1971, has also opened opportunities for research that simply were not available to earlier generations. So has the gradual opening of ecclesiastical archives. Oral history archives remain, unfortunately, grossly underdeveloped (Ferriter 1998).

It was truly ironic that Northern Ireland, which did indeed seek to neglect Irish history in the schools and even for a time at Queen's, devoted far more resources to its Public Record Office right from the start. It was no wonder that for long, until the latest round of Troubles in the north created its own difficulties, scholars in the south could only envy those whose work allowed them draw heavily on the far superior resources, and enjoy the far more congenial working conditions, of the PRONI. Lack of resources for the National Library of Ireland (NLI) has meant that many archival holdings, laboriously accumulated through the work of Edward MacLysaght and Sir John Ainsworth, which had already increased the number of manuscripts in the NLI from about 600 in 1940 to 18,000 by 1976, still lie uncatalogued, hopefully to surface in some future incarnation when the state remembers this institution still exists. The Irish Manuscripts Commission (IMC), under the chairmanship of Eoin MacNeill, began publishing an invaluable series, with James Hogan as editor, after its foundation in 1928. Unfortunately, the establishment of the Manuscripts Commission did not reflect any commitment by the official mind to the structured provision of historical source material. It is highly unlikely that, but for MacNeill's personal influence with his former colleagues in cabinet, the IMC would have emerged at that time. Likewise, but for de Valera's personal interest, it is highly unlikely that the Irish Folklore Commission would have been established in 1935, or the Dublin Institute of Advanced Studies, with a Celtic Studies School, in 1940.

In assessing the research output of individual scholars, it is, of course, necessary to know not only their workloads but how much access to sources they enjoy. Work requiring high travel and subsistence costs simply could not ordinarily be contemplated by staff, much less students, except perhaps by clerics enjoying a network of safe houses at home and abroad. Had David Quinn, for instance, not been appointed to Southampton in 1934, he could hardly have begun the work on the Sir Humphrey Gilbert material in the British Museum that would form the foundation of his prodigious contribution to the study of 'the westward enterprise'.

Perhaps it might be hazarded, if one considers relative staff-student ratios, historically more favourable in the north and in Trinity, with lighter teaching loads and greater opportunities for specialization, reinforced by their four-year degrees compared with three-year ones in other institutions, and their superior research conditions, that, by these criteria, Queen's and Trinity-based scholars, other things being equal, ought to have achieved 25% higher productivity than scholars in other Dublin institutions, who in turn ought to have achieved 25% higher productivity than those resident beyond commuting distance from Dublin and Belfast. (Since the UCD archives became a major repository for material on twentieth-century Irish history, it may be that this now compensates for Trinity's other advantages of location in this area.) There is obviously nothing sacrosanct about these estimates. Nevertheless, a full historical assessment by these criteria remains to be written, or even conceived. So of course does a full assessment of the basis of the degree of privilege in the background of individual scholars, in terms of family wealth and circumstances, location, gender and the like. In assessing the performance of Mary Hayden, for instance, Professor of Irish History in UCD for thirty years, how does one balance disadvantages which may have confronted her as a woman in a predominantly male environment (although this remains to be investigated), and which certainly involved calls on her time by women's organizations, to which she responded generously, with her class advantages as the daughter of a Dublin physician, which meant she did not have to find a job on graduation, allowing her travel to Greece, India and the USA, a privilege children of less-endowed parents in less-endowed places might not enjoy at the same age, or at all, half a century or more later (Macken 1942, 369)? Contrast that with the obstacles surmounted by Tony Stewart, who could not afford to take up a graduate scholarship because of the need to earn money immediately to support his widowed mother (Stewart 1993, 56). It is likely that the financial circumstances of the majority were far closer to those of Stewart than of Hayden.

To arrive at a total picture of the quality of research performance of Irish historians one would, therefore, need to know far more about the individuals themselves, about the opportunities available, about the alternative calls on their time in terms of teaching and supervision loads, administrative responsibilities in their own institutions and outside calls on their time. How attuned were their institutions to the idea of supporting research in terms, for instance, of Leave of Absence Schemes? Even T. W. Moody, within the privileged portals of Trinity, had only one sabbatical in his entire forty years as professor. It is a shade ironic to read that R. D. C. Black of Queen's collected 'much of the material' for his magisterial *Economic thought and the Irish question* (1960) during a leave of absence in the USA in 1950–1, supported by the Rockefeller Foundation. Research grants were then few and far between, even in Northern Ireland, and scarcer again in the south. A handful of scholars may have enjoyed virtual research institute conditions, while the many toiled with institutional loads that would seem virtually to preclude time or energy for research.

Certainly, few of even the most privileged Irish could enjoy the opportunities the French system permitted to François Furet, whose distaste for teaching, 'which he found both intimidating and exorbitantly expensive in time', impelled him to find 'shelter' in a pure research establishment, the CNRS (Kaplan 1995, 51). Furet, as it happened, contributed handsomely to the success of the joint Franco-Irish ventures pioneered by Louis Cullen at the Irish end, but many Irish historians must have ruefully wished to have been in a position to 'nourish their alienation' from the university world in Furetian style. Who would not have wished to have been in a position to have had written about them that their 'golden parachute from the Presidency of the EHESS consisted of a Research Centre named after Raymond Aron that was attached to the School but under his stewardship'(Kaplan 1995, 51)? Who would not even have settled for A. J. P. Taylor's predicament, who could celebrate his appointment to the Beaverbrook Library with the exultant reflection 'no more going to the British Museum', when most Irish historians would have given their right hand to have been in a position to go to the same British Museum? The closest to comparable research conditions any enjoyed is likely to have been at the School of Celtic Studies in the Dublin Institute for

Advanced Studies. What might not others have made of such Taylor-type conditions?

Far more representative for Irish historians than Furet or Taylor-type experience is the publication performance of Oliver MacDonagh, among the most productive, as well as the most incisive, of all Irish historians. The pattern of regular output throughout his career was interrupted only when he returned from Australia to take up the Chair of Modern History in Cork in 1968. Although 'he did manage to get some writing done also', he found the demands on his research time 'excessive', and not until returning to Australia was he 'to blossom again as a prolific writer' (Dunne 1990, 6–7). One may well hazard the conclusion that if a scholar of MacDonagh's stature and commitment found the obstacles so frustrating, what chance was there for others?

One can assume, happily, general improvement in the resources available in recent years, even if the pace of improvement has had to depend disproportionately, given the vagaries of leadership in the institutions, on the political skills of the heads of department, many of whom sacrificed much of their own scholarly time to the piranha-like struggle for resources. Their administrative responsibilities steadily increased with the growing scale and complexity of university administration, with staff-student ratios in the NUI colleges often still hovering well above 1 to 20, although more favourable in Trinity and Northern Ireland. Not all of his colleagues could emulate Louis Cullen's strength of will 'to shed adminis-trative commitments where possible' (Cullen 1994, 12). Indeed, where there were professors, as in the National University, obliged until the 1990s by statute to act as heads of department, little was possible in this direction.

It may be that the historians did not make matters any easier for themselves by the institutional structures they were involved in devising. UCD continues to operate with four departments in a combined Department of History — a veritable four-leaved shamrock! UCC went from one Department of History to three in the 1960s, before reverting to one in the 1990s. Trinity conjured two departments out of one in 1968. Queen's established an independent Department of Economic and Social History in 1962, only to merge it with History in 1999. Such variegated experience provided ample opportunity for a hundred flowers to bloom. To savour the full flavour of departmental life, a feel for the resultant profusion of gardening techniques, some decidedly rustic, would be essential. It might be premature to assume that the structures reflect the distilled wisdom of management organization theory, until specific investigation of the individual cases determines whether they fostered or squandered research opportunities, and to what extent apparently irrational organization actually contributed to achievement.

It would also be true to say that not all historians had to be hauled, kicking and screaming, into other activities, whether within or without their institutions. Many responded positively to what Leslie Clarkson has called 'the insidious allures of senior university management' (Clarkson, 1999, 1) in the forms of presidencies and provostships, vice-presidencies and vice-provostships, deanships, membership of senates, governing bodies and university committees, both useful and useless. Nor were historians notably reluctant when it came to varieties of public activity that required heads to be put above parapets, in everything from standing for public office to contributing to the media, and to resisting, like Frank Martin and Kevin Nowlan, the vandalization of our architectural and archaeological heritages.

Some historians are now deriving modest support from the university fund-raising activities that have become pervasive in recent years. Others are recipients of government assistance. But it has come passing slow. The acknowledgements in books by Irish historians, at least in the south, are rarely able to contain the lists of thanks to research councils, or to research assistants, that feature regularly in those of researchers elsewhere in the western world, including researchers on Ireland located abroad or in Northern Ireland. Some public funding for individual projects, as well as for the Irish Manuscripts' Commission, has certainly been of use, ranging from the small government grant for *The Great Famine* (1957), edited by R. D. Edwards and T. D. Williams, to the massive state support for *A new history of Ireland*, supplemented by a generous endowment from the Irish American businessman, John A. Mulcahy, a substantial government grant in 1995 for research to commemorate the one hundred and fiftieth anniversary of the Great Famine, state support for the 1798 bi-centenary and for women's history. But this type of support itself served further to emphasize how many scholars were still pursuing research with derisory resources.

Nevertheless, it should also be observed that state aid does not appear to have come burdened with any specific ideological baggage. While there may be cases to the contrary, de Valera himself, when urging that a research volume be published to commemorate the centenary of the Great Famine, also intimated that it should be undertaken by 'a trained historian'. It was scholarship, not hagiography, he sought. And the expla-nation, or at least excuse, offered by the Department of Finance in opposing support for specific historical projects was that it was inappropriate for the state to become involved in scholarly enterprise of this nature. However tongue in cheek the argument, it betokens a certain concept of opportunistic propriety.

The most important resource for many was their spouse, which until recently has mostly meant wives. If their time were to be costed, and not only in the unquantifiable but crucial area of emotional encouragement, but in the concrete area of direct research assistance, as expressed in acknowledgement after acknowledgement, from David Quinn's to his wife, Alison, for co-researching and indexing, to James Hogan's for the 'unwearying' secretarial services of his wife, Mary, to Gerard O'Brien's to his wife, Michelle, who 'deciphered some of the more daunting specimens of Fr. Gwynn's handwriting, and undertook typing where and when necessary', in preparing Aubrey Gwynn's *The Irish church in the eleventh and twelfth centuries* (1992) for posthumous publication, it would probably add up to far more than all direct government support for research during the entire twentieth century.

It is difficult again for the current generation to imagine how research could actually be physically conducted without secretarial assistance, or even the photocopier. Back-up facilities scarcely existed in many history departments, any more than others, until at least the 1950s, if not decades later. My recollection of UCD about 1960, just before major improvements in accommodation occurred, is of roughly ten staff members sharing a single office, with the solitary secretary, the wonderful Paddy Ann O'Sullivan, who would die tragically young, juggling a plethora of importunate demands while striving to instill a due sense of decorum into her sometimes boisterous charges. The idea that good secretaries, or even a room of one's own, might facilitate scholarly production was not then universally accepted. It is hard to know what history departments, as presumably most others, would now be doing without their secretaries. Certainly God knows where Cork history would be, for I unashamedly take the opportunity of paying tribute to the indispensable contribution our secretaries have made to sustaining the scholarship, not to mention the sanity, of staff and students alike. And yet they were rare indeed until about 1970.

The resources at research student level are among the poorest in the western world, although the introduction of the Government of Ireland Scholarships in 1998 brought welcome possibilities of improved support at long last. Research students were not generally in a position to avail of the uxorial services on which their elders relied, although I suspect that many a mother may, like my own, have been recruited, on a strictly non-profit basis, to put in hours of ancillary toil in the cause of research. The Travelling Studentship, sponsored by the NUI, in History, as in other subjects, about once every three years, has attracted high-quality applicants, the winners reading like a roll-call of the great, if not always of the good, over nearly a century. The studentship may have made the difference between following an academic career or not for many of the recipients, who simply could not have continued their studies without it.

The Institute of Historical Research in London in the 1930s, and Peterhouse, Cambridge, from the 1940s to the 1970s, thanks to the connections forged by Harold Temperley, Herbert Butterfield and Brian Wormald as External Examiners in the NUI, provided opportunities for Irish historians that in many cases would not otherwise have occurred. The Peterhouse connection, fostered most intently by T. D. Williams, would include, in a variety of guises, so diverse a range of personalities, in addition to Williams himself, as F. X. Martin, K. B. Nowlan, Hugh Kearney, Patrick Lynch, Oliver MacDonagh, J. C. Beckett, A. T. Q. Stewart, Gearóid Ó Tuathaigh, Ronan Fanning, Ian d'Alton, Tom Dunne, Gerard O'Brien and J. J. Lee.

RESEARCH ETHOS, PUBLICATION AND HISTORIOGRAPHY
It is clear that, despite the emergence of history as a formal, independent academic subject early in the twentieth century, lack of resources meant that research had to be residual for most academics until the present generation. How then did they approach such research as they were in a position to pursue? The approved version is a compelling morality tale of the triumph of virtue over the demons of sloth, slovenliness and surrender to the seductive charms of the capital letter. As with all the best morality tales, there has to be a knight in shining armour, in this case none other than T. W. Moody, initially accompanied in 1938 by R. Dudley Edwards as Joint Editor of *Irish Historical Studies* (*I.H.S.*), the flagship of the new 'scientific' history. Edwards would gradually prove, however, distinctly dubious company for virtue and would be duly jocked off in favour of presumptively more malleable, and hopefully more virtuous, editorial company. To vary the analogy, in the more extreme version, all was darkness until Moody said, 'let there be light', when the scales dropped from the eyes of the dullards and light flooded in to illuminate the contours of the historical landscape. In less biblical terms, one might say that, just as there was no sex in Ireland before the Late Late Show, there was no 'scientific' history before *Irish Historical Studies*. Biblical criticism too has advanced, to the point where scriptural studies are poised to enter a revisionist phase. But as the critical standards which *Irish Historical Studies* took pride in preaching stopped for a long while abruptly short at self-criticism, reality can only be tentatively reconstructed at this stage.

What *Irish Historical Studies* achieved in its early years was highly important, even making all due allowance for the Moody mythology. The very self-consciousness of its insistence that it was not as other men, that it had higher standards, did serve to focus attention on the rigorous use of evidence. It did strive to take politics out of history. Though aided by the gradual abatement of inherited political passions, it contributed significantly in its own right to the moderation of expression as well as to some extent to the conceptualization of historical writing. It succeeded in securing co-operation between north and south, as represented by Belfast and Dublin, through the elaborately contrived constitutional arrangements involving the co-operation of the Ulster Historical Society and the Irish Historical Society, both founded in 1936, on the initiative of Moody and Edwards, following the prompting of R. I. Best, the National Librarian. Given the potential for divisiveness in so sensitive an area, that was a truly striking achievement, which may not always receive the credit it deserves (Edwards 1978, 3–4). *I.H.S.* also introduced a much more focussed approach towards the organization of historical research aids, enhancing the supply of conveniently accessible information through bibliographies, reports on research in progress and an extensive review section.

These were significant advancements, even if they tended to relate more to the administration of research than research itself. Ireland was belatedly following a path pioneered nearly a century before on the continent. But Moody's constant insistence that *I.H.S.* marked the introduction of 'scientific' history to Ireland tended to denigrate earlier achievements, as well as those of contemporaries who toiled outside the *I.H.S.* orbit. In itself, the claim was simply 'unscientific'. For 'scientific' history was already firmly rooted before *I.H.S.* appeared, as McDowell rightly observes, however welcome an encouragement the launching of the journal gave to its advocates (McDowell 1993, 11). The main works of Moody himself, Edwards and Hayes McCoy — in all cases their only major books for many years to come — were already either published or in press at the time. However many significant contributions David Quinn would make to *I.H.S.*, he had already established his scholarly standing before *I.H.S* appeared. Jocelyn Otway-Ruthven, whose pen would also grace *I.H.S.*, had published her first substantial article, 'The King's secretary in the 15th century', in the *Transactions of the Royal Historical Society* in 1936. Aubrey Gwynn had been publishing regularly since 1920, his major work on Armagh owing nothing to *I.H.S.*, anymore than did the bulk of his subsequent prolific publications, which continued to appear in the UCD/Jesuit periodical *Studies*, or in the more specialized outlets of ecclesiastical history, or in local journals, without any sacrifice of scholarly standards because they dared appear beyond the 'scientific' pale. Fr Paul Walsh was already subjecting the unscholarly or the unwary to his 'austere professional standards' in early Irish history (Edwards and O'Dowd 1985, 205). At the other end of the chronological spectrum, Nicholas Mansergh had already published his two astoundingly precocious volumes, *The government of the Irish Free State* and *The government of Northern Ireland*, in 1934 and 1936, and would publish his short but seminal

Ireland in the age of reform and revolution in 1940, independently of any *I.H.S.* inspiration.

One result of this approach was a gross undervaluation, for all the no doubt legitimate criticisms that could be made, of the work of the 'earlier' generation, many of whom would remain active for many years afterwards, M. D. O'Sullivan's *Italian merchant bankers in thirteenth century Ireland* appearing in 1962, Aubrey Gwynn's final articles not until 1978. Moody was also largely oblivious to the existence of institutions outside Belfast and, later, Dublin. His tributes to Todd, while clearly well-deserved by a professor who opened doors for Moody himself, Quinn and Beckett, also reflected his own institutional localism. When Moody claimed that Queen's history department was by far the poorest in the 'British Isles' in the 1920s, he presumably referred to the United Kingdom. Had his passion for comparison stretched south of the border, he could hardly have failed to notice that the plight of the colleges of the National University, at least, and that of professors in the south struggling in even smaller departments with even more exiguous resources, could have placed Queen's predicament in more benign comparative perspective. The main difference between the reputations of Todd and those of Hogan, O'Sullivan, Hayden and even Curtis was that, through Moody's repeated tributes, Todd's name featured more prominently in *I.H.S.* than theirs, who not only carried at least comparable teaching loads, but had, except for Hayden, published vastly more on Irish history.

Another, and clearly unintended, consequence was the marginalization of local history. This was highly ironic, in that Moody's *The Londonderry plantation: 1609–41* (1939) could itself count as an example of the genre. But it was an inevitable consequence of the relentless refrain that 'scientific' history began in 1938. This tended to relegate all previous publication to inferior status. As much of that publication was in local journals, they were consigned at a stroke to the 'pre-scientific' age. Many of these journals were in fact quite vibrant on the eve of *I.H.S.* It was truly ironic to find exhortations of the late 1990s about local history echoing so many of the points made in the local journals sixty years before (Pender 1941, 110–22). *I.H.S.* was certainly not overtly hostile to local history, and indeed carried the contents of local journals for a time. But, as Denis Marnane puts it, the fact that the massive Curtis edition of the Ormond Deeds (1932) lay unused for years 'continues to be a reminder of the limited development of local studies' (Marnane 1997, 18). The remarkable series of country histories launched by Geography Publications under the auspices of William Nolan, and Kevin Whelan, an extraordinary publishing and editing feat, appears to have owed little to the inspiration of the flagship journal.

Yet another largely unintended consequence was the

undervaluation of teaching. Despite the fact that Moody himself was a conscientious teacher, and despite his tribute to Todd as a teacher, it would not be, apart from *Festschriften*, until the periodical *History Ireland* gave voice to other historians that debts to teachers would come to be acknowledged in a widely circulated periodical. *History Ireland*, launched in 1992 by Tommy Graham and Hiram Morgan, and predictably dismissed by the more supercilious as light-weight because it has the temerity to include illustrations, has, in fact, prompted a fundamental revision of Irish historiography through the interviews it has carried with a succession of senior scholars, at last invited onto the platform to tell it as they see it. *History Ireland* has given voice to the largely voiceless, and it has become crystal clear that many see it very differently from the Moody circle, salvaging, *inter alia*, the reputations of teachers outside the *I.H.S.* ambit.

In other respects, too, the *History Ireland* interviews, and other comments, place a rather different perspective on the whole Moody enterprise. The legendary R. B. McDowell, who saw it all, does not believe any revolution occurred in 1938 at all (McDowell 1993, 11). Aidan Clarke's coruscating obituary of Edwards proclaimed Moody the ideal man for the commas and capitals (or rather, non-capitals). It can hardly be claimed that Jim Lydon's refusal to conform to Moody's editorial dicta (Lydon 1995) has permanently damaged Irish medieval history, while the celebrated medievalist Otway-Ruthven had never been among Moody's cheer-leaders (McDowell 1993, 11).

It is clear at this distance that part of the Moody myth has to do with the packaging. The classic profile of Moody, the thirty-page account by Lyons in his *Festschrift*, is invaluable for both Moody and Trinity, especially between the lines, where Lyons did much of his best work. In contrast, Lyons devotes only two pages to the Foreword, admittedly as Provost rather than editor, to the Otway-Ruthven *Festschrift*. Yet Otway-Ruthven had been preferred to Moody by the electors to the Lecky Chair in 1951. Were they wrong? If so, why? If they were right, how do we account for the imbalance in the tributes? Any adequate appraisal of history in Ireland will have to address the issues involved.

Even at the purely organizational level, the effusive tributes to Moody's labours can come close to conveying the impression that no other Irish historian ever burned the midnight oil in this manner, virtually banishing out of sight the work of G. A. Hayes-McCoy as founder-editor of the *Irish Sword*, which gave military history a new standing, from 1949 to his death in 1976, of O'Sullivan, and later Síle Ní Chinnéide, as long-term editors of the *Galway Archaeological and Historical Journal* and/or *Galvia*, of Fr Benignus Millett as editor of *Collectanea Hibernica* for forty years, of James Hogan as editor of *Analecta Hibernica* for over thirty years, of Paddy Corish as editor of *Archivium Hibernicum* for thirty years, of Tomás Ó Fiaich as founder-editor of *Seanchas Ardmhacha* from 1954 until 1973, to confine oneself to Moody's contemporaries or near-contemporaries. This is not to denigrate Moody's dedicated editorial performance, either with *I.H.S.* or the monograph series *Studies in Irish history*, or with the *New history of Ireland*. But it is to seek rather more recognition for other labourers in the vineyard, and to suggest that the imputation that without Moody having brought with him to Dublin 'the work ethic of the north', the retarded creatures of the south would have slouched along at their slower and more rolling gait, may require reconsideration (Martin 1984, 6).

I.H.S. devoted substantial space to reviewing. Much of this was useful, and some contributions were outstanding. But the review section needs to be clinically appraised. Cormac Ó Grada has pioneered an illuminating approach by highlighting the inadequacy of the superficial, indeed supercilious, notice of Cecil Woodham Smith's *The Great Hunger* (1962) by F. S. L. Lyons. As Lyons was clearly the intellectual superior of many other reviewers, it is likely that a detailed analysis would reveal serious inadequacies in many cases. There is ample scope for sifting the genuinely perceptive reviews from those that confused pedantry with scholarship, or equated displays of arrested adolescent exhibitionism, intent on showing how much cleverer was the reviewer than the author, with 'scientific' reviewing. It would be misleading to imply that *I.H.S.* had, or has, any monopoly of those tendencies. But it matters more in the case of a journal that purported to raise standards through the 'scientific' quality of its reviewing.

The policy of *I.H.S.* on obituaries likewise contributed to the Moody myth. Irish historiography would have benefited greatly from considered critiques of the work of the great departed. But if *I.H.S.* was the birth of 'scientific' history in Ireland, there could, by definition, be no 'great departed' within Ireland, apart of course from Moody's own teacher, Todd, until the *I.H.S.* inner circle itself began to depart. Thus, no adequate analysis of the work of Curtis would appear. Moody's dismissive reference, despite his praise for his pioneering, that 'The meticulous scholarship inculcated by modern schools of historical research was uncongenial to him; and his works contain many errors of detail' (Moody 1942–43, 294), however factually valid, was historiographically uncomprehending. It would be an instructive exercise to compare Curtis and Moody as historians, placing both in their proper historiographical context. Moody, a fine scholar in his own right, deserves to be retrieved from his hagiographers. He will be better served by sympathetic, but scholarly, appraisals like Gillespie's assessment of *The Londonderry plantation* in *I.H.S*, the first of an admirably conceived series devoted to critiques of individual major works, and which, if handled with comparable discernment, could greatly enhance proper historiographical understanding (Gillespie 1994).

Eoin MacNeill, whom Edwards, less proprietorial than Moody, was later at pains to identify as the founder of the 'scientific' study of early Irish history, got as short shrift as Curtis, even though MacNeill had served as President of the Irish Historical Society since its foundation nine years before. *I.H.S.* did publish a bibliography of MacNeill, by F. X. Martin, prompted by Edwards, but it contained no critique. Neither did anything appear on Hogan or O'Sullivan, who scarcely existed in *I.H.S.* consciousness. What an opportunity was missed in Hogan's case, for instance, by the failure to provide a critique of an oeuvre that ranged from major articles on medieval Gaelic Ireland, as Francis John Byrne attested in his 1968 survey (Byrne 1968, 3), through his pioneering study on *Ireland in the European state system* (1920), which, for all the marks it bore of the extreme youth of the author — Hogan was twenty-two at date of publication — reflected a perspective that would take more than fifty years to be fully appreciated, through his Irish Manuscripts Commission editions of Walsingham (1959) and d'Avaux (1958) — was he right to take Macaulay so severely to task for his 'caricature of the French ambassador'? — and his seminal study of the relationship between electoral systems and political culture, *Election and representation* (1945).

The work of M. D. O'Sullivan would also have offered an opportunity for mature reflection on what 'doing history' in Galway, and on Galway, as a microcosm of the study of local history, had meant for nearly half a century. How would one reconcile the utterly dismissive review by H. W. Richardson in *I.H.S.* (1944–5, 361–7) of O'Sullivan's *Old Galway*, with the insistence of Edwards and Quinn in the same *I.H.S.* (16 [1968], p. 28) that it was invaluable for their period, and Jim Lydon's verdict that it was 'a superb book' (Lydon 1995, 11). Critiqued in conjunction with her *Italian merchant bankers in Ireland in the thirteenth century*, and a long series of articles on Galway history, it could have provided a window into an otherwise obscure area.

Hayes McCoy could congratulate himself on getting a page and a half obituary in 1977 which, though graciously composed by Gerard Simms, could hardly do full justice to the significance of his scholarly contribution, a misjudgement all the more glaring in the light of Nicholas Canny's verdict (Canny 1998, 52), that his *Scots mercenary forces in Ireland 1565–1603* (1937) survives better than either Moody's *The Londonderry plantation* or Dudley Edwards' *Church and state in Tudor Ireland* (1935). Simms himself would have to be satisfied with nothing, as would other regular *I.H.S.* contributors. There are no obituaries of even such stalwarts as Lyons

and Beckett, nor of such major scholars as Gwynn, Otway-Ruthven or Mansergh, all of whom offered opportunity for reflection about their impact on their field. For the obituaries of Lyons and Mansergh, it is to the assessments by Roy Foster and David Harkness in the *Proceedings of the British Academy* one has to turn, and for reference to Gwynn's 'learning, courtesy, and charm as a post-graduate Director' to Tomas Ó Fiaich's tribute in *Seanchas Ardmhacha* (**11**, 1983–4, ix–xi).

Useful bibliographical surveys were indeed published in *I.H.S.*, some of which included passages of deep thought, but they could not substitute for the historiographical perspective that the critique of the mind behind the word required. In this respect, the appraisals by Michael Drake of Kenneth Connell, Aidan Clarke of Dudley Edwards — Dudley's voice rings off the page — James Maguire of Desmond Williams, all in *I.H.S.*, as well as Liam Kennedy's of David Johnson in *Irish Economic and Social History*, mark major advances. Happily, appreciations did not always have to wait for obituaries. *Festschriften* contained appraisals, of admittedly widely varying scope and depth, not only of Moody and MacDonagh but of Quinn, Mansergh, Leslie McCracken, Paddy Corish, Dudley Edwards, Margaret MacCurtain, who has done so much to pioneer scholarly women's history, and historical geographers like T. Jones Hughes and John Andrews (Smyth and Whelan 1988; Aalen and Whelan 1992). Sadly, the Kenneth Connell *Festschrift*, like Todd's, had to be itself posthumous (Goldstrom and Clarkson 1988), Connell's untimely death at the age of fifty-six also leading to the unusual but correct decision of David Dickson and Peter Roebuck, the first editors of *Irish Economic and Social History*, to launch the new journal with Max Hartwell's notable obituary of him (Hartwell 1974).

And yet the Moody myth tells us as much about the profession as about Moody. If it be true that Moody's own surveys of Irish historiography are more in the nature of chronicle than critique, at least he provided or initiated regular surveys (Moody 1971, 1977). Other journals beginning with the *Irish Sword* in 1949 and subsequently including *Studia Hibernica* (1962–), *Éire-Ireland* (1966–), *Irish Economic and Social History* (1974–), *Études Irlandaises* (1976–), *Irish Studies in International Affairs* (1979–), *Saothar* (1980–), *The Irish Review* (1986–), *Eighteenth-Century Ireland/Iris an Dá Chultúr* (1986–), *Irish Studies Review* (1992–), *History Ireland* (1993–), *Bullán* (1997–), *New Hibernia Review* (1997–) and even the quite remarkable *Peritia* (1982–), have published occasional splendid surveys of individual topics, but not the regular overviews of *I.H.S.* vintage. Moody can hardly be blamed if, for many years, his was the only show constantly on the road.

It was a show that, at first, focussed heavily on the late medieval/early modern period. This made sense in that the initial research fields of Edwards, Hayes-McCoy and Quinn, as well as of Moody himself, clustered in this period, and a remarkable cluster it was, soon to be supplemented on the eighteenth century by Beckett, McDowell and Mc Cracken. It was also fairly common internationally. The convention that *I.H.S.* would publish nothing on the period after 1900 excluded contemporary history in principle until the 1950s when, in an editorial decision of glorious incongruity, it published two articles by Edwards' successor as joint editor, T. D. Williams, on the Anglo-Polish Agreement of 1939. So considerably has fashion shifted subsequently towards modern and contemporary history that Nicholas Canny can conclude his review of Ciaran Brady's *The Chief Governors: the rise and fall of reform government in Tudor Ireland 1536-1588* (1995) with the observation that 'his greatest contribution of all is to reveal just how understudied is the history of Ireland in the sixteenth century, what a wealth of sources remains to be examined' (*I.H.S.* **30**, Nov. 1996, 54).

Or at least *I.H.S.* was the only show, at national level, using mainly English-language sources, on the history of Ireland since the coming of the Normans. For a split quickly developed between early Irish history, where in many respects the most original developments of the previous generation, generally inspired by, if often challenging, the seminal work of Eoin MacNeill, had occurred, and the later period. How far this was the result of cultural, if not ideological, differences — even though MacNeill had encouraged the establishment of *I.H.S.* — and how far the largely unintended consequence of the establishment of the Dublin Institute of Advanced Studies, with its Celtic School, in 1940, would repay further inquiry. Whatever the reasons, the result, despite valuable contributions to early Irish history in the first issues of *I.H.S.*, was to create a chasm between the two. Only a handful of the references in, for instance, Donnchadh Ó Corráin's sparkling survey (1994) of the crucial issue of the early Irish laws (Bullán, **1**, 2), cite *I.H.S.*

This has unfortunate consequences for any attempt to see Irish history whole, and to discipline interpretation and imputation by subjecting it to the longest and widest possible range of evidence. Such central issues as the impact of the Normans cannot be adequately addressed on the assumption that 1169 constitutes some sort of year zero, at least until the assumption has been tested against evidence, as Michael Richter, has effectively argued (Richter 1984–5, 296–7), an approach pondered further by Art Cosgrove (1990) in a subtly argued meditation that also addresses contentious issues raised by Steven Ellis (1986). And the 'scientific' history of the impact of one culture on another can be written only by those familiar with the evidence pertaining to both cultures. Goddard Henry Orpen's pioneering enterprise

(1911), for all its research value, was vitiated from the perspective of culture contact by this one-eyed approach.

This constitutes a fundamental challenge — in many respects the fundamental challenge — for students of Irish history. The simplest, but very effective, technique, adopted by minds moulded on assumptions not only about the superiority of English culture over all things Irish, but on the belief that Irish culture was not only inferior, but so inferior as to be unworthy of historical inquiry, for dealing with the challenge of culture contact, was to apply a form of denial to the existence of the 'native' culture by simply ignoring it. This was a mind-set long widespread in Queen's, and it could also be found in Trinity. Even though Curtis had introduced Irish history onto the curriculum, it was still possible for students to graduate into the 1940s, as did F. S. L. Lyons, with scarcely any knowledge of the subject (Lyons 1980, 10).

There is nothing special about this. Similar attitudes can be found to such an extent in all cultures based on conquest that they may be deemed a psychological necessity for a particular type of mentality in those circumstances. Nor are they necessarily more emphatically avowed by English by birth than by English by adoption, again a world-wide experience against which the Irish example has to be assessed. English-born scholars in Northern Ireland, like Leslie Clarkson in Queen's and Peter Roebuck in the University of Ulster, as well as, further south, Hugh Kearney and Jack Watt in UCD, would bring refreshingly independent minds to bear constructively on Irish history, as would some of the historians of Ireland in Britain, not least the late Angus MacIntyre, although he himself had Irish roots — not that that provided any guarantee of fair-mindedness (Williams 1995).

Irrespective of the attitude of individual English historians, however, far and away the most important factor affecting the approach of Irish historians has been the influence of English culture in the widest sense, and of English ethnic images in particular. *I.H.S.* powerfully reinforced this orientation. It was not simply the modelling of virtually every aspect of *I.H.S.* on English examples, and especially on the periodical *History*, published at that time through the Institute of Historical Research where both Moody and Edwards studied. Most of these were sensible, and might even have occurred unaided. Nor was it simply the revelation of the assumption of Irish inferiority by Todd's eulogists, reverentially tracing the impact of this Oxford-trained, if Scottish-born, scholar on the awe-struck yokels of Belfast, their sectarian eyes suddenly opened to the eternal verities of 'scientific' history through the mouth of this Oxford oracle (Cronne *et al.* 1949, ix). Nor was it that the only guide to historiographical tendencies in any other country published in the early *I.H.S.* should have been on England (Butterfield 1944).

It was none of these things in themselves. Rather was it that the power relationship — no longer mainly the physical power, but the psychological, intellectual and cultural power relationship in the broadest sense between England and Ireland — was unique. Where historiography was concerned, this was no archipelago, with influence circulating rather than descending. Where intellectual relations are located in a specific power relationship, not only between stronger and weaker but between conqueror and conquered, the implications are quite different than when they exist at a purely scholarly level between equals. So much for the escapist vacuities of 'cultural relations'.

The innumerable ways, direct and indirect, in which English influence on Irish historiography exerted and exerts itself, remain to be fully reconstructed. The issue here is not one of right or wrong, good or bad. English historiography had enormous strengths — it was, and is, after all, one of the glories of the English mind — from which Irish historiography could profit. But it was itself naturally grounded in wider English world-views, which could often result in stereotype substituting for evidence on Irish matters, stereotypes which many Irish historians themselves either shared or internalized. This was not necessarily through uncritical acceptance, although that could occur. It was that even rejection of English attitudes towards the Irish often occurred within the modalities of thinking moulded by English influence, so that the debate remained anchored in terms of reference derived from English assumptions and stereotypes. What is striking is how little attention has been devoted to this entire question, which is absolutely central to proper understanding of the historiography as well as the history of Ireland.

It is in this area of assumptions that English influence remains most pervasive. The more unconscious it is, the more silently internalized, the more effectively it operates. How often do we exhort ourselves, for instance, to adopt a more comparative approach to Irish history? Greater familiarity with wider global history could, no doubt, usefully discipline generalizations based on Irish example alone. At a deeper level, however, one may wonder how many other national historiographies are so dominated by, indeed so saturated in, comparative perspective. Text after text by historians of Ireland is anchored in assumptions of Irish abnormalcy, or, to use a somewhat less pejorative term, Irish exceptionalism. But exceptional from what?

Time and again, it becomes clear that Irish conditions are 'special' or 'exceptional' by virtue of being different from English. They are 'special'. English conditions are not 'special'. They are normal. This is a very simple distinction at one level. But it is the single most influential, perhaps even the hegemonic, assumption in the way most Irish history since the coming of the Normans is written. It suffuses Irish historical writing in a way virtually unknown in the history of any western, or perhaps even eastern, European country. Indeed, it would be an interesting comparative inquiry to see whether there is any country on earth whose history is interpreted so pervasively in such terms. And yet the finest tribute that can be paid to its pervasiveness is that it has attracted only a fraction of the systematic attention devoted to far less central issues. What is truly 'exceptional' about Irish historiography is its failure adequately to address this aspect of its own exceptionalism. It is this too that, more than anything else, has prevented the immense potential of the Irish historical experience from being fully exploited for the construction of innovative rather than derivative conceptual frameworks.

Genuine comparison, on the basis of careful scholarly reflection, as distinct from the stereotypes of the street, can be enormously illuminating. And comparison with England, or with the experience of Britain more generally, can of course be instructive for the student of Irish history — but only when that comparison is itself located in its correct comparative context. When it is not, it can become a distorting mirror. It is precisely because of the failure of so much English historiography itself to think comparatively that a comparative approach to Irish history based on assumptions of English normalcy can be so misleading. One is tempted to wonder whether ever in the history of historical writing so many 'exceptions' have been based on comparison with one other case? It is not the lack of comparative perspective but the uncritical application of misleading comparison that is arguably the most pervasive, insidious and distorting of all the methodological inadequacies of Irish historiography.

English influence further worked its way into the psyche of Irish historians partly through close personal connections with English, or English-based, historians, including the recruiting of almost all external examiners in Irish history from England. These examiners, who are themselves usually Irish, have rendered sterling service to university examining as organized in Ireland, itself an imitation of the English examining system. The issue is not the quality of their service which, as far as my experience goes, has been outstanding, but the oddity involved, unusual if not unique in the western world, of a country drawing external examiners in its own history not only from abroad but from the former conqueror, and likely to be influenced, however unconsciously, by the silent assumptions of the profession in their own habitat. What is even more striking is that this does not, for the most part, make them much different from Irish historians in Ireland, who are generally steeped in the same silent assumptions.

All these factors conspired to place enormous

emphasis on satisfying an English image — a scholarly image, but a scholarly image which in turn was infused with popular stereotypes. In this respect, the role of scholars like Peter Alter, from outside the English sphere of influence, rooted in their own historiographical traditions, however familiar they may be with English assumptions, can be particularly salutary in stimulating a wider perspective (Alter 1989). So may the perspectives from scholars, Irish or other, associated with Centres for Irish Studies that have begun to flourish outside the orbit of English cultural power in the USA, in particular, which, in addition to the advantages of location in multi-cultural environments, attract a wide range of international scholars to discuss themes of potential relevance to Ireland but located in a world-wide discourse on topics like post-colonialism, subaltern studies and so forth, where discussion may be illuminated by a multiplicity of approaches and perspectives on the part of contributors unburdened by the various Irish and English emotional inheritances. The American Conference for Irish Studies has presided over a striking development of American interest in Irish history, if not without its own distinctive brands of emotional engagement (McCaffrey 1966–7).

The unthinking incorporation of English assumptions was surprising in some respects. True, Lyons unconsciously reveals his immersion in the observation that one had to go to England for graduate work — a sensible enough observation in purely pragmatic terms, but larded with assumptions about superiority and inferiority as well as wealth and poverty. But it was not as if all Irish historians were unfamiliar with other traditions. M. D. O'Sullivan studied in Marburg, as did Kevin Nowlan. Hogan studied in Paris, while J. F. O'Doherty took his doctorate in Munich. J. M. O'Sullivan, Professor of Modern History in UCD during 1909–48 and among the most interesting of all minds to apply itself to history in twentieth-century Ireland, but constantly diverted from sustained publication by his parliamentary career, had taken his doctorate in Heidelberg, duly published in Vaihinger's distinguished *Kant Studien* series. His successor, Desmond Williams, was deeply and widely read in German history, and would open doors for Michael Laffan and myself to research in Germany. From the 1970s, several graduates, including David Doyle, Nicholas Canny and Maurice Bric, headed for doctoral research towards the USA. The European University Institute in Florence has offered the possibility of new perspectives to Irish students, with Dermot Keogh the first student of any nationality to take a doctorate in history there in 1979. The ERASMUS programme of the European Union has offered opportunities for spending time in continental universities, while many clergy would continue to study in Louvain or Rome.

It was not, therefore, that Irish historians were unfamiliar with other historiographical traditions. But English cultural power was simply too strong for individuals to overcome. Desmond Williams launched *Historical Studies*, the proceedings of the bi-annual Conference of Historians, begun in 1954, whose prime purpose was to provide Irish historians with an opportunity of hearing foreign scholars, in non-Irish as well as Irish history. However, this actually reinforced English influence, for, despite valiant attempts to bring representatives of continental European traditions to Ireland, the bulk of the visitors were in fact English. Memorable though many of their contributions were, this was not quite what Williams had intended. Louis Cullen pioneered a valuable series of conferences involving Irish and French historians, as well as Irish and Scottish, which certainly helped alert the Irish participants to alternative perspectives, but have scarcely seeped into the more general mind-sets of historians.

The difficulty that minds steeped in the assumptions of English normalcy have in extricating themselves from this cultural inheritance can be glimpsed in the case of Seán Ó Faoláin. Few insisted more trenchantly than Ó Faoláin on the need for European perspective. Yet it was to England he turned, complaining that 'books like Trevelyan's *English social history* are unknown for Ireland'. What is striking is that for someone who so eloquently espoused 'European' comparison, his Europe turns out to be a mythical construct, designed for domestic polemic, rather than the Europe of historical 'reality', that favourite phrase of Ó Faoláin's, which he so rarely in reality applied to his imagined Europe, so strikingly anglocentric was his actual orientation, however imaginatively applied.

As with so much else in Irish historical writing, poverty must always be kept in mind. Even had more Irish historians, to say nothing of their students, mastered the languages, or in most cases even one language, of the major continental European historiographical traditions, Irish libraries could not have afforded substantial purchases in those languages. They found it impossible to buy anything like the full range of English-language books and periodicals, much less European publications. Only a limited range of English-language periodicals, to say nothing of those in other languages, are taken in even the best-endowed Irish universities to-day. The two main exceptions to this generalization are Celtic studies and much ecclesiastical history, sources for which were often more continental than English, and which involved far closer relations between Europe and Ireland. Whether this was a further factor in contributing to the divide between early and more recent history in Ireland requires further exploration.

The most obvious case of linguistic limitation, leading directly to the neglect of relevant original sources, is the poor knowledge of the Irish language among so many historians. F. J. Byrne would observe that it is 'with an irony surely unique' in the annals of scholarship that Irish historians apparently did not feel the need to tackle texts written in what was after all 'the language of their people throughout the greater part of recorded history' (Byrne 1968, 1). Many others, from MacNeill to Corkery to Curtis to Pender, made the same point. It made little impression on those steeped in assumptions about the inherent inferiority of all things Irish.

This bizarre neglect partly reflects deeply internalized assumptions in minds moulded by English images of the inferiority, and therefore of the irrelevance, or perhaps even the perniciousness, of anything involving the Irish language. This is not the place to probe the impulses, psychological even more than intellectual, underlying such perspectives. There is, of course, no more effective technique for promoting denial of a particular culture than to deny any value to the language, the essential carrier of culture. Even where a scholar like Constantia Maxwell was alert to the importance of Irish-language sources for social history, she did not, unlike Curtis, feel the need to learn the language herself. Instead, she complained that 'as for native sources, translations from the Irish are fairly numerous, but students of the language should provide the historian with more' (Maxwell 1949, 8). And this was long after Corkery's *The Hidden Ireland: a Study of Gaelic Munster in the Eighteenth Century* (1924) which, however contested subsequently, could only be contested by those capable of grappling with sources in Irish.

The enhancement of the possibilities of understanding the totality of Irish experience through the use of Irish-language material, apparent in the work of such scholars as Brendan Bradshaw, Neil Buttimer, Daniel Corkery, Tom Dunne, Steven Ellis, Seán Ó Coileáin, Donnchadh Ó Corráin, Louis Cullen, Kevin Whelan, Jim Lydon, Michelle O Riordan, Cormac Ó Gráda, Gearóid Ó Tuathaigh, Seán Ó Tuama, Liam de Paor, Nicholas Canny, Maureen Wall, John A. Murphy, Margaret MacCurtain, Gearóid Mac Niocaill, Tomás Ó Fiaich, Niall Ó Cíosáin and many more, has now surely been brought vividly home to even the most insular intelligence by Breandán Ó Buachalla's investigation of Gaelic Jacobite literature in *Aisling ghéar* (1996). Even after Ó Buachalla's magnificent achievement, it has been claimed that 'eighteenth century Gaelic literature has still many secrets to unfold to willing and able scholars' (Mac Craith 1998, 166). How many will be both willing and able remains to be seen. It may be hoped that women's history, which has made many illuminating recent contributions, may come to contribute significantly to the recovery of the history of the largely lost world of Irish-speaking women, for so long the majority of women in the country, asking here, as elsewhere, questions that can enrich genuine historical understanding.

The very fact that the mere knowledge of the language was for so long considered a statement of ideological loyalty rather than a simple scholarly requirement for the study of certain topics itself reflects the pervasiveness of English power assumptions. Knowledge of Irish, as of any other language, should be deemed, where the subject-matter requires it, an elementary criterion of scholarly qualification, not of ideological agenda. The issue in the use of Irish then becomes, as it ought to be in the use of all languages, fidelity to the evidence. The founding generation of *I.H.S.* showed, except for Edwards, scant appreciation of the possibility of using Irish-language source material, although this may have derived as much from the preoccupation with state policy, and therefore with official records, as the real stuff of 'scientific' history, as from dismissive cultural assumptions.

And yet, and yet. For all the criticisms that can be made of the *I.H.S.* school, and of Moody, its great strengths, and his, should never be lost from sight. It is doubtless true that he gave hostages to fortune with his unfortunate 'Irish history and Irish mythology' (1978), which, as Ciaran Brady delicately phrased it, 'was not greatly troubled by theoretical sophistication' (Brady 1994, 7), leaving him vulnerable to the type of assault launched by Seamus Deane (Deane 1997, 185–91). But for all the problems that confront the concept of historical evidence today, the rigorous use of evidence, however that may be defined, is central to the calling of historian. No evasion of that, under whatever banner, meta-historical, poetic, journalistic, novelistic, magic realistic, dramatic, memoirist, reincarnationist — or now Edmund Morris-type pre-incarnationist — can substitute for the historical study of the past. However important a quality imagination may be for the historian — and it marks one crucial difference between the chronicler and the historian — historians are not at liberty to imagine any old past they want. They have to satisfy the rules of evidence, however those rules may be cast and recast. That obliges a degree of self-restraint that historians can never fully achieve. But the closer historians can come to it, the better historians they will be. For all the limits of his imagination, Moody sensed that, and clove to it as closely as he could. However little *The Londonderry plantation* may now be cited even by specialists (Gillespie 1994, 111), however justified the strictures on his conceptualization of *A new history of Ireland*, it is not by repudiating the core scholarly values of the founder-generation of *I.H.S.*, but by refining their application, that the indispensable work of that generation can be soundly built on.

IMPACT

Moody cherished a deep belief in the potential of history for education for citizenship. Whatever criticisms may be made of the work rate of individual Irish historians —

and one of the conclusions of this survey is that no such criticisms should be levelled until the individual circumstances can be adequately reconstructed — the profession in general generated a substantial body of work, much of it of high quality, throughout the twentieth century. But what sort of impact has it had?

The *I.H.S.* school drew some of its inspiration from the conviction that they were telling the historical truth for the first time, rescuing the past from the charlatans and propagandists who had hitherto polluted it. Moody was instrumental in launching the Thomas Davis Lectures on Radio Éireann from 1954, and in promoting a lecture series, published as F. X. Martin and T. W. Moody (eds), *The course of Irish history*, which has been regularly reprinted since 1967. But views differ as to the influence exerted by the formal teaching of history in school. A Study Group on the Teaching of History in Irish Schools that included Margaret MacCurtain and Desmond Williams, and met ten times in 1966, shared an optimistic view of the potential influence of history, not only in the formation of 'mature and balanced citizens' but 'in giving a sense of unity to knowledge' in an age of the fragmentation of knowledge (Anon. 1967). David Fitzpatrick, on the other hand, concluded that it had virtually no influence (Fitzpatrick 1991, 182–3), while Gabriel Doherty detected a symbiotic relationship between the popular *Weltanschauung* and the school curriculum (Doherty 1996).

Despite this uncertainty, many historians will continue to hope that history has the potential, however rarely realized, to make some contribution. Whether it has or not, the observer at the beginning of the new millenium will note that it is being increasingly marginalized in the second-level curriculum, with little more than 20% of Leaving Certificate pupils now taking it, and that it was only the determined resistance of the profession, not least through the activity of teachers at second and third level, that prevented the then Minister for Education, Niamh Bhreathnach, from effectively eliminating it in the mid-1990s.

It seems possible, indeed probable, that more influence is exerted nowadays on popular perceptions by films — Neil Jordan's *Michael Collins* obviously springs to mind — TV documentaries, novels and newspapers, in the service of sundry causes, than by scholarly research. The systematic study of the influence of individual producers, writers or journalists has not yet begun. The scholarly assessment of these types of treatment of historical topics has itself begun to develop, however, with a growing sophistication emerging in the critical appraisal of the visual as a historical source for generations increasingly reared on cinema and television. The growing interest in issues of 'representation', and the associated 'literary' and 'visual' turns, for all the problems associated with them, offers one potentially fruitful way of deepening scholarly appreciation of these matters. (Bradshaw, Hadfield and Maley 1993; Gibbons 1997; Breathnach-Lynch 1997; Dodd 1999). If historians do not grapple with these issues, they may well find the rapid changes in recent Irish society creating a market for a more convenient past which media culture, or indeed more permissive academic cultures, appear eager to supply or even to create, unimpeded by inconvenient restraints imposed by scholarly values.

It was always likely that the conflict in Northern Ireland would spark reassessment of historical episodes. Once the Provisional IRA claimed legitimacy from the 1916 Rising, for instance, some of those who repudiated their campaign were likely to begin repudiating the Rising and its alleged legacy as well. Others seized the opportunity to give voice to latent instincts. The manner in which the reaction to Irish nationalism is working itself out has come to be called Revisionism.

It is through use of language that the assumptions underlying Revisionism most vividly reveal themselves. The classic case is the way the word 'nationalism' is habitually used by Revisionists. It invariably means 'Irish' nationalism. The possibility that English policy, or attitudes, or unionist ones, could in any way be described as 'nationalist' simply does not exist. A widespread English self-image, that 'nationalism' is a disease that afflicts others, and above all the Irish, but that it never infected the English, is absorbed uncritically into Revisionist discourse. In some cases, this may be a deliberate tactic by champions of nationalism — English or British, according to their taste — in its own right. Much of the time, it is more likely to be the unconscious derivative consequence of cultural power relations.

It is still too early to offer a final verdict on the impact of all this, though any discussion will have to build on Ó Tuathaigh's superb survey (1994, 306–26). One must, however, distinguish between Revisionism, with an upper-case R, and normal revisionism, of the lower-case type, that all vigorous national historiographies experience as a matter of course. *I.H.S.* itself represented this type of revisionism. But it did not invent it. Curtis had been a strong revisionist in many respects. So was Eoin MacNeill, who had been a relentless reviser in his day, in rejecting inherited assumptions, congenial to many Irish nationalists, about a centralized Gaelic state (Byrne 1973, 32). *I.H.S.* carried a section entitled 'Historical revisions' from the outset. But this in turn was modelled on a section of similar title in the English periodical *History*, which no-one understood as involving an ideological assault on the inherited English sense of national identity.

A new revisionism of this type began to be abroad in the 1960s, particularly with the growth in economic history which would lead to the launching of *Irish Economic and Social History* in 1974. R. D. C. Black's

Economic thought and the Irish question appeared in 1960, the challenging *Guinness's brewery in the Irish economy* by Patrick Lynch and John Vaizey in 1963, Raymond Crotty's iconoclastic assault on traditional assumptions, entitled *Irish agricultural production: its volume and structure*, in 1966, Austin Bourke's fundamental revisions of Famine historiography in several articles, while all the time Louis Cullen was building on his *Economica* article of as early as 1956, and his *Galvia* articles of 1957, to revise eighteenth-century economic history out of recognition, and to edit a revisionist Thomas Davis series in 1968. But this was normal revisionism, the scholars unimpeded by their political loyalties, their intellectual comradeship driven by shared commitment to methodological and theoretical innovation.

But this methodological revisionism came to be at least partly smothered by an ideologically driven Revisionism once the northern conflict erupted. For the timing of the northern 'Troubles' diverted energy from methodologically driven to ideologically inspired Revisionism, or from revisionism, lower case (RLC) to Revisionism, upper case (RUC) — or perhaps we should just call them scholarly Revisionism (SR) and ideological Revisionism (IR) (of course omitting stop after RUC).

No mental activity can be wholly impervious to ideological impulse. But there will nevertheless be a fundamental and irreconcilable difference between the use of evidence by those genuinely searching for truth by scholarly standards and those with eyes only for the ideologically correct conclusion. One should not exaggerate the purity of scholarly criteria even in the most austere days of *I.H.S.* The oft-trumpeted commitment of *I.H.S.* to 'scientific' history might have wilted before the changed circumstances. One need only compare the detached tone of Beckett's *Modern Ireland* of 1966 with the distinctly engaged tone of his *Anglo-Irish tradition* ten years later. In a manner reminiscent of Lecky, the perspectives of the 'liberal' founder generation of *I.H.S.* could change with changing circumstances, and the extent to which their 'liberalism' was a fair-weather ideology remains to be explored. Nevertheless, the emphasis on scholarly handling of source material still imposed certain restraints on the sustained misuse of evidence.

The irony is that ideological Revisionism imagined itself following in the footsteps of the founder-generation of *I.H.S.* through its 'scientific' use of evidence, whereas it in many cases marked a reversion rather than a progression. It was not only casualness in the use of evidence but also the tone of much Revisionism that was reminiscent of an earlier generation. How intelligent people could indulge such monumental self-delusion itself demands intense reflection.

It can only be hoped that ideological passions will not undermine the civilities that could subordinate ideological differences between, for instance, the Irish nationalist Curtis, the incarnation of Anglo-Irish ascendancy, Otway-Ruthven, and the later Irish nationalist Lydon, to a shared sense of participation in a common scholarly enterprise, reflected in the touching tribute from the unexpected quarter of the crustacean Otway-Ruthven, whose ability 'to conceal from casual observers, though never from those who know her well, the depth of her compassion', as F. S. L. Lyons coyly phrased it in his Foreword to her *Festschrift*, no less, had become legendary (xii). She concluded the Foreword to her own *History of medieval Ireland* (1968) with a tribute to a teacher twenty years in the clay: 'My primary debt is to my first teacher, the late Professor Edmund Curtis, to the honour of whose memory this book is dedicated. I have differed from him on many points, as my own pupils will no doubt differ from me: I should be well content if I could think that they would remember me with as much gratitude and affection as I do him'. In Jim Lydon, her successor, if not her pupil, she in turn would happily find a scholar of kindred spirit who, while indeed differing from her on many points, would in turn pay gracious tribute to her qualities (Lydon 1995, 12–13).

While many of the passions of the present are reminiscent of earlier conflicts, there is this difference. The battles then were largely conducted by non-academics, often snatching time from their day-jobs, with little time, training or opportunity either to conduct research or to ponder the meaning of historical truth. Latter-day academics have few such excuses. Has a century of scholarship, of developing history departments, journals, archives, research, made ultimately so little difference? Contrary to a naive earlier assumption of my own, formed in the days when one could be lulled by thirty years of *I.H.S.* taking politics out of history, into thinking of historical enquiry as a shared vocation among votaries of Clio, academic historians are not necessarily personalities of a different type from 'popular' ones, devoted to a search for truth. They may be simply more plausible propagandists, using the resources of scholarship to promote an ideological agenda, treating the past like a conquered colony, the men and women who lived there conscripted for causes they may have never known, and flung into battle with wanton disregard for their real convictions, all to buttress the ideological purposes of their puppet masters, and mistresses, of the present.

In the face of this mentality, plundering the past to find ammunition for the vendettas of the present, it is not only 'the deluded follower of Joanna Southcott' who has to be rescued, in the celebrated phrase of Edward Thompson, 'from the enormous condescension of posterity'. It is nothing less than the entire historical past, the very concept of historical understanding itself. To the extent that that is so, is it too pessimistic to wonder whether we are really much closer than we were a century ago, despite so much earnest scholarly endeavour, to rescuing the past from the pathetic parochialism of the present?

Bibliography

Aalen, F. H. A and Whelan, K. (eds) 1992 *Dublin, city and county: studies in honour of J. H. Andrews.* Dublin.

Akenson, D. H. 1988 *Small differences. Irish Catholics and Irish Protestants 1815–1922: an international perspective.* Kingston, Ontario.

Alter, P. 1989 *Nationalism.* London.

Andrews, K. R., Canny, N. P. and Hair, P. E. H. 1978 'Preface: David Beers Quinn' in *The westward enterprise* (Liverpool), pp. v–xi.

Anon. 1967 'The teaching of history in Irish schools' *Administration* 15, pp. 268–85.

Barnard, T. C. 1999 'British and Irish history' in G. Burgess (ed), *The new British history: founding a modern state 1603–1715* (London), pp. 201–37.

Beckett, J. C. 1972 'The study of Irish history' in *Confrontations: studies in Irish history* (London), pp. 11–25.

Bhreathnach-Lynch, S. 1997 'The Easter Rising 1916: constructing a cannon in art and artefacts,' *History Ireland* 5 (Spring), pp. 37–42.

Boyce, D. G. 1987 'Brahmins and carnivores: Irish history in Great Britain' *I.H.S.* 25 (May), pp. 225–35.

Bradshaw, B., Hadfield, A. and Maley, W. 1993 *Representing Ireland: literature and the origins of conflict, 1534–1660.* Cambridge.

Bradshaw, B. and Morrill, J. (eds) 1996 *The British problem, c. 1534–1707. State formation in the Atlantic archipelago.* London.

Brady, C. (ed) 1994 *Interpreting Irish history: the debate on historical revisionism 1938–1994.* Dublin.

Brown, J. 1981 'J. L. McCracken — an appreciation' in P. Roebuck (ed) *Plantation to partition: essays in Ulster history in honour of J. L. McCracken* (Belfast), pp. 1–13.

Butterfield, H. 1944–5 'Tendencies in historical study in England', *I.H.S.* 4, pp. 209–23.

Byrne, F. J. 1968 'Ireland before the Norman Invasion', *I.H.S.* 16 (March), pp. 1–14.

Byrne, F. J. 1973 'MacNeill the historian' in F. X. Martin and F. J. Byrne (eds) *The scholar revolutionary* (Shannon), pp. 15–37.

Canny, N. 1998 Interview in *History Ireland* 6 (Spring), pp. 52–55.

Canny, N. 1999 'Writing Atlantic history; or, reconfiguring the history of colonial British America', *Journal of American History* 86, 3, pp. 1093–1114.

Clarke, A. 1988–9 'Robert Dudley Edwards (1909–1988)',
I.H.S. 26, pp. 121–7.

Clarkson, L. A. 1999 'Closure of the Department of Economic and Social History at Queen's', *Economic and Social History of Ireland Newsletter* 10, pp. 1–3.

Comerford, R. V., Cullen, M., Hill, J. R. and Lennon, C. (eds) 1990 'Preface' in *Religion, conflict and coexistence in Ireland: essays presented to Monsignor Patrick J. Corish* (Dublin), pp. 1–5.

Connolly, S. J. (ed) 1999 *Kingdoms united? Great Britain and Ireland since 1500. Integration and diversity.* Dublin.

Corish, P. J. 1996 Interview in *History Ireland* 4 (Summer), pp. 17–20.

Cosgrove, A. 1990 'The writing of Irish medieval history' *I.H.S.* 27 (Nov.), pp. 97–111.

Cosgrove, A. and McCartney, D. (eds) 1979 *Studies in Irish history presented to R. D. Edwards.* Dublin.

Cronne, H. A., Moody, T. W. and Quinn, D. B. 1949 'Introduction' to *Essays in British and Irish history in honour of James Eadie Todd* (London), pp. ix–xv.

Cullen, L. 1994 Interview in *History Ireland* 2 (Spring), pp. 10–12.

Deane, S. 1997 *Strange country: modernity and nationhood in Irish writing since 1790.* Oxford.

Dodd, L. (ed) 1999 *Nationalisms. Visions and revisions.* Dublin.

Doherty, G. 1996 'National identity and the study of Irish history', *English Historical Review* 111 (April), pp. 324–49.

Drake, M. 1974 'Professor Kenneth Hugh Connell', *I.H.S.* 19 (March), pp. 83–5.

Dunne, T. 1989 'Memoir' in O'Brien 1989.

Dunne, T. 1990 'Oliver MacDonagh' in F. B. Smith (ed), *Ireland, England and Australia: essays in honour of Oliver MacDonagh* (Canberra and Cork), pp. 1–13.

Edwards, R. Dudley 1978 'An agenda for Irish history 1978–2018', *I.H.S.* 21 (March), pp. 3–19.

Edwards, R. Dudley and O'Dowd, M. 1985 *Sources for early modern Irish history, 1534–164.* Cambridge.

Ellis, S. G. 1986 'Nationalist historiography and the English and Gaelic worlds in the late Middle Ages', *I.H.S.* 26 (May), pp. 1–18.

Evans Estyn, E. 1996 'The Irishness of the Irish' in *Ireland and the Atlantic heritage* (Dublin), pp. 31–41.

Ferriter, D. 1998 'Oral archives in Ireland: a preliminary report', *Irish Economic and Social History* 25, pp. 91–5.

Fitzpatrick, D. 1991 'The futility of history: a failed experiment in Irish education' in C. Brady (ed) *Ideology and the historians* (Dublin), pp. 168–86.

Foster, R. 1997 'Angus Macintyre: historian of multiple identities' in L. Brockliss and D. Easterwood, *A union of multiple identities. The British Isles, c. 1750– ca. 1850* (Manchester), pp. xi–xviii.

Gibbons, L. 1997 'Framing history: Neil Jordan's *Michael*

Collins,' *History Ireland* **5** (Spring), pp. 47–51.

Gillespie, R. 1994 'Historical revisits. T. W. Moody, *The Londonderry plantation, 1609–41* (1939)', *I.H.S.* **29** (May), pp. 109–13.

Gleeson, D. F. 1941 'Sources for local history in the period 1200–1700', *Journal of the Cork Historical and Archaeological Society* **46**, pp. 123–9.

Goldstrom, J. L. and Clarkson, L. A. (eds) 1981 *Irish population, economy and society: essays in honour of the late K. H. Connell*. Oxford.

Harkness, D. 1976 *History and the Irish: inaugural lecture*. Belfast.

Harkness, D. W. 1999 'Ireland' in R. W. Winks (ed) *The Oxford history of the British Empire* **5** (Oxford), pp. 114-33.

Hayton, D. W. and OíBrien, G. 1986 'Introduction. The historical writings of J. G. Simms (1904–79)' in Hayton and O'Brien (eds) J. G. Simms, *War and politics in Ireland 1649–1730* (London), pp. ix-xiv.

Hartwell, R. M. 1974 'Kenneth H. Connell: an appreciation', *Irish Economic and Social History* **1**, pp. 7–13.

Kaplan, S. L. 1995 *Farewell, revolution: the historians' feud. France, 1789–1989*. Ithaca and London.

Kennedy, L. 1998 'Ireland in the light of the West Country: David S. Johnson (1943–98)', *Irish Economic and Social History* **25**, pp. vii–xii.

Lee, J. 1968 'Some aspects of modern Irish historiography' in Ernst Schulin (ed) *Gedenkschrift Martin Gohring: Studien zur Europaischen Geschichte* (Wiesbaden), pp. 431–43.

Lydon, J. 1995 Interview in *History Ireland* (Spring).

Lydon, J. F. 1999 'Historical revisit: Edmund Curtis, *A history of medieval Ireland* (1923, 1938)', *Irish Historical Studies* **31** (November), pp. 535-48.

Lyons, F. S. L. 1980 'T. W. M.' in F. S. L. Lyons and R. A. J. Hawkins (eds) *Ireland under the Union: varieties of tension* (Oxford).

Mac Craith, M. 1998 Review article of Breandán Ó Buachalla, *Aisling ghéar, Eighteenth-Century Ireland* **13**, pp. 166–71.

Macken, M. 1942 'In memoriam: Mary T. Hayden', *Studies* **31**, pp. 369–71.

MacNeill, E. 1921 *Celtic Ireland*, ed. D. Ó Corráin (1981). Dublin.

Marnane, D. G. 1997 'Writing the past: Tipperary history and historians', *Tipperary Historical Journal*, pp. 1–41.

Martin, F. X., 1984 'T. W. Moody', *Hermathena* (Summer), pp. 5–7.

Maxwell, C. 1949 *Country and town in Ireland under the Georges*. Dundalk.

McCaffrey, L. J. 1966-7 'The American Conference for Irish Studies', *I.H.S.* **15**, pp. 446–9.

McCaffrey, L. J. 1997 *The Irish Catholic diaspora in America*. Washington, D.C.

McDowell, R. B. 1993 Interview in *History Ireland* **1** (Winter), pp. 9–12.

McGuire, J. 1988–9 'T. Desmond Williams', *I.H.S.* **26**, pp. 3–7.

Moody, T. W. 1942–3 'The writings of Edmund Curtis', *I.H.S.* **3**, pp. 393–400.

Moody, T. W. (ed) 1971 *Irish historiography 1936–1970*. Dublin.

Moody, T. W. 1977 'The first 40 years', *I.H.S.* **20**, pp. 377–83.

Moody, T. W. 1978 'Irish history and Irish mythology', *Hermathena*, reprinted in Brady 1994, pp. 71–86.

O'Brien, G. (ed) 1989 *Catholic Ireland in the eighteenth century: collected essays of Maureen Wall*. Dublin.

Ó Corrain, D. 1994 'Early Ireland: directions and re-directions', *Bullán* **1** (Autumn), pp. 1–15.

O'Dowd, M. 1997 'From Morgan to MacCurtain; women historians in Ireland from the 1790s to the 1990s' in Valiulis and O'Dowd 1997, pp. 38–58.

O'Grady, J. P. 1998 'Irish archives in 1997 in the Republic of Ireland', *New Hibernia Review* **2**, 3 (Autumn), pp. 138–46.

Ohlmayer, J. 1999 'Seventeenth-century Ireland and the new British and Atlantic histories', *American Historical Review* (April), pp. 446–62.

Orpen, J. H. 1911 *Ireland under the Normans*. Oxford.

O'Sullivan, M. 1942 *Old Galway: the history of a Norman colony in Ireland*. Cambridge.

Ó Tuathaigh, G. 1994 'Irish historical revisionism: state of the art or ideological project?' in Brady 1994, pp. 306–26.

Pender, S. 1941 'How to study local history', *Cork Historical and Archaeological Society* **46**, pp. 110–22.

Richter, M. 1984–5 'The interpretation of medieval Irish history' *I.H.S.* **24**, pp. 289–98.

Smyth, W. J. and Whelan, K. (eds) 1988 *Common ground: essays on the historical geography of Ireland, presented to T. Jones Hughes* (Cork), pp. xiii–xvi.

Stewart, A. T. Q. 1993 Interview in *History Ireland* (Summer), pp. 56–8.

Valiulis, M. G. and O'Dowd, M. (eds) 1997 *Women and Irish history: essays in honour of Margaret MacCurtain*. Dublin.

Williams, P. 1995 'A. Macintyre (1935–94)', *English Historical Review* **110** (Sept.), pp. 829–31.

Historical/Cultural Geography

WILLIAM NOLAN

This chapter is concerned with the academic discipline of geography and in particular the sub-fields of historical/cultural geography which may be regarded as the areas which relate most to heritage studies. Probable genealogies for geography in Ireland are postulated and its incorporation into university curricula is discussed. Particular emphasis is placed on those regarded as the founders of geography as practised in third-level institutions in the 1900s, with some reference to their publications and research agenda. The paper also provides a brief account of certain ongoing research projects which are heritage-related. It concludes with a description of the role of local and national societies in the promotion of the subject.

Definitions of geography are becoming increasingly inadequate to incorporate rampant specialization within it. Geography locates and analyses the form and structure of bounded places; it connects places to processes and systems, spanning the natural and social sciences and the humanities. Such eclecticism can be a double-edged sword, fragmenting both the traditional core areas of the discipline and the 'political' power of geography brokers within universities. But geography's heterogeneity can also resuscitate the metaphor of the subject as bridge linking science and art. Irish geography in its formal academic dress is a creature of the twentieth century. Founding personnel came from the island of Britain and established departments according to the model with which they were familiar. Historical geography as taught in this country was coloured by the considerable influences of the French *Annales* school whose trademark was the regional monograph. Such detailed syntheses of man and land relationships were more appropriate to pre-industrial societies and foundered on the placelessness of urbanism. In some respects geography, like its collateral subjects, is overpowered by the density of detail which has made the global village a very complex place.

GEOGRAPHY'S PRECURSORS AND THEIR SOURCES

The best introduction to the theory and practice of Irish geography is the jubilee volume of the journal *Irish Geography* which was published by the Geographical Society of Ireland on the occasion of the fiftieth anniversary of its foundation in 1984 (Davies 1984). Its fifteen chapters, written by practitioners who focus on their respective sub-fields, though only sixteen years old, require updating and enlargement to take account of the scientific and intellectual changes in the subject since then. But is there an Irish geography or is there geography in Ireland in the same way as one can refer to Irish music or Irish Catholicism? What or who were geography's antecedents? Is it either necessary or worthwhile to rake over the ashes of history to make these connections? At an earlier stage *Irish Geography* in the 1970s thought it was, and began a series on 'the making of Irish geography' (Davies 1976). It was a short-lived exercise and petered out after presenting three founding fathers, William Petty, G. A. J. Cole and Sir Patrick Geddes, and one sponsoring institution, The Physico-Historical Society. Petty was, in J. H. Andrews' words, a 'youthful university professor, headline making anatomist, co-founder of the Royal Society, respected member of parliament to say nothing of pioneer economist and statistician', but 'in Ireland none of these achievements cuts any ice: Petty is famous only as director and beneficiary of the unprecedentedly extensive land survey that followed the Cromwellian confiscations' (Andrews 1997). Cole, professor of geology at the Royal College of Science and part-time director of the Geological Survey, was Ireland's first professional geographer and authored two significant texts, *Ireland: land and landscape* (1915) and *Ireland the outpost* (1919). Cole wished geography to proceed beyond the purely descriptive to become a challenging analytical discipline concerned with the interrelations of spatial phenomena. Reacting against the excluvisist cultural agenda in Gaelic League and Sinn Féin nationalist philosophies, he contested their claims for a pure Irish national stock in *Ireland the outpost* (Buttimer 1995).

Geography's precursors are invariably seen as coming from outside, as in the case of Petty and Geddes, or as belonging to the Protestant Irish nation such as Cole and the Physico-Historical Society did. It is apparent that the shape of geography as well as the shape of Ireland and much of its internal contents were delineated by Petty and his assistants in the seventeenth century. But there is always the lingering doubt that our knowledge, confined as it is to English-language sources, is limited and inadequate. However, geography does not carry this burden alone. On Thursday 14 May 1903 the German philologist Kuno Meyer delivered a lecture in the Rotunda, Dublin, on 'The necessity for establishing a school of Irish literature, philology, and history', in the course of which he proclaimed that 'without a knowledge of the Irish language in all its stages — Old Irish, Middle Irish, Modern Irish — no real advance in the knowledge of the various subjects mentioned above [history, philology, literature, archaeology] is possible, because the source, the documents are written in Irish' (Ó Lúing 1991). Geographers have not been unaware of the challenge posed by Meyer's words and such an injunction is particularly relevant in the context of historical geography. Estyn Evans, in the foreword to his influential *Irish heritage*, to be considered later, noted that

the vast field of Gaelic literature and legendary history remains almost unexplored as a source for the critical study of ancient geography, of economic and social history, in the light of present-day knowledge.

To demand, however, that a historical geographer working in Ireland should conform to Meyer's pronouncement is hardly realistic, but if geographers are to maintain parity of treatment it is as important when dealing with the seventeenth century, for example, to read the writings of Seathrún Céitinn as well as those of Petty. Céitinn, a priest on the run in the Glen of Aherlow in the 1620s, gathered the fragments of history for his *Foras feasa ar Éirinn* so that his people would have a memory. Some fifty years later Petty was mapping, counting and valuing Ireland; the future was for him more important than the past. We might say that Petty's geography bested Céitinn's genealogy. Petty's *Down* and *Civil Surveys* are exemplary sources for the historical geographer but are also very much instruments of colonization.

In the late seventeenth century and throughout the eighteenth various learned societies were formed to explore Ireland's internal geography. J. H. Andrews has elaborated on the Molyneaux surveys of 1683–1700 (Andrews 1976). As we have seen, the Physico-Historical

Society founded in 1744 to promote 'an enquiry into the ancient and present state of the several counties of Ireland', was recognized by a recent authority as one of the makers of Irish geography (Davies 1979). Significantly its surveys were motivated by the perceived necessity to correct misapprehensions concerning Irish society then prevalent in England. The volume on Waterford published in the Physico-Historical Society's series in 1746 was described by its author, Charles Smith, as a 'natural, civil, ecclesiastical, historical and topographical description thereof'. In the early years of the nineteenth century the Royal Dublin Society sponsored the county-based Statistical Surveys which were generally complemented by a mapping programme subsidized by the Grand Juries. These invaluable sources carry the hallmarks of geography: bounded places, detailed analysis and inventorization of both physical and human landscapes as well as the use of cartography.

Ireland's heritage was sundered by the Famine, but as the green potato stalks burned in the fields one of the most comprehensive cartographical/topographical inventories ever undertaken was under way. Enumerators, surveyors and valuators had traversed the country in the 1830s and in their wake came the great scholars John O'Donovan, Eugene O'Curry and George Petrie, who transferred to Thomas Larcom at headquarters in Dublin the rich paper harvest of the Ordnance Survey. By unlocking some of the secrets in the Gaelic manuscripts of the Four Masters and others, O'Donovan and O'Curry encouraged scholarship by George Petrie, James Hawthorn Todd and George Reeves in archaeology, history and literature (Kenney 1929). The quickening of interest in Ireland, its resources, people and landscapes, was intensified by the work of the Young Ireland movement in the early 1840s, inspired initially by Thomas Davis (Molony 1995). With the foundation of *The Nation* newspaper, its Library of Ireland publication series and the issuing of popular ballad collections, Davis and his collaborators captured their spirit of Ireland. Both the Young Irelanders and the Repealers of Conciliation Hall provided alternative data banks to the those of official government records. Each week at Conciliation Hall the death census of the Famine was collated from returns of parish priests. Written at the same time, Robert Kane's *Industrial resources of Ireland* can be regarded as the first comprehensive geography of Ireland's minerals.

In the second half of the nineteenth century land became the primary political agenda in Ireland. Revolutionary legislation fashioned a new countryside and massive data banks were assembled to facilitate the transfer from landlords to tenants. Perhaps the most geographical of all the documentation produced at this time are the Baseline Surveys of the Congested Districts Board, drawn up in the 1890s. Based on answers to a detailed questionnaire from central office in Dublin, the replies, from experienced fieldworkers who were the Board's inspectors, have not been surpassed, either qualitatively or quantitatively.

Geography in Ireland was now very much an auxiliary for both history and geology and a foundation for workers in the British Empire. But as the political agenda quickened in this country and Europe, new dimensions intruded to upset the tidy lists of commodity geography. Nationalist scholars, who in many instances were Catholic clergy, focussed on the pre-conquest landscape of Ireland as their foundation-stone for a new country. There is a curious similarity between the succession lists of priests assembled by many clerical authors and Burke's pedigrees which buttressed the landed gentry. The priests brooked no opposition and even looked beyond geographies:

'There is a knowledge', wrote the bishop of Derry in 1903, 'of greater importance than that which facts of history and scientific knowledge can impart. They seem to lose sight of the truth that man is not a mere animal, but he possesses an immortal soul, the salvation of which is the supreme good.'

Many diocesan studies, however, such as Carrigan's four-volume history of Ossory (1905–81), were benchmarks in the evolution of historical geography in Ireland. Apart from the diocesan historians there were others turning attention to the shape and substance of the island. Government commissions such as that on congestion in 1906 and the *Memoir on the coalfields of Ireland* published in 1921 carried forward into the new century the practice of state-sponsored data collection for pragmatic purposes.

TWENTIETH-CENTURY DEVELOPMENTS
There are only two histories of geography departments published to date — these are of Queen's University, Belfast (QUB) (Campbell 1978) and Trinity College, Dublin (TCD) (Davies 1986) — so that analyses of the development and content of the discipline have been largely based either on the 'gatekeepers' or on specialist investigations of the sub-fields of geography. A number of geographers have been given the special accolade of *Festschriften*; Estyn Evans has four dedicated to him, with Desmond McCourt, Tom Jones Hughes and J. H. Andrews having one each. T. W. Freeman deserved one but his teaching career did not end in Ireland. This section considers the life's work of some of the more influential of these guiding figures.

Academic geography entered the stage in Ireland in the person of Estyn Evans who was appointed to teach geography at QUB in 1928 at the age of 23 (Evans 1996). He was to suffer the fate of many pioneers — revered by his immediate followers but subjected to critical scrutiny

in later years both for the perceived absence of intellectual rigour in his work (Graham 1994) and his politicisation of the discipline (Stout 1996). But whatever the criticisms, his significance in the shaping of geography in Ireland and particularly in Northern Ireland cannot be discounted. Evans came to partitioned Ireland; through H. J. Fleure, his professor at Aberystwyth, he had been introduced to the divided country by Thomas Jones, adviser to the British Prime Minister, Lloyd George, during the Treaty negotiations and afterwards a key figure in the proceedings of the Boundary Commission in the mid-1920s.

Evans arrived in Belfast in 1928. In 1924 Daniel Corkery had published *The Hidden Ireland: a Study of Gaelic Munster in the Eighteenth Century*, to be followed in 1931 by his *Synge and Anglo-Irish Literature*. Corkery was asking who the Irish nation is and who is best qualified to write its life. He seemed to be saying that Ireland's secrets lay not in its cities nor landlord mansions nor in the wide plains of the east and south, but in the hard mountain lands facing Atlantic edges, the back places. Corkery also pronounced that the expatriate writers, as he termed Synge, Yeats and the historian Lecky, were either unable or unwilling to empathize with elements outside their own cultural consciousness. Therefore their work was exclusivist, unsatisfactory and ultimately offering a colonial perspective. The Kilkenny novelist and founder, with T. W. Moody, of the influential Thomas Davis series of Radio Éireann lectures, Francis MacManus, agreed that Corkery had grasped the fundamental problem of Irish history and by extension Irish geography: 'that relationship between the native tradition and people and the results of invasion.' He was critical, however, of Corkery's use of the word 'expatriate', noting that in the context of Yeats and others 'there was no expatriation of the heart, Ireland was fastened to these writers like flesh to the bone'. Paradoxically the expatriates had also made the pilgrimage to the back places: there they were joined by young writers such as Austin Clarke whose first major work was *The Vengeance of Fionn* published in 1917. Evans' preoccupation with the remote past and the Atlantic ends had, therefore, intellectual contexts. People were then engaged in retrieval exercises. The folklorist J. H. Delargy reconnoitered Ireland, particularly the Gaeltachtaí, through his cadre of schoolteachers in a mission which can be compared in its magnitude, though not its spatial coverage, to the Ordnance Survey work of the 1840s. Archaeologists and anthropologists from Harvard University excavated *crannóga* and went to the remote fastness of county Clare to find Ireland and measure crania (Arensberg and Kimball 1940).

So it was with Evans. Writing later about his early career and the fieldwork he initiated he remembered that we usually chose an area on the west coast, where the relics of many layers of history and pre-history were visible in the cultural landscape and where the soft climate and the easy pace of peasant life relieved the nerves. (Evans 1978)

Ireland for Evans illustrated 'the marginal survival of archaic elements of the Indo-European World' (Evans 1957). He was not alone in believing this. Listen again to Kuno Meyer, the German Celticist:

Ireland is in the fortunate position of having retained her dialects, while in other countries like England, they are now rapidly disappearing before a colourless and artificially polite standard, on the one hand, and the vulgar and debased speech of the great cities on the other. (Ó Lúing 1991)

For the outsider Ireland was a pure place, the scrutiny of which could reveal elements lost elsewhere to urbanization and the industrial world. Insiders like Pádraig Puirséal, historian of the Gaelic Athletic Association, had a rather different perspective. Comparing Ireland of the 1930s not to Europe but to the Ireland of the 1920s, he feared the tide of change and its impact on Mooncoin, county Kilkenny, and its dance:

The last Mooncoin dancer! Too soon, I fear, will it be danced and too soon will the last Mooncoin hurler hang up for ever his crooked stick of ash. But when the last of the old breed is carried in his oaken coffin to sleep with his forefathers in Mooncoin or Kilnaspic or Carrigeen, on that day you can bid farewell to the Suirside, as long ago Kickham bade farewell to Knocknagow. When that day comes Mooncoin will be Mooncoin in name only, differing in no other way from Little-Puddleton-under-the-Petrol-Pump, or Horner's Corner, Nebraska, or Sudbury Creek, New South Wales. The blight of civilisation will have done its work.

The insider, because he had a measure of change, grasped at the dynamic in Irish geography more so than those who saw Ireland as a place of stasis in contrast to their home societies. Yeats, for example, had portrayed the people of the east-Galway plains as 'a community bound together by imaginative possessions, by stories and poems'. But for Seamus O'Kelly, writing from Athenry, his native place told a different story: 'a barren land, a people scattered,' 'sagging thatched roofs and thick streaks of sodden rain downstripping its uneven mud walls'. For Yeats, looking from Thoor Ballylee, the Galway plains signalled community, consensual politics and unity of culture; for O'Kelly this lonesome empty world created by grazier landlords was a contested space full of bitterness.

Evans characterized the past in Ireland as a place being constantly replenished by immigrations, but in the following passage he suggested that there is an uncom-

fortable dichotomy between dynamism and stasis:

For many years I have studied archaeological and ethnographic evidence for the early diffusion and secular persistence of a cultural pattern which had its origins in pre-Celtic antiquity and which proved capable of absorbing and assimilating new elements brought in by successive intrusions, whether Celtic warrior, Christian missionaries or Anglo-Norman knights. (Evans 1978)

Although Evans published widely in geography and related disciplines, his paper in *Geography* in 1939 struck the deepest resonances among contemporaries and geographers since then. In it he claimed that a field and settlement complex he observed at Beltany townland in north-west Donegal was the key to Irish settlement history. This 'archaic survival' was characterized by open-field agriculture, nucleated settlement and communal land tenure. Individual strips of infield land of varying qualities were periodically allocated, and temporary cultivation of adjacent outfield wasteland supplemented arable production. Seasonal transhumance to upland boolies complemented subsistence tillage. This self-regulating complex had compelling attractions. Evans regarded it as the quintessential embodiment of man-land relationships in this *cul de sac*, a term which geographers such as Evans and Jones Hughes used as the equivalent of Corkery's back places. Allied to this material complex was the persistence of what Evans termed the 'elder faiths' which predated Christianity and governed behavioural patters as much as the dictat of the local Catholic priest. Fortuitously there was a Neolithic settlement site in the same townland. Evans proposed to call this complex a *clachan*. The term persisted and colleagues of Evans, like McCourt (who carried out a splendid countrywide survey of *clachans* and their associated rundale) and Buchanan extended the spatial range of the study. Kevin Danaher was wary of claiming national patterns on the basis of a specific regional distribution. He also criticised Evans' use of the term *clachan*, which in Gaelic means a 'thing of stone', and his uncritical application of the designation to refer to all nucleated settlement below the category of census town. J. H. Andrews found little to support Evans' model of settlement continuity from his analysis of cartographic evidence, while Kevin Whelan has recently dismissed his perception of the west as incompatible with the evidence and the recent date of *clachan* settlement there.

Evans has an impressive publications portfolio to his credit. In the foreword to his first major book, *Irish heritage: the landscape, the people and their work*, issued in 1942, he acknowledged his debt to his own students, the Swedish school of ethnology, the Harvard University mission to Ireland, Edward McLysaght's *Irish life in the seventeenth century* and the work of the historian Constantia Maxwell. Revised and re-published as *Irish folk ways* in 1957, he restated his credo 'that the crafts of arable farming, of animal husbandry and the home industries have done more to shape our instincts and thoughts than the trampling of armies or the wrangling of kings which fill the documents from which history is written'. *Mourne country* (1951) was the epitome of Evans' regional writing and is probably the finest regional monograph produced in Ireland in the last century. The book, beautifully written in elegant prose and full of wonderfully-evocative illustrations, demonstrates clearly that expatriates could possess Irish places. Apart from his archaeological output and measured contributions to a variety of local and regional studies, Evans' last major work, *The personality of Ireland*, first published in 1972 and reprinted in a revised edition in 1981, was his clarion call for the trilogy of habitat, heritage and history as the true interpreters of the Irish landscape. This book, however, was marred by massive generalizations which did him no justice. Evans' *Ireland and the Atlantic heritage: selected writings*, published posthumously in 1996, provides significant biographical contexts for his life's work.

Evans' participation in community and national affairs epitomizes the geographer as servant of the state comparable to Yeats' public man advising and counselling. He served on many committees concerned with urban and rural matters in the post-Second World War rebuilding phase. With the archaeologist Oliver Davies he revived the *Ulster Journal of Archaeology* in a third series which has continued since 1938. In 1958 he founded *Ulster Folklife* with R. H. Buchanan as first editor. Always pushing for a national/regional museum in Northern Ireland which would give Ulster people a common interest, he was instrumental in establishing the Ulster Folk Museum which in 1976 became the Ulster Folk and Transport Museum at Cultra, county Down. Evans had long promulgated the necessity for an Institute of Irish Studies and at one stage had proposed a School of Local Studies. The Institute became a reality in 1965 with Evans being appointed as its first full-time director in 1968.

Stout has claimed that Evans' archaeology and geography were motivated by a commitment to maintaining the Northern Ireland political entity, and that he used archaeological and geographical distributions to provide an origin in prehistory for a twentieth-century creation (Stout 1996). In his critique of Evans' work he maintained that the latter was particularly influenced by the decision of the Irish Free State government to remain neutral during the Second World War. Stout argues that his lack of objectivity, evident in references to Catholic nationalists in his *Personality of Ireland*, was a product of his distaste for the political violence in Northern Ireland which caused him great pain in the later years of his life. Certainly Evans became embroiled in controversies over the origin and distribution of archaeological artefacts such as horned cairns, going so far as to assert that the UCD archaeologist Ruaidhrí de Valera (son of Taoiseach Éamon de Valera) opted for a Mayo landing for their builders to compensate for the failure of invasion by the French at Killala in 1798. Whereas Stout has pointed to Evans' alleged unionist sympathies, Graham, writing from a Northern Ireland perspective, apart from being critical of Evans' lack of theory, his non-interest in urban places and his overall generalist approach — maintained that Evans and Tom Jones Hughes had been 'careless and insular in accepting particular nationalist posturing' (Graham 1994). He proposes that the historical geography they promulgated was 'derived from the Gaelic historiography developed in the nineteenth century to underpin the demand for Home Rule and eventual independence from England'.

In the context of geography and what has since become known as local studies, Evans and his fellow geographers at TCD and UCD brought a fresh perspective. Not distracted by the imperative of religion or pietas to ancestral places, they could set their own agenda, subject only to the restrictive practices of university administrators and bursars. Geographers, Evans' students, became key figures in Northern Ireland's intellectual landscape. John M. Mogey, whose early research was a field survey of human physical types in county Antrim, some of which he linked to Mesolithic people, published the pathbreaking though now neglected *Rural life in Northern Ireland* in 1947. This work had begun as a thesis in Evans' department. George Thompson, who completed a thesis on 'The distribution and forms of primitive types of farm transport in Northern Ireland', was the first director of the Ulster Folk and Transport Museum in 1977. Alan McCutcheon who became director of the Ulster Museum also in that year had worked on the collieries of county Tyrone for his postgraduate degree. Northern geographers centred on QUB, but including practitioners such as Desmond McCourt of Magee in Derry and subsequently the New University of Ulster at Coleraine, gave geography a public identity through collaborative publishing ventures with local authorities and tourism interests which did much to popularize the subject.

Tom Jones Hughes (Smyth and Whelan 1988), like Patrick Kavanagh, made the local universal. His academic training was at Aberystwyth but he came from farming folk, whereas Evans' origins were in a coal-mining community. Jones Hughes was appointed to UCD in 1950; the year 1960 was the foundation date of the chair of geography. The Catholic Church authorities who maintained a strict watch and apparently a veto over appointments in subjects regarded as sensitive, such as history, obviously found geography a less threatening discipline. They most certainly would not have countenanced the appointment of a Welsh non-conformist such as Jones Hughes to history. As Evans had done in Belfast, Tom Jones Hughes began constructing a geography department while at the same time getting to know Ireland. It was perhaps vital that geography in UCD was not taught in the prescriptive manner common in the secondary school curriculum, and it was also vital that the teacher was able to empathize with his students. Every pupil knew where the fishbones were on the map of Ireland and could rattle off the names of principal towns, islands and manufactures, but were unable to connect things. Coming from outside, Jones Hughes gave his students both a context and comparative knowledge. He was not as prolific a writer as Estyn Evans but was much more focussed, both in spatial and temporal senses. His work ranged from spatially circumscribed local studies, such as those of the distinctive micro-regions of Cooley, county Louth, and the Mullet, county Mayo, to larger regions such as east Leinster and individual administrative counties like Tipperary and Wexford. His measures of significance in an all-Ireland context were the distribution of place-name elements *baile* and town, medieval parish centres, farmers who held land above £100 in valuation and the variable scales and landscape features of the estate system of landownership. Thematically and historically open-ended, he eschewed the clutter of artefact and archaeological distributions which Evans considered as essential prerequisites of regional differentiation. Overall his geography as written and taught enabled his students to see their places from a distance. The shaping of Jones Hughes' Ireland was more influenced by the seventeenth-century land settlement than the distribution of megalithic tombs. Landlords rather than lazy beds were the diagnostic criteria through which he defined variations in settlement and society and regions. In a geography crowded with people he skilfully populated Ireland in a way reminiscent of Jack Butler Yeats' paintings. His cast told the story of Ireland: the east Roscommon landlords who had built up seemingly impregnable fortresses, the great graziers of Meath, the herdsmen and their dogs who lived out their lives in lonely plains, the hill communities driven to the limits by forced migration or the search for sustainability, the squatter on town commonages, the large farmer snug and secure in his fine house which one could pick out from a distribution map of medieval church sites. Towns to Jones Hughes were cultural and political statements. Their morphologies were patterned, not given. A colonial system superimposed on Ireland in the seventeenth century was everywhere obvious in arrangements concerning the ownership and distribution of land: townlands and estate cores had obliterated earlier traces.

Jones Hughes preached the significance of the documentary record which Estyn Evans generally, but not always, eschewed. For him the Primary Valuation of Tenements was the key locator of geographical truths which were as evident in 1960 as a century earlier. Significantly, in view of their importance in shaping curricula in other disciplines, his research focussed on the documents of enumerator, surveyor and valuator produced in the 1840–50 decade to facilitate taxation of the propertied for the relief of the poor. These documents — unknown to his students after some ten years immersion in primary and secondary schools — were given a new vitality in a series of key articles. In the records commonly known as the Griffith Valuation in deference to the polymath Richard Griffith (Davies and Mollan 1980), the names of owner and occupier of all tenements in town and country were written down for the first time and arranged by townland in the open countryside and by street in towns and villages. Irish society was revealed in all its manifest inequalities; landlord, strong farmer, tenant farmer, cottier, squatter, parson, priest, magistrate, miner were placed side by side. Jones Hughes could now surmise that Evans' *clachans* in the far west were not all symptomatic of continuity from prehistory but were more likely to be recent creations of refugees. Their seductive vernacular harmony had hidden both their age and the vulnerability that the Famine exposed. Jones Hughes' students were supposedly to ply the trade of the master craftsman but added significantly to the range of his documentation and spatial coverage.

T. W. Freeman, appointed from Manchester to TCD in 1936, epitomized the geographer as surveyor, analyst of statistical data and director of field studies. He made the censuses of population his Irish heritage — first tackling the census of 1841 to produce the valuable though now neglected *Pre-Famine Ireland* in 1957. Relying on cold figures, he revealed the many hidden Irelands of the nineteenth century with more precision than Corkery had, and in his coherent analysis read Ireland as a series of interlocking but distinctive physical entities. In 1950 his *Ireland: its physical, historical, social and economic geography* was published. Freeman's geography has a modern ring — religion, emigration, agriculture, employment, creameries were all part of his agenda. His regional text went through a number of editions and though now outdated has not been bettered. In his review of the latter book C. S. O'Connell, first professor of geography at UCC, opined that Freeman's work would only be superseded when a new generation of geographers had produced that accumulation of small local surveys necessary to inform the general picture.

J. H. Andrews taught historical geography at TCD from 1954 to 1990 (Aalen and Whelan 1992). He served as president of the Geographical Society of Ireland and has been closely involved with projects such as the Irish

Historic Towns atlas series, sponsored by the Royal Irish Academy. Andrews served as secretary to the editorial committee which, under the chairmanship of his TCD colleague Joseph Haughton, produced the first truly collaborative work by geographers in the Republic of Ireland, the *Atlas of Ireland* in 1979. He has been review editor of the map historical journal *Imago Mundi* and editorial advisor to the History of Cartography series published by the University of Chicago Press. Evans saw lazy beds as the key diagnostic factor in interpreting Ireland; Jones Hughes embraced the Griffith Valuation; T. W. Freeman mapped and analysed the census volumes; Andrews captured Ireland through the work of geography's creators, the cartographers. As his academic biography shows, he ably demonstrated that a geographer could devote a career to Ireland and secure in the process an international standing. His publications have been capably assessed by Kevin Whelan in the *Festschrift* volume dedicated to Andrews (Aalen and Whelan 1992). Suffice it to say here that his trilogy on maps and their drawers, *A paper landscape: the Ordnance Survey in nineteenth century Ireland* (1975), *Plantation acres: an historical study of the Irish land surveyor and his maps* (1985) and *Shapes of Ireland: maps and their makers 1564–1839* (1997) are benchmarks of knowledge and research integrity unlikely to be superseded. The prerequisites for the writing of historical geography, cited by Andrews in his review of Jones Hughes' contribution, factual veracity, correct and ample documentation, chronological as well as spatial precision, period specialization and concern for accuracy, are central tenets in his own work. He brought to Irish geography, as represented by its fragmented but rich heritage of maps, a great measure of style and substance. Andrews unfolds Ireland through the paper sheets of his cartographers. Shapes now accepted slowly evolve, names of places are negotiated to represent a linguistic compromise and the cartographers are placed in their spatial and temporal contexts. So vivid is Andrews' style and so thorough his reconstruction of so many elusive lives that we can imagine them living, working, canvassing and sometimes in the service of the state. Apart from Evans, who was the subject of a poem by John Hewitt, both Andrews and Jones Hughes have been celebrated in verse by the geographer-poet Patrick O'Connor who describes Andrews as *fear na mapaí* (O'Connor 1997).

Concluding his chapter 'Ireland in maps' in the Geographical Society of Ireland's jubilee volume, Andrews turned characteristically to the 'intellectual foundations of cartography'. He wondered whether 'map making may arguably be unsuited to the Irish predicament' because 'the theme of most maps is regional variation, whereas for many Irish people it is the unity of their island that needs to be emphasised'. But beyond the political argument he made a most acute observation which summarizes the dilemma of many geographers working in Ireland. Andrews considered that perhaps:

> Ireland's interior contrasts are less challenging to science and scholarship than the qualities that distinguish it from the rest of the world, and that many of these qualities are in any case too subtle and elusive to be trapped in the geographer's net. To capture them, the student must abandon both the Ordnance map and the Atlas of Ireland; he must even abandon the landscape itself, approach the farmhouse, pass through the door and sit down by the hearth.

THE CURRENT SITUATION

Geography as now practised is a new subject in an old country. The origin dates of its various chairs mark its formal acceptance in universities but obscure the protracted struggle for recognition. Queen's University, Belfast (1945), University College, Cork (1959), University College, Dublin (1960), Trinity College, Dublin (1966), The New University of Ulster (1967), University College, Galway (1968) mirror an uneven development which is by no means based on the east-west diffusion pattern highlighted in many geographical studies. St Patrick's College, Maynooth, established its chair in 1978 and new departments were founded in the Colleges of Education in the same decade. Geographers have contributed to the formulation and teaching of heritage/tourism courses in the Regional Technical Colleges, now Institutes of Technology.

Geography's greatest challenges are firstly to maintain the identity of the discipline which is threatened by its absorption into conglomerate departments in some institutions, and secondly to maintain its integrity and independence in research. Colin Thomas, reporting on the work of the Royal Irish Academy's National Committee for Geography, aptly proclaimed geography's mission thus:

> As geographers do the National Committee continue to uphold the necessity for maintaining a balance between ultra-specialisation in systematic research and the immense cultural benefits that derive from a holistic approach to complex problems not least through interdisciplinary research and international collaboration. (*Geonews*, November 1997)

This publication, which carried information on developments in research, teaching and travelling agendas of staff within the various universities, demonstrated the need for such a balancing act. A random sample of research interests and teaching programmes suggests that geographers may, in addition to core teaching courses, be involved in researching such areas as applied remote sensing, geographical information systems, cultural tourism, local and community studies, cross-border analysis of poverty indicators, overgrazing in upland areas, water resources, ethnography of everyday life in the suburbs, rural development and the flourishing investigation of sustainable development. New appointments mirror new directions, such as 'the political and cultural geography of national identity' and 'human behaviour with specific interests in the geography of disadvantage and discrimination', as well as 'the geographical application and implications of computing'.

Geography in Ireland has undergone several infusions over time as each new academic generation attempts to define and interpret its own world. In the 1960s geographers were focusing on urban places and spatial disparities in welfare. Regional planning was paramount and the technology and methodology of the quantitative revolution threatened to make many questions redundant. But it was a false dawn: universal laws, abstract geometry and borrowed economic models were difficult to apply in a discipline which was constructed on culture differentiation. Some historical geographers, influenced by the drift of politics, have proclaimed an agenda to establish 'a plurality of Irish identity, landscape and history', and to realign historical geography 'along a less disruptive and exclusive axis of representation, one mature enough to admit to an Irish diversity without recourse to a set of convenient and ambivalent assertions' (Graham and Proudfoot 1993). But it is at present difficult to identify any dominant school headed by individual geographers such as this chapter has done for the earlier years of the subject in Ireland.

Geography is now solidly established in the curricula of third-level institutions in the island of Ireland. It provides a broad education for its undergraduates and gives them a range of technical skills. Such a curriculum is rooted in the historical development of the subject. Up to the 1970s geography postgraduates and graduates generally took up teaching careers in third-level institutions or in second-level schools. For a variety of reasons employment in these areas was not as readily available in the 1990s. However, many more opportunities have opened up for geographers in positions related to environment, town planning, rural development, GIS, media and communication, administration, tourism, banking and overseas development.

GEOGRAPHY AND LOCAL/REGIONAL STUDIES

Estyn Evans pioneered the participation of geographers in regional or local studies, in collaboration with scholars from what may be termed collateral disciplines. Locally based historical and archaeological societies flourished countrywide and provided major fora for community-orientated research and its dissemination. Allied to the

societies were journals, and in some instances the ubiquitous summer school. These voluntary organizations brought university and people together in a way Evans had long preached and practised. 'I may add', he wrote in conclusion to his *Personality of Ireland*, 'that my own understanding of rural Ireland, such as it is, was enriched by a study, made many years ago, of a small *tuath* which keeps its old title in popular speech — the Kingdom of Mourne'. A project, commenced in 1987 with the publication of *Tipperary: history and society. Interdisciplinary essays on the history of an Irish county*, has now issued thirteen volumes in an Irish county history series under the imprint of Geography Publications. This venture gained much from Evans' precept and example and the teaching influence of Tom Jones Hughes. However, its immediate origins were derived from a wish to commemorate the foundation of the Gaelic Athletic Association in Thurles in 1884 by issuing a volume of essays on county Tipperary. Geographers have been heavily involved in an editorial capacity: Patrick O'Flanagan as principal editor of the Cork volume; Lyndsay Proudfoot, editor of the Down volume; Kevin Whelan, co-editor of the Wexford, Kilkenny and Dublin volumes; Fred Aalen, co-editor of the Dublin volume, and as contributors. Regional studies are central to the institutions in Northern Ireland, the Institute of Irish Studies, the Ulster Folk and Transport Museum, with which Evans was associated. The Ulster Local History Trust acts as an umbrella body in providing funding and direction for area based publications.

THE IRISH HISTORIC TOWNS ATLAS

Geographers have long enjoyed a positive working relationship with the Royal Irish Academy. Apart from the *Atlas of Ireland* published by the Academy in 1979 and *The atlas of the Irish rural landscape* (Aalen, Stout and Whelan 1997) the most noteworthy product of the collaboration has been the fascicles of the *Irish Historic Towns Atlas* series as mentioned above. This project is Ireland's contribution to an initiative taken by the European Commission in 1985 to establish a forum for the history of towns in Europe. The series editors include geographers Anngret Simms and J. H. Andrews, historians H. B. Clarke and Raymond Gillespie, with K. M. Davies as cartographic editor. Eight fascicles have been published to date *Kildare* (1986), *Carrickfergus* (1986), *Bandon* (1988), *Kells* (1990), *Mullingar* (1992), *Athlone* (1993), *Maynooth* (1995) and *Downpatrick* (1997) and *Bray* (1998). The series' success has emphasized that towns are as much part of the Irish heritage as the 'back places' and it has again stressed the influence of geographers as exponents of new methodologies.

THE GEOGRAPHICAL SOCIETY OF IRELAND

The Geographical Society of Ireland was founded in 1934

'to promote the study of geography in all its branches, particularly the geography of Ireland.' As part of its jubilee year celebrations in 1984 the Society published a supplement to its journal of that year in which G. L. Herries Davies provided a succinct account of the first fifty years, as noted earlier. The founders came from a variety of backgrounds and interests. Few were geographers in the narrow specialist sense, but their involvement with Ireland was paramount. Geography in Ireland has been shaped, like the country itself, by the coming together of native and immigrant, and both Society and subject have been invigorated by the interaction of insider and outsider. The publication of an annual journal, since published twice yearly and now known as *Irish Geography*, has been the Society's greatest achievement, but no less important were the field weeks and day excursions which gave new meanings to places. In 1977 the Society began the publication of the *Irish Geographical Newsletter* as an information forum for geographers; this became *Geonews* after issue 21.

Bibliography

Aalen, F. H. A., and Whelan, K. (eds) 1992 *Dublin city and county: from prehistory to present. Essays in honour of J. H. Andrews*. Dublin.

Aalen, F. H. A., Stout, M. and Whelan, K. (eds) 1997 *The atlas of the Irish rural landscape*. Cork.

Andrews, J. H. 1975 *A paper landscape: the Ordnance Survey in nineteenth-century Ireland*. Oxford.

Andrews, J. H. 1976 'Land and people, c. 1685' in T. W. Moody, F. X. Martin and F. J. Byrne (eds) *A new history of Ireland* (Oxford).

Andrews, J. H. 1985 *Plantation acres: an historical study of the Irish land surveyor and his maps*. Belfast.

Andrews, J. H. 1997 *Shapes of Ireland: maps and their makers*. Dublin.

Buttimer, A. 1995 'Gatekeeping geography through national independence: stories from Harvard and Dublin' in *Erdkunde*.

Campbell, J. A. 1978 *The Queen's University of Belfast Department of Geography Jubilee 1928-1978: geography at Queen's an historical survey*. Belfast.

Carrigan, W. 1905 *History of the diocese of Ossory*. Dublin (reprinted Kilkenny, 1981).

Cole, G. A. J. 1915 *Ireland: land and landscape*. Dublin.

Cole, G. A. J. 1919 *Ireland the outpost*. Dublin.

Davies, G. L. H. 1973 'Thomas Walter Freeman and the geography of Ireland', *Irish Geography* 6.

Davies, G. L. H. 1976 'The making of Irish geography, I, William Petty', *Irish Geography* 9.

Davies, G. L. H. 1977 'The making of Irish geography, II, G. A. J. Cole', *Irish Geography* 10.

Davies, G. L. H. 1979 'The making of Irish geography, IV,

The Physico-Historical Society of Ireland, 1744-1752', *Irish Geography* 12.

Davies, G. L. H. 1986 *This protean subject. The Geography Department in Trinity College Dublin 1936–1986*. Dublin.

Davies, G. L. H. and Mollan, C. (eds) 1980 *Richard Griffith 1784–1878: papers presented at the centenary symposium organised by the Royal Dublin Society*, September 1978. Dublin.

Davies, G. L. H. (ed) 1984 *Irish geography. The Geographical Society of Ireland golden jubilee 1934–1974*. Dublin.

Davies, K. M. 1973 'A bibliography of Mr T. W. Freeman's contribution to the geography of Ireland', *Irish Geography* 6.

Evans, E. E. 1942 *Irish heritage: the landscape, the people and their work*. Dundalk.

Evans, E. E. 1951 *Mourne country: landscape and life in south Down*. Dundalk.

Evans, E. E. 1957 *Irish folkways*. London.

Evans, E. E. 1973 (revised 1981, 1992) *The personality of Ireland; habitat, heritage and history. The Wiles Lectures for 1971*. Cambridge.

Evans, E. E. 1978 'Beginnings' in J. A. Campbell (ed) *Geography at Queens. An historical survey* (Belfast).

Evans, E. E. 1996 *Ireland and the Atlantic heritage. Selected writings*. Dublin.

Freeman, T. W. 1950 *Ireland; its physical, historical, social and economic geography*. London and New York.

Freeman, T. W. 1957 *Pre-famine Ireland a study in historical geography*. Manchester.

Graham, B. G. 1994 'The search for the common ground: Estyn Evans's Ireland', *Transactions of the Institute of British Geographers* 19, pp. 183–201.

Graham, B. G. and Proudfoot, L. J. (eds) 1993 *An historical geography of Ireland*. London.

Kenney, J. F. 1929, repr. 1979 *The sources for the early history of Ireland: — ecclesiastical an introduction and guide*. Dublin.

Molony, J. 1995 '*A soul came into Ireland'. Thomas Davis 1814–1845 a biography*. Dublin.

O'Connor, P. J. 1997 *A flow of feeling. Poems from home and abroad*. Newcastle West.

Ó Lúing, S. 1991 *Kuno Meyer 1858-1919. A biography*. Dublin.

Smyth, W. J. and Whelan, K. (eds) 1988 *Common ground. Essays on the historical geography of Ireland presented to T. Jones Hughes, M.A., M.R.I.A.* Cork.

Stout, M. 1996 'Emyr Estyn Evans and Northern Ireland; the archaeology and geography of a new state' in J. A. Atkinson and I. Banks (eds) *Nationalism and archaeology* (Glasgow).

Place-names

DIARMUID Ó MURCHADHA AND KEVIN MURRAY

The purpose of this chapter is to give a brief overview of Irish place-name research, to examine part of the theoretical framework behind medieval and modern naming practices and to attempt to put this work into its international perspective. It concentrates on place-names derived from the Irish (Gaelic) language which form the bulk of the country's toponomy. Place-name examples are generally cited in the Irish language with their modern-day equivalents following in brackets.

THE EARLY MEDIEVAL BACKGROUND

Irish place-names created before the end of the Old Irish period (*ca.* 900 AD) fall generally into two main categories. One relates to the population groups occupying specific areas on which they imposed their names, for example the Cairbre (Carbury in Sligo and Kildare), the Benntraige (Bantry in Wexford and Cork) and the Luigne (Lune in Meath and Leyny in Sligo). Three of our provinces are named from large population groups — Connacht (Connachta), Ulster (Ulaid) and Leinster (Laigin). The other category, probably older still, relates to prominent natural features, many of which use lexical items based on parts of the body to describe them, for example *ceann* 'head', *béal* 'mouth', *más* 'buttock' (Ó Maolfabhail 1987–88) as in *Ceann Muice* (Headborough, county Waterford), *Béal Átha Chomair* (Ballycumber, county Offaly) and *Más Ramhar* (Mausrower, county Kerry). Some mountain and river names may have been adapted from non-Gaelic speaking predecessors and are difficult to explain purely in terms of the Gaelic language. Even such a noted 'Irish' name as Blarney may perhaps be traced back to pre-Gaelic times (O'Rahilly 1964, 257). But for certain of our earliest chroniclers it soon became a labour of love to provide a meaningful exposition of many such celebrated place-names throughout Ireland.

Names of important sites were analysed into component parts around which elaborate legendary anecdotes were woven into what was called *dindshenchas* or 'place-lore'. However spurious the analysis may have been, the existence of an apposite story or poem often heightened both the significance of the site and that of the name itself. As Professor Proinsias Mac Cana remarks,

there can be little doubt that the Irish landscape and the *dindshenchas*, 'the history of places', which was its collective reflex in tribal myth and history served together as an effective mnemonic index and treasury of a great part of native tradition. (Mac Cana 1980, 27)

This wide-ranging miscellany of toponomic lore was assembled and committed to writing in the eleventh and twelfth centuries. These collections of *dindshenchas* are available in modern editions (Stokes 1892, 1893; Gwynn 1903–35), the best-known being the 'Metrical Dindshenchas', a series of 176 poems celebrating places as far apart as *Carn Uí Néid* (Mizen Head) at the south-west extremity of county Cork and *Coire Bhreacáin*, a whirlpool off the coast of county Antrim.

As already intimated, the etymologies assigned to the various names need not be taken too seriously. For example, what we now call the Galtee mountains were originally named *Crotta Cliach*, 'the humps of (the territory called) Cliú'. But in the relevant *dindshenchas* poem *Cliach* becomes a fairy harper and *Crotta* (which also means 'harps') the place where he made his music (Gwynn 1913, 224). Killarney's principal lake, *Loch Léin* (Gwynn 1913, 260–2), as celebrated then as now, became the underwater forge of a smith called Léan who each night would hurl his fiery anvil into the sky across Munster until it landed at *Indeoin na nDéise*, 'the anvil of the Déise' — which is an actual location still recalled in the name of the townland of Mullaghnoney (*Mullach na hInneona*) near Clonmel, county Tipperary.

The composer of the poem on *Luimneach*, the estuary

Fig. 14.1 An ancient island landscape, the abandoned settlement on Inishmurrary (Inis Muireadhaigh) off the Sligo coast, viewed from the early medieval monastic enclosure on the island.

of the Shannon, had two explanations of the name. One of the connotations of *luimneach* is 'cloaked', so he made it the site of a battle between the men of Munster and of Connacht where, when the tide turned, the estuary was strewn with cloaks. Or, he suggests, it may derive from *lumman*, 'a spiky shield', large numbers of which were borne by the opposing forces (Gwynn 1913, 270–4). In the case of the river Shannon itself, the poet first opted for Sinann, a golden-haired maiden of the mythological race known as the Túatha Dé Danann, as eponym, but prior to supplying an alternative derivation, wryly remarked: 'It is no better than the first version' (Gwynn 1913, 286–96).

Both names for Dublin are noticed. *Áth Cliath*, 'ford of the hurdles', proved too obvious for etymological speculation, so the poet contented himself with a legendary four-headed monster with four score feet who was slain in the Boyne valley and whose carcass, washed up in Dublin, provided the hurdles which gave the ford its name (Gwynn 1913, 101–3). The other name, *Duiblind*, 'black pool', was linked to a man named Rodub ('very black') whose daughter, a druid and poet, was slain there by a jealous rival (Gwynn 1913, 94).

The magnetism of place lore was by no means confined to the official *dindshenchas* but pervaded almost all aspects of early Irish literature, as Professor Brian Ó Cuív, among others, has shown (see also Kinsella, Kelleher and Haley 1975; Kinsella 1969, introduction). Referring to the epic saga of the Ulster Cycle, *Táin Bó Cúailnge*, Ó Cuív drew attention to the section where the hero Cú Chulainn on his first expedition was accompanied by his charioteer who, like his modern taxi-driver counterpart, was familiar with the name and fame of each place through which they passed. When questioned by Cú Chulainn, '... he told him the name of every chief fort between Temair and Cenannas (Tara and Kells, county Meath). He named, moreover, their meadowlands and their fords, their renowned places and their dwellings, their forts and their fortified heights' (Ó Cuív 1989–90, 92). And when Queen Medb's expedition set out from the Connacht headquarters at *Crúacha* (modern-day Rathcroghan, county Roscommon) to capture the famed brown bull, it did not suffice for the storyteller to recount that they arrived some days later in *Cúailnge* (now Cooley, county Louth). Instead, he introduced a litany of sixty-five names of places (all famous in their own right) through which the army passed on its march (Strachan and O'Keeffe 1904–12, 5–7).

Another example of this genre is to be found in the Fianaigheacht cycle. In *Acallam na Senórach*, 'the Colloquy of the Ancients', the storyteller ingeniously linked St Patrick with aged survivors of an earlier epoch, Oisín and Caoilte, who accompanied Patrick on a tour of famous sites, using each name as a key to unlock the wealth of lore attached to storied mountain cairn or ancient embattled fortress. In the course of their peregrinations they arrived at what is now Ardpatrick in county Limerick but was then known as *Fionntulach* or *Tulach na Féinne*. Patrick's query as to the reason for this name gave Caoilte the opportunity to describe an occasion when three battalions of the Fianna were preparing to march from there to fight the battle of *Finntráigh* (Ventry, county Kerry), and the vista of serried rows of spearshafts bound with enchanted cinctures caused Fionn mac Cumhaill to exclaim: *Is fionn an tulach* ('fair is the hill') — and what better name for it than *Fionntulach*! (O'Grady 1892, 110). Many place-names in Fianaigheacht lore, however, seem to exist only within the literature and the imagination (see Ó Coileáin 1993) and as actual place-names have lost (or never had) a locative function, a process that elsewhere has been referred to as 'de-onymization' (Baumgarten 1990, 121).

THE INFLUENCE OF THE CAMBRO-NORMANS

This zest for onomastic lore suffered a major setback in two respects following the arrival of the Cambro-Normans in Ireland in the late twelfth century. Firstly, the very fabric of romantic Gaelic-style names was rudely shattered in many areas where the landscape was transformed into clearly defined landholdings, most of whose names embodied the word *baile* ('town', 'homestead') with a personal name affixed, for example Barry's town / *Baile an Bharraigh* (Barrystown, county Wexford), Launder's town/*Baile an Londraigh* (Ballylanders, county Limerick) and Simon's town/*Baile Shíomóin* (Ballysimon, county Cork). Ancient Gaelic names were submerged in the flood of prosaic *bailte*: *Dún Cruadha* became *Baile Chaisleáin an Róistigh* (Castletownroche, county Cork) (Power 1932, 49 and 111) while *Dún na Séad* changed to *Baile an Tighe Mhóir* (Baltimore, county Cork) (O'Donovan, 1856, iii and 188). *Cill Ghobáin* yielded to *Baile na Tóna* (Bottomstown, county Limerick) (Ó Maolfabhail 1990, 46) and *Mairgheanán* became *Baile Bhaileanán* (Ballyballinaun, county Mayo) (Ó Murchadha 1994–5, 22). The Norman mode of land division, including the use of the word *baile*, became widespread in an Irish-speaking environment, as may be seen from a list of Roche lands in county Cork in 1461 (de hÓir 1967a) or from the descriptions of the lands of Uí Mhaine and Uí Fhiachrach in Connacht (O'Donovan 1843, 44).

Yet most of the old names were retained, albeit in a new mode of spelling. The Normans, and their Anglo-Irish successors, adapted Gaelic names within the sound systems of their own languages. In the early thirteenth-century *Song of Dermot and the Earl* (Orpen 1892) written in Norman French, *Áth Cliath* became 'Haythcleyth' (Dublin), *Gleann dá Locha* became 'Glindelath' (Glendalough, county Wicklow) and *Bearbha* became 'la Barue' (the river Barrow). From then on, 'anglicized' forms became the norm for official purposes — Tara (*Teamhair*), Armagh (*Ard Mhacha*), Tipperary (*Tiobraid Árann*) and so on. In some instances, through folketymology, this resulted in such peculiar forms as Tomregan, county Cavan (*Tuaim Dreacon*), Scaryhill, county Antrim (*Scarbhchoill*) and Vinegar Hill, county Wexford (*Cnoc Fiodh na gCaor*).

A second inauspicious factor was the cessation of creative onomastics. While *dindshenchas* continued to be copied by scribes, nothing new was added to the corpus. Because of the emphasis on land acquisition due to an increasing population, place-names now acquired an even more territorial dimension, linking to septs and sub-septs their ancestral lands and delimiting their boundaries. There are some tribal-oriented poems which reflect the Gaelic reaction to the take-over of large tracts of territory by lords of Norman descent. The best-known examples, the 'Topographical Poems' of Seaán Mór Ó Dubhagáin and Giolla-na-naomh Ó hUidhrín (O'Donovan 1862; Carney 1943), though compiled in the late fourteenth century, totally ignore the territorial changes wrought by the Norman incursions. A later production, Aonghus Ó Dálaigh's 'Tribes of Ireland' (O'Donovan 1852), lampooned indiscriminately lords both of Gaelic and Norman descent countrywide. Regional ownership tracts provide even more fruitful place-name sources, in particular those for Caoille (O'Keeffe 1928; Power 1932) and Corca Laoighdhe (O'Donovan 1849) in county Cork, Uí Mhaine in county Galway (O'Donovan 1843), Uí Fhiachrach in county Sligo (O'Donovan 1844), the Maguires of Fermanagh (Ua Duinnín 1917) and O'Reillys of county Cavan (Carney 1959). Then there is a sixteenth-century poem which rather than dealing with land ownership portrays the cattle-raiding exploits of Donnchadh Ó Ceallacháin of Duhallow, county Cork (de hÓir 1967b). That the composer of this remarkable poem relished the resonance of Munster place-names is obvious from the fact that in the course of 420 lines he managed to name over 200 different places.

THE BEGINNINGS OF MODERN PLACE-NAME SCHOLARSHIP IN IRELAND

In the seventeenth century the first stirrings of a renewed scholarly interest in toponymy became evident in the work of the Irish Franciscans at Louvain. Fr John Colgan wrote to many quarters in Ireland requesting lists of names of ecclesiastical sites for use in his great work on

Irish saints (Colgan 1645). He also hoped to publish an Irish ecclesiastical onomasticon but — mainly due to the failure of people in Ireland to reply to his inquiries — he never succeeded in this enterprise (Mooney 1946–50, a–b). The conflicts of the mid- and late 1600s inhibited further scholarship to a large extent, until the *pax Britannica* of the following century allowed a resumption. By then it was no longer native scholars who rose to prominence in the study of ancient Irish culture, but rather Anglo-Irish ones whose knowledge of the Irish language was meagre and whose etymological efforts were often misleading — people such as Mervyn Archdall, antiquary and rector of Slane, county Meath, author of *Monasticon Hibernicum* (Dublin 1786), Edward Ledwich, vicar of Aghaboe, county Laois, author of *Antiquities of Ireland* (Dublin 1789) and General Charles Vallancey, author of the six-volume *Collectanea de rebus Hibernicis* (1770–1804).

It was not until the establishment of the Ordnance Survey in Ireland in 1824, and in particular the appointment of Thomas Larcom as administrator four years later, that the study of Irish place-names was placed on a proper footing. Larcom's interest in the history and human ecology of the areas surveyed led to the assembling of invaluable data for most of the northern counties. He then appointed a team of scholars, including Eugene O'Curry, James Clarence Mangan, Patrick O'Keeffe, Thomas O'Conor — and in particular John O'Donovan — to decide upon the original Irish form of each name, so that a standard anglicized form could be provided for the Ordnance Survey maps. The pity is that the original Gaelic spelling was not retained, as it was in the case of many similar names in Scotland. In the course of frequent and arduous journeys to the four quarters of pre-Famine Ireland between 1834 and 1841 O'Donovan and the others amassed a prodigious quantity of topographical information, and not just in regard to townland names. The Ordnance Survey Letters, Name Books and Memoranda preserve copious details of named features on the landscape (such as hills, hollows, rivulets and so forth) along with meticulous recording of any ancient remains visible. In 1841 the work of the topographical team was terminated — sadly before county Cork was visited — and O'Donovan's employment was reduced. Not so his workload, however. Already, subsequent to the founding of the Irish Archaeological Society in 1841, he had edited for publication a series of important Irish historical and topographical works. His pioneering insight into these sources proved indispensable in his topographical work at the Ordnance Survey and, conversely, his familiarity with townland and parish names acquired there often helped to locate ancient sites referred to in manuscript sources. He continued until his untimely death to edit further significant works, his

Fig. 14.2 Prof. Edmund Hogan, seated centre, from A page of Irish history: the story of University College Dublin *(Dublin 1930).*

crowning achievement being the publication (by Hodges, Smith and Co., Dublin) of what is generally known as *The annals of the Four Masters* (O'Donovan 1848–51), a manuscript collection of annals from the earliest times to 1616, compiled by a seventeenth-century quartet of friars. In this formidable undertaking he had the assistance of Eugene O'Curry and George Petrie, but O'Donovan was the scholar whose annotations provided for each name in turn a comprehensive body of topographical evidence. Most of his identifications were extremely accurate, and even to the present day *The annals of the Four Masters* remain a treasure trove for researchers.

PATRICK WESTON JOYCE AND EDMUND HOGAN

Next we must touch upon two of the most important place-name publications ever in Ireland. Firstly, Joyce's *The origin and history of Irish names of places*. Many of those who edited Irish texts or collections of annals in the late nineteenth century depended almost entirely on O'Donovan for place-name identification, but Joyce, a self-taught scholar like O'Donovan himself, set a new course. Patrick Weston Joyce (1827–1914) grew up in a hamlet called *Gleann Oisín* (Glenosheen), not far from Ardpatrick (*Ard Pádraig*) in county Limerick, surrounded by mountains and glens bearing such names as *Suidhe Finn*, *Bearna Gaoithe*, *Gleann an Áir*, *Ladhar na bhFraochán* and *Ladhar na Gréine*, the last being the name he later gave to his residence in Rathmines, 'Lyre-na-grena'. Little wonder that from his youth he was imbued with an intense consciousness of those mellifluous names which were as much a part of his landscape as the very hills and valleys they designated. An indefatigable worker, in more than two dozen publications he illuminated many neglected areas of Irish culture — history (political and social), language, folk music and various aspects of education — but the work for which he is most renowned is his three-volume study mentioned above. Joyce was the first to realize the potential of the index of townlands, parishes and baronies which the labours of the Ordnance Survey had made available (Census 1861). Here was presented an alphabetical list of all the townland names in Ireland, a cornucopia overflowing with samples of place-name elements from every part of the country. When treating of the word *teamhair* ('elevated spot', 'height'), for instance, he was not confined to Tara in county Meath since the index lists townlands also named Tara in counties Down, Offaly and Wexford. Furthermore, Joyce found there townlands named Taur, Tower and Tawran, all of which he utilized to illustrate the semantics of the word (Joyce 1869, 295–6). In this way he built up a whole series of different categories to elucidate the system by which place-names were formed and the manner in which usage and pronunciation varied from one region to another. In concluding the preface to his final volume, written the year before he died, Joyce wrote:

And now, having finished my task, I claim that the account given in this three-volume work of the place-names of Ireland, their classification, analysis, and etymologies, is fuller, in the first place, and, in the second place, rests on surer foundations, than the history of the place-names of any other country. (Joyce 1913, viii)

This was no idle boast; Joyce's admirably comprehensive survey of modern-day townland names has never been surpassed in its field though it is best used in conjunction with Flanagan (1981–2).

In a different category, namely the collation and identification of original forms of place-names as found in Irish manuscripts, John O'Donovan's monumental edition of *The annals of the Four Masters*, mentioned above, provided the main inspiration for the single most important publication on the subject, Edmund Hogan's *Onomasticon Goedelicum* (1910). Fr Hogan, Todd Professor at the Royal Irish Academy (**Fig. 14.2**), spent

ten years of his life compiling this work, completing it in his eightieth year. He, along with his helpers whom he lists in the introduction, assembled nearly 700 pages (in double columns and closely-set type) of place-names excerpted from Irish manuscript sources, many of which were unpublished at the time, and added numerous place-name identifications to supplement those of O'Donovan and others.

A significant aspect of Hogan's work is its importance as a research tool for early and medieval Irish history. By following its references to the source, it often serves to link together information for the researcher that would otherwise remain unconnected. This has kept it central to medieval Irish studies as its references to sources have remained indispensable, whereas identifications of certain place and tribal names have been superseded by later scholarship. It is clear from Hyde (1917) and MacErlean (1917) that the debt that Irish studies owe to Fr Hogan and his *magnum opus* soon became considerable. The *Onomasticon* succeeded in putting place-name studies in this country on a new footing, especially with regard to the early written sources. Scholars of personal and tribal names owe a similar debt to Michael O'Brien for his *Corpus genealogiarum Hiberniae* (O'Brien 1962).

Because the *Onomasticon Goedelicum* was first published over ninety years ago, it is universally accepted that the time has come to update this standard work of reference. This is the remit of the LOCUS project, based in the Department of Early and Medieval Irish, University College, Cork. Under the direction of Professor Pádraig Ó Riain and with the aid of a very generous grant from Toyota Ireland Ltd, this work has been ongoing since October 1996. The project began ten years earlier as 'The Historical Dictionary of Irish Place and Tribal Names' under the auspices of the Royal Irish Academy and University College, Cork, but was transferred exclusively to Cork in 1986. At the moment the necessary groundwork is nearing completion and it is hoped that the editing stage will be well in train during 2000. It is envisaged that the end result will be a revised edition of Hogan's *Onomasticon* in fascicular form, along with a complete database of all collected place-names on CD-ROM.

INSTITUTIONS AND BODIES CONCERNED WITH PLACE-NAME RESEARCH

The Ordnance Survey of Ireland is an important source of information and publications on place-names (for its work see Andrews 1975; Ordnance Survey 1991; Ó Maolfabhail 1989, 1991, 1995). Building on a tradition that stretches back to O'Donovan, O'Curry and Petrie, among others, the Ordnance Survey has published (or facilitated the publication of) such important sources as the Ordnance Survey Name-Books, Memoirs and Letters.

The series of Ordnance Survey Memoirs published by the Institute of Irish Studies in Belfast (1990 to present) deserves special mention in this regard. An Coimisiún Logainmneacha (The Placenames Commission) was established by a warrant of appointment issued under the seal of the Minister of Finance in 1946. Its stated role was

(1) to investigate the place-names of Ireland;

(2) to establish the correct original Irish forms of those names, and

(3) to publish lists of those place-names, in Irish and English, for official use.

The Commission had no full-time paid staff at its disposal, however. Its duties were changed to advisory only in 1955 and the research work was left to a permanent body of professionals attached to the Ordnance Survey (Ó Maolfabhail 1992, 1998; Mac Giolla Easpaig 1992).

This body, the Placenames Branch of the Ordnance Survey, in association with An Coimisiún Logainmneacha, published a series of booklets entitled *Ainmneacha Gaeilge na mbailte poist* relating to the postal district names of each province between 1960 and 1964. These were eventually brought together and published as one volume in 1969. The Placenames Branch followed this with *Logainmneacha as Paróiste na Rinne, Co. Phort Láirge* in 1975. The publication of the *Gazetteer of Ireland/Gasaitéar na hÉireann* in 1989 was another important step towards establishing the correct Irish forms of population centres and physical features. This was followed by the *Liostaí logainmneacha* series which contains the official Irish and English forms of the townlands, civil parishes and baronies of each county. Six volumes, (Limerick, Louth and Waterford (all 1991), Kilkenny (1993), Offaly (1994) and Monaghan (1996), have been issued to date as well as one volume (that for county Limerick (1990)) listing the historical evidence for the townlands. What is so important about this work is that place-name evidence and cartography complement one another; the importance of maps in this area of study should never be underestimated. An Coimisiún Logainmneacha has also produced a book, T*he place-names of Ireland in the third millennium* (1992), which focuses on ways in which our rich place-name heritage can be preserved for future generations (see Ó Corráin 1992).

Part of the duties of the School of Celtic Studies, Dublin Institute for Advanced Studies, established by a special act of government in 1940, was 'the collection and study of Irish place-names'. Before work in this area could be organized, however, An Coimisiún Logainmneacha (mentioned above) had been formed and onomastic study remained an ancillary discipline to the School's main research, especially the editing of texts. An exception to this was the important work carried out by Liam Price resulting in the publication by the School of *The place-names of county Wicklow* in seven volumes (Ó Cuív 1977). Mention must also be made of their role as publisher of Fr Paul Walsh's *The placenames of Westmeath* (1957). In 1964 the journal of An Cumann Logainmneacha (The Place-names Association), *Dinnseanchas*, began to appear. Over the next decade, edited by Éamonn de hÓir, the chief place-names officer of the Ordnance Survey, *Dinnseanchas* pursued a vigorous publishing programme that resulted in articles on individual place-names and place-name elements as well as a series of important contributions from the staff of the Ordnance Survey itself entitled 'As Cartlann na Logainmneacha', based on entries in their archival holdings. After the premature death of Éamonn de hÓir (for an appreciation of whom see Flanagan 1978), only one more number of the journal appeared before it ceased publication altogether in 1977.

Another project deserving of mention here is 'Coiste Logainmneacha Chorcaí' (The Cork Place-names Committee) under the supervision of Dr Éamon Lankford. To date, this body, with assistance from Cork County Council, FÁS and the Heritage Council, has collected over 30,000 place-names, many of them field-names, boundary-names and other minor names which are in danger of being lost forever through urbanization, disuse and the loss of an older generation for whom these were living, functional names. This very worth-while, though labour-intensive, work should be dupli-cated in every county so that our living heritage will not disappear before our eyes. Guidelines for this type of study have already been laid down in Nicolaisen (1961).

PLACE-NAME RESEARCH IN NORTHERN IRELAND

One should not imagine that onomastic publication has been lacking in the north of Ireland. In the last century the first serial publication devoted to place-name research in Ireland was the *Bulletin of the Ulster Place-name Society* (*BUPNS*). Though the first series of this journal lasted for only six years (from 1952 to 1957), it managed to publish over seventy pieces, comprising articles on place-names and place-name elements, book reviews, selections from the Ordnance Survey name-books as well as a cross-section of Ordnance Survey letters, along with sundry articles on dialect, toponomy and cartography. Publication of the journal came to an abrupt end with the sudden death of its editor, co-founder and major driving-force, John B. Arthurs (Seán Mac Airt), a lecturer in Celtic Studies at Queen's University, Belfast (Buchanan 1959; Ó Cuív 1958–61; Mac Cana 1958–9, 1960–1). Mac Airt is best known among students of Irish history for his editions of *The annals of Inisfallen* (1944) and *The annals of Ulster* (1983) (with Professor Gearóid Mac Niocaill), though these represent only a fraction of his total scholarly output (Mac Cana 1958–9; Baumgarten 1986).

BUPNS remained defunct until 1978 when it was revived by one of Mac Airt's students, Deirdre Flanagan (née Morton), who had contributed much to the original volumes. It may be that the aforementioned demise of the journal *Dinnseanchas* inspired Flanagan to launch this second series of *BUPNS*, though it too was fated to have a short innings due to her untimely death in 1984 (for an appreciation and bibliography see Flanagan and Flanagan 1994, ix and 263–7). During the period of its publication (1978–82), however, it included important articles on all manner of subjects relating to name studies. The third coming of the Ulster Place-name Society was in 1986 with the launch of its new journal *Ainm*, under the editorship of Professor Ruairí Ó hUiginn. Seven volumes have been published with volume 8 promised for late 2000. Under Ó hUiginn, and present editor Dr Nollaig Ó Muraíle, it has actively encouraged place-name research in all parts of Ireland as well as ensuring that an outlet exists for the publication of this work. It is no exaggeration to say that Northern Ireland in general, and Queen's University, Belfast in particular, have led the way in onomastic publishing in Ireland.

Nowhere is this more evident than in the publications of the Northern Ireland Place-name Project, based at the Department of Celtic Studies, Queen's University, Belfast. It was established in 1987 to study the place-names of Northern Ireland appearing on the Ordnance Survey 1:50,000 scale map with a view to elucidating their origins, history and meaning. Under the general editorship of Professor Gerard Stockman (vols 1–6) and Dr Ó Muraíle (vol. 7) it has published seven volumes of detailed research on many of the place-names of counties Down, Antrim and Derry (see bibliography for further details). The invaluable archive of historical forms of Ulster place-names which has been built up during this work is stored at Queen's.

PERSONNEL AND PUBLICATIONS

Many other place-name workers deserve mention but only a selection of them may be named here. Along with the people enumerated above and in the bibliography, the following have all worked to various degrees on matters onomastic: historians (F. J. Byrne, E. MacNeill, K. W. Nicholls, and S. Ó Ceallaigh); linguists (G. B. Adams, L. Mac Mathúna, M. A. O'Brien, T. Ó Concheanainn, T. S. Ó Máille, T. F. O'Rahilly, O. Padel and J. Pokorny); professional place-name scholars (A. Mac An Bhaird, P. Ó Cearbhaill, S. Ó Cearnaigh and P. Ó Dálaigh); archaeologists (S. Ó Ríordáin and A. MacDonald), geographers (B.

Mac Aodha and P. O'Flanagan), and perhaps, most importantly, local historians and contributors to various local journals (S. Laoide, N. Lawless, M. Mac Cárthaigh, E. Mac Fhinn, D. Mac Íomhair, G. Mac Spealáin, H. Morris, L. Ó Buachalla, T. G. Ó Canainn, M. Ó Conalláin, B. Ó Dubhthaigh, R. Ó Foghludha, P. Ó Gallchóir, O. O'Kelly, P. Ó Niatháin, É Ó Tuathail, D. Piatt and M. Seoighe). The work of these scholars, among others, has increased our knowledge of Irish place-names and deserves to be read by all who are interested in Irish culture and heritage.

The mainstream Irish Studies journals, *Celtica*, *Éigse*, *Ériu*, *Journal of the Royal Society of Antiquaries of Ireland*, *Peritia*, *Proceedings of the Royal Irish Academy*, *Studia Hibernica* and their likes have all included important submissions on Irish place-names over the years. The contribution of regional journals should not be ignored either because many of them contain a wealth of detail on place-names pertaining to their local areas. This is especially true of the information garnered from native Irish speakers at the turn of the twentieth century or earlier regarding the folklore, meaning and pronunciation of certain place-names in districts where no native speakers now remain. Without the local journals these records might otherwise have been lost to us. Other important works on Irish place-names include Pádraig Ó Siochfhradha's *Triocha-céad Chorca Dhuibhne* (1939), Canon Patrick Power's *The place-names of Decies* (1952) and Breandán Ó Cíobháin's *Toponomia Hiberniae* (1978–85), of which four volumes relating to south county Kerry have already been published.

INTERNATIONAL DIMENSION

The last important onomastic periodical to be considered here is *Nomina*, which is published by the Society for Name Studies in Britain and Ireland. The nineteen volumes to date of this journal deal with personal and place-name subjects relating to England, Scotland, Wales, The Isle of Man, Guernsey, Ireland and Scandinavia, which represents a very wide range. It is also a very important source of critical reviews of work published on the subject of names. The Society for Name Studies holds an annual conference where ideas and opinions are freely exchanged; a recent conference was held in Maynooth in April 1998.

The work of societies such as the Society for Name Studies in Britain and Ireland and the International Committee of Onomastic Sciences (which produces the important journal, *Onoma*) helps to remind us of the international importance accorded to place-names. For example, the United Nations has held conferences regularly since 1967 on the standardization of geographical names. In an age of increasing communication, name standardization, which helps to avoid mistakes and yet preserves cultural differences, has become a necessary adjunct to governmental and international planning. The important legal position accorded internationally to place-names is also reflected in their position with regard to the law in Ireland. The *Towns Improvement Clauses Act* 1847; the *Public Health Acts Amendment Act* 1907; *the Local Government Act* 1946; the *Local Government Regulations* 1956; the *Road Traffic (Signs) Regulations* 1962 and the *Place-Names (Irish Forms) Act* 1973 all have legally enforceable aspects that deal with place-names (Ó Catháin 1992). For example, under the *Road Traffic (Signs) Regulations* 1962, all signposts most contain the Irish-language name forms along with their anglicized counterparts.

CASE STUDY

The history and descent of a particular place-name can often be quite complicated. On the face of it, a name such as Steeplestown (parish of Trim, county Meath) simply denotes a townland with a steeple. But when we look at its nineteenth-century Irish form, *Baile an Chloicthighe* (O'Donovan 1848–51, ii, 1182), we realize that the 'steeple', the last part of which fell around 1760, was an ancient round tower. The fact that an adjoining townland is named Tullyard enables us to identify the site as the *Cloictheach Telcha Áird* burned by Tighernán Ua Ruairc in 1171 (O'Donovan 1848–51, ii, 1180). After Ua Ruairc's raid it was garrisoned by 'foreigners' (presumably the Norman Hugo de Lacy's men) and *Gaill Tulcha Aird* feature in the 'Annals of Tigernach' (Stokes 1895–7) during the years 1175–7. But the round tower indicates an important early Christian settlement, and in the *Book of Leinster* (O'Sullivan 1983, ll. 51042–3) in a list of Irish saints are found the names *Ciaran Tulche Airdde* followed by *Ciaran Aird Heó*. The suspicion that one of the pair is a doublet of the other is borne out by versions of the same list in other manuscripts where the name reads *Ciaran Tulchi Airdde hEo* (Ó Riain 1985, 707.354–5 and fn.). Earlier in the same list we encounter *Brenaind Aird Eo* (Ó Riain 1985, 707.50).

So it appears that the original name was *Ard Eó* ('height of the yews') which later became *Tulach Airde hEó* and *Tulach Ard* ('high hillock'), part of which later became *Baile an Chloicthighe*/Steeplestown while the other part remained *Tulach Ard*/Tullyard.

CONCLUSION

The study of place-names contributes to our understanding of many different areas of human endeavour — cultural, historical, linguistic, legal, cartographic, geographic, to name just a few. It is an area of scholarship that combines the need for flair and precision to do full justice to the naming practices of bygone generations. Personal names and place-names are very much part of what we are, a genuine recognizable cultural link with our past. A recent publication, already referred to,

deals with names of places in Ireland in the third millennium (Ó Maolfabhail 1992), and it is worth remembering that many of those places still bear versions of names that were assigned to them around the beginning of the first millennium.

Bibliography

Andrews, J. H. 1975 *A paper landscape: the Ordnance Survey in nineteenth-century Ireland*. London.

Archdall, M. 1786 *Monasticon Hibernicum*. Dublin.

Baumgarten, R. 1986 (ed) *Bibliography of Irish linguistics and literature, 1942–71*. Dublin

Baumgarten, R. 1990 'Etymological aetiology in Irish tradition', *Ériu* **41**, pp. 115–22.

Buchanan, R. H. 1959 'Obituary of Seán Mac Airt', *Ulster Folklife* **5**, 5.

Carney, J. 1943 (ed) *Topographical poems by Seaán Mór Ó Dubhagáin and Giolla-na-naomh Ó hUidhrín*. Dublin.

Carney, J. 1959 *A genealogical history of the O'Reillys*. Dublin.

Census 1861 *Census of Ireland: general alphabetical index to the townlands and towns, parishes and baronies of Ireland*. Dublin.

Colgan, J. 1645 *Acta sanctorum veteris et majoris Scotiae seu Hiberniae*. Louvain.

Day, A. and McWilliams, P. (eds) *The Ordnance Survey memoirs of Ireland, 1830–1840*, 40 vols. Belfast.

de hÓir, É 1967a 'Liosta de thailte Róisteacha', *Dinnseanchas* **2**, pp. 106–12.

de hÓir, É 1967b 'Caithréim Donnchaidh mhic Thaidhg Rua Uí Cheallacháin' in E. Rynne (ed) *North Munster Studies* (Limerick), pp. 505–28.

Flanagan, D. 1978 'In Memorian: Éamonn de hÓir', *Bulletin of the Ulster Place-name Society* (2nd Series) **1**, pp. 56–7.

Flanagan, D. 1981–2 'Some guidelines to the use of Joyce's "Irish Names of Places"', *Bulletin of the Ulster Place-Name Society* (2nd Series) **4**, pp. 61–9.

Flanagan, D. and Flanagan, L. 1994 *Irish place names*. Dublin.

Gwynn, E. J. 1903, 1906, 1913, 1924, 1935 (ed) *The metrical Dindshenchas* (Todd Lecture Series, viii–xii). Dublin.

Hogan, E. 1910 *Onomasticon Goedelicum: locorum et tribuum Hiberniae et Scotiae*. Dublin.

Hughes, A. J. and Hannan, R. J. 1992 *Place-names of Northern Ireland, vol. 2: county Down II — The Ards*. Belfast.

Hyde, D. 1917 'A great Irish scholar: Rev. Edmund Hogan S. J.', *Studies* **6**, 24, pp. 663–8.

Joyce, P. W. 1869, 1875, 1913 *The origin and history of Irish names of places*, 3 vols. Dublin.

Kinsella, T. 1969 trans. *The Táin*. Portlaoise.

Kinsella, T. Kelleher, J. and Haley, G. 1975 'The Táin', *Ireland of the Welcomes* **24**, 6, pp. 19–29.

Ledwich, E. 1789 *Antiquities of Ireland*. Dublin

Mac Cana, P. 1958–9 'Obituary and bibliography of Seán Mac Airt', *Onoma* **8**, pp. 488–91.

Mac Cana, P. 1960–1 'Obituary of Seán Mac Airt', *Études Celtiques* **9**, pp. 244–5.

Mac Cana, P. 1980 *The learned tales of medieval Ireland*. Dublin.

MacErlean, J. 1917 'A bibliography of Dr. Hogan S. J.', *Studies* **6**, 24, pp. 668–71.

Mac Gabhann, F. 1997 *Place-names of Northern Ireland, vol. 7: county Antrim II — Ballycastle and North-East Antrim*. Belfast.

Mac Giolla Easpaig, D. 1992 'The Placenames Branch of the Ordnance Survey' in Ó Maolfabhail 1992b, pp. 76–87.

McKay, P. 1995 *Place-names of Northern Ireland, vol. 4: county Antrim I — The Baronies of Toome*. Belfast.

Mooney, C. 1946–50a 'Topographical fragments from the Franciscan Library', *Celtica* **1**, pp. 64–85.

Mooney, C. 1946–50b 'Colgan's inquiries about Irish place-names', *Celtica* **1**, pp. 294–6.

Muhr, K. 1996 *Place-names of Northern Ireland, vol. 6: county Down IV — North-West Down/Iveagh*. Belfast.

Nicolaisen, W. F. H. 1961 'Field-work in place-name research', *Studia Hibernica* **1**, 74–88.

O'Brien, M. A. 1962 (ed) *Corpus genealogiarum Hiberniae*. Dublin.

Ó Catháin, L. 1992 'Some thoughts on placenames and the law' in Ó Maolfabhail 1992b, pp. 71–5.

Ó Cíobháin, B. 1978–85 *Toponomia Hiberniae*, 4 vols. Dublin.

Ó Coileáin, S. 1993 'Place and placename in *Fianaigheacht*', *Studia Hibernica* **27**, pp. 45–60.

Ó Corráin, D. 1992 'A future for Irish placenames' in Ó Maolfabhail 1992 , pp. 33–46.

Ó Cuív, B. 1958–61 Obituary of Seán Mac Airt, *Éigse* **9**, pp. 202–3.

Ó Cuív, B. 1977 'The School of Celtic Studies in the Dublin Institute for Advanced Studies', *Nomina* **1**, pp. 14–15.

Ó Cuív, B. 1989–90 '*Dinnshenchas* — the literary exploitation of Irish place-names', *Ainm* **4**, pp. 90–106.

O'Donovan, J. 1843 (ed) *The tribes and customs of Hy-Many*. Dublin.

O'Donovan, J. 1844 (ed) *The genealogies, tribes, and customs of Hy-Fiachrach*. Dublin.

O'Donovan, J. 1848–51 (ed) *Annála Ríoghachta Éireann: annals of the Kingdom of Ireland by the Four Masters from the earliest period to the year 1616*, 7 vols. Dublin.

O'Donovan, J. 1849 (ed) 'Geinealach Chorca Laidhe', *Miscellany of the Celtic Society* (Dublin), pp. 1–144.

O'Donovan, J. 1852 (ed) *The tribes of Ireland: a satire by Aenghus O'Daly*. Dublin.

O'Donovan, J. 1862 (ed) *The topographical poems of John O'Dubhagain and Giolla na naomh O'Huidhrin*. Dublin.

O'Grady, S. H. 1892 (ed) *Silva Gadelica*. London and Edinburgh.

O'Keeffe, J. G. 1928 'The ancient territory of Fermoy', *Ériu* **10**, pp. 170–89.

Ó Mainnín, M. B. 1993 *Place-names of Northern Ireland, vol. 3: county Down III The Mournes*. Belfast.

Ó Maolfabhail, A. 1987–88 'Baill choirp mar logainmneacha', I, *Ainm* **2**, pp. 76–82; II, *Ainm* **3**, pp. 18–25.

Ó Maolfabhail, A. 1989 'An tSuirbhéireacht Ordanáis agus logainmneacha na hÉireann, 1824–34', *Proceedings of the Royal Irish Academy* **89** C, pp. 37–66.

Ó Maolfabhail, A. 1990 *Logainmneacha na hÉireann: Countae Luimnigh*. Dublin.

Ó Maolfabhail, A. 1991 'Éadbhard Ó Raghallaigh, Seán Ó Donnabháin agus an tSuirbhéireacht Ordanáis 1830–4', *Proceedings of the Royal Irish Academy* **91** C, pp. 73–103.

Ó Maolfabhail, A. 1992a 'The background and present role of the Placenames Branch of the Ordnance Survey' in Ó Maolfabhail 1992b, pp. 11–32.

Ó Maolfabhail, A. 1992b (ed) *The placenames of Ireland in the third millenium/logainmneacha na hÉireann sa tríú mílaois*. Dublin.

Ó Maolfabhail, A. 1995 'Eoghan Ó Comhraí agus an tSuirbhéireacht Ordanáis' in P. Ó Fiannachta (ed) *Ómós do Eoghan Ó Comhraí* (An Daigean), pp. 145–84.

Ó Maolfabhail, A. 1998 'The conception, birth and growth of a national placenames authority' in W. F. Nicolaisen (ed) *Proceedings of the XIXth International Congress of Onomastic Sciences*, 1 (Aberdeen), pp. 243–51.

Ó Murchadha, D. 1994–5 'A reconsideration of some place-names from The Annals of Connacht', *Ainm* **6**, pp. 1–31.

Ordnance Survey 1969 *Ainmneacha Gaeilge na mbailte poist*. Dublin.

Ordnance Survey 1989 *Gazetteer of Ireland / Gasaitéar na hÉireann: names of centres of population and physical features prepared by the placenames branch of the Ordnance Survey*. Dublin.

Ordnance Survey 1991 *Liostaí logainmneacha*, 6 vols. Dublin.

Ordnance Survey 1991 *An illustrated record of Ordnance Survey in Ireland*. Dublin.

Ó Riain, P. 1985 (ed) *Corpus genealogiarum sanctorum Hiberniae*. Dublin.

Orpen, G. H. 1892 *The song of Dermot and the Earl*.

Oxford.

Ó Siochfhradha, P. 1939 *Triocha-céad Chorca Dhuibhne*. Dublin.

O'Sullivan, A. 1983 (ed) *The Book of Leinster*, vol. 6. Dublin.

Power, P. 1932 (ed) *Crichad an Chaoilli*. Cork.

Power, P. 1952 *The place-names of Decies*, 2nd ed. Cork.

Price, L. 1945–67 *The place-names of county Wicklow*, 7 vols. Dublin.

Stokes, W. (ed) 1892 *The Bodleian Dinnshenchas*. London.

Stokes, W. (ed) 1893 *The Edinburgh Dinnshenchas*. London.

Stokes, W. (ed) 1895–7 'The Annals of Tigernach', *Revue Celtique* **16**, pp. 374–419; **17**, pp. 6–33, 119–263, 337–420; **18**, pp. 9–59, 374–90.

Strachan, J. and O'Keeffe, J. G. (eds) 1904–12 *The Táin Bó Cúailnge from the Yellow Book of Lecan*. Dublin.

Toner, G. and Ó Mainnín, M. B. 1992 *Place-names of Northern Ireland, vol. 1: county Down I — Newry and South-West Down*. Belfast.

Toner, G. 1996 *Place-names of Northern Ireland, vol. 5: county Derry I — The Moyola Valley*. Belfast.

Ua Duinnín, P. 1917 *Me Guidhir Fhearmanach: the Maguires of Fermanagh*. Dublin.

Vallancey, C. 1770–1804 *Collectanea de rebus Hibernicis*, 6 vols. Dublin.

Walsh, P. 1957 (ed) *The placenames of Westmeath*. Dublin.

Relevant websites

LOCUS Project, University College, Cork
http://www.ucc.ie/locus
Scottish Place-Name Project
http://www.st-andrews.ac.uk/institutes/sassi/spns/spnstop.htm

Genealogy

KENNETH NICHOLLS

The Irish genealogical texts constitute a body of material which is unique in Europe both for its chronological sweep — from the seventh to the eighteenth century — and, considering its date and the losses which it has sustained, its extent. The Welsh genealogical records, which testify to a similar interest in lineage, only coincide, apart from a small corpus of earlier material, with the later period of the Irish ones, from the fourteenth century onwards. However, while this process of recording genealogies preserved the same characteristics, and even forms, throughout this long era, it was not a continuous one. The genealogical texts fall into chronological groups, punctuated by periods — probably those characterized by extreme social and political change, as was certainly the case in that *ca.* 1130–1300 — in which they do not seem to have been scribally recorded, and following which the missing generations had to be recreated from fallible oral tradition. As has been noted in Africa (Richards 1966, 177–8), six, or at the utmost eight, generations seem to be the maximum that can be accurately preserved by oral transmission, and that under the most favourable conditions, when a lineage remained settled in the same area under relatively stable social and economic circumstances. Beyond this limit, and much sooner (as will be seen) in times of change, syncopation — the telescoping of generations — and confusion set in. The genealogists of the succeeding period will endeavour to reduce this confusion to a definitive written record.

The earliest stratum of the Irish genealogies was committed to writing, and so preserved in a definitive form for future generations, during the seventh and eighth centuries. Ó Corráin has argued cogently that the model for this redaction was provided by the genealogies of the children of Israel found in the Bible, and that even the two basic formulae used, the *geinealach*, tracing the single ancestral line of an individual, and the *craobh-sgaoileadh*, listing the offpring of a particular individual

with their descendants in turn, can be traced directly back to scriptural models (Ó Corráin 1999). There can hardly be doubt that the Irish literati of this period, familiar with the scriptural model, saw it as the perfect exemplar for recording the genealogies of their own elite. The forms they adopted, the *geinealach* and the *craobh-sgaoileadh*, remained the invariable ones down to the end of the tradition.

Since they record the descents of a society made up of patrilineages, Irish genealogies are strictly agnatic in form. The names of wives do not appear (in this they differ sharply from the late medieval Welsh genealogies) and, while in the fifteenth century a practice came in, in the case of important chieftaincy lines, of giving the names of mothers, this does not seem to have been persisted in to any great extent. In consequence, in the later period, it is often difficult, in the case of the larger lineages, to identify the particular individuals who occur in the Gaelic genealogies with those who occur in contemporary English records. Thus the tract called *Geinealaighe Fhearmanach* (1931), compiled in 1712 with later additions, names innumerable contemporary members of the Maguire lineage, but it would be difficult, if not impossible, given the constant repetition of forenames and the absence of any subsidiary information (such as regards their residences or marriages), to identify any of them with those whom we would find in contemporary records such as rentals. If the names of mothers, however, were seldom entered in the written genealogies, this does not necessarily mean that they were forgotten or ignored. There is evidence that in some cases they may have been present in oral tradition, and this raises an interesting point as to the extent to which the bare line of the written patrilineal genealogy operated as a framework to be fleshed out by oral tradition, for which it would provide a series of fixed points of reference. The late twelfth-century text known as the *Banshenchas*, 'The History (or rather, Genealogy) of Women' (ed. Dobbs 1930, 1931 1932; Ní Bhrolcháin 1998), records the names of the mothers of kings and of their children, largely for the eleventh and twelfth centuries but extending backwards over the previous centuries and, indeed, into legendary times.

The Gaelic Irish genealogical tradition operated in a society where there was a constant increase in the numbers of the ruling and dominant lineages parallel to that recorded, for example in the Bantu kingdoms of Africa, where, as in Ireland, there was a constant process of the replacement of commoners by members of the dominant lineage, and of the more distant members of the lineage by the sons of the ruling chief (Nicholls 1976). As the seventeenth-century Irish genealogist and antiquary Dubhaltach Mac Firbhisigh expressed it: 'as the sons and families of the rulers multiplied, so their subjects and followers were squeezed out and withered away'. An example of the process can be seen in the Maguire genealogies in the above-mentioned *Geinealaighe Fhearmanach*. By 1607 the members of the Maguire lineage, which had commenced to ramify at the close of the thirteenth century, were in possession of more than three-quarters of the soil of county Fermanagh, having displaced or reduced the clans who had formerly held it. In such a system, where there operates either a system of recognized polygyny or, as in Gaelic Ireland, an inclusive rule of legitimacy which ensures that those born outside recognized wedlock can nevertheless expect to share in the status and social advantages of their fathers, a woman optimizes the opportunity for her children by having them sired, whether within or outside formal marriage, by a member of a dominant lineage (cf. Ridley 1993), which will thus tend to increase in numbers at the expense of subordinate bloodlines. The rule of inclusive legitimacy ensured that children so conceived outside wedlock shared in the status and privileges of their fathers. When, from the Elizabethan period onwards, the Irish gentry and nobility adopted the English practice of making entails of their land to ensure its perpetuation in the patrilineage, it was normal — indeed invariable — for the illegitimate to be brought into them as successors in case of the failure of legitimate heirs. It is noteworthy that in Connacht, where a considerable proportion of native gentry managed to survive the seventeenth-century expropriations, the tradition of their fathering large numbers of illegitimate children remained strong, prompting the antiquary John O'Donovan to write from Mayo in 1839 that 'the curse of bastardy hangs over all this province'(!). Such illegitimate children of the gentry could expect to be well provided for with legacies or the tenancy of good farms, or even, in the case of legitimate heirs failing, with the inheritance of the estate itself (Nicholls 1980, 153–5; Mohr 1994, 114).

In this respect, the detailed descents provided by the Irish genealogies can be used to illustrate the capacity for expansion of particular patrilineages. While the multiple origins of the common Gaelic surnames — there are, for example, two other O'Brien lines of importance besides the descendants of Brian Boru and at least five major and unconnected lines of O'Connor — might inhibit research through DNA analysis of the claim of common descent of the kind which in Israel has validated the claim to a common ancestry of the Jewish priestly caste, the Cohens, this would not apply to the commonest surnames of Anglo-Norman origin, such as Burke and Fitzgerald.

This consideration, of optimizing the advantages for the children, was at the root of the strange Irish custom of the 'naming' of children, by which women would, often on their deathbeds, affiliate their children to fathers other than their husbands or those who had previously been reputed to be the fathers. The named or affiliated son will be denoted in the genealogies by the phrase *mac eile ar na chur chuige* ('another son who was put to him'), later abbreviated to the meaningless *mac eile*. The custom aroused not only the amusement of visiting English Elizabethans, such as Fiennes Moryson, but the furious indignation of contemporary English administrators, who saw clearly its effects in increasing the number of idle 'gentlemen' and swordsmen: one writer of the 1580s proposed drastic punishment for those women who practised it. Although in Gaelic law the affiliated son enjoyed, in theory, a lower legal status than others, this could be overcome by personal ability or other circumstances: one can instance the careers, at a wide remove in time, of Aedh Muimhneach O Conor, King of Connacht, 1278–9, and, most remarkably, of Mathew or Feardorcha O'Neill, Baron of Dungannon, affiliated son of Conn Bacach O'Neill, but chosen by the father as his heir on the death of an elder half-brother, and the father of the famous Hugh O'Neill, Earl of Tyrone.

SOURCES AND STUDIES

What survives to us of the Irish genealogical corpus, although extensive, is only a fragment of what formerly existed. Most of the manuscripts which contained the genealogies must have perished in the wars of the sixteenth and seventeenth centuries — when we are told that Gaelic manuscripts were deliberately targeted — or destruction by the English soldiery and the poverty and neglect of the eighteenth. The process of loss continued into the nineteenth century, as is shown by the survival of texts only in copies made at that period, the originals of which have since disappeared. The *Geinealaighe Fhearmanach* is preserved to us in a copy made in 1849 of a copy of 1809 from an original compiled in 1712. Ó Beacháin's genealogical poem on the O'Sullivans, which can be dated from internal evidence at around 1380, is only preserved (to my knowledge) in early nineteenth-century manuscripts. The mention of Ó Beacháin can be used to draw attention to a third form of genealogical text found in the Irish sources, and which continued right down to the end of the bardic tradition in the early seventeenth century, the detailed genealogy set out in bardic verse. The incessant copying of genealogical texts, and the disappearance of so many of the exemplars, has created the situation in which the date of a text does not depend on that of the manuscript in which it is recorded. Seventeenth-century manuscripts often preserve versions of texts, copied from exemplars now lost, which are older both in language and form than those to be found in the fourteenth-century codices.

Only a small proportion of the Irish genealogical corpus has been published in edited form. In this the early medieval period (the published portions of which are listed in Ó Corráin [1999], 179–81 nn) has been better served than the later. The only major genealogical text of the later period of which there is a satisfactory edition is the late (and often inaccurate) compilation known as *An Leabhar Muimhneach* (ed. Ó Donnchadha 1940), a model of scholarship in the editor's meticulous collation of the many manuscript version of the text and in his inclusion of appendices of related material from other sources. It can be contrasted with the edition of *The Ó Cléirigh Book of Genealogies* (Pender 1962), whose editor has made no attempt to collate the text with the parallel and better version of the greater part which exists in a Trinity College, Dublin manuscript (Nicholls 1975, 256). Mention may also he made of the eighteenth-century *Genealogical history of the O'Reillys* (Carney 1959), which again would have benefited from the inclusion as appendices of the earlier genealogical texts relating to that lineage.

More serious, perhaps, than the absence of published texts is that of adequate guides to the unpublished material. Pender's *Guide to Irish genealogical sources* (Pender 1935) can be described as almost worthless. Many compilers of catalogues of manuscripts seem to have regarded genealogies as so much useless lumber, unworthy of being recorded (Ó Corráin 1999, 179): the *Catalogue of Irish manuscripts in the British Museum* (1926) passes over their presence in total silence! Thus a researcher, say, on the sixteenth-century Magennises of Iveagh, county Down, would not learn from it (any more than he would from Pender) that his best source was Egerton MS 133. *The Catalogue of the Irish manuscripts in Trinity College, Dublin* (1921) does indicate the presence of genealogies, but without listing them individually. But even when the more recent catalogues, such as that of the Royal Irish Academy manuscripts, list genealogies in meticulous detail, such a list in itself is of little use in informing the researcher as to whether the genealogy in question merely repeats the standard version found in many other texts, or whether it contains additional or unique material. This is especially serious since the genealogies of many important lineages, although absent or present only in brief outline in the better-known collections such as Mac Firbisigh or *An Leabhar Muimhneach*, can be found in great detail in lesser-known sources. The O'Kennedys of Ormond and the Magraths are examples which spring immediately to mind.

The Irish genealogists of the so-called 'Gaelic revival' — the great upsurge of literary and historical activity which took place after the virtual collapse of the Anglo-Norman colonial regime in the fourteenth century, and following on a long period when a written genealogical tradition seems only to have endured in the case of a few ruling families of the west, such as the O'Briens — were faced with the task of filling the consequent gap by linking the ruling native lineages of their day with the written genealogies of their ancestors, or, in some cases, putative ancestors (cf. Nicholls 1998, 9–10), which they found in the earlier genealogical texts. A fortunate aid to tracing this process is provided by the earliest surviving genealogical text of this period, the collection (now National Library of Ireland MS G 2) made by Adam Ó Cianáin at dates between 1328 and 1350, which preserves versions of genealogies differing from those which become the accepted ones. From the late fourteenth century on, the genealogists manufactured the ancestry of the great house of O'Connor (Ó Conchobhair) of Uí Failghe (Offaly) by tacking on Muircheartach 'of Kilkenny', ancestor in the fifth degree of Murchadh who ruled from 1382 to 1421, as son of the Donnchadh (killed in 1134) who ended the earlier genealogy at their disposal. This however is flatly contradicted by the Uí Failghe king-list which dates from shortly after 1193, and which shows that Muircheartach ('who was slain by a sergeant at Kilkenny') was the son of a Congalach, and, indeed, Ó Cianáin, writing two generations earlier, provides a genealogy which in this agrees with the king-list (Nicholls 1984, 542).

The genealogies provided for the midlands lineage of the Mac Coghlans (Mac Cochláin) presents an extreme example of this process at work. The Mac Coghlans were the ruling dynasty, from the early eleventh century, of the ancient tribal group of the Dealbhna Bethra (or Ethra), and there is no reason to doubt their genuine descent from the earlier dynasty of kings of the Dealbhna Bethra, whose line was recorded in a genealogy probably dating from no later than the early tenth century. The genealogists of the later period were faced with the task of making the connection. Ó Cianáin interestingly recorded a genealogy of the then Mac Cochláin going back for thirteen generations to the eponym of the surname and no further, but showing clear evidence of oral transmission in the forms used for the names. A generation later, the great antiquary Seaán Mór Ó Dubhagáin (d. 1372) made the connection between the earlier and the later genealogies: dropping the first five generations of Ó Cianáin's genealogy (had they been forgotten in the intervening period?), he merely linked the remainder onto the line of early kings of the Dealbhna Bethra! Since this, however, left the line without an eponymous Cochlán, he doubly remedied this by inserting two Cochláns into the earlier line! But this was not the end. The great early seventeenth-century scholars known as the 'Four Masters' provided a genealogy (back to Adam!) for their patron Toirdhealbhach (Terence) Mac Cochláin by combining the Ó Cianáin descent (this time in its entirety) with the early genealogy of a quite different branch of the Dealbhna tribe, the Dealbhna Mór, who had disappeared at the time of the Anglo-Norman conquest. Finally, in 1644, two O Duigenan genealogists, realizing the fallacy in this version, reconnected the line with the Dealbhna Bethra but retained a few generations taken from the Dealbhna Mór (Nicholls 1983, 445–7)!

No doubt a detailed study of the later genealogies would uncover many more examples of such processes. But even the detailed *craobhsgaoileadh*, the tracing of the descendants of an individual, which we find in the collections of the 'Gaelic revival', may not be as reliable as their appearance would at first lead us to believe. That of the O'Kellys (Uí Ceallaigh of Uí Maine) traces all the descendants of the king of Uí Maine, Domhnall Mór (d. 1224), down to the 1380s; among them is the important line descended from an Eochaidh, a grandson of Domhnall Mór, who subsequently discarded the surname of Ó Ceallaigh for that of Mac Eochadha (Mac Keogh). There would be no reason to doubt the correctness of their descent as given but for the fact that an Eochaidh Mac Eochadha appears in English records as a prominent leader, in precisely the area of the Mac Keogh lordship, in the late thirteenth century. If he is one of the same lineage, then the descent as stated cannot be correct; at the best a generation has been omitted, but the connection with the chiefly O'Kelly line may in fact go back to an earlier, perhaps a much earlier, period. Among the same O'Kelly lineage, too, we find a seventeenth-century example of genealogical manufacture. In the closing years of the sixteenth century, a Colla O'Kelly of Skreen, a member of an obscure and minor branch of the lineage, rose to wealth and importance through service in the Elizabethan army; his son and grandson, John and Colonel Charles O'Kelly, were to rise to even greater prominence. In consequence of this, it was necessary for their ancestors to be brought close to the main chiefly line of the O'Kellys, and this was done by making the ancestor of the Skreen sept, Maghnus Cam, into a grandson of Maelsheachlainn Ó Ceallaigh (d. 1401), the ruler from whom all subsequent chiefs of the O'Kellys had descended. The detailed fifteenth-century

genealogies which are available to us in several manuscript sources show that this is a fiction, and that Maghnus Cam must presumably have belonged to a branch much more remote from the power centre: his insertion into the main chieftainly line was a retrospective validation of the high status achieved by his seventeenth-century descendants.

A lesser form of genealogical manipulation which, though not often provable — given that the majority of Irish genealogies consist of a single line — was certainly common, was the rationalization of genealogies. This takes the form, firstly, of the elimination from the genealogies of those individuals whose descendants had died out, and had consequently been forgotten by tradition — if X has left no surviving descendants, X will be forgotten (since he can only live through his descendants) and, when the oral genealogy comes to be written down, he will be omitted — and secondly, in late sixteenth- and seventeenth-century collections, the rearrangement of the order of seniority among brothers to give a spurious appearance of primogeniture. In the later texts, the son whose descendants ultimately managed to exclude their collaterals and secure a monopoly of the lordship will nearly always be made into the eldest son, although in fact he was not. Both these forms of editing can be strikingly illustrated by comparing the genealogies of the O'Carrolls (Uí Cearbhaill) of Ely (Éile) to be found in the late fourteenth-century *Book of Lecan* and in the seventeenth-century *Leabhar Muimhneach* (Nicholls 1975, 259–60).

But there are other forms of corruption. As an example, the seventeenth-century genealogies of the O'Molloys (Uí Mhaoilmhuaidh) trace the very important sept called Sliocht Mhic Teabóid to Teabóid (Theobald), a son of the Ruaidhrí who died as chief in 1383, and the Sliocht Coilín to Coilín, brother of Ruaidhrí. In fact, as a contemporary genealogical poem by Seaán Mór Ó Dubhagáin shows, the Teabóid in question was Ruaidhrí's elder brother, not his son, and Coilín was his uncle, not his brother. Such misplacings are endemic in many collections of genealogies.

The period between the 'Gaelic revival' of the fourteenth century and the destruction of the old Irish social order in the mid-seventeenth was perhaps the high-water mark of the Irish genealogical tradition, maintained by the professional learned families, the O Mulconrys, O Duigenans, O Duggans, MacFirbises, Magraths of Munster, O Dineens and O Luinins, who appear to have kept the genealogies of the Irish upper classes on a regular and continuing basis (Nicholls 1975). From the fifteenth century on the gaelicized families of Anglo-Norman descent were included in their work; the earliest surviving material of this kind is a group of de Burgo (Bourke) genealogies written, from internal evidence, *ca.* 1460 and included in a fragmentary but interesting manuscript dating from around 1500 (Dublin, King's Inns, Benchers' Library, MS G 11), but it is probable that there had been earlier examples. The missing leaves of the *Book of Uí Maine* and of the *Leabhar Donn* (RIA MS 23 Q 10) may possibly have contained such material. It is however notable that the Gaelic genealogies of the Anglo-Norman lineages of Munster (such as the Barrys or the Earls of Desmond) are, in general, totally unreliable for the period before the Gaelic revival. Whether this arises from the fact that it was not until after that period that these lineages adopted the use of Irish and became patrons of the learned families — as the fourth Earl of Ormonde (the 'White' Earl) was of the Magraths — or whether it is a consequence of the failure of oral tradition and so an indication that these genealogies were not written down before the sixteenth century, must remain uncertain. Nevertheless, the work of these professional genealogists, or such of it as survives to us, represents an extraordinarily valuable body of material which has hardly been discussed, let alone utilized. It must be stressed that the genealogies of even important lineages may only be found in a single obscure manuscript or in the compilations of the early eighteenth century, such as that found in a number of manuscripts (Nicholls 1975, 261, where I ascribed its compilation to Richard Tipper, the scribe of one of the copies in RIA MS P 41) or Roger O'Ferrall's *Linea Antiqua* (National Library of Ireland, Genealogical Office MS 155), written in English and arranged in the form of genealogical 'trees'. Both of these contain not only genealogies brought down to their own time but lines terminating at a much earlier date.

Another group of genealogical sources does not belong to the Gaelic but to an Anglo-Irish or English tradition. These have attracted, perhaps paradoxically, even less attention than the Gaelic ones, and this applies in excessive measure to one of the most important and interesting of them, Trinity College, Dublin MS 1212 (formerly E.3.2), compiled apparently by Christopher Ussher (later Ulster King of Arms), in the 1570s and early 1580s, but virtually unused by researchers (other than the present writer!). It would appear to have been formerly more extensive than now, since some material of the same type and date, but not now present in MS 1212, was copied by Dr Thomas Madden in the late seventeenth century into another TCD MS 1217 (formerly F.4.18). The contents include genealogies, in tabular form, obviously derived from oral sources, of many of the families of the Pale, along with various linkages of relationships, apparently drawn up for the purpose of challenging jurors and similar purposes; they exhibit the usual contradictions and faults to be found in orally preserved material, but are nevertheless of extreme value. To the same type of material belong the extensive genealogical collections, heavily but far from

exclusively of Munster interest, drawn up by the Elizabethan soldier and administrator Sir George Carew, afterwards Earl of Totnes (d. 1629). The main collections are in Lambeth Palace Library MSS 626 and (especially) 635, but there is also material in MS 599. Most of these were collected from oral informants (whose identity is occasionally stated) and, while of extraordinary interest in recording marriages, illegitimate children (and scandals such as incests), they tend to falter when they go back more than two generations. There is, however, some material in them of a *craobhsgaoileadh* nature, probably derived from Gaelic sources, dealing with the Kavanaghs, the Burkes and some Gaelic families of Connacht. Some fragments have been published in local journals and elsewhere, but again the collections have been little utilized. Some similar material, as well as English transcriptions of Gaelic genealogies, can be found in the collections of Daniel Molyneux, Ulster King of Arms (d. 1633), some of which, known to have existed in the 1790s have since been lost but which are still represented by National Archives, Dublin, MS M. 2550.

The seventeenth century saw not only the wholesale destruction of Irish manuscripts but also the complete break-up of the old order, with the dispossession of the majority of the old aristocracy and gentry, who were reduced to the alternatives of poverty or exile. In these circumstances the old genealogical tradition faded and died, but it took a long time to do so as families like the O'Duggans of county Galway and the O Luinins (or Lynegars, as they anglicized their name) in county Fermanagh continued to record genealogies into the eighteenth century. The former were probably the source of the detailed information on the O'Kellys which Roger O'Ferrall recorded in his *Linea Antiqua*; an interesting detail is that his mistake of 'Tuo Clery' for a hypothetical 'Tuo Clevy' (*Tuath 'tsléibhe*) shows that the exemplar had been transmitted to him in anglicized spelling.

A considerable amount of research has been done on the pre-twelfth-century genealogies and their compilers, most of that in recent years being by Donnchadh Ó Corráin (Ó Corráin 1999, where useful references will also be found to the work of earlier researchers), but the later ones, apart from the work of Nollaig Ó Muraíle on the great seventeenth-century scholar Dubhaltach Mac Firbhisigh (Ó Muraíle 1996), have remained virtually uninvestigated. The situation has not been helped by the intrusion into the field of well-meaning but ignorant amateurs, lacking the critical skills adequately to evaluate their sources. The most urgent need now is for a satisfactory guide to the later genealogies, especially those remaining uncatalogued in the British Library and Trinity College, Dublin — but this I fear is likely to remain a desideratum, at least in the immediate future.

Bibliography

Anon. 1931 'Geinealaighe Fhearmanach', *Analecta Hibernica* **3**, pp. 62–150.

Carney, J. 1959 *A genealogical history of the O'Reillys*. Cumann Sheanchais Breifne.

Dobbs, M. C. (ed) 1930, 1931, 1932 'The Ban-shenchas', *Revue Celtique* **47**, pp. 284-39; **48**, pp. 284-339; **49**, pp. 437-89.

Mohr, P. 1994 'John Birminghmam of Tuam: a most unusual landlord', *Journal of the Galway Archeological and Historical Society* **46**, pp. 111–55.

Ní Bhrolcháin, M. 1998 *An Banshenchas*. Dublin.

Nicholls, K. W. 1975 'The Irish genealogies, their value and defects', *The Irish Genealogist* **2**, pp. 256–61.

Nicholls, K. W. 1980 (ed) 'The Lynch-Blosse Papers', *Analecta Hibernica* **29**, pp. 113–218.

Nicholls, K. W. 1983 'The MacCoghlans', *Irish Genealogist* **4**, pp. 445–60.

Nicholls, K. W. 1984 'The land of the Leinstermen', *Peritia* **3**, pp. 535–58.

Nicholls, K. W. 1998 'Críoch Branach: the O Byrnes and their country' in *Feagh McHugh O'Byrne: the Wicklow Firebrand; Journal of the Rathdrum Historical Society* **1**, pp. 17–39.

Ó Corráin, D. 1999 'Creating the past: the early Irish genealogical tradition', *Peritia* **12**, pp. 177–208.

Ó Donnchadha, T. (ed) 1940 *An Leabhar Muimhneach*. Dublin.

Ó Muraíle, N. 1996 *Dubhaltach Mac Fhirbhisigh (ca. 1600–71), his lineage, life and learning*. Maynooth.

Pender, P. 1935 *A guide to Irish genealogical sources*, *Analecta Hibernica* **7**. Dublin.

Pender, P. 1959 *Ó Cléirigh book of genealogies*, *Analecta Hibernica* **18**. Dublin.

Ridley, M. 1993 'The rite of the genes', *Times Literary Supplement*, 16 July.

Richards, A. I. 1966 'Social mechanisms for the transfer of political rights in some African tribes', *Journal of the Royal Anthropological Institute* **90**, pp. 173–88.

Folklore and Ethnology

DIARMUID Ó GIOLLÁIN

This chapter will look at the history of the ideas from which folklore and ethnology emerged as well as their application in the Irish context. These ideas developed in various European countries under specific circumstances and prospered where conditions were politically propitious. The notion of folklore that crystallized envisaged an ancient cultural inheritance, a 'contemporary pre-history' in the unhappy phrase. But this notion was in fact a product of modernity, a result of the reflexivity that is part of all modern culture. Folklore was predicated on the death of tradition, a key concern of European thought since the end of the eighteenth century. It has been taken for granted for generations that modern society has no place for traditional ways of life, that modernity and tradition are incompatible. This has led both to a celebration of the onward march of humanity, unburdened by the dead weight of ancestors, and to a lament for the loss of a sense of continuity with the past, with all its moral and political implications.

THE INTERNATIONAL BACKGROUND

The emergence of empiricism and rationalism led to the undermining of tradition's claim to truth. Its value as precedent and as authority for significant human activities was reduced by the notion of progress and the concomitant rise of capitalism, which looked towards the future and to the consequences of actions. The growth of the absolutist state from the seventeenth and eighteenth centuries led to centralization and state encroachment on more and more domains of social life. The Enlightenment in the eighteenth century was explicitly hostile to tradition. Its project was a universal one, seeing a single path to progress. It despised the ignorance of the common people while at the same time saw them as the necessary symbolic legitimation for civil government (Gross 1992; Martín-Barbero 1993). The progressive bourgeoisie rejoiced at the end of tradition in part because tradition was an ideological support for the

ancien régime. The Industrial Revolution from the late eighteenth and early nineteenth centuries had a colossal impact on traditional life. The mechanization and rationalization of agriculture drove millions of peasants from their traditional world into industrial cities at home and abroad. At the same time consumer capitalism increasingly penetrated social life and made traditional arts and crafts redundant. Notions of rationality gradually extended into all aspects of public life and increasingly into private life, conflicting with inherited world-views (Gross 1992). All of these factors led to a greater distance between elites and the common people, both of which previously shared popular culture. By the nineteenth century popular culture was the sole preserve of the lower classes. The withdrawal of the elites from it lessened its integrative role for society as a whole and deprived popular traditions of a wider authority in society (Burke 1994; Muchembled 1991). A specifically Irish backdrop to these developments was the seventeenth-century destruction of the native elite, which caused the decay of all Gaelic learned traditions and a profound rupture in social and cultural life. Continuous oppression of the Catholic population led to a slow decline of the Irish language and popular Gaelic traditions. The Great Famine and its aftermath intensified the destruction of traditional life.

The 'discovery' of America had a deep impact on European thought, one aspect of which was the idealization of the 'savage'. This cultural relativism cleared the way towards the rehabilitation of that other savage, distinguished too by simplicity, virtuousness and lack of artifice: the European peasant. Cultural relativism was a useful way to criticize the European feudal and absolutist order as well as the universal pretensions of the Enlightenment. Jean-Jacques Rousseau (1712–78) was particularly influential in the spread of the notion of the Noble Savage and had an enthusiasm for rural life, disdaining the decadence of Paris. His famous letter to the Poles encouraged them to resist the Russians by being true to their own traditions (Cocchiara 1971). James Macpherson's *Ossian* (from 1760) had a sensational impact on contemporary European sensibility. Ostensibly translations of the third century Scottish bard (Oisín), the poems of Macpherson (1736–96) were loosely based on the common Gaelic tradition of the Fianna. The importance of *Reliques of ancient English poetry* (1765) by the English bishop Thomas Percy (1729–1811) was, as with Macpherson, in helping to initiate a new sensibility and in rehabilitating the 'Gothic' and the 'Celtic', previously synonymous with barbarism (Cocchiara 1971). Thus the 'revolt of poetry' encouraged a more positive evaluation of tradition by using popular poetry to renew a jaded art poetry. Celts and Goths, barbarian peoples who were enemies of classical civilization, were rehabilitated and an interest in them became fashionable (Chapman 1992).

The reaction against the abstract universalism of the Enlightenment was in full swing when Johann Gottfried von Herder (1744–1803), its most formidable adversary, came on the scene. Herder opposed the evolutionary idea of progress which saw France at the pinnacle of a supreme European civilization. He insisted that every nation was a separate organism with its own history and its own destiny, whose soul (*Volksgeist*) was expressed in its folk poetry. He opposed classicism and German imitation of foreign models (the Renaissance had much less resonance in central and northern Europe). He argued that the Germans had to return to their authentic origins. He was the first to use the word 'culture' in the plural, breaking with the notion of culture as a unilinear process culminating in contemporary European refinement. To him the people offered the means to renew the nation. The word *Volk* itself was productive in its very ambiguity, with connotations both of people and of nation. *Volkslieder* (also the title of Herder's famous collection published in 1778–1779) were both 'folk songs' and 'national songs': he referred to them as 'the archives of the *Volk*'. It was in these songs that the nation affirmed itself, which is why he could include in his anthology famous writers such as Goethe, who were true to the *Volksgeist* (Cocchiara 1971; Berlin 1976; Bausinger 1993). A pre-Romantic era characterized by sensibility, exoticism and the idealization of the primitive can thus be seen as coexisting with the Age of Enlightenment.

Romanticism flourished in the first half of the nineteenth century among the aristocracy and the middle classes in Europe. It reacted against the inheritance of the Enlightenment and critiqued that of the two revolutions, the French and the Industrial, which were transforming contemporary European society. It was contradictory in many ways, yearning for a utopian future and nostalgic for a past Golden Age. Its characteristics included a fascination with imagination, the

spiritual and the irrational, horror at the degradation and exploitation of capitalism and industrial society and reverence for nature and the countryside. It opposed universalism, arguing for the specificity and singularity of individuals, communities, places and situations; and the aesthetic implications of this conflicted with the notion of a classical canon (Porter and Teich 1988; Schenk 1979). Romanticism transformed the negative attitude to the popular and saw it as a major resource for artistic creativity. It embraced distant places, the exotic, the picturesque, the peasant, and found the antiquarian, focussed on the particular rather than the universal, particularly receptive (Ortiz 1992).

The Grimm Brothers, Jacob (1785–1863) and Wilhelm (1786–1859), helped to lay the foundations for folklore scholarship. Their collection of folktales, *Kinder- und Hausmärchen* (1812), was the second most widely read book in nineteenth-century Germany. They played a major role in establishing the notion of folklore as a collective and communal, rather than individual, creation. They saw folklore as a historical source with the continuity of tradition linking prehistory to the present. Jacob's *Deutsche Mythologie* (1835) was a key work in the development of comparative folklore scholarship. It used the evidence of comparative linguistics, Old Norse literature, the descriptions of classical writers, the poetry of the Christian Middle Ages and contemporary folklore to reconstruct Germanic mythology. Under the influence of comparative philology and the *Rig-Veda*, Wilhelm argued that folktales were a common Indo-European inheritance and were the end result of the long degradation of myths, two ideas that had a great influence on folklore scholarship. In the same way oral poetry was seen as the result of the fragmentation of the original epic. The brothers inspired vast collections of folklore, in Germany and elsewhere (Thompson 1971; Cocchiara 1971). From the middle of the nineteenth century evolutionism, particularly in the form of the 'social Darwinism' of Herbert Spencer (1820–1903), tended to dominate scholarly thinking, seeing unified processes of development in the world which operated strictly in accordance with certain laws. This thinking was positivistic, demanding the accumulation of hard evidence as the basis for conclusions. It helped folklore scholarship to develop in a more scientific direction. Nevertheless it shared a historical perspective with Romantic folklore scholarship. Evolutionists, however, saw folklore as a stage, now almost superseded, on the upward development to higher cultural forms while Romantics saw it as the decayed residue of a higher moral and cultural unity in the past (Ortiz 1992; Hautala 1968).

The notion of folklore as 'survivals' is associated with Edward Tylor (1832–1917), whose *Primitive culture* (1871) was both a foundational anthropological text and a major spur to folklorists. Tylor saw various marginal and residual cultural phenomena as 'survivals' (not 'superstitions'), the historical evidence of an earlier cultural state, maintained by inertia. He was thus able to compare 'primitives' and European peasants, who both preserved elements of primitive mentalities. Tylor's influence was particularly strong among folklorists in England, France and Italy, in which countries it was now possible to see folklore as cultural elements of those groups least exposed to progress, archaic survivals in the modern age (Ortiz 1992). The word 'folklore' was coined by the English antiquary W. J. Thoms in 1846 as an 'Anglo-Saxon' equivalent of 'popular antiquities', by which the field had previously been known. The first Folklore Society was founded in England in 1878 and its prestige was reflected in the hosting of the International Folklore Congress in London in 1891, the zenith of the influence of British folklorists (Dorson 1968). As a result of this prestige the word 'folklore' passed into many other European languages (the German *Volkskunde* is an older word, recorded before the last quarter of the eighteenth century, but in the context of statistical investigation into the common people). The study of folk culture, as folkloristics or as ethnology (the study of folklife, or, folk and popular culture), became well established in German-speaking, Nordic and central/eastern European universities, ethnology often having a close relationship with ethnographic and with local museums. The pioneering open-air folk museum, Skansen, was founded in Stockholm in 1891 and stands beside the Nordic Museum and the Ethnology Department of Stockholm University. The English and the French folklorists were less successful in establishing folklore as a scientific discipline, seeking a methodology which they never properly achieved. They tended to be provincial intellectuals, their field of interest supported by literary and antiquarian societies rather than by universities, which gave no space to them (Ortiz 1992).

The study of folklore was professionalized as an academic discipline above all in countries where it offered non-metropolitan intellectuals the means to 'de-provincialize' themselves by giving them the basis for a national culture. Finland gives a good example of that, though politically it had ceased to be a Swedish province when it was conquered by Russia in 1809. The wish to reconstruct the original epic was manifest in the work of Elias Lönnrot (1802–84), creator of the national epic, *Kalevala* (1835), which was synthesized from his extensive collection of oral epic songs. In Finland it has been seen, depending on various political conjunctures, as either history or myth. Julius Krohn (1835–88) and his son Kaarle (1863–1933), and the latter's student Antti Aarne (1867–1925), developed the Finnish or historical geographic method for studying the folktale which was to dominate folklore scholarship until the mid-twentieth century. It had its origins in Julius's study of the sources of *Kalevala* and is clearly evolutionistic in inspiration. Finland was one of the pioneers of folklore research: a department of folklore was established in the university in Finland as early as 1898 (Hautala 1968; Thompson 1971).

The ideas outlined above led to a clearly defined notion of the culture of the common people of the countryside, the 'folk'. Its specificity rested on its lack of contamination from modern high culture, the result of its isolation and distance from the metropolis. Its authenticity was the proof of that separation. Sealed off from modern social dynamics, the past was fossilized in folklore. The folk transcended history and was beyond social or historical analysis. One influential notion saw the common people simply as reproducers of what had been created in an earlier period by the upper social strata, thus denying their creativity, and helping to justify the lack of any 'sociological' interest in them. The culture of the people was not, paradoxically, 'popular culture' (Martín-Barbero 1993; Ortiz 1996). The philological approach which dominated the field of folklore study from the Grimms until the middle of this century was often in close alliance with nation-building projects. The Romantic notion of the folk was attractive to conservative political ideologies since it side-stepped real questions of power and social justice, refusing to explain cultural difference through differences in power and wealth. In many countries the interest in the folk is directly related to the rise of the urban proletariat, who became an object of dread and the inspiration for new scientific fields of enquiry such as crowd psychology and criminal anthropology (De Certeau, Julia and Revel 1993; Mattelart 1996). But the Romantics also legitimized forms of culture other than those of the elite. Imagining a past Golden Age as an inspiration for building a better future instilled a sense of pride in cultures traditionally associated with the common people. Symbols of national identity were provided for many European peoples by elements of folkore (Hofer 1991), both in their own right and as supposed relics of an earlier native high culture. The Romantic idealization of the countryside was a counter to the corruption, foreignness and inauthenticity of the city. The town was unworthy of interest, a place whose inhabitants, in Herder's words, 'never sing and compose, but only scream and mutilate'. Modern processes of industrialization, migration and democratization, however, led to the growth of large urban populations which could no longer be defined within the traditional social structure. The culture of these populations was the result of a complex process of transference, blending and transformation (Kaschuba 1995), but the challenge of investigating urban popular culture was not to be taken up by folklorists until the middle of the twentieth century. The Romantic autonomy of the folk is easily denied. The folk was in effect the peasantry, rural cultivators, raising crops and livestock, part of a wider society and in a symbiotic relationship with a larger outside world, with market towns and with the guidance of elites, who were mediators between local life and the wider world. It was neither isolated nor complete in itself, politically, economically nor culturally: it was subaltern. The folk *was* the product of a historical process, firmly within the framework of the state and in an unavoidable relationship with an official, or hegemonic, culture.

Lauri Honko (1991) talks about 'the first life of folklore' as its natural, unreflexive, almost imperceptible, existence in a community. The consciousness raising, the reflexivity, caused by the intellectuals who discovered folklore inevitably changed the way in which the 'folklore community' saw its own culture and heritage. The cultural elements in question now carried additional meanings: national, or indeed commercial. Singularity has always been taken to distinguish the work of art from the work of craft. The process of collecting creates scarcity, so scarce objects become singular by being removed from everyday life to be displayed as art in ethnographic and anthropological museums, despite being multiple objects in the ordinary context of their use (Kirshenblatt-Gimblett 1991). This is the danger of aesthetism, of dissociating objects on aesthetic grounds from their function and from social life. For the same reasons there was less interest in material folk culture in many countries because it quite clearly belonged to the prosaic and pragmatic realm of the basic necessities of peasant life whereas 'oral literature' was less obviously tied to function and belonged to a more poetic domain that seemed to transcend those conditions (Bausinger 1993). Hall (1981) argues that in every period the cultural process involves selecting what will be incorporated into high culture and what will not. García Canclini (1995) maintains that cultural heritage is used as a resource to reproduce social difference. The dominant groups determine which elements are superior and to be conserved, and invest them with refinement. The cultural products created by non-dominant groups may be of great creative value, but these groups have not the same possibility to turn those products into a widely recognized and accepted heritage. It may be difficult for them to accumulate such cultural products over time due to poverty or repression. Similarly, to convert them into an objective form independent of oral tradition and individual transmission demands resources available only to dominant groups. The selection of the cultural heritage is part of the process of identity. Honko (1991) defines identity as an ordering principle which selects elements from a group's culture and uses them to represent the group in its dealings with other groups. Honko uses the notion of 'the second life of folklore' to refer to folklore materials being used in different

contexts to the original one and makes a convincing case for the relativity of notions of inauthenticity in such cases in order to emphasize the unmistakable cultural importance of such phenomena. Is folklore 'national'? Folklore in the national Romantic frame was understood as representing in some way the *Volksgeist*, the spirit or genius of the nation. The process of recording, storing and archiving folklore helped to map the national territory, to nationalize the land, and presented it in microcosm in the ethnographic or folk museum or national folklore archive. The ethnographic museum, argues García Canclini (1995), by bringing together large numbers of artefacts in the capital, prioritizes the capital's pre-eminent synthesizing cultural role. He asks if national identity can be affirmed 'without reducing ethnic and regional peculiarities to a constructed common denominator'.

From the 1960s folklore reorientated itself in many ways and for a variety of reasons. The defeat of Fascism discredited one of its ideological foundations, the mysti-fication of the folk. Decolonization compromised evolu-tionist notions of the primitive. Traditional rural life continued to decline. There was an increasing engagement of folklorists with the social sciences and particularly with anthropology. And the rise of new social movements in the 1960s helped to create a new sensi-tivity to issues of power in society. The notion of mass-mediated culture has been usefully applied since the 1970s to all forms of culture disseminated through the mass media irrespective of their origin, whether in elite, folk, popular or mass culture. The folk is often associated with the premodern, but modernity does not necessarily suppress traditional culture. Indeed, it can be developed and transformed for different reasons, from continuity in traditional cultural production to the needs of the market to include traditional elements in order to reach particular groups, to political systems using folklore to help to legitimize themselves (García Canclini 1995). Folklore today is understood in various but related ways. For some it is 'oral literature' or 'verbal art', seen as being traditional and practised in small groups: 'the lore of the folk'. For other scholars the field of folklore includes oral literature, material culture, folk custom and belief and folk art (music, dance, drama), again being traditional and associated with small groups. In this case it has usually been associated with residual pre- or early modern agrarian or peasant society. In more recent times these definitions have expanded to take in the traditional informal and unofficial aspects of modern culture which fit into these categories. An over-arching definition, which owes much to the influence of the writings of the Italian political thinker, Antonio Gramsci, sees folklore as subaltern cultures, the cultures of groups who are removed from power. According to this view, subaltern cultures are heterogeneous, belonging both to the countryside and to the town, are informal and unofficial, and consist of elements generated from their own resources as well as those borrowed from outside, which are 'negotiated' with the dominant culture. This definition has the merit of reminding us that power relations are always a part of culture and that the popular is not defined by any *a priori* essence, but by its positioning in a complex socio-cultural system.

THE IRISH CONTEXT

An historical overview of Irish folklore should take cognisance of the varied definitions of what folklore is. Folklore was more easily isolated if seen as purely oral, traditional and rustic. To consider it ancient made it a historical source, of scholarly interest in the same way that historical documents or archaeological artefacts were, so that the notion of antiquities brought all three together. If the emphasis was on the native Irish aspect of it then folklore shared a common subaltern status with the language, so that traditional song and learned eighteenth- and nineteenth-century poetry in Irish both belonged to the same category. It is also worth mentioning the importance of sources for Irish popular culture such as the 'literature of confutation' (official religious catalogues of popular 'errors' from the seventeenth century), official enquiries (such as the Ordnance Survey, from 1824, and the 1835 Poor Law enquiry) and travel writing (the Breton Chevalier de la Tocnaye in the 1790s, the Anglo-Irish couple Mr and Mrs Hall and the Englishman Thackeray in the 1840s, for example). The 'first practitioner of ethnology in Ireland' (Ó Danachair 1983) was General Charles Vallancey (1721–1812), who wrote on traditional festivals in the twelfth volume (1783) of his *Collectanea de rebus Hibernicis* (1770–1804). Charlotte Brooke (1740?–93) was 'the first mediator of importance between the Irish-Gaelic and the Anglo-Irish literary traditions' (Leerssen 1996). Encouraged by Bishop Percy among others, she published Irish texts and translations from both oral and literary traditions in her *Reliques of Irish poetry* (1789) and in the only issue of *Bolg an Tsolair* (1795), the Gaelic journal published by the United Irish organ, the *Northern Star*. Edward Bunting (1773–1843) was the first collector of Irish music, from both the popular and the learned traditions. Enthused by the Belfast Harp Festival held in 1792, where he transcribed the music, he immediately afterwards set forth to west Ulster and Connacht to collect more music, publishing *A general collection of the ancient music of Ireland* in 1796. Since the words of the songs had not been transcribed, Patrick Lynch, an Irish scholar, was sent at the expense of the McCracken family to make good the deficit. To the same Belfast milieu of Irish studies belongs the contribution of Robert Mac Adam (1808–95), who made the first collection of Gaeltacht folklore. Travelling Ulster, selling the wares of his family's ironmonger's and saddler's business, he took advantage of the occasions to collect Irish manuscripts and oral traditions. His collections were entered in a book, often indicating the person from whom he recorded and the year of the recording, which consists of tales, proverbs, verses and songs (Ó Buachalla 1968). Mac Adam made the largest collection of proverbs in Ireland: 'Six Hundred Gaelic Proverbs Collected in Ulster' was published in the journal which he had founded and of which he was the first editor, *The Ulster Journal of Archaeology*, between 1853 and 1862 (Williams 1995).

The abiding interest of the Corkman, Thomas Crofton Croker (1798–1854), was in the popular tradition of Ireland, where he continued to visit during his holidays, having taken up a position as an admiralty clerk in London in 1818. He persuaded friends to help him by recording tales, which he was to edit, polish, refine, colour, and publish. In 1824 he published in London *Researches in the south of Ireland, illustrative of the scenery, architectural remains and the manners and superstitions of the peasantry with an appendix containing a private narrative of the rebellion of 1798*, a major source for contemporary Irish popular culture, with specific chapters devoted to 'History and National Character', 'Fairies and Supernatural Agency', 'Keens and Death Customs' and 'Manners and Customs'. In terms of the history of folklore research, Croker's second book is of especial importance. Published anonymously in London in 1825, *Fairy legends and traditions of the south of Ireland* was the first collection of oral tales to appear in the then United Kingdom. It was an immediate success and won the praise of such figures as Sir Walter Scott and the brothers Grimm. The latter had it translated into German as *Irische Elfenmärchen* within a year. A second and a third volume of tales appeared under Croker's name in 1828, the first dedicated to Scott, the second to the brothers, and the latter included a translation of an essay on Irish and Scottish fairy traditions which the Grimms had written for *Elfenmärchen*. In 1844 he published another book dealing with popular culture, *The keen in the south of Ireland*. Many commercially successful collections of tales were published in the nineteenth century following on Croker's work, and, like his, were edited into extravagant styles owing little to oral narration. Two figures stand out, the Wexford bookseller Patrick Kennedy (1801–73) and the Irish–American, Jeremiah Curtin (1838–1906). At the same time there was a continuous line of interest in the Irish language and Irish 'antiquities' from a linguistic, literary, historical, and archaeological perspective. Romantic historicism encouraged a fascination with the Celts, partly inspired by the success of Macpherson's *Ossian*, and it facilitated an enthusiasm for Celtic 'past and peasant'.

The speed with which the country changed in the nineteenth century was noted by many writers. It is clear that change had been hastened by the Great Famine. *Irish popular superstitions* (1853), by Sir William Wilde (1815–76), showed characteristic antiquarian concerns but, less typically, a deep sympathy for the peasantry in a period of intense change, which he saw as endangering traditional culture and which he attributed both to modernity and to the catastrophic Famine years. Similar concerns were to motivate Douglas Hyde in his agenda-setting lecture for Irish cultural nationalism, given in 1892. There he decried the influence of British popular culture — music hall ballads, popular literature and games — in the same way that a later generation in many countries would complain about the de-nationalizing influence of North American popular culture. The lecture, 'The necessity for de-Anglicising Ireland', shows that Hyde had assimilated contemporary ideas of the relationship between language and nation, and it seemed to him that Ireland was throwing away the very proof of its own nationhood (Hyde 1986). Hyde's challenge was answered in the foundation in 1893 of the Gaelic League, which set itself the task of reviving the Irish language and creating a modern literature in it. From the beginning the League published extensive collections of folklore, since it was the most obvious source for accessible texts in modern Irish (O'Leary 1994). The gatherings of the League and their cultural festivals promoted, in addition to creative writing (most often reworkings of folklore), traditional arts such as dancing, singing and storytelling (Ó Súilleabháin 1984). The Gaelic League and the work of the folklorists helped to legitimate the culture of the Irish-speaking west.

From 1890 Hyde began publishing songs with translations and commentary, firstly in *The Nation*, and they were to be collected as *Love songs of Connacht* (1893). The tales were published as *Leabhar sgéaluigheachta* in 1889. They were followed by a bilingual collection, *Beside the fire* (1890), and tales in a French translation published in 1893 in booklet form, and in an expanded Irish-French edition as *An Sgeuluidhe Gaedhealach* (1901). *Beside the fire's* 'Preface' gives a pioneering and influential historical overview of the collecting of Irish folklore. Hyde's methods were much more scientific than those of his predecessors, identifying his informants, giving their exact words, and scrupulously editing, translating and contextualizing. There is scholarly commentary on differences and similarities between the Irish and Scottish Gaelic traditions and on the orality/literacy question ('old Aryan traditions' and 'bardic inventions'), and explanations of the meaning of tales typical of the contemporary mythological school. He also gives portraits of storytellers.

Love songs of Connacht had a huge influence on writing in English, providing the example for Lady Gregory and Synge. Hyde is the key link between the literary revival in English and the Gaelic revival, between writing in English and writing in Irish, between the artistic use of folklore and the scholarly study of it. W. B. Yeats (1865–1939) was central to the role of folklore in the literary revival (Thuente 1980; Foster 1987). He published *Fairy and folk tales of the Irish peasantry* in 1888 and Irish fairy tales in 1892, both anthologies of stories and poems by various authors and collectors, including himself. *The Celtic twilight* (1893) is a mixture of oral testimony and tradition, his own spiritual experiences and his commentary and speculation, and was very influential, on the revival and much later on Lady Gregory's important collection *Visions and beliefs in the west of Ireland* (1920). Lady Gregory (1852–1932), through Hyde, was to experience popular culture as a revelation. *Poets and dreamers: studies and translations from the Irish* (1903) consists of essays on various popular themes and includes folktales, legends, verses and beliefs, as well as four of Hyde's plays on folk themes. *Poets and dreamers* does not give the names of her informants, nor does *The Kiltartan history book* (1909), which consists of a groundbreaking collection of oral historical accounts on a huge variety of subjects. John Millington Synge (1871–1909) had studied the Irish language and was particularly taken with *Love songs of Connacht*. He intensively studied comparative mythology and folklore and brought Hyde's *Beside the fire* and Campbell of Islay's *Popular tales of the Western Highlands* with him to Aran as a guide. Much folklore appears in various of his published writings and in his diary (Kiberd 1979). As with Yeats and Lady Gregory, Synge saw great artistic potential in folklore. Folklore, literature and Celtic studies came together in a particularly rich manner in the Blasket Islands through the influence of visiting scholars and Gaelic League enthusiasts, leading to a remarkable body of autobiographical writing, rich in ethnographic detail provided – uniquely – from the inside. Tomás Ó Criomhthain (1856–1937), a *seanchaí* who, as informant, was the source for the folklore collected by Robin Flower and edited by Séamus Ó Duilearga as *Seanchas ón Oileán Tiar* (1956), also wrote *Allagar na hInise* (1928) and the classic *An tOileánach* (1929), translated into English (*The Islandman*) and many other languages. The celebrated storyteller Peig Sayers (1873–1958), besides a large number of tales collected from her and deposited in the folklore archives, also left her own accounts of her life, dictated to (and thus in various ways mediated through) Máire Ní Chinnéide (*Peig*, 1936) and Peig's son Mícheál Ó Gaoithín (*Machtnamh seanmhná*, 1939, and *Beatha Pheig Sayers*, 1970).

The new Irish state helped to institutionalize the collection and archiving of folklore, under the leadership of Séamus Ó Duilearga (J. H. Delargy, 1899–1980), an assistant of Hyde's who, like his colleagues, had been formed in the Gaelic League. The stimulus partly came from eminent folklorists, the Norwegian Christiansen and the Swede von Sydow, who emphasized the importance of the Irish folk tradition. Both of them also learnt Irish and are an indication of the international contacts and broad perspective which were to be very much a part of Ó Duilearga's work. On 11 January 1927 the Folklore of Ireland Society (An Cumann le Béaloideas Éireann) was founded. It undertook to publish a folklore journal, and the motto of the Society was printed on the journal's cover: *Colligite quae superaverunt fragmenta, ne pereant*. Pádraig Ó Siochfhradha (An Seabhac) was elected president with Hyde as treasurer and Ó Duilearga as editor of the journal and librarian. Ó Duilearga's 1927 editorial in the first issue of *Béaloideas* gave practical and methodological advice to collectors of folklore while emphasizing the national importance of the task and the need for folklore to be the foundation of a new national literature in Irish. The Society began quickly to amass material donated by enthusiasts. The government, after continued representation, gave a small grant to establish the Irish Folklore Institute, headed by Ó Duilearga, in 1930. Further grants, from private sources abroad, followed and it was possible to make some collections and to publish three volumes. By 1935 some fifty thousand pages were in the possession of the Institute. In 1935 the government established Coimisiún Béaloideasa Éireann (the Irish Folklore Commission) to collect, catalogue and publish Irish folklore, with Ó Duilearga as honorary director and Seán Ó Súilleabháin (1903–96) as archivist. The latter spent three months training in Sweden at the Dialect and Folklore Archive of Uppsala University and part of the result was a handbook for folklore collectors — *Láimhleabhar béaloideasa* — published in 1937 (an enlarged version, as *A handbook of Irish folklore*, appeared in 1942).

The first full-time folklore collectors were appointed in 1935. They usually numbered from seven to ten, mostly natives of the areas in which they worked, and were all male. They were generally sent to Irish-speaking districts, equipped with an ediphone recording machine, the wax cylinders of which were transcribed into standard notebooks which were sent to the offices of the Commission. They kept a field diary of their daily activities, particularly valuable for the detailed descriptions of fieldwork and of individual informants. Evidence enough of how close collectors were to their informants is the fact that many collected from members of their own families and from neighbours. Hundreds of others collected folklore in a voluntary capacity, and sent it to the Commission. In the late 1930s there were between 100 and 150 part-time collectors. Perhaps not much more than one-eighth of the thousands who contributed in a part-time capacity and about six thousand out of forty thousand of the Commission's informants were female (Nic Suibhne 1992). Also in 1937–38 a scheme to record folklore with the help of schoolchildren was

carried out with the co-operation of the Department of Education and the Irish National Teachers Organization. The Department issued a guidebook to all the primary schools in the state. The circular issued by the Department of Education allowed schools in the cities of Dublin, Cork, Limerick and Waterford to opt out. The children were asked to collect folklore from family members and neighbours and to write it down in standard notebooks in school. The notebooks (of which there were some five thousand, amounting to half a million pages) were then returned to the Folklore Commission. Some six hundred of the teachers became correspondents of the Commission, replying to over one hundred questionnaires on specific topics of folklore and traditional culture over the years. The so-called Main Collection of the Commission covers much the same ground as the Schools' Collection, but much more comprehensively. Ó Súilleabháin's manuals guided the collectors, covering topics such as 'Settlement and Dwelling', 'Livelihood and Household Support', 'Communication and Trade', 'The Community', 'Human Life', 'Nature', 'Folk Medicine', 'Time', 'Principles and Rules of Popular Belief and Practice', 'Mythological Tradition', 'Historical Tradition', 'Religious Traditions', 'Popular Oral Literature' and 'Sports and Pastimes'.

Altogether, by the late 1970s the archives (since 1971 in the care of University College, Dublin) had at least two million pages, a valuable collection of some twenty-five thousand photographs (Caoimhín Ó Danachair in particular was a gifted photographer) and thousands of recordings: one of the largest folklore archives in the world and a national resource of inestimable value. The work of the Folklore Commission must be seen as one of the most important cultural projects in Irish history. In practice the remit of the Irish Folklore Commission covered the island of Ireland, with all the counties represented in the Main Collections. As already mentioned, this was not the case with the Schools' Collection (however, in 1955–56 a scheme modelled on that of 1937–38 was carried out under the auspices of the Committee on Ulster Folklife and Traditions and the Northern Ireland Ministry of Education). The Folklore Commission was a product of its time, of course. Its preoccupation with pastness, with Irish-speaking districts, with male informants, with folktales can all be questioned, but only by standards that have subsequently arisen. Similarly, it did not consider its own influence on the tradition, the role of the collectors in providing an audience of sorts and on the choices of individual informants, but that would be to ask for a reflexive ethnography before its time.

In Northern Ireland, folklore and folklife were institutionalized somewhat later than in the south. The pioneer was the geographer E. Estyn Evans (1905–89) who came to Queen's University in the late 1920s and developed an interest in folklife, publishing in that area from 1939. His publications, particularly *Irish folk ways* (1957), were widely read and established him as the best-known scholar in the field. His interests and his influence were particularly wide. The idea of a folk museum of the Skansen type was his, probably conceived before the Second World War. Although it was 1954 before a committee was established to investigate the matter, eventually the act establishing the Ulster Folk Museum was passed by Stormont in 1958 with the brief of 'illustrating the way of life, past and present, and the traditions of the people of Northern Ireland'. A site on 136 acres east of Belfast — Cultra Manor — was purchased in 1961 and the first house — an eighteenth-century cottage from near Limavady — was erected in 1963. Others followed, along with exhibition centres for the display of traditional artefacts. The first director, George B. Thompson, and his successor, Alan Gailey, were both geographers by training. From 1955 the journal *Ulster Folklife* was published and the recording of folklore was organized through the circulation of questionnaires and the employment of field-collectors. The Ulster Folklife Society was established in 1961 and worked closely with the Museum. In 1967 the Museum was merged with the Belfast Transport Museum to form the Ulster Folk and Transport Museum. The Museum is the major centre for folklife research and education in the island of Ireland, and is a major touristic and educational attraction. In the southern state folklife studies did not achieve the same institutional footing. The Irish Folklore Commission and its successor (from 1971), the Department of Irish Folklore in University College, Dublin, have both seen folklife as part of their brief, but in practice it has been somewhat overshadowed by folklore. The National Museum from the late 1920s set about assembling a folklife collection, later in co-operation with the field staff of the Folklore Commission and with the Irish Countrywomen's Association (who had surveyed traditional craft workers). A. T. Lucas (1911–86), who distinguished himself in folklife scholarship, was put in charge of the Folklife Collection in 1947, the first such full-time appointment. The Irish National Folk Museum is currently being established near Castlebar, county Mayo. There are a number of local museums of folklore and folklife interest. The study of folklore and folklife has been taught to degree and postgraduate level through English in the Department of Irish Folklore in University College, Dublin, since 1971 and through Irish in the Folklore and Ethnology Section of the Department of History in University College, Cork, since 1977 — since 1989 in English too. It is taught in other universities, north and south, as part of other subjects. Internationally, there is an overlap between folkloristics and ethnology in scholarly bodies and in journals. The strongest institutional basis for these disciplines is in central, eastern and northern Europe and North America, with growing co-operation with scholars in Asia and Africa. The closest contacts maintained by Irish folklorists and ethnologists tend to be with their colleagues in the Nordic countries and Britain (particularly Scotland).

Bibliography

Abrahams, R. D. 1992 'The past in the presence: an overview of folkloristics in the late 20th century' in Reimund Kvideland *et al.* (eds) *Folklore processed. Studia Fennica Folkloristica 1* (Helsinki), pp. 32–51.

Almqvist, B. 1977–79 'The Irish Folklore Commission: achievement and legacy', *Béaloideas* **45–47**, pp. 6–26.

Bausinger, H. 1993 *Volkskunde ou l'ethnologie allemande*, trans. by Dominique Lassaigne and Pascale Godenir. Paris.

Berlin, I. 1976 *Vico and Herder. Two studies in the history of ideas*. London.

Burke, P. 1994 *Popular culture in early modern Europe*, revised ed. Aldershot.

Chapman, M. 1992 *The Celts: the construction of a myth*. New York.

Cirese, A. M. 1982 'Gramsci's observations on folklore' in A. Showstack Sassoon (ed) *Approaches to Gramsci* (London), pp. 212–47.

Cocchiara, G. 1971. *Storia del folklore in Europa*. Torino.

De Certeau, M., Julia, D. and Revel, J. 1993 'La beauté du mort' in De Certeau, *La culture au pluriel* (Paris), pp. 45–72.

Dorson, R. M. 1968 *The British folklorists: a history*. London.

Dorson, R. M. 1972 *Folklore and folklife an introduction*. Chicago and London.

Foster, J. W. 1987 *Fictions of the Irish literary revival: a changeling art*. New York.

Gailey, A. 1986 'Creating Ulster's Folk Museum', *Ulster Folklife* **32**.

Gailey, A. (ed) 1988 *The use of tradition*. Cultra.

García Canclini, N. 1995 *Hybrid cultures*, trans. by Christopher L. Chiappari and Silvia L. López. Minneapolis and London.

Georges, R. A. and Jones, M. O. 1995 *Folkloristics: an introduction*. Bloomington and Indianapolis.

Gross, D. 1992 *The past in ruins: tradition and the critique of modernity*. Amherst.

Hall, S. 1981 'Notes on deconstructing "the popular"' in Raphael Samuel (ed) *People's history and socialist theory* (London, Boston and Henle), pp. 227–40.

Harvey, C. B. 1992 *Contemporary Irish traditional narrative: the English language tradition*.

Berkeley, Los Angeles and Oxford.

Hautala, J. 1968 *Finnish folklore research 1828–1918*. Helsinki.

Hofer, T. 1991 'Construction of the "Folk Cultural Heritage"' in 'Hungary and rival versions of national identity', *Ethnologia Europaea* **21**, 2, pp. 145–70.

Honko, L. 1991 'The folklore process' in F*olklore Fellows' Summer School Programme* (Turku), pp. 25–47.

Hroch, M. 1996 'From national movement to the fully-formed nation: the nation-building process in Europe' in G. Balakrishnan (ed) *Mapping the nation* (London and New York).

Hyde, D. 1986 *Language, lore and lyrics*, ed. Breandán Ó Conaire. Dublin.

Kaschuba, W. 1995 'Popular culture and workers' culture as symbolic orders: comments on the debate about the history of culture and everyday life' in A. Lüdtke (ed) *The history of everyday life*, trans. by William Templar (Princeton), pp. 169–97.

Kiberd, D. 1979 *Synge and the Irish language*. London and Basingstoke.

Kirshenblatt-Gimblett, B. 1991 'Objects of ethnography' in I. Karp and S. D. Lavine (eds) *Exhibiting cultures* (Washington and London), pp. 386–443.

Leerssen, J. 1996 *Mere Irish and Fíor-Ghael*. Cork.

Lysaght, P., O'Dowd, A. and O'Flynn, B. (eds) 1984 *A folk museum for Ireland*. Dublin.

Martín-Barbero, J. 1993 *Communication, culture and hegemony*, trans. by E. Fox and R. A. White. London.

Mattelart, A. 1996 *The invention of communication*, trans. by S. Emanuel. Minneapolis and London.

Muchembled, R. 1991 *Culture populaire et culture des élites dans la France moderne*, second edition. Paris.

Nic Suibhne, F. 1992 '"On the straw" and other aspects of pregnancy and childbirth from the oral tradition of women in Ulster', *Ulster Folklife* **38**, pp. 12–24.

Ó Buachalla, B. 1968 *I mBéal Feirste cois cuain*. Dublin.

Ó Catháin, S. and Uí Sheighin, C. (eds) 1987 *A mhuintir Dhú Chaocháin, labhraigí feasta!* Indreabhán, county Galway.

Ó Crualaoich, G. 1986 'The primacy of form: a "folk ideology" in de Valera's politics' in J. P. O'Carroll and John A. Murphy (eds) *de Valera and his Times*. (Cork), pp. 47–61.

Ó Danachair, C. 1983 'The progress of Irish ethnology, 1783–1982', *Ulster Folklife* **29**.

Ó Duilearga, S.1943 'Volkskundliche Arbeit in Irland von 1850 bis zur Gegenwart mit besonderer Berücksichtigung der "Irischen Volkskunde - Kommission"', *Zeitschrift für Keltische Philologie und Volksvorschung* **23**, pp. 1–38.

Ó Giolláin, D. 1996 'An cultúr coiteann agus léann an bhéaloidis', *Léachtaí Cholm Cille* **26**.

Ó Giollain, D. 2000 *Locating Irish Folklore: tradition, modernity, identity*. Cork.

Ó Muimhneacháin, A. 1977–79 'An Cumann le Béaloideas Éireann 1927–77', *Béaloideas* **45–47**, pp. 1–5.

Ortiz, R. 1992 *Romãnticos e folcloristas*. São Paulo.

Ortiz, R. 1996 *Otro territorio: Ensayos sobre el mundo contemporáneo*, trans. by A. Solari. Buenos Aires.

O'Sullivan, S. 1966 *Folktales of Ireland*. London.

Porter, R. and Teich, M. (eds) 1998 *Romanticism in national context*. Cambridge.

Schenk, H. G. 1979 *The mind of the European romantics*. Oxford, New York, Toronto and Melbourne.

Thompson, S. 1971 *The folktale*. Berkeley, Los Angeles and London.

Thuente, M. H. 1980 *W. B. Yeats and Irish folklore*. Dublin.

Ó Súilleabháin, D. 1984 *Scéal an Oireachtais 1897–1924*. Dublin.

Williams, F. 1995 'Six hundred Gaelic proverbs collected in Ulster by Robert Mac Adam', *Proverbium* **12**.

Irish Storytelling

GEARÓID Ó CRUALAOICH

This chapter discusses the cultural nature of heritage and the reality that all representations of heritage are culturally selective. Following on a somewhat theoretical exploration of these matters the traditions of Irish storytelling are examined to illustrate the issue in a concrete way and to highlight central aspects and central difficulties of immediate relevance to the management of heritage presentation. Questions such as how best to 'stage' what was, essentially, a spontaneous performance; how to locate authentic material that is still of appeal to the modern audience; how to compensate for the male bias in storytelling tradition in an equality-conscious era, are touched on. Certain principles for, or, at least, approaches to, the successful representation of Irish cultural heritage are suggested for implementation by heritage managers. These apply equally to storytelling and to most other aspects of Irish tradition, artistic or material, religious or social, and have an application to cultural heritages other than Irish. They comprise the contribution of the discipline 'ethnology' to the study of how to interpret and represent all cultural tradition.

Present-day ethnology is especially concerned with understanding the cultural processes whereby local, regional and national identities are constructed, contested, transmitted and transformed in a continual process of representation and re-interpretation. Formerly it was concerned in more general and more descriptive ways with the comparative and historical study of peoples. Today's ethnologists combine field study of culture with the historical and comparative approach. They are concerned that an acquaintance with first-hand details of the actual functioning reality of cultural tradition should inform all attempts at interpretation and representation. The acquisition, through fieldwork, of such first-hand, detailed, knowledge-on-the-ground is the aim of ethnography (literally 'the writing of culture'). Ethnography provides a platform of cultural knowledge on which the ethnologist builds up interpretation and analysis. Some ethnologists are their own ethnographers and some rely on the field collections of other and perhaps earlier workers and students of tradition. It is suggested here that heritage managers, in whatever corners of the heritage field, would do well to be aware of ethnology's implications for cultural representation.

TWO BASIC CONCEPTS

The application of an ethnological approach, which this chapter espouses, to any topic within the field of heritage management requires that two related ideas regarding the field itself be emphasized. These are;

(i) that heritage of any description is always to be regarded, first and foremost, as culture;

(ii) that heritage itself is invariably the product of a selecting out and a highlighting of aspects of culture in accordance with specific perspectives and specific interests. Some basic discussion of these ideas may be useful in the context of looking at one topic of Irish cultural heritage from the ethnological point of view as an example of the kind of approach to heritage and its management which is appropriate in an ethnological frame.

Firstly, let us look at the view that heritage of any description is always to be regarded, first and foremost, as culture. The term 'culture' has a long and varied history, not by any means confined to the humanities and social sciences. Indeed, its earliest associations are in the fields of husbandry (the culture of crops) and laboratory science (the culture of bacteria). Borrowed into the humanities and social sciences, culture has developed as a term with two separate ranges of connotation. The narrower of these has to do with what is sometimes though of as 'high culture' or 'elite culture';

such things as the 'fine' arts, 'classical' music and ballet and 'high-brow' or 'heavy' literature within the European tradition, together with similar 'high' or 'elite' examples in other non-western civilizations. The other, broader, connotation has developed from an appreciation of and a concern to understand the general human capacity and competence to adapt to environment, to reflect on life and find it meaningful and to represent and communicate this adaptation and meaningfulness in both material and symbolic ways.

Attempts to define in any exact or exhaustive manner this broader, albeit more technical, meaning of the human and social senses of culture have been dogged by the realization that since culture in this sense is as broad as human life in all its multifariousness, since in fact, in a sense, culture is the multifariousness of human life, then we can never hope to complete a list of its constituent elements. In place of such rag-bag definitions as have been attempted — seeking to enumerate all the aspects of human life involved (ideas, beliefs, art, morals, law, custom and so forth) — a definitional understanding of culture has been developing that regards it as comprised basically of knowledge: the kind of knowledge that an individual necessarily acquires in the course of growing up and being socialized into the adult human worlds of technology, social behaviour and meaning. Such 'knowledge' is not to be thought of as being simple or settled in its nature. Rather it is a shifting, dynamic, operational domain wherein each of us is continually making sense out of experience and adjusting our understanding, our behaviour and our communication in the light of prevailing circumstances and desired ends. Culture and cultural knowledge are thus properly understood as process: on-going process over time in which we all participate as cultural actors. Also it should be emphasized that cultural knowledge is not confined to the verbal or cognitive forms of knowing that we traditionally consider as being located in our 'heads', the alleged seat of intellect and reason. This knowledge also comprises what we know 'in our hearts', the supposed seat of the emotions and the traditional location of the values that inform our aesthetics and ethics. Likewise cultural knowledge includes the knowledge of 'how to do things', located by tradition in our fingers, in our feet, in our range of skills as put to work in technology, in art, in recreation.

Obviously no schematic model of culture, even culture-in-process, such as hinted at above, will comprehend the richness, the flow, the manifold and manifest wholeness and holistic nature of human cultural tradition as it is lived, yet some such model is conceptually valuable to those whose business it is to reflect on the nature of culture and cultural heritage. The model underlying the approach to heritage that this 'ethnological chapter' represents encompasses the afore-mentioned considerations of culture as knowledge-in-process. Furthermore, it takes the position that every individual, every group, every cultural community, whether on the local, the regional, the national or the global level, is continually engaged in giving external form (verbal, behavioural, symbolic) to shifting, dynamic transformations of those provisional formulations and realizations of knowledge — in all its 'locations' — that constitute the world-view and life-style of the individual, the group, the community at a given time and place. Kevin Danaher caught the sense of all this in his characterization of folklore as 'the sayings and the doings' of ordinary people, as long as we can understand that what people say and do is said and done within a never-ending process of adjustment and transformation in accordance with the dynamic of social transactions and the exercise of choice informed by the shifting meaningfulness of daily experience. Some forms of culture, some sayings and doings, in this process, come to be regarded as heritage.

The second idea to be emphasized here is that heritage is invariably the product of a selecting out and a highlighting of aspects of culture and culture process for specific purposes. This implies that the construction and promotion of heritage involve a kind and degree of conscious cultural choice that is additional to those group and community choosings and valuings that underlie the self-esteem and cultural pride stemming from that normal, spontaneous consciousness of cultural identity that is always part of the world-view and life-style of human groups. Such deliberate selection and deliberate highlighting as underlie the construction and promotion of heritage are themselves, of course, cultural in nature — though sometimes thought of as a kind of second-order cultural activity. They are to be understood as also subject to the dynamic play of adjustment and transformation that are at the heart of cultural knowledge. So just as culture is never a fixed or a finished quantum of knowledge or list of objects or prescription for behaviour or belief, so, too, heritage is to be understood as a field of cultural representation that is constantly responding to the adjustments and transformations and re-creations of social and cultural life and of social and cultural identity. That which is selected as heritage to represent the cultural traditions and the cultural identity of former times cannot comprise a fixed or finished entity. It offers, rather, the opportunity for an imaginative engagement with phases of a culture process that was dynamic in its nature and that yielded certain externalizations or realizations of the then world-view and life-style that are capable of representing to our time the cultural world of a former era in which they had their 'first life'.

Just as culture changes over time, so too does heritage, and there can be a history of heritage just as there is

172

culture history. A full representation of cultural tradition as heritage will try to address this issue and show the changing nature of heritage in respect of the cultural tradition in question, just as it will show the changes that have occurred in the tradition itself. Heritage management must thus be alert to what have been called 'the two lives' of cultural tradition. The first life is that of a relatively unreflective externalization of world-view and realization of life-style in artefact and repertoire, in custom and ritual and institution. The second life occurs when consciousness of the heritage status and potential of such externalizations and realization is raised either by threat from outside or by reason of the attentions and activities of scholars and others as part of some intellectual and/or political movement, for instance romantic nationalism in the case of so many 'small nations' in Europe — including Ireland.

In more recent times a third kind of life has been visited on cultural tradition under the pressures of the modern tourist industry, where the need to entertain has frequently taken precedence over considerations of authenticity or scholarship (Lowenthal 1985, 3–34, 263–362; Lowenthal 1987, 88–104). At its extreme this can lead to distorted visions of cultural tradition and heritage being constructed and exploited chiefly as a commercial resource whose value is seen exclusively in terms of contemporary consumer products and services. We can try to discern how each of these lives or phases or levels of cultural knowledge and activity pertains to the consideration of any heritage topic. By way of example, let us consider in some detail the case of Irish popular narrative tradition, that is 'stories and storytelling', as part of Irish cultural tradition and Irish cultural heritage. Given the emphasis in the ethnological perspective on processes of construction, representation and transformation, our initial concern will be to explore narrative heritage as a heritage of storytelling 'events' in the first instance, and then to consider also the contents or repertoires that were performed in the course of these events.

IRISH STORYTELLING TRADITION

The perceived heritage of Irish stories and storytelling, taken together, is regarded as having the status of a 'Grand Tradition'. Irish people and Irish culture are supposed to have a special talent, a special capacity, a special appreciation for storytelling and verbal art in general. The *Táin*, the epic account of the Cattle Raid of Cooley and the central saga of the so-called Ulster Cycle of early Irish literature, has a pre-eminent primary position in a canon of narrative excellence that stretches through the centuries to the prominent contemporary Irish novelists and short-story writers of the late twentieth century. As an element within this traditional heritage the figure of the traditional storyteller, the so-called *seannachie*, is taken as a representative person-

ality who has become something of a model for latter-day interpreters and performers of Irish storytelling tradition within the heritage field. The image of the *seannachie* — as promoted say in the stage and television performances of Éamonn Kelly — has established itself as something of a stereotype, fixing or freezing actual process in traditional narrative expression into a characterization that appears timeless and universal. Behind such a stereotyped characterization there is, of course, a rich ethnography of the incidence of actual storytelling in the popular culture of the Irish countryside in the last hundred years. It is to this ethnographic richness beyond the stereotype that here, as in all other cases of heritage, we must go for enlightenment. Actual Irish storytelling has been studied and described most famously by the scholars of the Irish Folklore Commission, whose Director, Professor Séamus Ó Duilearga, has published the seminal monograph entitled *The Gaelic storyteller* (Delargy 1945) and the seminal anthology of stories and lore from a single, talented, tradition bearer entitled *Leabhar Sheáin Í Chonaill/Seán Ó Conaill's book* (Ó Duilearga 1981). The impression of Irish storytelling tradition that these works convey is that of a kind of rural academy of verbal art where the well-known, gifted performers had a privileged, star-quality status in the eyes of the community and the eyes of the visiting, recording collector-scholars. Subsequent studies by such as Henry Glassie (1982), Clodagh Brennan Harvey (1992) and Máirtín Verling (1996) have shown how this rural academy/star-performer version of Irish storytelling tradition deviates from the cultural reality of storytelling in the Irish countryside of the early twentieth century where the forces of modernization — including the displacement of Irish by English — operated increasingly to transform the patterns of social and cultural life away from the somewhat idealized picture presented by earlier scholars of Irish storytelling.

That somewhat idealized picture draws fairly directly on one strand within the earlier history of Irish storytelling, the strand deriving from the medieval institutionalization of the *scélaige*, the professional storyteller as part of the entourage of king and chieftain. Such professional narrators operated in the context of the banqueting hall (entertainment) and the sleeping chamber (relaxation) among other customary locations, though in all such locations storytelling would frequently have had a quasi-political function also, in terms of praising the chief or king through recounting the glorious deeds of ancestors or famous antecedents and in propagandistic promotion of one faction over others. In fact the storytelling setting of nineteenth- and early twentieth-century rural Ireland was far more spontaneous and proletarian than the rural academy characterization — drawing on the medieval model — suggests. As such, however, storytelling continued into the last century as a central and valued expression of culture and heritage. Its importance is reflected in the ubiquity and variety of names for the commonest setting in which storytelling manifested itself. Some of these names are well known from media use of them in the context of presenting aspects of Irish tradition to a mass audience. *Áirneán, scoraíocht, céilí-house, rambling-house* are terms that have become generally familiar from the extensive list of local terms for the cultural phenomenon within Irish life whereby narrative performance within an assembly of people took on the quasi-artistic, quasi-religious, quasi-psychological functions capable of intensifying life experience for individual and group and giving externalization as verbal art to shared meaningfulness in terms of identity, memory and aspiration.

Another notable example of this kind of cultural phenomenon/heritage in popular Irish tradition in recent centuries is the funerary ritual of the 'Merry Wake' (Ó Crualaoich 1998; Ó Súilleabháin 1967). This was the gathering of relations and neighbours at the house of a deceased to wake or watch the corpse throughout the night hours. While the Merry Wake obviously cannot be regarded as constituting a storytelling event primarily, a combination of Christian prayers and ancestral verse-keening or lamentation formed an essential narrative accompaniment at the wake ritual. Both prayer and lament played their joint roles in the important social and sacred work that the traditional wake accomplished — namely the translation of the spirit of the deceased to the afterlife (conceived in both Christian and ancestral/fairy terms) and the cathartic release of the fear, sorrow and anger that is felt by individuals and community on the occasion of death. It should however be noted that 'storytelling' in the broader sense was also a feature of the Merry Wake, taking its place with other forms of recreation and activity, serving to realize and reinforce the intense, central preoccupations of the ritual over its two or three day course.

Other assemblies in which storytelling had a prominent, culturally intensifying role did not, by contrast with the wake assembly, depend on any dramatic occurrence, such as a death, to bring them into being. They were regularly formed and emerged in the course of ordinary daily life wherever people had the occasion or the opportunity to assemble — for a variety of purposes, some festive, some mundane. Examples of mundane occasions would be the occupational events and locations associated with potato and turf harvesting, night-fishing, bothy-herding or transhumance, child-minding, knitting and quilting parties. Other similar work groups of storytelling would include pattern-days at a holy well or other sacred site (Ó Giolláin 1998), *Lughnasa* or harvest outings, bonfire days or nights, for instance May Eve, Midsummer and life-cycle festivities

such as baptism or wedding parties as well as the wake ritual mentioned above (Danaher 1972). On each and all of these occasions in Irish tradition it was customary and normal for storytelling to 'break out', as it were, in a spontaneous expression of creativity and entertainment that was at once 'diversion', celebration and cathartic intensification of life-experience. The performers of narrative on all such occasions were not at all necessarily star performers but could be anyone with any ability to perform who was moved to or was prevailed upon to contribute to the narrative occasion. Of course there were degrees of competence and excellence recognized and shared by members of the assembly/audience. This evaluation encompassed factors of repertoire, of rhetoric, of performance — histrionic and aesthetic. Certainly there were occasional star performers who were more popular and more in demand, so to speak, but one must emphasize again the relatively informal and spontaneous nature of these storytelling events.

THE TYPICAL STORYTELLING EVENT

Apart from the above locations of storytelling in Irish tradition there remains to be considered the *locus classicus*, as it were, of the winter hearth in the farmhouse kitchen where friends and neighbours gathered to pass the long hours of darkness and inclement weather. This is the setting of the *áirneán* presented so vividly in the writings of Séamus Ó Duilearga (1945; 1981) and Henry Glassie (1982), the former treating of the community of the cliff-top village of Irish speaking Cill Rialaigh during the 1920s in south Kerry, the latter of the inland, English-speaking, border village community of Ballymenone, county Fermanagh during the 1970s. Each presentation is a reconstruction by an outsider of the structure and flow of the 'typical' storytelling event of local popular culture; each offers a rich tapestry of heritage to our later eyes. For Ó Duilearga the heritage issues most involved are those of illuminating and capturing a fragile remnant of the Middle Ages and bearing testimony to the noble and exemplary character of the bearers of that national heritage and of their way of life — lived in the teeth of modern misunderstanding, indifference and hostility. For Glassie the heritage issues involved relate in a more universal framework to a continual renewal and re-creation of human understanding and imagination by means of the intensification of the life experience out of the course of the daily round and the annual life-cycles of mundane community living, in bog and field and factory, in house and church and chapel, in utterance, in memory and in imagination. Glassie's account of the gradual intensification of communication in the course of the evening kitchen assembly, resulting eventually not only in story but also in music and song and food (for body and soul), is essential reading for all students of Irish storytelling and the heritage of Irish popular culture. Foremost among its virtues is the realization it brings that, even in the *scoraíocht* or the *rambling-house* (to use two other well-known appellations for the classic cultural site of the storytelling event), the telling of stories is not the unique, primary or professed reason for the coming together in assembly. Certainly there is an expectation that storytelling will occur, that stories will be told, that storytellers will perform — but only as a major and valuable incidental, so to speak, of the ostensible purposes of the assembly. These have more to do with desire for and delight in companionship (versus loneliness), the expression of neighbourly solidarity and group identity, a curiosity about local gossip and current affairs of an economic and political nature on the local and on wider fronts. Gossip and current affairs can lead to reminiscence or to make-believe; this in turn can eventually prompt the recounting of a recognized item of the storytelling repertoire. The patterned process of proceeding with the storytelling event can be a protracted affair and may, on occasion, be unsuccessful or unproductive of any good storytelling performances. What is certain is that it contrasts very greatly with the starting-from-cold stage performances of storytelling slotted into the concert or cabaret settings of contemporary entertainment events that purport to represent the heritage of Irish storytelling. While there are talented stage exponents who tell stories today, one must distinguish between them and the storytellers of actual cultural tradition.

SOME DIFFICULTIES IN REPRESENTATION

The challenge of how to represent Irish storytelling heritage in terms of contemporary cultural settings and contemporary media evokes a variety of responses that all, in various ways, attempt to capture the perceived essential character and flavour of Irish storytelling in its 'first-life' mode. The above discussion of certain limited aspects of that first life will, hopefully, enable the reader to draw conclusions regarding the viability — on historical and ethnographic grounds — of representing Irish storytelling tradition in the mode of Éamonn Kelly or the interpretative centre, of Kevin McAleer or the scholarly documentary. Apart from the characterization of the storytelling event itself, however, attention must also be paid to questions arising from the content or texts of storytelling and the gender bias that their traditional performance exhibited.

As regards the texts and genres that constitute the repertoire of Irish storytelling tradition, ample information and reasonably adequate anthologies are available for the chief categories as a result of the work of scholars over the last hundred years and especially the work of scholars associated with the Irish Folklore Commission. This scholarship has linked the Irish

popular storytelling repertoire into international storytelling scholarship. While a great deal remains to be accomplished — not least because of developments in the scholarly understanding of the role of storytelling in culture process that have given rise to new questions — there exists for heritage professionals a considerable amount of material that can ensure that excellent appropriate texts or items of repertoire can be utilized in any representation of popular narrative tradition — as a part of Irish heritage. A difficulty arises in repertoire terms from the fact that, historically, the type of story most highly valued and even most sought after, in the *áirneán* of the rambling-house, was the hero-tale of the 'Adventures of Fionn Mac Cumhaill' type with its stylized rhetorical features and its swashbuckling action. Neither this genre nor the other valued genre of the more international Wonder-Tale ('The Dragon-Slayer', 'The Quest for the Lost Husband', 'Cinderella' — known as *Móirín* or even 'Hairy Rucky' in Irish versions) are at all likely to appeal to modern general audiences. On the other hand, the humorous anecdotes and tall tales that prove popular in contemporary storytelling settings must be regarded as somewhat minor items of the narrative heritage. A real challenge exists here in regard to the adequate representation of the actual heritage of story within Irish popular cultural tradition.

As regards gender, the image conjured up by the term *seannachie* is inevitably male, and often, as in the Éamonn Kelly version, is replete with *caubeen*, *dúidín* and a penchant for spitting into the fire. The patriarchal, macho overtones of this image are best confined, in the light of ethnographic reality, to the domain of the native hero-tale or *Fiannaíocht* — named from the chief culture hero of popular Gaelic cultural tradition in Ireland and Scotland — though not all the hero-tales in the native repertoire concern the adventures of Fionn Mac Cumhaill and his warrior-band. The performance of hero-tales of this type, and, to a somewhat lesser degree, the performance of the international *Märchen*-type wonder-tale in its very plentiful Irish versions, was restricted to the male storyteller (*scéalaí* or *scéaltóir*). Indeed a taboo of sorts existed in relation to the performance of this type of material — especially the Fenian hero-tale — by females, in that it was held to be unlucky and even unnatural for a woman to narrate a story of this kind to an assembly — as unnatural, as the saying has it, as a hen crowing. The *seanchaí/seannachie* of Irish popular culture in early modern and modern times has, by contrast, been both male and female, the bearer and reciter of traditional lore rather than stories, lore comprising local genealogy, legends and history as well as prayers, verse, pithy sayings and the like. A certain female preponderance suggests itself in the ranks of known bearers and performers of certain kinds of *seanchas*/lore, for instance, prayers, lament verse, mythological legend. The degree to which these gender distinctions can or should be reproduced in heritage representations of storytelling tradition is a question to be taken into account in the light of issues deriving from the feminist perspective which has recently and very properly been added to the hitherto largely male scholarly gaze and scholarly voice in matters of cultural tradition and heritage. The stereotyped figure of the heritage *seannachie* needs radical alteration.

We now realize that our accounts of cultural tradition derive overwhelmingly from male sources and that attention in the study of these traditions has focussed more centrally and sustainedly on matters male. Large areas of traditional cultural knowledge and cultural life — those centred on female consciousness and realized in female life-style and life-forms — are all but invisible in the cultural record, that is, in our account, from scholarship and otherwise, of the first-life mode of popular culture in Ireland. Thus the second-life heritage representations of that popular culture are all too easily left equally biased against the equitable portrayal of the human reality of the former era in question and its culture process and patterns. This consideration applies to the world of storytelling in cultural tradition and in heritage as much as to any other part of the field. The site of storytelling tradition regarded as the *locus classicus* — the winter fireside with friends and neighbours assembled — turns out, on inspection, to be an almost exclusively male affair. We now realise that there are other *loci* to which women gravitated at different times and in different circumstances, and that at these female assemblies repertoires of traditional narrative other than the male assembly ones were performed and transmitted. In this regard especially, the responsibility of the student of heritage to engage in research as an integral prelude to and on-going integral part of representing cultural tradition adequately is paramount.

Finally, we can consider briefly the question as to what happened Irish storytelling tradition as represented by 'The Gaelic Storyteller'. Did it die? Did it stop? Did it change out of all recognition? Where is it, or its transformation, to be found today? These questions remind us of two fundamental facts. One, that storytelling is a universal human capacity and competence, a part of the human culture process in all conditions of society and history. Two, that in Irish cultural tradition a hundred years ago and more, storytelling was a kind of epiphenomenon arising from the social assemblies that occurred as a feature of the technical, economic, social, political and ritual symbolic sides of daily life. As society and social institutions change, we can be certain that cultural phenomena change also in their outward aspects, in their structure, in their function, in their meaningfulness. In the case of Irish storytelling tradition as we know it from descriptions of its operation in the

late nineteenth and early twentieth centuries, the historical and ethnographic reality is that technical and socio-economic developments were altering in radical ways the forms of companionship, entertainment and communication from those circumstances that had hitherto been a vehicle for the occurrence and performance of traditional narrative, whether story or lore. The storytelling assemblies or the assemblies that led to storytelling as a part of their proceedings were displaced by newer kinds of social arrangements in the work-place, in the home, in the local world in general. The newspaper, the motor-car and electricity all had a profound effect on the life-style of local communities; these are only three items from the many different aspects of the impingement of elements of modernity on Irish traditional life which those who would represent that tradition need to take into account. Harvey's discussion of the implications of just such factors of modernity for storytellers and their performances (Harvey 1992, 20–36) is an essential part of our understanding of all Irish traditional narration, medieval and modern. It throws much light on the process of culture and of culture change in relation to verbal art.

CONCLUSION

In the postmodern era in which, by the reckoning of some, we now find ourselves, our attempts at representing cultural heritage, including storytelling traditions, can benefit greatly from understanding as clearly as possible the cultural nature of stories and their performance in different eras of history and in different life modes as, over time, a consciousness of tradition as heritage develops. It is to be hoped that the points of view that the present ethnological chapter presents for consideration will prove of interest to those whose task it is to engage in the important cultural work of representing and recreating cultural tradition as heritage for the present day and, of course, for the future. In respect of storytelling itself, a recent report on the storytelling revival by Pat Ryan (1995) will be of particular interest. In respect of other areas of heritage — material, social and symbolic — the same general considerations apply.

Overall, the need is for heritage managers to be constantly alert to the necessity for further ethnographic research and further interpretation and analysis. In this, heritage management is yet another manifestation of that process which characterizes all phenomena of a cultural nature. Like all culture, heritage too is endlessly diverse and adaptive, continually remoulded to reflect the on-going dynamic of creativity in human life and its record.

Bibliography

Bruford, A. J. and MacDonald, D. A. 1994 *Scottish traditional tales*. Edinburgh.

Danaher, K. 1967 *Folktales of the Irish countryside*. Cork.

Danaher, K. 1972 *The year in Ireland*. Cork.

Danaher, K. 1972 *A bibliography of Irish ethnography and folk tradition*. Cork.

Delargy, J. H. [Ó Duilearga, S.] 1945 'The Gaelic storyteller', *Proceedings of the British Academy* **31**, pp. 3–47.

Finnegan, R. 1992 *Oral traditions and verbal arts*. London.

Gailey, A. (ed) 1988 *The use of tradition*. Cultra.

Glassie, H. 1982 *Passing the time*. Dublin.

Glassie, H. 1985 *Irish folktales*. Harmondsworth.

Hannerz, U. 1992 *Cultural complexity*. New York.

Harvey, C. B. 1992 *Contemporary Irish traditional narrative*. Berkeley.

Honko, L. 1991 'The folklore process' in *Folklore Fellows Summer School Programme* (Turku), pp. 25–47.

Lowenthal, D. 1985 *The past is a foreign country*. Cambridge.

Lowenthal, D. 1997 *The heritage crusade and the spoils of history*. London.

Ó Crualaoich, G. 1998 'The Merry Wake' in J. Donnelly and K. A. Miller (eds) *Irish popular culture 1650–1850* (Dublin), pp. 173–200.

Ó Duilearga, S. 1981 *Seán Ó Conaill's book*. Dublin.

Ó Giolláin, D. 1998 'The Pattern' in Donnelly and Miller (eds), pp. 201–21.

Ó Súilleabháin, S. 1967 *Irish folk custom and belief*. Dublin.

Ó Súilleabháin, S. 1973 *Storytelling in Irish tradition*. Cork.

O'Sullivan, S. 1966 *Folktales from Ireland*. Chicago.

O'Sullivan, S. 1967 *Irish wake amusements*. Cork.

O'Sullivan, S. 1977 *Legends from Ireland*. London.

Ryan, P. 1995 *Storytelling in Ireland: a re-awakening*. Londonderry.

Verling, M. 1996 *Gort Broc*. Dublin.

Folklore and Ethics

MARIE-ANNICK DESPLANQUES

In this section we shall explore the meanings and consequences of using folklore and ethnographic material for purposes other than fundamental research and more specifically related to a public-sector area referred to in Ireland as 'heritage management'. The material presented is defined in its international context and specifically illustrated with local examples. Ethical issues as they apply to the researcher's responsibilities to the community and the material involved are then identified and considered in relation to local and national contexts, with references to international guidelines. The outline of a case study on the Cork-based Northside Folklore Project illustrates a specific situation in which ethical issues relating to the interface between academia and the community become functional in terms of the applied dimension of ethnographic research.

As one can deduce from Diarmuid Ó Giolláin's and Gearóid Ó Crualaoich's contributions to this book, folklore and ethnographic material has never been the exclusive preserve of academics. Yet ethical issues arising from scholarly approaches and analysis have been and must continue to be examined as the discipline of ethnology takes on new dimensions and expands its contribution to the communities from which its study material originally derives. A clear and comprehensive understanding of the ethical issues associated with the collection, preservation and presentation of folklore and ethnographic material necessitates, however, the consideration of the processes that govern expressions of traditional and popular culture. Thus, such aspects as the learning and transmission, the performance contexts and the importance of traditional and popular culture in the formation and expression of world-views and collective identities are seen by folklorists and ethnologists as essential dynamics in the delineation of the processes which give traditional and popular culture meaning and continuity (Gailey 1988). Anthropologist Ulf Hannerz uses the metaphor of 'flow' to convey

similar ideas (Hannerz 1992). A further example of the metaphorization and application of 'process' as concept is illustrated in the title and indeed the content of the 1995 television series 'The River of Sound' (King and O'Connor 1995) which documents the history and dynamics of Irish traditional music.

Although it must be recognized that fundamental research is often viewed as an end in itself, results and findings would be of little use if the theories they serve to construct had no application in the real world. Yet it is also true that a dichotomy is likely to occur between 'pure' and 'applied' scholarship if bridges are not built to facilitate the translation of theoretical findings into practical implementation. In an article entitled 'Mistaken dichotomies', Barbara Kirshenblatt-Gimblett (1988, 141) illustrates the point by taking the American example where

academic folklore programmes have tended to maintain the dichotomy between pure and applied folklore and consistently refused to examine their own essentially and inescapably applied character .... Nor has the public sector really entered the intellectual life of the discipline.

As the examples below will show, issues concerning the nature of the relationship between the academic perspective — which has been rightly perceived to favour theoretical approaches, on the one hand — and the public sector or the 'community' which, on the other hand, has tended to concentrate on more immediate factors such as socio-economic potentials, are not restricted to the situation in the United States. Thus ethical considerations as they apply to uses of folklore and ethnographic material in the context of heritage management and the wider sector of the tourism industry may be contextually defined and have a local application, but ultimately they also have a global dimension in terms of principles. One could draw a parallel here with the concepts and principles attached to the respect of human rights.

THE GLOBAL DIMENSION AND ITS IMPACT ON LOCAL SITUATIONS

In the past ten years and since the publication of Kirshenblatt-Gimblett's paper in 1988, much progress has been made towards bridging the gap between academic perspectives in folklore and ethnology and the public sector at an international level. Folklorist Lauri Honko, who has been instrumental in this endeavour, points out that

The UNESCO process for the safeguarding of folklore is probably the most authoritative statement of the value of folklore and traditional culture the world has seen.
(Honko 1987, 4)

This process, which involved the participation of a majority of UNESCO member states, was initially triggered in 1979 by a questionnaire on the status of folklore from a general culture perspective. The questionnaire, which was sent out to member states, had itself emerged from a request from the Bolivian government regarding the status of folklore within the Universal Copyright Convention. Two succeeding committees composed of academics and public sector experts worked in consultation with over 100 member states on theoretical, practical, policy development and implementation issues. They produced a series of documents exploring the position of folklore from its local contexts to eventually define and derive an infrastructure encompassing these local issues within an international context. 1990 saw the publication of 'The Final Text of the Recommendation for the Safeguarding of Folklore adopted by the General Conference at its Twenty-Fifth Session, Paris, 15 November 1989'. This text identifies seven areas relating to the Definition of Folklore, its Identification, Conservation, Preservation, Dissemination and Protection, and finally advocates International Cooperation on the subject.

Thus the text in question is essentially concerned with issues which, while ethically oriented, remain nonetheless academic in their nature. It is only through the practical implementation of these recommendations that their effectiveness can be measured in terms of how they are ultimately experienced by those who are affected by them and how important their impact on the 'cultural flow' as such really is.

While such a document certainly promotes an awareness of traditional culture at an international level, it is the responsibility of each participant state and its institutions to ensure that these recommendations are effectively put in place at national, regional and local levels. As there are no documents indicating interna-

tional budget or funding provision, individual governments are therefore implicitly responsible for putting in place the financial resources to achieve this. On a national level in Ireland, institutions such as the Heritage and Arts Councils partially fulfil this function, although in a limited capacity.

To include aspects of folklore, traditional or popular culture in the notion of heritage enhances the latter's cultural dimension by introducing a human perspective. This in turn reinforces the core notion of collective identity at its basic elemental, and therefore essential, foundation level. In other words, without an appropriate representation of traditional and popular culture, one cannot fully comprehend heritage in terms of the socio-cultural legacy of a people. The inclusion of items of folklore and popular culture as part of a people's or a community's heritage therefore implies a high level of responsibility vis-à-vis those who are represented individually and collectively. As mentioned earlier, the dynamics of folklore and popular culture and their importance in terms of their role in contributing to a community's definition of its collective identity are essential factors to be considered when making the decision to introduce it into the wider notion of heritage and its representation.

Ethical concerns in this respect are therefore directly linked to the fact that expressions of traditional and popular culture beyond their potential artistic, communicative or educational functions, to name but a few, are also indicative of a system of values carried by the community whom they identify and which identifies with them. It is therefore important that these values be integrated into the philosophy which governs the collection, preservation and representation of defined items of traditional and popular culture as elements of a community's heritage. Ethical principles must then be considered and applied at each individual level of what ultimately becomes a selection process.

IDENTIFYING A COMMUNITY AND ITS CULTURAL TRADITIONS

There is no doubt that the notion of researching, developing and representing a community's cultural heritage, whether past or contemporary, is associated with acknowledging the fact that the community exists as a community with a sense of collective identity. The initial task of the heritage researcher in this respect will be to identify the community. Only then can we expect to look into more specific aspects of its traditional and popular culture. Identifying a community may seem an easy task, and we might think of geographical, occupational, linguistic or other common interests as criteria of belonging. Here it is important to consider our own perspective when identifying this community; which criteria are we applying to define the community and how do we define those criteria?

To illustrate the point, I shall take two geographical examples. One applies to a rural area in county Cork known as Sliabh Luachra, and another to an area in Cork city known as the Northside.

If one looks at a map of county Cork, there are no obvious specific physical or administrative boundaries which define the Sliabh Luachra area as such. However, people living in that north Cork district bordering on county Kerry identify themselves as Sliabh Luachra, and, rather than physically delineating the area, they tend to define it in terms of its traditional music, the intonation and the accent and the ways people living there interact. Local journalist Con Houlihan, once interviewed on the subject, described it as 'a state of mind' (Cranitch 1996). In other words, we have a name applied to an area which in fact cannot be defined solely in geographical terms.

The second example, Cork city's Northside, would again seem a simple area to identify. To the outsider the Northside implies the north side of the river Lee. To Northsiders, however, there are several Northsides. The most important being the 'real' Northside, whose location and boundaries are subject to where the person actually comes from. Moreover, there are areas geographically situated on the north side of the river which are not considered as part of the Northside by residents. Like Sliabh Luachra, the Northside, in which the case study presented below is based, is more than just a geographically defined community.

From these examples we can deduce that any community, whether geographically or otherwise defined, is heterogeneous in nature. Ethical principles with regards to defining a community therefore require that preliminary research be undertaken and that a rapport be established between researchers and members of that community (Goldstein 1964; Finnegan 1992). The case study described in the latter part of this chapter illustrates the various steps and the ethical principles taken into consideration during the establishment of a pilot urban ethnology research project and community archive. This project is the result of a cooperative effort to integrate academic and community interest in the study of traditional and popular culture at the local level in terms of its immediate impact, and at national and international levels in terms of the dissemination of data from selections published and used both in academic and non-academic publications, conference addresses and Internet applications. From the perspective of those directly involved in their activities, the success and sustainability of such community and/or academic projects are highly dependent on the integrity of the research policies. The latter benefit from being informed by the UNESCO guidelines mentioned earlier, and indeed, at a more practical level, from the integrity and the level of responsibility of the researchers themselves. Beyond this, however, success and sustain-

ability ultimately depend on local authority and government commitment in terms of resources made available. Excerpts from the UNESCO guidelines stipulate that member states should

train collectors, achivists, documentalists and other specialists in the conservation of folklore, from physical conservation to analytic work .... Provide moral and economic support for individual and institutions studying, making known, cultivating or holding items of folklore .... Encourage regions, municipalities, associations and other groups working in folklore to establish full time jobs for folklorists to stimulate and coordinate folklore activities in the region ... (Honko 1989, 8–9)

The following sections of this chapter will focus more specifically on ethical principles as they relate to role of the heritage worker in folklore-related cultural contexts, with special reference to material generated from ethnographic interviews.

THE RESEARCHER'S RESPONSIBILITIES
Research rapport

Establishing a research rapport with individuals or representatives of a community serves several purposes. This initial contact, preliminary to any substantial research, will determine the ethnographer's position and perspective. Regarding ethnographic interviews, two cases may then be considered. Either the researcher is an outsider to the community or a stranger to the individual interviewed or the researcher belongs to the community or knows the person interviewed and has a relationship with that person other than as a researcher. The position of the researcher must then be clarified so that a professional research relationship can take place. The nature and quality of this relationship will determine to a large degree the quality of the outcome of the research.

In the context of heritage-related ethnographic research, one would assume that the ultimate goal is to represent aspects of community life past and/or present by which the community can be identified, but also, and perhaps more importantly from an ethical perspective, to ensure that the community can identify with these representations as their own. These terms must be at the basis of the research relationship. One must remember that in ethnographic research, it is the individual or the community who are the carriers of tradition and therefore the experts on the way the tradition is performed, transmitted and perceived within that community. Consultation with the community is therefore essential prior to interpretation and public representation of that community's cultural heritage.

The onus is then on the researcher to consult the community and present it with a clear proposal which outlines the purpose of the research project, the interests to the researcher or research agency which he or she represents, the methodology and the degree of involvement of, and benefits to, the community. Many controversial and indeed abandoned projects could have been carried through successfully if ethical principles had been given more consideration from the start. Because of the heterogeneous nature of communities, it is also ludicrous to believe that total agreement can be reached at all time, but efforts must converge to ensure that ethical procedures are followed as exemplified in the case study discussed below. An element of reciprocity must exist between the researcher and the individuals or the community researched.

The collection phase

Consultation with the community is also important prior to the actual collection phase of a project. The selection process of tradition bearers who might contribute their knowledge to a project can be a difficult task if one considers the following variables of authenticity, aesthetics and competence. For instance, a village known for its singing or musical heritage will have several exponents of that tradition, otherwise the tradition would not be associated with that particular village. Yet the heritage researcher's position is to look for a representative sample of that tradition. Apart from archival research which provides references to and examples of past collections (Ó Súilleabháin 1970), a decision must then be made as to which exponent or what particular items of contemporary tradition will be used as the representative sample. The community's system of values must be taken into consideration when such a decision is made.

Once a research project is in place, when the nature of the material to be researched and presented has been identified, the collection phase can begin. Again from an ethical perspective, the researcher must keep in mind that the materials to be collected, whether stories, songs, traditional recipes or cures, or even artefacts such as tools or items of folk art, are all human productions. It is therefore important that this be acknowledged informally in the quality of the research rapport established with the individual contributor of this material by introducing an element of reciprocity in which, for example, the researcher may offer a gift or a favour which will facilitate the collection process. It is also essential that formal acknowledgement be given to the individual or community contributing the material. The most common type of formal acknowledgement begins with the 'contract'. The contract is an agreement between the collector and the contributor. It outlines briefly the purpose of the project, defines the form of contribution in terms of media (audio-visual material, artefact and the like), and indicates the copyright status of the material. Ultimately the contract serves to protect all involved, and also the material contributed. Material collected

without this explicit contract should not be made public in any form whatsoever.

Once, and not before, the terms under which the material is to be collected and used have been agreed upon, the actual collection can take place. Folklore material may be collected in a variety of ways using a variety of technologies. These include tape-recorded interviews, videos, photography and so forth. A number of fieldwork guides can be referred to as to the various techniques employed (Goldstein 1964; Ives 1974; Jackson 1979; Spradley 1979; Finnegan 1992), and most of them include a section on ethical principles. There are, however, a few general guidelines which are applicable and should be followed in most situations:

• The researcher and the contributor should always arrange to meet informally to discuss the format, the settings and the content of the collecting session before it actually takes place.

• The researcher or accompanying technician should always check the equipment prior to the collecting session.

• When possible, the collecting session should reflect the natural performance context in which the tradition documented usually occurs.

• Time should be allowed for the contributor to get used to the presence of recording technology or photographic equipment and for potential interruptions during the session.

• Within the context of the heritage 'industry', the contributor should be credited for his/her contribution and, where relevant, be offered at least one copy of the finished product.

Preservation

With regard to the use of folklore and popular culture, however, the heritage researcher must differentiate between the presentation of the material which is the end-product and the collection and preservation of the material which are necessary stages enabling presentation. Yet considering the fact that traditional culture and its expressions are not static entities, one must therefore view this in terms of a continuous process of defining identity. The preservation of items of folklore and popular culture therefore implies the documentation of the material and of the processes which affect it, but also the making available of these results to those interested in such dynamics. Folklorists and ethnologists working in academic contexts have generated archives of folklore and used those repositories as reference research tools in very much the same way as literary scholars have used libraries. Because of their location, mainly in universities, accessibility to the material they contain has been somewhat restricted. Yet while folklore archives are governed by policies which protect their holdings, and those who contributed them, from misuse and generally from commercialization, the advent of new technology has increased the level of accessibility, both in terms of the media used to store the material and in the dissemination of this material. Thus radio producers, film makers and playwrights use folklore archives to document their work. By so doing they have engaged in an interactive relationship where the result of their work itself enters the folklore and popular culture process by expanding the contexts of performance. However, the results of their work are rarely integrated into folklore archives, and often their preservation as such is overlooked.

In order to contribute to the preservation of folklore and popular culture, the heritage researcher's role should extend to encourage and participate in the creation of community archives and multi-media resource centres and thus guarantee accessibility and research facilities to a wide audience.

The collection and presentation of folklore material for public display and in the context of heritage belong to what ethnologists refer to as 'applied folklore'. The presentation of folklore in this context is not primarily intended for fundamental academic research. From the perspective of folklorists and ethnologists, however, their participation in this domain is an extension of their academic activities (Dettmer 1991). It is important then that although presented in a different context, the value of the primary material in terms of its authenticity is essentially retained. Moreover, these secondary contexts should not be regarded by ethnologists as denuded of academic interest in terms of their different performance dimensions, for example. To an extent, the presentation of folklore and popular culture material in a heritage context becomes a tradition in itself and certainly an integral part of popular culture. Folk festivals and traditional music summer schools are good examples of this. They become media by which traditional culture is preserved and transmitted.

The presentation phase

There are many different ways in which aspects of folklore and popular culture can be presented to a wider audience. In this respect, the re-presentation of folklore and popular culture becomes an integral part of a process where the communicative element prevails. Lauri Honko talks about the 'second life' of folklore when referring to non-original contexts such as those related to the concept of heritage (Honko 1987). Thus museums, interpretative centres and festivals, but also radio and television programmes, printed collections or websites on the Internet, may be used to re-present folklore and popular culture in its second life.

The awareness and promotion of folklore and popular culture from a heritage perspective also benefit greatly from being directly integrated into the community by way of utilizing existing physical and social structures as well as human resources. The notion of continuity in the processes governing traditional and popular culture as elemental aspects of everyday life can then be respected. For instance, the renovation of a building which once had a primary function would be preferable to the erection of an entirely new structure. The sense of identity associated with such a building may then be recognized even if the context in which it is used has changed. The case of the Butter Exchange in Cork city may be highlighted here. Once a major international trade centre, its focus of activity has changed due to historical and economic reasons (Rynne 1998). The buildings have now been turned into a museum and a craft centre where traders associated with traditional culture have workshops, practise their trade and train apprentices, and constitute such an example. Thus, the trades for which the building is being used have changed, yet it remains culturally significant as the processes inherent to the content, performance and transmission of traditional culture are maintained.

The function of these modes of re-presentation is to render the material accessible to a wide audience and therefore increase the awareness of cultural identities. Ethical concerns in this regard are not so much directed towards evaluating their merits but rather at general principles affecting the presentation of traditional or popular culture material in non-original contexts. Here again it is important that the material and the performers generate a sense of identity within their own community. Over-stereotyping may ultimately alienate the community from its own traditional heritage. To give a humorous example, traditional musicians have been known to refer to some tourism-oriented performances as 'dancing Books of Kells'. This in no way demeans the talents of the dancers who themselves would distinguish between this form of performance and traditional dancing by using the terms 'modern' and *sean-nós*. The jocular metaphor points to the fact that the design of the costumes or choreographed performances are not recognized by the musicians as a tradition with which they would readily identify, although music and dancing are inherent to Irish heritage (Hobsbawm and Ranger 1992). To an extent, the processes at work in the presentation and preservation of folklore as heritage are similar to those which govern the dynamics of folk revival movements (Rosenberg 1993).

The researcher must aim to achieve a balance which reflects the continuity of tradition in its transfer from an original to a secondary context. A presentation such as the one mentioned above would benefit from being integrated into a general context of traditional dancing, including, for instance, examples of set dancing with which people more readily identify. On its own, however, it is not reflective of a continuous and integrated traditional activity. It is also important that the community and the items of folklore and popular culture represented may identify with and receive appropriate credit for their contributions. The researcher must be conscious that traditional culture is a human production and must be acknowledged as such.

Aspects and elements of the previously cited UNESCO document are illustrated in the following case study. This emphasises the training of community researchers in collecting and archiving skills focussed on the management of their own cultural heritage primarily for their own community. The pilot project also has potential applications outside the community of origin.

THE NORTHSIDE FOLKLORE PROJECT:
A CASE STUDY IN URBAN ETHNOLOGY
This summary of the establishment of the Northside Folklore Project is based upon a series of unpublished reports and documents prepared by myself and Dónal Sugrue, project coordinator, with contributions from Gearóid Ó Crualaoich and Diarmuid Ó Gialláin from Folklore and Ethnology at University College, Cork. Further information has also been taken from the project's website (*http://www.ucc.ie/ucc/research/nfp*), established by Dónal Sugrue.

Rationale
In Ireland, urban culture is a relatively new concept. Until recently scholarly attention in folklore had concentrated on the rural environment. However, the use of ethnography as a method of ethnological investigation has much relevance for cultural research in urban contexts. The Urban Ethnology Project at UCC, through the Northside Folklore Project, is the first Irish application of these concepts and methods in a manner which fully integrates academic and the community, while promoting the importance of cultural research. The Northside Folklore Project pilot community-based collection project and community archive began in September 1996 as a joint venture between UCC and Northside Community Enterprises (NCE), which use training programmes to combat unemployment in the Cork's Northside. The primary aim of the Project is to create a substantial collection of material related to Northside identity by documenting the Northside's verbal folklore, its own account of its rituals, its sporting life and other recreations, as well as its music, material culture, religious life and so forth. The local insider's perspective is of particular importance in an endeavour of this kind. To that end, ten members of the Northside

community were initially recruited and trained by UCC staff in a variety of ethnographic research techniques, including interviewing, archiving and mapping. This resulted in a multimedia project featuring voice recording, music recording, photographic archive and video film. The material produced by the Northside Folklore Project has been made available on location and electronically through the Project's website and through an on-site repository.

Background research and rapport with the community
The Northside Folklore Project, which until September 1994 had constituted an element of UCC Folklore and Ethnology research interests and generated contributions from its students, received a UCC President's Research Fund grant and stepped up its activities to include active participation from the community in which the study is based.

In October 1995, I was appointed as research co-ordinator to Folklore and Ethnology at UCC. Part of my duty was to oversee the activities of the Northside Folklore Project and also to establish the Folklore and Ethnology Archive for which I had previously prepared a feasibility study (Desplanques 1994). Contacts between Folklore and Ethnology and representatives of Northside community groups were strengthened through a series of meetings called by staff members in Folklore and Ethnology at UCC. The possibilities of expanding the research project to take on a significant research input from the community were explored. A variety of ethical issues focussed along the same lines as those of the UNESCO document mentioned above were debated. Thus questions essentially relating to issues of control over the collection, preservation and dissemination of the material were discussed. In practical terms this translated into:

• evaluating the insider/outsider relationship in training non-academic collectors to gather Northside folklore and popular culture material;

• establishing the roles and functions of a folklore archive and developing an archive policy agreeable to all;

• ensuring that the material collected would be made available at an appropriate location and disseminated in suitable formats.

Eventually sufficient common ground was established to allow the research interests of Folklore and Ethnology to be considered of value both to the University and representatives of the Northside community. The project could then take on more visibility and status in the community, hence more credibility all around.

A series of field research workshops was organized by

Fig. 18.1 The interviewing process.

UCC for representatives of the community groups and a steering committee comprising an equal number of UCC and community group representatives was then put into place. Its primary tasks was to explore the possibility of a setting up a community employment scheme but also to establish an initial training programme and research agenda for what had now become the Northside Folklore Project. It also intended to facilitate research for students and members of the community by establishing relevant field contacts in the area.

In the spring of 1996 the proposed community employment scheme was approved and endorsed by the government agency FÁS (Foras Áiseanna Saothair / Training and Employment Authority). Contacts between Barry McCarthy, chairperson of the Northside Folklore Project Steering Committee, and Noreen Hegarty, manager of NCE, enabled the scheme to be co-sponsored by NCE, who would provide part of the equipment required and a base. In August 1996 candidates were interviewed for the positions of co-ordinator and researchers. The scheme was allotted one co-ordinator and 8 to 10 part-time researchers. An initial programme for the training aspect of the scheme was prepared by the Project Steering Committee. A team of nine people and a co-ordinator, Dónal Sugrue, who had an academic background in Folklore and Ethnology, were initially selected. The number of workers on the project has since increased to twelve per year.

In 1998 the Northside Folklore Project community employment scheme expanded its base to include a community archive and a library. The training part of the project is provided essentially by the staff of Folklore and Ethnology with contributions from other departments at UCC during three months each year. Trained researchers then conduct fieldwork in the community using a variety of collecting techniques and technologies, including questionnaire design, tape-recorded interviews, video and still photography. Emphasis in the collection to date has been on aspects of the calendar customs and popular culture of various groups.

Collection

A specific project on the Travelling community, for example, is aimed at breaking down cultural barriers through respectful and comprehensive research into Travellers' customs, oral literature and material culture. Results of this research conducted by workers from the Northside Folklore Project in tandem with members of St Finbarr's Training Centre, a Northside-based Traveller community group, will form an important database on aspects of Travellers' cultural heritage, to be stored in the project's community archive which is close to Travellers' halting areas and accessible to the public. Thanks to this particular research project, important links have been

Fig. 18.2 Editing video archive footage for the re-presentation of folk heritage material.

forged with settled Travellers at the local level.

It is obvious yet important to note that such research also implies the development of inter-community group dynamics contributing positively to the formation of an experienced sense of identity. This in turn may function as an ethnic advocacy tool, as illustrated by such publications as *A heritage ahead: cultural action and Travellers* (Pavee Point 1995).

Other areas of research at the community-based project include a schools project set up along the same lines as the 1937–38 Irish Folklore Commission endeavour and which aims to collect folklore in context from the point of view of school children. Several projects focus on the various sporting traditions popular on the Northside, such as drag-hunting and bowling, but also from a more contemporary perspective concentrating on international soccer player Roy Keane, who has achieved folk-hero status among young and old on the Northside where he originally comes from and where his family still lives. A fashion project has produced important visual records of the fashions and material culture of an urban community over a fifty-year period. From a similar perspective, a special project on tattooing as an expression of identity and popular culture is also currently being undertaken.

Occupational folklore is also documented through research into the textile industry, as the actual location of

the Northside Folklore Project is on the grounds and in the premises of the clothing factory Sunbeam Wolsey, once the major employer in the area. This research involves a series of life histories, including oral narratives, of former workers, complemented with visual documents. This particular research has also provided material for an EU textile history initiative called Arqueotex, of which the Irish contribution is entitled the Cork Textiles Project, co-ordinated by Dr Andy Bielenberg and Dr Colin Rynne of UCC. Other occupational folklore research focuses on various shops and traders of the area.

The musical heritage and popular culture of the community have been documented chronologically to include a folksong collection, an investigation of gramophone traditions and special interest groups who regularly meet to reminisce and exchange documents and operatic recordings, as opera-going was very much an aspect of popular culture in Cork in the first part of the twentieth century. A series of interviews with musicians involved in the showband era documents aspects of popular culture from the 1950s to the 1970s. A specific project looks at the music and the fans of Rory Gallagher, the recently deceased internationally known local blues musician who also has achieved folk-hero status in Cork city.

In all, over thirty major projects cover most aspects of

folklore and popular culture in the area and create a substantial collection of material related to Northside identity by documenting aspects of its traditional and popular culture.

Preservation

The material collected — audio and video as well as manuscript and photographic — constitutes an important collection of primary sources which is deposited in the Northside Folklore Project community archive and catalogued by a worker on the scheme who has been trained as an archivist. Together with the library section of the archive, it is an important resource for the community. This resource is based in and available to the public as opposed to being displaced to the University, access to which is perceived by the community as being restrictive, if only for geographical reasons. As mentioned earlier in this chapter, the project has retained its academic component. Thus material collected by the students in the Folklore and Ethnology research seminar differs slightly from the community-based resource in that these projects include an analytical perspective in the form of essays based on primary sources. This material is deposited in the UCC Folklore and Ethnology archive, strategically located on the periphery of University grounds for access reasons. The public may thus visit the archive without having formally to enter the campus. Location and access were among the points debated during the initial meeting between staff of Folklore and Ethnology and community groups. Both archives, however, share a similar cataloguing and classification system which is currently being incorporated into a specifically designed database compatible with Internet technology so as to increase accessibility.

Presentation

Mainly due to the establishment of this community-based archive and research project, the expansion of Folklore and Ethnology's activities, both from an academic and its necessary applied perspective, has attracted attention locally and internationally from various parties, including local and national media, local and national community groups with similar interests as well as the international academic community. Attention to the project's activities outside the immediate community has been generated through major travelling exhibitions supported by grants from the Heritage Council and prepared by heritage management students on work experience at the Project. The Project's newsletter, *The Archive*, features excerpts from its archive collection. *The Archive* is distributed free of charge to schools, libraries and community groups in Cork city. It is also available from commercial outlets on the Northside and copies are sent to folklore archives and

departments around the world. *Life journeys* (ed Hunter 1999), a collection of life stories and photographs — incidentally the last to be published in the twentieth century — was prepared entirely by researchers on the project, which also controlled all aspects of its publication.

It is clear that the Northside Folklore Project's activities, through its exhibitions and publications, values and enhances the cultural heritage of the community within which it is based. Beyond this, it also offers research facilities and services through its archives. Furthermore and perhaps most importantly, it provides training and employment in its area of expertise and for members of the community in which it is based. It should be noted here that several community workers employed at the Project have found permanent employment in heritage-related areas or have gone to third-level and post-graduate education. It would be presumptuous to assume that the Northside Folklore Project fully complies with the international guidelines outlined in 'The Final Text of the Recommendation for the Safeguarding of Folklore', although it certainly strives to do so. As mentioned above, the financial and resource assistance made available to the project has been limited. The resources provided by the academic institution should be increased; a budget and extra personnel should be made available. The Northside Folklore Project has recently benefited from Higher Education Authority funding, and has participated in 'Documents of Ireland', a major research project and database involving several UCC departments. The Irish government on the other hand might also provide full-time and permanent positions as well as adequate salaries. It is only through the provision of these necessary resources that such a project may be able to claim ethical viability and achieve an integral position in the heritage industry.

CONCLUSION

Although the ethical issues discussed above relate to important aspects of the integration of folklore and popular culture material into the wider notion of heritage, these are by no means exclusive. The development of heritage and the uses of folklore material in this context reflect a cultural reaction to other economic and social conditions (Dettmer 1991). It is important, therefore, that the heritage researcher does not lose sight of those parameters which are ultimately inherent in the overall dynamics of the folklore process within the heritage context.

Bibliography

Cranitch, M. 1996 'The Sliabh Luachra "Code"' in P. F. Devine and H. White (eds) *The Maynooth International Musicological Conference 1995: selected proceedings*.

Desplanques, M. A. 1994 *The archive of folklore and ethnology at University College Cork: a feasibility study*. Cork.

Dettmer, E. 1991 'Folklorism in Newfoundland' in G. Thomas and J. Widdowson (eds) *Community and process* (St John's, Breakwater).

Finnegan, R. 1992 *Oral traditions and the verbal arts*. London and New York.

Gailey, A. 1988 'Tradition and identity' in A. Gailey (ed) *The use of tradition: essays presented to G. B. Thompson* (Hollywood, county Down), pp. 61–7.

Goldstein, K. S. 1964 *A guide for fieldworkers in folklore*. Hatboro.

Hobsbawm, E. and Ranger, T. (eds) 1992 *The invention of tradition*. Cambridge.

Hannerz, U. 1992 *Cultural complexity: studies in the social organization of meaning*. New York.

Honko, L. 1987 'Possibilities of international cooperation and regulation in the safeguarding of folklore', *Nordic Institute of Folklore Newsletter* **15**, 1, pp. 4–21.

Honko, L. 1989 'The Final Text of the Recommendation for the Safeguarding of Folklore', *Nordic Institute of Folklore Newsletter* **17**, 2–3, pp. 3–12.

Honko, L. 1991 'The folklore process', *Folklore Fellows Summer School Programme* (Turku), pp. 25–47.

Hunter, S. (ed) 1999 *Life journeys: living folklore in Ireland today*. Cork.

Ives, E. D. 1974 *The tape-recorded interview*. Knoxville.

King, P. and O'Connor, N. 1995 *A River of Sound*, documentary series produced by Hummingbird Productions for BBC and RTÉ.

Kirshenblatt-Gimlett, B. 1988 'Mistaken dichotomies', *Journal of American Folklore* **101**, 440, pp. 140–55.

Jackson, B. 1979 *Fieldwork*. Urbana.

Pavee Point 1995 *A heritage ahead: cultural action and travellers*. Dublin.

Rosenberg, N. 1993 *Transforming tradition: folk music revivals examined*. Urbana.

Rynne, C. 1998 '*At the sign of the cow': the Cork Butter Market 1770–1924*. Cork.

Ó Súilleabháin, S. 1970 *A handbook of Irish folklore*. Detroit.

Spradley, J. 1979 *The ethnographic interview*. New York.

Science

GORDON HERRIES DAVIES

During August 1857 the British Association for the Advancement of Science convened in Dublin. The Association is a peripatetic body. Founded at York in 1831, it meets each summer in one of the cities within these islands, bringing science to the notice of the public and providing scientists themselves with a forum for the presentation of their latest research. The 1857 meeting was a significant occasion in Ireland's intellectual history. The Association's president for the meeting was Humphrey Lloyd (1800–81), the physicist from Trinity College, Dublin, and every one of the Association's eight sections — from Mathematics and Physics to Mechanical Science — had as its president an Irish scientist of distinction. It was a remarkable tribute to the achievements of Irish science. That science was then at its zenith. The hundred years between 1780 and 1880 represent for Irish science a memorable golden age.

A late eighteenth-century Irish surge of interest in science is reflected in the foundation of institutions such as the Dunsink Observatory (1785), the Royal Irish Academy (1785), the Belfast Reading Society (1788), the Armagh Observatory (1790) and the Royal Cork Institution (1803). But nowhere was the new interest in things scientific more strikingly apparent than at the (Royal) Dublin Society. There the Leskean mineral collection was purchased (1792), a new chair in chemistry and mineralogy was established (1795), a botanical garden was founded at Glasnevin (1795), and a chair in natural philosophy was inaugurated (1800).

During the first three decades of the nineteenth century the strength of the surge diminished somewhat. For that many will doubtless blame the Act of Union (1801), but some of those around at the time believed that Irish science had suffered through the diversion of overmuch energy into the struggle surrounding the cause of Catholic Emancipation (1829). It was nevertheless an hiatus of only brief duration. The 1830s and 1840s saw Irish science become a scene more lively than

ever before as there hatched a remarkable clutch of new scientific institutions. First there came the Zoological Society of Dublin, later the Royal Zoological Society of Ireland (1830), and then there followed the Geological Society of Dublin, later the Royal Geological Society of Ireland (1831), the Cork Cuvierian Society (1835), the Natural History Society of Dublin (1838), the Geological Survey of Ireland (1845), the Museum of Irish Industry, later the Royal College of Science for Ireland (1845), the science chairs in the Queen's Colleges at Belfast, Cork, and Galway (1849), and the Dublin Microscopical Club (1849). Irish science was truly effervescent, and it was this exciting Irish ambience which made of the 1857 Dublin British Association meeting the outstanding success which it so clearly was.

This heroic episode in the story of Irish science was of all too short a duration. Before the close of the nineteenth century Irish science had entered upon a decline. The reasons for that decline are here of no concern. What is of concern is that for one hundred years after 1780 Ireland was the scene of remarkable creativity across the entire spectrum of science. It was a creativity noteworthy even by the exacting judgmental standards of international science. This is the one aspect of Irish heritage of which the world should be reminded. It is another aspect of Irish heritage in which Ireland should take particular pride.

For many — certainly for non-scientists — the notion of an Irish heritage in science will perhaps seem strange and elusive. Is science not an amorphous entity, more akin to Hy Brasil that to a high cross? Other areas of human endeavour are easier to grasp. Should we wish to contemplate the creative achievements of Sir John Lavery, then we open the door of Ireland's National Gallery. Should we wish to admire the creative talents of James Gandon, then we stand upon George's Quay across from Dublin's Custom House. Should we wish to celebrate the genius of Sean O'Casey, then we reserve seats at The Abbey. But how are we to establish our contact with the creative achievements of Ireland's bygone scientists? Those achievements are now securely woven into the vast international tapestry which is modern science. How are we to unpick from the great tapestry those few disparate threads which are the Irish contribution to this most remarkable of all human accomplishments? How do we remind ourselves of Ireland's noble heritage in science?

IRISH SCIENTIFIC LITERATURE: SOURCES AND STUDIES

In seeking the answer to such questions we must first turn to our great scholarly libraries. There we have the opportunity of drawing close to the scientists of yester-year. There we may read the very words that they wrote. There, through sentences, equations, formulae and diagrams, we may explore the working of scientific minds long since departed.

Richard Helsham (1682?–1783) was a friend of Dean Swift and the first Erasmus Smith's Professor of Natural and Experimental Philosophy in Trinity College, Dublin. In the year following Helsham's death his prelections were published as *Lectures on natural philosophy*, and for many decades the book remained a standard text among Trinity's undergraduates. Its pages thus afford us with insight not only into Helsham's mind but also into the nature of the scientific education received by succeeding generations of Irishmen. Such is the interest of this corner of our scientific heritage that today there is talk of marking the millennium with the publication of a handsome facsimile of Helsham's work.

Richard Kirwan (1733–1812), second President of the Royal Irish Academy, was a scholarly polymath with interests ranging from chemistry and geology to meteorology and metaphysics. His *Elements of mineralogy*, first published in 1784, is today a collector's item, and somewhere in the world there is someone who clearly craved for an encounter with Kirwan amidst the 443 pages of the volume. At a Phillips auction held in Bath that somebody made the decisive bid of £460 when a copy of the *Elements* came under the hammer on 22 February 1999.

Éamon de Valera would have understood such a cash-backed interest in Ireland's scientific heritage. A mathematician himself, he idolized Sir William Rowan Hamilton (1805–65), that greatest of all Irish mathematicians. It was de Valera's insistence — he was then Taoiseach — which in November 1943 placed Hamilton upon an Irish postage stamp, but in the present context another, and hitherto untold, de Valera story is more apposite. During the 1960s Trinity College, Dublin, was raising money to allow the building of what today is the College's Berkeley Library. A scheme was devised (bibliophiles may consider it to have verged upon sacrilege) whereby those contributing more than a stated sum

might have their generosity recorded through the affixing of a commemorative label to any volume which they chose to name from within the Library's holding. During a visit to the College the scheme was explained to de Valera who was now become Ireland's President. He instantly offered to subscribe. When asked which book he wished to receive his commemorative label, he hesitated not a moment. He named Hamilton's *Lectures on quaternions* (1853).

Perhaps I convey the impression that the Irish literary heritage in science consists solely of book literature. Such an impression would be false. In science most research finds publication not in the form of books, but rather in the form of papers issued within scientific periodicals. Such periodicals have for long been a feature of the Irish scientific scene. Mention of just a few titles will suffice to illustrate this genre of literature within the fabric of our heritage in science.

The Royal Irish Academy issued its *Transactions* between 1787 and 1907, has published its *Proceedings* since 1836, its *Irish Journal of Earth Sciences* since 1984, and its *Biology and Environment* since 1993. The Royal Dublin Society published its *Transactions* between 1799 and 1810, its *Journal* between 1856 and 1878, its *Scientific Transactions* between 1877 and 1909, and its *Scientific Proceedings* between 1877 and 1980. Among others of our extinct periodicals there are the *Journal of the Geological Society of Dublin* and the *Journal of the Royal Geological Society of Ireland* (1833–89), the *Dublin Quarterly Journal of Science* (1861–66) and the *Irish Naturalist* (1892–1924). The latter periodical, based in Dublin, died amidst the turmoil surrounding the birth of what was then the Irish Free State but, happily, the periodical re-arose phoenix-like in Belfast in 1925 and it lives on as the *Irish Naturalists' Journal*.

Of course, by no means all the research conducted by Irish scientists finds publication within the pages of an Irish periodical. Much of the fruit from the branches of Irish science has fallen overseas. Here just two illustrations of the point fly to mind. First, many of the celestial discoveries made at Birr Castle by William Parsons (1800–67), the third Earl of Rosse, are to be found recorded within the pages of the *Philosophical Transactions of the Royal Society of London*. (The third Earl was President of the august Royal Society from 1848 until 1854, the only time when an Irish resident has held that office of high scientific distinction.) Second, in volume 18 (1862) of the *Quarterly Journal of the Geological Society of London*, we find a paper written by Joseph Beete Jukes (1811–69) and devoted to an analysis of the evolution of the river pattern of the south of Ireland. Jukes was then Local Director of the Geological Survey of Ireland, and his paper is today revered as one of the foundation stones of modern geomorphology. Indeed, the paper resulted in a case of geographical eponymy; a butte in the Henry

Mountains of Utah was named after Jukes in direct response to the brilliance of his Irish study.

This scientific literature, whether in the form of books or papers, whether published at home or abroad, forms the treasury of Irish science. It is a treasury which has to be explored by anybody seeking an appreciation of Irish creativity in science. But, sadly, it is a treasury which until the 1980s had attracted little scholarly attention. Even today growth within that field which is the history of Irish science is at a very early stage; the green shoots are still thin on the ground. Bookshelves bend under the weight of tomes devoted to Ireland's political heritage. Librarians wring their hands in despair at the arrival of further crates containing volumes to be catalogued under 'Joyce', 'Wilde' and 'Yeats'. But enquire in a Dublin bookshop for an introduction to Ireland's heritage in science, and the helpful assistant will be flummoxed by a VDU that insists upon indicating 'question not understood'.

No university within the Republic of Ireland employs an historian of science. Nowhere in the world do I know of a university course which is concerned with the history of Irish science. The Royal Dublin Society's series of historical studies devoted to Irish science and technology was inaugurated in 1980 and showed great promise, but it was murdered within the decade. And none of our scholarly libraries has seen fit to catalogue or assemble a special collection of works on the theme of science in Ireland.

The libraries of the University of Oklahoma have at Norman a superb special collection devoted to the history of science. It is a collection which draws scholars from around the world. Should I wish to read some of the manuscript letters of Jukes, Local Director and then Director of the Geological Survey of Ireland from 1850 until 1869, it so happens that it is to the University of Oklahoma I must go. What a boon it would be to every student of Ireland's heritage in science did some Irish library contain an Irish Science Room wherein there was assembled, upon open access, all the relevant literature reflective of Ireland's scientific heritage. To such a Room the Irish scientists of today and tomorrow might be encouraged to present their own germane manuscript materials. Such a Room (should I perhaps be a little more grandiose and term it a Resource Centre?) could become the internationally recognized focus for the study of the history of Irish science. I wonder, does any benefactor or librarian read me?

Manuscript sources such as those to which I have just alluded are yet a further element within our Irish heritage in science. The published books and papers represent the public edifice that is Irish science, but if we wish to know something of life among the builders of that edifice — something of their relationships, beliefs, ambitions, and weaknesses — then we must turn to

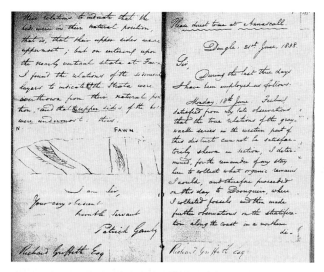

Fig. 19.1 Part of two letters written in June 1838 to (Sir) Richard Griffith, the 'father of Irish geology', by his field assistant, Patrick Ganly. The Dingle Peninsula of county Kerry was then the subject of Ganly's study, and here he explains how cross-stratification in a sedimentary stratum may be used to reveal whether the bed has been inverted by a subsequent folding. This was the first time that the technique had been used; today it is a technique in use the world over. The letters are preserved in the Library of the Royal Irish Academy.

those of their manuscript documents which survive to us. The manuscripts take us behind the published façade.

Despite the feebleness of past interest in the history of Irish science, the manuscript sources for its study prove to be surprisingly rich. The library of Trinity College, Dublin, for instance, contains the notebooks and letters of Sir William Rowan Hamilton together with an immense archive of documents relating to the history of the Royal Zoological Society of Ireland. In the same institution the College's Department of Geology holds the minute books of the Geological Society of Dublin and the Royal Geological Society of Ireland. The Royal Irish Academy possesses the manuscript catalogue of Richard Kirwan's library and three volumes of letters of Patrick Ganly (1809–99) to (Sir) Richard Griffith (1784–1878) written between 1837 and 1843 when they were working together to compile and then to improve the earliest large-scale geological map of Ireland, a map which was first published in 1839. The Geological Survey of Ireland possesses a quite remarkable treasure-trove of materials relating to the history of the Survey. The National Library of Ireland has the papers of Sir Thomas Aiskew Larcom (1801–79) which offer a multitude of fascinating insights into the life of Irish science as it climbed towards its mid-Victorian zenith. The National University of Ireland, Dublin, houses the records of the Royal College of Science for Ireland, that admirable institution which died amidst our political turmoil of the early 1920s. The National University of Ireland, Galway, has several of the actual field-sheets used by Patrick Ganly during his geological surveying. And so one might continue.

Some manuscripts evidently still await discovery. On 7 February 1999 I was invited to a party in county Tipperary. There a chance encounter and a fortunate comment revealed one of my fellow guests to be the owner of a small archive of material relating to Edmund Davy (1785–1857), professor of chemistry (later agricultural chemistry) at the Royal Dublin Society from 1826 until his death. He was a first cousin of that eminent man of science Sir Humphrey Davy. Other manuscripts have just as recently been lost. David Allardice Webb (1912–94) was professor of botany in Trinity College, Dublin, from 1954 until 1966. During the years immediately preceding his tragic death — he died in a road accident — he was engaged in the writing of an autobiography. That I know for certain. Some of the pages were written in my own home, and there the author gave me readings from his pencilled draft. But I am told that following his death the script was nowhere to be found among his effects.

IRISH SCIENTIFIC INSTRUMENTATION

Whether printed and published upon the pages of books and periodicals or scribbled in manuscript in the private leaves of letters and notebooks, words, and the ideas to which they give expression, form the very kernel of Ireland's heritage in science. But, happily, our scientific heritage does not consist exclusively of paper-borne verbiage. Our scientific heritage possesses other elements, and foremost amongst these is the great legacy of scientific instruments which has been handed down to us.

In their book 'Vulgar and Mechanick': the scientific instrument trade in Ireland, 1650–1921 (Royal Dublin Society 1989), John Burnett and Alison Morrison-Low have amply demonstrated that over the centuries many an Irish craftsman has been involved in the construction or sale of scientific instruments. Brass and glass, wood and wire are all durable materials, and in his splendid and compendious Irish national inventory of historic scientific instruments (1995) Charles Mollan has ably revealed to us the great wealth of historic scientific instruments which survives within this island. From abacuses, air-pumps and ammeters to X-ray tubes, yarn testers and a zoetrope (in the National Museum, Dublin), Mollan parades them all before us in review order. His list raises interesting questions — questions demanding of early investigation — as to the evidently high status enjoyed by science within some of our schools during the nineteenth century. In advance of Mollan's investigations, who would have expected to find within Blackrock College and Clongowes Wood College the rich collections

of Victorian instruments which Mollan has found to be there present? Presumably the instruments were originally acquired to serve didactic purposes. Clongowes Wood College even possesses an Atwood machine (it would have been used for studies in connection with the laws of motion) which is said once to have belonged to John Dalton, the great Manchester chemist.

All these instruments are fascinating in their own right as examples of craftsmanship generated by the scientific endeavour. Many of them are items of considerable aesthetic beauty, bearing ample testimony to the creative skills of the hands involved in turning and tapping metal or in compounding and polishing glass. But these instruments each contribute something else to our heritage in science. They are the very tools once used by the Irish scientists whose writings have bequeathed to us our literary heritage in science. To admire their instruments, to handle them, to read their vernier scales and to peer through their optics, is to be drawn close to the scientists of yore. A display-cased baton once waved by Arturo Toscanini at La Scala is inspiring, but it is no less inspiring to bring into focus a Dunsink telescope through which William Rowan Hamilton once gazed out upon the heavens.

It is sad that Richard Kirwan should so frequently have been dismissed as a freakish Irish eccentric. In reality he was one of the brightest stars ever to have arisen above Ireland's scientific horizon. His burning glass is today in the collection of the Royal Dublin Society. To stand beside the glass is to be transported back through time and into Kirwan's laboratory. Was he perhaps employing the glass in some experiment one day in May 1794 when there arrived from Paris that most frightful news? Antoine Lavoisier, the founder of modern chemistry and one of Kirwan's correspondents, had become a victim of the guillotine. To stand beside the glass is to remember those words of Joseph Lagrange uttered the day following the execution: 'only a moment to cut off that head and a hundred years may not give us another like it'.

The Physics Department of the National University of Ireland, Cork, possesses a balance reputedly constructed by John Boole, the father of George Boole (1815–64), first professor of mathematics in Queen's College, Cork. To gaze upon the balance is to be carried back to the humble home of the Boole family in the English city of Lincoln. There George Boole was self-educated in science. Did his mechanically inclined tradesman father perhaps construct this balance as a parental contribution towards the programme of scientific self-help embarked upon by a son possessed of so obvious a talent? Did the balance play its part in shaping the career of the man after whom there is now named a 'Boole Library' upon the campus where once he walked? Was this balance a factor in the intellectual evolution of the man whom John A. Murphy has recently hailed as 'the

Fig. 19.2 The Birr Leviathan. Reproduced from Sir Robert Stawell Ball's best-selling The story of the heavens, *first published in 1886 while he was Royal Astronomer of Ireland.*

most renowned professor in the history of the college'?

The Geological Survey of Ireland possesses the petrological microscope which was once the property of Grenville Arthur James Cole (1859–1924). He was professor of geology in the Royal College of Science for Ireland from 1890 until his death, and Director of the Geological Survey of Ireland from 1905 onwards. He was an outstanding man of science, being both a fine researcher and a prolific and most readable author. I presume that it was by means of this microscope that he drew the four thin-sections in variolite from Annalong in county Down with which he illustrated his paper read to the Royal Dublin Society on 17 February 1892. Later, his wife Blanche doubtless used the microscope, because she drew the two thin-sections — gabbro from Portsoy, Banffshire, and Torridonian sandstone from Ullapool, Ross and Cromarty — which formed the frontispiece to the later editions of her husband's *Aids in practical geology*. But I must confess that as I reflect upon the microscope I think not of gabbros and sandstones. I think of swollen and disformed fingers trying to turn knurled wheels in adjustment of the instrument's optics. In his later years Cole was seriously crippled by arthritis.

For anyone seeking an appreciation of Ireland's science heritage as revealed by the national stock of scientific instruments, there are two geographical

locations of paramount importance — two locations which simply reek of former scientific activity. One of the locations is in county Kildare and the other is in county Offaly. In county Kildare there stands St Patrick's College, Maynooth, where the Revd Nicholas Callan (1799–1864) was professor of natural philosophy from 1826 until his death. He was a major figure in the field of electrodynamical research and, happily, there survives a great deal of the apparatus which he devised and used. Today, perhaps somewhat strangely, the apparatus is all gathered in the College's Museum of Ecclesiology. There we may inspect induction coils, electro-magnets, Daniell cells, Grove batteries, a Voltaic pile and so much else, all of them instruments which were brilliantly employed by Callan in both the laboratory and the lecture-theatre. In 1994 Charles Mollan and John Upton together published a lavish catalogue of the entire Maynooth collection of scientific instruments, a catalogue which again serves to remind us of the remarkable richness of this aspect of our heritage in science. Thinking back to the nineteenth century — back to that memorable 1857 Dublin meeting of the British Association — Callan was there. To the Association's Section A (Mathematics and Physics) meeting in Trinity College he on Tuesday 1 September presented a paper 'On the electro-dynamic induction apparatus'.

The scientific heritage site in county Offaly is breathtaking in its scale and utterly captivating in the interest that it enshrines. This has to be acclaimed the *pièce de résistance* of Ireland's scientific heritage. This is a site of international significance. It stands within the gates of Birr Castle. It is the great 'Leviathan of Birr'. In 1834, William Parsons — he became the third Earl of Rosse in 1841 — resigned his seat in Parliament in order to devote himself to astronomy and, more especially, to the improvement of the reflecting telescope. He worked at Birr; he produced his own innovative designs; he trained some of his estate workers in the mysteries of telescope construction, and he built all the furnaces and machinery necessary for the task. By 1839 he had completed his first reflector, incorporating a 36-inch (91.4-centimetre) speculum, and this instrument Thomas Romney Robinson (1792–1882) of the Armagh

Observatory regarded as the most powerful telescope yet built anywhere in the world. But the new Lord Rosse was not content; he desired something larger. Between 1842 and 1845 he and his men therefore built a giant instrument containing a 72-inch (182.8-centimetre) speculum which was cast on 13 April 1842 in a turf-fired foundry built in the Castle's grounds. The speculum weighed over four tons (4,064 kilograms) and the barrel of the new telescope was 58 feet (17.17 metres) long and 7 to 8 feet (2.1 to 2.4 metres) in diameter. Robinson described the telescope when in a near vertical position as looking somewhat like an Irish round tower! The instrument is said to have cost £20,000 and until 1917 it remained the world's largest reflecting telescope.

Lord Rosse employed the telescope chiefly in studies of nebulae, and through a series of papers presented to the Royal Society he became the first to describe and

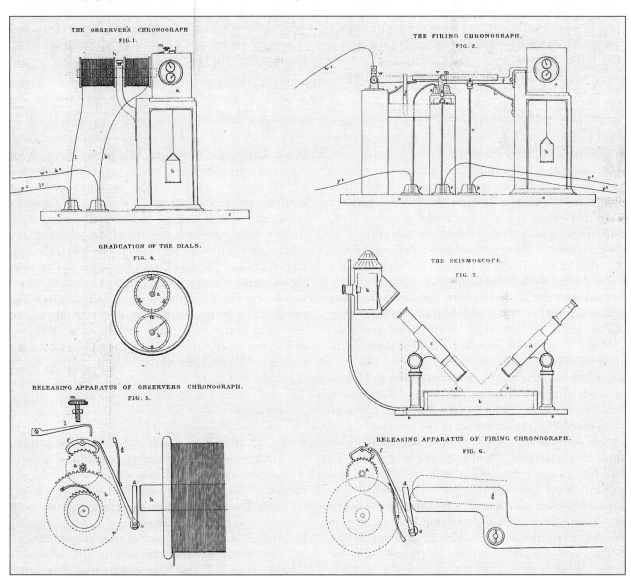

Fig. 19.3 Drawings for some of the instruments used by Robert Mallet during his experiments upon Killiney beach, county Dublin. None of the instruments is known to survive (from report of the British Association meeting held at Ipswich in 1851).

illustrate the spiral structure possessed by many of the nebulae. Following the third Earl's death in 1867, the telescope was less actively employed, and during the closing decades of the nineteenth century it fell first into disrepair and then into decay. For one hundred years 'Leviathan' stood forlorn and rotting. But, thanks to the energy of the seventh and present Earl, substantial financial grants were obtained during the 1990s, and the telescope has now been fully restored to become the focus of an imaginative Historic Science Centre located in the Castle grounds and in the very heart of Ireland.

At 10.00 a.m. on Thursday 3 September 1857 there steamed out of Dublin's Kingsbridge (Heuston) terminus a special train provided free of charge by the Great Southern and Western Railway. Aboard the train were members of the British Association. The Association's Dublin meeting was at an end, and these members were off on a two-day excursion to Birr to wonder at the 'Leviathan'. Their leader was a King's County man — George Johnstone Stoney (1826–1911), who later was to give us the term 'electron' — and their signatures are still to be read in the visitors' book preserved at the Castle. A less durable mark is perhaps left by the modern visitors arriving from every corner of our globe, but they, too, can only stand before 'Leviathan' in wonder and amazement. Lord Rosse's telescope is a truly remarkable artefact within our scientific heritage.

Even those who have difficulty in differentiating between a goniatite and a galaxy surely cannot fail to recognize in 'Leviathan' a piece of our scientific heritage. But there are many other sites where the relationship between science and some particular Irish locale is far from immediately apparent. Look, for example, at Killiney beach in county Dublin. Perhaps on a hot Saturday in July. Bare bodies brown. Paddlers picnic. Soaked setters shake. But where is the science? It was on this beach that in the October and November of 1849, Robert Mallet (1810–81) exploded charges of gunpowder in some of the earliest experiments on the transmission of shock-waves through the earth's surface. Mallet was one of the founders of the science of seismology. He gave to that science its very name. The studies commenced at Killiney were to culminate in his now classic investigations into the Naples earthquake of 16 December 1857.

Now we leave for Munster. Come down to Cappoquin in county Waterford. Stand upon the bridge over the River Blackwater. Note the course of the river. Just downstream of the bridge the river turns through a right-angle, abandoning a simple eastward course over a limestone-floored valley in favour of a complex southward course across a series of sandstone ridges. Jukes was here during 1861. He was perplexed by the river. He bestowed much thought upon the problem. Around the New Year of 1861–62 he had his solution, and when published in the *Quarterly Journal of the Geological Society of London* later in 1862 that solution was to transform our understanding of the processes responsible for the shaping of the earth's topography.

We remain in Munster. We go down to the Dingle Peninsula of county Kerry. The famed Conair Pass is our destination and there we pause by the shore of Lough Doon. This is a site associated with John Ball (1818–89). He came here around 1847. Earlier, Ball had been spending much of his time exploring the natural history of the Alps, but he returned home to play his part in grappling with the catastrophe of the Famine. He came to county Kerry as an Assistant Poor Law Commissioner. In the vicinity of Lough Doon his eyes opened wide in amazement. He was seeing the same suite of landforms as he had so often seen around glaciers in the Alps. Had these Kerry landforms been shaped by former Irish glaciers? Ball was convinced such was the sole rational explanation. At Lough Doon he became the first to adduce incontrovertible evidence that Ireland had experienced a recent Ice Age. At Lough Doon there was born the great Irish school of Pleistocene studies.

CONCLUSION

In emulation of the policy adopted in other nations, we might have erected roadside markers proclaiming to all the significance of scientific heritage sites such as Lough Doon, Cappoquin or Killiney beach. But I leave it for others to debate the merits or otherwise of our adoption of such a policy. It is time for me to conclude. As I lay down my pen I look up from my desk and gaze through the window. Out there, just across the road and standing derelict, is my own local, somewhat peripheral, and very minor, piece of Ireland's heritage in science. It is the little church in which William Rowan Hamilton and his wife, Helen, were married on 9 April 1833. It was not a happy marriage. I doubt whether his wife will have troubled herself to be present on the Saturday morning of that 1857 British Association meeting to hear her husband deliver his paper 'On some applications of quaternions to cones of the third degree'.

Bibliography

Bowler, P. J. and Whyte, N. (eds) 1997 *Science and society in Ireland: the social context of science and technology in Ireland, 1800–1950*. Belfast.

Burnett, J. E. and Morrison-Low, A. D. 1989 *'Vulgar & mechanick': the scientific instrument trade in Ireland 1650–1921*. Dublin.

Herries Davies, G. L. 1983 *Sheets of many colours: the mapping of Ireland's rocks 1750–1890*. Dublin.

Herries Davies, G. L. 1985 'Irish thought in science' in R. Kearney (ed) *The Irish mind: exploring intellectual traditions* (Dublin), pp. 294–310.

McKenna-Lawlor, S. 1998 *Whatever shines should be observed*. Dublin.

Mollan, C. 1995 *Irish national inventory of historic scientific instruments*. Dublin.

Mollan, C. *et al.* 1987 *Nostri plena laboris: an author index to the RDS scientific journals 1800–1985*. Dublin.

Mollan, C., Davis, W. and Finucane, B. (eds) 1985 *Some people and places in Irish science and technology*. Dublin.

Mollan, C., Davis, W. and Finucane, B. (eds) 1990 *More people and places in Irish science and technology*. Dublin.

Mollan, C. and Upton, J. 1994 *St Patrick's College, Maynooth: the scientific apparatus of Nicholas Callan and other historic instruments*. Dublin.

Gaelic Games

TOM HUMPHRIES

Another Saturday morning and the sod is wet, holding a week's rain in its heart. The sun is persisting, though, as the car park fills. There'll be play today. No doubt about it. Seven-year-old girls strap on their shiny blue camogie helmets, making themselves look like upright ants. They follow their coaches through the gap in a brick wall to the far field, dangling their ash hurley sticks in the wet grass behind them. Once this part of north Dublin was farms and prairies. Now between the houses and the schools these little aprons of playland exist. GAA pitches with their spiring posts in supervision. As quintessential an element of the Irish landscape as stone walls, grey rocks or green fields. Their coaches are intercounty stars in their own right, but on Saturday mornings Denise O'Leary, Mary Regan and the others roll the hurling balls into the paths of game seven-year-olds and wait patiently for them to strike crisply with their little hurleys. 'Brilliant. Brilliant. Do it again now.'

The intermediate football team is bustling about too. Grown men on another stage of their GAA journey. The manager is moving among them, having a quite word here, a joke there. Kevin Heffernan is a monument, a man who could have turned his brain to any other pursuit and become a millionaire, a celebrity or, at worst, a politician. He settled for being Chairman of the Labour Court and a GAA legend. Gaelic football and hurling were what seduced him most sweetly and completely. This his genius has flowed through more peaceful pastures. He's been walking out onto fields like this for fifty years now. Never thought to be tired of it. Perhaps single-handedly, he is the man who rescued the GAA in Dublin with his laser-like focus. This morning, though, he has his hands in his pockets and his head down as he heads to the main pitch. His brain is chewing over some football problem. His players run past him soloing footballs. 'Alright Hef?' 'Alright Twisty.'

This is Saturday and ritual is ritual. Pull out of the close-up study of Kevin Heffernan's thoughtful, lined face. Pull away, away up into the air. Wide shot: all over the fields on these verdant little ribbons of Dublin's northside, children and teenagers are swarming. Men and women move among them, regulating them, coaching them, inspiring them. Many of the mentors have faces which would be recognized in any house in the country but this is the giving back. Replacing what you took out of the games as a kid is glad duty. People do it for this. The games. The sheer drunk-making pleasure of hurling and football. So pull away from St Vincent's of Marino and away from Dublin and across the rugged landscape. The scene is being replicated everywhere. In suburbs, parishes and villages. On fields which they bought, begged or borrowed, GAA people are out, passing on the games which have entranced them to another generation. It is a lovely phenomenon, a social levelling and a social unifier, as distinctly Irish a ritual as you could imagine.

Gaelic games are the beautiful untranslatable song to which an entire country hums along. Football, hurling, camogie, handball, even the poor relation, rounders. Is there any other sport in the world which contributes so much fibre to the social fabric? Anything else which stirs up so much conversation? Harsh words are swapped in an intercounty teams' dressing-room. Well thirty players go home to their families and tell the tale. Thirty families go to work the next morning and pass it on. Hundred of workmates go home and to the pub and on the phone. So it goes. Twenty-four hours and the entire country knows.

Jacques Barzun once wrote that 'whoever wants to know the heart and mind of America had better learn baseball.' That was in 1954 when the pastoral rhythms of the great game still had strength enough to seize the popular American imagination. 1954. Before labour strikes, corporate cynicism and the NBA had weakened baseball's grip. Canadians worship their winter game in much the same way as the Irish love hurling and football, but ice hockey franchises have been migrating south of the border for some time now and the flavour of the sport is diluted slightly in the national culture when Gretsky no longer graces Edmonton but sets off for Los Angeles, then St Louis, then New York and retirement. That mobility, that following of the money, leaves tracks like scars. Australian Rules football, a hard professional game itself, is still essentially a regional phenomenon. Those countries which still swoon before the gods of professional soccer cannot have helped notice that their sport has become a soulless industry, its stars adopting the cool remoteness of the matinee idol. There is no need to list all the traduced and raped sports of the world. If drugs haven't deaded their souls, money or Murdoch or both have. There is just one corner of the earth where a big-time sport comes in a package with genuine passion, sheer for-the-love-of-it amateurism and the expression of local identity. Ireland. Gaelic games. There is no comparable phenomenon, no sporting organization which necklaces together the heartbeats of every village, every parish, every suburb and every county.

HISTORY

You can trace your finger back over a couple of routes if you need to know how we got here today to the stage where the GAA possesses the stadiums it does, commands the column inches it does, hogs the imagination in such a greedy way, yet stays meaningful in every parish and crossroads. The dry-as-dust version begins in the billiards room of a dowdy hotel in Thurles town when seven men met to form a sporting organization which from the beginning blended political theory with sporting romance. That was 1 November 1884 and ten days later, the GAA played its first official fixture, a hurling game at Macroom, near Cork. You couldn't say the GAA never looked back, as an organization it never does anything but look back, yet it grew exponentially. Now it is Ireland's prime distraction.

That is one route. It will take you through the history of this country since the late nineteenth century. Grieving men carrying hurley sticks at the funeral of Charles Stuart Parnell. Hopeful men piling up the rubble of Dublin 1916 after the Easter Rising and placing it in a corner of Croke Park as the foundation of the Hill 16 terrace. Dead men. Bloody Sunday 1920 when twelve spectators and a player, Michael Hogan, were killed when British forces opened fire during a football match in Croke Park between Dublin and Tipperary. Worried men gazing through the mirrors of Irish trade protectionism that existed in the GAA's ban on members playing foreign games. Suited men realizing that the Hill 16 terrace would soon have to become an all-seated area in keeping with the corporate tiered ambience of the new Croke Park. That's one history, a path littered with

documents and parched of colour now that we have left the twentieth century behind. It fascinates, though, to see a sports organization grow with a country, enjoying a relationship as symbiotic as conjoined twins. Sometimes, in all the love and squabbling, it is impossible to pry sport and country apart and see any light in between.

The games go way back right to the shrouded beginnings. In the heroic literature and bardic texts which survive from the eight century we read about hurling and the heroes who played it. Dating from this time is a grave slab in Donegal which is adorned with the picture of a hurler in action. Football came into existence later and is mentioned through the ages in its prior form as the game of *caid*. And what about handball, the independent-minded cousin? We are told that Buck Whaley, the legendary gambler and gamesman, once won a bet of one hundred guineas by playing handball on the walls of Jerusalem. That was in 1789.

There is that history mapped out by milestones and documents and landmarks and dates and underpinned always by the sense of the mythic which flavours so much of Irish life. It is the other history which sustains the games and glues them into the Irish psyche, though. The smaller fragmented history, each a mosaic tile in the big picture. County histories. Take the wild hunger of Clare people to bridge the gap between a hurling All-Ireland win in 1914 and their next win in 1995, the palpable sense that the county's well-being was somehow blood-bound to the county's hurling fate. Family histories. Michael Donnellan of Dunmore taking an All-Ireland football medal in 1998 and following the steps of his father and grandfather before him. Social histories. Teams and provinces being decimated by social factors like emigration. Galway and Mayo never win in bad times, their best players are working and playing in Chicago, Boston and New York. The GAA is about people. The fortunes of the Association ebb and flow with that of the country. Unlike other sporting organizations, there is no gulf of experience between audience and participants, between fans and stars.

A rookie in the NBA leaves behind the place he came from quicker than his feet return to earth after he sails above the rim. Money inserts itself between the star and his origins and gives rise to grotesque misunderstandings. During the 1998 NBA lockout, Patrick Ewing of the New York Knicks sought to explain why fans should dip into their pockets and attend a benefit game for locked-out players who made a minimum of $2 million a season. 'We may earn big', said Patrick, 'but we spend big too.' You could catch a cold in the draft as people spun and walked away. Ewing's crass misunderstanding of the relationship between professional sports and those who use professional sports as an entertainment or escape was not unique.

The sociological phenomenon which is the cult of

Manchester United raises questions about whether or not professional sports exist anymore as part of communities or merely as forms of mass entertainment, the modern opium of the masses. Manchester United's world-wide fan base represents a cult of self-perpetuating success. The more replica jerseys which are consumed by the faithful in Scandinavia or Tonbridge Wells or Cork, the more cash goes into keeping Manchester United successful enough to be on the television all the time, an end which in its turn produces more cash and which duly satisfies the cravings of the disconnected cult.

The GAA works differently. *It* has a perverse independence which has allowed it to survive and which lends the organization its character. It is nourished by immediacy, sustained by the fact that no programmes, books, analysis or media output will ever be as well-informed or gossip-laden as a good pub conversation. GAA people know the capillaries of their sport, the games are so local that the audience knows when an acorn drops, the media merely notes the felling of oaks.

It is a September Sunday, the same weekend as the national broadcaster, RTÉ, has opted to hand over a large chunk of Saturday evening prime time to the highlights of soccer matches from the English Premier League. The people of Ireland are tuned into a different wavelength, however. In the television studios three men in suits are discussing the fortunes of the millionaires of the English Premier league. Through the streets of Dublin men and women who have arrived in the city for the following afternoon's game are coursing like blood through veins. Tickets are being bought or haggled over, old friends are being tracked down, closing time in public houses is being negotiated with recalcitrant owners. Colours are worn and there is a sense of rivalry which exists nowhere else. Malice-free. Without spite. The All-Ireland finals in football and hurling are part sport, part ritual. This weekend is a social occasion, a trip to the capital where GAA people can speak their private language of insult and ribaldry, tall story and good gossip.

It gets passed on. Gossip, rumour and fact all swaddling history. Galway and Kildare are playing. You could trade three good stories about the consuming football obsession of the Donnellan family of Galway for an equal number of yarns about the cuteness of the O'Dwyers, Mick and Karl, the father and son who in turn managed and played for the Kildare team. Entire counties are judged by history and games. In Kilkenny they pissed in the powder and in Wexford they are still sore about it. The fact of a Wexford rebellion once having been quelled by Kilkenny men improvising to dampen the gunpowder has somehow fed into the hurling enmity between the two counties, and the insult is still hurled across touchlines. As for Tipperary? Stone-throwers. And so it goes.

IDENTITY

The Gaelic Athletic Association owes its very survival as a rare ethnic sport still intact, still vibrant, to the socio-political environment which it has grown up in. Without Ireland's historical cross-currents, Gaelic games might just be another sport of no more influence in Irish society than cricket or basketball. It has been a struggle to get here and the struggle has defined the character of the games. For years the GAA protected itself from the influence of foreign sports, determined that sport would not be erased from the Irish landscape as the Irish language and Irish music had been previously. The ban on foreign sports lasted so long that it became counter-productive, and in the seventies even the lingering resentment was still harming the Association.

The GAA freed itself of its own ban on members playing foreign games at a famous Congress in Queens University, Belfast, in 1971, but the insecurities of which the ban was a symptom have lived on as long as the resentments. In 1999 the GAA was still speaking sternly to clubs who permitted the facilities to be used by other sports. In Navan, county Meath, for instance, the local GAA club, O'Mahoneys, who have for a long time shared players with Navan rugby club, were asked to explain why they had lent their facilities to the rugby club while the neighbours were having their premises redeveloped.

The games rise and fall with the tide of Irish morale. Incidents like that in Navan are increasingly rare. The strength of the GAA in the late nineties could be seen as a by-product of increased national self-confidence. Enjoying wealth for the first time, benefitting from an unprecedented period of full employment and low emigration, the country began to value itself on new terms. We Irish are a people who have lived vicariously for many years. Validation traditionally came from elsewhere, from outside. Film stars who stopped over at Shannon on the way to somewhere more glamourous and more sunny were celebrated for their 'Irish connection'. American presidents with vaguely Irish names were on the fast track to sainthood, regardless of their politics. The coverage of any Irish achievement wasn't complete until we had read what the foreign papers (usually English) had to say about us. We yearned to be jet-set, space-age, with it. We embraced formica, leatherette and plastic with unseemly enthusiasm. We stampeded in the rush to get British television piped into our houses. We chuckled at the shameful harsh gutteralism of the Irish language and cringed at the stiff-backed formality of Irish dancing. Freed late in our history from foreign interference, we went through our national adolescence with a huge inferiority complex. The sooner we were just like everybody else the bloody better.

The GAA was always there and was always different. It represented a stubborn strain of Irish life. Unabashed, unself-conscious, self-absorbed, obsessional nation-alism. Sport as an expression of happy defiant Irishness. Imagine it. A huge national interest which no other country in the world gives a damn about. On the weekend of an All-Ireland final hours of television programming, acres of newsprint will be devoted to the nuances, the possibilities and the celebrations. In neigh-bouring England, not a line will appear in a national paper. For a long time that was an embarrassment, a well-spring of self-doubt. If nobody else cared for Gaelic games, where was the validity? When would we outgrow these enjoyably tribal occasions?

The GAA, though, had sown itself into the soul of Irish society. Physically it owned land in every town and parish. Even in times when the games were neither profitable nor popular, only the GAA offered a route to the celebratory sense of local pride and well-being which Irish people crave. The Gaelic Athletic Association was there being itself while the smart set tried their first martinis and their first continental holidays. For a time in the late sixties and early seventies, the games of football and hurling became mere rural curiosities. Then Dublin invented a glamourous team of its own and the world shifted slightly again as the city caught up.

The relationship between the GAA and the Irish people is almost too complicated for mere words to unravel. The Association has 800,000 members, but every Irish person considers themselves to be a stockholder. The most grotesque savageries may occur on rugby fields, unspeakable coarseness may have pervaded professional soccer, but only the affairs of the GAA can draw stern editorials from serious newspapers.

It is valid to ask what would county Kildare be without its football team. What would Tipperary be without hurling? What would Kerry be without football? The expression of the regional character is visible in the celebration of the games. Meath's sturdy farmers always play a suitably rugged game of football, roared on by a populace who will brook no argument till the game is over. If they win they depart in cackling triumph. If they lose they shake hands with graceful stoicism and depart quietly. Cork play hurling with a confident arrogance, a knowingness which is in the character of the second city. Northern teams play football earnestly and passionately. Teams from Connacht are suckers for a bit of flair and artistry.

Players live among the people who fashion them as stars and idols. The community is a gravity pull for the ego, yet the great men are permitted their small quota of hubris. An old teacher of mine once told me about asking a Kerry giant just what it meant to have an All-Ireland medal. 'Well', came the answer, 'I have five All-Ireland medals. Your man across the fields has four. There's a lot more thought of me than there is of him'.

There are always problems. Amateurism is a strain in a period where teams train like professionals and see sponsorship money flooding their own sporting environment. Take Jarlath Fallon. In September 1998 when Galway won the All-Ireland football title, closing the book on thirty-two years of heartbreak, it was Jarlath Fallon who made the difference. In a second-half perfor-mance of astonishing ferocity, it was he who pulled the balls down out of the sky, dipped his shoulder and cut into opposition territory, jinking and feinting. He is a postman. The next week he was back on the streets of Tuam delivering post. Within the Galway team it was felt that the All-Ireland final might have been his last game of Gaelic football. He has skills which the professionals of rugby have tapped into before. Now with a big name to sell, a wedding in the offing and his desire for an All-Ireland medal sated, they felt he would be lured away to rugby for good. The following season he was back busting his gut in a maroon jersey. Walking away isn't easy when you are a hero to every person you meet. The social pressure to stay within a sport that really matters was too much. Jarlath Fallon played on.

So did Martin McNamara, the goalkeeper on the team. He retired not long after the All-Ireland win to concen-trate on building the business of the pub which bears his name in Tuam. Endless nights paying people to work for him while he trained and travelled had taken their toll. But the success of Martin Mac's pub hinged also, he would discover, on his profile as a football player. People liked the association, liked the currency of the football talk they could have with him when he was behind the counter. During his brief sabbatical, a customer couldn't darken Martin Mac's door without urging him back into his goalkeeper's jersey.

If the games are bound up in the imagination of places they are linked inextricably it seems with politics too. The Irish evangelize on behalf of Gaelic games. Emigrants drag new neighbours to Irish bars to study the wristy wonders of hurling or the thumping energy of Gaelic football, but at home the nuance is different. Echoes of class and history still exist. It is hard to escape the other history of the Association, of course. The ties between the expressions of nationalism and the playing of Gaelic games seem to be unbreakable.

Anachronistic echoes. There is a bar on members of the security forces in Northern Ireland playing within the GAA. That prohibition, the infamous Rule 21, has outlasted the war in the north of Ireland. After almost half a decade of uneasy, frequently fractured peace, the GAA has held onto its ban like a cudgel. In the spring of 1998 the Association held a 'special' Congress in a Dublin hotel, called with the intention of deleting Rule 21 from its books. The debate preceding the Congress had been unusually open. The then president of the Association, Mr Joe McDonagh, had been unusually strident for a man occupying what is largely a ceremonial position which confines the occupant to club house openings and annual dinners. McDonagh pushed for the deletion of Rule 21 and hoped that the Association would recognize itself as big enough and confident enough to play its part in the changes which broader Irish society was experiencing. Those changes were dramatic and historic. The Good Friday Agreement between the two war-locked opposing traditions had raised the prospect that the country might enter the new century experiencing an unprecedented type of harmony. GAA memories are long, however, and attitudes were surprisingly slow to change. The Association sustained a tremendous public relations blow when delegates voted to keep the rule for the time being. Castigation was swift, harsh and in most cases justified. The GAA had given its traditional enemies, the agents of homogenization who find the rural-based passions of the GAA an uncivilized embarrassment, a stick to beat it with. Within the Association ranks closed relatively swiftly again. While the Irish Republican Army debated over whether or not to hand over the arms with which it had fought a thirty-year war, the GAA was unable to decommission the attitudes of many of its members.

It would be glib and irresponsible, however, not to examine the ingredients which go into such a mind-set. During the thirty years of strife, GAA members suffered as keenly as any sector affected by the Troubles. Members were murdered, often for merely being members of the GAA, club houses were burned down again merely because of their importance as symbols of nationalist confidence and culture. New pitches were strewn with glass so as to be made unplayable. In Crossmaglen, county Armagh, an entire pitch was annexed by the British Army for use as a base.

By the middle of the nineteenth century the Irish Republican Brotherhood, among others, were of the view that the cultural conditions needed to be right if political independence was to be in any way achievable or meaningful. It was the Young Ireland Movement which had first suggested using Gaelic sport as the battering-ram of a cultural renaissance. The Irish Republican Brotherhood took a similar stance and happily Dr Croke, a leading cleric of the time, took the lead by issuing a public letter decrying the decline in indigenous sports. The involvement of the church and the endorsement of many leading nationalist figures were crucial.

Three early rules were instrumental in developing the GAA and, ironically, their lingering influence are what most hampers the Association at present. The security forces were effectively banned from participation in the games. There was censure of sports events organized by the British federations. Players within the GAA were banned from participation or spectating in games which were not indigenous.

All the while the GAA served as a passive expression of nationalist identity. To play football or hurling was undoubtedly a political statement which covered a lot of issues. You followed your team in the All-Ireland championship, the sporting community of which you were a part operated on two levels, the sporting and the symbolic. 'It's recognized as a sport with political connotations', Chris McGimpsey, the moderate unionist politician, told the *Irish Times* in 1994, 'the flag, the tricolour, the refusal to let RUC men go on crowd control duty. There is a feeling of a state within a state.'

When the time came it was unimaginable to some people that the politics of exclusion which at one time had been necessary for the GAA to survive could be shed. Embedded in the history of the games. In 1903, O'Sullivan and Nash were concerned to rid the Association of what was perceived as the West British athletes. In January 1903, they persuaded the Congress of the GAA to pass a motion outlawing all future participation of policemen, soldiers and sailors in Gaelic games. The 1906 Congress declared any athlete ineligible for a GAA sports meeting if he had participated in any meeting sponsored either by the British military forces or the RIC.

The infamous ban on foreign games grew out of a reflex in the early part of the twentieth century which rejected the stated policy of anglicization of Irish society. De Búrca, in his history of the GAA, notes that 'far from being regarded as a purely negative rule the ban was to its early advocates and supporters a positive expression of loyalty to one form of native culture.' Undoubtedly by the time it was deleted from the GAA's rule book in 1971, the ban on foreign games had outlived its positive intent and had become counter-productive in that it was a cause of resentment among those outside the Association and even among those GAA members who wished to mix their sports.

The lesson is there but has been slowly absorbed by a cautious organization. For that curious period before 1998, in the weeks before the special Congress to discuss the ban, it seemed as if the crevices which opened up everytime the issue was discussed would consume the GAA. The motion to remove the ban was defeated, however, and smoothly the fissures disappeared. People got back to their fascination with the games.

MENTALITY

There is a class of person and commentator in Dublin who finds the earthed passion of the Gaelic follower an embarrassment in a modern Ireland which is told at every turn that it must embrace the philosophy of global homogenization. Yet stubborn as a wild flower, the GAA persists and thrives as the world grows smaller and the acid rain of mass media shrivels the harmless differences for which people once celebrated themselves. It is often said, sometimes perjoratively, that the GAA is a state of mind. As an organization it is conservative but classless, non-party political but political nonetheless.

In its spirit of communal co-operativeness it reflects a little of the old Soviet system. In Corofin, for instance, where Martin Mac, the aforementioned publican, hails from, the club has been a source of unity and pride which has transformed the local community. 'Oul fellas would have fallen out with each other years ago. You owe me twenty pounds for a heifer I sold you twenty years ago, you'll never have right of way over my land etc. When we play football it's the only time they are all together, all pulling for the one thing.' Fanciful? Look at the club house they built one Christmas week in the early nineties, gathering all the returned emigrants and everyone with a bit of holiday time on their hands to muck in and put the thing up in the space of a week.

Join them on the 26 March 1998, the night before the club played in (and won) its first All-Ireland club final. The entire community is jammed into the massive hostelry that is John Raftery's pub. Stories of great games and huge characters are told. They're all polished and familiar but they are the folklore of the town. This was once two parishes. Belclare and Corofin spread over miles and miles of unhelpful Connacht countryside. Football forced them to amalgamate. They played a football game to decide on the name of the new club and Corofin squeaked it by a point. Corofin it was. They have been united ever since.

Bring the camera back down on the far coast from Dublin, in the conjoined villages of Belclare and Corofin. Same Saturday, same green hue to the playing fields. Around here the walls are made of rocks piled upon each other and the houses are scattered higgedly-piggedly across the landscape. In the playing fields, through the arch, the kids are out playing. Great stars of Gaelic football are moving among them, tossing them footballs, asking them to concentrate on the leather, watch for the brand name, come and meet the ball. Putting it all back in. Martin McNamara is here, Galway's great and mythic goalkeeper. He has regraded himself to a junior team in the club so that his understudy, Glen Comer, can have some experience of the big time. He's doing the drills and taking the tumbles, making the jokes and showing the way. It's morning and he has his hood over his head. Keeps him warm as the pillow he's missing. But this Saturday morning the kids look at Martin Mac and they are saucer-eyed and awestruck. His soft dropped words of encouragement burn themselves into young minds. Fast forward now. Twenty years time and the odds are short that they'll be telling some interviewer, somewhere, about what kick-started the dream for them. Martin Mac on a grey day. And on Saturday mornings they'll be putting it all back in. The cycle of the games. Sowers. Reapers. Sowers. Reapers ...

Bibliography

Anon. 1984 *Cumann Lúthchleas Gael: a century of service*. Dublin.
de Búrca, M. 1999 *The GAA: a history*. Dublin.
King, S. J. 1996 *A history of hurling*. Dublin.
Ó Caithnia, L. 1980 *Scéal na hiomána ó thosach ama go 1884*. Dublin.
Ó Caithnia, L. 1984 *Báirí cos in Éirinn*. Dublin
Ó Riain, S. 1994 *Maurice Davin 1842–1927*. Dublin.

Local Studies

JOHN B. O'BRIEN

It may seem a contradiction in this era of globalization, with the world reduced to the click of a 'mouse', that interest in and promotion of local studies should be flourishing. Obviously instant global communication, with an apparently inexhaustible diet of information on a never-ending range of subjects, does not in itself fully satisfy. In fact it could be argued that the scale of the knowledge available can have the opposite effect, can be intimidating and induce a sense of helplessness and even feelings of inadequacy. Fortunately, however, this can be offset by the security which an appreciation of one's immediate circumstances provides, solid in the knowledge of one's own place in one's own environment. Once discerned, this in turn may actually enhance a person's understanding of and empathy with the wider global context.

It has always been the case that individuals have drawn sustenance from their perceived homeland. For some the country of their birth is sufficient; for others it may be a wider geographic region such as a continent, while yet for more it may extend only as far as a province, but, for all, identification with the immediate location of their birth and upbringing has been the most rewarding. The knowledge gleaned there and the values formed invariably provide the benchmarks by which people assess the wider world, so that the keener a person's insight into his or her local circumstances the greater the benefits from globalization; hence the growing appeal nowadays of local studies.

The outcome of local studies, however, is not uniform, mainly because of the increasing complexity of the subject-matter itself and also because of the multiplicity of approaches that can be taken to it. The number of disciplines involved in it has been expanding, with each of them introducing its own methodology and also delineating the nature of the basic unit under investigation. In the past, a wandering storyteller could meet the needs of his generation with accounts of great deeds of heroic local figures or with information on the interrelationships of parishioners within a limited area. Today, the range of knowledge available, either from history, archaeology, geography, folklore, linguistics, sociology and also from ballads, poetry, paintings, sculpture and so forth, has added enormously to our understanding of local environments. Needless to say, because of human constraints, it is not possible for any individual to grasp the full implications of these disciplines for their own areas. Nevertheless taken together they do allow for a heightened perception of the imagined community in which people find themselves.

In many ways the unit chosen for study is as much a function of the discipline employed as it is of the individual's own interests. The political scientist's units invariably coincide with constituency boundaries, while the sociologist, concerned with the existence of communities, looks for shared interactions and beliefs, so that his/her units may or may not be identical to electoral divisions. The archaeologist's units are determined by the survival of archaeological artefacts and monuments, and these usually extend beyond parish boundaries, while historian's and geographer's borders tend to oscillate, depending on historical events and changes over time. What may seem as a region today might have had quite different parameters in the past. For cultural and literary studies, shared language or dialects as well as common literary strands are the essential ingredients in the choice of units.

It should thus be obvious that local studies today are much more sophisticated than they were in the past and therefore provide a wider and also a significantly deeper insight into an individual's immediate circumstances. In suggesting markers for more globally based enquiries, local studies provide reference points that facilitate comparison and allow for deeper appreciation; in turn, the globalization of knowledge extends the range of the questions that can be asked, thereby enriching local studies themselves.

AN INSTITUTIONAL RESPONSE

In recognition of this complexity and to meet widespread public demand, University College, Cork, has made a number of extra-mural programmes in local studies available in recent years, and now also offers a masters degree in the area. This is in line with UCC's long-standing commitment, dating from the 1930s, to all forms of adult and continuing education (Murphy 1995, 255–56). In both its one-year certificate course and its two-year diploma course, UCC has provided insights into the archaeology, folklore, history, geography, language, politics and general culture of local areas in Munster and parts of Leinster. Starting in 1985, the University's Adult Education Department, in collaboration with academic departments and local interest groups, has arranged for such courses to be given in Cork, Killarney, Newcastlewest, Limerick, Tralee, Kilkenny, Bantry, Ennis, Mallow, Cashel, Clonmel, Listowel and Waterford. On average about 35 students have enrolled each year with on occasion as many as 55. To date nearly 500 mature students have taken the various programmes presented and in all instances satisfaction has been expressed. There now follows a brief description of the nature and objectives of these courses.

The range of material dealt with is extensive, covering the wider dimension of the individual disciplines taught while also focusing on the immediate environment of the participants. The chronology stretches from the Mesolithic era to modern times, with the archaeologists looking at Ireland from 10,000 BC onwards and the geographers concentrating mainly on the seventeenth, eighteenth and nineteenth centuries. Folklorists have ranged over a similar period and beyond, and the historians have dealt in part with the seventeenth century but also with political developments in the twentieth. The evolution of the Irish language during the last two millennia is also outlined.

The sources drawn on are varied and reflect the approaches taken by each teaching department. From the early period the archaeologists depend on digs, on the artefacts unearthed and on radio-carbon dating to determine the age of these sites and of the longevity of the specimens extracted. For later archaeological investigations, the students are referred, among other items, to monuments still extant and are also brought on a tour of Dúchas and the National Museum of Ireland. As might be expected, the geographers have introduced their classes to a wide range of maps which provide insights into topographical developments over time. In addition, students are made acquainted with censuses, especially the 1659 Census and the Civil Survey, but also the more comprehensive ones of the nineteenth and twentieth centuries. The main source for the folklorists are the collections of the Folklore Commission, 1935–70, and the Schools Collection of the winter of 1937–38. This is augmented by references to the material of cultural tradition which embraces the evolution of the normal artefacts of everyday life such as spades, ploughs and cottages as well as cooking utensils and clothing. Irish-language materials, especially those of pre-Famine Gaelic Ireland, are discussed by the lecturers in this discipline. Public records, newspapers and private collections are the principal sources for the historians and, at the opening session of each series, the students are given an insight into the peculiarities of each of these. In later lectures, they can observe how such documents are exploited by professional historians.

Generally speaking, all the disciplines concerned deal with the interplay of individuals and their environment over time within both the national, local, political and economic context. Lecturers' emphasis and their selection of topics depend on the nature of their own subjects. The main focus of the archaeologists in the early period is on the hunter-gatherer society of the early Stone Age, but on reaching the neolithic period this has been broadened to include considerations of settlement, houses, economy and burials. The course proceeds to explore the nature of the Bronze Age, the Iron Age and finally the early medieval era. In many ways the geography section takes up where archaeology ends, and the geographers' input is supplemented by case studies provided by historians. At the heart of the geographers' presentation is, once again, settlement and society, but now, because of the availability of more far-ranging sources, the characteristics of society over time can be more finely tuned. The evolution of villages and towns is addressed, while the geography of place-names is also treated. Following these analyses, the folklorists next take up society's memory and perception of these developments and provide insights into the traditions and practices that comprise the environment in which each generation live out their own lives. In addition to the physical settings and artefacts already mentioned, the students also learn of the rituals, both religious and profane, that contributed to ordinary life over the centuries.

Each of these fields introduces the students to their own distinctive techniques in handling their material. From the archaeologists the classes acquire a knowledge of digs, an evaluation of the artefacts and, in the later stages of these courses, opportunities are provided for the handling of ancient tools and even of examining human and animal bones. Next, students acquire an ability from the geographers to evaluate maps and also how to deal with vast quantities of complex census data, especially the assessment of that material over time. From the folkorists they learn how to distinguish between antiquarianism, romantic nationalism and the current academic practice of value-free assessment of the basic folklore tradition. Language teachers deal with issues such as the formation and distinctiveness of regional dialects. While not revisionist as such, the historians infuse a sense of objectivity in treating the facts, ensuring that the interpretation is based on a fair selection of these facts rather than requiring data to serve a pre-conceived view of the past.

Lest the reader by now conclude that the local aspects of the course are neglected, let me hasten to add that in each of the disciplines, the focus eventually returns to the immediate setting of the participants. Both in lectures and in field trips, the archaeologists cover the history of local monuments while the geographers do the same for a later period, but also with a concentration on more recent topography. Place-name lore is examined as well in language instruction. Drawing on the wealth of local material in the Irish Folklore Commission where for example in the case of Cork there were at least 300 collectors, the folklorists have fertile territory in which to direct their local enquiries. (This, as has been mentioned, is augmented by the Schools Collection of 1937–38 in which children in fifth class in every National School in the country collected data on their own localities — a veritable goldmine for local studies.)

Perhaps the most valuable undertakings of the local study course students are the projects they carry out under the supervision of their lecturers. Project work can be done in any of the disciplines provided. All of these are on a local topic, so that the students get a greater appreciation of local sources and of the uses to which they can be put. When completed they also have the satisfaction of having advanced, even in a small way, our understanding of one other locality; the students and their locality have been truly merged. It should therefore be obvious that in providing these courses, University College, Cork, has been satisfying an important need in the Munster area. Participants have acquired a deep and a diverse knowledge of their own environment which they are then able to relate to wider global issues.

Bibliography

Gillespie, R. and Hill, M. (ed) 1998 *Doing Irish local history: pursuit and practice*. Belfast.

Murphy, J. A. 1995 *The College: a history of Queen's/University College Cork, 1845–1995*. Cork.

Nolan, W. 1977 *Sources for local studies*. Dublin.

Traditional Music

Matt Cranitch

For many people, their first introduction to Irish traditional music is to its instrumental tradition, primarily dance-music with its lively rhythms and exciting melodies. The term 'Irish music' is frequently used to denote this instrumental tradition. The implication is that if the music is Irish, it must be traditional and instrumental at that! This instrumental tradition accounts for a very large proportion of the music as a whole. It is played and heard mainly in 'listening' environments, such as at sessions and concerts, even though very obviously it is dance-music. In the past, music and dance were linked more closely than is now the case: however, the revival of interest in set-dancing and step-dancing is reversing this trend to a certain extent. The instrumental tradition far exceeds the *sean-nós* singing tradition in terms of the number of performers, the size of the repertoire, accessibility and popularity. This is not, in any way, to deny the beauty, complexity and undoubted importance of this unique art-form. A great deal of traditional music is played at informal sessions which usually take place in public houses. In previous times, the music was played more in private houses, at house-dances and various social occasions. With the increase in its popularity, this music is now heard on concert platforms not only in Ireland but throughout the world.

The present chapter aims, therefore, to give a broad overview of Irish traditional music in approximately the last third of the twentieth century, with the primary focus being on the instrumental tradition. The form and structure of the music, as well as ornamentation and variation, will be discussed. Styles of playing will be considered, with Sliabh Luachra being used as an example of a region with particular stylistic features in its music. The revival will be examined, as will summer schools and the study of traditional music at university level. Various other developments and trends will also be outlined.

THE NATURE OF TRADITIONAL MUSIC

All types of music, particularly all kinds of traditional music, have elements in common, and to a greater or lesser extent. However, it is their differences which make them unique, in essence what they are. Irish traditional music has its own specific idioms, both melodic and rhythmic, which are the means by which it can be recognized and interpreted. It has its own special repertoire of tunes in a range of rhythms and forms, including jigs, reels, hornpipes, slides and polkas. The particular sounds of the various instruments used, such as fiddle, flute, accordion, concertina and *uilleann* pipes, are another characteristic feature. And of course, the sheer vitality, exuberance and beauty of the music are compelling.

Traditional music is passed from one generation to the next and from musician to musician primarily by the process of aural transmission. All traditional musicians learn and play from memory, or 'by ear'. Music notation is not used widely, and when it is, it tends to serve rather as an *aide-mémoire*. Even then, the spirit of the music is absorbed and learned aurally. In a sense, music can be considered a language, the sounds of which can only be acquired by listening. The tunes are being varied continuously as they move from one player to another, which means that there is no one 'correct' version of a tune. This is similar to the oral tradition of storytelling, where the details may change in transmission, but the core and spirit of the story remain the same. An indispensable link in the chain of music performance and reception is the listener. Music does not happen in a vacuum: it depends on the person who is hearing the sounds being produced as well as on the person who is creating them. And when the listener is informed about and knows the music, then the listening is much more than purely auditory, it becomes a thinking process. If the language of music is understood by the listener as well as by the player, then the music is more than just a matter of sounds. It has the capacity to become a deep and meaningful spiritual experience for both.

INSTRUMENTAL MUSIC

Traditional music is essentially a solo tradition, with the music based on a single melodic line. The various elements of a musical performance, particularly melody and rhythm, are very much present in solo playing. Even in group playing, the different melody instruments play the same melody line, albeit with slight variations and improvization. There is little counterpoint or harmony in the sense that there is in other forms of music. When accompaniment is provided by piano, guitar, bouzouki or *bodhrán*, the melody instruments still play the melody line as before, and with the same rhythmic articulation. With or without accompaniment, solo playing is at the heart of this music. It may be said that the 'highest' manifestation of this art-form is in its unaccompanied solo performance.

One of the most fundamental elements in dance music is rhythm. This particular feature contributes significantly to the overall result, and can be considered in a number of ways. The 'motor rhythm' is the ongoing cyclic pulse of the music, its constant regular beat with respect to time. Also, it is the rhythm that imparts the characteristic 'swing' to each of the various dance metres. Jig, reel, hornpipe, slide and polka, all have specific combinations of note values (durations), with distinctive accentuation, in each bar. For example in the jig, the note pattern consists of six quavers in two groups of three, with the accent or stress being placed on notes one and four — 1**23** 4**56**. Even though there are six quavers, the pulse of the music is a beat for each group of three, giving two beats per bar. At times, two or three quavers may be replaced by a crotchet or dotted crotchet, however the rhythmic impulse remains the same (**Fig. 22.1**). A bar, which is considered to be the primary metrical unit, is denoted on the musical stave by a vertical bar-line.

Fig. 22.1 Note pattern of jig.

Among traditional musicians, reels are undoubtedly most popular. At sessions and concerts, they are played much more than the other dance-tunes. For the majority of players, they are considered to be the most challenging type of tune and also the most enjoyable to play. In each bar, there are eight quavers (or their equivalent), with two quavers per beat. The accent is placed on beats 2 and 4 — 1**2**3**4** (**Fig. 22.2**).

Fig. 22.2 Note pattern of reel.

The extent to which the rhythmic accentuation is emphasized varies from one musician to another, and also can vary throughout a performance. It is influenced by a number of factors, including whether or not the music is being played for dancing, whether the playing is solo or accompanied, and the tempo. In many respects it is a matter of personal interpretation and to a great extent can be considered a feature of the individual style of playing.

To many people listening to traditional music, and probably other types of music, it 'all sounds the same'! However, there is a very definite form and structure to this music. Every tune has a number of parts, most usually two, each of which has eight bars. The parts are normally repeated, thereby giving a total of thirty-two bars in one complete round of the tune, and generally the tune is played three times through. Within the parts, there are subdivisions with recurring phrases and motifs. Consider, for example, *Jackie Coleman's Reel* (**Fig. 22.3**). The first part, also referred to as the A-part or simply 'the tune', consists of two four-bar phrases. Bars 5–8 are a repeat of bars 1–4 with a small change at the end of bar 8 as a cadence to the part. The note-pattern of bar 2 recurs slightly modified in bar 3, the low note descending and the upper notes rising. The second part (the B-part or 'the turn'), which is in a higher register, displays similar characteristics, and also features certain note-patterns from the first part, in bar 11 for example. Even though there is a very definite form to the music, traditional musicians are not consciously aware of these structures when performing. The music is not learned or thought of in this way, but rather it is memorized and played 'by ear' as a complete unit, like a story.

The fact that the music is centred on a single melodic line provides the player with the possibility and opportunity for ornamentation. Indeed the music derives much of its vibrant character from such decoration of the melody. Ornamentation can be achieved in a number of ways. For example in the 'roll', a note is ornamented with a group of five notes (**Fig. 22.4**). Conversely a number of notes may be replaced by one long note. The various ways in which ornamentation can be achieved in the case of one particular instrument, the fiddle, are explained elsewhere (Cranitch 1996).

Variation of the melody line itself is also possible, with a sequence of notes being replaced by a series of others. Ornamentation can also have a rhythmic dimension if a particular decoration, or the way in which it is played, enhances the characteristic swing of the tune. The

Fig. 22.3 Jackie Coleman's Reel.

instruments themselves, and the ways in which they are played, also have a major influence. For example on the fiddle, the left hand (fingering hand) provides the melodic ornamentation, and the right hand (bow hand) creates the rhythmic decoration. While ornamentation and variation certainly provide scope for improvization, they do so within limits. Clearly a thorough knowledge of the musical idiom is required. Also a high degree of technical skill and creativity are needed in order to achieve spontaneous and exciting results.

Fig. 22.4 Note sequence of 'roll'.

Although most traditional music is learned 'by ear', written collections play an important function in both the preservation and dissemination of the music. They provide a notated record of many pieces of music in the versions current at the time the particular collection was made. They also act as a very useful source of material and inspiration for those who are learning new tunes.

For many traditional musicians *The Dance Music of Ireland* by Francis O'Neill (1848–1936) is their 'bible'. This collection of 1,001 tunes was published in 1907 in Chicago, where O'Neill, a native of Tralibane near Bantry, county Cork, had been Chief of Police from 1901 to 1905. An extensive treatment of his life and work is available elsewhere (Carolan 1997). More recently, four volumes of *Ceol Rinnce na hÉireann* by Breandán Breathnach (1912–85) have been published. They contain 983 tunes in total, with very useful notes on names and sources. Volume 1 was first issued in 1963, and volume 4 was completed by Jackie Small in 1996 after Breathnach's death.

STYLES OF PLAYING

There are various styles of playing traditional music, as is the case with other types of music. The way in which a tune or a piece of music is played can differ significantly from one musician to another as well as from region to region. In this context, the term 'style' can have a number of meanings. It can denote the way in which one musician plays as distinct from another. It can refer to a particular way of playing a certain instrument, for example the 'open style' of piping or the 'press-and-draw style' of playing the accordion. It can also be taken to mean the distinguishing features of playing which identify musicians from a particular area. It is in this sense that the terms 'Clare style', 'Sliabh Luachra style' or 'Sligo style' are used. There is a parallel in this respect with the term 'dialect' used in the case of spoken language. In the past, regional styles of playing were confined primarily to their own geographic areas. However, with the advent of mass communication, recordings and competition, the differences between the regional styles may have become less obvious and the boundaries more diffuse.

As already stated, ornamentation and variation are special features of traditional music. The extent to which various kinds of ornament are used in order to create distinctive rhythmic nuances and colour varies from player to player, and from one style of playing to another. Repertoire can also be considered to be an element of style, in the sense that specific types of tunes and dance-rhythms may feature more prominently, or indeed only, in particular regions. Furthermore, there is no doubt that the personality of the musician, the very soul of the performer, contributes much to the creative process, and so may also be regarded as having a major influence on the style of playing.

SLIABH LUACHRA

Slides and polkas may well have been heard for the first time by many people on a Chieftains' record or from the playing of Jackie Daly and Séamus Creagh, or indeed on that wonderful recording *The Star above the Garter* by Denis Murphy (1910–74) and Julia Clifford (1914–97), brother and sister. Both Denis and Julia learned the fiddle from the legendary Pádraig O'Keeffe (1887–1963), often described as the Sliabh Luachra Fiddle Master.

Sliabh Luachra is situated on the Cork/Kerry border along the upper reaches of the river Blackwater. It extends over areas in east Kerry, north-west Cork and south-west Limerick, and includes places such as Bally-desmond, Brosna, Gneevguilla, Knocknagree and Scartaglen. While its exact location may be difficult to outline in geographic terms, its place on the musical landscape is much more clearly defined. Because the dancing of 'sets' has featured prominently in the area, the music is lively and rhythmic, with polkas and slides being predominant. Each of these has a very character-istic rhythm: polkas are single reels and slides single jigs.

In previous generations, the area was renowned for its Gaelic-language poets. The spirit of that era may well have passed on to the music of this century, a view expressed on a number of occasions by the broadcaster Ciarán Mac Mathúna. In the course of a four-part radio documentary by Peter Browne on the life and music of Pádraig O'Keeffe, he said

It was after all the country of poets in the Gaelic tradition,

Aogán Ó Rathaille and particularly Eoghan Rua Ó Súilleabháin and all that tradition. And I always felt that when the Gaelic tradition was dying out in that area in some strange way it survived through the music, in musical instruments, that where the language itself was losing ground that the tradition, the spirit of the tradition, in some way came into the instrumental music, and particularly into Pádraig O'Keeffe and people who came after him like Denis Murphy. (Ciarán Mac Mathúna, RTÉ Radio 1, 6 November 1993)

Fiddle and accordion are the dominant instruments in the Sliabh Luachra tradition, with a style of playing which has many distinguishing characteristics. These instruments have shaped to a great extent the music as we hear it today, particularly the fiddle, because of the influence of Pádraig O'Keeffe. For more than forty years, he travelled throughout the area teaching music, mostly the fiddle, but also the accordion. Although he was able to read and write standard music notation, he used two different systems of tablature in his teaching, one for the fiddle and one for the accordion. Numbers and special symbols were used to indicate the notes to be played (a detailed explanation of these notation systems, generally referred to as the 'Code', is given in Cranitch 1996). Many of O'Keeffe's pupils and also many of the musicians playing in the area would say that he was responsible to a great extent for the Sliabh Luachra style as it is known today. He is featured, with Denis Murphy and Julia Clifford, on the CD *Kerry Fiddles*. This music was recorded by Séamus Ennis for the BBC on 9 September 1952 in Castleisland. It was released on vinyl in 1977 and more recently has been re-issued on CD.

SEAN-NÓS SINGING

Sean-nós (old-style) singing is a highly complex and ornate way of solo unaccompanied singing in the Irish language. Frequently referred to simply as *sean-nós*, it is confined mainly to the Gaeltacht (Irish-speaking) areas. Like instrumental music, it is an oral tradition, with the songs being passed from singer to singer by the process of aural transmission. Among its principal exponents, some of whom are no longer with us but whose singing may be heard on record, are Seán de hÓra and the Begley family from the West-Kerry Gaeltacht, Seosamh Ó hÉanaí from Connemara, Darach Ó Catháin from Ráth Cairn in county Meath, Nioclás Tóibín and Áine Uí Cheallaigh from An Rinn in county Waterford, Iarla Ó Lionáird and the Ó Súilleabháin family from Cúil Aodha in county Cork, and Lillis Ó Laoire and Maighréad Ní Dhomhnaill from the Donegal Gaeltacht.

Melodic variation and ornamentation are important features of the music of *sean-nós*, with the phrasing following that of the text: there is not a pulse-like rhythm as in the dance music. The texts are often poems to which traditional melodies (tunes) are added. The subject-matter covers a wide range of topics including love, nature, people, places and disaster. For example the well-known song *Anach Cuain*, attributed to Antaine Raiftearí, laments the people from this village in Galway who were lost in a boating tragedy in the early nineteenth century. Occasionally the melody of a *sean-nós* song may be played as an instrumental piece: it is then generally referred to as a 'slow air'. The phrasing follows that of the song, and the ornamentation, which is obviously that of the instrument being played, aims to interpret the feeling and spirit of the song and of the singer. Slow airs do not feature to a great extent in the repertoire of most instrumental players; however, a small number of musicians do include them in their performances.

THE REVIVAL

A number of events, organizations and individuals have each made a major contribution to the revival of interest in traditional music from the late 1950s and early 1960s onwards. Also the general folk music revival which took place at about the same time had a very positive influence. This development has led to the point where Irish traditional music is now a significant force on the global stage. Irish music and Irish dance are now seen and heard on concert platforms throughout the world. Many visitors to Ireland seek to hear this music during their stay, and also to obtain recordings to bring home.

Comhaltas Ceoltóirí Éireann (approximately translated 'The Federation of the Musicians of Ireland') was founded in Mullingar in 1951, with its objective being to revive the playing of Irish traditional music. Since then Comhaltas, as it is generally known, has been involved in arranging classes, concert tours and *Fleadhanna Ceoil* (musical festivals/competitions), mainly through its network of local branches throughout Ireland: there are also some branches in England and the United States. Undoubtedly, Fleadh Cheoil na hÉireann ('All-Ireland Festival of Music'), now held on the last weekend of August, is their major annual event. Its central theme and focus are the competitions for solo playing, duets, trios and *céilí* bands, in a number of age levels, with All-Ireland titles being awarded in the various categories. Many thousands of people attend in order to hear the music at the competitions and sessions, as well as to partake in the general festival atmosphere.

In the 1950s, Ciarán Mac Mathúna began his collecting work for Radio Éireann, as it was known then. For close on forty years, he travelled to many places in Ireland, and also to some in the United States, and recorded an extensive collection of music and interviews. Some of this was featured throughout the years in his radio programmes *A Job of Journeywork* and more recently *Mo Cheol Thú*. These recordings have preserved a large repertoire of music in many different local styles of playing: they are an invaluable record of how the music was played, as well as being a source of repertoire for future generations of musicians.

In the opinion of many, the person to whom the major credit for the renewed interest in this music should go was Seán Ó Riada. Born in Cork in 1931, he graduated in 1952 from University College Cork with a B. Mus. He worked as Assistant Director of Music in Radio Éireann for a number of years and then as Director of Music at the Abbey Theatre in Dublin from 1955 to 1962. During his time there, he brought together a group of traditional musicians to play for a number of stage productions for which he had arranged and also composed music. This group, to become known as Ceoltóirí Cualann, continued to play together outside The Abbey. They were to be heard on *Reacaireacht an Riadaigh* and *Fleadh Cheoil an Radio* on Radio Éireann, and they also featured on the sound track of the film *The Playboy of the Western World*. As well as his involvement with traditional musicians, Ó Riada arranged and composed music for the orchestra: his score for the film *Mise Éire* in 1959 is probably the best known. His life's work, in both Irish music and in the European tradition, is examined in detail elsewhere (Ó Canainn & Mac an Bhua 1993).

Seán Ó Riada and his family went to live in the West-Kerry Gaeltacht in 1962. The following year, he took up a position as Lecturer in Irish Music at University College, Cork, and the family moved to Cúil Aodha. During this phase of his life, he became immersed in the life of the area, and established Cór Chúil Aodha, for which he wrote two masses. He travelled to Dublin from time to time to play with Ceoltóirí Cualann. By now, a number of these musicians had formed The Chieftains, who were quickly establishing a reputation throughout Ireland and who would go on to become one of the 'supergroups' of traditional music. Perhaps the most memorable performance given by Seán Ó Riada and Ceoltóirí Cualann with singer Seán Ó Sé was the concert in the Gaiety Theatre, Dublin, in the spring of 1969, honouring the memory of the eighteenth-century poet Peadar Ó Doirnín. This wonderful night of music, with Ó Riada directing the ensemble and playing the harpsichord, is featured on the landmark recording *Ó Riada sa Gaiety*.

Seán Ó Riada died in 1971, just 41 years of age. Although not everyone agreed with his arrangements of traditional music, and indeed some objected most strongly to them, there is no doubt that with Ceoltóirí Cualann he set a model of group performance and arrangement for others to try to emulate. He established a central place for traditional music and musicians on the performance stage, on radio and television programmes and on film scores. Since then, numerous groups have brought their music to concert platforms in many parts of the world, groups such as The Bothy Band, Planxty, Na Filí, Dé Danann, Stockton's Wing, Buttons and Bows, Altan, Patrick Street, Four Men and a Dog, Dervish, Nomos and many more. A number of these groups are probably as well-known abroad, if not even more so, than at home in Ireland. Another development which occurred during this revival period, and continues to do so, was the emergence of virtuoso solo performers, who travel world-wide playing their music. Many of them have become household names, and have achieved high levels of personal popularity, at home and abroad — players such as Mary Bergin, Joe Burke, Kevin Burke, Jackie Daly, Frankie Gavin, Paddy Glackin, Martin Hayes, Noel Hill, Seán Keane, Paddy Keenan, Seán McGuire, Matt Molloy, Máire Ní Chathasaigh, Gerry O'Connor, Máirtín O'Connor, Liam O'Flynn, Tommy Peoples, Sharon Shannon, Davy Spillane and many others.

The role of accompanying instruments, such as piano, guitar, bouzouki and *bodhrán*, became much more integral to the overall sound of many of the groups. In the case of each of these instruments, a number of highly rated players have emerged and are to be heard on many recordings, people such as Charlie Lennon, Carl Hession and Brian McGrath on piano, Stephen Cooney and Arty McGlynn on guitar, Alec Finn and Dónal Lunny on bouzouki, and Tommy Hayes, Johnny McDonagh, Mel Mercier and Colm Murphy on *bodhrán*. A further development was the huge increase of interest in Irish dance: this has also contributed greatly to raising the profile of traditional music. In particular during the last five years of the twentieth century, *Riverdance* and *Lord of the Dance*, through the phenomenal success of their stage shows, have brought Irish dance and music to many new audiences throughout the world.

Emigration, which touched communities in all parts of Ireland, has played an important part in the story of Irish traditional music. Many of those who left their families and friends in search of a better life, mainly in America and England, brought with them the music, songs and dances of home. In America particularly, emigrants had the opportunity to hear other kinds of music and other instrumentation, such as the piano, which has featured significantly on many of the recordings from there. Some of these people went on to become major figures in the world of Irish traditional music. Michael Coleman and James Morrison, both of whom had emigrated from Sligo, made many 78 RPM recordings of fiddle-music in New York during the 1920s and 1930s. Their wonderful playing set a standard for others to follow, and has been a source of influence for many traditional musicians in America as well as at home in Ireland: there are many further such examples. And of course Irish traditional music has had a significant influence on other musical genres and developments. For example, the influence on American Old-Timey music and Bluegrass is clearly audible. It has also played a central role in the whole folk-music revival. These and related topics were the subject-matter of the television series *Bringing it All back Home* (1991), and its accompaning book (O'Connor 1991).

And of course one must not forget the unsung heroes of the revival, and the role which they played in keeping the tradition alive through their own playing and through their willingness and generosity to share the music with those who followed. These men and women, throughout Ireland and in various parts of England and the United States, preserved for future generations the traditional styles of playing as well as a vast repertoire of tunes, and this at a time when it was neither popular nor profitable to do so. A small number of these people may have been featured on radio or commercial recordings, but the vast majority remain anonymous. To them must go a huge debt of gratitude and credit for the legacy which they have given.

SUMMER SCHOOLS AND UNIVERSITIES

The Willie Clancy Summer School was founded by Muiris Ó Rócháin in Miltown Malbay, county Clare, in 1973 to honour the memory of the local *uilleann* piper who died earlier that year. There were about eighty students at the first school, which lasted for a week. Since then it has expanded far beyond all expectations, and now runs for nine days each July, with many people from Ireland as well as from various parts of the world attending. There are classes, graded at various levels of ability, in all the traditional instruments, as well as in singing, set-dancing and step-dancing. Also there are concerts, *céilís*, lectures and of course numerous sessions. The number of people attending has increased greatly since the first year. In 1999 for example, over one thousand students registered for the classes and as many more for workshops and lectures; there were about one hundred and twenty-five teachers. This summer school has become the exemplar for others which have followed, and indeed it is the annual highlight in the traditional music calendar for many people.

'Blas' is the name of a summer school with a difference: it takes place on campus at the Irish World Music Centre (IWMC) in the University of Limerick. Like other summer schools, it features workshops, classes, lectures, concerts and *céilís*, but university study credits are available. IWMC was established by Mícheál Ó Súilleabháin on taking up the new position of Professor of Music there in 1994. Under his direction, a number of taught MA courses in specific disciplines, including ethnomusicology and traditional music performance, are offered, and research work on various topics in traditional music, leading to MA and PhD awards, is being undertaken. In addition to his academic work, Ó Súilleabháin has created a unique style of playing traditional dance-tunes on the piano, and of incorporating jazz elements in his music. He has also both composed and arranged music for the orchestra.

Prior to his appointment in Limerick, Ó Súilleabháin had taught Irish Music at University College, Cork, since 1975 when he succeeded Tomás Ó Canainn, who followed Seán Ó Riada in 1971. The present incumbent in this position is Liz Doherty. During all of this time, the stature and importance of traditional music in the B. Mus. course at UCC has grown and developed, to include areas such as ethnomusicology, taught by Mel Mercier. The reputation which followed has led to increased demand for admission to this course, not only from throughout Ireland but also from abroad. Gradually other academic institutions have begun to include similar courses of study, in light of the ever-expanding interest in this music. There is a view that such studies should feature in the curriculum of all B. Mus. courses, on the grounds that the music students of today will be the music teachers of tomorrow. Indeed there is a growing opinion that the study of traditional music and instruments should be featured much more actively in both primary and second-level education. To a great extent, such traditional music as is currently taught in many schools usually depends on the enthusiasm of individual teachers rather than on any official policy.

TRENDS AND DEVELOPMENTS

For many years, traditional music has featured on various radio programmes on RTÉ Radio 1 and Raidió na Gaeltachta. Since the establishment of commercially operated local radio stations, a number have included this music in their schedules. The arrival of Telefís na Gaeilge (TnaG), now TG4, in 1996 has led to an increase in the amount of traditional music on television, on this channel as well as on the established RTÉ channels. However, the traditional community would say that not enough coverage is being provided either by RTÉ, the national broadcaster, or the commercial radio and television stations, under the control of the Independent Radio and Television Commission (IRTC).

A number of newspapers and magazines provide some coverage of traditional events, including reviews of recordings and occasionally concerts. *Irish Music*, a magazine first published in 1995 and issued monthly, deals exclusively with traditional music matters. As in so many other facets of life, the Internet is also making an impact. There are many websites dedicated to various aspects of the music, including catalogues for both records and books, reviews, bibliographies, biographical information and much more. There are a number of active discussion groups, dealing with various issues in the music.

There has been a significant increase in the number of CD recordings being released, both by the established record companies such as Claddagh, Gael-Linn, Ossian and various others, and by groups and individuals on their own labels. In the past, the recording and issuing of a record was a large undertaking which involved considerable expense and expertise. Now, however, with ever-increasing technological innovation, recording equipment, particularly in digital formats, is becoming increasingly more portable and affordable. Also the companies which make and duplicate CDs offer a complete manufacturing service, including printing of the inlay booklet, as well as attractive prices for small quantities. These facts, coupled with increasing general prosperity, have led many groups and individuals to record and release their own CDs.

The era of mass communication has in many respects led towards standardization and homogenization in traditional music, as in other areas of life. However, it has also had the opposite effect in contributing to a renewed interest in regional styles and repertoire. The same technology which appeared to have threatened the existence of diversity is now playing a major part in reversing that trend. Modern sound-editing and electronic reproduction techniques have resulted in the availability on CD of music which had been lying dormant, and even decaying, in various sound collections. The opportunity to hear such unique recordings has led many people to re-discover and hear in a new light what is, in a sense, their own local music. The recordings of Pádraig O'Keeffe, Denis Murphy and John Doherty are examples.

The Irish Traditional Music Archive (ITMA) was established in 1987 as an archive and resource centre for Irish traditional music, song and dance. Currently located in Dublin, its work involves the collection, identification, cataloguing and archiving of all available material, such as recordings, videos, books and photographs, many of which are in private hands. It aims to make this information and material generally available to the public, especially to personal callers, as well as by phone, post and on-line access. It is likely that the growing availability of multimedia home computers will lead to a demand for an increase in such on-line facilities. ITMA also serves as a valuable resource and reference for the growing number of people who are engaged in research work.

The number of traditional music festivals which take place each year continues to grow. Generally each of these events is organized to honour the memory of some musician from a particular area. Increasingly they feature an 'educational' dimension by the inclusion of workshops or master-classes and occasionally lectures in the programme of events. This positive trend is also to be observed in the case of those folk-music festivals and arts festivals where traditional music activities are considered an important part, and in the programmes of which traditional events feature prominently. This development of the inclusion of 'educational' activities is generally welcomed, and usually receives the active encouragement and at times the support of the Arts Council.

An issue which emerged during the 1990s was that of innovation in traditional music. At one extreme were those who felt that the music should be played today exactly as it was done long ago, without the need for 'modern arrangements' or new instrumentation. At the other extreme were those who held the opposing view that only through such developments would the music continue to evolve. The debate was intensified following the television series *River of Sound* which was presented on RTÉ in 1995 by Mícheál Ó Súilleabháin. Even though these programmes received a mixed reaction, the series did stimulate debate on various aspects of the music. Many of these issues were addressed and examined at Crosbhealach an Cheoil ('The Crossroads Conference') which was held in Dublin in April 1996. This conference, with the sub-title 'Tradition and Change', considered the state of traditional music under various headings, including tradition and change, education and organizations, and commercialization. Most of the papers presented have been published in the conference proceedings (Valley *et al.* 1999). Needless to say, this gathering did not issue a definitive finding on one side or the other of the 'innovation' debate! For its survival, traditional music needs to be informed both by the past and the present, by the old as well as the new. The same may well be said of the musicians who create this music. By its very nature, traditional music changes with the passage of time; indeed it must do so in order to continue to exist. Perhaps it is the rate of change rather than change itself which is the central issue in this debate.

Several attempts have been made to combine Irish traditional music with other kinds, such as rock, pop, country and jazz, to create various kinds of 'fusion'. The resulting hybrid forms have met with some commercial success. However, as already stated, traditional instrumentation and musical ideas have definitely had an influence on some of these other genres of music, and indeed vice versa. Idiomatic features from traditional music may well be heard in other musics being created in Ireland as well as abroad. Traditional instruments, notably the *uilleann* pipes, have been featured in new areas of performance, particularly in orchestral arrangements and works. Probably the best known of these has been *The Brendan Voyage,* composed by Shaun Davey, with Liam O'Flynn as solo piper.

The recordings of all the performers referred to, both musicians and singers, contain a wide range of excellent traditional music. They will help to put into context the various points discussed and demonstrate particular features of the music. The sleeve (liner) notes accompanying the recordings, most of which are available

commercially, are generally sources of much useful information. There are a number of books which deal more extensively with many of the issues considered herein, and which provide valuable and contrasting insights to the world of traditional music. Both Breathnach (1971) and Ó Canainn (1978) discuss the structure of the music, the instruments used, the collectors of traditional music and, particularly in the latter, *sean-nós* singing. Ó hAllmhuráin (1998) traces the history and development of the music from early Ireland up to the present day. Vallely (1999) is a comprehensive reference book with many contributors covering a wide range of topics.

At the commencement of this millennium, Irish traditional music has reached new levels of exposure, acceptance and popularity: however it still remains a 'minority' interest. The music is now being created by ever greater numbers than before, in solo performances and in many combinations and groups of various sizes, each with its own distinctive instrumentation and sound. At sessions and concerts at home in Ireland and throughout the world, many many thousands of people are moved by this music. For some it is the sound, for others the rhythm, for more the haunting melodies, for still more it is all or none of these: it may just be the inexplicable magic. Whatever it is and for whatever reason, this music has had a profound impact.

Bibliography

Breathnach, B. 1971 *Folkmusic and dances of Ireland.* Dublin.

Carolan, N. 1997 *A harvest saved: Francis O'Neill and Irish music in Chicago.* Cork.

Cranitch, M. 1996 'The Sliabh Luachra "Code"' in *Irish Musical Studies volume 4: selected proceedings from the Maynooth International Musicological Conference 1995* (Dublin), pp. 343–53.

Cranitch, M. 1996 *The Irish fiddle book.* Cork.

Ó Canainn, T. 1978 *Traditional music in Ireland.* London.

Ó Canainn, T. & Mac an Bhua, G. 1993 *Seán Ó Riada: a shaol agus a shaothar.* Dublin.

Ó hAllmhuráin, G. 1998 *A pocket history of Irish traditional music.* Dublin.

O'Connor, N. 1991 *Bringing it all back home.* London.

Vallely, F. (ed) 1999 *The companion to traditional Irish music.* Cork.

Vallely, F., Hamilton, H., Vallely E. & Doherty L. (eds) 1999 *Crosbhealach an Cheoil: The Crossroads Conference 1996.* Dublin.

Irish Dance

JOHN P. CULLINANE

Irish dancing has never been as popular as it is at present. At the beginning of the twenty-first century, its popularity is not confined to Ireland but is world-wide. This is due to some extent to the fantastic stage productions of *Riverdance* and *Lord of the Dance*. A few minutes interval act during the 1994 Eurovision Song Contest brought the dance aspect of the culture exploding into millions of homes throughout the world. Even in this country, most viewers saw Irish dancing in a new light. However, its new-found popularity is due not just to *Riverdance* alone but to the work of dancing instructors and other organizations over the past two hundred years. Its reach extends far beyond the boundaries of the nation. It naturally involves members of the Irish diaspora, but many of those learning and teaching Irish dancing have either very tenuous Irish connections or none at all.

This work is, in turn, based on Ireland's extraordinary rich and diverse heritage of dancing that compares more than favourably with that of other countries. The present chapter attempts to define and classify what is meant nowadays by Irish dancing. It traces its origins from the references in early literature and also analyses the role in Irish dancing played by the Gaelic League since 1893 and its subsidiary body, the Irish Dancing Commission, founded by the League in 1930. The problems of legislating for Irish dancing on an international basis will also be discussed along with the impact of *Riverdance* on Irish dancing.

CLASSIFICATION

Irish dancing can be broadly divided into two major categories, namely:
(i) 'Solo' dancing, and
(ii) 'Figure' dancing.

SOLO DANCING

'Solo' dancing, as its name implies, is usually performed by one dancer at a time. However, two or more dancers can perform 'solo' dance simultaneously but without physical contact or interaction. The emphasis is almost completely on the footwork. The hands, if involved at all, are only used to a very limited extent. The footwork is among the most concentrated and difficult in existence as is illustrated by the fact that Michael Flatley has been recorded in the *Guinness Book of Records* as having the fastest feet in the world (McFarlane 1989). It is the intricacies of this footwork that attracted millions of people to *Riverdance* and *Lord of the Dance*.

The complete emphasis on the footwork demands absolute concentration. Non-utilization of the hands in solo/step dancing makes this dance form unique. In earlier times, when the dancing was less concentrated, a limited amount of freedom of hand movement was accepted. Hand movements were never prescribed in Irish solo dancing, such as seen in Scottish solo dancing, but then the latter does not involve the same concentration of footwork as does the Irish form.

There is a reference in literature from about 1800 to a dance master correcting a dancer for using his hands. The early dance masters of the eigheenth and nineteenth centuries, who also taught deportment and proper social behaviour as well as Irish dancing, were very strict about the execution of the dance and frowned upon the idea of the hands flying about. However, with the advent of competitive dancing in the 1890s, the Gaelic League disapproved of hands loosely flying around since it was the objective at that time to eliminate anything that could be seen as stage Irish. Nowadays, solo Irish dancing is performed with the hands held firmly by the sides.

Solo dancing includes 'step' dancing and a lesser-known form, usually referred to as *sean-nós* dancing. Step dancing consists of a series of eight bar steps. In each step, the dancer executes the first eight bars predominantly on the right foot. The next eight bars

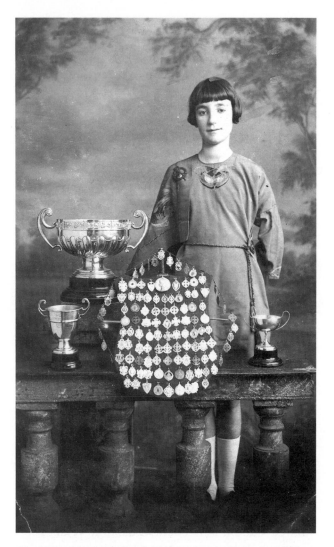

Fig. 23.1 Cora Cadwell, solo dancer champion, with trophies.

'tap' reel was very traditional but declined in popularity from the early to mid-twentieth century in Ireland. However, it was still danced in Australia up to the early 1960s. The heavy reel was frowned upon in competitions. Occasionally, spurious claims are still heard that the heavy tap reel was not traditional. Nonetheless, one-hundred-year-old-heavy reels were known and still danced in Cork, and many of these have been documented in handwritten sources. In recent times, the heavy tap reel has once again become very popular for exhibition work due to its audience appeal. While it is still not catered for by competition organizers, it is now the most popular form for exhibition display and is used extensively in the *Riverdance* genre.

The heavy dances (jigs, hornpipes and heavy/tap reels) are so called because of the use of heavy shoes equipped with toe-pieces made of leather covered with nails or fibreglass, so that the dancer can beat out the rhythm of the dance. Taps are not allowed on the shoes. Fibreglass is favoured nowadays both for toe-pieces and heels of the shoe, since this material allows the dancer to produce a nice clear sound, but, unlike nails, the fibre-glass does not mark the floor.

The advent of fibreglass had an effect on dancing and led to an increase in the amount of 'click' movements being performed. So great was the increase in the number and variety of click movements during the 1980s that the Commission had to introduce legislation to control them.

In heavy dances, the emphasis is on the beating or sound and rhythm (referred to as battering or trebling or rallying in different geographical areas). While these heavy dances did originate in the eighteenth century, they have become progressively more intricate, especially over the past half-century. The increase in intricacy involves both the introduction of more difficult movements in the steps, a major expansion in the number of beats in each bar of the step and the use of syncopated rhythm. The Scots do not appear to have any equivalent of heavy dances. The only other vaguely similar dance genres, are found in parts of Spain and in the old English 'Clog' dancing.

Light dancing (especially the reel and slip jig) became greatly altered during the last century. The advent, in the 1930s, of the light pump or ballet shoe led to a gradual modification of these dances and permitted the intro-duction of very balletic movements. The emphasis nowadays is on extreme lift and elevation and execution on the very tips of the toes. The best dancer is usually the one who travels most, up on the tips of the toes, and frequently executes leaps and jumps in which the dancer is frequently elevated two or three feet above the floor. This contrasts markedly with the style in the early decades of the twentieth century when a good dancer was one who could perform on the confined space of the

consist of the exact same movements performed on the left foot, so that the second eight are the mirror image of the previous eight. This rigid structure is known to have been in existence for at least two hundred years. 'Step' dancing originated with the advent of the travelling dance masters about 1750. It is a very disciplined form of dance. The steps were composed by the dance masters and taught with great emphasis on correct execution. Step dancing can be subdivided into (a) reels, (b) light jigs, (c) single jigs, (d) slip or hop jigs, (e) heavy jigs, also referred to as treble or battering or double jigs, (f) hornpipes and (g) solo set dances. These step dances can be danced as either 'light' dances, for instance reels, light jigs, single jigs, and slip jigs, or as 'heavy' dances, for example heavy reels, heavy jigs, hornpipes and all the solo set dances. The reel can be danced as either a 'light' or 'heavy' dance. Reels are in 4/4 or common time as are hornpipes, and so a traditional-style slow reel danced with heavy shoes and with trebling/battering shows a very strong resemblance to the hornpipe. This 'heavy' or top of a barrel or on the top of a dinner-plate. Even in the early 1950s, dancers were not allowed to travel more than two or three feet across the floor, and would be reprimanded for lifting the foot above the knee.

The slip jig, which was originally performed by both men and women in both solo and figure dances, has become so graceful and balletic that it is frequently described as 'not a man's dance' nowadays. However, in previous times, it was performed by men. *Feiseanna* (that is, dance competitions) in the early decades of the twentieth century, such as the London *Feis* in 1909, included competitions for 'slip jig in couples'. In the late eighteenth and early nineteenth centuries, most Irish figure dances were performed in slip jig time, that is 9/8 time. O'Keeffe and O'Brien (1902) and Sheehan (1902) both included figure dances in slip jig, which regretfully are no longer performed. Few if any folk dances in the world today are performed in slip jig 9/8 time, which is all the more reason for trying to resurrect those Irish figure dances executed in this time.

Of the solo step dancing, the reel is now by far the most popular dance, and most figure dances and *céilí* dances are also performed in reel time. The reel is, however, almost certainly not the oldest. Reels, as a form of dance music, appear unknown in Ireland until the end of the eighteenth century, and so the dance form only dates from early in the nineteenth century.

Step dancing also includes 'solo sets' which are commonly referred to simply as 'sets'. They should not be confused with those figure dances, usually performed by eight dancers (discussed below), also referred to as 'sets'. Solo set dances comprise such well-known dances as 'The Blackbird', 'Garden of Daisies', 'St Patrick's Day', 'Downfall of Paris' and many others. They are all 'heavy' dances and are performed either in jig time (6/8) or hornpipe time (2/4 or 4/4). They differ from the ordinary reel or jig or hornpipe, in which the steps always consist of eight bars, in that they have two parts (sometimes referred to as the 'step' and the 'set' part respectively, or simply the first part and the second part) which normally do not consist of eight bars. The first part frequently, but not in all sets dances, consists of eight bars, but the second part is usually a specific tune of an extended number of bars, namely, 12, 14 or 16 bars. The 'Garden of Daisies', for example, is in hornpipe 4/4 time and consists of a first part of 8 bars and a second part of 16 bars. The set dances require a specific setting of the dance specially designed for that tune and for that number of bars. For this reason, sets are more difficult than other solo dances and are the real test piece for the dancer.

Sean-nós dancing is essentially solo dancing, but it is usually less formal in the structure of the footwork and is not as disciplined as 'step' dancing. The repeat of the alternate eight bars on the right and left foot is usually not adhered to. This type of dancing is usually not taught in the formal sense, but rather learned simply by observation followed by trial and error. In recent times, some degree of formal teaching has been utilized in order that this rather 'primitive' style might be kept alive. The danger is that in teaching it so as to ensure its survival, it then becomes too structured and risks being altered too much from the original form. *Sean-nós* is performed largely by older males, and is found nowadays only in isolated rural pockets such as parts of Galway, Clare, Monaghan and Kerry. However, it is receiving increased exposure on national television and is undergoing a small revival.

FIGURE DANCES

This is a large anomalous category and embraces all those dances that are referred to as 'folk dances', 'national dances', 'country dances', '*céilí* dances' and 'set dances' (Cullinane 1998b). The term 'national dances' was used by authors such as Burchenal (1924) following the rise of nationalism and the foundation of the Gaelic League in 1893. Folk dances and country dances are words not used much nowadays in Ireland, but this is because the *céilí* was invented in 1897 following the Gaelic League revival (Cullinane 1987, 1997b), and only those dances performed at *céilis* are now fostered. The first *céilí* was organized by members of the Gaelic League in London in 1897. After that event, O'Keeffe and O'Brien (1902) and Sheehan (1902), all members of the London Gaelic League, published the first collections of Irish figure dances. Most of these dances have since come to be known as *céilí* dances. However, the term *céilí* dances was not actually coined until 1934 (Cullinane 1998b).

Apart from the very limited number of *céilí* dances and 'set dances', most Irish folk/national dances are completely neglected and in danger of extinction, if not already extinct. I have listed some 100 figure dances, of which only 30 are published and promoted by the Irish Dancing Commission (Cullinane 1998b), while the average *céilí* event consists of as few as six or eight figure dances. Some extinct figure dances are included in another account of mine (Cullinane 1990) in an effort to preserve them so that they might hopefully be resurrected.

Figure dancing is performed by groups of dancers, and the emphasis is on the intricacies of the movements or figures. Only basic footwork is employed. Well-known examples of such dancing are those dances that we refer to as *céilí* dances, of which the best known is 'The Walls of Limerick'. The distinction between the 'solo' and the 'figure' dancing is not as clear-cut as it might appear. Some dances performed by couples and by groups of three, and even groups of four, contain a mixture of solo-type step-dancing intermingled to a greater or lesser degree with figures, where the dancers interact with each

Fig. 23.2 Essie Connolly dance troupe at the Mantovani concert in 1938.

other by means of various hand movements. In fact, much of the dancing in *Riverdance* and in *Lord of the Dance* is essentially solo dancing but performed by the entire group in unison, the dancers are frequently executing solo footwork without any physical contact with each other. The majority of our figure dances are performed in reel time, although the oldest dances, such as the *rince fada*, were performed in jig time. Few if any of our present-day figure dances are performed in single jig or slip jig time and those that are, are extremely rare. While solo dancing, as known today, only dates from about the mid-eighteenth century and was introduced by travelling dance masters, figure dancing was popular long before that and was very much the social dancing of the country people.

'Set dances' or 'sets' are almost exclusively for four or eight dancers ('half-set' and 'set', respectively). For historical reasons, these sets are treated as being distinct from the *céilí* dances, although they both had a common ancestor. Sets were introduced into Ireland from France where they were known as a set of quadrilles. Sets have undergone a major revival since the 1970s and are enjoying enormous popularity at present. The set dance revival was largely due to the work of the Gaelic Athletic

Association from the 1970s onwards. The Gaelic League/Irish Dancing Commission, while proclaiming that its objective is to foster Irish dancing has, for historical/political reasons, ignored these dances. However, in the 1890s, at the time of the first *céilí* in London, the Gaelic League members in London, Dublin and elsewhere, performed set dances because the so-called *céilí* or figure dances were then almost unknown outside of Kerry and parts of Donegal. Subsequently, the Gaelic League discarded sets in favour of the newly discovered figure dances.

THE GENESIS OF IRISH DANCE
Having given a summary working definition of the most prominent types of Irish dance, there now follows a brief review of its historical development over time.

PRE-SIXTEENTH CENTURY
Many scholars have searched Old and Middle Irish literature and failed to find any reference to dance in Ireland in early times, for instance O'Curry (1875), O'Keeffe and O'Brien (1902), Joyce (1903), Ó Sé (1955, 1956), Fleischmann (1956) and Breatnach (1956). Thus Joyce (1903) stated that

Though we have in the old literature many other passages in which the several amusements at popular gatherings are enumerated, in no-one of them is dancing mentioned. There is, in fact, no evidence that the ancient Irish ever danced to music, or danced at all, i.e., in our sense of the word dancing; but very strong negative evidence that they did not.

The lack of references may be due to the fact that not sufficiently early literature is still extant, or that examination of early Irish documentation has not been exhaustive enough, or possibly that the terms used for a dance or for the act of dancing have eluded those scholars who have reviewed the literature. It should be noted that many primitive languages lack a specific term to describe the act of dancing, which is covered by a word having a more general, non-specialized meaning, such as jumping or leaping. Old Norse is an example of such a language.

Celtiberians were accustomed to dance all night in the open air worshipping the full moon, and it is believed that the British Celts danced around stones during religious ceremonies, but there is no evidence that such was the case in Ireland. Again, while it is known that continental Celts practised pre-battle 'dance' performances, there is no evidence that their counterparts in Ireland did so. The term *crónán* was mentioned in connection with the sixth-century St Coleman of Cloyne in east Cork, and this was interpreted as meaning a kind of singing accompaniment for dancing. But there is no evidence to support such a claim, and it probably referred to a type of nasal singing or humming. In the fifteenth-century Munster manuscript known as the Book of Lismore, there is a story relating to 'crooners' (*crónánuigh*) and 'croons' (*crónán*), and this has been interpreted as referring to dancers and to dances. If so, then the dance or *crónán* bore little resemblance to Irish dance as we know it today because the *crónán* was so exhausting and energetic that one of the performer's eyes was said to have shot out of his head!

The words *fer cengal* in the twelfth-century poem concerning the public assembly Aonach Carman (now Wexford) probably referred to an acrobat and not a dancer. Besides the terms are not found anywhere else in the literature and so it would be unsafe to build any theories on a once-off attestation. In a twelfth-century description of Salome dancing before Herod, the Irish scribe, in translating the Latin *saltavit* ('she danced'), used three different terms in Gaelic, namely *cleasaigecht*, *lemenda* and *opaireacht*. It appears that the scribe did not know the single Irish word for dancing, because dancing may have been more or less unknown. However, it could be that the writer simply used the full three terms to emphasize the point. The lack of references in early literature has been attributed to the Christian church's opposition to pagan religious dances and to the immorality of dancing. However, it is unlikely that the power of the early church was so great as to have abolished, not only the practice of dancing, but also all references to this activity. Regarding the current words for dancing in Irish, *damhsa* and *rince*, *damhsa* occurs in a text written early in the sixteenth century and can be interpreted to mean 'dancing', so it may be concluded that dancing in some form was probably familiar to our ancestors since 1500. The earliest use of the term *rince* appears to have been about 1588 in poetry associated with the Butler family.

'Come dance with me in Ireland': this is the final line of a little south-of-England poem dating from about 1300–50 that is frequently quoted as the earliest reference to Irish dancing, although not this time in the Irish language. The invitation is extremely vague and is not a dependable warrant for associating the pastime with the native Irish of the time. Even if it was accepted as evidence for contemporary dancing in Ireland, it gives no indication of the dance genre. In an incident involving the Mayor of Waterford on Christmas Eve at O'Driscoll's castle in Baltimore in west Cork in 1413, the Mayor informed the O'Driscolls to fear not, for all he wished to do was 'dance and drink and so depart .... The Mayor took up to dance O'Driscoll and his son, the prior of the Friary, O'Driscoll's three brethren, his uncle and his wife'. This is the earliest definite mention of dancing in Ireland, although again there is no indication of the dance genre in question.

1500–1750 AD: THE EMERGING PICTURE

References to dancing in Ireland in Anglo-Irish and English literature are numerous from the sixteenth century onwards. Many of these were written by English visitors touring here. Travellers were more concerned with the social conditions in the country. They only briefly mentioned the popularity of the dancing or the occasions on which dancing was observed. They rarely if ever give a satisfactory description of the actual dance. References for the period 1500 to 1750 are almost invariably to group or figure dances such as the 'Trenchmore', the 'Hey' or *rince fada*. According to O'Keeffe and O'Brien (1902), the 'Fading' or 'Rince Fada' and the 'Hey' were of Irish origin and imported into England, but these authors did not support their claims with any evidence. They also proposed that the *rince fada* was known in Ireland since 1549, based on a reference in the *Complaynt of Scotland* (1549). However, they were in error in that the piece that they quoted was not in the original 1549 work but was only added as an editorial comment in an 1801 edition.

Descriptions of the *rince fada* vary greatly. It is very likely that the term was a generic one, referring to a type of dance and not to a specific dance. The name appears to have been applied to almost any dance performed by a large number of people or any dance of an extended nature in that it took some time to complete. The *rince fada* apparently varied from place to place and also with time. The *rince fada* as published by the Irish Dancing Commission (1943) is not of any great antiquity, and neither it nor any of our present-day dances can be traced back to pagan times or even prior to the sixteenth century, as has been claimed by some authors.

In the seventeenth century there is a reference to an 'Irish Hey' in a 'West Country Jig'. There are many other references, in English literature, in the same century to the 'Irish Hay', but this cannot be taken to mean that the dance was of Irish origin and was conveyed from there to England. The so-called 'Irish Jig' as performed still by Scots has no Irish connections at all. Sometimes, the term 'Hay' or 'Hey' was used with reference to a dance itself, and in other contexts it referred to a figure or movement. However, there are no extant descriptions of this dance genre.

Fynes Moryson, writing about 1600, stated that 'the Irish delight in dancing', and referred to specific dances, namely 'Bulrudery' and 'The Whip of Dunboyne'. He described a type of sword dance performed by the native Irish and made reference to the 'Matachine dance' which was a type of sword dance popular in Spain. According to him, the Irish frequently danced around a fire in a room and some dances involved the use of naked swords. Sword dancing as practised by the Scots never formed a part of Irish folk dancing. Stick dances, as practised by the Irish, could be interpreted as degenerate forms of sword dances (Cullinane 1998a).

An engraved bone plate in the National Museum of Ireland is referred to as the first representation of dancing in Ireland. This plate of engraved whale bone dates from about 1620. From the coat of arms depicted, it has been concluded that the engraving came from Munster and belonged to some of the Desmond / Fitzgerald family. The plate depicts five figures that are 'possibly' dancers in the act of performing a 'Withy' dance, since three of them appear to be holding 'withies' (not cords). However, this depiction is open to interpretation.

Thomas Dineley (*ca.* 1680), writing about his journeys in Ireland in the seventeenth century, stated that 'the Irish on holidays are much addicted to dance after their country fashion, that is the long dance one after another of all conditions, masters, mistresses and servants'. He never actually referred to the dance by name, so comparisons with the dance known as the *rince fada* are unwise. It is my own belief that what Dineley meant by 'one after the other' was not necessarily a single line of dancers but rather the various social classes. The *rince fada* was apparently performed for King James II on his arrival in Kinsale in 1689 on the seashore, and was said to have pleased him greatly. Contemporary accounts of King

James' actual landing do not appear to contain any descriptions of the dance; the account in question probably dates from 1780 and was included in Walker almost one-hundred years later.

Ó Caoimh (1669) wrote bardic poetry realting to the dances performed by the county Cork-based family, the O'Keeffes, of which the following is a translation:

The withy dance by some of the company,
The sword dance which demands order,
The dance in ranks with changes in tempo,
The long dance with the sporting of maidens.

Dancing in the early eighteenth century was very popular within the Pale and this resulted in Neal (1726) publishing a book of country dances. This not only included the music for these dances but also diagrams of the opening formation and a description of each movement within the dance. The latter appears to have been the first attempt to describe the dance genre. However, there is no indication as to how 'Irish' these dances were or whether they were performed throughout the Irish countryside or only within the Pale, and if the latter, to what extent they remained distinctly Irish.

Accounts of the occasions on which dancing was performed first appeared about 1674 when Head stated that it was on Sunday, the day of most leisure, that the lasses are 'footing till they are all a foam'. Dineley indicated that it was on the holidays that the Irish were addicted to dance, and he also referred to dancers at wakes. Dunton, writing in 1695, confirmed that it was on Sundays or holidays that all the people resorted to the village green where the young folks dance 'till the cows come home'. He gave examples of dancing at weddings, at wakes and at a baptism. From these and subsequent descriptions right up to the nineteenth century, we can conclude that these were the main occasion on which the Irish celebrated and relaxed in dancing. Dunton referred to the dancing as being held in 'every field' which, even allowing for some exaggeration, gives some idea of the popularity of dancing. He also recorded a dancing competition held, over three hundred years ago, at a fair in county Westmeath, with a prize of a pair of brogues for the best dancer. MacLysaght commented that the practice of dancing at religious pilgrimages was an unsavoury feature of seventeenth-century Ireland. Sir Henry Piers reported the fact that the pilgrims, having completed their pilgrimage, retired to a green and there spent the rest of the day 'in lewd and obscene dancing — as if celebrating the Bacchanalia, rather than the memory of a pious saint, or their own penitential'.

The term 'cake dance' appears to have come into existence about 1680 and was in use at least up to the first decade of the nineteenth century (Cullinane 1998a).

It did not refer to a specific dance but rather to a cake which was presented in various ways for dancing. Sometimes, it was given to the (male) dancer who could dance the longest and who then presented it to the maiden of his choice, or else it was donated by the local baker to be shared out among all the village green dancers. Cake dancing was first noted in 1682 by Piers, who recorded the occurrence in county Westmeath. He described the usual happenings on a patron day in most parishes, or on Whitsuntide when a cake was provided by the 'alewife' for the dancers who performed in a big ring about a bush or garland. The prize was given to those who held out the longest.

Around 1808, Lady Morgan remarked that she had been 'at some of these cake (dances) and had invariably observed the inordinate passion for dancing, so prevalent among the Irish peasants'. William Wilde, writing in 1852 about his childhood, describes Sunday evening dancing at the cross-roads when a cake was presented, but he indicated that the dancing for the cake was also held indoors with the cake displayed outside to signal the happenings within. He also records a dance held on May Eve, in which the boys and girls performed 'Threading my Grandmother's Needle', during which they 'joined hands and danced a sort of serpentine figure up and down the roads sometimes for a mile in extent'. They carried wreaths of sloe and white thorn and posies of daisies and buttercups. He described a 'long dance' performed at the moat of Tibberoughny (Tibroughney) near Piltown, county Kilkenny, during which the dancers placed the 'May bush' on the top of the moat. The bush was adorned with golden balls provided by those who had been married the previous Shrovetide. The practice of dancing around a bush is not well documented in Irish literature but is remembered in the name of a village 'Skeheenarinky', which derives its name from the Irish words for 'a little bush' and for 'to dance'. This village is situated between Mitchelstown and Cahir, county Tipperary, close to the roadway that leads to the Mitchelstown Caves.

1750–1890: DANCE MASTERS AND STRUCTURED DANCE CLASSES

Up to the middle of the eighteenth century, dancing appears to have been reasonably simple and of a folk-dance nature, which was easily learned by observation. An extremely structured system of 'taught' dancing, which was very much an educational system and less of an entertainment one, began to evolve from about 1750 onwards. This more formal dancing was taught by a knowledgeable and professionally trained person who came to be known as 'The Dance Master'. During the eighteenth and nineteenth centuries, these were of no fixed abode, and so were sometimes referred to as itinerant or travelling dance masters. They existed in

parts of west Cork and Kerry up the early twentieth century. These paved the way for Irish dancing as we know it today, including all forms of solo/step dancing and those figure dances which became known as *céilí* dancing.

In all probability, dance masters came into existence in response to the enormous popularity of dancing among the peasant and middle-class Irish in the period 1700 to 1750. Some of the earlier instructors almost certainly arrived here from other European countries where such masters were popular at the courts and among the aristocratic classes for many years. Political unrest in Europe may have caused them to come to Ireland. The dance masters were held in high esteem and ranked above the peasants. They did not quite fit in with the aristocracy, even if they were hired to teach their children on occasions. The nature of their profession, their use of French terminology in teaching dancing and their high standard of dress further suggest that they originally did not rise up from among the Irish peasant classes but were, initially at least, migrants from other European countries. It is very probable that most of them came from France since, in addition to their use of French terminology, they introduced the sets of quadrilles.

Young, who was the first to remark on the dancing master, observed that during his travels in Ireland from 1776 to 1779, dancing was very general among the poor, and was almost universal in every cabin, noting that

weddings are always celebrated with much dancing, dancing is so universal among them, that there are every where itinerant dancing-masters, to whom the cottiers pay 6d a quarter for teaching their families.

Young described the method operated by the itinerant dance master as 'an absolute system of education'. This probably referred to the fact that the dance instructor taught deportment and the rudiments of proper social behaviour, and even fencing on some occasions, along with dancing.

By 1776–79, the masters appear to have been numerous and well-established, so that they must have originated as early as the first half of the eighteenth century. Carleton (1869) was the first to describe the character and profession of the Irish 'Country Dancing Master'. He included a detailed account of the dress worn by the instructor: 'Caroline hat and an ornamental staff, made of ebony, hickory, mahogany or some form of cane and which had attached a silver head and a silk tassel'. The teacher always wore 'pumps and stockings, seldom shoes'. From all of this, we can infer that the master was of a reasonably high social standing. 'His dress for instance was always far above the fiddler's — and this was the pride of his heart'. The dance master introduced the practice, early in the nineteenth century, of attaching hay and *súgán* (straw) to the dancers' different legs, and this was still in use up to the early decades of the twentieth century. They then referred to 'Hay foot' and 'Straw foot', which young country children were able to understand much better than 'right foot' and 'left foot'.

The dance masters appear to have originated in Munster, and Kerry seems to be the main point of origin. In that county, it is said that it was no use opening a hedge school for students unless a dancing school was associated with it. In some cases, the teacher was heard at one end of the room while the dancing master conducted his business at the other. Breathnach was of the opinion that the travelling dance master 'originated in Munster and were particularly numerous in Kerry'. He only mentioned three dance masters by name and they were all from Kerry, but he gave an account of a contest between two unnamed dance masters from Cork and Kerry as to who should 'own' Clonmel. Cormac O'Keeffe (pers. comm.) informed me that there were numerous travelling dance masters during the nineteenth century near the west-Cork/Kerry borders around the Ballyvourney area. Ó Cruadhlaoich's (1946) writing about his early childhood days in the area around Ballyvourney confirmed that there were dancing classes everywhere in that same district in or about 1880. He gave an account of one famous travelling dance master named 'Cleaver' who taught dancing about 1850. O'Keeffe and O'Brien stated that there were at least three great schools of dancing in Ireland around the year 1800, those of Kerry, Limerick and Cork. Others, if they existed, 'had not attained the renown of the three great Munster schools'.

Bryan MacMahon (in Cullinane 1987) documented the great Jerry Molyneaux of Kerry and traced his lineage back to 1820. Molyneaux lived at Coolard where he farmed during the summer months. During the off-peak periods, mostly in the winter, he travelled around, teaching dancing in different villages, one at a time, for a period of six weeks each. Molyneaux and other Kerry dance masters of the late nineteenth and early twentieth centuries differed from the earlier instructors in having a fixed abode and in the fact that they often had other professions as well as dancing. In some instances, the dancing school was attached to the hedge school, but this was not always the case. The west-Cork/Kerry dance masters tended to teach in one locality only for a fixed period of either six or nine weeks. In Wexford, a dance master often taught in at least five different adjacent villages at the same period, travelling to each village on a specified night in the week. One thing did not vary, that was the respect for the dance teacher and an acknowledgement of his high standing in the community.

THE LATE NINETEENTH CENTURY: IRISH DANCING AND THE GAELIC LEAGUE

The Gaelic League was founded in 1893. Its objectives were the promotion of the Irish language and literature. Douglas Hyde, its first president, was convinced that the way to recognition of distinct nationality was through a distinct cultural identity. He was therefore dedicated to promoting all aspects of Irish culture. Dancing was promoted by specially organized classes, by the introduction of competitions (reinventing the *feis*) and through social events that became known as *céilí*. The first national *Oireachtas* (or General Assembly) was organized by the League in 1897. It included a single competition for Irish dancing, and so introduced the concept of a national champion dancer.

At a more local level, the Gaelic League recreated the *feis*, at which competitions took place in various aspects of Irish culture, including dancing. The first *feis* was held in Macroom in 1898, followed very shortly afterwards by that of Ballyvourney. Within two or three years, *feiseanna* were being held throughout Ireland, but it does appear that west Cork pioneered the way. The Duhallow *feis* was inaugurated in Cullen, north Cork, in July 1899, and is still held annually. These early *feiseanna* usually included only one or two dancing competitions and usually attracted fewer than ten competitors. *Feiseanna* are still the most important means of promoting dancing and they are held in every country where Irish dancing is taught. In North America alone, there were 140 *feiseanna* in 1997, for example. The 1997 single day Chicago *feis* involved no fewer than thirteen platforms for the dancing alone. *Feiseanna*, especially in Britain and North America, play a very important role in the social life of the Irish diaspora and help to consolidate the Irish community. *Feiseanna* in North America are held outdoors throughout the summer and include a large variety of activities along with the dancing, so that they are very much family affairs (Cullinane 1997a).

Prior to 1893, Irish dancing was largely taught in rural areas, but following the foundation of the League, there was an enormous upsurge of interest in urban areas. Classes were established in major urban centres including London in 1897. Increased interest led to greater need for dance masters in the towns. In Cork, at least, this appears to have brought about the demise of the travelling dance masters, who found the security of teaching in the city in a fixed premises with ancillary facilities more attractive than the nomadic way of life. Many travelling dance instructors settled in Cork which then became a great centre for Irish dancing. By the end of the nineteenth century, the travelling dance master was more or less extinct, except in county Kerry, where he survived into the first decades of the twentieth century.

By 1895, there were sufficient numbers of settled dance masters in Cork to warrant setting up 'The Cork Dance Teachers Association', which is the oldest in the world. In 1897, the Cork Pipers Club was established and is also the oldest such club in the world. Din Moore, who had previously been a travelling dance master, was the first teacher at the Cork Pipers Club. A photograph taken in 1915 shows that there were over one hundred dancers learning at the Pipers Club alone (Cullinane 1996). The dance masters settled in the more urban areas, but in return for the security of teaching in the cities, they lost out on much of their prestige. They taught for a club, the committee of which more or less organized the dancing class, which was named after the particular club. Around the 1920s, the dance masters began to break away from the clubs and to establish their own independent dancing classes which they organized and named after themselves. These were the prototypes of the present-day 'dancing classes'.

Prior to the Gaelic League Revival of the 1890s, Dublin was lacking in dance teachers since the travelling dance masters had not been part of the city's life-style. It was mostly Cork dancers such as Morley and O'Leary who brought the dancing to the capital about 1900. Two of the earliest dancing classes in Dublin were run by a husband and wife team by the name of Brewers, and a second class was run by Wheeler, all of whom had learned their dancing in Cork. Throughout the 1920s and up to the early 1950s, teachers from various parts of Ireland, but especially Dublin, including such well-known dance teachers as Lily Comerford and Essie Connolly, travelled to Cork to improve their dancing repertoire. However, by the 1950s, the old Cork and Kerry styles were in decline, overtaken by more modern and more progressive forms such as the Belfast style.

After 1893, there was also a great revival of interest in the Irish figure or folk dances, especially for social purposes. The London branch of the Gaelic League, which was one of the most vibrant and active, set about organizing social evenings based on the Scottish role model of the time. The London Irish, in fact, introduced the first ever Irish céilí. This was held in Bloomsbury Hall in London on 30 October 1897. The céilí phenomenon spread from there to Ireland and then to various other countries (Cullinane 1997b).

While sets were danced at the first céilí in London in 1897, these were not altogether approved of by the Gaelic League, since the manner in which they were performed was held to reflect badly on the Irish, so the London Irish set about collecting other Irish dances. They travelled to west Cork and Kerry in the late 1890s. In Kerry, they collected a number of dances that we now refer to as céilí dances. The term 'céilí dances' was not used until 1934 when Seán Óg Ó Ceallaigh published a number of figure dances suitable for dancing at a céilí on a weekly basis in a Sunday newspaper. As stated, Kerry appears to have been the home or place of origin of most of what we now call céilí dances. They probably originated from the set dances and were modified into a more Irish form and set

to traditional Irish dance music by the Kerry travelling dance masters of the eighteenth and nineteenth centuries. From the early decades of the twentieth century onwards, the Gaelic League promoted those newly discovered figure/céilí dances and discouraged set dancing.

The London Irish not only collected such figure dances but published the first two collections of these as early as 1902 (O'Keeffe and O'Brien 1902, and Sheehan 1902). The next collection of Irish figure dances was published in 1924 in America by an American anthropologist, Elizabeth Burchenal. It was not until 1939 that a collection (Ar rinncidhe fóirne) was published in Ireland, and even that relied heavily on the 1902 London publications

THE TWENTIETH CENTURY: THE IRISH DANCING COMMISSION/AN COIMISIÚN LE RINCÍ GAELACHA

Throughout the early decades of the twentieth century, there was a great increase in both the number of dancers and in dancing competitions (feiseanna). There were, however, no overall national guidelines, and this led to large degree of dissatisfaction. In 1924, a 'Control Board' was established jointly between the newly founded Leinster Dance Teachers Association and the Gaelic League. Although this Control Board has not previously been recorded in any publication, it was in fact the first joint venture between the League and the dancing teachers.

In 1928, the Gaelic League set up a 'Commission of Enquiry'. In 1930, the League established the Commission as a permanent body with the mandate to foster and legislate for all aspects of the Irish dancing. The Commission was not active until the year 1932–33, when a register of 32 teachers and 27 adjudicators was compiled and a set of rules established and distributed to all feiseanna. The Irish Dancing Commission continues to legislate for all aspects of Irish dancing, only now it does so on a global basis and not just in Ireland alone. Up to the mid-1960s almost all the teachers (TCRGs) and adjudicators (ADCRGs) registered by the Commission were resident in Ireland. During the late 1960s and early 1970s, representatives from the Commission visited England, Australia, New Zealand and North America and held examinations to qualify people in those countries. From that time onwards, the Commission gradually changed from being a national Irish body to being an international body.

In 1997, the Commission registered a total of 1,050 TCRGs among which were 340 in Ireland, 370 in North America, 178 in England, 108 in Australia, 28 in Scotland, 20 in New Zealand, along with others in Wales, Africa, Argentina, and Holland. At present, there are more registered teachers in North America than in Ireland. They teach in thirty-three different American states and seven

Fig. 23.3 The Dunell family of Melbourne, Australia, holders of the record for number of children learning at one time.

Canadian provinces. The Commission conducts examinations in Ireland twice a year, in America on an annual basis, and in other countries less frequently. It also organizes the All-Ireland and World Championships in Ireland annually, along with legislating for Irish dancing world-wide.

All-Ireland Dancing Championships have been organized each year by the Irish Dancing Commission since the 1930s. The event now takes some six full days to run since it involves some two to three thousand competitors. Adjudicators are hired from England, Scotland, Ireland and America. In 1998, the event was held in The West County Hotel, Ennis, county Clare, and a striking feature was the big increase in the number of American and Canadian dancers who not only competed but won a number of the championships. The World Championships are organized at Easter in Ireland and take some eight days of non-stop competition to complete. Some two and a half thousand competitors take part, making it the largest competitive cultural festival in Ireland. The numbers have to be strictly controlled by means of qualifying rounds, held in various regions in some eight countries. Competitions take place in solo dancing, *céilí* dancing, figure dancing and dance drama.

Both the All-Ireland and World Dancing Championships are major economic benefit to the area where they are held. The World Championships were estimated to have brought £2.5m of business to Ennis in 1998. The conference centre at the West County Hotel had to be enlarged to house the event, resulting in the development of the largest conference centre in Ireland outside of Dublin. An additional marquee/tent had to be erected in the hotel grounds to cater for the overflow and to hold up to five hundred competitors who took part in some *céilí* competitions. The North American championships, held in a different city each year on the 4 July weekend, likewise attract some two thousand competitors. Only the largest hotels in North America are capable of catering for the event.

The Commission itself consists of some fifty members, elected by either the Gaelic League or by the various dance teacher bodies in the relevant parts of the world. Meetings of the Commission are held once every month or so in Dublin, are attended regularly by delegates from England, Scotland, America and Canada, and less frequently by delegates from Australia and New Zealand. In between the main meetings, the Commission functions through a number of smaller-sized 'committees' (The Standing Committee, Oireachtas Committee, Examination Authority, Office Management and Finance Committee). The Commission works in conjunction with such organizations as The Irish Dance Teachers Association of North America (IDTANA) and the Australian Irish Dance Teachers Association (AIDA), but membership of these organizations is conditional on being qualified and registered with the Commission in Ireland. The Irish Dancing Commission has its own office situated at 6 Harcourt Street, Dublin. This office employs three full-time staff and at the height of activities (such as the annual registration of teachers and adjudicators or the receiving of entries for the All-Ireland or World Dancing Championships), additional part-time workers and a large number of volunteers are involved.

Financial costs of the office, office staff salaries and costs of meetings are largely covered by the annual registration paid by teachers and adjudicators in all countries. This is the main source of income. Supplementary funding is derived from a registrations fee levied on all dancing competitions held throughout the world. Events such as the All-Ireland and World Championships may or may not make a profit. Losses have to be met out of Commission funds. The Commission does not receive any financial assistance from the Irish government either directly or through the Arts Council, although the World Irish Dancing Championships are the largest Irish cultural event held in Ireland. Irish dancing is not only a major cultural phenomenon but is also a big economic affair. There are many spin-off industries from the Irish dancing. The designing and manufacture of dancing costumes, shoes and accessories, including music tapes and CDs, are all major businesses and are carried on in several countries.

CONCLUSION

In recent times, Irish dancing has become much more of a world-wide art form and its expression of national identity has greatly diminished. Dancers of various ethnic origins throughout four continents learn and enjoy it, many of them even oblivious of where Ireland is located. The most recent development has been the establishment of a South African Irish Dance Teachers Association. I myself have taught Irish dancing to Australian aboriginal children, North American Indian children, children of all colours and various ethnic backgrounds in some seven different countries. You do not have to be Irish to take part in the St Patrick's Day parade and you do not have to be Irish to be an Irish dancer, as some of the greatest champion Irish dancers in the world have proven.

Irish dancing has been evolving and changing very much since the middle of the twentieth century. This involved greater elevation and an ever-increasing variety of movements, along with more intricacy of footwork with a greater number of beats per bar of music and the use of syncopated rhythm. These features, along with the innovation shown in newly composed figure dances, have all helped to make dancing attractive all over the world. Much of this development remained rather hidden until it exploded on an unsuspecting audience at the 1994 Eurovision Song Contest. The macho image of

male dancers, freed from the constraints of the kilt and the rather flamboyant use of the hands in *Riverdance*, have all contributed to the popularity of the performance. The brilliance of some of the most intricate and precise footwork the world has seen is so enjoyable that dancers are no longer asked why they do not smile. Dancers who have spent almost all their lives dedicated to Irish dancing lessons now find that there is a lucrative profession awaiting them in their later teenage years doing what they love most of all — Irish dancing.

While some dancing teachers express some slight reservations because those dancers whom they have spent years training for competition are now finding alternatives to competition in these shows, Irish dancing teachers around the world are proud of the exposure that Irish dancing is finally receiving. All the dancers in *Riverdance* and *Lord of the Dance* were trained by those Irish dancing teachers who are registered with the Commission, and those dancers received their early formal training in those competitions/*feiseanna* organized by the Commission and its representative bodies. Teachers registered with the Commission are wholeheartedly behind both the *Riverdance* genre and the dancers in the shows, for it was they who promoted the evolution of this dance genre and it was they who initially trained these dancers.

The dance teaching profession itself is big business, especially for those who carry it on as a full-time profession. Top-class teachers and adjudicators are in demand in four continents. Teachers and adjudicators regularly fly between Europe, North America and Australasia to conduct workshops and master classes or adjudicate Irish dancing. In America, some teachers get around to as many as ten different states, covering distances between classes that are greater than from Ireland to America. Armed with airline tickets, hotel reservations, tape recorders and video cameras, they continue the two hundred and fifty-year-old profession of the travelling dancing master. It is the ability of Irish dancing and Irish dancing teachers to evolve and to adapt that has made Irish dancing as popular as it is today.

Bibliography

An Coimisiún le Rinncí Gaelacha 1997 *Liosta oifigiúil.* Dublin.
Anon. (*ca.* 1549) *Complaynt of Scotland*, J. Leaden (ed) (London 1775).
Anon. 1939 *Ar rinncidhe fúirne Part 1*. Dublin.
Anon. 1943 *Ar rinncidhe fúirne Part 2*. Dublin.
Anon. 1969. *Ar rinncidhe fúirne Part 1, 2 and 3*. Dublin.
Breatnach, R. A. 1956 'The evidence for dancing in ancient Ireland', *Journal of the Cork Historical and*

Archaeological Society **60**, pp. 88–94, **61**, pp. 59–60, 65–7.

Breathnach, B. 1971 *Folkmusic and dances of Ireland.* Cork.

Burchenal, E. 1924 *National dances of Ireland.* New York.

Carleton, W. 1869 *The Poor Scholar — Frank Martin and the Fairies — The Country Dancing Master — and other Irish Tales.* Dublin.

Cullinane, J. 1987 *Aspects of the history of Irish dancing.* Cork.

Cullinane, J. 1990 *Further aspects of the history of Irish dancing.* Cork.

Cullinane, J. 1994 'Irish dance world-wide' in P. O'Sullivan (ed) *The creative migrant* (Leicester), 3.

Cullinane, J. 1996 *Irish dancing costumes: their origins and evolutions.* Cork.

Cullinane, J. 1997a *Aspects of the history of Irish dancing in North America.* Cork.

Cullinane, J. 1997b 'Contribution of the London Irish migrants to Irish dancing — 100 years of *céilí* dancing', paper presented at 'The Scattering' conference, UCC (September).

Cullinane, J. 1997c 'All set for the *céilí*', *Cork Hollybough*.

Cullinane, J. 1998a 'Of swords, sticks and cakes', *Irish Dancing Magazine* **1**, 2 (March–April).

Cullinane, J. 1998b *Aspects of the history of Irish céilí dancing.* Cork.

Dineley, T. 1870 *Thomas Dineley — Observations in a voyage through the Kingdom of Ireland in the year 1681.* Dublin.

Fleischman, A. 1956 'The evidence for dancing in ancient Ireland — 1, further evidence', *Journal of the Cork Historical and Archaeological Society* **61**, pp. 58–9.

Joyce, P. 1903 *Social history of ancient Ireland.* London.

McFarlane, D. (ed) 1989 *The Guinness Book of Records.* London.

Moryson, F. 1566–1630 *Manners and customs of the Irish.* Glasgow.

Neal, J. and Neal, W. 1726 *A choice collection of country dances with times*, edited by R. Jackson and G. Fogg (Boston, 1990).

O'Curry, E. 1873 *On the manners and customs of the ancient Irish.* Dublin.

Ó Cruadhlaoich, P. 1946 *Cuimhne sean-leinibh.* Dublin.

O'Keeffe, J. G. and O'Brien, A. 1902 *A handbook of Irish dances.* London.

Ó Sé, M. 1955 'Notes on old Irish dances', *Journal of the Cork Historical and Archaeological Society* **60**, pp. 57–63.

Ó Sé, M. 1956 'Evidence for dancing in ancient Ireland', *Journal of the Cork Historical and Archaeological Society* **61**, pp. 60–5.

Sheehan, J. J. 1902 *A guide to Irish dancing.* London.

Walker, J. 1786 *Historical memoires of the Irish bards.* Dublin.

Wilde, W. 1852 *Irish popular superstitions.* Dublin.

Young, A. 1780 *A tour in Ireland.* London.

Theatre and the Performing Arts

MARK MULQUEEN

Culture is important to the Irish, they just do not always show it. Culture that reassures notions of the stereotypical national identity is appreciated, but, as a source of radicalism that acts as a sort of mirror to society, it is scarcely welcome. The public outcry at Synge's *The Playboy of the Western World* in 1907 is the classic example of this attitude.The state has not had an unequivocally proud history of supporting the cultural or artistic life of the country in the past. Until recently, it could be argued that it could not afford such luxuries, although we still continue to under-perform in comparison to other supposedly equally 'disadvantaged' European nations. The arts are often a secondary activity in the education system, something to be endured when the important lessons have been learned. Yet despite all of that apparent gloom, culture is an essential element in Ireland's development. There is an irony in the fact that our fastest-growing indigenous economic sector, tourism, is dependent on two of the most neglected natural assets in Ireland, our civilization and our environment. The national tourism agency, Bord Fáilte, can justify annual increases in its multi-million pound marketing budget by pointing to the continuing expansion in visitor numbers, while all the time it is the nation's cultural reputation created by a host of artists that achieves more than any glossy advertizing campaign. Of course, pop music reaches out to vast markets via the likes of MTV, but dancers, poets, writers, dramatists and actors have also been making headlines for at least one hundred years. Ireland's theatre tradition has been at the source of much of this success, as the names Wilde, Yeats, O'Casey, Shaw, Behan, Beckett, Keane, Friel and so on indicate. Theatre in Ireland has changed many times through the intervention and influence of such key figures.

Change is constant in theatre and the performing arts and in many ways it is this constant evolution, tempered by established traditions, that allows for an animated and creative environment. These regular implosions and re-inventions have been particularly intense throughout the last century. In the approach to theatre each country has distinct characteristics, whether in design, direction or writing. Ireland is internationally recognized as having had particularly brilliant writing for the stage. In Irish theatre the central figure of the writer has gained continued renown through the works of individuals such as the aforementioned Brian Friel, Hugh Leonard and John B. Keane or, latterly, Jim Nolan and the remarkable Martin McDonagh. It is only in very recent times that the more physical and visual approaches to drama have become a common feature of the country's dramatic output. As just one 'attraction' in the increasingly crowded entertainment sector, theatre and the performing arts are therefore showing a versatility and consistent appeal some may not have believed possible. However, there are a number of major challenges to their relatively healthy state and to drama in particular. We shall look at certain of these factors in due course, but first let us consider our theatre in terms of its historical evolution, social context and innate identity.

DRAMA: ORIGINS AND RECENT DEVELOPMENTS

Tyrone Guthrie believed that

The Theatre is the direct descendant of fertility rites, war dances and all the corporate ritual expressions by means of which our primitive ancestors, often wiser than we, sought to relate themselves to God, or the Gods, the great abstract forces which cannot be apprehended by reason but in whose existence reason compels us to have faith.

The visually and physically extravagant performances created in the late 1980s and early 1990s by the Catalonians El Comediants and Galway's Macnas are contemporary cases of these timeless human impulses for expression, impulses evident before them in the work of

Siamsa Tíre in north Kerry. The need to convey emotions, convictions and moral dilemmas and to portray them and express them physically is a characteristically human urge. The performing arts — music, dance, drama, and film — are our outlets in this regard. Today the physical is joined with the mechanical to create synthesized music, fantastic light and computer-generated virtual reality. We sometimes use the term 'multi-media' when identifying non-traditional practices. Many theatre companies are now able to move with ease between 'cutting-edge' technical effects and more traditional formulae. But a review of the recent history of Irish theatre shows a long-standing capacity to innovate by linking the past with the present.

In the mid-nineteenth century the 'Stage Irishman' came to prominence as the standard portrayal of the Irish character. This is due in part, to the public awareness of figures such as Conn in *The Shaughraun* (1881), a play by Dion Boucicault (1822–90), one of the most prolific and successful Irish dramatists of the time. Dionysius Lardner Boucicault is generally attributed with inventing the 'hop, leg and jump, school of Irish theatre, in which a grand-natured dolt is forever saving the life of the Heroine and in which the cads and miscreants give themselves away by the cut of their eyebrows and the arrogance of their swagger', to quote Fintan O'Toole. However, his thesis is that if Boucicault had been an American dramatist he would also be remembered as 'the prodigious orchestrator of spectacles and special effects, as the founder of the global mass media event, as the first major playwright to come to grips with new technology, as a key figure in the development of the notion of intellectual property'.

In 1850s he wrote a play called *The Streets of New York*. It was designed to accommodate the world market by being adaptable to local circumstances wherever it toured, so it became in time *The Poor of Liverpool*, or *The Streets of London* and, of course, *The Streets of Dublin*. This was during a time of intense nationalism, and his notion that such a distinct product could easily be adapted to tell a story of general relevance was quite bold.

O'Toole believes 'Boucicault anticipated the development of cinema by trying to create moving pictures on stage. He envisaged the "sensation scenes" for which his play became famous as a film director would imagine a big, climatic sequence'. Boucicault's melodrama *The Octoroon* had a remarkably modern visual plot device whereby the villain is unmasked by the camera which catches and preserves the evidence of his misdemeanour. This astute recognition of technology's potential also manifested itself in his approach to production management. His work as a writer, producer and actor had a huge impact on the creation of the Broadway theatre. His method had influenced David

Belasco, who invented and controlled Broadway, as he had spent time as Boucicault's secretary. The latter's decision to take a share of profits rather than a flat fee as author of *The Colleen Bawn* paved the way for the system of author's royalties that is now taken for granted. He was particularly capable in a style of characterization that was a central feature of popular theatre of the time. The fact that this was a period when emigration from Ireland was at an all-time high, contributing to the increasing racial mix in the New World, cannot be forgotten. Theatre was mirroring real life where people sought reassurance in their individuality and 'native' nationality. The Abbey Theatre's production of *The Colleen Bawn* in the summer of 1998 was both critically acclaimed and enjoyed a successful box office. After all, using a traditional Irish rural setting and a host of what could be considered stage-Irish characters as devices to explore contemporary Ireland is exactly what today's Irish playwrights are doing again in their own distinctive way.

The stage Irishman would soon have had his day and Irish theatre was about to acquire respectability, as it has continued to do to the present. A route by which this often farcical one-dimensional character could, in the course of a generation, be freed to play a role in the new indigenous tradition of theatre was provided by writings of two of the other of the most eminent Irish figures of the time. George Bernard Shaw (1854–1950) and Oscar Wilde (1845–1900) had by the 1890s begun to establish themselves in the Irish 'stage comedy tradition'. They were not overtly 'Irish' in their style of work and, with the exception of Shaw's *John Bull's Other Island* (1909), neither dramatist's work made explicit use of Irish themes. However, they do mark a point from which today's theatre tradition can claim certain of its roots.

The Irish theatrical heritage owes much to what is commonly known as the 'Gaelic Revival' of the 1890s and 1900s. Irish political and cultural movements were never so intertwined as they were in this era of cultural regeneration and 'new' nationalism. A common misconception in recording history is to see the period immediately after the death of Charles Stuart Parnell (1846–91) as a political vacuum. It is true to say that political energy was focussed in a way not previously so closely linked to the national question. Without forgetting the considerable parliamentary success achieved by Mr John Redmond, an unusually high level of effort was being diverted mystically into the channels of 'culture'. To quote W. B. Yeats in a famous passage:

The modern literature of Ireland and indeed all that stir of thought which prepared for the Anglo-Irish War, began when Parnell fell from power in 1891. A disillusioned and embittered Ireland turned from parliamentary politics; an event was conceived: and the race began, as I think, to be troubled by that event's long gestation. (cited in Foster 1988, 43)

Augustine Birrell, Chief Secretary for Ireland, was of a similar mind, stating 'there was a leap to the front rank of thought and feeling altogether novel'. Irish literature and drama were by far the dominant artistic modes by which this will was carried forth. This was the overall context which led to the birth of our modern dramatic tradition. Much is attributed to the meeting and friendship of W. B. Yeats (1865–1939) with Lady Augusta Gregory (1852–1932) and Edward Martyn (1859–1924) (see Gregory 1913). From the 1890s on a distinctively Irish dramatic movement was well under way, led by Yeats, marked by his interest in Irish folklore, peasant life and Irish mythology (Owens and Radnor 1990). Together they founded the Irish Literary Society — the precursor to the National Theatre (The Abbey; see Hunt 1979). The movement gambled — successfully — on its power to inspire Irish writers to create suitable scripts, trusting, as the first manifesto said, 'that the Irish audience would allow dramatists that freedom to experiment which is not found in theatres in England'. Such gutsy confidence, with a clear broadside at the English theatre tradition, must have helped endear this predominantly Anglo-Irish 'National Theatre Society' to the mainstream nationalist movement. Unfortunately for them, they found Irish audiences to be much like their English counterparts, expecting entertaining and often humorous storylines matched with colour and pace in the production.

The establishment of the National Theatre Society (or The Abbey) and equally importantly the willingness of the first Free State government to provide annual grant - aid to the Society (Mr Ernest Blythe, Minister for Finance in the initial Free State administration, became Managing Director of The Abbey in the 1950s), making it the first country to provide direct funds for such a purpose, meant that professional theatre had a permanent home in the new state. From the outset, The Abbey has had a special obligation of cultivating Irish identity, and that remains the case today. It has also maintained a unique if ambiguous relationship with the state. To quote the present Artistic Director, Patrick Mason, 'With all the high ideals and great ambition that they had, Yeats and Lady Gregory ran very quickly into the hard facts of the market. So they gave the theatre to the State. And to everyone's surprise, they took it!' (Fitzgibbon 1997, 62). It is this involvement with the state and a sometimes lofty notion of its place in contemporary Irish theatre that gives rise to the often taut relationship The Abbey has had with the independent theatre sector. The Abbey now has an annual commitment to bringing its production on tour to the main venues through the country. But for many years, its sphere of influence seldom extended beyond 'the Pale', and similar levels or standards of dramatic production were not to be found in other urban centres in Ireland.

Around the same time as the Irish National Theatre Society was being conceived in Dublin, there were also moves a-foot in Ulster to integrate cultural and political identities into a literary theatre movement (Bell 1972). The Ulster Literary Theatre was founded in 1902 by two young Belfastmen, Bulmer Hobson and David Parkhill. This was created above all as a weapon of propaganda for a united Ireland. Both men were first and foremost followers of Wolfe Tone and the principles of the United Irishmen. The notion that there would be a 'school' separate to that espoused by the Irish National Theatre Society met with considerable resistance. The editorial in the first edition of the new literary review *Ulad* (meaning 'Ulster') set out the aims of the new Ulster Literary Theatre. It was clear that Ulster wished to go its own way. It met with a protest in its second issue from a contributor 'Conula', a pen-name said to be that of the Irish Labour leader, James Connolly. 'Conula' saw a danger in the idea that the Ulster Literary Theatre should set up a 'school' in Belfast, such as Dublin had but with a difference. 'Ulster has not yet sufficiently assimilated the rudiments of national culture on which she must base the development of her best provincial characteristics.'

However, the amateur movement was instrumental in the development of drama in Ulster early on in the twentieth century. The Northern Drama League, formed in 1923, was one of the most influential amateur drama societies active throughout the townlands of the province. It is difficult in a brief survey to give due recognition to the very many societies which were on the one hand still working at pieces that one would have thought were forgotten, while other societies were presenting with professional finesse plays from contemporary theatre on the other. The Belfast Repertory Theatre were actively producing contemporary Ulster dramas such as *The Early Bird* by James Douglas throughout the 1930s.

In the 1920s and 1930s, after The Abbey plays became widely known in rural Ireland, a new indigenous amateur movement took shape where many of the country's best professionals got their first experience of the stage. An Amateur Drama Association of Ireland was formed in 1932. This was followed by the establishment of the Amateur Drama Council of Ireland in 1953. It was successful in creating a national network of local festivals where hundreds of groups competed annually, and from which a winner would go forward to the national finals in Athlone. The work of such notable writers as Bryan McMahon, M. J. Molloy, Walter Macken and John B. Keane contributed to this development. John B. Keane (born 1930) is a native of the north-Kerry town of Listowel where he has spent a life as one of Ireland's most popular writers. It was the 1959 performance of the play *Sive* by the Listowel Drama Group which set him on his way to becoming one of the most successful Irish playwrights of his generation. Much of the success of *Sive*, in addition to the authenticity of its theme and native pagan resonances, must be attributed to the national amateur award-winning production by the Listowel Drama Group. It was common in the 1950s for an emerging dramatist to be closely connected with an amateur group, as in the latter half of the nineteenth century the popular melodramas of Boucicault were frequently staged by local companies in country towns. The amateur movement was central to the advancement of rural Irish writers like Keane and it continues to be a breeding ground for much of today's new talent. Much as Keane is indebted to the amateur movement, they owe even more to him. The Southern Theatre Group, which was based in Cork on a semi-professional basis, reaped a rich harvest from *Sive* and other Keane plays. This enabled the Cork company to stage seasons of plays in commercial theatres in Cork, Limerick and occasionally in Dublin. *The Field*, widely regarded as the Listowel-man's best play, tells the story of greed, frustration and violence resulting from 'land hunger', the Irish obsession with ownership of land and property. (Unfortunately, the feature film adaptation of *The Field* fails to capture this particularly Irish trait. It focuses instead on the struggle between the individual spirit and the dominant Catholic ethos of the time.) Keane's strength lies in an ability to use drama formed out of the commonplace and weave rich authentic dialogue and humour into what was in fact a tragic situation.

The staging of plays in Irish was closely related to the same amateur movement. At the beginning of the last century, the Gaelic League oversaw the production of dramatic pieces in Irish and later groups such as Na hAisteóirí and An Comhar Drámaíochta continued its development. The only permanent theatre for plays in Irish, An Taibhdhearc in Galway, survived with the benefit of state grant assistance. It has helped ensure, along with other venues such as Siamsa Tíre in Tralee, that a stage is available for Irish-language playwrights. *An Giall* by Brendan Behan (1923–64) became *The Hostage* in translation and was produced by Joan Littlewood at the Theatre Royal, Stratford East, London, in 1958. This must have been a relatively unique transition for an Irish-language composition and probably owed as much to Behan's infamous ebullient personality as to theatrical qualities.

Although incomparable to any of the other new Irish writers to come on the scene in the 1950s and 1960s, Samuel Beckett's *Waiting for Godot* was expected to be another 'shocking' new play by a reclusive *émigré*. Samuel Beckett (1906–89) was born in the Dublin suburb of Foxrock. He grew up in an atmosphere of material comfort, 'surrounded by tennis-courts, conservatories and clumps of pink hydrangrea'. His upbringing and education were integral to the formation of his unique dramatic style. He went to Portora Royal School, Enniskillen (where Oscar Wilde had been a pupil fifty years before), and to Trinity College, Dublin, where he won a Foundation Scholarship in Modern Languages. After taking his moderatorship in Trinity, Beckett taught at the École Normale Supérieure in Paris and then returned to Trinity as lecturer in French from 1930 until 1932. He later settled in Paris, which remained his home for the rest of his life. Since 1945, he wrote chiefly in French, although he is quoted as describing English as a 'good theatre language' because of its concreteness, its close relationship between thing and the vocable.

En Attendant Godot (1953), translated *Waiting for Godot* in 1955, *Fin de Partie* (1957), rendered in English as *Endgame* (1958), and *Happy Days* (1961), in French *Oh, les Beaux Jours* (1963), were not conceived of as a trilogy, but they are early plays which take up a full theatre evening, and all, in some way, are concerned with the condition of waiting. The critic Alec Reid said Beckett's art is the 'art of involvement … the thing itself not something about the thing, creation not description, first hand not second, that is what makes Godot far more than a brilliantly original solution to a problem in play-writing …'. It is accepted that *Waiting for Godot* changed the course of western theatre. The play was first produced in 1953 at the Babylone Theatre in Paris. French actor Jean Martin who played Lucky 250 times at the tiny Paris venue described the audience's reaction: 'At the end of the first act, some of them would yell "bravo, bravo". Others just looked at each other'. *Le Figaro* had published a front-page opinion piece by the playwright Jean Anouilh, hailing *Godot* as a masterpiece. Upper-middle class Paris was flocking to the Babylone; within six months the play was world-famous and its notoriety brought Beckett a renown that stayed with him for the rest of his life. However, Ireland in the nineteen fifties and sixties was a very conservative, repressed nation, poor and not able to afford time for the works of Beckett. He stayed away from what he knew had become an alien place to him.

It was not until the 1950s and afterwards that regionalization really took place in the Irish theatre. In Cork the Group Theatre provided a platform for both local and visiting companies to perform. The re-building of the Opera House in 1965 as well as the opening of the Everyman Theatre Playhouse in 1972 gave Cork city the choice of both medium- and large-size performance houses. The Belltable Art Centre has provided a stage for theatre in Limerick City since 1981. The Hawkswell in Sligo represented the mainstay of drama in the northwest for many years. Other centres such as Athlone and Waterford also have a tradition of local and regional theatre production. In the late 1970s and early 1980s new 'professional' theatre companies appeared in most of the major towns throughout the country. Waterford's Red Kettle Theatre Company and the Island Theatre of Limerick have been central to the consolidation of regional theatre as well. Probably the most successful of all of these has been the Druid Theatre Company. Druid was founded in western city of Galway in 1975. It began in a location which had little in the way of a theatre tradition, except for An Taibhdhearc, the Irish-speaking semi-professional playhouse established in 1928. Unlike a centre such as Cork, Galway does not have a strong amateur drama heritage. The company probably owes more to the city's university and the tradition of hard graft and dependence on self in the west of Ireland. Druid's choice of productions cannot easily be pigeon-holed. Although they have always been conscious of their location in the west, the early repertoire was made up of works by Ibsen, Buchner, Wilde and others. It was not until the late 1970s and early '80s that they began to develop productions of the classic Irish repertoire which brought them to the forefront of Irish theatre at that time. What does appear to be common to all their presentations is the central role of the writer: 'Druid has succeeded because it set about creating not a "writers theatre", but a theatre that could be good for writers to work in, that could have the skills and the clarity of vision to be able to produce new plays', according to one commentator.

The 1982 production of *The Playboy of the Western World* by John Millington Synge (1871–1909) was considered the greatest achievement of the early years. The *Irish Times* described it as 'definitive'. The Synge classic became the company's signature production and stayed in the repertoire throughout the 1980s. Directed by Gary Hynes and including Mick Lally, Maelíosa Stafford, Bríd Brennan, Marie Mullen and Sean McGinley in the cast, it toured the Edinburgh Festival and came back to the Bedlam Theatre where it was described by one reviewer as 'nothing less than perfection, leaving the audience quite breathless at the wonder of true theatre'. The *Playboy* toured Ireland to packed houses and even made the unusual trip to the hall on the Aran Island of Inis Meáin where Synge had stayed so often. There the physical challenges came both in the shape of the theatre, which required adaption to accommodate the production, and the gale-force winds, which tested the company's boat on the journey to the island. Any fears of an island audience being uninspired by a play which had brought the house down in urban centres was unfounded. The reception accorded the *Playboy* by the islanders was outstanding. Gary Hynes went on to win 'Director of the Year' in the inaugural *Sunday Independent* Arts Awards. It was also around this time that Druid produced new plays by the writer Tom Murphy. These included *Conversations on a Homecoming* and the magnificent *Bailegangaire*.

In 1991 Gary Hynes left the company to become Artistic Director of The Abbey Theatre. In her absence, Maelíosa Stafford as Artistic Director had a number of successful productions with works by writers such as Paul Vincent Carroll and Frank McGuinness, and his tenure will be best remembered for his direction of Vincent Woods' *At the Black Pig's Dyke*. Hynes returned as Artistic Director in 1995 and instituted a new writing programme which culminated in the 1997 presentation of *The Leenane Trilogy*, three plays by Martin McDonagh. McDonagh's first production with Druid was in 1996 with *The Beauty Queen of Leenane*. This went on to Broadway in 1998 where it provided the company with possibly its greatest achievement to date, winning four Tony Awards, including Best Director for Gary Hynes, best actress for Marie Mullen, best supporting actress for Anna Manahan and best supporting actor for Tom Murphy.

INFRASTRUCTURE AND AUDIENCE DEVELOPMENT

One of the major developments brought about by the then Department of Arts, Culture and the Gaeltacht (established in 1992) was the implementation of the Cultural Development Incentive Scheme (CDIS). This has provided substantial capital funding to assist the improvement of the national arts infrastructure. In most cases, CDIS monies have been matched by local authority and Arts Council financing. The scheme has enabled very necessary improvements to the country's performing arts framework to take place. The recently opened 400-seat municipal theatre, the Town Hall Theatre in Galway city, was one of its most positive outcomes. For years, Galway's theatre-going public had to make do with a variety of temporary venues, including a 'big top' tent during the annual Arts Festival. With a rapidly growing population and a number of award-winning production companies based in the city, CDIS could not have come at a better time.

The advent of CDIS and the general increase in funding for capital schemes from both the Arts Council and local authorities might retrospectively be looked upon as a case of putting the cart before the horse. Maybe we should be getting the basics right first — education and training in theatre, audience development and the like (of which more later). But to turn down any kind of investment in the arts in a country not particularly renowned for state support in this area would have been unwise and probably impossible. However, there is no clear strategy to provide for additional funding to service these new centres, and although the likes of Galway's Town Hall Theatre can state, with validity, that it was responding to a growing and demanding market, many other similar ventures may turn out to be white elephants. A physical, visible and thus far more tangible return is received from 'building' initiatives in the arts compared to relatively invisible schemes such as Aosdána. Moreover, there is no guarantee of a return from investing in an individual. In this connection, the case in favour of being market-led and responsive to audience and demand may be justified. The Cultural Development Incentive Scheme has, at any rate, led to many very necessary improvements in theatre halls throughout the country, at Galway, Macroom and elsewhere, such that there is now a stage fit for the finest in every corner of Ireland for the benefit of the next generation of talented writers and performers. While these monies do not come with additional resources for the performing arts or general administrative requirements, the noticeable improvements they have created throughout the country must be acknowledged.

Today, theatre in Ireland has diversified into many forms. In particular, it has endeavoured to embrace a broader social spectrum. Theatre-in-Education (TIE) is being delivered in particular by two versatile and prolific companies, namely Graffitti and TEAM. Graffiti Theatre Company was established in 1984. It was founded as an educational theatre company, catering for the south of Ireland. The company's TIE programmes have been seen by over 500,000 young people in every part of the country. TIE is a theatre experience that harnesses the dramatic event as a catalyst for learning. The teachings of Augusto Boal have informed the genre, though its practices are as varied as the professionals who strive to educate and entertain young audiences or 'spectators'. In Dublin, the ARK is the first cultural centre exclusively intended for children to have been set up in Europe. Martin Drury, its Director, has declared 'A six-year-old is not a third of an eighteen-year-old, or a quarter of a twenty-four-year old. A six-year-old is a fully formed six-year-old — a citizen with needs, rights and a contribution to make. Theatre provision for children should not be about "preparing a new audience for the future". It should be about responding to the cultural needs of the child now'. TEAM Education Theatre Company has been in Dublin since 1975 and is now based in the ARK. TEAM and Graffiti have been the primary TIE activators in Ireland, but they are now being joined by other regional initiatives, for example the Kilkenny Theatre Project and, in Dublin, Very Special Arts and Sticks and Stones, who run a school's drama programme focusing on bullying.

If TIE is to function as the main experience of live theatre for young people during compulsory education, then some measures have to be taken to ensure that this experience is of a high artistic and educational standard, relevant (as opposed to reduced or patronising), exciting, challenging and enjoyable. Poor standards and inappropriate work can only lead to a 'turn-off effect' (Arts Council 1995, TIE section, *passim*). My own experience of TIE productions has been one of consistently high levels of realization. This consistency might also be attributed, at least partly, to the small number of practitioners present in Ireland and so to the relative ease with which they can communicate regularly and maintain an evenness to the development of this theatre experience.

Either way, its impact is unlikely to be fully appreciated for a number of years to come, when hopefully it becomes a commonplace experience for all school-goers. Youth theatre is therefore possibly the most successful of the newer dramatic practices. Almost every town in Ireland now has a youth theatre group. This development has benefited from the role played by the National Association of Youth Drama. Although still catering primarily for the middle classes, youth theatre is laying the foundations for a new generation of practitioners and audiences.

Is it unrealistic to think that theatre can become as central to people's lives as television and film? Is there an over-expectancy that youth and community drama schemes can create a more central role for theatre in contemporary Irish society? Paul Mercier of Passion Machine Theatre Company posed these and related questions in the Arts Council's *Dialogues* (1995) document: 'Are we [the producers] playing to the converted? Is theatre for the drama literate? Is it for the artistic community? Is it for the Irish media, for the Arts Council, for London or for New York? Is there a conscious or unconscious concern among theatre companies about winning this constituency first?' Although these are difficult questions to answer, they do expose the unclear and undefined relationship that production companies have with the public. There is a degree of competence in theatre appreciation that is shared by a small body of theatre-goers. These are what Paul Mercier refers to as the 'drama literate'. Whether they have been educated in the arts or are actually working in the performing arts, they have become equipped with the know-how and reference points necessary for them to be able to judge a production for its 'artistic worth'. They can appreciate production values and are informed enough to be alert to any fashionable comment or reference that may arise in the course of a performance.

An audience that is in tune to your message is a pleasure to play to. Theatre companies are creating new productions which are heavily reliant on audience figures, both to provide direct-box office income and equally to justify the funding support being provided to them by state agencies and government departments. Although a situation where art is judged on purely aesthetic grounds may be aspired to, it is in everyone's nature to consider the level of interest in and support for a production as something very important to its success. But in the conception of new works, the audiences' needs or tastes are not central to the creators. Instead, marketing is sometimes perceived as a tool by which an unattractive or irrelevant piece of theatre art can be packaged in a manner whereby a customer can be either deceived or simply convinced to buy into something they do not want. This is not genuine marketing, and it is not the role of marketing in theatre. 'Marketing, in the true sense of what marketing professionals mean, is shaping your product to suit your audience and the arts rarely do that. It is more a case of publishing the product on offer', according to Jerome Hynes, Chief Executive of the Wexford Opera Festival. I do not believe a play could be conceived of with a proper marketing 'ethos' driving its creation. The Irish audience is fickle and probably impossible to define. The public's taste is very particular and tends towards one type of theatre. 'I have a suspicion that there may be many people involved in theatre and drama in the country — amateur, youth and community drama — that never set foot in a professional venue', said Peter Mason of Hampshire County Council during the Galway meeting of the 1995 theatre review. 'Popular culture is culture on the audiences terms (Gans 1974). It is therefore the public and not the producer who transforms something into popular culture on the artists terms', as Dag Bjorkegren stated in an excellent publication (1996). He says 'the public has to be educated if it is to grasp and understand the artist's meaning', and that 'popular culture products (unlike high arts) aim at attracting the widest possible audience'. Bjorkegren directly connects one's level of education with one's ability to appreciate and understand the arts: 'Academic knowledge is often required. For this reason, it is rare for high culture to succeed in becoming popular culture'. If this is the case, are exercises such as marketing and advertising a waste of resources, and can the exact audience potential be ascertained simply by examining Department of Education statistics? Can we target one art-form at Leaving Certificate holders and another for those lucky enough to have a third-level degree? I do not think so, but education remains central to the business of long-term arts audience development.

The public are entitled to choose a theatre event on the basis of personal interest. Unfortunately, they are missing performances by artists who are sincere and often very talented individuals. Yet many of the needs and shortcomings of the Irish performing arts sector relate either directly or indirectly to inadequate levels of finances. It is true that the Arts Council is not able to supply the scale of funding that is being requested of it, but as they provide public funds, one might wonder how much would be available if theatre-goers were directly deciding the total sum of arts financial support? I ask this as I believe the public to be far more likely to provide the finances deemed necessary by professional practitioners through the box-office rather than through taxes.

Therefore the public must be embraced and listened to. The work of Grafitti and TEAM TIE companies is of such a consistently high standard that it can have the effect of enhancing its audiences' attitude towards and perception of theatre. Youth theatre, Theatre-in-Education, community drama and forum theatre all have an advantage over the 'professional' theatre producers in

that their performances were designed for a specific audience. Similarly, an amateur theatre company adapting or simply presenting an already established play is not having to create a whole new 'market'. With these points in mind, one could take a solely developmental view of funding for professional theatre companies and consider a grant as 'risk capital' and 'research and development', with the same parameters for assessment as applied in industrial product development. There is a price to be paid if a nation wants a living and innovative theatre tradition and thus perpetuate the dynamic dramatic legacy it has inherited from the past.

Although these are important matters to those in the performing arts, it does appear that the latter 'have never had it so good'. The Arts Council's annual budget has been expanded considerably in recent years. In 1998, for example, the government provided an increase of £5m, bringing the total budget of this agency to £26 million. A report titled *The employment and economic significance of the cultural industries in Ireland* was commissioned by Temple Bar Properties in 1994. This document informed the national theatre review sessions implemented over the following year, and it was found that 'a comparison of aggregate attendance in 1994 and in 1981 shows that overall attendance at art events among the population rose from 60% to 78% in the intervening period. Theatre is one of the art-forms in which the increase is significant with attendance rising from 30% in 1981 to 37% in 1994. It now ranks third after films and popular performances in attendance at arts events'.

CONCLUSION

I conclude by returning to the people who create theatre and the performing arts, in this case the much-lauded writers who have ensured that the international perception of us remains that of an island of scholars of particular quality. Tom Murphy is one of these contemporary writers. In an interview in the *Irish Times* (15 January 1998) he stated: 'I have seen over 3,000 plays. Of that there has been some 15 magical evenings, maybe 60 really good nights and a lot of stuff that left me cold'. One might ask what theatres he is attending so that they can be avoided but, to be serious, the fifteen magical evenings would probably have made up for the rest. Murphy has immense respect for the actor, and points to the hardship attached to the trade. 'Even a busy actor working here [in Ireland] is lucky to make say £10,000 a year'. Indeed his sympathy for the many unemployed actors could well be extended to aspirant writers. In general, there appears to be a strong case to re-direct arts funding back towards the creators also. If all of these arguments and reasons fall on deaf ears, maybe the views of an educationalist might be considered as being of greater import. According to Paddy Walley (1993), creativity is said to be the principal ingredient for our long-term economic prosperity. Creativity needs to become the core of our culture and not seen as an aberration or a fringe activity:

A central aspect of creativity lies in the ability to make fresh perceptions and produce new ideas. This requires that one steps outside one's accustomed and inherited ways of viewing the world. The nature of the human process of perceiving and thinking is such that we do not perceive reality directly, but filter it through the traditional assumptions learned in our upbringing and culture. Creating new ways of seeing the world involves stepping outside this conditioned prison of perception, outside of the basic assumptions underlying our thinking; this process is helped by becoming aware of the assumptions we make about the way life should be which we normally take for granted ... Our future wealth will be intimately linked with our ability to co-operate in organisations in the creative process of inventing and selling new products and services.

So for no other reason than our economic prosperity, the arts, and especially the performing arts, may be considered intrinsically important.

Bibliography

Arts Council 1994 *The arts plan: 1995–1997*. Dublin.

Arts Council 1995 *Views of theatre in Ireland*. Dublin.

Arts Council 1999 *Dialogues*. Dublin.

Bell, S. H. 1972 *The theatre in Ulster*. Dublin.

Bjorkegren, D. 1996 *The culture business: management strategies for the arts-related business*. London and New York.

Fitzgibbon, M. 1997 'Speaking for themselves part two: interview with Patrick Mason' in M. Fitzgibbon and A. Kelly (eds) *From maestro to manager: critical issues in arts and culture management* (Dublin), pp. 52–66.

Foster, R. 1988 *Modern Ireland: 1600–1988*. Harmondsworth.

Gans, H. J. 1974 *Popular culture and high culture: an early analysis and evaluation of taste*. New York.

Gregory, Augusta Lady 1913 *Our Irish theatre: a chapter of autobiography*. London.

Hunt, H. 1979 *The Abbey: Ireland's national theatre 1904–1979*. Dublin.

Hynes, J. *ca.* 1985 *Druid: the first ten years*. Galway.

Owens, C. D. and Radner, J. N. 1990 *Irish drama 1900–1980*. Washington, D.C.

Walley, P. 1993 *A brief guide to the knowledge society*. Galway.

The Visual Arts in Ireland

PETER MURRAY

Apart from the dire and unfortunately accurate prognostications of Irish scribes and illuminators during the Viking raids, there has been at almost every stage in the history of the visual arts in Ireland a compulsion to affirm that never before has talent been so much in evidence, never before the arts so vibrant and never their progress so irresistible. In these points, the rhetoric of cultural promoters of the late twentieth century differed little from the optimistic prose of the great art and industry exhibitions of the 1850s, or indeed the high-minded pronouncements of the Palladians of the previous century, save perhaps that in recent times a more sincere attempt has been made to base rhetoric on statistics and audience research. Putting aside the vauntings and puffs of the past, much credence has been attached to the notion of a recent renaissance in the visual arts in Ireland, the physical evidence for which, in the form of publicly funded exhibitions, studios, galleries and museums, is undeniable. Also undeniable is the steady increase in the willingness of the state to support individual Irish visual artists financially. However, somewhat less attention has been paid to how these artists and institutions (much of the capital funding for which was provided by European tax payers) may fare in the future. Their basis of popular support, their anticipated income from cultural activities — these issues are defined more by optimistic predictions than by hard facts. The considerable achievements of previous centuries being largely overlooked for political reasons, for many years Ireland projected the self-image of a country deficient in the visual arts, with emphasis being placed upon the country's rich music and literary traditions. But with increasing awareness among historians of the usefulness of visual resources, and a new appreciation of the value of art and architecture art in society, much is emerging to contest the generally held notion that it is·only of late that the visual arts in Ireland have been so popular, or interest in them so widespread.

In spite of recent progress, the visual arts here may still make some claim to be undervalued when compared with literature or music. The international success of contemporary Irish singers, song-writers and musicians is well known and does not need elaborating. Similarly, the popular storytelling tradition, such an important part of rural society in Ireland through the years, has also contributed to the emergence of generations of Irish writers whose works are translated and read by millions world-wide. There may well be a sound basis for this success as regards the relative quality of these arts in Ireland but, in political terms, popular music and literature have an instant democratic appeal, so perhaps this emphasis is inevitable. Access to and participation in the visual arts are seen as more difficult issues, and charges of elitism are not uncommon. However, the recent provision of subsidised artists' studios in many cities, the upgrading and expansion of art galleries and museums, the development of a network of commercial galleries and the publication of a range of academic and popular texts have begun to change this perception, bringing the visual arts to a wider audience in Ireland and abroad. Along with the development of public holdings and institutions, private galleries and art collections are increasingly a factor in the visual arts. The burgeoning Irish art market and current commercial interest nonetheless reflect in many cases a somewhat narrow understanding of the evolution of the visual arts in Ireland over the centuries. In spite of widespread current interest in 'Irish' art, it can be argued that there are many more points of connection and comparison than there are points of difference between the art of Ireland and that of Europe and the United States, particularly over the past four hundred years. A correct classification of Irish painters during this period might far more convincingly associate them, not with preceding and succeeding Irish artists, but with their contemporaries and counterparts in other European countries, particularly England, the Netherlands, France and Italy.

The paucity of material evidence in the form of paintings, sculptures and other artworks acts as a brake on the building of any coherent argument. Works by nineteenth- and twentieth-century Irish artists not in private collections or churches are for the most part housed in public museums, principally, in Dublin, at the National Gallery of Ireland, the Hugh Lane Municipal Gallery and the Irish Museum of Modern Art; in Cork at the Crawford Municipal Art Gallery and in Limerick at the City Art Gallery and the University of Limerick. Apart from these major collections, there are municipal collections in several other cities, notably Kilkenny, Sligo, Drogheda and Waterford. The Ulster Museum in Belfast has important holdings of Irish art, mainly nineteenth- and twentieth-century. Tellingly, one of the most important collections of twentieth-century Irish art has been formed not by an organization funded by the Irish state but by one of its leading financial institutions, Allied Irish Bank. This corporate collection presents a broad range of paintings and sculptures, but there is little which can be described as challenging. The Office of Public Works has a good collection of contemporary Irish art, as has the Arts Council, but in both cases these collections are widely dispersed and are shown in a variety of public buildings such as hospitals and libraries. Outside the state and Northern Ireland there is a very sparse representation of Irish art in public collections in Europe or America. Works by James Barry, William Mulready, Daniel Maclise, John Lavery and William Orpen can be found in museums and galleries in Britain, but, as these artists were essentially *émigrés* living in London, this is not surprising. Jack B. Yeats is the only Irish resident artist to have achieved significant representation internationally. In more recent times, Francis Bacon and Sean Scully, both born and raised in Ireland, are represented in many fine museums overseas, but both left Ireland in their teens and pursued their careers in Britain or America.

Within Ireland, collections of Irish art are few enough and contain many gaps. There is, for instance, no major work by Francis Bacon in any public holding in the Republic of Ireland (although his studio has recently been acquired by the Hugh Lane Gallery, and is to be 're-created' in Dublin). The National Gallery concentrates almost exclusively on works of art created between 1600 and 1950 and the great strength of its collection is in Dutch and Italian paintings, while the new Irish Museum of Modern Art is hampered in building up a representative collection of Irish material by limited funds and an acquisitions policy that is world-wide. Because of this patchy representation in public collections, the history of the visual arts in twentieth-century Ireland, a somewhat insular saga of competition between progressive art groups and a reactionary academy, is for

many people a forgotten one. The passion for the Modern that led to the establishment of the Society of Dublin Painters in 1920, the White Stag Group in the 1930s and the Irish Exhibition of Living Art in 1943, is recorded, for the most part, only in textbooks and journals of art history. Yet the story is an interesting one.

The following chapter sets out to look at the ways in which the current renaissance of the visual arts has both fulfilled and betrayed the promises of earlier generations. It examines the use of the visual arts to underpin the developing concept of Ireland as a self-sufficient political entity in the late nineteenth and early twentieth centuries, and it provides an overview of the institutions that have served both the Republic of Ireland and also the arts in Northern Ireland through the course of the twentieth century. Perhaps most importantly, the essay focuses on the work on individual artists, providing, through their biographies and a brief analysis of their output, an insight into their expectations and achievements.

ART, POLITICS AND PROGRESS IN EARLY TWENTIETH-CENTURY IRELAND

The pre-historic and monastic periods of Ireland's visual arts have been well known for many years. In the eighteenth century Francis Grose, Gabriel Beranger (fl. 1765–72) and other antiquarian watercolourists began the process of identifying and depicting antiquities in Ireland. Beranger's *The Cromlech at Kilternan* is one of a number such watercolours preserved in the Royal Irish Academy in Dublin. Throughout the nineteenth century, fine gold jewellery from the Neolithic era, illuminated manuscripts such as the Book of Kells, enamelled reliquaries and other artifacts were acquired by the Academy and Trinity College, Dublin. The excavation and study — frequently by amateur archaeologists — of Neolithic, Bronze Age and Early Christian sites led to a reappraisal of the quality of art in ancient Ireland. The founding of an antiquities museum at the Academy in the mid-nineteenth century consolidated this reappraisal. The accepted wisdom of the time, that the country had had a very impoverished cultural life and economy prior to the English colonization of the sixteenth and seventeenth centuries, was thus effectively eroded. The antiquities and works of art collected by the Academy throughout the nineteenth century now form the basis of the National Museum of Ireland's collection, which has since grown considerably. These works have been reproduced and published widely, providing both metaphor and symbol in the creation of a visual and a political identity for Ireland over the past one hundred years.

In the mid-to late nineteenth century, amid growing excitement at the high quality of ancient Irish artworks being collected in museums and libraries around the

THE VISUAL ARTS IN IRELAND

country, a new sense of national identity was forged for an emerging affluent middle class, as indeed was also being done in Scotland, England and many other European countries at the time. The visual arts became associated in many cases with the quest for political independence, and images which reinforced the creation of a national self-awareness were highly popular. The visual arts in late nineteenth-century Ireland became politicized, with interlace motifs from thousand-year-old Celtic manuscripts reappearing in a variety of forms, on book-bindings, stained-glass windows, furniture and jewellery. However, artists who chose to celebrate the cultural achievements of Celtic and Early Christian Ireland were entering a contentious area. The artist and antiquarian George Petrie, whose Romantic watercolour paintings often depicted Irish monasteries, high crosses and holy wells, was accused of being hostile to the Tory government of the day. More adroitly, the artist Daniel Maclise, again conscious of the symbolic importance of these motifs, attempted to create works which re-inforced the political status quo. *The Marriage of Strongbow and Eva*, a gigantic painting dating from the middle of the nineteenth century, is an interesting example of an image that, while recognizing the strength of nationalist feeling, also sought to validate the political union of Britain and Ireland. An Anglo-Norman soldier of fortune who was invited over from Wales in 1170 to assist Dermot MacMurrough's bid for political supremacy in Ireland, Strongbow is shown standing on a fallen high cross, symbolizing the defeat of Celtic, or Gaelic, Ireland.

Painters in Ireland in the nineteenth century who concentrated on landscapes rather than historical repre-sentations were very often drawn, consciously or uncon-sciously, to depict the ruined monasteries and castles which dotted the landscape and which provided a reminder of the fall of the Irish Celtic civilization. The fact that many of these religious establishments were of continental inspiration and quite distant from Irish Celtic culture was neither here nor there. The landscape, never a neutral ground, became in Ireland synonymous with the quest of a newly affluent Catholic middle class for the restitution of political power in the country. Following European and American precedents, attempts were made, some convincing, others verging on the absurd, to embody the spirit of the resurgent Irish nation through images of heroic warriors and noble women. The most successful of these was probably John Lavery's portrait of his wife Hazel, painted in the 1920s, which was incorporated into the design of the banknotes of the newly constituted Irish Free State. Allied to this were the efforts of sculptors such as Oliver Sheppard, whose late nineteenth-century public works cast in a heroic mould figures from Irish history. Shepherd's figure of a 1798 rebel pikeman, versions of which can be found in

Wexford and Enniscorthy, can be directly compared in style and content to Henry Kitson's bronze *Minuteman* in Lexington, Massachusetts. Similarly, the Aran Island paintings of Seán Keating, Charles Lamb and Maurice MacGonigal, in attempting to provide a visual corollary to de Valera's concept of an enduring Gaelic nation which derived its values and mores from rural west of Ireland communities, closely echo the American distinction between an east coast corrupted by European influences and the moral innocence of the untamed west.

One of the hazards of linking art closely to the political idealism of an era is that it dates quickly. So it is in Ireland, where the figure paintings of Keating today appear staged and theatrical. Keating's paintings are nowadays nowhere near as highly regarded as the works of Jack B. Yeats who, like his brother, the poet William Butler Yeats, took extraordinary care to avoid overt refer-ences to current political issues in his work, but instead allowed a highly developed poetic imagination to define his creativity and perhaps even to veil his political beliefs. Early woodcuts by Jack B. Yeats published around the turn of the century in the *Manchester Guardian* show a direct sympathy with the Irish peasant, forced to emigrate to England or take steerage passage to America. His later paintings, however, have moved away from reality and seem almost dreamlike, often depicting scenes drawn from memories of his childhood stays in county Sligo. Both Yeats brothers had a horror of poverty, genteel or otherwise, and were no strangers to the scramble for material success. In Ireland, the inter-connection between the visual arts and politics has always been a complex one. As with Yeats, the work of the other great Irish painters of the twentieth century, William Orpen, Louis le Brocquy, William Leech and William Scott, are practically devoid of any overt political commentary. A factor that may be relevant to this conscious avoidance of politics is that these artists were by and large born and educated into a class which, in spite of its progressive, artistic and liberal posturings, was facing potential annihilation in the revolutionary ferment of Irish public affairs. As with the men, so with the women. Most Irish women artists of the early twentieth century, such as Mainie Jellett, Mary Swanzy, Hilda Roberts, the Hamilton sisters and Evie Hone, came from relatively privileged backgrounds. They epitomized the choice of art as a recreation or leisure activity rather than a career move. Certainly, the male artists of the early 1900s, Orpen, Yeats, Lavery, Touhy, Keating and MacGonigal, had more professional opportunities, but either their own conservatism or the conservatism of their clientele held them back from moving forward from that nineteenth-century academic realism which continued to dominate the visual arts in Ireland up to the 1970s.

The contemporary understanding of Ireland allows for a far more complex picture of cultural interdependencies than was the case when Keating was painting his views of heroic islanders and fishermen. Similarly, while scant regard is paid by contemporary Irish artists to the Celtic past, the most convincing interpretations of interlace patterns are provided by the American veteran of Abstract Expressionism, Ellsworth Kelly. Art historian Barbara Novak has also suggested that the simultaneously heroic, aggrandising and self-destructive tendencies which mark the career and work of Jackson Pollock may well be rooted in his Irish Celtic ancestry. However, this is to anticipate.

Until the mid-century, the teaching and exhibition axis of the National College of Art and the Royal Hibernian Academy, with its emphasis on academic realism, had dominated the artistic establishment in Ireland. The hegemony of the Academy had been regularly challenged, but never seriously damaged, until the founding by the government of the Arts Council in 1951 legitimized and supported the more avant-garde and Modernist artists who were gradually ousting the academicians from their exalted position as the 'official' artists of the state.

Academic realism had a long and distinguished history in twentieth-century Ireland, and in many ways the image of the people and landscape of the Irish Free State was formed both for a national and an international audience through the paintings of academicians who followed in the footsteps of William Orpen. Although Orpen pursued his extremely successful career as a society portrait painter in London, he regularly visited his native Dublin where he retained a professorship at the Metropolitan School of Art. In the early years of the century, a generation of Irish students studied under Orpen — Seán Keating, Patrick Tuohy, Leo Whelan and others — and their paintings of people and landscapes became the popular and accessible images which, for many, defined the route that Irish art should take, regardless of the new styles and fashions of the Modern movement. Their students continued this tradition. Maurice MacGonigal, who attended the Metropolitan School in 1923, was not tutored by Orpen personally but by Touhy and Keating. However, through his thirty-five years teaching at that same school (re-named the National College of Art), MacGonigal continued Orpen's traditional approach, an approach based on the atelier system and maintaining at its core the primacy of the life-drawing class. It was this style, which can be referred to as 'Academic Realism', which came to be adopted as the 'official' artistic style of the new Irish Free State, a relationship which ultimately helped neither the state nor the artists it professed pride in supporting. The paradox of course was that the immediate source of this style — adopted by a country which had just broken centuries of political connection with Britain — was one of the most prominent British art schools, the Slade School of Art in London.

Ultimately, it was increasing student agitation and resistance to these academic teaching methods which forced Maurice MacGonigal's resignation in 1969 and should also have signalled the end of the dominance of the academic tradition which he had inherited from Orpen. But such was not the case — the opportunities presented to that radical student generation of the late 1960s were never fully exploited. Neither were the rifts exposed ever properly addressed, and so an uneasy relationship between progressive and conservative traditions in art education still lingers. The National College of Art and Design has largely outgrown these divisions, facilitated by the move from Kildare Street, Dublin, to new premises in Thomas Street.

The image of 1950s' Ireland as a dark era, with economic deprivation, state censorship and a conservative audience for the arts, is certainly true, but this characterization is somewhat belied by the steady progress made in a number of areas in the visual arts. The Irish Exhibition of Living Art, founded in 1943, in response to the conservative policies of the Royal Hibernian Academy, held annual exhibitions and promoted the work of more progressive artists. Those artists who had come to maturity in the difficult but electrifying years of the founding of the Irish Free State — Keating and MacGonigal, also Mary Swanzy, Evie Hone, Charles Lamb, Paul Henry, Harry Kernoff — were still working, but in most cases they had established their styles in the 1920s and since then had been content, for the most part, to settle into a pattern of producing paintings that broke little in the way of new ground. The social and political instability of the early 1920s had acted as a stimulus to the production of art, but in the 1930s there was a growing sense of disillusionment among artists about the role they were being asked to play in the creative life of the country. By 1950 much of the youthful energy of this generation had been dissipated, and artists such as Paul Henry, Keating and MacGonigal, although still working steadily, were no longer producing their best work.

Seán Keating was professor of painting at the National College of Art from 1934 through to the 1960s. During that period, his trenchant opposition to Modernism and other recent art movements grew steadily, to such an extent that it hindered the development of the contemporary visual arts in Ireland and, ultimately, encouraged much that was second-rate, simply because it followed academic precepts. His intolerance was all the more unfortunate as he had displayed, in a giant mural painting commissioned by architect Michael Scott for the Irish Pavilion at the 1939 New York World's Fair, a zest for the modern world and a strong sense of design and abstract composition that were in no way retrogressive. However, the public, on both sides of the Atlantic, seemed to prefer Keating's traditionalist approach. His *The Race of the Gael*, a prizewinner at an exhibition organized by IBM in New York also in 1939, showing a group of Irishmen in profile, has something of the feeling of a Norman Rockwell set piece. Maurice MacGonigal trod a more ambiguous path, occasionally experimenting with Modernist styles, adventures that were not welcomed by his admirers or his colleagues at the Academy.

Whatever about the rivalries which existed between the (mainly) male academic painters, much of the vitality in Irish art between the wars was provided by a group of talented women artists who dominated the annual exhibitions of the Society of Dublin Painters. The Dublin Painters, founded in 1920 by Paul Henry and the ardent Cubist painter Mainie Jellett, had exhibited the work of moderately progressive artists such as Hilda Roberts, Lilian Davidson, Stella Frost, Joan Jameson, Brigid Ganly and Beatrice Glenavy. In many cases these women had either independent means or were married to prominent men. Jellett came from a wealthy Dublin medical family; Glenavy's husband was a director of the Bank of Ireland; Joan Jameson's a director of the family distillery; Roberts' the headmaster of Newtown School. Under such circumstances, the artistic careers of these women were

Fig. 25.2 Mainie Jellet's Composition, ca. *1935.*

inevitably hampered by social constraints, and, while they were resolute in their commitment to painting, the fact that they were not dependent on sales to support themselves had a defining influence on their self-esteem as artists. Mary Swanzy remarked, with some justification, that if her name had been Henry she would have been taken far more seriously as an artist in Ireland, for the academic realists of the Royal Hibernian Academy, over which MacGonigal and Sleator presided, regarded themselves as 'professional' artists and greeted the experimental progressive art styles of the Dublin Painters, in general, with derision. Sleator himself had been a founder-member of the Dublin Painters, but had only shown once and then withdrew after the first exhibition, presumably because of the non-academic approach of most of the members. Swanzy's description of her childhood environment, growing up in a house on one of the finest Georgian squares in Dublin, is revealing: 'It was a wonderful education to live where everything was in proportion: the size of the squares related to the width of the streets and the height of the houses even to the balustrades and the doors, a world of art. You learned about structure from it' (Robinson 1988, 26).

The era of the independently wealthy woman artist drew to a close with the Second World War, when the

Fig. 25.1 Seán Keating's Economic Pressure, *1936.*

funds that had sustained the affluence of Edwardian upper-middle class life in Ireland began to peter out. In the 1950s, when women such as Camille Souter and Nano Reid opted to become full-time painters, they were more often obliged to rely for a meagre income on the sale of their work. The early death of the proselytising Mainie Jellett, whose lantern slide talks to the Irish Countrywomen's Association on the virtues of Synthetic Cubism had been influential in changing public opinion, was a blow to those who wished to promote Modern Art in Ireland. Her friend and companion, Evie Hone, who had also studied with Andre Lhote and Albert Gleizes, lived until 1955 but was less influential.

The second generation of progressive artists that had emerged in the 1930s — painters such as Anne Yeats, Fr Jack Hanlon, Ralph Cusack and Patrick Hennessy — were far less influential, and merged quickly with the artists of the 1920s. Intimidated by the powerful social and political changes which swept Europe in the 1930s, the Irish government had pursued an increasingly isolationist and xenophobic policy, culminating in the country's neutrality in the Second World War, a period known as 'The Emergency'. This policy had a silent, insidious and ultimately damaging effect on the country's cultural and artistic life, the years after the war being something of a doldrum period. There were some unexpected benefits, however. Sales at the Irish Exhibition of Living Art in 1943 were brisk; during the war people had little opportunity to spend money on imported luxury goods. Fleeing the Blitz in London, a group of progressive British and European artists who called themselves the White Stag Group formed an expatriate community in the safe haven of Ireland. Nonetheless, in spite of several exhibitions held in Dublin during the war years, their presence does not seem to have had a lasting effect, apart from launching the career of just one progressive Irish artist, Patrick Scott.

Scott had worked for fifteen years as an assistant to architect Michael Scott (no relation), before deciding to become a full-time painter in 1960. His influence on and presence in the visual arts in Ireland should have been considerable in the following decades but, as Brian O'Doherty has pointed out, because of the hegemony enjoyed by MacGonigal and Keating at the National College of Art, Scott was never invited to teach and so has remained a respected but somewhat isolated figure in the contemporary Irish art world (O'Doherty 1971, 10–11). Scott's works, large tapestries with abstract designs — very influenced by Japanese art — are displayed in several universities and banks throughout Ireland. His work as a designer in a wider sense — the orange, black and white livery of Irish trains, for instance — has also had a considerable impact in shaping artistic consciousness in Ireland in recent decades.

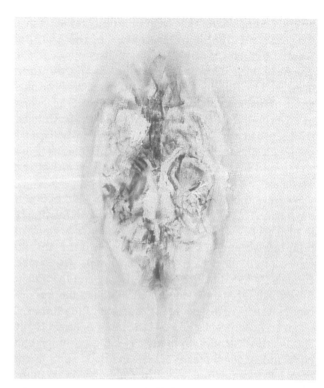

Fig. 25.3 Louis le Brocquy's Image of James Joyce, *1994.*

The inspiration of the White Stag exhibitions led to the establishment of the Irish Exhibition of Living Art in 1943 by Louis le Brocquy, Norah McGuinness, Mainie Jellett and Jack Hanlon. The rejection of le Brocquy's painting *Spanish Shawl* by the selectors of the annual RHA exhibition in 1942 shocked even supporters of the Academy and led to a controversy about its continuing hostility to new forms of art. The Exhibition of Living Art, with its Fauvist-inspired paintings by Norah McGuinness, the Cubist paintings of Doreen Vanston and Mainie Jellett and works in a variety of progressive styles by Ralph Cusack, Nano Reid, Patrick Scott and Gerard Dillon, demonstrated that there were many artists working in Ireland outside the academic realist tradition (Kennedy 1991, 115–46). In 1972, Norah McGuinness, who had been chairperson of the Exhibition of Living Art since the 1940s, dissolved the original organizing committee and a new committee took over. However, things had changed in the intervening years, and with the growth in support for contemporary art practice, both in the art colleges and in the Arts Council, the reasons for the existence of the Living Art Exhibition had were simply disappearing.

In November 1950, the Irish government debated a new *Arts Bill*, which passed into law in 1951 and provided for the establishment of an Arts Council, to dispense government funds to the arts. The first Arts Council was appointed in 1951 and while it predictably enough included the directors of several institutions, such as Thomas MacGreevy of the National Gallery, also, and more interestingly, it numbered Muriel Gahan, founder of the Irish Countrywomen's Association and the Country Shop, on Stephen's Green. While Dublin's famous pubs such as McDaids and the Palace Bar had long served Ireland's writers well, it was in the back room of the Country Shop, furnished by Gahan with chairs by Alvar Aalto and Cubist paintings by Mainie Jellett, that discussions on new movements in the visual arts took place between Louis le Brocquy, Patrick Scott and other avant-garde artists (as indicated in conversation with Patrick Scott in January 1998).

The establishment of the Arts Council came paradoxically at the beginning of one of the most depressed decades of twentieth-century Ireland. For many artists there seemed little point in remaining in the country. In 1946, the Advisory Committee of the Hugh Lane Municipal Gallery in Dublin, of which Seán Keating was a member, had rejected as blasphemous a George Rouault painting, *Christ and the Soldiers*, offered as a gift by the Friends of the National Collections. Louis le Brocquy wrote a letter of protest to the *Irish Times* and shortly afterwards left Dublin for London, beginning years of peripatetic existence which led to London with many visits to the European mainland and finally, in 1960, to a house in Carros in the Alps Maritimes, which has remained his principal home until recently (le Brocquy 1996, 10).

In spite of having quit his native shore, Louis le Brocquy continued to exhibit in Dublin — unlike Ralph Cusack, a co-founder with le Brocquy of the Irish Exhibition of Living Art who, suffering from that mix of arrogance and self-loathing which seems to have reached a peak among Irish artists and writers during these years, emigrated with his family to France in 1954, vowing never to set foot in Ireland again. Le Brocquy and Cusack left behind their friends and family, a closed society, mainly Protestant, in which devotion to European culture had become almost a fetish: gramophone evenings — and even concerts — before private audiences; discussions on art, accompanied by tea and scones, in the back room of the Country Shop on Stephen's Green; the works of Schopenhauer and Kierkegaard held as talismen against the scholastic Jesuits (Plunkett 1997). It was a world too in which there was a significant contribution by Irish artists of Jewish faith or background. Harry Kernoff's animated cityscapes and portraits, the strange surreal tableau paintings of Beatrice Glenavy, prints by Stella Stein (one of the few Irish artists to have studied at the Bauhaus) and talented portraits and landscapes by Estella Solomons who, like Jellett and Swanzy, had come from a leading Dublin medical family.

Le Brocquy and Cusack both ultimately settled in France, as did Michael Farrell over a decade later. Patrick Swift, one of the most interesting Irish *émigré* painters of the period, settled in Portugal. Swift, born in 1928, gave up his job in the Dublin Gas Company to become a full-time painter in the late 1940s (Ryan 1971, 100). Moving to London, he settled easily into the artistic and bohemian life of Soho, where he was friendly with Lucien Freud and Francis Bacon, and edited an influential literary magazine called *X*. He then moved to Portugal in the early sixties where he played an important role in the revival of the traditional pottery industry of the Algarve. A retrospective exhibition held at the Irish Museum of Modern Art in 1995 revealed him to have been a painter of consistent strength and vision.

Fewer artists, surprisingly, chose to emigrate to America. In 1957, with the aid of a Fulbright Scholarship, a young medical student and painter from Roscommon, Brian O'Doherty, moved to the United States, where he quickly began to make a name for himself as a progressive artist and art critic. Along with Sol le Witt and Joseph Kosuth, O'Doherty (who changed his name to Patrick Ireland in 1969) was one of the pioneers of the Conceptual art movement in New York in the 1960s. His friendship with Edward Hopper, Marcel Duchamp and other leading artists influenced his own development, while the enthusiasm evident in his writings on Hopper, Pollock, de Kooning, Rothko and Rauschenberg was undoubtedly driven by memories of the rather insular art scene in the Dublin he had left behind. Commenting on the efforts of the Society of Dublin Painters and the Irish Exhibition of Living Art, O'Doherty wrote:

All this took place outside the official Dublin art world, represented by the pleasant body of men who make up the Royal Hibernian Academy. The Academy controlled ... the National College of Art, where the teaching was, and is, splendidly irrelevant to its students' needs. The floating complex of dealers (Waddington was joined by the Dawson Gallery in 1944 and by the Hendriks Gallery in 1956), artists and collectors thus had no access to the institutions. This explains the peculiar lack of influence by many of the best artists, such as Patrick Scott — they never got the opportunity to teach. One would have expected Jellett's demanding ideas to affect some of the younger artists, but the only painter who shared her tough-mindedness was Thurloe Connolly. His loss — he abandoned painting for design and went to live in England — further testifies to the lack of response to anti-romantic ideas in Irish art. Jellett's failure to give Irish art a firm cubist underpinning (apart from the work of Nano Reid) is easily understood. A suggestive form of painting with a particular atmospheric complexion, a product of the interaction of the artists and the audience created by and for their art in the forties and fifties, gathered force. Owing to the war, something 'local' in the best sense had the opportunity to develop. To call it a national quality could be an exaggeration, though all the paradoxes and misunderstanding of that idea were in operation. (O'Doherty 1971, 10–11)

The painters O'Doherty was referring to in this revealing text, written in 1971 — Patrick Collins, Nano Reid (Ruane 1986, 46), and Camille Souter — had each evolved an art that was in no way 'International' but which also avoided clearly the cul-de-sac of academic realism. A student of Keating at the Metropolitan School of Art in the same years as Maurice MacGonigal, Nano Reid's paintings — for the most part quasi-abstract landscapes and interiors with figures, loosely painted in tones of browns and greens — have nowadays become emblematic of that somewhat dismal era in Irish life. The recurring motifs of glasses, bottles on tables, dark pub interiors, rain-sodden landscapes and tinkers are presented in her work with a sense of humour and lack of pretentiousness that is honest and appealing (Hutchinson 1971, 90).

Patrick Collins made the decision to become a full-time painter in the 1940s, after working for twenty-two years in an insurance company. Apart from some part-time classes at the National College of Art, he was largely self-taught. In some ways Collins was the inheritor of the tradition of Jack Yeats — both artists also hailed from county Sligo. However, the literary and autobiographical strains which recur frequently in the works of Yeats remain muted in Collins' soft and evanescent landscapes, which hover on the fringes of figuration.

Although born in England, Camille Souter grew up in Ireland. She embarked initially on a nursing career (as had Nano Reid), but contracted tuberculosis and returned from Guy's Hospital to Ireland in the early 1950s. Inspired by paintings of Pierre Bonnard she had seen in London in 1947, Souter decided to become a full-time painter. Showing great tenacity and single-mindedness, and in the face of many difficulties, she worked steadily at developing a lyrical and painterly style. There is an inverted hierarchy of quality in Souter's subject-matter; she is more at home portraying a discarded and rusting bed in a ditch than the interior of a neat bedroom. The power station chimney that would have appalled the aesthetic sensibilities of most Irish landscape painters is celebrated in Souter's work (Dukes 1997, 159–68).

In many ways, Souter's career and style of painting can be compared to that of Kilkenny artist Tony O'Malley, forced also by tuberculosis to quit his job as a bank clerk, and electing as well to become a full-time painter. His early paintings, generally on panel, became increasingly abstract as he came into contact with the work of Ben Nicholson, Peter Lanyon, Alfred Wallis and other artists in Cornwall in the 1950s. These early works are often sombre and dark. In more recent years, O'Malley has combined these formative elements with a lyrical abstract quality in which colour, tone, shape and form are laid, incised and scratched into the surface of the panels on which he almost invariably works, with a sure and elegant sense of balance and harmony.

The Exhibition of Living Art after a number of years came to be dominated by a group of northern painters which included George Campbell, Gerard Dillon, Nevill Johnson and Daniel O'Neill. Born in Belfast, Dillon left school in 1930 at the age of fourteen. His keen interest in art led to his becoming a full-time artist, but from time to time, in order to earn a living, he returned to his trade as a house painter. During the war years he worked in Belfast, where he was friends with Johnson and O'Neill (who gave up working as a shipyard electrician to become an artist), and also in Dublin, where he showed with the White Stag Group and with the Irish Exhibition of Living Art. Dillon's *Self-Contained Flat*, painted around 1955, is a complex work inspired by Gauguin and Van Gogh, and contains clues also to the artist's troubled sexuality. From the beginning of his career Dillon portrayed aspects of life in Connemara and the Aran Islands. Like Keating and Charles Lamb, he was interested as much in the life of the people of the west of Ireland as in the landscape. One of the most outstanding painters in the next generation of northern artists is Basil Blackshaw. Born in Belfast in 1932 and trained in the art college of that city, Blackshaw travelled rarely, preferring to paint local landscapes of county Down, horses and other animals and the occasional portrait. What comes through most strongly in his work is an honesty and lack of pretension, qualities he shares with Patrick Collins and Souter. Like these artists, Blackshaw's work shows the influence of the Irish countryside and climate (Hunter 1971, 40). A painter of very considerable talent who in recent years has moved to Ireland and established a studio in Kilkenny is Hughie O'Donoghue. O'Donoghue's international reputation as a painter is formidable and his renown within Ireland was quickly established with the exhibition at the RHA gallery, in 1999, of a series of paintings which had been commissioned by a private collector and which were subsequently presented to the Irish state.

Another accomplished painter whose influence, particularly in the Kilkenny and Sligo areas, is evident among younger artists, is Barrie Cooke. Although born in Cheshire, Cooke's parents shortly afterwards emigrated from England and most of his childhood was spent in the United States, Jamaica and Bermuda. An early enthusiasm for marine biology led Cooke to Harvard University, but shortly after enrolling he switched to art history. He later studied art at Skowhegan in Maine before deciding to settle in Ireland, in 1954, in a small cottage at the edge of the Burren in county Clare. Over the past thirty years or so, Cooke has immersed himself in the landscapes of Ireland, particularly in counties Clare, Kilkenny and more recently Sligo. From the days of his childhood, Cooke has been a keen naturalist, his art taking inspiration from Heraclitus, 'All existence flows in the stream of creation and passing away'. Living in an island swept by rain-clouds and traversed by rivers, the artist has focussed this philosophical meditation on Irish landscapes and wildlife, elements which are an important part of Irish legend and mythology.

Cooke's interest in the Irish countryside is reflected in his paintings — not the countryside of sedate farms and ploughed fields, but the wilder and more remote areas where streams, lakes and mountains retain a primordial atmosphere. He is also inspired by Irish myths, his painting *Dawn/Dusk — Sweeney Affrighted by the Stag* (Collection, University College, Cork) juxtaposes a stag's antlers silhouetted at the top left of the painting with the crouching figure of Sweeney at the bottom right corner. Sweeney, a curious figure from ancient Irish mythic history, was a man who came to believe that he was a bird and thereafter led a harried and quixotic life, attempting to nest in trees and meeting with various adventures on his travels through the countryside. A powerful metaphor for the life of the artist, Sweeney has been a fertile source of inspiration for several other Irish painters and writers, including Brian Bourke, Alicia Boyle, Flann O'Brien, John Montague and Seamus Heaney. It was Heaney's translations of the story of Sweeney, published in the early 1980s, that directly inspired Cooke to paint both this series and also produce a limited edition series of monotypes (published in 1983 by Farar, Strauss and Giroux, New York). Cooke's figure of Sweeney is in no way heroic and represents the hapless bird-man being terrified by a belling stag on a hillside. The forces of nature are suggested by the artist's use of liquid flowing colours, both staining and running across the surface of the canvas.

Cooke's presence in Kilkenny, along with that of artists such as George Vaughan, director of the Grennan Mill Craft School, ensured that the Butler Gallery in Kilkenny maintained an exceptional exhibition programme through the 1990s. The annual Victor Richardson award exhibition at the Butler Gallery has acknowledged and rewarded some of the most promising younger artists in Ireland in that same period.

DISTANCING THE PAST

The tradition of lyrical, textured, quasi-abstract painting established by artists such as Barrie Cooke and Tony O'Malley has been carried on in recent years by a younger generation of Irish artists including Cecily Brennan, Eithne Jordan, Robert Armstrong, Michael Mulcahy, Gwen O'Dowd, Janet Pierce and Seán Fingleton. It is a style which has wide regional distribution, with practitioners pursuing their careers in different parts of the country, among them Elizabeth Cope in Kilkenny, Seán McSweeney in Sligo, Tim Goulding in west Cork and Jill Dennis and Billy Foley in Cork.

However, any attempt to establish a coherent 'school'

of these artists is confounded by their individuality and concern for personal authorship. Their work is characterized by an interest in colour, mark-making and an expressionism which ranges from the gentle to the fervid. A parallel expressionist vein, based largely on the human figure, can be followed through the work of Paul Funge, Brian Bourke, Michael Kane, Brian Maguire, Patrick Hall and Patrick Graham. Sexuality, trauma and disfunctional relationships are evident in the output of these male artists. Contemporary Irish women artists tend to approach the same issues in a more oblique way. Alice Maher, Colette Nolan, Briged Flannery and Louise Walsh have addressed questions of sexuality and the role of women in society, but the direct male anger evident in the work of Graham, Kane and Maguire tends to be subliminated within a more aesthetic and exploratory consciousness. This suggests that censorship may be still very much a living, albeit unacknowledged, force in Irish visual art.

While landscape and figurative painters were to dominate the artistic life of the country through the decade of the 1950s, they were somewhat overshadowed by the arrival in the 1960s of an internationalism which made great claims to be the true art of its day. In general, one must admit, there were few enough Irish artists who consciously set out to adopt the 'international' look. Common sense dictated that, with few gigantic lobbies or skyscrapers requiring a clean, hard-edged art on a large scale, such art was unlikely to be produced. But when a number of modernist office blocks, banks and new university buildings did come to be constructed in the late 1960s and early 1970s (many of the best designed by architects Scott Tallon Walker), there was an immediate response from painters. These buildings were fitted out with art of a type and scale that accorded well with their impressive Modernist surroundings, by artists such as Brian Henderson, Michael Farrell, Patrick Scott and Eric Van Der Grijn, whose large, abstract, hard-edge paintings were partly inspired by the vivid yellow and black diagonals of road signs. Scott, whose early training as an architect is clearly evident in his carefully constructed canvases, won a considerable number of commissions for the new bank and university buildings which were springing up all over Dublin. In retrospect, some of the creative potential in his work was restricted by his strong sense of design, the elegance consequent on his use of raw linen with gold leaf overlaid, holding his work in an aesthetic sense close to the world of Japanese interiors and furnishings.

In recent years, the introduction of the per-cent-for-art schemes in virtually all publicly funded building and road construction projects has led to a considerable number of commissions to young artists. A percent for art scheme apportions a percentage — ideally 1% — of the cost of capital projects such as roads, bridges and hospitals to be used for works of art to embellish these projects. For example, the county of Cork contains 2,878 square miles traversed by 11,730 km of roads. Since 1989, over £150m has been spent in upgrading these roads, with funding coming from the Department of the Environment, the National Roads Authority and the European Regional Development Fund. In ideal circumstances, one percent of the budget for a roads project should be devoted to art. However, while in the period 1989–93 around £150m was spent on road improvements, a ceiling of £20,000 was imposed on the per-cent-for-art schemes, which meant that considerably less than £1.5m was spent on commissioning artworks. This limit has now been raised.

Some of the most outstanding of these roadside sculptures have been carried out by artists such as Eileen McDonagh, Jackie McKenna, John Burke, Rachel Joynt, Michael Warren and Michael Quayne. A characteristic of this recent upsurge in contemporary public sculpture works is the lack of any one identifiable recognizable style or theme. The sculptures are fabricated in a wide variety of private or publicly funded studios and workshops, with a geographical spread across the country. Some of the more prominent sculptors, such as Michael Warren, have their own fabrication workshops. Maud Cotter, Vivienne Roche and Eilis O'Connell, three graduates of the Crawford College of Art and Design in the mid-1970s, have all availed of the facilities at the National Sculpture Factory in Cork to fabricate large-scale public commissioned work. Indeed the existence of the Sculpture Factory in Cork, used by a wide variety of artists, is due to the energy and vision of these artists. Increasingly, sculpture is also being fabricated in the Factory by international artists who have no access to comparable facilities in their own countries.

In ways, the recent upsurge of interest and state support for the visual arts has by-passed some of the older generation of artists. It is the up-and-coming painters, sculptors and others who seem to have achieved most success in benefiting from bursaries, travel grants and other support mechanisms offered by the Arts Council. In the 1960s, when a new generation of artists began to emerge, the range of awards was far more limited: the Taylor Travelling Scholarship, the Carroll Award at the Exhibition of Living Art and some Fulbright Scholarships.

Michael Farrell, who studied at St Martin's School of Art in London, received the Carroll Award a total of four times during the 1960s. His early abstract paintings and sculptures combined geometric and organic elements, and were perfectly in tune with the hard-edged abstraction then current internationally. One of the finest of these works was a large mural commissioned by the Bank of Ireland in 1967. Like Robert Ballagh, Farrell found himself in hostile opposition to many social and political aspects of life in Ireland in that decade. Speaking at the opening of a Living Art exhibition in Cork in 1969, he declared his intention of never exhibiting in Northern Ireland until the political situation there had been resolved. Perhaps prompted by this new-felt need to express his personal convictions, Farrell's work moved away from purely formal concerns and towards figuration. In 1971 he emigrated to France, a path favoured by many radical Irish intellectuals over the years. Although the career of Michael Farrell flourished in France and he continued to exhibit regularly in Ireland, in some ways he fell victim to that cultural paradox of moving from a gradually liberalizing social agenda to seek intellectual freedom in a country where conservatism is almost unrecognizable, so closely is it woven into the matrix of society. His response in the ensuing years was to withdraw from the international stream of art to a more personal style, in which figurative elements again reappear, but one in which, predictably, the dominant consciousness was of his own particular status and condition, linked with that of his native country (Barrett 1979). This attitude is expressed clearly in the painting *Madonna Irlanda, or, The very first Real Irish Political Picture* painted in 1977, which satirizes the burgeoning commercialization of Ireland (it borrows from Boucher's famous sexy portrait of Louise O'Murphy, the Irish mistress of Louis XV), the voyeuristic role of much figurative art, and the dilemma of a committed Modernist seeking some sort of detente with the academic tradition.

Another Irish artist who studied at this time (albeit briefly) at St Martin's School of Art was Brian Bourke, whose figurative portraits and landscapes, first shown in Dublin in 1965, gained an immediate following. The painting *Seated Nude* dates from this year. *Woman with an Umbrella* dates from two years later. Bourke's style, combining elements of German Expressionism, an appreciation of African sculpture and literary themes such as Don Quixote, is individualistic and energetic, but the artist's development since the sixties has been curiously tentative (Hunt 1989).

Robert Ballagh, born in Dublin in 1943 and initially trained as an architect, is one of a number of Irish artists whose enthusiasm for international Modernism in the sixties was quickly tempered by the realization that it was a style that married uneasily into the Irish experience. Apart from his paintings, since the mid-1960s Ballagh has produced a wide range of theatre designs, stamp and currency designs for the Irish government (including the present banknotes) and various public art projects. His firmly held political views require that his works, in whatever media, contain little mystery and leave little to the imagination. In 1969 he began a series of paintings which, while stylistically paying homage to the appropri-ations of Roy Lichtenstein and the black-edged interiors of British Pop artist Patrick Caulfield, draw their iconography from the great history paintings of the nineteenth century. One of the most important of this series *The Rape of the Sabine Women* (Crawford Gallery, Cork) is based on the famous work by Jacques Louis David in the Louvre. However, the excessively simplified motifs and evident Pop Art origins lend an uneasy ambivalence to these works, which were intended by the artist to be read both by art critics and the general public as serious commentaries on the political situation in the north of Ireland. The artist's response to this ambivalence was to paint a work, *My Studio 1969* (Gorry Gallery 1992), which explicitly juxtaposes, on the artist's drawing table, a simplified image of Delacroix's *Liberty at the Barricades* with a contemporary Irish newspaper bearing news of rioting in Derry. The 'Starry Plough', the flag of Irish socialism, has replaced the French Tricolour in the hands of Liberty (Gorry Gallery 1992, 17). From the outset, Ballagh consciously fettered himself in this way to the world of outward appearances and material possessions. His photo-realist portraits and urban interiors, as with the *Portrait of Bernadette Greevy* (1978), can be seen as late twentieth-century transpositions of the proto-Marxist paintings of Ford Madox Brown, a Victorian sensibility revealed most tellingly in the profusion of objects and possessions which clutter up the paintings.

The northern Troubles provide a backdrop for a number of figurative artists. Rita Duffy's scenes of life in Northern Ireland continue the tradition established by William Conor, but her paintings are more satirical and barbed in their commentary on the situation. This commentary is repeated, albeit obliquely, in the work of Leo McCann, Jack Pakenham and Dermot Seymour. Willie Doherty's photographs of street scenes have been shown widely and evoke well the unease and fear which have been a part of everyday life in the north. This sense of fear and unease is conveyed also by the photographs of urban peripheries and borders taken by Paul Seawright.

The leading abstract painters in Ireland in the twentieth century include Mainie Jellett, a founding member of the Society of Dublin Painters in 1920; Theo McNabb, one of the group of artists inspired by Nevill Johnson in the 1940s; Cecil King, a largely self-taught hard-edge abstractionist, and William Scott, whose simplified forms of kitchen utensils on plain backgrounds are frequently cited as combining successfully a northern puritanism with a more Mediterranean sensuality of paint and colour. Tony O'Malley's abstract paintings, dark and severe during the years he spent in St Ives in the 1960s, have in recent years been light in colour and feeling, in atmosphere not unlike Monet's late paintings at Giverny. Of the contemporary generation, Felim Egan and Ciaran Lennon have established considerable reputations with their accomplished abstract

paintings, while both Oliver Whelan and Micky Donnelly have explored the ways in which imagery interplays with the process of painting. A loose grouping of sophisticated minimalist painters and printmakers has also emerged in recent years, which includes Brian Kennedy, Fergus Martin, Fergus Feehily, Ita Freeney and Willie McKeown. Brian Kennedy was born in 1958 and studied at the Crawford School of Art in Cork and also at the Chelsea School of Art in London where he did a postgraduate year in printmaking. Curiously, although he has worked almost exclusively with printmaking techniques over the past ten years, his initial training in Cork was as a sculptor. After spending a year or so teaching printmaking in Newcastle-on-Tyne, he returned to Ireland in 1983 and took up a teaching post at the Crawford School of Art. In many ways, Kennedy is a classic abstract artist. He juxtaposes simple shapes which generally remain flat on the surface of the paper, and he rarely attempts to introduce illusions of depth. The prints are generally quite large (and have become increasingly so in recent years) with the colour saturated into the paper and bled, or extended, right to the edge of the sheet. He prefers to work not just on isolated prints but in series or sequences. Latterly the sequencing of prints, and particularly monoprints, has become an important part of his work. In addition, his interest in formal concerns and an increasingly confident command of printing techniques have led to a steady development in his work over the past decade.

Shane Cullen is one of the few contemporary Irish artists exploring the interplay between the state and the private individual with his H-block series, which memorializes in a very formal way letters written by hunger strikers in Northern Ireland prisons in the 1980s. Shown at the Venice Biennale in 1995 and at P.S.1 in New York three years later, this is one of the most challenging works of art, from both a political and conceptual point of view, to have been created in Ireland in recent decades.

Performance art, a more common art form during the 1970s and 1980s, when it was brought to almost a popular art form by Nigel Rolfe, Alistair MacLennon, Nick Miller, Alanna O'Kelly and Danny McCarthy, has been largely replaced by the installation, a form of art where a total environment in created within which the viewer can engage with the work. Possibly the greatest exponent of this art form in Ireland is James Coleman, who lived for many years in Milan and who has just recently returned to live and work in Ireland. Coleman's works vary in size and complexity, but a typical installation might take a year to prepare. Coleman employs actors, musicians and set designers in constructing elaborate *mise-en-scène* audio-visual installations which deal, among other things, with the alienation of the individual and the relationship between art and life.

INSTITUTIONAL SUPPORT: TEACHING ART

The teaching of art in primary and secondary schools in Ireland was one of the main casualties in the flight from poverty that characterized Irish society for much of the last century. With memories of famine still vivid in the popular imagination and mass emigration until recently a fact of life, training for any occupation that did not carry with it a guarantee of life-long financial and social security was regarded as folly. Allied to an almost universal social snobbery that made the Indian caste system look like a model of democracy, the value of the visual arts as anything other than a method of attaining desirable refinements for the scions of middle-class families was simply ignored. Art as a profession was regarded with an even greater horror than in England or France, where at least there were recognized opportunities for painters and sculptors to make a living. From the days of Mulready and Maclise, graduates of Irish art schools had been accustomed to pursuing their vocation in London, Paris, New York and other major art centres. As has been seen, the visual arts in Ireland were dominated by the twin pillars of the Royal Hibernian Academy and the Metropolitan School of Art which, in the interests of their members, and following the honourable tradition of the Royal Academy in London, essentially operated as closed shops. The status accorded to art education in primary and secondary schools reflected and supported this neglect, and the consequent erosion of visually based conceptual thinking has had ramifications throughout Irish society. To the uneducated eye can be attributed an uncaring and haphazard approach to rural and urban building development, confused notions of visual identity in both government and semi-state organizations, and low levels of discerning support for the visual arts amongst private collectors. The visual identity of the Irish Free State itself benefited initially from the work of graduates of the period before independence, and the design of Ireland's coinage and official publications in the early years was acclaimed internationally. The apogee of this period was the Irish pavilion at the New York World Trade Fair in 1939. Thereafter, art colleges became increasingly marginalized and the pursuit of excellence more and more a private affair, focussed on a handful of galleries such as Victor Waddington's. The really outstanding artists of this period, Jack B. Yeats, William Scott, Louis le Brocquy, were essentially self-taught or remained distant from the art school system.

Recent years have brought changes, however. The swift movement since 1990 in Irish education towards a more technologically based curriculum, and the equally rapid transformation of Regional Technical Colleges into fully-fledged Institutes of Technology, were not motivated primarily by a revolution of social mores in Ireland, but resulted directly from the high level of demand within new industries setting up in Ireland for technology and computer graduates. Art education, in Ireland an area traditionally allied to vocational or technical institutes, has in some ways been an accidental beneficiary of this changed academic landscape. When the College of Marketing and Design was absorbed into the new Dublin Institute of Technology, and the Crawford College of Art became a constituent college of the Cork Institute of Technology, fears were voiced that these colleges would be subsumed and downgraded within a new and competitive environment. However, these fears have proved groundless, as the Institutes of Technology have forged ahead rapidly, developing teaching programmes and resources in new media that are more relevant to contemporary visual art than the more traditional art historical studies of the older universities. Along with these technological advances there have been improvements in the academic status of art colleges. After decades of awarding diplomas, degrees were first awarded to students at the National College of Art and Design in the early 1980s, while the Crawford College of Art attained degree status a decade later. The attainment of degree status was an important step forward for Irish art education and removed an anomaly that had existed between colleges in Ireland and Britain since the 1960s. However, the unfairness of this anomaly had been recognized within the art school system for decades, with art schools in Britain, knowing well the quality of Irish art school education, would routinely accept diploma graduates from Irish art colleges onto post-graduate courses.

The National College of Art and Design (NCAD), formerly the Metropolitan School of Art, was originally founded as the Drawing Schools of the Dublin Society in 1746. It has always been the pre-eminent art college in Ireland, although, as with any such national institution with expectations placed upon it from all sectors of society, NCAD has often been criticized for failing to meet such burdens. Art colleges in the regions, perhaps protected more from these expectations and from the political and economic pressures of a capital city, were able to preserve a stronger teaching ethos and sense of continuity in the years of transition from the Academic to the Modern, and beyond. MacGonigal's resignation in 1969, although hailed as a victory by the radical young students, in reality brought NCAD to a low ebb. The period of unrest in the late 1960s culminated in the occupation of the college building by dissatisfied students and the deliberate smashing of a number of plaster casts that had formed the basis of the didactic teaching system that stretched back to the days of William Orpen and to the Dublin Society's Schools. However, the wounds of those years have substantially healed in the ensuing decades, and many fine artists have been employed on the teaching staff at NCAD,

244

including Brian King, Charles Cullen, Michael O'Sullivan and Theo McNabb. The art college in Limerick, as in Cork, has a good reputation for producing graduates who are successful in establishing themselves as artists and who frequently move on to do post-graduate degrees in fine art.

The crisis in third-level art education which occurred in 1969 at the National College of Art was confined to Dublin, although its revolutionary influence was felt throughout the country. In Cork, the Crawford School of Art (now the Crawford College of Art and Design) was able to benefit both from the electric atmosphere of the time but also from the relatively stable and protective management of the City of Cork Vocational Education Committee. One of the most outstanding students to enter the Crawford in the twentieth century was John Burke, who was born in 1946 in Clonmel, county Tipperary, and who enrolled at the Crawford School as a student at the age of eighteen. Burke's talents as an artist were recognized quickly by his teacher John O'Leary (ob. 1999), himself a graduate of the Crawford School. A sensitive painter and draughtsman, O'Leary's interest in finely crafted abstract art carried through to the young student from Clonmel. In 1967 Burke won the Student of the Year Award and three years later a McCauley Fellowship. Encouraged by O'Leary, Burke moved to London in 1970 where he studied for a year under Bryan Kneale at the Royal College of Art. Here he was introduced to welded steel sculpture and in particular the work of Anthony Caro and Philip King. After a period of travelling through Europe, North Africa and the Middle East, Burke returned to Cork where he had his first one-person exhibition in 1973. Three years later, he exhibited his work in New York and encountered first hand the monumental public sculptures of Alexander Calder and other American sculptors. From Calder, he learned the importance of revealing in his works the process of construction, and the sculptures he made on his return to Ireland, particularly the large public piece outside the Bank of Ireland on Baggot Street, Dublin, were distinguished by exposed bolts and visible welded seams.

In 1969 Burke had taken up a part-time lectureship at the Crawford School of Art to which he returned in 1972 and where he remained for five years. During this time he established a reputation as a dedicated, if sometimes fiery, teacher. He was the first tutor in the Crawford Sculpture Department to work in a serious way with welded steel, and contemporaries recall his struggle to convince the school authorities of the need for arc welders and power tools in the Sculpture Department. Up to that time, sculpture had been taught in the more or less traditional method established in Cork in the mid-nineteenth century, where the predominant tradition was in carving stone and modelling clay from sculpture casts and the human figure.

In the early 1970s, the Sculpture Department of the Crawford School of Art enjoyed a considerable renaissance. Among the outstanding students who enrolled in 1970 were John Gibbons, Vivienne Roche, Eilis O'Connell and Maud Cotter. Robbie McDonald joined the class shortly afterwards, while James Scanlon signed on as a full-time student in 1974 after attending night classes for two years, and Jim Buckley enrolled the following year. The majority of these students were to win the Cork Arts Society's 'Student of the Year' award. In reviewing their progress over the ensuing quarter century, it is clear that, whatever the disparities in their individual approaches to art, these artists have been united in their resolute, determined and professional approach to the development of their careers. It is tempting to ascribe their success to the tuition and inspiration they encountered at the Crawford in the early 1970s, although clearly there are many other factors to consider.

Burke, just a couple of years older than Gibbons, Roche and O'Connell, was also a practising artist and between students and teacher there was both a sense of competition and also of shared discovery. Gibbons himself had spent six months in London in the autumn and winter of 1970, during which time he had seen the McAlpine collection of contemporary sculpture at the Tate Gallery. This collection focussed on sculptors like William Tucker, Tim Scott and David Annesley, artists associated with St Martin's School of Art, whereas Burke's inspiration had derived largely from the rival tradition of Brian Kneale and the Royal College of Art. To the untutored eye, the work of sculptors from both these schools could appear startlingly similiar, but there were fundamental differences in terms of the way they dealt with formal values as against narrative content in their output. Cork was to some degree isolated from this debate but, through visits to Dublin and London, Burke was able to experience it. Burke was a passionate and dedicated teacher who, although committed to his own personal vision of abstract steel sculpture, did not adopt a rigid or doctrinaire attitude. Gibbons recalls 'You had to fight him, but he made you believe in yourself'. The strength of the Sculpture Department at the Crawford during this period became legendary; there was nothing similar happening in Limerick or Dublin, in which latter city the National College of Art was wracked by crises at the time. For a brief period, with Burke and his students there was a shared confidence that the art school system, and indeed society in a wider sense, could be changed by engaging in student activist movements and through marching, sit-ins and demonstrations.

In the Crawford Sculpture Department itself, McDonald recalls Burke's teaching style as 'critical, but in a positive sense'. However, he could also be abrasive and cutting with those who were unclear in their intentions or lacking in motivation. He forced his students to take seriously what they were doing, but in return his loyalty to them was legendary, particularly in terms of fighting for improved library and workshop facilities. With his encouragement, O'Connell and Cotter took specialized courses in welding at the Cork Regional Technical College. However, his single-minded and sometimes confrontational approach distanced him from other staff and from the school administration, and, with the introduction of a new Diploma course in the mid-1970s, his style of direct and engaged teaching began to be replaced by a more planned and structured course development. New teachers, Ian Bibby, Roger Hannan, Patrick O'Sullivan and Peter McTigue among them, were recruited and Burke's influence began to wane. He ceased teaching at the Crawford School of Art around 1977. Burke himself is characteristically honest in his assessment of his own accommodation, or lack of it, for the increasingly important academic side of the Crawford's educational programme. John O'Leary and Con Lynch also left the Crawford during this time and settled in Sligo.

Although distanced from the academic side of the Crawford School of Art, Burke took a prominent role in organising the Sculpture and Drawing Exhibitions (SADE '82 and '87) at the Crawford Gallery in Cork, thereby ensuring a continuing national and international focus on Cork as a centre for excellence, particularly in the area of sculpture. The Triskel Arts Centre was also founded at this time and is now one of the leading art centres in Ireland. The establishment in 1992 of the National Sculpture Factory in Cork, under the leadership of Crawford graduates O'Connell, Cotter and Roche (along with sculptor Danny McCarthy), was the most significant development in the visual arts in Cork in the last century.

The achievement of Crawford sculpture graduates has extended beyond the setting up of the National Sculpture Factory. In reviewing their progress over a ten-year period, what is interesting is the way in which Gibbons, Cotter, O'Connell, Roche, Scanlon and Buckley are united in their increasing awareness of and concern for what might be described as 'essential form'. There is little which can be termed as superfluous or arbitrary in their work. The objects they create give the impression of having been stripped of all non-essential or extraneous matter, but still retain a rich, almost organic or crystalline, essence. Another factor which might be said to unite these artists is an affinity with Nordic countries, as evidenced clearly in the exhibition of work by O'Connell, Roche and a third artist, Kathy Prendergast, which toured to Finland and Sweden through 1990 and 1991. Both Roche and O'Connell have worked at the Nordic Arts Centre in Helsinki and have travelled extensively in Scandinavia. Roche's recent bronze sculptures represent a relatively new departure in her work; for years after graduating from the Crawford, she had been more associated with large, welded steel work, typically located in Irish town centres, parks and other public areas. In latter years her output has acquired a more personal idiom and a specific aesthetic which derives in part from her travels in Scandinavia.

Maud Cotter studied at the Crawford School of Art from 1972 to 1978. In the early 1980s her work in stained glass established her as one of the most original and interesting artists in Ireland. Along with James Scanlon, she was responsible for the virtual re-invention of an artistic tradition of stained glass which had been one of the great achievements of Irish art in the first decades of the twentieth century. Cotter's recent work, incorporating steel and glass into a sculptural facade for a new building in Temple Bar in Dublin, brings her output in a new and exciting direction. In recent years she has travelled in Iceland, and her response to the landscape of that country, still in the process of geological formation, has influenced her pieces. The sculpture Cotter created for the touring exhibition '0044' in 1999 again shows a new departure in the artist's work, combining as it does the fragility of translucent sections of corrugated card supported on a slender iron framework that hints both at strength and fragility.

Although equally informed by these forces of growth and change, Eilis O'Connell takes a slightly different route in that the artist seeks to combine a sense of a physical presence as well as an intellectual quality in her material. The scale of her work is a response to the scale of the human body, and while her sculptures may seem at first glance impersonal and abstract, they also have an organic quality that prevents them from being seen as too machine-like. Like her contemporaries Roche, Scanlon, Cotter and Buckley, O'Connell responds to the challenge of public commissions with a confidence and determination that, as with her counterparts, speaks of a confidence in both her ideas and in her ability to translate those ideas from drawings and sketches through maquettes, to the final product. As with John Burke, she is accustomed to having occasionally to defend the integrity of these public works against criticism. Considering its controversial history, a case can be made that O'Connell's accomplished Modernist sculpture, *The Great Wall of Kinsale*, suffered the principal misfortune of being sited in Kinsale, an historic seaport whose many resident writers and artists have too few opportunities of airing their views on Modern art. Acclaimed by some, and with equal enthusiasm condemned by others as a 'monstrosity', the unveiling of the 179 ft long work on 22 July 1988 included, the *Cork Examiner* noted, 'a background of placard-carrying protesters, angry about the cost and what they saw as a danger to the children who are already using part of the sculpture as a slide and a bicycle ramp.' In spite of the efforts, including paving and perimeter walls, to make the sculpture an integral part of its surroundings, the controversy continued through the following year, with motions being put before the Urban District Council to have the piece removed. Eventually, the UDC ordered the sculpture painted grey, a compromise reluctantly accepted by the artist. Changes were also made in the paving and wall, and safety rails were set in place to prevent children climbing onto the sculpture. These insensitive alterations compromised the original artistic integrity of *The Great Wall of Kinsale*. Nonetheless, O'Connell's recent very large-scale public sculpture commissions in Cardiff, Bristol and London, along with successful exhibitions in London and New York, have established her as one of the foremost contemporary artists working in Britain as well as in Ireland.

Like O'Connell (and more recently Cotter), Jim Buckley has moved to live and work in Britain. Since 1988 he has been based in Glasgow where he has continued to develop his art in welded steel sculpture and where he was also a founding member of the Glasgow Sculpture Workshop. As with Roche and O'Connell, Buckley has found an affinity with a Nordic tradition and worked for a period in Denmark. His recent exhibition at the Triskel Arts Centre in Cork showed his output developing strong metaphorical overtones, with the artist displaying a series of strong-boxes with grille-covered slits on their heavily riveted metal skins.

James Scanlon has also continued to work in stained glass and sculpture in a brilliant and innovative way. Among his most recent commissions has been a large stained-glass window for the Crawford Art Gallery; in 1995 he was included in an exhibition of Irish art organized by the Crawford Gallery and touring to five venues in the United States. In that year also he was awarded a commission for a stained-glass window in the headquarters of the European Commission in Brussels.

Of Burke's former students, it is perhaps John Gibbons who in many ways has remained closest to what he learned at the Crawford in Cork, and subsequently at St Martin's in London. Gibbons follows this tradition with a magisterial and unwavering confidence, building tall pieces of sculpture, sometimes immensely heavy, with a concern for the processes of working with steel, grinding, cutting and welding, that harks back to the exhortations repeated again and again by Burke to his students in Cork, 'there is no excuse for bad delivery'. However, from the outset, Gibbons' art was more concerned with narrative rather than purely formal qualities, and he is opposed to the characterization of his output as being constructed from 'found' steel shapes. There is an immense amount of original construction and fabrication in his pieces, and although on first sight they appear to be made of found girders and other elements, this appearance is deceptive. One of his most recent works, a tall stainless steel sculpture commissioned for the new headquarters of the Environmental Protection Agency in Wexford, was completed at the National Sculpture Factory in 1997.

If there is one facet of these Crawford graduates' work which can be said to be held in common, it is most likely that duality which reappears in their sculptures in many different guises, a duality between the organic and the mechanical, between the human body and the built environment, between the psychic and sexual life of the individual and the constraints and pressures imposed by society.

THE INTERNATIONAL DIMENSION — CONTEMPORARY IRISH ARTISTS OUTSIDE IRELAND

The tradition of Irish artists emigrating, some to the European Continent and North America, but most to Britain, has continued to the present day. London in recent years has reasserted its position as an important centre internationally for the visual arts. Responding to this new vitality in the British capital, an increasing number of Irish artists, many of them graduates of the National College of Art and Design, the Crawford College of Art and other art schools in Ireland, have settled in London in order to avail of opportunities both for employment and exhibition. Many graduates of the Belfast College of Art also make their way to the British capital.

The cross-over that takes place with these artists is interesting. Because of their cultural and historic identity, Irish artists quickly become assimilated into the London art world. Indeed, in recent years some Irish artists have been chosen (as part of group shows in most instances) to represent Britain internationally, benefiting both from historic links between the two countries and from a mutually accepted policy of both British and Irish governments that regards domicile as 'belonging' (not forgetting that artists from Northern Ireland are UK citizens). Perhaps because of certain qualities in their work, Irish artists are often singled out for notice by critics in London, who are interested in and curious about Ireland and Irish art. What makes it interesting to British critics may be the fact that it is simultaneously familiar and strange, as when they travel to Ireland with pre-conceived notions, find something that is recognizable and yet acknowledge that it is somehow different from their own country.

In spite of the positive developments in Dublin, it is evident that many artists whose work is at the cutting edge of contemporary Irish art at the beginning of the twenty-first century prefer to live in or near London. Evidence of this can be found in the high proportion of artists selected by the Cultural Relations Committee to represent Ireland at the Venice Biennale or at the Sao Paulo Bienal, who are in fact resident in London. This is true of Kathy Prendergast (Venice 1995), Jaki Irvine

(Venice 1997), Anne Tallentire (1999) and others. The painters among this loose group include Mark Francis and Elizabeth Magill. Francis' recent paintings are large abstract canvases, often featuring black spots and smoky trail marks, while Magill, also from Northern Ireland, both pays homage to and critiques the conventions of Romantic landscape painting. A number of Irish artists have moved to Britain in response to teaching opportunities.

It is clear that for many of these artists, questions of national identity which were of key importance to an earlier generation are now disregarded or ignored. The photographer Paul Seawright responds thus to the question, whether he would identify himself as Irish, Northern Irish or British, as Protestant or Catholic? 'I really wouldn't try to identify myself using any of those terms because I think that kind of terminology led us to where we are. The fact that people have to label themselves in certain ways as British, Irish, Northern Irish, English, whatever, is wholly problematic. The idea of labelling is a real problem, because as soon as you adopt any of those labels you ostracize and exclude people'. Siobhán Hapaska, also from Belfast, concurs with this strongly: 'My name, for instance, has always provoked people to try and identify my origins. I don't know why they bother. I've always hated that tendency, especially growing up in Belfast where your surname was a means to identify religious affiliation through the ties we have with names. My name always backfired. It was something else'. Hapaska showed at the ICA in London in 1990, and was also included in the 1997 Documenta at Kassel. Her sculptures are characterized by the use of disparate materials, and often juxtapose 'natural' elements with high-tech or synthetic materials. She also won the 1998 IMMA Glen Dimplex prize, a valuable financial award made each year to an artist who has exhibited in Ireland.

As well as being selected to represent Ireland at Venice, a number of Irish artists resident in London have been chosen (as part of group shows mainly) to represent Britain in international exhibitions. This transfer of identity tacitly acknowledges a relational understanding of identity formation, and of the relationship of the individual to society. The artists develop different strategies to deal with this problem of identification. Again Paul Seawright is determined to avoid being 'tagged' with national labels — 'If you say Northern Irish, it's like you're making a political statement. If I say I'm British, which is what I would have felt growing up — again, another political statement. So it is very, very difficult. I quite often say that I'm an artist born in Belfast who lives in Wales. My identity is something, I don't think, that can be summed up by some kind of geographic label. I always resist it and the joke I often hear is that your nationality depends upon who's giving you the grant'. Anne Carlisle, also from Belfast, sums it up when she points out that irrespective of political posturing, the issue of not really belonging is so deeply embedded in the Northern Irish psyche that it has become a physical and mental state in its own right. Echoing the sentiments of Mo White and Nicky May, she finds it liberating to be nowhere: 'I can ask am I Irish or British, or both? Now that's what I call a real "free state". When you perceive yourself positively as being nowhere, even though you may not have chosen but inherited that position, you become comfortable about the idea of making connections, because you've got no place to defend'.

What has happened with many of these artists is that the experience of moving from Ireland to Britain has made them consider themselves anew, consider their own identity, their sense of belonging, of being. This quality is clearly evident in the drawings and sculptures of Kathy Prendergast. Prendergast, born in Dublin, a National College of Art graduate, moved to London in the mid-1980s to complete an MA at Camberwell School of Art. She has represented Ireland at several international events, including the 1995 Venice Biennale, where she was awarded the Primo Duomilia — the prize for 'the most outstanding young artist' at the Biennale. Cities, terrain, bodies, represented in map drawings or sculptures, have formed a recurring motif in her work. A retrospective of Prendergast's work at the Irish Museum of Modern Art in 1999 places her firmly in the first rank of contemporary Irish artists. Prendergast's direct answer to questions about life in a trans-global, cross-cultural world suggest that nationality can be as misused as a map. She finds identity nowhere, everywhere, or in some liminal 'in-between' place. There is a suggestion that identity may most easily found in the search itself. Prendergast's elegant commentaries on the eternal human search for a map that will show a way — and the impossibility of that quest — is reiterated by the artist in her extraordinary series of delicate map drawings and related works.

These same questions appear in Siobhán Hapaska's highly finished and unsettling sculptures, which are resistant both to fixed viewpoints and attempts at definition. 'I am not a perfectionist just for the sake of it', Hapaska points out. 'The reflective surfaces safeguard against a saturation of memory and overload. I wanted to keep them fresh. I wanted them to be self-contained and self-sufficient. The surface creates a sensual boundary between the internal life of the object and the person. It was important to eradicate my presence from these objects. They are not meant to be about me. I wanted to give them their own life as if they had just arrived from somewhere'. This confluence of distance, strangeness and memory recurs in Liadain Cooke's *21 Balls of Clay dug up from a Field at Closscregg*, where the transformation from one material to another — from mud to aluminium — is counterpoised against the geographical distance from the field where the clay was dug in Ireland to the artist's studio in London. Cooke, who was born and raised in Kilkenny, moved to London in 1990. She is an artist whose work seeks to make whole again a world in a state of constant fragmentation. She takes objects and materials, re-examines them minutely, then transforms them into works of art in which fictional attributes and narratives are interwoven with reality, acknowledging the impossibility of making whole again that which cannot be re-constructed. Although they are deeply informed by a sense of place, the lumps of clay transposed into aluminium also deny that sense of place and assert a more universal truth about humanity, an assertion echoed in the large-scale photographs of Paul Seawright, where he locates the viewer literally in a no-man's land, on the borders between different communities in Belfast, Catholic and Protestant. These images of wastelands between housing estates are a powerful critique, without any accompanying text, of the dead-end attitudes which separate these neighbours one from the other.

A sense of slippage or a lack of fixed reference points comes through in the work of several Irish artists in Britain. Cooke refers to insecurity as one of the key elements in her work, while Mark Francis equates the blurred finish of his paintings with a sense of uncertainty about existence and place. Hapaska expresses this notion clearly: 'The inability to identify the origin or the precise meaning of a work creates an acute sense of dislocation, which is important to me. It's not about affirming what you know already. It's about enabling people to register that maybes can have greater value'. Nicky May describes his paintings as being about the whole notion of chance, of 'hitting on something and making it work, that notion of attraction to strangeness'. However, artists Cecily Brennan and Maud Cotter stress the sense of liberation they felt on moving to London, a sense of liberation less to do with national tags than with being transported into a neutral environment. London was a place where they knew nobody and were not known. The feeling that they were at liberty to re-invent themselves as artists, and strike out in new directions, was perhaps the most positive aspect of their move, and is reflected in their recent work which shows a clear change in direction and focus. Cotter refers metaphorically to taking out parts of her own consciousness in London, and examining them in a way that, publicly, she would never have done in Ireland. This sense of distance from Ireland is important also in the work of Jaki Irvine. Irvine, who showed at the Venice Biennale in 1995 (in the young British contingent) two years later represented Ireland at the next Biennale. Originally from Belfast, Irvine showed a complex video and film installation at the Frith Street Gallery in 1997 which explored issues of identity and alienation, an exploration continued in her installation two years later in the Douglas Hyde Gallery in Dublin.

Viewing Ireland in a retrospective way, from the distance of Britain, is important to John Gibbons, who went from Cork to St Martins and is now head of sculpture at Winchester School of Art. He puts it graphically: 'For me being in Ireland is like being in the fire. It's hard to get distance. Being in London gives me distance. London is an international sculpture centre. The stimulus allows me to exist as an artist'. Paul Seawright, before moving to Britain, had never made photographs of the political situation in Northern Ireland. He affirms that moving away from Belfast gave him a perspective and made him suddenly aware that he knew very little about the political background of the Troubles. 'I started collecting political books, texts, all kinds of stuff. Reading material I would never have read if I had stayed in Ireland. When you're close to something you're not interested in it'. For Seawright, there has been a sense of implosion throughout the conflict, 'a sense that we have destroyed ourselves, mentally as well as physically'. His fire pictures talk about the scars of that destruction and the burning away of the past. However there is a sense also of cauterizing wounds, of the potential for new growth.

In common with several of the artists, Seawright has had to deal with negative attitudes towards the Irish in Britain. It must be somewhat ironic for the descendants of seventeenth-century lowlands Scots who colonized Northern Ireland to find themselves responding defensively to the cultural stereotypes of Irishness created as a means of justifying that same colonial enterprise. The realization that the world at large does not care much for delicate nuances of caste and class which define life in 'the Province' is coupled with the knowledge that even Protestants from Northern Ireland can expect little in the way of a sentimental welcome in Britain. Partly this is due to the media in Britain, which have portrayed the conflict or political situation in Northern Ireland in simplistic and reductive terms. However, through their art, several of the artists feel that they have the freedom to address these complex issues in a more sophisticated way. John Carson has also had to confront simplistic British views of Northern Ireland, having been roughed up on occasion in bars for having the accent of an IRA man, while Tina O'Connell has also experienced racist slights. But as O'Connell puts it: 'I take no more notice of them than the man in the moon. In comparison to other people, it's the tip of the iceberg, because basically I'm white and middle class and if I don't open my mouth I can get away with an awful lot'. Tina O'Connell's installations generally form a dialogue between the work of art and the space within which the work is shown. She operates with diverse materials, plastic sheeting, rivets, iron bars, liquid bitumen and found materials. Her output is thoughtful, profound, occasionally satirical and always original. Daphne Wright's installations in the 1990s at Artforms in London and the Temple Bar Gallery in Dublin showed the artist creating room-like spaces with delicate filigrees of plaster, concrete and tin foil. Wright's work addresses issues of nature and culture and is closely bound up with her own experiences as an Irish artist living for the past number of years in England. Mo White, with a Northern Irish background although actually born in England, brings an extra dimension to a discussion of Irish art, as she addresses in her work issues of sexuality and identity very much in the context of her own life and her own family background in Ireland.

With the realization that in London there is limited interest in, and comprehension of, the realities of the situation in Ireland, comes again a sort of slippage, where realities and certainties are upset. The racist attitude that in the past coloured much of the political and social transactions between the two islands is disappearing steadily. This attitude was essentially a residue of the dysfunctional but close relationship that has existed between Britain and Ireland for centuries. Carson's early performance, Men of Ireland, played on these stereotypes, with wooden cut-outs and the artist mimicking the roles of clergyman, workman, Orangeman, leprechaun with a shillelagh and a paramilitary with beret, dark glasses and combat jacket. The ability of artists like Carson to confront and subvert negative stereotypes through humour and informed critical comment, can legitimately be read as part of the peace process — a process that has entailed in both islands an honest re-appraisal of values and traditions once held to be sacred and inviolable.

In his installations, which often involve an element of surveillance or spying, Andrew Kearney has also played on the uneasy relationship between Ireland and Britain. Kearney, who studied at the Limerick College of Art and afterwards at Chelsea, received the 'Barclay's Young Artist of the Year' award in 1992, and was shortlisted for the Glen Dimplex prize in 1995, where his installation consisted of a darkened room with small video monitors, each showing an electrical storm. A sound and light installation created by Kearney for the exhibition '0044' (shown at P.S.1 and also at the Albright Knox Museum in 1999) contained three hundred pulsating light bulbs and speakers on metal shelves connected to microphones outside the gallery space. His installation in '0044', while incorporating an element of surveillance, also deals with memory and the stacked shelves of history. This is a feature found also in previous work by Anne Tallentire and John Seth, whose strategic approach to making art is perhaps the most complicated of all the artists, but is

again informed by their ardent desire to avoid being labelled or tagged in a reductionist way. Tallentire, an artist born in Armagh who moved to London in 1984 to study, and then teach, at St Martin's School of Art, has been very influential to a younger generation of artists, a number of them Irish, who have followed that same academic route. She represented Ireland at the forty-eighth Venice Biennale in 1999 with a work entitled Instances. This consisted of three separate parts. In one darkened room, a video projection showed dawn in an unknown sector of an unknown city. The dawning was filmed, and projected, in real time, in a piece lasting thirty minutes. In another room, a video monitor showed the artist carrying out a series of enigmatic actions linking geometry, memory and the domestic interior. The third part of Instances was a large colour photograph, an extract from Trailers, a work which Anne Tallentire and John Seth, in their collaborative practice work seth/tallentire, had presented in Dublin in 1998. It would be disingenuous to suggest that Tallentire's creation can be appreciated on a quick viewing. On one level, the images used in Instances are simple and direct. However, the work contains within itself elements which make any attempt at simple appreciation or interpretation difficult. During the course of the Biennale, Tallentire continued to make and film 'actions', which were introduced into the work in the Nuova Icona. Thus the piece by its very nature exposed the insubstantiality of constructs upon which people base their sense of reality. Tallentire's work represents a partial view of the trail left by an artist whose every waking minute is to some extent an examination of the nature of the artifices and constructs that underpin contemporary society. In her thoughtful and considered negotiation of contested ideas — particularly about art and the form it should take — Tallentire also embodies characteristics which have a particular resonance within an Irish context.

Over the past century, the history of Irish emigrants living in Britain has been one of social transition. Their movement in economic terms has been steadily towards prosperity, and with that prosperity has come assimilation into the dominant culture. Paradoxically, along with prosperity in these areas has also come a renewed pride in being Irish, which complicates the process of assimilation. For the so-called dominant culture in Britain is in itself a highly artificial and eclectic construct, which has always relied to a great extent on the contribution made by the regular influxes of immigrants from other countries. Something of a sea change in attitudes to Ireland has occurred in recent years. In contrast to Francis Bacon who lived in London in the 1950s and 1960s and repudiated his Irishness, Seán Scully, a Dublin-born painter who maintains studios in New York, Barcelona and London, now asserts his Irish roots with confidence, perhaps gauging it to be an advantage rather than an impediment to maintaining success in the international mainstream.

INSTITUTIONAL SUPPORT: GOVERNMENT AND GALLERIES

The visual arts in Ireland receive financial assistance mainly from from the public sector. Support from the private sector comes primarily through the purchase of artworks by companies and private individuals, or through the sponsorship of exhibitions and arts festivals by commercial organizations. Government aid is primarily channelled through government departments, local authorities such as corporations and county councils and one quasi-autonomous agency, the Arts Council, which is based in Dublin. The Arts Council is quasi-autonomous in the sense that, while it operates quite independently of politicians and most civil servants, its members, whose term of office is five years, are political appointees, nominated by the Taoiseach of the day.

The government departments providing the bulk of support to the visual arts are the Department of Education and Science, the Department of Arts, Heritage, Gaeltacht and the Islands and the Department of Foreign Affairs. There is also a substantial subsidy to the visual arts through the operation of FÁS schemes (government-subsidized work for long-term unemployed people) in galleries and art centres throughout the country, while the Office of Public Works (OPW) provides maintenance for public buildings and exhibition centres such as Kilkenny Castle and the Butler Gallery. OPW often commissions works by contemporary artists for prestigious locations such as Dublin Castle and government buildings, as well as possessing a sizeable art collection which is shown in various offices and locations around the country.

The Department of Education and Science may well be the single most important supporter of the visual arts in Ireland. Of its budget of some £3 billion per annum, a substantial portion goes to assist the 1,000 teachers of art at primary and secondary level, as well as a range of third-level institutions dedicated to art and design. These include the National College of Art and Design in Dublin, the Crawford College of Art and Design in Cork, Limerick College of Art, as well as sizeable art departments in the Institutes of Technology in Sligo, Galway, Letterkenny, Waterford and Dún Laoghaire. The art history departments at University College, Dublin, and Trinity College, Dublin, are also important elements of the visual arts in Ireland. Both departments provide undergraduate and post-graduate courses and are responsible for training many museum and gallery personnel, and indeed some artists working today in Ireland. In addition, UCD runs a *Diploma in Arts Administration*. University College, Cork has developed both a heritage management course and a fledgling art history diploma course.

The Department of Arts, Heritage, Gaeltacht and the Islands (DAHGI) through Dúchas, the Heritage Service, directly supports national visual art institutions including the National Gallery of Ireland, the Chester Beatty Library, the Irish Museum of Modern Art and the National Library of Ireland (an institution with a visual arts remit insofar as it has holdings of watercolours and prints). The National Museum, both at Collins Barracks and at Kildare Street, possesses important collections of pre-historic Irish art, Early Christian metalwork and other visual arts material. DAHGI has also administered the allocation of EU funds for the development of Ireland's cultural infrastructure, and many galleries have received European funding in recent years to assist in capital development projects. Broadcasting and film, the latter an important area of the visual arts not covered in this essay for reasons of space, also fall within the remit of DAHGI. Exhibitions of Irish art abroad receive support from a small annual budget (currently around £1m) administered by the Cultural Relations Committee (CRC) of the Department of Foreign Affairs. The Cultural Relations Committee, like the Arts Council, is composed of voluntary experts, and is re-appointed every two years by the minister of the day. Ireland's participation at the Venice Biennale and the Sao Paulo Bienal is funded and organised by the CRC.

The Arts Council consists of a secretariat based in Dublin which works under the direction of a group of seventeen voluntary experts — the Council — appointed for a five-year period. These experts, arts practitioners, administrators and academics, for the most part, are drawn from a wide variety of arts organizations and backgrounds. Officially, the policies and decisions of the Council are implemented by a staff of seventeen — headed by a director appointed by the Council. In reality, over the past two decades, the Council has more often been driven by energetic and visionary directors and dedicated staff. The Arts Council has higher visibility than the other agencies mentioned above, but its increased budget (now £35m), is intended also to cover drama, literature, music and film. The achievement of the Arts Council in securing a virtual doubling of its government funding between the years 1993 and 1999 is all the more remarkable when compared with cuts in funding which were imposed in other European countries during the same period. However, the overall percentage of public funding allocated to culture in Ireland remains well below the European average. In 1984, the Arts Council announced a crisis in arts funding in Ireland, basing its argument on the fact that amount spent in Ireland was a mere .09% of per capita government expenditure. However, fifteen years later the percentage had not changed dramatically and even in the most recent report issued by the Council in March

2000, *A comparative study of levels of arts expenditure in selected countries and regions* this same figure of .09% (excluding tax breaks) is cited for Ireland. The study compares the Irish figure, which includes museum and arts expenditure, with the equivalent expenditures of Australia (.19%), England (.14%) and Scotland (.21%). The figures are significantly higher in Scandinavia, where Finland spends .27% and Sweden .35% respectively on the arts. In Northern Ireland, the figure is .19%. These figures indicate a serious failure on the part of the Irish state to take culture seriously, a failure compounded by the lack of reliable statistical data upon which policy and funding decisions can be made. The accuracy of the Irish GDP figures can be questioned: factors such as income tax exemption offered to visual artists, or tax relief offered to film investors should be included if a true picture of public investment is to emerge. However, the fact remains that in countries such as Finland, per capita spending on the arts by government is nearly three times that of Ireland.

Looking at the visual arts budgets of the Arts Council gives a clearer idea of trends in funding. In 1990, expenditure by the Council on visual arts amounted to just over £1m. This included Aosdána *Cnuas* grants to visual artists of £230,000. By 1995, however, Arts Council expenditure on the visual arts and architecture had risen to £1.8m, an increase of £323,000 (22%) on 1994. (This figure included Aosdána *Cnuas* awards to 44 artists, totalling £336,221.) The increases went mainly on awards, residencies and support for artists' studios, including the Fire Station Studios and Temple Bar Galleries in Dublin, the National Sculpture Factory, artists collective studios and workshops in the larger cities, such as Artspace in Galway, Backwater Studios in Cork, Cork Artists Collective, New Art Studios in Dublin, Visual Arts Centre, Dublin, and Wexford Sculpture Studios. In 1998 the total grant to the Council had risen steeply to £26.1m, of which only £2.01m was allocated to the visual arts, with grants to arts centres, not-for-profit galleries, exhibitions and arts festivals forming the main avenues of disbursement. This expenditure of £26.1m should be compared with the level of expenditure by local authorities, which in 1997 totalled less than £4m. Putting it simply, local authority support of the arts is equal to less than one-sixth of the amount provided by central government. The Arts Council also provides financial support for a number of significant open submission exhibitions, including Iontas at the Sligo Art Gallery, EV+A at Limerick and the Claremorris Open. EV+A, the exhibition of contemporary visual art held in Limerick every year since 1977, has grown in size and reputation to be one of the most important visual arts events in Ireland. The roll-call of EV+A curators is impressive: Sandy Nairne, Rudi Fuchs, Nabuo Nakamura, Ida Panicelli, Germano Celant, Jan Hoet,

Maria de Corral and Guy Tortosa are among those who have been invited to curate. Apart from Brian O'Doherty (1980) and Jeanne Greenberg Rohatyn (1999), the selectors have been mainly drawn from Europe.

Compared with grants to exhibitions such as EV+A, Arts Council grants to individual practising artists are small. The percentage of Council funding allocated to the visual arts has declined over the years and now hovers at around eight per cent. Most of this funding goes to painters and sculptors: funding for interdisciplinary projects is rare. The existence of the state agency Bord Scannán na hÉireann (the Irish Film Board), which receives annual funding of around £5m from DAHGI, as well as commissions to film-makers by the state-run television services, affects how film and video are recognized as media for artists. There are currently few demands placed upon visual artists in return for Council funding, nor is their work subjected to any measurable form of critical assessment. This lack of a critical environment extends to the national media, and, by extension, to Irish society in general.

A national academy of artists, writers and musicians called Aosdána is administered by the Arts Council. In some cases, artists who are members of Aosdána receive an annual stipend (*Cnuas*). Aosdána is a self-electing and self-regulating organization, with membership in 1998 totalling one hundred and seventy-four. Of these, eighty-one were visual artists. Of these, fifty-one received *cnuas*, totalling just under half a million pounds. Such income is important in providing financial support for visual artists, whose earnings are often meagre. Under the *Finance Act* of 1969, artists in Ireland do not pay income tax. However, as the average income of visual artists frequently keeps them outside the tax net, this exemption is of limited advantage. The exemption notably benefits a relatively small number of high-earning writers. Visual artists in ireland do not benefit from the *droit de suite* — a percentage of the re-sale of their work.

Architecture is another area of the visual arts that merits a degree of attention impossible in the present text. Over the past decade, the annual awards exhibition of the Royal Institute of Architects in Ireland and the Architectural Association of Ireland have highlighted the extraordinary range and quality of contemporary Irish architecture. Many new buildings which have received AAI and RIAI awards serve the visual arts; architect Shea Cleary designed the remodelling of the seventeenth-century Royal Hospital Kilmainham, Dublin, into the Irish Museum of Modern Art. He also designed the multi-media Arthouse in Temple Bar, while O'Donnell and Twomey designed the new Gallery of Photography and the National Photographic Archive, also in Temple Bar. These buildings show the high standard of contemporary Irish architecture. The Irish Architectural Archive preserves thousands of photographs, drawings and other material relating to the history of architecture in Ireland.

In some cases, visual arts institutions dependent upon Arts Council funding may receive subsidies from more than one source. For instance, the Douglas Hyde Gallery, a leading contemporary art gallery in Dublin, obtains part of its income from the Arts Council, with the remainder coming from Trinity College, Dublin, which in turn receives substantial funding from the Department of Education and Science. Similarly, a touring exhibition, shown at a number of diversely funded venues around Ireland, would bring to these venues an element of Arts Council support. In terms of overall government expenditure on the visual arts, it is extremely difficult to estimate the proportion of funding which is directed towards contemporary visual art, as opposed to historic (that is eighteenth- or nineteenth-century) art. The policy of the Arts Council has been firmly accented towards the contemporary visual arts since its foundation, leaving the acquisition, study and promotion of the arts of other eras to a small and very underfunded public sector. The irony of this is that in spite of the rarity of retrospective or survey exhibitions covering Irish art of the eighteenth or nineteenth centuries, interest amongst private collectors in these areas is very considerable. A figure of approximately 80% of government expenditure goes on the support of contemporary art, as opposed to heritage art, the National Gallery of Ireland being virtually the only institution in the country with any realistic purchasing budget to acquire works by artists working prior to, or in the early part of, the twentieth century.

Residencies available for artists in Ireland include the IMMA works programme, the Tyrone Guthrie Centre in county Monaghan, the Ballinglen Arts Foundation in county Mayo, Cill Rialaig in county Kerry and the Sirius Arts Centre in county Cork. Working jointly, the CRC and the Arts Councils of Ireland and Northern Ireland support the P.S.1 residency fellowship, awarded annually to two promising young contemporary artists to enable them to live and work in New York for a year.

Apart from the Arts Council, but dependent on it for funding, there exist several support and information services for artists. The Association of Irish Art Historians provides a forum for lecturers and museum employees to exchange information. The Artists Association of Ireland (AAI) has over 400 members, and provides information on rights, social welfare, exhibition payment entitlements and other aspects of importance in artists' lives. The Sculptors Society of Ireland (SSI) has 350 members. Both the AAI and the SSI publish magazines which give detailed information on the work of their membership, while the area of Irish contemporary art is covered in greater detail by the monthly magazine *Circa*. A significant number of art books dealing with the contem-

porary visual arts and architecture are published annually by Gandon Editions, based in Oysterhaven in county Cork. *The Irish Arts Review*, published annually, is a high-quality publication, edited by former National Gallery director Homan Potterton, that presents scholarly research in a popular and accessible format.

While acknowledging the increase in Arts Council research and expenditure on the arts and the presence of an arts ministry at the cabinet table, in contrast with other European cities the development of Dublin's cultural infrastructure in recent years has been hampered by a lack of strategic thinking. Decisions have been made which reflect expediency and crisis management rather than considered and rational forward planning. That this is in such marked contrast to the cultural infrastructure in the nineteenth century is perhaps regrettable. The core of the problem lies in the decision taken in the 1920s to locate the Dáil (parliament) of the new Free State in Kildare House. Up to that time this large Palladian residence, designed in the mid-eighteenth century by Richard Cassels, had been the headquarters of the Royal Dublin Society, a cultural and scientific institution. Kildare House was the hub of the cultural and museum quarter of Dublin. At its four corners were established the National Gallery, the Natural History Museum, the National Library and the National Museum. The Metropolitan School of Art, originally the Drawing School of the Royal Dublin Society, was also part of this complex of buildings. In the surrounding streets were galleries and artists' studios.

The conversion of Kildare House into the seat of government brought with it demands for office and administrative space. Over the years, this resulted in the steady sundering of Dublin's nineteenth-century cultural quarter, with today only the National Gallery surviving and thriving on its original site. The National Library remains in Kildare Street but faces almost insurmountable pressures on space, the College of Art has been relocated to Thomas Street, while the National Museum has substantially relocated to a converted military barracks, some two miles west along the river Liffey. However, Collins Barracks, a huge building dating from the beginning of the eighteenth century, is not suitable for the entire collection and therefore just part of the National Museum — the decorative arts section mainly — has been relocated there. The early Irish goldwork, artefacts central to that sense of national identity that eventually led to the formation of the Republic of Ireland, remain at Kildare Street, while the ethnographic, industrial and other material was removed.

This sundering of the cultural heart of the city was compounded by the decision taken in 1989 to locate the new Irish Museum of Modern Art (IMMA) at the Royal Hospital Kilmainham, not far from Collins Barracks. It was evident even at that point that the Royal Hospital, a magnificent seventeenth-century building designed along the lines of Les Invalides in Paris, would make an ideal new home for the National Museum if the latter was to be forced out of its original buildings in Kildare Street. There was considerable advocacy of the idea that a new contemporary art museum should be located in one of the huge docklands buildings then becoming available in the city centre close to the new Financial Services Centre. In the event, the decision to locate IMMA at the Royal Hospital Kilmainham went ahead, and its opening by An Taoiseach, Charles J. Haughey, in 1991 was the crowning moment of Dublin's year as European Cultural Capital. It has been a successful move in many ways, and has vindicated those pragmatists who rightly doubted that IMMA could do better in terms of the magnificence of its new home. The National Museum has faced the difficult move to Collins Barracks, a far more utilitarian building than the Royal Hospital, where the spaces and facilities are less than ideal.

All this leaves IMMA and the National Museum at Collins Barracks physically remote from the city centre and with a consequent difficulty in attracting audiences. Lacking a public transport connection with the centre of Dublin, their ability to function effectively at a popular level is hampered. The present exhibitions programme at IMMA concentrates on bringing an interesting variety of international contemporary displays to Ireland, including much work which would not otherwise be shown in this country. The building has been put to imaginative use over the past few years, challenging the traditional notion of a museum and developing a range of community, education and outreach programmes which interact with a wide spectrum of social groups whose access to contemporary visual culture would otherwise be limited or non-existent. Criticisms of the failure of IMMA to develop and exhibit a broadly based twentieth-century Irish collection were addressed in 1998, while exhibitions such as the Andy Warhol have succeeded in drawing more people to visit the museum.

Tradition and conservatism, even in the promotion of contemporary art, still play an important role in Dublin. The major contemporary commercial galleries, the Kerlin, the Taylor, Green on Red, the Rubicon, remain clustered around Kildare Street. The Hallward and the newer Peppercanister are also located in this quarter of the city — the traditional haunt of the arts in Dublin since the eighteenth century. The lyrical abstractionists — those influenced by what was termed in the 1950s 'the School of Paris', and also by the St Ives School — tend to be represented by the Taylor Galleries in Dawson Street, a long-established commercial gallery founded by John Taylor (who previously worked for Leo Smith in the Dawson Gallery). This gallery therefore provides a linear and almost uninterrupted tradition of over fifty years of showing work by moderately progressive Irish painters

and sculptors such as Conor Fallon, Tony O'Malley, Breon O'Casey and others.

Attempts to induce these galleries to move to the newly revitalized Temple Bar area have had virtually no success, nor have any moved to Thomas Street, where the National College of Art, housed since 1982 in a converted distillery, remains in virtual isolation, cut off from both the commercial galleries which are clustered around Kildare Street, two miles to the east, and the Museum of Modern Art, a mile to the west. The situation has not been helped by the social deterioration in recent years of the Thomas Street and the adjoining inner-city public housing complexes, where heroin addiction is now as common as was alcoholism twenty years ago. Closer to the city centre, a substantial public investment in arts and building infrastructure has successfully transformed Temple Bar into an energetic and bustling tourist quarter. However, this social transformation has also encountered problems as result of that same failure to take into account the basic realities of everyday life in Ireland. The disenchantment of artists as they are forced out of the area by high prices is countered by the enthusiasm with which public houses have doubled and tripled their floor area, and the unbridled enthusiasm which has been a feature of the streets of Temple Bar at night. These problems are accentuated by the high degree of expectation placed on the Temple Bar district to provide a home for the visual arts. Visual arts institutions in Temple Bar supported by the Arts Council now include the ARK (a children's art and theatre centre), the Design Yard, the Irish Film Centre, the Project Arts Centre, a centre for new technology in the arts called Arthouse (which is also a home to the Artists Association of Ireland), the Black Church Print Studios, the Graphic Studio, the Gallery of Photography and Temple Bar Gallery and Studios.

Dublin's municipal art gallery bears the somewhat cumbersome and inaccurate title 'The Hugh Lane Municipal Gallery of Modern Art'. Born in 1875, Hugh Lane was one of a group of talented Irish middle-class Protestants which included Jack B. and William Butler Yeats, J. M. Synge, Oscar Wilde and George Bernard Shaw. Lane, from a Cork family, was brought up in Cornwall. Trained as an art restorer, he began his career as an art dealer in London by buying and selling paintings in and around Bond Street in a small way. Within a few years, he had attained considerable success as a dealer, with clients on both sides of the Atlantic, and had himself amassed a sizeable collection of paintings, including works by Monet, Renoir and Fantin-Latour. His house on Cheyne Walk in Chelsea was the last word in Edwardian elegance. Lane considered artists like Monet and Renoir to be the best of Modern Art, and evidently had little time for those who were pioneering new developments in his own era such as Picasso, Matisse or

Braque. He was also easily seduced by the flashy portraits of fashionable painters such as Boldoni. Lane wanted to make a gift of this collection to the city of Dublin to found a Gallery of Modern Art. After vacillating, he succeeded, but his untimely death in 1915 — he was among the passengers of the ill-fated *Lusitania*, sunk by a German submarine — left an uncertain legal situation, with the National Gallery in London and the Hugh Lane Gallery both claiming ownership of his collection. An awkward but workable solution to this legal dispute was found which has the core of the Lane Bequest alternating between the two museums, spending seven years in London, then seven years in Ireland. The Hugh Lane collection was shown for a number of years in Harcourt Street before moving to its present home, the magnificent Palladian town house of the Earl of Charlemont on Parnell Square.

In the seventy years or more since its establishment, the collection at the Hugh Lane Gallery has grown considerably. However, its mandate to be representative of Modern Art is somewhat skewed by the astonishing quality of the original gift — *Les parapluies* by Renoir, Monet, the *Portrait of Eva Gonzales* and *La musique aux Tuileries* by Manet. The recent acquisition of an adjoining eighteenth-century townhouse will enable the Gallery further to develop its range of services and exhibition spaces in the future. After a few somewhat moribund decades, enlivened by the occasional touring exhibition, the Hugh Lane has in recent years been revitalized with a refurbishment of the existing building and a greatly increased programme of temporary exhibitions.

In recent decades, the number of spaces devoted to touring exhibitions has increased, with the establishment of the Douglas Hyde Gallery within the campus of Trinity College, Dublin. The completion of the RHA Gallagher Gallery on Ely Place in the mid 1980s also provided a fine space for contemporary exhibitions, while the Guinness Hopstore, located within the giant Guinness brewery on James's Street, continues to provide an occasional venue for visual art exhibitions. The programme at the Douglas Hyde Gallery has tended over the past two decades to be a straightforward reflection of the interests and predilictions of its directors. However, it has built up a solid international reputation as one of the leading European galleries to show new art of a challenging nature by European and American contemporary artists. The world of the visual arts in this country has always tended to be dominated by a small coterie of critics, curators and gallery directors. Even with the recent growth in the number of art centres and exhibition spaces, this is still the case. This coterie does not act in a concerted or strategic way. Each institution has the freedom to determine its own programme and to schedule, occasionally in direct competition, those

artists considered the most interesting.

While the Hugh Lane, the Douglas Hyde and the Irish Museum of Modern Art have had an active temporary exhibition programme in recent years, the National Gallery of Ireland has concentrated on a building and refurbishment programme, with mixed results. The building structure is now in better shape than it has ever been, with full air-conditioning being introduced to many galleries. However, the sensitivity of the interventions has been questionable, with an inappropriate lift now installed in the centre of a fine cantilevered stairwell and an unprepossessing entrance lobby. The grandeur of the original nineteenth-century galleries has not been interfered with, and a range of new exhibition galleries shows to perfection the collection which is particularly strong in Italian and Dutch seventeenth-century paintings. Almost before the paint was dry in the existing and new sections, plans have been carried forward to build a new wing which will give the National Gallery a totally new street frontage and public entrance onto nearby Clare Street. Although the present entrance is not architecturally distinguished, being a great pile of rusticated granite facing onto Merrion Square, it has clear presence and a comfortable feel, facing onto one of the greatest eighteenth-century urban squares in Dublin. Its new identity, when a second entrance is introduced onto Clare Street, is more difficult to predict. However the move to provide a high-quality exhibition space on Clare Street is a well-considered one that will reap benefits in terms of public accessibility and visitor figures.

Outside the capital, the scene is far more patchy. Three cities in Ireland have dedicated municipal art galleries, Dublin, Limerick and Cork. In both Dublin and Limerick, these galleries receive an annual grant from the corporation, while in Cork the Crawford Municipal Art Gallery is the responsibility of the City of Cork Vocational Education Committee. The arrival in Cork in 1818 of a collection of classical sculpture casts from the Vatican Museum prompted the founding of the Cork School of Art. Consistently espousing through the course of the nineteenth century solid middle-class values, the Cork School of Art found itself somewhat adrift amidst the political and civil turmoils of the early twentieth century, but recovered in the nineteen sixties to re-establish itself as one of the leading art schools in Ireland. The art collection associated with the School of Art had for many years been the *de facto* municipal art collection, and when the art school moved to new premises in 1979, the old north-lit studios were incorporated into the exhibition spaces of the Crawford Municipal Art Gallery. With the assistance of European Union funding, a new temporary exhibitions gallery has been constructed for the Crawford Gallery, while improvements are being made in the existing building, which dates from 1720 and 1884. The City Art Gallery in Limerick is also undergoing refurbishment and redevelopment of its galleries in the old Carnegie Library on Perry Square, while the Model Arts Centre in Sligo is destined to become the municipal art gallery of that city.

The commercial galleries that one might expect associated with municipal galleries are hardly to be found. Outside the commercial gallery network of Dublin, there are few galleries selling art in Ireland. One reason for this is that state-subsidised galleries and art centres generally conduct and encourage the sale of art, in contemporary exhibitions particularly, with an enthusiasm equal to private commercial spaces. This skews the market and makes it uneconomical for all but a few select commercial galleries to exist alongside the slew of state-subsidized spaces for whom selling art is an important part of their income. It may be said that these state-subsidized spaces would be unable to survive if they did not sell art but, by so doing, they erode the viability of the private sector and create unfair competition.

Most commercial galleries outside Dublin are subsidized by ancillary enterprises such as framing, sales of antiques or furniture, or through subsidy by private patrons. In Dublin itself, the leading commercial galleries are supported by a relatively small number of serious collectors. A survey carried out in 1994 by Paula Clancy and Martin Drury for the Arts Council highlighted some of the difficulties facing commercial galleries. Although the percentage of the population purchasing works by living Irish artists had increased from 2% in 1980 to 6% in 1994, this still meant that original works of art were never purchased by 92% of the public. Attendance at exhibitions was 23% as opposed to 37% attending plays (Clancy and Drury 1994, 113). The report pointed out that while there was perhaps a modicum of comfort to be taken from the fact that in 1993 6% of the population had bought original works of art by Irish artists, as compared with 2% in 1980, it was clear that there was 'a massive market failure and every need for intervention from public funds. Such a market failure of course reveals a problem of public cultural competence with its roots in education, broadly defined. Therefore policies of public subsidy to close the market gap must be matched by cultural and educational policies which are committed to the long-term alleviation of that market failure' (Clancy and Drury 1994, 93).

The 1994 Clancy and Drury survey highlighted the extreme disparity in terms of access to the arts that exists between those living in Dublin and in other parts of the country. The authors of the report were unequivocal in their assessment of this imbalance:

The survey revealed that living in Dublin is a discrete factor, irrespective of class, age, education or gender. As such a singular factor, Dublin has favourable impact upon attendance, partici-

pation, purchase and home-based engagement with the arts. We emphasise that this is not simply an urban phenomenon. Indeed with the exception of the more traditional arts, the profiling treatment reveals that there is not an enormous disparity between rural and urban audiences *per se* and that it is class, education, age and region that are the critical factors.

In a necessarily speculative mode, we suggest that the Dublin factor can be accounted for in a number of ways. Certainly there is the existence of a range of permanent facilities and the occasional opportunities in the capital city not available elsewhere in Ireland. To that must be added that many of those facilities are of very long standing, embedded into the traditions and habits of the city and its citizens to a degree not to be found even in other cities like Cork and Limerick.

There is the location in Dublin of most of the national cultural institutions which though in Dublin are not of Dublin. In addition, the vast majority of the working arts community and the greatest proportion of the cultural industries like television, film and popular music are based in Dublin. Large cities like Dublin have a very high proportion of their population who are not native to the city. Away from home and from the social patterns of small and medium scale communities, there is a greater reliance upon culture and entertainment for distraction and social intercourse.

It remains the case that the survey reveals that all else being equal, Dublin is the place to be, if you have, or wish to develop, an interest in the arts. (Clancy and Drury 1994, 96)

The report did contain some grounds for optimism, however. In the case of the visual arts, the authors pointed out that the trend since the 1980s had been away from the large annual exhibitions and towards more small- and medium-scale exhibitions. Together with the development of studios in many towns, and of arts centres with galleries, the dominance of Dublin in the visual arts has not been diminished, but at least there is recognition of the problem. Though the figures are as yet modest in absolute terms and appear dwarfed by those for film and popular music, there is an achievement of some significance to be recorded here, and one to be built on for the future, with due regard, as already noticed, for rural areas away from large conurbations (Clancy and Drury 1994, 97). Whether the Arts Council will be able to react to the findings of this and other reports which highlight graphically the imbalance between funding for the arts in Dublin versus other parts of the country is debatable. Complaints from provincial cities that they are given inadequate funds to sustain programmes of excellence are countered with the accusation that, compared with counties in the midlands of Ireland, provincial centres such as Galway, Limerick and Cork do comparatively well. This rebuttal effectively silences opposition from these cities' arts communities and enables the Arts Council, having paid lip service to the development of art centres in areas of low population, to continue to direct the great bulk its resources towards the capital city.

THE ARTS COUNCIL AND THE FUTURE OF THE VISUAL ARTS IN IRELAND

As has been seen, the future of the visual arts in Ireland lies substantially in the hands of the Arts Council. The department which provides funding to the Arts Council, the Department of Arts, Heritage, Gaeltacht and the Islands, is probably more circumscribed in its freedom of action, being obliged primarily to fund national institutions. The Arts Council has more latitude and in its *Arts Plan 1999–2001*, published in 1999, it was apparent that the ground was being laid for the Council to assume a leadership role in the development of the visual arts, rather than being merely a responsive agency.

The new plan was both a catalogue of failures and a wish-list for future success. How the word 'failure' could have been appended in 1999 to an organization whose grant-in-aid from government had nearly doubled over the past five years is something of a mystery, but the chairman's preface, littered with phrases such as 'time to make a new start', 'the preserve of the few' and 'reduce the barriers', seemed steeped in a sense of present failure and future opportunity, although it should be remembered that the plan's purpose was largely to convince the Minister for Arts, Síle de Valera, and her department, that the annual grant to the Council should be increased handsomely, and in that respect the plan succeeded in its initial objective.

The preparation of the plan was informed by a series of consultative meetings which the Council undertook around Ireland in the two years preceding its publication. Although well-intentioned, the meetings were not a great success. The fear of those attending, many of whom were clients of the Council, that their funds would be axed if they expressed views critical of the Council, was palpable. However, some key issues were raised. The Council was seen as too remote, too centralized and too obscure in its decision-making. Client organizations experienced great difficulties in planning ahead as they were unable to predict the level of forthcoming grant aid. There was a clear wish that the Council should become less paternalistic, draw back from the minutiae of small decision-making, devolve some of its responsibilities and functions to local and regional level and leave the practice of the arts to professional arts practitioners.

Little of this was reflected in the plan, which nevertheless stressed the need for a dialogue with the arts world that was 'more open, more purposeful'. The language and thinking of the plan was far more informed by the government's Strategic Management Initiative, introduced by Taoiseach Albert Reynolds at the beginning of the 1990s, that required all publicly funded state agencies to justify and rationalize their procedures, methodologies and aims for the future. The purpose of the plan was essentially to enable the Council to secure further budget increases, recruit more staff, augment its centralized control of the arts, and involve itself more in the detail of what was being done by arts practitioners. Tiring of its passive role, the Council announced its intention of transforming itself from a simple funding agency into a more aggressive 'development agency for the arts'. This is not to say that the plan did not contain many admirable elements and worthy aspirations. Artists were promised every help towards realizing their full potential. Excellence and innovation were accorded handsome rewards. Research was to be funded and new audiences for the arts developed. The arts would be available to all. That these aspirations hardly differed from those articulated twenty years before by the Council was not referred to.

No matter how worthy the aspirations, history has shown that when in the past the Council has become unduly prescriptive, things have not quite worked out as planned. When the Council begins to prepare 'strategic objectives', tensions arise. Intellectual property, no less than any other sort of property, brings with it responsibilities as well as privileges. One example from the recent past was the well-intentioned scheme whereby the Council commissioned a public sculpture for the winner of the annual Tidy Towns Award. After a series of public relations disasters, where contemporary sculptures were placed in towns that did appear to want them, and artists' reputations were damaged, the scheme was dropped. Similarly, in the late 1980s and early 1990s, the Council became directly involved in the initiation of several projects, such as the Fire Station Studios and the Irish Film Centre, from the management of which it was only later able to extricate itself with considerable difficulty.

Warnings of the dangers of this 'hands-on' approach were clearly sounded in 1976 in the Richards Report, which recommended that 'The purpose of the Arts Council is not to impose art on anyone or to propagate its own views. Councils and other bodies who try to do so destroy spontaneity and substitute for it some kind of social or moral obligation. The Arts Council should remain in the background in the sense that it should seldom become involved in directly promoting the arts' (Richards 1976, 94). But times had changed, moral obligations abound and the Council of 1999 did not seem content to remain in the background. The then chairman, Brian Farrell, put his views trenchantly:

'Confident, more developed economically, more socially critical and aware, Ireland is ready for new policy departures in all areas of life ... This is an entirely opportune time to re-evaluate, re-organise and radically re-invigorate the place of the arts at the heart of Irish society and the larger world.'

The reality was that things were going quite well for the Arts Council and it had accomplished a great deal over the years. Looking back to 1978, under the directorship of Colm Ó Briain, the Council's grant was increased from £1.5m to £2.3m and the staff expanded to seventeen. In the year 2000, with thirty-two staff members, the grant voted was approximately £35m.

The most important element of the plan, and the element that contained the most promise for the future development of the visual arts in Ireland, was the concept that particular organizations would be selected by the Council and given financial resources that were both adequate and assured over a number of years. This was one issue raised at the consultative meetings which was clearly articulated in the resulting plan. For the first time in the history of the Arts Council in Ireland, this provision enabled selected arts organizations to plan ahead in a proper and strategic way, with consequent benefits in terms of quality. The plan also contained a clear listing of the criteria under which the performance of arts organizations would be judged. For the first time, the international dimension of the arts in Ireland was clearly acknowledged.

The plan also recognized the differing handicaps under which arts organizations worked, particularly the differing problems facing urban and rural arts groups, which perhaps may provide reassurance that the decisions made by the Council might also reflect these realities. Given the imbalances that already exist in Ireland, there should be on the part of any contemporary Irish Arts Council a sense of absolute obligation that its influence and support be evenly and fairly spread across the entire country. Too many of the strategic objectives in the plan seem predisposed towards favouring the capital city, where, as has been shown in this essay, a disproportionate amount of national resources are already expended. It is to be hoped that the aspirations contained within the plan will be achieved and that access to, and participation in, the visual arts can become recognized as a birthright. The pursuit of excellence, so long overlooked, rejected or marginalized in past years in Ireland, will hopefully be given the proper support and encouragement it deserves.

Bibliography

Arnold, B. 1977 *A concise history of Irish art*. London.
Arnold, B. 1991 *Mainie Jellett 1897–1944*. Dublin.
Arts Council of Ireland 1990–98 *Annual reports*. Dublin.
Barrett, C. 1971 *Irish art in the nineteenth century*. Cork.

Barrett, C. 1975 'Irish nationalism and art 1880–1921', *Studies* (Winter).
Barrett, C. 1979 *Michael Farrell* [exhibition catalogue, Douglas Hyde Gallery]. Dublin.
Butler, P. 1990 *Three hundred years of Irish watercolours and drawings*. London.
Campbell, J. 1984 *The Irish impressionists — Irish artists in France and Belgium 1850–1914*. Dublin.
Campbell, J. 1993 *Onlookers in France — Irish realist and impressionist painters*. Cork.
Catto, M. 1991 *Art in Ulster 2 1957–1977*. Belfast.
Clancy, P. and Drury, M. 1994 *The public and the arts: a survey of behaviour and attitudes in Ireland*. Dublin.
Crookshank, A. and The Knight of Glin 1978 *The painters of Ireland c. 1660–1920*. London.
Crookshank, A. and The Knight of Glin 1994 *The watercolours of Ireland — works on paper in pencil, pastel and paint*. London.
Dukes, G. 1997 'What are you doing here with that pencil?: the integrity of Camille Souter', *Irish Arts Review Yearbook 1997*, **13**, pp. 159–68.
Dunne, A. 1986 *Barrie Cooke*. Dublin.
Dunne, A. 1990 *Irish art — the European dimension*. Dublin.
Dunne, A. 1992 *Barrie Cooke — claochló*. The Hague.
Dunne, A. Fowler, J. and Hutchinson, J. 1990 *A new tradition — Irish art of the eighties*. Dublin.
Fallon, B. 1990 *Contemporary artists from Ireland* [catalogue essay]. London.
Fallon, B. 1992 *Tony O'Malley — work from the sixties* [catalogue essay]. Kilkenny.
Fallon, B. 1994 *Irish art 1830–1990*. Belfast.
Fitz-Simon, C. 1982 *The arts in Ireland: a chronology*. Dublin.
Fuchs, R. *et al.* 1991 *Jack B. Yeats — the late paintings*. Haags Gemeentemuseum.
Garner, W. 1983 *Ireland: a cultural encyclopedia*. London.
Gorry Gallery 1992 *Irish paintings* [exhibition catalogue]. Dublin.
Hewitt, J. 1991 *Art in Ulster 1 1557–1957*. Belfast.
Hunt, J. 1989 *Brian Bourke* [Arts Council touring exhibition]. Dublin.
Hunter, M. 1971 'Basil Blackshaw' in *The Irish imagination 1959–71* [Rosc exhibition catalogue, Hugh Lane Municipal Gallery of Modern Art] (Dublin), p. 40.
Hutchinson, P. 1971 'Nano Reid' in *The Irish imagination 1959–1971* (Dublin), p. 90.
Hutchinson, J. 1991 *Inheritance and transformation*. Dublin.
Kelly, A. 1998 'Irish visual culture: a policy review', *Éire-Ireland* **23**, **24**.
Kennedy, B. P. 1993 *Irish painting*. Dublin.
Kennedy, S. B. 1991 *Irish art and modernism 1880–1950*.

Belfast.

Knowles, R. 1982 *Contemporary Irish art*. Dublin.

Le Brocquy, L. 1996 *Louis le Brocquy: conversations with the artist*. Oysterhaven.

Marten, B. *et al.* 1982 *Seamus Murphy 1907–1975* [catalogue essays]. Cork.

McConkey, K. 1990 *A free spirit — Irish art 1860–1960*. London.

McConkey, K. 1993 *Sir John Lavery*. Edinburgh.

Morgan, G. (interviewer) 1995 *Louis le Brocquy — the head image*. Kinsale.

Murray, P. 1990a *GPA awards for emerging artists 1990* [catalogue essay]. Dublin.

Murray, P. 1990b *William Crozier — paintings 1949–1990* [catalogue essay]. Cork.

Murray, P. 1992 *Illustrated summary catalogue of the Crawford Municipal Art Gallery*. Cork.

O'Doherty, B. 1971 Introductory essay in *The Irish imagination 1959–1971* [Rosc exhibition catalogue, Hugh Lane Municipal Gallery of Modern Art] (Dublin), pp. 10–11.

O'Regan, J. (ed) 1990 *Edge to edge — three sculptors from Ireland*. Kinsale.

O'Regan, J. (ed) 1991a *Works 1 — James Scanlon: Sneem* [introduction by Patrick Reyntiens; interview by Shane O'Toole]. Kinsale.

O'Regan, J. (ed) 1991b *Works 2 — Vivienne Roche* [introduction by the artist; interview by Vera Ryan]. Kinsale.

O'Regan, J. (ed) 1994a *Works 14 — Tony O'Malley* [interview by John O'Regan]. Kinsale.

O'Regan, J. (ed) 1994b *Works 15 — Charles Tyrrell* [interview by Brian Fallon]. Kinsale.

Plunkett, J. 1997 'Ralph Cusack in exile', *The Recorder: Journal of the Americal Irish Historical Society* **10**, nos 1–2.

Pyle, H. 1975 *Irish art 1900–1950* [catalogue essay]. Cork.

Pyle, H. 1992 *Jack B. Yeats*. Dublin.

Richards, J. M. 1976 *Provision for the arts*. Dublin.

Robinson, K. 1988 'Mary Swanzy' in *Critics choice* [exhibition catalogue, Hugh Lane Municipal Gallery of Modern Art] (Dublin), p. 26.

Ruane, F. 1980 *The delighted eye — Irish painting and sculpture of the seventies, a sense of Ireland*. Belfast.

Ruane, F. 1986 *Twentieth-century Irish art*. [catalogue essay]. Dublin.

Ruane, M. 1990 (ed) *A new tradition — Irish art of the eighties*. Dublin.

Ryan, J. 1971 'Patrick Swift', *The Irish imagination 1959–1971* (Dublin), p. 100.

Ryan, V. 1985 *Cork art now '85* [catalogue essay]. Cork.

Ryan, V. 1994 *Tony O'Malley, a personal choice*. [catalogue essay]. Cork.

Sheehy, J. 1980 *The rediscovery of Ireland's past — the Celtic revival 1830–1930*. London.

Smolin-Ryan, W. (ed) 1987 *Irish women artists from the eighteenth century to the present day*. Dublin.

Stewart, A. M. 1985 *Royal Hibernian Academy — index of exhibitors 1826-1979*. Dublin.

Stewart, A. M. 1990 *Irish art loan exhibitions 1765–1927, index of artists*. Dublin.

Strickland, W. G. 1913 *A dictionary of Irish artists*. Dublin.

Walker, D. 1981 *Louis le Brocquy*. Dublin.

Turpin, J. 1990 'Oliver Sheppard', *Irish Arts Review Yearbook 1990–1991*. Dublin.

Walker, G. 1990 *Charles Tyrrell — the borderland paintings* [catalogue essay]. Cork.

White, J. 1994 *Gerard Dillon — an illustrated biography*. Dublin.

The Irish Film Industry

HELEN GUERIN

Films were first screened in Ireland in April 1896, a mere four months after the emergence of cinema as we know it today, the credit for which is attributed to the Lumière brothers' first public screening of *La Sortie des Ouvriers de l'Usine Lumière* in Paris in December 1895. By the end of that year, audiences in Cork, Dublin and Belfast were experiencing the new invention, silent film. The first great impresario of cinema in Ireland was James T. Jameson, who came to film from his book-publishing business in Cope Street, Dublin. He screened films at the Rotunda, the Rathmines Town Hall and the Pavilion in Dún Laoghaire (then Kingstown). He acquired a huge library of films from abroad, which he rented out to provincial exhibitors, sending both his operators and his equipment to these venues, as was common practice at that time.

While Dublin had several venues for screening films, it did not boast a fully dedicated cinema. In an attempt to redress this deficiency, the internationally renowned writer, James Joyce, persuaded some Italian entrepreneurs to invest in a cinema in Dublin, as a sister to the Volta Picture Palace in Bucharest. This would allow Italian films to be screened in Ireland, as well as adding to the box-office revenues of the Italian investors, and, in return, Irish audiences would have the benefit of experiencing world cinema. On the 20 December 1909 the Volta Cinema opened in Dublin. The following day, two cinemas open in Cork, the Cork Electric Theatre and the Assembly Rooms on the South Mall.

The only films screened in the new Volta cinema, therefore, were silent Italian films, with Italian subtitles. The audience were given printed handbills carrying a synopsis of the stories in English. However, audiences were not completely satisfied with the bill of fare, and within twelve months the Volta had been taken over by the British Provincial Cinematograph Theatres, who later built the Sackville and Grafton cinemas. By 1910 cinemas were custom-built and spread throughout the country,

with Belfast boasting a total of five. Moreover, the supply of films from Europe and America became increasingly available, as distributors found it profitable to operate in Ireland.

Unfortunately, in Ireland the process of film production got off to a much slower start. When it eventually did get going, it was characterized by a stop-start style of production, which impeded the development of the type of coherent film infrastructure which accompanies continuity of production. In the early years Ireland became popular as an off-shore location for foreign films. The Kalem Film Company was one of the most prolific of these, filming a number of popular dramas based on the 1798 Rebellion and the 1803 Rising, and focussing on the attempts of Irish republicans to establish an independent Irish state. Indeed the company's principal director, the Irish-Canadian Sidney Olcott, is credited with having made the first fiction film in Ireland, *The Lad from Old Ireland* (1910). This was followed swiftly by *The Colleen Bawn* (1911), *Arrah Na Pogue* (1911), *Ireland the Oppressed* (1912) and *The Irish Rebel* (1916), as well as numerous other productions.

The first indigenous feature film made in Ireland was produced by the Film Company of Ireland, whose leading directors, Fred O'Donovan, *The Eleventh Hour* (1916), and J. M. Kerrigan, *O'Neil of the Glens* (1916) and *A Girl from Glenbeigh* (1917), dominated early Irish cinema. In the three years leading up to 1920, the Film Company of Ireland made almost twenty films, including *Knocknagow* (1918), *Paying the Rent* (1919) and *Willy Reilly and his Colleen Bawn* (1920). The predominant theme for the next thirty years of film-making in Ireland, for both indigenous and off-shore productions, was the War of Independence. In addition to the films of the Film Company of Ireland, many feature films were attempted by individuals and short-lived enterprises, among whom one of the most notable was James Power, a Bray barber who directed *Rosaleen Dhu*, which reportedly has the unique claim of having been shot by a blind cameraman and processed by the barber-shop lather-boy. Outside of Ireland the plays of Boucicault had accustomed foreign audiences to an image of Ireland which owed little to reality, and, while proving popular abroad, they received short shrift at home and were derogatorily termed 'stage Irish'.

One of the most famous Irish directors of the early 1920s was Rex Ingram, who filmed the *Four Riders of the Apocalypse*, with Rudolph Valentino and Alice Terry (whom he later married), *The Prisoner of Zenda* and *Scaramouche* (which launched Ramon Novarro's career). Another internationally renowned Irish director of the time was Herbert Brenon, who directed, among others, *A Kiss for Cinderella*, *Beau Geste* and *Peter Pan*. Several Irish film-makers chose to work abroad, especially in America, Canada and Australia, where funds for production were more freely available. Some of the most notable film-makers with Irish roots were Robert Flaherty, the father of the documentary, John Ford of *The Blue Eagle* (1926) and *The Informer* (1935), *The Plough and the Stars* (1936) and *The Quiet Man* (1952), Raoul Walsh, *Gentleman Jim* (1942) and John Huston, *The Mackintosh Man* (1973), *The Maltese Falcon* (1941) and *The Dead* (1987). It is also worth noting here that the very first feature film produced in Australia, *The Story of the Kelly Gang* (1906), was based on the Irish bush ranger Ned Kelly.

The appearance of *The Singing Fool* at the Capitol Cinema in Dublin in April 1929 marked a new era in the cinema. The talkies had arrived and people flocked to see them. While the addition of sound was undoubtedly a welcome development, it had far-reaching consequences, the extent of which can only be seen in hindsight. The talkies were eventually to contribute to the monopoly of English-language films, and thereby unwittingly precipitated the demise of the other so-called 'foreign-language' film industries. Indeed the initial rumblings of this demise were already being heard in the 1920s when one takes stock of the full effects of World War One. Throughout Europe emerging film industries were decimated, as national industries increasingly felt the effects of lost personnel, lost resources and lost markets. Of the major film-producing countries only the United States remained intact. Moreover, in the lean years between the two world wars, America was the only country with the necessary resources to build a strong international film infrastructure. Ironically, it was the advent of the talkies that put an end to the popular catch-cry, originally cited by the father of American cinema, D. W. Griffith, that 'film was the language that would unify the world'.

At home in Ireland the lack of resources was blindingly evident. Indeed, one could argue that Ireland was one of the countries that suffered most as a result of English-language film's dominance of the international marketplace. Due to our proximity to Britain and our close ties with America, it was virtually impossible to halt the relatively cheap English-language films pouring into the Irish market. Their ready availability, compounded by the lack of both public and private funds to support indigenous film production, meant that Irish film-makers found it next to impossible to find the resources to make a film, either in the English or the Irish language.

Those entrepreneurs who did risk investing in film production found a very poor return on their investment, as the limited capacity of Irish audiences could not ensure an adequate return, while audiences abroad were more accustomed to 'stage Irish' productions and cared little for the more gritty perspective. This stymied any attempts to create a critical mass of Irish-made films to secure a presence on the international stage. This in turn prevented the indigenous industry from reaching fruition. Indeed the 1920s and 1930s were a time of great change in Ireland as the country tried to recover from hundreds of years of British rule, followed by a brutal civil war. The government's primary concern was with setting up a new state, and little attention was given to the emerging art-form of film.

With the increasing popularity of the cinema, material that may be considered 'indecent or subversive to public morality' proved disturbing to Irish social mores. The *Censorship Acts* of 1923 and 1929, and the subsequent *Emergency Powers Act* 1939, gave the censor the power to reject a film if he was of the opinion that its exhibition would be 'prejudicial to the maintenance of law and order or to the preservation of the state or would be likely to lead to a breach of the peace or to cause offence to the people of a friendly foreign nation'. Probably the most famous victim of Irish censorship was *Gone with the Wind* (1939), which was actually withdrawn by the distributors following demands by the Film Censor, James Montgomery, for so many cuts as to render the film almost meaningless. Regrettably, Montgomery's successor, Dr Richard Hayes, shared his conservative views, a fact which was aptly captured in a *Dublin Opinion* news article entitled 'We had films before our eyes, now we have only Hayes'. Unfortunately, cuts and bans were as much a part of the cinematic experience as the opening credits on the film. The emergency powers measures were eventually lifted in May 1945, but censorship, influenced in no small way by the Church, continued to play a role, to a greater or lesser extent, in dictating what could and could not be seen in Irish cinemas. This had obvious implications for the development of indigenous film-making, both in terms of what stories might be told and the attitudes of the government towards public investment and support for the emerging industry.

In 1936 the Irish Film Society was formed in Dublin by

a number of film aficionados, including Liam O'Leary. Its objectives were to screen classical and foreign films; to establish a Film School, designed to encourage people to make films and learn about cinema art; to oversee the development of suitable programmes for young people, including the introduction of films into schools through *Comhairle na nÓg* (the first flying film squad) and organize film-related lectures, discussions and disseminate film literature, including the magazine *Scannán*. The key person behind the Irish Film Society was Liam O'Leary (1910–94) who was born in Youghal, county Cork, and emerged as Ireland's premier Irish film historian and film archivist. His work led to the eventual establishment of the National Film Archive. Unfortunately, the development of the Irish Film Society was hampered both by the mores of Irish society (the showing of Eisenstein's *Battleship Potemkin* by the Dublin Little Theatre Guild in 1936 drew headlines of 'Spreading Deathly Poison' and 'First Soviet Propaganda Film in Ireland') and the fact that films had often to be rented from England where renters were reluctant to risk the delay in return. In an article in the *Leader* newspaper (15 June 1946) in which he criticized the production of government propaganda films and lack of realism, Liam O'Leary asked: 'Would we stomach the making of films which reveal our less attractive characteristics — our unemployed, our slums, our emigration, our escapism, our trusted educational system?' The Film School collapsed around 1948 as a result of difficulties in sourcing suitably qualified teachers. This was compounded by the assumptions of members of the organization that silent films were better than 'talkies', that American and British imports were generally rubbish, and that excess of money encouraged bad cinema art.

Throughout the 1940s and 1950s the Irish government pursued a policy of attracting foreign investment into Ireland as a reaction to the conservatism and protectionism of the de Valera era. During this period it finally began to address issues of heritage and cultural identity. At last, after years of lobbying, in 1958 the authorities decided to establish the three-stage National Film Studios (Ardmore) facility in Bray, county Wicklow. The Studios were designed to attract bigger-budget films, which were seen to be lucrative sources of state revenue. In 1959, the first international feature, *Shake Hands with the Devil*, starring James Cagney in a Michael Anderson production, was made in Ardmore. This was the beginning of a number of films which, using Ardmore as their base, shot in and around the Studios locations as diverse as Cold War Berlin in Martin Ritt's *The Spy who came in from the Cold* (1966) and World War One air battles in John Guillerman's *The Blue* (1966). Ardmore got off to a running start, and between 1958 and 1963 twenty-seven films were made at the Studios. However,

government policy still did not support the individual film-makers, and this made it extremely difficult for lower-budget indigenous film-making to develop.

As Ardmore was geared specifically towards off-shore productions, its pricing structure reflected this, which resulted in indigenous film-makers finding the Studios financially prohibitive. As a result the Studios were extremely under-utilised, which resulted in a legacy of indebtedness and bankruptcy right up until the 1980s, both under public and private ownership. Fortunately the downward spiral at Ardmore Film Studios was reversed in the mid-1980s and its future secured. The turning-point occurred during the two-year period of ownership between 1986 and 1988 by the Mary Tyler Moore organization. As 'MTM Ardmore Studios', a \$1 million refurbishment programme was carried out, building on the existing infrastructure and facilities, expanding the number of sound stages to four, part of a continual upgrading that has continued to this day. Recently a water tank for the sea battle scenes in *Kidnapped* (1995) was constructed. The studio has continued to accommodate many foreign feature film productions, such as John Boorman's *Excalibur* (1981), Ron Howard's *Far and Away* (1989) and John Schlesinger's *Sweeney Todd* (1997).

The event that made the greatest impact on indigenous film-makers during the 1960s was the expansion of the national broadcasting agency, which had been providing a comprehensive service on radio since 1926, to television production in 1961. Radio Telefís Éireann (RTÉ) presented an opportunity to aspiring film-makers to work in television, thereby providing them with their first chance to engage in continuous production. Moreover, it provided the opportunity available for actors and technical crew to actually earn a living making television programmes.

However, during the 1960s the predominant film activity in Ireland continued to be off-shore productions which, while contributing to the development of skilled technicians, did little to help the indigenous film-making community. As a result of much lobbying, the government agreed to commission a report on the state of Irish film in the 1960s. The Huston Report of 1968 recommended the setting up of a Film Board to support indigenous film-making. This would mean a move away from investing in fixed assets and towards the support of film-making, through a grants system for specific projects. However, this report was not acted upon until 1980 when Bord Scannán na hÉireann/The Irish Film Board was established.

Ironically, the need to constantly lobby government brought the indigenous film community closer together and fuelled their determination to kick-start the Irish film industry. Some of these film-makers had worked in RTÉ and had decided to set up their own production companies in order to give themselves more creative freedom. Others had worked on a freelance basis on off-shore productions. While others had little or no production experience, they were driven by a single-minded desire to fulfil their creative vision.

Films such as Bob Quinn's *Caoineadh Airt Uí Laoghaire* (1975) and *Poitín* (1978), Cathal Black's *Wheels* (1976), *Our Boys* (1982), and *Pigs* (1984), Joe Comerford's *Down the Corner* (1977) and *Traveller* (1981), Kieran Hickey's *Exposure* (1978) and *Criminal Conversation* (1980) and Pat Murphy's *Maeve* (1981) and *Anne Devlin* (1984) sought to examine and explore elements of Irish culture and politics hitherto considered taboo. Most of these films dealt with issues relating to different aspects of social marginalization, such as the exploration of incest in *Traveller*, alcoholism in *Down the Corner* and drug abuse in *Pigs*. However, the production of these films often proved to be an unrelenting struggle for funding as there was no coherent infrastructure in place to support them. The only source of financial support available, the national broadcaster, shied away from seemingly controversial film-making.

Eventually, the film-makers demands were met and the first Irish Film Board was established in 1981 under the chairmanship of the acclaimed helmsman, John Boorman. An Bord Scannán was the first sign that the Irish government recognized the contribution of film-making to Irish culture and representation, as well as to the economy, both directly and indirectly through tourism, support services and the like. During the six years of its existence the Film Board was allocated £3.06 million in capital for investment in films. This was a revolving fund whereby the money invested in projects would be re-invested in future productions. The Film Board part-funded ten feature films, twenty short films and documentaries and fifteen experimental shorts during its brief time in office. It also provided development funds and grants to approximately sixty other projects to assist in script development and pre-production work. One of the most memorable of these projects was Neil Jordon's *Angel* (1982), which was the forerunner to the internationally acclaimed *The Crying Game* (1992), a film which achieved phenomenal success, both financially and artistically.

However, in 1987, in a desperate attempt to cut government spending, the Film Board was dissolved. Of the £1.247 million advanced to the ten feature films only 8.5% was repaid by February 1987. The poor financial return was given as the reason for cutting off the Film Board's funding. But the government failed to consider the additional revenues to the exchequer which these projects generated, including Irish investments of £1.615 million and foreign investments of £3.295 million.

The Irish film community responded with anger and utter disbelief, as they were well aware of the indirect benefits to the exchequer from the government's limited investment in film production. The film community set up an action group to lobby the government and established FilmBase, a film and video resource organization set up to provide access to reasonably priced equipment and facilities to low-budget film-makers. FilmBase was supported by the Arts Council of Ireland, which appreciated the plight of indigenous film-makers. Shortly afterwards the Galway Film Centre was set up and the Cork Film Centre followed some years later. These three film resource organizations bridge the gap between student films and bigger-budget films which receive public or private investment funding.

Almost as swiftly as it was dissolved, An Bord Scannán was re-constituted in 1992, to coincide with the Academy Award for Neil Jordan's *The Crying Game*. (Michelle Burke also won an Oscar on the day in the 'Hair and Make-up' category.) The re-constituted Bord Scannán was chaired by the first lady of Irish cinema, Lelia Doolan, and given a budget of £1.1 million. Today the budget of Bord Scannán exceeds £4 million. Moreover, there are over 4,000 people working in the industry, and the estimated tax revenues generated for the exchequer exceeded £32 million in 1997, for example.

Starting from a modest base, Bord Scannán, often with the support of the Arts Council of Ireland, RTÉ, BBC Northern Ireland and Channel 4, has supported the development of the fledgling industry, which attempted to do a century of growing in a decade (total turnover in the sector increased 3,400% between 1992 and 1997). Over thirty feature films were made in the 1990s, a huge improvement on the production levels of the preceding ninety years. Also, several television series, documentaries, short films and scripts have been produced. Almost more importantly, the quality of Irish film-making continues to improve, as film-makers increasingly appear more comfortable with representing themselves on screen. Film-makers have also moved away from the age-old themes of oppression, emigration and rebellion which dominated early Irish cinema.

Probably the best known contemporary Irish film-makers are Jim Sheridan, *My Left Foot* (1989) and *In the Name of the Father*, Neil Jordan, *The Crying Game* (1992) and Pat O'Connor, *Circle of Friends* (1995). Indeed it could be argued that Jim Sheridan's 1989 film marked a critical turning-point in Irish cinema. *My Left Foot* does not deal with the traditional themes of the Civil War, the War of Independence or the 'Troubles', but rather it celebrates the individual and lauds a person's power to overcome whatever obstacles emerge throughout one's life. Moreover, the phenomenal success of this film, which was nominated for five Academy Awards and five BAFTAs, brought the spotlight onto the emerging Irish film industry and thereby secured a place for Irish cinema on international screens. Some other notable film-makers who emerged during the 1990s and who have received development support from Bord Scannán include Paddy Breathnach for *Ailsa* (1994), Barry Devlin, *All Things Bright and Beautiful* (1994), Mary McGuckian, *Words upon a Window Pane* (1994),Thaddeus O'Sullivan, *Nothing Personal* (1995), Gerard Stembridge, *Guiltrip* (1995), Geraldine Creed, *The Sun, the Moon and the Stars* (1996), Trish McAdam, *Snakes and Ladders* (1996), Tom Collins, *Bogwoman* (1997).

Probably the most promising sign for the future of the Irish film industry is the establishment of a number of vibrant production companies witnessed throughout the 1990s. This will enable new film-makers to get their projects off the ground without the heartache and torment endured by previous generations. Such companies include Noel Pearson's Ferndale Films, Ed Guiney's Temple Films, David Collins' Samson Films, Tim Palmer's Parallel Films, Marina Hughes' Venus Productions, Liam O'Neill's Paradox Pictures and Brendan McCarthy's Blue Light Productions, to name but a few. (A full list can be found at *http://www.iftn.ie* or from Film Makers Ireland.)

Apart from the aforementioned public sources of funding which support indigenous film-making, namely Bord Scannán na hÉireann/Irish Film Board, the Arts Council of Ireland and Radio Telefís Éireann, over the years Irish film-makers have relied heavily on additional funding from BBC NI and Channel Four. More recently Irish film-makers have also benefited from private sources of funding through the tax incentive scheme Section 481 (formerly Section 35 of the *Finance Act*). It would be true to say that access to these funds has been primarily confined to the more established film-makers and off-shore productions. However, the importance of this tax incentive should not be underestimated, as it provides an important cornerstone to support the infrastructure of the industry, both in terms of hiring of post-production facility houses and as regards providing continuity of employment to the high-calibre technical crews available in Ireland. One of the final pieces of the jigsaw was put in place recently with the establishment of the Irish Screen Commission to promote Ireland as a location for film production as well as maintaining a presence at international festivals and markets.

Bibliography

Ó Drisceoil, D. 1996 *Censorship in Ireland: 1939–1945.* Cork.

O'Leary, L. 1945 *An invitation to film.* Dublin.

Rockett, K., Gibbons, L. and Hill, J. 1988 *Cinema and Ireland.* London and New York.

Rockett, K. and Finn, E. 1995 *Still Irish.* Dublin.

Rockett, K. 1996 *The Irish filmography.* Dún Laoghaire.

Film and Northern Ireland

JOHN HILL

The peculiar status of Northern Ireland — geographically a part of the island of Ireland but politically a part of the UK — has meant that the history of film-making in Northern Ireland has been modest, confined to the margins of both the British and Irish film industries. Indigenous film-making in the north began with the appearance of Ireland's first sound film, *The Voice of Ireland* (1932). The film starred Northern Ireland singer and actor, Richard Hayward — the first man 'to use the Ulster dialect on the screen' according to the publicity at the time — and a number of features involving Hayward and the Belfast Repertory Players followed: *The Luck of the Irish* (1935), *The Early Bird* (1936), *Irish and Proud of it* (1936) and *Devil's Rock* (1938). While these were all relatively unambitious, low-budget musical comedies they proved immensely popular with local audiences, not least because of the rare opportunity they provided to see Northern Ireland locations (mainly the Glens of Antrim) on the big screen. Audiences queued to see *The Luck of the Irish* in the Picture House on Royal Avenue in Belfast while *The Early Bird* opened one of Belfast's most famous cinemas, the Broadway cinema in the Falls Road (with a capacity of 1,500). Although there were plans to build on these successes, and even establish a film studio in Northern Ireland, these did not come to fruition.

As a result, there was virtually no feature film production in Northern Ireland in the period between the 1930s and the 1980s, although a few British films did make use of Northern Ireland locations. The most famous of these is undoubtedly *Odd Man Out* (1947), a gloomy *film noir* tracing the demise of James Mason's wounded IRA man. However, while set in Belfast, most of the film was actually shot in England where the interior of the Crown Bar was faithfully reproduced in the studio at Denham. Ironically, given the current competitiveness among film commissions, an official at the NI Ministry of Commerce wrote prior to the start of the film's shooting that 'a film with Belfast as a background has no

commercial significance whatever, direct or indirect'! This would hardly be true today.

REVIVAL AND DEVELOPMENT IN THE 1980s AND 1990s

It was not until the 1980s that indigenous film production in Northern Ireland began to revive. Of particular significance, in this regard, was the role played by television, especially Channel 4. Channel 4 was launched in 1982 and had a particular remit to complement the other three UK channels and encourage 'innovation and experiment'. A distinctive feature of the Channel's activities was its financing of film production, mainly through the Drama Department (and 'Film on Four') but also via the Department of Independent Film and Video which was committed to funding less orthodox film and television material. This involved support for a number of film workshops and the first feature to be made under the workshop agreement was *Acceptable Levels* (1984), shot mainly in Belfast by Belfast Film Workshop in collaboration with London-based Frontroom Productions. Dealing with an English television crew filming a documentary in Belfast, it also proved a challenging reflection upon the ways in which the — primarily British — media had covered the conflict. Channel 4 subsequently funded Belfast Independent Video (which evolved out of the Northern Ireland section of the Independent Film, Video and Photography Association) as well as Derry Film and Video which was responsible for a further feature, *Hush-a-bye Baby* (1989). Along with Pat Murphy's *Maeve* (1981) which was partly shot in Belfast with British Film Institute (BFI) Production Board support, this was a key film in bringing feminist concerns to bear upon traditional perceptions of the 'Troubles' and represents something of a milestone for local film-making. At the beginning of the 1990s, however, the channel's Department of Independent Film and Video abandoned its separate budget for workshops and moved away from

265

the funding of low-budget features. Independent producers have continued to benefit from Channel 4 commissions for television material (such as the 'Violent Britain' series). However, the channel's contribution to feature production in Northern Ireland has been less significant than in the '80s and the main feature with which it has been involved is the romantic comedy *Old New Borrowed Blue* (2000) which was partly funded by FilmFour.

However, if the seeds of Northern Irish film production were sown in the 1980s, it was in the 1990s that a sustained growth of Northern Irish film-making occurred. Three main factors contributed to this development: the establishment of the Northern Ireland Film Council (later Commission), the growing involvement of BBC Northern Ireland in film production, and the use of Lottery funds to support film. During the 1980s, there was growing dissatisfaction with the lack of public support for film and video activities in Northern Ireland and the NI Independent Film, Video and Photography Association commissioned a report *Fast forward* (1988), which identified the disadvantaged position of the north in relation to the rest of Ireland and the UK and called for the establishment of a Media Council. The following year, the Northern Ireland Film Council was launched in order to encourage support for film and television production, distribution and exhibition as well as the promotion of media education and training and the preservation of Northern Ireland's film heritage. In 1991, the Council produced detailed strategy proposals in all these areas and, partly on the basis of this document, secured funding from the Department of Education for Northern Ireland (DENI) in 1992. In subsequent years, this grant was routed through the Arts Council of Northern Ireland (ACNI). At this time, the only local source of production finance was the money provided by the Cultural Traditions Media Group (of the Community Relations Council) which supported film and television projects that contributed specifically to an understanding of cultural diversity within Northern Ireland. In 1993, the Council launched a new production fund (amounting to £100,000 in 1994) which provided development funding and production assistance to film and television projects of artistic and cultural relevance to Northern Ireland. One of the earliest and biggest awards was for John T. Davis' feature-length documentary, *The Uncle Jack* (1995), a fascinating semi-autobiographical work inspired by the film-maker's cinema architect uncle.

In 1994, the NIFC also launched, in collaboration with the BBC, a drama shorts scheme, 'Northern Lights', intended to develop the creative talents of Northern Irish film-makers. This scheme entered its fifth series in 1999 and has provided budgets of around £45-50,000 for three shorts per year, the first of which was writer John Forte's directorial debut, the amusing *Skin Tight* (1994). Since then Forte has gone on to write *Old New Borrowed Blue* (2000) as well as write and direct *Mad about Mambo* (2000), a comedy dealing with teenage obsessions, which was partly shot in Northern Ireland in 1998. The second series of 'Northern Lights' also included the Oscar-nominated *Dance Lexie Dance* (1996), dealing with a young Protestant girl who, inspired by *Riverdance*, takes up Irish dancing with the bemused support of her widowed father. This was produced by the multimedia arts centre in Derry, the Nerve Centre, which has not only played a significant role in training but also in the development of animated work, such as the television series *Cuchulainn* (1994), animated and directed by John McCloskey. Also, at this time the sheer energy and determination of local young film-makers was becoming manifest in the emergence of a 'no-budget' ethic. It was this spirit that underlay the do-it-yourself philosophy of Enda Hughes whose feature-length schlock horror film, *The Eliminator* (1996) was made for only £8,000. It was also apparent in the 'Six-Pack' initiative, a loose collective of young film-makers responsible for an eclectic collection of shorts typified by experiment and innovation, made in 1996 for virtually nothing.

Responding to this growing level of activity, the Film Council, in 1997, set up a second shorts scheme, 'Premiere', in association with Ulster Television, Belfast City Council and the London-based British Screen (a state-funded private company with a responsibility for supporting British film-makers). Under this scheme three series of five films have so far been funded with budgets of around £18–23,000. Once again, the Nerve Centre was responsible for one of the most striking of these, *Surfing with William* (1998), an amusing look at a Derry girl's infatuation with Prince William and her attempts to contact him via the Internet, written by Lisa Burkitt and directed by Tracey Cullen. However, while the Film Council played a key role in stimulating low-budget production and assisting new talent in Northern Ireland, it was severely restricted in the scope of its activities by its low levels of public funding. A significant breakthrough occurred when the Council succeeded in securing funding (£1 million over a 30-month period) from the EU Special Support Programme for Peace and Reconciliation to establish a screen commission and development fund. Although the Film Council had been lobbying for a film commission for a number of years, it was only with the availability of EU (and matching Department of Economic Development) funding that it became economically viable. It was partly to signal this new role that the Council changed its name to the Northern Ireland Film Commission in 1997.

The NIFC continues, however, to be more than what is conventionally meant by a screen commission (which helps to attract film-makers to a country or region) and has retained much of the Film Council's commitment to training and exhibition. In the case of training, for example, the NIFC was recognized by the Northern Ireland Training and Employment agency as the Sector Training Council in 1995 and has continued to work alongside Skillset (the UK training organization) in Northern Ireland since then (setting up a NVQ Skillset Assessment Centre in 1999). The establishment of the Northern Ireland Film Development Fund has also led to substantial sums of new money becoming available for film and television production in the north. The NIFC's policy in establishing a substantial development fund was designed to complement the production funding becoming available through the Lottery and, in line with its 'industrial' remit, to attract not just features but television series and serials with a potential for repeat business. Accordingly, the Fund offers production companies, rather than individuals, loans of up to fifty per cent of the estimated costs of developing projects — normally up to £40,000 for television series and £15,000 for feature films — that will be primarily produced in Northern Ireland. By the end of 1999, the NIFC had committed nearly half a million pounds to the development of around forty film features and television series to a mixture of companies based in Ireland, both north and south, as well as London and Canada. In 1999 the NIFC was also allocated a further £500,000 under the EU Special Support Programme to establish a one-off production for feature films. Following the expiry of EU funding, the Department of Economic Development (subsequently the Department of Enterprise, Trade and Investment) committed to an annual allocation of £250,000 while the new Department of Arts, Culture and Leisure has taken over from the Department of Education as the Commission's other key funder.

In addition to the NIFC, the BBC in Northern Ireland has been another key player on the local scene. During the 1980s, the BBC Drama Department in Northern Ireland produced a number of one-off dramas, often shot on film but shown only on TV (including, in the late 1980s, a number of pieces directed or produced by Danny Boyle). In line with BBC policy more generally, BBC NI began, in the 1990s, to move more in the direction of drama series (most notably the hugely successful *Ballykissangel*) and films with theatrical potential. This policy was initiated with Barry Devlin's *All Things Bright and Beautiful* (1994) and the Devlin-scripted *A Man of no Importance* (1995), both of which opened in cinemas. Like *Ballykissangel*, both of these features were shot mostly in the south in order to take advantage of Section 35 tax benefits and, in the case of the two features, financial support from the Irish Film Board. With the availability of Lottery funding in the north (and changes to the UK tax regime), there has now been a certain 'levelling of the playing field' between north and south and, as a result, it has become much more financially attractive for BBC NI to film in the north. This is evident, for example, with *Divorcing Jack* which was supported by the Lottery, and has been BBC NI's highest profile feature to date. The Lottery has also, since the third series, cooperated with the BBC in funding the 'Northern Lights' scheme (as a replacement for the NIFC's share).

FUNDING

UK Lottery funding for film began in 1995 following agreement that film production could be regarded as capital expenditure. Lottery funds are administered by the Arts Councils of England, Wales, Scotland and Northern Ireland and, in the case of Northern Ireland, there has been evidence of a desire to rectify the traditional underfunding of film and video production within Northern Ireland (such that in 1997–8, over 13% of total grants awarded went to film development and production). During the 1970s and early 1980s, the Arts Council of Northern Ireland did support small-scale film and video production, but it discontinued to do so on the grounds that it considered this to be more properly the responsibility of the London-based British Film Institute. Although Northern Irish film-makers could apply to the BFI Production Board (which at that time supported low-budget and experimental work), the BFI's charter did not extend to Northern Ireland and it was argued that it could not provide separate funding to the region. The BFI did change its charter in 1991 to include Northern Ireland, but no extra funding for NI production followed. The BFI maintained that, despite the extension of its charter, it had received no additional funding for Northern Ireland and that it was the job of local government agencies, such as DENI (whom the NIFC was lobbying), to support film production. During the early 1990s, therefore, the support of the Arts Council for film was, with the exception of the NIFC, largely confined to exhibition: the main NI arthouse, Queen's Film Theatre (opened in 1968), the Foyle Film Festival in Derry (established in 1987 with seed money from the University of Ulster), Cinemagic (the children's film festival set up by the NIFC in 1990), and the West Belfast Film Festival (launched in 1995). With the change in the NIFC's status in 1997, however, ACNI transferred its existing financial responsibilities for film to the Commission which became funded directly by DENI and the Department of Economic Development (the conduit for EU finances). Nevertheless, under Lottery legislation, the Arts Council continued to play a major role in film funding. While this has involved support for both buildings (such as the Orchard Cinema in Derry) and equipment (such as the grant of £370,274 to Derry's Inner City Trust for equipment for the Nerve Centre), the most substantial slice of expenditure in this area has been on film and video production and development.

Under criteria developed in association with the NIFC, Lottery funding is available to film companies producing a film in Northern Ireland and intended for distribution or broadcast in Northern Ireland and elsewhere. Funding includes development monies (up to a maximum of £20,000 or 75% of total development, whichever is less) and production grants up to £200,000 (and normally not more than 25% of the overall budget). Under these terms, the Arts Council had, by the end of 1998, allocated over £1.5 million to production — to eight feature films, ten short films, four animated works and three documentaries — as well as a further £120,000 on nine development awards (including seven features). Of the eight features receiving production awards, six had been completed by the end of 1998: Tommy Collins' *Bogwoman* (1997), following a young Donegal woman's experiences in Derry at the start of the 'Troubles'; the allegorical *Sunset Heights* (1998), set in a violent Derry of the future; a film adaptation of Mary Costello's semi-autobiographical novel of the 'Troubles', *Titanic Town* (1998), set in Belfast; a romantic historical drama, *All for Love* (originally *St Ives*) (1998); and two adaptations of novels by the local comedy thriller writer Colin Bateman, *Crossmaheart* (1998) and *Divorcing Jack* (1998). A seventh — *A Love Divided* (originally *Wild Horses*) (1999), a drama about a mixed marriage in 1950s Ireland — was in post-production. In terms of amount, the biggest awards went to *Divorcing Jack* and *Sunset Heights*, both of which received £200,000, while *Titanic Town*, *Crossmaheart* and *Bogwoman* were each awarded £150,000. In terms of percentages, however, these last two were actually the most substantial, amounting to 29% of *Crossmaheart's* budget and about 24% of *Bogwoman's* (compared with 7% of *Divorcing Jack's* budget and 4.6% of *Titanic Town's*).

A number of observations can be made about these awards. First, despite the involvement of the Northern Ireland Arts Council, these are 'Northern Irish' films to differing degrees. Although ACNI has been concerned to develop 'new, local talent', the basic requirement for funding is that a film is, at least partly, shot in Northern Ireland. This has meant that the amount of filming that occurs in the north has varied. So, while most of *Divorcing Jack* was shot in Northern Ireland, others have shot for comparatively short periods. *Titanic Town*, for example, filmed in Northern Ireland for two weeks, while the bulk of the film was shot in England. *Bogwoman*, *Sunset Heights*, and *A Love Divided* were all cross-border ('all-Irish') projects, involving substantial amounts of shooting in the south. And, although most of the films were actually set (at least partly) in Northern Ireland, *All for Love* simply used NI locations as a 'substitute' for elsewhere. The degree of involvement of NI personnel has also varied. Although NI people contributed to the

making of all of these films at different levels, only two (*Bogwoman* and *Sunset Heights*) of the six films were made by NI-based production companies and only three involved NI directors. In this respect, the strategy of the Lottery has been to reinforce the Commission's work in encouraging outside production companies to shoot in Northern Ireland and not just support what might be regarded as 'indigenous' production. This, however, is almost inevitable, given the relatively modest levels of funding at ACNI's disposal (particularly in comparison to the Arts Council of England which has awarded as much as £2 million to a single film) and the cross-national character of contemporary film financing and (co)production.

Another characteristic of the financing of these films is that, while one of the aims of the Lottery fund has been to 'encourage the production of commercially successful feature films', these are all films that have depended heavily upon public support. So, while the Lottery is not prepared to be the sole investor in projects and requires partnership funding before it makes awards, additional sources of finance have tended to come from other parts of the public sector in Ireland, UK or Europe. *Bogwoman* and *Sunset Heights* both received funding from the Irish Film Board, *Titanic Town* was funded by the Arts Council of England (ACE) and British Screen while *Divorcing Jack* was funded jointly by ACE and BBC NI, a public service broadcaster. *A Love Divided* received funding from two public service broadcasters — BBC Scotland and RTÉ — as well as from the Irish Film Board while *All for Love* was an elaborate European coproduction involving (state-supported or regulated) British, French and German TV companies as well as German public finance. It is, of course, the case that this is one of the strengths of the system: in a situation where sources of finance are limited, risks are spread across a number of agencies. However, it may also be a weakness insofar as films are then made through a combination of various forms of 'soft' public finance (rather than commercial investment). This issue is given added significance when the difficulties these films have faced in securing distribution and exhibition are taken into account.

DISTRIBUTION AND EXHIBITION

As in Ireland and the UK more generally, there has, in recent years, been a significant growth in the number of cinema and cinema screens in the north, especially in the Belfast area, as a result of the opening of multiplexes. Thus, there are now roughly 26 cinemas with 114 screens in Northern Ireland which, per head of the population, compares favourably with both the rest of Ireland and Britain. However, this expansion of exhibition outlets has tended to benefit Hollywood productions rather than local films which still find it difficult to secure a distribution deal and proper exhibition. So far only *Divorcing*

Jack has received widespread exhibition within Northern Ireland and elsewhere, with the result that Northern Ireland audiences have so far had few opportunities (outside of festivals and specialist cinemas in Belfast and Derry) to see the Lottery-supported films (long after they have been completed). *Bogwoman*, the first of the films to be finished, provides one of the most striking examples of this. Moreover, even *Divorcing Jack*, the most overtly 'commercial' and heavily marketed of these films, only did modest business at cinemas outside of the north.

The assessment of the performance of these films, however, is complex. Problems of distribution and exhibition are not, of course, restricted to NI films but extend to Irish and British (and indeed European) films more generally. Thus, according to a survey in *Screen Finance*, over 30% of British films made between 1991 and 1996 failed to secure a cinema release and many more were subject to delays. As a result, the Arts Council of England Lottery Film Department (shortly to become part of a new 'super-body', the UK Film Council) has seen very low returns on its loans and plans to use Lottery money to support distribution as well as production (as is already evident from its policy towards franchises). Similarly, it is likely that ACNI will have to consider how it can help support the exhibition and distribution of the films in which it invests as well. Given the massive domination of the distribution sector (in both film and video) in Ireland and Britain by subsidiaries of the Hollywood majors and the general decline in more specialist outlets for European films, there is, however, no simple solution to this problem.

Nevertheless, it would be a mistake to over-emphasize the significance of cinema exhibition (desirable though this must be). Given the importance of international television sales, the economic viability of film features does not necessarily depend on box-office performance, and local audiences will eventually get access to local films through television. Moreover, from the point of view of overall public policy, the economic benefits that accrue to Northern Ireland in terms of employment and spend will probably outweigh the lack of return on individual films. Furthermore, it is hard to underestimate the significance of recent levels of film production in Northern Ireland when there has been no sustained tradition of film-making and violent conflict has been a characteristic of social life for so long. In this respect, the economic costs of public support for film production must be weighed against the cultural value of nurturing creative talent and promoting new and challenging forms of cultural expression. As in Britain and Ireland more generally, there is inevitably a certain tension between industrial and cultural goals. From an economic point of view, the NIFC's recent emphasis upon television series and serials and attraction of 'offshore'

productions makes considerable sense. However, in relation to local 'indigenous' film production, there is a danger that an over-emphasis upon the industrial or commercial element will lead to work that simply falls between two stools: films that are still too modest in scale to compete effectively in the international market-place (given Hollywood's huge economic advantages) yet which, in conforming to what are believed to be 'commercial' imperatives, fail to be of real artistic and cultural significance (or to serve, in the words of the Lottery requirement, a genuine public good).

CONCLUSION

For what is significant about much of the best work coming out of Northern Ireland is the evident determination to avoid some of the conventional signifiers of the 'Troubles' and explore new ways of representing the north. While a number of the features have continued to be 'Troubles' dramas, displaying varying degrees of originality in the way they represent the conflicts, many of the shorts in particular have sought to break out of the 'Troubles' paradigm, either by attending to other matters or rendering problematic the traditional binaries — British and Irish, Protestant and Catholic — that have historically governed perceptions of Northern Irish life. By attending to issues of age, gender and sexuality, such films have begun to question the traditional construction of identities in Northern Ireland and suggest how these are rarely 'pure' or unidimensional but multiple and hybrid. Although, quite rightly, much of the support for film in Northern Ireland by government has been predicated upon the economic benefits that television and film production brings (in the form of a commercially focused industry, jobs, tourism spin-offs and so on), it is ultimately this willingness to provide fresh ways of looking at one's own culture that will ensure the vitality of the current film-making revival.

Bibliography

Hill, J., McLoone, M. and Hainsworth, P. (eds) 1994
    Border crossing: film in Northern Ireland. London.
Hill, J. and McLoone, M. (eds) 1996 *Big picture, small
    screens: the relations between film and television*.
    Luton.
McLoone, M. (ed) (1996), *Broadcasting in a divided
    community: seventy years of the BBC in Northern
    Ireland*. Belfast.
Moran, A. 1996 *Film policy: international and regional
    perspectives*. London.
Rockett, K., Gibbons, L. and Hill, J. 1988, *Cinema and
    Ireland*, revised ed. London and New York.

The Library Tradition

HELEN MOLONEY DAVIS

The purpose of this chapter is twofold: firstly, to establish a context for libraries overseas and in Ireland; secondly, to focus attention on their potential as a primary heritage resource. Accordingly, it falls into two sections: the first gives a brief sketch of the growth of libraries from antiquity to those of France, Germany, Switzerland and Italy where, during the Middle Ages, wandering Irish scholars and pilgrims, the *Scotti peregrini*, had a significant influence. The second deals with libraries in this country from earliest times to the present day. The latter section will also outline the past, contemporary and future role of the profession of librarianship. This review indicates that the evolution of libraries in Ireland is an essential though neglected component of Irish intellectual history. The library network is probably the most extensive form of institutional contact members of the public have with information and learning apart from their interaction with the educational system, and yet its background and workings remain comparatively unknown. Accordingly, awareness of our library tradition is important in the ongoing management and enhancement of Ireland's cultural inheritance. Libraries are continually changing entities which have evolved and developed in an unbroken continuum over five thousand years in response to the stimulation they receive from society, of which they are a vital record.

THE INTERNATIONAL BACKGROUND

Scholars throughout the ancient Near East had such respect for the written word that the period which preceded the emergence of writing was conceived of as chaos. The denizens of the era were monstrous titanic races for whom no literature existed. Writing signalled the emergence of humanity: it ensured not only the permanence of records but the possibility of multiple copies, their sale and acquisition by the learned classes. Large databases were quickly accumulated. Retrieval from this growing amorphous bulk of literature required

classification of the subject/intellectual matter. Description of the physical format also was soon found to be desirable. The organized collection of literature or books was called a library; the people who arranged it, cared for it and ensured its growth and preservation were the librarians. As if to symbolize the centrality of these functions, the work which we now know as the Bible was for St Jerome (*ca.* 345–420) the *Divina Bibliotheca*, the Sacred Library. Western culture has been largely shaped by this unique collection of writings, itself one of the chief witnesses to ancient Near Eastern civilization.

The earliest library which still exists today is that of Telloh of Mesopotamia. Dating from 2500 BC, it consists of over 20,000 cuneiform clay tablets now in the Louvre. One of the first references to the library as a resource for education comes from an inscription in the Palace of Sardanapalus, King of Assyria *ca.* 650 BC, which reads: 'I have written [in cuneiform writing] upon clay tablets, signed it, put it in order and placed it in the midst of my palace for the instruction of my subjects' (quoted in Edwards 1859, 16). As for books among the Jews, in II Mach., ii 13–15 we read 'in these writings and in the Memoirs of Nehemias how Nehemias founded a library and made a collection of the books dealing with the kings and prophets, the writings of David and the letters of the kings on the subject of offerings. Similarly, Judas made a complete collection of the books dispersed in the late war and these we still have. If you need any of them, send someone to fetch them'. Although the literature of the ancient Egyptians has come down to us in considerable quantities, and Rameses II had a library of twenty thousand papyrus rolls *ca.* 1250 BC, only the library of Alexandria, founded by Ptolemy I Soter in the third century BC, captured the popular imagination; it is probably best known of all the libraries of antiquity. Legend tells that it was here that the Septuagint, the Greek translation of the Hebrew Old Testament, was made by the seventy-two translators employed by

Ptolemy Philadelphus (285–46 BC), who gave it its basic name (LXX or Seventy). Comprising the Musaeum and the Serapeum, the library survived many vicissitudes including damage by fire during the Egyptian campaign of Julius Caesar in 48 BC until its ultimate destruction by Theophilus, the Christian patriarch of Alexandria, in AD 391. It is generally agreed that the loss of this institution was one of the greatest disasters to befall civilization.

The best-known Greek equivalent of the Alexandrian library was the library at Pergamum which reached the height of its glory in the reign of Eumenes II (197–59 BC). Ptolemy Epiphanes (205–182 BC) of Egypt wished to hamper the growth of this rival library and placed an embargo on the export of papyrus. Pergamum responded by inventing the alternative writing medium *pergamena carta* or parchment. Aristotle's Lycaeum, founded in 336 BC, was the first library to receive legal deposit as decreed by Alexander the Great. In 40 BC this library was transferred to Rome where the foundations of this city's contribution to library history had begun only in 168 BC with the capture of the Macedonian royal library after the Battle of Pydna. Seneca, Roman senator and philosopher, observed *ca.* 50 AD, in his *De tranquilitate animi*: 'You will find in the libraries of the most arrant idlers all that orators or historians have written — bookcases built up as high as the ceiling. Nowadays a library takes rank with a bathroom as a necessary ornament of a house'. Fourth-century AD sources credit Rome with thirty public libraries, and there is evidence for the existence of libraries throughout the provinces.

Our first reference to collections of books among the early Christians comes from St Paul in his Second Letter to Timothy. Eusebius (*ca.* AD 260–340), bishop of Caesarea in Palestine, used and described a large important episcopal library at Jerusalem. St Jerome is one of our sources for the excellence of the library at Caesarea. Pachomius (*ca.* 290–346), the Egyptian father of Christian monasticism, in his Rule identified the collection, care and reading of books as one of the responsibilities of monks. Subsequently all the great monastic rules incorporated this exhortation, including that of Cassiodorus (485/90–*ca.* 580), who was explicit about the *raison d'être* of the library: 'to ensure the engagement of the monks in research'. With the decline of the Roman Empire, libraries existed mainly in monastic and episcopal foundations, many established by Irish missionaries in France, Italy and Germany, including Saints Columbanus, Gall and Virgil of Salzburg. Columbanus (*ca.* 550–615) founded monasteries at Anegray, Fontenay, Luxeuil and Bobbio, where his first concern was the scriptorium. Most of the manuscripts from the Bobbio library (some of which may date from the seventh century) are now in the Vatican Library, the Ambrosian Library in Milan and in Turin. His erstwhile companion, St Gall, established a hermitage at St Gallen in Switzerland. On this site was founded the great monastery and library bearing his name, which still houses many Irish manuscripts. One of the most important documents for the history of libraries is the ninth-century manuscript Plan of St Gall (Stiftsbibliothek MS 1092). Scholars generally agree that it was intended not merely for the St Gall foundation but as the ideal layout for the reformed monastery. It is clearly evident that the scriptorium and library were the nerve-centre of the monastery, located as they were next to the high altar on the side opposite to the sacristy. It has been suggested that 'Without the cultural activities carried on in these spatially relatively modest facilities, western civilization would not be what it is today' (Horn and Born 1979, 147). In St Gall, books had been kept in presses and in medieval England in a chest, as shown in British Library (BL) MS Cott. Claud. E. iv (Gesta Abbatum) (Savage 1970, 49). In the later period printed books and manuscripts were displayed flat on shelves with the shelf number written on the fore-edge. As bindings became more elegant, fashion gradually demanded that the decorated spine should face the viewer (Barnard 1998, 216).

The most famous protagonist of learning and libraries during the early Middle Ages, Charlemagne (742–814; Roman Emperor from 800), had as his mentor Alcuin of York (*ca.* 740–804), himself believed to have been a pupil of Colgu of Clonmacnois in county Offaly (Kenney 1929, 534). Alcuin who, while at York, had been engaged in the care, preservation and enlargement of that already famous library, established the palace library at Aachen for Charlemagne. In twelfth-century Germany and Austria the Irish Benedictines set up monasteries which became known as *Schottenklöster*. Twelfth-century Irish liturgical music and other manuscripts are still in the library of the *Schottenkloster* in Vienna (Ó Riain 1997). When these and other monasteries were dissolved during the Reformation, their manuscripts were often moved to the nearest large library, which was almost always on or close to historic pilgrim routes. Although Charlemagne's encouragement and patronage monastic libraries had flourished, the true renaissance of libraries did not happen until the mid-fourteenth century when the Bibliothèque Nationale, Paris, was founded. This was followed by the University Library of St Andrews, Scotland, in 1411, the Vatican Library 1450, St Mark's Venice 1468 and Cambridge University Library in 1475. These are still some of the great modern libraries of our own day.

The book, even prior to the introduction of printing, was one of the catalysts which marked the emergence of the Renaissance and the break with the medieval world. With the Renaissance a new awareness of book-collecting, the preservation and reproduction of written materials as well as their exploitation for new ideas came about, beginning roughly in the mid-fourteenth century.

Petrarch's (1304–74) collection of books is regarded as archetypal of the period. His friend Boccaccio assembled and copied manuscripts in the Vatican. At his death Boccaccio's collection had grown to one thousand two hundred items. Nicholas V (1397–1455; pope from 1447) inherited three hundred and fifty manuscripts from Pope Eugenius IV (1383–1447). The influence of books after the introduction of printing by Johann Gutenberg *ca.* 1450, as shown by reformers such as Martin Luther (1483–1546), Philip Melanchthon (1497–1560) and Desiderius Erasmus (1466/9–1536), led to the 1522 decree by the Duke of Pomerania that all unsuitable books from the monasteries should be sold for scrap. This decree and the Peasants' Revolt (1524–26), during which the contents of seventy monasteries were destroyed, occasioned the loss of thousands of books.

It is suggested that the founding of the University of Leiden in 1575 marked a new chapter in librarianship, that of serving researchers in a gradually evolving tradition of analytical scholarship comprising meticulous attention to detail. Resources had been provided by the great collectors, the methods and standards set by Erasmus and Reuchlin. Gutenberg's revolution provided cheaper, faster and more widespread access to literature in a way which put new demands on librarians and emphasised the importance of the retrieval of relevant information. In view of the attention currently being focussed on the availability of library catalogues through electronic media, a sketch of the history of the library catalogue appears relevant. In this connection, it should be noted that the story of libraries is the record of writing and literature and therefore of society. The term 'literature' covered all subjects, from agriculture to zoology, until the eighteenth century when the word began to imply *belles lettres*. Stone, clay, papyrus, skins, paper, ink, palaeography, type design, the book trade, book illustration, binding: the use of these media, the sequence and pattern of the employment of each category reflect the economy of a locality, its taxation, customs and taboos, advertising, the organization of the scribes' or printers' offices, a region's reading tastes, the censorship exercised. It should be possible to assess all of these aspects through a district's library. These are also the fields which provide the broad background for the study known as historical bibliography.

FINDING AIDS

The Chaldeans catalogued their collections by inscribing the contents of each room on its walls. They subsequently invented the fore-runner of the card catalogue: cuneiform inscriptions on clay tablets. When palaces were burnt and destroyed, the clay tablets were baked in the fires. Consequently, we have the catalogues of some of these libraries: that of the great library at Nineveh formed by Sargon, King of Assyria (722–05 BC), much

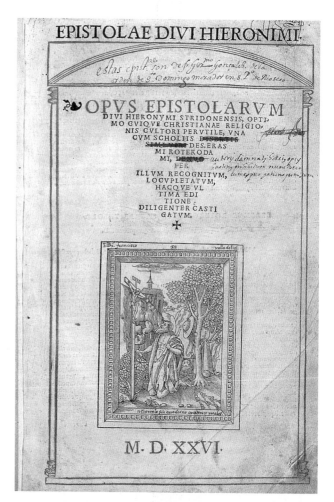

Fig. 28.1 *Early printed copy of Letters of St Jerome in the Cathedral Library, UCC.*

enhanced by his great-grandson, Assurbanipal (668–28 BC), and now in the British Museum, as well as several in the Louvre. Some of the 'catalogue walls' have also been recovered and are preserved. It is generally agreed that the Greeks first decided on the idea of the author as the main catalogue entry. The poet and scholar Callimachus (340–270 BC) was appointed by Ptolemy Philadelphus to undertake the task of providing a catalogue of the great library at Alexandria. It was known as the *pinakes* (Latin *tabulae*), which suggests it was a list of the books on each shelf. It contained biographical information about the author as well as bibliographical details of the books, the *incipit* (index of first lines) and, in the case of drama, dates of production. This information was attached to each roll on a label known as a *sillubos*. The catalogue was destroyed along with the library, although excerpts from it survived in several sources. While it was seen primarily as a list of the property of the library, it was consciously prepared by scholars to ensure a record of contemporary leading literary works for future generations. Cleopatra VII, understanding the significance of the catalogue of the library at Alexandria, initiated and

272

funded research, which continued for many centuries, to recreate it. Scholars still mourn its loss.

A mid-ninth-century manuscript at St Gall, MS 728, contains a page which bears the title *Libri scottice scripti* ('books written by the Irish'). This, the oldest list of books at St Gall, has its importance in respect of library history and that of education, not only for St Gall and Ireland but for the period as a whole. The thirty entries, mostly biblical and ecclesiastical, dated from a much earlier period and could no longer be understood by the monks, so they formed a special collection within the library. Other catalogues, including the catalogue of the Bobbio library, also testify to the holdings of books written by Irish monks (Kenney 1929, 19). The contents of one hundred and eighty-three English monastic libraries were later recorded in the Franciscans' *Registrum librorum Angliae* 1250–1296 (Bodleian Library, Oxford, Tanner MS 165; Savage 1970, 58–9, pl. x). This is the first known attempt at a union catalogue, that is a single catalogue of all books in a defined group of libraries. Trade catalogues subsequently developed as a result of the proliferation of printed books, and Andrew Maunsell's *Catalogue of English printed books*, published in 1595, was one of the more important examples. In this catalogue the author was used as the main entry for the first time and has continued to be so ever since (Gneuss 1996). Harvard University Library afterwards played a major role in the development of cataloguing. It has the distinction of issuing the first printed library catalogue in 1723. The first national code for cataloguing was formulated by the French in 1791; it provided simple but comprehensive rules, beginning with the numbering and assembling of books with cards which were mailed to the Bibliothèque Nationale, Paris, for the purpose of forming the first modern card catalogue. Trinity College, Dublin, introduced a card catalogue in 1827 and the British Museum introduced eleven-by-four inch slips of paper in 1841. The physical format of the card catalogue was refined by Ezra Abbott who in 1846 also introduced the idea of subject headings based on the content of the book as opposed merely to the title. In 1787 the British Museum had published its first catalogue, *Librorum impressorum qui in Museo Britannico adservantur catalogus*, which appeared in two volumes. The next catalogue, compiled by Antonio Genesio Mario Panizzi, was based on the rules formulated in 1834 by Henry Baber, Keeper of Printed Books at the British Museum. Several editions later, the British Library Catalogue, which developed from its British Museum fore-runner, continues to be one of the most basic requirements for any library, whether available in hard-copy or on-line.

Throughout the nineteenth century, several cataloguing codes were developed, mainly in England, Germany and America, culminating in the Anglo-American Code in 1908. These evolved on the basis of empirical data and pragmatic research, as no fundamental laws of library science had yet emerged. In 1924–25 the famous Indian pioneer of library scholarship Shiyali Ramamrita Ranganathan (1892–1972), graduated from the School of Librarianship at University College, London. During his studies he had been struck by the lack of uniformity in classifying and making available books, particularly by '... the sense of revolt induced in the mind while learning cataloguing ... No attempt [was made] to present the rules [of the Anglo-American code of 1908] as a system ... not a word was said about ... differences between catalogues ... the discrepancy between the rules taught in the theory class and those prescribed for adoption in the practical class ... the bibliographical details about format, collation and imprint were overemphasized in the practical class. The revolt made one say within oneself "When I go back home"' (*ELIS* 1974, 365–6). On his return to India he was appointed librarian at Madras University and immediately set to work on his ideas. He summarized the essential attributes of a library catalogue: 'it should be so designed as

(1) to disclose to every reader his book;

(2) to secure for every book its reader;

(3) save the time of the reader; and

(4) for this purpose save the time of the staff' (*ibid.* 366–7).

On the basis of this framework, a moment of intuition revealed the fundamental five laws which now provide the starting point for *a priori* research in the different branches of library science as a whole. These laws, as published in 1931, are

(1) books are for use;

(2) every reader his book;

(3) every book its reader;

(4) save the time of the reader;

(5) a library is a growing organism.

The Five Laws and Ranganathan's insights into the role of the library demanded critical assessment of the physical as well as the intellectual content of the catalogue. Through pragmatic research based on his Five Laws, Ranganathan deduced that the card catalogue was the most desirable physical format and a classified catalogue was equally necessary to enable readers to gain a full panorama of material on a specific subject. Further research in cataloguing resulted in the recognition of a set of nine canons of cataloguing enunciated by Ranganathan in 1969, relating to choice of information for a catalogue entry, the entry's uniqueness, updating, consistency and other considerations. The Anglo-American Cataloguing Rules (AACR) were revised and provided the International Standard for Bibliographic Description (ISBD) in 1967, followed by another revision in 1988. The 1967 edition paved the way for Machine-Readable Cataloguing (MARC), the standard description format for the electronic age.

The story of classification is similar. Over the last hundred and fifty years a number of systems have gained international popularity. Librarians had been aware of the potential for centralized cataloguing and classification for many years. The idea was first published by F. Max Müller, librarian at the Bodleian Library, Oxford, in March 1876. The advent of automation greatly enhanced the concept's attractiveness, so it was inevitable that one or two systems would win international recognition. The Dewey Decimal Classification (DDC) system, first introduced in the United States of America by Melvil Dewey (1851–1931) in 1876, gained widespread currency in the western world, not because of its superiority to others but because of the financial and organizational backing it received at the Dewey Foundation headquarters in Lake Placid. Its acceptance by the British Library was a major affirmation. Its numerical sequence, 000 to 999, is based at the broadest level on the sixteenth-century thinker Francis Bacon's chart of the main elements of human learning, with basic subdivisions reflecting later, nineteenth-century concepts. At its more specific levels, however, because of its continuous development on the basis of current publication, DDC usually follows contemporary scientific and educational consensuses. It is now in its twenty-first edition. The Library of Congress (LC) classification scheme is an alpha-numeric system, that is it employs a combination of letters and numbers to reflect the subject-matter of the book, and is also widely used. DDC and LC references are usually given in the Cataloguing in Publication (CIP) data on all books published since 1980. It is worth mentioning also that the International Standard Book Number (ISBN) and International Standard Serial Number (ISSN) were introduced in 1978 to refine the acquisition process even further. These numbers reflect the language, title, publisher's name and format of the item. The ISBN is assigned by the publishers Whittaker in the UK and in Ireland the ISSN is assigned by the National Library of Ireland. The modern computerized library catalogue is generally treated as a mechanism for discovering whether a book is in the library, on loan or available, in other words, it is perceived simply as a record of the property of the library. It may not convey to its users the complex history and intellectual endeavour outlined above which underlie its own development and that of its fore-runners (Baker 1994).

Many libraries produced their own in-house classification schemes. The basic aim of all was ease of retrieval for readers, although the inevitable idiosyncrasies provide interesting glimpses of social and cultural history. For UCC Library, of which he was also Director, Dr Alfred O'Rahilly (1884–1969), President of University College, Cork (1943–54), developed a classification system in the 1950s. Mnemonically based on Aristotelian categories, it was an alpha-numeric scheme, for instance having L for Literature followed by the initial of the language (LE, English Literature, LI, Irish Literature), followed by a numeric subdivision: 5, history; 10, general works; 15 anthologies; 100 individual writers, and so forth. It gained notoriety on several points, which reflected not merely the author's prejudices but also those of much of Irish society in his day: MT (Moral Theology); 25 Sex Instruction, Catholic; MT 30 Sex Instruction, Non-Catholic; MT 40 Sexual and Marital Morals — Catholic; MT 50 Natality and Sex — Non-Catholic. Interestingly, this unit of the scheme was never actually used, and had a line drawn through it! The substitute which was employed was quite simple: MOR for Ethics, with a few subdivisions. The Church History section is also noteworthy. One curiosity was CH 370 Converts (those who had converted to Catholicism) as well as CH 380 Perverts (those who had converted from Catholicism to another religion). Some writers including Chateaubriand were classified in Church History at CH 790 Catholic Writers, while H. G. Wells and Voltaire among others were placed at CH 890 Protestant Writers.

IRISH LIBRARIES
THE MEDIEVAL BACKGROUND

While Ireland's reputation as the 'Island of Saints and Scholars' is well attested throughout early medieval Europe, no library from this period has survived in any form in this country. Although references to individual books abound in early Irish literature, those to collections of books are few, like that in the seventh-century enigmatic Hiberno-Latin poem the *Hisperica Famina*, which gives some information about the making, binding, covering, carrying and storing of books:

Hang your white booksacks on the wall,
set your lovely satchels in a straight line,
so that they will be deemed a grand sight by the rustics ...
This white satchel gleams,
it has thick bristles that provide a rather small cover;
the aforesaid container is sewn in the shape of a square;
the upper rim surrounds a single opening,
which is closed by a tight covering with many-angled turning knobs,

then is bound by twelve cords,
and the curved load is born[e] on the necks of the scholars.
I shall describe the excellent construction of this book satchel:
not long ago it protected the fattened flesh of a sheep;
a butcher flayed the hairy hide with a sharp knife;
it was stretched on the wall between thick stakes
and dried with fiery smoke.
A proud craftsman cut out the aforesaid container,
drew taut the skin covering with tight laces,
fashioned the four angles,
and finished the leather container with a choice strap.
(Herren 1974, 84–5, 104–7; quoted in O'Neill 1997, 78–9).

The desire for the ownership of books is attested in the well-known sixth-century legend of St Colmcille's copying of a manuscript belonging to 'St. Finnen of Druim Finn' [Dromin, county Louth] (O'Kelleher and Schoepperle 1918, 177–8), who has been suggested to be Finnian of Moville (Ó Riain 1977, 65). The scholar or scholars who compiled the early seventh-century corpus of church law texts entitled *Collectio canonum Hibernensis* certainly had access to a collection of canon law and exegetical material. Certain manuscripts of the text may have been used as episcopal handbooks, offering advice on Christian living. The *Collectio* appealed not only to clerics, but also, possibly, to educated rulers in eighth- and ninth-century Europe. A selection of the texts in one manuscript was dedicated to a queen, possibly the Empress Judith, second wife of Louis the Pious (Davies 1999). Further evidence of the early availability of literary sources comes from the writings of the Irish on grammar, travel and scientific subjects. We know that Irish monks were familiar with the sixth-century Isidore of Seville's *Etymologiae*, Book VI ch. 3 of which is entitled 'De bibliothecis' and ch. 9–14 'De librariis et eorum instrumentis'. The instructions regarding the care, arrangement and handling of books and ink as detailed in the St Gall Library beg the question as to whether the same guidelines had been followed in Ireland. It is only at the very end of the Middle Ages, in the Welsh scholar Edward Lhuyd's *Archaeologia Britannica*, printed at Oxford in 1707, that the Gaelic word *leabharlann*, 'library', first occurs in print, having been borrowed from Richard Plunket's manuscript dictionary which he completed in September 1662 (Ua Súilleabháin 1995). In his general Preface, Lhuyd remarks that Archbishop Narcissus Marsh (of whom we shall learn more shortly) had bought the manuscript dictionary of one 'Richard Plunket a Franciscan of the Abbey of Trim, a Person of Laudable Industry ... the great use that Manuscript has been of, is particularly mentioned in the Preface to the Irish Dictionary'. He acknowledges the words, including *leabharlann*, which he took from Plunket with 'Pl'. The autograph is still in Marsh's Library, Dublin, MS Z.4.2.5.

Returning to the later Middle Ages, in 1336 the Pope ordered that each Franciscan convent should compile a list of books and that this list should be kept up to date. Archbishop FitzRalph of Armagh (d. 1360) complained to Pope Benedict XII that the Franciscan friars bought up every useful book on the market and furnished their foundations with magnificent libraries. The only catalogue of an Irish Franciscan house which exists, however, dates from the latter half of the fifteenth century and constitutes a unique window on a later medieval monastic collection. Written on two blank pages at the end of a thirteenth-century vellum MS, 'Usuardi Martyrologium', which in the mid-nineteenth century belonged to the celebrated English book collector Sir Thomas Phillipps and is now in Tübingen University, Germany, it is an inventory of the books which were in the Franciscan library at Youghal in 1491. Further titles were added to the catalogue in 1523. The list was written in very contracted Latin by the Sub-Prior, Brother William O'Hurrily, 'lest perchance, by carelessness or neglect, or, which is worse, want of conscience ... they might be completely destroyed and no memorial of them remain' (Brady 1863, vol. 3, 319–23). There were one hundred and forty-five items in the collection. In some cases several items were bound together, for instance *The meditations of St Bonaventure* with other meditations was bound with a history of the Welsh-Norman Irish family the Geraldines, which seems to be the only secular item in the holdings. There were several multi-volume works, for example those of Nicholas of Lyra, an authority on biblical exegesis. Most were probably manuscript, but some were 'printed on paper'. All were in Latin, except for a German-language dictionary. Not a single Irish-language text is listed. Apart from three categories, sermons, canon law and 'books for the use of Maurice Hanlan', the books do not seem to have been classified, although they may now be divided into liturgical, scriptural (including exegesis, especially Nicholas of Lyra), works of the Fathers and Doctors of the Church (Jerome, Gregory, Bonaventure, Aquinas) and lives of the saints. Of the titles added in 1523, it is interesting to note that a borrowing record of several is given: 'now in the hands of David Ronan', 'now in the hands of John O'Connor' and the like. This is the first library record of books being borrowed in Ireland. At the dissolution of the monasteries, the Youghal Franciscans took refuge in county Waterford, but what happened to the library is not known. Could the fifteenth-century martyrology and breviary MS 19,954, recently acquired by the National Library of Ireland and believed to have been written in Waterford, be one of the liturgical books from Youghal? Only for the foresight of Bro. William O'Hurrily we should only have had a limited impression of what was contained in an Irish monastic library before the Reformation (Laistner 1935, cited in O'Loughlin 1994; Herbert 1988).

Two catalogues of books have come down to us from the library of a secular aristocratic family, that of Garrett Óg FitzGerald, 9th Earl of Kildare, after the death of his father the Great Earl in 1513. Both are listed in BL Harleian MS 3756, which has recently been published for the Irish Manuscripts Commission (Mac Niocaill 1997). The list, undated and occurring on f. 190 v., which has always been regarded as the earlier, gives fifty-seven books. They were classified according to their language: twenty-one in Latin, ten in French, seven in English, nineteen in Irish. Among the Latin books were a breviary and an ordinale or guide to the breviary, two psalters and commentaries on the New Testament (including Nicholas of Lyra). In common with Youghal, Garrett Óg had lives of the saints, a copy of the philosopher Boethius and the dialogues of St Gregory the Great. As a Renaissance man he also possessed copies of the works of Virgil, Juvenal and Terence. His French books included the Chronicles of France and Sir John Mandeville's Travels. Among his Irish books, all titles of which are translated into English, were a copy of the Psalter of Cashel, the life of St Kathryn [of Alexandria], the Deeds of Cú Chulainn and the History of Clane Lyre (Oidhe Chlainne Lir) (Gilbert 1879, pl. 63; App. 9, pp.32–3). On ff. 96 v.–7 r., the 'Books remaining in the library of Gerald FitzGerald' in February 1526 are listed. There were eighty-seven books in all. Among the 'new accessions' were the Utopia of Sir Thomas More and his book 'against the new opinions that hold against pilgrimages', St Augustine's De civitate dei, the Roman de la rose, and the King's answer to Luther. The Irish books are not itemized, but a blank page then occurs in the manuscript. Does this mean that the scribe intended to write them in later or could it signify that they were not there in 1526 and that he acquired them subsequently? Can it mean that he had disposed of them, and if so why? A possibly interesting connection between the two libraries discussed so far is that it was one of Garrett Óg's forebears who introduced the Franciscans into Ireland when he founded the friary at Youghal in 1203. The cultural milieu in which these libraries existed, that of the fourteenth, fifteenth and sixteenth centuries, also produced great Gaelic manuscripts like the Book of Ballymote, the Leabhar Breac, the Yellow Book of Lecan, the Book of Lecan, the Book of MacCarthy Rea (now known as the Book of Lismore), the Book of Fermoy and Laud Miscellany 610, many of which were compiled in the Cork area alone. These are only the better-known manuscripts; many lesser-known or minor works were also created.

UPHEAVAL: THE SIXTEENTH AND SEVENTEENTH CENTURIES

Sixteenth-century Europe saw the dawn of a new era. The old order had changed, Empire and Papacy had become diminished. The discovery of the New World meant that Ireland lay across new lines of trade and communication; she refused to give up the old Gaelic customs or join in the Protestant revolt, asserted national rights, allied herself with Spain and ended the century with defeat at Kinsale, thus completing the Tudor conquest of Ireland. 1540 saw the dissolution of the monasteries by Henry VIII and the subsequent dispersal of monastic libraries. A contemporary graphic description of their wholesale destruction was provided by John Bale, Protestant Bishop of Ossory, in his preface to Leland's New Year's Gift to King Henry VIII:

A greate numbre of them which purchased those superstychous mansyons, reserved of those librayre bookes some to serve theyr jokes, some to scoure theyr candlestycks, and some to rub theyr bootes; some they sold to the grossers and sopesellers, and some they sent over the sea to the bookbynders — not in small nomber, but at tymes whole shippes full, to the wonderynge of foren nacyons; yea, ye universyties of this realme are not all cleare in this detestable fact, but cursed is that bellye which seeketh to be fed with such ungodlye gaynes, and so depelye shameth his natural conterye. I know a merchantmanne, which shall at this time be namelesse, that bought ye contents of two noble libraryes for forty shillings price: a shame be it spoken. Thys stuffe hath he occupied in the stedde of grey paper by the space of more than these ten years, and yet he hath store ynoughe for as many years to come. (O'Leary 1892, 239)

The field of scholarship known as historical bibliography allows us to trace what happened to the contents of some monastic libraries in greater detail, for instance items which later turned up in Mornington, county Meath, from church sources. Henry Draycott, originally from Denby in Derbyshire, acquired Mornington through marriage to Joan Becke. He was appointed comptroller of the pipe in the Irish Exchequer on 21 May 1545 and master of the rolls from June 1565 to his death in May 1572. He collected a personal library at Mornington which comprised many manuscripts, including the Register of the Hospital of St John's in Dublin and the Black Book of Llanthony. These were 'acquired in the confusion following the closing of the monasteries' (Barnwell 1977, 70). The library was added to by his grandson, Sir John (d. 1639), who had access to the records held by his neighbours (McNeill 1923, 274), among whom were the Bellews of Barmeath, county Louth, whose descendant, Miss Teresa Mullalley, was a friend, religious sister and correspondent of Nano Nagle (1716–83), foundress of the Presentation Order. Mornington was burned by the troops of the English garrison at Drogheda in March 1642. 'His [Draycott's] Library (what could be preserved from the Fire) was brought in hither [to Drogheda] and sold us at very easy rates; a very fair parchment Manuscript of an old Missal consecrated to that Church of Marlington came to my hands, the loss of which I presume they valued more than their houses' (Dean Nicholas Bernard, *The whole proceeding of the siege of Drogheda* 1642, quoted in McNeill 1923, 274). This is apparently how Sir James Ware, the seventeenth-century antiquarian, acquired the Register of the Hospital of St John's in Dublin. The copy of Leicester's *Commonwealth* now in Cambridge belonged to the Draycott library, but the editor of the modern edition did not know about the looting of the library (K. W. Nicholls pers. comm). It should also be noted that non-monastic libraries of the period were equally subject to dispersal and an uncertain future. A detailed inventory of the estate of Henry O'Brien, fifth Earl of Thomond, was compiled at the time of his death in 1639 (Huntingdon Record Office Manchester MSS dd. M7/23, cited in Perceval-Maxwell 1994, 39; O'Brien 1995). ' ... because this was done by four men who were not members of his family it is more reliable than the inventories found in the depositions ... [there were] 200 books surely an impressive number, but also a tantalizing entry as the inventory takers did not list the titles' (Perceval-Maxwell 1994, 39). The library may have been started by the fourth Earl of Thomond after 1603. However, 'The books taken away by his Lordship [Thomas FitzMaurice, Thomond's nephew and executor] [are] esteemed to be worth £200, but cannot be expressly charged by reason his Lordship hath the catalogue which he found of them at Bunrattie' (Petworth House Archives Bundle C.6.2 unsorted; K. W. Nicholls pers. comm). The present whereabouts of the catalogue is not known.

Although monastic libraries had been largely scattered, sixteenth-century writers refer to other collections of books available to them in Ireland. Edmund Campion (1540–81), the Jesuit martyr and historian, thanked 'Iames Stanihurst, Recorder of Dublin ... [who] by the benefit of his owne Library, nourished most effectually mine endeavour'. James Stanihurst was the father of Richard Stanihurst, author of the historical tract *De rebus in Hibernia gestis*, and Edmund Campion had been his tutor in Oxford. Raphael Holinshed (d. 1580), the self-effacing editor of *Chronicles of England, Scotlande and Irelande* (1577), about whom very little is known, provided a list of 'The Authors out of whome this Historie of Irelande hath been gathered', and cites them in marginalia. Campion refers to his in footnotes. Although the catalogues of these libraries are not extant, at least we know the books that were available to such writers.

Printing was introduced into this country in 1550 with the arrival in Dublin of Humphrey Powell, mainly to serve the advancement of the Reformation. An entry in the Acts of the Privy Council of England under the date of 18 July 1550 records that a warrant was issued 'to deliver twenty pounds to Powell, the printer, given by the King's Majestie, towards his setting up in Irelande'. The first

book issued by him and still extant is the *Book of Common Prayer*, dated 1551. In mid-century an attempt was made to establish a university at St Patrick's Cathedral, Dublin, but this came to nothing. In 1591 Henry Ussher was sent to the Privy Council in England with Letters of Recommendation requesting royal assent to the founding of a college as a means 'to plant religion, civilitie, and true obedience in the hearts of this people'. The Queen granted a warrant to the Lord Deputy and Council for the erection of a college and in 1592 it was incorporated by charter, declaring it 'the Mother of an university' under the style and title of the 'College of the Holy and Undivided Trinity near Dublin founded by Queen Elizabeth'. The establishment of Trinity College, Dublin, was obviously a major event in the ensuing history of libraries in Ireland, as the TCD library has since become one of the country's foremost, and has holdings of international as well as national significance. The library was first endowed in 1593 but the earliest catalogue is dated 1600 when there were thirty books, classical, biblical and patristic texts, all in Latin. There were ten manuscripts in the library, nine of these were similar in subject-matter to the books, but the tenth was on French history. The next catalogue, begun in 1604, shows the library to have held four thousand nine hundred volumes, and by 1610 the College had a very respectable library, thanks to the addition of libraries of great collectors such as bishops Thomas Challoner and James Ussher (Boran 1998). Like the libraries of Oxford and Cambridge, books were chained and not for borrowing (Fox 1994).

Despite the dispersal of monastic libraries, Irish Catholics either created or had access to libraries in continental Europe as part of their church's Counter-Reformation drive in the early seventeenth century, for instance the library of the Irish Franciscan foundation of St Anthony's College at the famous contemporary seat of learning, Louvain in Belgium. Much of this library was returned to Ireland in the nineteenth century and is now in the Franciscan Library, Killiney (Mooney 1959; de Brún 1969). We see here the recovery and transcription, particularly by Fr Stephen White, SJ, of Irish manuscripts of lives of the Irish saints held in the libraries of the *Schottenklöster* already referred to, which contributed to his colleague Fr John Colgan's hagiographical collection *Acta sanctorum Hiberniae* (1645) and *Triadis thaumaturga acta* (1647), the latter containing the biographies of Patrick, Brigid and Colum Cille. Among his confrères at Louvain was Brother Michael O'Clery, one of the Four Masters, as Colgan called them (the others were Conary O'Clery, Cucogry O'Clery and Ferfeasa O'Mulconry). In 1636 they had produced the compendium of medieval and contemporary historiography known as *Annála Ríoghachta Éireann*. The combined work of this group coincided with the great enterprise of the Bollandists, the collection of the lives of the saints from throughout Europe entitled *Acta sanctorum*, the purpose of which was to enhance Catholic spirituality. The first Bollandist volumes were published in 1643, and the series has continued, with only a relatively short break, to the present day. All of these hagiographical items have been reprinted, reedited or both since they were first produced in the seventeenth century. It is worth noting also that, whereas the Louvain Franciscans concentrated on the spiritual and political history of Ireland, their counterparts at St Isidore's, the Irish College in Rome, were working on the story of the Franciscan order. There was a large library here also.

Emphasis on the emergence of a new Ireland after the Flight of the Earls and the political turmoil which accompanied it has tended to obscure scholarly achievements which crossed the sectarian divide. The common cause seems to have been the indignation aroused by the attempt made by Scottish historians like Dempster 'to affix the historical label *Scotia*, without even a duplicate to their portion of Britain, and transfer to its annals all the celebrity of ancient Ireland' (Reeves 1861, 29). Jesuits (Henry Fitzsimon and Stephen White), Franciscans (Hugh Ward, Patrick Fleming, John Colgan and the Four Masters), David Rothe, Catholic bishop of Ossory, and even the Protestant Primate of Ireland, Archbishop James Ussher, the antiquarian Sir James Ware, son of the Adjutant-General of Ireland, as well as the scholarly medic, Dr Thomas Arthur, cooperated by sharing their knowledge and libraries while attempting to assert the chronological priority of Irish history over that of Scotland in a manner which cannot fail to impress those interested in Irish heritage (MacLysaght and Ainsworth 1959; Sharpe 1991, 39–74; O'Sullivan 1994–5; Thornton forthcoming). Writing in reply to three letters of Colgan, White, while acknowledging the hospitality he had received from Ussher, remarked that the lack of access to a good library had nonetheless hampered his research.

The upheavals of the seventeenth century did not result in the absolute decline of a library tradition within the Catholic community. As one commentator on this section of the population has remarked, 'We may talk of the penal times but not (if this list be any guide) of a penal culture' (Fenning 1976, 76). The particular library inventory referred to in this case was the early eighteenth-century holding of the Drogheda-based Dominican Fr James Donnelly. However, the comment applies equally to the contents of three late seventeenth-century libraries owned by other Irish Catholic ecclesiastics: Bishop Luke Wadding (1628–91) (Corish 1970), Archbishop Piers Creagh (1640/1–1705) (Mooney 1955) and Bishop William Daton (1644–1713) (Fenning 1978, 30–57). In the first twenty-one pages of his Notebook, Bishop Wadding gives us a list, or catalogue, of almost seven hundred books which he had in 'Rosse and Wexford'. Many of the entries carry bibliographical notes, for instance on size, provenance and price. The list is classified by subject. In a preamble to it he had noted 'the best part of my bookes are marked at the end of each booke for whom they are' (Corish 1970, 54). Wadding also owned a bass viol and enjoyed gardening! The library of Bishop Creagh, censor for the Irish catechism of Fr Francis O'Molloy, *Lóchrann na gCreidmheach, Lucerna Fidelium* (Rome 1676), Bishop of Cork during 1676–92 and later Archbishop of Dublin from 1692 until his death in Strasbourg in 1705, probably never came to Ireland (he had left it for safe keeping in St Isidore's in Rome). Bishop Daton of Ossory owned one hundred and seventy books, all but seven in French. Of the seven English books, two were dictionaries. It is interesting to compare the contents of these libraries of Catholic churchmen with that of a Protestant gentleman, Mr Robert Taylor, probably of Ballinort, county Limerick, who had a library of seventy-nine books. These were listed for probate purposes by a James Wilson in 1672. The books of the churchmen compare very favourably with Taylor's (Mac Enery 1947, 30–4).

THE EIGHTEENTH CENTURY: CONSOLIDATION AND EXPANSION
The closing years of the seventeenth century set the scene for the eighteenth. When the Irish Parliament met in 1695 it initiated a series of Penal Laws under which Catholics suffered severely for more than a century. The 1697 session of this parliament ordered that Catholic clerics and all Jesuits and friars should leave the country before the following May, which had grievous effects on their libraries, although it did not curtail this tradition, as we shall see. The conversation, correspondence and foreign travel which had distinguished the seventeenth century continued and grew in the eighteenth. Consequently primary sources abound (Dickson 1983, 715–95). 'The spectacular expansion of Irish publishing in the English language in the course of the eighteenth century has created a pool of books, newspapers, and pamphlets of great historiographical value' (*ibid.* 714). Family and personal correspondence, diaries, directories, almanacs, contemporary accounts by travellers and eyewitnesses, surveys, inventories, catalogues and book sale catalogues can be added to these as direct records of library history in the period. Individual monographs and numerous scholarly articles (references to which will be given below) have chronicled the story of most important libraries and aspects of librarianship dating from this century onwards, and particularly those of the dominant Ascendancy.

We have already encountered one of the library pioneers of the early eighteenth century, Archbishop Narcissus Marsh (1638–1713), Provost of TCD from 1679, who complained of the difficulty of using the library there. He also believed that Dublin bookshops were furnished with 'new Triffles and Pamphlets and not well with them ... [it was] this consideration alone that at first moved me to think of building a library in some other place (not in the College) for publick use, where all might have free access, seeing they cannot have it in the College', said Marsh (McCarthy 1980, 17). Building of the library commenced around 1701. Its rules were based on those of the Bodleian Library in Oxford and the first librarian was the Huguenot Dr Elias Bouhéreau (1643–1719), whose qualifications met with Marsh's strict instructions (White 1908). In 1685 Louis XIV revoked the Edict of Nantes which had given relative religious freedom to the Huguenots since 1598. Consequently large numbers of highly skilled Huguenot refugees arrived in Ireland and England. The rules laid down for use of Marsh's Library were that 'All Graduates and Gentlemen shall have free access to the said Library ... provided they behave themselves and give place and pay due respect to their Betters' (McCarthy 1980, 36). The library is made up of four collections of books. Archbishop Marsh brought his own volumes with him from Oxford, Bouhéreau his collection of over two thousand books (which included his late father's), the library of Bishop Edward Stillingfleet (1635–99), Bishop of Worcester from 1689, which was purchased in 1704, and subsequently that of John Stearne (1660–1745), Bishop of Clogher. Bouhéreau compiled a superb shelf catalogue of the items in Marsh's which is still in use to-day. Robert Dougatt, Bouhéreau's successor, commenced work on a catalogue which is now bound in twelve volumes. It is written in three different hands, and was probably completed by John Wynne, the third librarian of Marsh's (MacCarthy 1980, 49–50; (www.kst.dit.ie/marsh/library.html). There are official records of the Library right from the very beginning. *The Calendar of Treasury Books Vol. XVI* for 11 June 1701 notes a Royal Warrant to Lords Justices to insert in the Civil List the salary of two hundred pounds for Elias Bouhéreau. *Vol. XIX* of the same series for 24 April 1704 records the reduction of his pension from two hundred to one hundred pounds, but later entries suggest that he continued to receive the two hundred pounds. The earlier *Calendar of Treasury Papers Vol. LXXXVI* for 11 July 1703 had contained a letter from the Bishop of London to the Lord High Treasurer describing Archbishop Marsh's pathetic financial circumstances as well as Marsh's petition appealing for the rent due to him in his diocese of Armagh. An act of the Irish Parliament of 1707 (6 Queen Anne 1707), incorporating Marsh's Library as a public library, was passed, despite initial opposition from the Irish House of Lords. It gives details relating to 'settling and preserving a publick library for ever, in the house for that purpose built by his grace Narcissus, now lord archbishop of Armagh, on part of the ground belonging to the archbishop of Dublin's palace,

near to the city of Dublin' (McCarthy 1980, 228–9). Marsh's Library is currently funded by the Department of Arts, Heritage, Gaeltacht and the Islands and by private donations.

Church of Ireland cathedral libraries which have come down to the present largely date from this time. The holdings are not confined to philosophy and theology but generally reflect the interests of educated gentlemen of the period: law, medicine, literature, travel, history and science (Tallon 1959; Woodworth 1970; Carson 1998). One of the best known in this category is probably the Cashel Diocesan Library, which was brought to Cashel in the 1730s by Bishop Theophilus Bolton on his translation from the bishopric of Elphin. Sometime after Archbishop King's death in 1729, Bolton acquired the bulk of King's books, and these constitute the library's greatest treasures. Bolton had been identified by Primate Boulter as being 'as dangerous an Irishman as any on the bench'. It is housed in the Chapter-house at Cashel, built in 1837 when Henry Cotton was archdeacon of the diocese (Woodworth 1994). A catalogue was published in 1973 during the deanship of Charles W. Wolfe (Cashel Diocese Library 1973).

The first mention of a library at St Fin Barre's Cathedral, Cork, occurs in the Chapter Book under 4 November 1627, when Richard Owen, Prebendary of Kilnaglory, 'Presented towards the erection of a Library in the Cathedral Church £20, said Richard to have the use of the Library during his life, and at his death to remain for the use of the Prebendaries' (Coleman 1905, 97). The Cathedral Library as it is now known was founded in 1720 by Bishop Peter Browne and endowed in 1723 by Archdeacon John Pomeroy, who bequeathed to it books of his own to the value of £60. In 1727 the library of Bishop Charles Crow of Cloyne was purchased for £115. In 1805 the collection was further enhanced by the acquisition of the library of Bishop Thomas Stopford of Cork. At a later stage, long runs of parliamentary journals and statutes as well as some early encyclopedias were obtained from the Earl of Bandon. University College, Cork, purchased the collection in 1982 and it is now housed there. In 1996 a project to clean and catalogue the entire holdings was initiated and is nearing completion. It is the first Irish cathedral catalogue to be available on-line and is accessible via UCC's Boole Library Catalogue (www.ucc.ie/services/ library.html). There are also cathedral libraries in Lismore (still housed in the Church of Ireland Cathedral there), Waterford (the collection is now in the Representative Church Body Library in Dublin), Kilmore, Elphin and Ardagh and also Tuam (Tallon 1959).

The library of Armagh was founded in 1770 by Richard Robinson, Archbishop of Armagh, 1765–94, successor to Dr George Stone who had succeeded Dr Boulter on his death in 1742. In 1771 he endowed it as a public library and the building was erected at a cost of three thousand pounds. It was built to the design of Thomas Cooley and the inscription over the public entrance in Greek describes the institution as 'the medicine shop of the soul'. *An Act for Settling and Preserving the Publick Library in the City of Armagh for ever* (13 & 14 George III c. 40) was passed in 1773. This was the last statute to address the availability of public libraries in Ireland until 1850. The position of Keeper of the Library was created by this measure and his appointment vested in the Primate for the time being. It was laid down that he must be a Presbyter of the Church of England or Ireland and be a Master of Arts of one of the universities or colleges of England or Ireland. The Keeper was required to take an oath to protect the books and observe all the statutes, rules and constitutions 'already made, concerning the said Office of Library-keeper, while the same shall continue in Force, and I shall continue in the said Office' (Weatherup 1975). Dr William Reeves (1815–92), a native of Charleville, county Cork, and a renowned authority on early Irish history, was probably the most famous Keeper, which position he held from 1862 until 1886.

Among Archbishop Robinson's collections given to the Library, as well as books, were numerous engravings, coins, seals, medals, sculptures and prints. Gifts have been a major source of the Armagh Library's acquisitions, both from Keepers, individuals and institutions. The income for the Library is derived from the land with which it was endowed by its founder. There are references in the records to grants for special purchases, including the manuscripts of Bishop Reeves and the Gaelic scholar John O'Donovan's copy of Colgan's *Acta sanctorum*. The records are unique, being the earliest from a public lending library in Ireland. A catalogue of the library was already in existence in 1799. This was updated in 1815, but when Reeves became Keeper in 1862 he 'found no catalogue, but an interleaved copy of old Robert Fisher's Bodleian one, in which many books common to both libraries were marked for Armagh in the margin and every item without a counterpart was entered on the interleaf. This was a cumbrous and unpleasant makeshift'. In 1867 the new catalogue, 'in two volumes, of 650 pages each, containing about 25,000 titles', was completed by Reeves, assisted by Mr Edward Rogers, his Deputy Keeper. A further catalogue of the books in the Keeper's room was completed in 1921 and in 1926 a listing of the pamphlets. *A catalogue of the manuscripts in the Public Library of Armagh* has already been published (Dean 1928). The library has recently been computerized in a joint project with the Southern Education and Library Board of Northern Ireland, and the catalogue will be available on-line in the near future.

The late seventeenth-century Charity School Movement in England led to the establishment of several charity schools in early eighteenth-century Cork. One of these was the Green Coat Hospital. It was set up by the leading advocate of charity schooling, the Rev. Henry Maule. Situated in what is now Skiddy's Almshouses, the foundation stone was laid on 6 March 1715 and the schools were finished 12 August 1716. In his tract *Pietas Corcagiensis*, Maule describes the reasons for the establishment of the school: to advance the glory of God, the welfare of fellow-Christians, to educate the poorer classes who were leading lives of immorality, poverty and ignorance. No less was the desire to 'prevent the growth of Popery amongst us' (Maule 1721). It has been suggested that the school was 'an object of admiration for the whole country, and a model to be emulated by other charity schools during the first half of the eighteenth century. Thereafter its fortunes declined, and it was in serious financial difficulty before the end of the century' (McCann 1973, 102–11). The library, consisting of about five hundred items now deposited in University College, Cork, was very well supplied with valuable and erudite books on all subjects, not only in English but also in Latin, Greek, French, Spanish and Portuguese.

Protestantism, education and library history converge in the case of one further unique early eighteenth-century initiative. Bishop Francis Hutchinson arrived in Ireland from Derbyshire in 1721 as Bishop of Down and Connor. In England and subsequently in Ireland he had specialized in the study of witchcraft. Between Wing's *Eighteenth-century short-title catalogue* and Walter Harris's edition of Ware, it has been possible to compile a bibliography of twenty-six titles attributable to Hutchinson, most of them pamphlets, in the majority of which his 'theological shortcomings' and 'his partisan and authoritarian attitude [spill] over into his social contributions' (Wheeler 1996, 144). However his *Defence of the Antient Historians* (1734), in which he sets out to review and assess Irish historiography, demonstrates 'his familiarity with the printed sources, most of which were in his own library' (*ibid.* 147). His interest for us lies in two libraries: his own of seven hundred and eight titles in seven hundred and twelve volumes and the small library at his proposed school on Rathlin Island off the north-Antrim coast for the island's Irish-speaking population of four hundred and ninety, up to that time served by neither priest nor minister. In setting up this parochial library he was imitating the pioneering work of James Kirkwood in Scotland (1704/5) and Thomas Bray in England, Wales and the Isle of Man between 1705 and 1730. He wished to provide bilingual primers, catechisms, psalters, prayer books and bibles, and himself published one such catechism, *The Church Catechism in Irish. With the English placed over against it in the Same Karakter.* Printed in Belfast, the octavo-sized volume contained fifty-six pages of text, as well as sixteen preliminary pages, and cost him £15. Wheeler points out that the catechism is 'of special interest because it does

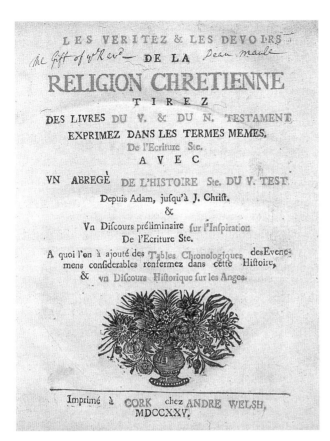

Fig. 28.2 Copy of Huguenot New Testament, Green Coat Library, UCC.

not employ an Irish type but instead uses a fairly defective half phonetic spelling to reproduce the sounds of the Scottish form of Irish spoken on the island at that time' (*ibid.* 145–6). His aim was, however the anglicization as well as the proselytization of the people. Among many others, Lord Charlemont and Archbishop King of Dublin donated books for the library. While Hutchinson's own catalogue of his library is important, the octavo auction catalogue 'is a unique survival for its time in that it is the copy actually used by the auctioneer [Wiliam Ross of Dublin], or his clerk, in the course of the sale' (*ibid.* 148). It records the lot number, selling price, name of buyer and record of payment, further underlining the importance of the book trade for historical bibliography (O'Kelley 1953; Munter 1988; Pollard 1989).

Two medical libraries date from earlier years of the century: that of Sir Patrick Dun (1711), Dublin, bequeathed to the Royal College of Physicians of Ireland, of which he had been President, and Dr Edward Worth's (1723), preserved in the cases which he had made for them in the boardroom of the former Dr Steevens' Hospital, in the same city. In 1733 Worth bequeathed his library to Dr Steevens' Hospital, of which he had been appointed trustee in 1717. Most of the book collectors of the period were working scholars and their libraries reflected this. Worth 'decided to take a totally different

approach. Unlike many famous collectors, he does not seem to have been interested in having the first edition of every book. He was more inclined to collect editions which were masterpieces of typography and which were also superbly bound' (McCarthy 1986, 29). Worth bought books at important auctions in England, Holland, Ireland and at one German sale. His volumes were bound, and many rebound, to his specifications, probably in Dublin. Sir Edward Sullivan in his *Decorative bookbinding in Ireland* (1914), said 'With the volume containing the Journal of the House of Commons for 1707 begins a more luxuriant form of ornamentation, which in the years that followed blossomed into an astounding magnificence' (*ibid.* 32). Worth's books were bound in 'the finest polished plain, or speckled or mottled calf or in superb red morocco. Moreover, although most of the spines and the upper and lower covers have been tooled in gold, in some cases where the covers have not been decorated, the spines have been, and this gives a uniform look to the whole collection'. The library contains works on all aspects of medicine, but also books by French, English and Italian authors on philosophy, politics, history, classics and *belles lettres*. It has been argued that 'Worth may have hoped that his collection would stimulate doctors, as well as the clergy, to collect books, and may well have intended his collection to be a model for others in early eighteenth-century Ireland. Perhaps it was for this reason that he donated it to Dr Steevens' Hospital' (*ibid.* 29). There are three manuscript copies of the library catalogue. Worth's library is currently being catalogued by Vincent Kinnane of Trinity College, Dublin.

While notable libraries were formed by grandees such as Conway, Ormonde and Orrery, as well as by dignitaries of the Church of Ireland, it would appear that libraries were 'still uncommon in early eighteenth-century Ireland' (Barnard 1998, 213). By the mid-century, however, this had changed and an unprecedented flowering of personal collections occurred in this country. The records of one hundred and ninety-eight private libraries have come down to us. The profession and social class of the owners and their contents have been examined (Cole 1974). In size these libraries ranged from fifty books to over six thousand, although most were in the five hundred to one thousand range. Contemporary catalogues, newspaper reports of sales and actual sale catalogues provided the relevant sources of information. Despite the penal era, it is interesting to note that we know of twenty-five Roman Catholic priests (including bishops) who owned libraries. One of these was John Wickham, parish priest of Templeshannon and Edermine, county Wexford, from 1760 until his death in 1777. He bequeathed his books to the Franciscan Friary, Wexford, where an inventory was made by Fr John Broe, then guardian of the friary. Fr Wickham had been a student of philosophy in Louvain during 1751–52, and his books reflect this interest. He had approximately one hundred books, amounting to two hundred and sixty volumes: twenty in French, twenty-five in English and fifty-five in Latin (Ó Suilleabháin 1963–4). The large library of the Gaelic aristocrat Charles O'Conor of Bellanagare, county Roscommon, deserves special mention. O'Conor's collection of manuscripts was brought to Stowe, Buckinghamshire, by his grandson, Rev. Charles O'Conor, who was librarian there as well as Catholic chaplain to the Marchioness of Stowe, Mary Elizabeth, daughter of Sir Robert Nugent of county Westmeath. They were returned to Ireland in 1833 when the Ashburnham Collection of Irish manuscripts was deposited in the Royal Irish Academy by the British Government (Ó Catháin 1989). The library of printed books owned by Charles O'Conor is now in Clonalis House, county Roscommon, and is currently being catalogued.

Apart from ecclesiastical, educational and private libraries, the eighteenth century also witnessed the formation of a number of other distinctive institutional holdings. The Dublin Society for Improving Husbandry, Manufactures and Other Useful Arts (it became the Royal Dublin Society when it received the patronage of George IV in 1820) was founded in June 1731. Its library was the forerunner of the National Library of Ireland. The establishment of the Royal Irish Academy in 1785 to promote the study of 'science, polite literature and antiquities' shows that a change in attitudes to learning and books had certainly taken place (Ó Raifeartaigh 1985; Dolan 1985). The Cork Library Society was founded in 1790 and the Cork Institution, later the Royal Cork Institution, in 1803. This society was the forerunner of Queen's College, Cork, founded in 1845 (McCarthy 1989; Murphy 1995). In 1788 the Belfast Reading Society had been set up. Its library seems to have been modelled on Benjamin Franklin's Library Company of Philadelphia. The Belfast Reading Society (later the Linen Hall Library) became a model of a reading society library which truly developed as the memory of the community it serves, given the unbroken continuity from its establishment to the present day. Founded in May 1788 by a group of 'worthy plebeians who would do honour to any town, [with] not among them one of higher rank than McCormick the gunsmith or Osborne the baker' (McTier to William Drennan, 1792, quoted in Killen 1990, 7), it became in 1792 the Belfast Society for Promoting Knowledge and in 1802 moved into the White Linen Hall. It stayed there until 1892 when it moved into the Linen Warehouse in Donegall Square North where it has since remained. The institution's primary manuscript sources include personal papers, minute books of various societies (including the Irish Harp Society), grand jury lists and verdicts, registers of committee members, account books, state papers, in other words the full range of available archival sources. Official publications include acts and reports of parliamentary committees. Apart from the complete range of Linen Hall Library catalogues, dating from 1793 on, there are also several theses, newspaper and journal articles on this important institution (Killen 1990). Secondary sources are equally extensive (*ibid.* 252–55). The Hawnt Report (1966) had earlier recognized the important contribution made by the Society's Library in the field of library provision and education. Accordingly, 'For the first time an official body recommended the propriety of an annual grant from public moneys to the society' (*ibid.* 108). The special collections of the Library range from the Belfast Printed Book Collection to the Traditional Irish Music Collection (Killen 1996). The most recent and current special holding, the Northern Ireland Political Literature Collection, is a notable example of the importance of ephemeral material as a primary heritage and historical resource (Gray 1996). In 1968 the then librarian, J. W. Vitty, recognizing 'that here was history in the making', had started to assemble 'the ephemera of the Troubles' — handbills, newspapers, posters, stickers, post-cards and the like published by the current political parties and pressure groups. Microfilming of the collection commenced in 1986, thus ensuring preservation of the originals and providing a revenue source for the Library. In 1987, funding was secured to undertake the cataloguing and digitization of over five thousand political posters (Killen 1990, 133–91).

The first circulating library in Ireland was probably that of James Hoey of the Dublin family of printers and booksellers. The library was advertised in the Dublin *General Advertiser* for 13 January 1737, as having 'a large Collection of Histories, Romances, Novels, Memoirs, etc,' that could be rented for 8d for a large book, 6d per week for a small one (Cole 1974, 112). On the basis of newspaper advertisements and lists of subscribers to books published in Ireland by subscription, it is possible to identify twenty-four community circulating libraries and eleven book clubs in addition to the non-profit subscription libraries, most of which date to the second half of the eighteenth century. Some of the libraries issued catalogues from time to time, although few are known to have survived, for instance Conoly's *Catalogue of books* (Galway [1799?]) and Conoly's *Catalogue of books in the Galway Circulating Library* (Galway [1795?]), both in the Special Collections Department of the Library at University College, Dublin, and Dowling's catalogue of 1794 in the National Library of Ireland (Traxler-Brown 1990, 86–102.). This last was issued by a Vincent Dowling, founder of the Apollo Circulating Library *ca.* 1792, who had the temerity to identify himself as the 'Manager of the British Library, London for many years' (Cole 1974, 111–23). His library consisted of two thousand titles, according to an undated one hundred and seventeen-page catalogue. He specialized in non-fiction. His advertisement in the *Hibernian Chronicle* newspaper stresses the advantages of membership of his library: 'The Fund of Information and Amusement which this Establishment presents, must strike every discerning Mind, friendly to the Improvement of Knowledge and refined Taste, especially in the rising Generation, while the terms of Subscription [16s 3d like the others] unite these Advantages with the strictest Economy, and point out a rational and most advantageous Source of Amusement to those who prefer "The Feast of Reason and the well stored Mind" before Recreations of a much more expensive and less advantageous Nature' (Cole 1974, 115). The English, French and Italian Circulating Library in Cork, and the later Cork Library, founded in 1792, have been described elsewhere (Kaufmann 1963), and in particular the Cork Library's rules and catalogues (Coleman 1905, 82–93).

TOWARDS A PUBLIC LIBRARY SYSTEM (1800–1922)

Despite the enlightenment, increased literacy and the availability of books, by 1800 there was only one large public library in Britain and Ireland, the British Museum. The story of the nineteenth century is that of the development of more widespread access to information from which arose the establishment of public libraries throughout these islands from 1850 onwards (Neylon and Henchy 1966). The beginnings of this process emerged in somewhat unexpected circumstances. Organized adult education was introduced for the first time in 1816 by the London Hibernian Society, one of several Protestant proselytising societies operating in Ireland. It had 347 schools in this country, catering for children and adults. Within six years, 1818–24, the number of adults had increased from 1,250 to 10,117. To counteract these societies, many Catholic parishes set up parochial libraries. At first they contained only devotional literature but later held secular works and books for children also. Typical holdings towards the end of the century were of approximately 'five hundred volumes, all having the *imprimatur* of the P. P.' (C. 1894). The Young Men's Catholic Association would later provide similar small if uninspiring libraries (Griffith 1891). The education of the masses was equally regarded as essential by Daniel O'Connell and Richard Lalor Shiel, although for different reasons. In 1824 they founded the Catholic Association to address the grievances of Catholics. An educational programme was designed to politicize the people through awareness of current affairs. Texts of political speeches were published in a *Weekly Register*, which was funded by the collection of 1d per month from members. In its heyday, about 6,000 copies were sent out to country areas, and church-wardens read it aloud at the church door after Sunday Mass. Its contribution to the achievement of Catholic Emancipation in 1829 gave the Catholic population a new sense of purpose and self-reliance.

In 1840 O'Connell subsequently founded the Loyal National Repeal Association of Ireland (known as the Repeal Association) to achieve repeal of the Act of Union. It attracted a huge membership, Protestant and Catholic. Thomas Matthew Ray, Secretary to the Association, initiated 'Repeal missions' in 1842 with the purpose of inculcating the principle of nationality and organizing local agitation in various districts. In the same year, Thomas Davis, John Blake Dillon and Charles Gavan Duffy joined the Association. Around this time they also founded *The Nation* and became known as Young Ireland. Figures published by Thomas Davis during 1844 in *The Nation* newspaper claimed that of a national population of 8.5 million, 3.7 million were illiterate. Reading rooms, which became known as Repeal Reading Rooms, were therefore established to 'diffuse among the people useful information and early intelligence on all subjects of public interest, especially on the great national question of repeal' (Rules, 1844). The objectives were to collect and combine popular opinion in aid of the latter; to afford a source of rational occupation for the leisure hours of the industrious classes, where they might be instigated to increased patriotism, temperance and virtue; to promote the weekly collection of the Repeal Fund and to extend the Repeal organization. These quasi-libraries were unique in that their particular purpose was the education of the poorer classes (Barnes 1965). Repeal Reading Rooms were the brain-child of Ray, although Young Ireland, and especially Thomas Davis, displayed such enthusiasm for the idea that they, not Ray, were often given credit for their establishment. The first opened in Newcastle, county Limerick, in 1844. By 14 April 1845 there were at least seventy-one reading rooms in operation, by 28 April eighty-five and eventually there were some three hundred.

Thomas Davis had a huge influence on the Reading Room holdings, not least through *The Nation*, the popularity of which secured over £1,000 per year for Repeal funds. The concept of the heritage of Ireland as we know it to-day was largely his, although he rarely receives credit for it. He recognized that the essence of heritage and nationhood lay in every conceivable aspect of human activity:

To be able to keep it and use it and govern it the men of Ireland must know what it is, what it was and what it can be made; they must study her history, perfectly know her present state, physical and moral, and train themselves up by science, poetry, music, industry, skill and by all the studies and accomplishments of peace and war. If Ireland were in national health, her history would be familiar, by books, pictures, statuary and music, to every cabin and shop in the land; her resources, as an agricultural, manufacturing, and trading people, would be equally known, and every young man would be trained and every grown man able to defend her coasts, her plains, her towns and her hills not with his right arm merely, but by disciplined habits and military accomplishments. These are the pillars of independence. (Davis [n.d.], 84–5)

It is arguable that, in Ireland, Davis was uniquely aware not merely of the developments in libraries worldwide but also of the significance of these developments. He pleaded for a fair trial of the library system, and urged a true and full classification of books. He was quite emphatic about the knowledge which he desired his countrymen to possess. He did not propose to lay down a censorship as to what were good and what were bad books, but appealed to the good sense and noble ambition of young men to make the right choice. The Repeal phenomenon lasted for about five years. The Great Famine, the death of O'Connell in 1847, the abortive Tipperary uprising of 1848 and quarrels among the members caused the final extinction of the Repeal Movement. However, the Reading Rooms had made a significant contribution to the advancement of literacy and the creation of a reading public, a foundation on which developments involving librarianship would soon build.

In 1832 Mechanics' Institutes were established in England to create and foster a desire for learning in scientific and literary fields, a move which led to an increase in technological invention and improvement for the operative classes. These Institutes and a wide range of literary societies provided reading rooms towards this end. Although Ireland did not experience an industrial revolution, the increased desire for education is well attested by the growth of similar bodies. The Dublin Mechanics' Institute was founded in 1835 with 110 books in the library, and already by 1855

A subscription of ten shillings per annum, payable yearly, half-yearly, or quarterly, constitutes a member, and entitles him to the privileges of the News and Periodical Rooms, a Lending Library of eight thousand volumes, and access to the lectures (with power to introduce a lady), free. Members have also the advantage of getting tickets at reduced prices to nearly all the public exhibitions that take place from time to time in the city. They can join any of the undermentioned classes at the very low premium attached per quarter: — Evening Classes, Mathematics, English, etc., 2s.6d; Drawing, 2s.6d.; French, 5s.; Dancing, 5s.; Instrumental Music, 5s.; Vocal Music, 5s.; Gymnastics, 5s.; Day Classes for Ladies, French 5s.; Italian, 5s.; German, 5s.; Singing, 5s. (Thom's *Irish Almanac and Official Directory*)

Mechanics' Institutes quickly spread throughout the country (Byrne 1976). The desire for learning among the middle classes continued to increase during the nineteenth century also. Charters had been granted for the establishment of Queen's Colleges in Belfast, Cork and Galway. Histories of the libraries of these institutions have not yet been written, although articles about them in various journals are available, and aspects of the story are taken up again below. The history of antiquarianism in Munster, but especially Cork, which has often been eclipsed by that of Dublin, is now receiving more scholarly attention (Ó Conchúir 1982; Shee Twohig 1987; McCarthy 1987 and 1997; Harrison 1999; Rockley 1995 and in progress; Ireland forthcoming).

The growth of Mechanics' Institute libraries, among other factors, motivated the authorities to investigate the broader issue of public provision of library services. In 1849 a Select Committee of the House of Commons on Public Libraries was set up, under the Chairmanship of William Ewart, MP, assisted by Edward Edwards (1812–86), a library historian on the staff of the British Museum. This resulted in the first of six acts, culminating in the 1902 *Library Act*, the net effect of which was finally to accord the authority to establish public libraries throughout the country. It is on this legal basis that Ireland's present public library system is ultimately founded. An act of 1850 allowed town councils in England to levy one half-penny in the pound on the rates (Hansard for 13 March, 10 April and 16 May 1850). In 1853 the first *Public Libraries and Museums Act* was passed. The 1854 *Towns Improvement Act* (17 & 18 Victoria c. 103) extended the 1853 measure to Ireland, but only to boroughs with a population of over 10,000 people. Under this act, the 1850 rate could be levied by town councils. In 1855, the *Public Libraries Act* (18 & 19 Victoria c. 40 s. 8) raised the rate to 1*d* in the pound, and extended the 1853 act to towns with town councils and a population of 5,000 inhabitants. It also laid down that 'all libraries and museums established under this Act shall be open to the public free of all charge', thus allowing access to those who could not afford to pay the subscriptions for the Mechanics' Institutes Libraries. The 1855 measure was amended by the *Public Libraries (Ireland) Amendment Act* 1877, which permitted libraries to borrow money on interest, and use as security a mortgage or bond on town funds or rates. The method of borrowing was regulated by the earlier *Companies Clauses Act* 1845 (ss 38–55), which is incorporated into the *Public Libraries Act* 1855. It also allowed library committees, the governing authorities for local libraries, to have members who were not necessarily commissioners or other regional representatives. Subsequently the *Public Libraries (Ireland) Act* of 1894 attempted to confer the privileges of the 1855 act on rural districts, stating that 'when the library district is a parliamentary polling district not within the control of an urban authority ... then the rural sanitary authorities should have the same powers'. But as several parliamentary polling districts comprised two or three sanitary authorities, the idea was unworkable. However, the act provided that urban authorities might grant the use of their free libraries to persons who were not resident in the district, either gratuitously or upon payment of a specified charge. Eventually the *Public Libraries (Ireland) Act* of 1902 extended the power of the 1855 act to any rural district council, and allowed a library authority to enter into agreements with the manager of a school to use it as a library. Under this statute also, county councils (recently established in 1899) were allowed to make grants to library authorities in their areas for the purchase of books or towards the maintenance of public libraries from funds available for technical education.

There were three other possible sources of revenue referred to in the acts. A library might accept any grant from the Department of Science and Art for various purposes, including the purchase of a site. Monies were allowed to come from the charges levied on non-residents for the use of the library, from fines, sales of catalogues and so forth. Any lands or houses vested in the library authority which were not required for the time being might be let, but all rents and profits arising therefrom had to be applied for the purposes of the acts. If these methods proved insufficient, the statutes allowed for the authority to fall back on voluntary subscriptions and donations from public-spirited citizens. Due concern was also expressed in the legislation regarding the availability and suitability of sites and premises. Accordingly, the urban authority could (with the approval of the Treasury) appropriate for the purposes of the acts any lands that happened to be vested in them. They might also (with like approval) purchase or rent any land or suitable buildings by mutual agreement, the library authorities having no powers of taking land compulsorily. They were permitted to erect appropriate buildings, rebuild, repair or alter any structures already in existence, intended for public libraries, public museums, schools for science and art or art galleries. They could take a grant or conveyance by way either of gift, sale or exchange of any land held by trustees for any public or charitable objective, provided that it did not exceed one acre, and only with the consent of the Commissioners of Charitable Donations and Bequests (or of the Board of Works, in the case of charitable property), which was charged with the repayment of advances made under the *Glebe Loan Act (Ireland)* 1870.

Only one city and two towns attempted initially to adopt the 1855 act until in the 1880s greater use began to be made of the aforementioned legislative measures. Cork was the first Irish city to implement it, but the rate to support a library was not levied until 1892. Dundalk adopted the measure in 1856, and it was here that the first public library was opened. Ennis implemented it in 1860, but the sum of money raised was insufficient to make the establishment of a library realistic. In 1884 two municipal libraries opened in Dublin, and the Belfast library was founded in 1888. Waterford adopted the act in 1894 and opened its Library two years later (Jones 1970). Other libraries available to rural populations in the nineteenth century including lending libraries, circulating libraries and library societies. Accounts of these, their management and holdings, were published in contemporary journals such as *The New Ireland Review* and the *Dublin Builder* (later the *Irish Builder*). The establishment of the Gaelic League in 1893 gave fresh impetus to the library movement in Ireland. By 1902 there were over 400 branches throughout the country, many with their own book collections. The desire to revive the Irish language resulted in an intense interest in everything pertaining to Irish history and the promoting of Irish industry. The Irish Rural Libraries Association was founded in April 1904 with the objective of implementing the provisions of the 1902 act (Boland 1902). The founding of a professional body, Cumann na Leabharlann, in June 1904 supported the Association and emphasized the value of public libraries, particularly the stimulus they provided to the educational, social and economic life of the country. Between 1904 and 1909 five issues of its journal, *An Leabharlann*, were published, containing articles on Irish history and literature as well as on library history and administration. Among its better-known contributors were Patrick Pearse, Douglas Hyde and T. W. Lyster. The records and papers of John P. Whelan, former librarian at Kevin Street, Dublin, and founder-member of Cumann na Leabharlann, were donated to the Library Association of Ireland (to be discussed later) in 1995. Among the records are minute and agenda books of An Cumann, including those for its first meeting in 1904.

Many scholars continued contributing to research into the various intellectual aspects of librarianship around this time of development and innovation, thus providing a solid foundation for similar work which persists to the present day. The Bibliographical Society of Ireland was set up in 1918 to enquire into the history of Irish bibliography in all its various aspects. Its *Papers* were produced irregularly in pamphlet form until 1958, and contained seminal studies, covering topics such as local printing, periodical publications and scientific publications, by E. R. McClintock Dix, P. S. O'Hegarty and several others. The Society produced an annual report as well. A journal also associated with it, *The Irish Book Lover* (1909–57), was later printed and published by the distinguished scholar printer Colm Ó Lochlainn. It covered a broader spectrum by including literary works. On its demise, an attempt was made to continue this type of investigation in *The Irish Book*, volumes 1–3, printed by Liam Miller at the Dolmen Press, but formally published by the Bibliographical Society of Ireland. The School of Librarianship at UCD then initiated the publication of the *Irish Publishing Record* in 1967/8. Since 1970, *The Long Room*, the journal of the Friends of the Library of Trinity College, Dublin, edited by Vincent Kinnane from 1992 onwards, has continued to provide a forum for bibliographic discussion. In 1971 *Irish Booklore* was first published in Belfast by the Blackstaff Press and was incorporated into the *Linenhall Review* in 1986.

Between 1897 and 1913, grants amounting to £170,000 were given by the American philanthropist, Dale Carnegie (1835–1919), for the provision of eighty library buildings to facilitate the local authorities which had adopted the 1855 *Public Libraries Act*. In 1913 the Carnegie United Kingdom Trust (CUKT) was founded and a large number of library buildings throughout Britain and Ireland were endowed by it. Although not all the libraries intended for this country were built, sixty-two of them still survive and form an essential component of our existing library system (Grimes 1998, 17). Sir Horace Plunkett, George Russell (AE) and their associates in the Co-Operative Movement, like Carnegie, also identified the library as the intellectual centre of the community, providing access to education for all. In 1915, a report commissioned by CUKT and carried out in Limerick by Cruise O'Brien, father of the well-known historian Conor Cruise O'Brien and librarian at the Co-Operative Movement Reference Library, together with another in 1917 carried out by Lennox Robinson, The Abbey playwright, showed that lack of resources and competent supervision led to administrative difficulties and that the rural district scheme instigated by Carnegie had not been entirely successful (Ó hAodha 1998). In 1918, CUKT established a Book Repository in Harcourt Street, Dublin, to help libraries acquire new books on easy terms. It continued until 1928 when it was closed down, but by that point following the events of 1916–22 a new Ireland had come into being.

LIBRARIES IN INDEPENDENT IRELAND

The story of the post-1922 period is in large measure a continuation of that of the nineteenth and early twentieth centuries. Improvements under the new political dispensation were slow at first, perhaps in response to the degree of caution surrounding publications generally. One administrative development was set to have a profound effect on library management from mid-century onwards. Closer to the present, libraries, like other institutions have had to come to terms with rapid transformations in technology. The profession has been equipping itself by means of its associations and organizational structures to deal with these and other challenges. The remainder of the chapter now outlines these important aspects of the subject under review. The focus is on the south, because, despite close professional

and co-operative links (particularly through the North/South Liaison Committee, a joint committee of the Library Association of Ireland and the Library Association, Northern Ireland Branch), the story of the Northern Ireland library system is inevitably interwoven with that of the broader United Kingdom narrative, which perforce puts it largely outside the remit of the present chapter (Ronayne 1995, 43; Parker *et al.* 1996)

A Conference of Library Officials held in 1923 at University College, Dublin, shortly after the creation of the new southern political order, urged government support for library services and identified the need for a forum to discuss policy and professional problems from an Irish point of view. The first aspiration of the conference was realized when government assistance was provided in 1925 by the passing of the Irish Free State *Local Government Act* 1925. This gave powers to the county authorities to levy a rate in aid of public libraries and to extend the powers of library authorities to cover free lectures and other educational work. The *Local Government Act* of 1935 formally empowered county councils to adopt the *Libraries Act* of 1855. It also raised the rate limitation from 1*d* to 3*d* in the pound. The County Librarian, in consultation with a Library Committee, under the 1935 act was responsible for the provision of a library service in each county. The County Librarians had five aims: to assemble and administer books, provide reliable information, facilitate education, optimize leisure and serve those who were aiding in the advancement of knowledge and technical skills. Under the subsequent *Local Government Act* of 1940, County Managers were appointed to administer local government legislation in all counties where county councils had been functioning. When this act was applied to the county libraries in 1942, the Library Committee ceased to function and the County Librarian became responsible to the County Manager for the administration of the library. Under the 1940 act, the County Manager had discretion to appoint a Library Committee to function in an advisory capacity. Accounts of meetings between the County Manager and Librarian and other details regarding the running of the libraries are available in local newspapers. The appointment, promotion, remuneration, travelling expenses and other matters relating to rate-supported library staff were provided for within the Local Government (Officers) Regulations 1943 (SR & O No. 161 of 1943). The keeping of accounts and records by library authorities is based on the Public Bodies Order 1946 (SR & O No. 275 of 1946).

These largely positive measures contrast with a more negative underlying reality. The evidence of censorship in the inter-war period and afterwards is reflected in the many obvious lacunae within library holdings at the time. It has been remarked that eighteenth-century scholarly gentlemen regarded books 'as essential armour against bucolic indolence' (Bernard 1998), but the new public libraries were viewed as 'seed beds of filth' which needed to be kept under control by all right-minded citizens (Casteleyn 1984, 215). The new Irish state had taken over British legislation in this regard, and the main statute dealing with indecency was the *Obscene Publications Act* 1857. The *Customs Consolidation Act* of 1876 also provided for powers to prevent the sale of obscene books, pictures, prints and other articles. Pressures from groups such as the Irish Vigilance Association, founded in 1911, dissatisfied with the type of periodicals and newspapers in circulation, eventually led the Minister for Justice of the Irish Free State to set up a Committee of Enquiry on Evil Literature. The report of this committee resulted in the *Censorship of Publications Act* 1929, enabling a Censorship Board to ban publications that in its opinion were 'in their general tendency indecent or obscene'. The writer/essayist Hubert Butler, who had himself been a librarian, claimed 'it is largely the spread of the free libraries that has made censorship important' (Butler 1949). Furthermore, he suggested 'The pressure towards censorship does not principally come, as Seán Ó Faoláin and his adversaries think, from either Church or State. It is entirely democratic and comes from the people' (*ibid.* 50). However, the combination of all three explains the emergence of a closed introverted society with 'an even more closed system of government' (Keogh 1995, 11) in the 1930s and 1940s and even later. 'Censorship became an important mechanism of control in this environment, a measure designed, in its various manifestations, to maintain the security of the state and protect the (narrowly defined) morals and culture of 'the nation' (Ó Drisceoil 1996, 1). While the librarians were drawn chiefly from the class to which Barnard had referred, Library Committees exerted great influence over stock selection and had a particular interest in fiction. Librarians were trying to raise the educational standards of the readers; the Library Committees, representatives of people who were not ready for what libraries could do for them, were insisting on providing low-quality reading matter. This largely restrictive mentality may be at least also partially responsible for the relative underfunding of the library system. The report on public library provision in the Irish Free state (1936) was the result of a survey financed by the Carnegie Trust and carried out in 1935 by Miss Christina Keogh, Librarian of the Irish Central Library for Students (ICLS) (Keogh 1936 ; Hall 1980). The ICLS was one of three such libraries established in 1923 by the CUKT (the others were the National Central Library London and the Scottish Central Library, Dunfermline, Fife). Their aim was 'to facilitate the more serious reader particularly in isolated areas' (Hall 1980, 125). Three conditions were laid down:

(1) to supply books to libraries, urban and rural, not to individuals (except in areas where no public library system existed);

(2) to devise a basis of contribution for services rendered;

(3) in due course to expect state assistance. The 1936 report pointed to the significant lack of financing for libraries. No further meaningful increase in fiscal support would in fact be made available to public libraries until the creation of Public Library Grants Scheme of 1961.

AN CHOMHAIRLE LEABHARLANNA AND LIBRARY ADMINISTRATION

There was one major evolution in library management in mid-century, however. This was the setting up, in 1947, of An Chomhairle Leabharlanna, the library advisory authority. The professional forum, Cumann Leabharlann na nÉireann (the Library Association of Ireland (LAI)), founded in 1928 and to be described later, among its first proposals looked for a government commission on libraries in 1933, a suggestion which ultimately bore fruit over a decade later. An Chomhairle Leabharlanna's functions were those of 'accepting from the Carnegie Trust the gift of the Irish Central Library for Students, of operating a central library and of assisting local authorities to improve their library services, and to provide for other matters connected' with the *Public Libraries Act* of 1947, under which this advisory body had been legally instituted. Its membership consisted of a Chairman, appointed by the Minister for Local Government in consultation with the Minister for Education, and twelve other members also appointed by the Minister for Local Government; five nominated by the universities; five by the local authorities; one by the National Library of Ireland and one from an 'approved association', which was and currently is the professional body, the Library Association of Ireland. The *Public Libraries Act* of 1947 also laid down that An Chomhairle 'be deemed to be a local authority, local body, county council or public body, according to the context of the enactment'. In providing financial aid to local authorities for the improvement of their library services, An Chomhairle was required to gain the sanction of the Minister for Local Government. An Chomhairle was to assist library co-operation and development, promote, facilitate, aid and participate in carrying out research, studies and surveys. Half of all other expenses incurred by An Chomhairle, or two thousand five hundred pounds, whichever was less, was to be reimbursed by government.

Apart from these provisions, there were several significant shortcomings in the setting up of this organization. No reference was made to the guidelines set out in the United Nations Educational Scientific and Cultural

Organization's (UNESCO) Public Library Manifesto of 1945 which later became the foundation for the Standards for Public Library Service proposed (but not published) by the International Federation of Library Associations (of which more below) between 1956 and 1958. No provision was made for other standards, and public libraries were not formally represented on the board of An Chomhairle, despite its stated purpose. It has therefore been suggested that the legislation which set up the authority 'was hurried and unbusinesslike' (Ó Conchubhair 1970, 79). However, over time the organization took a number of significant steps on behalf of libraries, and it is now a key component of the direction and administration of the system. These considerations require that we examine its progress over the past six decades in some further detail.

The stock of the ICLS, which consisted of fifty thousand volumes, was taken into care by An Chomhairle, and, although no longer maintained as such, it is still in existence and available in its premises at 53 Upper Mount Street, Dublin. Immediately on its foundation, An Chomhairle established the Irish Association for Documentation (IAD) to secure the recording, organization and dissemination of specialized knowledge in Ireland. Most of the chief librarians and scientific institutions became members, and committees were set up to deal with a number of projects, among the best known being the *The union list of current periodicals and serials in Dublin libraries* which went through three editions and was the basis for the cumulative listing of articles in Irish periodicals (Hayes 1970). In 1967, this body changed its name to the Irish Association for Documentation and Information Services (IADIS). Under its aegis, a union list of current periodicals and serials was published, as was a directory of special libraries.

After undertaking a two-year study of Irish libraries in 1951–3, An Chomhairle produced a report on the library services in Ireland in 1955. It can be summarized in one sentence: 'the library is still regarded in many quarters as the least essential of our public services' (Clarke 1956, 95). The *Public Libraries Act* 1947 (Grant) Regulations 1961 (SI No. 265 of 1961) was subsequently introduced in response to the annual report of An Chomhairle for 1958 (An Chomhairle Leabharlanna 1958). This authorized An Chomhairle to make grants available (from 1961 onwards) 'in the form of contributions towards the annual loan charges of the local authorities in respect of expenditure incurred in the exercise of their powers under the *Public Libraries Acts* 1855 to 1947 in

(a) the erection, acquisition, reconstruction, alteration, improvement and furnishing of any building;

(b) the purchase of books;

(c) the provision of vehicles for the transport of books;

(d) such other matters as may from time to time be approved by the Minister' (SI No. 265 of 1961).

This development resulted in book stocks being renewed, branch libraries being opened and the introduction of mobile libraries. The publication in 1969 of the twenty-first annual report of An Chomhairle provided a timely forum for a review of its first two decades of existence. The extent to which the grants scheme was availed of in the seven years up to 31 March 1969 is seen in capital projects to a value of approximately one million pounds: £203,000 for book-stocks, £59,000 for mobile units and delivery vans and £780,000 for new buildings and conversion of existing premises. The twenty-third annual report for the year ended 31 March 1971 gives an overview of library expenditure over a three-year period commencing in April 1968, together with the estimates for 1971–2. This provides useful background information for evaluating observations and recommendations made by the organization in a document on library development presented to the Department of Local Government in June 1971.

The International Federation of Library Associations (to be discussed again below), finally revised and published standards for the public library service in 1972. These were still based on the UNESCO 1945 document, but were again ignored by the Irish government, despite the publicity given them by An Chomhairle and the LAI. The next significant government contribution however was the *Public Libraries Act* 1947 (Grants) (Amendment) Regulations 1977 (SI No. 321 of 1977), by which the scope of the *Public Libraries* Act 1947 (Grants) Regulations 1961 was extended 'to enable the Minister for the Environment to pay grants to An Chomhairle Leabharlanna in respect of financial aid to local authorities towards the cost of leasing premises for the improvement of their library services'. This resulted in increased dependency on central government finance, and the majority of library authorities experienced cuts in their book funds in the turbulent economic conditions of the 1980s. A stern response to the recession of that decade saw an embargo on appointments and recruitment in the public sector and the introduction of charges for users of the library service. Up to 1982, most public library authorities had token charges for membership, generally ranging from £0.05 to £1.25. The *Local Government Financial Provision No. 2 Act* 1983 conferred discretion on local authorities to make charges for services, but it gave the minister power to exclude any particular service from the scope of the act and stated that at that stage no order had been made under this section. As the power to levy a library charge now rested with local authorities, An Chomhairle decided to convey its disapproval of charges to the county and city managers. Their appeal was ignored, and by 1983 twenty-two library authorities were charging registration fees ranging from £0.12 to £5.00 (Martin 1997, 102). In spite of the charges, 'In 1984 [whereas] £3.26 million was spent on acquisitions ... In 1988 the equivalent figure was £2.285 million, a 30% decrease. If the relevant totals for Dublin City and County are excluded the figures show a 47% decrease over the remaining twenty-nine public library authorities' (*ibid.*). Finance for stock funds in 1990 was less than in 1982, yet the cost of books had increased by 75% in that time.

Automated circulation systems were introduced in 1988, a year of considerable change for the library authorities. The Department of the Environment (the department which had subsumed Local Government) provided a small incentive grant to encourage local authorities to begin library computerization, considering automation a priority over stock. National Lottery funds were refused for this purpose. The Minister for the Environment revised the procedures for attracting grant-aid for all new public library projects, taking into account the recommendations of the Public Library Service Review Group which had reported to him in the previous year (1987). One of the recommendations in this review referred to the need for the integration of library authority proposals and the elimination of duplication. It was also suggested that proper standards for the appraisal of proposals, cost control and financial management be evolved. The new procedures required that in future formal submissions on library projects would be made directly to the Department of the Environment, while preserving the statutory role and responsibilities of An Chomhairle. An Chomhairle would continue to be fully involved in the examination of proposals and 'advise, consult and generally liaise with library authorities and make recommendations to the Minister in relation to such proposals and on matters generally relating to the public library service' (An Chomhairle Leabharlanna 1988, 5).

In 1991 An Chomhairle published *Public library statistics 1979–1988: an analysis of trends*. A second analysis, for the period 1988–1994, was issued in 1996. These consist of a series of six summary tables with accompanying illustrative charts, covering public library income, expenditure, personnel, collections, issues and membership, service points and services to primary schools, to which the reader is referred for a wealth of minute detail on topics having a direct bearing on outlays in heritage areas. Complementing these nationally based overviews there are some noteworthy studies of individual local library services, for instance that of Donegal (Byrne 1997), which give particular insights into their libraries' contribution to heritage at a regional and local level. In addition, in 1994 An

Chomhairle put out a twelve-year survey entitled *Irish public library service statistical analysis 1982–1993*. This provides statistics for each public library authority regarding membership, issues, total expenditure and bookfunds/acquisitions. While charges are still levied, a recent UNESCO Public Libraries Manifesto, published in 1994, declares 'The public library shall in principle be free of charge' (quoted in Martin 1997, 101). The Irish government endorsed this in its policy document *Public library development: public libraries 2000*, stating 'The library service should be available to all without charge' (*ibid.*). Arising out of the *Local Government Act* 1994, each library authority now has a legal duty to adopt programmes for the operation and development of its library service. Section 65 of the act places a statutory responsibility on local authorities to preserve and manage their archives and make them available to the public, but does not make any provision for this service, apart from suggesting that it would be 'somehow grafted on to the public library system' (Helferty 1997, 45).

Public libraries are still engaged in significant and wide-ranging business and community-centred projects which were largely initiated in the early 1990s and may have a direct heritage-related focus (for instance Browne 1995): the scholarly research work of the Donegal County Librarian (such as Ronayne 1981 and 1995), the South West Action Project (S.W.A.P.), adult literacy and the Consumer Health Information Research Project. The S.W.A.P. project began in 1994 and is based in Cork Central Library and the Bantry and Clonakilty branch libraries of the County Library. It is a model for the implementation of a business information service in public libraries in Ireland. An Chomhairle is represented on the Steering Committee by the Assistant Director, and the Project Officer is the Assistant Librarian (O'Mahony 1997, 123–27). Teltec Ireland at University College, Dublin (UCD-CS), was commissioned to evaluate S.W.A.P. during August 1997 (Clissman 1997). The Department of Education has also made funds available to An Chomhairle to carry out research into the role of public libraries in improving adult literacy. Two action research projects commenced during 1997: one in Limerick City Library, the other in Offaly County Library, with the aim of formalizing the library's role in adult literacy provision. Both schemes planned to strengthen and further develop partnerships with existing literacy projects. The Department of Health provided funds for the Library Association of Ireland to initiate the Consumer Health Information Research Project, and An Chomhairle is represented on the Committee by the Research and Information Officer. The research was undertaken by Jennifer MacDougall and the report, *Well read: developing consumer health information in Ireland*, was launched in June 1998. It acts as a comprehensive reference book on the current provision and providers of consumer health information in Ireland. Information on other new and on-going projects is published regularly in the periodical *An Leabharlann.*

A project team was established by the Minister for the Environment and Local Government in 1997 to review public library policy in Ireland. It held its first meeting on 10 September 1997, met a further ten times until 8 October 1998 when its report, *Branching out, a new public library service*, was agreed and submitted to the Minister by the Chairman, Tom O'Mahony. The report includes a comprehensive analysis of the service, as suggested by Hubert Butler as early as the 1940s. It summarizes the way forward for the future development of the public library service by:

(1) ensuring a clear focus and direction for the service;

(2) improving the service through better opening hours, investment in staff, equality of access to service, improving specialized services, improving library information services, developing life-long learning services;

(3) providing properly staffed and equipped service points through the whole country;

(4) developing new service delivery methods to areas of low population;

(5) improving the range and quality of stock;

(6) enhancing local and national marketing of the library service;

(7) furthering co-operation with other library and non-library organizations and playing a full role in local government reform;

(8) improving schools library services;

(9) maintaining the library as a centre of culture, and

(10) strengthening the service through library research.

The project team proposed that 'the Minister should make arrangements for the review of the Department's library investment programme to commence as soon as possible. This review should involve consultation with library authorities and An Comhairle Leabharlanna' (DELG 1999, 106).

The activities of An Chomhairle are not confined to public libraries. *Serial holdings in Irish libraries (SHIRL)* is a finding list of serial titles held in a variety of libraries throughout the country. It was first issued in 1982 and comprised two listings per annum on microfiche. In 1994 An Chomhairle commissioned a study of *SHIRL*, and on the basis of its finding it was decided to cease publication, as its enhancement would be too costly in terms of finance and commitment. It is still a useful, even if not fully comprehensive, tool for locating information about serials in Ireland. *Serials Information News (SIN, www/iol.ie/~libcounc)* is an occasional publication of An Chomhairle which contains more recent information on serial acquisition, cancellation and retention policies and supplements information on the now defunct *SHIRL.* There are twenty-seven subscribers supplying relevant data via e-mail and fifty-seven postal subscribers. Since September 1977, An Chomhairle has published *Irish Library News.* It disseminates news and information on libraries and librarianship in Ireland and the activities of An Chomhairle, and is published six times a year. Another publication, *Tips*, is a current awareness service for public library authority staff.

While the focus of this section has been mainly on the workings of An Chomhairle and particularly the public library sector, there is another strand of the library network, namely third-level and other special libraries, which should also be considered. The third-level sector has expanded hugely from the 1960s on, so that there are now significant holdings of resources in natural and cultural heritage in upwards of twenty geographically dispersed institutions. Dealing with them is complicated by the fact that they all fall under the aegis of different administrative bodies; there would appear to be no statutory equivalent of An Chomhairle to co-ordinate their operations. Third-level institution administrators are ultimately accountable to the Higher Education Authority (HEA) through their president/director, and the reader is directed to this organization *(www/hea.ie)* and its publications for overall information on this area. The Committee of National and University Librarians (CONUL) was established in 1972 by the librarians of TCD, UCC, UCD, UCG, St Patrick's College, Maynooth and the Director of the National Library of Ireland. At a later stage, the librarians/directors of the University of Limerick, Dublin City University and the Royal College of Surgeons in Ireland became members. In 1993 the name was changed (but not the acronym) to the Consortium of National and University Libraries, to emphasize that the institutions, rather than the individual librarians/directors, were acting in collaboration. Their aims are:

(1) to promote co-operation among member libraries;

(2) to provide a forum for discussion for matters of mutual interest and concern;

(3) to represent the collective views of the membership. The objectives are fulfilled through regular meetings, the collection and exchange of statistical and other information, the establishment of working groups of CONUL

library staff to address specific problems, propose recommendations or share experience, and through occasional briefing meetings with decision-makers outside the CONUL libraries (S. Phillips pers. comm). From 1972 to 1981, the Committee published the CONUL list of theses accepted for higher degrees held in Irish university libraries edited by library staff at University College, Cork, as a contribution towards the IFLA aim of bibliographic control of theses. These data are now supplied by individual libraries to the organization Aslib (discussed below) and published in the *Aslib index to theses accepted for higher degrees in the universities of Great Britain and Ireland.* (The non-acceptance of dissertations submitted in partial fulfillment of higher degrees by most university libraries and by Aslib increases the difficulty of achieving full bibliographic control.) The Committee of the Heads of Irish Universities (CHIU) Committee of Librarians was recently established by CHIU to advise the university presidents, registrars and other administrators on library matters. Another body which helps co-ordinate the work of university libraries is the Standing Conference on National and University Libraries (SCONUL) *(www.sconul.ac.uk/about.htm),* which works to improve the quality and extend the influence of the university and national libraries of the UK and Ireland. It exists to promote and advance the science and practice of librarianship and to improve the standards of its member libraries (S. Phillips pers. comm). Like CONUL, it achieves its aims through meetings, conferences, staff development and publications.

There is no single in-depth study of any Irish university library. Currently, university and special libraries are engaged in publishing strategic plans, some of which are already available through the worldwide web, for instance those of Dublin City University *(http://www.dcu.ie/~library/lib_pubs/94plan.htm)* and University College, Dublin *(http://www.ucd.ie/~library).* There are many opportunities here for the investigation of collection management and development, not least the presentations and donations which have enhanced the holdings of all university libraries, for instance the Douglas Hyde collection at NUI Galway, the Salamanca Papers (Richardson 1995a) and others at NUI Maynooth (Neligan 1995; Richardson 1995b), the Anglo-Indian and Friedlander collections presented to University College, Cork, the Feirtéar and Zimmer collections at University College, Dublin, and the Norton Collection in the University of Limerick. The library of the Royal Irish Academy *(http://www.ria.ie)* recently mounted an exhibition of significant donations to the Royal Irish Academy collections received between 1997 and 1999 (O'Rafferty 1999). The Chester Beatty Library, Dublin *(http://www.cbl.ie)* deserves special mention as a major resource in a distinctive area of library heritage. This unique collection 'has enabled us to view, in one place, the history of civilization from 2700 B.C to the present century' (Henchy n.d.; Smith 1994). It comprises over 15,000 volumes and papyri, which 'in geographical provenance encircle the globe from Ireland, on the fringe of western Europe, to Sumatra and Japan' (Henchy n.d.). Each of these items was acquired by Beatty as 'the best or only copy in existence' (Horton 2000). Among its Western holdings, the early Christian and Manichean papyri make it one of the premier centres for Old and New Testament scholarship. The Islamic collection contains many copies of the Holy Qur'an. Over forty catalogues and monographs of the collections have been published (for instance Chester Beatty Library 1996). It was left in trust to the Irish nation in 1951 by Sir Alfred Chester Beatty (1875–1968), an American of Irish ancestry (his father was from county Armagh and his mother from county Laois). The most valuable bequest of any kind to this country, it is administered by a Council of Trustees and financed by a state grant from the Department of Arts, Heritage, Gaeltacht and the Islands. It has recently been moved from its original premises at 20 Shrewsbury Road to a new development in the eighteenth-century Clock Tower Building at Dublin Castle, which now contains two modern exhibition areas.

The rich stories which remain to be told in relation to specialist and third-level libraries may be glimpsed further in the case of law libraries. As we have seen above, some of the earliest literature of this country is concerned with law, its interpretation and applications. In 1542 Henry VIII granted the property of the recently dissolved Dominican monastery, which lay on both sides of the river Liffey, to a number of judges and senior law officers. On the north bank they established their Inn and adopted the title of King's Inn in recognition of the royal grant. Among the latter's archives for the years 1607–1917, which are now in the custody of the librarian of the Honourable Society of King's Inns, is the 'Black Book' or 'Liber Niger' of King's Inn, which contains admissions, accounts and council minutes from 1607 to 1730. Prior to the passing of the *Attorneys and Solicitors (Ireland) Act* 1866, admission to apprenticeship and subsequent admission to the solicitors' branch of the profession was governed by the Benchers of King's Inns, and records of these memorials formally addressed to the Benchers are an important source of genealogical research (Keane, Phair and Sadlier 1982; Byrne 1990). The earliest record of a professional law library dates from 1787 when, on the death of Mr Justice Robinson, the Honorable Society of King's Inns purchased his law books (then valued at £700), by which time the Society had moved to Constitution Hill/Henrietta Street, where in 1800 the architect James Gandon was commissioned to design a library, dining-hall and chambers. A new library, adjoining the main building, was erected between 1826 and 1830 and enlarged by annexe in 1892. Under the provisions of the *Copyright Act* 1801, this library and that of Trinity College, Dublin, became deposit libraries for every book, pamphlet and periodical published in the United Kingdom. The act as it applied to the King's Inns was repealed in 1836, but compensation of £433 6s 8d, equal to the average annual value of books received during the previous three years, was to be paid annually. This sum is still made over to the library by the Irish exchequer. The librarian of King's Inns provided the penultimate edition of all leading textbooks in that library for the Bar Library in Belfast. Under the provisions of the *Government of Ireland Act* 1920, members of the Bar in Northern Ireland set up their own Bar Council in 1922 and appointed a Library Committee on the same principles as the Law Library in Dublin. As well as law material, the King's Inns' library *(http:// www.kingsinns.ie)* holds an important collection of fifteenth- to nineteenth-century Gaelic manuscripts (de Brún 1972; Cochrane 1986; Byrne 1990).

The Law Library in the Four Courts *(http:// indigo.ie/~gregk)* is said to have evolved from the activities of booksellers on the nearby quays who conducted lending libraries, as discussed earlier. One of these is believed to have gone bankrupt in the early nineteenth century, and members of the Bar in Dublin acquired his stock and set up their own library, whose management is vested in a Library Committee which is now an integral part of the Bar Council (Byrne 1990). In the mid- and late nineteenth century, several law societies were formed. The Society of Attorneys and Solicitors of Ireland was established in 1841 in succession to the Law Club of Ireland (founded in 1791) and the Law Society of Ireland (1830). The Annual Reports of the Society and Minutes of the Benchers of King's Inns refer to a grant of £500 by the Benchers and the provision of surplus books to the Society's library. The Society was incorporated by charter in 1852 and in 1888 its name was changed to the Incorporated Law Society of Ireland *(ibid.)*. Local societies were formed in Belfast (1843) and Cork (1953). The Northern Law Society library was initially accommodated in the Linen Hall Library and later in the Royal Courts of Justice until it moved to its present premises in Victoria Street, Belfast in 1983. The Southern Law Association benefitted from the presentation of a valuable library to the legal profession in Cork in 1878. Formerly held in the Courthouse, Cork, it is now housed in the Boole Library, University College, Cork *(ibid.)*. Law libraries at Queen's University, Belfast, and Cork date from the early to mid-nineteenth century. The holdings of these libraries constitute a major heritage resource in their own right (for instance, Furlong 1996). However, as they have kept pace with the electronic and other developments currently taking place in all libraries, they can now provide a further easily accessible resource for

heritage management as they continue to furnish 'the highly special kind of service to the somewhat exacting readers identified by Sir Frederick Pollock in 1886' (Byrne 1996; Gleeson 1996; Clinch 1999).

THE PROFESSION OF LIBRARIANSHIP AND ITS ASSOCIATIONS
The Library Association (LA) was established in Britain in 1877 and incorporated by Royal Charter in 1903 *(http://www.la-hq.uk/directory/about.html)*. It has a membership of 25,000 who work in all sectors, including business and industry, further and higher education, schools, local and central government departments and agencies, the health service, the voluntary sector and national public libraries. The maintenance and improvement of standards of service is central to its mission. Professionalism is encouraged through the accreditation of library and information courses at degree level. The association confers chartered status and awards for professional achievement. There are twenty-two special interest groups within the organization which provide fora for debate, communication and training in specific areas of the profession. As well as publishing monographs dealing with bibliography (for example, Eager 1980) and other aspects of the profession, the LA also publishes the *Library Association Record* monthly, *Library Technology* which has five issues per year, as well as the *Library Association Year Book*.

In the later years of the nineteenth century, the question of the work done by and the education required for librarians and library staff was raised and discussed by the Library Association in Britain, American Library Association and the Carnegie Trusts (*ELIS* under 'Education for Librarians'). It was generally agreed that a postgraduate qualification was desirable. In 1928 a new Cumann Leabharlann na hÉireann, the Library Association of Ireland (LAI), was founded to provide a forum where library workers and other interested persons could come together to promote the better administration of their institutions, improve the status and qualifications of librarians and help provide a unified nation-wide service administered in accordance with the needs and ideals of the country. The insignia of the LAI, designed by the above-mentioned Colm Ó Lochlainn, are the torch of learning, the flame being a monogram of the three letters 'LAI'. 1928 also saw the establishment of the School of Librarianship at University College, Dublin. It provided a one-year post-graduate course which led to a *Diploma in Library Training*. L. R. McColvin's *Report on library work in England* (1938) emphasized the word 'service' in connection with this activity, believing that in few types of work was the quality of the service more closely related to the calibre of the individuals providing it, stating:

This is not a pious platitude, for the keynote of effective

librarianship is individual service. No amount of mechanical organization, no mere efficient machine, can serve. They can help. Without organization and efficiency the individual cannot function. Yet ultimately it is a case of men dealing with men (*sic*). One has only to consider the enormous range of human requirements for information and the vast accumulation of knowledge contained in millions of pages of printed matter to understand that mechanical slide-rule practice cannot apply. If readers are to obtain the best from their libraries there must be people on the staff who can understand their needs, who have a wide knowledge of material and who have developed the right technique for using it — who can find their way about books better, perhaps, than the subject-specialist himself.

This argument was quoted in 1956 by S. Ó Conchubhair, County Librarian of Longford-Westmeath, when he described the qualities and qualifications required for all levels of library staff (Ó Conchubhair 1956). He pointed out that 'Far too many consider that County Librarians spend part of the day reading books and the remainder discussing them, and that the staff in between handing out books at branches and making odd trips to centres spend the remainder of their time browsing through the bookstocks in order that they may be able to talk brightly of the latest treasures added to the bookshelves' (*ibid*. 101). Although referring specifically to law librarians, the former Attorney General, Mr Dermot Gleeson, endorsed the entire profession when he stated 'My own conversion to appreciating the central role of a modern law librarian has been recent, direct and complete ... prospective clients ... when assessing law firms ... [should] enquire as to the quality and range of the firm's law library services and the extent to which those services are run by professional law librarians' (Gleeson 1996). The Department of Local Government promised in 1964 that professional qualifications would be essential for the office of County, City or Borough Librarian. This promise was not fulfilled until industrial action was threatened in 1969 (Cumann Leabharlann na hÉireann 1970, 24–30). In 1970 the School of Librarianship at University College, Dublin, inaugurated a course leading to a *Certificate in School Librarianship*, open to qualified teachers with five years' teaching experience. Currently, the Library Association of Ireland and the Library Association have accredited several courses in library and information studies. They are the *Diploma* and *M.Sc. in Information Management* delivered by Queen's University, Belfast, the *B.Sc. Econ. in Information and Library Studies* by distance learning offered by the Department of Library and Information Studies at the University of Wales, Aberystwyth; the University of Wales, Aberystwyth degree programme in distance learning, with contributions on local issues from the Department of Library and Information Studies at University College, Dublin, and the *Diploma, M.Sc. in Information Management* and *M.Phil. in Information*

Management delivered by the Department of Library and Information Studies at University College, Dublin.

The Chartered Librarian's qualification, Associate of the Library Association (ALA), is obtained when five years' post-diploma working experience under the supervision of a chartered librarian have been completed. It is necessary to have this qualification to practice as a librarian in the UK, but not in the Republic of Ireland. Fellow of the Library Association (FLA), the higher qualification, may be achieved on completion of a thesis on some aspect of librarianship. The Irish equivalent is FLAI. Since 1995, new qualifications for Library Assistants and Library Assistants (special) in Ireland's local authority public library services have come into force. Candidates must now have five Leaving Certificate passes in higher or ordinary level, including Irish and/or English, or the equivalent. A sufficient knowledge of Irish and English to enable them to perform their duties in both languages is required also. The five passes must be in subjects from the approved Department of Education and Science list. Library Assistant (special) applicants will have to be registered, or entitled to be registered, with the National Rehabilitation Board and 'be free from any disability which would interfere with the proper discharge of the duties of the office and be in a state of health such as would indicate reasonable prospect of ability to render regular and efficient service' (Hanrahan and Kinter 1995–6, 86).

Since its foundation, the LAI has constituted the professional forum for the centralization, provision and promotion of a library service throughout the country. It is affiliated to the International Federation of Library Associations and to the UK Library Association, by which the Code of Conduct for Professional Libraries has been drawn up (*Library Association Yearbook*). Evidence of this work is recorded throughout its journal, *An Leabharlann* (1930–), and in its annual report. Librarians influence the professional development and orientation of their associations through membership of the various section and group committees within the LAI. Eleven groups and sections are currently in existence; they comprise the Library Staff Training Committee, Audio Visual and Information Technology Section, a Cataloguing and Indexing Group, a Government Libraries Section, a Munster Regional Section and a Rare Books Group. Several of these publish newsletters during the year and summarize their activities in the LAI's annual report. As well as the publications referred to above, the LAI issues a *Directory of libraries and information services in Ireland*. In 1996 it published the proceedings of the Rare Books Group Annual Seminar for the previous year (Long 1996). The proceedings of the 1997 seminar held jointly with the Economic and Social History Society of Ireland on books and reading has also been issued (Cunningham and Kennedy 1999).

Cumann Leabharlannaithe Scoile (The Irish Association of School Librarians) was founded in 1962 to foster the development of school libraries. In 1993 the LAI and the Association of Secondary Teachers, Ireland (ASTI) launched *A library information pack for second level schools* which contains the policy of the ASTI on school library services, a position statement of the LAI, a guide for libraries at second level, a resource list of helpful organizations, a list of thirty-four basic reference books which a school should have and sources for further information. In 1996 the Policy Statement of the LAI on School Library Services was adopted by the LAI annual general meeting. In 1998 the Department of Education and Science funded a research project, under the auspices of the LAI, which will assess the nature and extent of the current provision of information services to this sector, determine the perceived needs of all members of the school community as well as other recent developments in provision, review best practice internationally and consider the most appropriate routes towards delivery of effective information services into the primary school library sector. An Expert Committee, consisting of nominees from the Department of Education and Science, the National Parents Council, the Irish National Teachers Organisation and An Chomhairle Leabharlanna as well as the Library Association of Ireland, will manage it. The resulting report will be the first piece of comprehensive countrywide research in this area.

On the European front, the LAI is involved in the European Bureau of Library, Information and Documentation Associations (EBLIDA), which enables it to keep abreast of developments at a European level. Through this forum, the LAI's views on issues such as the cultural programmes, copyright and censorship are expressed. A European Parliament Forum on books and reading, in which it plays an important and active role, has been established. The LAI is also affiliated to the International Federation of Library Associations (IFLA). Founded in Edinburgh in 1927 during the International Congress of Libraries, IFLA was established as a small gathering of mainly national and academic library associations. It was one of the first international non-profit, non-governmental organizations aiming to further the cause of librarianship. IFLA's primary function was to provide librarians throughout the world with a general forum for international contacts and exchange of ideas and experiences, principally in the field of bibliography. IFLA has facilitated intellectual and cultural interaction between nations afflicted by two world wars and confronted by the latest technological revolutions. According to its statutes, IFLA will 'undertake, support and coordinate research and studies, collect, collate, publish and otherwise disseminate information relating to library, bibliography, information and training activity, organize

general and specialized meetings and conferences, collaborate with international organizations in the fields of information, documentation and archives'.

LIBRARIES AND INFORMATION TECHNOLOGY

As this chapter has sought to indicate, libraries have long been involved with contemporary developments in various forms of technical and mechanical innovation. Organizations linking both domains were already being formed in the early twentieth century. They include the Association of Special Libraries (Aslib, *http://www/aslib.co.uk/aslib.html*), a charity registered in 1924 concerned with the efficient management of information resources. Its key roles are threefold: to stimulate awareness of the benefits of good management of information resources and its value; to represent and lobby for the interests of the information sector on matters and networks which are of national and international import, and to provide a range of information-related products and services to meet the needs of the information society. To fulfill these aims, Aslib developed four main functions: consultancy, publications, training and recruitment.

Developments in all these areas gathered pace in the second half of the last century with the rapid evolution in information technology (IT). The United States of America led the way in library automation with the *Library Systems and Construction Act* and the *Higher Education Act* of 1965 which made millions of dollars available to support library expansion and research projects in universities and libraries. One of the objectives of these grants was to 'create totally integrated in-house systems that use a single bibliographical database to support multiple library functions (i.e., on-line public catalogue, circulation, acquisitions, serials control, catalogue)' (De Gennaro 1976). In the late 1960s, the Library of Congress developed the machine readable cataloguing (MARC) format, and in 1969 introduced a magnetic tape database which allowed for standardized on-line cataloguing. In 1971 the US Online Computer Library Center (OCLC) shared cataloguing system commenced, and was followed by a host of regional networks. The British Library adapted the MARC format to suit their own needs and established UK MARC. Their network was known as BLAISE (British Library Automated Information Service) and others which grew up around the same time include the South-West Co-operative Project (SWALCAP), and the Birmingham Libraries Co-operative Mechanization Project (BLCMP). In Ireland, the universities were to the forefront with the introduction of computerized cataloguing, first in Trinity College, Dublin, soon followed in 1977 by University College, Cork. On-line searching for current medical and scientific research through BLAISE and the European Space Agency (ESA) was introduced into University

College, Cork, as soon as it became possible in 1977–78, and by 1982 on-line searching for the humanities and social sciences was feasible through databases like Datastar, Eurolex and Dialog.

The depressed economy of the mid- to late 1970s and the rising costs of higher education forced libraries world-wide towards these co-operative networks and shared resources, as income could not keep pace with demands. As Terry (1998, 25) points out, 'while libraries were devoting their attention to cooperative networking efforts, commercial vendors applied the newly developed technologies to create marketable automation products' which targeted labour-intensive circulation functions. Most libraries invested in these as finances were no longer available to support research into developing integrated systems, that is systems which catered for the whole library. In the US, Northwestern University and Virginia Polytechnic and in Canada State University and Université de Quebec à Montréal developed their own individual integrated systems. The DOBIS/LIBIS system was created by the University of Dortmund and the Catholic University at Leuven, Belgium, using its own proprietary version of MARC, D-MARC, and supported by IBM. DOBIS/LIBIS 1.2 was introduced into UCC in 1982 and provided an integrated database system for technical processes, circulation control and information retrieval from the library catalogue using Boolean search functions. Simultaneously, the commercial vendors introduced their own integrated systems, for instance Dynix (purchased by Trinity College, Dublin, and later by several other university libraries as well as by public libraries). As open public access terminals (OPACs) became the norm, the Z39.50 standard was developed as a mechanism to expedite multi-OPAC searching. There are still problems with this, but research and development are on-going. New systems have recently been introduced into Ireland. Among these are the Innovative product, designed specifically for academic libraries. As INNOPAC, it was acquired by University College, Cork, in 1995. The following year Trinity College, Dublin, acquired Geac and the National University of Ireland, Maynooth, is currently introducing Aleph, a product designed in Israel.

CONCLUSION

The librarians of the twenty-first century are fully engaged in the continuing evolution of libraries (*http://www/ukoln.ac/services/elib*). The term 'hybrid library' (Cimbala 1988), the notion of which was once 'ruled out as a viable possibility, ... is gradually gaining in acceptance' as librarians realize the networked information environment is here to stay (Garrod 1999, 187). The hybrid library aims to provide information in any format, from traditional print to multimedia, with access to data not physically held in the library, 'thus minimizing the risk of redundancy. Neither the bath water nor the baby is thrown out — both are needed in times of drought or epidemic' (*ibid*. 192; Ellis-King 1997). Governments and funding bodies will thus have to be as receptive to the imperative for the preservation of documentary evidence as Bro. William O'Hurrily was over five hundred years ago when, as we have seen, he listed the contents of the Youghal Franciscan library 'lest perchance, by carelessness or neglect, or, which is worse, want of conscience, [it] might be completely destroyed and no memorial of [it] remain'. It is fervently to be hoped that as a result of the later twentieth-century information explosion and the unprecedented access to higher education, the concerns of librarians to preserve and make available the records of our natural and cultural heritage will now be better understood, appreciated and supported.

Bibliography

An Chomhairle Leabharlanna 1958 *Eleventh annual report: year ended December 31 1958*. Dublin.

An Chomhairle Leabharlanna 1988 *Forty-first annual report: year ended December 31 1988*. Dublin.

Baker, N. 1994 'Annals of scholarship: discards', *New Yorker* (4 April), pp. 64–86.

Barnard, T. 1998 'Learning, the learned and literacy in Ireland, 1660–1760' in T. Barnard, D. Ó Cróinín, K. Simms (eds) *A miracle of learning: studies in manuscripts and Irish learning. Essays in honour of William O'Sullivan* (Aldershot), pp. 209–235.

Barnes, M. 1965 'Repeal Reading Rooms', *An Leabharlann* **23**, pp. 53–7.

Barnwell, S. B. 1977 'Henry Draycott and the Draycotts of Mornington, Co. Meath', *Ríocht na Midhe* **6**, 3, pp. 68–81.

Boland, J. P. 1902 'Rural libraries in Ireland', *New Ireland Review* **17**, 4, pp. 193–202.

Boran, E. 1996 'Aspects of the early history of TCD — building up a library', doctoral dissertation, TCD.

Boran, E. 1998 'The libraries of Luke Challoner and James Ussher' in H. Robinson–Hammerstein (ed) *European universities in the age of Reformation and Counter Reformation* (Dublin), pp. 75–116.

Brady, W. M. 1863 *Clerical and parochial records of Cork, Cloyne and Ross*. Dublin.

Brown, B. T. 1987 'Three centuries of journals in Ireland: the library of the Royal Dublin Society, Grafton Street' in [Anon. ed] *300 years of Irish periodicals* (Dublin), pp. 11–28.

Brown, B. T. 1990 'Library history research in Ireland: 1918–1988', *Libraries and Culture* **25**, 1, pp. 86–102.

Browne, K. 1995 'Heritage awareness', *The Kerry Magazine* **6**, pp. 43–5.

Butler, H. 1949 'The county libraries: sex, religion, and censorship', reprinted from *Irish Writing* **8** in D. Murphy (ed) *Grandmother and Wolfe Tone* (Dublin, 1990), pp. 50–63.

Byrne, K. 1976 'Mechanics Institutes in Ireland before 1855', M.Ed. thesis, UCC.

Byrne, M. 'Law libraries in Ireland', *The Law Librarian* **21**, 2, pp. 53–58.

Byrne, P. J. 1997 *'Vanity enough': the story of the origins and development of Newry Public Library*. Armagh.

[Byrne, P. J.] 1997 *75 blian ag fás 1922–1997: a history of the Donegal County Library*. Letterkenny.

C. 1894 'From the study chair: what our country folk read', *New Ireland Review* **1**, 1, pp. 65–7.

Carson, H. 1998 'Cathedral libraries in Ireland', *An Leabharlann* **14**, 2, pp. 59–64.

Cashel Diocese Library 1973 *Catalogue of the Cashel Diocesan Library, county Tipperary, Ireland*. Boston, Mass.

Casteleyn, M. 1984 *A history of literacy and libraries in Ireland: the long traced pedigree*. Aldershot.

Cimbala, D. 1987 'The scholarly information center: an organisational model', *College and Research Libraries* **48**, 5, pp. 393–8.

Clarke, D. 1956 'The public library: a reassessment', *An Leabharlann* **14**, 3, pp. 95–100.

Clinch, P. 1999 'Academic law libraries in Britain and Ireland', *The Law Librarian* **30**, 1, pp. 47–55.

Clissman, C. 1997 *The South West Action Project: an evaluation on behalf of An Chomhairle Leabharlanna — the Irish Library Council*, unpublished report.

Cochrane, N. 1986 'King's Inns Library, Dublin', DLIS dissertation, UCD.

Cole, R. C. 1974a 'Community lending libraries in eighteenth-century Ireland', *Library Quarterly* **44**, 2, pp. 111–23.

Cole, R. C. 1974b 'Private libraries in eighteenth-century Ireland', *Library Quarterly* **44**, 3, pp. 231–47.

[Coleman, J.] 1905 'Dr. Caulfield's antiquarian and historical notes ... The library of St Fin Barre's Cathedral, Cork', *Journal of the Cork Historical and Archaeological Society* **11**, pp. 93–8.

Coleman, J. 1905 'The Cork library in 1801 and 1820', *Journal of the Cork Historical and Archaeological Society* **11**, pp. 82–93.

Corish, P. J. 1970 'Bishop Wadding's notebook', *Archivium Hibernicum* **29**, pp. 49–114.

Cumann Leabharlann na hÉireann 1970 'Report of the Executive Board for the year 1969/70', *An Leabharlann* **28**, pp. 24–30.

Cunningham, B. and Kennedy, M. (eds) 1999 *The experience of reading: Irish historical perspectives*. Dublin.

Davies, L. 1999 'The *Collectio canonum Hibernensis*',

paper to the 11th International Congress of Celtic Studies, Cork, July.

Davis, T. [n.d.] 'The history of Ireland' in *Selections from his prose and poetry; with an introduction by T. W. Rolleston* (Dublin), pp. 83–91.

Dean, J. 1928 *Catalogue of manuscripts in the Public Library of Armagh*. Dundalk.

de Brún, P. 1969 *Catalogue of the manuscripts in the Franciscan Library, Killiney*. Dublin.

de Brún, P. 1972 *Catalogue of the Irish manuscripts in the King's Inns Library Dublin*. Dublin.

De Gennaro, R. 1976 'Library automation: changing patterns and new directions', *Library Journal* **108**, 7, pp. 629–35.

DELG (Department of the Environment and Local Government) 1999 *Branching out: a new public library service*. Dublin.

Dickson, D. 1983 'Bibliography' in T. W. Moody and W. E. Vaughan (eds) *A new history of Ireland Vol. 4 The eighteenth century 1691–1800* (Oxford), pp. 715–95.

Dolan, B. 1985 'Learned society libraries', *Library Review* **34**, pp. 102–7.

Eager, A. 1980 *A guide to Irish bibliographical material: a bibliography of Irish bibliographies and sources of information*. London.

Edwards, E. 1859 *Memoirs of libraries including a handbook of library economy*. London.

ELIS (Encyclopaedia of Library and Information Science) 1968– New York.

Ellis-King, D. 1997 'Mumlib — multimedia methodology in libraries: a user-centred approach' in *Elvira 4: electronic library and visual information research* (London).

Fenning, H. 1976 'The library of a preacher of Drogheda: John Donnolly O.P. (d. 1748)', *Collectanea Hibernica* **29**, pp. 72–104

Fenning, H. 1978 'The library of Bishop William Daton of Ossory, 1698', *Collectanea Hibernica* **20**, pp. 30–57.

Fox, P. (ed) 1994 *Treasures of the Library: Trinity College Dublin*. Dublin.

Garrod, P. 1999 'Survival strategies in the learning age — hybrid staff and hybrid libraries', *Aslib Proceedings* **51**, 6, pp. 187–94.

Gilbert, J. T. (ed) 1879 *Facsimiles of national manuscripts in Ireland Part 3*. London.

Gleeson, D. 1996 'Foreword' to *The Law Librarian* **27**, 3, p. 138.

Gneuss, H. 1996 *Books and libraries in early England*. Aldershot.

Gray, J. 1996 'Documenting a community in conflict: the Northern Ireland political collection at the Linen Hall Library, Belfast', *The Law Librarian* **27**, 4, pp. 216–22.

Gray, J. and McCann, W. (eds) 1996 *An uncommon bookman: essays in honour of J. R. R. Adams*.

Belfast.

Griffith, T. B. 1891 'On Catholic lending libraries', *Irish Ecclesiastical Record* 13, pp. 1004–10.

Grimes, B. 1998 *Irish Carnegie libraries: a catalogue and architectural history*. Dublin.

Hall, T. 1980 'Christina Keogh: pioneer — the Irish Central Library for Students and the foundation of the Library Council', *An Leabharlann* 9, 4, pp. 123–9.

Hanrahan, F. and Kinter, M. 1995/6 'Information matters', *An Leabharlann* 12, 2 and 3, pp. 79–91.

Hayes, R. (ed) 1970 *Sources for the history of Irish civilization: articles in Irish periodicals*. Boston, Mass.

Helferty, S. 1997 Review of Department of the Environment *Report of the steering group on local authority records and archives 1996 (Dublin)* in *An Leabharlann* 13, 1, pp. 41–5.

Henchy, P. [n.d.] *Chester Beatty Library Dublin*. [Dublin].

Herbert, M. 1988 *Iona, Kells and Derry: the history and hagiography of the monastic families of Columba*. Oxford.

Herren, M. 1974 *The Hisperica Famina: 1 The A-Text*. Toronto.

Horn, W. and Born, E. 1979 *The plan of St. Gall: a study of the architecture & economy of, & life in a paradigmatic Carolingian monastery*. Berkeley.

Horton, C. 2000 Lecture delivered to the Book Collectors' Circle of the Library Association of Ireland.

Ireland, A. forthcoming *Some Cork antiquarians*.

Jones, G. 1970 'Irish local authorities and the Public Libraries Acts 1855–1914: a check list of adoptions', *An Leabharlann* 28, 4, pp. 118–9.

Kaufmann, P. 1963 'Community lending libraries in eighteenth-century Ireland and Wales', *Library Quarterly* 33, 4, pp. 299–312.

Keane, E., Phair, P. B., and Sadlier, T. U. (eds) 1982 *King's Inns admission papers*. Dublin.

Kenney, J. F. 1929 *Sources for the early history of Ireland: ecclesiastical; an introduction and guide* (reprinted Dublin 1979). New York.

Keogh, C. 1935 *Report on Irish library provision in the Irish Free State*. Dublin.

Keogh, D. 1995, 'Irish democracy and the right to freedom of information', *Ireland: a Journal of History and Society* 1, 1, p. 11.

Killen, J. 1990 *A history of the Linen Hall Library*, Belfast. Belfast.

Killen, J. 1996 'John Templeton, the Linen Hall Library and the preservation of Irish Music' in Gray and McCann 1996, pp. 199–212.

Laistner, M. L. W. 1935 'The library of the Venerable Bede' in A. Hamilton-Thompson (ed) *Bede* (Oxford).

Long, G. (ed) 1996 *Books beyond the Pale: the provincial books trade in Ireland before 1850: proceedings of the Rare Books Group Seminar 1994*. Dublin.

Mac Enery, M. 1947 'A seventeenth-century Anglo-Irish library', *Irish Booklover* 30, pp. 30–4.

MacLysaght, E. and Ainsworth, J. 1956 'The Arthur Manuscript', *North Munster Antiquarian Journal* 8, 2, pp. 79–87.

Mac Niocaill, G. (ed) 1997 *Crown Surveys of lands 1540–41 with the Kildare Rental begun in 1518*. Dublin.

Martin, B. 1997 'Double trouble: public library registration fees and cutbacks, 1982–1993', *An Leabharlann* 13, 3 and 4, pp. 101–6.

Maule, H. 1721 *Pietas Corcagiensis, or a view of the Green Coat Hospital*. Cork.

McCann, P. 1973 'Cork city's eighteenth-century charity schools: origins and early history', *Journal of the Cork Historical and Archaeological Society* 84, pp. 102–11.

McCarthy, J. P. 1987 'Dr. R. Caulfield: antiquarian, scholar and academic librarian', *Journal of the Cork Historical and Archaeological Society* 95, pp. 1–23.

McCarthy, J. P. 1995 'In search of Cork's collecting traditions: from Kilcrea's library to the Boole Library of to-day', *Journal of the Cork Historical and Archaeological Society* 100, pp. 29–46.

McCarthy, M. 1980 *All graduates and gentlemen*. Dublin.

McCarthy, M. 1986 'An eighteenth century Dublin bibliophile', *Irish Arts Review* 3, 4, pp. 29–35.

McNeill, C. 1923 'Some early documents relating to English Uriel, and the towns of Drogheda and Dundalk', *County Louth Archaeological Journal* 5, pp. 270–82.

Mooney, C. 1955 'The library of Archbishop Piers Creagh', *Reportorium Novum* 1, 1, pp. 117–39.

Mooney, C. 1959 'Fr. John Colgan, O.F.M., his work and times and literary milieu' in T. O'Donnell (ed) *Fr. John Colgan: essays in commemoration of the tercentenary of his death* (Dublin), pp. 7–39.

Munter, R. 1988 *A dictionary of the print trade in Ireland 1550–1775*. New York.

Murphy, J. A. 1995 *The College*. Cork.

Neligan, A. 1995 *Maynooth Library treasures: from the collections of St Patrick's College*. Dublin.

Neylon, M. and Henchy, M. 1966 *Public libraries in Ireland*. Dublin.

O'Brien, I. D. 1995 'An inventory of the property of the late 5th Earl of Thomond', *The Other Clare* 19, p. 33.

Ó Catháin, D. 1989 'Charles O'Conor of Belanagare: antiquary and Irish scholar', *Journal of the Royal Society of Antiquaries of Ireland* 119, pp. 136–64.

Ó Conchubhair, S. 1956 'County library staffs', *An Leabharlann* 14, 3.

Ó Conchubhair, S. 1970 'Gnó na leabharlannaíochta', *An Leabharlann* 28, pp. 77–83.

Ó Conchúir, B. 1982 *Scríobhaithe Chorcaí*. Dublin.

Ó Drisceoil, D. 1996 *Censorship in Ireland, 1939–1945:*

neutrality, politics and society. Cork.

Ó hAodha, M. 1998 'Irish rural libraries — glimpses of the past', *An Leabharlann* **14**, 2, pp. 71–9.

O'Kelleher, A. and Schoepperle, G. (eds) 1918 *Betha Colaim Chille: life of Columcille; compiled by Maghnas Ó Domhnaill in 1532* (reprinted Dublin 1994). Illinois.

O'Kelley, F. 1953 *Irish book-sale catalogues before 1801*. Dublin.

O'Leary, P. 1892 'Notes on the Cistercian Abbey of Graignamanagh', *Journal of the Royal Society of Antiquaries of Ireland* **2** (5th series), pp. 237–47.

O'Loughlin, T. 1994 'The library of Iona in the late seventh century: the evidence from Alomnán's *De Locis Sanctis*', *Ériu* **45**, pp. 33–52.

O'Mahony, N. 1997 'SWAP the South West Action Project: a business information service to a rural community', *An Leabharlann* **13**, 3 and 4, pp. 123–7.

O'Neill, T. 1997 'Columba the scribe' in C. Bourke (ed) *Studies in the cult of Saint Columba* (Dublin), pp. 69–79.

O'Rafferty, S. 1999 *Catalogue of the exhibition of significant donations to the collections of the Royal Irish Academy 1997–9* (unpublished). Dublin.

Ó Raifeartaigh, T. 1985 *The Royal Irish Academy: a bicentennial history 1785–1985*. Dublin.

Ó Riain, D. 1997 'Ireland's oldest music manuscript?', *History Ireland* **5**, 3, pp. 11–3.

Ó Riain, P. 1977 'St. Finbarr: a study in a cult', *Journal of the Cork Historical and Archaeological Society* **82**, 2, pp. 63–82.

Ó Riain, P. 1997 *'John Colgan's Trias Thaumaturga'* in J. Colgan *Trias Thaumaturga;* with an introduction by Pádraig Ó Riain (Dublin).

Ó Súilleabháin, P. 1963–4 'The library of a parish priest of the penal days', *Collectanea Hibernica* **6/7**, pp. 234–44.

O'Sullivan, W. 1995 'Correspondence of David Rothe and James Ussher, 1619–23', *Collectanea Hibernica* **36–7**, pp. 72–49.

Parker, L. *et al.* 1996 'Crossroads? a symposium on the future of public libraries in Northern Ireland', *An Leabharlann* **12**, 4, pp. 129–43.

Perceval-Maxwell, M. 1994 *The outbreak of the Irish rebellion of 1641*. Dublin.

Pollard, M. 1989 *Dublin's trade in books, 1550–1800*. Oxford.

Reeves, W. 'Memoir of Stephen White. With a copy of a letter, in Latin, dated 31 January 1640, dealing with antiquarian matters, sent by him to John Colgan', *Proceedings of the Royal Irish Academy* **8**, pp. 29–38.

Richardson, R. W. 1995 *The Salamanca letters: a catalogue of correspondence (1619–1871) from the archives of the Irish colleges in Spain in the library*

of St Patrick's College, Maynooth, Ireland. Maynooth.

Rockley, J. 1995 'Antiquarian activity in Cork 1803–1881', MA thesis, UCC.

Rockley, J. in progress 'Towards an understanding of the development of antiquarian and archaeological thought and practice in Cork up to 1870', doctoral dissertation, UCC.

Ronayne, L. 1981 *Seandlithe na nGael: an annotated bibliography of the ancient laws of Ireland*. Glasgow.

Ronayne, L. 1995 'A select bibliography' in W. Nolan, L. Ronayne and M. Dunlevy (eds) *Donegal history and society: interdisciplinary essays on the history of an Irish county* (Dublin), pp. 839–77.

Ronayne, L. 1997 'Presidential address' in *Annual Report of the Library Association of Ireland* (Dublin).

Savage, E. A. 1911 *Old English Libraries: the making, collection and use of books during the Middle Ages* (reprinted New York 1970). New York.

Sharpe, R. 1991 *Medieval Irish saints' lives: an introduction to Vitae Sanctorum Hiberniae*. Oxford.

Smith, A. 1994 'The new directors: [interview with] Michael Ryan', *Irish Arts Review Yearbook 1994*.

Tallon, M. 1959 'Church of Ireland diocesan libraries', *An Leabharlann* **17**, 1 and 2, pp. 177–27 and 45–63.

Terry, J. L. 1998 'Automated library systems: a history of constraints and opportunities', *Advances in Librarianship* **22**, pp. 21–38.

Thornton, D. forthcoming *'Vita Sancti Carthagi* in the seventeenth century' in J. Carey, M. Herbert and P. Ó Riain (eds) *Studies in Irish hagiography*.

Twohig, E. S. 1987 'Pitt-Rivers in Munster 1862–1965/6', *Journal of the Cork Historical and Archaeological Society* **95**, pp. 34–46.

Ua Súilleabháin, S. 1995 'A closer look at the Latin and Irish sources of Pluincéad's *Vocabularium* (1662)', paper to the 10th International Congress of Celtic Studies, Edinburgh.

Weatherup, D. R. M. 1975 'The Armagh Public Library 1771–1971', *Irish Booklore* **2**, 2, pp. 268–99.

Wheeler, G. 1996 'Bishop Francis Hutchinson: his Irish publications and his library' in Gray and McCann 1996, pp. 40–58.

White, N. J. D. 1908 'Elias Bouhéreau of La Rochelle, first public librarian in Ireland', *Proceedings of the Royal Irish Academy* **27 C**, pp. 126–44.

Woodworth, D. 1970 'St. Canice's Library', *Old Kilkenny Review* **22**, pp. 5–10.

Woodworth, D. 1994 *Cashel's museum of printing and early books: a short history of the GPA-Bolton Library*. Clonmel.

Library Collaboration and Collection Policy

MÁIRE DOMHNAT KIRAKOWSKA

The aspiration to the 'universal library', whereby the reader would have access to all the world's literature and scholarly publications, has informed the development of many of the great libraries throughout the history of civilization. The library at Alexandria is reputed to have had a copy of every existing scroll known to its administrators. The acquisition of the world's written literature was the ideal of the Bibliothèque Nationale in Paris and the British Museum under Sir Antonio Panizzi. The Library of Congress in the United States established field offices in many countries whose function was to collect, catalogue and archive indigenous literature. In the same spirit, university libraries aimed to assemble and provide access to balanced holdings extending over the totality of knowledge; to be self-sufficient, able to satisfy the educational and research needs of their users from their own stock. To have to borrow from another institution was at first seen as a mark of inadequacy. The concept of 'universality', however, in a library collection was limited to the acquisition of publications and works of literature for the scholarly and professional classes. But even within these parameters, libraries were eventually forced to be selective in what they obtained, beset as they became by inadequate funding, among other constraints. In the nineteenth century, for example, the British Museum had to cut back on its purchasing of American literature and it is still trying to fill some of the major gaps in its holdings. The problems associated with this philosophy of collection development were exacerbated as the rate of publication increased, the focus of scholarship was enlarged to include popular material, grey literature and ephemera and as the numbers and types of people being educated expanded. It was more and more difficult for individual libraries, having regard to their budgets, space and administration costs, to serve their users from their own holdings.

Few institutions would now regard self-sufficiency or comprehensiveness in terms of their own collections as either attainable or desirable. Various strategies have evolved to cope with these emerging realities. In the context of their economic, social, cultural and educational environment, libraries, in planning collection development, are seeking to balance access to information against ownership of collections, holdings of hardcopy against electronic or multimedia resources, serials versus monographs. Local holdings are accordingly complemented through cooperative schemes and electronic access to bibliographic data or full text sources. This diversification of sourcing and of format or media has raised questions for libraries about commitment to preservation and the archiving, storage and access to multimedia materials. The present article briefly outlines two of the more important approaches to the availability of library resources. These issues are of particular relevance to Ireland and its traditions. Much of our cultural inheritance is not held in libraries in this country. While our library history is rich, it has also suffered from various degrees of fragmentation, discontinuity and partial development. We can often illuminate aspects of our heritage by seeking support from other library networks whose holdings are richer in areas of special concern to us. As our library systems strengthen, we are in a position to provide assistance in fields where we enjoy existing unique capacities or are ensuring a growing competence.

INTERLIBRARY LOAN

The value of interlibrary co-operation in terms of resource sharing between libraries has been appreciated throughout history. In Alexandria a rather forced form of interlibrary loan (ILL) was practised. Books and manuscripts found on board any ship calling at the port were brought to the city's Library, where copies were made before being sent on to the owners. In medieval Europe many monasteries kept exchange catalogues to record books lent to other monasteries and in the seventeenth century, for example, attempts were made to establish an ILL agreement between the Royal Library in Paris and the Vatican and Barberini libraries in Rome.

More formal arrangements of resource sharing, whereby materials are made available by one institution to another, are largely a twentieth-century phenomenon, driven by the ideal of democracy and equity, increase in literacy arising from education and growth in the rate of publication. Interlibrary loan schemes can be based on geographical areas such as national or regional libraries; or around subjects such as medicine or agriculture; or by library type, for instance research libraries or university libraries.

The efficiency and effectiveness of an international ILL service depends on a developed library system, bibliographic control in the form of bibliographies and union catalogues and a recognized process for the management of ILL requests at national level. The Principles of International Lending agreed by national libraries and the Standing Committee of the International Federation of Library Associations' Section on Interlending state that 'Every country should accept responsibility for supplying ... copies of its own publications', and that 'each country should aim to develop an efficient national lending system, since national lending systems are the essential infrastructure of international lending'.

These international aspirations and plans depend on an information infrastructure within each country which is designed to collect, record, archive and provide access to its own publications. National libraries have tended to fulfil this role. The national bibliographies produced by them serve a number of functions, including that of being the archival records of the national imprint. However, the rate of publication has increased dramatically. (Between 1973 when the British National Bibliography came into the British Library and 1987 there had been an 80% increase in the national output of publications and this trend has continued.) The range of formats collected has been expanded, national library functions have been extended in many countries to other organizations. Both the British Library and the Library of Congress have had to accept that it is not possible for one library to carry the high costs of collecting, cataloguing and archiving material and have involved other specialist libraries, such as the National Library for Medicine in the United States and the legal deposit libraries in Britain, in these activities. The British Library in its Co-operation and Partnership Programme is exploring ways of collaborating with other libraries in collection development; preservation; and retention; access; bibliographic services and cataloguing. For example Cranfield University is leading a project on the management of access to grey literature, while the National Library of Wales is collaborating on a feasibility

study to investigate and make recommendations for a collaborative approach to mass de-acidification as part of a national preservation strategy for the cultural written heritage. The EU has also been concerned with the economics of collecting, cataloguing and archiving and has funded research projects to look at ways of improving the interchange of bibliographic records between European national agencies and of providing better access to European national bibliographies. CoBRA is one such project, which was set up in 1993 to explore and promote initiatives that would facilitate national bibliographic services at European level. Later the CoBRA project broadened its scope to include electronic publications, looking at, amongst other aspects, the bibliographic descriptions, implications of legal deposit, long-term storage of and access to electronic publications and digital collections. There are many instances of major world libraries playing a key role in this regard. The British Library, already mentioned, was established in 1973 but was made up from five much older libraries, including the British Museum Library. In the nineteenth century, as we have seen, under the direction of Sir Anthony Panizzi, the latter institution aspired to the complete acquisition of printed works in all areas of knowledge in all languages. One aspect of the British Library's collection policy has been to acquire all significant serials, irrespective of language and subject, so that, as well as making back-up available for the networks of regional libraries, subject collections and academic libraries, it provides a helpful international service for serial requests. The Bibliothèque Nationale in Paris and the Lenin State Library in Moscow had similar policies, and this is reflected in the size of their collections. In the US the Library of Congress had a long-standing practice of exhaustive acquisition of foreign material. The Scottish Confederation of University and Research Libraries co-operates on collecting and disposal policies. The Scottish Books Exchange circulates lists of duplicates and items for disposal, first to the National Library and then to the other participating libraries. Last copies from collections are notified to the Scottish Union Catalogue, and if it has the last copy in Scotland for that particular title, the library which holds it is asked to retain it.

From its beginning in 1877 the National Library of Ireland saw its particular function as being the national institution with the responsibility to collect, catalogue and make available material of Irish origin and of Irish interest. The next chapter sets out its activities in this regard in greater detail. Attention may be drawn here to one special aspect of its undertakings involving international collaboration. The retrospective collection of the literature of a country or the assembling of material relevant to it can be challenging. In ex-colonies, records of past history may be held in the libraries of other countries. During wars collections are dispersed and lost, or 'trophy literature' can be taken. In more recent times, for example, the end of the Cold War, the reunification of Germany and the fall of the USSR have been marked by the finding of collections outside their countries of origin and by subsequent negotiations for their return. The National Library of Ireland has been involved in projects such as the sourcing, microfilming and listing of manuscripts relating to Ireland in foreign libraries.

An Chomhairle Leabharlanna in this state and in Britain the British Library have for long coordinated the national and international interlibrary lending functions. Together they produce, for example, the regional location list of non-fiction holdings available for lending which is based on ISBNs submitted by public libraries. The Irish Joint Fiction Reserve Scheme, which consists of adult fiction held in reserve for ILL, is linked to the Provincial Joint Fiction Reserve and the London and South-East Region (LASER) Joint Fiction Reserve in Britain.

The Committee on Library Cooperation in Ireland (COLICO) was set up in 1977 to promote the ideal of an interdependent coordinated library and information network on the island of Ireland, and to encourage collaboration between libraries of all sorts. Its functions were amended in November 1986 and then became

(a) the promotion of interlibrary cooperation and exchange of information between libraries;

(b) the examination of all aspects of library collaboration in Ireland and formulation of proposals for action where necessary;

(c) the coordination of cooperative activities between libraries, ensuring that, as far as possible, these arrangements between different kinds of libraries in Northern Ireland and the Republic are compatible;

(d) the monitoring of the above-mentioned Irish Joint Fiction Reserve Scheme operated by An Chomhairle Leabharlanna on the Committee's behalf, and

(e) the provision of liaison between Irish libraries, the British Library and other similar bodies.

COLICO has a budget to undertake research into library cooperation in Ireland, and meets three times a year, the venues rotating between the Republic and Northern Ireland. The chairmanship also alternates between persons from both jurisdictions, with the chairman from one part of Ireland and the vice-chairman from another; both serve for two years. Membership of the Committee consists of five representatives of LISC NI, one from the Library Association,

Northern Ireland Branch, seven representatives from An Chomhairle Leabharlanna, two from the Consortium of National and University Libraries (CONUL), one from the Library Association of Ireland and one from the British Library Document Supply Centre (BLDSC). An Chomhairle provides the secretariat to the Committee.

In 1994 COLICO set up a working group to review its functioning and objectives. As a result of this, the organization produced a strategic plan for the following five years. The Committee recommended that the action plan include these cooperative library activities: preservation/conservation, resource sharing, research and development, staff training and development, development of library information policy at national level, information dissemination and the operation of the Irish Joint Fiction Reserve Scheme. A study was commissioned and carried out between March and August 1996 to review resources, resource sharing and its effectiveness and to make recommendations up to the year 2000. The resulting report was not published. COLICO compiles the *Directory of libraries and information services in Ireland*. During 1994 it became the advisory body to both An Chomhairle and the Library Information Services Council (Northern Ireland) (LISC NI).

Libraries in Ireland rely heavily on the resources of the British Library to service their ILL requirements. In 1992 some 85% of Irish interlending traffic was satisfied by the BLDSC. The desire was therefore expressed to seek a solution which would more fully exploit the resources of Irish libraries themselves. A proposal for funding from the Commission of the European Communities under the TELEMATIQUE Programme was approved. The latter, supported by the European Regional Development Fund, aims at developing advanced telecommunications services for Small and Medium-Sized Enterprises. The terms of TELEMATIQUE require that 50% of the co-funding comes from the participant libraries. The proposal was for an invisible network linking a number of major library databases in Ireland. A consortium consisting of six libraries, those of Dublin City University, Forbairt, Trinity College, Dublin, University College, Dublin, University College, Galway and the University of Limerick, agreed to proceed with the scheme. This service, IRIS, was largely based on the compatibility of the software and hardware platforms in use in these locations.

Some subjects, like medicine or agriculture, require specialist collection, cataloguing and ILL administration. In the US the collection of medical and agricultural material is the particular responsibility of the National Library of Medicine and the National Library of Agriculture and ILL administration is based on regions using these national repositories as libraries of last resort. In Britain and Ireland the British Medical Association offers an ILL service to health libraries and medical practitioners. As an instance of a collaborative development within Ireland itself one might mention the scheme set up by University College, Cork's Medical Library, which has forty-six member libraries contributing to a union list of holdings and arrangements for reciprocal ILL facilities. The EU also runs its own document delivery service EUDOR (*http://www.eudor.com*) to cover documents in the *L* and *C* series of the *Official Journal*, merger decisions, consolidated legislation and COM documents. Similarly different formats such as film and sound require specialist collection, cataloguing, storage and administration including ILL services. In Britain the British Film Institute Collections (*http://www.bfi.org.uk*) house the largest collection of films and television titles in Europe and the Institute offers a retail and lending service.

Resource sharing based on types of libraries such as university or research libraries, as well as facilitating ILL, may also seek to rationalise collection development, cataloguing, storage, preservation and access. After the First World War a group of academic libraries in Germany agreed on acquisition and access policies; thus Bonn was responsible for the collection, cataloguing and preservation of Romance philology and literature while in Gottingen the specialism was English. The Center for Research Libraries in the US collects potentially important material, such as outdated textbooks and foreign dissertations, for which there is no immediate demand. In Britain and Ireland twenty research-based university libraries, national libraries and other institutions with major research collections have formed the Consortium of University Research Libraries (CURL) (*http://www.curl.ac.uk*) to develop co-operative solutions to the acquisition, processing, storage, preservation, and delivery of information and library materials for research. The consortium database COPAC (*http://copac.ac.uk*), of approximately 13 million MARC records, supports a record retrieval and reference service. However as most of the contributing libraries did not have on-line catalogues until the early 1980s, over 50% of the records on the database represent material published since 1980. Special efforts are being made to convert the records currently held on card and microform catalogues and so improve the proportion of the libraries' records of older materials available on-line. CURL is also engaged in a feasibility study to investigate how a national programme of retrospective conversion of catalogue records could contribute to broadening access to the heritage of printed books in Britain. The success of COPAC and other virtual union catalogues, notably the UK Electronic Libraries Program (eLib)-funded Clumps projects such as Music Libraries Online (*www.musiconline.ac.uk*) has prompted a feasibility study into a national union catalogue for the UK. This study will look at the problems and issues involved in the creation

of such a catalogue for monographs, serials, archives, manuscripts and other formats. The Ligue des Bibliothèques Europeenes de Recherche (LIBER) is an association of the major research libraries in more than thirty countries in Europe. It is active in supporting a functional network across national boundaries so that the preservation of European cultural heritage is ensured and that access to the collections is improved.

The creation of the Internet and electronic publishing has greatly facilitated access to information and material not held locally. The catalogues of many libraries are available and many journal articles and monographs are accessible electronically in full text. The Online Computer Centre (OCLC) (*http://www.oclc.org*), based in the US, by integrating electronic resources under one web interface can provide flexible access to information for both libraries and library users. Individuals can now have direct access to OCLC's WorldCat and ILL service as well as First Search which gives access to 85 on-line databases and more than 5 million full-text articles. Document delivery is arranged through e-mail, ILL, fax or post. OCLC has recently formed the Global Sharing Group Access Group to foster international resource sharing initiatives. An EU Libraries project, Europagate (*http://europagate.dtv.dk*), set out to build and operate a pilot service through which users get on-line access to library catalogues by a standardized server interface with the spin-off effect of better use of library stock through ILLs.

Libraries and other organizations are also making texts available via the Internet. Examples of the variety of material available in Ireland include the Transportation Records Database of prisoners sent to Australia 1791–1868 set up by the National Archives (*www.national archives.ie/*) while the site for CELT (*http://ucc.ie/celt/*) is described elsewhere in this volume. The full texts of the acts of the Oireachtas are on the website of the Office of the Attorney General (*www.irlgov.ie.ag*). The Regional Media Bureau of Ireland (RMBI) is a consortium of Irish newspapers and through their website (*www.rmbi.ie*), it is now possible to access many local Irish newspapers.

In Britain the Higher Education Resources ON-demand (Heron) project is working to provide key articles and book extracts, material usually associated with off-print and short loan collections for undergraduates, electronically on a national scale to the higher education community.

Historically union catalogues were library-oriented tools, indispensable for the administration of an ILL service. Now, however, with so much information available electronically and the emergence of virtual union catalogues available through the world-wide web, end users have direct access to information and information sources. While libraries and other information providers are working to facilitate this shift in emphasis from ILL towards direct end user services, many practical problems such as authorization and costing still need to be overcome. The Tolimac Project (*www.tolimac.ulb. ac.be*) in the EU Telematics for Libraries programme is addressing the problems of security of transactions on open networks, authorization and cost recovery in electronic document delivery.

LEGAL DEPOSIT

While there are references to forms of legal deposit going back to the library at Alexandria, it was the introduction of printing and the beginnings of mass communication which prompted many countries to legally formalize the deposit arrangements. In France in 1537 François I by royal decree established that printers and booksellers had to deposit copies of any book published in the realm with the Royal Library at Chateau de Blois. Other states soon implemented similar measures. Statutory obligations were introduced in Denmark in 1623, while in England a Star Chamber decree of 1637 stated that one copy of every work had to be deposited with the Stationers' Company before publication, and that this copy should be preserved at Oxford University. In 1707 the Library of the Old Academy of Turku, now Helsinki University Library, was granted the privilege of receiving the publications of the Danish and Swedish printers on legal deposit. In Britain the current statutory arrangements are contained in the *Copyright Act* of 1911 and in Ireland in the *National Cultural Institutions Act* 1997. In both the United Kingdom and Ireland the publisher is obliged to deposit one copy of each publication with the British Library and on request to the National Libraries of Scotland and Wales, the University Library at Cambridge, the Bodleian Library at Oxford and the library of Trinity College, Dublin. Irish publishers must also deposit with the National Library and on request to the libraries of the National University of Ireland, Dublin, Galway, Maynooth, University College, Cork, the University of Limerick and Dublin City University.

Originally, legal deposit extended only to published works in print, and in many countries this remains the case. Ambiguity in the definition of 'published' material has proved problematic in the collection and management of grey literature. The limitation to printed works excludes non-print media such as sound recordings, film, computer software and on-line information. Countries such as France and Canada have extended their legal deposit requirements to include audio-visual material, computer software and electronic publications in physical formats, and in some other states separate voluntary arrangements have been made for other formats such as broadcast material and film and sound recordings. The British Library's National Sound Archive and the collections of the British Film

Institute have relied on purchase and voluntary donation. These new formats present fresh problems in terms of their collection, storage and preservation. Non-print items such as feature-length films can be more expensive to produce than printed materials and deposit is very costly. Preservation of these non-print media has implications for the maintenance of appropriate technology and upgrading of the format. The storage of sound recordings on cylinders requires equipment necessary for playing. It is important too that the originals of these recordings be copied to a current format to allow user access to them while protecting the originals and their technology. Many national libraries are not well provided for in dealing with audio-visual and electronic media, and responsibilities for these have been given to other organizations and libraries with the necessary expertise to collect, archive and make the data available to the general public. In Denmark it is the State Media Archive at the State and University Library at Aarhus which assembles and preserves commercially produced sound recordings as well as Danish broadcast programmes. In Britain a scheme for the national deposit of non-print materials is being piloted by publishers and deposit libraries in anticipation of legislation being extended to cover these formats. The code of practice agreed covers microform and off-line electronic media such as tapes and CDs or products also available in print. Legal deposit, as presently constituted, has worked towards the conservation of the national imprint and thereby the intellectual inheritance of the state. However, the global nature of electronic information and the world-wide web are raising many issues for the limited state-bound view of legal deposit. For example, how will original material held in single copy on the web be collected or the on-line work of international consortia? How will databases published on-line in which information continually changes be captured and stored as part of the international intellectual inheritance?

The pressures of economics and the electronic availability of information have shifted the balance for many libraries in the access versus ownership of holdings debate. At the same time, however, the increase in material published and the accessibility of information available on what has been published on the Internet, through abstracts and indexes, on-line networked catalogues and so forth have resulted in raising expectations of library users. They now expect their libraries to provide higher levels of service and to make more material available, and this has led to an increase in the use of interlibrary loan or document delivery services. Between 1985 and 1995 ILLs in Britain and Ireland grew by 17% but, interestingly, in the same time-span the number of unsatisfied requests increased by almost 25%. These factors highlight for governments and libraries that they, the libraries, can no longer be autonomous units. National information strategies are necessary to bring about collaboration in collection development, cataloguing, preservation, storage and access on a national scale, so that all published material in any format, whether held in public or private collections, legal deposit libraries, public libraries or those of private institutions and universities is considered to be the national heritage, and subject to concern for its preservation.

Bibliography

Barwick, M. M. 1990 *A guide to centres of international lending and copying.* Boston Spa.

Cornish, G. P. 1994 'Copyright issues in legal deposit and preservation', *IFLA Journal* **20**, 3, pp. 341–49.

Day, A. 1998 *Inside the British Library.* London.

European Commission, Directorate General X 111–E4, 1996 *Telematics for libraries: synopsis of projects. Telematics applications programme 1994–1998.* Luxembourg.

Gibson, P. 1996 'Preserving a digital heritage', *Library Manager* **18** (May), p. 8.

Harrison, K. C. 1963 *The library and the community.* London.

Hielmcrone, H.v. 1995 'Access to the intellectual heritage', in conference proceedings of *Networking and the future of libraries 2, Bath,* 19-21 April 1995 (London), pp. 165-173.

Hoare, P. 1996 *Legal deposit of non-print material: an international overview.* London.

Kenny, A. 1996 'Beyond the printed word', *Library Association Record* **98**, 2, p. 201.

Lerner, F. 1998 *The story of libraries.* New York.

Line, M. B. 1988 *Lines of thought.* London.

Oppenheim, C. 1997 'United Kingdom moves towards legal deposit of nonprint publications', *Information Management Report* (July), pp. 16–9.

Phillips, S. 1994 'Copyright law in the Republic of Ireland: an overview', *An Leabharlann* **11**, 2, pp. 31–33.

The National Library of Ireland

GERARD LONG

The National Library of Ireland's (NLI) objectives were defined in the mission statement which appeared in its *Strategic Plan 1992–1997*:

The National Library of Ireland aims to collect, preserve and make accessible materials on or relating to Ireland, to provide an accurate record of Ireland's output in manuscript, print and other media for present and future users and to provide timely and free access to those with genuine research needs. It aims to acquire reference material to support its collections and to maintain a basic collection of reference material suitable for a National Library in a European context and to carry out those functions in the most cost effective manner.

Its purpose is to fully exploit its resources through research and publications and to encourage co-operation both nationally and internationally in the public and private sector. It aims to respond sympathetically to users' needs and to be open and alert to new media and technology. (p. 5)

The first part of this article traces the development of the National Library from its origins in the library of the Royal Dublin Society to the present day, combining a brief history with an overview of the legal framework within which the Library operates. The nature and extent of the Library's collections are then considered. The financial and staffing arrangements of the Library are described, and finally there is a synopsis of the services offered (for which see also *http://www.nli.ie* and the quarterly newsletter *National Library of Ireland News/Nuachtlitir Leabharlann Náisiúnta na hÉireanan* [Autumn 1999–]).

HISTORY, DEVELOPMENT AND LEGAL FRAMEWORK
The Dublin Society was founded in 1731 as 'The Dublin Society for improving husbandry, manufactures and other useful arts and sciences'. A royal charter was granted in 1750. Though a private institution, the Society's motives were altruistic, being concerned with the improvement of the country in matters such as agriculture, manufactures and the applied arts. Government acknowledged the Society's usefulness by an annual grant. The use of public funds to help support a private institution was likely to lead to controversy, and in 1836, William Smith O'Brien, Conservative M.P. for the County of Limerick, proposed that a Committee be appointed

to inquire into the administration of the Royal Dublin Society, with a view to the wider extension of the advantage of the annual parliamentary grant to that institution, without reference to the distinctions of party or religion.

The Select Committee, under the chairmanship of Smith O'Brien, prepared a report on the Society, which recommended that

In the opinion of your Committee the Library of the Dublin Society ought to be considered as intended, not solely for the advantage of a comparatively few individuals who belong to the Society, but as a National Library, accessible under proper regulations to respectable persons of all classes, who may be desirous to avail themselves of it for the purpose of literary research. (*Report from the Select Committee on Royal Dublin Society*, H.C. (445), xii, 355, p. xii)

From 1836 onwards, the Library (hitherto available to the public only in a very limited manner) became more accessible, largely due to the efforts of the Society's Library Committee to provide increased accommodation and longer opening hours. The Library's stock in 1836 was largely scientific and technical, reflecting the Society's aims, but over the following decades, the acquisitions policy became more general, and an emphasis was placed on acquiring material of Irish interest. In 1863, the Royal Dublin Society Library received a valuable donation of books, prints, music, manuscripts

Fig. 30.1 Late nineteenth-century exterior view of the National Library of Ireland.

and other material from Jaspar Robert Joly. This added significantly to the Irish holdings of the Society. The collection was given to the Society on condition that

... if at any time hereafter a public library should be established in the city of Dublin under the authority of Parliament ... analogous to the library of the British Museum in London the Joly Library would be transferred to it. (*Dublin Science and Museum Act* 1877 40 41 Vict., ch. ccxxxiv, p. 10)

Negotiations between the Royal Dublin Society, the Department of Science and Art (London) and the Commissioners of Public Works (Ireland) led to the passing of the *Dublin Science and Art Museum Act* of 1877 establishing a National Library and National Museum. This act enabled the transfer of most of the Society's library, including the Joly Library, to the new National Library, which in fact remained on the Society's premises in Leinster House until 1890. The Library was funded by, and reported to, the Department of Science and Art (London), and formed part of the Dublin Institutions of Science and Art, comprising the Library, the Museum, the Natural History Museum, the Metropolitan School of Art and the Royal Botanic Gardens. The Library was superintended by the Council of Trustees, eight of whom were appointed by the Society and four by the Department. The Council of Trustees held its first meeting on 21 February 1878, and appointed William Archer (librarian of the Royal Dublin Society, and author

of *Suggestions as to public library buildings*) as the first Librarian. Relations between the Society and the Department were not invariably cordial, and some controversial points regarding authority and administration were clarified by the *Agreement between the Science and Art Department, the Commissioners of Public Works, and the Royal Dublin Society. March 1st, 1881.*

The present building was designed by Thomas N. Deane and Son, following two controversial competitions, and opened on 29 August 1890. It was one of the first libraries to implement the new Dewey Classification System. Under Archer and his diligent successor, T. W. Lyster (described by W. B. Yeats as 'the most zealous man I know'), Librarian from 1895 until 1920, the collections grew steadily, and the institution's popularity is reflected in the very high number of readers. Effectively, it was acting as a large public reference library, and was particularly popular with the students of the nearby National University. Unlike most national libraries, it did not benefit from any legal deposit legislation, nor did it compile a national bibliography. In April 1900, responsibility for the Library was transferred to the Department of Agriculture and Technical Instruction, under which the Library remained until 1923–24. After the foundation of the Irish Free State, the Department of Education became the parent body, from 1924–25 to 1986.

Robert Lloyd Praeger, better known as a botanist, served as Librarian from 1920 to 1922, taking early retirement upon the establishment of the Free State.

Over the following decades, the institution gradually developed into a centre of Irish bibliography and studies. In 1904, Richard Irvine Best became the first Celtic scholar to join the Library staff. His *Bibliography of Irish philology and of printed Irish literature* (1913) and its companion volume covering the years 1913 to 1941 (1942) are standard works. He became Librarian in 1924. During the following decades, due to Best's diligence, the collection of Gaelic manuscript material grew significantly, many of the most important items coming from the Sir Thomas Phillipps collection in 1931. Coverage of Irish printing was greatly augmented through the generosity of E. R. McClintock Dix, who presented the main part of his remarkable collection of early Irish imprints to the Library over a period of years.

The *Industrial and Commercial Property (Protection) Act* 1927 gave the NLI legal deposit status for the first time. (The Library is entitled to a copy of every book and serial, including newspapers, published in the Republic of Ireland.) A significant increase in the newspaper collection is evident from this time. The *Copyright Act* 1965 (section 56) subsequently amended this, and is presently in force.

Richard J. Hayes joined the Library in 1924, and became Director in 1940. He made a huge contribution to Irish bibliography, through his compilation and editorship of catalogues of Irish manuscript material and indexes to Irish periodicals (Hayes 1965, 1970, 1979; de hAe agus Ní Dhonnchadha 1938–40). In 1943, the Office of Arms was transferred to the control of the Library, and renamed the Genealogical Office. This was located in Dublin Castle until 1981.

Though the collections had grown steadily in size over the years, there had been no commensurate increase in the accommodation available to the Library, and a severe shortage of space was the main problem which faced Patrick Henchy, who succeeded Hayes as Director in 1967. Dr Henchy was responsible for acquiring further premises in the vicinity — notably nos 2 and 3, Kildare Street (previously part of the premises of the Kildare Street Club), which now house the Manuscripts Department, Genealogical Office and Heraldic Museum, and nos 4 and 5, Kildare Street. The accommodation problem was the recurrent concern of Alf Mac Lochlainn, who served as Director from 1976 to 1982, and his successor, Michael Hewson. Refurbishment of the Kildare Street premises began in 1982, and the Manuscripts Reading Room at nos 2–3, Kildare Street,

Fig. 30.2 Original reading rooms, National Library of Ireland.

was formally opened in 1991.

In July 1986, the Library was transferred to the Department of An Taoiseach. The Department of Arts, Culture and the Gaeltacht (now Arts, Heritage, Gaeltacht and the Islands) was established in 1992, and assumed responsibility for the Library. Patricia Donlon became the first woman Director in 1989. This was also the first time that the post was filled by open competition. In the same year, the Library took over responsibility for the compilation and publication of the *Irish publishing record*, the national bibliography. In 1992, the Library published its *Strategic plan 1992–1997*, a blueprint for development. Dr Donlon retired in 1997. The position is now held by Brendan O Donoghue.

The implementation of the *National Cultural Institution Act* 1997 would alter the statutory and administrative framework of the Library, effectively turning it into a semi-state organization. The most significant provisions of the act (references to the relevant sections of which are given in square brackets here) to affect the Library relate to a broad definition of 'library material' to include new categories [Section 2 (1) (b)]; the establishment of Bord Leabharlann Náisiúnta na hÉireann (in place of the Council of Trustees), its principal functions being

... to conserve, restore, maintain and enlarge the library material in the collection of the Library for the benefit of the public, and to establish and maintain a record of library material (including material relating to the Irish language) in relation to Ireland and to contribute to the provisions of access by members of the public to material relating to other countries [12 (1)].

The Board would have the power to lend library material [12 (2) (d)], to dispose of library material (by sale, exchange or gift) [18 (2)], and to borrow money [34]. Staff would become members of the staff of the Board [31 (1)]. A register of cultural objects would be established and maintained [48 (1)], whose export from the state would constitute a serious loss to the heritage of Ireland, and for the export of which a licence is required [50]. New legal deposit provisions would significantly expand the entitlement of the library [65]. At the time of writing (March 2000), the act has not yet been implemented.

BUDGETARY AND STAFFING TRENDS
The Library is largely funded by its parent department, which is responsible for paying the salaries of the permanent staff (£1.737 million in 1999). In addition, the parent department provides two annual grants:

(i) a grant to cover routine administration costs,

(ii) a grant-in-aid to cover services (such as conservation

and ICT) and the purchase of library materials (including books, periodicals, manuscripts and other items for the collections). Figures for the last eleven years are as follows:

	GRANT-IN-AID	ADMINISTRATION
1990	£146,000	£68,000
1991	£182,769	£127,505
1992	£200,000	£90,000
1993	£310,000	£174,196
1994	£400,000	£237,000
1995	£440,000	£250,000
1996	£482,000	£255,000
1997	£670,000	£320,000
1998	£855,000	£360,000
1999	£980,000	£396,000
2000	£1,177,000	£500,000

Source: *Revised Estimates for Public Service*

A steady increase is evident. Additional special grants have, on occasion, been allocated to assist towards the purchase of particularly important items or collections. Such grants amounted to £176,000 in 1999. Furthermore, the Library generates a certain amount of income (through publications, copying services, reproduction fees, grants of arms and so forth) which is retained for Library use. Such income totalled £247,000 in 1999.

All permanent staff are civil servants, though their status would change upon implementation of the *National Cultural Institutions Act*. The number of permanent staff has increased from 51 in 1989 to 84 in 1999, a significant increase in a period of public service embargoes on recruitment. Two trends are evident in the recent past:

(i) the redeployment of personnel from other branches of the civil service, and

(ii) the employment of staff on fixed-term contract or consultancy assignments, usually for specific tasks or projects. The annual *Report of the Council of Trustees* gives, as an appendix, the names and grades of permanent staff.

NATURE AND EXTENT OF THE LIBRARY'S HOLDINGS
The library collection of the Royal Dublin Society (with the exception of the scientific periodicals) formed the basis of the National Library collection. In 1836, the Society's holdings were largely of a scientific and technical nature, reflecting its aims. Over the following decades, the acquisitions policy developed a broader base. Material was acquired in the humanities as well as

the sciences, and efforts were made to improve the collection of books of Irish interest. For example, an important collection of pamphlets dealing with seventeenth-century Ireland was purchased from the London bookseller, Thomas Thorpe, in 1840. The donation of the Joly Library was particularly important in adding to the Irish holdings. Official publications were also acquired. By 1877, when the National Library was established, the holdings constituted a comprehensive general collection in the sciences, applied sciences and humanities, with an emphasis on Irish material. Initially, the National Library served principally as a printed book and periodical collection. The collection of other forms, such as manuscripts and photographic material, came later in its development. In practice, the National Library is now a library of Irish studies, predominantly in the humanities rather than the sciences. The concept of collecting everything published in the Republic of Ireland (for which legal deposit legislation is a necessity) is relatively recent. Most of the collections are housed in the main Library building, with the exception of the Manuscripts Department, which is located at 2–3 Kildare Street. There follows a brief account of the various sections into which the collections are divided, with a description of the finding aids available. All of the sections are under the charge of a Keeper or Assistant Keeper.

PRINTED BOOKS
The Library's aim is to acquire all material printed and published in Ireland, and all material of Irish interest published abroad. This includes books by Irish authors (on any subject-matter) and on Irish subjects. The Library has a particular responsibility to collect publications in the Irish language. The main strengths of the printed books collection are in the area of literature (in Irish and English) and history, including local and family history. The collections contain many printed genealogical resources as well as microfilm copies of Roman Catholic parish registers up to the year 1880. The holdings of national and provincial newspapers and periodicals are particularly important, as many of these are unavailable elsewhere.

Books are listed in the General Catalogue of Printed Books, and in the On-line Public Access Catalogue (OPAC) as follows:

Author Catalogue
(i) Guard-book catalogue: accessions to 1969;

(ii) Card catalogue: accessions 1969–1988;

(iii) OPAC : accessions 1988 to present.

Subject Catalogue
(i) Guard-book catalogue: accessions to 1977;

(ii) Card catalogue: accessions 1977–1988;

(iii) OPAC: accessions 1988 to present.

There is very little overlap between these three sequences.

It is possible to search OPAC under author, title, title keyword, subject, subject keyword and ISBN/ISSN. A project to convert the entire card catalogue to machine-readable form, and to integrate these records into OPAC has just been completed. OPAC, representing a considerable part of the Library's printed book collection, will be made available on the Internet by mid-2000. Work on the conversion of the Guard-book Catalogue has been initiated. It is hoped to have records of all of the Irish collections available on-line by mid-2002.

PERIODICALS AND NEWSPAPERS
Periodicals are listed by title in the Author Catalogue, and Hayes (1970) as well as de hAe and Ní Dhonnchadha (1938–40) contain useful indexes.

The Library attempts to acquire all current Irish newspapers (approximately 200 in number). These are either bound or microfilmed. As both of these processes take some time, current issues are not made available. The Library's list of its newspaper holdings is available in the Reading Room. These holdings, along with Irish newspapers held in the British Library Newspaper Library and other institutions, are listed in the publication *Newsplan* (London: British Library; Dublin: National Library of Ireland, second edition, revised, 1998). The Newsplan project, in co-operation with the British Library Newspaper Library and libraries in Ireland, aims to ensure the preservation of Irish newspapers, these being a particularly important and fragile form. Towards this end, an in-house dedicated newspaper microfilming unit has been established in order to film titles from the Library and other collections to archival standards; it is hoped to copy all extant Irish newspapers eventually. This means that the information is preserved, multiple copies can be made available, and the hardcopy original can be removed to an off-site store, thereby liberating valuable storage space. A significant recent development has been the establishment of the Newsplan Office, which became operational during 1998, as did the Binding and Conservation Unit. The Binding unit has implemented the 'flush-binding' procedure, ensuring that material is bound to archival standards. It is a quick and cost-effective process. The above units are located in the Technical Services Building (a conversion of the nineteenth-century Racquet Hall of the Kildare Street Club).

ISSN Centre: The Irish ISSN Centre, based at the Library, undertakes the issuing and recording of International

Standard Serial Numbers for serial publications published in the Republic of Ireland. An information leaflet, *What's in a name*, and application form are available on request.

OFFICIAL PUBLICATIONS

Official and government publications include legislation (statutes, acts, bills, statutory instruments), parliamentary debates, reports of government departments, parliamentary commissions and committees, and statistical data. The Library's collection contains Republic of Ireland official publications (1922–); the Irish Parliament (pre-1801); a comprehensive collection of British official publications, including much material relating to Ireland (1801–1979/80); Northern Ireland official publications (1921– , incomplete), and the publications of a number of international organizations.

PRINTS AND DRAWINGS

The Library has a large collection of prints and drawings. The collection is founded on the Joly Library of approximately several thousand albums and 70,000 individual prints. This collection contains much European material, and a very fine collection of Napoleonic images. Since the foundation of the Library, additions have been mainly of Irish topographical and historical interest. There are also some architectural drawings and designs. (Elmes 1938 and 1975; Butler 1997; Harbison 1998)

There is much additional material in the collections, and constant new acquisitions, not listed in the above. Specific enquiries may be sent to the Prints and Drawings librarian. It is advisable to make a prior arrangement if you wish to consult material in these collections.

MAPS

There are approximately 120,000 items in the Map Collection including 22,000 in the Manuscripts Department, although some of these are printed maps. There is a catalogue in the Reading Room. A list of Ordnance Survey maps is held at the Reading Room counter, and manuscript maps are listed in the manuscripts catalogues listed below.

PRINTED MUSIC

Much of the collection of printed music dates to the eighteenth and nineteenth centuries, and forms part of the Joly Collection. There is a card catalogue of individual items of sheet music in the Reading Room; collections in book form are to be found in the Printed Books Catalogues.

EPHEMERA

This catch-all term refers to items such as posters, handbills and leaflets. The NLI has a collection of such items, many relating to political events such as elections and referenda. Catalogued items appear in the Printed Books Catalogues.

MANUSCRIPTS

The Manuscripts Department is housed in the converted premises of the Kildare Street Club, at 2–3, Kildare Street. The collection consists of over 65,000 catalogued manuscripts, representing more than 750,000 individual items. There are also about 28,000 deeds. The collections contain the personal papers of many significant literary and political figures, including Sir Roger Casement, James Joyce, William Smith O'Brien, Seán T. O'Kelly, George Bernard Shaw, Hannah Sheehy Skeffington and William Butler Yeats. Of considerable interest to economic and social historians are the records of landed estates, which usually include maps, correspondence, rentals and leases. Such items can also be of great value to genealogists. The Library also has a large collection of microfilm copies of Irish manuscript material held abroad. Microfilms are consulted in the main Library building. Manuscripts are listed in Hayes (1965 and 1979).These are union catalogues; as well as listing National Library of Ireland holdings, they list manuscript material held by other institutions. The Card catalogue of National Library material processed in the period 1975 is in the Manuscripts Reading Room. OPAC contains recent records. Irish-language manuscripts are included in the above; more detailed information on them is available in Ní Shéaghda *et al.* (1967–).

PHOTOGRAPHIC COLLECTIONS

The National Photographic Archive opened in Meeting House Square, Temple Bar, in October 1998. The Archive houses the Library's collections and has a permanent exhibition space, a reading room (with a back-up collection of printed material relating to the photographic collections) and a reference area where the collection may be viewed. An imaging project, involving the digitization of images from the collection, is ongoing. The photographic collections contain several hundred thousand images, dating from the 1850s to the present, representing the output of professional and amateur photographers, and mainly relating to Ireland. The most famous collections are those of the Lawrence, Eason and Valentine studios. There are separate indexes available for specific collections (Rouse 1998).

GENEALOGICAL OFFICE

The Genealogical Office, incorporating the Office of the Chief Herald, has been part of the National Library since 1943. It is the state authority for design and issue of heraldry, including coats of arms. Grants of arms are made to individuals and to corporate and professional bodies including local authorities. Family history is one

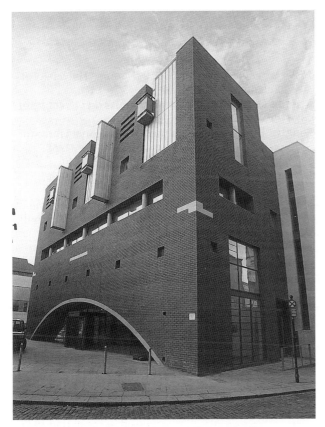

Fig. 30.3 Photographic Archive, Temple Bar, Dublin.

of the largest single areas of research among readers in the National Library. In response to the great demand for specialist advice, a Genealogy Service, based in the main Library building, is available free of charge for people wishing to undertake genealogical and family history research. Several information leaflets are available, as is a list of professional researchers. Readers are, of course, welcome to carry out their own research, and many important sources are available in the Library, of which the most important are microfilm copies of most surviving Roman Catholic parish records up to the year 1880; valuation records, including Tithe Applotment Books (microfilm) and Griffith's Valuation (microfiche; index on CD-ROM); many collections of estate records (available in the Manuscripts Reading Room) and various printed family histories.

NATIONAL LIBRARY OF IRELAND SOCIETY
The National Library of Ireland Society is a voluntary support group founded in order to publicize the Library's resources and to highlight its needs. The Society arranges an annual programme of lectures, and organizes an annual outing.

SERVICES PROVIDED IN THE AREA OF CULTURE AND HERITAGE
In collecting and making available library material, the Library provides a service to the general public.

Additional services are available which will be of interest to exhibition organizers, curators, publishers and others working in the area of culture and heritage. It is important to stress that staff numbers are limited, and that staff have many responsibilities. Therefore, persons wishing to avail of services should plan ahead, and make appointments with staff members well in advance. This is particularly important where copies of Library material will be required.

The Library has the responsibility of collecting and preserving the written record of the nation. Consequently, the Library has a policy of promoting public awareness of its collections and services. A number of publications (books and folders of facsimile historical documents) are available, based on the collections. The Education Officer provides tours of the Library (by appointment) to groups, and can arrange lectures on the Library. Exhibitions are held in the Library on a regular basis. There is usually an accompanying publication. Travelling versions of these exhibitions are usually available for loan to outside venues.

COPYING SERVICES
Copies (usually photographic) of items in the Library collections may be ordered, and are often requested by cultural organizations and commercial publishers for use in exhibitions and/or publications. Prior notice is required.

AVAILABILITY OF LIBRARY PREMISES
The Library foyer is available for occasions such as book launches.

FUTURE DEVELOPMENTS
Within the Library itself, a major building programme is in train. The Library has acquired the main part of the Leinster Lane premises of the National College of Art and Design, and these will be converted to provide additional reading rooms and a lecture theatre. Further elements of the building programme include the refurbishment of the main Library building, the construction of a new storage block, and the refurbishment of nos 4 and 5, Kildare Street.

On a broader front, developments in the field of information technology affect the manner in which information is stored and retrieved. Old catalogue forms such as card catalogues are being replaced by machine-readable versions, and the catalogue will soon be made available to a global readership via the Internet. This allows for faster and more comprehensive search facilities.

Increasingly, fragile hardcopy forms will be copied digitally, and replaced by surrogate forms. This will allow for ease of access and use, cheaper copying facilities and the possibility of remote access. A case in point is the

Imaging Project, presently in progress in the Prints and Drawings and Photographic Sections. Imaging, essentially, is the digitizing of an image (print, drawing, photograph), in order that it may be stored electronically and that the viewer can see it on screen. The image can be linked to the catalogue record. Thus, visual resources can become accessible via the Internet. The Library is likely to extend its collection policy to include audio-visual and other new forms.

CONSTRAINTS AFFECTING THESE MATTERS

Libraries, like most cultural institutions, are subject to the normal economic constraints which are part and parcel of the public service. In comparison with many European national libraries, the National Library of Ireland is inadequately staffed and funded. The additional responsibilities placed on the Library under the terms of the *National Cultural Institutions Act* would have further staffing implications. The amount available annually for the purchase of material has been a matter of concern. We may justly be satisfied with the remarkable achievements of Irish writers in the English language; their very success, however, has meant that, when their manuscripts appeared at auction, or were offered for private sale, they were often beyond the reach of the National Library, which simply could not compete with analogous institutions abroad. In more recent years, however, there has been a greater willingness on the part of successive governments to make special grants available so that the Library could acquire collections of manuscripts of special importance. In addition, the Library has been able to exploit the tax credit scheme for donations of heritage items to acquire some valuable and historical material.

Bibliography

Best, R. I. 1913 *Bibliography of Irish philology and printed literature*. Dublin.

Best, R. I. 1942 *Bibliography of Irish philology and manuscript literature: publications 1913–41*. Dublin.

Butler, P. 1997 *The Brocas collection: an illustrated selective catalogue*. Dublin.

de hAe, R. agus Ní Dhonnchadha, B. 1938–40 *Clár litridheachta na Nua-Ghaedhilge 1850–1936*. Dublin.

Elmes, R. M. 1938 and 1975 *Catalogue of engraved Irish portraits* (revised ed. by M. Hewson [Dublin, 1975]). Dublin.

Harbison, P. (ed) 1998 *Drawings of the principal antique buildings of Ireland, by Gabriel Béranger*. Dublin.

Hayes, R. J. (ed) 1965 *Manuscript sources for the history of Irish civilisation*. Boston.

Hayes, R. J. (ed) 1970 *Sources for the history of Irish civilisation: articles in Irish periodicals*. Boston.

Hayes, R. J. (ed) 1979 *Manuscript sources for the history of Irish civilisation: first supplement 1965–1975*. Boston.

Henchy, P. 1986 *The National Library of Ireland 1941–1976: a look back*. Dublin.

Irish University Review 1977, **7**, 2 [National University of Ireland centenary issue].

Kissane, N. (ed) 1994 *Treasures of the National Library of Ireland*. Drogheda.

Long, G. 1991 'The foundation of the National Library of Ireland, 1836–1877', *Long Room* **36**, pp. 41–58.

Ní Shéaghdha, N. *et al.* 1967– *Catalogue of Irish manuscripts in the National Library of Ireland*. Dublin.

Rouse, S. 1998 *Into the light: an illustrated guide to the photographic collections in the National Library of Ireland*. Dublin.

Archives

VIRGINIA TEEHAN

Ireland has a great wealth of archival material. Contained within these archives is unique and irreplaceable information about our past and current lives. Physically the archives and records are found in many formats, some conventional text-based documents, other records are in the form of photographs, drawings, architectural plans, compact disks, computer tape, postcards, photographs and so forth. Collectively such material represents a major strand of our national memory. It is one base upon which our society defines itself and re-defines the actions of previous generations. Archives thus make up a central part of our cultural heritage. They have significant relationships with other types of evidence of past and present human activity. Similarly archivists have a central role in the framework of Irish cultural services. Archivists are equipped with specialist skills, the application of which is vital in safeguarding Irish heritage. The significance of their contribution to the preservation of heritage demands that they must be included, and include themselves, in the professional cultural community and are not seen as something separate. Within the context of contemporary Ireland, new perceptions of tradition as a complex multi-layered background from which our understanding of ourselves as a people evolves demand that archivists be full participants in cultural discourse as one anticipates the evolution a new phase in Irish life.

This chapter attempts to define current understandings of the terms 'archives' and 'archivists'. Secondly, information is presented regarding the care of archives which attempts to provide *very general* practical guidelines for those who are entrusted with the custodianship of archival material. It must be emphasized here that archival material is unique and frequently irreplaceable. Its care demands the specialist skills of archivists and conservators. In the absence of such professional services, efforts to preserve and or conserve material can permanently damage it. The welfare of the intellectual and physical properties of archival matter is best realized within a dedicated archival institution. Finally, the role of archives and archivists within the context of the changing landscape of Irish cultural management and administration is examined.

WHAT ARE ARCHIVES?

Archives are documents made or received and accumulated by a person or organization in the course of the conduct of affairs and preserved because of their continuing worth. Historically, the term has often referred narrowly to records which are no longer of value to the creator but are deposited in an archival institution. In its singular form, 'archive' refers specifically to the whole body or group of records, a vital resource also known by the French word *fonds* or the term *Archiv* common to many European languages. People and organizations create records employing whatever technology is available to them. Therefore such items can be in any medium, paper, microfilm, film, magnetic tape or disk, optical disk, video or audiotapes. As mentioned above, they come in various formats, including letters, files, diaries, registers, index cards, maps, plans, microfiche, aperture cards, photographs, video cassettes, computerized databases, electronic mail and all forms of electronic media.

Individuals keep personal records of their activities and relationships with other individuals and organizations. They comprise personal financial records, legal records, our records as consumers, as citizens, as the beneficiaries of public service and taxpayers. Birth, death and marriage certificates, passports, visas, statements of educational qualifications, plans, titles, wills, deeds and employment histories document our status, property rights and other entitlements. Letters, records relating to our membership of clubs and societies, diaries, photographs, home videos, postcards, invitations and the like express our social and community involvement.

Most records are discarded. Some are kept for longer periods. All capture our experiences, support our memories, and for each individual they form the history of a life.

ORGANIZATIONAL RECORDS

Organizations of all kinds — governments, businesses, churches, societies — keep records of their interaction within the business world. Financial records, employment records, share registers, policy and precedent files, the agenda, minutes and papers of decision-making processes, drafts and internal memoranda, annual reports, taxation returns, project or research and development files, maps, plans and contracts all document an organization's legal and financial obligations and entitlements as an employer, provider or receiver of goods and services, debtor or creditor and owner of property. Such material documents processes showing how transactions are performed; they also encapsulate administrative activities and account for the actions of the organization. Organizational records may be of short- or long-term value to the entity that created them. Those of continuing worth form the organization's archives.

THE CHARACTERISTIC OF ARCHIVES

Records are the informational products of social and organizational activity. They are defined by their creation in the context of this activity, of human interaction. Key attributes of records of social and organizational functioning are their links to their creator, the activity itself and other records accumulated as part of the undertaking. Usually they are unpublished. Records are most likely to be part of an accumulation of documentation, although they may also be discrete items. As well as their relevance to the people and organizations that produced them, records of social and organizational activity may be of lasting importance to the wider community, to other people and organizations or for broader social purposes.

ARCHIVES IN CONTEXT

Together with other records of social and organizational ventures, archives are part of the wider cultural world. This includes oral tradition, the natural and built environments, natural objects, artefacts and works of art. The distinction between records of activity (as administered by archivists) and information products (as administered by librarians) is not always absolutely clear-cut. Literary manuscripts, that is outlines of notes and drafts of published works on paper or word-processing files accumulated by an author in the course of producing a novel, may be considered records of activity and evidence of the author's business or work. Copies of the published work, on the other hand, are information

products, consciously created and designed for the public. A similar distinction can be made between unedited film and the commercial product of a television broadcast. Alternately, records of activity may be incorporated into an information product, such as through the publication of a diary, personal correspondence or selected records of a government or business enterprise, or the inclusion of a home video in a television broadcast.

Archives relating to manufacture and construction projects, their use and associated people and events, may contribute to our understanding of artefacts or the built environment. Similarly, interpretation of the evidence provided by archives may be enhanced or modified by the consideration of the built environment or artefacts. Oral history programmes or projects aiming to record oral tradition are often supported by extensive research into other sources and in turn add another dimension to the interpretation of the archival record. The user gains understanding from different types of evidence in a variety of different ways, intellectually, experientially and through sensory perception. In some countries, for instance Canada and Australia, service providers such as archivists, librarians and museum curators have encouraged users to examine sources in a dynamic interdisciplinary fashion to study past activity and its current relevance. The results demonstrate how much richer our understanding can be if the user is encouraged to draw on all available forms of evidence and explore their interrelationships. Combining sources together in this way is not yet the general practice in this part of the world; nonetheless the development of strong communication links across professional boundaries may encourage a more productive research landscape.

THE PRINCIPLES OF ARCHIVAL WORK

The meaning or value of archives derive from the social and organizational context in which they were created and used and from their links with other records. Used or interpreted out of context, their significance is lost or compromised. Therefore, to provide for their continuing value, archivists ideally manage archives from their creation onwards in a manner which helps to preserve their worth and meaning and ensures their long-term physical survival.

Sir Hilary Jenkinson identified the moral and physical defence of the archives as being the archivist's primary duty. By moral defence Jenkinson means that archives must be cared for in a way that safeguards their authenticity and preserves their context and links to other records. This ensures their value as primary sources, their capacity to fulfil and give expression to the administrative, legal and social roles defined above. By physical defence he meant the physical care and security required for sustained preservation. In their moral defence of archives, early archivists established two interconnected principles which continue to guide the management of archives today. They emphasize particularly the processes which document the records and their context and the development of systems for their physical and intellectual control, including their arrangement and description, storage and preservation. These measures have in turn had a significant influence on archival finding aids and guides.

The two principles are those of provenance and original order. The principle of provenance is closely associated with the notion of *respect des fonds*, respecting the integrity of the whole body of records of continuing value associated with an organization or individual. It therefore relates to the preservation of the context of the records, that is their links to purpose, function and activity, to the individual or section within the organization that produced them, and to other records created by that individual or within that organization. Historically *respect des fonds* and adherence to the provenance principle were achieved by keeping the body of records of continuing value physically together following transfer to archival custody. In some cases the application of the principle of provenance resulted in the records of an organization being kept physically in ways which reflected organizational structures and record-keeping practices. In modern systems the setting of the records is often preserved on paper or intellectually by describing the archives, their administrative and organizational context-related purposes, functions and activities as well as record-keeping processes and the inter-relationships between records.

The principle of original order involves keeping records in the sequence in which they were accumulated as they were created, maintained or used, and not rearranging them according to some imposed order or classification scheme. Such rearrangement may suit the needs of one group of users but not another. It may compromise the integrity of the records and destroy the evidence provided by their original arrangement and relationship to one another. Keeping records in their original order also facilitates access using their own indexes and registers. Determining original order is not always straightforward. Some may never have been kept in a systematic way, they may have been rearranged as changes occurred in organizational structures or the way an organization does business. What stage in the creation, accumulation, rearrangement and use of records should then be captured in the archival arrangement? This question is increasingly being resolved by using the last active order or the order in which the records were found as the basis for arranging records, and then describing all other stages in guides and finding aids.

The guiding principles for archival work can be contrasted with those which inform the work of librarians. As they have dealt mainly with consciously created information products, librarians have developed collection-building techniques based on knowledge of subject specializations, bibliographic and reference tools suited to the discrete items which they manage. Archivists have developed different approaches centred on the relationship between an activity and its record. Provenance-based archival systems of arrangement and description preserve context and relationships because they are essential to the integrity and research value of the archives. In 1948, Jenkinson described the archivist's career as

... one of service. He exists in order to make other people's work possible, unknown people for the most part and working very possibly upon lines equally unknown: some of them perhaps in some quite distant future and upon lines as yet unpredictable. His Creed, the Sanctity of Evidence; his Task, the conservation of every scrap of Evidence attaching to Documents committed to his care; his Aim, to provide, without prejudice or afterthought, for all who wish to know, the Means of Knowledge.

These sentiments, old-fashioned though they may sound, nonetheless capture the spirit of what was then a relatively new profession.

THE WORK OF THE ARCHIVIST

Archivists are professionally qualified specialists responsible for the management and administration of archives and/or records. They do so by appraising and identifying records of continuing value, by documenting and preserving archives in their context and by enabling and facilitating their continuing use. The work of the archivist is not limited to older documents. Record and information management also involves the archivist in decision-making about the disposition of modern records, the extent to which information should be maintained in an electronic format and about those systems which integrate textual and electronic data. The purpose of these procedures is to manage information appropriately and to achieve greater economy and efficiency in administration. They also ensure the more effective identification of potential archives. The work of the archivist, therefore, often entails close co-operation with and integration into modern administration — public, private and commercial.

The electronic age brings distinctive new challenges and opportunities for archivists. In the paper environment, information provided by the content of records, their form and structure, their links to other records and their context is physically present in the records themselves or in their association with other records. This is not the case with electronic systems. For example, in electronic mail systems, the form and structure of a document and its links to other documents are not physically present, but result from software applications. One of the greatest challenges for archival professionals is to capture and preserve information content and contextual information of continuing value in electronic systems and provide for long-term accessibility to and usability of these sources.

THE CARE OF ARCHIVES

The responsibility assumed by the custodians of archival material is considerable. In taking charge of archives, custodians accept long-term legal and moral obligations to the material, its donors/owners, the creating agency and the research community. Archives by their very nature have a value and currency far beyond the lifetime of those interested in them. The collection and care of archives needs to be undertaken in a responsible, responsive, thoughtful and committed way, and certain basic guidelines in this regard will be examined here. Overriding the latter consideration must be a further guarantee that the physical and intellectual custody of the material will be safeguarded by the employment of relevant specialists such as archivists and conservators.

Administering, collecting and maintaining archives costs money; it is not an enterprise that can be entered into lightly. If there are no sources of assured income, the venture should not proceed. Neither the material nor its users are well served by archival facilities that are established on a flimsy financial basis. Almost inevitably they will close because monetary support dwindles or is withdrawn, leaving the collections unusable and/or vulnerable to dismemberment or loss. None of these results is desirable. Similarly, personal enthusiasm, although commendable, obviously cannot sustain an archival service in perpetuity.

ACQUISITION

Acquisition is the process by which archival institutions add to their holdings by accepting material as a donation, transfer, loan or purchase. All acquisitions of archival material must be governed by the wishes of both the donor/creator/depositor and the archival service, as expressed in a legal deposit agreement. Deposit agreements protect the interests of both the depositor and owner and those of the archives. The conditions expressed in such agreements must always be fulfilled. Acquisition is a crucial activity in the development of an archival collection. It should be carefully documented, not only to provide the archival institution with directions for present activity but also to provide guidance for future generations of archivists to assess the evolution of the collection. The process of acquisition is not static but continuing. Review of the type of material accepted by institutions is become increasingly important, especially as archives must justify their expenditure and holdings.

PHYSICAL PRESERVATION

In general, the priorities for the physical care of archival material demands that there are facilities which ensure:

- a suitable and stable environment;

- that the environment is secure and safe;

- that there is adequate space to store material;

- that space is available for administrative work.

The preservation of archives demands their physical protection. The building in which archives are kept must be secure from the dangers of fire, flooding, environmental damage and unauthorized access. It must contain dedicated areas for the storage of archives and suitable facilities for the conduct of professional functions. Security within an archives facility is a major factor. Because archives are unique materials, they require more stringent protection than individual published items, which can normally be replaced if lost or damaged. Thus the use of archival records must be confined to the archives itself. It is not acceptable practice to allow material to leave the building for purposes other than conservation or exhibition. When they are made available for use, the archivist must ensure that the archives are not physically damaged or abused. Areas where archives are stored should be locked and records in use supervised to avoid loss or damage. Access to the storage area must be limited to staff only. A record should be made when each item of material is taken form the shelves for use by researchers or for processing or conservation work. Facilities must be provided in which fragile documents can be strengthened and repaired, and the process of deterioration and decay reversed. Ideally, there should be a supervised place where all persons entering and leaving the archives, be they staff, researchers or tradespeople, register their presence. All keys to storage areas should be surrender to security staff at night. After-hours patrols and alarm systems are necessary.

The general environment within the archives is also important. The physical protection of records demands a stable, cool and clean environment. Proper containers, storage equipment and handling procedures are vital, and every care must be taken to control levels and changes in temperature and humidity. A number of hazards must be avoided and minimized throughout the archives facility, but particularly in the storage area where the archives spend most of their time. It is not possible to set out at length here the physical requirements for the storage of archival materials, but general indicators are outlined in **Table 31.1**. However, it is important to emphasize that the physical demands of

Table 31.1 Recommended Archival Storage Conditions

MATERIAL	TEMPERATURE (C)	RELATIVE HUMIDITY	STORAGE
Paper	20º	55%	Acid-free folders and boxes on baked enamel coated steel shelving.
Animal skin	10–200º	45–55%	As above.
Photographs (general)	20º	35–40%	Store individually in chemically inert mylar envelopes.
Photographs (colour)	-180º	25–30%	Refrigerate and store individually in moisture-proof inert plastic envelopes.
Microfilm	20º	< 40%	Shelve vertically in acid-free boxes in purpose-built cabinets.
Nitrate film	< 100º	30–40%	Store in purpose-built vaults. *Highly dangerous. This medium can self-combust.*
Disks, including CDs, floppy disks, etc.	18º	35–40%	Shelve vertically in dustproof envelopes.

archival materials require day-to-day preventative conservation procedures. In many instances individual items need the skills of specially trained conservators.

Furthermore, the archivist must try to minimize the potential damage caused to archives by a major disaster. If a disaster does occur, the archives service should be in a position to implement a comprehensive recovery plan.

INTELLECTUAL PROTECTION OF ARCHIVES

The availability of archival collections necessitates the careful description and arrangement of each collection and the production of a range of finding aids. Finding aids help researchers to locate those archives that are relevant to their interests and to assist them in assessing their evidential value. The archivist must balance accessibility, however desirable, with the protection of the depositor and the creator of the archives. Not all archives are automatically made available for research if their content is sensitive, confidential or potentially embarrassing to an individual or to that person's family, as noted again in the next section.

The description and arrangement of archives are interdependent activities forming part of the overall processing of archival collections. This activity, processing, is supported by the basic archival tenet of provenance and original order. Unlike books, which are usually individual items, archives draw their meaning from their context, as observed earlier. They are organic products of continuing work or life activities, and can only be fully understood through knowledge of why and

how they are created and used. Each archival collection is different and the amount of arrangement and description that is necessary will vary. In processing archival holdings the archivist discovers much about the creation of the material and the relationships between its various parts. Users cannot be expected to be able to examine the whole collection to determine how and why individual sections were created and what function each part records. This information is vital if the records are to be fully understood.

The arrangement and description of archives produce descriptions of records set out according to provenance. Findings aids, the bridge which leads researchers to archival material, present these data in a variety of ways, supplementing them with additional information and indexes to help users locate records. Physically, the system of finding aids for an archival institution can consist of a variety of formats, including printed publications, optical disks, microfilms, card indexes, computer databases and so forth. If finding aids are effective, they assist in the preservation of material by reducing the handling of archives needed to locate information. Finding aids are important tools to ensure the secure protection of collections when in use. It is unacceptable to make collections of archival material available unless they have been fully processed and recorded in the form of suitable finding aids.

ACCESS

The fundamental reason for keeping archives is to enable

them to be used. To this end, each archival service must design policies and procedures which cater for research, while at the same time ensuring the physical protection of the records it holds. The access policy should be clearly explained and properly regulated. To design an access policy to suit the needs of the organization, one must consider a range of factors, some of which will be more significant than others depending on the context in which the archive is operating. Archives whose access provisions are laid down by statute may need to develop specific procedures to support the general principles in the legislation. Others need to draft policies in which the following points are addressed:

- sensitivity or confidentiality of records;

- protection of individual privacy;

- restrictions placed on records by depositors;

- clientele;

- equality of access to records;

- levels of access;

- physical condition of the records;

- security of records;

- fees.

Administering access to records demands the completion of access forms by each individual user. These record basic details about the user and his or her research interest. It provides the information relating to the institutional policy regarding conditions for access, including the rules for use of the research room. It is useful to give information in this form about citation practices, copyright and reproduction of records. The administration of the research room is significant in preserving the overall security of the records. **Table 31.2** outlines suggested regulations for use in a research room.

EMERGENCY CARE

The care of archival material demands the skills of specially qualified archivists and conservators. However, situations arise where individuals find that they are given responsibility for archival collections without the help of specialist staff. In all circumstances it is advisable that the archival collections are transferred to a suitable repository equipped with the facilities and personnel to administer the material responsibly. In the short term institutions or individuals can seek advice from

---

Table 31.2 Recommended Guidelines for Reading Room Supervision

(1) Researchers may use the search room only after they have completed the access application form and the archivist has authorized the form.

(2) Access to records is governed by the archive's access policy, and the material is issued to researchers subject to any specific conditions relating to individual collections.

(3) No bags, brief-cases or coats are allowed in the research room.

(4) No smoking, eating or drinking is permitted in the research room.

(5) Pencils only are to be used for writing. Biros, fountain pens, felt-tip and other pens and correction fluid are not permitted in the research room as they contain substances which can cause serious damage to records.

(6) Researchers must handle all records carefully and must not mark, fold, tear or otherwise harm the sources in any way. Any damage found in material issued should be reported immediately to staff.

(7) Researchers must not rearrange or interfere in any way with the order of archival material.

(8) Usually only one volume or folder at a time will be issued to each researcher.

(9) No archival material is to be removed from the research room by researchers.

(10) Researchers must respect research room conventions relating to courtesy and, where possible, silence. Equipment such as lap-top computers and tape recorders may be used only with the express permission of the archivist.

---

consultant archivists and thus take the best steps to guarantee the proper care of the material. In the interim the following actions are appropriate.

It is important to remember that archives by definition are unique; they are also probably very fragile and usually contain the seed of their own physical destruction. For all these reasons, great care must be taken when handling records. Always clean your hands before beginning any work that requires you to touch records. Keep work surfaces clean and do not handle records more than is necessary. It is advisable to wear cotton gloves at all times. When physically transferring records from one place to another, all material should be boxed. A simple box list that records the contents of each box, including an exact number of items and covering dates, should be composed. Each box should be clearly numbered and labelled. Very simple conservation measures such as removing pins, clips, staples and other metal fasteners from the records can be undertaken. However, measures should be taken to indicate the fact that certain items were previously fastened or pinned together, for instance by placing these items in folders. Anything more complicated should not be attempted. Do not attempt to place an order or sequence on the records. It is essential that no effort is made to sort or re-organize the material, as valuable evidence inherent in the undisturbed order may be destroyed. Do not write on any record; a simple record of the contents of each folder can be written in pencil outside each folder. Do not attempt to repair any item and do not use sellotape or any paste or adhesive on the archives as this action can permanently damage the records. Store the records in a safe secure clean area that is free from dampness and potential threat of fire, flood or intrusion, until the advice of a professional archivist is available.

ARCHIVISTS IN IRELAND

Having examined the general background, this chapter now concentrates on archival work in this country. It examines a number of key issues and concludes with an overview of possible future developments.

TRAINING

Most professional archivists working in Ireland are graduates of the University College, Dublin, postgraduate diploma course in archival studies. The objectives of the course as defined by the course director are to provide professional training

• for those who wish to work as archivists in archives services and in other institutions which require professional expertise in the administration of their records;

• for archivists who will be able to contribute to the expansion of the profession in Ireland by establishing and managing new archival posts;

• for archivists who will have high professional standards and who will respect the integrity of archives;

• which balances and integrates both theoretical and practical elements in the course syllabus;

• which results both in a professional qualification and in an educated approach to archives;

• which will ensure that the future of Irish archives is broadly based and not restricted by any narrow archival perspective or tradition.

The syllabus is divided into three sections. The core section is entitled 'Archival science and the management of the archives service'. The two ancillary sections are entitled 'Ancillary sciences' and 'History, administration and sources'. The purpose of the core element is to provide professional expertise in all matters relating to archives, to the management of the archives service and to the work of the archivist. It includes the following subject areas:

Fundamentals of archival science: the basic principles of archival science; analysis of definitions of archives; implications and use of terminology.

Fundamentals of the archives service: its objectives and role in society and in the modern state; the identity and work of the professional archivist; the nature and prioritization of professional functions; establishment and constitution of the archives service.

Introduction to the career of archivist: career opportunities; contract and consultancy work; professional development and information sources.

Management techniques and professional standards: basic management techniques; policy and planning; corporate plans and annual reports; sources of finance and budget administration; staff recruitment and deployment; in-service training and professional development; professional standards and codes of practice; public relations and marketing.

Law and legal issues: analysis of the requirements and objective of archives legislation; current archives legislation in Ireland and the UK; nature and implications of laws dealing with copyright, data protection and privacy, export control, tax concessions for archives, freedom of information and company records; legal problems encountered by archivists; admissibility of evidence.

Acquisition and appraisal of archives: methods of acquisition; nature of surveys and fieldwork; collection reception, accessioning and coding; deaccessioning; nature of deposited collections; deposit implications, incentives and procedures; deposit agreements; services to depositors; appraisal objectives; techniques, procedures and criteria; appraisal of specific types of records; nature of bureaucracy; reappraisal.

Architecture: design objectives and siting of archival repositories; external features and construction; internal features; storage, professional, technical and public facilities and their interface; electrical, engineering and technical services; standards; fire detection and extinction; contemporary trends in European archives architecture; design objectives and siting of records centres; records centre features and construction; conversion of non-purpose built buildings for archives.

Non-written archives: acquisition, administration, processing, preservation and use of cartographic, photographic, sound and film archives.

Archival history and practice: history and development of archival practice to the present day; archival practice in Ireland, United Kingdom, France, Germany, United States, Canada, Australia; archives in the European Commission and European Union; international archives organizations and issues; archives in relation to museums and libraries.

Processing of archives and finding aid production: finding aid network; method of descriptive list production and the structure, format and nature of descriptive entries; description standards; arrangement principles and collection characteristics; collection structure, identity and arrangement and coding; structure, format and nature of descriptive entries in the guide, general index and small collections' index; specialized description of maps, photographs, sound recordings and other non-written archives; other finding aids; description of literary papers, legal documents and other archives; reference sources.

Preservation and conservation preservation: practices, responsibilities and policies; physical composition and storage requirements of archives; deterioration causes; administration, control and design of dedicated storage areas; movement and handling of archives; preservation resource implications; damage treatment, conservation techniques and documents repair; disaster prevention strategies and recovery techniques.

Information technology and computer applications: microfilm technology, systems and uses, electronic information management systems; integrated microimaging systems; computer applications in archives services and in records centres.

The auxiliary sciences are as follows:

Diplomatics: development of science; medieval chanceries; genesis of public documents and their characteristics; analysis of public and private documents; diplomatics of contemporary documents; contemporary forgeries; sigillography; chronology.

Palaeography: origins of handwriting and emergence of the alphabet; writing surfaces and inks; abbreviations;

scribal conventions and expedients; handwriting in Roman antiquity; medieval hands; Carolingian miniscule; hands of the later Middle Ages; early Irish manuscripts and palaeography; abbreviations and other scribal conventions; English handwriting after 1550; the hands and conventions of public and private documents in the English language, in Ireland and England; reading classes in secretary, italic and mixed hands.

Administrative, legal and constitutional history: administrative legal and constitutional history before the Act of Union and during the nineteenth and twentieth centuries; British constitution; Irish constitution before and after 1800; the constitutional position in Ireland in the period form 1920–1922; the constitution of 1937 and the *Republic of Ireland Act* 1949; judicial review; the courts and constitution since 1937; constitutional amendments since 1937; legal administration before and after 1877; judicature acts and nineteenth-century reforms of the judicial system; nineteenth-century Irish administration; Dublin Castle and the Chief Secretary; the Grand Jury system; Poor Law administration and the *Local Government Act* 1898; the police; the structure and basis of administration since 1922; sources for research in Ireland.

Information technology: introduction to computers: an overview of the range of processes and equipment which enable information to be stored, retrieved, organized, communicated and used; basic theory of computer representation of data, of hardware and software, and of data communication; human, social and ethical issues associated with computerization; microcomputers — hardware and software: the evaluation of software and hardware for the organization of information on microcomputers and larger computer facilities; the theory underlying the practical software implementation of database management systems, full text retrieval, expert systems, spreadsheets and integrated software packages.

Records management and services to administration: theory of records management; administrative procedures and structures; establishment of records management programmes; surveys; management of current records and standard filing systems; document management and control; administration of records centres and records centre services; schedules and other methods of dispositions; vital records protection; electronic information management; micrographics in administration; corporate archives services; record management systems.

User services: administration of researcher services and the research facilities; admission procedures and implications; reprographic services; research methods and

Table 31.3 Employment of Archivists Working in Ireland, including Northern Ireland

	PERMANENT EMPLOYEES	CONTRACT EMPLOYEES
Banks, Insurance Companies and Private Business		2
Broadcasting		3
Private Consultancy Firms	9	
Hospitals		1
Libraries	2	4
Local Authorities	5	14
National Archives	9	4 (one vacant)
Private Archives		1
Public Record Office of Northern Ireland	9	5
Second-level Schools		1
Religious Bodies	3	3
State Services (Garda, Army)	2	
Theatre and Film		2
Universities	9	5
Totals	48	45

Source: *Society of Archivists' membership list (May 2000)*

techniques; user education; production of guides calendars catalogues and other publications. Administration of services to the non-researching public; exhibition organization and display techniques; educational services; outreach.

EMPLOYMENT

Irish employment patterns as summarized in **Table 31.3** indicate that most archival work concentrates on central government and official archival collections. Geographically, most archival activity is centred in Dublin, as is indicated in **Table 31.4**. Within a European context this dearth of archival services available to the public places Ireland at the very end of the scale. In fact many of the developing eastern European states have a more comprehensive national archival network.

Only archival services based in the universities and National Library of Ireland can cater for unofficial or private collections. Accordingly, there is an urgent requirement to develop these existing services and establish new services to cater for the unofficial records. Little is known about the extent of private paper collections — many remain unidentified, unprotected and physically disintegrating at a rapid rate. Their possible loss to Irish heritage cannot be underestimated.

Given the potential richness of these collections, their care is a great worry to the archival and research communities. The network of local libraries has been invaluable in the protection of some private paper collections, but libraries have already limited resources

and a very different role to that of an archival repository. Moreover, libraries may not necessarily have the skills to deal with archival material. Already a considerable amount of our Irish archival heritage has been irretrievably lost. Many significant private archives have left the country for safe homes in American universities, British repositories or the Public Record Office of Northern Ireland where there is a guarantee of permanent care. It is universally accepted that archival material is best preserved within the context of the locality from which it came. Its intellectual worth is of greater significance and importance to that community. It is sad that the some owners of valuable private collections have, in the past, been forced to deposit their material outside the state because of the absence of suitable local repositories.

LEGISLATIVE DEVELOPMENTS

The *Public Record Act* 1867, the first Irish archival legal instrument, established the Public Record Office as the repository for official records, the other main government repository being the State Paper Office. The *Public Record Act* was extremely effective in the context of colonial administration. However, its provisions did not account for changes brought about by the creation of the new state early in the twentieth century. Coupled with this, innovations in modern administrative, legal and political practices during the last century rendered the 1867 act totally unsuitable for modern requirements. Until the passing of the *National Archives Act* 1986 and

Table 31.4 Places of Employment of Archivists Working in Ireland, including Northern Ireland

	PERMANENT EMPLOYEES	TEMPORARY EMPLOYEES
Belfast	9	8
Clare		1
Cork(City)	3	2
Derry (City)		1
Donegal		1
Dublin City and Counties	36	23
Galway		2
Mid-East Region (Counties Kildare, Wicklow and Meath)		1
Midland Region (Counties Laois, Offaly, Longford and Westmeath)		1
Limerick (City Council)		1
Louth		1
Mayo		1
Waterford (City)		1
Waterford County		1
Totals	48	45

Source: *Society of Archivists' membership list (May 2000)*

the establishment of the National Archives, legal provisions for the preservation of the public records and their accessibility to the wider community did not in any way meet required needs.

The excellent services provided in Northern Ireland have their origins in the *Public Records Act (Northern Ireland) 1923*. This act defines the role of the Public Record Office of Northern Ireland (PRONI) as being that of the agency responsible for identifying and preserving 'certain public records pertaining to Northern Ireland' and for preserving 'any [privately owned] deeds or documents ... deposited in the Public Record Office of Northern Ireland'. The act, and the absence of any subsequent provision for county or local record offices in Northern Ireland, places on PRONI the unique threefold responsibility of being a public record office preserving official papers, the equivalent of an archival agency which acquires private paper collections, and the British equivalent of a county record office for the six counties.

The development of services to protect local authority records in the Republic was initiated by legislation passed in 1994. The *Local Government Act 1994* demands that local authorities preserve their records and expresses the belief that these records should be accessible for public inspection. When introducing the measure the then Minister of the Environment, Mr Michael Smith, T.D., stated:

There must be a priceless heritage of archival material throughout the country, deriving from the archives of our local authorities and the bodies that preceded them. In the absence of any formal statutory provision and with out a co-ordinated programme for the development of local archive services much of this material could be lost or destroyed. A network of fully fledged local archival institutions cannot be developed overnight, but we can not afford to delay in taking the basic steps. Five years from now, in April 1999, our county councils will be 100 years old. What better way could the councils mark the centenary than by resolving now to put in place a phased programme for recording, preserving and making available for inspection the records of their own activities over the years? (Dáil Éireann, 14 April 1994)

The minister went on to outline why he had included a separate section for archives as follows:

It is not appropriate that we should rely any longer on the local librarian or local history society to see to the collection, safeguarding and presentation to the public of local records and archival material. It requires the skills of professional archivists. That is the reason section 67 of the bill contains a new provision relating to the keeping of records and archives, modelled on the law applying to the National Archives ... (*ibid.*)

Local authorities are increasingly responding to the act

and many new archival posts have been created. It seems though they wish to preserve their archives within the geographical boundaries of the county. It is interesting to note that many authorities did not respond to the Department of the Environment offer (in 1997) of monies to help support the establishment of regional archives services.

CONCLUSION

It cannot be denied that Ireland has a remarkable wealth of extant archival material throughout the country. Poignantly, much of that material remains unknown and uncared for despite the many advances in the Irish archival world in recent decades. It is unfortunate that Irish archival tradition, particularly in the early decades of the twentieth century, did not mirror European practice. The established European emphasis on the cultural and historical role of archives, dating from the eighteenth century, largely by-passed our new state.

Undoubtedly, culture, in the broad sense, has been hugely important in twentieth-century Ireland. For many decades emphasis was placed on what was understood to be indigenous culture, such as the collection of oral history and traditions, the recognition of the importance of traditional music, dance, sports, literature, painting, sculpture and artefacts. Their attractions in the search for the definition of an Irish cultural identity greatly overshadowed any steps for professionally preserving archival records. Moreover, the absence of adequate provision for the training of professional archivists until 1972, when the training course at the Archives Department, University College, Dublin, was established, was a subtle statement that the skills of such professionals were deemed largely irrelevant to Irish needs and circumstances.

Many of the positions available for archivists in Ireland are new ones. Irish archivists are, therefore, individually given a responsibility to establish standards of professional service and conduct. Furthermore, many archivists work alone within the institutions to which they are attached, frequently in professional and geographical isolation. Archivists in Ireland must be willing and equipped to make almost all their working decisions alone without the support or stimulation of colleagues. This isolation is forcing archivists to negotiate their role and definition and that of archival services in the future framework of Irish cultural services. It demands that archivists must become more closely associated with the professional cultural community and are not seen as being apart. It is hoped that the inclusion of archives and archivists will transform the Irish cultural landscape in the new millennium.

Bibliography

Enwere, J. C. 1992 'Archival Europe and the archival world', *Janus* 2, pp. 327–335.
Society of Archivists, Irish Region 1997 *Standards for the development of archives service in Ireland*. Dublin.
Helferty, S. and Refaussé, R. (eds) 1999 *A directory of Irish archives*. Dublin
Department of the Environment 1996 *Guidelines for local authority archives services* (unpublished report). Dublin.
Pederson, A. 1997 *Keeping archives*. Sydney.

The National Archives

DAVID V. CRAIG AND AIDEEN M. IRELAND

The chapter begins by outlining the historical background to the National Archives and the legislation governing its operations. This is followed by an account of its premises, management and staff. The statutory functions and archival holdings of the National Archives are then summarized, and this is succeeded by a discussion of the services provided to the public. We conclude with a brief description of arrangements for the preservation of the archives of the Defence Forces and local authorities. A select bibliography is appended.

The National Archives is the largest and most important institution in the Republic of Ireland with responsibility for the preservation and public availability of archives. However, this responsibility is shared with the Military Archives, the Manuscripts Department of the National Library of Ireland, university archives and manuscripts departments, local authority archives services and many other cultural and academic bodies. There are now various city- or county-based local authority archival services like the Cork Archives Institute which caters for Cork city and county, Dublin City Archives, Fingal County Council Archives covering north Dublin, Limerick Regional Archives for Limerick city and county, and Waterford City Archives. The number of such services is likely to increase significantly over the next few years, with archivists currently employed on short-term contracts in various regions and counties. The archival profession in Ireland remains small, but it is growing steadily in both size and influence.

HISTORICAL BACKGROUND AND LEGISLATION

The National Archives was created in 1988 through the amalgamation of the State Paper Office and the Public Record Office of Ireland. The Public Record Office was by far the larger of the two offices, and from the late nineteenth century the State Paper Office was, in effect, a sub-office of the Public Record Office. The State Paper Office was established in 1702 as a repository for the records of the Secretary to the Lord Lieutenant (later known as the Chief Secretary). Until that date, records had been removed to England on the completion of the term of office of the Secretary, and the absence of papers from the previous administration had made the governance of Ireland unnecessarily difficult. After 1922, the State Paper Office also became the repository for the records of the Department of the Taoiseach. From the beginning of the nineteenth century until 1990, the State Paper Office, along with the state papers, was situated in a medieval tower in Dublin Castle.

The Public Record Office of Ireland was established in 1867 to house records of the courts which were over twenty years old, records transferred from the State Paper Office and the records of all defunct commissions and bodies. Later, the office also became responsible for the parochial records of the former Established Church. The office was located at the Four Courts complex, Dublin, primarily in order to facilitate legal research. In April 1922, the Four Courts complex was seized and occupied by anti-Treaty forces. Mines were laid in the Public Record Office, and following bombardment by pro-Treaty forces at the beginning of the Civil War, a fire started which resulted in a major explosion on 30 June 1922. The record repository and almost all the records stored in it were destroyed.

Later in the 1920s, the record repository of the Public Record Office was rebuilt and the Irish Manuscripts Commission was established. During the 1920s and 1930s, both the Record Office and the Commission made attempts to identify replacements for records which had been destroyed. In the 1940s, the Commission established a Survey of Manuscripts in Private Custody, which subsequently became the responsibility of the National Library of Ireland. The National Library commenced a major programme of surveying records of Irish interest held in other countries, and the Public Record Office began accessioning records of government departments and offices. In the 1960s, access to records in the State Paper Office was liberalized, and the records of Dáil Éireann for the period 1919-22 were released to public inspection. Nevertheless, it was not until the 1970s that archives in the Republic of Ireland began to escape from the shadow of 1922.

In 1970, the Public Record Office and State Paper Office recruited professional staff for the first time since 1945. The staff numbers employed in the Public Record Office and State Paper Office doubled over the years 1973–76, and the release of government minutes and associated files on the basis of an informal thirty-year rule began in 1976. Other significant developments in the same decade included:

(a) the establishment in 1970 of the Cork Archives Council (later renamed the Cork Archives Institute) as the first of Ireland's new local authority archives services;

(b) the establishment in 1970 of the Business Records Survey by the Irish Manuscripts Commission (the Business Records Survey is now a responsibility of the National Archives);

(c) the introduction in 1972 of formal training for professional archivists in the Archives Department of University College, Dublin (which had been established in 1970);

(d) the setting up, in November 1970, of the Irish Society for Archives as a forum bringing together archivists and other people with an interest in archives (the Society also publishes the journal *Irish Archives*);

e) the establishment, in May 1979, of the Irish Region of the Society of Archivists (the professional association for archivists working in Britain and Ireland).

There was no legislation governing the establishment and operation of the State Paper Office. The Public Record Office was established by *The Public Records (Ireland) Act* 1867 which was subsequently amended by the *Public Records (Ireland) Act* 1867, *Amendment Act* 1875 and the *Parochial Records Act* 1876. This legislation remained in force after 1922. However, it was silent on the subject of the growing mass of records held by government departments and offices.

Proposals for new legislation were made as early as the 1930s, but it was not until the 1970s that the matter received serious attention from the government, and it was not until the early 1980s that a decision was made to proceed with new legislation. As Taoiseach, Dr Garret FitzGerald took a strong personal interest in the drafting of the legislation, and piloted it through the Oireachtas

to its enactment as the *National Archives Act* 1986. The act provided for the amalgamation of the State Paper Office and the Public Record Office to form the new National Archives, and gave the National Archives new responsibilities with regard to departmental records (the records of government departments, the courts and other state bodies listed in the schedule to the act). Most sections of the act, including the section establishing the National Archives itself, came into operation in June 1988.

Section 65 of the *Local Government Act* 1994 provided statutory protection for records of local authorities and a legislative basis for local authority archives services. Section 92 of the *Harbours Act* 1996 did the same for the records of harbour authorities. The *Freedom of Information Act* 1997 gives the public a right of access to the current records of government departments and offices, health boards and local authorities, and gives individual members of the public a right of access to records relating to themselves, regardless of date (Mc Donagh 1998). Other relevant legislation comprises aspects of the *Data Protection Act* 1988, the *Statistics Act* 1993 and the *National Cultural Institutions Act* 1997.

PREMISES AND STAFF

For nearly two centuries the State Paper Office was housed in a medieval tower (the Record Tower) in Dublin Castle which had been enlarged, floored and shelved for the purposes of a repository. The building was inconvenient to use and the retrieval of documents stored at a high level was potentially dangerous. The building was also a fire hazard. Research facilities for the public were limited by space constraints. The Public Record Office was housed in a mid-nineteenth century purpose-built record repository in the Four Courts complex. Unfortunately, the Record Treasury (which housed all the records) was totally destroyed during the Civil War. It was rebuilt in the late 1920s, but with consequent loss of storage space. In the 1960s, the building of an extension to the Land Registry in the Four Courts complex deprived the Public Record Office of the space for expansion which had been left deliberately unused in the 1920s.

By the 1980s, the State Paper Office and the Public Record Office had long outgrown their allotted storage space. Even with the use of some storage space in the basement of the main Four Courts building and the acquisition, in 1988, of off-site storage in a former factory building, the problem of storage had become critical. With the coming into operation of the *National Archives Act* in 1988, it was decided that new premises must be found for the amalgamated State Paper Office and Public Record Office. Consequently, in 1989, the government assigned a large office and storage complex at Bishop Street in Dublin to the National Archives as its new

Fig. 32.1 Modern storage facilities in the National Archives' Bishop Street premises; static shelves in the strong-room.

headquarters. The fact that the building is close to the city centre ensures that it is easily accessible to researchers.

In January 1992, seventy years after the destruction of the Public Record Office, the new public Reading Room (**Fig 32.2**) on the fifth floor of the Bishop Street building was formally opened by the then Taoiseach, Charles J. Haughey. In July 1993, the Reading Room was dedicated to the memory of the late Mr Justice Niall McCarthy, the first Chairman of the National Archives Advisory Council, by the then President, Mrs Mary Robinson. The Reading Room has seating for 68 people, with extra seats for those consulting finding aids only; it contains microfiche and microfilm reader/printers and is wired for personal computers. Works of art from the state's collection adorn the walls. In 1992, the Reading Room was the Royal Institute of Architects of Ireland winner in the category of commissions over £200,000; the award was for 'an awkward space converted in a dignified and restrained manner with great feeling for materials and colour'.

The front block of the building at Bishop Street is eight floors high (including basement), but it is the much

larger warehouse to its rear which will make it big enough to meet the needs of the National Archives well into the twenty-first century. In December 1997, the Minister for Arts, Heritage, Gaeltacht and the Islands, Ms Síle de Valera, announced that the government had approved the expenditure of £13 million on the redevelopment and extension of the warehouse in accordance with international standards for the storage of archives. It is expected that this major building development will commence late in 2001 or early in the year 2002, and that the new building will be ready for occupation in late 2003 or early 2004.

At present, the collections of the State Paper Office, some of the records formerly held at the Public Record Office and most modern departmental records are stored in the Bishop Street premises, and can normally be produced to researchers in the Reading Room within 15 minutes. Court records and some other less frequently used records are still stored in the former Public Record Office building in the Four Courts, and are available for research in Bishop Street 24 hours after they are ordered by a researcher. Some records which are closed to public inspection or are infrequently used have had to be stored temporarily in the unadapted warehouse in a way which makes it impossible to produce them without lengthy delays. Following the adaptation of the warehouse at Bishop Street, the premises at the Four Courts will be totally vacated, the premises in Bishop Street will be the sole storage and research facility, and all records will normally be available on the day they are ordered.

The National Archives is headed by its Director who has statutory responsibility for its management. It is a separate agency within the civil service, and answers to the Department of Arts, Heritage, Gaeltacht and the Islands, having moved from the Department of the Taoiseach in 1993. Its annual budget for the year 1998, for example, was about £1.2 million, about half of which was spent on pay and other staff costs. The equivalent

Fig. 32.2 The new Reading Room at the Bishop Street headquarters of the National Archives, formally opened in 1992.

figure in 1993 was about £0.85 million. During the 1990s, the financial allocations made to the National Archives increased in real terms from year to year, but these increases did not include any provision for additional staff.

Under the *National Archives Act* 1986, a National Archives Advisory Council was established, consisting of 12 members. These are drawn mainly from the ranks of professional archivists, academics and administrators. The present Chairman is Dr Margaret MacCurtain, an eminent historian. Her predecessors were Mr Justice Niall McCarthy (1987–92) and Mr Justice Hugh O'Flaherty (1992–97).

The main function of the Council is to advise the Minister for Arts, Heritage, Gaeltacht and the Islands on matters of policy relating to the National Archives and, more generally, on the archives of public bodies in Ireland. The Council publishes an annual report on its activities and in 1996 it published *A future for our past: strategic plan for the National Archives, 1996–2001*. The present Council was appointed in June 1997 and is the third Council. The original Council (which, apart from its Chairman, retained the same membership for two five-year terms) was appointed in January 1987. The Council meets about six times a year.

The staff of the National Archives comprises thirty-five people, of whom four are employed on short-term contracts. In the professional archivist grades there are thirteen members of staff; the rest of the staff is made up of clerical staff and services officers. The Reading Room is staffed primarily by clerical officers, but archivists also devote a considerable amount of time to reader services.

In the *Strategic plan*, the National Archives Advisory Council reported that the level of staffing in the National Archives was seriously below that required and needed to be at least doubled. The priorities for additional staff include specialized posts in the conservation and information technology areas, the extra clerical posts needed to allow the Reading Room to be opened in the evening and/or at the weekend, and the additional archivists required both to tackle the backlogs of unlisted archival collections and to respond adequately to requests for authorization for the disposal of records which do not warrant permanent archival preservation.

STATUTORY FUNCTIONS AND ARCHIVAL HOLDINGS
The *National Archives Act* 1986 is primarily concerned with departmental records (the records of government departments, the courts, and the other state bodies listed in the schedule to the act). The main provisions of this act with regard to departmental records may be summarized as follows:

(a) All departmental records must be preserved, unless their destruction is authorized in writing by the Director of the National Archives or another officer of the National Archives designated by the Director for the purpose.

(b) In general, all departmental records which are more than 30 years old must be transferred to the National Archives to be made available for inspection by the public. Particular records may be retained by departments and/or be withheld from public inspection only if they are covered by certificates stating either:

(i) that they are in regular use by a department or are required in connection with its administration, or

(ii) that they should not be made available for public inspection on one of the grounds specified in the act.

The major achievement of the National Archives since 1988 has been the transfer and release to public inspection of enormous quantities of departmental records. Most records of government departments for the period 1922–69 are now held in the National Archives, although most records of the other bodies listed in the schedule to the act have yet to be transferred, due to lack of storage space.

Since the *National Archives Act* came into operation relatively little attention has been paid to the disposal of records. There is no doubt that many departments are having to preserve records which do not, in fact, merit permanent preservation simply because the National Archives does not have the staff time needed to examine them. Another major challenge for the National Archives is the preservation of records in electronic form. It may henceforth be assumed that most departmental records will be created and preserved electronically. The National Archives is working closely with the Department of Finance in seeking to address the problems arising from this development.

With regard to records other than departmental records, the *National Archives Act* enables the National Archives to give advice to state-sponsored bodies, local authorities and other public service organizations on records under their control, and to acquire records from them. It also provides that the Minister for Arts, Heritage, Gaeltacht and the Islands may, at the request of a public service organization which is not a local authority or harbour company, declare its records to be departmental records.

The National Archives also accessions records from private sources, for example records held by solicitors (partly in order to make up the losses of legal material suffered in 1922), business records and family and estate papers. Some of these categories of record are also accessioned by the National Library of Ireland, by the Manuscripts Department of Trinity College, Dublin, and by other university archives departments, so care is taken not to accession records which would more appropriately be accessioned by one of the latter.

In 1875, consequent on the disestablishment of the Church of Ireland in 1871 (which had been the state church up to that date), the Public Record Office of Ireland was also made responsible for its records of baptisms and burials up until 31 December 1870 and marriages up to 1 April 1845. Control of Church of Ireland records is now shared by the National Archives and the Representative Church Body Library.

The records acquired by the National Archives are referred to in the act as 'archives'. The statutory functions of the National Archives with regard to archival material in its custody include the following:

(a) the preservation, restoration, arrangement and description of archives;

(b) the preparation of guides, lists, indexes and other finding aids to archives;

(c) making archives available for public inspection;

(d) making and providing copies of archives;

(e) the publication of archives, finding aids and other material relating to archives, and

(f) the provision of education services relating to archives.

Due to shortage of staff, the National Archives has had to concentrate to date on those functions relating to archives which involve the direct provision of a service to the public. The lack of an in-house conservation workshop to carry out the repair of damaged archives is a major problem. However, in recent years, the National Archives has had very small quantities of archives repaired commercially and, more importantly, has made considerable progress in packing its holdings in archival quality boxes which minimize the risk of future damage. It has also recently initiated a programme of preservation microfilming, running in parallel with an existing programme of microfilming of genealogical sources by the Genealogical Society of Utah. The National Archives has also begun to address the huge challenge of listing archives which currently either cannot be made available to the public because they are unlisted, or are very difficult to use because of the inadequacy of the existing finding aids. Unfortunately, the scale of the problem is such that it will never be fully solved without a very large increase in resources.

Sadly, almost all the archives accessioned by the Public Record Office of Ireland before 1922 were destroyed in

June 1922. Consequently, the archives now held by the National Archives date mainly from the nineteenth and twentieth centuries, although some date back as far as the thirteenth century. They may be summarized as follows:

(a) archives of government departments relating mainly to the period 1922–69;

(b) archives of the Chief Secretary's Office and its associated offices for the period 1790–1922;

(c) archives of other state agencies operating mainly in the nineteenth and twentieth centuries, but including some archives from the seventeenth and eighteenth centuries;

(d) archives of the courts and probate registries dating mainly from the late nineteenth and twentieth centuries, but including a few items dating back to the fourteenth century;

(e) archives acquired from other sources, including Church of Ireland parishes, harbour boards, health boards, hospitals, schools, charities, trade unions, business firms, solicitors' offices, estate offices and private individuals, relating especially to the nineteenth and twentieth centuries, but including material for the seventeenth and eighteenth centuries, and

(f) transcripts, calendars, abstracts and indexes of archives dating from the thirteenth to the nineteenth centuries which were destroyed in 1922.

The most frequently used archives are those consulted principally by genealogists: the Census of Population returns for 1901 and 1911, the Tithe Applotment Books of the 1820s and 1830s, the Primary Valuation (Griffith's Valuation) of the 1840s–1860s, and wills and other testamentary records. The records most used by historians are now the files of the Department of the Taoiseach and the Department of Foreign Affairs for the period since 1919, while the Chief Secretary's Office Registered Papers for the period 1818–1922 are arguably the single most important body of source material for the history of Ireland in the nineteenth century. The National Archives holds the equivalent of about 210,000 boxes of archives. Each box has a capacity of about 0.67 cubic feet, so the holdings amount to about 140,000 cubic feet, or about 4,000 cubic metres.

SERVICES TO THE PUBLIC

The National Archives receives visits from an average of 80 readers per day, who read about 50,000 documents a year. First, in terms of numbers, come the genealogical researchers who carry out family research on a professional or personal basis, and other private researchers who carry out historical, local and other non-genealogical research. Next come the academic community who may be undergraduates, post-graduates or those in permanent positions who carry out a variety of historical and other academic work. Finally come those from the legal profession, who need access to certain classes of testamentary records and to other legal records for assistance in legal work. While research periods tend to peak at various times during the year, the summer months bring an influx of foreign visitors, most of whom are undertaking genealogical research.

The Reading Room in Bishop Street has seating for 71 researchers, but on very busy days this is not adequate to cater for all. A planned expansion of the Reading Room will increase the number of tables available to researchers and so cut down the queuing for seats which happens at busy periods. It is also hoped to improve the system for ordering photocopies, so that copies may be made available to researchers on a same-day basis for small orders, and to cut down the delay in producing larger orders. Readers will also be encouraged to make greater use of the reader/printer microform machines and so be able to generate on-the-spot copies for themselves.

At present, the Reading Room is open only from 10 a.m. to 5 p.m., Monday to Friday, although it is hoped that it will prove possible to open it on at least one evening a week and/or on Saturdays. In order to maximize the time available to researchers and to reduce the unnecessary use of staff time, it is intended that visitors will soon be able to help themselves with self-service microfilms as is the practice in other research institutions. It is also intended to increase the number of computer terminals available in the Reading Room so that eventually researchers will have access to most finding aids in computerized form.

In order to facilitate research and advance planning for visits, especially by those based abroad, the National Archives maintains, and updates regularly, a site on the world-wide web. The address is *http://www.nationalarchives.ie*. This has proved to be enormously popular. The *Draft short guide to the National Archives* will soon be added to the site, and in the longer term it is intended to add most finding aids to the site.

At present, although some finding aids can be accessed on the world-wide web, access to records held in the National Archives is by manual means only. Very few of the finding aids to record classes have been computerized. However, a database of those sentenced to transportation to Australia for the period 1788–1868 is available on a designated terminal in the Reading Room, and this will shortly be augmented by making available in the Reading Room the recently created databases concerning the Famine Relief Commission in the period 1845–47 and penal servitude in the period 1881–1922. (These databases are already available on the National Archives website.)

The National Archives is developing a publication policy, but constraints put on professional staff time mean that very little has been published in recent decades. This deficiency on the part of the institution has, to some extent, been made up by the Irish Manuscripts Commission which was established in 1928. This is a body consisting mainly of academic historians, the main role of which is to publish transcripts and calendars of archival material, both in its journal *Analecta Hibernica* and in separate volumes. During 1998, the Royal Irish Academy began publication of a new series, *Documents on Irish foreign policy*, based largely on archives held in the National Archives. The *Reports of the Deputy Keeper of the Public Records in Ireland and Keeper of State Papers* were published from 1869 until 1962. A final report covering the period 1962–88 is in preparation. Publication of the *Reports of the Director of the National Archives* has commenced. Several *Reports of the National Archives Advisory Council* have already been issued since 1990.

In the 1980s, packs of facsimile documents on a given theme were produced — often to accompany a travelling exhibition — and it is hoped to resume publishing of this kind. At present, exhibitions capable of travelling are being created along with extensive catalogues containing the exhibition captions, photographs and references. Two recent exhibitions were 'A nation and not a rabble', an exhibition covering Ireland in the period July 1921–June 1922, and 'The calamitous fire', an exhibition covering the establishment, destruction and regeneration of the Public Record Office of Ireland from 1867 until 1929.

The public are kept informed of developments within the National Archives by means of public lectures which are generally delivered to local societies and to students of university departments. Visits of special-interest groups are also arranged to the National Archives itself, generally when the Reading Room is closed, so that detailed discussions on record classes held by the Archives and viewing of sample records can take place uninterrupted. The public are also kept abreast of developments within the National Archives through the production of inexpensive information leaflets which may be updated readily. The most important of these are *Reading Room information* and *Sources for genealogy and family history*, but others are produced to deal with specific classes of records.

MILITARY AND LOCAL ARCHIVES
Under the *National Archives Act* 1986, the Minister for Arts, Heritage, Gaeltacht and the Islands may approve

places other than the National Archives for the deposit of specified categories of departmental records. The most important place of deposit is the Military Archives, which holds the records of the Department of Defence and the Defence Forces for the period since 1919. At present, it is situated in Cathal Brugha Barracks in Rathmines, Dublin. Here members of the public may consult records, by appointment, between 10 a.m. and 4 p.m.

Many official records of great importance are created at local level. The local administration of the Republic of Ireland is carried out by 29 county councils, 5 county borough corporations (cities) and a much larger number of smaller urban bodies, and also by harbour authorities, health boards, vocational education committees and a variety of other local administrative bodies. This complexity of administration has led to the creation of a vast amount of records, the survival of which is unfortunately haphazard. *The National Archives Act* 1986 included a provision allowing for the voluntary transfer of the records of local authorities from local custody into the care and custody of the National Archives in Dublin. However, no local authority removed its records to Dublin, and the National Archives never encouraged this development. The provision has been repealed by the *Local Government Act* 1994, Section 65. Under the latter section, local authorities are now obliged to make proper arrangements for the management, custody and care of their records and to make them available for inspection. To fulfil this requirement, many county councils are co-operating on a regional level in the employment of archivists to begin the work of bringing the archives under control.

In the light of the new legislation, it was decided that the Department of the Environment should determine what local authority archives exist in different areas, what work has been done to date in relation to those archives, what the immediate priorities are and how a uniform and consistent programme of development could best be put in place. To advise and assist the Department in this work, a Steering Group representative of the different interests in local authority records and archives was appointed. To establish what local authority archives exist and what condition they are in, the National Archives carried out a survey of local authorities on behalf of the Department of the Environment. The Steering Group's *Report* was launched by the Minister for the Environment in July 1996. On the same occasion, the minister announced new funding arrangements to assist local authorities in establishing archives services.

In 1992, the Irish Region of the Society of Archivists started work on the preparation of standards for archives services which would take account of the fact that most archives services in Ireland must inevitably operate on a very small scale. This initiative led to the publication of *Standards for the development of archives services in Ireland* (1997) by the Irish Region. In parallel with this development, the Department of the Environment and the National Archives prepared guidelines dealing more specifically with the needs of local authority archives services; these *Guidelines for local authority archives services* were published by the Department of the Environment in December 1996.

Bibliography

Connolly, P. 1996 'The destruction of the Public Record Office of Ireland in 1922: disaster and recovery', *Archivum* **42**, pp. 135–46.
D'Arcy, F. A. and Hannigan, K. (eds) 1998 *Workers in union: documents and commentaries on the history of Irish labour*. Dublin.
Darwin, K. 1963 'The Irish record situation', *Journal of the Society of Archivists* **2**, 8, pp. 361–6.
Griffith, M. 1950 'The Irish Record Commission 1810–30', *Irish Historical Studies* **7**, 25, pp. 17–38.
Griffith, M. 1964 *A short guide to the Public Record Office of Ireland*. Dublin.
Helferty, S. and Refaussé, R. (eds) 1999 *Directory of Irish archives*. Dublin.
McDonagh, M. 1998 *Freedom of information law in Ireland*. Dublin
Wood, H. 1919 *A guide to the records deposited in the Public Record Office of Ireland*. Dublin.
Wood, H. 1930 'The public records of Ireland before and after 1922', *Transactions of the Royal Historical Society* **13**, pp. 17–45.

The Public Record Office of Northern Ireland

DAVID LAMMEY

The Public Record Office of Northern Ireland (PRONI) was established under *the Public Records Act (Northern Ireland)* 1923, and opened in March 1924 in temporary premises in Murray Street, Belfast. It was created against the background of partition and of extensive destruction of the Public Record Office of Ireland, Dublin, in 1922. The first Deputy Keeper, Dr D. A. Chart, who had been on the staff in Dublin, was well acquainted with the records that had been lost. Duplicates, copies and abstracts were assembled as surrogates for many of the destroyed documents through application to other repositories, government departments, private collections, solicitors' offices and individuals who had worked with the originals. It is a tribute to the success of Dr Chart and subsequent deputy keepers and their staff that PRONI has in its custody such a comprehensive accumulation of genealogical material and historical records relating to Northern Ireland and further afield, dating from the plantation of Ulster to the present day. PRONI now has 53 shelf kilometres of records. During the financial year 1997–98, for example, 15,999 visitors (including 902 from North America) came to the office in order to carry out research, and more than 60% came to compile their family tree. In addition, just over 4,000 'remote' accesses were recorded, including 2,200 visits to the Royal Commission on Historical Manuscripts in London which provides access to catalogues supplied by PRONI, 803 visitors attending 'outreach' lectures conducted by PRONI staff, and 1,008 visits to the Ulster American Folk Park which provides information on emigration records held by PRONI using a stand-alone PC.

THE NATURE OF THE RECORDS

The bulk of the 1923 legislation is concerned with the establishment of the Record Office, and the creation of administrative procedures by which governmental and legal records were to be deposited in and processed by it. Provision was also made for the deposit of 'imperial' records: records which, although relevant to Northern Ireland, for instance the records of the higher courts, were created by administrative or legal bodies under Westminster control. And, as the Northern Ireland government was aware in 1923 that the new state's archival heritage from official sources was limited, it gave PRONI authority to accept records from private depositors. Northern Ireland records were placed under the ' ... charge and superintendence of the Minister of Finance for Northern Ireland ...', who was to appoint a Deputy Keeper.

The act has given PRONI virtually a monopoly responsibility for every aspect of Northern Ireland's archival heritage. It receives records ranging from those of government departments, courts, local authorities and non-departmental public bodies to those of landed estates, businesses, churches, societies, community groups and private families and individuals. Following the introduction of direct rule from London in March 1972 and the passing of legislation re-organizing central government functions in Northern Ireland, a new Department of Finance took over the role of 'Keeper of the Records' from the outgoing Ministry of Finance. Then, in April 1982, responsibility for PRONI and Northern Ireland records transferred from the Department of Finance to the Department of the Environment (DOE NI).

PRONI has from its creation carried out a wider range of functions than its English (and Welsh) equivalent, the Public Record Office in London (Kew), and than its Scottish equivalent, the Scottish Record Office in Edinburgh. What particularly distinguishes PRONI from other archival institutions in the United Kingdom and, indeed, the British Isles, is the unique combination of private and official records. PRONI combines the functions and responsibilities of a whole range of institu-

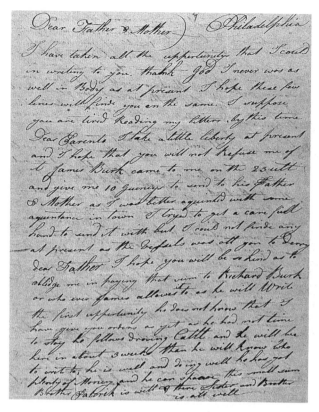

Fig. 33.1 Portion of emigrant letter from James Horner, Philadelphia, USA, to his father and mother, Boyvevagh, county Londonderry, 1801.

tions: it is at once Public Record Office, Manuscripts Department of a National Library, and County Record Office for each of the six counties of Northern Ireland and for the boroughs of Belfast and Londonderry.

PRONI holds millions of documents which relate chiefly, but by no means exclusively, to present-day Northern Ireland. The earliest record dates from 1219, with the main concentration of records covering the period 1600 to the present day. PRONI's landed estates archives include those of the great private owners (the Dukes of Abercorn in county Tyrone, the Marquesses of Downshire in county Down and the Earls of Antrim in county Antrim, for example), and those of many institutional owners like the London Companies (the Drapers and Salters Companies, for example), who were granted almost all of the re-named county of Londonderry at the Plantation. PRONI also holds what is probably the largest collection of business records in the British Isles. Among them can be found the names that have made Northern Ireland famous for linen, ships and engineering. The most extensive holdings of business records relate to the linen industry — more than 250 companies are represented. One of PRONI's outstanding resources in the sphere of economic and social history are its 'emigrant letters' — many of them components of archives, many of them the result of a deliberate collecting policy

pursued by PRONI on both sides of the Atlantic.

Records relating to central government include the files of the principal departments of government from the 1920s — Home Affairs, Finance, Commerce, Agriculture and, most recently, Economic Development, Environment and so forth. And, documenting the decision-making process at the very heart of government are the papers of the Northern Ireland Cabinet from 1922 — the Cabinet Conclusions. Records of local government running from the seventeenth century to the present day are available for consultation in PRONI. They include the records of Manor Courts, Parish Vestries, Grand Juries, Corporations, Town Commissioners, Boards of Guardians, County and District Councils, and, in more recent times, the records of other public bodies such as the Northern Ireland Housing Executive, the Education and Library Boards, the Health Boards, the Hospitals and so forth.

Collections deposited by private individuals or private institutions have reference letters **D** or **T** or **MIC** or **DIO** or **CR**. The reference letter **D** indicates an original document; the letter **T**, a transcript or photocopy; the letters **MIC**, a microfilm copy; the letters **DIO**, diocesan records, and the letters **CR**, church records. The records of a government department are catalogued according to the department where they originated, and their reference is normally the first three letters of the name of the department or ministry, for instance, records of the Ministry of Finance have the reference letters **FIN**. The same referencing system applies to the records of non-departmental public bodies, courts of law and so forth, for example, the records of the Boards of Guardians — workhouses — have the reference letters **BG**.

There have been shifts of emphasis over the period 1924 to the present. During the 1950s and 1960s there was in the private sphere an energetic policy of document acquisition, as a result of which a large number of family, estate and business archives were gathered in. By the early 1970s, it was estimated that the holdings of PRONI were approximately 50% official and 50% non-official. Since then the balance has tipped towards official records — a reflection of the post-1945 expansion of government services, and of the fact that an increasing number of official papers are being deposited in PRONI through the departmental records management system which governs relations between PRONI and the Northern Ireland departments. Intake of records from non-departmental public bodies has increased significantly over the last twenty years. For example, PRONI took in the records of the local authorities abolished in 1973 following a radical re-organization of local government. Moreover, PRONI has also had to accommodate the records of around 150 statutory bodies and quangos which have been established over the last decade.

Fig. 33.2 Lithograph of Muckamore Bleach Green, York Street Spinning Company, Belfast, by R. Welch, ca. 1900.

STORAGE

The successful acquisition of records over the years created a storage space problem. As far back as 1964, there had been concern about the fact that the Record Office was not centralized under one roof, with records being stored in various locations in unsuitable conditions in Belfast and at Gosford Castle, county Armagh. There were other problems too. Search Room facilities for the public wishing to consult documents were inadequate, and the public was subjected to long delays in obtaining access to documents when they were housed in out-stores. However, in 1965 the Ministry of Finance approved the building of a new Record Office on a site formerly occupied by Balmoral Hall, the Stranmillis College Hall of Residence. Building began in 1969 and the new Office was opened in February 1972. The first phase of storage accommodation provided for twelve strong-rooms, but in the summer of 1972 work commenced on erecting an additional nine strong-rooms.

The twenty-one air-conditioned and fire-proof strong-rooms with roller-racking soon filled up, and by the early 1990s, PRONI faced another major accommodation problem. However, the availability of public money was an even bigger problem. In November 1992, PRONI was formally told what had become increasingly apparent, namely that resources simply did not permit the £2-3,000,000 permanent extension to Balmoral Avenue for which successive bids had been made. It was against this background that a decision was taken to establish for the year 1993/94 a Reappraisal Team (consisting of 5 curatorial and 2 administrative staff). The remit of the team was to ease the Office's storage space problem by identifying for elimination material already in PRONI's custody but which might not by today's standards and criteria be deemed worthy of permanent preservation. Material which survived the reappraisal and was considered of historical or other research value was to be listed and made available to the public.

The work of the Reappraisal Team has gone a long way towards alleviating PRONI's storage problem, but it is a problem which will inevitably return again. With the storage question successfully shelved, at least in the short term, attention focused on making permanently preserved material more accessible. As the 'team' concept proved such a success in the case of the reappraisal exercise, it was used again in the drive to improve reader services during 1994/95. A Cataloguing Action Team (CAT) and a List Indexing Team (LIT) were established. CAT dealt with a substantial backlog of unlisted material which had been in PRONI's custody for several decades, and which had been left unprocessed through a lack of resources. LIT strove to remedy the deficiencies in the subject indexing of official records. As a result of LIT's input, and follow-up work carried out by the newly established Access Standards Section (created April 1995), the number of subject index entries on PRONI's computer database, PROMS (Public Record Office Management System), rose from *ca.* 50,000 (April 1995) to *ca.* 90,000 (April 1996), for instance.

AGENTIZATION

In February 1992 a feasibility study was commissioned with the terms of reference 'to examine the different responsibilities of the Public Record Office of Northern Ireland and to consider a range of options: abolition, privatization, contracting out in whole or in part, public corporation status, executive agency status or a combination of the options'. The feasibility study was completed in October and reached the conclusion that, on the analogy of the Public Record Office (Kew) and the Scottish Record Office (which became Executive Agencies on 1 April 1991 and 1 April 1992 respectively), and in accordance with PRONI's own particular situation and statutory and other functions, it would be appropriate for PRONI likewise to assume agency status.

Pending a decision on this study, PRONI pursued a vigorous market-testing programme and undertook other restructuring measures helpful in the short term to its functioning as a division of the DOE NI, and necessary in the longer term if it was to stand alone as an executive agency. On 19 July 1994, it was formally announced in the House of Commons that PRONI would become an executive agency and, soon after, a departmental working party was set up to steer PRONI towards agency status.

PRONI began operating as an executive agency within the Department of the Environment for Northern Ireland on 1 April 1995. The 'agentization' process seeks to improve the business of government. PRONI's *Annual Report 1994–95* explains:

By focusing executive functions within clearly defined business areas, and giving Agencies increased management discretion, government expects to enhance quality, customer orientation and the delivery of services. Agentisation is thus expected to bring benefits to the public.

Agency status has brought with it a plethora of corporate documents. PRONI's 'agency pack' includes a Framework Document, a Corporate Plan, a Business Plan (published annually), an Annual Report and Financial Statements (published annually), and a Citizen's Charter Statement. Dr A. P. W. Malcomson was appointed Chief Executive of the new PRONI Agency (and Deputy Keeper of the Records of Northern Ireland, the Department remaining the Keeper). The Chief Executive is responsible, under the Agency's Framework Document, for day-to-day management and is accountable to the minister for achieving the objectives and targets set and reviewed each year.

The fundamental aim of the agency is to identify and preserve Northern Ireland's archival heritage and to ensure public access to that heritage which fully meets Open Government standards. In support of this aim and in fulfilment of the *Public Records Act (Northern Ireland)* 1923, the agency's strategic objectives during the first five years were to:

• ensure the selection and acquisition of records of historical importance and to give particular attention to those records unique to the Northern Ireland situation by liaising systematically with bodies generating Northern Ireland records and with potential private depositors;

• arrange, catalogue and index such records in an orderly and efficient manner, taking advantage — where it represents best value for money — of a modern system of information management;

• preserve all records selected for permanent preservation to the standard and in the format which gives full weight to both good archival practice and economic cost;

• co-ordinate arrangements for access to Northern Ireland public records and improve effectiveness in the release of such records by identifying all material due for sensitivity review in accordance with Open Government standards, and

• provide a public service which enables customers to use the records in conformity with the standards of the Citizen's Charter and improve public understanding of that part of the national heritage held by PRONI.

PRONI's activities are reflected in its organizational structure. There are five sections:

Acquisition Section — responsible for the professional archival function of PRONI in the appraisal, selection, acquisition and cataloguing of all records deemed worthy of permanent preservation and in the provision of records management advice to official bodies;

Preservation Section — responsible for ensuring that the proper conditions exist within the Agency for preserving records. The section comprises the three main areas of preservation: Conservation, Repository and Reprographics;

Access Section — co-ordinates the annual sensitivity review under which all non-sensitive official records are released to the public on 2 January every year, and also the Northern Ireland response to the white paper on Open Government. In addition, the section is responsible for dealing with access-related enquiries from official bodies and members of the public. It ensures that newly listed material is indexed for inputting onto PRONI's computer database, and has responsibility for developing PRONI's fully integrated computer project,

PROMS;

Reader Services — responsible for most services to readers and other members of the public, including the giving of talks and lectures on- and off-site, as well as for producing PRONI's statutory report each year and publishing guides and leaflets;

Corporate Services Branch — responsible for the provision of the support services, including personnel, finance, registry, typing and accommodation, which enable the agency to perform as efficiently as possible.

The agency operates under gross expenditure control through the Parliamentary Vote system. A sum of £2.2 million was granted for the first year of the agency; however, financial pressures reduced that figure to £1.8 million for the 1996–97 Business Plan year. For 1997–98, £1.9 million was granted, a slight increase which, with salary pressures, was in effect a reduction. For the foreseeable future, it is expected that the parliamentary vote will hover around the £2 million mark. Most of PRONI's budget is expended on staff salaries and therefore any cutbacks have a direct impact on staff numbers. The number of professional and administrative staff employed by PRONI dropped from 93 in 1995–96 to 81 in 1996–97 and to 69 in 1997–98.

ACCESS, INFORMATION TECHNOLOGY AND READER SERVICES DEVELOPMENTS

The '30-year rule' — introduced in 1976 by the then Secretary of State by means of a Commons written answer — governs access to official records in Northern Ireland on the same basis as elsewhere in the United Kingdom. In essence this means that a record — file, minute book and the like — is eligible for release thirty years from the date of its last paper. The *White Paper on Open Government* (Cm 2290), published in July 1993, confirmed the '30-year rule', placed great emphasis on release of material and laid down stricter criteria for any extended closure. Files may be closed to the public only for one (or more) of three reasons:

(1) public interest;

(2) breach of good faith, and

(3) protection of individuals.

PRONI has been heavily involved in the implementation of additional measures to release more records as laid down by the white paper. The additional measures include the re-review of all material currently withheld for longer than thirty years to see whether its sensitivity has passed, and the identification of 'blocks of records' of long-term historical or other research value which could be released at earlier than thirty years. Since 1994, PRONI has co-ordinated the release of over 12,000 departmental files which had been closed for an extended period under the old sensitivity criteria. PRONI has also co-ordinated the early block release of over 4,000 official records.

The application of Open Government principles concerns not only official records. These same principles are being extended to cover private records in PRONI's custody, and the implementation of this policy is one of PRONI's Business Plan targets. In the main, PRONI has been establishing terms of access where they do not exist, rationalizing terms of access so that a myriad of time-bounded closures is avoided, eliminating any terms of access which might be perceived as discriminating against particular individuals or against a particular section of the community, and generally making private records more accessible to readers. For example, PRONI has taken steps to make some solicitors' archives more accessible by re-sorting bundles which are closed for sixty years from the terminal date of the most current document in the bundle. The material which is over sixty years old is being identified and listed so that it can be ordered out and consulted.

The potential of computerization was first raised as a management issue in 1968 by the then Deputy Keeper, Kenneth Darwin. However, the first practical signs of automation did not appear until 1985, when a word-processing system was installed for the sole use of the Typing Unit. The flexibilities offered by this system were quickly recognized, and within two years a Data Processing Committee was set up to discuss the way forward. In 1987 a 'small projects team' from the Department of the Environment's Information Systems Unit (ISU) visited PRONI to view its operations and consider its potential for computerization. The following year an Initial Project Appraisal took place and problems inherent in the existing manual system were identified. PRONI, at this crucial stage, avoided the temptation to aim simply at capturing the manual data accumulated over seventy years for a speedier handling of the same data in essentially the same format. It was decided that nothing should be outside the project's terms of reference, and that a fresh look should be taken at all archival processes.

A team from ISU arrived at PRONI in 1989 and began discussions with senior staff to find out what they wanted from a computer system. Mandatory and optional requirements were discussed and a Project Initiation Document was produced. A full-blown Business Systems Options case followed shortly afterwards and PRONI's computer system was given its name — PROMS (Public Record Office Management System). The business case was formally accepted by the Department of Finance and Personnel's Supply Branch in 1992.

While the financial details were being considered, serious work had already begun towards a transformation of the way in which PRONI did its archival business. An IT Branch was established to carry out a massive data take-on exercise. Data capture involved the taking-on of piece (or reference) numbers and related data, thus creating the spine of the computer system. Sophisticated hardware and software alone would not make PROMS an efficient tool — the accuracy of the data was vital. Therefore, an enormous effort went into the checking of the data. Eliminating basic errors involved staff going into the strong-rooms and checking again the details gathered. It also involved recognizing the deficiencies in the archival numbering systems employed over the seventy years of PRONI's existence, and imposing the consistency demanded by 'logical' software programs. And that has meant physically renumbering thousands of individual documents.

Both PRONI management and the ISU computer experts recognized that PROMS would only be a success if it met the everyday needs of PRONI's staff. Consequently, a reviewers' team, composed of curatorial staff representing each section of PRONI, was also set up, and training in Structured Systems Analysis and Design Methodology (SSADM) followed. The SSADM reviewers read the computer documentation prepared by the ISU's PROMS project team, individually and then collectively. It took between 10–15 man days to carry out this review per function (for example, listing, indexing, accessioning, and so on). Finally, the reviewers would meet with the ISU staff to thrash out any points of concern — of which there were many! After the consultative process had run its course, the documentation was signed off and handed over to the computer programmers to begin their work.

Further consultations, screen-by-screen evaluations and 'dry runs' have taken place in recent years and today the end-product is very much in sight. PRONI will soon be the first British national archival institution to operate an interactive, on-line multi-user computer system. As presently constituted, PROMS boasts many useful features. An automated document ordering system went 'live' in January 1996 and currently around 80% of all document orders are processed by this system. Only post-1900 wills and grants (of which there are approximately 4 million) have to be ordered using the manual system. All visitors to PRONI are registered on the readers' database. At the reception desk the member of staff on duty inputs the following details: name, address, occupation, subject of research, name of organization/institution (if applicable), payment of a business user's fee (if applicable), and reader category status (solicitor, genealogist, local historian). Once these details have been captured, readers are simply logged in

and out during subsequent visits. Only those persons logged in are permitted to use the automated document ordering system. Behind the scenes, the Annual Sensitivity Review exercise has benefited considerably as a result of computerization. A once labour-intensive 'cut and paste' operation carried out by clerical officers is now a matter of running a software program which scans through the piece (or reference) number database, sifting out official files with an appropriate terminal date (for example, for the January 1997 release of records, official files with a terminal date of 1966 were selected).

In line with government Information Technology initiatives, PRONI has been very active in embracing new computer technology to improve the efficiency of its services and facilitate public access. The development of PROMS was one important manifestation of this policy; the establishment of an Internet website at PRONI is another. PRONI was quick off the mark in identifying the world-wide web as having the potential to fulfil, in whole or in part, many of its objectives. Indeed, PRONI's website, which was launched in December 1995, was prominent in seminars and demonstrations organized by the Department of Finance and Personnel's Business Development Service, which was tasked with promoting the use of the Internet's facilities in providing government services.

In its early stages, PRONI's website was used primarily as a publishing medium, and effort concentrated on displaying existing public-information leaflets and documents. A big step forward was taken in early 1997, when PRONI appointed a consultant to work on both the content and presentation of its website. PRONI's web pages (*http://proni.nics.gov.uk/index.htm*) now give general information about the Office's facilities, and how to use its finding aids and records. They also provide extensive introductions to major private archives. The emphasis is on information which will prepare any researcher thoroughly before he or she steps across the threshold of PRONI. And, recognizing that the Internet was more than just a publishing medium, e-mail provision alongside the website marked a first step towards exploiting the medium's two-way communications possibilities.

With the emphasis very much on the quality of public services since the publication of the Citizen's Charter for Northern Ireland in 1992, PRONI has responded by harnessing new technologies and by opening up new lines of communications. An inter-active touch screen video is available to the public at PRONI's headquarters. It is designed to assist the first-time visitor in particular. One can discover what services are available, the range of records in PRONI's custody, how to order documents, and how to handle original documents or, in the case of the 'Mr Bean' clips, how not to handle them. PRONI's library has been open to the public for consultation purposes between 2.00 p.m. and 4.00 p.m. on weekdays since April 1997. The newly refurbished library, situated at the rear of the Exhibition Hall, is fully computerized. Details of 4,500 books have been captured on a specially designed system. The range of subjects covered is wide, with biography, church, local and legal history being exceptionally well served. Books based on research in PRONI or relating to some of the major historical figures whose papers are held in PRONI's custody (Lords Castlereagh and Carson, the 1st Marquess of Dufferin and Ava, and Earl MacCartney, for example) are another strong point. Many of the books are rare and would be difficult to obtain from any other source. Communication with the public has been formalized in recent years by the setting up of a Users' Group, composed of representatives from the Ulster Museum, the Ulster Folk and Transport Museum, the Federation for Ulster Local Studies, various organizations involved in genealogical research on a commercial basis, postgraduate students, among others. Readers' 'Comments and Suggestions' are reviewed every three months and a response is drafted (copies of which are made available in the Public Search Room), indicating that ameliorative action has been taken and, if it has not been taken, why not.

Following the launch, in February 1999, of its first regional studies (outreach) centre, based in the premises of the of the Border Counties History Collective in Blacklion, county Cavan, PRONI continues to be actively engaged in negotiations to establish other centres in Armagh, Ballymena and Londonderry. The aim of the centres is to raise the awareness of people in these areas of the work of PRONI. It is envisaged that the computer hardware and software installed in the centres will enable access to PRONI's subject, geographical and prominent persons name indexes only available at PRONI's headquarters at the moment. PRONI's website pages will also be available, plus the interactive touch-screen video. Hard-copies of PRONI catalogue lists, guides, leaflets and books relating to the areas in which the centres are based will be supplied and appropriate exhibitions erected. All these facilities will provide an impressive backdrop to lectures, seminars and workshops organized by PRONI staff with a view to inducting users and priming them for a visit to PRONI's headquarters to inspect the original documents.

CONTINUOUS IMPROVEMENT, INVESTORS IN PEOPLE AND CUSTOMER CARE

In May 1995, Sir David Fell, then Head of the Northern Ireland Civil Service, launched a service-wide 'Continuous Improvement Programme' (CIP). As part of the DOE NI response to this initiative, PRONI was required to take stock of, and report on, CIP-type projects which were already under way or indeed had been completed. These, essentially, are projects in which

members of staff at different levels and often from different disciplines consider on a team basis how various business processes could be shortened, streamlined or eliminated altogether — the re-thinking of old manual systems, which PROMS had stimulated, being a particularly good example in PRONI's case. Later in the year, more precise guidance on how CIP was to be implemented was provided by the Department. Granted the small scale of PRONI, it was thought appropriate to give to the PRONI Management Team the role of CIP Quality Council and to establish a procedure whereby CIP was an agenda item at every Management Team/Quality Council meeting. In 1996 the first CIP project was concluded; this was an examination of whether service to the public could be improved by allowing payment by credit card and in Irish currency, without derogation from accountability standards.

In 1996, PRONI embarked on the road to achieving accreditation to the Investors in People Standard. Throughout the United Kingdom, the public sector is committed to seeking accreditation to the Standard, to improve delivery of service to the customer by targeting staff development on organizational needs and business objectives. This is a major initiative which takes an average of eighteen months to two years to complete successfully. The appointment of PRONI's Project Team to liaise with the Training and Employment Agency's CIP Unit was the first step towards this.

In 1994 a Customer Care Quality Team was set up to examine how the care of PRONI's customers, both external and internal, could be improved. It was quickly recognized that how PRONI staff treat each other is reflected in relations with external customers. Indeed, PRONI's corporate documents emphasize that 'it is important to remember that PRONI's most valuable resource is its staff'. The documents commit the Chief Executive to 'develop and sustain ... a personnel policy which will help promote a culture of good customer care'.

A Customer Care Charter which had been endorsed at the final meeting of the Customer Care Quality Team in April 1995 was devised and produced for staff. Composed of a representative cross-section of PRONI staff, the Team's function was to examine and make recommendations for all aspects of staff relations. These include mutual accountability, the role of the Chief Executive and Senior Management Team in setting the culture, communications in PRONI, job satisfaction, and training and development. The Charter established a Customer Care Group to represent all staff, its members annually elected by section/discipline/grade on a *pro rata* basis. The Group meets quarterly, although more frequently if required, and is attended by a Charter Officer as observer. The Customer Care Charter for staff is not just a set of recommendations on how to behave towards colleagues. It is a formal document, providing a mechanism for redress of breaches of the Charter, initially through line management. Where this does not resolve the issue, the Charter Officer (Head of Corporate Services) is empowered to investigate the grievance and report to the Chief Executive. The Charter was formally launched in May 1995 with a small reception for staff to mark the occasion. Customer care remains a vital and ongoing area of personnel management in PRONI.

DISASTER PLANNING

Care of the documents is, of course, one of PRONI's principal statutory functions and, unfortunately, PRONI's archives have, in recent times, experienced just about every pestilence an archive can well do without: fire, flood and theft. Therefore, during the 1990s much attention was paid to the drawing up of contingency plans to cope with a disaster. A Disaster Plan was formulated, and a Disaster Reaction Team (DRT) was set up and trained in disaster response procedures. Both were brought into active service following the fire at Parliament Buildings which broke out on 2 January 1995. Although the fire did not reach PRONI's strong-rooms in the basement, where Northern Ireland census enumerators' returns and other important records were housed, most of the water used to douse the blaze found its way into two of PRONI's stores. Almost 3,000 boxes of public records, papers and preservation microfilm had to be removed from the flooded area. No boxed records were irreparably damaged, thanks mainly to the protection given them by archival boxes. However, over 1,100 boxes were too damp to re-use and many hundreds of documents had to be transferred to new boxes. The census enumerators' returns presented an even more serious problem. Over 2,500 volumes, unboxed because of their size, were either drenched by water pouring through the ceiling, or partially immersed by rising floodwater. All required air-drying and around 10% needed urgent conservation treatment. Altogether it took the DRT eight full days to carry out the salvage operation. Two points emerged strongly from a subsequent internal review of events. Firstly, the Stormont fire provided proof of the effectiveness of PRONI's Disaster Plan. Secondly, and more importantly, it was clear that had it not been for the speedy and effective response of the DRT, there would have been losses of important public records.

CONCLUSION

The future looks exciting for PRONI and its readership. Nearly thirty years after moving into its purpose-built Balmoral Avenue headquarters, PRONI is now seeking new premises. Inadequate records out-storage, the cramped conditions in both the public and staff areas of the Office, the urgent need for major refurbishment of the existing building at Balmoral Avenue, and the need to find alternative uses for the Crumlin Road Courthouse and Prison, together have been the impetus for a wide-ranging examination of the various options for PRONI's future accommodation. To this end, an economic appraisal of all possible options was completed in October 1998. A 'do minimum' together with extensive and modest extensions on the present site, build new on a single or split green-field sites, and occupation of the above-mentioned Crumlin Road sites were all examined and costed, taking into account PAFT (Policy Appraisal and Fair Treatment), TSN (Target Social Needs) and Equal Opportunities. Only new-build on a green field site and the Crumlin Road options could meet all of the requirements. However, the economic appraisal concluded that the single green-field site option would be the most cost effective and was the best in weighting and scoring of non-monetary factors.

Much encouragement for PRONI's drive for new accommodation has come from its Advisory Board. As most executive agencies had advisory boards, PRONI took advantage of this dispensation to create one for itself that was representative of total 'customer interests' — which means not simply readership, but private and official depositors. Its membership, which includes senior public servants from local government, can provide PRONI's Chief Executive with advice on funding matters, for example, as well as giving moral support and encouragement. PRONI will need such well-directed advice as the organization continues to navigate an ever-changing world. However, the future should hold no fears for PRONI because its main strength lies in its archives. Indeed, its present Chief Executive states in a paper entitled 'The major research strengths of PRONI', and which is available on the Internet: 'for most areas of research relevant to PRONI, the records held by it are important, well-catalogued, easily accessible and greatly under-utilised'.

Bibliography

PRONI 1924–89 *Reports of the Deputy Keeper of the Records*. Belfast.
PRONI 1990–95 *Annual reports*. Belfast.
PRONI 1991 *Guide to the Public Record Office of Northern Ireland*. Belfast.
PRONI 1995–98 *Statutory reports*. Belfast.

The CELT Corpus of Irish Texts

Donnchadh Ó Corráin

CELT (Corpus of Electronic Texts) is a project designed to exploit advanced telecommunications for humanities studies by developing an on-line text-base source of Irish history and literature and by giving scholars, students and the general public, nationally and internationally, access to these materials. It makes available on-line down-loadable texts of high quality for consultation, searching and onward processing by individual scholars (*http://www.ucc.ie/celt*). It serves the cultural needs of the public, of public authorities, of heritage and tourist interests as well as the scholarly requirements of academics. It provides textual resources for teaching, for special topics, student projects and individual research, and is constructing an IT virtual library to meet the anticipated demands of Irish education. It provides the textual material for future multi-media developments in CD-ROM and DVD publishing. CELT has 2.5 million words of text on the Internet. These comprise the Irish annals (text and translation), poetry and prose in medieval Irish, the output of modern Irish writers of creative literature or political commentary, for instance Horace Plunkett, the complete works of James Connolly and Oscar Wilde, as well as documents of modern Irish history, including 250,000 words of the Treaty Debates. The site has had almost 900,000 visitors at the time of writing.

The project's primary aim is to bring the wealth of Irish literary and historical culture (in Irish, Latin, Old Norse, Anglo-Norman French and English) to the Internet as a scholarly undertaking, and to make it available to any interested user. In other words, it intends to migrate the materials of Irish culture from hardcopy (often in scarce, out-of-print and expensive editions rarely found outside large research libraries) to a freely available digital form, but without dilution of rigorous academic standards. This first and fundamental objective is, of necessity, a long-term one, because of the sheer size of the corpus involved. Old Norse and Anglo-Norman French may be finished in a short time, but the writings in Irish and English are vast. A second ambition is to publish selections of these materials (for example the complete Irish annals) in CD-ROM or other suitable media as such media become available. The third aim is to collaborate with multi-media projects (especially in education and training) by providing academically sound digital text with bibliography and annotation as a major component of the multi-media product.

CELT was initiated by the present author and evolved, in the first place, as a collaboration between the Department of History, University College, Cork, UCC's Computer Centre and the Royal Irish Academy. It has subsequently become an independent UCC undertaking. The project uses state-of-the-art technology. It is fully ISO conformant, employs Standard Generalized Mark-Up Language (SGML) as the text descriptive language of its primary files, and adheres strictly to the protocols of the Text Encoding Initiative, an internationally agreed set of conventions for the encoding of multi-lingual, multi-genre scholarly texts. This is an evolving set of protocols and CELT has played an important part in the great advances made in the creation of platform- and software-independent corpora over the past six years. Its texts have a limitless life-span as cultural artefacts, and textual acquisition is indefinitely cumulative. Special sorts and diacritics (which are important for all medieval and many modern literatures, as well as in textual and metrical analysis) are rendered as SGML entities and may be effortlessly adapted to any desired platform. There are strategies for the creation of the scholarly multivariate text (in fact, first fully tested and realized by the CELT project), and text may be cumulatively enhanced and enriched with annotations and other materials, for instance bibliography, scholarly emendation, additional variant readings and the like. From this SGML base text any other view of the text can be generated on an automated basis, including the

Hypertext Mark-Up Language (HTML) versions which are also provided on the Internet, by browsing, downloading and printing.

On the humanities side, CELT uses the most rigorous proofing and textual editing. Digital editing is about as labour-intensive as hardcopy editing, and the output of high-quality digital texts is a direct function of the availability of qualified editors and funding. Enhancement of the hardcopy text in the CELT digital form often represents a significant improvement on the base text. All digital texts are provided with a header that details the text history, lists the editorial conventions, and provides (usually) a listing of manuscript sources and (always) an up-to-date bibliography of scholarly work on the text. Digital text enables the investigation of text in a quite different way (search, indexes, concordances, lexico-statistics and other forms of enquiry). When texts are enhanced with deep-level mark-up (as are centrally important documents like the *Annals of Ulster* in the CELT project), the interrogation of text is proportionately facilitated. Therefore the CELT digital text is a new scholarly tool in its own right.

The CELT project has trained humanities graduates in computerized text handling and editing techniques to both masters and doctorate level. Many other humanities students who were involved with it have subsequently found full-time employment in the computing field. CELT cooperates and shares experiences and techniques with other projects in the humanities, both within UCC and farther afield. It is negotiating a long-term venture with the University of California at Berkeley, which seeks to produce the Berkeley–Cork Digital Corpus of Early Irish Law (1.4 million words). It collaborates with the School of Celtic Studies, Dublin Institute for Advanced Studies, the largest holder of copyright material in the field of early and medieval Irish language and literature, and has secured the rights to the School's copyright texts. CELT obtained competitive funding under the Higher Education Authority's Humanities Research Awards Scheme for the period 1999–2002 AD. It is, therefore, in Irish terms, a pioneering project in humanities/IT and has built up a body of expertise in the handling of complex, multi-lingual academic documentation. It has solved problems associated with the generation, standardization and manipulation of such material and their wider communication. It is currently the largest scholarly corpus available freely on the Internet. The digital editions (as we know from our log of users) have a broad appeal to a very wide range of readers and researchers — academics, students at all levels and the general public in Ireland and overseas. They are also used by software authoring companies to test their software, because CELT provides the most complex, difficult and lengthy SGML texts (with appropriate and scrupulously corrected Document Type

Descriptions or DTDs) publicly available, and are thus excellent test material. Our project greatly facilitates the productive capture and manipulation of data essential for a full understanding and appreciation of Irish civilization, and represents, in our view, a significant advance in the storage, retrieval and consultation of vital sources.

The Professional Conservator/Restorer

MAIGHREAD MCPARLAND

As there is much confusion relating to the words 'conservation', 'restoration' and 'preventive' or 'passive' conservation as they refer to artefacts, it may be helpful to explain them. *Conservation* always implies an active or 'hands-on' intervention by the conservator to stabilize an artefact which has deteriorated for whatever reason, to redress the damage insofar as it is permissible to do so and, finally, to ensure that it does not get damaged again. *Restoration* is the process by which the conservator 'makes good' an area of total loss. An oil painting or fresco, for example, may be so badly damaged in some parts that the image has lost its cohesion. These areas will be infilled or retouched sympathetically to restore the visual integrity of the whole, but no attempt will be made to recreate the original. The infills must be recognizable as such. *Preventive* or *passive conservation*, or simply 'Caring for Collections', involves firstly undertaking a survey of the collection to establish how many of the artefacts are in good, fair or bad condition. The next step is to identify the factors (probably environmental) which are responsible for causing any damage which may be occurring, and then to attempt to halt or at least minimize their effect. The building itself as the envelope of the collection should be included in the survey, and note taken of whether or not it is well maintained. Whereas conservation is object-specific, preventive conservation addresses the needs of a collection *in toto*. Thus it is important that all museums draw up and implement a preventive conservation or 'Caring for Collections' policy. Such a policy should be complemented by a training programme for staff which would address such issues as security, how best to handle artefacts, health and safety matters, emergency procedures, fire prevention, packaging and transport (Corr 2000).

THE ART OF THE CONSERVATOR

Following a meeting of conservators in Pavia in October 1997, organized by the Istituto Giovanni Secco Suardo, it was decided that the professional should be referred to as a 'conservator/restorer'. Throughout this article the word 'conservator' will be used. When artefacts such as the Derrynaflan chalice in the National Museum or Michelangelo's frescoes in the Sistine Chapel are exhibited for the first time after major conservation work, very few of the viewers would be aware of all the preliminary investigations which were undertaken before treatment began or that, once conserved, they will have to be 'preserved' on an ongoing basis if they are not to deteriorate again. The preliminary investigations will reveal what the artefact is made of, how it was made and why it is no longer in good condition. This knowledge will help to decide how best to conserve it. The conservator will not work in isolation but will call on the expertise of the librarian/curator and possibly of the conservation scientist to assist in this task.

The importance of liaising closely with the librarian can perhaps best be illustrated in the case of a rare book which, as part of the conservation treatment, has to be disbound or 'pulled'. All of the bibliographical details, including the structure of the binding and the arrangement of the gatherings, will be recorded. The conservator will number all of the pages in pencil so that they can be collated again, and will also be aware of the importance of retaining labels and remnants of the old binding. Quite often a minimalist approach will be adopted. Rather than undertake a major intervention, such as that involved in disbinding a rare book, the conservator will recommend that it be protected in a box of archival quality. However, the decision to do so will be dictated to some extent by usage, and the librarian will have access to such information. The conservator will record all of the details relating to the artefact, catalogue number, size, technique, provenance, its present condition, the results of the investigative techniques and the conservation treatment it received. It is most important that all of this documentation is retained. To facilitate the process, the conservator may design a report sheet with a series of boxes for the various headings which can then be ticked off 'yes' or 'no', with space to indicate the extent of the damage and where it has occurred, also to record the treatment the individual item has received and recommendations for its preservation. Similar sheets, but less detailed, are used to record the condition of an artefact which is to be lent to another institution. The condition will be checked out again and recorded on arrival, before departure, and on arrival home again. Thus if the artefact has been damaged, it should be possible to say when and where it happened.

The role of photography as a tool in the documentation process is indispensable, not only as a record of the condition before conservation but also during treatment and finally when work is completed. It should be as comprehensive as funds, permit and include shots in raking light. It is at this point that the distinction is blurred between recording and investigating the object in greater detail. Techniques such as x-ray radiography, infra-red reflectography, ultra-violet and microscopic examination will reveal more about the artefact than the naked eye, or perhaps confirm what the conservator already suspects. Among the growing number of investigative techniques available to the conservator, the choice of which one to use will be made on the basis of whether or not it is non-destructive or at worst micro-destructive to the artefact. Fibre analysis of paper requires such a tiny sample as to be considered acceptable. In well-endowed institutions such as the British Museum and the National Gallery London (Bowman 1991), it is the scientific department which carries out this testing in addition to researching new materials and techniques for use in conservation. In Ireland, the State Laboratory undertakes analyses for conservators.

In trying to find the reason or reasons why an artefact has deteriorated, the conservator will have quite a selection to choose from. It may have been caused by vandalism such as was the case with Leonardo's cartoon in the National Gallery London, and Michelangelo's Pietà in St Peter's Basilica, Rome. Flawed craftsmanship may be another reason, or the damage may have been caused by exposure to damp conditions promoting mould growth, or light resulting in fading and weakening textile fibres. Sulphur in the atmosphere will tarnish silver and blacken the lead white pigment used by artists as highlights. Another possibility, encountered very frequently in nineteenth- and twentieth-century papers, is that the deterioration is the result of factors inherent in the object itself.

Having thoroughly investigated the artefact and decided how best to conserve it, the conservator will

adhere to a code of ethics which stipulates that, in the course of treatment, no adhesive or consolidant which will become chemically cross-linked and hence insoluble in the future will be used; neither will any irreversible process be undertaken. Preference will be given to using a pure substance, such as an adhesive made from potato starch, rather than a proprietary brand product which may contain an unknown additive. It is also a prerequisite of the *National Monuments Acts* 1930 to 1994 that a licence be obtained to alter an archaeological object. Of all the many different artefacts which are no longer in good condition and require treatment, paper is a very good example of what the conservator must know beforehand in terms of its composition and how it was made. This knowledge will explain why the paper may have become yellow and embrittled, and also provides the rationale for the various remedial procedures.

CONSERVATION, PAPER AND THE HISTORY OF PAPER-MAKING: *A CASE STUDY*

For many centuries in Europe the source of cellulose, the basic constituent of paper, was provided by rags of linen, later cotton. Cellulose is a polymer composed of carbon, hydrogen and oxygen in the proportion $C_6 H_{10} O_5$. In association with other substances such as hemicelluloses and lignin, it forms the skeletal structure of the higher plants. In rags, most of these other constituents have been eliminated, in the case of linen by the retting process, so that the cellulose is relatively pure. It itself is fairly stable chemically, being insoluble in water for which, however, it has great affinity. It is unaffected by dilute alkali, but if subjected to prolonged treatment with acid, will break down ultimately by hydrolysis into its basic sugar molecule, beta D-glucose (McParland 1982).

To make paper, rags were collected, sorted and wetted to allow some fermentation to take place, facilitating the beating process later on. For the production of white paper of the finest quality, the selection and sorting of rags was very carefully controlled and the sorters highly skilled. Beating the softened rags was the next step in the process. It macerated the rags still further and, if efficiently carried out, ensured that the ends of individual fibres split longitudinally into fibrils, thus assisting the bonding process between the fibres, contributing to the strength of the paper. The resulting pulp or stock was fed into a vat. The operator or vat man dipped a sieve-like structure called a mould into the vat, and withdrew a mixture of stock and water which was allowed to drain away. The resulting web of fibres was turned out on to a felt, and when a certain number of felts accumulated, they were placed in a press and more water extracted. Finally, the sheet of paper thus formed was peeled off and hung in an airy loft, known as a *salle*, to dry. Paper for writing purposes was made more receptive to ink by sizing it, that is dipping it into a warm bath of gelatine, then allowing it to dry and possibly burnishing it to produce a sheen. The manufacture of the mould itself required great skill. A design was sometimes attached to the wire of the mould which left its impression on the sheet formed on it. This was known as the watermark. Once the printing process became widespread, the demand for rags for making paper became acute. Experiments using grasses as the source of cellulose were carried out in France in the late eighteenth century and in England using straw at the beginning of the nineteenth century. None was successful. In the 1840s in Germany, a process was developed whereby debarked logs were ground down mechanically and the resultant pulp used to make paper. Known as groundwood or mechanical pulp, it contains not only cellulose and hemicelluloses but lignin also, which rapidly discolours and embrittles.

Newsprint contains about 80%–85% of this mechanical fibre. Its presence in paper can be detected microscopically using a staining technique. In the last half of the nineteenth century, chemical processes were developed for extracting cellulose from trees and eliminating the lignin. It is now possible, using trees as the source, to extract cellulose with a very high degree of purity. Such cellulose will be used in the manufacture of archival quality papers.

Another factor responsible for the deterioration of paper was introduced by Moritz Friedrick Illig in Germany. In 1807, he published an account of how sizing could be accomplished with considerable economy using rosin instead of gelatine. The rosin was dissolved in an alkali, then added to the stock while it was undergoing beating.

The subsequent addition of alum precipitated the rosin on to the fibres. Rosin does not strengthen paper as gelatine does, and alum is acid. Alum-rosin sizing became increasingly popular from the 1830s onwards. Its introduction made one of the biggest contributions to the deterioration of paper. Researchers working in America in the 1920s proved that there is a correlation between acidity and the deterioration of paper, but no sustained effort was made to apply these findings. Then in 1939, W. J. Barrow, working in Richmond, Virginia, confirmed that deteriorated documents usually have a high acid content (that is, a low pH). As a result of these observations, he developed a method of first washing, then de-acidifying, such papers with solutions of calcium hydroxide and calcium bicarbonate, that is washing out the soluble impurities, then neutralizing the acidity, and finally affording the paper some 'buffering' or protection against contamination in the future. Today washing and de-acidification are two of the most important techniques used in the conservation of paper.

There may be other factors inherent in paper, such as excessive bleaching of the pulp or the addition of mineral fillers, which result in its deterioration, but acidity and fibre content are the most significant. It is also acknowledged that the discolouration from poor-quality paper can migrate into good-quality paper in contact with it. This explains why it is so important to use paper and mounting board of archival quality to preserve documents, books or works of art on paper and maps.

Armed with this information, however, the conservator may discover that even though washing and de-acidification would be very good for the paper, the paper is but the support for what has made it of historic or artistic value. Certain inks and pigments may be fugitive in water, and these will have to be tested beforehand. Signatures will have to be checked for solubility and 'fixed' so as to withstand immersion. Pastels and chalks cannot be immersed. Decisions will have to be made at every stage. Iron gall inks are acid and in time will eat into the paper, so that the text becomes suspended like lace. Washing followed by de-acidification is likely to alter the colour contrast between the ink and the paper, but otherwise the text would be lost, so is intervention justifiable? The conservator of archival material believes that the text itself is of paramount importance and will do what is necessary to save it. The conservator of works of art on paper, on the other hand, will be very conscious of aesthetic considerations, and these may impose limitations as to what can be done. Parchment, used for so many centuries before paper became widespread, is animal in origin. (Paper was first made in England in 1493, in Ireland in 1693.) Its characteristics, therefore, are quite different, and it requires different skills to conserve it.

Modern works of art present the conservator with incredible difficulties because of the diversity of materials used and the artist's use of them. The philosophical basis for attempting to prolong their life is on a rocky foundation too, as the artist may intend them to crumble away. But what if the owner has paid a fortune to acquire such a work? An interesting subject for debate!

ENVIRONMENTAL FACTORS

As mentioned earlier, in carrying out the pre-treatment assessment of an artefact, the conservator will be looking out for damage which may have resulted from exposure to inappropriate environmental conditions. Too dry an atmosphere will cause parchment to cockle, and if it is an illuminated manuscript, for example, the pigment layer may be under stress and flaking off. Furniture may have split or distorted for the same reason. On the other hand exposure to a damp atmosphere will promote mould growth and cause metals to corrode. An elevated temperature will accelerate the deterioration of photographic materials. Light will not only fade furniture, miniatures, watercolours and textiles, but will also weaken textile fibres. Pollutants such as sulphur dioxide in combination with water will erode stone; not so obvious is the fact that they also weaken cellulosic material, such as paper, and canvas which is the support of oil paintings. Artefacts may occasionally deteriorate because of the materials used in the construction and fitting out of display cases and storage cupboards. For example, oak is well known to 'off-gas', that is, it exudes acids such as acetic which corrode metal. Composite boards may 'off-gas' formaldehyde, and wool contains sulphur which tarnishes silver.

THE MUSEUM ENVIRONMENT

Generally speaking, it is the moisture in the atmosphere which is of most concern. This is expressed as the percentage relative humidity (% rh), that is, the extent to which the air is saturated at a given temperature. If the relative humidity is 100% at 20°C, it would be fully saturated and could hold no more moisture. If the temperature dropped to 19°C, some of the moisture would fall out as condensation. This relationship between the relative humidity and temperature has a practical application. If the temperature increases, the air can hold more moisture, so the % rh falls correspondingly. If the temperature falls, the air can hold less moisture, and so the rh increases. If humidistats, which respond to the relative humidity, are fitted to heaters and set at a rh of 50%, they will turn the heat off if the rh falls below 50% rh, on again if the rh rises above 50%. It is interesting to note that in 1747, Lafont de Saint Yenne wrote expressing concern for the safety of the king's paintings stored in Versailles (Sitwell and Staniforth 1998), and in 1777, Anton Rafael Mengs, in his report on the condition of the paintings in the Escorial, said 'they are all affected by a very subtle humidity which they absorb, which makes them all appear sunken and damaged since they hang against walls of stone' (*ibid.*).

Many artefacts, including paintings, have survived for centuries in conditions which are not ideal. The explanation for this is that they can adapt to slow variations in relative humidity such as may occur on a seasonal basis, but cannot withstand a sudden change or rapid fluctuations even within an otherwise acceptable range of relative humidity. Artefacts have survived in the ground or under water for many centuries but, once excavated, will have to be dried out gradually if they are to survive. Similarly, the introduction of central heating into an old house or church will result in an elevated temperature, with consequent lowering of the relative humidity. Unless precautions are taken, such as raising the temperature very slowly and using a humidifier, panelling and furniture will split and panel paintings will be put under stress. It is accepted that mould growth will develop if the rh rises above 65%. Metals corrode if the rh is above 40%. For many objects, however, a rh between 40% – 65%

is acceptable. (A compromise may have to be found for composite objects.) The temperature may be dictated by the requirements of 'people comfort' in exhibition areas and reading rooms; it may be lower in storage areas, but not so low as to allow condensation to form on cold surfaces. Rapid removal of objects from one set of conditions to which they have acclimatized to a different one should be avoided, for example from storage to reading room.

With the introduction of air-conditioning plants, the possibility of having tighter control of the relative humidity and temperature became a reality. Moreover, the air which is drawn into the plant from outside to be treated and later distributed throughout the building via ducting could be filtered, not only to exclude the dust or 'particulate matter' but, if activated carbon filters were also incorporated into the system, the concentration of pollutant gases in circulation could be reduced. Thus it became 'best practice' to specify a very narrow range for the relative humidity and temperature, and for the concentration of dust and gases to be reduced to very low levels.

In the second edition of his book, *The museum environment* (reprinted in 1999), Garry Thomson (1986) gives the following specification for a Class 1 situation, that is for a major national museum, old or new, also for all important new museum buildings:

rh day and night throughout the year
50% or 55% ±5%
Temperature
Winter 19°C ±1°C
Summer up to 24°C ±1°C

Air Pollution
Particulates removed to 80% efficiency on Eurovent 4/5
Sulphur dioxide and nitrogen dioxide each removed to below 10 g/μ³
Ozone removed to below 2 g/μ³

These conditions will be maintained while having a certain number of air changes per hour, which in turn will be related to ceiling heights and possibly occupancy. (Reference should always be made to external conditions, including the level of pollutant gases, before specifying internal conditions.)

It would not be difficult to incorporate an air-conditioning plant into a new building, but to introduce it into an existing building with the ancillary ducting could be much more difficult, not only mechanically but also aesthetically. An added complication in old buildings is that, because of their construction, it might be difficult to sustain a plenum (that is, the slightly positive pressure which is required to keep untreated air out), and also, unless precautions are taken, moisture vapour could migrate into the walls where a cycle of repeated thawing and freezing would start, ultimately damaging the fabric of the building itself. Even in a modern well-insulated building, the cost of maintaining the relative humidity and temperature within a narrow range is considerable. Because the cost of cooling is so high, the temperature in summer is now allowed to rise to 24°C ± 1°C (it had been 20°C).

An additional energy-saving mechanism is achieved by reducing the number of air changes at night time, and also by 'zoning' the building so that the highest control is maintained in exhibition and storage areas; greater tolerance is permitted elsewhere, such as bookshops, restaurants, entrance halls and cloakrooms. The life expectancy of an air-conditioning plant is twenty years. Thus many factors have to be considered when planning to install one (Cassar 1995). Those responsible, the curator, conservator and engineer, each have their own specialisms. Nevertheless, it will be assumed that this triumvirate will have but one objective, the provision of an efficient, cost-effective, safe environment for the preservation of the collections in accordance with statutes, especially the Code of Professional Ethics, International Council of Museums, UNESCO (Paris 1987). The reservations which conservators now have about specifying a very narrow range of environmental conditions, such as air conditioning might provide, have received additional support from the research carried out by Dr Jonathan Ashley Smith, who has proved that artefacts are more resilient than we once thought (McParland 1997).

Where air conditioning is not an option, it is important to look at the building housing the artefacts, not only as the envelope for what is inside, affording security, on the one hand, but also, on the other, acting as a buffer against the elements. It is essential that it be well maintained, that dampness does not get in through a broken slate or gutter, that birds do not nest in the chimneys. Birds' nests are a serious source of insect infestation. Windows and doors should also be well-fitting. As a general rule, whether there is air conditioning or not, it is useful to have adequate cloakroom facilities, double doors with an intervening lobby at the entrance and large mats so that visitors do not bring in too much grit or dirt on their shoes.

The presence of hygroscopic materials such as upholstery, drapes and wallpaper will take up some excess moisture. As mentioned earlier, the installation of heaters with humidistats may keep the relative humidity within an acceptable range but, if this is not possible, it may be necessary to use dehumidifiers if the atmosphere is damp, or humidifiers of the evaporative type if the atmosphere is too dry. It is important to monitor the conditions before making any financial outlay, and then to continue to do so, preferably on a continuous basis.

In some museum situations, a stable environment can be achieved for very vulnerable artefacts by incorporating pre-conditioned silica gel into a sealed case. By 'pre-conditioned' is meant ensuring that the silica gel has a certain moisture content which will depend on the relative humidity it is required to sustain within the sealed container. Silica gel has the ability to soak up moisture if the rh goes above the specified limit, and to release it again if the rh falls. The rh should be checked, however, as the efficacy of the silica gel falls off eventually. It should also be handled with care as the dust from it is harmful. There is an interesting account of an archive storage building designed for the Regional Archive of Schleswig-Holstein, Germany, given in a paper read to the tenth Triennial Meeting of ICOM. The mass of the building itself is such that it is a major contributory factor in the maintenance of a stable environment without air conditioning (Christofferson 1993).

As artefacts are vulnerable to rapid fluctuations in relative humidity, it is essential to protect them in transit, not only from mechanical damage, but also from changes in rh. This is most likely to occur in air travel as the rh may be as low as 12% even in the cabin of a plane (Mecklenburg 1991). Before agreeing to lend a work of art to another institution, the conservator will examine it carefully to see if it is fit to travel. If so, the results will be recorded in a special condition report which will travel with the artefact. The borrowing institution will have to prove that its own arrangements measure up to certain criteria, relating not only to security and fire precautions but also to light levels, relative humidity and temperature. If these reassurances are satisfactory, the artefact will be packed, note taken of how this was done and, on arrival at its destination, it will be left unopened for at least twenty-four hours. It will be checked again before leaving the borrowing institution. On arrival home, it will be left to acclimatize before being opened and checked again. It is usual for a courier to accompany the loan. Such precautions are necessary, not only to ensure the safety of the artefact, but also to qualify for indemnity and insurance cover.

LIGHTING

Most cultural material which is organic in nature is susceptible to damage caused by light, natural or artificial. Textiles, works of art on paper, especially water-colours and miniatures, and natural history specimens are the most vulnerable, paintings rather less so. The most obvious way in which this damage is manifested is in fading or colour change, but fibres such as textiles may be weakened and paper degraded. Daylight and some sources of artificial light such as fluorescent tubes have an ultraviolet component, that is rays of very short wavelength which are considered to be very damaging and so must be excluded. However, this is not the only problem. The strength or intensity of the light is also important or, more accurately, the intensity of the light and the duration of exposure to that light.

Glass does not afford complete protection against ultra-violet radiation. This may be achieved by the application of a special ultra-violet absorbing film to the windows or display cases, or the use of ultra-violet absorbing Perspex or Lexan, which is a polycarbonate, for 'glazing' where static will not create a problem. Pastels, for example, must not be 'glazed' with these, as the static would lift off the pigments. Fluorescent tubes can be fitted with an ultra-violet absorbing film. This film does not last indefinitely and will require renewal. Tungsten incandescent bulbs emit small amounts of ultra-violet radiation, tungsten-halogen and metal halide emit a lot and must be used with the appropriate filter. The recommended level for ultra-violet content has been reduced to less than ten microwatts per lumen.

As with other environmental factors, such as temperature and relative humidity, so too with light there is a 'high-tech' approach appropriate in some buildings, but for other institutions a good-housekeeping or common-sensical approach will be perfectly adequate. The use of blinds on windows will reduce the amount of daylight coming in. There is a range of acrylic films available which will reduce the total amount of light as well as excluding ultra-violet radiation. Their effective life-span may be quite short. Their application to period glass is not recommended. Remembering that the duration of exposure is also important, display cases might be covered except when viewing, or the light on a timer switched on by the viewer, the exhibits changed frequently — the scope for ingenuity is unlimited. It is useful to avail of the flexibility provided by spot-lights on tracks, especially if fitted with dimmer-switches. However, not only must precautions be taken to ensure that the spots are not a source of ultra-violet radiation, as stated above, they must not throw heat forward onto the exhibit, but allow it to dissipate out at the back of the lamp. Lighting within show-cases, unless well designed and controlled, is hazardous.

There are other considerations associated with lighting which relate more closely to aesthetics. Some of these are comparatively easy to resolve, such as the importance of ensuring that the light sources have good colour rendering or balance across the spectrum, in other words the light is not too blue, green or red. In addition, the colour temperature should be suited to the display area. For example, a light source with a very high colour temperature will emit a cold light which will not be pleasant in an area lit solely by artificial light. Some art lovers believe that paintings should be viewed in sunlight or daylight, but this is damaging and must be controlled. Nevertheless, it is pleasant to have some visual contact with outside while walking through a gallery. In an air-

conditioned building, especially one which is top-lit, the heat gain from sunlight entering will put an unnecessary strain on the plant. In this situation, the only effective way of handling it is to stop the sunlight gaining entry, perhaps by fitting blinds externally. The introduction of fibre optics for museum lighting has several advantages. It is excellent for modelling three-dimensional objects and, as the light source is outside the display case, the optic fibres do not transmit heat or ultra-violet to the bulbs themselves. However, the light source itself must be adequately ventilated as it gets hot.

PROTECTION AGAINST POLLUTANTS

Whether an institution has an air-conditioning plant or not, good house-keeping procedures will greatly assist in preventing dust accumulating on artefacts (Sandwith and Stainton 1991). Reference has already been made to the desirability of having double doors with an intervening lobby at the entrance and adequate cloakroom facilities. Additional protection is afforded by covering artefacts in storage with dust sheets. They can also be stored in boxes or folders of archival quality. Backing paintings with an inert board protects them from mechanical damage and ensures that they are less exposed to gaseous pollutants.

HOW TO CHOOSE A CONSERVATOR

The owner of an artefact may have decided that it should be conserved. As a first step, it is always wise either to have some idea of its value or, if one does not, to have it valued. Of course the decision to have an artefact conserved or not may be influenced by non-commercial considerations such as its historic importance or its sentimental value. Having established, for whatever reason, that the artefact should be conserved, the owner has then to choose a conservator to give an estimate and, if acceptable, to commission the work to be undertaken. How is this choice to be made?

Check the qualifications of the conservator. Training may have been by means of the older apprenticeship scheme or through a formal course at one of the recognized training institutions. The experience gained is also important, not only in terms of the number of years but also its diversity. Ask if he/she is a member of one of the professional organizations such as the Irish Professional Conservators' and Restorers' Association (IPCRA), Institute for the Conservation of Historic and Artistic Works in Ireland (ICHAWI), Institute of Paper Conservation (IPC), United Kingdom Institute of Conservation (UKIC), Association of British Picture Restorers (ABPR), British Antique Furniture Restorers' Association (BAFRA). Some of these bodies, such as ICHAWI, ABPR and BAFRA, now confer accreditation. Although inclusion in the conservation register kept by the Conservation Unit of the Museums and Galleries

Commission, London, is not an accreditation, the criteria for registration are quite exacting and could be taken as a guide to the conservator's professional status. If possible, visit the studio where the work on your artefact will be carried out. Note its layout, location, security precautions, equipment, organization and conformity with Health and Safety regulations.

Check that the conservator will either carry out the work or, if undertaken by an employee, that the employer will supervise it and accept overall responsibility for the result. Ask what other commissions have been undertaken and for whom and, if possible, check with the clients to know if they were satisfied with the work the conservator has done for them. Having checked these points to your satisfaction, you can then expect:

(1) A report assessing the artefact's present condition with some idea of what the causes of deterioration were. (It may be necessary to carry out some investigative techniques to assist in the formulation of this report.)

(2) A proposal as to what treatment is recommended. A good practitioner will be prepared to discuss alternatives with the client. For example, it may prove too costly for full conservation/restoration treatment to be applied and, as an alternative, the artefact may be treated to slow down its deterioration, that is preserved rather than redressing it. Listen to what is being said and if, for example in the case of a work of art on paper which is badly stained, the conservator advises against bleaching, it would be better not to insist as this procedure can be quite damaging to the paper itself. In other words do not expect a miracle!

(3) An estimate of the cost and the time involved to carry out the work. The client should expect to pay for a consultation and for written reports even though the work may not be commissioned, and also to pay travel expenses if these were incurred.

Once a report on the proposed treatment and an estimate of the cost are furnished, it would be considered unethical for another conservator to base an estimate on the same job specification. Before going ahead, the client should check such details as packaging, transportation and insurance for which he may be responsible while the artefact is being conserved (McGuinne 1998).

CONSERVATION IN IRELAND
THE NATIONAL MUSEUM OF IRELAND
As has been the case in many institutions in these islands, until very recently artefacts have been repaired by staff who have received in-house training and are graded as technicians, and so it has been in the National Museum. In 1997, a trained conservator was appointed as Head of Conservation at keeper level. This appointment was followed by the formation of a conservation department, an up-grading of some of the conservation staff, and the continuing development of new facilities in the museum in Collins Barracks. The staff numbers five.

THE NATIONAL GALLERY OF IRELAND
In 1964, Dr James White, Director of the National Gallery, consulted the Director of the Istituto Centrale del Restauro, Professor Pasquale Rotondi. As a result of this meeting, the Instituto became effectively the National Gallery's 'Restorer'. This supervisory role, which lasted for several years, covered the period when the Gallery's studio was designed, and the first appointments made were of conservators who were graduates of the Istituto Centrale. During these early years also, many of the Italian paintings in the collection were treated by a team of Italian conservators from the Istituto Centrale who were supervised by Professor Paolo Mora and his wife Laura. The oil painting section of the department has two trained conservators. The paper studio, which is responsible for the collection of works of art on paper and also for the environmental aspects of the Gallery, was set up in 1970. The studio functions in an advisory capacity to many other institutions. Both sections accept interns occasionally. Except for a three-and-a-half-year period when the staff numbered two, it has one conservator (O'Connor and McGuinne 1998).

THE NATIONAL LIBRARY OF IRELAND
For many years, the National Library and National Museum shared a book-binder. In 1993 the book-binder was appointed to the post of preservation officer in the National Library. In 1994 a trained conservator and an assistant were appointed on a contract basis specifically to conserve the map collection. Many of the maps were in such a parlous state that they had to be withdrawn from consultation by the public. The initial staffing levels are unchanged.

THE LIBRARY, TRINITY COLLEGE, DUBLIN
In June 1999, the conservation laboratory attached to the Library of Trinity College celebrated its twenty-fifth anniversary. When overseas funding, donated to assist the rescue operation in Florence after the floods of 1966, came to an end, the non-Italians working there had to leave. At this point, Anthony Cains, who had been in charge of the rescue operation in the Biblioteca Nazionale, was appointed to set up a conservation laboratory in TCD. Thus he became responsible for the care of one of the world's great libraries, housing many early Irish manuscripts, including the Book of Kells. The department advises other institutions including the

National Library, the Royal Irish Academy and the Delmas Bindery attached to Marsh's Library. Interns who are already graduates of a conservation programme are accepted occasionally. There is a staff of five.

MARSH'S LIBRARY (DELMAS CONSERVATION BINDERY)
This facility, which has a staff of four, undertakes commissions for the National Library and the National Archives as well as for members of the public.

COUNTY MUSEUMS
Monaghan, Donegal, Louth and Tipperary South Riding County Museums have conservation facilities and staff.

OTHER CONSERVATORS IN IRELAND
The second edition of *The Irish conservation directory*, published by the Irish Professional Conservators' and Restorers' Association (IPCRA), lists almost one hundred members in many disciplines working in Ireland, north and south. Some are listed as individuals or institutional.

ORGANIZATIONS REPRESENTING CONSERVATORS IN IRELAND
In March 1982, a small group of conservators met in the Joint Conservation Laboratory of the Ulster Museum/ Queen's University in Belfast and, as a result, the Irish Professional Conservators and Restorers Association (IPCRA) was founded. It now has a membership of more than 150, most of whom are conservators, while others, termed 'associates', support the aims of the association. These are to promote the practice of conservation and restoration in Ireland to internationally acceptable standards, to provide a forum for discussion, and to disseminate technical information. After the publication of the first edition of *The Irish conservation directory* in 1988, it was decided to establish a more formal structure in order to be in a better position to attract the financial support needed to develop training programmes in conservation, and also to be in a stronger position to represent the profession in Ireland. An *ad hoc* committee of IPCRA members founded the Institute for the Conservation of Historic and Artistic Works in Ireland (ICHAWI) as a limited company, without share capital. Its main objective is 'to promote for the benefit of Ireland the preservation and conservation of historic and artistic works therein'. The subsidiary objectives relate to how this is to be achieved, mainly by education. The institute organizes courses, some of which are of interest to conservators, others such as 'Caring for Collections' of more interest to curators/administrators. Because it fulfills an educational role, the Institute has charitable status.

In the 1990s, the issue of accreditation became of great concern to the profession, not only in Ireland but also in the UK and in Europe. ICHAWI, which at this point comprised the founding members only, formulated a Code of Conduct. Dr Marc Laenen, then Director General of the International Centre for the Preservation and the Restoration of Cultural Property, Rome (ICCROM), was contacted and asked to recommend an expert with multi-disciplinary skills who would come to Ireland to assess the members with a view to accreditation. Subsequently in March 1996, Sir Bernard Feilden, Director Emeritus, ICCROM, and Dr Peter Cannon-Brookes came to Dublin and spent five days visiting the studios and sites for which each founding member was responsible, and interviewing the candidates individually. After this rigorous assessment, the assessors sent a favourable report to the Director General of ICCROM. The founding members felt confident that, having written a Code of Conduct, been assessed themselves and also agreed the criteria for membership, the Institute was now in a position to accept new members. In order to ensure that potential candidates conform to internationally accepted standards, an external assessor is appointed to the interview panel. The Institute has organized, since its foundation, lectures or seminars such as Chemistry in Conservation, Photography, Caring for Collections, Electronic Environmental Monitoring, Caring for Historic Houses and their Contents, Conservation Framing, Moulding and Casting, Preserving the Cultural Heritage: An Holistic Approach, Collections in Storage, Wood Structure and Identification. In the absence of facilities to train conservators in Ireland, ICHAWI gives small bursaries to students wishing to pursue an accredited course abroad.

The Institute was represented on two sub-committees of the Museum and Archive Committee of the Heritage Council, one relating to standards and accreditation, the other to training. As a result of their deliberations, a report on *The introduction of a standards and accreditation scheme for Irish museums* was presented to government in June 1999. Under the provisions of the *Heritage Act* 1995, the functions of the Heritage Council are defined as proposing policies for the identification, protection, preservation and enhancement of the national heritage, including heritage objects. As defined by the Standards and Accreditation sub-committee: 'Museums are not-for-profit institutions that collect, safeguard, hold in trust, research, develop and interpret collections of original objects and original objects on loan, for the public benefit. They function publicly as places where people learn from and find inspiration and enjoyment through the display and research of original objects'.

INTERNATIONAL LINKS
Both IPCRA and ICHAWI are represented on the National Council for Conservation-Restoration which is a body of UK conservation organizations in partnership with the conservation unit of the Museum and Galleries

Commission. Ireland has been affiliated to ICCROM since the late 1980s. Irish students avail of the various training courses run by ICCROM in paper and stone conservation, scientific principles of conservation, non-destructive and micro-destructive methods of analysis. Ireland renewed its membership of International Council on Monuments and Sites (ICOMOS) in 1994. Ireland has been represented at three meetings convened to agree at European level a full range of professional competencies for the conservator/restorer. A workshop entitled 'Centres of Excellence', held in Amsterdam in 1997, was followed by a meeting in Pavia in 1997 which resulted in the 'Document of Pavia', and in Vienna in 1998 which produced the 'Document of Vienna'. The issues raised are diverse and complex and by no means resolved.

Bibliography

Bowman, S. 1991 *Science and the past.* London.
Cassar, M. 1995 *Environmental management guidelines for museums and galleries.* London.
Christoffersen, L. 1993 'Resource-saving storage of historical material', *Preprints,* ICOM Committee for Conservation. Paris.
Corr, S. 2000 *Caring for collections: a handbook of preventive conservation.* Dublin.
McGuinne, N. (ed) 1998 *The Irish conservation directory.* Dublin.
McParland, M. 1982 'Book conservation workshop manual, part two: the nature and chemistry of paper, its history, analysis and conservation', *The New Bookbinder* 2, pp. 17–28.
McParland, M. (ed) 1997 *Preserving the cultural heritage: an holistic approach.* Dublin.
Mecklenberg, M. (ed) 1991 *Art in transit. Studies in the transport of paintings.* Washington
O'Connor, A. and McGuinne, N. 1998 *The deeper picture: conservation at the National Gallery of Ireland.* Dublin.
Oddy, A. (ed) 1992 *The art of the conservator.* London.
Sandwith, H. and Stainton, S. 1991 *The National Trust manual of housekeeping.* London.
Sitwell, C. and Stainforth, S. (eds) 1998 *Studies in the history of painting restoration.* London.
Thomson, G. 1986 *The museum environment.* London.

Conservation and Restoration: The Built Environment

GRELLAN D. ROURKE

We seek to preserve buildings because they have some intrinsic value. This is not solely an artistic or cultural value; they are also a historical document of the past and a record of technological innovation and development. There is a wealth of information contained within, not all of it immediately apparent. Historically, the focus has been on individual monuments, but in recent years a more holistic approach has been adopted and to-day it is recognized that entire groups of buildings are important. The historic monument is now not necessarily the individual building but its setting, be it a landscape or an urban environment.

APPROACHES TO CONSERVATION AND RESTORATION

In the past there have been fundamentally different approaches to the preservation of historic buildings. At one end of the spectrum there was the minimalist intervention, repairs to retard the process of natural decay, supported by the Society for the Protection of Ancient Buildings (SPAB), founded by William Morris, and set out in his manifesto (Harvey 1972, 210–12). This was a strong reaction to the over-restoration and re-working of historic buildings, particularly during the nineteenth century by Viollet-le-Duc and others. In the last century there was much concern about how one should proceed, and at an international level there were attempts to work towards a standard for good conservation and restoration practice. The Charter of Athens (1931) attempted to define the basic principles, and these were given further study and enlarged in the more recent Charter of Venice (ICOMOS 1965) which superseded it. The latter charter presents an internationally agreed set of guidelines on how to proceed and covers definitions, conservation, restoration, historic sites, excavations and publication. The sub-sections below examine these areas in greater detail.

Preservation of historic buildings is very different to preserving a museum artefact, as it is more dynamic. At one end of the scale a ruinous mediaeval building might only require a conservation process; at the other, the preservation of an urban Georgian terrace house may require restoration which might include an element of adaptation to suit contemporary needs. In this case preservation may demand a new use or function to sustain the long-term viability of the historic building. However, it is important that this new function should respect the integrity of the structure and its applied decoration.

But when presented with an historic building which is a composite from different periods, can one ever remove more recent parts? This question has generated a lot of heated debate. Clearly in dealing with a mediaeval building, say a thirteenth-century abbey which was much altered in the fifteenth century, both periods must be retained in any project of conservation or restoration. But it will not always be possible to proceed in this way, 'preserve as found', according to the strict SPAB view. A Georgian building, with its sash windows replaced by mid-twentieth-century aluminium windows, needs another approach. It would be desirable to remove these and replace them with sashes to the original pattern. Paul Drury (1997) put the case very clearly when he states 'restoration to the last period of considered change may be justified. By this is meant a phase of adaptation which although probably in the style of its own day was undertaken with obvious regard for both the final appearance of the building and the integrity of its structure'. It is important that any recent part removed should have no significance, architectural or historic, and that speculative restoration is avoided. In general, though, a building should not be restored to some earlier period of its development with the attendant removal of later essential aspects of its overall integrity.

To insist on a clear distinction between new and old work is not always the best way forward. Integrating the work into a coherent whole makes sense when we look at the development of historic buildings. Many are from more than one period, building up several historic layers; the new works are the latest layer. To the trained observer, these changes will be visible under inspection and, in any case, all works should be fully recorded and preferably published. When a distinction does need to be made, it should be done in such a way that it is not detrimental to the visual appreciation of the whole.

Restoration has moved more to the fore in recent years, and sometimes the word has erroneously become synonymous with the preservation of historic structures, leading to the view that a building can only be preserved if it is restored. Unless there is a very good body of documentation, it is impossible to restore a building without elements of conjecture; then a decision must be made on the level of such conjecture. This brings us into a very grey area indeed, and one has to tread very carefully. A sound level of judgement is necessary and certainly nothing should be done which in any way falsifies the artistic or historic evidence; no part of the existing historic building which has worth should be altered or removed. The patina it has acquired through time must also be respected.

Restoration allows us to experience the building as it would or might have been in its original state. The restoration process may require the use of traditional techniques of construction and decoration, or it may be considered desirable to use a more modern approach. Whatever path is taken, it is essential that the overall integrity of the building should not be compromised. Restoration can often present the possibility of experimentation with materials and methods of construction, and this can give new insights into and broaden our perspective on and understanding of the past. In undertaking a project of conservation or restoration to an historic building, it is essential to employ professional advisers with relevant experience in conservation and restoration. The following headings should be carefully considered.

RESEARCH
The age of the historic building will dictate what might be available. With early buildings one must rely on brief historic reference and, more importantly, on detailed site study and investigation; but by the seventeenth and eighteenth centuries, however, more documentation was made. Where this has survived, much information can be found relating to the construction of the building and later alteration where this has occurred. Prints and drawings may also be of help, particularly where loss has occurred in the interim. Antiquarians recorded early and late-mediaeval sites, particularly in the nineteenth century, and these can be important sources of material, although not everything recorded is necessarily accurate.

In more recent times there has been a greater interest in preserving past records. The Irish Architectural Archive in its brief existence has already amassed an important body of records. Other important repositories of historic documentation include the National Archives, the National Library, the Royal Irish Academy, the Royal Society of Antiquaries of Ireland and local libraries. Every possible source of historic documentation should be exhausted at the outset of the project.

SURVEY AND RECORDS
A survey can never be too detailed, but it is important that it be accurate, as it will reveal a lot about the building and, more particularly, what may be happening to it. A detailed survey will permit one to get to know the building intimately; time spent at this stage will repay itself many times over and will certainly allow for a smoother-running project.

The architect personally responsible for the project should be involved in the survey. There are different types of survey for different situations, but hands-on recording will often yield more information about the building. It is possible to commission a set of wonderfully detailed photogrammetric drawings, but that will often give little feeling or understanding for the structure. Each type of survey has its own place and value. It is important to remember that recording and surveying do not stop once the job starts on site; they are an ongoing process. Not all features will present themselves at the outset and exciting discoveries are often made during the course of a project, so provision must be made to accommodate such an event. A flexible approach is fundamental in undertaking any work to an historic building; everything cannot be set in stone at the outset and the building contract should reflect this fact.

ARCHAEOLOGICAL INVESTIGATION
Very often work to an historic building will require the services of an archaeologist, especially where it is necessary to strengthen foundations, investigate original ground floor levels or install services. If possible, this work should be undertaken during the investigative period so that the findings can more easily be incorporated into the overall project before the main contractor begins on site.

STRUCTURAL CONSIDERATIONS
This can be one of the most important factors. It is no use embarking upon a costly restoration or conservation project to an interior or decorative work when there is a fundamental problem with the structure. Appearances can be very deceptive. An historic structure may look fine and show little outward sign of underlying structural problems, but in the course of an intervention difficulties can appear with alarming rapidity, resulting in possible irretrievable loss of historic fabric or, worse, loss

of life. Throughout the project, any cracks or deformation should be monitored very regularly.

Part of the initial investigative process must be a structural analysis; this will more often that not require some opening up to reveal the true picture. Perfectly sound-looking walls may no longer be capable of doing what they were originally designed to do. Solutions to deal with structural problems in historic buildings need to be sensitive, but occasionally the problems will be so serious that the intervention may need to be invasive if the building is to be saved. Innovative solutions should be sought so that they will impinge on the building as little as possible.

Restoration of structures which have been roofless for a considerable period requires particular attention. They may be structurally sound as ruins, but once a restoration is attempted, the equilibrium is being interfered with and new stresses are being introduced; the building may not be able to adapt to its new role and it might be necessary to upgrade its structural capability. Grouting may be required. If so, it is important to remember that the grout used must be compatible, so that the walls still retain an element of flexibility; they must never become rigid.

SCIENTIFIC INVESTIGATION

Before any work should start on site and preferably before the specification stage, a certain amount of scientific investigation must be undertaken. Detailed analytical laboratory work will be required to ascertain the make-up of mortars or internal plaster finishes or the processes involved in the deterioration of stone. If the historic building uses more than one external building material, as is often the case, it will be necessary to know if there is some undesired interaction which will require resolution.

SPECIALIST WORK

Science has come to play a much bigger role in conservation work and new developments and techniques are constantly coming on the market. The architect must be informed about up-to-date scientific research and be able to make value judgements on a variety of treatments. It will often be necessary to call in the expertise of specialists and it is important to ensure that such specialists have the necessary experience to undertake the work; previous examples of their work should be examined. The effectiveness of a conservation process is only as good as the person doing the work.

It is important to realize that the process of deterioration cannot be halted, but conservation is an invaluable aid in slowing down this rate. Different materials will present different problems and consequently different solutions. Interventions should be reversible; the concept of reversibility in conservation is considered essential, but it is important to be realistic. While it may be theoretically possible to reverse a process under laboratory conditions, this will not be quite as successful out of doors on a building site. The least invasive intervention should be chosen where possible.

RECORDING THE AFTERMATH OF AN INTERVENTION

Once the specialist conservation process has been completed, particularly if there has been a chemical intervention, it is essential that monitoring be continued afterwards to ascertain if it is indeed doing what it is supposed to do. If there are subsequent problems, at least others can be alerted and so, hopefully, similar problems could be avoided in future at other sites. There is a need for a constant exchange of such information between professionals, and this is sadly lacking.

MONITORING AND SUPERVISION

This is an essential tool in the practice of conservation and restoration. No amount of preparation in term of drawings and detailed specifications can compensate for bad on-site supervision. Much destruction has been visited upon unfortunate defenceless historic buildings due to a lack of a suitably qualified and experienced supervisor. Time spent on site during the works will pay dividends; problems can be anticipated more easily and resolved before irredeemable damage is caused. It will also lead to improved working practices and relations on site.

EXPERIMENTATION

It may be necessary for some experimentation to be carried out prior to working on the building. The recreation of historic mortars will be quite a new concept to most masons, and they should spend some time familiarizing themselves with mixing and using suitable lime mortars. Sample panels for pointing stone and brickwork should be executed until the correct mix and finish is achieved. Repairs to building materials should only be attempted by suitably qualified personnel.

SITE SAFETY

In recent years safety legislation and regulations have been introduced (*Safety, Health and Welfare at Work Act* 1989), and it is a legal requirement to be familiar with them and implement them on site. Particular care must be taken with an historic building as there can be so many unknowns; risks must never be taken. Appropriate safety measures should be observed; there should be standard safety procedures in operation on site at all times.

MAINTENANCE

Many problems could be avoided if buildings were

consistently maintained; in Ireland, we have a very poor record in this regard. As an integral part of the project, a follow-up programme of maintenance should be put in place by the client/owner to ensure that the conservation or restoration work will not have been in vain; consequently, the life of the building will be greatly extended.

DOCUMENTATION AND PUBLICATION

Once the project has come to a conclusion on site, there is one further step which must be taken, one which is so often neglected. All the pre-works research and survey material, together with the records made throughout the duration of the project, specialist reports and the like, should be put together in a coherent way and kept so that they will be accessible in future years to architectural historians and those who will work again on the historic building at some future date. Ideally, the work should be published so that it more freely available for record and comment. The Irish Georgian Society *Bulletin* has made a start in this regard.

CASE STUDY: ROSS CASTLE, KILLARNEY, COUNTY KERRY

This project began its life as the consolidation of a ruinous medieval building in serious structural condition, and it was probably the most dangerous project ever undertaken by the National Monuments

Service. However, its position in one of the most picturesque locations in Ireland on the shores of Lough Leane, its romantic place in the imagination of so many people and its potential as a visitor attraction all influenced the development of the project into a full restoration proposal. The EU Structural Fund programme facilitated this transformation.

The project has been chosen as a case study because of its complexity, the opportunity it presented with regard to possible research and scientific investigation and because, like so many such undertakings, it is not always possible to abide by the strict codes outlined in the various charters, especially when a major structural intervention is necessary. In recent years there have been a number of restoration projects; EU funding has helped facilitate this. While it can be seriously argued that a small number of well-chosen buildings should be restored, given our history which has rendered almost all our mediaeval buildings roofless ruins, we must be careful that the current restoration mania does not get out of hand. There must be very good reason to go down the road of restoration, and very few projects will be ideal candidates.

HISTORIC BACKGROUND

Ross Castle, a fine tower house defended by a fortified

Fig. 36.1 Ross Castle, Killarney, county Kerry, before consolidation and restoration.

Fig. 36.2 Ross Castle, Killarney, county Kerry, after consolidation and restoration.

bawn with circular flanking towers, was constructed by the O'Donoghues on the shores of Lough Leane in the later fifteenth century. Like many mediaeval buildings, it was altered many times to accommodate new ideas. The first changes occurred in the sixteenth century with the addition of larger windows at upper levels and modifications to the existing battlements to insert musket loops. A house was constructed against the keep on the lake side in 1688, by which time it had passed into the ownership of the Browne family. The castle itself is a rectangular keep with the larger chambers located at one end and the spiral staircase and small chambers at the other. It is austere, with few decorative features. A barrack, constructed against the south side in the middle if the eighteenth century, caused major structural alterations to the castle; the internal crosswall and lower stone vault were removed and six Georgian sash windows were inserted into the east wall

PREVIOUS ATTEMPTS TO HALT STRUCTURAL DETERIORATION
The later barrack alterations fundamentally undermined the structural integrity of the castle, and much effort was made during the nineteenth and early twentieth centuries to counteract the resultant structural problems:

• metal plates were fixed to the east and west facades and tied together with metal bars;

• two walls (*ca.* 1.2 m wide) were constructed internally to support the collapsing upper stone vault;

• the six large sash windows were removed and the opes blocked up in an attempt to consolidate the east wall which was by then falling outwards;

• a large buttress was constructed against the north-west corner of the castle;

• a roof of metal 'I'-sectioned beams and precast concrete was added to waterproof the interior of the building and,

• more recently (1930s), part of the east wall was grouted in pure cement to stop it from collapsing.

All in all the building was in a very sorry state when taken into care, many of the earlier attempts to halt collapse having failed, and one of the major concerns during the project was keeping the castle from falling apart while it was 'restructured'.

HISTORICAL RESEARCH
As with so many historic buildings of this period in Ireland, there is virtually no documentation of importance in relation to the construction or fabric of this castle. Due to its romantic and picturesque location, Ross Castle was much recorded in print and drawings, most of this material dating from the late eighteenth and nineteenth centuries. However, the detail is very

inaccurate and in many cases there is so much artistic licence that these documents were of little help for restoration purposes. Most of the written historic documentation related to the later barrack building. A detailed knowledge of the building and its construction could only be gleaned from detailed *in situ* survey and study.

INITIAL INVESTIGATION

The alterations made access into the interior space very difficult and, in places, impossible, so all the internal features could not be recorded before works began. From the outset it was necessary to adopt a very flexible approach, and the survey was built up as one went along. However, the survey of the exterior was completed together with the basic outline for the plans and the accessible interior features. Archaeological investigation within part of the interior was undertaken and this gave the base of the original internal crosswall of the castle; it was essential to reconstruct this structural feature if the castle was to be saved from collapse. Site investigations were undertaken early on to establish the condition of the foundations, particularly with respect to rock, and, fortunately, these investigations confirmed that most of the castle had been built on rock outcrop.

THE CONDITION OF THE CASTLE BEFORE COMMENCEMENT OF WORKS

At the commencement of works, despite all the interventions, the castle was probably not very far from partial collapse. The ties and plates had badly rusted and were no longer effective. The upper vault had collapsed in part onto the later internal supporting walls, and the east wall had continued its movement outwards. The grouting had only penetrated into the wall in certain areas, forming large 'floating' masses of walling which had become very dangerous. The large buttress at the north-west corner had added so much weight that this section of the castle had begun to separate, two large cracks forming at either end of the buttress and running the entire height of the castle. The steel and concrete roof structure had deteriorated with much of the steelwork rusted away; it was a wonder that some of the concrete slabs actually remained *in situ*.

RESEARCH, SCIENTIFIC INVESTIGATION AND EXPERIMENTATION

A project such as this presents an ideal opportunity to experiment and in doing so to find out more about the building and its construction. Analytical work was undertaken on both the mortar and internal render so that we could formulate materials which would be compatible with the original. A wide variety of historic mortars exists and conducting this research each time a building project is undertaken adds to the greater picture. Hopefully this will eventually yield a greater understanding of the diversity and development of historic mortars in Ireland.

The internal render had been applied in more than one coat, all but the final one with animal hair mixed through it to give extra strength and prevent cracking during the drying process. Investigation showed that the hair came from cattle or cows' tails and, surprisingly, this was not an easy material to come by. Once the mixing formulae were known, operatives experimented with them so that they became accustomed to the mixes and acquired a competency to work the material in a satisfactory way.

Experimentation also took place with wicker-work to reproduce the original patterns. The woven material was placed on sand and then removed. The pattern on the sand was then compared with that on the remaining vaulting within the castle to make sure it was correct.

INITIAL WORKS

When the project commenced, works were limited to conservation and repair; later, however, it developed into a major project of consolidation and restoration when sufficient funding became available and the full extent of re-structuring became evident. Initially it was decided to consolidate the north end of the castle by reconstructing the original crosswall found in excavation and reinstating the small chambers. Though these features had been removed in the restructuring, following the construction of the adjacent barrack, much of the evidence had been left cantilevered out from the inner wall faces, and most of the internal features were intact. In addition, the spiral staircase was intact, together with the doorways into each chamber, so it was possible to make a very accurate reconstruction of this part of the castle.

MONITORING MOVEMENT AND INTERIM STRUCTURAL INTERVENTION

During this time, the rest of the castle was monitored for movement to try to build up an accurate picture of what was happening. It took some time to do this, otherwise the wrong conclusions might have been reached. Monitoring of cracks needs to be done, if possible, over a long period. There are two types of cracks, those which are moving in a constant way and those which have a cycle of movement, so that at particular times they are opening while at others they are closing. It is important to differentiate between these two types of movement.

Crack monitors were fitted to all cracks, and these were recorded at regular intervals throughout the life of the project. In areas where active work was taking place monitoring was undertaken very frequently. Some of the cracks were active, particularly in the east wall and the upper stone vault, so it was decided to introduce an independent steel and timber structure into the castle in order to give essential support to the three outer walls — by this time the north wall had been stabilized — and the upper vault. This support consisted of raking shores on three sides of the castle tied through the building onto an independent steel frame standing within. This was very awkward and slow to achieve, given very limited access within the castle and the risks of possible collapse.

THE 'RESTRUCTURING' OF THE CASTLE

Once the internal rebuilding of the small chambers had been completed, this end of the castle had been stabilized, and works then started on the main structure. The east wall was repaired and consolidated to a height of the springing of the lower vault, which had been removed when the barrack had been constructed; the west wall needed only minor repair at this level. The stone vault was reconstructed following the outline of the original which was clearly visible on the interior of the south wall. Due to the deteriorated structural state of the walls, it was necessary to introduce an additional reinforced structure above and in the haunches of this vault. Fortunately, there was enough height to achieve this without raising the floor level above the vault.

Just before this vault was constructed there were two collapses, both from areas which looked perfectly sound. An infill panel approximately 2.0 m high, which blocked up a later ope in the south wall, presented a well-pointed face showing no deformation. However, within the blocking there was only rough dry rubble, and the walling had been built on a sharply sloping base, so the whole infill just slipped outwards and onto the timber formwork set in place for the construction of the vault. The second collapse occurred at the top of one of the two thick (1.2 m) crosswalls built to support the upper vault. Again the wall showed no deformation and looked in perfect condition, but the interior was roughly constructed of coarse rubble with very little mortar. Luckily, these areas had been monitored for safety reasons, and there was a warning, albeit very short. However, it brought home the necessity for constant monitoring and vigilance throughout the project. It also demonstrated that one can never undertake too much investigation, even in areas which have the outward appearance of stability.

Once this lower vault was reconstructed, further investigation took place. The buttress at the north-west corner was taken down; it soon became clear why it had been placed there. This corner of the castle had been undermined, the rock outcrop having been removed, when a house had been built against the castle in 1688 (the roof outline of which was still visible on the west wall). The buttress had been added after the house had been demolished to give support to this corner; however, in addition to providing lateral support, its own self-weight

had added to the problems of the castle. To remedy the situation, a reinforced concrete 'crutch' was inserted into the rock outcrop to support the re-made corner; large sections of rock were excavated further along the lake shore and these were positioned to mask the 'crutch' where the rock had been originally removed.

The consolidation of the outer wall progressed up the castle. Bands of walling about 2.0 m high were stabilized and repaired in short lengths. It was necessary to proceed in this fashion given the precarious nature of the walls, particularly on the east side. At the springing of the upper vault large segments of this walling had been cement grouted, and, as work progressed, these unstable sections needed constant monitoring as they were liable to fall out onto the scaffolding.

As debris and later failed supports were removed from the interior many complete and partial features were revealed. It was most fortunate that in all cases there was enough of the medieval feature to effect a reconstruction with little or no conjecture. It was surprising there had not been more loss, given the extent of the later interventions. The next level brought us up to a timber floor; the wall-plates and large oak beams were adzed in the traditional way. It took time to develop the correct action in using the adze but the final result made the effort worthwhile. All the planks were adzed and pegged to the joists beneath to create an uneven floor. From examination of an intact timber floor in a castle in county Kilkenny and from the detailed evidence of levels on site, it would appear that there was originally a layer of compacted earth on this floor.

The upper vault had collapsed onto the temporary support beneath it, so reluctantly much of it had to be taken down, although we did save the springing on either side. The upper stone vault was then reconstructed in the same manner as the one below using reinforced concrete ties in the haunches and above the stone vault. Once this level had been reached, it was possible to remove some of the temporary steel and timber bracing and shoring. This gave much more room to work on the repair of the interior. Unfortunately, the ingress of water over the years had removed much of the internal plaster, but wherever it was sound it was retained.

RESTORATION OF THE ROOF AND BATTLEMENTS

Most of the uppermost floor of the castle was conserved, although it was necessary to rebuild a section of the west wall containing the flues which had been interfered with. While all this work had gone on, the remnants of battlements had been netted as they were very close to collapse and, given the extreme exposure of the site, this was also necessary for reasons of safety. The masonry used in the construction of the battlements was of very poor quality and at this stage the mortar had so degraded that it no longer functioned. It was necessary to record in detail what remained, numbering the stones; the walls were then taken down and reconstructed. The actual outline of the battlements had fallen away, but there were various remains of features which gave some hint to what must have been originally there.

At this stage a survey was undertaken in the south of the country of other tower houses of the period where sections of battlement remained intact; there was not a great number of them. In time the different patterns were tried on the castle — each side of the castle was quite different because of the diversity of battlement features, so it was a hard fit. Only one worked with any success, that of Ballycarbery Castle about 40 miles south-west of the site, in fact the nearest one! Our parallel for the later machicolations with musket loops was Coolhull Castle in county Wexford; the remains of the originals at Ross were uncannily identical to these.

At roof level, the remains of stone corbels on the lateral walls indicated the location of the original timber trusses. There was a caphouse which created a complex roof geometry; it was necessary to construct a detailed model of the roof and battlement features to resolve possible problems and create a roof which was not only convincing but one which actually worked. The roof design was based on the only known example from this time, that of Dunsoghley Castle near Dublin. All the oak roof members were roughly adzed and the whole construction pegged in the traditional way. Large heavy Valentia slate was used. The possibility that thatch had been employed was examined but, given the details of the interface of the roof structure and battlement features, it would have been impossible to circum-navigate the wall-walk. In addition, fragments of slate had been found during the works and research had shown that slate quarries had existed in the locality early on. The water from the roof was taken away down the garderobe chute so downpipes would not appear on the external walls. Fine bronze frames were used for the windows to maximize the area of glass and make the glazing as unobtrusive as possible.

All these works were undertaken by trained craftsmen of the National Monuments Service, and this was of enormous help in achieving a high standard of work; it also facilitated the possibility of experimentation which is a vital element of a project like this.

SERVICES

The introduction of services into an historic building can be difficult; they need to be hidden away as much as possible. Fortunately, there was enough space throughout to use underfloor electric heating and it was possible to bury all the electrical conduit within the plaster thickness of the walls. Where possible electrical points were located where furniture would be positioned and all light switches were centralized at the reception

desk to minimize modern intrusion.

TIMESCALE AND FINANCING

Works began at Ross Castle in the late 1970s. The project was not sufficiently defined at the outset and was funded directly by the exchequer. Serious structural problems inhibited progress and the number of workmen who could work on the building at any given time was limited, so progress was slow. Funding was inadequate for the scale of the project and for some years works were halted due to commitments to other projects in the district. In a task of such magnitude the full scope of the undertaking should be agreed at the start and a detailed works programme prepared in advance of going on site. This was not the case here; the project evolved gradually. Ideally, the complete restoration should have taken possibly three years; in reality it took very much longer. It was not until the latter stages that additional resources became available through the EU Structural Funds programme and this made a huge difference to progress. The restoration was completed in early 1993 and the castle opened to the public that summer. During the previous five years a collection of early oak furniture was put together and facsimiles of ceramics and pottery were made which are now on display in the castle.

Bibliography

Ashurst, J. and N. 1989 *Practical building conservation.* London.

Ashurst, J. and Dimes, F. G. 1990 *Conservation of building and decorative stone.* London.

Brereton, C. 1991 *The repair of historic buildings: advice on principles and methods.* London.

Denslagen, W. 1994 *Architectural restoration in western Europe: controversy and continuity.* Amsterdam.

Drury, P. 1997 'Conservation techniques: the built environment' in R. Harrison (ed) *Manual of heritage management* (London), pp. 196–201.

Harvey, J. 1972 *Conservation of buildings.* London.

ICOMOS 1965 *The International Charter for the Conservation and Restoration of Monuments and Sites* (The Charter of Venice). London.

ICOMOS 1990 *Guide to recording historic buildings.* London.

Insall, D. W. 1975 *The care of old buildings today: a practical guide.* London.

Conservation and Industrial Archaeology

FRED HAMOND

The present chapter highlights the many issues which arise in the conservation of industrial heritage in the Republic of Ireland. Although this heritage ranges from landscapes to documents and oral records, the paper will focus on built forms and, to a lesser extent, machinery and artefacts. An introductory section outlines the concept of industrial heritage in an Irish context and highlights the urgency of its conservation. The statutory legislation for its protection is reviewed and its effectiveness assessed. Practical conservation by recording and physical retention are then discussed, with an extended presentation on site restoration. Capital and revenue funding issues are also addressed. The paper concludes by highlighting the value of conservation plans to such work.

IRELAND'S INDUSTRIAL HERITAGE

Industrial heritage comprises those vestiges of past industrial activities which have survived to the present day. As such a wide range of activities is embraced, some form of classification is required if only to grasp its scope. As is evident from **Table 37.1**, industry is not confined solely to manufacturing, but also extends to the extraction of raw materials and the provision of public utilities. Because it is necessary to move people, raw materials and finished products, communications are also an important aspect of this heritage as well. Moreover, because of their importance to mechanization, prime movers (especially steam engines) also have thematic interest, even though they are subsets of the other four categories too.

Industrial archaeology is the study of all material manifestations of past industries, not just those which now survive, in order to form an overview of industrial development and its impact upon past societies. Although it could be regarded simply as a theoretical framework for understanding and interpreting a particular facet of our past material culture, the fact that it also embraces a host of techniques relating to research, recording and interpretation makes it of real practical relevance to the conservation of what currently survives. The relevance of such techniques becomes apparent when one considers the wide variety of forms in which this heritage can be manifest (**Table 37.2**).

During the formative years of the development of industrial archaeology in Britain in the 1950s and 1960s, many of the subject's practitioners focussed on those sites which emerged as a consequence of the so-called Industrial Revolution, which took place between 1750 and 1850. This period is characterized by quantum changes in the nature, scale and organization of Britain's agriculture and industry, all of which had a profound impact on its society. Outside Britain, however, such revolutionary changes generally came about later and progressed at a slower pace. In Ireland, large-scale, factory-based urban industries are found, but are generally confined to a few specific localities. However, the countryside abounds in vestiges of numerous small industries which formed part of the agricultural cycle and were integrated into the domestic mode of production. This contrast with Britain is partly due to the fact that Ireland has no significant deposits of coal and iron to form the basis of large-scale heavy industries. Its economy has therefore been, until very recently, predominantly rural in character, with its industrial focus on the processing of agricultural products.

The first nationally significant industry in this regard was flour milling during the later eighteenth century, followed by brewing, distilling and linen production during the nineteenth. Much of the impetus for Ireland's industrial flowering at this time was due to political events in Britain (for instance, the Napoleonic Wars) and the development of trading and commercial centres such as Dublin and Cork. This progressive trend was, however, halted on account of the Great Famine in the 1840s. The countryside became depopulated and the towns expanded, necessitating the eventual establishment of public utilities to support their growing populations, many of which were now engaged full-time in manufacturing, trade and commerce. Steam power, mechanization and factory labour became the norm, although only of real consequence in the larger urban areas such as Belfast, Cork, Dublin, Dundalk and Limerick. The coming of the railways in the second half of the nineteenth century also enabled these town-based industries to extend their spheres of influence beyond their immediate hinterlands, often to the detriment of more local enterprises. However, only in Belfast, with its linen mills, tobacco factories, rope works and shipyards, can industrial development be said to have been on par with British industries in terms of its magnitude and significance.

THE LOSS OF IRELAND'S INDUSTRIAL HERITAGE

On the basis of various industrial heritage surveys which have been carried out throughout Ireland since Green's pioneering work in the 1950s and McCutcheon's in the 1970s (Green 1963; McCutcheon 1980), it is estimated that over 100,000 sites of industrial interest have operated at one time or another. Unfortunately only a small fraction — less than 5% — has been recorded by fieldwork. Where field survey has been carried out, it was invariably found that a high proportion of sites had been demolished and many of the survivors were defunct and falling into ruin.

There are, of course, many reasons why industrial sites in particular become obsolete. Most were designed for very specific purposes and cannot be cost-effectively re-equipped, enlarged or adapted to new uses. Many sites, especially those in rural centres, are further disadvantaged by poor location and difficult access. It is also inevitable that many buildings erected in the late eighteenth and early nineteenth centuries will incur escalating repair costs as their fabric comes to the end of

Table 37.1 Scope of Industrial Heritage and Examples of Subject-Matter

CATEGORY	ACTIVITIES ENCOMPASSED	EXAMPLES
1. Extractive industries	Extraction of naturally occurring raw materials.	Mines, quarries, gravel and sand-pits.
2. Manufacturing industries	Processing of raw materials into usable forms.	Limekilns, brickworks, saltpans, flax scutching mills.
	Transformation of materials into finished products.	Glass-works, foundries, corn-mills, textile mills, breweries, engineering works.
3. Public utilities	Power production — gas and electricity.	Coal and oil gasworks, hydro-electric plant.
	Sanitary provision — water supply and drainage, waste and sewage disposal.	Reservoirs, wells, hand pumps, refuse depots, sewage pumping stations.
4. Communications	Transportation of materials, products, people and animals by road, water, rail and air.	Roads, bridges, mileposts, harbours, coastguard stations, lighthouses, canals, railways, tramways, airfields.
	Transmission of information by post, telegraph, telephone, radio, television and electronic means.	Postboxes, post offices, telegraph offices, telephone boxes, radio and television masts, satellite tracking stations.
5. Prime movers	Renewable energy: motive power — human, animal, wind and water.	Treadmills, horse gins, windmills, watermills, tide-mills.
	Fossil energy: motive power — steam, internal combustion and electric.	Steam engines, gas, oil, petrol and diesel engines, electric motors.

Table 37.2 Physical Forms of Industrial Heritage and Examples Thereof

ARTEFACT/MONUMENT	PHYSICAL FORM	EXAMPLES
Built forms	Earthworks	Railway embankments, dams, roads
	Excavations	Railway cuttings, canals, mine shafts, quarries
	Non-mechanical structures	Bridges, chimneys
	Mechanical structures	Lifting bridges, dockside cranes, water pumps
	Buildings	Mills, factories
	Houses	Workers' and factory owners' dwellings
Machinery	Prime movers	Steam engines, electric motors
	Appliances	Milling equipment, spinning frames
Artefacts	Tools	Stone dressing equipment, engineering tools
	Products	Slates, bricks, glassware, bread, shoes
Transport	Externally powered	Horse-drawn and electric trams
	Self-powered	Road vehicles, rail locomotives, boats, airplanes
Documents	Primary records	Photographs, ledgers, architects' drawings
	Secondary records	Parliamentary records, local history articles

its useful life. As retention becomes less viable, the site's worth becomes increasingly perceived of in terms of salvageable materials (for instance ashlar stone) and the redevelopment value of the ground on which it sits, especially if this near a town centre. It is for these reasons that many vestiges of past industries have recently succumbed to the ravages of the ubiquitous 'Celtic Tiger'.

STATUTORY PROTECTION

In the Republic of Ireland, the two principal legislative measures for the protection of archaeological and architectural heritage (of which industrial heritage is a significant element) are the *National Monuments Acts* and the *Local Government Planning Acts* respectively.

NATIONAL MONUMENTS ACTS

This legislation was originally implemented by the Office of Public Works but is now administered by Dúchas, the state's Heritage Service. In theory it embraces all types of built form, irrespective of date, but in practice it has mainly been applied to defunct sites (generally ruinous or buried) of pre-1700 date. The acts encompass five measures which offer varying levels of statutory protection to the built heritage.

Register of Historic Monuments. This was established under Section 5 of the *National Monument (Amendment) Act* 1987 and contains the name, location and brief description of each site. It is a criminal offence to alter a registered site without giving two months' advance notice to Dúchas of any intended works. This gives the department the opportunity to negotiate with the developer and stipulate whether an investigative assessment, full excavation or watching brief on the work is necessary. Where such works are deemed inappropriate but the site is still threatened by development, a Preservation Order can be made (see below). However, as Dúchas must notify the site's owner of its inclusion in the Register, only a small proportion of all known archaeological sites are thus protected. Only three are of industrial interest: bog tracks in county Roscommon, a watermill at Killogrone (county Kerry), and a nineteenth-century signal tower on Clear Island (county Cork).

Record of Monuments and Places. The impracticality of the Register was rectified by the creation, under the *National Monuments Act* 1994, of the Record of Monuments and Places (RMP). Sites included in the RMP are afforded the same degree of protection as those in the Register, but site owners do not have to be individually notified. The application of this legislation is achieved under articles 32 and 132 of the *Local Government (Planning and Development Regulations) Act* 1994 which obliges planning authorities to notify Dúchas of applications which may affect such sites directly or threaten their amenity value by encroaching on their immediate surrounds. At the time of writing, the RMP contains some 110,000 sites, of which 3% (3,322) are industrial.

Preservation Orders. Under section 8 of the *National Monuments Act* 1930 and Section 4 of the 1954 amendment, the state can place a temporary (six-month) or permanent Preservation Order (PO) on a monument which is considered to be 'in danger of, or actually being, destroyed, injured, or removed, or is falling into decay through neglect.' One important proviso is, however, that it must be a national monument, this being defined under the 1930 act as 'a monument, or the remains of a monument, the preservation of which is a matter of national importance by reason of the historical, architectural, traditional, artistic, or archaeological interest attaching thereto'. There are, however, no explicit criteria by which a site is adjudged to be of national importance, it being left to the experience and opinion of the appraising archaeologist. Once a PO is applied, interference with the monument becomes a criminal offence and can result in a fine and/or imprisonment. A PO is, therefore, a valuable procedural device to avert unauthorized site works, but only where these are known in advance. To date, some 420 POs are in place, of which six relate to shipwrecks and four to conventional industrial sites: Bronze Age copper mines at Derrycarhoon and Mount Gabriel (county Cork), a nineteenth-century lead mine and chimney at Ballycorus (county Dublin), and Newmills corn and flax mills (county Donegal).

Sites in Guardianship. Under the *National Monuments Act* 1930, the owner of a national monument can transfer responsibility for its upkeep to the state or local authority. Although the site's ownership still resides with the individual, for practical purposes it can be regarded as a monument in state care. To date, Guardianship Orders have been applied to 177 sites. Two are of industrial interest: an eighteenth-century windmill shell at Vinegar Hill (county Wexford), and Tacumshin windmill (county Wexford).

Sites in state ownership. Most of these sites have been acquired by negotiation, but some have been compulsorily acquired as a last resort. This is the ultimate form of protection in that only the state can interfere with them. There are presently some 425 state-owned sites, of which three are of industrial interest: medieval bridges at Garfinny (county Kerry) and Tintern Abbey (county Wexford), and Newmills corn and flax mills. The state also maintains an extensive inland waterway network comprising the Shannon-Erne, Barrow and Shannon navigations and Grand and Royal canals.

It is evident that, although the RMP has afforded statutory protection to the largest number of industrial sites, relatively few of post-1700 date have been protected. Given that the vast majority of Ireland's industrial sites only came into existence after 1750, this is a major shortcoming, not of the *National Monuments Acts,*

but of their application to this facet of the built heritage.

PLANNING ACTS

The *Local Government Planning Acts* relate to the protection of the built heritage by local planning authorities. Their intent is to retain the special character of sites by imposing pro-active controls on their alteration or demolition. These acts relate not only to archaeological sites (which also come within the scope of the *National Monuments Acts*) but also to structures and buildings of post-1700 date.

The *Local Government (Planning and Development) Act* 1963 obliged local authorities to formulate plans indicating development objectives for their respective areas. Section 21 (1c) empowered them to include provision for the preservation of structures because of their 'artistic, historic or architectural interest', and for the preservation of 'caves, sites, features and other objects of archaeological, geological or historical interest'. Where a structure was included in a Development Plan, it was deemed to be 'listed' and required explicit permission from the planning authority to alter or demolish it. This measure thus enabled the extent and nature of such work to be controlled and permission could, in some instances, be refused.

Between 1973 and 1978, the industrial heritage of 19 counties was surveyed in whole or in part by An Foras Forbartha, the Republic's National Planning Institute. However, because of time, manpower and financial constraints, only the more obvious sites were inspected. Those regarded by the surveyors as being of special significance were recommended to the planning authorities for inclusion in their respective development plans. During the 1980s and '90s, several planning authorities also commissioned their own industrial surveys, notably in county Dublin (Scally 1998), county Kilkenny (Hamond 1998a) and the Dublin docklands (McMahon 1998).

Although most of the listed industrial sites are of post-1700 date, they are mainly structures, buildings and houses which are upstanding, of special architectural merit and which are in use or could be re-used. Industrial earthworks, excavations and defunct sites which are ruinous, buried or destroyed (but which may still contain buried material) have largely been ignored. Moreover, those industrial sites which are listed typically comprise less than 15% of the listed building stock in each planning area. In the author's view, this is not a fair representation of what is potentially listable, but more a reflection of the limited scope of the initial fieldwork. Only in the case of county Kilkenny, where an opportunity existed to carry out an extremely detailed survey, is there an appreciable number of listed industrial sites (comprising 27% of the 596 listed sites).

To date, planning restrictions have generally been

applied only to the exteriors of listed buildings and the maintenance of their visual character (particularly front elevations). Interiors received little protection until section 43 (1) of the *Local Government Act* 1976 deemed that plasterwork, staircases, woodwork and other internal features 'of artistic, historic or architectural interest' could also be listed. Unfortunately, the legislation did not give inspectors powers of entry, so the explicit listing of such interiors was dependent on the owners' goodwill. This is obviously highly unsatisfactory in the case of industrial buildings, many of which are of no particular architectural character but which may be of special interest because of their internal machinery.

A particularly contentious issue is that of site maintenance. Where an owner wished to demolish a listed building, it was usually left to deteriorate to such an extent that the local authority was forced to serve a Dangerous Buildings Notice under the *Local Government (Sanitary Services) Act* 1964. This allowed it to be demolished for reasons of public safety. Although the *Derelict Sites Act* 1990 enabled local authorities to prevent buildings falling into decay, they were reluctant to use this power. This has been to the detriment of those industrial sites which are long defunct and for which a suitable reuse has not yet been found.

Some of the shortcomings of the 1963 act are addressed in the *Local Government (Planning and Development) Act* 1999 which was to come into effect on 1 January 2000. The salient features of the new statute and their likely consequences for industrial sites are as follows:

• Local authorities will now have a mandatory responsibility for the protection of the built heritage through the inclusion of listed sites in Development Plans. This should ensure a substantial increase in the number of listed industrial sites.

• The definition of a 'structure' is extended to include its internal and external fixtures and features. If a structure is listed, protection will be automatically given to these additional items without having to specify them explicitly. Planning permission must be sought for works to any of these elements where they will affect the character of the structure. In theory, this should enable items such as external water wheels and internal machinery to be protected.

• The definition of a structure also extends to the land and structures lying within its curtilage. The protection afforded a listed building automatically extends to these other items. This is of particular relevance in the case of dispersed multi-component industrial sites, where the value of the group as a whole may be greater than the sum of its individual components.

• Features which lie in the attendant grounds of listed structures which add to the interest of the latter may also be listed. This issue has special relevance in the case of listed industrial structures associated with long linear features (for instance watermills, races and weirs).

• On the basis of the National Inventory of Architectural Heritage (NIAH), Dúchas is empowered to recommend specific structures and buildings to the authorities for listing. Although the NIAH has been in existence since 1991, it has only recently been placed on a statutory footing with the passing of the *Architectural Heritage (National Inventory) and Historic Monuments (Miscellaneous Provisions) Act* 1999. To date, upwards of 1,000 industrial sites have been recorded. Because of the systematic nature of the survey on which this inventory is based, a more representative selection of listed industrial sites should ensue.

• Applications for works which involve removal, alteration or replacement of any element of a listed structure must be made to the relevant planning authority which will then refer the matter to Dúchas. As before, unauthorized works may result in imprisonment and/or fine.

• Local authorities are empowered to grant-aid owners or occupiers of listed structures to carry out approved works to listed structures, whether these be instigated by the owner or demanded by the authority. Although most grants will probably be targeted at the adaptive reuse of buildings, some may be directed towards maintenance.

• Local authorities can demand that an owner of a derelict building make it structurally sound and weatherproof. If this request is ignored, the authority will have powers to carry out the work and recoup its cost from the owner. As a last resort, it will also have the power of compulsory purchase (except in the case of private dwellings).

• In those cases where a local authority has approved the alteration or demolition of a listed structure, it is empowered to insist that a record be made in advance of such works. Moreover, it can also insist that items be salvaged where appropriate. This is particularly pertinent in the case of machinery, which is usually the first item to be removed during renovations.

• All existing listed structures will be protected under the new act unless their owners or occupiers can convince the planning authority otherwise.

• Financial assistance will be given to local authorities to appoint county Conservation Officers for the purpose of monitoring and enforcing the regulations.

CONSERVATION BY RECORD

Although statutory legislation can play an important role in slowing down the disappearance of Ireland's industrial heritage through redevelopment, reversal of this trend will only come about through deliberate intervention in order to secure the future survival of selected sites. This is, in essence, what conservation is about. Given the wide-ranging nature of the industrial heritage, it is not surprising to find the concept applied in many different ways (Brisbane and Wood 1996, 35–39; Cossons 1975). For the purposes of this chapter, however, it is regarded as having two basic forms. Where the physical retention of a site is not viable, conservation by record is probably the only realistic option. The detailed recording of a site's physical attributes will thus conserve for posterity the knowledge of what will eventually disappear. However, actual retention of some sites may be possible under certain conditions, this action being termed 'physical conservation'.

A thorough understanding of a site is essential if its significant features are to be conserved, whether by means of a paper record or actual physical retention. This entails finding out when it was established, by whom and for what purpose, how and why it developed and functioned in the way it did, and recording what now survives. Such knowledge, which can only come about through documentary research and field survey, enables a site's special features to be recognized and its heritage significance evaluated. The results are of value in not only being a record in their own right but also a firm basis for any future programme of physical conservation.

DOCUMENTARY RESEARCH

A useful starting point in examining a site's historical development is the Ordnance Survey map. Between 1829 and 1845, some 1,600 maps were published on a county-by-county basis at a scale of six inches to a mile (1:10,560). A resurvey was completed in 1891 and at periodic intervals thereafter. Detailed town maps are also available at 1:1,056 and 1:500 scales, and 1:2,500 maps have covered most of the country since the early 1900s. Individual buildings are clearly discernible on these maps and the functions of most industrial sites are also explicitly captioned. Using the various editions of such maps for a particular area, one can readily gauge a site's evolution — in terms of its number of components, spatial extent and changing function — from the early nineteenth century to the present day.

Additional background information may also be obtainable from published and manuscript documents such as eighteenth-century county and estate maps, nineteenth- and twentieth-century Valuation Books, drawings, paintings and photographs, local history publications and street directories. More detailed data can sometimes also be found in business and estate records.

FIELD SURVEY

The above documentary research, or 'paper survey' as it is also known, will not only generate a useful body of data in its own right, but also enable more effective field survey in that one will have some inkling of a site's nature, extent and content. Field inspection will probably also reveal features not apparent from the paper survey, particularly later modifications, additions and demolitions. It furthermore affords the opportunity to make descriptive notes, take measurements and photographs and ascertain the site's present condition, uses and likelihood of destruction.

As was evident from **Table 37.2**, industrial sites usually present a combination of different physical forms in various states of completeness. A defunct mining site, for example, might comprise numerous shafts, spoil heaps and an assortment of mechanical structures and buildings dispersed over a wide area. Upstanding industrial buildings such as mills and factories may be associated with substantial earthworks like ponds, and also contain machinery and artefacts. Moreover, those sites which have remained in use for many decades are likely to have done so only by a process of continual adaptation. This will be reflected in the addition of new buildings and the adaptation, demolition and obliteration of existing ones. Likewise, equipment is also likely to have been upgraded or scrapped in favour of new technologies, particularly where the site has changed use. The demise of the site after it closes will also give rise to changes in form and content as buildings deteriorate and machinery is removed. The net result is a rich, but usually very incomplete, palimpsest of visual evidence. The recording of such sites therefore demands both archaeological and architectural recording skills, some specialist knowledge and experience in interpreting what is being observed.

The extent to which a site is recorded in the field will obviously depend on the purpose of that survey (Hamond 1998c, 41–43). For a preliminary assessment, a basic qualitative description, dimensions of the principal structures and general photographs may well suffice. This will enable one to establish what now exists and the practicality of restoration in the light of the site's completeness and physical condition. When combined with the results of the paper survey, it should also be possible to arrive at an understanding of how the site evolved and enable one to highlight the salient surviving features which are indicative of this process. If physical conservation is a certainty, a much greater level of detail is obviously required in terms of written text, photographs and measured drawings. In some instances, archaeological excavation may also be necessary to understand the site's past development. Not only will such a 'baseline' survey be a definitive record of the site in its unrestored state, it will also provide a sound basis for the preparation of specifications, costings and drawings for the intended works.

SITE EVALUATION

Most industrial sites were of social and economic importance to their respective localities, and many are still of cultural relevance as a historical memory. The beneficial impact on the local community may be reason enough physically to conserve a site. However, given the costs entailed in restoring all but the smallest of sites, support from enabling agencies is more likely to be forthcoming if the heritage significance of a particular site can be shown to transcend its purely local context.

An assessment of a site's intrinsic merit entails a consideration of many criteria apart from local sentiment. Physical attributes include scale, form, composition, decoration, materials and quality of workmanship. Such attributes are not restricted to formal architecture — vernacular and industrial character may be of equal interest. However, these attributes may be tempered by later modifications and the site's current physical state.

It is unfortunate, however, that industrial sites are often judged solely on the basis of their aesthetic quality as this is often of little merit compared, say, with a large country mansion. Many other physical qualities can also be of interest. Thus a site may be a good example of a particular type of structure, have an unusual function, be built in a certain way, exhibit a distinctive and unusual internal spatial arrangement or have a high technical content in terms of plant and machinery. Moreover, whilst individual structures within a site may be of no particular merit, they may have group value in the context of the site as a whole.

Aside from a site's intrinsic physical attributes, its historical context may also be of interest. It may contain physical evidence of successive adaptations to different uses or illustrate the evolution of a single function. It may also demonstrate a particular period of development with regard to that industry (for instance innovatory or climactic). Age and rarity may be other considerations in that the older and rarer the site, the greater its perceived historical importance. In some instances, a site may have an association with a nationally important person or event. A site's spatial context should also be considered. Is it, for example, demonstrative of a particular regional variant of a particular class of site? It might also have landscape value where it forms a particularly important visual element to its surrounding area. By taking all these criteria into consideration, it should be possible to rate the site's industrial heritage significance in terms of its local, regional, national and international significance. One will then be in a much stronger position to argue for its physical conservation than if basing one's argument on sentiment alone.

PHYSICAL CONSERVATION

There are three basic ways in which the physical elements of a site may be retained:

(1) stabilization of the site in its existing state (*preservation*);

(2) reinstatement to a former state (*restoration*), and

(3) alteration to some new use (*adaptive reuse*).

Irrespective of what type of physical conservation is enacted, the challenge is to intervene in such a way that a site's significant features remain unchanged insofar as is practically possible. This is especially difficult with industrial sites as many comprise not only buildings and structures but also topographical features, machinery and artefacts. This difficulty is compounded by the fact that there are, as yet, no national or internationally agreed guidelines for conserving industrial sites. However, the 1964 International Charter for the Conservation and Restoration of Monuments and Sites (known as the Venice Charter) sets out some basic general principles which are also relevant to industrial sites:

• Monuments should be preserved *in situ* whenever possible and their visual setting maintained.

• Whilst it may be desirable to put monuments to new uses, their original character, internal layout and setting should be respected.

• Restoration must be based on sound archaeological, historical and field research. All phases of construction should be retained, except where the importance of revealing an earlier construct greatly outweighs the value of the later material.

• The emphasis should be on minimal and reversible intervention.

• Where possible, the retention and repair of original elements using matching traditional materials and techniques is preferable to outright replacement.

• Reconstruction of missing parts must be in keeping with the original, but clearly distinguishable and stop short of conjecture.

• New additions must respect the character and setting

of the original structure.

• All works to an historic site should be properly documented before, during and after intervention and this record should be placed in a public archive.

• A maintenance plan is essential if the site is not to deteriorate in the future.

This charter was adopted by the International Council on Monuments and Sites (ICOMOS UK 1995) and is recognized by the Royal Institute of the Architects of Ireland (RIAI 1997, 1998) and the Department of the Environment (Pearson 1998). Its principles have recently been adopted as a British Standard (1998), and similar recommendations are likely to govern conservation work to listed buildings as a result of the 1999 *Planning Act* (discussed above). In applying these principles, one must, of course, also comply with planning requirements (especially if the site has statutory protection) and the regulations relating to buildings, fire, health and safety (Arnold and Ó Cofaigh 1999).

PRESERVATION

The preservation of a site in its existing form essentially entails the retention and repair of what survives, and usually also the introduction of new appropriate materials to extend the durability of the surviving original fabric (*consolidation*). In all cases, high-quality traditional materials should be used as appropriate, taking care to match like with like, for example natural slates (not artificial or imported southern European ones), natural stone (not reconstituted or concrete), native timber (not imported hardwoods), lime putty (not sand-cement), lime wash (not masonry paint), red lead paint (not lead oxide) and cast- and wrought-iron (in preference to mild steel).

In the case of the preservation of a small and durable monument such as a milestone, such repair work is usually straightforward. In the case of buildings, walls may require capping (particularly if their roofs have gone) and possibly also underpinning or the insertion of additional piers (due to shallow foundations). Substantial outdoor metal structures (such as gasholders) require considerably greater expenditure and a continuing commitment to regular maintenance. Machinery and artefacts are particularly problematic as they can deteriorate rapidly because of the nature of their materials (wrought-iron, steel and wood, and the like) and their attractiveness to thieves (especially cast-iron, brass and bronze components). This problem can be further exacerbated if their enveloping structure is not in itself weatherproof.

It is essential that expert advice be sought on the proper course of action. No one approach is universally applicable, as circumstances will vary according to the scale and number of items to be preserved, the skills and finance at hand, and resources available for subsequent upkeep. In many instances, mothballing may well be the best action, at least in the short term. This will usually entail removing the principal causes of deterioration (for instance cutting back vegetation and repairing leaking roofs), arresting further decay (treating wood with a clear preservative and applying heavy-duty grease, oil, wax and proprietary rust inhibitors to metalwork; paint is to be avoided if it was not used originally), and securing the site (to counteract vandalism and theft).

It is not unusual to remove machines and artefacts to museums so that greater control can be exercised over their future well-being, particularly with regard to climatic control and public access. Although contrary to the Venice Charter, due to the loss of setting, it may sometimes be the only viable option, as at the Straffan Steam Museum where a number of engines destined for scrapping were re-erected and are now operational. In a few instances, whole buildings have been removed, as at the Ulster Folk and Transport Museum (Cultra, county Down), where three watermills which would otherwise have been demolished are preserved in an operational state.

RESTORATION

Over the past two decades a number of defunct industrial sites have been restored as visitor attractions, many to full working order (**Table 37.3**). The vast majority of these sites are relatively compact and contain a manageable number of features. Nevertheless, restoration costs have generally been beyond the means of private individuals, and most are the result of efforts by public bodies, commercial companies and charitable groups.

Most industrial sites have evolved over many years and are likely to have undergone changes in both form and function. Their restoration will therefore entail some or all of the following:

(1) removal of those components deemed inappropriate to the period of the restoration (*demolition*);

(2) retention, repair and consolidation of selected items (*preservation*, as discussed above);

(3) the copying of existing machinery (*replication*), and

(4) the recreation of missing items (*reconstruction*).

The period of restoration is particularly problematic and has a direct bearing on what is retained or demolished. Should the site be returned to its state when last in use or to an earlier incarnation? If to the latter, what

Table 37.3 Restored Industrial Heritage Sites in the Republic of Ireland

Newmills Corn and Flax Mills, Letterkenny, county Donegal	ST
Clonmacnois and West Offaly Railway, Shannonbridge, county Offaly	ST
Ballincollig Gunpowder Mills, county Cork	LA
Skerries Wind and Watermills, county Dublin	LA
Blennerville Windmill, Tralee, county Kerry	LA
Lifeforce Mill, county Cavan	CO
Midleton Distillery, county Cork	CO
Guinness Hop Store, county Dublin	CO
Foxford Woollen Mills, Foxford, county Mayo	CO
Mizen Head Signal Station, Goleen, county Cork	VG
Donegal Railway Heritage Centre, county Donegal	VG
Fintown Railway, county Donegal	VG
Tuam Mill Museum, Tuam, county Galway	VG
Tralee and Blennerville Railway, county Kerry	VG
Cavan-Leitrim Railway, Dromod, county Leitrim	VG
Elphin Windmill, county Roscommon	VG
Locke's Distillery, Kilbeggan, county Westmeath	VG
Kilmore Quay Maritime Museum, county Wexford	VG
Glengowla Silver-Lead Mine, Oughterard, county Galway	PR
Ballytore Watermill, Crookstown, county Kildare	PR
White River Mill, Dunleer, county Louth	PR
Croom Mill, county Limerick	PR
Kylecrue Mill, Thurles, county Tipperary	PR
Newtown Mill, Nenagh, county Tipperary	PR
Craanford Watermill, Gorey, county Wexford	PR
Tacumshin Windmill, county Wexford	PR

Key:

ST = state/semi-state owned;

LA = local authority;

CO = commercial company;

VG = voluntary/community group;

PR = private individual

justification is there for removing an element of the site's later history which may be of potential future interest, for example an electric motor installed in place of a waterwheel and without which the site may not have continued to operate for so long? One must therefore balance the loss of what is being removed by the gain of what is revealed as a consequence.

The question of copying existing material in a more durable and maintainable form must also be considered. This dilemma often arises with restoration to working order, particularly in the case of engines and vehicles which it is intended to operate. Copying, if taken to extremes, can result in what is essentially a replica, faithfully reproducing the original's form and function but not its fabric. Where replication is the best course of action, like should, where possible, be replaced with like in material, form and finished appearance.

The reconstruction of missing items and where exactly they should be positioned may prove problematic and usually require careful analysis of alternative possibilities. This will entail examining features of the surviving structures and making oneself aware of the site's historical development. Here the detailed documentary research and field survey, outlined above, becomes especially relevant. Comparison with functionally similar sites elsewhere may also be necessary, although one should bear in mind that regional variations may occur which are not directly translatable to another area. Obviously the more intact the site and the fuller its past documentation, the more accurate will be the reconstruction.

Sometimes suitable replacement equipment may be available at nominal cost from a site elsewhere. However, care should be taken to establish that its removal does not compromise the latter's eventual restoration (no matter how keen an owner might be to sell the items!). If replicated anew, the cost may be such that inferior materials must be used (steel instead of wrought- and cast-iron). In all cases, it is imperative that the original detailing on which the reconstruction is based is fully recorded and that the context of any salvaged items is also noted.

Ballincollig Gunpowder Mill is a prime example of almost total reconstruction. Little physical evidence of this early nineteenth-century mill survived apart from the watercourses, water-wheel pit, bearing support blocks and edge runner stones. Subsequent archaeological excavation uncovered the outline and fabric of the mill building, while documentary research revealed the materials of the machinery and the water wheel. From field observations, it was possible to calculate the size of the wheel and the most likely size and configuration of the gears. Some of the finer detail was provided by Faversham Gunpowder Mill, Kent, this being the nearest site with intact original machinery. Combining all this information enabled the author to draw up plans for a workable reconstruction, all of which were subsequently executed.

Similarly detailed fieldwork and comparative analysis was also undertaken by the author at Blennerville and Elphin Windmills, both of which survived as empty shells. However, as little or no documentary evidence could be found, their resultant machinery installations were but one of several operational possibilities. In all these cases, the principles of mill repair as laid down by the Wind and Watermill Section of the Society for the Protection of Ancient Buildings were followed as far as possible (SPAB 1983 and n.d.). Nevertheless, the purist could argue that such reconstructions were speculative and thus counter to the Venice Charter. However, they might also be regarded as exercises in experimental archaeology, particularly as Irish millwrighting traditions no longer survive. As a result of this work, one can also appreciate more fully the skill of the millwrights who built such mills without recourse to electrical power tools and heavy lifting cranes.

Restoring machinery to working order presents particular challenges. On the one hand, there is the potential wear and tear on original materials and, on the other, the need to comply with modern health, safety, hygiene and insurance regulations. These factors must be set against the benefits of demonstrating and understanding the actual process for which the machinery was devised and the passing on of traditional operating skills (Ball 1997, 24–28). Moreover, where a site is restored to full commercial production, traditional methods may prove incapable of coping with demand, and additional machinery may be required to sustain production. This was the case at Lifeforce Mill, where wholemeal flour is produced. Here it was necessary to introduce an oil-powered engine and electricity to augment the erratic power of the water turbine.

The need to accommodate visitors in order to sustain the running of the site once restored also makes internal alteration inevitable. Changes may include the removal or relocation of machinery and the introduction of additional stairs, electric lighting, fire doors, safety barriers and warning signs. However, where sites are worked by experienced operators and visitors are accompanied by trained guides, such intrusive changes can usually be kept to a minimum, as is well demonstrated at Locke's Distillery and White River Mill.

ADAPTIVE REUSE

Most industrial buildings are virtually impossible to reuse in their existing form and for this reason are vulnerable to unsympathetic alteration or demolition. Many were built for a specific purpose and their design may therefore restrict modern reuse on account of their internal plan forms, low ceiling heights, poor light levels and narrow doorways. Restricted reuse and the need to comply with modern building regulation therefore make such buildings more expensive to adapt than to replace with new purpose-built ones.

Because of the close relationship between an industrial building's function and form, they are particularly fragile in terms of adaptive reuse. Machinery is especially vulnerable as it may impede internal reuse. Given that such assemblages of equipment were once working entities in which the whole was greater than the sum of its parts, even partial removal may compromise what is left. This problem is exacerbated by the fact that protective legislation is often perceived as being relevant only to the visible external elements of buildings and structures. Buildings are usually gutted and no record is made of the machinery before it is scrapped. This often happens, for instance, when watermills are converted to dwellings and only the water wheel is retained for purely decorative purposes. In considering a change of use, one must therefore ask whether the building can accommodate it without a significant loss of character. In answering this question, it is necessary to differentiate between two types of feature (English Heritage 1997):

• *Critical features*, the disappearance of which would be a greater loss than the benefit gained by their removal (for instance a prime mover, power transmission system and principal machinery in a factory).

• *Tradable features*, the loss of which would be outweighed by the benefits of reuse (for instance window resizing on rear elevations).

Dividing the 'historical capital' into these two forms is not always straightforward, and each site must be considered on its individual merits. For example,

Fig. 37.1 Thomas St Windmill, Dublin, is the tallest extant windmill in Britain and Ireland. Erected ca. *1810, it survives as an empty shell, the interior being protected by an ogee copper cap. Now owned by Arthur Guinness & Son, it could find eventual reuse as a* camera obscura.

expansive multi-storeyed floors are an essential characteristic of many later nineteenth-century textile mills, but such spaces are only rarely retained in modern usage. Likewise, in re-watering a canal for recreational use, one would have to weigh up the long-term economic benefits of allowing large cruisers to use it against the permanent loss of historical integrity and heritage value brought about by widening the locks and raising the bridges. This latter course of action was adopted on the Erne-Shannon waterway and entailed the virtual obliteration of most original features on the Ballinamore and Ballyconnell Canal, the course of which is followed.

Elements of an original design which do not make a functional contribution to a new use should also be retained where possible (for instance chimney stacks, kiln vents). However, the introduction of spurious features more relevant to some other type of building or region should be strenuously avoided. Efforts should also be made to mothball structures and buildings which contribute to the site's historical integrity even if they do not lend themselves to immediate reuse. An excellent example of this approach is to be found at the Thomas

Street Windmill, Dublin (**Fig 37.1**).

Unfortunately, it is often the case that only the facade of a building is retained, everything else being demolished. However, there are also many examples of the successful adaptive reuse of smaller buildings such as watermills for dwellings, restaurants and craft shops. Some watermills have also been adapted to generate electricity using modern water turbines in place of the original water wheels. Larger buildings and multi-component sites are more problematic. Although some have been converted to workshops and industrial estates, this transition is not always successful owing to the alteration of fabric and layout. Many large sites still lie derelict, not only because of the high conversion costs but also due to lack of demand for industrial and commercial space at those particular locations. Fortunately, the potential of such sites for a multiplicity of simultaneous uses is being increasingly demonstrated at countless sites in Britain (Binney *et al.* 1990), and it is to be hoped that this will increasingly be the case in Ireland as more architects come to appreciate the cultural significance of the built heritage.

FUNDING CONSERVATION — CAPITAL

Unlike new buildings, it is extremely difficult to quantify precisely the cost of conserving a defunct industrial site. It is invariably the case that extras will arise which only become apparent once work has started. Moreover, it is often well-nigh impossible to estimate how long a particular task will take until one embarks upon it and becomes aware of the practical difficulties to be resolved.

The key to arriving at a reasonably precise estimate of the cost of a conservation project is a detailed survey of the site's existing state prior to any work being undertaken. Ideally, this requires someone with both an understanding of such sites and practical conservation experience. Initially, a qualitative survey may suffice in order to determine the site's structural condition, degree of completeness and conservation options (for example restoration as a static exhibit or to a working state). On this basis, one should then be able to determine whether it is worthwhile to invest more effort in a detailed quantitive survey. This will then provide a firm basis for specifying the precise nature and extent of the conservation work and the materials, manpower and skills required.

Costs can be estimated in one of two ways, or a combination of both. On the one hand, a contractor could be engaged on a time and materials basis. Whilst this procedure may suffice for small projects with definable boundaries and of modest cost, it may prove unsatisfactory for more complex works, as the timescale and expenditure will be open-ended. The alternative procedure is to prepare working drawings and a bill of quantities in which as much of the work as possible is

Table 37. 4 Approved Leader II Industrial Heritage Projects up to October 1998

(Not all will necessarily have been implemented.)

LEADER GROUP	PROJECT
Arigna	• Administration of marketing of Arigna Valley mining trail (funded by Peace and Reconciliation programme). • Feasibility study on mining museum at Arigna, county Leitrim.
Ballyhoura	• Funding for a structural assessment and feasibility study into the restoration and reuse of a community-owned mill at Castletownroche Mill. Restoration is now taking place with FÁS input. Likely to be used as an enterprise centre.
Blackwater	• £50,000 granted for the conversion of Glanworth Mill, county Cork, for tourist accommodation and restoration of water wheel.
Comhdháil Oileáin na hÉireann	• Restoration of dwelling houses associated with Aranmore lighthouse as two self-catering units by a private developer. Approval given for 40% of cost (£11,400). • Marketing grant of £2,278 (50% of total cost) to promote a privately run folk museum at a disused lighthouse at Inis Mór.
Donegal	• Grant approval for £4,480 for a feasibility study on restoration of dam at Convoy Mill, for electricity, water and tourism. • Feasibility study into the creation of a motor museum at Ramelton. £1,920 grant aid given (80% of total). Approval given for a further £50,000 of funding.
Galway	• Development of a nineteenth-century forge as a heritage centre and museum.
Kildare	• Feasibility study into development of an old distillery as a visitor attraction.
Laois	• Restoration of a disused road as a tourist trail. • Development of tearooms at old mill.
Longford	• Grant aid up to 80% of cost (£3,776) towards feasibility study into preserving Ballymahon Mill.
Mayo/Sligo	• Canopy over railway carriages at museum.
Offaly	• An Dún transport and heritage museum, Ballinahown, Athlone (vintage and classic cars, and farm machinery). £1,500 given towards marketing campaign.
South Kerry	• Restoration and display of a locomotive as a tourist attraction. • Feasibility study into development of old railway building in Castlemaine.
South Mayo	• £5,000 grant towards research into Irish coastguard stations. • £30,000 approved for restoration of a coastguard station at Rosmoney as an educational resource and for displaying curraghs.
Tipperary	• Approval given for grant to restore a limekiln.
West Limerick	• Restoration of a limekiln. • Restoration of a forge. • Restoration of railway station into self-catering units.
Westmeath	• Feasibility study into reuse of Mullingar railway station and reopening of line to Athlone as a tourist attraction. • Grants for exhibition of distilling equipment (£10,000), upgrading of tearoom, and restoration work (£55,000) at Locke's Distillery, Kilbeggan. • Approval given for the preparation of a development plan for Kilbeggan Canal.

specified in detail, including the size and treatment of the materials. Daily manpower rates for unforeseen extras can also be included in this specification, as well as provisional sums for more specialist work. Although more costly to begin with, this procedure is preferable for large projects as one will have a better idea of timescale and final costs.

Whatever method is used for estimating, the services of an experienced quantity surveyor may well prove cost-effective. Once the specifications are drawn up, at least three tenders should be sought from contractors experienced in conservation work in order to determine the actual likely costs. One can thus amend the project to fit a specific budget, or seek out additional finance in order to realise it fully. Project costs should take into account not only manpower and materials for the actual conservation work, but also some or all of the following: visitor provision (toilets, car parking, interpretative panels), statutory fees (for instance, planning permission), professional fees, inflation uplift, Value Added Tax, bank borrowing charges (grants are generally only payable after the money is spent) and contingency (at least 10%). Needless to say, tight budgetary control should be maintained during the execution of the works.

Having costed the project, the next task is to obtain the finance to enable it to happen. Because of the weakness of the 1963 *Planning Act*, local authorities gave very few grants to listed buildings, notable cases being Newtown and Kylecrue Mills, both by Tipperary County Council. The 1999 *Planning Act* gives such authorities greater powers to grant-aid restoration projects, but it remains to be seen how this measure will be implemented in practice; advice should be sought from the relevant authority's Planning or Conservation Officer. Dúchas, the Royal Irish Academy and the Heritage Council can give discretionary grants in support of the built heritage, but only exceptionally are these for site restoration. The Heritage Council has been particularly active, assisting with the restoration of Locke's Distillery and financing the preparation of conservation plans for limekilns at Proleek Acres (county Louth), Delaney's Mill (Ashbourne, county Meath) and Old Ross Mill (county Wexford). Other agencies have also assisted, both directly and indirectly, with capital funding. The International Fund for Ireland funded the restoration of White River Watermill as a commercial flour mill. Sites such as Blennerville Windmill, Elphin Windmill, and Locke's Distillery have relied heavily on FÁS training schemes for their restoration. A few sites have also benefited from business initiatives such as the AIB Nationwide 'Better Ireland' Award. In recent years, the European Union has become the main source of funding for schemes involving the built heritage. Conservation projects undertaken by local authorities and community groups have benefited from initiatives such as the Local Urban and Rural Development Programme (1994–99). However, it has been the smaller-scale funds such as Leader II and Agri-Tourism which have been most relevant to the conservation of the industrial heritage.

LEADER II

The 1994–99 Leader II programme was administered by the Department of Agriculture, Food and Forestry and implemented by 34 approved Local Action Groups (DAFF 1995; 1997). Each group instigated its own community business initiatives and also assisted individuals, small firms and other groups within their respective areas. Approved initiatives have included the development of heritage trails, historic sites and museums, and the identification and preservation of local architectural heritage and making it accessible to the public. Much of the funding has gone towards feasibility studies and some towards restoration or adaptive reuse (**Table 37.4**). It is anticipated that the present programme will be continued along similar lines within Leader III.

AGRI-TOURISM

Under this scheme grant aid is available to farmers and other rural dwellers outside the major conurbations for the provision of tourism facilities relating to leisure activities and for the marketing thereof. The scheme is administered by the Department of Agriculture, Food and Forestry in conjunction with Bord Fáilte and Shannon Development. It focuses primarily on the provision of accommodation, whether through the conversion of traditional farm buildings of character or the refurbishment of existing accommodation. There is also scope for the provision of other visitor facilities such as theme farms and farm museums where there is an identified shortfall. There is scope for conservation of the industrial heritage, although only a few sites have benefitted to date (**Table 37.5**).

Table 37. 5 Approved Agri-tourism Industrial Heritage Projects

BORD FÁILTE OFFICE	PROJECT
Cork	• Refurbishment of water wheel and building at Bealick Mill, Macroom.
Waterford, Wexford and South Tipperary	• Conversion of Hook Head lighthouse, county Wexford, to a tourist facility by Hook Heritage Trust.

As well as direct grant aid, there is also indirect assistance through tax relief. This is potentially available to owners or occupiers of approved buildings in respect of expenditure on their repair, maintenance or restoration. Under section 19 of the *Finance Act* 1982, such a building is one which Dúchas considers to be 'intrinsically of significant scientific, historic, architectural or aesthetic interest to which the public has reasonable access'. A shortcoming of this act was that there was no control on what works were carried out except in the case of listed buildings. This was rectified under section 4 of the *Finance Act* 1989, which states that all works were to be consistent with the building's original character and fabric.

Owners may apply to Dúchas for an assessment of eligibility, and each application is considered on its own merits. It is not necessary for a building to be listed or to appear on the RMP to be eligible. If the application is successful, a 'Certificate of Determination' is issued for tax purposes. However, no relief is given on any element of expenditure which is wholly grant-aided by a public body. Should the building be altered or allowed to deteriorate, the certificate can be revoked.

FUNDING CONSERVATION — REVENUE

Depending on the size and complexity of the site, maintenance costs can be substantial, particularly with large industrial structures made of non-durable materials. Added to this are the costs of operating the site. Before embarking on any project involving physical conservation, it is therefore imperative that a comprehensive analysis be made of its long-term financial viability.

Aside from routine maintenance, expenditure will include some or all of the following: wages (manager and staff), heating and electricity, office costs (stationery, telephone/fax, postage), marketing and publicity (printing and distribution of brochures/leaflets; creation and maintenance of Internet homepage), travel, rates (if applicable), insurance (buildings/contents, employee/third party/public liability), site maintenance, bank charges (capital and interest repayments) and miscellaneous sundry items.

As most restored industrial sites cannot work, or do so only for demonstration purposes, they are unlikely to yield a salable product. Lifeforce Mill and White River Mill are exceptional in this respect as both grind wheat for commercial sale. In most cases, the bulk of the income will be from ticket sales and ancillary trading activities such as shops and tearooms. A particularly good example of the latter is Croom Mill, county Limerick, where a fine display of working prime movers is subsidized by ancillary visitor facilities.

To gauge what tickets sales are likely to generate, it is necessary to forecast visitor numbers through the year, having set a realistic admission price. This task will be facilitated if statistics are available from nearby attractions and similar sites elsewhere. Some guesswork is inevitable, but it is preferable to err on the conservative side rather than be over-optimistic and constantly fail to meet unrealistic targets (as is so often the case with many commissioned studies). This expenditure/income exercise should be repeated over a five-year period (at least), allowance being made for inflation and anticipated visitor growth. In this way, one can gauge the likelihood of breaking even or better. Unfortunately, it is more likely that a recurrent deficit will be the norm. Only in exceptional circumstances, as at the Guinness Hop Store and Blennerville Windmill, are visitor numbers likely to be sufficient to sustain the enterprise.

In the case of sites operated by the state and local authorities, this deficit can be underwritten from the public purse. The justification for pubic subvention is two-fold. First, there is a public duty to preserve selected examples of our built heritage, as has long been demonstrated by the Office of Public Works and Dúchas and their involvement with archaeological monuments. Second, the existence of these sites may attract visitors to the area who might not otherwise have come. This can only be to the benefit of the local economies. For sites operated by voluntary and community groups, indirect financial assistance may be forthcoming for staffing through FÁS training schemes; this has been the case at Elphin Windmill. In the case of privately run sites, deficit support will probably be extremely difficult to obtain, although this may be mitigated if the operator does not cost their own time. Ideally, the state and local authorities should be empowered to grant-aid the upkeep of community and privately owned industrial sites which are significant to the nation's industrial development. However, given the many demands on public funds, such a proposal is unlikely ever to be a priority. In any event, Dúchas, the Heritage Council and Department of the Environment should all be contacted for the latest information on heritage-related grants.

SUSTAINING OUR INDUSTRIAL HERITAGE

Industrial heritage is but one element of the built environment which gives individuals, groups and communities a direct perspective on their past and also provides them with a sense of their identity and place in the nation. However, this heritage will only continue to be relevant if conserved in a sustainable way, not only by central government and local authorities but also through the direct involvement of local communities (Streeten 1998).

The notion of communities being involved on a statutory basis in sustaining their built heritage is enshrined in Integrated Area Plans (IAP), an initiative

Fig. 37.2 Blennerville Windmill, county Kerry, was reconstructed within an existing shell in the 1980s. It is one of the best Irish examples of heritage-led development and has had a far-reaching impact on the local economy.

administered by the Department of the Environment (DOE 1997). These have been in operation since late 1998, having replaced the previous programme of Urban Renewal Schemes. Local authorities desiring IAP status must submit development plans to the Department and their formulation must involve local community input. The Department's guidelines on IAP applications specifically demand the compilation of an inventory of buildings of architectural, historical and industrial archaeology interest at the outset of the project in order to develop an integrated conservation policy for that specific area.

Without doubt, conservation of the industrial heritage can be a catalyst in the economic regeneration of local communities. Good examples in the UK include New Lanark near Glasgow (recently nominated as a World Heritage Site), London's dockland, Liverpool's Albert Dock, and Manchester's G-Mex Centre (formerly the city's central railway station; English Heritage 1998). Nearer to home, an excellent example of such heritage-led development is Blennerville Windmill, near Tralee (**Fig 37.2**). This mill was erected in 1800 and after a short working life fell into disuse and eventual dereliction. In the mid-1980s, Tralee Urban District Council restored the site to a fully operational state as a visitor attraction. Craft units and a visitors' centre were subsequently erected on an adjacent site, followed by the recon-

Fig. 37.3 The building and water wheel at Glanworth Woollen Mill, county Cork, were restored by Cork County Council in 1989. None of the internal machinery survives and the building has recently found reuse as tourist accommodation.

struction of the Dingle steam railway between Tralee and Blennerville. The restoration of the Tralee canal is nearing completion and the *Jeanie Johnston*, a full-scale replica famine ship, was to set sail for North America in June 2000. These developments have been of considerable benefit to the local economy and raised Tralee's profile as a worthwhile long-stay tourist destination. Perhaps most importantly of all, they have restored the community's belief in its own capabilities.

Such success relies on the economic potential of the existing built heritage being recognized by local communities and the provision of adequate public and private funding for its redevelopment. Affirmative and sustained action are essential to a project's realization and success. A role model in this respect is 'Regeneration Through Heritage', an initiative of the UK-based Business in the Community. Its aim is to link private developers to development opportunities involving the reuse of industrial buildings for employment, training and social and cultural activities. The project is funded by the Heritage Lottery Fund and supported by English Heritage and the Architectural Heritage Fund; full details are to be found on the Internet homepage (*http://www.bitc.org.uk*).

THE CONSERVATION PLAN

The key to bringing any conservation project to a successful conclusion is the formulation of a conservation plan prior to interfering with the site (Kerr 1996; Clark 1999a). This plan should state the reasons for conserving that particular site, identify its salient features meriting conservation, and demonstrate how these are to be integrated into a sustainable end-product.

Unfortunately, it is all too common for such a plan to be implemented in reverse, starting with the offer of a fixed amount of grant aid. This is then translated into what can be done rather than what should be done and there is little thought as to how the site will be financed once the capital is expended. Applications for grant aid should come only *after* a plan has been developed and are also more likely to succeed as a consequence.

At the outset, a preliminary feasibility study should be carried out. This will entail researching the site's historical development and a field survey to ascertain what survives, its completeness and present condition. Its industrial heritage merit should also be evaluated as well as its potential for various levels of conservation (consolidation, restoration, reuse and combinations thereof). Ideally, a number of conservation options should be explored and an assessment made of their strengths, weaknesses, opportunities generated and threats thereto (SWOT analysis). Their economic viability should also be addressed, both in terms of estimated capital expenditure (and where this will be sourced) and revenue support once conserved. On this basis, the most

promising option can then be explored in more detail.

The final conservation plan should present a historical analysis of the site, details of its current state and highlight its key features of interest, their heritage significance and vulnerability to loss or change (Clark 1999b). It is also vital to state explicitly the conservation strategies to be adopted, the cost of this work (and the basis thereof) and how the work will be funded, implemented and managed. Where physical conservation is intended, a business plan should also be drawn up for the site's sustainable management.

Bibliography

Arnold, P. and Ó Cofaigh, E. 1999 *Regulatory environment for the management and repair of historic buildings*. Dublin.

Ball, S. 1997 *Larger and working objects: a guide to their preservation and care*. London.

Binney, M., Machin, F. and Powell, K. 1990 *Bright future: the re-use of industrial buildings*. London.

Brisbane, M. and Wood, J. 1996 *A future for our past? An introduction to heritage studies*. London.

British Standard 1998 *B.S. 7913: 1998 — guide to the principles of the conservation of historic buildings*. London.

Clark, K. (ed) 1999a *Conservation plans in action: proceedings of the Oxford conference*. London.

Clark, K. 1999b 'Introduction to the Heritage Lottery Fund guidance' in Clark 1999a, pp. 27–40.

Cossons, N. (ed) 1975 *Transactions of the First International Congress on the Conservation of Industrial Monuments, Ironbridge 29 May–5 June 1973*. Ironbridge.

DAFF (Department of Agriculture, Forestry and Food) 1995 *Operational Programme for the implementation of the EU LEADER II initiative in Ireland 1994-1999*. Dublin.

DAAF (Department of Agriculture, Forestry and Food) 1997 *Leader II in Ireland*. Dublin.

DOE (Department of the Environment) 1997 *1998 Urban Renewal Scheme guidelines*. Dublin.

English Heritage 1997 *Sustaining the historic environment: new perspectives on the future*. London.

English Heritage 1998 *Conservation-led regeneration: the work of English Heritage*. London.

Green, E. R. R. 1963 *The industrial archaeology of county Down*. Belfast.

Hamond, F. 1998a 'The industrial archaeology of county Kilkenny' in Hamond (ed) 1998b, pp. 20–28.

Hamond, F. (ed) 1998b *Taking stock of Ireland's industrial heritage*. Dublin.

Hamond, F. 1998c 'Ireland's industrial heritage — where

now?' in Hamond 1998b, pp. 40–44. Dublin.

ICOMOS (International Council on Monuments and Sites) UK 1995 *Guidelines for the recording of monuments, groups of buildings and cultural sites.* London.

Kerr, J. S. 1996 *The conservation plan: a guide to the preparation of conservation plans for places of European cultural significance.* Sydney.

McCutcheon, W. A. 1980 *The industrial archaeology of Northern Ireland.* Belfast.

McMahon, M. 1998 'Recording the industrial heritage of Dublin's docklands' in Hamond 1998b, pp. 8–11.

Pearson, P. 1998 *Conservation guidelines 1: conservation principles/general information.* Dublin.

RIAI (Royal Institute of the Architects of Ireland) 1997 *Guidelines for the conservation of Buildings.* Dublin.

RIAI (Royal Institute of the Architects of Ireland) 1998 *Conservation guidelines for local authorities in the preparation of Development Plans.* Dublin.

Scally, G. 1998 'Industrial archaeology survey of county Dublin' in Hamond 1998b, pp. 4–7.

SPAB (Society for the Protection of Ancient Buildings) 1983 *A philosophy of repair of windmills and watermills.* London.

SPAB (Society for the Protection of Ancient Buildings) n.d. *Some principles and practice in windmill repair.* London.

Streeten, A. 1998 'Public access to England's industrial heritage', paper presented on behalf of English Heritage to Association for Industrial Archaeology conference, Devon.

The Principles of Interpretation

PAT COOKE

TOURISM PROGRAMMES AND HERITAGE

Within the space of a single decade, the presentation of Irish heritage, both natural and man-made, has undergone something of an interpretational revolution. The cause of this radical change has been singular: since the late 1980s, as part of the EC's Regional Development policy for tourism, unprecedented levels of capital funding have been directed towards the provision of visitor facilities at heritage sites in Ireland. Under the Operational Programmes for Tourism 1989–99, a total of £140 million was spent or committed on heritage projects. By 1997, 143 projects involving the provision or improvement of interpretative facilities had received funding (see Appendix A). The list comprises forty national monuments, with analysis in the same Appendix, thirteen museum projects and ninety others, ranging from historic houses and gardens, heritage parks and centres to nature and wildlife centres. In addition, twenty-one towns in the Republic have received support under Bord Fáilte's Heritage Town scheme. Clearly, then, the Tourism Development Programmes have provided a turbo-charger to the whole mission and business of heritage presentation. Those visitor facilities that have been completed frequently combine a bold architectural statement, state-of-the-art-graphics and multimedia presentations in a manner that suggests a renewed confidence in the value of the heritage they interpret.

That, to begin with, is the broad picture in quantitative terms, but how should we go about assessing the qualitative value of what has been achieved? The task is not an easy one. The change has been at dizzying pace, is still in flux and has taken place against a background where, prior to the 1980s, cultural institutions and other heritage agencies had largely considered the presentation of their collections, buildings and landscapes as very much secondary to conserving, collecting, researching and recording. (There were, of course, exceptions. In particular Dr James White, Director of the National Gallery of Ireland in the 1960s, displayed not only an exceptional talent for interpreting works of art, but a clear understanding that communicating with its audience was a primary function of a national institution. He deserves recognition as a pioneer of the art of interpretation in the Irish context.) While there had always been a certain level of interpretative activity associated with the presentation of aspects of heritage, it had been at a relatively modest scale in technical and financial terms. On the whole, it is fair to say that our indigenous resources of skills and experience in the field of interpretation were ill-prepared and scarcely adequate to meet the sudden and massive demands imposed by the coming on stream of the First Programme in 1989. This condition of ill-preparedness forms a critical baseline in any evaluation of the interpretative achievement of recent years.

In particular, there was a scarcity of appropriate, natively based skills in the design area to call upon. While Ireland did possess a first-class graphic design tradition, very few Irish-based designers possessed the kind of specialized three-dimensional design experience that the exhibition and museum environment demands. Given the time constraints associated with the Programmes, agencies responsible for delivering projects by specified deadlines felt compelled to make up the deficit by seeking abroad for the appropriate expertise. That expertise was sourced almost exclusively in Great Britain, to the extent that one of the hallmarks of the new generation of interpretative facilities created under the Tourism Programmes has been the involvement of British-based consultancies in a preponderance of these centres. Any genuine attempt to assess the impact of what has been achieved over the past twelve years must reckon with the cross-cultural implications of this very distinctive form of Anglo-Irish co-operation. It should be acknowledged that many of these consultancies have brought a high level of technical competence to the task and have shown considerable sensitivity and imagination in the way they have presented the various subjects. However, there was considerable scope for cross-cultural misunderstanding and confusion, and sometimes this manifested itself in a less than organic relationship between the story and the way it was told.

If a heritage presentation is to work as a valid cultural exercise, the closest possible sympathy between designers and concept developers is needed to ensure the imaginative truth of what is being presented. With the best will in the world, both parties can misunderstand each other, and when you add in significant differences of culture and background, the opportunity for the resulting display to add up to a less than integrated whole is magnified. In practical terms, one ends up with a technically sophisticated but formulistic presentation, an elaborate but recognizable house style of design overlaying a dry rehearsal of facts that have been barely interrogated for their emotional content or meaning.

However, the latter failings can by no means be ascribed exclusively to cross-cultural confusion of an Anglo-Irish kind. Even a society so comparatively homogeneous (until recently) as Ireland's is now experiencing the kind of debate about cultural values that is typical of post-modern society everywhere. The attempt to interpret heritage has increasingly to deal with disputation arising on such grounds as the power relations between the centre and the periphery, feminist perspective, differing ecological values and historical revisionism. Thus, for example, the extraordinarily bitter levels of controversy aroused over the Burren and Wicklow National Park visitor centres showed traces of the first three of these forms of dispute. All of this indicates that the interpretative path to be pursued in constructing heritage is an increasingly complex and tortuous one. Three key features of the Tourism Programmes have not been helpful in smoothing that path.

The first is the tight five-year time-frames attaching to the Programmes. Quite suddenly, state agencies, local authorities and voluntary organizations were faced with the challenge of devising and implementing sophisticated interpretative presentations on a scale previously only dreamt of. Some projects, in the rush to meet either feasibility or funding deadlines, were compelled to take what in interpretative terms is the shortest distance between two points: they fell back into the dry rehearsal of fact rather than wrestle with the time-consuming issues of value and meaning. (Why is this story so important? Why should it mean anything to a viewer, native or foreign? Does it have an emotional level of appeal? Is this an accurate representation of the historical truth? Is there an unpleasant or problematic dimension to the story and should it be avoided or revealed?) These are not issues which are easily explored

or resolved from a standing start. As a result, some projects ended up being ripped untimely from the womb of history, compelled to bypass or telescope the kind of critical analysis and in-depth research that would have added cultural resonance to them.

The second was the advance designation of such unprecedented levels of funding for heritage projects. This left the application procedure open not only to well-conceived and properly researched projects, but also to ones which were hastily contrived, more with the objective of attracting funding to a locality or region than telling a tale that cried out to be told. While in most cases the outcome has been projects with a compelling story to tell and a self-evident quality of popular appeal (the Foynes aviation and the Cobh maritime stories are good examples), in some cases there was an irresistible temptation to resort to time-saving generic formulae. In particular, some of the local heritage and visitor centres suffer from what could be called 'mini-national-museum-syndrome' — the rehearsal in well-trodden categories (archaeology, folklore, the fight for freedom) of the story of Ireland from the local or regional angle. This is not to say that local perspectives on issues of nationality are not both valuable and worthwhile — in fact this is a job that has for years been well done, and is generally best done, by local and county museums — merely to point out that, when resorted to as an expedient means of attracting funding labelled 'heritage' into a region, the result is likely to be more formulaic than illuminating.

The third was the overwhelming bias in the Programmes towards capital funding, with not nearly enough attention being given to the financial viability of projects in the longer term. While well and often grandly designed visitor facilities have been developed as turnkey projects, a serious question mark remains over the sustainability of many. Conceived of primarily as capital projects and as single-purpose tourist attractions, many of them failed to put in place a feasible long-term management plan, allowing for flexible or multiple use, to facilitate, for instance, a dimension of local cultural and community use of the building in the off-peak season. To compound the problem, many are lumbered with expensive and inflexible exhibitions that are purely the product of high levels of initial capital funding. Given normal wear and tear, the average lifespan of such presentations is between five and fifteen years (much less for costly audio-visual components). Replacement and renewal are likely to prove extremely expensive and unlikely to be met from revenues.

There was a broader cultural dimension to this ill-preparedness as well. The attempt to interpret heritage is the projection of a set of propositions about its value and meaning into the field of public discourse. Such projections are always and necessarily contestable. However, the relative absence of a vigorous interpretative dimension to Irish heritage in the preceding decades meant that there had been little opportunity for the growth of a critical environment to support and inform it. This may seem paradoxical in a country so renowned for its preoccupation with what Frank O'Connor called the 'backward look', but that tradition had been almost exclusively oral and literary in nature. The widespread projection of narratives about our past into three-dimensional space, mixing 'authentic' historical objects with imagery filtered through multimedia techniques of simulation and reconstruction, only became possible with the proliferation of sophisticated video and graphic reproduction technologies in the 1970s and 1980s. The advent of this novel multimedia form required a new kind of criticism that could adjudicate the complex amalgam of aesthetic effects and moral-philosophic values it presented. In this regard the Irish experience was not exceptional. Britain's heritage boom had begun many years earlier than ours, and the first signs of critical reaction did not emerge until the mid-1980s when the proliferation of heritage facilities cried out for a critical response. A landmark in the critical reaction to the British heritage boom was Robert Hewison's *The heritage industry* of 1985.

It is hardly surprising, therefore, that initial responses to the heritage boom in Ireland had an air of bewilderment. At the journalistic level, conservative categories of critical review left this new phenomenon in limbo: was it art, or theatre, or media, or environment? At the academic level, the failure to develop proper interdisciplinary approaches to the complexity of modern culture, and especially popular culture (significantly, no Irish university has a fully-fledged cultural studies department), left the traditional academic professions warily regarding this new upstart with a mixture of bemusement and hauteur. Historians, in particular, have shown remarkable indifference or reluctance to engage with a phenomenon that impinges directly on their own field of interest.

Only relatively recently have there been signs of an emergent critical capacity to engage with the specific implications of the heritage phenomenon in the Irish context. David Brett's *The construction of heritage* (1996) marks an important landmark in the way it brings a serious intellectual analysis to bear upon the cultural implications of heritage presentation in Ireland. Particularly valuable also has been the attempt in Cronin and O'Connor's earlier *Tourism in Ireland: a critical analysis* (1993) to bring out the latent ideological assumptions of tourism and to stress the need to develop an adequate critique of how tourist ideology works both to alter and condition local and national forms of identity. For similar reasons, it is vital that those responsible for delivering interpretative projects develop a sense that what they are

about is inherently problematic, contingent and contestable — whose identity is being interpreted by whom and for whom? Heritage interpretation needs to be opened up to a process of negotiation if it is to be valid as a cultural exercise in our complex modern world of pluralistic identity and competing value systems. In this regard, the very idea of 'interpretation' as a specialized conceptual tool developed for the purpose of heritage presentation is in need of revision, and it is to this more philosophical issue I would like to turn in the second part of this survey

TILTING AT TILDEN: THE LIMITS OF INTERPRETATION

The roots of the idea of interpretation in the specialized context of heritage are relatively shallow. In 1957, Freeman Tilden, a freelance journalist who had joined the US National Parks Service in 1941 as a literary consultant, brought out a book called *Interpreting our heritage*. Though National Parks had existed since the 1870s (the first was Yellowstone, formed in 1872), it was only with the boom of affluence and leisure in America after the Second World War that the challenge of communicating the philosophy and values of nature conservation to unprecedented numbers of visitors from a wide variety of backgrounds became a major priority for those who managed the parks. The concept of interpretation which Tilden distilled for this purpose rapidly became central to the management of heritage resources of all kinds. Indeed, so influential have Tilden's ideas become that it is hardly an exaggeration to describe him as the father of heritage interpretation, and his book as a kind of bible for practitioners. Tilden attempted to capture his idea of interpretation in the following core principles:

(i) Interpretation should relate to something within the personality or the experience of the visitor.

(ii) Information, as such, is not interpretation. Interpretation is revelation based upon information. However, all interpretation includes information.

(iii) The chief aim of interpretation is not instruction, but provocation.

He was here describing an act of communication, the value of which is crucially dependent on its spiritual or imaginative content and its inspirational effect. He is careful not to present it as a definition, because interpretation can only exist in the particular enactment or context and is coloured by the inspirational talent of the interpreter.

However, it would be a mistake to conclude that his idea of interpretation is either morally or culturally relativistic. For Tilden, the contingent aspect of interpretation lay in the performance, not in the nature of the reality to be interpreted. The tenets of his interpretational 'faith' were rooted in a specifically American tradition of nature worship. Ralph Waldo Emerson is quoted more often than any other source in his book. It was Emerson, along with his disciple Henry David Thoreau, who conjured up for the non-conformist American conscience the vision of the solitary, contemplative individual sublimely uplifted in the presence of nature's grandeur. That the grand spectacle of nature has the power to inspire and transform us, and that the knowledge gained thereby is spiritual in essence, is an Emersonian axiom. The same faith lies at the heart of Tilden's definition. The interpreter's role is to moderate in a group context what Emerson had initially envisaged as a solitary experience. The role is hieratic; it is, he says, to reveal 'something of the beauty, and wonder, the inspiration and spiritual meaning that lie behind what the visitor can with his senses perceive;' it is 'the revelation of a larger truth that lies behind any statement of fact' (Tilden 1957). The key word is 'revelation'. The function of the interpreter is to lay bare a body of truth that is stable, and a meaning that is at once hidden and self-evident; it is finally to mediate nothing less than the universal grand design behind all things. It is worth noting that Tilden does not make clear how his first principle — that interpretation should relate to the personality or experience of the visitor — would work when, for example, the visitor is an atheist or, like journalist P. J. O'Rourke, holds values hostile to what he sees as ecological sanctimoniousness.

Epistemologically, this set interpretation on a path where it would be an encounter with truth rather than a quest for meaning. And from this followed a powerful emotive corollary: interpretation would always be the act of bringing the Good News; determined optimism was one of its defining features. Thus Tilden (without blushing) could define interpreters as 'middlemen of happiness'. He clearly saw the role of such middlemen as dealing in reassuring certainties rather than corrosive doubts; 'generally speaking,' he says, 'certainties contribute towards human happiness' while 'uncertainties are a source of spiritual loneliness and disquietude' (Tilden 1957, 13).

But while such rhetoric holds up plausibly enough in the escapist context of wilderness, when applied to human history its optimism is exposed as both willful and naive. Indeed, it verges on the morally obtuse. Tilden's insistence that in human history the interpretative emphasis should be on 'the beauty of human conduct' is extended even to the battlefield; the story of the battlefield, he says, 'is the story of how in such a tragic environment the human being finds the path to beauty of behaviour' (Tilden 1957, 115). This appeared in the second edition of his book, which came out in 1967

at the height of the Vietnam War and amidst a growing realization amongst his fellow-citizens that a battlefield could be a hellish, futile and far from ennobling place.

To criticise Tilden in this way is not to undermine the central value of his idea of interpretation (namely, the need for the act of communicating the values inherent in heritage to be an engaged and engaging activity), but to point up the historical and philosophical limitations of his thinking. What makes this exercise all the more necessary is that these principles have over the years been reduced to a foundation text by those whose ambition it is to see interpretation and the role of the 'interpreter' recognized as a profession in its own right. It has thus become customary for professional interpreters to cite Tilden, deferentially and uncritically, as a canonical source of wisdom on the subject. Thus Larry Beck and Ted Cable in *Interpretation for the 21st century* (1998), endorse all of Tilden's principles, adding nine of their own which complement rather than challenge any of his. This is not only unfair to Tilden in that it ignores his sense of interpretation as a contingent and non-expert form of human expression, but it has also arrested the refinement of the concept and left it intellectually inert. As David Lowenthal has recently observed, 'worship of a bloated heritage invites passive reliance on received authority, imperils rational inquiry,' and 'saps creative innovation' (Lowenthal 1997, 12).

The major philosophical weakness in Tilden's thinking about interpretation is the assumption that it is about communicating a given understanding of the past or of the nature of heritage. Increasingly, we are having to reckon with the fact that in our contemporary world all values are open to contestation. The most effective way to deal with these relativities is to change the emphasis in interpretation from *revelation* to *exploration*. It means asking open rather than leading questions and avoiding the temptation to beg them.

It is in this critical sense that received wisdom on interpretation has proven such an inadequate conceptual tool in the Irish context. The latent Good News optimism of Tilden's interpretative faith rhymes far too conveniently with the more commercially motivated celebratory intent driving the presentation of Irish culture as a tourism 'product'. I recall a number of years ago listening to a marketing manager enjoining an audience of heritage professionals to ensure that the visitor was sent away 'happy'. However difficult the subject, it was always important to seek out and emphasize the upbeat note. It seemed to me that not only would this be a preposterous goal in the case of one of the sites I managed (Kilmainham Gaol), but that it made no sense in marketing or any other terms. When people stand in the execution yard at Kilmainham Gaol and are told that fourteen men were put to death on this spot in 1916, almost all are moved in some way, some to

378

tears. Far from repelling visitors, it seems to create a magnetism: the visitor numbers to Kilmainham have been going upwards relentlessly from year to year. The point is that the story does not need to be happy (it is a boon of course when it genuinely is) but to be compelling. It is tempting to see the urge to put the best possible gloss on our history in Ireland as connected in some way to a post-colonial complex, but it is perhaps more accurate to see it as an aspect of the heritage syndrome at work in all modern societies; as David Lowenthal has again pithily asserted, 'self-congratulation for inherited virtues is the global norm' (Lowenthal 1997, 68).

Yet the ghost at the table of all presentations of Irish heritage is our unresolved history, most obviously in relation to the northern conflict. The test of how successful we are at communicating the value of our heritage to others is largely a function of our capacity to articulate its depth, richness and complexity to ourselves. Wordsworth wrote that the best poetry is not heard but *overheard*. He meant that if, as he wrote, the poet had the reader foremost in mind, he would inevitably strike a falsely accommodating note. There is, I believe, a valuable lesson here about how natives should go about presenting themselves to the tourist gaze. The essential requirement is self-confidence in the intrinsic value of the story to be told rather than anxiety about how it is being received and understood.

The opening of the Famine Museum at Strokestown in 1995 was rightly praised as marking a new sense of maturity in our presentation of the past. Here was a subject on which any attempt to exercise the celebratory impulse would have been immediately exposed as trite and insensitive. The Famine of 1845-52 demanded a serious treatment and got it. And even though the exhibition has some obvious flaws in interpretational terms (the acres of text being the main one), the tough, uncompromising impulse behind the presentation is right. The Famine is a central traumatic event at the heart of modern Irish history; no matter how 'visitor friendly' the presentation, the subject remains difficult to comprehend, both imaginatively and emotionally. There are few ways of simplifying the story that do not run the risk of being trite and facile. At Strokestown, the viewer is not patronized. The intimation of difficulty is sometimes vital to the cultural and moral integrity of heritage presentation.

There will, of course, always be the need to clarify messages directed at a popular audience, insofar as it is eminently sensible interpretative practice to keep the use of language clear and concise, to avoid obfuscation and to ensure that the visual presentation is crisp, lively and engaging. These values are not peculiar to heritage, but are typical features of effective communication in any form, be it in literature, the audio-visual media or

dramatic performance. But modern interpretative practice does have to tread a very thin line between being faithful to the complexity of a subject on one side and the banality of oversimplification on the other. An overweening desire to simplify meaning, an anxiety to be entertaining at the expense of difficulty and a terror of the ever-receding boredom threshold of putative viewers can tip the balance into bland and hollow presentation.

Thus a dilemma facing contemporary heritage practice is how to strike a balance between market-oriented entertainment concerns and moral-philo-sophical values of meaning and identity. Again, a contradiction in Tilden's idea of interpretation helps to illuminate the nature of this dilemma. On the one hand, Tilden clearly exalts the imagination, and the appeal to the imagination, as the essence of interpretation. Yet, as we have seen, directly in conflict with the value placed on imagination is an implicitly prescriptive sense of the reality to be interpreted. The key to this contradiction lies in his third principle, where he states that 'the chief aim of interpretation is not instruction, but provocation'.

As a kind of secular evangelist, the interpreter stands between a body of knowledge and the person who is to be 'provoked'. The distinction between 'instruction' and 'provocation' is (ironically) instructive. Abjuring 'instruction' means avoiding teaching, informing, directing or commanding. Yet most of the dictionary definitions of 'provoke' are, if anything, more negative in connotation (to 'rouse', 'incite', 'irritate', 'instigate', 'tempt', 'allure'). 'Instructing', we might conclude, is overtly directive, 'provoking' covertly so. The manipu-lative potential of this notion needs to be recognized. Recently, some writers on interpretation have become attuned to the manipulative potential of the message. Don Aldridge sees the challenge as 'to communicate with the public about conservation ideas, to stimulate them to think about values, without telling them what to think' (Aldridge 1989). If the nature of reality is given, then the role of interpretation is to steer the unseeing towards a realization of it. To 'provoke' an audience requires some predisposing knowledge of it, a behaviouristic model of some kind.

Where Tilden leaves off in quasi-religious terms, the secular discipline of marketing is more than willing to take up in behaviouristic terms. Thus many interpre-tative practitioners have taken comfortably to themselves ideas about knowing your audience and their needs and about pitching the message at such dubious phenomena as 'the intelligent twelve-and-a-half year-old'. Of course visitors do have real needs that can be anticipated and planned for. We know that in any encounter that lasts more than half an hour people get tired and need rest-points, to go to the toilet or drink cups of tea and coffee. We know that it is mentally fatiguing to read large tracts of text while standing and moving. We can identify special needs, such as those of the disabled or visually and aurally impaired. We can determine whether and how certain cultural expectations should be built into the presentation (for example, bilingualism in the Gaeltachtaí, or multi-lingualism where there is a high proportion of European visitors, or even certain themes where there is a clearly expressed expectation on the part of a local or sub-cultural group). All of these we can accommodate within a presentational strategy, and they make sense both in marketing and interpretational terms. But there comes a point, admittedly not always easy to define, when we have to leave off on this elaborate anticipation of the visitor and reckon with the fact that he or she is in possession of a sovereign imagination. There is a point after which the story we have to tell cannot be modelled psychologically in terms of customer needs and expectations.

One cannot have it both ways: the ambition to devise a rigorous predictive model of visitors' needs and behavioural patterns is ultimately in conflict with the desire to appeal to their imagination. In his description of the interpretation at Tower Bridge, for example, Richard Harrison stresses the importance of 'understanding who the visitors are now and are likely to be in the future, their characteristics, interests, needs and level of knowledge' (Harrison 1994, 315). He writes enthusiastically of a total visitor experience that is scheduled to last 72.5 minutes, allowing a 'dwell time' of four minutes on each floor of the towers. But what is actually happening to the visitor here? Are they the subjects of an imaginative experience or the objects of a rigorously planned processing system designed to cope with 500,000 visitors a year?

A feature of good interpretation is that it has no imaginative prepossession on its audience; what it offers is an essay on or an exploration of the subject that at some vital point *leaves* it to the imagination of the viewer. There is one group in society who understand the nature of this kind of process profoundly and who, I believe, can contribute vitally to the interpretation of heritage — artists. All artistic creations are contingent in nature; we are free either to like or dislike, agree or disagree with whatever propositions art posits in visual or other terms. Works of art create of themselves an intellectual and emotional space in which the viewer is free to respond. Artists, therefore, can bring not only a level of visual sophistication, subtlety and irony to bear on the interpretation of heritage, they can help counter what Matthew Arnold called the 'tyranny of fact', that dry rehearsal of information which is typical of much heritage interpretation. One of the difficulties we face in Ireland is a tendency to think more rigidly of heritage as a distinct cultural category. The distinction is enshrined in the way we have developed separate bureaucratic paths for dealing with arts and heritage: we have an Arts Council and a Heritage Council, courses for arts administrators and for heritage managers.

The drift of the best contemporary museological thinking is towards ways of envisioning the visitor's autonomy. When Charles Saumarez Smith of the National Portrait Gallery is convinced that 'visitors bring a multiplicity of different attitudes and expectations and experiences to the reading of an artefact, so that their comprehension of it is individualized,' he is no longer talking the language of visitor needs but of visitor autonomy. Thinking through strategies that reinforce rather than compromise the visitor's freedom also involves taking a much closer look at the relationship between interpretation and the space in which it occurs. To Smith the relationship is symbiotic: 'the design of galleries is thought to be a problem independent of the way that artefacts are viewed and understood by visitors', he says, whereas 'the environment conditions and codifies the visitor's expectations.' The same point has been somewhat differently expressed by David Brett when he speaks of paying close attention to the 'narrative topology' of the heritage exhibition environment. This he defines as 'the arrangement of spaces and the connections between them such that they set up, suggest or assert relationships between whatever is displayed in those spaces.'

It is significant that this new thinking has occurred in the context of museums and not of heritage interpretation generally. What distinguishes museums from other forms of heritage presentation is the possession of authentic objects. The role of authentic objects in establishing realms of imaginative freedom cannot be overstressed. Ludmilla Jordanova asserts that museum objects 'are triggers of chains of ideas and images', such that 'the "knowledge" that museums facilitate has the quality of fantasy because it is only possible via an imaginative process'. She contrasts this with the total heritage experience, achieved through technologies of reconstruction and simulation. She cites the Jorvik Centre at York as an example, a place where the appeal is to all the senses, the stress on mimicking experience in a way that 'allows audiences to cultivate a quite unrealistic belief in their own knowledgeability'. She describes such 'experiences' as 'technologies of enforced meaning' (in Vergo 1991, 22–40).

Certainly the Tourism Programmes could not be accused of overenthusiasm for museums. Of the 143 projects listed only thirteen can be described as such. There has been a tendency to view museums as representing an old-fashioned mustiness. In Britain, the best museums are consistently among the top visitor attractions. Well-presented museums, combining authentic collections with the best modern display techniques, offer one of the most sustainable options in heritage presentation. By contrast, revamping pure 'experience' presentations requires a scale of capital re-investment likely to prove increasingly onerous in the post-Structural Funds era. Museums, on the other hand, have in their collections a means of augmenting, revising and refreshing their presentations at much lower cost.

In the longer term, the test of whether our current level of enthusiasm for heritage is enduring and serious will be our willingness to re-invest, refine and improve upon the many fine interpretative facilities put in place under the fair wind of Euro-funding in the last decades of the twentieth century.

Bibliography

Aldridge, D. 1989 'How the ship of interpretation was blown off course in the Tempest: some philosophical thoughts' in Uzzell 1989.

Beck, L. and Cable, T. 1998 *Interpretation for the 21st Century.*

Brett, D. 1997 *The construction of heritage.* Cork.

Cooke, P. 1992 'A modern disease: art and heritage management', *Circa* **61** (January–February), pp. 30–33.

Cronin, M. and O'Connor, B. (eds) 1993 *Tourism in Ireland: a critical analysis.* Cork.

Hewison, R. 1987 *The heritage industry.* London.

Karp, I. and Lavine, S. 1991 *Exhibiting cultures: the poetics and politics of museum display.* Washington, D. C.

Lowenthal, D. 1997 *The heritage crusade and the spoils of history.* London.

Tilden, F. 1957 *Interpreting our heritage.* Chapel Hill, N. C.

Uzzell, D. 1989 *Heritage interpretation (Vol. 1).* Belhaven Press.

Vergo, P. (ed) 1991 *The new museology.* London.

Harrison, R. (ed) 1994 *Manual of heritage management.* London.

APPENDIX A: PROJECTS FUNDED UNDER OPERATIONAL PROGRAMMES FOR TOURISM, 1989–99

The deductions listed on the following pages are derived from information supplied by Bord Fáilte, Shannon Development and the Department of Arts, Heritage, Gaeltacht and the Islands. The list does not include grant aid to the recent refurbishment of Collins Barracks on behalf of the National Museum. Phase 1 designates the First Operational Programme, Phase 2 designates the Second.

DISTRIBUTION OF PROJECTS BY COUNTY

County	
Cavan	1
Clare	9
Cork	12
Donegal	3
Dublin	18
Galway	15
Kerry	16
Kildare	5
Kilkenny	3
Laois	1
Limerick	11
Louth	1
Mayo	2
Meath	3
National	1
Offaly	6
Roscommon	6
Sligo	2
Tipperary	7
Waterford	7
Westmeath	3
Wexford	6
Wicklow	3

PROJECTS CLASSIFIED BY NATURE OF FACILITY

Monuments	40
Museums	13
Visitor Centres	90

PROJECTS CLASSIFIED BY DEVELOPMENT AGENCY

Local Authority (la)	18
State-funded (st)	67
Semi-state (ss)	11
Private (pr)	41
Tourism Org. (to)	6

ABBREVIATIONS
la — local authority
mon — monument
mus — museum
pr — private
ss — semi-state
st — state-funded
to — tourism organization-funded
vis — visitors centre

HERITAGE PROJECTS FUNDED UNDER EU STRUCTURAL FUNDS, 1989–99

PROJECT	COUNTY	CLASS	AGENCY	PHASE	STATUS
Visitor Facilities, Source of Shannon	Cavan	vis	Cavan CoCo.	1	la
Milling Interpretative Centre, Ennis	Clare	vis	Clare CoCo./Ennis UDC	1	la
Ballincollig Gunpowder Mills	Cork	vis	Cork CoCo.	1	la
Rural Life Museum, Newbridge House	Dublin	mus	Dublin CoCo.	1	Ia
Battle of Aughrim Interpretative Centre	Galway	vis	Galway CoCo.	1	Ia
Kerry County Museum, TraIee	Kerry	mus	Tralee UDC/Shannon Her.	1	Ia
Blennerville Windmill	Kerry	vis	Kerry CoCo./Tralee UDC	1	la
Visitor Service, Medieval Precinct	Limerick	vis	Limerick Corp./Sh. Dev.	1	la
Lough Gur, Visitor Facilities	Limerick	vis	Limerick CoCo.	1	la
Adare Heritage Centre	Limerick	vis	Limerick CoCo.	1	la
Adare Castle	Limerick	mon	Dúchas	1	st
Dundalk Museum	Louth	mus	Dundalk UDC	1	la
King House Military History Museum, Boyle	Roscommon	mus	Roscommon CoCo.	1	1a
Roscommon Heritage Centre	Roscommon	vis	Roscommon CoCo.	1	la
Restoration of two Watermills	Tipperary	vis	Tipp. NR CoCo.	1	la
Waterford Visitor Centre	Waterford	mus	Waterford Corp.	2	la
Athlone Castle	Westmeath	vis	Athlone UDC	I	Ia
1798 Centre, Enniscorthy	Wexford	vis	Private/Enniscorthy UDC	2	la
Wicklow Gaol	Wicklow	vis	Wicklow CoCo.	1	1a
Barryscourt Castle, Carrigtwohill	Cork	vis	Barryscourt Trust	1	pr
1796 Visitor Centre, Bantry	Cork	vis	Armada Trust	1	pr
Interpretative Centre, Midleton Distillery	Cork	vis	Irish Distillers Group	1	pr
Women's Gaol, Cork	Cork	vis	Private	1	pr
Cork Heritage Park, Blackrock	Cork	vis	Private	1	pr
Penn Castle	Cork	vis	Private	2	pr
Millstreet Heritage Park	Cork	vis	Private	2	pr
Glencolmcille Folk Village Museum	Donegal	mus	Private	2	pr
Viking Adventure	Dublin	vis	Temple Bar Properties Ltd	1	pr
James Joyce Cultural Centre	Dublin	vis	Private	1	pr
Museum Complex, TCD	Dublin	mus	TCD	1	pr
GAA Museum	Dublin	mus	Private	2	pr
Doctor Steevens' Medical Museum	Dublin	mus	Private	2	pr
Dublinia, Synod Hall, Christchurch	Dublin	vis	Medieval Trust	1	pr
Provision of Working Steam Train	Galway	vis	Westrail Ltd	1	pr
Kilronan Visitor Centre, Inismór	Galway	vis	Fiontar Oidhreachta Inismór	1	pr
Inis Oírr Visitor Centre	Galway	vis	Private	1	pr
Kylemore Abbey, Interpretation	Galway	vis	Private	1	pr
Galway Irish Crystal, Visitor Centre	Galway	vis	Private	1	pr
Kerry Country Life Experience	Kerry	vis	Trustees Muckross House	1	pr
Cahirciveen Heritage Centre	Kerry	vis	Acard Ltd	1	pr
Crag Cave, Showcave, Castleisland	Kerry	vis	Private	1	pr
Tralee/Dingle Steam Railway	Kerry	vis	Private	1	pr
Dingle Sealife Centre	Kerry	vis	Private	2	pr
Transport Museum, Straffan	Kildare	vis	Private	1	pr
Kilkenny Heritage/Genealogy Centre	Kilkenny	vis	Kilkenny Arch. Soc.	1	pr
Foynes Aviation Museum	Limerick	mus	Private	1	pr
Water Wheel and Milling Museum, Croom	Limerick	mus	Private	1	pr
Foxford Woollen Mills Interpretative Centre	Mayo	vis	Foxford IRD	1	pr
Crank House, Bannagher	Offaly	vis	Private	1	pr
Famine Museum, Strokestown	Roscommon	mus	Private	1	pr

HERITAGE PROJECTS FUNDED UNDER EU STRUCTURAL FUNDS, 1989–99

PROJECT	COUNTY	CLASS	AGENCY	PHASE	STATUS
Brú Ború Exhibition Centre, Cashel	Tipperary	vis	Comhaltas Ceolteoirí Éireann	1	pr
GAA Interpretative Centre, Thurles	Tipperary	vis	Private	1	pr
Celtworld	Waterford	vis	Private	1	pr
Waterford Crystal, Visitor Centre	Waterford	vis	Private	2	pr
Restoration of Farmstead, Tagoat	Wexford	vis	Tagoat Community Council	1	pr
Irish National Heritage Park, Ferrycarrig	Wexford	vis	Wexford Heritage Trust	1	pr
Powerscourt House, Visitor Centre	Wicklow	vis	Private	2	pr
Bunratty Folk Park, Expansion of Facilities	Clare	vis	Shannon Dev.	1	ss
Lough Derg Interpretative Centre, Killaloe	Clare	vis	Shannon Dev.	1	ss
Dunguaire Castle	Clare	vis	Shannon Dev.	1	ss
Ailwee Cave	Clare	vis	Shannon Dev.	2	ss
Fenit Sealife Centre	Kerry	vis	Shannon Dev.	2	ss
National Stud	Kildare	vis	National Stud	1	ss
King John's Castle	Limerick	vis	Shannon Her.	1	ss
Hunt Museum	Limerick	mus	Shannon Dev.	2	ss
Birr Science Centre	Offaly	vis	Shannon Dev.	2	ss
Lough Key Forest Park	Roscommon	vis	Coillte	2	ss
Avondale House	Wicklow	vis	Coillte	1	ss
Iniscealtra Church	Clare	mon	Dúchas	2	st
Mooghaun Hill Fort	Clare	mon	Dúchas	2	st
Scattery Island	Clare	vis	Dúchas	1	st
Dromore Forest	Clare	vis	Dúchas	1	st
Barryscourt Castle	Cork	mon	Dúchas	2	st
Doneraile Wildlife Park	Cork	vis	Dúchas	1	st
Lough Hyne Nature Reserve	Cork	vis	Dúchas	2	st
Glengarriff Nature Reserve	Cork	vis	Dúchas	2	st
Donegal Castle	Donegal	mon	Dúchas	1	st
Newmills Cornflax Mills	Donegal	mon	Dúchas	2	st
St Audeon's Church	Dublin	mon	Dúchas	1	st
Rathfarnham Castle	Dublin	mon	Dúchas	1	st
Waterways Visitor Centre	Dublin	vis	Dúchas	1	st
Ashtown Castle, Visitor Centre	Dublin	vis	Dúchas	1	st
Interpretative Panels, Dúchas	Dublin	vis	Dúchas	1	st
St Enda's Park, Nature Study Room	Dublin	vis	Dúchas	1	st
Botanic Gardens Visitor Centre	Dublin	vis	Dúchas	2	st
Portumna Castle	Galway	mon	Dúchas	1	st
Athenry Castle	Galway	mon	Dúchas	1	st
Dún Áengus	Galway	mon	Dúchas	2	st
Aughnanure Castle	Galway	mon	Dúchas	2	st
Glebe House, Kilmacduagh	Galway	mon	Dúchas	2	st
Coole Park	Galway	vis	Dúchas	1	st
Connemara NP	Galway	vis	Dúchas	1	st
Ross Castle	Kerry	mon	Dúchas	1	st
Derrynane House	Kerry	mon	Dúchas	1	st
Ardfert Cathedral	Kerry	mon	Dúchas	1	st
Deenagh Lodge, Information Service	Kerry	vis	Dúchas	1	st
Muckross House	Kerry	vis	Dúchas	1	st
Killarney NP	Kerry	vis	Dúchas	1	st
Ionad an Bhlascaoid	Kerry	vis	Dúchas	1	st
Maynooth Castle	Kildare	mon	Dúchas	2	st
Castletown House	Kildare	mon	Dúchas	2	st

HERITAGE PROJECTS FUNDED UNDER EU STRUCTURAL FUNDS, 1989–99

PROJECT	COUNTY	CLASS	AGENCY	PHASE	STATUS
Grange Castle	Kildare	mon	Dúchas	2	st
Gowran Church, Museum	Kilkenny	mon	Dúchas	2	st
Kilkenny Castle	Kilkenny	vis	Dúchas	1	st
Desmond Hall	Limerick	mon	Dúchas	2	st
Sarsfield House	Limerick	mon	Dúchas	2	st
Céide Fields	Mayo	vis	Dúchas	1	st
Mayo National Park	Mayo	vis	Dúchas	2	st
Knowth	Meath	mon	Dúchas	2	st
Trim Castle	Meath	mon	Dúchas	2	st
Brú na Bóinne	Meath	vis	Dúchas	1	st
Clonmacnoise	Offaly	mon	Dúchas	1	st
Durrow Abbey	Offaly	mon	Dúchas	2	st
Improved Visitor Facilities, Bannagher	Offaly	vis	Dúchas	1	st
Clara Nature Reserve	Offaly	vis	Dúchas	2	st
Boyle Abbey	Roscommon	mon	Dúchas	2	st
Carrowmore, Visitor Facilities	Sligo	mon	Dúchas	1	st
Sligo Abbey	Sligo	mon	Dúchas	2	st
Roscrea Castle	Tipperary	mon	Dúchas	1	st
Ormonde Castle	Tipperary	mon	Dúchas	2	st
Rock of Cashel, A/V	Tipperary	vis	Dúchas	1	st
French Church	Waterford	mon	Dúchas	2	st
Dunmore Caves	Waterford	vis	Dúchas	2	st
Hill of Tara	Westmeath	mon	Dúchas	1	st
Fore Abbey	Westmeath	mon	Dúchas	2	st
Tintern Abbey	Wexford	mon	Dúchas	2	st
Wexford Wildlife Reserve	Wexford	vis	Dúchas	1	st
Monument and Wildlife Signs	National	vis	Dúchas	1	st
G. B. Shaw House	Dublin	vis	Dublin CoCo. & RTO	1	to
Joyce Tower	Dublin	vis	RTO	1	to
Malahide Castle, Visitor Facilities	Dublin	vis	RTO	1	to
Newman House	Dublin	vis	RTO	1	to
Yeats Interpretative Centre, Thoor Ballylee	Galway	vis	Western RTO	1	to
Skellig Experience	Kerry	vis	SW RTO	1	to
Cruachan Aí Visitor Centre	Roscommon	vis	Private	2	pr
Spirit of Ireland Experience ('Dunbrody')	Wexford	vis	Kennedy Trust	2	pr
Dungarvan Castle	Waterford	mon	Dúchas	2	st
Reginald's Tower	Waterford	mon	Dúchas	2	st
Mainguard, Clonmel	Tipperary	mon	Dúchas	2	st
Dunamase Rock	Laois	mon	Dúchas	2	st
Newcastlewest Castle	Limerick	mon	Dúchas	2	st
Iveagh Gardens	Dublin	vis	Dúchas	2	st

The Process of Interpretation

JOHN HARRISON

The word 'interpretation' has been thrown around in discussions and articles on Irish heritage for the past fifteen years or so. At first it was touted as the solution to all our heritage problems; it seemed that local authorities or private investors only had to buy interpretation from the most convincing consultant and their greenfield site would be a money-making heritage magnet.

'Cultural tourism' was on the increase in Ireland of the 1980s and 1990s and interpretation was seen as a means to attract new visitors. After the boom years of the 1980s for the heritage industry in Britain, several large and persuasive design firms fixed their sights on Ireland. As 'heritage' and 'cultural tourism' became buzz-words, money flowed in from Europe and we witnessed the birth of the cloned exhibition where overseas designers transported their favourite media techniques to Irish topics. The result was a series of designer exhibitions in which, if you suddenly woke up in one without knowing where you were, you would instantly recognize the house style of the designer, regardless of the subject-matter. As content sank beneath waves of 'design', the effect was either that of a high street jeweller's shop or a chamber-of-horrors collection of hoary, 'life-like' figures and third-rate talking heads. The transplanted design details had the calculated effect of drawing visitors' attention away from the subject of the exhibition and into an imagined golden age of history.

And then the interpretive bubble burst. In 1992, in the wake of the Burren Centre controversy, Fintan O'Toole — misunderstanding the essence and aims of interpretation as blatantly as the cloned exhibition designers — wrote the following in the *Irish Times*:

To hire an interpreter is to admit that we cannot be spoken to directly. It is an acknowledgement of incomprehension. The rash of interpretive centres is the first public admission that we are now abroad in Ireland, that we have become tourists in our own land.

As a result of the bad publicity, 'interpretive centre' became a four-letter word. O'Toole, branded all 'interpretation' as a conspiracy against the common man (an odd position for someone who had made his name through interpreting the labyrinths of our political, judicial and beef-producing systems for readers of the *Irish Times*). In the public consciousness, interpretation had moved from being the Holy Grail of the tourist industry to a destroyer of landscapes and a sign that we had lost touch with our past.

WHAT IS INTERPRETATION?

We now seem, mercifully, to have reached a middle ground between these polar views, and are coming to appreciate just what interpretation is and how it can help us in the presentation and preservation of our heritage. Interpretation is not an expensive building or a fancy exhibition or an audio-visual show, or a sign that we do not understand our history. It is not just the provision of information; it is an educational technique used to bring visitors closer to a specialized subject than they could normally get. The aim of interpretation is to reveal the inner world of a subject in a simple and meaningful way and then to inspire people to find out more for themselves.

The beginnings of interpretation lie in the history of collections and the perception that environment and landscape are themselves artefacts, as much as are a stone axe or a renaissance painting. Primitive people began to collect unusual stones or crystals, or the heads of their enemies, and people have been assembling material and exhibiting ever since. Renaissance collections were the beginnings of museums as we know them. Owned by educated people, they represented the status of their proprietors, their travels, culture and disposable wealth. But the owners felt no need to make them intelligible to the general populace — abstruseness was seen as a virtue.

Nineteenth-century scholars, such as those who inhabited the British Museum and our own National Museum of Ireland, had entirely different motives. They collected to broaden their own knowledge and, often, to display their erudition to their peers in an age of the popularization of science. But there was rarely real effort, beyond rudimentary labelling, to help visitors understand the collection. The aim seemed to be to have the biggest, most diverse, most academically remote collection possible.

As more people were educated, more began to visit museums and exhibitions, and it became clear that the simple provision of information, usually couched in technical language, was not enough. The word 'interpretation' seems to have been coined by Freeman Tilden (Tilden 1957) in his writings for the United States National Park Service. It was at first directed at educating people about the landscape and the environment, but gradually came to be adopted by those working in history and archaeology. Later, the word and the discipline would be applied to any of an infinite number of subjects which would come under the general term 'heritage'.

INTERPRETATION IS EFFECTIVE ON-SITE EDUCATION

We can now see that the process of interpreting our heritage is simply about moving knowledge from specialists to the general public in a clear and effective way. The natural and man-made world is a hugely complex system, and it is often very difficult for specialists to venture outside their area of expertise — and the jargon associated with it — to talk intelligibly with non-specialists.

Freeman Tilden (1957) defined heritage interpretation as:

An educational activity which aims to reveal meanings and relationships through the use of original objects, by first-hand experience, and by illustrative media, rather than simply to communicate factual information.

This was in an age when museums presented objects with the minimum of information; a time when Hugh Casson of the British Museum maintained that:

Too many museums are still hardly more than heavily subsidized play-pens for squabbling misers, pedants, and fuss-pots, where skill in presentation is regarded as unscholarly and therefore to be deplored.

The Centre for Environmental Interpretation at Manchester has since written that:

Interpretation should be designed to complement first-hand experience of a site, not to usurp or duplicate or interfere with the visitor's experience of that site. It should focus on what makes a place special.

Effective interpretation should stimulate an interest and encourage people to discover for themselves. It should be applied sparingly — much needs to be left uninterpreted for this discovery to be made and owned.

One of the key points about interpretation is that it is a *process* and not a commodity which can be bought off the shelf. Often the best way to interpret a particular subject is to leave it as it is or to present it in a very simple way. Many of our modern cloned exhibitions only manage to obscure historical or environmental heritage and replace it with a well-lit changeling. True interpretation is based firmly on content and authenticity.

HERITAGE

Interpretation is effective communication. But what of heritage? It seems that it could be just about anything that we inherit from the generations who came before us. In speaking to students, I have been asked if the way single mothers were treated in Ireland in the 1950s was part of our heritage — and I had to say that it was. The field of heritage interpretation can include World War II concentration camps such as Dachau and Auschwitz (sometimes unfeelingly, and in the jargon of the advertizing world, referred to as sites of 'hot interpretation'), centres of immense religious importance such as the Jewish Wailing Wall, battlefields, ruined churches, old mills — in fact practically anything you care to mention which is now at a safe distance in time can be classed as heritage. The following is a short list of subjects of developed Irish heritage sites open to the public:

Large military castles
Small castles
Large country houses
Small farmhouses
Shops and the type of goods once sold in shops
Town houses
Environment
Geology
Archaeological remains
Folk stories and legends
Industrial remains (such as mills and gunpowder factories)
Social remains such as gaols (Kilmainham and Tarbert)
Flying-boat ports and old airports
Remnants of colonial days (such as an exhibition of Maori or Egyptian artefacts in the National Museum)
Political figures (such as Collins and de Valera)
Literary figures (James Joyce's tower and Shaw's house)
History of science (Birr Castle)
History of medicine (the College of Surgeons Museum)
Secret societies — The Mason's Museum, Dublin

Textiles
Artefacts made of precious metal and jewels
Trades and crafts
Landscapes (National Parks)

This list contains only a small sample of the huge variety of subjects which we call our heritage. Heritage, it appears, can mean anything.

THE INTERPRETIVE PLAN

The basis of all good interpretation is a logical, prior examination of why the facility is needed and what its aims are. This procedure, called the *interpretive plan*, is the blueprint for a museum, exhibition or visitor information point. It will describe the general storyline, the main sub-themes within that storyline, the types of physical spaces required, levels of visitor facilities, staff requirements and the most suitable media to communicate the information.

The interpretive plan should answer the following questions:

• *Why* is the site being developed?

• *Who* are the potential visitors?

• *What* will be communicated in the displays?

• *How* will the information be made available?

The best approach is to begin with a broad view of the planned function of the site and to use that as a base for architecture and media planning. The following is an outline of the more important aspects of the interpretive plan. Much of this relates to small exhibitions or museums, but many sites will need only minimum interpretation, such as signage or guides, and would be ruined by anything more elaborate.

WHY? — INTERPRETIVE FUNCTION

The proposed function of the development must be clearly stated. Often there is a only a fuzzy, general feeling that interpretation for visitors would be good and useful to have; but it is not clear exactly why. The function of the interpretation can be crystalized in the answer to the question 'why is the facility being developed?'

The quest for an answer can cause much soul-searching. Some possible answers are as follows:

• Because visitors are attracted to a site already and something is needed to cater for them.

• Because visitors have asked for some facility to be provided.

• Because certain people in an organization would like to have their efforts appreciated by a wider public.

• Because interpretation can help regenerate the economy of an area which once depended on industry or farming but which now sees its future in tourism.

• To make money.

• To help local people and visitors appreciate their heritage and thereby take care of it and preserve it for future generations.

• For 'soft' visitor management. This is the management of visitors to delicate archaeological or ecological sites through education of the visitors. It is the hope of this philosophy that, once visitors come to realise the full importance of a site through interpretation, they will treat it with respect and help in its preservation. This is the kernel of the motto of the United States Parks Service — *through interpretation, understanding; through understanding appreciation; through appreciation, conservation.*

• For 'hard' visitor management. This is where visitors are physically led away from fragile areas by the provision of interpretive walks, panels and exhibitions. This was the philosophy behind much of the planning for the ill-fated Burren Visitor Centre mentioned above.

• Because money or a building has suddenly become available and 'interpretation' to attract tourists seems like the best thing to do with it.

• For propaganda. Totalitarian — and other — regimes have often used interpretation, in the form of folk museums, military exhibitions and so on, to alter people's view of the past to suit a particular political philosophy. This is also common in the world of industry where large corporations use the past in the form of exhibitions of objects to give a feel-good quality to their product. A good recent example of this is the use of a nineteenth-century steam train to take people to see the visitor centre at the Sellafield nuclear reprocessing plant in Cumbria, England.

• For entertainment. Many displays, particularly those in the private sector, make no bones about using the past as simple entertainment to attract visitors and ultimately make a profit.

• By a public body as part of its civic duty. Many state and local government agencies have a duty to provide interpretation to the public about the work they do and the heritage for which they are responsible. These include county councils and the Department of Arts, Heritage, the Gaeltacht and the Islands.

• As part of a museum display function. The four main functions of a museum can broadly be said to be collection, conservation, study and presentation.

It is as part of the fourth museum function that interpretation is relevant. In the minds of many museum professionals, however, it is this function — the only one which is seen by the public — which is the most annoying and which takes them away from, as they see it, the much more important job of the first three museum functions. This is why we need professional, specialist heritage interpreters.

WHO? — POTENTIAL VISITORS

One of the most difficult things to know about a new development is who it should be aimed at. Sometimes the answer will be 'anybody we can get to visit it'. But what kind of visitors a site can expect will often depend on the proposed function. For example:

• If the interpretive site is in a medical college and is intended to be used as part of the training of medical personnel, it would have a completely different orientation to a facility which is intended for the general public.

• If the development is intended to appeal mostly to children, displays will be specially focussed at that age group.

• If the function of the exhibition is to act as a marketing ploy for a certain commercial product, then it may have to be aimed at specific age groups.

• If visitors are mostly expected to come in coach tours, allowances will have to made in the car parks and displays will have to be designed so that they can accommodate large groups who will move through the exhibition at the same time.

• If overseas visitors are expected, there must be provision for several languages.

• Displays and facilities should be made accessible to older or disabled people if it is to become possible for them to visit the site.

• If the site is going to be marketed to school tours, specially trained guides will often have to be provided to deal with large groups of children. Teachers who accompany these groups usually look on the visit as time off for themselves and often do not see it as their respon-

sibility to control their charges while they are at your site.

In general we can say that as much as possible should be known about potential visitors. This knowledge can then be augmented by visitor surveys once the site is operating.

WHAT? — RESEARCH AND THEMES

Basic research of the subject in question is the foundation of the interpretive plan and is the beginning of the answer to the question '*what* will be communicated in the displays?'. Research should be done meticulously but should not be pedantic. Most of the material found will not be used in the exhibition, but it must be available to decide what *will* appear and also to be used as back-up information for specialists. Depending on the subject-matter, varying levels of research will be necessary. Some subjects will need a great deal of primary research into original documents and photographs, other topics will have been well covered already by scholars working in the area and the relevant information will have been published.

Once the basic research is complete, you must decide what elements of this information will be included in the exhibition and how they will be grouped logically to make them more intelligible to non-specialist visitors. The overall *theme* or *storyline* which makes the exhibition special must be stated. This can then be divided into sub-themes which — while having their own internal logic — should always relate clearly to the main theme. This approach will give visitors a memorable and unified impression of the subject rather than a vague recollection of a mass of unrelated information. The number of possible themes for any particular subject can be daunting, but a process of consultation with any interest groups, amateur or professional, will help to narrow the field considerably.

AUTHENTICITY

Whatever area of heritage we are dealing with, there is one characteristic which is vital — authenticity. In his collection of essays *Eight little piggies*, the historian of science Stephen Jay Gould tells of an experience he had at the Smithsonian Institute:

Authenticity comes in many guises, each contributing something essential to our calm satisfaction with the truly genuine. Authenticity of object fascinates me most deeply because its pull is entirely abstract and conceptual. The art of replica making has reached such sophistication that only the most astute professional can now tell the difference between, say, a genuine dinosaur skeleton and a well-made cast. The real and the replica are effectively alike in all but our abstract knowledge of authenticity yet we feel awe in the presence of bone once truly clothed in dinosaur flesh and mere interest in fibreglass of identical appearance.

If I may repeat, because it touched me so deeply, a story on this subject told once before in these volumes: A group of blind visitors met with the director of the Air and Space Museum in Washington to discuss greater accessibility, especially for the large objects hanging from the ceiling on the great atrium and perceptible only by sight. The director asked his guests whether a scale model of Lindbergh's Spirit of St Louis, mounted and fully touchable, might alleviate the frustration of non-access to the real McCoy. The visitors replied that such a solution would be most welcome, but only if the model were placed directly beneath the invisible original. Simple knowledge of the imperceptible presence of the authentic can move us to tears.

The presentation must be authentic. But this raises a tricky problem for professionals trying to present heritage to the visiting public — 'how much do we tell them?' Is it the function of heritage sites to present an idealized past which will take visitors away from hard reality to a mythical golden age, or should we present everything in stark colours? Folk parks and museums which include reconstructions of houses and farm buildings rarely have reconstructions of children's graveyards; but infant mortality was an ever-present reality in our society before the advent of twentieth-century medicine.

Even those heritage sites such as prisons and concentration camps can never tell the whole truth about the lives of their inmates. The very act of trying to present the reality of tragedy can cheapen the memory and turn it into crass voyeurism. I shall never forget the sight of visitors jostling to get photographs of themselves, summer-clothed and smiling, outside the ovens of Dachau concentration camp.

INTERPRETATION AND INFORMATION

As we have said, interpretation is not just information. On its own, information frequently alienates visitors by frightening them with obscure terms or boring them with tracts of detailed text (sometimes this is seen as a great success by the academic or museum curator who provided the information to ward off an inquisitive public). The interpretive approach is based on converting information into a form which is accessible to the people who will visit the site. Technical terms should be avoided or clearly explained. The ideal is to appeal to as many of the five senses as possible — sight, sound, smell, taste and touch (this ideal is often unattainable, and certainly should not be taken to outlandish lengths, but should be borne in mind). The old educational dictum 'I see, I forget; I do, I remember' is particularly relevant here.

A good interpretive approach can be achieved in many different ways, but it is vital to remember that people are mostly interested in other people. The general thrust of

the exhibition should relate to the visitor's everyday life or to the common factors in human experience which are relevant to the subject. Technology, art or archaeology without people are normally of interest only to technologists and specialists. These will probably constitute about 1% of visitors. For the remaining 99%, the story must be told from a human perspective.

When providing an interpretive facility, the most difficult decision is often not what to put in, but what to leave out. Although more detailed information should be available to experts, it should be provided so as not to obscure the subject for non-specialists. This can often be achieved by providing layered information which uses type-size, colours, models and other techniques to present the subject on several different levels of detail.

HOW? — INTERPRETIVE MEDIA

The answer to the final basic question of the interpretive process — how will the information be made available? —tells us which media should be used in the exhibition. One of the commonest mistakes of museum or visitor centre design is to have made a decision on a range of media before the basic interpretive plan has been completed. For example, an elaborate audio-visual-theatre might be provided for a subject which is not suited to treatment by that medium, or which would be more effectively treated by including smaller audio-visual elements as part of a general exhibition. Over-emphasis on a particular medium must also be avoided. There are several visitor centres in Ireland today which consist of just four or five AV shows one after the other; others are simply a string of 'life-like' models. The medium must suit the subject. Cartoons are effective when dealing with some subjects, but would be totally out of place with others. There are occasions when an empty room can be the most appropriate medium. The range of media to be used should reflect the theme of the exhibition — the theme should not be changed or adapted to suit a certain medium.

ARTEFACTS

In general, we can say that artefacts should function as part of the overall storyline. Many museums care for collections of artefacts which will never be shown to the public. The care and conservation of historical objects for their own sake are a vital part of museum policy, but as a *function* they must be distinguished clearly from the use of artefacts as part of an exhibition. Though artefacts should be the principal component in any exhibition — without objects it tends to be just an illustrated book on a wall — their primary role is to substantiate some piece of information about a subject or to evoke the atmosphere of a particular event or practice. Artefacts as an element of an exhibition should be viewed as part of the overall storyline and great care must be taken in what is included and how it is presented.

Some objects will need no extra interpretation; they will already have a strong enough historical resonance and a clear enough function. Others will need to be explained — though this might simply be a question of placing an obscure item next to one that everyone is familiar with, and thereby suggesting that they have the same function. Artefacts have their own problems: they will be placed in an environment that is not natural to them, people will want to touch them and may even try to take souvenirs. Delicate or small objects must be protected while keeping them accessible to visitors. As well as restoration work, some items may need special exhibition environments — such as atmospherically controlled show-cases — which will help to slow natural deterioration.

ARCHITECTURE

Sir Roy Lankester — one-time director of the British Natural History Museum — told a museums conference in 1879 that:

> It is always extremely difficult to erect a museum with proper attention to the requirements to which the building is erected. That enemy of the human race — the eminent architect — is always lying in wait. He deliberately and habitually perverts the funds entrusted to his discretion, so as to produce a showy and expensive building, whilst ignorantly and shamelessly neglecting the essential purposes for which the building is required.

The more things change ...

In general, building design should be a direct response to exhibition design. The physical spaces which are occupied by a museum or exhibition have a dramatic effect on presentation. Spaces must be integrated with the exhibition plan — and the themes to be communicated to visitors — rather than be designed as a building which will just happen to contain a museum.

The exhibition should firstly be planned and outlined. The themes will fall into natural categories and sub-categories; some will need to be physically near or in communication with others, some might be clearer if they were isolated. The architect must also take into account visitor flow through the building, the entrance desk, storage space, staff rooms, and any necessary visitor facilities such as toilets, tearooms and shops. There should be a continuity of design throughout the building as well as exhibitions and publications which will create an immediately recognizable style in the minds of visitors. The most effective approach to providing exhibition buildings is for the exhibition designer and the architect to work together in the following way:

(i) The exhibition designer should prepare a complete interpretive plan and arrange themes and sub-themes as they will appear in the exhibition.

(ii) A rough, preliminary, media design should then be drawn up — including artefacts, working and non-working models, dioramas, interpretive panels and so forth.

(iii) A flow diagram of the spaces required in the building — including visitor and staff facilities — can then be drawn.

(iv) The architect can now be given these documents in the form of a brief which will enable him to respond to the requirements, with due consideration to the integrity and function of the exhibition, but which will still leave ample room for creative architecture. The subsequent planning of the building and exhibition design should then proceed together to produce a single integrated design.

CHILDREN AND SPECIAL ACTIVITIES

Children, as part of school tours or family groups, will comprise a considerable proportion of visitors. Interpretation for children is not just a dilution of that for adults — exhibits, or parts of exhibits, should be provided which will appeal directly to children (and to the child in many adults). All show-cases and artefacts must be within a child's range of vision and steps and handrails should be provided where necessary. Exhibits for children should be physically interesting and, if possible, pose a problem which can be answered immediately and clearly. Cartoon characters appearing regularly and reinforcing the storyline can be useful to both children and adults. Humour in an exhibition is particularly appealing to children. Special guide-books or work-books could be designed — possibly in association with local schools — for young people to use at home and as a simplified guide to the exhibition.

As well as permanent exhibitions, a planned series of special events will keep any exhibition active and alive in the minds of both public and staff. They will also help gain valuable publicity on a regular basis. These need not be very elaborate, and could simply be the demonstration of certain pieces of equipment or some physical phenomenon basic to the subject of the exhibition. Other ways of doing this are to have temporary exhibitions of items on loan from other museums, or special work-days for schools. Special activities like these have worked well in other museums, particularly in those with an emphasis on the physical sciences.

LIGHTING

Lighting is one of the most important elements of exhibition design. In general, light directed at exhibits, artefacts and pieces of text which also provides enough ambient light for the room is more effective than using general house lights. It will make panels and exhibits stand out clearly and dramatically in relation to the walls of the room. A house light system — on a separate circuit to the exhibition lighting — should be provided for special uses of the spaces, but should be well hidden. All lighting should be switched back to a central switching point. Whatever lighting system is decided upon, the safety and comfort of visitors is the most important consideration. Emergency lighting is mandatory.

MANAGEMENT AND MAINTENANCE

Regardless of what facilities, artefacts or interpretive techniques you provide, staff will often create the strongest impression in the minds of visitors. They are the most significant resource at any visitor attraction, and it is important to prepare a detailed staffing plan at an early stage of design. Even if only a small number of staff is involved, the earlier you know who they are, what they do and how they relate to each other the better. The following are the most frequent staff categories:

• Manager — the manager will handle all administrative duties, accounts, salaries, staff rotas and all the other day-to-day tasks involved in running what is essentially a business.

• Curator (at a small site this could be the same person as the manager) — the curator will be responsible for the acquisition and maintenance of all artefacts and displays and also for all interpretive material.

• Receptionists.

• Exhibition guides.

• Security personnel.

• Restorers and conservators.

• Maintenance and cleaning staff.

It is important to think about staffing early so as to provide any necessary staff facilities in planning the building — such as cloakrooms, toilets, an office or phone point — as part of the interpretive plan. It creates a bad impression for people to see staff coats or bags in the public area. Early staff training is also important. Regardless of the number of staff, they must be trained properly and be fully aware of visitors' needs for facilities and information. There must also be a strict mainte-nance programme for the whole exhibition. Setting up a museum or exhibition is one thing; maintaining and managing that new resource is quite another. The impact of thousands of people every year will quickly become all too noticeable if there is no maintenance programme.

PUBLICATIONS AND ARCHIVES

There will probably be a need for a number of small publications such as publicity flyers, free leaflets at reception and a general guide-book to the exhibition. Though it is not vital that they are produced for the opening day, the design of these publications should fit in with the overall design of the museum so as to create the impression of continuity of function. Logos, colours, design features and the like should all be carried on into publications.

The vast majority of visitors to the exhibition will probably be non-specialists who do not wish to go into the subject in any great detail. But it is always useful to have a separate space where people who are particularly interested in certain aspects of the subject can obtain more detailed information. An archive and reading room which houses historical documents as well as general textbooks is often a very useful secondary function of a good exhibition.

VISITOR FACILITIES

Though people visit exhibitions for a variety of different reasons — education, entertainment, specialist interest — it is often the total experience which attracts them. It is important to make sure that visitors can arrive and park their cars easily and be physically comfortable during all stages of their visit. The following are some of the more common visitor facilities:

• *Car parks* — though city-centre visitor attractions are less dependant on parking than are those in rural areas, some provision for parking is a great advantage.

• *Toilets* — there must be sufficient toilets for the number of people you are expecting. If coach tour business is expected, there must be enough toilets to cater for groups of about 60 arriving at one time. Wheel-chair toilets should also be provided.

• *Shops* — though it is wise to avoid over-commercial-ization, people like to buy small souvenirs from the places they visit, so a shop can help to make a visit more memorable as well as being a good source of revenue.

• *Refreshments* — a tearoom serving light snacks and tea and coffee is often very welcome at a visitor attraction where people spend a long time on their feet. Both this and the shop could be franchised to an external operator.

• *Disabled access* — access for disabled and elderly people to as many areas as possible is expected at all modern museums and visitor centres.

• *Languages* — though the majority of your visitors will be English-speaking, many people will come from non-English speaking countries. Probably the best way of catering for these is to provide written translations of texts and descriptions of artefacts which they can return to the reception before they leave the museum premises. Though these may be only a synopsis of all the text in the exhibition, they will be very much appreciated. Foreign-language guides can be brought in to deal with special groups.

ADMISSIONS

A decision will have to be taken on whether or not the exhibition needs an admission charge or whether it will be seen as a public service. In general, admission charges should pay for day-to-day operation costs of the exhibition, but should never be expected to recoup the capital costs of the investment. Whether or not it is decided that the museum will need an admission charge to pay for an operations budget, there should be some nominal admission fee. This will act as a control to people entering and help to prevent misuse of the facility. Admission charges should be scaled so as not to exclude the less-well-off. Special arrangements should be made for old-age pensioners, students, the unemployed and other disadvantaged groups.

PUBLICITY

The most effective form of publicity is that which costs least — people talking to each other in glowing terms about your fascinating exhibition. But, apart from an initial curiosity factor, this will only happen after you have established yourself in the market-place. This normally takes a number of years. The level of marketing will depend on the function of the exhibition and the nature of the exhibits. Some institutions will do all they can to attract as many visitors as possible — others will try to limit the number of visitors in order to avoid damage to fragile artefacts or buildings. It is a good idea to look at the proposed function of the museum, decide the optimum number of visitors and then work to that figure. One simple form of publicity is general signposting. A large proportion of visitors to many exhibitions are casual visitors who have seen road signs and then decided to visit the site.

BENEFITS OF INTERPRETATION

As was pointed out above, the concept of interpretation has received a lot of misguided attention from people who wished to promote it, as well as from those vigorously opposed to it. Approached rationally, interpretation can be a great aid to both visitors and managers at many heritage sites. The following is a short list of some of the benefits of interpretation.

• It helps people to enjoy their visit through education.

• It encourages local residents to value their environment.

• Interpretation increases general understanding of heritage, thereby creating a sense of place and concern for conservation.

• It attracts more visitors to an area to support the local economy.

• It helps environmental improvement, regeneration and employment.

• It compliments other services designed to encourage care of heritage and the environment.

Bibliography

Gould, S. J. 1983 *Eight little piggies: reflections in natural history*. New York.

Tilden, F. 1957 *Interpreting our heritage*. N. Carolina.

Harrison, R. (ed) 1994 *Manual of heritage management*. London.

Design and Layout of Museum Exhibitions

Ann Scroope

The role of a museum is to preserve and foster its collection, to record it, build upon it and register it in the context of time, to present selections from this to the public for their education and entertainment. However, many questions arise from this apparently simple definition. It is clear that the most pointed question is in relation to the nature of the public, an issue already identified in the late nineteenth century by the American museologist, George Brown Goode, who claimed:

The museum of the future in this democratic land should be adapted to the needs of the mechanic, the factory operator, the day labourer, the salesman and the clerk, as much as to those of the professional man and the man of leisure ... In short, the public museum is, first of all, for the benefit of the public.

The public is no longer an implicitly understood conglomerate; we have to talk about different 'publics', and ask at whom precisely the exhibition message is aimed. This questions the operational approach of museums. While its immemorial house-keeping role has not changed, the emphasis has shifted from the collection to the visitors and their perception of the value of the museum experience in the context of their own lives. Life-styles are constantly changing; museums must recognize and manage these changes.

The shift of emphasis from collection to public has been accompanied by a radical shift of power. The curator is no longer the sole decision-maker on what is presented or how it is presented. Decisions about what to display and how to display it are now less the function of a singular scholarly whim: they are made by a greater group of collaborators, each with their own particular talent, voice or expertise to bring to bear on the final presentation. The realization that the museum must now compete for the public's attention with an unprecedented variety of educational and entertainment alternatives has driven the shift in direction. At the same time

wise voices like that of Rudi Fuchs, Director of the Stedelijk Museum (speaking on its centenary), cautioned the museum from straying too far in the direction of courting popularity at the expense of its overall mission:

the ability to compare everything with everything is the museum's last defence against fashion — the more museums are judged on the basis of attendance, the more they will be inclined to give precedence to that which is fashionable, and neglect and forget the rest. The authority of the museum is founded on its remoteness from fashion.

The challenge, therefore, is to engage the public without succumbing to the fluctuations of transient concerns. In this chapter, I specifically address the presentation of museum collections in the form of exhibitions. In particular, I try to shed light on what my particular area of expertise, design, contributes to the process.

DEFINITIONS

There are three main design stages to the implementation of exhibition: briefing to concept design; design development to documentation, and construction. Design is an evolutionary and objective process of learning, negotiation, interrogation, selection and interpretation. The final presentation does not spring from a single mind. It results from a complex set of interactions among a group of people whose skills, experience and ideas are significant only in relation to the contributions of others. The process of preparation, production and final presentation is organic. The designer, in other words, never acts alone, but in concert with others. To initiate the process, a sound basis of understanding between the designer and the client is crucial. This is often no easy matter, as the client is often a 'composite'. The client, for example, could include all or any of the following: councillors, curators, architects, development managers, writers, academics and educational advisors.

Also the clients' motives may be mixed: they may want an exhibition to reflect values of scholarship or entertainment or, indeed, in some cases, a marketing strategy may be a driving force behind an exhibition.

Whatever the motive, it is crucial that the client group begins with a clear vision of the institution, its philosophy and the role they want a particular project to fulfil. There is currently a great deal of rhetoric about 'the vision' phenomenon. It forms a virtually indispensable basis for a museum with the ambition to engage a contemporary audience. A somewhat extreme example from a 1994 architectural preliminary brief for the new Museum of Victoria, Australia, may be quoted at length in this connection:

the museum of the future will be a store house of ideas ... [and] will not merely see things as they are and ask why, but (rather) will explore things as they might be and ask ... why not? [The] focus will not be on objects alone but on the people and the stories behind the objects .... visitors will feel a sense of excitement and discovery ... Programs will stimulate enthusiasm and knowledge and engender optimism in the future ... collections [are] to address issues of debate to interest, mystify and amuse ... the museum will provide means to overcome barriers of language, culture, age and interests ... It will be full of chatter with the joy of discovery and learning: there will be laughter, parents conversing with children and vice versa, the old will mix with the young, the infirm and the disabled will be at home, and school children will not want to leave.

All those aspirations were supported with a budget of A$250 million, allowing $30 million for exhibition fit-out and the project to be completed no later than mid-2000.

In Ireland we may not share this 'Billy Graham' style of approach, but the clarity of the vision for the museum's future is unmistakable. One can see how a whole range of functional operations, from conservation policy to design, can be orchestrated around it. If the museum of the future is to face the challenge of a changing society, it will aim, through its exhibitions, to be engaging and provocative, to promote respect for natural and cultural heritage, to influence attitudes, opinions and actions. It will be a forum for discussion and debate.

Therefore, the design brief should acknowledge the challenge facing museums and heritage presentations and attempt to find a fresh way of articulating it. The brief begins with the clients addressing their ambition for the exhibition. The design process then moves forward to embrace in detail the character of the visitor, the narrative of the exhibition and the physical environment. However, this will only happen if the client is prepared to enter into a genuine dialogue with the designer or the design team. Regrettably, a misunderstanding frequently occurs whereby the client views the design process as merely a technical one of adding visual

flesh to ideas contained in the initial brief, however well- or ill-defined those ideas may be. If the designer remains in the role of technician, there is a strong possibility that the end result will be superficial.

The design process has to be more than an exercise where the designer has to guess the right answer, which the client already has in his or her head. The process has to be about the client and the designer together trying to map the imaginative territory of the exhibition, with the brief providing a set of co-ordinates to guide them. In this way, the client who takes an active part in the creative process can exert considerable influence on the design style and content of the finished product. For this creative process to be truly exploratory, the relationship between the commissioning body and the designer must be vigorous and candid. The collaboration must be thorough and sustained. It must not cloud the responsibilities of the design team or the client, but should get behind the hand-holding exercise these relationships often fall into. With a sound basis of understanding and trust between the designer and the client, the development of the brief can move forward.

BRIEFING TO CONCEPT

The concept stage is about ideas — brainstorming is a key word here. This is an informal, wild, speedy and often witty romp through all the possibilities of the project. It involves everyone who may wish to take part: cleaners, accountants, the secretary, the designers (of course) and the client. There is no assessment or judgement of the ideas to be made during this session. The purpose is to open every possible avenue of thought on the project. Once all the ideas are brought together, they are studied broadly to see if a particular pattern is emerging. Like the hands of the potter moulding the clay, the parameters of the brief — the physical space, the narrative of the exhibition, the character of the institution, the collection and the visitor — are then applied to the ideas, and the concept begins to emerge.

The principal designer is ultimately responsible for the aesthetic of the exhibition, translating the ideas into the physical environment. This role includes the day-to-day planning of the project, negotiating budget details, supervising changes and refinements to the design, preparation of working drawings, design detailing, the supervision of contracts and the co-ordination of other skills to ensure visual integration. The designer has creative influence from the start, generating the vision and adapting the client's vision to the limitations of time, budget and physical space.

The creative input is never limited to one person, but the principal designer shapes and guides the creative contributions of other key personnel — researchers, designers, model-makers, artists, technicians — determining their input and roles. The main design team establishes all information pertaining to the building and the conceptual framework of the brief in order to determine both the physical and philosophical parameters of the project. The research information available is studied in the context of the space and themes for the exhibition. This includes the list of objects, photos, dimensions and any known display requirements. Information on the objects is essential in order to calculate the physical requirements for their display. During this phase, the freedom should exist to relocate objects, juxtaposing them with each other and even deselecting them. This process, of course, is subject to discussion amongst all interested parties.

PHYSICAL LAYOUT

The physical layout of displays on the floor may itself serve as a metaphor for the exhibition. The motive for the metaphor must be clear. The deliberate time tunnel of the United States Holocaust Memorial Museum in Washington D.C., for example, reinforces the message of the exhibition. The visitors are controlled and herded silently through the horror of the holocaust as the victims of the Nazi camps were in the 1940s. This layout would not work so well for an exhibition presenting the complex development of a society from 10,000 years ago to the present. In this situation themes embracing the time-frame may be considered so that the visitor can choose individual interests and revisit displays in order to make comparisons between time horizons, technologies or social developments.

SELECTION OF MEDIA

The assessment of various media is based upon a number of factors, the primary one being the 'message'. While one still hears echoes of 'let the object speak for itself' down the hallowed halls of some institutions, most recognize that inanimate objects do not in fact speak. Media are employed to support the focus of the exhibition, to serve, not determine or control, the exhibition. There are two pet hates in the briefing stage of a project. One is the demand for 'state-of-the-art technology', the other is the demand not to employ 'multimedia'— meaning computer-based — technology. There is the assumption that the techniques used in interpretative design are the essence of interpretation. It is not unfair to say that this assumption is sustained because of recent historical continuity rather than by an ongoing assessment of the validity of employing these techniques.

'Bringing the past to life' through recreations, wax figures, mechanical mice, smells and other 'fakesimilies' can result in a lesson on wax sculptures or mechanics while the focus of the exhibition is lost to the curiosity of the illusion. The mission is not to bring the past to life but to enable a better understanding of the past.

Presenting a sense of the past can only be achieved through the senses. Thus in the stories of Kilmainham Gaol, Dublin, solitary confinement and hard labour were to be represented in the exhibition. The various narrative threads running through the Gaol were studied in preparing the exhibition. Solitary confinement can drive a person mad. Hard labour can break the emotional spirit. These messages are not relegated to history, they are relevant to the here and now. The depiction of this reality is, therefore, not the reconstruction of the past but the articulation of a contemporary emotional response.

Obviously, the budget determines to what extent any particular technology will be employed, but selection or deselection must be determined by first deciding what has to be said. How a message is imparted follows from this. The choice of media available comprises the physical space, light, colour, spoken and written word, mechanical and sculptural models, audio, images and computer-generated programmes, to list but a few. The study of objects, their multi-faceted complexities, what they represent, the stories and people behind them, also shapes the detail of presentation. The material that is used, the design style that is adopted and the technologies that are selected, all send messages to the visitor. The employment of the different media in presentations must recognize varying physical, intellectual and emotional responses on the part of the visitors, their idiosyncrasies (among young and not so young), and encourage interaction on these levels. It is a critical part of the design process that there is a formal analysis of the media being chosen to ensure that the message we are imparting to the visitor is right.

THE VISITOR

In addressing the character of the visitor, the team investigates how the exhibition will engage visitors. Essentially, this means finding ways in which the imagination of the visitor will be stimulated and provoked. Imagine you are part of a group to be photographed. Copies of the photograph are made and given to everyone in the group. Each person will look for himself or herself first. Imagine you have been cut out of the group. Your are now alienated and no longer interested in the photograph.

This happens within exhibitions when the character of the visitor is not part of the assessment criteria throughout all stages of the design. How the visitors 'see' themselves in the exhibition may take the form of posing questions and encouraging them to seek answers for themselves, inviting the visitor to respond to the subject-matter through reaction cards or reflection on their own lives by using contemporary imagery and language.

With continuing input from all personnel, the principal designer generates the overall plan for the exhibition. This involves an exhibition pre-write document supported with spatial and editorial plan drawings, models and sketches. Quantification is an essential part of this stage to ensure the project is steered within budgetary limits. It is particularly important that, as precisely as possible, estimation of elements such as graphic panels, showcases, audio-visual elements and special effects media is established. A broad budget breakdown is presented and the programme further refined. The presentation of this stage is subject to review by everyone involved. A response in writing is critical. A deadline is set for this response and for making any amendments.

DESIGN DEVELOPMENT TO DOCUMENTATION

Once the concept is approved, the design programme involves sourcing the specialized contractors — model-makers, audio-visual contractors, sculptors and illustrators — required to implement the works. Their contribution is guided by the exhibition pre-write document. The selection of specialized contractors is based on interviews and credentials. It is often required by the client to get comparative quotations also, but lowest price is not the sole determining factor in making a selection. This exercise is more valuable than seeing how the overall budget for the exhibition is breaking down prior to the main construction contract being finalized.

When commissioned, both the researcher and the principal designer brief the specialized contractors. During this development, the full team meets with the client to resolve in detail the editorial content, use of language and presentation of images. The design researcher provides all the edited text and pictures and this material is shared between the graphic and audio-visual presentations. General scripting for programmes, materials, images, film footage and so forth is issued, and the details of the physical spaces available for their hardware in the exhibition are determined. Decisions are made regarding the length of time programmes will operate and regarding the choice of language for instructions to the user.

GRAPHIC DESIGN

The collation of all graphic material is the first priority at this stage: the draft editorial, the sourcing of images, copyrights and references material. If not part of the in-house design team, the graphic designer is usually one of the first to be brought on board. The choice may simply be the preference of the principal designer. The graphic designer takes an active part in the choice of styles, materials, visuals and the task of conferring with researchers about themes and narratives. Closest collaboration is with the principal designer — meeting the constant assembly of choices, each choice creating and defining the next step. Where special illustrations or images must be commissioned, all reference material and specific guidelines are provided by both the main designer and the graphic designer. Legibility, emphasis on word identity and multiple languages are issues addressed by the graphic designer. Though often ignored or at best considered as a last attachment to the process, the title for the exhibition and the themes within it are in fact keys to the panel layout. The right title and the right image can reduce the text appearing on the panel to a simple statement.

A major criticism of many exhibitions has been expressed as 'I should have just bought the book and not bothered going to the exhibition'. This is such a disappointing outcome to a long and considered design process. So, what goes wrong? At the beginning of every project, most clients say they do not want the 'book on the wall'. As the project progresses and more detailed facts come to light, it is extremely hard for the design group to argue the benefit of editing the content of panels by countering the suggestion 'but it is all so important'. The fact is an exhibition serves a limited function in the overall educational endeavour of a museum. It serves to bridge the gap between the expert and the novices, but should not try to turn all novices into experts. So a balance must be struck somewhere between the 'switch-off' factor and the 'turn-on'.

Hearing, seeing and doing, all are important. The graphic design (as is the case with the printed word and image) element of an exhibition is not to be considered independently of the three-dimensional or structural elements of the exhibition.

Both skills must meet, overlap and become interdependent within the exhibition environment. Both share the responsibility of imparting the message to the visitor, but how it is done and at what level it is carried out differ. As an image can replace a thousand words, the same principle can apply to a physical structure. When the message is clearly defined, its expression is shared between all elements employed in the design. We can create a hierarchy of information and legibility. For example, at primary level, a question may be posed to the visitor in large text on a panel; the snappy answer may be found in the object on display or the 'game' the visitor is invited to partake in. More detailed information such as historical or technical background to the subject may then be accessed via captions on a database or within the showcase.

In the County Museum at Dundalk, county Louth, 14,000 years of natural evolution is presented in a space measuring 9 metres long, 3 metres high and a depth of about one metre. The key question being presented is 'Evolution or Extinction?' Flora, fauna and man's exploitation of the landscape form the messages. The exhibition design team here agreed the medium to be employed would be a mural, but we were also concerned that this, at a first glance, would 'switch off' some visitors, particularly those who did not have a leaning towards natural history. The design result is a three-dimensional mural as interpreted by an artist. The artist played with scale and composition within the parameters of academic correctness and proposed a monochromatic finish. The display is a work of art that engages the visitor immediately by virtue of its material expression. Positioned in front of the mural are three computer touch-screen data units presenting a colour rendering of the same mural. The visitor scrolls across the mural on screen, selects images of the relevant flora and fauna and navigates through levels of information on each species. The last feature of the mural is that of an 'Eco quiz'. Here the visitor is asked questions on current ecological issues, but before doing so is presented with the arguments made by conservation groups and industrialists. Graphic design guides the mural imagery and the screen conventions.

CAPTIONS

Call it the showcase dance step. You take one step forward, put on your glasses to read the caption, take one step back, take off the glasses to see the object, take one step forward, put on the glasses and repeat until fatigue sets in. If every object on display in a showcase has to have a caption, and therefore the caption is a small card positioned with each object, then make it worth the visitor's while to study this gem of information. What cannot be seen from the object itself may be of particular interest — where the object was found, who found it and what its 'life story' has been before ending up under a high-security, environmentally controlled case in a museum. The catalogue or archive reference number can actually appear on the back of the caption card.

CONSTRUCTION

Once the 'vision' is shaped into a physical space, the creative environment can be built. This stage of the process can be summarized briefly here as it is more a role of project management for the team rather than design. The overall structures and displays are drawn up in detail for construction. Lighting is planned with careful attention to conservation requirements as well as supporting the mood, pace and ambience of the exhibition spaces. Technical and material specifications are drawn up and tender packages prepared. Once the tenders are returned and the successful contractor is appointed, the designer makes any amendment necessary if costs are above budget. The contractor draws up the programme for the main construction works, and this details both on- and off-site works. The principal designer only gives instruction to the contractor. It is essential to note that the client does not deal with the contractor directly on any issue. To do so can negate any legal responsibility the designer has towards the implementation of the works and more than likely will add extra expense to the construction contract. If the client wishes to amend any aspect of the works, a request or instruction must be made in writing to the designer. The designer then seeks costs from the contractor for any proposed changes and issues these to the client for approval. If approved, the designer instructs the contractor in writing to proceed. All this must be clearly documented so that there is no dispute at the end of the project with regard to responsibilities or costs. During the construction phase, the graphic design proceeds to the production of artwork. For this, all final editorial copy for the graphic panels must be confirmed. The graphic works will then be prepared for tendering to photographic reproduction houses. It is usual that a defect period of six months is written into the main construction contract with a retention sum of an agreed percentage. After six months, the designer returns to site to check that all the work is still good.

WHAT DO YOU WANT, HOW MUCH WILL YOU SPEND AND WHO IS GOING TO DO THE WORK?

Prior to commissioning a design team to implement a project, it is advisable for the client to identify the various points of reference by which an exhibition will be judged successful, commercially and culturally. This does not mean requesting a certain amount of touch-screens or models. It is about identifying the target visitor group, the character of the exhibition and clearly articulating the rationale for the project.

Finding out how much time was spent on research, design and the financial spend on existing exhibitions is also a very valuable exercise. Depending on the character and purpose of the exhibition, a number of specialist advisors may be required to assist with its implementation: industrialists, environmentalists or academics. This expertise may not be available within the proposed production time, so adjustment must be made to the schedule before commencing work. Delays in production cost everyone.

Finally, putting to paper what type of relationship the client would require with the design group is probably the most difficult but most desirable element. This is for the benefit of the designer as much as for the client. Designers have different styles of practice, some wish to address exclusively the exhibition aspect and all that relates to it, other studios address the operation and management of the centre, marketing issues and sponsorship of the exhibition as part of their brief. The client and the designer must have a clear understanding of the roles and responsibilities each will have within a project. These affect the running of the project and, of course, the fees being proposed by the designer.

Commissioning a design team can be quite a challenge for a client who has never handled an exhibition project before. The commission itself implies a certain element of trust on behalf of the client. This trust must be returned by the design team and developed. It means listening to the client and responding with positive and effective solutions to problems that arise throughout the process. While every project is different and every solution is unique, the process demands one constant: collaboration. All the parties who contribute to this process claim ownership of a successful exhibition.

THE RESULT

Allan Bennett recalled the following experience after his visit to the 'Age of Chivalry' exhibition at the Royal Academy: '"You've only an hour", says the ticket lady. More than enough for me, who finds shovelling coal slightly less exhausting than traipsing around an art gallery'. What makes a good exhibition so good or a bad one so bad? As a designer of exhibitions, my criteria of assessment are probably different from those of the client group. As a regular visitor to museums and exhibitions, my judgement starts with questions like — how easy is it to get there, how much to get in, what is the person at the desk like, where can I go (I do not want to be told where I cannot go), how much can be seen in one hour, where is the cloakroom and the way out? In between these essentials I look for a unique identity to the exhibition and an acknowledgement of why I am there. This must go beyond the need to get out of the rain, use the washroom facilities or worse still if I have been shuffled off a coach for 45 minutes.

Over the past twelve years Ireland has invested in heritage centres 'helicoptered' into the landscape, so much so that the country is marketed as 'Heritage Ireland'. Get off a plane in Shannon or Dublin, travel twenty miles in any direction and you will hit one of these centres, if not four, all promising a unique insight into the culture and history of the country and the thrilling fifteen-minute audio visual show. Unrealistic time-scales and restrictive budgets being applied to projects by funding authorities, without due consideration for the process involved in creating an exhibition, have led to an element of formulaic design. The public is simply not buying the formula any more. This is reflected in the empty galleries, half-day opening times and the general 'no comment' response from visitors. In a constantly changing world of new media, changing technologies and promises of new experiences, human emotional responses are probably the most stable. We all have egos and we all look for some reassuring image of ourselves framed in a positive and progressive context. It is about being included.

'Interpretative design' is design that enables and welcomes the visitor to interpret. Exhibitions within museums and heritage centres, being for the benefit of the public, must clearly address the publics out there and adopt the language which enables dialogue. Whatever the motives for people visiting an exhibition, if by going they have found what they want (and hopefully more), have had positive expectations met (and hopefully more) and simply believed at the end that the visit was worth it, as recent visitors to the Kilmainham Gaol Museum did, calling it 'Honest ... intelligent ... emotive ... provocative ... magnificent ... splendid ... brilliant ... I intend to go back ... I intend to bring people along with me ... That a museum can do this is wonderful ....', then one can say one has created a success.

Bibliography

Eco, U. 1987 *Travels in hyper-reality*. London.

Friedman, A. J. 1984 *The clockwork universe*. Chicago.

Saumarez Smith, C. 1986 'The philosophy of museum display — the continuing debate', *Victoria and Albert Album* **5**, pp. 31–38.

Thomson, G. 1986 *The museum environment*. London.

Exhibiting the Great Famine

JOHN CROWLEY

1995 marked the beginning of the one hundred and fiftieth anniversary of the Great Famine (1845–52). During the course of that year, a number of exhibitions were organized both at local and national level to commemorate those who died during that fateful event. An exhibition held at University College, Cork, in November 1995 looked at the Irish experience in a global context, with a key aim being to try 'to bear witness to the thousands of men, women and children who perished during the Famine and lie in unmarked graves, never buried properly, never mourned properly, and never remembered properly' (Smyth 1995). It was felt from the outset that a university or certain departments within it could make a distinctive contribution to the commemoration on the basis of their particular expertise. This chapter tells how the wish to make these intellectual resources available was fulfilled. It summarizes the nature and scope of the UCC exhibition, the guiding principles which underpinned it, as well as outlining the coordination and effort required to see the project through to a conclusion. In addition, it describes the possibilities and challenges of organizing a display in what was essentially a non-museum setting.

THEMES, SOURCES AND PLANNING

Over one million people died in the Great Famine while thousands more were dispossessed and displaced. In the context of the exhibition, it was necessary not only to remember but also to examine the dark landscapes and hidden histories of those who perished during the period. Any narrative which tries to comprehend and explain the Famine years must deal with the particular silence which pervades the archives. It is the silence of those who suffered the torment of hunger and the indignity of death by starvation in a largely undocumented manner. The final resting place of many who died behind workhouse walls is marked by mass graves. For those who perished by the roadside or in fields and

ditches, there is little which bears witness to their scattering. Countless thousands arrived on foreign shores bringing with them what one contemporary in Glasgow described as 'pestilence on their backs and famine in their stomachs'. Many died anonymously in transit or in quarantine stations such as that at Gross Ille in Canada. While few social classes emerged unscathed from the calamity, it is clear that the Famine — as with all famines — had a disproportionate impact in terms of mortality on the most vulnerable and least adequately recorded in society, the cottiers and landless labourers. As Ó Gráda (1994, 10) points out, recognition of this fact alone challenges a 'version of Famine history in which the descendants of those who survived all become vicarious victims.'

Historians have debated the scale of the disaster in Ireland. The causes and effects have been analysed and reinterpreted. The governance of Ireland during the period is the subject of much recent scholarly attention. Kinealy (1997) has examined the motivations of those in Whitehall who were vigorously opposed to any sustained measures of relief for Ireland. Because real people suffered the consequences of such opposition, the human tragedy which unfolds would have to become the cornerstone of any exhibition. Few historians tackle this human dimension, the pain felt by a mother unable to feed her children, the psychological scars left by the death of a parent or sibling in terrible circumstances, the residual guilt associated with survival or the unspoken horror of cannibalism (Lee 1997).

The trauma of the Famine has come to light in the oral tradition (Póirtéir 1995, 1996). That tradition was very much locally focussed, covering the landscape with words and meanings which revealed the calamity as a local phenomenon removed from the world of high politics. The survival of a number of manuscripts in the Irish language which relate to the Famine period confirms the view that the culture associated with the greater part of that section of the population most in distress 'did not depart in unbroken silence' (Buttimer 1996, 109). Literature, whatever the genre, novel, poem or play, allows the creative artist the opportunity to explore what Pine (1990) has referred to as the 'deeper drama of emotional history'. 'To the creative artist may have fallen the task of explaining what no historian has fully illuminated', according to one commentator (Kiberd 1996, 646). The desperation of those trapped at the extremities of the Famine experience is spelt out in Tom Murphy's play *Famine*, while Eavan Boland clears a space in her poetry to deal with the human truths of death, despair and humiliation. The desolation of Mother's death in 'Famine' along with her plea to her husband — 'Where is a woman with children when nature lets her down?' — allows for a fuller understanding of the effects of famine, similar to what Toni Morrison's novel *Beloved* achieved for slavery. It became necessary, then, to create an aesthetic platform as a means of exploring the trauma, guilt and defensiveness associated with the Famine and its aftermath.

Initial planning began in January 1995 when Professor W. J. Smyth of the Geography Department, UCC, convened a series of meetings with interested parties to discuss the possibilities of organizing an exhibition for the following November. A committee was subsequently formed which discussed the content of the proposed display, the time-frame involved as well as the practical requirements of such an undertaking. It was agreed from the outset that the intellectual content of the exhibition would be based on specialized 'Famine Maps' and the unique perspective which they would bring to bear to our understanding of the Great Famine. The idea for mapping the 1841–51 census originated with Professor W. J. Smyth as part of his ongoing research on the historical geography of nineteenth-century Ireland. The maps themselves were unique in that they detailed for the first time the intensity of population loss at parish level between 1841 and 1851. While the Famine was island-wide in scale, it was very much regional in terms of its impact. The maps illustrated the extent of the disaster in a visually effective way. They would also prove valuable in providing the visitor with an insight into the social and economic conditions which prevailed in Ireland on the eve of the Famine as well as documenting the state of the country as the disaster took its toll. Other key information contained in them included literacy levels, housing classifications as well as Poor Law valuation per parish. The emotional counterpoise to cartography would be achieved through the use of poetry, sculpture and music. 'It would have been inappropriate to attempt to deal with the subject of famine without providing this emotional and intellectual balance. Maintaining that balance was seen as integral to the success of the whole exhibition' (Teehan 1995).

RESEARCH AND FIELDWORK

A great deal of effort was expended during the summer months of 1995 in trying to establish an accurate picture of what unfolded in Ireland during the Famine years. A number of visits to key sites in the Munster region revealed the extent of the devastation in some of the worst effected areas such as the Mizen peninsula. Relic features in the landscape like the paupers' grave in Clogheen, county Tipperary, or the famine pits (mass graves) in Skibbereen, county Cork, were visible reminders of the horrors of the time. Historians such as Pat Hickey, C. C., and Edmund O'Riordan provided detailed descriptions of events in their respective localities, the Mizen and Clogheen-Burncourt, as well as access to important primary sources. It is clear from the records that contemporaries struggled at times to find terms capable of expressing the awful scenes they had witnessed. Yet their testimony is vital to our understanding of the years in question. Hence there was broad agreement that the story of the Famine should emerge, where at all possible, in the words of those who experienced it. The committee decided to include a wide range of voices, however humble, from the period, in the knowledge that in allowing only certain witnesses to speak we had suppressed others.

A visit to the Skibbereen Sculpture Symposium in mid-July had again underlined the significance of the artistic response to the Famine. Seven artists had previously been commissioned by the West Cork Arts Centre to explore the theme of famine in a rather unique setting, an old sawmill in the centre of Skibbereen which had formerly been the site of an auxiliary workhouse during the Great Famine. Two artists represented there, Annette Hennessy and Alannah Robins, were invited to participate in the UCC exhibition. In his autobiographical account *The Drowned and the Saved* (1988), Primo Levi described the people who perished in the concentration camps as the true witnesses to the horrors of the Holocaust. His comment had a certain relevance as regards Annette Hennessy's sculptural installation which in its own reflective way was making a similar statement in relation to the Famine. It drew attention not only to the silence of the victims but also the hurt, pain and sorrow which lie at the heart of the Famine story.

In the initial planning stages, it was also acknowledged that, in the rush to commemorate the Great Famine, there was a danger of ignoring the plight of more recent victims of famine. The inclusion of this global perspective was deemed to be both important and necessary. In coming face to face with the terrible suffering endured by victims of the Irish Famine, it was critical not to lose sight of the scale of suffering in many parts of today's developing world. The eventual title of the UCC commemorative exhibition, *Famines Yesterday and Today: the Irish Experience in a Global Context*,

Fig. 41.1 President Mary Robinson at the opening of the exhibition in 1995 with artist Annette Hennessy (right).

reflected these early concerns. Photography was seen as a creative medium which could be used to link the Irish story with contemporary hardship. Contact and discussion with the Magnum Photographic Agency resulted in the inclusion of over twenty black-and-white photographic prints depicting world famine today. In some of the Agency's images one glimpsed a faint trace of life, in others one 'had life looking more and more like death'. The air of weariness and loneliness which pervaded the photographs was appropriately both haunting and disturbing. The choice in many respects demonstrated a need to challenge the visitor. As Susan Sontag (1973, 23) has pointed out, 'the ultimate wisdom of the photographic image is to say, there is the surface — now think, or rather feel and intuit beyond it, what the reality must be like if it looks this way'. A number of our exhibition panels would also deal with the causes and effects of world famine.

CONTENT AND PRESENTATION

The exhibition proper was composed of two parts. The main display area was located in the concourse of the Boole Library at UCC. This section was conventional in format (display panels with text and images mounted on walls) and presented for the first time the original computer-generated maps based on the 1841–51 census returns. It also included the series of photographs which conveyed in a poignant way the terrible suffering endured by more recent victims of famine. The central exhibit, a sculptural piece by the artist Annette Hennessy, consisting of over 250 hand-made wax figures which symbolically came to represent the many victims of famine who suffer in silence, was also located here (**Fig 41.1**).

The second exhibition area was a self-contained space, *Oileán an Uaignis* ('Island of Loneliness'), which was located in a specially designated room in the North Wing of UCC's central Quadrangle. This space acted as a retreat from the rest of the exhibition. It included a sculptural installation by Alannah Robins as well as a fifteen-minute audio-visual presentation on the diverse voices of the Famine. This presentation was accompanied by a specially commissioned piece of music, *Cuimhnímis siar/Remembering, not Forgetting*, composed by Marion Ingoldsby.

It was acknowledged from the outset that while the maps would provide the visitor with a unique way of interpreting the Famine, they did not in themselves tell the whole truth. Eavan Boland's poem, 'That the science of cartography is limited', draws attention to the selective nature of the map-maker's art and was included in the display. The poet reflects on the failure of maps to represent 'the line which says woodland and cries hunger', designating a Famine road. The map-maker's pen is mute in relation to the pain endured by the many thousands employed on such relief schemes. The absence of a line delineating a Famine road is in keeping with the tendency to ignore the experiences of those who toiled endlessly on such schemes and who had largely been effaced from the historical record. A number of these roads led nowhere in particular, but remain a fitting testimony to the punitive nature of such public relief measures. Boland (1997, 216) recently described her initial experience of a Famine road: 'the bleakness had hit me there and then in a way statistics never had, small, bitter trails in the woods, giving out into a nothingness that made as true a comment on the Famine as any other visible sign of it'.

One of the key aims of the audio visual presentation *Oileán an Uaignis* was to shift the emphasis away from statistics and to deal with the crisis at a more human level. The Famine is an emotive issue and hence lends itself to an artistic response. A number of themes were selected and appropriate images and text were chosen to represent these topics. For instance, a folklore account of evictions in the townland of Kilgalligan in county Mayo names the families who were evicted. The prolonged nature of the crisis along with government legislation had increased the likelihood of such eviction scenes (Donnelly 1997). While no photographic record of the

Famine exists, a conscious decision was taken to use photographs of eviction scenes which, although post-dating the Famine period, nevertheless conveyed the despair of those driven from their homes.

Against the backdrop of the Knockmealdown mountains stands a cross which marks the site of the paupers' grave in Clogheen, county Tipperary. The cross casts its pale shadow over scrub and overgrown grass. It was erected by locals to the memory of those who perished in the Clogheen workhouse. The term 'pauper' itself was part and parcel of a system designed to humiliate. During the cruel winter months of 1848, bodies were despatched there with regular monotony. The dead too cast their shadow over this place. There are no inscriptions on monumental headstones: those who are buried are nameless. A slide of this paupers' grave introduced a section on workhouses. A number of images were used to convey the awfulness of life within these institutions. Paupers had to abide by the strict rules and regulations which governed each house. These were often designed to chastize. When one views the cold interiors of what remains of the workhouses, one gets an immediate sense of the degradation endured by their inmates. Suddenly, one enters what Eavan Boland (1997, 214) again refers to as 'that terrible parish of pain and human suffering'. The report of the Fermoy Board of Guardians details the extent of the mortality between January and March 1847. In that period 543 paupers died in its workhouse. The abject state of the thousands of paupers who lined the wards and sheds can only be glimpsed at in the Minutes of the various Board of Guardians:

A pestilential fever is now raging through the house, every room of which is so crowded as to render it impossible to separate the sick from the healthy ... All the horrors of disease are aggravated by the foul air engendered by a multiplicity of impurities unavoidable where fifty patients are crowded into a room too much for twenty ... On the first day of January the number in the house was 1377, from which date to the eight of March, the admissions exceeded the discharges by 917, making a total of 2294 of whom 543 died .... (MacKay 1990, 244)

Overcrowding accelerated the spread of disease. It is hardly surprising that such institutions reeked with pestilence during the Famine years. Built to cope with destitution in normal times, they were incapable of dealing with the levels of hardship in a period of crisis. The countless thousands who clamoured at their gates regarded the workhouse as their last refuge and only hope of escape from the torment of hunger. Doctor O'Connor, a physician in the Cork workhouse, reported such scenes:

Death amongst them was divested of many of its most painful associations: there was no sorrowing, no tears, no wailing of even mothers for their children. To many death came as a relief; and if they had any tales of sorrow to tell about the past, of children or wife dead or separated, they let it rest near their hearts, and troubled no-one with the recital. (O Mahony 1997, 156)

A slide of an installation created by the Swedish artist Lotte Pile on the site of an auxiliary workhouse in Skibbereen captured the loneliness of death behind workhouse walls.

The final section of *Oileán an Uaignis* dealt with the issue of absence. It included a slide of an installation by the artist Annette Hennessy which addressed the theme of death and emigration. Many emigrants who left Ireland during the Famine years were aware of the finality of their leaving. There would be no going back. For the shipowners there was much to be gained from this trade in human cargo. There are many graphic accounts of the privations endured by emigrants bound for the New World. Disease, especially in the form of typhus, would take its toll. The inhumane crowding accelerated the spread of sickness. Thousands would die in transit. During 'Black '47' the vessels carrying Irish emigrants to Canada literally 'reeked with pestilence': at least 20,000 died en route to British North America or shortly after arrival, and of those bound for the United States, between 8,000 and 9,000 perished (Miller 1985, 316). The sequence of slides concluded fittingly with an extract from Seamus Heaney's poem 'At a potato digging',

and where potato diggers are
you still smell the running sore.

The feeling of despair was evoked in the haunting music which accompanied the series of images and text by Marion Ingoldsby's *Cuimhnímis siar/Remembering, not Forgetting*, was first performed and recorded at UCC's Honan Chapel in late October 1995. An intense period of work followed as the images had to be placed in sequence and adapted to the music. The Audio-Visual Services unit at UCC were instrumental in completing this task. In addition to the music, the sculptural installation, *Excavated Space,* by Alannah Robins succeeded in creating an appropriate atmosphere for the visitor. Replete with hand-beaten bowls, Robins' installation commemorated the individual lives lost during the Great Hunger, with each bowl embodying a sense of individual being.

A technical supervisor, Tony Balfe, was employed to coordinate the main exhibition. All the maps and photographic prints had to be mounted separately on boards before being attached to the specially prepared velcro walls. Refurbishment work was carried out in the exhibition areas. This involved painting of the walls, the erection of temporary velcro supports and the re-arranging of the existing exhibition space. Perhaps, in hindsight, it would have been preferable to have had both exhibition areas located in the same building, but this was not feasible, given spatial constraints. College archivist, Virginia Teehan, played a role in making sure that the material which was exhibited was of the highest professional standards. In the final days leading up to the opening of the exhibition, the determination of all concerned was evident in the hours spent making certain that these standards were attained. Much of the work involved was voluntary and carried out against a background of other commitments, both teaching and research.

An exhibition is no longer accepted as being an entirely neutral space. Decisions are made not only in relation to the choice of themes but also the most appropriate means of representing them. Acknowledging this fact puts paid to the notion of letting the story speak for itself. The UCC exhibition in the end reflected the knowledge, skills and concerns of those who participated in it.

CONCLUSION

Over 5,000 people visited the exhibition during the three weeks it was open. These ranged from members of the academic community to second- and third-level students as well as the general public. Drawing conclusions from the visitor books, it was clear that the exhibition succeeded in addressing the needs of these various kinds of audience by striking a balance between insight, information and feeling. The display had communicated original research into the Great Famine to both a wider and a scholarly public. It had also, by the inclusion of photographs which represented world famine, reinforced the need to understand the contemporary implications of Ireland's historic tragedy.

Famine Exhibition Organizing Committee

Professor W. J. Smyth (Geography Dept, UCC), Ms Virginia Teehan (College Archivist, UCC), Mr Michael Murphy (Cartographer, Geography Dept, UCC), Mr Charlie Roche (Visiting Lecturer and European Field Officer, Microsoft), Patrick Hickey C. C. (Historian), Dr Neil Buttimer (Roinn na Nua-Ghaeilge, UCC), Dr John Tyrell (Geography Dept, UCC), Mr John Crowley (Geography Dept, UCC), Mr Tony Balfe (Technical Supervisor), Ms Fidelma Mullane (Údarás na Gaeltachta and Geography Dept, UCC).

Bibliography

Boland, E. 1995a *Collected poems*. Manchester.

Boland, E. 1995b *Object lessons*. London.

Boland, E. 1997 'Famine roads' in T. Hayden (ed) *Irish hunger: personal reflections on the legacy of the Great Famine* (Dublin), pp. 212–23.

Buttimer, N. 1996 'A stone on the cairn: the Great Famine in later Gaelic manuscripts' in Morash and Hayes 1996, pp. 93–109.

Donnelly, J. S. 1996 'Irish property must pay for Irish poverty: British public opinion and the Great Famine' in Morash and Hayes 1996, pp. 60–76.

Heaney, S. 1970 'At a potato digging' in B. Kennelly (ed) *The Penguin book of Irish Verse* (London).

Hickey, P. 1993 'Famine mortality and emigration: a profile of six parishes in the Poor Law Union of Skibbereen' in P. O'Flanagan and C. G. Buttimer (eds) *Cork history and society: interdisciplinary essays on the history of an Irish county* (Dublin), pp. 873–918.

Kiberd, D. 1995 *Inventing Ireland: the literature of the modern nation*. London.

Kinealy, C. 1997 *A death-dealing famine: the Great Hunger in Ireland*. London.

Lee, J. 1997 'The Famine as history' in C. Ó Gráda (ed) *Famine 150 — commemorative lecture series* (Dublin), pp. 159–75.

Levi, P. 1988 *The drowned and the saved*. London.

MacKay, D. 1990 *Flight from famine: the coming of the Irish to Canada*. Toronto.

Miller, K. 1985 *Emigrants and exiles: Ireland and the Irish exodus to North America*. New York.

Morash, C. and Hayes, R. 1996 *'Fearful realities': new perspectives on the Famine*. Dublin.

Morrison, T. 1988 *Beloved*. London.

Murphy, T. 1977 *Famine*. Dublin.

Ó Gráda, C. 1994 'Satisfying a great hunger for guilt and self-pity', *The Sunday Tribune*, 15 May.

O Mahony, C. 1997 *In the shadows: life in Cork 1750–1930*. Cork.

O'Riordan, E. 1995 *Famine in the valley*. Tipperary.

Pine, R. 1990 *Brian Friel and Ireland's drama*. London.

Póirtéir, C. 1995 *Famine echoes*. Dublin.

Póirtéir, C. 1996 *Glórtha ón Ghorta*. Dublin.

Sontag, S. 1973 *On photography*. New York.

Smyth, W. J. 1995 *World famine 150 — famines yesterday and today: the Irish experience in a global context*. Cork.

Teehan, V. 1995 *Minutes of the UCC Famine Exhibition Committee*. Cork.

The National Museum of Ireland

NIGEL T. MONAGHAN

The National Museum of Ireland (NMI) was established well over a century ago with roots in earlier museums dating back to the late eighteenth century. In that time, it has been influenced by major political events and has also exercised a significant influence on the Irish public. In facing up to the challenges of a modern museum, it is undergoing a period of considerable change. New premises, evolving staff structures and a more enlightened approach to funding by the state have combined to put the Museum on a sound footing for many years to come.

HISTORY

No comprehensive history of the National Museum of Ireland has been published to date but a number of aspects have been covered by different authors. Articles on the natural history collections include general background to the Museum (O'Riordan 1983; Monaghan 1992), and there are also publications on parent museums as far back as the eighteenth century in the Royal Dublin Society (Berry 1915; Meenan and Clarke 1981), the Royal Irish Academy (Ó Raifeartaigh 1985) and the Museum of Irish Industry (Herries Davies 1983, 1995). A full history is long overdue and will be an exciting challenge for future scholars.

The Museum of Science and Art, Dublin, was founded on 14 August 1877 by act of parliament. The decision to establish a state-run museum arose from requests by the Royal Dublin Society (RDS) for continued government funding for its expanding museum activities (Mac Lochlainn *et al.* 1977). A number of developments led to the *Science and Art Museums Act* of 1877 which had the effect of transferring the buildings and collections of the Royal Dublin Society to state ownership. These were further enhanced by the transfer of other notable collections from institutions such as the Royal Irish Academy and Trinity College, Dublin (Bantry White 1911).

The state support for the institution was manifested in the form of the construction of a new building in Kildare Street which was opened to the public in 1890. The new museum housed coins, medals and significant Irish antiquities from the Royal Irish Academy, including the Tara brooch and Ardagh chalice, ethnographical collections with material from Captain Cooke's voyages on loan from Trinity College, Dublin, and the collections of the Geological Survey of Ireland (Herries Davies 1996). These were joined by material from the decorative arts and ethnographical collections of the RDS and their Irish collections of antiquities, minerals and plants. The old RDS museum on the Merrion Street side of Leinster House was devoted to natural history, dominated by zoology throughout much of its subsequent history, with an annex devoted to geology.

The new building in Kildare Street was designed by Thomas Newenham Deane and used to demonstrate Irish craftsmanship in its construction. It is one of the best surviving examples of Irish decorative stonework, wood carving and ceramic tiling. It has suffered to an extent over the years from decay of the sandstone sections of the exterior (Wyse Jackson 1993), and is currently being restored by the Office of Public Works.

The state involvement in the running of the Museum allowed for steady funding, and the connection with other state museums in London and Edinburgh was also of considerable benefit (Jarrell 1983). A standard registration system made all departments accountable for their collections which swelled with material acquired through purchase, public donation and shares of significant collections acquired by the state and dispersed by the London museums. Catalogues were prepared by leading experts in various disciplines and printed at the Museum's own press.

The emergence of the Irish Free State in 1922 had a significant impact on the predicament of the Museum beyond the change in name to National Museum of Ireland. Traditional seats of power such as the current

Bank of Ireland building in College Green, used for Grattan's Parliament in the late eighteenth century, were excluded from use for the new Dáil by conditions of the treaty with Britain. Michael Collins was given the task of locating a suitable place for the new assembly and chose the old RDS buildings of Leinster House, which had been transferred to state ownership along with their museum collections in 1877.

The RDS abandoned Leinster House in favour of new developments on their Ballsbridge site and the organs of state began a long-running war of attrition on Museum space in the Leinster House area. The first impact of the Dáil on the Museum complex was felt when the 'fossil hall' annexe at the side of the Natural History Museum was partly commandeered and closed for security reasons in 1922, hiding the geological exhibitions from the public except by special arrangement (it was demolished in 1962). The Geological Survey of Ireland collections, then on display in the Curved Gallery beside the Natural History Museum, were evicted in 1922 and their space taken over by the Dáil (Sleeman 1992).

New gates and railings were erected for the Kildare Street buildings of the new Museum and the National Library. These were replaced in the 1980s to increase the security of the complex. The Natural History Museum was given a new entrance directly onto Merrion Street and the architecture was altered to allow the present opening at the east end and the development of new staircases. The original entrance was through Leinster House, and the grand stone staircase within the Natural History Museum is now hidden from public view in the Museum office block at the west end of this building. Space had to be found for staff formerly housed in Leinster House, and a number of exhibition galleries in Kildare Street were taken over for this purpose.

The loss in space and facilities was matched by ever-expanding collections and a decline in resources as a new state struggled to fund other priorities. Reorganization of the Museum followed a number of official reports (O'Brien et al. 1927; Lithberg 1927), but these were not successful in solving all Museum problems or coping with the rapid growth of the collections (Bodkin 1949). The reduction in space was catalogued in 1973 by the Museum's staff association, showing a loss of 18,500 square feet (1,700 square metres) of office and collections accommodation and 31,400 square feet (2,900 square metres) of exhibition space (Institute of Professional Civil Servants 1973). Their appeal to the Department of Education, their government department since 1924, had little effect at the time, and the decline continued.

Numerous internal reports over the last eighty years have echoed these problems and a variety of solutions have been proposed for accommodation, management and staffing. These included plans to develop a stately

home in a suburban Dublin park at Cabinteely into an Earth Science Museum in 1980 for which funding was not secured. The geological collections remained crated in Daingean, county Offaly, along with the Irish folklife collections, some eighty kilometres from Dublin city in a dilapidated set of buildings. These had been occupied as a temporary measure in 1979 when the Museum vacated stores at The Royal Hospital in Dublin to allow refurbishment of that old military hospital complex.

Following the transfer of the National Museum, along with other state cultural institutions, to the Department of An Taoiseach in 1984, these problems received fresh attention. A new proposal was developed to utilize the old army buildings of The Royal Hospital, Kilmainham (Hall 1986), which had been refurbished with European funding of over £20 million without a clear future for the building having been established. The complex could have accommodated the Museum collection of decorative arts, but not solved other long-standing issues. It has since become the Irish Museum of Modern Art. A subsequent proposal for housing the decorative arts and historical collections in the new Custom House Docks development in Dublin was explored in 1988. Work on a proposal for a folklife museum also took place, with a number of potential venues being investigated on a countrywide basis (Strategic Plan Team 1992).

The establishment of the National Lottery led in 1988 to funds becoming available to address many issues, and building works allowed refurbishment of a number of existing premises. Re-wiring of the Natural History Museum allowed removal of the original twisted copper cables sheathed in waxed paper which had served the timber-floored building since its original wiring in 1895 as one of the first public buildings with electric lighting. An old barracks building at Beggars Bush, Dublin, was also refurbished as a store for zoological and geological collections. In 1993, the Museum was transferred to a new government department set up to tackle Arts, Culture and the Gaeltacht (now Arts, Heritage, Gaeltacht and the Islands). The key remaining problems for the National Museum were the possession of enough suitable space for exhibition and storage of its collections (Office of Public Works 1992) and the necessary staff to care for the collections and provide public services.

Reorganization of the armed forces led to a decision in 1988 to close Collins Barracks, Dublin (Comptroller and Auditor General 1996). The complex started out in 1702 as 'The Barracks', changed in the early nineteenth century to the 'Royal Barracks' and was named Collins Barracks in 1922 when it was handed over to the troops of the Free State. The initial buildings were designed by Col. Thomas Burgh and the complex, which includes eighteenth- and nineteenth- century buildings, housed troops continually for three centuries. It was assigned to

Museum use in 1994 and an initial cash injection of £10 million, recouped during a tax amnesty, allowed the government to provide the first step on a long road to recovery for the Museum. The detailed progress of the Collins Barracks Project has been studied by the Comptroller and Auditor General (1996) and continues now that European Union funding has been added on to produce a £28 million development budget. The first phase of exhibitions on the site opened in September 1997 and includes 2,500 square metres of space devoted to introductory exhibitions outlining the Museum's chequered history and showcasing some of the prime collections long hidden from public view.

CHANGES IN THE ADMINISTRATION OF THE MUSEUM

Under the terms of the act of 1877, a Board of Visitors was established to ensure the safety of the collections and protect the interests of the stakeholders in the Museum. It comprises representatives of the state, the Royal Dublin Society and the Royal Irish Academy. One of the long-standing items on their agenda has been addressing an outmoded staff structure which has changed little in over a century. Recent internal studies have been augmented by work carried out by specialist Museum consultants reporting to a board appointed by the minister (Lord 1994).

The first 'Interim Board' was appointed in 1994 to oversee the development of the Collins Barracks site and to prepare the Museum and its staff for the necessary changes in the institution to address the challenges of this development. A successor 'Caretaker Board' has continued this work and is the advisory body to the minister during the preparations for semi-state status.

The staffing levels and structures have been addressed in a number of reports, but most significantly by the Department of Finance, which started a review in 1994 which has unfortunately never been finalized and only partly implemented (Management Services Unit 1995). Changes in staff structures have taken place, however, and in 1997 six new posts were established which were the first steps in a major reorganization of the institution.

SEMI-STATE STATUS

The implementation of legislation in the form of the *National Cultural Institutions Act* 1997 (Ireland 1997) will have wide-ranging implications for the Museum and related institutions. One interesting effect of this is to make the introduction of general admission charges an issue which would have to be approved by both houses of the Oireachtas. This vexed question has been addressed elsewhere at some length (Duffy 1991). Few elements of this legislation were enacted in the first year after it entered the statute books (under Irish law the commencement date for legislation is a matter for ministerial decision after legislation is passed and acts may be enacted in instalments). The primary step of setting the Museum on a semi-state footing has yet to be taken. This would see the transfer of staff out of the civil service and necessitate the establishment of a statutory board and the institution taking over duties from its parent department, such as personnel, payroll and pensions.

There should also be greater policy decision-making powers under a Board and some freedom granted to staff the Museum in ways which are difficult within the strict confines of civil service procedures. Successive governments have placed limits on staff numbers which are part of wider policies designed to rationalize the public sector. These are applied unilaterally and somewhat blindly. While some efficiencies have resulted, the policy has been particularly damaging to specialist areas of employment where the loss of an individual member of staff through retirement may leave a gap in expertise. The Museum has lost numerous specialist staff over the last twenty years without replacements; the decline in permanent staffing levels in the Museum may continue to be a handicap to its ability to develop its true potential.

MUSEUM DEPARTMENTS

The Museum is headed by a Director who is responsible for the running of the Museum and reports to the minister and Caretaker Board, comprising eleven members who are appointed by the minister. Of the twelve Directors since the foundation of the Museum in 1877, most in the twentieth century were appointed from within the institution with a background in curation, the last four being archaeologists. Thirteen years were spent without a Director when the Museum was run by civil service administrators, and twenty years were under 'Acting' Directors. The present Director was the first to be appointed by open competition.

The Director is responsible for staff management, fund-raising, budgetary matters and planning, and liaises with the Caretaker Board and the Cultural Institutions Section of the Department of Arts, Heritage, Gaeltacht and the Islands (as renamed in 1997). He (it has yet to be 'she') provides advice to ministers and other government departments on heritage and tourism issues and holds the office cited in various items of heritage legislation which incur particular duties, especially in relation to Irish archaeological objects.

The Museum is organized under three main subdivisions at present, only one of which is currently headed by a senior member of staff. This is the new Services department which includes Conservation, Education, Graphic Arts, Marketing and Photography. Also included is the Department of Documentation /Information Technology which takes care of information technology as well as centralized collections documentation, archives and library. The Head of

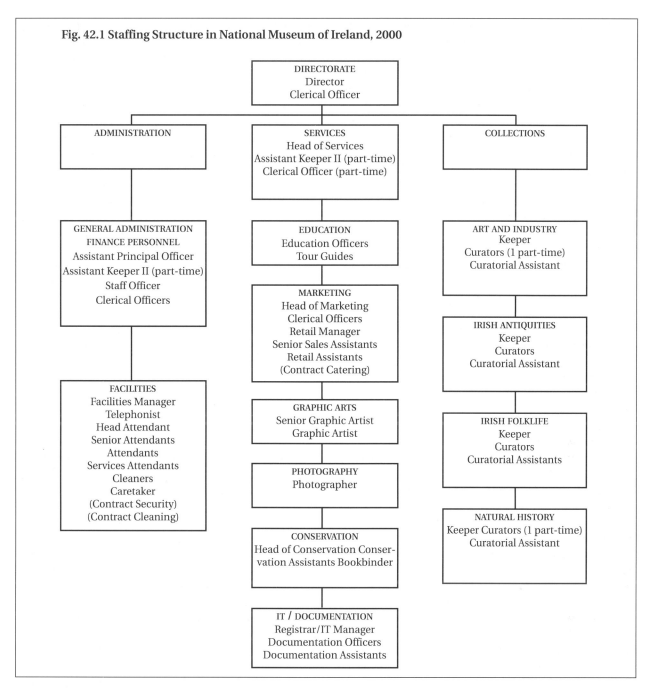

Fig. 42.1 Staffing Structure in National Museum of Ireland, 2000

Services is also responsible for managing the further development of Collins Barracks as a Museum headquarters.

The Administration Department is headed by an Assistant Principal Officer and comprises accounts, personnel and administration. Included in this Department are the security staff and cleaners who are managed by a Facilities Manager who is also responsible for buildings maintenance, health and safety and accommodation issues.

The third main sub-division of the Museum is an amalgam of the four long-standing Divisions, each of which is headed by a Keeper and staffed by curators responsible to the Director for particular sectors of the collections. Reorganization of duties in 1998 involved re-allocation of five technical staff to the fledgling Conservation Department. These staff were formally dispersed through the four curatorial Divisions.

ART AND INDUSTRIAL DIVISION AND ITS COLLECTIONS

The Division includes collections which span the range of decorative arts and Irish history. It is a large and diverse collection, some parts of which are now being seen in the new exhibition galleries at Collins Barracks. The decorative arts collections reflect largely the trades, crafts and industries operating in Ireland over the past three centuries and include material from other countries which was acquired to introduce new ideas to an Irish audience. The fine and decorative objects in the collections largely reflect the lives of the more affluent members of Irish society, particularly in the areas of glass, ceramics and silverware. The objects in the historical collections are defined by their relevance to documenting the events and people from Ireland's complex and colourful history. Arms and militaria from several centuries of conflict will be augmented in exhibition terms through collaborative galleries in Collins Barracks, to be developed with the Defence Forces. The collections of approximately 250,000 objects are cared for by a staff of six, including a Keeper.

IRISH ANTIQUITIES DIVISION AND ITS COLLECTIONS
The Division is the national repository for portable archaeological material from Ireland, and since 1930, all archaeological objects found in the state must be reported to the Director of the National Museum. Archaeological curators are involved in inspection of find sites and assessing the significance of artefacts which may be added to the Museum's collections at their discretion. Conservation of artefacts and their export outside the state are controlled by a licensing system administrated by the NMI staff. Some sites are excavated by Museum archaeologists, the most notable being a series of excavations of Viking and medieval Dublin, at Wood Quay and adjoining streets, from 1962–81.

Abuse of the national monuments legislation involves illegal trading or export of artefacts and the use of metal detectors. Staff work with An Garda Síochána and other agencies in Ireland and abroad to ensure the enforcement of such legislation. There is also liaison with staff in the National Monuments and Historic Properties Service section of Dúchas (the state Heritage Service) regarding archaeological sites.

The Irish collections of the Division are significant in extent, diversity and quality. Few national museums of this size have such an impressive array of archaeological objects which in this case span the last eight thousand years or so since Ireland was first settled. Many of the high-profile collections have been popularized through exhibitions and publications, some of which are listed in the bibliography

Foreign archaeology includes classical material from the ancient Mediterranean as well as an Egyptian collection. The latter was re-displayed in a permanent gallery in 1996 and, as with most exhibition preparation, was accompanied by extensive curation of reserve material and research into the collection.

The ethnographical collections of the Division date from the period between 1760 and 1914 and represent a vast range of cultures. There is material from Polynesia, Melanesia, Micronesia, North and South America, West and Southern Africa and South and East Asia. Related material from India and southern Asia is also included in the 'non-Western' collections of the Art and Industrial Division. Only a small part of the collection has been seen in recent decades, with two exhibitions representing Maori culture (Cherry 1990).

The size of the archaeological collection has been estimated as being in excess of 1.5 million artefacts and there is a substantial archive. It is cared for by a staff of six, including a Keeper.

IRISH FOLKLIFE DIVISION AND ITS COLLECTIONS
The Division evolved from a collecting strategy and a series of exhibitions stimulated by a late nineteenth-century Scandinavian approach to studying the people of a region through their life and culture. The original acquisition policy was to gather 'objects illustrative of the domestic life of times which have passed away recently', and led to active collecting under Dr Adolf Mahr in the 1920s when Keeper of Irish Antiquities. In the 1930s, an Irish Folklore Commission was set up by the state in order to record the facets of a largely rural culture which was fast disappearing as Ireland adapted to a modern western economy and culture. This was paralleled within the Museum by a significant effort in acquiring relevant artefacts by staff such as the former Director, Dr A. T. Lucas, who is responsible for a significant proportion of the artefacts now in the collection and their detailed contextual documentation.

Exhibitions since 1937 have been successful though sporadic; there was no regular exhibition venue from 1962 to 1997 when a new gallery opened in Collins Barracks. Numerous plans for a regional folk museum have been investigated and in 1996 a ministerial decision was taken to establish a branch of the National Museum with a folklife theme at Turlough Park, Castlebar, county Mayo. This project, funded by the European Union together with state and local authority support, is currently under development.

The three curators and two technical staff of the Division look after a collection of approximately 50,000 objects as diverse as ploughs, lobster pots and Halloween masks. Most objects are made from materials available locally in the landscape and many show great ingenuity and resourcefulness on the part of their makers.

NATURAL HISTORY DIVISION AND ITS COLLECTIONS
The Division cares for the state collections in the disciplines of zoology and geology. The botanical collections of the Museum, together with some staff, were transferred in 1970 from the top floor of the Kildare Street building to the National Botanic Gardens, where a new herbarium and library building was opened in 1997 to provide these collections with a suitable home. The collections in the Division and their histories have been

studied previously in some detail (O'Riordan 1983; Monaghan 1992).

The collections include approximately two million specimens cared for by a staff of five, including a Keeper. The largest of the collections in terms of numbers is the extensive insect collection, which accounts for approximately half of all specimens. As with all of the natural science holdings of the Museum, there is a surprising amount of material from outside Ireland. Much of this is a legacy of the nineteenth-century British Empire when Dublin was one of its most significant and populous cities and Irish scientists and keen amateurs staffed the largest navy in the world and were involved in numerous expeditions to far-away places.

The early origins of the collections in 1792 (Vaccari and Monaghan 1993) and the nature of science in the nineteenth century have ensured that the Division holds a significant proportion of type specimens in zoology and geology. Such specimens are the individual examples of particular species of animals or fossils which are used by scientists from all over the world when they encounter similar species and wish to establish their true identities.

The collections are used as a reference resource by staff and research visitors, and play an important role in the identification of specimens, such as insect pests, which may have considerable economic significance. Staff carry out field work, publish their own research and assist visitors who are also involved in scientific publications. Time is also spent acquiring new examples of the Irish fauna through regular fieldwork (O'Connor 1997).

FUTURE DIRECTIONS FOR THE NATIONAL MUSEUM OF IRELAND

The Museum staff developed a statement of purpose in 1994, adapted from the original declaration by the Committee of Enquiry (O'Brien *et al.* 1927), in order to define the modern role of the NMI and to form the guiding principles to which all policies should adhere (Lord 1994):

The purpose of the National Museum of Ireland is to accumulate, document, preserve, study, display and interpret in both official languages such objects as may serve to increase and diffuse the knowledge of Irish civilisation, of the natural history of Ireland and of the relations of Ireland in these respects with other countries; and to encourage other institutions in Ireland to do the same.

In addition, a number of ways of fulfilling this purpose were articulated in the form of a mission statement. The mission of the National Museum of Ireland is:

• to preserve and make accessible the portable natural and cultural material heritage of Ireland;

• to communicate to the people of Ireland, and visitors to Ireland, a vision and understanding of that heritage and to act as a major educational resource;

• to deepen cultural ties both within Ireland and with other countries;

• to deepen cultural ties throughout Ireland, and

• to open a 'window' on the world's material heritage through which the Irish people may appreciate their own culture in its European and global context.

PUBLIC SERVICES

The main involvement of the public is through exhibitions which attract over three quarters of a million visits a year on the three sites. It is important to distinguish between visits and visitors, as up to one-third of visits may represent a visitor making more than one visit. Annual visit figures for the Kildare Street building average 450,000, which reflect its long-standing image as the premier museum in the country. The visitor patterns were studied in 1986 by the firm Behaviour and Attitudes, and confirmed the general impression that it was a popular venue for foreign tourists, with only 40% of the summer visitors being Irish as opposed to 80% in the Natural History Museum. The annual visits figure for the Natural History Museum is 200,000, and with the development of Turlough Park and increased awareness of Collins Barracks (which had 200,000 visitors in its first year of operation), the total should soon reach a million visits a year to National Museum premises.

All visitor services and amenities are being regularly assessed and steady improvements have been made possible through building works and increases of staff in the Education Service. Advertizing and corporate functions have seen significant growth over the years and are being developed through the Marketing Department established in 1997. The Education Service is responsible for guided tours, lecture series and activity days in addition to providing a general information service. Staff arrange for school and group bookings and advise teachers and other group leaders on how to make the most of their visit. The Museum also operates a photographic service, supplying images of objects in the collections to publishers and scholars. In addition, the Museum is responsible for its own publications, from scholarly texts to popular pamphlets, exhibition guides and a calendar.

SERVICES TO THE HERITAGE COMMUNITY
Loans
The Museum has substantial collections which are used in a variety of ways. In addition to making collections available for study on Museum premises, it is possible to

arrange research loans for some categories of objects. On a larger scale the Museum is also responsible for lending objects to other museums for exhibition to the public, either in temporary exhibitions or as major contributions to long-term exhibition galleries.

In all cases, the museums, whether in Ireland or abroad, must meet the Museum's needs regarding safety and security of the artefacts on loan. Local authorities in Ireland have played a growing role in the development of local museums throughout the country. Major collections are currently on loan for exhibition in the City or County Museums of Cavan, Cork, Kerry, Limerick, Louth, Monaghan and Tipperary. It is hoped that similar museums of quality will be founded in other local authority areas, allowing wider public access through exhibitions to the objects held on behalf of the nation. Collaborative exhibitions include the restored Georgian residence at No. 29 Fitzwilliam Street in partnership with the Electricity Supply Board and the 'Down to Earth' geological exhibition with the Geological Survey of Ireland.

Advice

The Museum is a large national institution with a variety of specialist staff whose expertise is called on throughout a wide range of disciplines. Staff have advised on the setting up of museums and helped other centres and members of the public in the care of objects held in private hands. Many hundreds of objects are identified each year, although valuations are not given as part of this service. Specialist advice is given in health and scientific matters by zoological staff, who use the collections and library to identify pests. Many of these pose a significant hazard to Irish crops or to personal health. Staff represent the Museum on a variety of academic and other committees of state bodies, institutions and societies. The NMI has a formal role under a number of areas of legislation and may advise the state on many aspects of heritage. In particular, there is a key role under the terms of the *National Monuments Acts* and amendments, the *Heritage Act* and the *National Cultural Institutions Act*.

FUTURE EXHIBITION STRATEGIES

In 1997, the Museum employed the services of museum consultants to develop a strategy for the Collins Barracks exhibition galleries. This was designed to allow planning of the building works to determine the location of galleries as well as to develop an overall programme of exhibitions for the general public. Studies by the consultants included a plan for the re-use of Kildare Street following its vacation by the Art and Industrial collections and other departments, allowing for its improved use for archaeological exhibitions. A plan was also developed for the exhibition of Folklife in Turlough Park.

It is intended to retain the Natural History Museum in its present style and to exhibit the geological collections at Collins Barracks. There is not sufficient space at the former site to treat all aspects of natural history and in particular the Earth Sciences, whose gallery space was lost in 1962.

The greater proportion of the Kildare Street building will be used for exhibitions. The design of the building indicates that it was built primarily as an exhibition centre. At the time, the other functions of the Museum were accommodated in Leinster House, but when this was lost in the early twentieth century much of the Kildare Street building was turned over to offices. Restoring many of these spaces to exhibition use has been allowed by the developments at Collins Barracks. A programme of re-organization of the archaeological exhibits will result in a sequence of galleries along an 8,000 year time line from the first known settlements through to the period of recorded history. The riches of the Museum in certain artefact types will be placed in context with such theme galleries as Bronze Age gold and early Christian art. Feature galleries will include the popular Egyptian gallery opened in 1997.

Collins Barracks will be the venue for exhibitions placing Irish history in context, together with a number of theme galleries. These will incorporate collections from all curatorial Divisions, particularly Art and Industry and Irish Folklife, telling the story of Ireland's development over the last four centuries. In addition, there will be temporary exhibition spaces and permanent galleries devoted to Ethnography and the Earth Sciences.

Turlough Park will be devoted to the story of Irish folklife. This will be done through the rich collections of artefacts crafted from materials available locally and used by a largely rural population employing techniques which can be traced into pre-history.

FUTURE BUILDINGS STRATEGIES
CURRENT PREMISES

The Museum has grown steadily since its foundation and currently occupies buildings on no fewer than ten sites, most in Dublin but including premises in county Offaly and county Roscommon. Many have been occupied as short-term measures which have lasted well beyond any initial plans. A modest strategy for rationalization was developed in 1992 by the Office of Public Works (OPW), the state body responsible for Museum accommodation. This study identified many problems which were later addressed by the acquisition and development of Collins Barracks.

As an example, in 1981, the geological collections were to be found in five buildings (Kildare Street, Merrion Street, Merrion Row, Fenian Street, Dublin, and Daingean, county Offaly). Minor collections and the main crated collection from outlying stores were assembled in Beggars Bush in 1991 where, by 2002, all geological material should be housed.

In addition to the OPW survey, a more detailed collections analysis which included all collections of the Museum was carried out in 1997 by consultants. This is being used as the long-term plan for collections accommodation, but will still take many years to implement. Apart from reorganization of collections, there have also been numerous projects to improve storage environment, proper furniture and micro-environments for a number of specific collections in all Divisions in recent years.

FUTURE RATIONALIZATION
Early in the twenty-first century the National Museum of Ireland should be located on a total of four public sites. The layout of facilities should be as follows.

COLLINS BARRACKS
This site has long-term potential for growth, but this will be limited by the available budgets for development. In the medium term, a detailed 'functional brief' was agreed in 1997 following thorough analysis. The available budget will see this site house the headquarters of the institution with all central departments and major facilities. The Directorate, Administration and Services will be based on this site, together with the Art and Industrial Division staff and collections and the Geology staff from the Natural History Division. Included in this development will be the main conservation laboratories and staff, although minor facilities will be found on other sites as dictated by the needs of the collections. A significant proportion of the site will be devoted to public services, including exhibition galleries, lecture theatre and education spaces.

KILDARE STREET
This site is being developed as an archaeological museum and will continue to house archaeological collections and archives, together with staff of the Irish Antiquities Division. It will also act as a local centre where services for education and administration will be based, serving the building and the neighbouring Natural History Museum. Building works will include the installation of a lift and upgrading of public facilities. The exhibitions will tell the story of Ireland from the arrival of the first settlers up to the period of recorded history. The space made available by removing functions to Collins Barracks will allow a proper showing of the collections for the first time in decades.

MERRION STREET
The Natural History Museum will be retained as an exhibition venue with little alteration apart from the provision of additional public services, including a lift connecting the four floors. Staff are keen to retain the atmosphere of the 'museum of a museum' which has been a major attraction of the zoological exhibits for over a century, being very popular with visitors. Collections storage at Beggars Bush will continue for zoological and geological collections.

TURLOUGH PARK, CASTLEBAR, COUNTY MAYO
The Irish Folklife Division staff and collections are to be relocated to a site where additional buildings will provide exhibition space for artefacts which have not been seen for a generation. The country house is set in gardens and some green space which will allow for development of a major tourist attraction. The distance from the Museum headquarters will necessitate some local services, including conservation and administration.

CONCLUSION
The National Museum of Ireland is in the early stages of major reform and significant improvements in its facilities. Much of this is a response to long-term neglect of the organization and lack of appreciation of its collections or potential throughout the mid-twentieth century. It is the aim of the institution to strengthen its own human resources through an increase in staff within a more effective structure, combined with improvements in training and career development. The current building programme is aimed at providing adequate exhibition space and collections accommodation combined with much improved visitor facilities. For the first time in a generation, there are detailed strategies for all aspects of the Museum's activities which are being progressed in a collective fashion by a management and civil service which is committed to setting the institution on a firm footing for the twenty-first century. It may take some years for all elements of the current programmes to be completed in full, and it will be a matter for future generations of staff to assess their impact.

Public attitudes towards and expectations of museums have suffered along with our neglected collections. Apathy is one of the greatest threats to their future. The recent adoption of 'heritage' as a flagship of national identity within a homogenous world is to the benefit of museums. The National Museum of Ireland, like all museums, must endeavour to use this public support for our ideals and turn it into support for our institutions. This can only happen if we are seen to embrace change and deliver a service which they, as our principal financial backers, are entitled to expect. Part of this process is the education of our visiting, and, more importantly, our non-visiting, public. They must learn to appreciate what we can offer in terms of real objects and real experiences of our world, and through this appreciate our desire to preserve our collections. The National

Museum of Ireland is but one of many museums where a lack of appreciation of its value resulted in neglect. In some instances, museums have disappeared and their collections have been lost as a result. The current changes at the Museum are planned to reverse that pattern.

Bibliography

Bantry White, H. 1911 'History of science and art institutions, Dublin', *Museum Bulletin of the National Museum of Science and Art*, **1**, 4, pp. 7–34.

Bantry White, H. 1912 'History of science and art institutions, Dublin', *Museum Bulletin of the National Museum of Science and Art*, **2**, 3, pp. 41–44.

Berry, H. F. 1915 *A history of the Royal Dublin Society*. London.

Bodkin, T. 1949 *Report on the arts in Ireland*. Dublin.

Brindley, A. 1994 *Irish prehistory*. Dublin.

Cherry, S. 1990 *Te ao Maori/the Maori world*. Dublin.

Comptroller and Auditor General 1996 *Report on value for money examination, Department of Arts, Culture and the Gaeltacht, the National Museum at Collins Barracks*. Dublin.

Duffy, C. 1991 'The public funding of museums: a case study of the National Museum of Ireland', doctoral dissertation, TCD.

Hall, M. 1986 *The National Museum of Ireland at the Royal Hospital Kilmainham: a concept study*, unpublished report. National Museum of Ireland, Dublin.

Herries Davies, G. L. 1983 *Sheets of many colours: the mapping of Ireland's rocks*. Dublin.

Herries Davies, G. L. 1996 *North from the Hook*. Dublin.

Interim Board of the National Museum of Ireland 1985 *Report of the Interim Board of the National Museum of Ireland presented to the Minister of Arts, Culture and the Gaeltacht, Mr Michael D. Higgins T.D.*, unpublished report, National Museum of Ireland. Dublin.

Institute of Professional Civil Servants 1973 *Fóntas Músaem d'Éirinn/Museum service for Ireland*. Dublin.

Ireland, A. 1997 'National Cultural Institutions Act, 1997', *Museum Ireland* 7, pp. 42–55.

Jarrell, R. A. 1983 'The Department of Science and Art and the control of Irish science in the nineteenth century', *Irish Historical Studies* 23, 92, pp. 330–47.

Kelly, E. P. 1993 *Early Celtic art in Ireland*. Dublin.

Kenny, M. 1993 *The road to freedom*. Dublin.

Kenny, M. 1994 *The Fenians*. Dublin.

Kenny, M. 1996 *The 1798 rebellion*. Dublin.

Lithberg, N. 1927 *Report on the National Museum of Ireland*, unpublished report, Ministry of Education. Dublin.

Lord, B. 1994 *National Museum of Ireland strategic plan*, unpublished report, National Museum of Ireland. Dublin.

Mac Lochlainn, A., O'Riordan, C. E. and Wallace, P. F. 1977 *Science and Art 1877–1977*. Dublin.

Management Services Unit 1995 *Revised draft report on the future structural, managerial and administrative arrangements in the National Museum of Ireland*, unpublished report, Department of Finance. Dublin.

Meenan, J. and Clarke, D. (eds) 1981 *RDS the Royal Dublin Society 1731–1981*. Dublin

Monaghan, N. T. 1992 'Geology in the National Museum of Ireland', *Geological Curator* 5, pp. 275–82.

O'Brien, D., Adams, J. M., McNeill, C. and Bodkin, T. 1927 *Report of the Committee of Enquiry into the working of the National Museum*, unpublished report, Ministry of Education. Dublin.

O'Connor, J. P. 1997 'Insects and entomology' in J. W. Foster and H. C. G. Chesney, *Nature in Ireland: a scientific and cultural history* (Dublin), pp. 219–40.

Office of Public Works 1992 *Report on accommodation at National Museum of Ireland*, unpublished report, Office of Public Works. Dublin.

Ó Floinn, R. 1994 *Irish shrines and reliquaries of the Middle Ages*. Dublin.

Ó Raifeartaigh, T. (ed) 1985 *The Royal Irish Academy: a bicentennial history 1785–1985*. Dublin.

O'Riordan, C. E., 1983 *The Natural History Museum, Dublin*. Dublin.

Quane, M. 1947 *Report on the National Museum of Ireland*, unpublished report, Ministry of Education. Dublin.

Ryan, M. 1993 *Metal craftsmanship in early Ireland*. Dublin.

Sleeman, A. G. 1992 'The palaeontological collections of the Geological Survey of Ireland', *Geological Curator* 5, pp. 283–91.

Strategic Plan Team 1992 *National Museum of Ireland Strategic Plan [Folklife]*, unpublished report, National Museum of Ireland. Dublin.

Teahan, J. 1994 *Irish furniture and woodcraft*. Dublin.

Vaccari, E. and Monaghan, N. T. 1993 'E minerali di Giovanni Arduino nella collezione geo-mineralogica di Nathanael Gottfried Leske: verifica di un caso di comunicazione scientifica nell' Europa del tardo Settecento', *Geologica Romana* 26, pp. 547–65.

Wyse Jackson, P. N. 1993 *The building stones of Dublin, a walking guide*. Dublin.

County Museums

PATRICK HOLLAND

Since I took up the post of curator of Tipperary S.R. County Museum in 1983, the intervening busy years have passed very quickly. I have seen many changes in my institution and its staff, in the extent of my duties and in the situation of county museums in this country. Our collection has grown from some 900 specimens to a total of over 20,000. We have now secured a major advance, the construction of a completely custom-built museum premises. None of this would could have taken place without the presence of four elements:

(i) the personal commitment of all those working in the museum;

(ii) the constant support of Tipperary S. R. County Council;

(iii) encouragement and donations from the people of the county, and

(iv) financial and administrative support from central government and statutory bodies, four crucial elements for any county museum (Holland and Deaton 1998).

COUNTY MUSEUMS: THE CURRENT POSITION

Today there are nine county museums, defined by the Local Authority Curators Group as an institution set up as a section of the local authority with a curator appointed by open competitive interview and reporting to a member of the council management team as a section head of a separate and distinct component of the council with an established budget. Some of the nine county museums are linked to county borough councils, but all collect, record, preserve and display the history of a county. My museum is unusual in being based within a local authority which serves an administrative county that is one of two parts of a geographical county. The nine museums (in order of foundation are) Cork,

Limerick, Monaghan, Tipperary S.R., Donegal, Kerry, Louth, Cavan and Clare.

Tipperary S.R. County Museum was apparently founded as Clonmel Museum in late 1947/early 1948. Three elements were instrumental in its establishment:

(i) the Clonmel and District Historical and Archaeological Society (founded in 1944);

(ii) the South Tipperary Fine Arts Club (founded in 1940), and

(iii) Clonmel Corporation and the development of its library service.

It would appear that there was a small but vocal campaign for the creation of public collections in the 1940s. The present collections of the County Museum are based upon these foundations: the small collection of some 900 specimens assembled by Clonmel Museum and the small but notable collection of mostly modern Irish works of art formed, as one of their stated objectives, by the Fine Arts Club. While the membership of both societies seems to have been quite limited, they did contain influential persons. When Clonmel Corporation decided to acquire an old bank building for their developing library service in 1944, it was agreed that it should also house a museum and the art collection. A committee was set up and cases were acquired by 1949. Mentions of donations and exhibits to the members of the historical society are common in their minute book. Requests for the appointment of a curator begin to appear in the early 1950s and in 1954 Mr R. J. Long, retired Art Master in the Clonmel Technical Institute and a prime mover in the Fine Arts Club, was appointed as curator. It would appear that the museum went into a decline in the 1960s, probably as the Historical Society itself faltered. The Fine Arts Club was already defunct and Mr Long had died at the beginning of the decade. The Historical Society was revived in 1971, and one item which it discussed was the re-opening of the museum. However, the administrative structure supporting the museum had changed. The institution was, in effect, left behind and parentless when responsibility for the corporation's library service passed from it to the county council and thence to the Joint Library Committee. It would appear that the museum remained closed until the early 1970s when there was a good deal of public unease. The county council then decided to reopen it as a county museum with an advisory committee and appointed a retired official, Mr Kevin Fennessy, as curator. Advice was sought from the curator of Monaghan County Museum, some special exhibitions were held and acquisitions were added to the collection. In November 1983, the author was appointed curator and the museum's development entered a new phase.

In hindsight, the museum can be seen to have been in a weak position from the start. The two societies which were active in its foundation were comparatively small and eventually faded away, and the administrative background shifted. The need for a solid placement within a local authority of sufficient size and resources to support a museum is clear. Similar ebbs and flows in the tides of support and prosperity can be seen in many of the other county museums. Limerick Museum opened to the public in 1916, having been founded in order to increase the rates levied for the support of the library (Herbert 1940). In 1947, the museum specimens were packed away to provide additional space for the library. The museum was revived in 1974 with the appointment of a curator and reopened to the public in 1979. It is interesting to note that Limerick, like many towns in Ireland, had at least two previous unsuccessful attempts at the foundation of a museum. While a great deal of research has yet to be undertaken into the history of museums in Ireland, the apparent number of such abortive institutions makes the task of provenance reconstruction a huge one. It should act as a warning as to the fact that, like children, museums are very easy to start but very hard to maintain. Limerick also points out the reality that in times of financial restrictions on the activities of a library service, any museum function within that service may come off worst in comparison with core library functions. Other county museums have been founded in response to a need to have a tourist facility, or as a result of the representations of a small but influential group who found a favourable response among the county's councillors and senior management team. The need to save an important collection has also been cited.

The collections of Tipperary S.R. County Museum now number some 20,000 specimens and are, with the exception of the holdings of modern works of art, based upon the acquisitions policy of the museum, that is to collect the history of Tipperary's South Riding. Restrictions of space have meant that, as yet, very few large items such as pieces of furniture have been acquired. Otherwise the collection is very varied with specimens ranging in date from the Stone Age to modern times. Like some of the other county museums, we spend a good deal of time assembling contemporary items, specializing, in our case, in political posters and related ephemera. Our collections of photographs and posters are noteworthy and we are building up small but useful holdings in many other spheres such as the War of Independence and the local involvement in the First World War. We also hold the Kiely collection of sporting prizes associated with a local Olympic gold medal winner.

Unlike some of the other museums which were founded many years ago, we have very few foreign, classical, ethnographical or natural history specimens. Such material would have come to a museum in times when collections of this kind were more easily available at lower or no cost from families which had had the means and opportunity to acquire them and when collection policies were less strict. We are similar to the other museums in having a large percentage of paper-based specimens such as photographs and documents. Historical accidents can give each county museum's collection a distinct flavour. Limerick Museum has, for example, a fine collection of silver, clocks and other pieces of craftsmanship made in the town, while similar items made in the smaller towns of our county are very rare. Archaeological artefacts are generally under-represented in the collections due to their scarcity, except where a museum has been in existence for several decades or where the curator has accepted excavation finds.

A commitment to a documentation project over the last several years by both our respective councils and the Heritage Council has meant that our museum has now recorded over 70% of our collection on our computer database for speedy data retrieval, with most of the other county museums having comparable percentages in a similar format. This is a huge collective resource. The next step for most of us is to have the collections electronically recorded so as to be able to use them more easily for a large variety of purposes and audiences, both actual and virtual.

THE PLACE OF THE COUNTY MUSEUM IN THE DEVELOPMENT OF IRISH MUSEUMS

The total number of county museums is small, but there has been a slight but definite increase in the rate of creation in recent years (Holland 1994, 50). It is likely that the nine county museums could shortly become ten or eleven. In 1983, there were only three other county curators in the state. Now we have become a small but recognized grouping within the museum profession. In past years, county museums were founded by enlightened local authorities within a national policy vacuum. Now we not only have a government department dealing with heritage, we also have the Heritage Council with a museums sub-committee and its museums officer. County museums have received substantial grants from the Heritage Council to computerize their collections records to a unified standard, to purchase some important specimens and, in the case of Tipperary S.R. County Museum, to commission a multimedia computer-based presentation as a prototype for the other museums. The curators of the county museums are increasingly working together to create common positions and understandings, so much so that if we did not have our curators' group to represent us, we would have to invent it very fast.

The next ten years will see a continuation of trends already emerging. The Heritage Council and the Departments of Arts, Heritage, Gaeltacht and the Islands will continue to have an increased impact upon county museums and museums in general. Much of their agenda will coincide with ours and we welcome, and shall hopefully assist, their efforts to speed up the pace of development in aspects such as museum education and conservation services. A museum registration scheme, based upon a voluntary striving towards agreed basic standards, will be a crucial move forward. It will encourage museums either to reach basic minimum standards in 'behind-the-scenes' work or to publicize the fact that those standards have been achieved. Once sufficient momentum is reached, then the possession of these basic standards should become a qualifying factor for grants from official bodies, ensuring that better climate of official approval for well-founded museums and an incentive for others to improve. Collections should be better served also, as basic conditions of care and recording must be part of such a scheme. This prospect must not evoke needless fears of a stifling, centralized and external control so long as a proper consultation process is undertaken and the potential benefits of membership are made clear. A registration scheme will highlight the necessity to assist those museums which have threatened collections or which have had to retrieve such endangered collections. The foundation of a museum service by the Heritage Council would be a critical step forward, but great discretion in terms of a realistic and strategic selection of its objectives will be required of its staff and guiding committee, since there is so much to be done that it could easily be swamped or seem ineffective. Ideally, the first aim for a museum support organization is to guide as many museums, their staff and governing bodies, as possible towards successful approval under a museum standards

scheme. Training for all, the facilitation of intense discussions among the governing body and the staff, as well as some financial assistance with basic requirements such as physical infrastructure and collection care and documentation, will probably be the agenda for the museum service for the first few years. Relationships between the county museums and the National Museum of Ireland will hopefully result in a greater degree of mutual understanding and an integrated partnership approach based upon an objective implementation of the 'designated museum' sections of the *National Cultural Institutions Act*.

The county museums are likely to form an important foundation for the future development of museums in Ireland. We are well spread geographically, we have regular budgets and trained staff and we enjoy the backing of our stakeholders. We could achieve so much more if we were to work cooperatively as institutions, pooling resources, ideas, exhibitions and problems. We have grown over the last fifteen years or so, not only in numbers but in confidence and achievement. The challenge now is to create a synergy which will move us, and others, onto another level of development in which we not only help ourselves but other museums, both larger and smaller, throughout our counties and beyond.

PUBLIC EXPECTATIONS AND COUNTY MUSEUMS

Roger Weatherup, retired curator of Armagh County Museum, has written that 'museum work can be compared to a game of golf because as much as playing against competitors, one is striving to improve one's own game. There are, I say, only twenty people in Ireland who can judge whether I am doing my work properly and I can bluff nineteen of them — the twentieth is myself' (Weatherup 1980, 16). Looking at the county museum from the outside, from the point of view of our public, can provide us with a better view of our achievements. Simply put, if our users think that we are doing well, then we are doing so, at least in those parts open to scrutiny. In parallel to the requirements of the stakeholders upon us are those of the museum on the stakeholders.

STAKEHOLDERS: IDENTITIES, EXPECTATIONS AND RESOURCES

The stakeholders in a county museum are many and varied. The county council, the primary funder and employer, is of course the most immediate one. Other institutional stakeholders include the Departments of the Environment and of Arts, Heritage, Gaeltacht and the Islands and the Heritage Council. The management and staff of the county council and the curator and staff of the museum must also be stakeholders. The public is, of course, the most important stakeholder, in all its manifestations, from the schoolchildren to the casual visitor, the researcher to the tourist to neighbours down the street. We must recognize that there are emotional stakeholders who feel that they should be consulted with regard to the museum but who may never have visited it at all. There are also those who value the museum not for its aims but simply for the use to which they can put it to, as a location for a function, for example, or to see it solely as a positive economic element in an area.

The fundamental issue here is how we communicate with these constituencies and how much notice we take, if any, of their needs and aspirations for us. We have to ask ourselves whether we have surveyed each stakeholder to see what they want of us. Do we hope that by a form of telepathy, we shall absorb, by constant close presence, what we presume are their desires? Could it be that we only know what the stakeholders want by a museological form of aversion therapy, whereby we simply learn by hard experience when what it is they do not want is made abundantly clear to us? Could it be that we do not really know what our stakeholders require? Have we ever asked them? If we do know what their expectations are, how do we respond to them and how should we respond? What do we expect in return and what do we actually get in return?

A most basic requirement for each of the stakeholders is that the museum should be a success. This assumes, of course, that the stakeholder is not a hostile one. Unfortunately this is not as simple as it might seem in that each group could have a different definition of success, which might conflict with that of another group. Thus, for example, the museum staff might define success as an up-to date documentation programme for the collection, while the public will surely far prefer interesting and attractive exhibitions to numbers in a database. In some cases, the stakeholders may have no real expectations or completely unreasonable ones. The challenge facing the museum and especially the curator is to recognize and reconcile these varying wishes, to seek to influence those with impracticable or frankly unwise expectations and to awaken a sense of involvement and ownership among those stakeholders unaware of their responsibility, so as to arrive at a position where the museum now has a coherent mission, aims and consistent supporters to guide it in its work.

Some requirements are common to many stakeholders. The museum building and the institution in general should look successful, be sound, suitable and well maintained. The appearance of a museum is the first clue as to how healthy it is. Even with restricted finances, it is possible to keep a museum looking well-kept, prevent nature or litter-louts getting an upper hand. Less attributable to finance is the attitude of the museum to maintaining a business-like approach in its public face. If the public noticeboard is covered with old tattered papers, the door has crudely written or misspelt notes stuck to it, if the toilets are grubby, then the museum may be sinking towards apathy and unacceptable standards. We must strive towards high standards of presentation so that our users will recognize that we care about what they think of us and about how we are seen to do our job. Commercial services to the public today are of a very high standard and the stakeholders, if they care and know about museums, are no longer happy to accept the easy-going ways of yesteryear. If we do not have modern, bright structures, as our competitors in the leisure industry have, then our old buildings should, at least, be well kept and well presented. A recurring and adequate maintenance budget and a proactive maintenance programme are essential.

The county council, our employer, is the most important stakeholder. There is at present no legal requirement on it to provide a museum. It could be accused of diverting finance and resources from other services if it founded and supported a museum. It is crucial, therefore, that the members of the council and the management team be convinced of the value of the museum to ensure their continued support. The members of the council will expect a return in several forms on their investment. In the most basic terms, the museum must be something which reflects well upon the council. It must be seen to be a public service which is of benefit to the county. It should provide, in varying amounts, depending on location, size, mission and original brief, a return in educational, economic, social and cultural terms. It should be seen to be active and successful in preserving the history of the county and should never be an embarrassment to the council, the major stakeholder.

Our response as curators of the county museums should, of course, be to seek to fulfil as many of these expectations as possible. We must be honest, however, and say that we may not be as aware of these wishes as we should be. We might be conscious of them informally or implicitly. We may have taken some surveys of visitors, but I doubt that any of us have gone so far as to ask the tourism bodies in our area, for example, what they require of us. This is understandable insofar as the answer we could receive might not be palatable to us, and to respond might require other aspects of the museum's work to be neglected. If the choice, in a restricted budget, is between facilities for tourists and the preservation of the collection, our core value, then each curator would find it very hard to do anything other than take care of the specimens. However, we cannot deny that if we do not satisfy at least a majority of our stakeholder supporters, then our institution will not prosper. In return, we must ask for the resources and their support to fulfil their expectations of us. We cannot be expected to perform miracles without even some loaves and fishes to begin with. In many ways, the relationship between us and our stakeholders, especially those who directly fund us, is a cause and effect one. We fulfil some expectations by simply existing. Having been given certain resources, we fulfil more expectations or even create more. If we do our job well, then we may be given more resources. Hopefully, this cycle proceeds until it reaches a balance created by the drying up of revenues caused by the fact that either all expectations are fulfilled or by the more usual cause that, despite our successes, the stakeholder cannot afford any more resources. A third factor may be our exhaustion, whereby we cannot achieve any more objectives, even with additional resources.

THE CURATOR'S ROLE

A vital part of the duties of the curator is to fulfil the stakeholder's expectations, both of him or herself and of the institution. The council will expect their curator to have the vision to see where the museum should be going, the commitment and energy to ensure that it gets there, the managerial and leadership skills to motivate and lead the staff, the tact and diplomacy to ensure that their aspirations and those of the public are fulfilled, the integrity to have the museum be trusted and respected and the skills of persuasion successfully and diplomatically to seek support and assistance for their institution. Common sense, presence of mind, commitment, a business-like attitude and a realistic appraisal of the aims and functions of the museum are other qualities required by a curator. It is also his or her responsibility to encourage and allow a low-key but positive self-criticism, to harness it for the betterment not only of the institution as a whole but also to allow each of the staff to develop professionally and personally. The council will also expect curator and staff to have an appropriate attitude to the local authority which employs them. The curator should regard himself or herself as a member of a public-service organization.

Trust is fundamental to the relationship between a county museum and its stakeholders, who rely on the museum to take adequate care of the specimens which it holds and to behave in a professional and ethical way. Unethical actions by the museum would destroy that trust and the relationship which sustains the museum. Unethical methods or policies could include inappropriate or illegal collection, faulty recording, inadequate provision for preservation, biased or inaccurate displays, poor management and the breaking of confidentiality agreements. As the person who leads, the curator is the individual responsible for setting the tone of the institution and its work. It is up to him or her, therefore, to be trustworthy and to ensure that the museum is similar.

The skills and qualifications thought to be appropriate for a curator of a county museum have not been clearly defined. Relevant experience is very important, but it should be accompanied by an appropriate attitude. The competition for posts is such that the successful candidate will have at least one qualification, if not two. There is not, as yet, any third-level course devoted exclusively to museology in this country, though a number of post-graduate courses do deal with it, among other topics. It has been the practice in the past to appoint persons who have a primary degree which includes archaeology, but this need not necessarily be the case in future. It is important, however, that the person appointed has a basic knowledge of archaeology so as to appreciate the significance of any object brought in or already among the collections. Stakeholders such as the National Museum and the archaeological profession would expect this. Stakeholders from other professions or expertise would equally expect the curator to have sufficient knowledge of their subject to appreciate the importance of relevant items in the collections.

A general awareness of the importance of a museum object, no matter how insignificant, in its own right, rather than simply as a piece of corroborative evidence for the written record, is crucial. Each specimen in the collection must be cared for equally, to the best of the museum's ability. A basic knowledge of archaeology is vital since the museum will be, and indeed should be, seen as a place to seek information regarding sites and discoveries. Even with the present boom in contract archaeology and the growth in employment of archaeologists, county museums can form a vital link in the thin and uneven archaeological coverage of the country. Indeed, we can regard the university Departments of Archaeology as a stakeholder, as one of the traditional career paths for graduates is in curatorship.

Today, a curator of a county museum will need an extremely wide range of skills and knowledge, ranging from an acquaintance with all types of artefacts varying in date from the Stone Age to modern craft items, to management and public administration matters, including an appreciation of the benefits and pitfalls of information technology, as well as a knowledge of the county, its people and history, and so on. The list is endless because, in a small institution, one does not have the luxury of being a specialist. This can, however, lead to a crisis of identity where curators who have pursued an academic course of research can become extremely frustrated when they realize that there is no time available during work hours and little energy afterwards for private research if they are doing their job properly. It can be argued that one of the essential tasks of a local museum is to research aspects of its theme. However, the reality is that if a local museum curator, working on his or her own (with no assistant curator), is able to use more than a very small percentage of his or her working day to undertake research, then it is likely that either the museum or the curator is not working to their full shared potential. There is simply not sufficient time to be able to undertake intensive research. It is the responsibility of the curator to decide how much time can be spent on research without interfering with the museum's other functions as expressed in the development plan. In any event, it is more than likely that any research undertaken will be related to forthcoming exhibitions, possible acquisitions and registration of items in the collections. Ideally, we should aim at a multiplicity of uses for any particular piece of data. Research undertaken so as to create a better register entry should be retained for re-use in exhibition labels, exhibition catalogues and booklets and even in the captions for published booklets and postcards.

At a basic level, most stakeholders will expect that the curator will manage the museum to a high standard. The general public will not be particularly worried if our filing is not up to date; our colleagues in the service of the council, our counterparts in other museums or institutions will expect our office procedures to be efficient and for us to be an effective part of the local authority and museological team. It would be severely detrimental to the museum's long-term prospects for it to become isolated from the council or its staff. The staff of the museum should do whatever is possible and sensible for it to become an accepted and normal part of its parent organization. Suppliers and contractors will also expect prompt service and payment of invoices. The museum must be aware of the museological issues being debated in the wider world, if only to spot opportunities for itself.

Museums must have access to modern office equipment such as computers. They should be moving forward at the same rate as the institution to which they belong, albeit some distance behind the lead section. The staff should be seeking to maintain progress in the technological current, but ought not become so besotted as to neglect other aspects of the museum's work and so let the institution become diverted from core functions. They should not be hiding from the future by refusing to upgrade (Hogenboom 1995). They must be aware of the more important issues involved with information technology such as the threat of viruses, the issue of copyright and access to the collections.

The council and other major institutional stakeholders will expect the museum to be seen publicly as a positive, progressive and relevant centre of which they can be proud. This requires the curator and staff to present positive images of the museum to the public and the governing body. Does the museum's staff care about how they are seen? Are members of the museum's staff seen as appropriate persons to receive invitations to speak at meetings and events? Is the curator, as a local public official, invited to events and, if so, does he or she try to attend? Have the curator and the museum succeeded in convincing the members of the governing body of the

validity of all of its aims, educational, social and preservation-orientated, or is it regarded primarily as an economic asset?

This is not to deny that museums have an economic role. However, expectations can sometimes be more than optimistic, with visitor levels appropriate to a long-standing national institution with a renowned collection being expected from brand-new centres with constructed themes, 'off-the-shelf' displays and an unknown public reaction to an aesthetic experience still in embryo. Brand-new institutions, like cinema films, may not succeed with the public no matter how much is invested in them. Charm, interest and quality are not synonymous with big budgets. A museum must attempt to convince stakeholders not to view it on economic terms only since that is an impoverished impression of its functions and aims, and because museums find it hard to compete against many other more effective economic revenue-creating elements. We must always try to have museums appreciated on their own terms since our distinct aims are our strengths.

Each curator will do what he or she considers possible or necessary to fulfil their employer's expectations. However, that may vary as widely as do personalities, personal circumstances, skills and resources. It would be surprising but gratifying if such superhuman curators as described above existed. The reality, of course, is that it is pointless to define the characteristics of the ideal curator since we do not want a clone approach to appointments. Each museum will gain part of its character from the staff who work there, and each will and should be different, while based on similar principles. Each curator will have strengths and weaknesses. Some will excel at public relations while others will ensure that the behind-the-scenes work is done thoroughly, but shy away from publicity. In the main, curators have not lacked for commitment to their work and to their expectations of what the museum should be achieving. The pressure of deadlines, whether imposed externally or internally, can result in stress illnesses. Sometimes, to prevent illnesses caused by the frustration of conflicting and/or unachievable needs and expectations, curators can withdraw into fulfilling one particular perceived requirement, for instance research, with poor performance in another such as public relations. When staff and other resources are so scarce or non-existent that essential functions are not carried out, then a curator may simply give up, leading to a disillusioning acceptance of inability to deliver basic standards. Were there to be adequate resources, then the curator should have sufficient confidence and self-awareness to allow suitable members of staff to fulfil those roles which they themselves are either too busy or unsuitable to discharge. Faced with several years of being refused necessary resources, a curator can give up and concentrate on those matters which can be achieved. However, it would be placing the museum in a very vulnerable position for the curator or any other member of staff to move into an introspective withdrawal from proactive promotion of the institution and its aims. A museum that drifts into an apathetic or arrogant attitude and then fails to fulfil stakeholder expectations is open to dramatic and possibly damaging change imposed by an impatient outsider.

Without the protection of a statutory provision, as has recently been secured for local authority archives, a county museum must constantly work at being relevant, valued and appreciated by both the public and the councillors and management. If this is achieved, then the museum may secure additional resources and facilities. This constant need to be seen to achieve, to be an advocate for itself, might be daunting, but it is a healthy tension which ensures that the institution does not fail. Museums which have had to fight for survival have this creative tension in abundance, but when times get better can fall into a torpor. A constant and pressing desire to listen to one's stakeholders and to be positively self-critical about one's achievements is vital. One of the few positive benefits of charging the public for admission has been the fact that the museum has to provide the customer with value for money. It is simply not enough for a museum to think that it deserves support or visitors because it exists. Institutional names and titles are not a very good bargaining point. Museums must come out from the shadows and present themselves to the funding bodies in a persistently and politely positive way, always being unafraid to publicize their good points while diplomatically reminding their superiors of their needs and the validity of their cause.

Museum curators find themselves advancing from an initial bewilderment in dealing with a variety of roles to an enriching and very broad accumulation of skills and knowledge. It is very important that the museum be an independent section of the county council with the curator as a section head, having access to the management of the council to argue the case for increased funds or facilities. The level of access by museum staff to those in senior management is a measure of the museum's standing within the council. Such access need not be sought very often, as the museum is generally not a section which requires constant supervision by management, assuming that it is being managed properly, but access of this kind is important. It is the responsibility of the curator to keep management informed so that they are aware and approve of the direction in which the museum's development is progressing.

PLANNING

It would be highly unrealistic to expect that a small, non-statutory section of the council or indeed any section would succeed in having a budget sufficient for all that it would like to do. However, a county museum should have adequate finance to pay for an adequate staff, to maintain and run the museum building and to collect a representative sample of the history of the county in accordance with its collection aims, to cater for the recording and preservation of the collection, a regular programme of visiting and special exhibitions, a modest but effective outreach and education programme and the provision of a reasonable number of visitor services, including some catering services and a select range of museum shop goods. A budget which allows for the consistent, albeit modest funding of the needs just listed is of far greater potential than a once-off very large capital grant. It is not uncommon for a private, community or commercial heritage institution to start off in a blaze of publicity, with a large injection of capital funds, but to falter in a few years under the pressure of constant revenue demands and/or interest charges.

To undertake its job properly, a county museum requires the following basic staff compliment. It needs a curator to manage and lead the institution as well as to perform specific curatorial functions, an assistant curator with specific responsibility for life-long education and exhibitions, a clerical officer to run the museum office and administration, a museum assistant to deal with day-to-day curatorial matters and enquiries, including acquisition cataloguing as well as exhibitions, a conservator to undertake responsibility for the preservation of the collection and a cleaner/caretaker to clean and maintain the building. In addition, the museum should have access to external professional and technical expertise (preferably they should be on the staff) and also the opportunity to employ additional staff on contract to deal with specific projects such as a documentation backlog or a special exhibition.

Each of the major institutional stakeholders such as the county council, the Heritage Council and the Departments of the Environment and Arts, Heritage, Gaeltacht and the Islands will (or should) expect the curator and the museum to have a definite written plan, agreed to and supported by all stakeholders, and used as the framework within which all possible avenues of action are decided upon. A detailed and honest examination of the museum's strengths, opportunities, threats and weaknesses by the staff should form the basis of the development plan within which the institution moves forward. The plan, and the long-term and short-term objectives and tactics it contains, should be based upon the mission statement which details the aims of the museum. Central to the statement will be a vision of what the institution should strive to become, for the benefit of the stakeholders and the assets it contains. The place of the museum in the county and the country, in terms of the development of museums, must also be clear. The possession of this long-term view is essential as the day-to-day grind of paperwork, registration and endless public queries can obscure the far-off horizons towards which we are all struggling. The pace of progress in the development of the museum can vary but ideally should be balanced. Slow, steady development will eventually grind to a halt because resources have become outstripped by needs. The museum will require a large input of funds to allow it to break out of the restrictions facing it. A museum set up in a blaze of publicity in a new building and with new displays should have one or two years of steady progress after the frantic activity of the initial phase in order to settle down administratively, to acquire friends and allies among the stakeholders and, above all, to begin to build up the collection. A successful museum must fill many roles. Its main one, of course, is educational, but it will also have social, cultural, economic and artistic functions. It should have a role in the general development of the county by assisting the other museums within it. We would expect some stakeholders to have an input into the creation of the plan and others, having endorsed it on completion, to support it.

THE PUBLIC

The general public in the museum's area is the most important stakeholder since no matter how well we might think we are doing, surely the most basic test is whether we are popular with the public. Do people 'go out feeling better than when they go in', to use Kenneth Hudson's query about a good museum (Hudson 1997)? We might, perhaps, say that popularity is not the only indicator of success, that we could put on displays which would be popular but which could also be unethical or improper. Conversely, there have been exhibitions which have not been popular but which were a great success in their own terms and highly regarded by those interested in the particular topic. Popularity is not, of course, the only criterion, but I believe that our greatest achievement would be to reach a standard of work and service which conforms to our internally generated professional criteria and which is viewed as a success by our stakeholders. Of course we have to ask ourselves how we know whether the museum is popular with the public. A simplistic use of visitor numbers can be misleading. This year's figures may be very high because of a popular exhibition, but unless an exhibition of similar appeal can be presented next year, the visitor totals for that period will inevitably be lower, although that does not mean that the museum staff are not working just as hard. An exhibition might attract only a small number of visitors, but those that do see it may regard it as a valuable experience. The quality of a visitor's experience must always be considered. Never-

theless, a consistently declining visitor total must be a matter of concern and has to be analysed by the museum's staff to see if its cause can be uncovered. The curator should always be conscious of the need to monitor visitor numbers and to wonder whether the questions they pose can be answered for the benefit of the museum. Why are there peaks and troughs in the graphs of visitor numbers? Do children and adults come in different proportions at different times? Which exhibitions were most popular and with which groups? Has the museum undertaken a marketing survey of its visitors and non-visitors? Where do visitors come from and how did they find out about the museum? What methods of publicity are the best? More crucially and fundamentally, what do visitors think of the museum and its displays? Does the visitor understand the display? Do they enjoy their visit? Are they happy with the facilities? What suggestions have they made? I am not proposing that taking marketing seriously means that the museum should automatically spend vast sums on generating visitor numbers. A free admission museum has to balance the need for a satisfactory number of visitors against the fact that, unless it has a very carefully chosen range of shop goods or other means of income generation, it may not actually recover much of the funds spent on marketing. The funds could have been better expended on actually caring for the collection. The crucial point is whether or not the museum is curious about its visitors, their expectations and attitudes towards the institution and how to improve their frequency and numbers.

Having surveyed the public's expectations, one has to ask what the museum's attitude towards the public is. First impressions can tell a lot. If, on entering, one is greeted with a friendly welcome or at least in a business-like way by a staff member who seems reasonably happy, then morale and the concept of visitor service in the museum are probably healthy. If, on the other hand, the person at reception is falling asleep, bored or downright unfriendly, then something is wrong. If the telephone is answered with an inarticulate grunt by someone who obviously has no interest in the caller, if letters go unanswered in the long term, if there is an air of tension and an obvious fear among the staff of somebody or something, then the institution or that staff member may be ill or completely unmotivated. In a similar fashion, it is vital for the curator and his staff, no matter how wearying it may be, to regard each visitor as a potential donor, a potential sponsor and a potential carrier of good publicity. A county is a relatively small space and word-of-mouth is a very efficient means of publicity, especially when dealing with bad news.

Today's visitor deserves and expects a pleasant welcome, an interesting display with technology-based features as appropriate, a range of services such as a shop, catering facilities, access to historical data, multi-lingual guides and labels, clean toilets, comfortable places to sit and rest and, above all, a satisfying experience. We must never forget that we are judged by criteria other than those we might prefer to use, such as the richness of the collection or the scholarship of the staff. We are compared with other visitor facilities by our visitors and often come off second best. The reality is that, for example, there are very few cafes, while displays are often traditional and unexciting. It is not that we do not see the need to improve our services to the public but, rather, that funds are scarce and, given a choice between visitor services and the preservation of the collection, we have tended to choose the latter. In the long term, putting funds into front-of-house activities might be more to the collection's benefit as it may encourage investment in an institution clearly doing its best.

More generally, we must work to achieve a high level of 'public quality', to use Kenneth Hudson's term, so that we satisfy the needs and wishes of our visitors. I cannot do better than quote from the summary of a recent lecture delivered by him:

Does it [the museum] look and feel like a place which puts the customer first? Is the presentation and interpretation of objects attractive and understandable ? Is it calculated to appeal only to people who know a great deal already, or does it meet the requirements of its visitors in a more realistic and democratic way? Second, does it employ people who are genuinely interested in the art of communication and who see a museum as an important medium for the two-way transmission of ideas, talents and experience, as a valuable meeting ground of the small world and the big world, as a source of mutual inspiration? And, third, are the communication tools adequate? What kind of language does the museum use in order to build bridges between itself and those who come to see what it has to offer? How far is it prepared to go towards meeting the public halfway? (Hudson 1997)

What is clear is that while museum staff are generally very diligent, they have a long way to go in meeting visitor expectations.

A museum which is attempting to make itself relevant and essential in the community should be open when the community is able to visit. Most museums are open during the week when it suits the staff. An institution which does not open when the public want to visit it can hardly be regarded with approval by them. Lunchtime and weekend opening must be introduced.

The question of having to pay for admission to see the historical artefacts belonging to one's own community has been strongly debated for several years. In this country, admission to most of the national and county museums is free and many curators are strongly opposed to fees (Cooke 1995). On the one hand, there are plenty of examples of museums in the UK where visitor numbers dipped after the introduction of admission charges, but there are other points to be considered. On the other hand, there can be no doubt but that the introduction of admission charges at institutions faced with otherwise unavoidable redundancies has brought about a culture change in museums which were not focused on visitors, their needs and interests. However, this does not necessarily translate directly into higher visitor numbers and higher income.

We must also consider the meaning of 'access'. If we support the idea of free access to all those who cannot afford a visit, should this be at all times and for all exhibitions? Should access be free for those who can easily afford the charges? There is also the reality that many of those groups whom we would like to see visiting for free rarely come even if they can afford a visit. In many ways, the real access problem for museums is not to convince those who can afford to visit to actually do so, whether it costs them or not, but rather to persuade those who never visit a museum to come inside our doors. These would include not only the less-well-off or deprived, for whom entering a cultural institution is a visit to a 'foreign country', but also groups such as the elderly and the disabled. Charges, if they must happen, should never be imposed as a knee-jerk reaction, therefore, but as a properly researched and considered policy. It ought to be noted that several county museums have been exempt from paying rates to the local authority within whose area they are sited on the basis that they are a free admission institution devoted to educational aims. It may be possible, indeed, for a county museum with relatively small visitor numbers to raise more finance by being a free admission museum with an active secondary income-generation policy (shop and other sources) than by trying to realize funds directly from a visitor total which could be reduced by reason of the entrance charge, as well as having a rates bill to pay.

If, however, charges have been imposed, has the institution considered and monitored their impact upon the visitors, their number and origin (schoolchildren, lower-income families and so forth)? Has the museum researched and considered an alternative approach to income generation or even different ways of imposing admission charges, for instance 'optional' or seasonal charges? Were stakeholders canvassed or were the charges imposed by one stakeholder only as a simple and perhaps self-defeating answer to a complex need? Do museum curators and the members of their governing body care about public access to a publicly funded facility? Conversely, has the museum refused to consider the question of admission charges at all and ignored the need to raise finance from what may be a ready-made income stream?

Following on from the previous point, has your museum a policy on the generation of income? Some stakeholders might like to see the museum charging for admission. If they are opposed to admission charges, it is unlikely that they and other stakeholders would be opposed to the museum generating revenue from other sources. Some of the economic players in the area may not be acting in the best interests of the museum. In recent years, we have the unfortunate policy of heritage attractions being established as commercial concerns, often with what seemed to be inflated prospective visitor numbers. As many of them have begun to falter, we have heard them say that the free museums constitute unfair competition. In effect, they are realizing what we have been saying for years, which was that museums are not purely commercial organizations, and require subsidy to fulfil their aims. Having seen funds go to them to create modern means of communication and not to us to do the same, at a time when we are being criticized for having out-of-date displays, we now have them trying to reduce us to commercial institutions when it is clear that commercial heritage centres find it difficult to survive. Free admission museums are not in the commercial world, being primarily educational establishments. If commercial heritage centres cannot survive it is because they entered a very small market with a product which is either over-priced, is unchanging or unappealing.

Income-generation is certainly encouraged in many county museums. We are all aware of the need for additional finance to cater for increased needs, but how many of us have seriously looked at the possibilities for revenue? Has your museum decided which would be better, to seek a once-off major donation or a smaller steady income from sales? Have you considered how much it will cost, in terms of staff time, to sell shop items? Have you considered the design of your shop and the space necessary for storage? Has your museum made a comprehensive study of the fund-raising possibilities, their associated costs, benefits and disadvantages?

Having succeeded in raising additional funds from various enterprises, we should not be penalized in effect by having our finances further reduced by our funding body on the basis that the income should replace our grant. Income-generation funds should be kept by the institution as a reward for initiative and hard work, to be used as it sees fit, but mostly on the unattractive behind-the-scenes work while retaining a sufficient amount of seed capital for further revenue raising.

A small but important sub-group among the public is that of the researcher. The latter expect access to the collection with a minimum of delay and impediments. A county museum should be able to offer them a desk and chair in a designated room or area which is reasonably quiet, comfortable and conducive to study. Availability of basic historical works is desirable, as is the use of equipment such as microscopes and photocopiers. In relation to the collection, the museum should be able to identify efficiently and locate a particular object and its records within a reasonable time. The opinion of researcher stakeholders of the museum can be seen in the number of enquiries made to it. While the staff of a museum may, at times, wish that there were not so many requests for historical information from so many sources, the absence of enquiries is surely an indication of a lack of public appreciation of the resource that is the museum. Do those making enquiries receive a satisfactory service? Do members of the public even know of the museum? Is there a range of pre-printed information sheets on various topics, including the nature and extent of the collections, which the public can buy? Does the museum pride itself on being an institution which is consulted by the local authority and the public, or does it regard visitors and enquiries as nuisances to be tolerated, who take from the more enjoyable and rewarding pursuits such as research and scholarship and knowledge of the collection? Stakeholders expect us to make our collections open for inspection and research. Sometimes we have to work to explain why they cannot be as accessible as would be wished.

DISPLAYS AND COLLECTIONS

The displays of a museum are the primary interface between it and the public, and we must therefore ask whether the stakeholders think we are doing a good job in this regard. What are their expectations? We could suggest that they expect our displays to be professional, interesting, balanced, accurate, colourful, intelligible, easily comprehensible and satisfying. We do respond by working very hard to make our exhibits conform to these wishes, but also go further to try to create challenging displays which fulfil our own expectations. We must also recognize the varying expectations of different stakeholders. Researchers or experts would like more detail, some institutions feel happier with certain styles of display rather than others, local stakeholders might prefer local themes and so on. Again a delicate balancing act has to be undertaken. Throughout this process of compromise between different expectations and physical realities such as the finance available, we should try to bridge the gap between display and viewer. Events such as guided tours, lectures, workshops, organized school visits, are all necessary to evoke a sense of comprehension and maybe even wonder and enlightenment in the viewer. In return, we hope to receive a sense of satisfaction from the stakeholders which will eventually translate into additional resources.

Fundamental to our attempts to satisfy our stakeholders is a display policy guiding us in our work and complimenting the collection policy. Both policies should integrate so that the display needs of the museum

Fig. 43.1 Choices in the Creation of a Museum Display

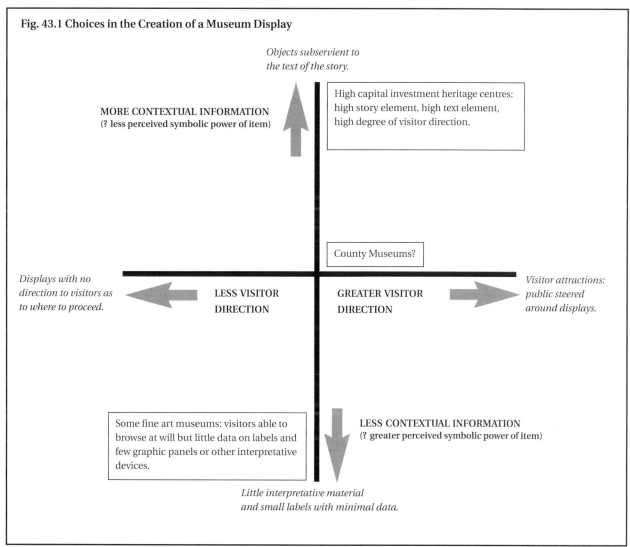

Objects subservient to the text of the story.

MORE CONTEXTUAL INFORMATION
(? less perceived symbolic power of item)

High capital investment heritage centres: high story element, high text element, high degree of visitor direction.

County Museums?

Displays with no direction to visitors as to where to proceed.

LESS VISITOR DIRECTION

GREATER VISITOR DIRECTION

Visitor attractions: public steered around displays.

Some fine art museums: visitors able to browse at will but little data on labels and few graphic panels or other interpretative devices.

LESS CONTEXTUAL INFORMATION
(? greater perceived symbolic power of item)

Little interpretative material and small labels with minimal data.

inform the collection policy and the collection policy influences the displays. A curator should set a priority on the collection of those specimens which will fill gaps in the array of the material available for the display and promotion of the museum's theme. The standing exhibits should be primarily based upon the museum's aims and theme, though with some allowance for interesting 'sidelines'. Temporary exhibitions can range even farther afield, allowing the museum to answer more of the stakeholder expectations but without diluting its aims so as seriously to alarm other stakeholders.

The arrangement of displays is ultimately a matter of personal taste, but one preferably founded on certain basic principles. The safety of the public and of the collection is paramount. Neither should be threatened by inadequate planning, design or display construction or environmental control. The purpose of the exhibit must also be considered. Some displays seem designed to show how much the label writers know about some esoteric branch of antiquity, but how little attempt is being made to communicate with the public. Art

historical displays often present specimens in such rarefied terms that even the most basic and utilitarian of objects can become sanctified, whether they deserve it or not. Others are so cluttered as to indicate either the confused mind of their designer or the theatrical effects sought by display specialists.

A museum curator seeking to design a display has to make conscious decisions as to how it will communicate, to what extent and to whom. I have attempted to schematize some of the main decisions in the above illustration (**Fig. 43.1**). The upright arm is an index of the information available to the visitor regarding the contexts, social, cultural, economic, historical, of the specimen on view. At the top of the scale is the heritage centre approach where the specimen becomes increasingly powerless and subservient to the theme, the story told in graphics, text panels ('books on the wall') and other media. We can imagine this line fading out as it proceeds upwards into the realms of the heritage and amusement industry, where the distinctions between the real and the reconstructed become blurred and reality eventually vanishes. The other end of the scale proceeds downwards, with the symbolic power of the object, whether seen by the public or imposed or suggested by the curators, growing larger all the time. Midway along the downward leg is the local museum where labels are used to explain the collection on display. Further down, the amount of information begins to drop, either because the museum is professionally parochial or assumes that the displays of local glories will be intelligible to all. Lower again comes the art display where it is thought sufficient simply to display rooms full of paintings in different 'schools' for contemplation by the awe-struck visitor. Labels are generally discreet, so small that visitors have to crane and peer to read them, and rarely offer much information. Suggestions on possible interpretations of the scenes, especially in the case of modern art, are generally not given by label writers. Interpretative material on the period, the artist, the social conditions, are rare, though occasionally, as a great concession, some furniture of the period is added to the room.

At right angles to the information axis is the direction axis which indicates the degree to which a visitor is directed around the displays. At the right outer end one is visiting a visitor attraction, where your stay in an area and even rate of movement is determined by a human guide or a 'time car'-type conveyance which deposits you into the shop area at a constant and programmed rate. More crucially, from our point of view, the displays will present a single story with separate messages at each point. One starts at 'A' and proceeds through the message alphabet to finish a programmed length of time later at 'Z', the end of the circuit, having hopefully absorbed the message of the exhibits. But while the visitor may feel happy in that he realizes that there is a framework to operate within or perhaps even to enjoy, is that message accurate? Does a display with a simple message convey the complexity of the past? Could there be another route through the message? Would a single simple forceful opinion on a complex contemporary issue be regarded as adequate or acceptable by society today? If not, can we allow ourselves the same luxury with the past?

As museum display designers, we have a tremendous responsibility to our public to erect exhibits which are ethical, balanced, thoughtful, honest and truthful. They must be accurate reflections of our environment and our history in the context of the museum's theme. For a museum to be only an entertainment is a failure of its aim. To manipulate a visitor's emotions or opinions in a dishonest cause is more than a failure. We can design a display which can affect a visitor deeply. The presentation of German modern history in the Haus der Geschichte in Bonn opens with the end of the Second World War and the occupation of Germany by the Allies. Immediately inside the first gallery, however, is a display

dealing with an aspect of the preceding period. A large, black, tomb-like cube has exhibits within it dealing with the Holocaust. While one might say that it is out of context chronologically, it is appropriate in that it tackles the dilemma faced by the German people after the war as they attempted to come to terms with crimes committed against humanity. The colour, shape, sense of enclosure and even placement of this display are all carefully chosen, it is clear, to evoke a sense of mourning, serious thought and hopefully an effort at comprehension and maybe catharsis. It was noticeable to me that very few people spoke as they stood within the black walls of the cube, in contrast to the frequent comments from persons chatting about their shared past in all of the other displays.

Even a lecture describing an exhibit can be so strong as to render an audience speechless, as the members of the Irish Museums Association found when they received a deeply thoughtful and thought-provoking lecture from Jette Sandahl at their annual seminar in 1996. She argued very strongly that, as exhibition designers, we are not objective or emotionless, nor should we be (Sandahl 1996, 17–30).

Mid-way along the direction axis one is in the area of a museum where it is possible to wander from room to room but where each room and case topic are clearly marked and briefly explained. A framework of orientation but not a strait-jacket is provided. At the left end of the axis is the extreme where the visitor is not directed at all. Here the visitor is completely free to wander through the displays at will, without any indication by the designer as to where to go next. This can occur as the result of the careless or unaware evolution of a museum where cases, rooms or themes are added on haphazardly. It may be due to the over-familiarity of the staff with their topic, so that they assume that all others understand it. It may be a deliberate choice by the curator or designer where they do not want to impose their view of the theme upon the visitor, or where they want to give an impression of the chaotic nature of the historic episode they are dealing with, as in the amazing local history displays in the Berwick-on-Tweed Barracks Museum. It may also be a deliberate attempt to emphasize the artistic value of the objects in showing that they are timeless works of art which do not require a context. There is a severe danger that visitors will be confused and lost without some element of direction. They may experience a thrill when they find something that excites their imagination, but they may leave the museum, having missed some important item, and will then become irritated when they realize that they have not been provided with the cues to follow it up.

Perhaps we could place many of the high-investment heritage centres high in the right upper quadrant of the graph described above? Indeed, they often direct their visitors around the displays, frequently for commercial reasons and also because the story they present and the text and other methods used to illustrate it are often more important than the objects. Context is all-important, even if the specimens are not. The upright axis could also be taken as an index of the perceived symbolic power of the object, with the upper end being where the object is seen only as a prop and the lower end being where it is so laden with power that it is often not interpreted or placed in context at all.

Fine art museums can be placed in the lower part of the figure and generally in the lower left quadrant, as visitors are free to wander in quiet contemplation among the images in the 'artistic temple'. Personally, I feel that a local museum's displays should be in the right upper quadrant, but not at a great distance from both axes so as to indicate a sufficient amount of direction and contextual data to guide but not overwhelm the visitor.

It is important for a local museum to stick to its specified display themes. Very early in its existence comes the first critical moment when a donation is offered which has absolutely nothing to do with the exhibit and collection guidelines. If it is accepted, the museum has begun its slide down the long slippery slope to the point where it will consist of a collection of objects thought to be of importance to the donors but not to the museum. Display galleries will be littered with the permanent traces of donor-directed displays. Wholly inappropriate and often trashy pieces of modern junk will have to be retained on display simply because the person responsible for the museum could not say 'no'. In effect one stakeholder, the donating public, has been allowed to take precedence over the wishes of the others. The county council, for example, might not want precious resources to be expended on specimens which do not accord with the museum's aims.

Museum staff themselves often deviate from the paths of curatorial righteousness. Many a small museum is displaying generic items of agricultural and folk history and ignoring themes unique to the area. It may be that the history of the town gasworks, dog-racing track, iron-works or other local industry is not seen as interesting. Perhaps there is an implicit or unchallenged idea that the museum should show the history which tourists are believed to expect, an Arcadian view where our ancestors all lived happily in tidy thatched country cottages except when they were being evicted by cruel landlords. This view of history could be seen as an exercise in nostalgia or an assertion of a simplistic approach where we are reflecting in our own museum displays a marketing image created over many years for consumption by foreign customers. This is not simply a tourism interest overpowering other stakeholders. It is a deeper concept within us as to what is historically interesting. If we have come to accept a marketing image of ourselves in

preference to the far more varied and often brutal reality, what does it say about us? A local museum should reflect local history within the context of its collection, rather than accept a homogenized view of the past imposed upon its holdings.

Personal collections of no local relevance whatsoever can often break from cover in a museum which is losing its focus. I have visited a local museum where a new display of modern American militaria occupied a prominent room, while important nineteenth-century trade banners from the area were stacked in a small storeroom at the furthest end of the building. Though the militaria were of interest, they had no apparent link with the area (the labels did not note any) while the banners are a crucial piece of evidence for the region's industrial history. While there may be perfectly good reasons for this choice of displays, I must admit that it made me uneasy as to the direction in which the museum is apparently going. Here again the balance between the expectations of the various stakeholders may be upset. In trying to achieve or keep that equilibrium, constant contact with all of the stakeholders is necessary, if only to balance opposing pressures. We can expect that each stakeholder will have to take account of the other stakeholders and their wishes, even if we have to make them apparent ourselves.

Taste and fashion can also interfere. While we might seek to move beyond a simple and partisan view of Irish history, we should not be so revisionist as to deny that violence and oppression, from many sources, were a constant element of life in the past. Unpalatable realities must be faced up to, in a mature fashion, and the history of our areas revealed without preference or prejudice insofar as we are able.

A properly managed county museum should have a clear and definite attitude and commitment towards life-long learning. This is not only in relation to welcoming bored schoolchildren but, rather, being far more proactive. Each section of the community, such as the ICA or day-care centres for the elderly or schools, deserves an individual approach to see if their educational needs can be catered for. It is no longer enough to say that 'we provide worksheets'. We should be seeking out the opinion of our visitors and all other stakeholders, indeed those of our non-visitors, to see what they want us to do to bridge the gulf of comprehension, of imagination, between them and our collections. Education in all its aspects, and in the broadest sense of the term, must become a core function and attitude of the museum, rather than something to be 'bolted on' to an exhibition after it has been designed. Each exhibition should be examined in an evaluation process to see if it has achieved its aim and to see whether the public understand it and what they are taking from it. However beautiful the collection is, it is not enough to say that the display exists simply to show it. If exhibitions work, then we should expect a vibrant relationship between the public and ourselves, an opening out of the museum towards the community and an acknowledgement of this by our institutional stakeholders.

The staff are a vital stakeholder in the museum. They must feel that the institution is well-managed and is a place where they enjoy working and gain a sufficient measure of personal satisfaction. A well-managed museum is one where the staff are trusted to do a professional job, where matters proceed within a plan and procedures with which they are familiar, where they have as much responsibility devolved to them as is possible, where the essential tasks of collecting, recording, preservation, education and display are all considered equal and have an appropriate and fair share of whatever financial budget is available devoted to them and, finally and most crucially, where targets are set and achieved. The curator, while probably coming to the museum with an academic training, must be able to adapt and become an efficient manager of staff, of finances, of administration and of the buildings under his or her control. County museums are lucky in being small institutions where every staff member has to be multi-skilled and willing to take on several different roles. Such centres cannot ever allow themselves the luxury of demarcation lines, wasted resources in the form, for example, of attendants forbidden to do anything other than sitting in bored contemplation of the potted plants or a class structure where only the curatorial 'gods' may approach the 'sacred objects'.

The collections themselves can be regarded as an inarticulate stakeholder in the museum, with the curator and staff acting as their legal counsel and guardian. The collections, if they could speak (and is it not the museum's job to make them speak to the public?) would surely demand their own preservation and survival as a basic requirement. Left unbalanced, some stakeholders's expectations might be to the detriment of the holdings. The building housing the collection should be structurally sound, without leaks or floods, and secure against determined attack. It should be functional so that it can actually be used as a museum with a minimum of steps and stairs not bypassed by a lift, have large, clear galleries, sufficient offices, workshops and collection stores and pleasant public spaces. The conservation needs of the museum's collection must take precedence, in display areas, over the desire to have the building made impressive and lightsome to visitors. Our institutions are potentially threatened by many emergencies. Fire, flood, vandalism, terrorism, theft, assault are all possible and must be considered and planned for. The curator should have consulted with a security advisor in advance of any major development or exhibition.

It is a failure of the museum profession that most of the population, and especially some of those who are our superiors, still think that an old building is the most obvious and appropriate location for a museum. This is sometimes carried to unfortunate lengths where a curator has to struggle with a building which is totally unsuitable and may be in the wrong location, away from the public it seeks to serve. Thus churches, castles, warehouses, town houses all need to be examined critically to see whether they can be used successfully and whether their adaptation will not totally destroy their architectural integrity. I have sometimes said, not totally in jest, that the ideal museum is a large warehouse with a pleasing front. In all cases, whether adaptation, extension or construction, the task of creating a museum building requires a brief clearly and knowledgeably stating the functional needs of the museum, and a curator and an architect both committed to the open discussion of these needs. Closed minds create practical problems or unaesthetic solutions. The aesthetic needs of the building cannot be ignored: indeed they should create a structure appropriate to its location, but they should not overwhelm functional needs.

It is surely a fundamental tenet of a museum, an institution which seeks to collect and preserve, that the long-term survival of the collection is a basic aim, and that the degree to which a museum succeeds in passing on its holdings to the next generation is a measure of its success or failure. However inadequate the general public's, and other stakeholders', understanding of our aims is, it at least includes a belief that museums should take care of the collections. Yet I believe that we would be deluding ourselves were we to say that the health of the nation's portable heritage, in terms of preservation, is beyond reproach. It is true that great advances have been made in the last several years, with specific appointments and projects in national institutions and similar moves in the county museums, but conservators are still a very rare species. Training courses and meetings organized by both the Irish Professional Conservators and Restorers Association and the Irish Museums Association have resulted in a greater awareness, but we need to move forward to a position where the conservation of a museum's collection is acknowledged as a core activity and the profession of conservation respected by all. The relationship between conservator and curator must be one of shared responsibility and mutual respect. Each profession ought to acknowledge the responsibilities and obligations and professional standing of the other. Cross-professional feuds do not impress the other stakeholders. Proper care of a museum's collection must include a programme of preventative care to ensure proper handling, environmental control and storage. Active conservation care should be available to bring about more effective and routine intervention for specimens requiring greater care. It is no longer simply enough to curate the specimens and to bemoan the lack of conservation advice, to let the collection slowly and almost imperceptibly slide into a trough of dissolution. Professional advice is now available and, while voluntary local museums might not be able to afford any funds for conservation, a properly established county museum with a yearly budget should be ashamed if it is not spending a sizeable proportion of it on conservation. If it has not succeeded in having a conservator appointed, then it should certainly have access to one. As curators, one of our main roles should be not simply to subscribe to a general desire to preserve the collections but actively to promote conservation and the employment of conservators.

A far more basic question in relation to the preservation of the collection is whether the museum is economically and institutionally secure. Will it, and more crucially the collections, survive into the next generation? Has there been sufficient capital investment to carry the museum forward? Is the revenue provision sufficient? Far too often museums are set up by one stakeholder group without the full and confirmed involvement of other stakeholders. It is also common for museums to be established without a proper examination of the whole stakeholder issue, ensuring that the institution is isolated from the start, making its sustainability even more unlikely.

Many of the stakeholders expect us to fulfil our aims of collecting the history of the county in an effective, ethical, economical and systematic way. There can be conflicts here. One stakeholder may applaud a purchasing 'coup' while another might worry about the money spent to acquire the specimen or the space to store it. As with so many other features of museum management, a balance must be struck between conflicting needs, and each museum should have a collection policy which assists the museum by indicating what it should and should not collect. The museum will be constrained not only by its theme but also by its pre-existing collection, its strengths and weaknesses. Resources such as space, staff, conservation assets and finance are all crucial too. Collection policies are a framework upon which to hang the character of the museum and its collection, not a straitjacket. There must be space for the museum to develop a distinctive collection, derived from the local environment, the interests of the staff and their public. Collection policies must also not be allowed to prevent the once-in-ten-years opportunity to save an item or set of items which might strain the resources of the museum but which are an irreplaceable and rare part of the county's heritage.

However, it is vital for a museum not to stray too far from the guidelines in collecting. A concern for historical matters, an awareness of the passing of time and tradi-

tions or even a desire to increase the tourism potential of an area or business can all lead to the casual or planned acquisition of museum objects. The natural generosity of the Irish people, at least up to recent years (there does now seem to be a greater general awareness of the possible financial worth of specimens than existed ten to fifteen years ago) means that once the doors are open, specimens will come in steadily. A local museum without a critical collection policy will soon end up as a glorified tip-heap of unwanted items with nothing in common but their place of deposition. The concomitant implications of conservation and recording costs and the difficulties of creating a display showing something other than the lack of discretion in collecting must mean that we should exercise a general prudence while not failing to acquire vital objects.

Having attempted to resolve conflicting stakeholder expectations and constricting physical resources with a collection policy soundly based upon the strengths and weaknesses of the existing collection and the institution, then we can also ask how well the museum is actually collecting. How many specimens did it acquire in a given year and from how many donors? Were the donors' expectations fulfilled? This, of course, is a very crude method of quantification, and the correct answer could be either very low or high depending on the policy. More searching questions could be how well the museum has collected those items 'targeted' in the policy as being especially desirable, or how many offers of specimens were followed up to a conclusion. One might also include the regularity with which the curator makes visits and inspections to possible donors around the county. The relevant performance indicator here is how successfully the museum actively collects, according to a set plan agreed with the stakeholders, rather than simply and passively accepting what comes in the door. Having collected according to plan, we should be able to return to our stakeholders for support in the light of the consequences of collecting.

Collection without the recording of a specimen's provenance is, from a museological perspective, pointless. Some of our stakeholders will be very conscious of this need, especially our colleagues in other museums or institutions which set museological standards. The public may not see a huge amount of value in recording information unless the information is directly relevant to themselves in some way. Researchers will always see the point of data collection. The Heritage Council has now set a benchmark in regard to documentation by insisting that the Local Authority Curators Group, representing the curators of county museums, adopts a minimum standard, having examined other standards such as Spectrum (Museum Documentation Association, UK) and the UK Museums and Galleries Commission Registration Scheme. This we have done, with some curators adding in more data in the cataloguing process, while others, with much larger collections, have decided to work with the minimum standard only. The potential for computerized museum records, however, is far greater. An astute and considered cataloguing process by an experienced museum assistant can add a good deal of associated information without an excessive amount of time-consuming research. This converts an acquisitions register database into a catalogue. The associated data, together with a social and historical classification system tailored to the county in question or at least to Irish conditions, would allow us to apply the databases to a much wider body of research needs. It would be appropriate to keep the collection data separate from general historical data derived from reference library material, for example, but together these two types of information could create, if only on a small scale initially, a county archaeological and historical database resource. A county museum would become even more relevant and be able to meet so many needs with the formation of such a resource. However, it is possible to become so besotted with the creation of the perfect database that progress can slow down to a crawl while subjects and specimens are researched. We owe it to our funding stakeholders to achieve timely and efficient conclusions to documentation projects. We must also ensure the security and safe-keeping of the collected data.

CONCLUSION

Museums cannot exist in isolation, either from their communities, their counterparts or, most crucially, from their stakeholders. If we are to develop successfully, we must seek out, canvass and listen to those who have a stake and an interest in the results of our work. If we do not, how can we expect support?

Bibliography

Cooke, P. 1995 'A charged issue: admission to museums', *Museum Ireland* 5, pp. 19–30.

Herbert, R. 1940 'The City of Limerick Public Library and Museum', *North Munster Antiquarian Journal* 2, 2, pp. 76–89.

Hogenboom, J. 1995 'Spot the museum guerilla (or on-line databases and internal communications structures)' in *Information: the hidden resource, museums and the Internet* (Cambridge), pp. 203–10.

Holland, P. 1994 'Rational regionalism and the county museum', *Museum Ireland* 4, pp. 38–53.

Holland, P. and Deaton, J. 1998 'A museum is a machine for collecting, recording, preserving and displaying', *Museum Ireland* 8, pp. 24–34.

Hudson, K., 1997 'Summary of lecture: A museum's public quality', *International Committee for Regional Museums, Newsletter* (Winter) Austria .

Sandahl, J. 1996 'Emotional objects', *Museum Ireland* 6, pp. 17–30.

Weatherup, D. R. M. 1980 'Premises, staff and security' in B. S. Turner (ed) *Museums in Ireland: present and future.* Dublin.

Local Authority Museums

STELLA CHERRY

The present chapter will review the origins and development of local authority museums in Ireland, and focus in particular on day-to-day working and administrative considerations. These museums play a major part in the collection, preservation and conservation of a large percentage of the national material heritage. They maintain sizeable holdings with the assistance of local government funding, are repositories of regional history, memories and culture, and a major, if often under-used, educational resource. In the vast majority of cases they are run by professionally trained staff, and are effectively administered, despite the scant financial resources at their disposal. Nonetheless, local authority museums in Ireland have steadily expanded the services they offer to the public, especially within the last decade. This growth has been and continues to be assisted by EU funding. In no small way, however, the professionalism of museum staff itself has initiated these developments, through successful grant applications and by convincing local government of their relevance as well as of the importance of museums to local communities. It is not generally realized that museum collections are organic entities that can grow exponentially through the zeal of the curatorial staff in convincing potential donors that their institution is the best possible repository for items of local importance. Collection is often a matter of opportunity rather than choice. A museum's potential to collect is, therefore, not something that can be easily quantified. Thus, a museum is something that develops in tandem with the community. Traditionally, however, it has been difficult for curatorial staff to get this message across to the authorities that control and finance.

HISTORY AND ROLE

There are eight functioning local government-funded museums in the Republic, with one in the process of being created (Ennis, county Clare). Of the eight established museums, four are located in Munster, one in Leinster and three in Ulster. There is, as yet, no local authority museum in Connacht. Ireland's first local authority museum was established in Cork in 1909. The latter had closed by the 1930s, and the museum as it now exists was opened in 1945. A collection was established in Limerick in 1916, but it was not until 1977 that the museum proper came into being. Monaghan County Museum was set up in 1974 followed by Tipperary South Riding in 1983, Donegal in 1987, Kerry in 1992, Louth in 1993 and Cavan in 1994. Local authority museums in Ireland are, therefore, a relatively recent phenomenon.

In the early 1990s, all the curators of local authority museums formed a group not surprisingly called the Local Authority Curators Group (LACG), which meets every two months and holds an annual general meeting. The group has an elected chairman, secretary and treasurer. The incumbents keep their positions for a two-year term. In 1993, the group prepared a consultative document which states that 'the primary function of a local authority museum is to collect, preserve, conserve, document and display the material culture of the county'.

A museum should ensure that, if possible, it assembles a good representative sample of its region's material culture. Collections can be acquired through donation, loan or purchase, and once a museum obtains an object it has a responsibility to ensure its survival well into the future. Thus, if individuals give an object to a museum, they have a right to expect it to be well cared for. The museum, for its part, will record the object in great detail, in addition to thoroughly examining it to assess its conservation needs. The item will then either be placed on exhibition or stored in the museum's reserve collection: in either case, its long-term preservation will be ensured by the institution. The environmental conditions of both display and storage must also be to a high standard, so that the object is not in any danger of being damaged. Documentation records are crucial to the efficient running of the museum, particularly when an item is on loan. For example, if somebody gives you an artefact on loan, you must ensure that at a future date a descendant of the donor can retrieve the object in the same condition in which it was taken in. To this end, museum records are scrupulously maintained, not only to ensure that items entrusted to it are recorded, but also so that the requisite information is easily retrievable. This activity is one of the 'hidden' costs of museums, as it is labour-intensive and is, along with securing expanding storage facilities, one of a museum's principal expenses.

A museum is obliged to make its collection accessible to the public, a fact which also holds true for the material on display and in storage. Museum collections are widely used for academic research, but their overall educational potential, curiously enough, is not being utilized. This is unfortunate, especially as a large percentage of museum visitors in Ireland are made up of school children. Indeed, school groups are the main source of 'repeat' visits, but, arguably, financial constraints have prevented local museums from enabling school children to make the most of their visits. Temporary exhibitions are thus extremely important to museums, as they ensure that return visitors will always have something new to see. They are also a means whereby such an institution can introduce its visitors to its reserve collection. This latter contains all items not on exhibition, primarily because the space or resources for doing so are unavailable, or either because the items themselves are not germane to the history of the locality or are additional examples of items already on display. A local museum can also serve as a community resource, particularly when the exhibition is generated by local people and displayed in the museum.

Collection care and display are primary functions of a local authority museum, but museums are about a lot more than this. The large archive of archaeological and historical information stored within each museum helps provide members of the public with information they seek, be it for a school project, local history or academic thesis. The number of requests for information by phone, correspondence and personal visit that museums handle on an annual basis is quite substantial. The role of the local authority museum is much wider than a description of its functions. Museums help provide a community with a sense of identity and help to harness local pride. They are also economically important, particularly from a tourism perspective.

Utilizing state-of-the-art technology and modern display techniques, the advent of heritage and interpretative centres in Ireland has created a new expectancy and approach to display design. Visitors to these centres now expect the same level of presentation from museums. Those museums with the financial resources to do so have responded accordingly by employing professional designers to work on their exhibits. Monaghan, Tralee, Cavan and Louth Museums all employed professional designers when preparing their original displays, as has the recently designed museum extension in Cork. Indeed, within the last decade major changes have occurred within museums and their approach to display. Prior to this, curators did their utmost to achieve good exhibition standards, but with very limited resources at their disposal this was not always possible.

PLACE WITHIN LOCAL GOVERNMENT

Local authorities are responsible for a wide variety of areas within the community including housing and building, roads and transportation, planning, water supply, sewage, environmental protection and recreation, to name but a few. Within local authorities, museums normally come under the 'Recreation and Amenity' heading, along with libraries, archives, public parks, swimming pools, golf courses and sports centres.

The work of the local authority is divided into executive functions and reserved functions. In practice, it is the city/county manager who performs executive functions and the elected council perform reserved functions. The manager is responsible for the day-to-day running of the county council or county borough corporation. The executive functions undertaken by the manager include decisions relating to staff, planning, fixing rents, making contracts and accepting tenders. Reserved functions are defined as all of the functions of the local authority except those performed by the manager. The elected council decides all local authority policy and has ultimate financial control of the authority.

Most curators report directly to the manager or assistant manager of their respective county council/corporation. There are, however, curators who have to report to the county librarian or the town clerk who, in turn, reports to the manager on their behalf. Every year, each curator prepares an estimate of the finance required to operate the museum for the coming year. This includes calculating staff salaries, day-to-day running costs such as heating, electricity, phone bills, stationery as well as funding for acquiring artefacts, conservation, photography and the like. In effect, all potential expenditure is listed and calculated, and the curator's estimate is ultimately submitted to council who vote on whether to accept or reject it. Thus the council decides on the allocation of funding to the various local authority departments. Naturally, larger sectors get the greater allocation of funds, and understandably curators are sometimes disappointed with their annual funding allocation. Nonetheless, they must be realistic and recognize that within the local authority museums are not a major priority and will never have the same public profile as a multi-million-pound engineering project or a new motorway. Overall, local authority museums receive adequate funding for day-to-day operations.

Local authority museums are funded entirely by the local authority but can, nonetheless, occasionally benefit financially or in kind from other organizations. The Heritage Council, for example, has been generous in funding a computerization project that will ensure each museum has a complete database of its records. The Heritage Council provided the hardware and software for this and has continued to finance the project for several years by providing monies to enable museums to employ personnel to input the records. The Council has also furnished many museums with financial assistance to purchase artefacts and equipment. In addition, the Friends of the National Collections have purchased artefacts and donated them to several local authority museums. Furthermore, many museums have recently benefited from European funding, and those museums situated in the border region have benefited from cross-border monies.

The fact that the local authority funds such museums ensures their continuity and survival. It also allows museums to be run by a professional staff. The museum has at its disposal advice, expertise and assistance from other departments within the authority. This is invaluable in areas such as building maintenance, finance, law, planning, health and safety and so forth. The museum is also seen as an important addition to the services the local authority provides, while the knowledge and experience of museum staff is an asset to the authority, and many curators are members of local authority committees such as National Monument Committees and Arts Committees.

STAFFING

In general, staffing levels within local authority museums are low. This becomes very obvious when comparisons are made between similar-sized museums (in terms of collections) in Northern Ireland and Britain. Most museums function with a core staff ranging from two to six permanent members of staff. A total of forty-one people work permanently in the eight local authority museums in the Republic of Ireland. Of these, some thirty-two are full time and nine are part-time employees. Many museums augment their staff through employing personnel on contract or on various social or student employment schemes or by relying on volunteers.

The staff make-up within the eight museums differs widely. The one position common to all the museums is that of curator. In theory there are no special education qualifications needed to become a curator. In reality, all present curators are graduates and most have postgraduate qualifications. Not all museums have clerical staff, cleaners or attendants, and in such cases it is the curator, or another member of staff, who ends up doing this work. Most museums do not have the specialist staff to handle areas like conservation (only three museums have conservators), education, marketing, public relations, exhibition design, research and photography. Again, it is the curator who undertakes much of this work despite having little training or skills in these fields. Moreover, only one of the eight existing museums employs an education officer. This is a major deficiency and leaves one of the major educational resources in the country greatly under-used. In general, the staff of a local authority museum is multi-faceted, working on a wide variety of diverse tasks at any given time.

There is no existing or recognized qualification in museology in this country. None of the third-level institutions provides a museum studies course and only one of the heritage management and arts administration courses available includes a module on museology. Not surprisingly, most people working in Irish museums learn on the job. Some of the curators of local authority museums had no prior museum experience before taking up their employment, although three curators had worked in the National Museum of Ireland. At present, only one of the eight local authority curators has a qualification in museology, obtained from an English university.

BUILDINGS

Until recently, there have been no purpose-built museums in the country. All museums are located in old buildings whose former uses include a workhouse, a convent, a Georgian residence and an industrial building. Naturally, none of these buildings is ideally suited to house valuable artefacts, and providing optimum environmental conditions can be very difficult. Many have problems with dry rot, dampness and even flooding. Curators are faced with the task of adapting these buildings to provide an adequate environment in which to store and exhibit their irreplaceable collections. Many of the buildings do not have public toilets, cafés or adequate disabled access.

In 1999, major structural developments were taking place at Tipperary South Riding County Museum and at the Cork Public Museum, both developments being funded by the European Regional Development Fund. The Tipperary Museum in Clonmel became the first purpose-built museum in the country, while a large modern extension was constructed at the existing museum in Cork.

DEVELOPMENTS IN COLLECTION POLICY

The collections of the local authority museums are predominantly of a general nature. They contain a little bit of everything, from various disciplines such as geology, archaeology, folklife, history and ethnography.

Naturally each collection reflects the history of the particular region in which the museum is located. Collection policy, depending on the individual museum's resources, is either active or passive, but most museums tend to have very active collection policies. Some, however, are restricted by lack of storage space and finance, and are therefore not in a position to collect as they would wish. The size of the collections is also varied; in general the longer-established museums tend to have the larger holdings. The number of artefacts within the museums' collections ranges from about 800 to over 35,000.

While most museums have their own holdings, some rely on loans of artefacts from the National Museum of Ireland. Until November 1999, legislation prevented local authority museums from collecting archaeological artefacts. Under the 1994 amendment to the *National Monuments Acts*, all newly discovered archaeological artefacts are henceforth considered state property, and are to be housed in the National Museum of Ireland. Only designated institutions are now to be allowed to collect archaeological material on behalf of the state. Section 6, subsection (1) of the *National Monuments (Amendment) Act* 1994 provides for designation by the Director of the National Museum of Ireland of persons to exercise a number of the Director's functions (in this instance the collection of artefacts). Under Section 68, subsection (2) (a) of the *National Cultural Institutions Act* 1997, provision has been made for a procedure whereby local authority museums can collect and hold archaeological objects on behalf of the state. All local authority museums applied for this designation in 1994, and in November 1999, at a ceremony in the National Museum, the Minister for Arts, Heritage, Gaeltacht and the Islands, Ms Síle de Valera, presented the curator of each local authority museum with a certificate of designation.

TOWARDS THE FUTURE

There have been substantial changes within local authority museums within the last two decades. More authorities are also investigating the possibility of setting up museums in their areas — in many ways a very positive move — where museums are increasingly recognized as an asset to a community. The standard of museum display has improved within the last decade and the individual museums' approach to their self-presentation has also evolved. Significant improvements have been made in conservation awareness and practice. The role of the museum within the community has expanded and the museums themselves are more conscious of their identity and function.

The Heritage Council is in the process of introducing a scheme of Standards and Accreditation for all museums within the country, an approach which will hopefully lead to the universal adoption of high professional standards. The concept of having a minimum standard to achieve or, indeed, aspire to, is a very welcome development for local authority museums. The Heritage Council is also currently preparing a report on the need for training within the museum sector. It is still unclear how the proposed alterations in the nature of local government itself will impact on museums. It seems, however, that the changes will have a positive rather than a negative effect. There can be no doubt that local authority museums have expanded and improved considerably since they were first established almost a century ago. There are, however, several areas that need to be enhanced if the country is to have a truly satisfactory local authority museum service. Funding, first and foremost, is always a vital issue. Needless to say, the more enlightened local authorities will always ensure their museum has sufficient funds to provide a good service. Yet in all of Ireland's local authority museums, staffing levels, conservation and education services need to be improved. Overall, this is an exciting time of change and development for local authority museums, as new museums are established and older ones revamped. The continued support of local authorities will ensure that our museums will flourish and survive for future generations to enjoy.

Folk Museums

JONATHAN BELL

Interest in recording Irish rural customs and beliefs goes back at least as far as the eighteenth century, when travellers such as Arthur Young occasionally noted practices which they found unusual or bizarre (Young 1780). By the nineteenth century, it had become common for writers to present Ireland as a country where exotic and archaic ways of life survived, unchanged by the international culture of modernization. This often took the form of reinforcing colonial stereotypes of the Irish as primitive, barbaric and irrational (**Fig. 45.1**). More important for the development of folk museums, however, were the equally inaccurate, but positive, stereotypes that were also developed, which presented Irish society as a survival of a heroic and mystical era:

A significant factor in ... the essential unity of Ireland ... has been the retention, persisting in many areas into modern times, of certain attitudes towards the world and the otherworld ... which had their origins in the Elder Faiths of pre-Christian times. (Evans 1992, xi)

Fig. 45.1 Ploughing by the tail. An inaccurate caricature of a practice which was alleged to reveal the primitive barbarism of the Irish. From Edward Dubois, My Pocket book *(London, 1808).*

As elsewhere in Europe, the academic study of rural life-styles became serious as elite cultural groups committed themselves to the values of romantic nationalism. Some of the leaders of this movement postulated a natural, organic relationship between a nation, its landscapes and the culture of its people. Each national culture was believed to have its own essence. It was vital for countries attempting to achieve political and cultural independence from powerful neighbours that this essence should be identified and cherished (Ó Giolláin 2000). It was often asserted that the essence was most clearly seen in 'unspoilt' rural culture and landscapes, which had escaped the erosion of 'traditional values' by urban, industrial society.

The identification of some rural people as the 'folk' was to some extent part of this project. Rural people have presented special problems for social theorists, past and present. They are part of large-scale society and culture, and yet they are in important ways distinct. One difference often identified is between the warmth and closeness of country life and the impersonal sophistication of the city. A poem by Belfastman, John Hewitt, written in 1950, summarizing the richness of experience which he found in the Glens of Antrim, provides an excellent example of this:

Or is it that the unchristened heart of man
still hankers for the little friendly clan
that lives as native as the lark or hare?
And, though to keep my brain and body alive,
I need the honey of the city hive,
I also need for nurture of the heart,
the rowanberries and the painted cart,
the bell at noon, the scythesman in the corn,
the cross of rushes, and the fairy thorn. (Hewitt 1969, 11)

The apparent independence of country life from the movements transforming wider, especially urban, society is emphasized by the concept of 'folk'. In many early studies, we can see a range of assumptions about the nature of the folk. They were seen as living in 'communities', close-knit groups held together by bonds of kinship and neighbourliness, where conflict was uncommon and short-term. This model of rural society is very close to that described by social scientists of the Functionalist School:

The sociology of Irish rural life and small-farm subsistence is largely a matter of the anatomy of two institutions ... These are the family and the rural community ... a framework of longstanding customary relationships uniting people. (Arensberg and Kimball 1961, 311)

These communities were in some sense seen as unchanging, ruled by 'tradition'. Estyn Evans, for example, saw Irish rural life as profoundly influenced by a 'prehistoric substratum', going back to neolithic times, which still shapes cultural practices, attitudes and beliefs (Evans 1992, 66). If culture could indeed be shown to have an essence, the folk were the most likely people to exhibit it.

The west of Ireland, with its spectacular scenery, its remoteness and rich centres of Gaelic culture, was opened up to scholars and artists from the east of Ireland during the late nineteenth and early twentieth centuries, with the spread of rail and later motorized road transport. Many of these people found their discovery of the west an overwhelming, sometimes life-changing event:

Oldest Ireland lives along the western seaboard of Donegal, in Connemara, Kerry, and Cork. It is Gaelic speaking and for that reason preserves the customs of the antique world. It is so different from the rest of Ireland that even the rest of Ireland hardly knows it ... I write of a deeply buried substratum which only the most devoted and trained folk-lorists can, with patience ..., touch. (Ó Faoláin 1947, 4–9)

Until recently, some folk scholars in the Republic of Ireland continued to view the west as the main area in which one could find 'untainted' 'tradition bearers'. The study of folk life as an academic subject developed in Ireland during the early twentieth century with the establishment of the Irish Folklore Commission in 1935, and during the 1940s and 1950s in the work of scholars such as Estyn Evans and A. T. Lucas. The energy and vision of these researchers shaped the folk museums which have been established throughout Ireland.

FOLK MUSEUMS

Small folk museums have proliferated in almost every county during the last two decades, from Sneem in Kerry to Kilmacrennan in Donegal. These are often intended to

Fig. 45.2 Cottage in the Outdoor Museum at Muckross House, Killarney, county Kerry.

appeal primarily to tourists, but the rise of interest in local history has meant that even in areas where tourism is not so important, such as Fivemiletown in county Tyrone, local artefacts have been collected and displayed. Some of these developments include outdoor museums. This kind of museum presentation was first developed in Scandinavia in the late nineteenth century. The core of the display is a collection of buildings, usually illustrating local vernacular architecture, which are either replicas of buildings situated elsewhere or ones which have been removed from their original sites and rebuilt in the museum's grounds. In Ireland, the scale of outdoor museums varies greatly. A small, but particularly evocative, outdoor museum has been established at Glencolumkille, county Donegal, while a potentially major development has been sited in the grounds of Muckross House, Killarney (**Fig. 45.2**), which also houses one of the most important indoor exhibitions of Irish folklife material. The largest outdoor museum in the Republic of Ireland is situated in Bunratty Folk Park. This Park is commercially run and has had to cope with particular problems arising from its success, which has resulted in very large visitor numbers. Bunratty has dealt with this well, so far, and has an international reputation as a museum as well as being one of Ireland's best-known tourist attractions.

The largest publicly funded institutions dealing with Irish folklife are the Folklife Department of the National Museum in Dublin, the Ulster Folk and Transport Museum and the Ulster American Folk Park, the latter two institutions now forming part of The National Museums and Galleries of Northern Ireland. The development of the national museums has reflected changes in the evolution of both the theory and practice of folklife in Ireland. The National Museum of Ireland holds the most important collection of rural artefacts in Ireland. The Museum's Department of Folklife has produced displays of significant parts of the collection, in the Museum's Merrion Row building and, more recently, in the Collins Barracks galleries. Perhaps the most

Fig. 45.3 A byre dwelling house from Gaoth Dobhair, county Donegal, re-built in the grounds of the Ulster Folk and Transport Museum.

important achievement of the Department to date, however, has been in the research published by staff. Folklife scholars have often dealt with aspects of life which were previously undocumented, and in folk museums, collection and research have been particularly closely linked. Curators have had to identify the significant aspects of the life-styles which they have been charged with interpreting before making collections. The published work of a number of curators in the National Museum has made a major contribution to the understanding of Irish rural history. The Museum is now engaged in the development of an Irish Folklife Museum at Turlough Park House, near Castlebar, county Mayo. This uses formal indoor galleries to display and interpret the significance of the Museum's magnificent collections.

The largest folklife institution in Northern Ireland is the Ulster Folk and Transport Museum, which was established originally as the Ulster Folk Museum by act of parliament in 1958. This act charged the Museum with the task of interpreting the way of life, past and present, and the traditions of the people of Northern Ireland. The Museum was consciously modelled on Scandinavian prototypes, which has meant that a major element of its

display is an open-air museum, occupying a site of about sixty acres of the estate at Cultra, nine miles outside Belfast. The outdoor museum has been developed to illustrate both urban and rural life in Ulster around the turn of the twentieth century. Early development concentrated on reconstructing a range of vernacular dwellings moved from their original sites (**Fig. 45.3**). The large size of the site has allowed these to be placed in landscapes which have been modified in an attempt to recreate those in which the houses were originally located. From its inception, it was also planned to include some craft workshops in the outdoor museum, and in more recent decades representations of non-residential buildings have been developed to show a range of occupational and social functions: mills, forges, workshops, shops, churches, schools and community halls. The Museum attempts to bring these exhibits 'to life' by an increasing programme of activities, including craft demonstrations, role play and major events days. The development of a town area in the outdoor museum has allowed representations of urban houses and some small-scale displays on industrial activity.

Development plans for the Ulster Folk and Transport

Fig. 45.4 Medb, *one of the four largest steam locomotives built at Inchicore, Dublin, the locomotive works of the Great Southern and Western Railway. The engine is on display in the rail gallery at the Ulster Folk and Transport Museum.*

Museum have also included the construction of galleries, which were intended to complement the outdoor museum, examining particular aspects of life in detail, showing change through time. To date, only one folk gallery has been built, the major developments in this area having been concentrated on displaying the Museum's large collections related to transport history (**Fig 45.4**). The problems of interpreting the Museum's extensive rail and road transport collections have led staff to examine some of the assumptions underlying many folk studies. This will be discussed below. As in the National Museum, curators in the Ulster Folk and Transport Museum are expected to publish research. The Museum issues an annual journal, *Ulster Folklife*, and curators are expected to publish a wide range of interpretative material, from academic research to educational and popular publications aimed at school groups and the visiting public.

The Ulster American Folk Park was established by the Mellon Trust in 1976. The museum undertook the ambitious task of showing the world left by emigrants from Ulster during the eighteenth and nineteenth centuries, and the American world which they helped to create. As at Cultra, a central element of the display is an outdoor museum which includes vernacular buildings from both Ulster and the United States. This has presented the museum with particular problems in creating appropriate environments — how to make a county Tyrone landscape look like the New World. As at Bunratty and Cultra, the museum recognizes the importance of role play and demonstrations in enriching interpretation. Its success can be seen in its growing visitor numbers and in its being taken over as a publicly funded national museum. The museum now emphasizes its role as a centre for migration studies, and a large database has been developed which will ensure its central importance as a research institution.

The museums mentioned above are funded in a wide variety of ways. The finances of some are entirely dependent on the fund-raising efforts of local community groups and historical societies, although many of these can take advantage of grants from Europe and especially the internal resources generated by lotteries, both north and south. Local councils also fund a range of museums, including a number, such as Fermanagh County Museum, which have significant collections relating to rural life. The national museums, north and south, are funded by central government, but here there has been an ongoing drive towards increasing generated income. The security of government funding has allowed the national museums to develop infrastructures appropriate to their status, and especially the background work of storage, documentation and conservation. The Ulster Folk and Transport Museum has the largest curatorial staff dedicated to studying social life and popular culture. Individual curators have responsibility for agriculture, crafts, domestic life, maritime history, music, road and rail transport, social life and textiles. The increasing importance given to practical interpretative activities will probably lead to the employment of more practically skilled staff. The national museums also employ education and marketing officers, the latter increasing with the awareness that the museums must reach people who previously did not know what these institutions have to offer.

PRACTICAL AND THEORETICAL DEVELOPMENTS
In the early 1980s, the national museums in both the north and south of Ireland began to respond to government policies which increasingly emphasized 'performance targets' and 'value for money'. This push, with its emphasis on performance indicators, was sometimes condemned as an extreme example of the commodification of culture, but it also forced museum staff to place service to the public at the centre of strategic planning. To this extent, it marked a healthy departure from a tendency to elitist mystification within museums, which could provide a front for rather mediocre and limited outputs. The need to provide a directed programme of interpretation which fulfils the museum's educational and research roles, and at the same time enables it to perform well as a leisure and tourist amenity, led to consideration of museum display techniques. These in turn were related to a changing perception of the issues which concerned visitors to museums dealing with rural life. By the 1990s, the public's view of the countryside and of country people was, in general, no longer one of unchanging harmony. This coincided with an increasing uneasiness among researchers with the models of rural society implied by the notion of 'folk'.

The achievements of the folklife movement must, however, be properly acknowledged. Early scholars had to combat the contempt with which their learned peers often viewed anything associated with peasants. This elite contempt can be found in Gaelic texts, such as the seventeenth-century *Pairlement Chloinne Tomáis* (Williams 1981), and typified many of the writings of the Anglo-Irish ascendancy in the eighteenth and nineteenth centuries. The attitude persisted well into living memory. Estyn Evans records that, in 1932, 'in my enquiries into ... rural customs and sociology ... I got no encouragement from [The Queen's] University [Belfast]. Indeed I faced open hostility from professors who regarded "local studies" ... [as] beneath their notice' (Evans 1967, 5). Folk studies can be seen as the precursor of local histories and 'people's histories', which have rightly attempted to redress the entrenched notion that the proper concern of history is the lives of ruling minorities. The strength of vision of scholars such as Evans not only overcame this prejudice but has led to the foundation of university and museum departments which are now accepted as vital parts of the world of scholarship.

The folk movement also led to the development of research and display techniques which are still used to great effect. The fact that folklife researchers usually worked with people who were either not literate or whose lives had never been considered valuable enough to record in detail led to an emphasis on field recording. This was a precursor to the development of oral history as one of the most important sources for local historians. Folklife researchers also emphasize the importance of context. This is particularly important in studies of artefacts. In Irish rural life, the artefacts used by the poorest people were often very simple in construction. Hand tools used in tillage and harvest, for example, were often made from one, or two, pieces of wood and metal. The brilliance that underlay their construction only becomes apparent when the refinement of the techniques in which they were used are examined. An awareness of this has meant that curators exhibiting these artefacts have tended to escape the pitfall of presenting material simply as a technological or typological series. The development of outdoor museum displays has also put context at the centre of interpretation (Gailey 1986, 60). Presenting an artefact in relation to others with which it was used, in the building in which it was used, goes a long way towards showing its significance. As emphasized above, outdoor museums also allow the development of practical demonstrations and performances which are increasingly expected by museum visitors as aids to understanding. Practical experiments in the context of outdoor museums have proved valuable for research, leading to discoveries of the implications of the use of techniques for both people and the environment.

The poetic vision of early folklife researchers has to be recognized also. In part, this seems to have arisen from a particular aesthetic taste, which delighted in the use of local natural materials and handcraft techniques. Visitors to the rural area of the outdoor museum at the Ulster Folk and Transport Museum, for example, can still delight in the beautiful model of harmony between humans and nature created by this vision. Unfortunately, this vision also imposed limits on what could be studied or interpreted in displays. As with the collection of folklore, non-local material tended to be regarded as an intrusion, which to some extent spoiled the aesthetic whole. However, an examination of the dwellings in Irish outdoor folk parks, and especially of their contents, raises questions as to the adequacy of a model of rural life which accepts only the local. The houses are full of imports: sponge-ware bowls made in Scotland, cast-iron pots made in England and clocks made in the United States of America. Many of the skills and activities shown, which at first sight seem to be part of an unchanging rural cycle, use the products of heavy industry: threshing machines, cooking ranges, cast-iron mill gears. The inadequacy of the folk model of society to assist understanding of the past became very obvious to curators at the Ulster Folk and Transport Museum when the museum inherited large collections of artefacts illustrating the development of transport systems in Ireland. The models of the past provided by folk scholarship could not deal with the global, industrial culture represented by these collections.

The concepts of 'folk' and 'tradition' have to some extent become barriers rather than aids to understanding. The notion that there are people in the countryside who carry ancient knowledge and who, to some extent, live by an older wisdom, and even an older faith, is very attractive for people confronted with the uncertainties of the uncaring, impersonal world which can be represented by mass international culture. Artistically, the evocation of such a world still has enormous appeal. A programme produced by Siamsa, the National Folk Theatre in Ireland, summarizes its delight:

The entire dependence was ... on the elements ... The seasons became friends, each one bearing a different bounty, each one a welcome caller for a different reason. And bound up as they were in this elemental circus, people lived together. Nobody was any different from anybody else; the same winds blew warm or cold on each family. This led to a wonderful and human tangibility, a community, a neighbourliness, which had to find expression somehow or other. It did, in co-operation, in neighbourly interest, in the helping with harvests and the delivering of children. (Siamsa Tíre 1975, 3–4)

This is a normative view of rural life — how it should have been. However, historians know that Irish rural people, and especially those in the west, were not permitted to live in this way. The Penal Laws, the Great Famine and mass emigration meant that local ways of life were brutally disrupted. Nor is there evidence that the local people always lived in harmony when possible. Artists and writers have presented us with another vision of rural life, where gombeens bled the poor and where the poor lived in a world of faction-fights and feuds over the inheritance of land. Such a model, fortunately, is no more accurate historically than the rural idyll presented in some versions of folklife.

Categorizing some rural people as 'folk' who live by 'tradition' can be seen as belittling to both the 'folk' and their non-folk fellow citizens. The notion of people who do things because they have always been done that way suggests a group of rather uncritical people who are not so aware of the problems and opportunities presented by the modern world as the rest of us. Ireland has had a literate element in its culture for at least 1,500 years. Cultural influences from abroad have revolutionized Irish society for the entire historic period. The coming of Christianity is an obvious example. Irish cultural influence abroad has been immense during the same period. Excluding part of our population from all this ferment is not only historically untenable, it is in some sense demeaning to the people so excluded. On the other hand, people who are not categorized as 'folk', many country people from the rich farming counties of Ireland, and almost, by definition, all city dwellers, are by implication less in tune with the essential spirit of the country.

The human warmth of Irish rural society, its cultural riches of language and music and the ingenuity of its people in overcoming poverty are vital, and sometimes ancient, realities. However, these are part of history, not separate from it. The concept of folklife can obscure this. In even such a highly regarded institution as Monaghan County Museum, 'Traditional Life' is treated separately from 'Local History'. The same distinction is found at the national museum level in Northern Ireland, where the Ulster Folk and Transport Museum has been charged with dealing with 'tradition', while the Ulster Museum has a Department of Local History.

It is very doubtful whether the model of rural life implied by folklife approaches can remain satisfactory to people attempting to comprehend our history and the present state of the countryside. Few people living in our world of pollution and destruction of landscapes by intensive farming would find a model of rural society which emphasizes unchanging harmony of much relevance in helping their understanding of how things have gone so badly wrong. Museums can help in increasing appreciation of these and other issues, and here the holistic approach advocated by early folklife scholars still has great value. Our exhibitions should show the changing relationships of people with their environment and with each other. They can reveal the achievements and tragedies which these changing relationships produced, and in an area of museum work where performance and demonstration have an established place, they can also celebrate the musical and linguistic expressions of the people's experiences. In this way, folk museums can keep a place at the cutting edge of museum interpretative work.

Bibliography

Arensberg, C. M. and Kimball, S. T. 1961 *Family and community in Ireland.* Gloucester, Mass.

Evans, E. E. 1967 *The Irishness of the Irish.* Armagh.

Evans, E. E. 1992 *The personality of Ireland.* Dublin.

Gailey, A. 1986 'Creating Ulster's Folk Museum', *Ulster Folklife* **32**.

Hewitt, J. 1969 'Sunset over Glenaan', *The day of the corncrake* (Belfast).

Ó Faolain, S. 1947 'Magical Ireland' in *Countrygoer: introducing Ireland* (London).

Ó Giolláin, D. 2000 *Locating Irish folklore tradition, modernity, identity.* Cork.

Siamsa Tíre 1975 *Publicity brochure.* Finuge.

Williams, N. (ed) 1981 *Pairlement Chloinne Tomáis.* Dublin.

Young, A. 1780 *A tour in Ireland.* London.

The European Union and Heritage

VALERIE C. FLETCHER

Various interlinked points are covered in this chapter in respect of the European Union and heritage. Firstly, the origins of the European Community and its institutions are examined, paying particular attention to the Commission and explaining the regulatory framework. Secondly, the article introduces some of the information relays of the EU as well as national and other organizations involved in the provision of EU-related data. Thirdly, the paper summarizes certain funding mechanisms of relevance to the subject area of this book. Fourthly, natural and man-made and cultural heritage topics are reviewed in their own right. Issues related to the preservation of sources of information regarding the EU are addressed in conclusion. Documents of the European Union as well as journals and pamphlets which are easily read and attractively presented have been utilized in compiling the account. References to material accessible via the Internet have been incorporated within the main narrative at appropriate points.

The presentation of bibliographic information differs in this chapter from others because of the complex nature of publications relating to the EU. Where the publisher is the official publisher of the Union (discussed again below), the place of publication only (Luxembourg) is given. The acronym 'C.E.C.' denotes the 'Commission of the European Communities', on whose behalf a considerable number of publications are issued. Both the publisher and place of publication are mentioned in other instances, particularly to avoid creating the impression that the relevant titles may reflect official EU policy. A separate section on 'Journals' has been included. This largely comprises entries where an entire issue of a publication has been given over to the treatment of a particular topic, often including contributions from many authors. The Bibliography includes material not specifically cited in the text which nonetheless parallels information within the main narrative and can act as a guide to more detailed reading

in the areas in question.

The European institutional creations discussed here are unprecedented in the continent's modern history. Much of the development is experimental in nature and as such is continuously evolving. The reader should appreciate that constant innovation and transformation are a necessary part of the history of this intricate supranational and intergovernmental endeavour. It is not always possible to predict outcomes, even in the short term, and keeping up with new approaches and unfolding situations requires a persistent scrutiny of print and non-print material and media. It is hoped that the chapter will furnish a guide to the story of the past thirty years, an impression of how matters stand at present and some glimpse of trends in European affairs over the medium term. During the period of Ireland's contact with it, the EU has had a perceptible influence on Irish identity and on the physical surroundings in which we live. It is likely to continue to mould these factors in important ways in the years to come.

ORIGINS AND DEVELOPMENT OF THE EUROPEAN UNION

The Second World War ended in 1945, leaving Europe severely weakened and no longer in a central position on the world stage. France and Germany, having experienced two major wars in quick succession, had been devastated, while other countries which had been involved had also suffered severely. Europe confronted two questions: how could it be restored economically and how could it be given new political strength and stability, together with the self-respect and confidence which would prevent the re-emergence of aggressive nationalism? During the period 1947–52, various European states attempted, in differing groupings, to form bodies to create political unity, economic stability or defence cooperation. These efforts were not always successful, but the multiplicity and intensity of thought and action underlying them illustrated the profound desire for lasting peace and cooperation. The energy and creativity that had been subsumed into waging war were now devoted to the establishment of united international organizations. In a speech in Zurich in 1946, Winston Churchill declared 'We must build a United States of Europe', and this became a concept which expressed the common aspiration in a non-controversial way.

Several attempts were made to realize this goal. Firstly, in 1947, to encourage economic recovery, the United States offered Europe generous financial aid in the shape of the Marshall Plan on condition that Europe itself allocated the aid and organized the recovery. The British and French governments, together with other countries, collaborated with the US in the implementation of this European Recovery Programme, which was to put Europe back on its feet by the end of 1951. Eventually sixteen countries formed the Organization for European Economic Cooperation (OEEC) in April 1948 to ensure free trade and to distribute this assistance efficiently. A European Payments Union (EPU) was set up to help countries pay for the increased imports needed to get back on their feet. In 1960, the OEEC added development aid for the third world to its activities and evolved into the Organization for Economic Cooperation and Development (OECD). In the same year, the USA and Canada became members.

In May 1948, over 700 delegates from sixteen countries had attended a 'congress of Europe' in the Hague which called for a United Europe and, in particular, for a European Assembly, a Charter and a Court of Human Rights. These proposals were developed by the European Movement, an unofficial organization set up after the Hague Congress. They were submitted to the governments of Belgium, France, Luxembourg, the Netherlands and the United Kingdom, which had earlier formed the Brussels Treaty Organization providing for military, economic, social and cultural co-operation. In March 1949, Denmark, Ireland, Italy, Norway and Sweden were invited to help these countries prepare a constitution and on 5 May 1949, ministers from the ten countries met in London to sign the statute of the Council of Europe. There was unanimous agreement that the headquarters of the new organization should be in the French Rhineland city of Strasbourg to symbolize post-war reconciliation. The membership of the Council has since expanded to over forty states and it remains the largest political institution in Europe. The Council's aims are to work for greater European unity, to improve living conditions and human values and to uphold the principles of parliamentary democracy. Each member state had to recognize the principle of the rule of law and guarantee its citizens the enjoyment of human rights and fundamental freedoms. In addition to a Committee of Ministers, the Council of Europe has a Parliamentary Assembly made up of politicians from national parliaments in the member states. Its aims and objectives are broader and more general than those of the European Community and it does not cover defence. The emphasis is on the individual, as is clearly shown by the work of the Council's European Court of Human Rights, which is based in Strasbourg.

However, at the beginning Germany was not a member state and economic reconstruction was not part of the Council of Europe's brief, so that to meet the conditions required in these areas another solution to building up post-war Europe had to be found. In 1950, the French Foreign Minister Robert Schuman (1886–1963) read the proposals drafted by Jean Monnet (1888–1979), the French Planning Commissioner, making unification open to all European countries. The Schuman Declaration of 9 May 1950, as we know it today, was one of the most constructive acts of the twentieth century, providing a blueprint for the integration of Europe and giving the aims and methods to be used for the whole structure of European unification. It was founded on the ideal that 'we are not [only] forming a coalition between states, but a union among people'. Political discussion between governments began immediately to draft a treaty based on the principles laid down in the Declaration. It was soon accepted officially by Germany and Italy, as well as Belgium, the Netherlands and Luxembourg (the Benelux countries) and France. Even today, agreement between France and Germany is seen as the axis on which European unity is built. On 16 April 1951, the six signed the Treaty founding the European Coal and Steel Community (ECSC) known as the Treaty of Paris. (European treaties have usually been called after the location in which they are signed.) It was ratified and entered into force in July 1952, and it is interesting to note that Jean Monnet was the ECSC's first President. Thus was born the first European Community of what is now the European Union.

The six governments made an attempt at creating a European Defence Community (EDC) Treaty, but this was rejected by the French National Assembly. Instead a plan for a European Political Community was drawn up, but without the defence element this also foundered. The ECSC was, by itself, a limited attempt at economic integration, and was applied in only two industrial sectors. The ECSC foreign ministers decided in 1955 to launch a much more comprehensive proposal. The result was the Treaty of Rome, founding the European Economic Community (EEC), which was signed on 25 March 1957, ratified later that year and entered into force on 1 January 1958. The Common Market, as it was to be known, was to create a single market for all goods, services and people. Also that year, the EURATOM Treaty, called the Treaty of Rome as well, creating a European Atomic Energy Community, came into force.

In June 1961, Ireland applied for membership of the European Communities and a document was laid by the Irish government before each house of the Oireachtas on the EEC. It was concerned chiefly with Ireland's trading position and the economic considerations relating thereto, and made clear that the national interest would not be served by joining the EEC if the United Kingdom remained outside. In Europe the so-called 'Merger Treaty', the Treaty of Brussels, entered into force on 1 July 1967 and created a single Council, a single Commission and a European Assembly as the common institutions of the three Communities. A more comprehensive document on the Communities was published in Ireland in April 1967. A consultative publication on the implications of membership for Ireland was then issued in April 1970, and a statement of policy (a white paper) followed in January 1972. The 'Accession Treaty' under which Ireland, Great Britain and Denmark entered the EEC was ratified on 18 October 1972 and came into force on 1 January 1973. It should be noted that treaties of this kind are termed the primary legislation of the European Communities.

Under what conditions did these new members join? Firstly, they had to be democracies and were obliged to obey the rule of law. Secondly, they had to have the regulatory structure capable of taking on the community *acquis*. The *acquis communautaire* is the body of common rights and obligations which binds all member states together within the European Union. It relates mainly to the single market and the four freedoms inherent in it (freedom of movement for goods, persons, capital and services), the common policies which underpin it (agriculture, trade, competition, transport and others) and measures to support the least-favoured regions and sections of the population. Thirdly, aspirant members needed to be accepted unanimously by the existing member states. Up to 1973, no English-speaking (or Gaelic-speaking) country had joined, and therefore until that year most Community documents were only in the languages of the other member states. The Irish language was given a special position when this country joined. It was recognized as an official language of a member state. All primary legislation, namely treaties and conventions, are translated into it. It has been recognized for the purposes of grants by the LINGUA programme and by the Bureau of Lesser-Used Languages, based in Ireland and Brussels, both of which are examined below. However, it was agreed, uniquely at that time, that correspondence to the Dublin Office and directly to the Commission only (not the European Parliament) made in Irish should be replied to in Irish. It can be used in the Court of Justice as a working language if the plaintiff cannot understand any of the other official or working languages of the EU. If the Irish President wishes to address the European Parliament, adequate notice has to be given in advance. There is no simultaneous translation available because there are usually no Irish-language interpreters in the Parliament.

The Single European Act (SEA) of 1986 modified and extended the EEC Treaty and in particular ushered in a Single Market by providing for the removal of the barriers to free movement of goods by 1 January 1993. However, one of the biggest changes in recent years occurred when the European Union (replacing the term European Communities) came into being on the 1 November 1993 following the ratification of the Maastricht Treaty. The Treaty on European Union (TEU), as it is officially titled, was structured in three sections or 'pillars', symbolically representing a Greek temple. The three original European Communities, ECSC, EURATOM and EEC, thus constitute what is commonly called the 'first pillar' of the European Union or the 'Community' pillar, which has a high degree of integration between member states. It is in the Maastricht Treaty that culture (including heritage) was first given proper status. It is in this treaty also that the principle of 'subsidiarity' is enshrined. In general terms, this means that a higher authority may not and must not act if an objective can be achieved satisfactorily at a lower level. One consequence of subsidiarity is that it is up to the appropriate authorities at national level to select projects to be financed and also to supervise their implementation. The most recent treaty to be signed by the fifteen states of the EU came into force on the 1 May 1999, namely the Amsterdam Treaty. It was passed in 1998. It has four main objectives:

(i) to place employment and citizens' rights at the heart of the Union;

(ii) to remove the last obstacles to freedom of movement;

(iii) to give Europe a stronger voice in world affairs, and

(iv) to make the Union's institutional structure more efficient, because of the advent of a large number of new member states.

There were three further enlargements in the years after 1973. Greece joined the European Communities on 1 January 1981, followed by Spain and Portugal together on 1 January 1986, bringing the number of member states to twelve. No formal accession was required when in October 1990 the former German Democratic Republic was integrated with Germany. Three countries, Austria, Finland and Sweden, became members of what is now the European Union on 1 January 1995, bringing the total to fifteen. It is to be emphasized that any amendment to the treaties (including enlargement of membership) must be by unanimous agreement. Some of the most interesting and demanding stages of enlargement are currently in prospect, involving ten Central and Eastern European countries which have what are called 'Association Agreements' with the EU, as do Turkey, Cyprus and Malta. These agreements are a prerequisite to full membership. At the Copenhagen European Council (June 1993), not only was the approval in principle agreed to embrace the associated countries of Central and Eastern Europe, but also the criteria which applicants would have to meet before they could join were defined. These include

(i) the stability of institutions guaranteeing democracy, the rule of law, human rights and respect for minorities (political criterion);

(ii) the existence of a functioning market economy as well as the capacity to cope with competitive pressure and market forces within the European Union (economic criterion);

(iii) the ability to take on the obligations of membership, including adherence to the aims of political, economic and monetary union (the 'community *acquis*' criterion).

In this connection one should note that the European Commission (to be discussed later) published *Agenda 2000* on 16 July 1997. This policy document looks at

(i) the future of the main areas of Community policy;

(ii) the European Union's financial profile for the period 2000–06, and

(iii) the Union's enlargement.

Of the ten applications from Central and Eastern Europe, the Commission decided to start negotiations with five, the Czech Republic, Estonia, Hungary, Poland and Slovenia. The situation of other countries would be reviewed annually. In 1997, Cyprus was added together with the other five, Bulgaria, Latvia, Lithuania, Romania and Slovakia. The accession of these new countries, each with its own culture, heritage and, in some cases, language, will have a huge impact and create further diversity in this aspect of the Union's policy.

THE COMMISSION

As we saw when discussing the origins of the European Communities, the 'Merger Treaty' effectively fused the higher executives of the original three Communities to create a single Commission. What is the Commission? It is a corporate body of approximately 16,000 people, consisting of a President, at present twenty Commissioners, over twenty Directorates-General (DGs) plus another dozen or so specialized Services, based in

Brussels. About one-fifth of the Commission's staff work in the translation and interpretation services. Each DG is headed by a Director General, who is equivalent in rank to the top civil servant in a government ministry. The Directors General report to Commissioners, each of whom has the political and operational responsibility for one or more DGs. The Commissioners are chosen by their national governments. They are usually people who have held senior posts in their own countries, or have sat in their national parliaments or in the European Parliament before coming to Brussels. Of the twenty Commissioners, two at present come from each of the large member states (Germany, Spain, France, Italy and the United Kingdom) and one each from the smaller ones (Belgium, Denmark, Greece, Ireland, Luxembourg, the Netherlands, Austria, Portugal, Finland and Sweden). They normally enjoy a five-year mandate and had been due to stay in office until 2000, but because of the conclusions of the report on fraud, mismanagement and nepotism by the Committee of Independent Experts, set up in January 1999, the then Commission decided on the dramatic night of 15 March 1999 to resign *en bloc*. A new President has since been selected, Romano Prodi from Italy, and the twenty new Commissioners were appointed and accepted by the European Parliament on 15 September 1999. A radical reorganization of Directorates-General and Services also took place around this time (**Table 46.1**). This chapter reflects the new administrative structures, but also refers — to ensure comprehensiveness of coverage — to their predecessors (**Table 46.2**), which were distinguished from each other by being numbered as well as named (the reconstituted DGs have not been assigned numbers).

Before taking up office, each Commissioner has to take an oath of independence, distancing himself or herself from partisan influence from any source. They are charged to act in 'the general interest of the Community' and are to be completely independent in the performance of their duties. The feasibility of each country having is own Commissioner is at present under scrutiny as part of the proposals for institutional reform. The Commission represents the common interest of the Union's 370 million citizens and embodies to a large degree the personality of the Union. Each Commissioner has a private office, called a *cabinet*, with six to eight senior advisors (officials chosen by the Commissioner) and some support staff. Their role is to assist the Commissioner and serve as a bridge between him or her and the DGs, and also between him and political interests, consumers, trade unions, businesses and lobbying groups. They brief the Commissioner on policy papers, are his/her eyes and ears, draft proposals prepared by other Commissioners and are headed by the *chef de cabinet*. The work of the Commissioners is coordinated by the Secretariat General. The Commission

Table 46.I Services and Directorates-General (DG) of the European Commission (after September 1999)

GENERAL SERVICES	POLICIES	EXTERNAL RELATIONS	INTERNAL SERVICES
EUROSTAT	Agriculture	Common Service for External Relations	Budget
Publications Office	Health and Consumer Protection	External Relation	Joint Interpreting and Conferencing
Press and Communications	Competition	Development	European Anti-Fraud Office
Secretariat General	Information Society	Humanitarian Aid Office-ECHO	Legal Service
	Economic and Financial Affairs	Enlargement	Finanacial Control
	Internal Market	Trade	Personnel and Administration
	Education and Culture		Inspectorate General
	Joint Research Centre		Translation Service
	Employment and Social Affairs		
	Justice and Home Affairs		
	Energy and Transport		
	Regional Policy		
	Enterprise		
	Research		
	Environment		
	Taxation and Customs Union		
	Fisheries		

© **European Commission** Source: *http://www.europa.eu.int/comm/dgs/_en.htm*

interacts closely with the other institutions of the EU, particularly the European Parliament and the Court of Justice, but also, obviously, with the Council of Ministers (of which more shortly). The Committee of Permanent Representatives (COREPER) are the ambassadors of the member countries to the EU. They also have an important advisory role in the preparation of legislation. The Economic and Social Committee and the Committee of the Regions are also advisory bodies in this process. The President of the Commission is chosen by the EU heads of state or government meeting in the European Council, but the choice has to be endorsed by the European Parliament which also subjects prospective Commissioners to parliamentary approval by means of an individual vote of investiture before they can take office.

The Commission fulfils three main functions:
(i) It is the sole institution with right to make *proposals* for all new legislation (that is to say, it has the 'right of initiative'). However, under certain circumstances, member states (or a member state) may make proposals on their own initiative (see Article 67 of the EC Treaty as amended by Amsterdam Treaty). The Commission must do so by balancing the interests of the EU as a whole rather than those of individual countries or sectoral parties. It must take the principle of 'subsidiarity' into account. Decisions on legislation, however, are taken by the Council and the Parliament.
(ii) The Commission acts as guardian of the treaties to ensure that EU legislation is applied correctly. It takes action against those in the public or private sectors who

fail to respect and implement their treaty obligations. For instance, it can institute legal proceedings against member states or private individuals who do not introduce EU Directives (dealt with separately below), bringing them before the European Court of Justice.

(iii) As the executive body of the EU, the Commission administers policies and negotiates international trade and cooperation agreements with outside countries and groups of countries on behalf of the Union. It manages the annual budget and runs the Structural Funds (also discussed in what follows). The Commission is represented at both the European Parliament and at the Council of the European Communities. The Commission is an administrative machine, as can be seen from the structure of its DGs and Services. As stated above, one-fifth of its staff work from the translation and interpretation services. The Union has at present eleven official languages and, as the laws adopted in Brussels are often directly applicable in the member states, texts must be available to citizens in their own vernaculars.

The Council of the European Union (sometimes referred to as the Council of Ministers) is the institution in which the member states *negotiate* and *adopt* community legislation; it is 'the decision-maker'. Unlike the Commission, each member state in the Council has one representative for its country, the minister in that country who represents the area under discussion. Depending on the subject and the provisions of the Treaty under which it falls, the Council decides, voting by qualified majority or unanimity. The Amsterdam Treaty

Table 46.2 Services and Directorates-General of the European Commission (to September 1999)

SECRETARIAT-GENERAL

FORWARD STUDIES UNIT

INSPECTORATE-GENERAL

LEGAL SERVICE

SPOKESMAN'S SERVICE

JOINT INTERPRETING AND CONFERENCE SERVICE

STATISTICAL OFFICE

TRANSLATION SERVICE

INFORMATICS DIRECTORATE

DG I	External Relations: Commercial Policy and Relations with North America, the Far East, Australia and New Zeland
DG IA	External Relations: Europe and the New Independent States, Common Foreign and Security Policy and External Missions
DG IB	External Relations: Southern Mediterranean, Middle and Near East, Latin America, South and South-East Asia and North-South Cooperation
DG II	Economic and Financial Affairs
DG III	Industry
DG IV	Competition
DG V	Employment, Industrial Relations and Social Affairs
DG VI	Agriculture
SCR	Joint Service for the Management of Community Aids to Non-Member Countries/Service commun des relations extérieurs
DG IX	Personnel and Administration
DG X	Information, Communication, Culture, Audiovisual
DG XI	Environment, Nuclear Safety and Civil Protection
DG XII	Science, Research and Development Joint Research Centre
DG XIII	Telecommunications, Information Market and Exploitation of Research
DG XIV	Fisheries
DG XV	Internal Market and Financial Services
DG XVI	Regional Policies and Cohesion
DG XVII	Energy
DG XIX	Budgets
DG XXI	Taxation and Customs Union
DG XXII	Education, Training and Youth
DG XXIII	Enterprise Policy, Distributive Trades, Tourism and Cooperatives
DG XXIV	Consumer Policy and Consumer Health Protection

European Community Humanitarian Office

Task Force for the Accession Negotiations (TFAN)

EURATOM Supply Agency

Office for Official Publications of the European Communities

© **European Commission** Source: *http://www.europa.eu.int/comm/archives/dgs/_en.htm*

was supposed to contain proposals for changing this one minister/one country representation, in light of enlargement, but this remains a nettle still to be grasped. The Presidency of the Council is assumed by each member country for a period of six months, January to June or July to December. The country concerned chairs all important meetings and has the responsibility of ensuring that the programme and agenda it sets for that six months are negotiated and carried out to the highest possible standard. In 1999, Germany and Finland respectively held the Presidency. In the year 2000, Portugal and France in that order were the holders.

The European Council or summit of the heads of state or government of the European Union provides the Union with the necessary impetus for its development and defines general political guidelines for it. These summits are usually held at least twice a year (in the final month of a Presidency), and are named after the city in which they take place. The leaders discuss matters of prime importance directly with each other, and all the Community institutions must follow the conclusions which they reach. The President of the Commission is *ex officio* a member of this body. The Council is assisted by foreign affairs ministers of the member states and by one other member of the Commission. They usually meet in the country holding the Presidency.

EU LEGISLATION

To understand the workings of the EU, one must be aware of its different kinds of legislation and have at least a summary appreciation of the processes involved in its implementation. The type of legislation at issue in this sub-section comes in four forms. *Regulations* apply to and are binding on all member countries as soon as they are adopted by the Community. They are uniform in content (unless exceptions are made by introducing a special one for a particular country) and are directly applicable without the need for additional national implementing measures. They supersede national law. Regulations often contain diagrams, charts or tables in their annexes, and are cited by Regulation number first and year second. Thousands of these are produced and brought into force in any one calendar year in subjects as diverse as transport, internal market, business, pollution, trade, food and drink, emergency signs and so forth. An example is Commission Regulation (EC) No. 2473/98 of 16 November 1998 suspending the introduction into the Community of specimens of certain species of wild fauna and flora (*Official Journal [OJ] L* 308, 18.11.1998, p. 18). *Directives* set objectives, but it is up to the member states to apply them at national level. They are binding on the member states in terms of the result to be achieved, but leave to them the choice of form or means to be used. When checking Directives, it is necessary to be aware that a country may have added national legis-

lation which is binding as well as the Directive, so it is imperative to verify both of these at the same time. Directives are cited by year first and by number second. Usually hundreds of these are produced per year. An example is Council Directive 85/337/EEC of 27 June 1985 on the assessment of the effects of certain public and private projects on the environment (*OJ L* 175, 5.7.1985, p. 40). Directives can be amended by a later Directive, as in this case, so the enquirer must check that he/she has the most recent Directive in force. *Decisions* address specific issues and are binding in all respects on those to whom they are addressed. A Decision can thus be addressed to any or all member states, businesses or even individuals. Decisions are cited like Directives, year first and number second, for example 93/389/EEC Council Decision of 24 June 1993 for a monitoring mechanism of Community CO_2 and other greenhouse gas emissions (*OJ L* 167, 9.7.1993, p. 31). They do not need national implementing measures. A Directive and a Decision, however, can have the same number and the same year, yet be about totally different subjects and addressed to different countries or people, so it is wise to check these references carefully to make sure they are accurate. *Recommendations* and *Opinions* are instruments with no binding legal effect. They simply indicate the institutions' position on a given subject. *Common Positions* are also not binding; they are the Council's bargaining statement before the second reading of measures proposed in the European Parliament, taking account of the changes suggested in the first reading. *European Parliament Decisions* are not binding on a given subject. *Resolutions* give general policy on a subject, which are not always followed by legislation and are often promises to do something, which may not always be fulfilled. Regulations, Directives and Decisions are called secondary legislation (and are normally published in the *Official Journal of the European Communities L* Series) because, as we saw above, treaties are the foundational primary legislation of the Union. Lists of them in numerical and alphabetical order appear in the annual *Index to the Official Journal of the European Communities, alphabetical index and methodological table*. Proposals for legislation usually come out as Commission Documents (hereafter abbreviated as COM Documents). These are issued separately, with their own numbering sequence. They also appear as part of the *Official Journal C*, but this version does not contain the 'explanatory memorandum', usually a statement of scope and purpose contained in the COM Document itself. It is wiser, unless specifically requested otherwise, to consult, refer to and produce the full version. Annual reports, white papers (statements of official policy) and green papers (discussion documents), together with communications from the Commission (and sometimes other advisory bodies) can, but do not always, appear as Commission Documents.

INFORMATION

We now consider some of the European Union institutions, organizations, agencies and other bodies and sources which make information available, with particular reference to those based in the Republic of Ireland. The Commission has treaty obligations to inform the public of its activities by Article 55 of the Treaty of Paris (ECSC) and Article 2 of the Treaty of Rome (EURATOM). All major EU policies can be traced back to specific articles or ideas expressed in the Treaties. The European Union produces a prodigious amount of information on its central website (*http://www. europa.eu. int/*): presentation and portfolios of the new Commission, work programmes, a history of the EU, links to information sources, databases, European Community legislation, governments on-line and the sites of the other institutions of the EU. The Scadplus site of the Commission, which has linked information sources on its homepage, gives access to information on a number of key policies of the European Union. The Scad database (*http://www.europa.eu.int/scad/en-warn.htm*), a simple free subject, title, domain or author search giving access to bibliographical references in over 3,000 journal titles, is an excellent resource. Links are also provided to the various information bodies which the EU has set up in the different member states. In 1978, the Central Library of the European Commission was computerized, leading to the development of the database called the European Commission Library Automated System (ECLAS). It covers the Union's official publications and documentation as well publications and documents of many intergovernmental organizations, commercial, academic and government presses, and selected journal articles of lasting interest. It was made available to the public shortly after its inception and can be accessed on the Internet (*http://www.europa.eu.int.eclas*). This multilingual database is updated weekly.

It was originally up to each of the EU institutions to make decisions about its publications policy. The cost of publications was charged to these specific institutions. The Secretariat did this for the Commission, both of which were based in Brussels. The Office for Official Publications (now known as EUR-OP), established in 1969, is to be found in Luxembourg (*http://www.eur-op.eu.int/*). It is a specialized service of the Commission and is the Union's official publisher. As such, it must meet the challenge which now exists of publishing EU publications in the eleven official languages, and prepare for the new languages which will become official during the enlargement process. EURODICAUTOM is the multilingual terminological database of the European Commission's Translation Service. Initially developed to assist in-house translators, it is today consulted by an increasing number of other EU officials as well as by language professionals, thanks to the MLIS (Multilingual Information Society) Project formerly monitored by DG XIII. The information it contains is drafted in twelve languages and is constantly updated. It covers a broad spectrum of human knowledge, although the core relates to EU topics. It can be accessed via the Europa site.

Throughout the history of the Community, the European Commission has had a particular leadership responsibility to provide information relating to European integration and the working of the Community's unique pattern of decision-making. It set up its own press office for this purpose. The Spokesman's Service (SSP) is in charge of the Commission's relations with the press. Some 900 journalists are accredited to the Commission in Brussels and a daily bilingual briefing in French and English is held at noon. A formal press conference in the Commission's eleven official languages takes place following its regular mid-week meeting. Formal press conferences are broadcast live on 'Europe by Satellite'. The full texts of the press releases are published by the Commission's spokesman and are accessible in eleven languages in a special database named RAPID (*http://www.europa.eu.int/rapid/start/welcome.htm*). A summary of the most important releases is available on the Europa site under Midday Express, covering the most significant news items in the previous twenty-four hours (*http://www.europa.eu.int/rapid/start/midday*). These can be in French or English and are excellent brief sources of current information. Links with the most important of these are also provided (*http://www.europa.eu.int/news-en.htm*).

The Council of the European Communities is the decision-maker on legislation, and it is important to be aware of any recent information available relating to it. Information on the current Presidency of the Council is always to be found on its website (*http://www.ue.eu.int/en/summ.htm*). The European Parliament (EP) provides its information on the Internet also (*http://www.europarl.eu*). The progress of legislation database (L'OEIL) lists EP Information Offices, parliamentary questions, Members of the European Parliament (MEPs) and political parties. All these and other sites can be accessed using the Europa site as a gateway. When searching for individuals or the hierarchical structure of employees in the institutions of the EU, the IDEA database, updated fortnightly (*http://europa.eu.int/idea/ideaen.html*), is the appropriate source. The annual official *Interinstitutional directory* lists all the main institutions, Directorates-General and organizations under the EU's aegis, giving addresses, websites, fax numbers, heads of sections and so forth. At times of significant change of personnel, the official electronic sources are usually the most up-to-date.

EUROSTAT is the official statistical office of the European Communities. It was established in 1953 and is based in Brussels. Its mission is to provide the European Union with a high-quality statistics information service. It uses uniform rules to collect all statistical data from the National Statistical Institutes (NSIs) of each of the fifteen member states of the European Union. Up to 1989, EUROSTAT supplied the major information relays with a wide variety of statistical material which encompassed the following subject areas: general statistics, social and economic statistics, industry and energy, agriculture, trade, transport, services, environment and statistical investigations. Since 1990, most of the extensive journal runs have been replaced by two editions of some of the statistics in CD-ROM format. The data shop in Brussels accepts requests for information made by letter or via e-mail. Details of the publications and services including electronic services it offers are available on its website, found under Information Sources on the Europa site. EUROSTAT has a particularly significant input into the Structural Funds decisions, discussed in the section on funding below. The NSI for the Republic of Ireland is the Central Statistics Office, based in Dublin and Cork, which provides links to the official statistical organizations of other EU member countries on its website (*http://www.cso.ie*). It issues a wide variety of statistical information, as can be seen from its annual publication *Guide to CSO publications and information services* and also the *Statistical abstract of Ireland*. National and international sites do not necessarily provide anything more than very recent statistics on subjects that are usually of wide public or economic interest. It is well to note too that statistics are not always uniformly available, even in EU countries, or to one's own specific requirements, so that in the case of information produced by national or international statistical organizations, it is always wise to check with one's national statistical office, information relay or national representation, as appropriate.

As each member state joins, the EU opens an Office or Representation, usually in its capital city. These delegations play the following role:

(i) representing the Commission in the member state;

(ii) promoting the Union's policies;

(iii) developing relations between the Commission and its political and special interest partners, including the media, and meeting public information needs relating to the Community.

The Commission Representation in the Republic of Ireland is at European Union House, Dublin, which has a European Public Information Centre (EPIC) (*http://www. euireland.ie*). The European Commission has for many years disseminated its published information through a number of designated information agencies, targeted to different audiences. These are often referred to by the Commission as 'information relays'. The Representations in member states refer a wide range of inquiries to the general and special information relays with which they have close partnership, which will be mentioned later in this section. These relays have the advantage of being readily accessible to the inquirer, and can provide information locally. A list of Irish relays os on the Irish Representation site, while EU relays can be found at *http://www.europa.eu.int/comm/dg10/relays/all_lang/*.

Before exploring these, the existence must be noted of two EU Depository Libraries in the Republic of Ireland: the Oireachtas Library (available only to the members of the Oireachtas) and the National Library of Ireland, both in Kildare Street, Dublin. Depository Libraries are usually national repositories of material published and printed in the state to which they belong, and provide (under certain conditions) access for the public to the documents and collections which they hold. Their most important function from the point of view of our study is that as EU depositories, they retain, conserve and preserve the material deposited with them *ad infinitum*, and since national depositories are entitled to more extensive EU information than any of the other information providers mentioned below, they are an invaluable resource for ourselves and our legislature. They are a national and international resource of inestimable value, a point which becomes very obvious in times of extreme national unrest when irreplaceable material can be, and often has been, destroyed for ever.

European Documentation Centres (EDCs) were established from 1963 onwards and are usually located in universities. Their aims are to help universities promote and consolidate their teaching and research on European policies and the process of European integration. EDCs are available to lecturers, researchers and students as well as all other accredited users of the university library. They provide limited access and consultation to the public. They hold a wide range of EU books and journals, provided and distributed by the Union free of charge, which individual EDCs supplement with CDs and commercially produced back-up material according to their needs. They are often, but not always, under the remit of the librarian dealing with Official Publications or Law. EDCs hold comprehensive sets of the *Official Journal L* and *C* Series, debates of the European Parliament and European Court of Justice cases. There is now a move to produce and distribute the Official Journals in CD-ROM format only. The EDC network has been established in both member and non-member states on a world-wide basis to make available for consultation, as widely as possible, comprehensive, well-managed collections of EU official publications. There are currently over 500 centres, mainly in universities, 313 of which are in member states. The five EDCs in the Republic of Ireland are at the University of Limerick, Trinity College, Dublin, the National University of Ireland at Cork, Dublin and Galway and a partial EDC at NUI Maynooth. They participate in an electronic bulletin board restricted to EDC librarians and EU staff, entitled *Eurodoc*, through which information relevant to EDCs is circulated. This network, instigated by Richard Caddel, former EDC Librarian of the University of Durham, is of particular assistance to EDCs worldwide. The EDCs come under the remit of the Education and Culture Directorate-General (formerly DG X, Unit X, A 6, Libraries and European Documentation Centres).

Innovation Relay Centres (IRCs) are advisory offices located in fifty European regions. Their goals are to promote innovation, to encourage the exchange of research results throughout Europe and to promote advice, consultancy and training support to meet the specific needs of companies in their region. IRCs are primarily devoted to helping companies, although universities and research institutes may also benefit from their services for transferring results to industry. A team of professionals staffs each Centre. In the Republic of Ireland, this role is fulfilled by Enterprise Ireland (*http://www.enterprise-ireland.com*). The Rural Information and Promotion Carrefours were set up to bring information on the EU into rural communities. They are available to individuals, local and regional authorities, economic operators, non-profit associations and public-interest organizations. They are located within pre-existing agencies which have experience in rural development. They play an active part in the economic and social life of their area, produce newsletters and magazines, work with schools, media and other associations, organize symposia to allow various local partners to meet and help project promoters to prepare their funding applications. They operate as part of a network. 114 of them are distributed across Europe. In Ireland there are three: Carrefour Galway (*http://www.ucg.ie/ecn/carrefour*), Carrefour South-West Rural Ireland (*http://www.kerrygems.ie/carrefour/*) and Carrefour South-East Ireland (*http//www.amireland.com/waterfor/*).

Urban Forums for Sustainable Development are designed for people living in towns, public authorities, businesses and non-profit organizations. They keep these bodies informed about all the decisions and practices which make for better management of the urban environment. They help to promote the EU's strategy for sustainable development and provide the information on the Union's environment policy decisions and measures, as well as the implementation of these in national law. They are active in the town in

which they are situated, provide a consultation service and most carry out specific experiments. There are 34 in Ireland, under the responsibility of Local Development Boards. Europe Info Centres form a network which provides specialized information, advice and assistance to Small- and Medium-Sized Enterprises (SMEs) in all Community matters. Totalling 275, they are to be found throughout the European Economic Area. The network is represented by nineteen Correspondence Centres (EICCS) in Central and Eastern European countries as well as in the Mediterranean area. They are under the remit of the Enterprise Directorate-General (formerly DG XXIII). There are seven Centres in Ireland, based in Athlone, Cork, Dublin, Galway, Limerick, Sligo and Waterford. Euro Info Points (EIPs) are established within facilities which are visited frequently, for instance national or community facilities and so forth. They provide information to the general public. Ireland has three, in Dundalk, Mullingar and Athlone, but there are over thirty-two centres in EU countries. EIPs provide general information on the EU and direct specific queries to the appropriate sources. They distribute publications of general interest concerning all Community policies, make available for consultation various official publications (*OJ L* and *C* Series and reference works), present videos on certain policies and provide a question-and-answer service.

The Information Centres on Europe are set up by a joint initiative of the Commission and the national government of a member state to keep the general public informed, respond to requests for information from special interest groups and to provide a permanent forum for meetings, training and other events relating to Europe. They are located in capital cities and formerly came under the remit of DG X. Three have been established, namely 'Sources d'Europe' in Paris, the Jacques Delors in Lisbon and the Berlin Information Centre at Jean Monnet House in that city, but there is none yet in Ireland. The European Consumer Infocentres (Euroguichets) were established after a pilot phase in 1991; these were previously under DG XXIV, co-financed by the European Commission, and were originally set up for a five-year duration. There is one Centre in each of the following cities: Barcelona, Bolzano, Gronau, Kiel, Lille, London, Luxembourg, Vienna, Vittorio and Dublin (*http://www.ecic.ie*). These Centres provide advice to people who face difficulties linked to the completion of the Single Market. They distribute information on legislation and case-law both at European and member-state level and foster cross-border studies. They assist and advise on mediation and information concerning procedures, and provide a first point of reference for legal aid as well as approaches to local authorities. There is at least one Centre per member state and an additional Centre in countries characterized by major linguistic and cultural differences.

As stated at the outset of this section, the EU itself and its information relays are only some of the many sources to which we go to seek European Union data. Official facts are now well supplied by governments, and the Irish government website (*http:www.irlgov.ie*) has, in its many departmental areas, a great deal of information on the Union and how its policies and programmes are implemented and regulated. Press releases and statements are liberally provided, and many departments have lists of their recent publications on their web pages. One should also investigate the links which these pages give. The Irish government has supported the centre entitled the Economic and Social Research Institute (ESRI) (*http://www.esri.ie*), founded in 1960. It publishes a *Quarterly Economic Commentary*, the journal *Economic and Social Review* and a *Medium-Term Economic Review*. The ESRI also issues research projects undertaken by its staff in its *General Research Series*, *Broadsheet Series* and *Policy Research Series*, some of these being of direct interest to those studying European Union matters. The National Economic and Social Council (NESC) (*http://www.nesc.ie*) was established in 1973 and is based in Dublin. Its main task is to provide a forum for discussion of the principles relating to the efficient development of the national economy and the achievement of social justice, and to advise the government, through An Taoiseach, on the applications of these principles. NESC reports are produced in the areas of industrial policy, agricultural policy and social services priorities; they are submitted to government, laid before each house of the Oireachtas and then published. Some reports have direct relevance to EU policies, and membership of the Council includes an observer from the European Union.

Turning to voluntary organizations, the European Movement (Irish Council) (*http://www.european-movement.ie*), based in Dublin, was formed in 1954 and has produced timely publications to explain current developments in the EU for the general public. The Movement has three main functions: it acts as an umbrella group for all political parties and socio-economic entities which support European unification. It functions as a lobbying organization which presents its views on important issues affecting Ireland's future in Europe to government, and provides a forum for debate and discussion at national and regional level. It is also a campaigning body, seeking to bring information on the European Union to the public. It has produced several important publications to inform readers in a comprehensive way on current matters of national and EU significance, and issues a newsheet entitled *Europe Newsline*. It organizes regional seminars on a regular basis on specialized topics, as well as providing courses of instruction with the aim of promoting peace and prosperity in Europe by means of an ever-closer union. The Institute for European Affairs (IEA) (*http://www.iiea.com/*) is located at European House in Dublin. It is an independent, self-governing body which promotes the advancement and spread of knowledge on the process of European integration and on the role and contribution of Ireland within Europe. Its main aim is to provide objective analysis of the key political, economic, social and cultural issues for those charged with representing Irish views within the European policy-making structures. It facilitates policy discussion, assembles information on important topics and disseminates research results. The IEA produces the quarterly journal *European Document Series*, which reproduces contemporary and historic European Union documentation, *IEA News*, research papers, interim and final reports, seminar reports and occasional papers on subjects of EU interest, among which *A European cultural identity: myth, reality or aspiration?* (Tonra and Dunne 1997) is of particular relevance to this book.

The European Information Association (EIA) in Great Britain has a very informative website (*http://www.eia.org.uk*) and produces a journal, *European Information*, written and edited by practitioners (usually librarians and documentalists) in the EU or by related information professionals. Its origins are described in the January 1997 issue of its journal *EIA Review*, the forerunner of *European Information*. It also runs courses on various aspects of EU policies, legislative and electronic sources and services, and reviews new publications and services, including those provided by the European Union.

The European Bureau of Library Information and Documentation Associations (EBLIDA) is based in the Hague (*http://www.eblida.org/about.htm*). It produces a journal entitled *Information Europe* and several frequently published newsheets. Subjects which the journal covers comprise copyright, conferences, culture, telematics, Central and Eastern Europe and so forth. The bibliographic journal *European Access*, produced six times a year, provides detailed information on EU sources, covering books, journals, bibliographic snapshots of specialized areas, funding and electronic data. It also contains a chronology of events and review articles of topical EU interest. Each issue lists useful addresses as well as sources of EU information in Great Britain and Ireland.

An electronic service called European Access Plus (*http://www.europeanaccess.co.uk*) provides even more detailed information and bibliographic snap-shots, but this has now become subscription-based. Eurotext (*http://eurotext.ulst.ac.uk*) is another new electronic service; it offers a resource bank of the full text of early or difficult to trace EU policy documents, but again has also recently become subscription-based.

FUNDING: AN OVERVIEW

In order to understand how heritage or, for that matter, any of the sectoral areas have been advanced in the European Union, it is important to have some appreciation of the policies, structures and major funding mechanisms which the EU has adopted and implemented. Funding, of course, in an essentially practical way creates the dynamic and systematic foundation on which successful projects are promoted. Co-operative and parallel evolution in many different subject areas is vital if balanced development is to be achieved. Resources are targeted at actions which help to bridge economic gaps and which promote equal employment opportunities between the more and the less developed regions and between social groups, according to certain priority objectives.

EARLY FUNDING SCHEMES

The first funding mechanism to be set up was the ECSC in 1951, which was to support the coal and steel industries in the European Community after the damage wrought by the recent war. In 1958, the European Agriculture Guidance and Guarantee Fund (EAGGF) Guidance Section was initiated. The early policy embodied a set of measures aimed at making lasting improvements to agricultural production and processing mechanisms. In the establishment of the EAGGF, part of its mandate was to finance structural modifications required for the proper working of the common market. The policy for the modernization of agricultural structures was thus conceived of as a necessary concomitant of market policy and therefore vital to its functioning. It is from this usage that the concept of Structural Funds in the sense that we now understand it would gradually evolve.

The financing of these structural actions was to correspond as far as possible to one-third of the amount fixed for EAGGF. The idea of a programming framework, containing individual projects, was there from the start (Regulation [EEC] 25/62). The objective of the Guarantee Section is to stabilize the prices of Community products using mechanisms which provide the community preference (import levies), outlets on external markets (export aids, called 'refunds') and price supports provided by national intervention agencies which store or sell products when prices fall. These mechanisms are managed by national government departments (for instance, agriculture or fisheries) and intervention agencies for each sector. In 1964, a distinction between the EAGGF Guarantee and Guidance sections was introduced (Regulation [EEC] 17/64) and clearly delineated the latter's field of intervention. The Guidance Fund's brief was to finance the adaptation and improvement of

(i) the production structures of agricultural holdings, and

(ii) the structures and conditions for processing and marketing agricultural products.

The Guidance Fund support was given for individual, public or private projects. Requests were made by the end beneficiary and channelled through national authorities to the EEC Commission. The principle that these public and private projects should support the programming framework, however, was not fully implemented for some time. The Community's structure's policy became more evident in 1971 when it was agreed that the Guidance Section could be used to promote the construction and modernization of inshore and middle-water fishing vessels, for example. In 1978, this was replaced by a series of annual interim packages of wider scope. By 1981, this scheme had received 1,052 applications for aid to construct fishing vessels and 123 applications for fish farming, nearly three times the aid available. The assistance tended to be in coastal areas where the local population was heavily dependent on fishing, principally Scotland, Southern Italy, Greece, Ireland, Northern Ireland, Brittany and Greenland. Since the 1992 reform of agricultural policy, the Guarantee Section has been funding measures to slow down the increase in production, setting aside land, promoting afforestation of agricultural land and early retirement (Regulations (EEC) 2078/92, 2079/92, and 2080/92; *OJ L* 215, 30.7.1992). There are also specific projects for promoting products, some managed directly by the Commission, others by national governments. The scheme now aids the adjustment of agricultural structures and rural development measures supporting farmers, producers and, of particular interest to us, the development of rural infrastructure, village renewal, the protection of rural heritage, the development and exploitation of woodland and the protection of the environment and countryside. The EAGGF Guidance Section is managed by the European Commission's Directorate General for Agriculture (formerly numbered DG VI) and in Ireland by the Department of Agriculture, Fisheries and Food.

Related to the foregoing, although somewhat later in time, is the Financial Instrument for Fisheries Guidance (FIFG), which dates from 1983. This assists structural measures in that sector, including fish farming, promotion of products, fish processing, modernization of fleet and landing areas, aquaculture, marketing, protection of some marine areas and the development of ports. Its legal foundation is Council Regulation (EC) No. 3699/93 (*OJ L* 346, 31.12.1993). The task of FIFG is to help the fisheries sector solve the problem of over-capacity within the Community fleet, to improve the structures of the European fishing and aquaculture industry and to enhance its international competitiveness. In Ireland, the sea-fishing, aquaculture and processing industries are vitally important for coastal regions, supporting the employment of nearly 16,000 people. The Common Fisheries Policy (CFP) is at the core of the European Community initiative in this area. It is managed by the European Commission's Directorate General for Fisheries (formerly DG XIV), and in Ireland by the Department of the Marine and Natural Resources.

In 1975, following the first enlargement of the Community, the European Regional Development Fund (ERDF) was established. It introduced the concept of redistributing resources between the rich and poor regions of the Community. Its assistance is limited to less-favoured or less-developed areas and is focussed mainly on productive investment, infrastructure and development. In Ireland, we have seen huge investment in infrastructure in particular. There is also investment in education and health linked to the environment. The Fund concentrated assistance on four priority objectives corresponding to four kinds of regions:

Objective 1, regions whose development was lagging behind;

Objective 2, converting regions or parts of regions seriously affected by industrial decline;

Objective 5b, facilitating the development and structural adjustment of rural areas, and

Objective 6, development and structural adjustment of regions with extremely low population density. Lists of these areas are given in the DG XVI website (*http: //www.inforegio.cec.eu.int/*). (The Inforegio database gives up-to-date information on projects and programmes supported by the ERDF and the Cohesion Fund, the latter to be discussed shortly.)

The Regional Policy Directorate-General (formerly DG XVI) is responsible for Community action to promote economic and social cohesion aimed at reducing the gaps in socio-economic development between the different regions of the European Union. Its work is focused on the management of the two major funds which give financial assistance to the programmes and projects in the more disadvantaged regions of the Union, ERDF and, as discussed below, the Cohesion Fund. Funding comes in the form of non-reimbursable assistance, as opposed to the repayable loans that are available from the European Investment Bank (EIB). The financial assistance is channelled through development programmes, which are packages of measures eligible for support. Between 1981 and 1982, for instance, this fund granted ECU (the European monetary unit of account) 9.5 million to fishing projects involving harbour improvements, processing factories and research

centres. The European Social Fund (ESF), established in 1958, was formerly managed by the European Commission's Directorate-General for Employment, Industrial Relations and Social Affairs (DG V), the DG most recently the responsibility of the Irish Commissioner, Padraig Flynn, up to mid-1999 (now entitled Employment and Social Affairs), and in Ireland by the Department of Enterprise, Trade and Employment. ESF concentrates on vocational training and employment aids, occupational integration of those searching for employment, equal opportunities, adaptation to industrial change, strengthening human resource development in research, science and technology and strengthening education and training systems (*http: //www.inforegio.cec.eu.int/*). Funding is granted in different kinds of geographical regions which correspond to criteria set up by the European Community assisted by figures supplied by EUROSTAT. Taking once more an area already mentioned under various other funding headings, in the fishing sector, the Social Fund has financed training programmes for fish farms in Ireland and Scotland.

STRUCTURAL FUNDING AND THE SINGLE MARKET

The communication *Making a success of the Single Act — a new frontier for Europe* (1987), called the 'Delors Plan' after the then President of the Commission, Frenchman Jacques Delors, suggested the reform of the Structural Funds so that they could be made instruments of economic development. Leading up to the completion of the internal market in 1992, with the recent addition of Spain and Portugal as members, these policies were intended to enable all the Communities' regions to share increasingly in the major economic benefits derived from the frontier-free market. The aim was to secure closer consultation between the Commission, member states and the competent authorities designated by them at national, regional and local level, with each party acting as a 'partner in pursuit of a common goal'. Consistency was sought, with the member states' policies at all levels directed towards achieving economic and social cohesion and improved administration of the funds. The reform involved a switch from a project-based to a programme-based approach which would give the Community action the necessary depth and width, at the same time allowing greater flexibility. Organizations active in social and economic life (local authorities, associations, enterprises and so forth) could propose projects and apply to receive the relevant Structural Funds. The selection of projects was carried out by national or regional authorities, not by the Commission. Community structural measures are 'programmed' on a multi-annual basis (three or six yearly) which allows for coordination of the various European funds. The principle of 'additionality' is adhered to, that is action taken by the Union must be in addition to, and never replace, resources already deployed by national and local authorities for regional development and job creation. The principle of 'partnership' implies the closest possible co-operation between the Commission and the appropriate authorities at national, regional or local level in each member state, from the preparatory stage to the implementation of measures.

The Community Support Framework (CSF) is the document approved by the Commission, in agreement with the member state concerned, following appraisal of the development plan submitted by the member state and containing the strategy and priorities for Structural Funds action in that state, their specific objectives and the contribution of the Funds and other financial resources. This document is divided into priority areas and implemented by means of one or more Operational Programmes. The member state may present draft Operational Programmes at the same time as the plan. The Single Programming Document (SPD) is one single document approved by the Commission which contains the same information provided in both a Community Support Framework and an Operational Programme. However, whereas in all regions accorded Objective 1 status, the Commission will establish CSFs, in general, under the new Objective 2 and 3 Regions, SPDs may be required. If a Single Programming Document is to be used, the regional development plan submitted by the member state will be treated as a draft SPD. Whether initiated at national or Community level, all programmes part-financed by the Structural Funds are put together by the appropriate authorities in the member states.

Once approved and adopted by the Commission, plans are then implemented by the competent national or regional authorities. Implementation is supervised by monitoring committees, which are made up of representatives of the regions, the member state, the responsible bodies and the Commission. These committees oversee the implementation of the programmes on a regular basis and set guidelines where necessary. Once the programme has been approved, the member state authorities are responsible for informing potential project promoters of the assistance that is available through, for example, public calls for tender. Such calls are advertised in the *Official Journal S* Series on the Europa site (available on the Internet through the Tenders Electronic Daily (TED) database *http://www/ted.eur-op.eu.int.*). Following agreement reached at the European Council meeting in Brussels on 13 and 14 February 1988, commitment to the appropriation of the three Structural Funds (excluding FIFG) was doubled in real terms from ECU 7 billion to ECU 14 billion.

In 1993, Ireland's contribution to the EC Commission's white paper on *Growth, competitiveness and employment* gave this country's vision of the role of the Structural Funds and the National Development Plan (NDP) for 1994–99. Operational Programmes were produced under the headings Environment, Rural and Urban Development, Fisheries, Agriculture and Forestry as a result of the NDP. In total, EU and national interventions in that period averaged some 5% of Gross Domestic Product (GDP). In Ireland in 1996, the Irish EU Structural Funds Information Unit, based in Dublin (*http://www.csfinfo.com*), established a newsheet called *EU Structural Funds News*. This small but extremely informative publication is still being issued, and is a concise and authoritative data source on Irish developments and specific funding projects in this complex area. An information office is available to the public. Concise overviews are also given in the *European Monthly Newsletter* of the Irish Business Bureau (*http://www.ibb.be*).

THE COHESION FUND

Cohesion is the clearest expression of Community solidarity, involving the redistribution of large sums of money to help the least prosperous countries, regions and groups. This funding instrument was formally set up in 1994, exclusively for countries whose Gross National Product (GNP) was less than 90% of the Community average, that is Greece, Ireland, Portugal and Spain. The purpose of the fund is to contribute to investment in transport infrastructure and environmental improvements and to help the states in question control their budget deficits — one of the requirements for the single currency due fully to come into operation in 2002, known as the Maastricht criterion. Assistance from the Cohesion Fund is only to be given to countries that satisfy the European Monetary Union (EMU) convergence criteria and follow the economic convergence programme. Projects must belong to one of two categories. Firstly, environment projects: those which matched the Community's environmental objectives as outlined in the Maastricht Treaty and the Fifth Environmental Action programme (examined again later), namely preserving, protecting and improving the quality of the environment; protecting human health and assuring prudent and rational use of natural resources. The Fund gave priority to ensuring the supply of drinking water, waste-water treatment and solid waste disposal. Re-afforestation, erosion control and nature preservation actions were also eligible. Secondly, transport infrastructure projects (*http//www.inforegio.cec.eu.int/*.) A 50–50 share-out between these two categories was decided on by the Commission, although in Ireland the proportions did not quite end up that way. This country has benefited enormously from this Fund, as can be seen from the many projects, particularly road and motorway ones, which were undertaken, far beyond our national budgetary resources. Ireland received 7–10% of it, ECU 144.4 million, in 1993 and an indicative allocation of ECU 1.3 billion for 1994–99.

Two kinds of programme are funded from the Cohesion Fund which are administratively distinct, National (or Operational) Programmes and Community Initiatives. Community Initiatives (CI) were launched for the first time in 1989. They are intended to support operations which help solve problems of particular importance at a European level, comprising these elements:

(i) the development of trans-national, cross-border and interregional cooperation;

(ii) a 'bottom up' method of implementation, and

(iii) a high profile on the ground through expanded partnership.

Each CI goes through the following stages. Firstly, the Commission adopts draft guidelines setting out the Initiative's objectives, the main kinds of measures involved, the regions targeted and financial provisions. The draft is then submitted for opinion, most notably to the Advisory Committees of the member states' representatives, the European Parliament and the Economic and Social Committee. The Commission adopts the final guidelines, which are published in the *Official Journal*. The relevant authorities of each member state are then invited to submit programmes translating the Community guidelines into measures adapted to national and regional conditions, following approval of which these same authorities then implement the plans. Community Initiatives have been among the most highly-valued forms of assistance at local level. This is particularly true of INTERREG (cross-border cooperation), LEADER (rural development), NOW (equal opportunities for women in the labour market), HORIZON (access to the labour market for the disabled and disadvantaged groups), ENVIREG (environmental protection and regional development), REGIS (integration of the most remote regions), TELEMATIQUE (the promotion of advanced telecommunications services) and REGEN (energy networks, under which the Ireland-UK gas interconnector project was funded), a number of which will be mentioned again at appropriate points below. The first funding period was from 1989–93, in which CIs were allocated ECU 5.8m, almost 10% of the Structural Funds, monies which supported fourteen Initiatives. The remaining 90% of the Structural Funds budget was used to finance measures proposed by the member states under the CSFs (which, unlike CIs, are generally confined to measures within an individual state). The second CI funding period was for 1994–99.

Up to and including 1999, the whole of the Republic of Ireland was eligible for Structural Fund support under Objective 1, regions whose development is lagging behind, which gave us the maximum funding available. This, however, was destined to be changed in the next round of funding. The eligibility criteria are calculated on the basis of the level of GDP per inhabitant. The *per capita* GDP must be below or close to 75% of the Community average. The territorial unit used for definition purposes is usually what is known as Nomenclature of Territorial Unit for Statistics (NUTS). These were established by EUROSTAT, to provide a single uniform breakdown of territorial units for the production of regional statistics for the European Union. This form of measurement has been used in Community legislation since 1988 (Council Regulation [EEC] No. 2052/88 on the tasks of the Structural Funds; *OJ L* 185, 15.7.1988). For the period 2000–06, a guidance document has been issued by the EU on the Structural Funds and what will now be their closer linkage with the Cohesion Fund entitled *The Structural Funds and their co-ordination with the Cohesion Fund: guidelines for programmes in the period 2000–06* (COM [1999] 344 final). It gives as the structural and analytical basis for guidance three priorities:

(i) regional competitiveness,

(ii) social cohesion and employment, and

(iii) the development of urban and rural areas.

In addition, it takes into full account the analysis contained in the *Sixth periodic report on the social and economic situation and development of the regions* which is being adopted simultaneously with this document. It lays emphasis on decentralized effective and broad partnership. In Part 3 on urban and rural development and their contribution to balanced territorial development, the working paper states the new Community Initiative for rural areas will provide opportunities for complementary actions to mainstream programmes by supporting actions conceived and carried out by partnerships operating at a local level.

Following the conclusion reached by the heads of state and government at the Berlin Summit, the Council of Ministers adopted the draft Regulations on the reform of the Structural Funds for the period 2000–06. The final texts were forwarded to the European Parliament on the 14 April 1999 for discussion in its final plenary session from the 3–7 May 1999. The approval of these texts ensured a smooth transition towards the new programming period. Once this was done, the texts were returned to the Council, formally to adopt the new Regulations. The European Commission informed the member states of

(i) the list of eligible Objective 1 regions, including those with transitional status;

(ii) population coverage per member state for Objective 2 regions (on the basis of proposals by member states and

(iii) the amounts for each Objective.

Final adoption of guidelines for Objective 1, 2, and 3 programmes were completed by the end of 1999. Structural Funds programming for these Objectives were to be determined by the presentation of development or restructuring plans by each member state. With regard to Objective 1, the plans had to be forwarded to the European Commission not later than four months after the establishment of the list of eligible areas. Based on the appropriate national and regional priorities and the Commission guidelines, each plan included:

(i) an analysis of the regional situation relative to the Objective concerned;

(ii) an analysis of priority needs;

(iii) the strategy and envisaged priorities for action, and

(iv) an indicative financing plan.

The plans were to be drawn up by responsible authorities designated for this purpose by each member state. Before submitting the plan to the Commission, the member states had to consult all relevant regional partners (for example, regional or local authorities, the economic and social partners and interest groups). At this point, the member states could submit a regional development plan and, if required for Objective 1 areas, draft operational plans. An example of a regional submission to government towards the Ireland's National Development Plan (NDP) was the publication, in June 1998, of *Údarás Réigiúnach an IarDheiscirt/South-West Regional Authority Regional Submission for the 2000–06 European Community Support Framework*. The Inforegio site, referred to earlier, also offers access to official texts of a technical nature which covered the proposals for programming for the period 2000–06.

On 9 February 1999, the Irish government announced details of the new regional structures which it proposed to put in place on foot of the application made to EUROSTAT to divide the country into two regions for Structural Funding after 1999. Two new Group Regional Authorities were be established with the task of

(i) promoting the coordination of local authority and public services in their areas;

(ii) advising the government on the regional dimension of the NDP;

(iii) monitoring the general impact of all EU programmes for assistance, and

(iv) managing regional programmes in 2000–06, this previously always having been done entirely by government departments.

The new regions were called 'Southern and Eastern' and 'Borders, Midlands and West' (BMW) respectively. Ireland's geographical area covering BMW still has full Objective 1 status. The Southern and Eastern Region has been changed to Objective 1 Transitional Status, which means that the latter's funding will be tapered off towards the end of the funding period. The Irish government NDP was published in October 1999. This plan allows for a total spending of almost £40.6 billion. Of this, £13.5 billion will be invested in the BMW Region and £27 billion in the Southern and Eastern Region. Almost £21 billion will be spent on infrastructure, and, of particular interest, £6.7 billion will be expended on measures to support rural development. The objectives are fourfold:

(i) continuing sustainable national economic growth;

(ii) consolidating and improving Ireland's international competitiveness;

(iii) fostering balanced regional development, and

(iv) promoting social inclusion.

The plan comprises three national or inter-regional Operational Programmes, two regional Operational Programmes and a separate Peace Programme which operates in the border counties and in Northern Ireland. Other allocations include £10 billion being made available for the employment and human resources Operational Programme, water and waste water (£2,495 million), coastal protection (£35 million) and energy (£146 million). In the productive sector Operational Programme, agricultural development is allocated £278 million and fisheries £45 million. Regional infrastructure will include investment in non-national roads, rural water, urban and village renewal, seaports, culture, sport and recreation. Investment in the productive sector will be made in tourism, fisheries, forestry and rural development. In this funding period, four Community Initiatives will be financed as opposed to the former thirteen (for further details, see the sections on natural and man-made and cultural heritage below). With regard to the Cohesion Fund, a review of eligibility will be carried out in the year 2003, at which stage it is likely that Ireland will cease to be eligible for funding. Negotiations in Ireland on the new CSF were to be completed in summer 2000.

Two more funding mechanisms should be considered by way of conclusion. Firstly, 'Calls for Proposals' which appear in the *Official Journal C of the European Communities*, offering partial or more rarely total funding to support development in particular sectoral areas or to support specific topic-orientated programmes. Usually, these require cooperation between three or more other EU member states, giving deadlines for applications and guidelines as to aims and requirements. Secondly, there are the Framework Programmes. Framework Programmes have embraced the European Communities' Research, Technical Development and Demonstration (RTD) activities. The Single European Act which entered into force in July 1987, established a genuine European RTD community, formally institutionalized the concept and laid the foundation for a second Framework Programme covering the years 1987–91. There were three more such programmes, the third for 1990–94, the fourth for 1994–98 and the fifth and present one for 1998–2002. These programmes provide policy and direction for funding from the EU to universities, research institutes and SMEs, as well as the opening up of national public and private contracts. The programmes seek to ensure the availability of venture capital, the protection of intellectual property rights, the development of human resources and the encouragement of technology transfer. What distinguishes the Fifth Framework Programme from its predecessors is greater selectivity in EU research activity and the attempt to make this effort more visible to European citizens. Areas covered by this programme include the quality of life and management of living resources (QUALITY OF LIFE), user-friendly information society (IST), energy, environment and sustainable development (EESD). The Fifth Framework Programme guidelines for applications and funding appeared on the CORDIS website (*http://www.cordis.lu*) and in the journal *Cordis Focus* (4 June 1999). The details of the programme appeared in print in the *Official Journal L* 26, 1.2.1999, pp. 1–61 (available on EUR-Lex at (*http:// europa.eu.int/ eur-lex*). Marie Curie Fellowships are another action funded by the Fifth Framework Programme. They offer postgraduate training and exchanges, and are advertised in Ireland in the newsheet *Innovation Relay Centre Update* produced by Enterprise Ireland (*http://www. forbairt.ie/funding/rd/irc*). The newsheet also offers and undertakes partner searches for funding for European Union and RTD programmes.

EVALUATION

Monitoring exists for the purpose of carrying out regular checks on the progressive and effective physical and financial implementation of assistance from the Structural Funds and their impact in terms of the objectives laid down. The main statutory provision are Article 6 of the Framework Regulation of 1988, as amended in 1993, and articles 25 and 26 of the Coordination Regulation (as amended). These articles set out the principal concepts of monitoring and evaluation, comprising:

(i) effective honouring of commitments;

(ii) adjustment of measures where necessary;

(iii) evaluation of impact and arrangements for partnership, and

(iv) the levels of monitoring and evaluation.

They provide for evaluation of terms of assistance (CSF), indicate the responsibilities of the Commission, member states and monitoring committees, respectively, and stipulate the means of evaluation to be used, reports, indicators and so forth. The rules imply monitoring at three levels. Firstly, the Commission is responsible for monitoring of the Structural Funds as a whole for all the aims referred to in Article 10a. It must report to the other institutions (Council, Parliament, Economic and Social Committee and Committee of the Regions) through annual reports on the implementation of the funds and a three-yearly report made on progress towards economic and social cohesion (see Article 16 of the Framework Regulation and article 31 of the Coordination Regulation). Secondly, at CSF level, monitoring is carried out principally by the Monitoring Committees for the CSFs set up for that purpose. These committees define the factors to be taken into account in monitoring. The monitoring of the CSFs and items of assistance to which the guidelines relate relies on the authorities and bodies responsible for implementing the assistance granted from the Funds. They report to the Monitoring Committees, which in turn report to the member states and the Commission. In the CSF, there is no provision for annual reports at this level, but the frameworks are revised or adjusted where necessary. Thirdly, at assistance level (programmes or global grants), evaluation is undertaken by a Monitoring Committee set up for that purpose, which must produce annual reports and a final report on the progress of this assistance (Article 25 [4] of the Coordination Regulation). Such reports are drawn up according to procedures jointly agreed by the member states and the Commission (Article 25 [1] of the Coordination Regulation). In the case of a measure lasting less than two years, only one report within six months of completion is required.

The operational nature of SPDs means they should be monitored in the same way as items of assistance.

Initially, operational monitoring takes place at the beginning of the process (or programming stage) to identify, in the following order,

(i) general objectives, then

(ii) specific objectives, and

(iii) the physical completion of a number of measures.

The project's aim is to produce results which permit the specific measures to be achieved. However, when the ongoing operation is being assessed by the Monitoring Committee, the specific objectives are examined and monitored first, and then the data and measures, in order to assess the overall impact on the general objective. *Interim* evaluation involves the critical analysis of all the data collected, particularly those collected through monitoring and measuring, to ascertain whether the objectives sought are being achieved. It gives room for explanation of discrepancies, forecast of results, corrective measures, validation of assistance and reassessment of the relevance of objectives originally selected. The main purpose of interim evaluations is to improve the monitoring mechanism and provide a useful tool for decision-making and effective management. The second stage is a *mid-term* evaluation after three years' work (for six-year assistance), or at the end of the first period (three-year assistance). There will be several stages in this, including a critical analysis of the Communities' policies involved, particularly those relating to the environment and public procurement. The third stage is intended to continue proposals for adjustments to programmes and prepare for *ex-post* evaluation. The practical arrangements for implementation, particularly the timing of reports, will be agreed between the two parties concerned.

NATURAL AND MAN-MADE HERITAGE

We now turn to the two issues of principal interest to this book, natural and man-made heritage and cultural heritage. These are the sectors in which the types of funding just discussed are applied and regarding which certain of the information agencies described earlier furnish data and assistance. The two main topics are treated in a similar way in what follows. The chapter identifies key areas of interest and relevance within each. The subject-matter of these sections is then explored in chronological sequence, starting with developments occurring close in time to the point when Ireland joined the EEC, and taking the narrative down towards the present. Within the relevant sectors, we shall look at policies, their implementation, modification, abandonment or renewal as the case may be. Factors both internal and external to the European Union

affecting these issues are highlighted. Here, it will be seen that a number of considerations remain remarkably recurrent, for instance adjusting for currency fluctuations between states, absorbing the impact of enlargement, reconciling the differences between an ideal situation and what is achievable in reality, among other factors. EU-supported agencies founded to serve the interests of the various sectors, or elements within them, are also briefly treated. The account is mainly based on the types of official EU information sources previously mentioned in this paper. References are indicative only and not absolutely comprehensive, as the provision of full coverage would extend the chapter substantially beyond its present confines. Nevertheless, it his hoped that the data will reveal how a reader wishing to learn about a specific theme can pursue his or her enquiries relating to areas of major significance by basing this research on centrally produced data sources in the first instance. The approach may also underline the fact that individual topics are most fruitfully examined as part of the broader context in which they occur. Exploring the material over time should recall issues we may have now forgotten but which were of central importance in their own day and have left a lasting legacy in the various domains to which they apply. Little attempt is made to estimate the appropriateness or otherwise of measures taken in the individual sectors, as this is a task for those better placed to judge these developments. It should be finally noted that there is often a degree of overlap between natural and man-made and cultural matters, despite the fact that they are treated separately here.

AGRICULTURE

When Ireland joined the European Communities in 1973, it was predominantly an agricultural country, and the effect agriculture has had on communities and landscapes is integral to a study of heritage. We therefore look at this area of natural heritage first. As Ireland's major industry, the prospects offered by entry into the EEC for the development of Irish agriculture were among the determining factors in the decision to accede. It was hoped that new remunerative markets for farm produce would bring overall gain to the Irish economy and lessen dependence, at that time, on the UK market. The sector is now the responsibility of the Agriculture Directorate-General (*http://www.europa.eu.int/comm/dgs/agriculture/index_en.htm*), previously DG VI.

Agriculture was the first common policy to be formulated by the Community. The Treaty of Rome (1957) laid down the five basic objectives of the Common Agricultural Policy (CAP): to increase productivity by promoting technical progress; to ensure a fair standard of living for farmers; to stabilize markets; to assure the availability of supplies, and to ensure reasonable prices for consumers.

When the CAP was agreed in 1962, a primary objective of the Commission and the six original member states was to attain self-sufficiency in food production. 'In working out the common agricultural policy ... account shall be taken of the particular nature of agricultural activity, which results from the social structure of agriculture and from the structural and natural disparities between the various agricultural regions' (Treaty of Rome, article 39, para. 2). From this assertion, echoed by Commissioner Sicco Mansholt in his closing speech to the Conference of Stresa and reaffirmed in the memorandum he would present to the Council of Ministers in December 1968, was born the concept of a policy geared to the ongoing modernization of agriculture through structural improvement. The intention of the Mansholt Plan was to set in motion a global reform of the sector. He warned that non-market and price support policies alone could not solve the fundamental difficulties for farming. The memorandum emphasized the inter-relationship between the two aspects of agricultural policy: markets and structures. The new Council Regulation on the financing of the Common Agricultural Policy (Regulation 729/70) formalized the regulatory framework of the structure's policy. The Community's structural policy formally started in 1971, and in 1972 the Mansholt Memorandum was given concrete underpinning by the approval of three 'socio-structural' Directives, one concerning the modernization of farms (72/159/EEC of 17 April 1972), a Directive concerning measures to encourage the cessation of farming (known as the early retirement scheme (72/160/EEC) and a third on qualifications for people working in agriculture, Directive 72/161/EEC (*OJ L* 96, 23.4.72, pp. 1 ff.). To these provisions were added successively regional and sectoral measures: the first concerned the constitution of producer groups in the fruit and vegetables sectors (Regulation 1035/72), the second laid down a series of criteria enabling the delineation of territories eligible for special measures. The aim was to stop the agricultural and rural exodus which threatened the social integrity of rural areas and the survival of the natural environment. The Directive represented an important innovation for agricultural structural policy: for the first time, an explicitly territorial approach was brought to bear for reasons of economic, social and environmental balance.

On 1 February 1973, the common organization of agricultural markets became applicable in three new member states, Denmark, Ireland and the United Kingdom. Compensatory amounts provided for in the Act of Accession were fixed for most agricultural products, although common prices were applied immediately to certain products. European agriculture was strongly influenced by external factors, the need to expand markets, the inflation and unstable exchange rates which affected all economic sectors and increased or decreased world commodity prices, and the uncertainty of the weather in any given year. The floating of the Irish and English pounds was a factor as soon as the relevant countries joined the Community. For conversion of agricultural prices, the pound was converted, not at the theoretical parity declared to the International Monetary Fund (IMF), but at a representative market rate and representing a devaluation of some 10%. This was the first step towards basing Common Agricultural Policy conversion rates on more realistic data, making it possible to re-establish the single market. But since the pound continued to float, monetary compensatory amounts (MCAs) were also provided for subsidizing imports and taxing exports, this being necessary in a downward float (Regulation EEC No. 222/73, *OJ L* 27, 1. 2.1973; Regulation No. 270/73, *OJ L* 30 of 1.2.1973). The object of MCAs was to maintain the value of agricultural price guarantees at times of monetary instability and to permit free movement of foodstuffs at fixed prices. MCAs compensate for the difference between market rates of exchange and the representative agricultural (or 'green') rate used in price guarantees. The rates of exchange on the agricultural market differed from the rates quoted on the member state national exchange markets. The MCAs were subsidies levied (taxed) or granted (subsidized) on trade between member states and also trade with third countries. For countries with revalued currencies, they were levied on imports and granted on exports, and for countries with devalued currencies, they were levied on exports and granted on imports. The ultimate ideal was to bring the green currency levels closer to the actual exchange rates in the Community but, in the interim, to compensate for the differences in prices between member countries in inflationary or deflationary situations. In monetary crises, the EEC effectively established Community markets inter-linked by a system of Compensatory Amounts. The Commission remained convinced that in order to achieve Economic and Monetary Union (EMU), the MCAs should be gradually phased out. As we shall see later, in the event, EMU had to be achieved first.

By the end of the 1970s, for the first time international prices for certain agricultural products exceeded Community threshold prices. The market in beef and veal was also strained owing to shortages. The increased Monetary Compensatory Amounts widened the gap between the CAP unit of account and the German agricultural currency (agri-monetary) system. The Council increased milk prices by 5% and adult bovine prices by 10%. Consumer subsidies were also granted for butter. The Commission made proposals for 1973/74 prices, but also put a memorandum of suggestions for the CAP before the Council on proposed reorganization for the period 1973–78 (*Bulletin of the European*

Community Supplement 17/73). The Commission, convinced as to the basic principles of the CAP, felt that agricultural incomes policy had to be seen within the political and economic context of developments of the CAP and other areas of Community policy. On 27 February, the Commission proposed a Directive on agriculture in mountain and hill farming and farming in less-favoured areas. The aim was to improve agricultural income and enable an increase in agricultural activity in those areas, thus preventing depopulation and preserving the natural environment. Member states were to communicate lists of the regions in question to the Council. For the first time since 1962, there was a cutback for supplies of wheat which cause considerable price rises. The Commission brought in a short-supply Regulation to try to control this. The Accession Treaty provided a policy for sugar for application to new member states, with a system of production quotas, where the sugar industry picked up the cost on market losses. Attempts to negotiate a new sugar agreement with the United Nations Conference on Trade and Development (UNCTAD) failed. Monetary instability continued in 1973, and the Single Market, to be created by applying common prices fixed in units of account, was gradually fragmented due to changes in European currency parities. The differences between common agricultural prices expressed in national currencies was 30% between German and Italian markets, with the Benelux, Irish, German and Danish markets in between these two extremes. Eventually, member states (with the exception of Italy, and in 1973 the exception of Ireland and the UK at accession) decided to float their currencies jointly, agreeing to maintain a gap of only 2.25% between them, a situation known as 'the snake.'

Widespread inflation due to the energy crisis and high import prices had several consequences for agriculture in 1974. Firstly, production costs rose because of the increase in energy costs, motor oil, fuel oil and fertilizers and of feedstuffs. Secondly, there was an overall increase in agricultural prices of up to 1% and in the economy as a whole. The floating of the French franc in January 1974 and changes in the representative rate for the Italian lira for CAP brought in MCAs. This was effectively a subsidy to compensate for the effect of the fluctuating currency rate. The valuation of the agricultural lira and the British and Irish 'green' pounds was similarly adjusted. In spite of these setbacks, the Commission made proposals for Directives in measures on hill farming and farming in less-favoured areas. Under the Directive (72/160/EEC) mentioned above, the rate of Community financing of eligible national expenditure was increased to 65% for Ireland and Italy. From now on, the elements which would make up the future European rural policy were gradually put into place. Variable co-financing rates were introduced as part of this process. On the 2 October

1974, the Council requested the Commission to prepare by 1 March 1975 a full-scale review of the CAP entitled *Stocktaking of the Common Agricultural Policy (Bulletin of the European Communities Supplement 2/75)*. In this review, the Commission took account at a given moment in time of the past history of the CAP, the extent to which the instruments used by this and related policies had contributed to the aims stated in the Treaty (Part 2), summarized the main problems which had arisen and indicated principal improvements to be made. In 1975, the Directive (75/268) on mountain and hill farming and farming in certain less-favoured areas was intended to halt the steady decline in agricultural incomes in those areas as compared with other regions of the European Community (*OJ L* 128, 19.5.1975, p. 1).

In 1976, once again European agriculture faced problems arising from events beyond its control. The general economic crisis was felt to varying degrees in the individual sectors and in the member states, and was compounded by some exceptional natural disasters and extreme drought, the worst in over a century, which affected farmers' incomes severely. In spite of this, the persistence of dairy surpluses confirmed that they were a structural problem, and stocks of milk and skimmed milk products were extremely high. Efforts were still being made to achieve integration and expansion of markets. The main external problem remained the widening economic gap between member states with appreciating currencies and those with depreciating currencies. This gap grew wider still in 1976, coupled with a trend towards further disparity in the exchange rates of their currencies. MCAs were now placing such a heavy financial strain on the Community budget that the Community was forced to rethink this option. The Directive (75/268) on hill farming was brought into effect. Having assessed national draft provisions and measures on the implementation of the reform of the agricultural policy, the Commission adopted thirty-three decisions, most being dependent on this Directive. The Commission presented proposals on the 1976/77 prices, taking into effect economic recession, price and income developments and inflationary trends. These efforts were to achieve economic stability and budget austerity in the CAP, disrupted since 1971 by monetary events. In the plant health sector, the Council brought ten years of discussion to a close by adopting an important Directive which lays down comprehensive health requirements for trade in vegetable products and a Directive for fixing maximum levels of pesticide residues in fruit and vegetables. A strengthening and tightening up of veterinary Regulations to combat animal diseases also took place, leading to the establishment of an Advisory Veterinary Committee (*OJ L* 171, 30.6.1976). As far as imports were concerned, Ireland was allowed derogations from Regulations under the Act of Accession. This country was permitted to maintain traditional rules on meat imports for a further five years. In 1976, the price of beef and veal rose slightly for the first six months of the year. Faced with serious imbalances in the milk market, and the overproduction of skimmed milk, the Commission proposed to the Council an action plan covering 1977–80. Ireland, as with several other EU member countries, ended the year with a further downward trend financially, and its green pound (like that of the UK) was further devalued.

From the point of view of weather, the next year, 1977, was a better one for agriculture. Compared with the rest of the economy, which suffered recession and high unemployment, the CAP supplied some protection. Three fundamental problems, however, dominated. Firstly, the economic and monetary divergence between states was reflected in the MCAs, which threatened to break up the Single Market. There was a 40% price difference between British and German markets. The Commission proposed dismantling the MCAs. Secondly, the imbalance on certain agricultural markets became increasingly severe. There were large surpluses of sugar, beef, veal, milk and other commodities. A 1.5% co-responsibility levy on milk surpluses was introduced. It was used to finance direct expenditure in the dairy sector, the most costly of the Community policies, and a cautious price policy with a whole range of measures designed to restore a balance in the markets. Thirdly, many regions of the Community suffered from economic and structural under-development. To reduce income disparities, the Commission proposed intensive revision of the socio-structural policies in the Mediterranean Region, known as Integrated Mediterranean Programmes (IMP). Funding for a five-year period was to be provided from the European Regional Development Fund and the European Social Fund. On 15 February, the Council adopted a Regulation on common measures to improve conditions under which agricultural products were to be processed and marketed, and on 31 May, the Commission presented to the Council a new proposal for a Regulation concerning producer groups (*OJ C* 146, 22.6.1977, p. 2). A common measure had been adopted in 1978 to improve the acceleration of drainage in the west of Ireland (Directive 78/628/EEC), and this region was to be helped by an overall economic development programme (*OJ L* 206, 19.6.1978, p. 5). On the 6 February 1979, the Council adopted a Directive on the programme to promote drainage in catchment areas including land on both sides of the border between Ireland and Northern Ireland (*OJ L* 43 6.2.1979, p. 23). The European Monetary System (EMS) became operative on 13 March 1979 and the ECU, the new European monetary unit of account, was introduced into the agricultural policy of eight member countries. It was now feasible to dismantle the MCAs over a period of two years, precipitating

neither an increase nor a decrease in national currency prices. Price increases for agricultural products were to be applied by the Community in parity within each member country. It was a year of good harvests, but inflation returned, mainly due to soaring energy prices. The pound sterling and Italian lira were further devalued. Serious disparities in regional incomes continued. A series of Directives and proposals for Directives were introduced, including one for farming in mountain, hill and less-favoured regions, and another specifically aimed at regions in greatest difficulty, for example the west of Ireland. In November, the Commission put forward new proposals for the CAP, to provide a better market balance and limit the expenditure incurred by the Community (*OJ L* 192, 31.7.1979). Surpluses in the milk and sugar sectors above the agreed level were to be disposed of, and the cost paid by the producers themselves. Savings were to be made in the support systems for beef and veal.

From the beginning of 1980, the CAP was affected by world events, economic and political instability and increased conflict, which led to a rise in oil bills and an awareness that too much dependence on unstable regimes was unhealthy and uneconomic for industry. In response to the Soviet military intervention in Afghanistan, the United States decided to stop exports of agricultural produce to the Soviet Union, whereupon the Council decided that supplies from the Community to the Soviet state should not directly or indirectly replace those from the US. The modernization of the CAP was proposed by the Commission in response to the mandate assigned to it by the Council of Ministers on 30 May 1980, amongst measures to regenerate Community policies. To secure a better balance of demand and supply, limited price increases were proposed for milk, sugar, beef and veal. Nevertheless, the Community achieved the establishment of a common market in sheep meat. Consumer objections to certain farming methods led the Council to consider the protection of intensively reared stock, and the use of hormones in animals. On 24 June, the Council amended its Directive on hill farming in less-favoured areas. On the 30 June, the Regulation to give aid to the west of Ireland was adopted (*OJ L* 180, 4.7.1980, p. 1). Northern Ireland was encouraged to speed up agricultural development (*OJ C* 179, 17.7.1980).

In *Reflections on the Common Agricultural Policy*, the new principle that producers take financial responsibility for disposal of their surpluses was promulgated (*Bulletin of the European Community Supplement* 6/80, p. 13). On 31 July, the Commission adopted a Regulation laying down detailed rules for the formation, activity and economic expenditure of producer groups. Again, production surpluses, control of budgetary expenditure and safeguarding of farmers' incomes were considered.

Practical solutions for additional co-responsibility levy was added to the milk sector (*OJ C*, 182, 21.7.1980, p. 36). The arrangements for the common organization in sheep meat came into force (*OJ L* 275, 18.10.1980, p. 2). A new proposal for the Community's market in sugar for a five-year period (*OJ C* 271, 18.10.1980, p. 2) was initiated. Tightening up on brucellosis and tuberculosis and measures for the control of swine fever were key points in public health provision, a ban on hormones in animal feedstuffs for domestic consumption and on the marketing of fresh meat with hormone residues was also proposed. Monetarily, the UK pound (not fully part of EMU) appreciated steadily, to such an extent that MCAs had to be introduced. The French and Italian representative rates were brought in line with their central rates, so that MCAs were consequently eliminated. The production of butter and skimmed milk fell, with the result that intervention stocks fell. Milk production continued to increase and the buying-in of beef by intervention agencies continued.

At the beginning of 1981, Greece joined the Community. With 30% of its workforce in the farm sector, almost half of its input, its admission increased the diversity of European Community agriculture. During the year, the agricultural policy was discussed at length in the Community institutions. In its report of 24 June on the May mandate, the Commission made specific suggestions on how to adapt the CAP and integrate it into general economic recovery. Their guidelines proposed:

(i) a prudent price policy, taking into account incomes and market balance aspects, and

(ii) modulation of price guarantees by a set of multi-annual production objectives combined with provision for participation by producers if these thresholds were exceeded.

Nonetheless, the Commission recognized that in the absence of alternative employment for some sections of farm population, a fair standard of living should still be guaranteed.

Northern Ireland benefited specifically in the acceleration of agricultural development and jointly with the Republic in a common measure for beef cattle production and an additional premium for maintenance of suckler herds (*OJ L* 111, 23.4.1981, pp. 1 and 6). Amendments to Directive 72/159/EEC and 72/161 EEC (see above) were introduced, and a list of eleven measures were adopted (*OJ L* 197, 20.7.1981 pp. 41 and 44). On 27 July, the Council adopted two special provisions to assist Ireland, concerning the amount of interest-rate subsidy provided for in Directive 72/159/EEC on the modernization of farms and the

special drainage programme in the less-favoured areas of the west of Ireland. Larger price rises (12%) were agreed by the Council after deliberation by the European Parliament and the Economic and Social Committee, together with a substantial reduction in MCAs. The generalized applications of the co-responsibility principle was rejected, but it was kept for cereals and increased in milk. Green currencies were eliminated and representative rates were aligned with national currencies in the Benelux countries, France, Denmark and Ireland. The MCAs were phased out for the Benelux states (and for the other countries kept at zero) and reductions were made in Germany and the UK. The market in sugar was reorganized and rules (including production quotas) were made applicable for a five-year term. The basic Regulation on wine was also amended. With reference to animals, the Council approved measures on the protection of animals during international transport, and minimum standards for the protection of laying hens in battery cages were proposed. The economic recession, high interest rates and the high cost of concentrates, coupled with a cautious price policy and in April an increase of the co-responsibility levy paid by producers, slowed down the growth rate of milk production to 0.4%. Increased export demand for milk products and an increased domestic demand for butter led to the virtual elimination of butter stocks. Production of beef and veal reached a peak in 1980 and thereafter declined, and domestic consumption being low any surplus was exported. Work on information and training in rural areas was increased, especially for young farmers.

In 1982, many of the difficulties of the previous nine years having been resolved, the Council adopted some of the guidelines for European agriculture proposed by the Commission in May 1980. The United Kingdom was unhappy about its financial contributions to the Community. Dispute settlement procedures under the General Agreement on Tariffs and Trade (GATT) were initiated between the United States and the Community, because of the latter's difficulties in the export markets and the use of export refunds. Output was high, but prices were good. The sale of 120,000 tonnes of Christmas butter for direct human consumption helped ease the surplus in that area. Farm incomes improved. High interest rates led to a rise in the level of interest rate subsidies, (*OJ L* 193, 3.7.1982, p. 39). The milk-quota system was introduced in 1984 to prevent over-production (*OJ L* 90, 1.4.1984, pp. 10 and 13). It lays down that when the quotas are over-run, an additional levy, over and above the co-responsibility levy, is imposed. The production of cereals reached a new record, mainly due to exceptionally good weather in the growing season.

The accession of Spain and Portugal as new member

states in 1985 created a period of adaptation in the agricultural situation. Special arrangements had to be made for Portugal, which had the most vulnerable agriculture in the entire Community. Even before it joined, Portugal received Community aid for the modernization of its agriculture and for ten years after its accession, a major specific programme for the improvement of its agricultural structures would have to be implemented. Integrated Mediterranean Programmes (IMPs) had to be applied in the south of France, part of Italy and in Greece to restructure the economies of the rural areas of these regions by means of massive investments enabling them to compete effectively with the Spanish and Portuguese farmers. The year 1985 was also marked by the adoption and publication of plans and ideas which had been in the pipeline for some time. The new long-term guidelines for agriculture were drawn up. In view of the challenges facing the CAP, the Commission outlined a number of options in its green paper, entitled *Perspectives for the Common Agricultural Policy* (COM [85] 333 final), which was to serve as a basis for consultation with all parties concerned. It suggested the following:

(i) balance in agricultural markets;

(ii) a search for new products which were not in surplus and for new outlets for existing production;

(iii) action to be taken with regard to agricultural imports and exports;

(iv) the establishment of a relationship between agriculture and the environment;

(v) rural and regional development, and

(vi) income aids.

Having gathered together the various opinions expressed, the Commission presented the Council with a policy document entitled *A future for Community agriculture*. Discussions on improving the efficiency of agricultural structures led to a Regulation which superseded the socio-structural Directive of 1972 and would apply for ten years from 1985–94. The milk quota system achieved its objective of reducing milk production. Production of butter and skimmed milk powder declined by 6% and 9% respectively, and intervention stocks for skimmed milk powder fell, but there was still a surplus of butter. One of the major features of the beef/veal market was a cyclical downturn in cattle numbers, particularly in the case of female breeding animals. Slaughtering of dairy cattle triggered by the milk quotas made the downturn even sharper. Production did remain high, and

the Community became one of the chief world exporters in this commodity. The supply of sheep meat outstripped demand, growth occurring in Ireland and the UK. The pig meat market improved during the year, but African swine fever made terrible depredations in Flanders (Belgium). Egg prices failed to reach the high of 1984, but poultry meat demand outstripped the supply. World sugar prices fell to an all-time low since 1982, but made a modest recovery. Sugar-beet demand both rose and fell between 1982 and 1985.

From the mid-1980s, there was a change in trends in the relationship between the Community and CAP. With greater internal economic stability, policies tended to become wider in approach and more interrelated with other Community policies, and the Community, as a cohesive unit, tended to make more international agreements. In 1986, Community institutions were again faced with the urgent situation posed by the combination of accumulating surpluses of stocks and acute budgetary difficulties. They devoted themselves to securing implementation of the guidelines for restructuring the CAP drawn up in 1985 (price restraint, adjustments to certain market organizations and socio-structural measures). The imbalance between supply and demand was felt to be the key to the problem. The Commission kept the institutional prices of some products which were in surplus (milk, sugar, meat) at the same level and reduced the prices of food and wheat. The producer co-responsibility was extended to the cereals sector. Intervention returned to its role as a safety net, and could not be used as surplus storage for a saturated market. The intervention scheme was to be more flexible for cereals, milk and beef products. In the milk market, the Commission supported the buying-up of quotas but also decided the quotas were to be cut by 3% at the end of a two-year period. By the end of 1986, all the member states including Spain and Portugal, adopted the new policies on agricultural structures. They sought to grant investment aid to farmers in order to reduce production costs, to improve living and working conditions, raise product quality and direct production with reference to market outlets. The Commission felt that quotas should only be used as a last resort, and strengthened implementation measures. The socio-structural policy was to be allowed to develop as follows:

(i) support for efforts to adjust;

(ii) support for disposal of produce;

(iii) the maintenance of farming in certain areas and help for the reduction of production potential, and

(iv) support for young farmers entering farming.

In February 1987, the Council presented *The Single Act: a new frontier for Europe* (COM (87) 100 of 17 February 1987). In the context of agriculture, the achievement of a united economic area made it imperative to reduce the differential between backward areas burdened by structural handicaps and the more successful regions, and in particular to help foster rural development. Substantial progress in the reform of the CAP was realized in 1987. Further changes were made in market organization with a view to achieving better balance and greater control of spending. Weaker farms were facilitated in decisions on initiative and adjustments. The accession arrangements for Spain and Portugal were extended for a year. In the milk sector, guaranteed quantities for milk were reduced by 8.5% within a year. The Commission presented a report on the milk-quota system with proposals for its future (COM [87] 452 final) and on the sheep meat sector. The Community was the leading world beef exporter because of the large import requirements of non-member states such as Brazil, Egypt and the USSR. Severe restrictions on the buying of products for intervention were implemented for milk powder and cereals. Even for beef it was more selective and less automatic, although beef premiums were introduced for the first 50 cattle on a holding. Under price restraints nearly all the institutional prices were frozen at Community prices, and nationally by less than the rate of inflation. It contained *inter alia* measures in favour of environmental protection and an annual premium per hectare repayable by EAGGF to farmers using environmentally favourable production methods (*OJ L* 903, 30.3.1995). It also included an extension of allowances to cover certain crops and an increase in the maximum compensatory allowance. The Commission adopted rules for the application of two Council Regulations on the protection of forests against fire and atmospheric pollution and granted financial assistance of almost ECU 6.5 million towards 68 projects in the 1987 programme.

In 1987, for the first time a co-responsibility levy on cereals was introduced. A large surplus still existed in world sugar markets and the price continued to be very low since 1981. The beef/veal market was again depressed,

(i) because of competition from other meats, but, significantly,

(ii) as a result of the glut of dairy cow meat following the reduction of milk quotas.

The main event was the introduction of firm arrangements for the dismantling of MCAs. In September, the Commission adopted two aid codes that would in future apply to all existing or projected national aids for the promotion of agricultural and certain allied products,

and for investment in the production and marketing of certain milk and milk substitute products.

In 1988, the price restraint policy continued and further measures to improve the flexibility of intervention were taken. New 'stabilisers' were intended to step up producer co-responsibility. The harvest was poor due to bad weather in the northern hemisphere. On the socio-structural front, schemes were introduced for the first time for the set-aside of farm land. This scheme was intended to encourage reduction in the area under cultivation. To qualify for aid, the reduction had to equal at least 20% on an individual holding over a period of five years. The extensification scheme aimed at a 20% reduction in actual production, and included measures to assist diversification (*OJ C* 51, 23.2.1988, p. 6). The measures provided for a cessation of farming (early retirement) by farmers over the age of 55 (*OJ C* 236, 1.9.1988, p. 10). These measures were voluntary, not compulsory. The Commission suggested further ways to integrate the development of agriculture with the environment, though there had been a slow take-up on the first phase (COM [88] 338 final). Commission papers were prepared on the future of rural society (see below). Rural society in Ireland faced social and economic problems as a result of the changes it had undergone, comprising depopulation, reduction of small farms and uneconomic holdings, increased dependence on imported fruit and vegetables, population moves to urban areas, and the growth of tourism. *The Future of rural society* aimed to restore the vitality and environmental balance of rural areas, based on analysis, well-defined strategy, guidelines and measures (COM (88) 501 final, 28.07.1988). Direct specific development and greater account of rural problems in all the actions and programmes of the Community were essential. The measures of the CAP had to be more adaptable to regional and local conditions, yet develop the regions cohesively. Diversification, encouragement of local initiatives, participation in research and development and adaptation to information and telecommunications systems would assist in the encouragement of new industries and the improvement of living and working conditions. The Council reduced the milk quotas for 1988–89 by a further 9% to dissuade production increases and to reduce unlimited buying of intervention butter and skimmed milk powder, but the quota system was extended to March.

The CAP focused on four main areas in 1989: market prices, structural funding, forestry for rural development and international developments. In the markets, a common approach to sheep meat and goat meat was suggested, and a new beef and veal regime was introduced in a major reform of the market organization. Prices for most products were frozen, allowances being made for less-favoured areas. In their communication of

18 October on the guidelines for rural development actions linked to the functioning of agricultural markets, the Commission studied the possibility of 'modulation' of the market arrangements so as better to concentrate the available funds on small family holdings, a new direction in policy. Aid to young farmers was also provided. Internationally, 1989 and early 1990 were dominated by GATT Uruguay Round multilateral trade negotiations. The interim negotiating agreements on textiles, agriculture, safeguards and intellectual property, concluded by senior officials following the special meeting of the Trade Negotiations Committee in Geneva in April, completed the mid-term review undertaken by the ministers four months earlier in Montreal. The Community played a particularly active part, aiming to encourage a real liberalization of all the markets, at the same time strengthening the multilateral trading system. In suggesting new practices for products not yet regulated, the Community proved the value of its experience in this field. The set-aside measures for agricultural land were beginning to take effect. In the dairy sector, additional quotas had to be allocated to certain producers, whose situation gave cause for concern because of a 7% reduction in collection over a two-year period, whereas in a more balanced economy, the price of dairy products rose. The crisis in the egg sector in the UK in 1989 (due to salmonella poisoning) led to a drop in prices. Relatively stable currencies led to the complete dismantling of MCAs in all member countries that were full members of EMS.

In 1990, the CAP was fully adapted, applied and reformed for the first time. The decisions included the possibility of granting the suckler cow premium to small milk producers with mixed herds, and gave member states the opportunity to buy back milk quotas with a view to re-allocating them to small producers in mountain, hill and less-favoured areas. On the 6 and 27 June, the Commission formally adopted the 44 Community Support Frameworks for the regions eligible under Objective 5b (development of rural areas). Five priorities were concentrated on, developing other sections of the economy, particularly SMEs, tourism and recreation, environmental protection and human resources. The Council adopted a Regulation on improving the efficiency of the set-aside provision to encourage the use of set-aside land for non-agricultural purposes. On 7 June, the Commission adopted a proposal to set up a network of rural development information centres dealing with rural development initiatives and agricultural markets, called MIRIAM (COM [90] 230 final). It also adopted a communication on rural tourism that emphasized the need to assist the development of high-quality tourism products as the alternative to mass tourism. On the 25 July, 1990 a new programme 'Community Initiative for Rural Devel-

opment — LEADER (Links between rural economic development action)' was proposed by Ray McSharry, the Irish Commissioner (Spokesman's Service P52/1990). The necessary merger between heritage policy and the 'bottom up' approach to local development (based on the principle of subsidiarity) was at the heart of this programme. It was aimed essentially at Objective I and Objective 5b regions. Tourism generally receive priority in rural development programmes (over 42% of the amounts invested in LEADER I went into this area). Emphasis was placed on the innovative and demonstrative nature of the rural development actions, the latter being implemented by Local Action Groups (LAGs). The programme, with the help of local communities and chambers of commerce, has sought to promote and disseminate innovation in rural areas. It is a prime tool for the exchange of experience and know-how. It has been a flagship initiative in the Republic of Ireland.

However, the Mac Sharry Report (1991), entitled *The development and future of the Common Agricultural Policy*, highlighted the problems of costly storing of food surpluses in intervention in cereals, dairy products and beef. Even with a 30% increase in the farm budget from 1990–91, farmers incomes were set for decline. Large numbers of farmers were leaving the land, and 80% of resources were going to 20% of farmers because of the systems' linkage of price support to food volume. Eleven proposals were suggested in this report, which followed in broad outlines the Commission's Reflection paper (COM [91] 100 final). One of the main keys for reform was in the pricing strategy. This year marked increasing overlap between the policies of tourism, regional development, environment and agriculture. In this report, an agri-environmental action programme was also proposed. The agri-monetary situation improved, the Council was able to dismantle the remaining agri-monetary gaps in currency values between the member states, apart from Italy. Continuing agricultural negotiations of the Uruguay Round increased Community assistance to the countries of Central and Eastern Europe, and in this year, German unification and the extension of the CAP to cover the territory of the former German Democratic Republic as well as the beginning of the second transitional stage in the accession of Spain and Portugal were key factors.

In 1991, the situation regarding overproduction on several agricultural markets, the rapid increase in budgetary expenditure and the need to ensure competitiveness of European agriculture while safeguarding social and economic equilibrium in rural areas led the Commission to propose a fresh general discussion on the future of the CAP and to present to the Council a series of guidelines for amending the policy as currently applied (COM [91] 100 final). The Commission proposed a general reduction in agricultural prices and adjustments to the current quota and intervention arrangements, in order to adapt production better to market requirements and to encourage more widespread preferential use of Community products. Compensation schemes to offset price reductions would no longer be based on the quantities produced but on the areas under cultivation. The Commission was trying to prevent increased production, safeguard the income of farmers, and take account of specific situations. The Commission adopted a series of Regulations in October in relation to various commodities (*Twenty-fifth annual general report on the activities of the European Communities* [1991], p. 168). It also adopted proposals for Regulations on accompanying measures dealing with the countryside, environment, the afforestation of farmland, and aid for early retirement (*OJ C* 300, 21.11.1991). The GATT negotiations broke down in December, but the search for agreement had continued during the year, and the Community had started to secure cooperation agreements with the countries of Central and Eastern Europe, particularly Hungary, Poland and Czechoslavakia. A new emphasis in the latest reform measures for agriculture in 1992 was competitiveness, internal and international, achieved by guaranteed price reductions in some, but not all, products. Quality of production was emphasized, lower prices for consumers, protection of the environment, and stability of farm incomes (*OJ L* 180 and 181, 1.7.1992; 215, 30.7.1992; 221, 6.8.1992). In view of the final completion of the Single Market, the Community adopted a series of measures designed to eliminate all border controls linked to the implementation of the transitional arrangements for Spain and Portugal.

In the sustainable towns project launched by the Commission in 1993, LEADER II was allocated some ECU 1,400 million for the period 1994–99. Activity in 1993 and 1994 centered on the proposal and putting through of measures in the reform programme. There was a good start where production fell, internal consumption rose and farm incomes improved, particularly in the arable sector. In addition, the Council adopted several Regulations aimed at intensifying efforts to combat fraud. There was a greater variability in exchange rates because there was an increase in the fluctuations of the EMS exchange rate mechanism to 15%. On the international front, agricultural questions formed an important part of the accession negotiations with the EFTA countries. One of the main elements in the agreement reached was that the applicant countries would apply the CAP as from accession. On 20 July 1994, the Commission also proposed the negotiation of a new bilateral agricultural agreement with Switzerland. With the accession of Austria, Finland and Sweden in 1995, the European Union had 15 member states and as a result nearly 370 million citizens. The new member countries accepted all the provisions of the treaty and the *acquis communautaire* without derogations. The CAP was therefore applied to them as from this date without transition arrangements. Various factors (primarily the weather) had caused problems (floods in the north of the Union and drought in the south). The reform of the CAP reached its third and last stage, the final phase for many areas, cereals, oilseeds, beef and veal. Again, improvement overall in the agricultural situation was reported; along with improvements of the last year being maintained, public stocks had gone down, farm incomes had improved and the use of fertilizers and plant health products had been reduced. A single set-aside rate reduced to 10% was therefore adopted for the next marketing year. With regard to rural development, the Commission continued to implement LEADER II and to approve CFS and SPDs and Objectives 1 and 5b Operational Programmes for 1994–99. At the invitation of the European Council in Essen in December, the Commission made a study of alternative development strategies for the future integration into the CAP of the Central and Eastern Europe agriculture sectors.

The main feature of the year 1996 was the serious crisis in the beef and veal sector of Bovine Spongiform Encephalopathy (BSE or Mad-Cow Disease), possibly linked to the Creutzfeldt-Jakob disease which affects humans. Health protection steps were taken, and the measures ensured only safe beef and veal were on sale were restoring consumer confidence. However, this was an issue which dominated the last years of the twentieth century, particularly in the UK. British beef exports to France are still frozen, in spite of strenuous negotiations. The Florence European Council decided in June to provide a total of ECU 850 million to help stock farmers affected by the crisis. Particular attention was given in 1996 to product quality through the adoption of a Regulation extending community rules on organic production methods to include livestock, as well as the first lists of geographical indications and protected designations of origins. The common organizations of the markets in fruit and vegetables were reformed, with a greater role for producer organizations. The monitoring of the ban on the use of certain substances in livestock was enforced, for example hormones and beta-agonists. On 26 May, the Council adopted Directives 96/32/EC and 96/33EC on pesticide residues. The Delors II document affirmed that rural development policy 'has become a key element in economic and social cohesion, enhancing the threefold function, productive, social and environmental, of all rural areas'. In particular, it opened the debate on how best to strengthen rural Europe's competitiveness. In Chapter 2, the complex relationship between rural areas and agriculture and between landscape and environment were addressed. In Part II of the report, maps produced by the Geographical Information Systems (GIS) team of the former DG VI served to illustrate the different characteristics of rural Europe.

In 1996, the 500 delegates who took part in the Commission's discussions at a conference in Cork entitled 'A living countryside' (7–9 November) were policy-makers, professionals and others whose deliberations led to what is now known as the 'Cork Declaration', emphasising once more the need for a 'bottom-up' approach to rural development. In its *Agenda 2000* communication, *For a stronger and wider Union*, published in July 1997, the European Commission set out its vision for Europe's future which included a reflection on its agricultural and rural development policies. The communication proposed sustainable growth and employment to improve the living conditions of European citizens and to deepen the commitment to economic and social cohesion, to which the reform of structural policies of the CAP and of rural development would contribute. It stressed the need to deepen the 1992 reforms by continuing the move to world market prices and providing partial compensation for the resulting lower institutional prices by increasing direct income aid (COM [97] 509 final). A high priority of these reforms is a deepening of the Union's commitment to maintaining viable rural communities and to protecting Europe's rural heritage. EU aid for rural development (outside the horizontal measures) is delivered through three priority Objectives of the Structural Funds Objective 1 (least developed areas), Objective 5b (fragile rural areas not covered by Objective 1) and Objective 6 (extremely sparsely populated regions). The challenge was to maintain a 'living' countryside. Rural areas of the European Union, defined as those with a population density of less than 100 people per square kilometre, were inhabited by 17.5% of the total EU population but accounted for 80% of the total territory. The population density of rural areas varied considerably across the Union. Although agriculture remains the major user of available land in rural areas, it is no longer the backbone of the rural economy, producing only 2% of GDP.

In *Agenda 2000*, the Commission responded with a rural development policy founded on two principles:

(i) a recognition of the multi-functional role of agriculture, and

(ii) a need for an integrated approach to developing rural areas, so that Europe's rural heritage does not decline in parallel with its traditional economic base.

Farmers already play an important role in the preservation of biodiversity and the protection of the countryside. The potential range of occupations adaptable to the rural countryside can either be conducted using the farm, for example agri-tourism, or perhaps be unrelated to it, for instance, leisure, culture, environment, nature conservation, information technology, communications or teleworking, all of which are growth industries in Ireland. It was hoped to streamline existing framework actions by bringing them into a single, flexible, simple, decentralized framework. In the accompanying measures, too numerous to mention individually here, the Commission has proposed to maintain a Community Initiative, building on the success of the previous LEADER programmes, which would develop capacities amongst local people in Europe's rural communities. Among these strategies were agricultural restructuring, setting up and training young farmers, renovation and development of villages, protection and conservation of local heritage, developing and improving rural infrastructure, promoting tourism and craft activities and improving the processing and marketing of agricultural products. Community Agencies would advise on how to take the measures required to protect the environment, to assess the results of these measures and to ensure that the public is properly informed about the state of the environment. Measures of this kind are examined in further detail below in the discussion on the environment.

The BSE crisis continued in 1997 and, after investigative work had been done by the European Parliament, the Commission produced a report on the measures adopted to eradicate the disease, protect public health and restore confidence to the consumer. The Commission adopted a report on the applications of the Regulation on agricultural production methods compatible with the requirements of the protection of the environment and the maintenance of the countryside (COM [97] 620 final). The Luxembourg European Council in December also stressed the need to extend the reform of the CAP to Mediterranean products and to develop the existing model of European agriculture, while seeking greater competitiveness inside and outside the Union.

In 1998, as part of *Agenda 2000*, the Commission tabled proposals for the CAP which were designed to strengthen competitiveness, stress product quality, food safety and the environment. However, there was a firm commitment to guarantee equitable standard of living for the farmer, to promote economic diversification of the Union's rural areas in advance of the introduction of the single currency. It rectified a Directive to provide better welfare protection for livestock on farms. The proposal for support for rural development from the EAGGF provided for agri-environment schemes, early retirement schemes, woodland management schemes and aid for farming in less favoured areas for non-Objective 1 regions. The Guidance Section of the EAGGF was to fund Objective 1 areas. The proposal for a

Regulation drawing up common rules for direct payments under the CAP, presented by the Commission as part of *Agenda 2000*, provided for aid to be made conditional on compliance with environmental criteria.

FISHERIES

In Ireland, the native consumption of fish in the 1970s was low, and there was at that time the added disadvantage of lack of appropriate storage, fish processing facilities, serviced landing areas and infrastructure. Unlike its Scandinavian neighbours, fishing was an industry that had failed to capture adequate funding or policies, and fish as gourmet food or as part of a healthy diet took some time to become established in the national consciousness. In coastal waters renowned for their unpredictability, it was a livelihood that was more dangerous than profitable. There has been some improvement in the catching, storing and marketing of fish, as well as in the creative policies and funding, but, as in agriculture, fishing will always be subject to the influences of international monetary policies and markets, quotas, prices and the weather. The fishing industry in Ireland and the EU has been dogged by the over-fishing of certain species, the increasing sparsity of resources, the lack of up-to-date and appropriate fishing and surveillance vessels, as well as the dependence of some coastal regions, and their fishermen on the industry as the sole source of income. The sector is the responsibility of the Fisheries Directorate-General (*http://www.europa.eu.int/comm/dgs/fisheries/index_en. htm*), formerly DG XIV.

Prior to Ireland's accession, in the fishing industry Community prices were increased to take account of the price trends. With the exception of plaice, these prices were applicable throughout the enlarged Community. On entry formulation of prices was supplemented by a list of representative wholesale markets and ports in the new member states, Ireland, Great Britain and Denmark (*OJ L* 266, 25.11.1972, pp. 21 and 23). A measure adopted in December 1972 allowed the financing by the EAGGF of conversion of the salt cod fishing fleet and on-shore facilities (drying plants) over a period of five years under certain criteria (Regulation [EEC] No. 2722/72 of 19 December 1972; *OJ L* 291, 28.12.1972, p. 30).

Considerable success was achieved in the fisheries market following the Community's decision to establish 200-mile economic zones. In the fisheries sector at the beginning of 1976, several non-member countries decided to extend their fishing areas with effect from 1 January 1977 to 200 miles off their North Sea or North Atlantic coasts (*Bulletin of the Economic Communities* No. 10, 1976, Par. 1501). However, there was a serious depletion of stocks of herring in the North Sea and off the west of Scotland, and of sole and other North Sea species. At the same time, there were potentially undeveloped fisheries markets for species such as blue whiting, horse-mackerel, ling and blue ling. This drastic situation had been brought about by cut-throat competition. Increased fishing resulted not in increased catches but in a dangerous drop in resources, reducing the profitability of the industry and hitting fishermen's incomes. The starting-point for ensuring that stocks were not over-fished was the setting annually of Total Allowable Catches (TACs) for each stock. Two international organizations, the International Council for the Exploration of the Seas (ICES) and the Northwest Atlantic Fisheries Organization (NAFO), provided the scientific input and calculated the level of catches possible at different levels of fishing from each of the stocks during the year. A balance had to be struck by the Commission between the long-term objective of replacing stocks and the short-term obligations of ensuring fishermen a suitable income. The technique for dividing up the Community's share was devised in three stages. The first set of criteria was laid down at The Hague in 1976, where the Community recognized the particular situations of regions highly dependent on fishing, with little alternative employment, for example, Ireland (principally at Killybegs), Greenland and the UK. It agreed that, for Ireland, the TAC could be doubled between 1975 and 1979.

As result of the introduction of the 200 mile fishing limit in 1977, the Commission decided to protect the sea-fishing zones and gain access to locations outside them in four ways:

(i) the preparation of a common policy on conservation and management of resources mainly decided on determination of maximum authorized catches (quotas);

(ii) defining conditions for fishing in non-member country waters or Community waters;

(iii) a socio-structural policy to help the fisheries sector adjust to catch possibilities and definitive arrangements after research on stock controls, and

(iv) management of the Community market (*OJ L* 48, 19.2.1977, p. 28).

The proposed allocation of catch quotas (TACs) took into account the interest of the coastal populations of Ireland and UK. Technical measures were introduced for the conservation of fish species and control of fishing, and Directives on structural adaptations of fishing fleets to new conditions for exploitation of resources were proposed. The fishing of endangered stocks of herring was banned or reduced. Strenuous efforts were made between 1977 and 1980 to implement a Common Fisheries Policy (CFP) with 200-mile zones, but there was a lack of agreement among member states.

The second stage of dividing the fishing share was elaborated by the Community's foreign ministers in May 1980. They stated that

(i) traditional fishing activities of the shipping boats should be taken into account, as should

(ii) the heavy dependence on the industry in some regions and

(iii) the losses which would be suffered by Community boats in third-country waters after the introduction of the 200-mile zones.

In interpreting these criteria, the Commission took the catches between 1973 and 1978 as a base to determine traditional fishing activities. In calculating third-country losses, it was not possible to grant full compensation from stocks in Community waters due to insufficient resources, because to do so would disrupt traditional fishing patterns, so it was suggested that they be compensated for on a percentage basis. During the year, the Commission amended an improved proposal to the Council, on the basis of the European Parliament's resolutions, to enable the Council to adopt overall fisheries policies. The proposal covered

(i) access to fishing zones;

(ii) conservation and exploitation of resources;

(iii) relations with non-member states;

(iv) re-organization of production structures, and

(v) a review of the organization of the market.

However, the Council remained divided on conditions of access to fishing zones and on the allocation of catch quotas among member states.

Though efforts were made in 1982 to agree a new fisheries policy before the expiry date of the exceptional fishing arrangements set down in the Act of Accession, the proposals were rejected by Denmark. The Commission reminded member states of their right and obligation to take responsibility for national measures particularly as regards fish conservation. The Council extended the validity of the existing fishery arrangements with certain non-Community countries and interim measures for inshore fishing were again prolonged. Therefore, it was not until 25 January 1983 that 'blue' Europe came into being when the Common Fisheries Policy (CFP) was agreed. Its principles were the common management of the economy of coastal areas,

the common organization of the market in fishery and aquaculture products, the creation of catch quotas and the collective management of fisheries agreements with non-member countries. A comprehensive set of measures of technical conditions for fishing in EEC waters was adopted. The legislation set standards for minimum mesh sizes to protect young fish, minimum landing sizes and established permanent levels of by-catches of edible fish which may be scooped up with other (usually industrial) fish. It also listed zones where fishing was prohibited or restricted to certain times of the year to protect spawning grounds and nursery areas. Temporary conditions were attached to TACs and used to protect stocks. The TACs lapse if they are not renewed and reviewed each year. Each member country's inspectorate is obliged to check up on Community fishing vessels in its own ports and maritime waters, to ensure compliance with conservation and Regulations. The governments themselves had to take administrative or punitive action against skippers who violated these measures.

The Community approved multi-annual guidance programmes for fisheries and aquaculture drawn up by the member states in 1985. On 20 December, the Council adopted the TACs, together with the new rules and amendments made necessary by enlargement (*OJ L* 363, 3112.1985). The new fisheries policy was fixed for a ten-year period with the approval of the relevant structural Regulation (*Bulletin of the European Communities* No. 12 1986, pp. 94 ff.). This policy was based on the specific programmes which the member states had to submit to the Commission for approval. Some amendments to the control Regulations facilitated surveillance and assisted the implementation of the conservation of fishery resources. Changes to the TAC Regulations allowed for the incorporation of Spain and Portugal for the first time (*Bulletin of the European Communities*, 1987 Par. 601).

In 1987, the new structural policy provided for in December of the previous year came into force; the Commission approved a multi-annual guidance programme for the fishing fleet and aquaculture, thus setting the structural targets for the period 1987–91. Adoption of the research programme for the period 1988–92 would, it was hoped, enable better use to be made of the results of data compiled in marine science and technology. In the field of external relations, various fisheries agreements were concluded, in particular an agreement with Morocco which was significant in terms of catch possibilities. In view of the political and economic difficulties facing fishermen and undertakings in certain member states with regard to the TACS and quota arrangements, the Commission subsequently adopted a Community frame of reference (*OJ C* 224, 31.8.1989, p. 3). Mechanisms for management of fishery resources, supplemented by rules governing their use, lined up with the objectives of the CFP and the basic principles of the treaty. The adoption of a series of Regulations in December 1989 enabled not only the fishing possibilities in the Community zone to be fixed for the next year but also those in the waters of Norway Sweden, the Faroes, Greenland and the area covered by the Northwest Atlantic Fisheries Organization. The Council decided that the Community should help finance the expenditure of the member states in the enforcement of the provisions relating to the management of fishery resources.

In a discussion paper on the outline of a common fisheries system in the Mediterranean, the Commission sought to implement a common policy of conservation and management suitable for that region. On 28 November 1990, it also adopted a communication on the Common Fisheries Policy (*Bulletin of the European Communities*, No. 11). The marked imbalance between available stocks and existing fishing capacity, a recurrent problem, and the high degree of dependence of third countries on access to Community waters, short-comings in the structures and the need for better management and control, were salient points. It proposed an amendment to Regulation EEC No. 4028/86 which gave priority to exploratory fishing, and adjustment of capacity.

In March 1991, the Commission formally adopted the Community Support Framework (CSF) for the improvement of the conditions under which the fishery and aquaculture products are processed and marketed in various member states (*OJ L* 99, 19.4.1991). On 4 December, the Commission adopted a report on the situation of fisheries in the Community, the economic and social development in coastal areas and the state of stocks and their probable development. The report laid down the guidelines for the policy for the period 1993-2002. Striking the proper balance between resources and fishing effort was to bring about the socio-economic changes to which the Community would have to find solutions, especially the social problems, as a contri-bution to economic and social cohesion. In 1992, the Commission had two main objectives:

(i) to guarantee sustainability of the activities of the sector while

(ii) ensuring its economic and social viability through the stable and rational use of resources.

This was accompanied by proposals for the reform of the monitoring system. The Council also decided, in 1993, while adapting the arrangements for fisheries for the accession of Spain and Portugal, to introduce identical arrangements for the vessels of all the member states from 1 January 1996. The Commission arranged a conference for all the member states bordering the Mediterranean. It also presented a communication on the use of large drift nets in the framework of the CFP. The ecological impact of fishing had now been fully integrated into Community activity; therefore, measures were being taken to protect marine biodiversity and the rational pursuit of fishing on a sustainable basis. A crisis in the Community fisheries sector led to a communi-cation adopted by the Commission on 19 July 1996. The decline in prices in the main species of fish meant that the Community was dependent on 50% imports for its supply. The Commission adopted conclusions on the situation and outlook in the industry in 1996.

Criteria and procedures for the introduction of a system for the management of fishing effort aimed at bringing fleet capacities and catches under control in certain fishing areas were adopted by the Council on 27 March 1995 (Regulation [EC] No. 685/95). They covered Community waters in the Atlantic and were aimed at a spatial distribution of fishing effort while preserving the existing balance between different areas. At its sixth meeting in August that year, the United Nations Conference on Straddling Stocks and Highly Migratory Species adopted an agreement by consensus on the implementation of the Convention of the Law of the Sea (1982) as regards conservation and management of these species. Within the Food and Agriculture Organization (FAO), an agreement was drafted on a code of conduct for responsible fishing which covered all sea areas and fishing, but the agreement was not binding.

In 1997, the Council adopted a decision on the objec-tives and detailed restructuring of the Community fisheries sector for the period 1997–2002, with a view to achieving a balance on a sustainable basis between resources and their exploitation (Decision 97/413/EC). Further reduction of the fleet was envisaged. On 16 December, the Commission adopted multi-annual guidance programmes covering the period January 1997–2001. The adoption of a Regulation banning the use of drift-nets from 1 January 2002 by all vessels in Community, other than the waters of the Baltic, the Belt and the Sound, and in other waters by all Community vessels, was the most important measure of 1998. The implementation of this Regulation was to be accom-panied by social measures and compensation for the fishermen concerned. The involvement of fishermen, administrators and scientists in solving the difficulties associated with single-species fisheries started the previous year for all types of fish and was continued at regional meetings (COM [1998] 145). On the 5 June 1998, the Commission adopted a working plan entitled *Improving the implementation of the Common Fisheries Policy — an action plan* (COM [98] 92 final). It was more hopeful of the intention of member states to protect their own resources, given the receipt of over 40 plans for fishery conservation from these states.

ENVIRONMENT

The Directorate-General responsible for environment was formerly DG XI and is now simply called Environment (*http://www.europa.eu.int/comm/dgs/ environment/index_en.htm*). It is based in both Brussels and Luxembourg. Its mission is

(i) to secure a high level of environmental protection;

(ii) to improve the quality of life;

(iii) to increase environmental efficiency;

(iv) to preserve the rights of future generations to a viable environment, and

(v) to ensure equitable use of our common environmental resources. Europe's environment can be divided into the natural environment, comprising rivers, lakes, the atmosphere, wildlife, vegetation, and the man-made environment, towns, cities, architecture, art and so forth.

As we are currently more fully aware, 'pollution knows no frontiers'. The Rhine, for example had been a convenient dumping ground for industrial (and domestic) wastes in Switzerland, Germany and France, so that by the time it reached the Netherlands downstream, it was extremely heavily polluted, a situation which was then foisted on the last country in the chain. In the urban environment, economic growth policies, industrial expansion and increased urbanization, transport and energy requirements, the consumer society, threatened much of what we value in our culture, heritage and society, our living and working conditions, our quality of life (Article 2 of the Treaty of Rome 1957). This growth was based on the consumption of non-renewable resources, and the corollary that man-made pollution inevitably finds its way into the environment. The pragmatic need to create a common industrial base to further the internal market meant that joint action in the environment was essential if distortion of competition was to be avoided. More stringent and expensive anti-pollution measures in one member state would disadvantage its industry in the common market. The cost of combatting or preventing such pollution is high and unattractive to governments, who have limited financial resources and uncertain political futures. When one reviews the progress of European Union policies, it is clear that even before Ireland joined, funds for these policies were limited, because the number of contributing states was also restricted. The policies themselves were clearly separable, and in some areas actually contravened each other's provisions. The reader

will accordingly note that Directives of an environmental nature can also be found under such headings as agriculture, industry, structures, regional development, consumers and so forth.

The growing unease about the environmental state of the world, particularly as regards pollution, urged the European Community to adopt a first communication on Community policy concerning the environment in 1971, and to encourage constructive comments from international trade unions and industrial organizations (SEC [71] 2616 final; SEC denotes documents of the Office of the Secretary-General of the Commission. These internal working documents represent an earlier stage in the operations of the Commission than COM documents, and are not systematically available.) The main impetus in the early days came from political engagements as well as from the provision of Article 30 of the Treaty of Rome guaranteeing the free movement of goods and services between member states, to which certain exceptions, including measures capable of justification on environmental grounds, are now accepted.

The need for a formal EEC policy was recognized at the Paris Summit (19–20 October 1972) and internationally at the United Nations Conference on the Human Environment held in Stockholm in June 1972. Subsequently, the Commission plan was published. General principles were endorsed and were worked out by EEC environment ministers at their meeting in Bonn on 31 October 1972. Heavy emphasis was laid on the prevention of pollution (as well as its control), the safeguarding, measurement and monitoring of its effects on the environment, be it water, air, land or atmosphere, from industry (and industrial products, including cars), energy and waste. Just over a year later, on 22 November 1973, the Council of Ministers adopted the Community's First Environmental Action Programme (*OJ* C 112, 1973, p. 1). All Community institutions were called on to establish this policy, and to implement a programme of action accompanied by a precise timetable before 31 July 1973. The objectives were:

(i) to prevent and eliminate pollution and nuisances and maintain a satisfactory ecological balance so as to ensure the protection of the biosphere;

(ii) to avoid exploitation of natural resources and significant damage to the ecological balance, and to provide sound management, guide development in accordance with quality requirements, especially by improving working conditions and the quality of life.

Finally, it was to be ensured that more account was taken of environmental aspects in town planning and land use and to seek common solutions to environmental problems with states outside the Community, in particular international organizations.

However, in the closing months of 1973 (the year of Ireland's entry into the Community), a series of external events, monetary crises, rising commodity prices and incidents in the Middle East resulting in the energy crisis had blown the Community off course. These developments emphasized how heavily the EEC had become dependent on outside sources of energy and raw materials to sustain production, economic growth, competitiveness, employment, tourism and trade. Only 40% of its energy was actually produced inside the Community. The years 1974 and 1975 were ones of uncertainty and of united work to overcome these adverse circumstances. In December 1974, a recommendation was introduced concerning the protection of architectural and natural heritage (*OJ L* 21, 28.1.75, p. 22). Between 1973 and 1976, a series of Directives, Decisions, Resolutions and Recommendations was adopted in relation to detergents, waste, energy, dangerous substances (including their packaging and labelling), ionizing radiation, cosmetics, quality of bathing waters, marine pollution, foods for human consumption and so forth and, on the pro-active front, sources of information, technical progress and research. Of particular significance was the recommendation to public authorities of applying the 'polluter pays principle' (*OJ L* 194, 25.7.1975). Also implemented were steps to protect the environment in relation to agricultural policy and the urban context. Harmonization of measures across the member states was considered vital, providing it did not effect the implementation of the Single Market. Cooperation with international organizations already involved in the area was encouraged, for example OECD, the United Nations, the Council of Europe, the World Health Organization and NATO.

The Second Environmental Action Programme, agreed by environment ministers on December 9 1976, basically provided for a continuation of measures set out and initiated under the First Programme. This five-year programme (1977–81) forged a more comprehensive environment policy with emphasis on preventative action, particularly as regards pollution, land use and the production of waste. Special attention was also paid to the protection and rational management of space, the environment and natural resources. (It was drafted against the backdrop of the energy crisis, which had demonstrated Europe's dependence on external resources.) It involved a method of mapping combining environmental data with space management, endeavours to solve environmental problems arising from intensive farming, management of urban space and coastal and mountainous regions, protection of flora and fauna and of natural resources. Of particular importance was the study of anti-wastage measures, prevention, reclamation and disposal, still problems today, and the

importance of recycling and re-use. It also considered how Environmental Impact Assessment (EIA) procedures (the prevention of pollution at source) might be introduced. In 1979, the Directive on the conservation of wild birds (the Wild Birds Directive) was promulgated (*OJ L* 103, 25.4.1979, p. 1). A report was issued in 1980 entitled *Progress made in connection with the Environment Action Programme and assessment of the work done to implement it* (COM [80] 222 final). Many Directives had been passed in 1980, for example Council Directive 80/68/EEC on the protection of groundwater against pollution caused by certain dangerous substances (*OJ L* 20, 26.1.1980, p. 43), Council Directive 80/778/EEC of 15 July 1980 relating to the quality of water for human consumption (*OJ L* 229, 30.8.1980, p. 11), Council Directive 80/779 on air quality limit values and guide values for sulphur dioxide and suspended particulates (*OJ L* 229, 30 8.1980, p. 30) and so forth. The main feature of the first generation of policies was their highly restrictive approach towards the environment and the action to be taken in areas such as air, water and waste, which tended to be viewed in isolation. The emphasis fell mainly on counteracting pollution and the resources given to support this policy remained fairly limited.

The Third Action Programme issued in 1982 was scheduled to run from 1982–86, and sought to complete the shift of emphasis away from efforts simply to contain environmental damage to action to prevent it from occurring in the first place. The 'Seveso' Directive on the major accident hazards of certain industrial activities laid the responsibility on the management of industry to protect workers, the public and the environment against major industrial accidents (*OJ L* 230, 5.8.1982, p. 1). The Community sought to integrate concern for the environment through the wider use of the EIA mechanism at the planning stage, particularly in agriculture, industry transport, energy and tourism. EIAs were first adopted in the USA within the framework of the *National Environment Policy Act* 1969. Their objective is to ascertain as far as is feasible the full range of impacts on human activities in the environment so that optimal decisions can be taken and adverse consequence avoided. Their application varies (in relation to terms and conditions) according to the type of project, when it is in the planning process and the manner of their use (what kind of assessment). The Community had to agree on the principles to be followed while leaving the member states free to incorporate them in their legislation and practice in the most appropriate way.

The problems to be confronted in the 1980s were the economic recession, unemployment, lack of competitiveness in industry and raw materials shortages. Environmental policy could play its part by creating jobs in environmental protection, by reducing pollution through the employment of non-renewable raw materials, recycling of waste and reducing negative effects of using oil by the employment of coal and nuclear power. The pollutants tackled were those from motor vehicles, lead in petrol, exhaust fumes, chemicals, noise abatement and in particular the link between noise reduction and energy savings. Examples include the Council Directive 82/884 on limit values for lead in the air (*OJ L* 378, 3.12.1982, p.15) or Council Decision of 25 November 1982 on the consolidations of precautionary measures concerning chloro-fluorocarbons in the environment (*OJ L* 329, 25.11.1982, p. 29). The rational use of land and natural resources was also of great importance. Special attention would be paid to environmental problems in the Mediterranean because Spain and Portugal were to join the Community during this programme.

The year 1984 was distinguished by a plethora of Directives aimed at the reduction of noise, be it the sound level and exhaust system of motor vehicles, compressors, tower cranes, welding and power generators, concrete mixers or lawnmowers. In 1985, the Commission was involved in the implementation of the Third Action Programme while preparing for the Fourth. The Council adopted a Directive abolishing lead in petrol by 1989 (85/210/EEC) and on the approximation of the laws of the member states concerning the lead content of petrol (*OJ L* 96, 3.4.1985, p. 25). The publication of *Europe's green mantle: heritage and the future of our forests* coincided in 1985 with the Commission Directive for assessing the environmental impact of major public and private development projects (85/337/EEC of 27 June 1985; *OJ L* 175, 5.7.1985, p. 40). For the first time, a Directive required the Commission itself and the European Investment Bank to take environmental factors into account before approving aid for infrastructure and other developments.

In acknowledgement of the need for information, the Community initiated the CORINE programme in 1985 to establish a coordinated information system on the state of the environment and natural resources. Noxious emissions from motor vehicles were also considered and agreement reached in the Council. The Commission amended its proposal for a Directive on the emissions of pollutants into the air from large combustion plants. As part of its work on an inventory of existing chemicals entitled European Inventory of Existing Commercial Chemical Substances (EINECS), the Commission drew up a provisional inventory which was sent to member states to be checked. Secondly, thanks to its action, the system introduced for processing notifications of new chemicals worked satisfactorily. The Luxembourg Council reached agreement in principle on the subject of confirming the Community's responsibility in the environment field (*Bulletin of the European Communities* No. 11, 1985, point 2.1.104).

The year 1986 was marked by the Single European Act (SEA), a fragile economic recovery and by the preparation for the European Year of the Environment (EYE). Public opinion had played a major role in galvanizing governments and the Community into making the environment a high-priority policy area. This Community Initiative in 1987 was marked by a series of public events, from trade fairs and exhibitions to nature conservation camps, clean-up campaigns in canals, rivers, forests and on beaches and coastlines, not excluding urban areas. The Community stepped up its efforts to ensure that a full account was taken of environmental matters in all the Community's policies. The third report on the state of the environment was published by the Community. Previous reports in 1977 and 1979 tended to look at activities undertaken to implement polices rather than to evaluate the state of the environment. It was a sweeping evaluative report and an excellent foundation for the creation of a future policy. The role of the environment as an essential component of economic, industrial, agricultural and social policies would be further enhanced in the SEA. The Commission formally adopted a resolution on the Fourth Action Programme for the Environment which set out the framework for this activity from 1987–92 (*OJ C* 63, 18.3.1986). To incorporate the environment in all stages of planning and economic and social policies was a key objective. The Council also adopted Council Regulation No. 3582/86 of 17 November 1986 on the protection of the Community's forests against atmospheric pollution (*OJ L* 326, 21.11.1996, p. 2). In 1987, with the adoption of the SEA and more recently the Treaty on European Union (Title XVI, Article 130 r), protection of the environment became a recognized part of Union policy and a key element of its objectives.

Perhaps one of the more remarkable achievements of the EC policy in this area was that, prior to the SEA taking effect in 1987, there was no explicit legal provision for Community environmental actions. In spite of that, more than 100 instruments, mainly Directives, were adopted in the fifteen years after the heads of state or government took the first steps to protect our environment. The Community's Fourth Programme included several sub-programmes covering the four objectives for the year:

(i) promoting the use of clean technologies and good environmental practice;

(ii) encouraging local community activities;

(iii) providing support for the organization of advanced training courses and education, and

(iv) taking specific measures in non-member countries

to increase environmental awareness.

The signing of what was to be known as the Montreal Protocol in September by twenty-four countries, including most of the member states of the Community, was a significant event. This is the Protocol on Chlorofluorocarbons (CFCs) to the Vienna Convention for the Protection of the Ozone Layer. It provided for a freeze in the consumption and production of CFCs at 1986 levels. Production was to be cut to 80% and further in future years, and also a halt to the production and consumption of halogens was to be included. The Commission continued with work on the classification and labelling of dangerous substances, in particular carcinogens, mutagens and teratogens.

The European Year of the Environment ended on 20 March 1988. EYE showed that Community policy would have to concentrate on three main areas: legislation and its enforcement, the raising of public awareness and practical projects to improve the existing situation. Monitoring the applications of Community law was an onerous task. A substantial increase occurred in the number of complaints made to the Commission on environmental matters. On 14 October, the Council formally adopted the aforementioned Montreal Convention, which would come into force in the beginning of the following year. On 31 October, the Commission sent to the Council a proposal for a Directive on freedom of environmental information. The Commission adopted a Directive on measures taken against air pollution by exhaust gases from private cars powered by diesel engines. In 1989, the European Council's Madrid and Strasbourg meetings were more global in the range of their concerns; in them and at the Western Economic Summit in Paris, significant attention was paid to issues such as the protection of the ozone layer, the conservation of tropical forests and climate change. On 8 June, the Council adopted a Resolution on the greenhouse effect known as global warming (*OJ C* 183, 20.7.1989). At its June 1990 meeting in Dublin, the European Council agreed on the need for a more determined and systematic approach to environmental management in the Community. In its statement, it called for action by the Community and its member states to be developed on a coordinated basis, in keeping with the principles of sustainable development, and to give precedence to preventive measures. The European Council also defined areas of activity to which priority should be given, thereby determining the direction of Community environmental policy in the years ahead. A Regulation was adopted establishing the European Environment Agency (EEA) (Regulation 1210/90 of 7 May 1990) and the European Environment and Observation Network (EIONET) (*OJ L* 120, 11.5.1990, p. 1). Also in May, Directives on the deliberate release into the environment of genetically modified organisms and on the freedom of environmental information were adopted. On 6 June, the Commission adopted the green paper on the urban environment (COM [90] 218 final). It adopted guidelines for the initiatives on the protection of the environment in coastal areas (ENVIREG). On 17 December, the Commission ratified a proposal for a Regulation to protect the environment of the Irish Sea, the North Sea, the Baltic Sea and the North East Atlantic (NORSPA).

By 1991, environment policy had become inextricably linked to the overall economic policy of the Union, and was seen to be an integral part of policies such as agriculture, internal market, transport and energy. In its response to the Council's conclusions to stabilize carbon dioxide emissions in the EC by 1990, the Commission adopted a strategy to limit carbon dioxide emissions and to improve energy efficiency. This communication outlined a comprehensive strategy to meet the stabilization target by means of voluntary regulations, research and development programmes on carbon dioxide and energy taxes and national programmes. Significant progress was made in the environmental field when the Commission adopted or agreed measures in the NORSPA project, waste water, Community eco-labelling, the protection of natural habitats and pollution by lorries. The Council adopted a series of measures to reduce pollution by inputs in agriculture, including Regulation 2092/91 (*OJ L* 198, 22.7.1991, p. 1) of 24 June on the organic production of agricultural products and a Directive concerning the placing of plant protection products on the market (91/414/EC; *OJ L* 230, 19.8.1991, p. 1). It also agreed on a Directive concerning the protection of water against pollution from agricultural nitrates. At this stage in the development process of environmental policy, one finds environmental-type legislation in many areas such as tourism, transport, energy, agriculture, regional development, industry structures, economic and social cohesion, so wide had its scope become.

When the Treaty on European Union was signed (1992) and later ratified, the protection of the environment became a fully recognized part of the Union and its objectives. Other key events in 1992 were the Fifth Action Programme on the Environment and the holding of a United Nations Conference on Environment and Development in Rio de Janeiro in June 1992. In Rio, the Community and the member states recognized their wider responsibilities in promoting environmental action at a global level. The introduction of the Directive on the conservation of natural habitats and of fauna and flora, known as the 'Habitats Directive', was a key step forward (*OJ L* 206, 22.7.1992, p. 7). The Fifth Environmental Action Programme adopted by the Council in March 1993 for a period of eight years is entitled *Towards*

Sustainable Development (*OJ L* 275, 10.10.1993). Its objective is no longer to protect the environment in a restrictive way, with corrective actions, but to reconcile it with necessary economic growth. This integrationist and long-term view of the central theme emphasized coordination and a long-term approach, together with a full participation at all levels of society. This theme underlies the various initiatives undertaken by the Commission. The Council adopted measures on titanium dioxide, pollution, cross-frontier movement of waste and the conservation of habitats. The Commission adopted a green paper on the impact of transport on the environment and a communication on industrial competitiveness and protection of the ozone respectively.

Arising from the Fifth Environmental Action Programme and the CAP reform of 1992 came the Rural Environment Protection Scheme (REPS), established under Council Regulation (EEC) 2078 on Agricultural production methods compatible with the requirements for protection of the environment and maintenance of the countryside (*OJ L* 215, 30.7.1992, p. 85). The scheme's objectives are to establish farming practices and controlled production methods which reflect increasing public concern for conservation, landscape protection and wider environmental problems, to protect wildlife habitats and endangered species of flora and fauna, and produce quality food in an extensive and environmentally friendly manner. It also sought to give recognition to farmers as guardians of the countryside. REPS was open to part-time or full-time farmers, those owning or leasing at least 3 hectares (7.5 acres), excluding areas under associated tourism and craft activities. Farmers had to follow an agri-environmental plan, with recommendations in eleven different areas, for a continuous period of five years. These included waste management, liming, fertilizing and grassland management plans. Watercourses and wells were to be protected from livestock and maintained, wildlife habitats were to be retained, together with field margins, woodlands, wetlands and natural vegetation. Maintenance of farm and field boundaries was essential, tillage crop production was subject to certain restrictions, agri-chemicals and fertilizers could not be used in and around hedgerows, lakes, rivers or streams. Features of archaeological or historical interest were also to be protected. The programme was to be jointly funded by the European Union (75%) and the national exchequer (25%), and administered in Ireland by the Department of Agriculture. REPS came into operation in this country on 1 June 1994 and there have been various accounts and studies of its implementation to date (for instance Bell 1996, TEAGASC 1998).

Another recent fiscal measure to assist the environment was entitled *The financial instrument for the environment*, for which the acronym LIFE is employed. It was initially established for a three-year period (1993–95) with a global budget of some ECU 400 million. The programme was organized to cover several priority fields, the two principal ones being

(i) the promotion of moderate development and the quality of the environment (LIFE-Environment, 40% of resources), and

(ii) protection of habitats and of nature (LIFE-Nature, totalling 45% of resources).

The latter field saw the development of actions for financing incentive projects under the implementation of the Habitats Directive and a Corrigendum to it (*OJ L* 176, 20.7.1993, p. 29) and under the Birds Directive (amended by a Commission Directive 97/49/EC of 29 July 1997). LIFE-Nature, relating essentially to the safeguarding of natural heritage and biodiversity, stems from an understanding of culture which is different to that adopted by this report, specified by Article 128 of the Maastricht Treaty. In LIFE-Environment, projects are supported within the context of rural development; some will fall into the 'restoration of historical landscapes' category (archaeological or historical, urban or vernacular sites) which acquire their cultural dimension owing to interaction between the natural environment and its inhabitants, as well as the tourism-related opportunities which they create. The priority was to improve the quality of the environment in urban areas and included projects aimed at the sustainable management of access to and of the quality of the environment at important tourist sites.

In 1995, the Commission depended more strongly on the provision of information and the raising of awareness to provide greater protection for the environment. In the legislative field, it continued to rely on framework Directives and instruments. The control of trans-boundary wastes and their disposal (Basle Convention) and the Montreal Protocol (see above) were discussed internationally, and the EU was involved in more discussion with its Central and East European neighbours.

In 1996, the Commission, having reviewed implementation of the Fifth Action Programme, was not satisfied, and took stronger measures to enforce it. Water policy, ground water and environmental agreements were made between public authorities and industry, and it adopted a further Directive to prevent major industrial hazards (97/42/EC). Flora and fauna were protected by a Regulation. Framework Directives were introduced for integrated pollution control and ambient air, showing how seriously the concept of Sustainable Development was being taken. Internationally, preparations were being made for a special United Nations Assembly on Sustainable Development, as a sequel to the Rio de

Janeiro Conference. The Commission followed up its communication the previous year on water by proposing a framework Directive on water in 1997.

To combat acidification, it proposed a Directive to limit the sulphur content in certain fuels. It proposed three Directives on waste management, now a subject of debate in Ireland because of pending local-authority decisions to locate landfill waste dumps in certain areas. The European Consultative Forum on the Environment and Sustainable Development was an environmental consultation body created by the European Commission in 1997 under the Fifth Action Programme on the Environment, and is located at the Environmental Directorate-General. It covers all issues relating to sustainable development and has members from the European Economic Area (EEA; this comprises the remaining EFTA states added to EU states already in EFTA, and was established in January 1993 to coordinate relations in the wake of the Single Market) and the associated countries of Central and Eastern Europe. The Forum advises the Commission on policy development. The members are appointed in a personal capacity on the basis of suggestions from European interest groups. Members of the Forum come from trade unions, non-governmental organizations (NGOs), business, industry, consumers, farmers, local and regional authorities, scientific communities and other parties. The principles on enlargement and environment are what bind them together. In the publication *Natura 2000 — managing our heritage* (1997) a brief overview is given of the natural heritage situation.

Substantial progress was made in 1998 with regard to greenhouse gas emissions to meet the commitments given at the Kyoto conference in Japan on climate change, including air pollution from motor vehicles. Particular attention was paid to taking environmental concerns into consideration in other policies by broadening the instruments used and enforcing the legislation. Raising awareness and international cooperation in environmental matters were the concepts which the Commission undertook until 2000. When one considers that in Ireland in the 1970s, those interested in environmental matters were either in government or comprised only a handful of individuals or groups, the evolution and international acceptance of the importance of this relatively new policy has been remarkable.

Certain Community Agencies are particularly important in informing the public about the environment and natural heritage. A Community Agency is a public authority set up under European law and enjoying legal personality. While not provided for under the treaties establishing the European Communities or the Treaty on European Union, they are initiated by Community secondary legislation which details the very specific technical, scientific or administrative task they are expected to carry out. As indicated above, the European Environment Agency (EEA) was established in 1994 in Copenhagen to ensure the supply of objective, reliable and comparable information at European level. It enables member countries to take measures to protect the environment, to assess the results of these measures and to ensure the public is kept *au fait* about the state of the environment. Membership is open to countries which are not EU members but share in its concern for the environment, like Iceland, Liechtenstein and Norway. It ensures the supply of objective, reliable and up-to date data. The EEA has produced a wide range of reports and studies and has its own Internet site (*http://www.eea.dk*). It supports EIONET, its extended information network, and its European Reference Centre on Environmental Information (the latter service being available to the public). It creates and monitors environmental information aimed at sustainability both for the EU and the citizen. The *Dobris Assessment*, a well-known comprehensive report issued in 1995, was followed by *Europe's environment: the second assessment* (1998) and a more comprehensive report entitled *EU's environment outlook* (1999). These are all valuable contributions to a comprehensive understanding of the state of recent EU environmental policy and cultural heritage. The Community Plant Variety Office, based in Brussels, administers plant variety rights, a specific form of industrial property relating to new plant varieties. Every two months, the Office publishes information entered in the registers, and every year it produces an annual report listing valid Community plant variety rights. In the Republic of Ireland, one must also consult the Department of the Environment website for current information and its *Environment Bulletin* for recent information. ENFO, The Environment Information Service, based in Dublin (*http://www.enfo.ie*), was established by government in 1990 to promote knowledge of and care for the environment. It provides access to wide-ranging and authoritative information by means of a query-answering service, information leaflets, a library with a computerized database, access to INFOTERRA, video lending facilities, lectures and exhibitions.

CULTURAL HERITAGE

When starting to look at heritage as a keyword in EU information, one should realize that it was often the responsibility of 'culture'. Culture was previously under the aegis of Directorate-General X, Information, Communication, Culture and Audiovisual, of the Commission, now Education and Culture under the direction of Commissioner Vivianne Reding (*http://www.europa.eu.int/comm/dgs/education_culture/ index_en.htm*). The EU is built on the recognition of both individuality and diversity of the heritage of each state, the need to create structures, policies and financial incentives to enhance them individually and collectively and, where possible, to make them available to each other to achieve mutual recognition and co-operation. Some member states had constitutional or political reservations about general culture being 'subsumed' under Community policy. The early attempts to consider culture were therefore defined in a more limited way than at present. Most Community action in the cultural area was nothing more than the application of the EEC Treaty to this sector. However, in the late 1960s, there were several significant developments internationally and within the Community itself. The Council of Europe Agreement on the Protection of Archaeological Heritage was signed in London in May 1969. At The Hague in early December of the same year, the Community heads of state declared that they regarded Europe as an exceptional centre of development, culture and progress, and that it was important to preserve these characteristics. The Community adopted a UNESCO convention on 14 November 1970, under which the following issues were addressed:

(i) freedom of movement and establishment of cultural workers;

(ii) removal of tax barriers to the development of cultural foundations and patronage, and

(iii) copyright and related rights; literary translators and the social effects of these measures.

At the first summit conference of the enlarged Community held in Paris on 19–20 October 1972, attended on Ireland's behalf by An Taoiseach, Jack Lynch, it was stated in the final declaration that 'particular attention will be given to intangible values'. In the communique on European identity adopted at the Cophehagen summit in December 1973, culture was recognized as being one of the foremost elements of this identity. Following the European Parliament's Resolution on behalf of the Liberal and Allies Group entitled *On measures to protect the European cultural heritage* (*OJ C 62*, 30.5.1974, p. 5), adopted unanimously on 13 May 1974, and also its Resolution of 8 March 1976 on cultural exchanges (*OJ C 79*, 5.4.1976), preparations for additional policies and publications were set in train.

One of the earliest documents on the subject was *Community action in the cultural sector: Commission communication to the Council* sent on 22 November 1977 (*Bulletin of the European Communities Supplement 6/77*). In accordance with the proposals contained in the Commission's European Action Programme on the Environment of 17 May 1977, the Community could contribute to the preservation of architectural heritage by promoting training for restorers and developing new

conservation and restoration techniques. This memorandum endeavoured to describe the state of progress of Community intervention in the cultural domain and to indicate further targets to be aimed at. It encouraged support for cultural events which could be evaluated, as well as the formation of university research teams. The communication also stressed the need for co-operation between the cultural institutes of the then nine member states and the promotion of socio-cultural activities at European level.

There appears to have been a widening and awakening interest in various aspects of culture in the late 1970s and into the 1980s. The Parliament's Cultural Affairs Committee had identified many problems. In 1982, the European Commission published a statement on 'stronger Community action in the cultural sector' (*Bulletin of the European Communities Supplement 6/82*), and this year saw the first informal meeting of the ministers responsible for culture in the Community. In March 1983, the Commission produced a further pamphlet entitled *The Community and culture* (*European File 5/83*). In it, the Community recognized these often conflicting needs: to promote economic and social betterment and deepen the quality of life by creating structures that improved co-operation and freedom of movement, and yet at the same time protected the individuality and diversity of each culture. It proposed a Regulation to allow the temporary export of cultural or other goods, even though the Treaty of Rome allows member states, under certain conditions, to forbid or limit the export of national treasures of artistic, historic or archaeological importance. The publication *Towards a community television policy* (*European File No. 19/84*) considered the protection of copyright for creative artists, television rights, reproductions of records and cassettes and increased time-span for claiming royalties. The European Social Fund (discussed above) was to support training of cultural workers and creation of jobs. Funding was to be given to enlarge audiences and support live performances of plays, poetry and so forth. A European network of museum directors had been initiated. In 1985, the European Commission produced proposals on a tax regime for the cultural sector, intended to promote investment and initiatives in this area (*Europe documents*, English edition, Brussels, no. 1355, 15 May 1985, pp. 1 ff.). A more exciting series of events launched by the Council of Ministers on 13 June of that year on the initiative of Melina Mercouri was the European City of Culture, designed to demonstrate the rich cultural diversity of European cities and highlight their shared inheritance. This measure gives rise to artistic events and cultural exchanges of the highest standard which have been selected up to 2000, and in this special year nine cities hold the honour.

In the leaflet *European Community and culture* (*European File* 14/85), the Commission stated that there was a 'European dimension' or identity based on a common cultural heritage. It did, however, recognize that it was still dealing with a complex subject and the jealously guarded individuality of its component member states. Since the protection of architectural heritage would also give a boost to tourism in underdeveloped regions, this led to a Resolution on the part of the ministers with responsibility for cultural affairs, meeting with the Council on 13 November 1986, on the protection of Europe's architectural heritage (*OJ* C 320, 13.12.1986, p. 1). In 1987, the European Parliament passed a Resolution on the languages and cultures of regional and ethnic minorities (Doc. A2–150/87/Corrigendum 3) and the ARCHIPELAGO initiative was set up to provide EU support for minority languages. There was also a Resolution on the conservation of the Community's architectural and archaeological heritage (*OJ* C 309 1988, p. 423; *European Parliament Report* PE Doc. A2–192/88). In the run-up to the completion of the Single Market, the Council and the ministers responsible for cultural affairs, in their conclusions of 27 May 1988 on future action in the cultural field (*OJ* C 197, 7.7.1988, p. 1), singled out vocational training as one of the four areas for priority attention. From this came the Commission communication on *Vocational training in the arts field* (COM [90] 472 final). Events really began to move in tandem when the statement *New prospects for Community cultural action* (COM [92] 149 final) was adopted on 29 April 1992 by the Commission and approved by the Council on 12 November. This stated that specific proposals and programmes in the cultural field would be presented after the entry into force of the Treaty on European Union. Proposals for the KALEIDO-SCOPE Programme and the ARIANE Programme, both examined below, were contained in that one document.

The most significant development, however, was that Article 128 of the Treaty on European Union (known more familiarly as the Maastricht Treaty), at last provided a Treaty basis for the inclusion of culture (and heritage) as a sphere of activity. This was the start of the first phase of cultural action over the period 1994–99. It said 'the Community shall contribute to the flowering of culture of the Member States, while respecting their national and regional diversity and at the same time bringing their common cultural heritage to the fore'. It required on the one hand that the Council reaches its decisions unanimously and on the other that the Committee of the Regions be consulted. The Community was also to foster co-operation with third countries and competent international organizations in the sphere of culture, in particular with the Council of Europe. Now, for the first time, the Commission was obliged to take cultural aspects into account in its actions under other provisions or in different subject areas of the same Treaty. The areas Maastricht concentrated on were

(i) knowledge and the dissemination of the culture and history of the European peoples;

(ii) conservation and safeguarding of the cultural heritage of European significance;

(iii) non-commercial cultural exchanges, and

(iv) artistic and literary creation, including the audiovisual domain.

The entry into force of the Treaty thus brought significant changes in the action undertaken by the Community in the cultural sector. Achieving an ever-closer union of the peoples of Europe, notably via the introduction of a citizenship of the Union, was given substance through the conferment of specific powers in sectors such as culture, books, reading, translation and research.

We mentioned earlier Community Initiatives, and we now look at Community Initiative programmes with a regional aim and a cultural orientation. Thirteen Initiatives were adopted for the 1994–99 period, eight of which come under a balanced regional development approach. These have a structural purpose, are supported by the Structural Funds and have the same assistance procedures, but the areas, concepts and priorities are established by the Commission itself. They generally apply to regions eligible for the objectives of economic and social cohesion, though special exceptions can be made for other areas. INTERREG II is concerned with cross-border co-operation, with eligible areas including some maritime and certain external border areas. It offers joint financing for economic, cultural, educational and training activities, comprising certain infrastructures for geographically contiguous regions which historically have been part of different states. In Ireland north and south, it has been used in the Wexford-Waterford regions, in border areas and of course within Northern Ireland itself. The cultural dimension is estimated to represent 1% of the total allocation. These amounts are to finance actions linked to forms of 'cultural co-operation', or arising from the promotion of 'tourism and agri-tourism' or rural development. ADAPT covers vocational training and job-creation measures in industries undergoing change. Its main aim is to provide joint financing for Europe-wide projects in all regions. PESCA offers funding for economic diversification operations for isolated areas dependent on fishing which would apply particularly in north-west Ireland. URBAN offers funding for run-down urban sites, and EMPLOYMENT-NOW equal opportunities for women and access to future-orientated occupations and management positions. EMPLOYMENT — HORIZON seeks to improve employment prospects for disabled people, EMPLOYMENT — INTEGRA the integration of people threatened with social exclusion and measures to combat racism. In 1994, Title IX Article 128 of the Treaty on European Union was studied in depth within the context of the Commission's Communication to the European Parliament and to the Council of the European Union entitled *European Community Action to promote culture* (COM [94] 356 of 27.7.1994). This served as a framework for the adoption of three action programmes, KALEIDOSCOPE to promote artistic and cultural activities, ARIANE devoted to books and reading, and for our purposes, the most important, RAPHAEL, the Community action programme in the field of cultural heritage (Decision No. 2228/97 of the European Parliament and of the Council of 13 October 1997; *OJ L* 305, 8.11.1997, pp. 31–41).

The RAPHAEL Programme ran from the 1 January 1997–31 December 2000, with an overall budget of ECU 30 million. It defines 'cultural heritage' and 'preservation', followed by six objectives. One of the elements not seen in any previous communication is 'to help develop good practice in regard to the conservation of cultural heritage'. The programme is based on three main areas of action:

Action 1, conservation, safeguarding and development of the European cultural heritage through European co-operation;

Action 2, co-operation in the field of exchanges of experience and techniques applied to heritage, and

Action 3, access, public participation in and awareness of cultural heritage.

This whole programme is a landmark in the encouragement of activities in the cultural heritage sector. As a result, the *First report on the consideration of cultural aspects in European Community action*, adopted by the Commission on 18 April 1996 (COM (96) 160 final), was introduced and covers four broad areas. These are

(i) culture and the Single Market regulatory aspects. This includes reference to Directives pertinent to freedom of movement and professionals in the cultural sector, copyright, cultural assets and so forth;

(ii) culture in the Community's internal policies, including regional development and funding, social and human resources, advanced information and communication technologies, research, SMEs, tourism, social economics, environment, and town-twinning;

(iii) audio-visual policy, and

(iv) culture in community foreign relations.

The Maastricht Treaty provided for the convening in 1996 of an Intergovernmental Conference which is the formal mechanism for revising the treaties on which the Union is based. The scope of the Conference's work had been set out by previous European Councils. The Conference was to analyse the challenges which confronted the Union in the years ahead. The Conference formally began its work at Turin on 29 March 1996. The Italian Presidency examined the issues and explored the delegations' positions and priorities. It reported on the outcome of its work to the Florence European Council in June 1996. The Florence European Council requested the subsequent Dublin Presidency (July-December 1996) to prepare a general outline of a draft revision of the treaties. What followed this detailed examination was the Communication from the Commission to the European Parliament, the Council and the Committee of the Regions entitled *First European Community Framework Programme in support of culture (2000–2004)* (COM [1998] 266 final, pp. 2–12), to enter into force on 1 January 2000. This programme was to set up a guiding and transparent approach to culture. The document included a proposal for a European Parliament and Council Decision establishing a single financing and programming instrument for cultural co-operation (pp. 13–22), the Commission Orientation Document entitled *Explicit integration of cultural aspects into Community action and policy* (pp. 23–43) and a Financial Statement. The aim of this Operational Programme is to encourage creative activity and the dissemination of knowledge of European culture, notably in the fields of music, literature, the performing arts, fixed and moveable heritage and the new realms of culture (mass culture) by fostering co-operation between cultural organizations and operators and the cultural institutions of the member states, and by supporting measures which, by their European scope and character, promote the spread of European culture, both inside and outside the Union. New web pages were launched in 1998 on the electronic journal *I'm Europe* (*http://www.echo.lu/milia98/*) covering EC Research and Development (R & D) activity in the area of trading cultural heritage assets. Many of the EC's R&D programmes have strands directly or implicitly relevant to the task of getting Europe's cultural heritage on-line, especially ESPRIT, ACTS, TAP, Language Engineering, MLIS, ISIS and so forth. The site highlights steps that help cultural heritage players bid for funds and help companies which wish to work with them to solve new problems or exploit the results of solved ones. The site is expected to be a first point of reference for funding culture and the information society.

Finally, one may mention the Commission's green paper on *Copyright and related rights in the Information Society* (COM [95] 382 final), a discussion document which identified the issues at stake, discussed the legal framework of the Information Society, including the internal market, specific rights and general rights. The amended proposal for a Copyright Directive was presented by the Commission on 21 May 1999 (*http://europa.eu.int/comm/dg15/en/intprop/copy2.htm*), but it was expected that the Council of Ministers would not discuss the draft directive in detail until much later in 1999. Meanwhile, some countries including France, Luxembourg, Ireland and Germany have drafted or are drafting updates on their national legislation on copyright, taking into account the delay in adopting and implementing an EU Directive.

The EU also supports a number of organizations active in the cultural heritage sphere. These include the European University Institute (*http://www.iue.it/*), which was founded in 1972 by the EEC member states to provide advanced academic and cultural training on a European basis and to make an intellectual contribution to the life of Europe. Its mission is to promote through its activities the development of Europe's cultural and academic heritage in its unity and diversity. The Institute facilitates academic training and research projects (fundamental, comparative and Community research) in the area of the social and human sciences, including law. It does so under the leadership of professors assisted by research associates, research fellows and Jean Monnet Fellows. It is responsible for the administration of the European Historical Archives, opened to the public under the thirty-year rule, for the institutions from 1952 onwards and also for some individuals, associations or private organizations involved in the process of European unification. These can be accessed through its website. It established a European Cultural Research Centre in 1987 to concentrate on socio-cultural themes. In 1990, it established Jean Monnet professorships in several universities. Its current principal is Patrick Masterson, formerly President of University College, Dublin.

The European Foundation for the Improvement of Living and Working Conditions (*http://www. eurofound.ie*), established in 1973 in Dublin, is run by a board on which there are representatives of trade unions, employers organizations, national governments and the European Commission. Its remit is to contribute to the planning and establishment of better living and working conditions by developing ideas on their medium- and long-term improvement and identifying factors leading to change. Two of its six important themes are employment and sustainable development. It is responsible for the European Industrial Relations Observatory

(EIRO) which was set up to meet the needs of the Commission. It serves a wide public of national organizations, individuals and the research community through its database (*http://www.eiro.eurofound.ie*). EIRO collects and disseminates information and analysis on developments in industrial relations. EIROnline, the on-line database, carries news features and authoritative information provided by the EIRO network. The Foundation issues a wide range of information on living and working conditions, as well as publications on cities, the urban environment, and so forth which are useful sources of information.

The European Centre for the Development of Vocational Training (CEDEFOP) (*http://www.cedefop.gr*), established in 1975 by decision of the Council of the European Communities, based in Thessalonika, Greece, is also run by a board similar to that of the European Foundation in Dublin. Its aim is to promote at Community level vocational and continuing training, and the work programme tends to focus on the issues of trends in qualifications and training systems. The Youth Forum of the European Union was established in 1978 in Brussels to promote the interests of young people in the European Community. It brings to the attention of the Commission, the Council of Ministers and the European Parliament the main political, cultural and social concerns of young people in the European Union, including those of national youth councils and international youth organizations.

In 1981, on the occasion of the first European Council in Maastricht, the Dutch Prime Minister, Mr van Agt, inaugurated the European Institute of Public Administration (*http://www.eipa.nl/*). It is an international institute supported and governed by national administrations of the EU member states and the European Commission. The objectives of the Institute are to provide civil servants and other interested parties with training courses of a European character relating to public administration in the European Union and the collection and development of knowledge regarding public administration in the European Community. Its website gives up-to-date information on forthcoming conferences and developments, and the Institute issues a variety of publications including a journal *Eipascope*.

The European Bureau for Lesser-Used Languages (*http://www.eblul.org*) came into being at a colloquium held in Brussels in May 1982 to consider the implications of the Arfe Report which the European Parliament had adopted the previous October. Its constitution defines the general aim as being 'to preserve and promote the lesser used auctocthonous languages of the members of the European Communities, together with their associated cultures'. Originally based in Dublin, it produced the first issue of its journal *Contact Bulletin* in November 1983. Among the Bureau's 1999 publications is a multi-lingual CD-ROM covering 3,500 local administration terms in thirteen European languages, including Irish. The Secretariat-General has recently moved from Dublin to Brussels, in order to facilitate daily contacts with the main EU institutions, but the Bureau still retains a Dublin office.

EDUCATION

In the first few years of the Community's existence, little thought was given to education, which was due in part to the volume of other work which needed to be concluded at that time. International law specialists were also unable to agree on whether the Community could take action in the education field. Each of the founding treaties permitted steps in certain restricted areas, but no treaty contained an overview of the whole topic. This fragmentation ended in 1973 when a member of the Commission, Mr Ralf Dahrendorf, was entrusted with the newly created Research, Science and Education portfolio. A proposal for a policy was then put forward (*Bulletin of the European Communities Supplement* 10/73). It is interesting to note that the European Centre for the Development of Vocational Education and Training (CEDEFOP), discussed above, was set up in 1975. The need to develop a strategy of cooperation in education and to promote a systematic exchange of information and experience was recognized as a priority at that time. Also in that year, a Directive on the mutual recognition of qualifications in medicine was adopted which facilitates the right of establishment for doctors, the first of many such Directives. The Council and Ministers of Education ratified an action plan in a European Parliament Resolution on 9 February 1976 (*OJ C* 38, 19.2.1976, p. 1). The programme covered six topics:

(i) better facilities for the education and training of nationals and children of national, of other member states of the Communities and non-member countries;

(ii) promotion of closer relation between educational systems in Europe;

(iii) compilation of up to date documentation and statistics on education;

(iv) cooperation in the field of higher education;

(v) teaching of foreign languages, and

(vi) achievement of equal opportunity for the free access to all forms of education.

In 1977, a Directive was adopted on the education of children of migrant workers (77/486/EEC; *OJ L* 199, 6.8.1977, p. 32). The exchange of experience amongst teachers was encouraged. A students' handbook in higher education was introduced, reflecting the efforts to enable students to enter higher education more easily in other member states by means of joint-study programmes. A plan on the teaching of foreign languages was devised in 1978.

Grants for research projects at the European University Institute were increased. Towards the end of the 1970s, the topics of transition of people from school to working life and vocational education, as well as adult education, were given greater emphasis. In September 1980, EURYDICE, the network needed for rapid exchange of information by education policy makers in the Community, was established. In 1981, the Commission strengthened its links with the European University Institute by financing extensively its research and training and sending representatives to the newly established research committee. It also met with representatives of the European Trade Union Committee recently set up at Community level. With the assistance of the Kreyssig Fund, the Commission continued to promote the teaching of European Studies in schools. The Commission proposed a five-year action plan on vocational training in the early 1980s (*OJ C* 306, 1982, p. 6). It also proposed a new Community Initiative on vocational training and new information technologies for the period 1983–87 (*OJ C* 162, 29.6.1982, p. 7). The Commission joined with the Council of Europe in producing EUDISED, an educational thesaurus. In September 1983, the Council and the Ministers for Education adopted a resolution concerning vocational training in relation to new technologies, the impact on small businesses and on young people in job restructuring and re-training (*OJ C* 166, 25.6.1983). They adopted a resolution on the introduction of new information technology in education which focuses on pooling the experiences of the member states (*OJ C* 256, 24.9.1983). In June 1985, the Council and the ministers for education adopted an action programme on equal opportunities for boys and girls in education and on the importance of the European dimension in education (*OJ C* 166, 5.7.1985). They emphasized the importance of the European dimension in education and of cooperation in higher education. On 5 December, the Council approved an action programme for education and training in technology entitled COMETT (*OJ C* 234, 13.9.1985), covering the years 1986–89. COMETT was to support initial and ongoing training initiatives between universities and enterprises in response to technological and social change, and was intended to assist young people to enter the labour market. In vocational education, there was a decision on the equivalence of these training programmes and the establishment of a new programme for the period 1985–88 on vocational training and new technologies (*OJ L* 199, 31.7.1985, p. 56). The ERASMUS programme on student mobility was proposed around this time also (*OJ C* 73.2.4.1986, p. 4). Mobility was to be assisted by grants and by the creation of a network of inter-university cooperation schemes.

The decision on COMETT was formally adopted in 1986 (*OJ L* 222, 8.8.1986, p. 17). A Resolution on consumer education in primary and secondary schools was also adopted, which seems very forward-looking (*OJ C* 184. 23.7.1986, p. 21). In 1987, the Commission finally adopted the ERASMUS programme (*OJ L* 166, 25.6.1987, p. 20), and automatic credit for course transfer was introduced in 1988–89. In 1988, the Council ratified the decision to establish the 'Yes for Europe' action programme to promote youth exchanges in the Community. The Commission communication, *Education in the Community: medium-term prospects 1988–1992* (COM [88] 203 final) led to discussion of the most appropriate measures to be taken leading up to the Single Market in 1992, and a communication on the teaching of foreign languages (the proposed establishment of the LINGUA programme) to encourage the study and the teaching of foreign languages (*Bulletin of the European Communities* 12, 1988). Ministers adopted resolutions on environmental education and promotion of innovation in secondary education. The subject of education now passed from employment to human resources education, training and youth. The Commission adopted a communication entitled *Education and training in the European Community — guidelines for the medium term 1989–1992* (COM [89] 236 final). It also gave an account of the measures it proposed to take in various fields, including, for the first time, quality improvements in the educational systems through cooperation, and additional training in the light of technological change. In 1989, the Commission approved the 'Jean Monnet' programmes, designed to assist European integration studies at universities and the promotion of youth exchange schemes. Courses on European integration were established in the universities. A workshop on higher education was held in Louvain from 21–23 June 1989 to bring together ideas on the future of education in Europe. The year was marked by the development of Community action in the fields of initial and continuing vocational training and by the provision of assistance in the countries of Central and Eastern Europe. Two important instruments were devised towards this end. The first, PHARE (an acronym for 'Poland and Hungary Action for Restructuring of the Economy'), aimed to provide financial and technical support in key areas to the governments of the states in question, in order to help create conditions for a marked-orientated economy based on private ownership and initiative. Former Soviet republics later also became beneficiaries under the scheme (*OJ L* 257, 21.9.1990, p. 1). The second, TEMPUS, a trans-European mobility

scheme for university studies, was established in 1990 and applied to countries eligible under PHARE (*OJ L* 131, 25.5.1990). The establishment of the European Training Foundation was also helpful in this regard. The Council and ministers adopted a resolution on the integration of young people with disabilities into ordinary systems of education (*OJ C* 162, 3.7.1990) as well as conclusions on the equality of opportunity in the training of teachers. The importance accorded to vocational education was reinforced by the work of both sides of industry in social dialogue, and the comparability of vocational qualifications was discussed at length, both in agriculture and in relation to training based on Article 128 of the EEC Treaty. Vocational training was strengthened by the development of the PETRA programme. Guidelines were adopted by the Commission in higher education, vocational training and distance learning.

In 1992, the implications of the Treaty of Maastricht were studied. For the first time, education in its entirety became the responsibility of the Union. Attention among the ministers for education and the Commission was given to health and the environment, the status of the teaching profession, the quality of teaching and the wider concept of European citizenship. Moves were being made towards a specific policy for youth and for youth training. A decision was adopted on the FORCE programme on vocational training (89/657/EEC). The Commission endorsed a new generation of Community programmes on vocational training (LEONARDO DA VINCI and YOUTH FOR EUROPE III). In 1994, following the entry into force of the Treaty on European Union and in accordance with the white paper on growth, competitiveness and employment, a third youth programme was added called, SOCRATES. It is to some extent based on ERASMUS and LINGUA, but is intended to strengthen trans-national cooperation in higher and school education. A communication on education and training and education in the face of technological, industrial and social challenges was also introduced (COM [94] 528 final). 1995 was the actual year of the adoption of SOCRATES covering the whole of the educational field (*OJ L* 87, 20.4.1995). The white paper entitled *Teaching and learning in the knowledge-based society* was adopted by the Commission in November and set out the Community approaches to the challenges of the twenty-first century. 1996 was European Year of Lifelong Learning, and there was a debate on the Commission's white paper *Teaching and learning: towards the learning society* (COM [95] 590). The Florence European Council underlined the potential of the information society in terms of education. The Commission adopted an action plan entitled *Learning in the information society*, which sought to integrate the use of multi-media tools in teaching practice and the espousal by schools of the information society. A green paper on the obstacles to transnational mobility was also adopted by the Commission on 2 October (COM [96] 462 final). One of the key points made in these publications was that lifelong education is essential for employment and social integration. In 1997, in a communication called *Towards a Europe of knowledge*, the Commission presented more guidelines for education training and youth for the period 2000–06 (COM [97] 563 final).

Fresh impetus was subsequently given to the SOCRATES, LEONARDO DA VINCI and YOUTH FOR EUROPE programmes by opening them up to the countries of Central Europe and Cyprus. In 1998, the Commission adopted proposals for new Community programmes in the fields of education training and youth for the years 2000–04. The three major programmes, SOCRATES, LEONARDO DA VINCI and YOUTH, were to receive greatly increase funding. A common framework composed of six broad elements would link the three programmes, namely

(i) physical mobility for people;

(ii) different forms of virtual mobility (use of new information and communications technologies);

(iii) development of cooperation networks;

(iv) promotion of linguistic and cultural skills;

(v) development of innovation through pilot projects based on transnational partnerships, and

(vi) ongoing improvement of Community references, databases, exchanges of good practice for systems and policies in education, training and youth in member states.

In connection with the Commission communication *Learning in the information society — action plan for a European education initiative*, the Internet-based schools network was inaugurated on 8 September 1988 in collaboration with the education ministries of the member states. The education policy of the European Union, after a relatively slow start, due to its lack of legislative provision, had come of age.

CONCLUSION

It would have been possible for this chapter to address other topics relating to heritage or expand on any of those dealt with. Thus forestry has only briefly been touched upon despite the appreciable impact of policies in this area on the Irish landscape. Among the former, for instance, is information technology (IT), Europe's approach to it and its employment to make data on the EU and its various concerns available to as wide a range of users as possible. This is demonstrated by the creation of a new DG on the Information Society, and by various recent EU Initiatives, including those of the Lisbon European Council of 23–24 March 2000. Neville Keery's *Reflection* paper also underlined the concerns of the Commission in relation to EDCs. Many developments in this domain are only gradually unfolding and await the necessary distance in time to look at them in proper perspective. One aspect of the use of IT should be noted in conclusion, however. As stated at the outset, the information presented here has been derived from both printed and electronic sources. In the race to provide more and more facts, statements and literature via IT, much information seems to be dropped from the electronic system, often for no other reason than to provide access to more current data. There would appear to be no meaningful obligation on providers to evaluate the importance or accuracy of information or to create archival files. Consequently, the urgent need to archive EU information on the web has been recognized and advocated. In this connection, one may again recall that the Union already holds key historical archival material relating to the ECSC, the EEC and EURATOM, for example, at the European University Institute in Florence. The likely accession of ten additional countries will make the establishment of an electronic archive even more imperative. Indeed at national level itself, growing volumes of data are also being discarded from the web on a regular basis. This information might not necessarily be issued elsewhere or in other formats, as governments may not have the physical space in which to store increasing quantities of published material. Since lifetime employment in any post is no longer guaranteed, one cannot now depend on employees such as librarians developing archival memories, as used to be the case. It would therefore seem opportune to create both national and international policies for the maintenance of our electronic heritage before it is eliminated forever. Access to such a resource is vital for the economic, legal, social and cultural fabric of our society. Its loss would inevitably curtail opportunities for writing studies like this one, and leave us with an imprecise understanding of our shared inheritance from the past as we attempt to navigate and shape both the present and the future.

Bibliography

Bell, P. 1996 *Environmental farming: a guide to the Rural Environment Protection Scheme (REPS)*. Navan: Philip Farrelly.

C.E.C. 1987 *The state of the environment in the European Community*. Luxembourg.

C.E.C. 1989 *Guide to the reform of the Community's*

structural funds. Luxembourg.

C.E.C. 1991 *Pollution knows no frontiers*. Luxembourg.

C.E.C. 1992 *Report of the Commission of the European Communities to the United Nations Conference on Environment and Development. Rio de Janeiro-June 1992*. Luxembourg.

C.E.C. 1996 *The agencies of the European Union*. Luxembourg.

C.E.C. Directorate-General for Information, Communication, Culture 1992 *New vitality for the countryside*. Luxembourg.

C.E.C. Directorate-General for Information, Communication, Culture, Audiovisual 1995 *The European Commission 1995–2000*. Luxembourg.

Conference of the Representation of the Governments of the Member States 1996 *The European Union today and tomorrow. Adapting the European Union for the benefit of its peoples and preparing it for the future. A general outline for a draft revision of the Treaties* (Dublin II) (Conf. 2500/96 CAB).

Council of Europe 1969 *European Convention on the Protection of the Archaeological Heritage. London 6 May, 1969*. Strasbourg: Council of Europe (European Treaty Series No. 66).

Council of Europe Directorate of Press and Information 1982 *The Council of Europe: a concise guide*. Strasbourg.

Council of the European Union General Secretariat 1994 *Texts concerning culture at European Community level*, first edition. Luxembourg.

Council of the European Union General Secretariat 1998 *Texts concerning culture at European Union level*, Supplement No. 1 (1993–97) to the first edition. Luxembourg.

Cuddy, M., Ó Cinnéide, M. and Owens, M. (eds) 1990 *Revitalising the rural economy: how can it be done?* Proceedings of the European Conference on Rural Development, Galway. Galway: Centre for Development Studies, UCG.

Deckmyn, V. 1998 *Guide to official information of the European Union*, third edition. Maastricht.

Department of Agriculture, Food and Forestry 1994 *Rural Environment Protection Scheme (REPS) introduced by the Minister for Agriculture, Food and Forestry in implementation of Council Regulation (EEC) No. 2078/92*. Dublin: Department of Agriculture, Food and Forestry.

Dooge, J. and Barrington, R. (eds) 1999 *A vital national interest: Ireland in Europe 1973–98*. Dublin: Institute of Public Administration/The European Movement.

Dower, M. 1998 'An asset for local development: heritage as a resource', *Leader Magazine* **17**.

E.C. 1994 *Guide to Community legislation applicable to the industry processing fishery and aquaculture products*. Luxembourg.

E.C. 1995a *Grants and loans from the European Union: a guide to Community funding*. Luxembourg.

E.C. 1995b *Guide to innovative actions (European Regional Development Fund — ERDF, Article 10) 1995–99*. Luxembourg.

E.C. 1996 *France: Single Programming Document 1994–99*. Luxembourg.

E.C. 1996 *Structural Funds and Cohesion Fund 1994–99. Regulations and commentary*. Luxembourg.

E.C. 1997a *Agenda 2000. Vol. I. For a stronger and wider Union. Vol. II. The challenge of enlargement* (COM [97] 2000). Luxembourg.

E.C. 1997b *Caring for our future: action for Europe's environment*. Luxembourg.

E.C. 1997c *Glossary: the reform of the European Union in 150 definitions*. Luxembourg.

E.C. 1997d *Situation and outlook: rural developments*. Luxembourg.

E.C. 1997e *Statements on Sustainable Development: the General Consultative Forum on the Environment, 1993–96*. Luxembourg.

E.C. 1998 *Investing in culture: an asset for the regions*. Luxembourg.

E.C. 1999 *Better management through evaluation. Mid-term review of Structural Funds programmes: Objectives 1 and 6 (1994–99)*. Luxembourg.

E.C. Directorate-General for Information, Communication, Culture and Audiovisual 1996 *How does the European Union work?* Luxembourg.

E.C. Directorate-General XI Environment, Nuclear Safety and Civil Protection 1996 *European Community environment legislation*. Luxembourg.

E.C. Press and Information n.d. *Uniting Europe: the European Community since 1950*.

Economic and Social Research Institute/DKM Economic Consultants 1993 *EC Structural Funds. The Community Support Framework: evaluation and recommendation. Summary of report to the Department of Finance*. Dublin: ESRI.

European Commission 1985 *Common guide for monitoring and interim evaluation*. Brussels.

European Commission 1997 *Guide to programmes: education, training and youth*. Luxembourg.

European Commission Secretariat General 1994 *Archives in the European Union: Report of the Group of Experts on the Coordination of Archives*. Luxembourg.

European Consultative Forum on the Environment and Sustainable Development 1998 *Statement on environmental legislation*. Luxembourg.

European Consultative Forum on the Environment and Sustainable Development 1999 *Enlargement and environment: principles and recommendations from the European Consultative Forum on the*

Environment and Sustainable Development. Luxembourg.

European Environment Bureau 1985 *Ten years of European Community environment policy, 1974–83.* Luxembourg.

European Parliament, Directorate-General for Research and Documentation 1979 *The effects on Ireland of membership of the European Communities.*

EUROSTAT 1995 *Regions Nomenclature of Territorial Units for Statistics (NUTS)* (March). Luxembourg.

EUROSTAT 1998 *European Union database directory 1999: a guide to EU on-line information services.* Luxembourg.

Honohan, P. (ed) 1997 *EU Structural Funds in Ireland: a mid-term evaluation of the CSF 1994–99.* Dublin: ESRI.

Institute of European Affairs 1999 *Agenda 2000: implications for Ireland.* Dublin: IEA.

Ireland Government 1948 *The European Recovery Programme: basic documents and background information. White paper.* Dublin: Stationery Office.

Ireland Government 1961 *European Economic Community.* Dublin: Stationery Office.

Ireland Government 1967 *European Communities 1) European Economic Community (EEC). 2) European Atomic Energy Community (EURATOM). 3) European Coal and Steel Community (ECSC).* Dublin: Stationery Office.

Ireland Government 1970 *Membership of the European Communities: implications for Ireland.* Dublin: Stationery Office.

Ireland Government 1972 *The accession of Ireland to the European Communities.* Dublin: Stationery Office.

Ireland Government 1993 *EC Commission white paper on growth, competitiveness and employment: contribution by Ireland.* Dublin: Stationery Office.

Ireland Government 1994a *Community Support Framework 1994–99. Objective 1 Development and structural adjustment of regions whose development is lagging behind.* Luxembourg.

Ireland Government 1994b *Community Support Framework 1994–99. Operational Programme for Environmental Services 1994–99.* Dublin: Stationery Office.

Ireland Government 1994c *Operational Programme for agriculture, rural development and forestry, 1994–99.* Dublin: Stationery Office.

Ireland Government 1995a *Operational Programme for fisheries 1994–99.* Dublin.

Ireland Government 1995b *Operational Programme: Local urban and rural development 1994–99.* Dublin: Stationery Office.

Ireland Government 1999 *National Development Plan 2000–06.* Dublin: Stationery Office.

Irish Business and Employers Confederation (IBEC) 1995 *Ireland, the European Union and economic integration: a business perspective.* Dublin: IBEC.

Keatinge, P. (ed) *Maastricht and Ireland: what the Treaty means.* Dublin: IEA.

Keery, N. 1998 *Rethinking the EDCs: a DG X reflection paper,* unpublished.

McArdle, E. 1995 'An evaluation of an Irish rural community's capacity to diversify its natural resource base in light of new approaches to rural development', M.Sc. thesis, UCC.

McMahon, B. M. E. and Murphy, F. 1989 *European Community law in Ireland.* Dublin: Butterworths Ireland.

National Economic and Social Council 1992 *The impact of reform of the Common Agricultural Policy.* Dublin: NESC.

Nugent, N. (ed) 1997 *At the heart of the Union: studies of the European Commission.* London.

O'Donnell, R. (ed) 1999 *Europe: the Irish experience.* Dublin: IEA.

Ó Riagáin, D. (ed) 1998 *Vade-Mecum: a guide to the legal, political and other documents pertaining to the lesser-used languages of Europe.* Dublin: An Biuró Eorpach do Theangacha Neamhfhorleathna.

TEAGASC 1998 *Protecting Ireland's national heritage,* Proceedings of REPS Conference, Johnstown Castle, Wexford, December. Dublin: TEAGASC.

Thomson, I. 1989 *The documentation of the European Communities: a guide.* London: Mansell.

Tonra, B. and Dunne, D. 1997 *A European cultural identity: myth, reality or aspiration?* Dublin: IEA.

Journals

Adjustment of the common agricultural policy 1983 *Bulletin of the European Communities Supplement* 4/83.

The Agricultural Situation in the Community (Annual) 1975–98.

The Agricultural policy of the European Community 1979 *European Documentation* 2/79.

The Agricultural Policy of the European Community 1982 *European Documentation* 6/82.

Borchardt, K. 1995 'European integration: the origins of the European Union', *European Documentation.*

Browning, H. and White, S. 1999 'Rethinking European Documentation Centres — is a regional network of repositories really the way forward?' *European Information* **6** (April), pp. 21–23.

Caddel, R. 1997 'European Documentation Centres: the development of a UK information relay', *Journal of Government Information* **24**, 2, pp. 103–12.

C.E.C. 1999 *Sixth periodic report on the social and economic situation and development of the regions of the European Union.* Luxembourg.

C.E.C. Directorate-General for Information, Communication and Culture 1988 'Jean Monnet: a grand design for Europe', *European Documentation* 5/88.

Chase, S. 1999 'Navigating the sea of EU information', *European Information* **8**, pp. 6–13.

A community programme concerning the environment 1972 *Bulletin of the European Communities Supplement* 5/72.

Community action in the cultural sector 1977 *Bulletin of the European Communities* 6/77.

Cultural action in the European Community 1980 *European Documentation* 3/1980.

Davies, E.1998 'Information and communication in the EU', *European Information* **3**, pp. 2–14.

An education policy for Europe 1982 *European Documentation* 4/1982.

Environment programme 1977–81 1976 *Bulletin of the European Communities Supplement* 6/76.

Environmental policy in the European Community 1990, fourth ed. *European Documentation* 5/1990.

The European Community and the environment 1987 *European Documentation* 3/1987.

The European Community's environmental policy 1977 *European Documentation* 1977/6.

The European Community's environmental policy 1984 *European Documentation* 1984/1.

The European Community's fishery policy 1985 *European Documentation* 1/1985.

The European Community and the energy problem 1975 *European Documentation* 1975/2 (Trade Union Series).

The European Community and the energy problem 1978 *European Documentation* 1978.

European Environment Agency *EEA Annual Reports.* Luxembourg.

European Monthly Newsletter February 1999, No. 120 and May 1999 No. 123.

The European Social Fund: a weapon against unemployment 1984 *European File* 2/84.

European unification : the origins and growth of the European Community 1987 *European Documentation* 1987/2.

For a Community policy on education 1973 *Bulletin of the European Communities Supplement* 10/73.

From the Single Act to Maastricht and beyond — the means to match our ambitions. 1992 *Bulletin of the European Communities Supplement* 1992 (Delors II).

General Report on the Activities of the European Communities Annual Reports 1973–98.

Improvement of the common agricultural policy 1973 *Bulletin of the European Communities Supplement* 7/73.

MacSharry, R. 1991 'The development and future of the Common Agricultural Policy', *Green Europe* **2**.

'Memorandum forestry: discussion paper on the Community action in the forestry sector', *Green Europe* **36**.

Mutual recognition of diplomas and professional qualifications *European File* 20/80.

A new impetus for the common policies 1981 *Bulletin of the European Communities Supplement* 4/81.

Ó Cléirigh, A. 1999 'National Development Programme (NDP) 2000–06 ', *EU Structural Funds* **10** (Winter 1999–2000).

Perspectives for the Common Agricultural Policy: the green paper of the Commission 1985 *Green Europe* **33**.

Programme of environmental action of the European Communities 1973 *Bulletin of the European Communities Supplement* 3/73.

Recognition of diplomas and professional qualifications 1984 *European File* 13/84.

Relaunching Europe: agricultural policy target 1988 *European File* 4/82.

Report from the Commission of the European Communities to the Council pursuant to the mandate of 30 May 1980 1981 *Bulletin of the European Communities Supplement* 1/81.

Secretariat-General of the Commission 1969 *Memorandum of the reform of agriculture in the European Economic Community [Mansholt Plan]. Supplement to Bulletin No. 1–1969 of the European Communities.* Luxembourg.

Stocking of the Common Agricultural Policy *Bulletin of the European Communities Supplement* 2/75.

Sevetson, A. 1998 'The European Union on the Internet: a vanishing record?', *European Information* **1** (January), pp. 6–12.

Thomson, I. 1995. 'European Union information developments: challenges facing European Documentation Centres', *European Access* **6**, pp.16–19.

Towards a new energy policy strategy for the European Community *Bulletin of the European Communities Supplement* 4/74.

Towards a common agricultural and rural policy for Europe 1997 *European Economy* **5**, 1977 (Reports and Studies).

Towards a European education policy 1977 *European Documentation* 1977/2

Trading cultural heritage information assets *Info 2000 Echo facts for users,* 1/98, p. 1.

Irish Heritage: The State's Involvement

NUALA REARDEN

The purpose of this chapter is to introduce the reader to the work undertaken by certain government departments in their efforts to implement policies, agreed by government, in relation to heritage protection and promotion. To help understand how policy is decided, there will be a brief look at parliament in Ireland and how it works, together with the role of the Houses of the Oireachtas in the enactment of legislation. A closer examination will then be made of the operations of the departments in question, which will include the Department of the Marine and Natural Resources, the Department of Agriculture and Food, the Department of the Environment and Local Government, the Department of Tourism, Sport and Recreation, the Department of Education and Science and the Department of Arts, Heritage, Gaeltacht and the Islands. These are the relevant departments as they are entitled at the time of writing. Their nomenclature and profile are subject to change, but the essential areas for which they are responsible remain relatively constant.

THE OIREACHTAS

Ireland is a parliamentary democracy. The parliament is known as the Oireachtas, and consists of a President and two Houses — Dáil Éireann (Lower House) and Seanad Éireann (Upper House). The President is universally elected by Irish citizens over eighteen years whose names appear in the register of electors. Voting for the 166 members of the Dáil, representing 41 constituencies, is done by the same electorate but, in addition, resident British citizens may also vote. The term of office of a Dáil is not fixed, though by law the maximum length is five years. An election for the Seanad must take place not later than ninety days after the dissolution of the Dáil. The work of the Dáil falls into four main categories. The House considers proposals for legislation initiated by ministers or by private members; it considers expenditure proposals presented by ministers; it debates

motions, and it is a forum in which questions may be addressed to ministers (Dooney and O'Toole 1992, 54). Members of the Dáil are referred to as TDs, an abbreviation of their title in Irish, Teachtaí Dála. The sixty members of Seanad Éireann are elected as follows:

• 43 are elected by the members of the Dáil, members of the outgoing Seanad and members of the county councils and corporations around the country;

• 6 members are elected by the universities, three by the National University of Ireland and three by the University of Dublin (Trinity College);

• 11 members are nominated by the Taoiseach (Prime Minister).

As most members of the Dáil and Seanad and members of county councils and corporations are members of political parties, usually the forty-three members they elect are members of political parties also. The Taoiseach's choice of eleven individuals also tends to reflect the interests of the parties in power, so the six members elected by the universities are generally the only independent candidates in the House.

The main function of the Seanad is to review legislation passed by the Dáil. Its powers, however, are limited. It can reject, and thereby delay, a bill for ninety days, a power which is rarely used as bills passed by the Dáil are almost invariably passed by the Seanad. If there is disagreement between the Dáil and the Seanad on any aspect of a bill, the position of the Dáil prevails (Mulcahy 1996, 37). The fact that a bill initiated in the Dáil must also be examined by the Seanad is a safeguard against legislation being enacted too quickly. The Seanad is also a forum where important issues can be debated and, as the government is constitutionally responsible to Dáil Éireann, such issues can be debated with greater freedom in Seanad Éireann because the fate of the government will not be at stake.

Article 15 of the Constitution gives the Oireachtas exclusive power to make laws governing the Republic of Ireland, which many would argue is perhaps its most important function. Though in theory legislation can be introduced in either House, the vast majority of bills are introduced in the Dáil by the government. Bills to amend the Constitution and money bills, that is financial legislation, can be initiated in the Dáil only. The Seanad is allowed only twenty-one days to consider money bills; it cannot amend such bills, it can only make recommendations.

The first step in the preparation of legislation is the drafting of a bill. This is done by civil servants in the relevant department in consultation with the minister and appropriate legal advisers. Once it reaches parliament, the bill will go through five stages in each House, and when it has been passed by both Houses will be signed into law by the President. Sometimes a minister will publish a green and a white paper before a bill is drafted. A green paper usually contains an outline of proposals concerning what might be contained in the forthcoming bill. Its purpose is to encourage discussion on the topic, and it gives interested parties and pressure groups an opportunity to make submissions to the minister on what they think should be contained in the bill. When he or she has considered the submissions, the minister publishes a white paper, which is a more definite statement of what the bill is likely to contain.

The role of the President as part of the Oireachtas in the enactment of legislation is signing into law and promulgating bills which have already been passed by the Dáil and Seanad. He or she can act as a check, but does not have a veto, on legislation. There are, however, two occasions on which the President may refuse to sign a bill. The first is when a petition, signed by a majority of senators and at least one-third of the members of the Dáil, is presented to the President requesting that a bill not be signed without submitting it to the people in a referendum, although it has been passed by both Houses of the Oireachtas. On such an occasion, the President, after consultation with the Council of State, may submit the bill to a referendum. The second occasion is where the President may refer any bill (with some exceptions, principally money bills), to the Supreme Court for a judgement on its constitutionality, even thought the bill has been passed by both Houses of the Oireachtas. This again requires that, before acting, the President must consult with the Council of State. The president is not compelled to act on their advice.

The meetings of the Dáil and Seanad are held during three terms, September to Christmas, January to Easter and Easter to July. During these periods, meetings of the Dáil take place on Tuesday, Wednesday and Thursday of each week while Seanad meetings are generally held on Wednesday and Thursday only. However, the members of the Seanad sometimes meet on Tuesday or on Friday if the volume of work before the House so demands. When the Houses are not in session, the business of the Oireachtas continues in parliamentary committees which only go into recess for the month of August.

The government consists of no fewer than seven and not more than fifteen members. It is frequently referred to as the cabinet, though this term is not to be found in the Constitution. The members are selected by the Taoiseach and appointed by the President. The Constitution provides that no more than two Senators may be members of the government, but this provision has been exercised only twice in the last sixty years. Collective cabinet responsibility is an important fundamental principle underlying the operation of government in Ireland. What this means, in effect, is that while ministers may hold different views about matters under discussion at the cabinet table, once a policy decision has been taken they are obliged to support it in public. The title 'minister of state' was first introduced in 1978. A minister of state, or junior minister, is not a member of government, and does not have the right to attend cabinet meetings. He/she is assigned by the Taoiseach to a particular department and will work with the cabinet minister for that department.

THE CIVIL SERVICE

Before looking in detail at the work of particular government departments, it is timely to comment on how the administration of a department is organized. The term used to describe those who work in government departments is the civil service. The secretary general of a department is the highest grade within the civil service. Unlike other civil servants who are recruited by the Civil Service Commission, he is appointed by the government and retains his position if the minister is changed because of a cabinet reshuffle or a change in government. This is an extremely powerful position as adviser to the minister. The secretary is responsible for the management of a department and the administration of all money voted to the department by the Dáil. Because of this continuity, it is fair to say that the secretary of a government department is likely to have a far greater understanding of the issues and problems of a department than any minister can have.

There are several grades within the civil service. These include clerical ones which are mainly involved in regular office work within the department. The tasks of executive and higher executive officers include writing reports, preparing briefs, analysing material and summarizing accounts of issues for presentation to superiors. Preparing answers to Dáil questions is work which is also frequently undertaken by these grades of civil servant

(Mulcahy 1996, 94).

The term 'higher civil servants' refers to four grades in particular, those of assistant principal, principal, assistant secretary and secretary general in ascending order of seniority. Mulcahy explains that, within a department, these grades take responsibility for large units of administrative work, for the formation of policy, the preparation of legislation and the examination of proposals for change and development. It is from this group that advisers and assistants to the minister are drawn when he or she goes to meet a delegation or deputation.

THE DEPARTMENT OF THE MARINE AND NATURAL RESOURCES

As an island nation, the sea is an integral part of our heritage. For generations, families have earned a livelihood through harvesting its resources, while, in addition, it has been the source of leisure activities — swimming, sailing and boating — for others. It has provided valuable access routes to the country for visitors and for trade alike, and has proved itself a resource to be utilized and protected. In recognition of this, a Department of the Marine was established in 1987, bringing together all responsibilities for marine matters. The scope of the department was extended in 1997 to include forestry functions of the former Department of Agriculture, Food and Forestry, and the earth resources (mining and hydrocarbons) functions of the former Department of Transport, Energy and Communications, and the department title was changed (DMNR 1998, 12).

The roles and functions of the department, as outlined in its *Strategy statement 1998–2000*, include:

• to support and facilitate the availability of efficient and competitive sea transport and port services;

• to maximize the long-term contribution of the fisheries sector to the national economy;

• to foster sustainable and environmentally friendly development for the forestry service;

• to promote minerals and hydrocarbons exploration and development for the optimum benefit to the Irish economy, consistent with the highest standards of safety and environmental protection;

• to support the sustainable management and development of the marine coastal zone;

• to promote the sustainable development of marine tourism and leisure;

• to prevent, as far as possible, the loss of life at sea by establishing and enforcing high safety standards and providing effective emergency response standards;

• to preserve and protect the quality of the marine environment;

• to support and facilitate the development of the marine and natural resources through effective research and technology development.

SEA FISHERIES

Apart from its pivotal responsibility for maritime access transport and the development and expansion of the indigenous shipping sector, the department has overall responsibility for the regulation, management, protection and development of the Irish sea fisheries industry. In this particular area it lists as one of its key objectives 'to ensure efficient and effective conservation of fish stocks and management and control of fishing activity' (DMNR 1998, 29).

INLAND FISHERIES

The department has overall policy responsibility for the conservation, management, regulation and development of this resource. Its principal economic value is in the context of tourism, but it is imperative that adequate conservation measures are taken to protect it. The Central and Regional Fisheries Boards are responsible for policy implementation.

AQUACULTURE

The Irish aquaculture sector now accounts for over 25% of total fish production, reflecting global trends. The department is responsible for the strategic and economic development, as well as the regulation, of the aquaculture sector within the framework of the EU's Common Fisheries Policy and the *Fisheries (Amendment) Act* 1997.

FORESTRY

It has been identified that there is considerable scope for the expansion of forestry in Ireland. At present, about 8% of available land is under forestry, compared to an EU average of 33%. Forestry is a complex activity, providing an alternative agricultural land-use, a wildlife habitat, an environment for recreation, an agent of landscape change and a source of raw material for a wide range of timber-based industries. The strategy of the department is to develop the forestry sector via a range of financial incentives by increasing planting and the range of species planted, facilitating the development of the forest processing sector and training farmers and others in forestry management.

MINERALS EXPLORATION AND MINING

The department regulates and promotes two areas of the minerals industry: exploration and mining. The exploration sector is small in a world-wide context, with approximately £7 million a year being spent in Ireland. There is also increasing pressure from conservation and environmental lobbies for more stringent controls on mining developments in the EU which are invariably in greenfield sites. The department's awareness of this is evidenced from their statement of overall goal: 'to stimulate discovery of economic mineral deposits and to maximize the contribution of the mining sector to the national economy, with due regard to its impact on the environment' (DMNR 1998, 34).

PETROLEUM EXPLORATION AND PRODUCTION

The department is responsible for the promotion, regulation and monitoring of the exploration and development of oil and gas in onshore and offshore Ireland. It also acts as co-ordinator of all the state's requirements regarding the operations of the exploration and production companies here.

THE DEPARTMENT OF AGRICULTURE AND FOOD

Traditionally, one of the main focuses of this department has been agricultural production. In more recent years, the general concern for the environment and the impetus to put in place a range of environmental policies, which has come mainly from the European Union, has led it to becoming more deeply involved in attempting to reconcile traditional agricultural policy objectives with increasing demands for environmental protection (The Heritage Council 1996, 12). The need for such measures was confirmed recently within Birdwatch Ireland, where the organization's Countryside Officer, who was appointed to two Advisory Committees in Brussels, made the point that farming and conservation traditionally worked in harmony, and many birds thrived best in the type of non-intensive mixed farming environment that was widespread up to the 1950s and '60s. Changes in land use during the latter half of the twentieth century, however, were accompanied by substantial pressures on Ireland's wildlife and natural habitats (Murphy 1998, 18).

As part of the reform of the Common Agricultural Policy agreed in May 1992, an agri-environment programme was put in place. Under this programme, the department introduced a Rural Environment Protection Scheme (REPS) in June 1994. Agri-environmental specifications were revised in May 1996. REPS main objectives are to establish farming and controlled production methods which reflect the increasing public concern for conservation, landscape protection and wider environmental problems; to protect wildlife habitats and endangered species of flora and fauna, and to produce quality food in an extensive and environmentally friendly manner (DAFF 1994, 5).

Farmers who wish to be involved must have plans drawn up by an agency approved by the minister, and a basic premium of 125 ECU per hectare is payable up to a maximum of 40 hectares. There is a range of measures in REPS that have to be complied with on the total area of the farm. These measures include:

• following a waste management liming and fertilization plan prepared for the total area of the farm;

• adopting a specific grassland management plan;

• protecting and maintaining watercourses and wells;

• retaining wildlife habitats;

• maintaining farm and field boundaries;

• ceasing to use herbicides, pesticides and fertilizers in and around hedgerows, ponds, rivers and streams;

• protecting features of historical or archaeological interest;

• maintaining and improving the visual appearance of the farm (including farmyard);

• producing tillage crops without growth regulators;

• become familiar with environmentally friendly farming practices, and

• keeping such farm and environmental records as may be prescribed by the minister

REPS payments are annual for a period of five years, though the department is seeking the approval of the European Commission to extend the application of REPS in overgrazed areas from five to fifteen years. The figure for the national uptake of farmers in REPS in December 1996 was 14%. In that year, agri-environmental specifications were revised, as stated above. In addition to the basic REPS premium, farmers who undertake supplementary steps, such as rearing animals of local breeds in danger of extinction, taking measures to rejuvenate degraded areas, organic farming and other measures, are entitled to additional payment. Extra allowances are also provided to farmers who are following a REPS scheme whose land also comes within lands designated as a Special Protection Area (SPAs) under the Conservation of Wild Birds Regulations 1985, or Special Areas of Conservation (SACs) under the European Communities (Natural Habitats) Regulations 1997. Both of these sets of Regula-

Table 47.1 Bodies under the Aegis of the Department of the Environment and Local Government

QUASI-JUDICIAL/REGULATORY	An Bord Pleanála — The Planning Board
	The Rent Tribunal Body
	The Environmental Protection Agency
	The Medical Bureau of Road Safety
ADVISORY/PROMOTIONAL	The Building Regulations Advisory Body
	An Chomhairle Leabharlanna — The Library Council
DEVELOPMENTAL	The Custom House Docks Development Authority
	The Housing Finance Agency*
	The National Building Agency*
	Temple Bar Properties*
	Temple Bar Renewal*
SERVICES FOR LOCAL GOVERNMENT	The Local Government Computer Board
	Local Government Staff Negotiations Board
	The Fire Services Council

These are regarded as commercial bodies and must as a general rule operate without subvention.

tions resulted from EU Directives. The uptake of the REPS Scheme is increasing every year and earliest figures available from the department (September 1997) indicate that by that stage a total of 28,931 participants had been accepted, and approximately 1,300 further applications being processed at local level.

While acknowledging that the agriculture and food sectors are vital to the economic and social fabric of rural areas, the department also takes a wider view of rural development which includes both farm and other enterprises in rural Ireland. It focuses on addressing the issue of rural poverty and the promotion of a vibrant economy in rural areas. There has been a fall in the farming population as a proportion of the overall rural community, and the share of farm household income coming from non-farming sources has increased. Schemes like the LEADER Programme and Agri-Tourism have been put in place. LEADER is an EU initiative which enables groups in rural areas to implement their own multi-sectoral business plans for the development of their areas (DAF 1992, 52). Agri-Tourism, which is another EU co-financed scheme, makes grant aid available to farmers and other rural dwellers to provide tourism facilities and for the support of marketing. Though supplementary measures such as these exist, it may now be opportune for the department to take a closer look at the vital part farmers play as protectors of the environment and be mindful of this when negotiating the future direction of agricultural support measures.

THE DEPARTMENT OF THE ENVIRONMENT AND LOCAL GOVERNMENT

Though we have just seen how, in certain ways, the Department of Agriculture and Food has responsibilities for safeguarding the environment in rural areas, the Department of the Environment and Local Government has overall responsibility for the protection of the environment. This department began life as the Department of Local Government and Public Health in 1924. When health and welfare activities were assigned to two new departments in 1947, the Department of Local Government assumed responsibility for local government matters, roads, housing, water/waste water services. In the thirty years to follow, and particularly in the 1960s, the range of functions expanded to include the need for physical planning legislation to cope with the phenomenon of urban development. This arose as a consequence of the Industrial Revolution, which was taking place here a little later than in other countries. Moving into the 1970s, the impetus to put in place a range of environmental policies came mainly from Europe. 1977 saw the title of the department change to the Department of the Environment. The most recent change came with the twenty-fifth Dáil in 1997.

In line with national policy and international developments, a whole new area of environmental protection and protection activity has come into being. The traditional focus on the local government system remains a primary, though no longer an exclusive, concern of the department, and its role in relation to infrastructure also remains but with new emphasis on both economic development and environmental effects (DOE 1996, 4).

Most of the services for which the department is responsible are ultimately provided through a network of public sector agencies, local authorities and semi-state bodies. Until recently, the department has exercised considerable control, particularly over local authorities, in the amount of funding and also the way in which it has been disbursed. Seventeen semi-state bodies operate under its aegis. They fall into four different categories, set out in **Table 47.1**.

Three state-sponsored bodies which play a particularly active part in protecting our heritage include An Bord Pleanála, the Environmental Protection Agency and the Library Council, and so they are discussed at greater length below.

AN BORD PLEANÁLA

Under the *Local Government (Planning and Development) Act* 1963, physical planning was made a compulsory function of local authorities. Under this act, appeals against the decision of a planning authority were made to the Minister for the Environment. By 1976, it was generally accepted that the Board ought to be set up because political parties at the time agreed that an independent tribunal should deal with appeal decisions in an area as controversial and sensitive as land development. Under the *Local Government (Planning and Development) Act* of that year, a statutory Planning Appeals Board, An Bord Pleanála, was set up.

The Board comprises a Chairman, Deputy Chairman and four other members who carry out their duties on a whole-time executive basis. The Board is responsible for the determination of appeals, references and certain other matters under the *Local Government (Planning and Development) Acts*. It also has responsibility for dealing with appeals under the *Building Control Act* 1990, the *Local Government (Water Pollution) Acts* 1977 and 1990 and the *Air Pollution Act* 1987 (An Board Pleanála 1995).

The main characteristics of the appeal system are that it is independent, designed to be fair and impartial and open. Unlike most planning appeal systems in Europe, third parties can make appeals. The Minister for the Environment and Local Government has the power to issue general policy directives relating to planning and development, and the Board is required to have regard to such directives. The law does not, however, enable the minister to exercise any power in relation to any particular appeal.

THE ENVIRONMENTAL PROTECTION AGENCY

This Agency was established in July 1993 under the *Environmental Protection Agency Act* 1992. It is an independent public body, managed by a full-time Executive Board consisting of a Director General and four directors. The Executive Board is appointed by the government following procedures laid down in the act. The Agency is assisted by an Advisory Committee of twelve members. The members are appointed by the Minister for the Environment and Local Government and are selected principally from those nominated by organizations with an interest in environmental and developmental matters. The Agency's main responsibilities include:

• the licensing and regulation of large/complex industrial and other processes with significant polluting potential, on the basis of integrated pollution control (IPC) and the application of best available technologies for this purpose;

• advising public authorities in respect of environmental functions and assisting local authorities in the performance of their environmental protection functions;

• the promotion of environmentally sound practices through, for example, the encouragement of the use of environmental audits, the establishment of an eco-labelling scheme, the setting of environmental quality objectives and the issuing of codes of practice on matters affecting the environment;

• the promotion and co-ordination of environmental research, and

• generally overseeing the performance by local authorities of their statutory environmental protection functions.

AN CHOMHAIRLE LEABHARLANNA

An Chomhairle Leabharlanna, the Library Council, was established under the *Public Libraries Act* 1947. The Council consists of a chairman and twelve ordinary members who are appointed for five-year terms. The chairman is appointed by the Minister for the Environment and Local Government following consultation with the Minister for Education. The ordinary members are appointed by the minister on the nomination of bodies specified in the act, University College, Cork, University College, Dublin, and University College, Galway (1 each), Trinity College, Dublin (2), the National Library of Ireland (1), the Irish County Councils' General Council (3), the Association of Municipal Authorities of Ireland (2) and the Library Association of Ireland (1).

Under the 1947 act, the functions of An Chomhairle are to accept from the Carnegie Trust the gift of such books, equipment and other assets of the Irish Central Library for Students as may be offered to it, to establish, maintain and operate a central library and to assist local authorities to improve their library services. An Chomhairle is empowered to consult with and advise local authorities as to the improvement of public library services, assist them (including financial aid) to improve such services and make recommendations to the minister in relation to such services. An Chomhairle also advises the department on all stages of library proposals submitted by local authorities for sanction. Apart from a statutory grant of just £2,500 from the Minister for the Environment and Local Government, and some minor sundry receipts, the cost of running An Chomhairle Leabharlanna is borne by the county councils and county borough councils in proportion to the rateable valuations of their respective functional areas.

THE DEPARTMENT OF TOURISM, SPORT AND RECREATION

Irish tourism has full ministry status, and the industry makes a significant contribution to the country's economy. 'Thanks to tourism Ireland can support three airlines, a large ferry company, hundreds of hire pleasure boats, many dozens of quality golf courses, and thousands of world-class restaurants, hotels and guest-houses. There are magnificent art galleries, museums, interpretive centres, wildlife refuges, national parks, and a host of other visitor attractions' (Bord Fáilte 1997, 3) The department is responsible for the formulation of national policies connected with tourism. A number of state-sponsored bodies and executive agencies are charged with implementing these policies.

THE TOURISM COUNCIL

This Council, which is made up of representatives of the industry, Bord Fáilte, the Regional Tourism Authorities and the Department of Tourism, Sport and Recreation, acts as a forum for consultation between the constituent sectors. It also advises the minister and provides guidance in the formulation of tourism policy to be implemented by state agencies.

BORD FÁILTE

Bord Fáilte is a body corporate which began life in 1951 with a developmental role alongside Fógra Fáilte, which was tourism's marketing arm. In 1955, the new Bord Fáilte assumed both roles. Over the next forty years, Bord Fáilte was involved in registration and classification functions. During 1995, following the recommendations of the A. D. Little Report (1994), Bord Fáilte was significantly reorganized. Its new focus is aggressively, professionally and in close partnership with the Irish tourism industry, to market the Irish tourism product worldwide.

REGIONAL TOURISM ORGANIZATIONS

There are seven tourism regions, of which six are admin-

istered by Regional Tourism Authorities (RTAs). These include Dublin covering Dublin City and County, South-East (Carlow, Kilkenny, South Tipperary, Waterford, Wexford), South-West (Cork and South Kerry), West (Galway, Mayo, Roscommon), North-West (Cavan, Donegal, Leitrim, Monaghan, Sligo), Midlands East (Kildare, Laois, Longford, Louth, Meath, North Offaly, Westmeath, Wicklow). The seventh, the Shannon Region, covering counties Clare, North Kerry, Limerick, South Offaly, North Tipperary, is administered by Shannon Development. The membership of the RTAs and Shannon Development consists of local authorities and individuals, associations and firms whose combined activity and interests cover the tourism spectrum of their regions. The RTAs and Shannon Development provide tourism services in four main areas: planning, servicing, development and marketing (Bord Fáilte 1997, 29).

CERT

CERT is the state tourism training agency. At every level within tourism, CERT provides training to create the best practices critical to a quality product. Working in partnership with the industry itself and with the educational sector, the agency delivers courses which are industry driven, recognized by employers and lead to national qualifications. As the state tourism training agency, CERT is governed by a Council which reports to the Minister for Tourism, Sport and Recreation (Bord Fáilte 1997, 30).

As indicated in the latter report on tourism's role in economic growth, it appears that outstanding artefacts from a nation's history can play a major role in attracting tourists. Research shows that more than half of all visitors to this country include a visit to at least one place described as being of natural, cultural or historical interest during their stay.

THE DEPARTMENT OF EDUCATION AND SCIENCE

The Department of Education and Science is responsible for the administration of public education, primary, post-primary and special education. State subsidies for universities and colleges are channelled through it also. The primary education sector comprises primary schools, special schools and non-aided private primary schools. In all, it services almost 500,000 children in just over 3,200 primary schools and 116 special schools. The primary schools, which account for the education of 98% of children in the primary sector, are staffed by 21,000 teachers. The current and capital costs of primary schools, including the full cost of teachers' salaries, are predominantly funded by the state and supplemented by local contributions.

The second-level sector comprises secondary, vocational, community and comprehensive schools. There are roughly 370,000 students in this sector, attending a total of 768 publicly aided schools; 445 of these schools are secondary, 246 are vocational and 77 are community or comprehensive. There are also 30 other aided and non-aided schools. Sixty percent of second-level students are educated in secondary schools which are privately owned and managed. The majority are conducted by religious communities and the remainder by individuals or Boards of Governors. Over 95% of the cost of teachers' salaries are met by the state. Allowances and capitation grants are paid to the 95% of secondary schools which participate in the free education scheme. Twenty-six percent of all second-level students are educated in vocational schools which are administered by Vocational Education Committees. These schools are funded up to 93% provision with the balance being generated by the Committees. Individual budgets are provided for community and comprehensive schools where 14% of second-level students are educated (DES 1998).

Apart from acting as its major financier, the Department of Education and Science acknowledges the critical role of education in making people aware of the actual disciplines of heritage, Irish, English, History and so forth, through the school curricula put in place. At a national level, curricula are formulated by the Minister for Education and Science, on the advice of the National Council for Curriculum and Assessment, and the department oversees their implementation through its inspectorate. One of the proposals contained in the *Education (No. 2) Bill* 1997 was to establish the National Council for Curriculum and Assessment on a statutory basis.

Third-level education is provided in the Republic of Ireland in four universities, twelve Institutes of Technology, five Teacher Training Colleges and a number of independent business and professional training colleges. The four universities comprise the National University of Ireland (NUI), the University of Dublin (Trinity College), the University of Limerick and Dublin City University. The National University of Ireland is organized on a federal basis comprising NUI Dublin, NUI Cork, NUI Galway and NUI Maynooth, each of which enjoys a large measure of autonomy. The National College of Art and Design and the Royal College of Surgeons are also recognized colleges of the NUI. The Institutes of Technology are located in Athlone, Carlow, Dundalk, Dún Laoghaire, Galway, Letterkenny, Limerick, Sligo, Tallaght, Tralee and Waterford. The National Council for Educational awards (NCEA) has statutory award-giving authority for non-university higher education qualifications. It also sets and monitors standards in the colleges. Primary school teachers study for a Bachelor of Education (B. Ed.) degree at one of the five Teacher Training Colleges, which include St Patrick's College, Church of Ireland College, St Mary Marino and

Froebel College of Education — all of which are located in Dublin — and Mary Immaculate College which is based in Limerick. Two Colleges of Education for Home Economics provide training leading to a Bachelor of Education (B. Ed.) degree level at St Angela's, Sligo, and St Catherine's, Sion Hill, Dublin. Along with the publicly funded third-level sector, there are a number of independent private institutions, mainly involved in the provision of business and professional training. Many of the programmes offered by these colleges are validated by NCEA and some have liaisons with universities and/or professional associations through which the courses on offer are validated (DES 1998, 27).

The Higher Education Authority (HEA) is a statutory body under the aegis of the Minister for Education and Science. Among its functions, all of which are noted in the last document referred to, is the role of paymaster, insofar as it allocates among these institutions grants approved by the Oireachtas. It is interesting to note that funding was available from the HEA, under the Advanced Technical Skills Programme, to initiate the graduate *Diploma in Irish Heritage Management* at University College, Cork, from 1990–91 to 1994–95. Several other courses in the area of heritage, rural development and culture have been approved for funding since then. These include the Masters Degree in Rural Development in NUI Galway, an M.Sc. in Rural Development in NUI Dublin and a *Higher Diploma in Cultural Tourism* at NUI Maynooth, to mention but a few.

THE DEPARTMENT OF ARTS, HERITAGE, GAELTACHT AND THE ISLANDS

This is the new title given, following a change in government, to the Department of Arts, Culture and the Gaeltacht which was formed in 1993. The department was initially established by amalgamating the Department of the Gaeltacht with elements of the Department of the Taoiseach (in relation to arts, the cultural institutions and film), the Department of Tourism, Transport and Communications (in relation to broadcasting policy) and the Office of Public Works (in relation to heritage policy) — a Heritage Policy division was established in the department the same year. This department's functions were further expanded with the transfer of operational responsibility for the Heritage Service (Dúchas), including national monuments and historic properties, national parks and wildlife, and waterways, from the Office of Public Works. All statutory functions in relation to the built and natural heritage, including property ownership, which were formerly vested in the Minister for Finance and the Commissioners of Public Works in Ireland, are now the responsibility of the Minister for Arts, Heritage, Gaeltacht and the Islands (DACG 1996, 6). The title of the department was changed to the Department of Arts, Heritage, Gaeltacht and the Islands in 1997 when responsibility for the islands was added.

The collection of all those functions within one department was a very cogent step, providing a means whereby policy, decision-making and practical arrangements in relation to culture and heritage could be brought under one roof, facilitating a more integrated approach. The broad functions of the department as outlined in its *Statement of strategy plan* include the promotion of the cultural, social and economic welfare of the Gaeltacht and the preservation and extension of the use of Irish as a vernacular language. Providing employment is obviously essential to maintaining the population in Gaeltacht areas, and there was a considerable increase with the provision of 1,285 new jobs in 1996, for example, in projects assisted by Údarás na Gaeltachta. Gaeltacht harbours benefited from some £7 million being provided under the EU Operational Programme for Industrial Development and Fisheries.

Formulating national policy in relation to the arts is another important function of this department. The government approved *The arts plan 1995–99*, the co-ordinated plan for the arts prepared by the Arts Council. The plan adopted an area-based approach to the development of the arts in Ireland. A Cultural Development Incentives Scheme was put in place which is designed primarily to assist the four main categories of the visual and performing arts: arts centres, theatres, galleries and museums.

The *National Cultural Institutions Act* 1997 provided for the establishment of statutory boards to care for and manage collections in the National Museum and in the National Library, and make wide-ranging and extensive changes to the governance structures of these institutions. The conservation of our built and natural heritage is also the responsibility of this department. Developments in these areas include changes under the *National Monuments Act* 1994 and the transposition of the Habitats Directive (92/43/EEC) into Irish law through the European Communities (Natural Habitats) Regulations in February 1997.

LOCAL GOVERNMENT

Various forms of local government were put in place under British rule, but the principal landmark in the development of Irish local government is the *Local Government (Ireland) Act* 1898, which introduced the structure and constitutions of county and county borough councils. After this, the institutions of local government were:

• County Councils

• County Borough Councils

• Borough Corporations

• Urban District Councils

• Rural District Councils

• Town Commissioners

There have been some changes in the intervening years which include the abolition of Rural District Councils in 1925 and the transfer of their functions to county councils, the upgrading of Galway from Borough to County Borough status in 1985, the creation in 1991 of three new administrative counties, namely Dún Laoghaire/Rathdown, Fingal and South Dublin (each with its own Council) to replace Dublin County Council, Dún Laoghaire Corporation (and Dean's Grange Joint Burial Board) which were dissolved under the act. The most recent change was the addition of eight Regional Authorities by ministerial establishment order in December 1993 pursuant to the *Local Government Act* 1991. The Regional Authority areas include Dublin (City and County), South-East (Kilkenny, Carlow, Wexford, Waterford City and County, Tipperary SR), South-West (Cork City and County, Kerry), Mid-West (Clare, Limerick City and County, Tipperary NR), West (Galway City and County, Mayo, Roscommon), Border (Donegal, Leitrim, Cavan, Monaghan, Louth, Sligo), Midlands (Offaly, Longford, Westmeath, Laois), and Mid-East (Kildare, Meath, Wicklow). Membership of the Regional Authorities consists of 'persons who are members of a council of a County or County Borough, the functional area of which is included in the region' (*Local Government Act* 1991).

The main purpose of the Regional Authorities is to promote the co-ordination of the provision of public services within the region and, in addition, the co-ordination and planning of certain public services at local level. It is also a function of these Authorities to monitor and give advice on the implementation of EU funding by the constituent local authorities with support from the Department of Finance in respect of EU-related functions.

There are now 114 directly elected local councils in five separate legal categories as follows:

• County Councils (29)

• County Borough Councils (5)

• Borough Corporations (5)

• Urban District Councils (49)

• Town Commissioners (30)

Before outlining the specific functions of local authorities, we shall take a brief look at how the system operates.

Local authorities comprise two elements, a democratically elected council and a chief executive or manager. Local elections are scheduled to be held every five years, but under the *Local Elections Act* 1973, the minister was given power to extend this period. This is just one example of the considerable level of control which has been exercised over local authorities by the department over the years. Local elections have been postponed on several occasions, but the power was removed under Section 20 of the *Local Government Act* 1994, which stipulated that 'An election of members of every local authority shall be held in 1999 and every fifth year thereafter.'

MANAGEMENT

The management system was introduced under the *Cork City Management Act* 1929, when the first City Manager was appointed for Cork city. Managers were appointed to the cities of Dublin, Limerick and Waterford under separate acts in 1930, 1934 and 1939 respectively, and the system was extended to the counties in 1942 under the *County Management Act* 1940. The county manager also acts as manager for every elective body whose functional area is completely within the county. In the initial act, a clear distinction was drawn between 'reserved' and 'executive' functions. Reserved functions are the functions performed directly by the elected members. These involve principally policy decisions.

Membership of local authorities is open to persons aged eighteen years or over. Sitting TDs and Senators may at the same time act as members of local councils. The *Local Government Act* 1991 excludes ministers and ministers of state from local authority membership, and this exclusion was extended to MEPs, the Chairman of Dáil, the Chairman of Seanad and the Chairmen of Select Committees of the Oireachtas under the *Local Government Act* 1994. Other categories of person disqualified from being a member of a local authority include Gardaí and civil servants not permitted by their conditions of employment. Quite a large proportion of Oireachtas members are either currently or at some stage have been members of a local authority. The franchise for voting in local elections is not confined to Irish or British citizens but is extended to those over eighteen years of age on the date the electoral register comes into force (15 April each year), irrespective of nationality.

Neither the Free State Constitution of 1922 nor the Constitution of 1937 made any special provision for local government. Local authorities have derived their powers from acts of the Oireachtas and have, by international standards, a narrow range of functions. Unlike many European countries, they have no role in policing, public transport, personal social services and very little in health and education. However, as recently as June 1999, in conjunction with the European and local government elections, a referendum was held on whether local government should be given recognition in the Constitution. The response of the people was positive.

Prior to the passing of the *Local Government Act* 1991, local authorities in Ireland were restricted in their actions by an archaic *ultra vires* rule. Desmond Roche's explanation of this rule was that 'if a local authority purports to do something in exercise of its powers but is acting beyond these powers it is said to be acting *ultra vires* and can be restrained by the High Court' (Roche 1982, 184). In other words, they were precluded from doing anything for which they did not have statutory responsibility. This compared badly with the 'general competence' enjoyed by other European local authorities which allowed them to take initiatives and act in the interest of their area. The 1991 act granted a 'general competence' to Irish local authorities, although they will have a statutory duty to take cognisance of government policies and the availability of resources. A government Action Programme for the Millennium 'included a commitment to the restoration of real decision-making and power to local authorities and local people, as well as the enhancement of efficiency and customer service in local government' *(http://www.environ.ie/dept/strategy 1998-2000.html)*.

FINANCE

Another major limitation to the autonomy of local authorities has been the level of financial control exercised by its government parent department over the years. Local government has traditionally been financed in three ways: through rates, government grants and other sources. Rates are a local tax, payable on immovable property and generally considered local government's 'own tax', and at this stage were payable on commercial property, domestic dwellings, agricultural land and the like. They are an independent source of revenue, and in 1924 provided the major proportion of local authority receipts.

The *Local Government (Financial Provisions) Act* 1978 totally abolished rates on domestic dwellings, secondary schools, farm buildings and community halls. Until 1981, while the minister retained a power of limitation on rate increases, the amount lost in income to local authorities was recouped in full by a Rate Support Grant. This generosity, however, was not to last, and since 1982, when this limitation was dispensed with, a grant which is an ever-reducing fraction of the rates yield was paid to the local authorities. The *Local Government (Financial Provisions) (No. 2) Act* 1983 enabled local authorities to levy charges for services, namely water, refuse collection and sewerage services. There was widespread resistance to these charges, and the attempt to restore some financial flexibility to authorities was described by Basil Chubb as 'a failure', as 'the amounts raised were small and, clearly, this was a political hot potato that some local authorities could not handle' (Chubb 1992, 174). Further trouble lay in store for local authorities' independent sources of funds when, following a Supreme Court decision, agricultural rates ceased to be a source of income in 1982.

Funding arrangements were to change in January 1997 with the abolition of the Rate Support Grant and revenues generated from domestic water and sewerage charges. In lieu of these, the local authorities were to receive the full proceeds of motor taxation as an independent source of revenue. A recent change in January 1999 saw the establishment of an independent Local Government Fund which amounted to about £590 million in 1999, financed from two sources: an amount of £270 million in 1999, increased annually to take account of inflation and changes in the functions of local councils, and the proceeds of motor tax. Ostensibly this change in financing arrangements would appear to give more financial independence to local authorities which, coupled with the 'general competence' referred to earlier, may mark a new era of autonomy.

The work of local authorities is arranged into eight programme groups:

• Housing and Building

• Road Transportation and Safety

• Water Supply and Sewerage

• Planning and Development

• Environmental Protection

• Recreation and Amenity

• Agriculture, Education, Health and Welfare

• Miscellaneous

All of these programmes have an important part to play in maintaining the image of the country, but three should be identified as having a special significance in contributing to the protection of Ireland's heritage in various ways.

PLANNING AND DEVELOPMENT

The importance of tourism as Ireland's leading internationally traded service is widely recognized, and a quality natural environment, boasting of scenic landscapes of world renown, which is fortunately our heritage, is probably the foundation stone of this industry. Prior to 1963, local authorities' involvement with tourism was extremely limited, being confined to an annual contribution to approved bodies 'engaged in advertising health resorts' as early as 1925, and to contributing up to a rate of one penny in the pound (counties and cities) or three pence (urban authorities) since 1931. The passing of the *Local Government (Planning and Development) Act* 1963 signalled a revolutionary change in the attitude and powers of local authorities, not only in relation to tourism but in a much wider context. The local authorities were now to become the planning authorities for the entire country, whether county, city or town, and the appearance of the whole countryside was in their hands.

There were a number of shortcomings in the 1963 act. One was the granting of 'exempted' status to development by state bodies and planning authorities. This was corrected by the *Local Government (Planning and Development) Act* 1993. The act provides a new framework for regulating development by or on behalf of state authorities and was in response the the Supreme Court ruling concerning development at Mullaghmore, county Clare, and Luggala, county Wicklow. The act also provides for the establishment of a new procedure for public consultation for developments proposed by planning authorities.

The process of 'listing' as dealt with under the act has also attracted criticism. 'Listing' refers to the process of selecting buildings for inclusion in a list, the contents of such list then being subject to legal protection and rights. Under the 1963 act, this is not a mandatory function and the listing of buildings of artistic, architectural or historical interest in a County Development Plan is, therefore, entirely at the discretion of the local authority. The planning legislation, though it allows a building itself to be listed, at the same time leaves the interior of that listed building with no protection. This alarming gap has been highlighted for many years by voluntary organizations like An Taisce.

In March 1995, the Minister for Arts, Culture and the Gaeltacht, together with the Minister for the Environment, established an interdepartmental working group to address the limitations of the procedures which are in place. In preparing the report, the working group invited submissions from planning authorities and a wide range of interested organizations, resulting in a very comprehensive publication entitled *Strengthening the protection of the architectural heritage* (1996). The report is a powerful document, with very practical and imaginative recommendations covering the listing system, a National Inventory of Architecture, financial incentives and a training, education and advisory service. A tangible result of the report is the *Local Government (Mandatory Listing of Historic Building and Protection of Historic Interiors) Act* 1999. A fund of £3.9 million has also been made available to local authorities for protected buildings and structures. This will be an annual ongoing fund, hopefully increasing with time.

ENVIRONMENTAL PROTECTION

Generally speaking, it is only in recent years that there has been recognition of the fact that the environment is an endowment to each generation, an undisputed part of our heritage, and that it is the duty of each generation to ensure it is not damaged irreparably for the future. Therefore, there is a challenge to law makers to facilitate sustainable development in industry, agriculture and other sectors.

In 1992, at the UN Conference on Environment and Development held in Rio de Janeiro, the concept of Sustainable Development was given international recognition. Sustainable Development is defined as development into the twenty-first century which is referred to as 'Agenda 21'. The Department of the Environment issued guidelines on Sustainable Development to local authorities in June 1995. During Ireland's presidency of the EU, an Environmental Action Programme was launched to indicate the steps being taken by Ireland to clean up the environment. Some of the principal initiatives outlined in this programme included:

• ENFO — the Environmental Information Service;

• Air quality — measures taken to deal with smog in Dublin;

• Inland water — the government was to spend £300 million between 1990 and 2000 on new and improved public water supplies;

• The marine environment — sewage discharges: it was planned to eliminate untreated discharges of sewage from major coastal towns by the year 2000;

• Dumping at sea — a ban on all dumping of industrial wastes at sea from 31 December 1995;

• Waste disposal in harbours — harbour authorities would be required to install facilities for receiving ships' waste in all ports;

• Agriculture and the environment — grants available for pollution control works. Other initiatives included the promotion of organic farming;

• Forestry and the environment — Environment Impact Assessments (EIAs) to be carried out for individual developments of 200 ha or more and where it is proposed to replace more than 10 ha of broadleaf with conifers;

• Industry and the environment — the EIA system has been mandatory for certain major categories of development since 1 February 1990;

• Waste recycling and disposal — each local authority to prepare a recycling scheme for its area — grants provided to voluntary bodies and local authority;

• Wildlife Habitats — Protection of Habitats — under the *Wildlife Amendment Bill* 1997, the Minister for Arts Culture and the Gaeltacht designated Natural Heritage Areas (NHAs). The designated areas were estimated to cover approximately 11% of the national territory. Designation as a NHA is intended to protect important habitats. There are two specific implications arising from this:

(i) In deciding whether to grant planning permission, local authorities must take into account the designated status of the area.

(ii) Grant aid would not be available for projects which were incompatible with the conservation of the habitat in a designated area, for instance, grants for tree planting.

• Protecting the ozone layer — grants for the provision of CFC recycling facilities.

Under this general programme of environmental protection, local authorities have statutory powers in relation to waste disposal/refuse collection, litter, water pollution, air pollution, noise pollution, derelict sites and dangerous buildings/places.

RECREATION AND AMENITY

This is the third local authority programme which has particular relevance to the current discussion. The activities covered include the provision and maintenance of public libraries, museums and related arts facilities. The *Public Libraries Acts* and the *Local Government Act* 1960 had provided various powers in relation to schools of music, science and art, the establishment of concert halls, theatres and museums. The *Local Government Act* 1994 repealed these acts and defined library authorities in Section 32 as the council of a county, the corporation of a county borough, and certain joint library committees. Section 33 empowered library authorities to 'take such measures, engage in such activities or do such things in accordance with law (including the incurring of expenditure) for the provision of library services as it considers necessary or desirable'. This is consistent with the 'general competence' allowed to local authorities under the *Local Government Act* 1991.

Local authorities have had statutory power to provide

arts support under the *Arts Act* 1973. The level of arts activity has increased considerably over the past ten years or more, due to the appointment of Arts Officers. These posts are mostly jointly funded with the Arts Council and nearly thirty county councils/local authorities have appointed an Arts Officer. In 1997, a joint report from the Combat Poverty Agency and the Arts Council noted that the work of arts officers in local authorities and county councils was 'broad-ranging and varies from place to place, depending on the budget allowed and the amount of local interest in the arts'. The report also referred to a further area of arts-related activity by local authorities — the One Percent Scheme. Under this scheme, local authorities may allocate one percent of a capital project (housing project, roads, water services and the like) or £20,000, whichever is the lesser amount, to an artistic feature which must be related to the scheme, sited close by and permanent.

CONCLUSION

It is encouraging to note the considerable raft of legislation, much of which was as a result of EU Directives, which has been put in place to protect our heritage in various forms, built, natural and other, in recent years. However, having legislation in place is only the beginning, enforcing it involves considerable commitment, financial and otherwise. It will involve co-operation between state departments and local authorities. In a relatively recent report on better local government, it was acknowledged that the 'small scale of local authority operations has made it difficult for them to employ personnel with the expertise necessary to cope with increasingly complex environmental issues' (DOE 1996b). It is also worth noting that much local authority expenditure is discretionary, and the Recreation and Amenity Programme which involves expenditure on arts activities, libraries, museums and the like must compete for funding with housing maintenance, road maintenance and other major projects.

Ireland's accession to the EEC in 1973 may have served to sharpen the focus of our concern in maintaining our individual 'Irish' identity. This is not, however, the first generation to acknowledge the importance of protecting our heritage. In Seanad Éireann on 10 June 1925, during his contribution to the debate on the *Shannon Electricity Bill*, 'where it was proposed that whenever any monument of antiquarian interest was to be disturbed in the course of the electricity scheme, the Board of Public Works should be notified', Dr W. B. Yeats, who, just two years previously had been awarded the Nobel Prize for Literature, showed precisely the same concern and indeed considerable foresight when he observed: 'There are many monuments which we should respect and which will become of great importance to this country, not only to the education of our own people, but to the tourists who come here. Therefore, they will be of financial value' (Pearce 1960).

Bibliography

An Bord Pleanála 1995 *Report and accounts*. Dublin.
An Chomhairle Ealaíon — The Arts Council 1995 *Annual report*. Dublin.
Bord Fáilte 1997 *The Fáilte business — tourism's role in economic growth*. Dublin.
Chubb, B. 1993 *The government and politics of Ireland*, 3rd ed. New York.
Combat Poverty Agency/The Arts Council 1997 *Poverty, access and participation in the arts*. Dublin.
DACG (Department Arts, Culture and the Gaeltacht) 1996a *Statement of strategy*. Dublin.
DACG (Department Arts, Culture and the Gaeltacht) 1996b *Strengthening the protection of architectural heritage*. Dublin.
DAF (Department of Agriculture and Food) 1992 *Schemes and services in agriculture*. Dublin.
DAFF (Department of Agriculture, Food and Forestry) 1994 *Rural Environment Protection Scheme*. Dublin.
DAHGI (Department of Arts, Heritage, Gaeltacht and the Islands) 1998 *Statement of strategy*. Dublin.
DES (Department of Education and Science) 1998 *Brief description of the Irish education system*. Dublin.
DMNR (Department of the Marine and Natural Resources) 1998 *Making the most of Ireland's natural resources: strategy statement 1998-2000*. Dublin.
DOE (Department of the Environment) 1996a *Operational strategy*. Dublin.
DOE (Department of the Environment) 1996b *Better local government, a programme for change*. Dublin.
Dooney, S. and O'Toole, J. 1992 *Irish government today*. Dublin.
Little, A. D. 1994 *Review of the roles and responsibilities of Bord Fáilte Éireann: proposal*. Dublin.
Mulcahy, B. 1996 *Government in Ireland: a study of the political make-up of the Republic of Ireland*. Dublin.
Murphy, J. 1998 'Europe tackles unsustainable farming, the EU's new farming policy should benefit wildlife', *Wings* **10**, 18.
Pearce, D. R. 1960 (ed) *The Senate speeches of W. B. Yeats*. London.
Roche, D. 1982 *Local government in Ireland*. Dublin.
The Heritage Council 1996 *Evaluation of environmental designations: Ireland*. Dublin.

Government and Tourism in Northern Ireland

Neil Collins and Rosalind Beggs

Northern Ireland is probably better known internationally for terrorism than tourism. Nevertheless, tourism has remained, despite the 'Troubles', an important part of the economy. It contributes significant employment and earnings to Northern Ireland. Perhaps just as importantly, tourism acts as a barometer of politics — the lower the political tension, the higher the tourism figures. In this account, the institutional background to tourism policy is underlined before some of the most salient policy issues are examined.

GOVERNMENT STRUCTURES IN NORTHERN IRELAND

Northern Ireland became a separate political entity in 1921 because of the *Government of Ireland Act* 1920. A wide range of responsibilities — education, health, personal social services, home affairs (including law and order), housing, planning and economic development — were devolved to the regional parliament and government in Belfast. Responsibility for certain other matters, such as foreign affairs, defence, taxation, government publications and the postal service, was reserved to the sovereign parliament in London and continued to be administered in Northern Ireland by UK civil servants. A separate civil service, the Northern Ireland Civil Service (NICS), was set up to administer the devolved functions. This structure survived until 1972 when the Northern Ireland parliament was prorogued; the NICS has remained in place, but the Secretary of State and a number of junior ministers in the Northern Ireland Office (NIO) directed the work of Northern Ireland departments. As well as this quasi-supervisory role, the NIO is itself responsible for the contentious area of law and order, and for what is described as political development — the search for a long-term solution to the Northern Ireland problem. In 1998, as a result of the Belfast (Good Friday) Agreement, a local assembly was elected from which a regional executive was formed on 2 December 1999. These arrangements were suspended on 11 February 2000 but re-instituted on 29 May 2000. The new agreement may have long-term advantages for tourism if it provides an enduring political settlement.

THE NORTHERN IRELAND ASSEMBLY

The Assembly meets in Parliament Buildings, Stormont, Belfast. It is the prime source of authority for all devolved responsibilities, with full legislative and executive authority. In other words, the Assembly has the power to make laws and take decisions on all functions of Northern Ireland departments. The Assembly has elected a First Minister, Deputy First Minister and ten ministers (Ministers of Legislative Assembly, MLA) have been appointed on a cross-community basis with responsibility for the new Northern Ireland departments. Together, twelve ministers make up the Executive Committee. The Committee meets to discuss and agree on issues that cut across the responsibilities of two or more ministers and therefore acts on a cross-community basis. The Executive will seek to approve each year and review as necessary a programme of governance within an agreed budget. This will be subject to approval by the Assembly after examination in Assembly Committees. These Committees are also formed on a cross-community basis.

Ministers and their departments

The First Minister and Deputy First Minister have appointed two junior ministers to assist each of them in their responsibilities. These include a wide range of issues comprising economic policy, equality and liaison with the North/South Ministerial Council, the British-Irish Council, British-Irish Intergovernmental Conference, the Civic Forum (see below) and the Secretary of State for Northern Ireland.

Departments

Ten departments have been set up, each with a breadth

499

of responsibilities. **Table 48.1** details them and their major remits.

It is interesting to note that many of the core areas of previous responsibility have been split across the new departments. In particular, those matters relating to the management of tourism within Northern Ireland are included within the remits of the Departments of Enterprise, Trade and Investment and Culture, Arts and Leisure. Additionally, other departments will play a peripheral role in tourism. This illustrates the cross-departmental and community approach to the Northern Ireland Assembly. Perhaps significantly, the Northern Ireland Tourist Board (NITB) is no longer mentioned by name in the official description of departmental responsibilities, rather the term 'tourism' is used. The NITB's sister organizations responsible for economic development, however, all receive a mention.

Departmental Committees

The Assembly has ten statutory Committees. Positions as chair and deputy chair are allocated using the proportional d'Hondt System. Membership of Committees is in broad proportion to party strengths in the Assembly to ensure that the opportunity of having Committee places is available to all members. Each Committee has a scrutinizing, policy development and consultation role in relation to its department and a role in the initiation of legislation. Committees have the authority to:

• consider and advise on departmental budgets and

Table 48.1 Departments of the Northern Ireland Government with their Major Responsibilities

DEPARTMENT OF ENTERPRISE, TRADE AND INVESTMENT
Economic development policy, tourism, industrial safety, consumer affairs, energy policy.

DEPARTMENT OF REGIONAL DEVELOPMENT
Transport planning, public transport, roads, rail, ports and airports, water, strategic planning.

DEPARTMENT OF CULTURE, ARTS AND LEISURE
Arts and culture, sport and leisure, libraries and museums, inland waterways, inland fisheries, language policy, Lottery matters, visitor amenities.

DEPARTMENT FOR SOCIAL DEVELOPMENT
Housing policy, Northern Ireland Housing Executive, voluntary activity, urban renewal, community sector, Housing Benefit Review Boards, Social Security Agency, Child Support Agency, Lands Division, social legislation.

DEPARTMENT OF THE ENVIRONMENT
Planning control, environment and heritage, protection of the countryside, waste management, pollution control, wildlife protection, local government, sustainable development, mineral resources (planning aspects), road safety, transport licensing and enforcement.

DEPARTMENT OF FINANCE AND PERSONNEL
Finance, personnel, IT and common services.

DEPARTMENT OF EDUCATION
Schools funding and administration.

DEPARTMENT OF HIGHER AND FURTHER EDUCATION, TRAINING AND EMPLOYMENT
Higher education, further education, vocational training, employment services, employment law and labour relations, teacher training.

DEPARTMENT OF HEALTH, SOCIAL SERVICES AND PUBLIC SAFETY
Health, social services, public health and safety, health promotion, Fire Authority.

DEPARTMENT OF AGRICULTURE AND RURAL DEVELOPMENT
Food, farming and environment policy, agri-food development, veterinary matters, science service, rural development, forestry, sea fisheries, rivers.

annual plans within the overall budget allocation;

• approve relevant secondary legislation and take the Committee stage of relevant primary legislation;

• call for persons and papers to advise and assist Northern Ireland ministers in forming policy;

• initiate enquiries and make reports, and

• consider and advise on matters brought to the Committee by its minister.

THE NORTH/SOUTH MINISTERIAL COUNCIL

The North/South Ministerial Council brings together ministers from Northern Ireland and the Irish government. The Council will meet on a regular basis to develop consultation, co-operation and action on an all-island and cross-border basis on matters of mutual interest. Under the North/South Ministerial Council, six new North/South Implementation Bodies came into being on 2 December 1999. The new bodies include Waterways Ireland and the Trade and Business Development Body. These bodies will implement policies agreed by ministers in the North/South Ministerial Council. In addition to the six Implementation Bodies, an initial six areas, of which tourism is one, have been identified for co-operation between existing government departments and other bodies in the two jurisdictions.

THE BRITISH-IRISH COUNCIL

The British-Irish Council aims to promote the harmonious and mutually beneficial development of relationships among peoples of the United Kingdom and Ireland. It is made up of representatives of the British and Irish governments, of the devolved institutions in Northern Ireland, Scotland and Wales and of the Isle of Man and Channel Islands. This Council has decided as a priority to examine and develop policies for co-operation on drugs, social exclusion, the environment and transport. In addition, other areas will include agriculture, culture and tourism.

BRITISH-IRISH INTERGOVERNMENTAL CONFERENCE

The British-Irish Intergovernmental Conference will replace the Anglo-Irish Intergovernmental Council and the Intergovernmental Conference established under the 1985 Anglo-Irish Agreement. It aims to promote bilateral co-operation on matters of mutual interest to the British and Irish governments, particularly issues in relation to Northern Ireland.

THE CIVIC FORUM

The Civic Forum will consist of sixty representatives of the business, trade union, voluntary and other sectors of

---

Table 48.2 Local Authorities in Northern Ireland

Antrim
Ards
Armagh
Ballymena
Ballymoney
Banbridge
Belfast
Carrickfergus
Castlereagh
Coleraine
Cookstown
Craigavon
Derry
Down
Dungannon
Fermanagh
Larne
Limavady
Lisburn
Magherafelt
Moyle
Newry/Mourne
Newtownabbey
North Down
Omagh
Strabane

---

the Northern Ireland community, and a chairperson appointed by the First Minister and Deputy First Minister. It will act as a consultative mechanism on social, economic and cultural matters.

EXCEPTED AND RESERVED MATTERS

The Secretary of State for Northern Ireland remains responsible for Northern Ireland Office policy areas not devolved to the Assembly. These include issues such as policing, security policy, prisons, criminal justice, international relations, taxation, national insurance, and the regulation of telecommunications and broadcasting. The Secretary of State will represent Northern Ireland interests in the United Kingdom cabinet.

LOCAL GOVERNMENT

The *Local Government (Northern Ireland) Act* 1972 provided for the creation of twenty six local authorities (LAs) with responsibilities for relatively few executive functions (**Table 48.2**). These include certain regulatory services such as cinema and dance hall licensing, building regulations and health inspection. Councils also provide a limited range of direct services to the public: street cleaning; refuse collection and disposal; burial grounds and crematoria; public baths; recreational facilities and tourist amenities. Added to these recently has been the freedom to engage in certain local industrial development activities.

Refuse management together with leisure and community services represent the only major items of expenditure by local authorities in Northern Ireland. As a consequence, local government is responsible for less than 3% of total public expenditure. In addition to these executive responsibilities, local authorities have representative and consultative functions. They are entitled to representation on certain public agencies and advisory councils. Local councils are also consulted about matters for which they have no executive responsibility, such as proposed housing schemes, planning applications and road developments within their area. It is probable that the representative and consultative role of local government will decrease as the Northern Ireland Assembly's powers increase.

BACKGROUND TO TOURISM IN NORTHERN IRELAND

Prior to 1969, tourism from all areas, domestic, national and international, to Northern Ireland grew steadily. The advances experienced in Northern Ireland during the 1960s were dramatically halted with increased civil unrest during the early part of the 1970s. In particular, tourism from the two main traditional sources, Britain and the Republic of Ireland, declined to half its normal levels. Although the latter part of the 1970s witnessed a short recovery in total tourist traffic, greater political tension during 1981 brought about a downturn in visitor levels. Whilst there had been erratic fluctuations during the 1980s, the advent of the ceasefires in late 1994 gave a tremendous boost to the industry. In 1995, the first summer after the IRA and Combined Loyalist Military Command ceasefires, Northern Ireland tourism enjoyed a record 461,000 tourists, which was a massive 67% rise on the previous year. This confirmed to many that, given the right conditions, the tourism industry had the potential to grow at similar rates as Scotland and the Republic of Ireland.

TOURISM IN NORTHERN IRELAND: PUBLIC POLICY

Despite the importance of tourism in Northern Ireland, public policy has historically been criticised for the lack of co-ordination, purpose and direction. Traditionally, UK government involvement in tourism has been a product of wider policy aims relating to the balance of payments and regional economic development. The present position in NI is quite different. At the Northern Ireland Assembly level, matters relating to tourism are the responsibility of the Department of Enterprise, Trade and Investment. The Department of Culture, Arts and Leisure, amongst other responsibilities, is concerned with arts, culture, leisure, museums and the Armagh Planetarium. In addition, the North/South Ministerial

Council, the British-Irish Intergovernmental Conference and the Civic Forum each have a peripheral role in the administration of tourism.

The NITB is a non-departmental public body, constituted under the Tourism (Northern Ireland) Order 1992. It has responsibility for developing tourism in Northern Ireland and for promoting the area as a tourist destination. As part of the Belfast (Good Friday) Agreement, the matter of future arrangements in relation to the NITB as well as the promotion and marketing of tourism on an all-island basis is to be reassessed. Bord Fáilte and NITB have worked in close co-operation in recent years, particularly in joint promotion and marketing of the island. All developments in this respect will, of course, require agreement by the Northern Ireland Assembly, the Oireachtas and both governments. Some commentators suggest that an inevitable consequence of the Agreement is an all-island tourism body.

As well as NITB, a series of bodies at local authority level have responsibility for tourism matters within Northern Ireland. Local councils play an important statutory role in tourism development. In particular, the *Local Government (Northern Ireland) Act* 1972 gave councils functions such as responsibility for the attraction of tourists to their respective areas; provision and maintenance of each area's tourist amenities, and services and the provision of advisory and information services. In recent years, the twenty-six LAs have participated in regional marketing consortia. These are typically comprised of an amalgamation of local authorities and, in some cases, private-sector interests, which have played an important role in the marketing of Northern Ireland abroad, in conjunction with NITB. The current regional tourism organizations include the Belfast Visitor and Convention Bureau and Causeway Coast and Glens. A number of local councils and associated bodies decided to 'opt out' of these joint arrangements. These include the Armagh Marketing Initiative, the Banbridge and Craigavon District Councils (The Linen Homelands), Dungannon District Council and the Sperrins.

In addition to governmental involvement in Northern Ireland tourism, it is estimated that there are more than fifty associations representing resources which the tourist industry uses. These are diverse and wide-ranging. They involve other elements such as accommodation, entertainment, attractions, transport, sport and recreation activities.

THE NORTHERN IRELAND TOURISM PRODUCT

An analysis of the value and relevance of the tourist industry requires some discussion of the industry's economic context. When considering tourism in Northern Ireland, therefore, it is useful to compare it with Britain and the Republic of Ireland, because of their geographical proximity and similar physical characteristics.

Tourism in Northern Ireland has undergone significant change. Market conditions have altered dramatically between 1995 and the present, with consequences for anticipated visitor numbers and economic impact. Visitor tourism is taken to mean visitors from outside Northern Ireland who spend at least one overnight stay. According to NITB published figures, tourism generates around £200 million revenue per annum from out-of-state visitors. In 1998, there was a 2% growth in revenue in real terms, injecting an estimated £217 million into the local economy. In addition, the domestic market generates some £63 million revenue from Northern Ireland residents and overall the sector sustains 15,000 full-time equivalent jobs. It contributes 1.6% to GDP. It is hoped to raise this to 5%, close to the level enjoyed in Scotland and the Republic. Visitor numbers increased during 1998 by 4% on 1997, reaching 1.48 million and including some 27,700 (19%) pure holiday visitors. Visitor numbers from the Republic increased by 4%, with the holiday element rising by 12.5% to 90,000.

Tourism within Northern Ireland remains heavily reliant on those visiting friends and relatives. In addition, business traffic is ensured by close economic links with Britain. While opportunities for development and growth exist, a recent study undertaken by the Northern Ireland Economic Council (NIEC 1996) identified a number of important, wide-ranging recommendations for tourism within Northern Ireland. These have been summarized in **Table 48.3**.

At present, the NITB's approach is based on establishing a brand strategy for Northern Ireland and its five regions as defined by the Tourist Board. The overall strategy aims to sell Northern Ireland on the basis of the characteristics of its people, its rich history, environment, spirit, culture and its unique qualities and relationship with the rest of Ireland. There will be an increasing emphasis on product marketing groups with a focus on six activity and special interest areas, namely walking, cycling, angling, golf, equestrian and cultural tourism.

The NITB strategy to raise the contribution of the tourism sector to 5% of GDP and thereby secure approxi-

---

Table 48.3 Important Issues to be addressed within Northern Ireland Tourism

ATTRACTIONS — an increased demand in visitor traffic requires a need for private-sector involvement in the provision of attractions;

ACCOMMODATION — increase in demand for accommodation, in terms of both visitor numbers and length of stay;

SUSTAINABILITY — careful consideration should be given to the continued development of tourism which is to be managed in a manner which protects the environment and the long-term viability of the industry;

HUMAN RESOURCES — expanding demand will create a need for more job opportunities and career progression within the industry, a need for a high skill base and opportunities for the entrepreneur;

MARKETING — in a peaceful environment, the marketing of Northern Ireland will progressively become the key function of the governmental agencies responsible for tourism;

ORGANIZATION — an increase in demand would alter the environment in which the NITB has operated, which may create a need for organizational change and a greater role for the private sector;

FINANCE — a reduction in public resources for tourism projects;

TRANSPORT — the development of access to routes across Northern Ireland, in terms of frequency, range and costs;

SEASONALITY — the development of business conferences, events and the short break market to lengthen the tourist season, and

DIVERSITY — to attract a diversity of visitors from a wider geographical market.

Source: *NIEC 1996, pp. 9–13*

Table 48.4 Cultural Tourism Sector Benefits

CAN PROVIDE TOURISM WITH:	TOURISTS CAN BRING TO THE CULTURAL SECTOR:
a magnet to increase visitor numbers in certain specialized markets;	increased audience potential;
a means of defining a destination and adding to the overall appeal and sophistication;	distinct programming opportunities and the opportunity for a wider range of events;
a means of adding value to a visit and increasing customer satisfaction, and	the opportunity to put on minor events;
a means of generating off-peak visitor traffic.	an audience during periods when local residents consider themselves on holiday, and
	exhibition and performing opportunities as well as souvenir income sales.

Source: *Arts Council et al. 1998*

---

mately 20,000 new jobs is based on a number of assumptions outlined below:
• there must be sustained peace and summer disturbances must be resolved;

• economic and monetary conditions must place Northern Ireland in a more competitive position (for instance, movement is needed on the value of sterling against the Euro and on high VAT and fuel costs);

• an increase in overall economic activity in the area;

• continued partnerships with the Republic and the British Tourism Authority (BTA) to sell the island of Ireland and Northern Ireland internationally;

• exploit world-wide brands with unique Northern Ireland links, including the *Titanic* and St Patrick, and

• continued EU funding for development and marketing in addition to mainstream government expenditure and private investment.

The overall tourism strategy for Northern Ireland has three strategic themes: 'Strategy for All', 'Effective Partnerships' and 'Flexibility'. This is translated into three core elements. The first is to raise the profile of tourism so that it is recognized as an important part of the overall economic development strategy for Northern Ireland — attracting public- and private-sector investment. The second relates to the ability to attract visitors by creating and implementing marketing plans and encouraging regional co-operation. The third strategy aims to develop the capacity to deliver by ensuring that the infrastructure and product base are in place and that there is capacity in the workplace to provide the quality of service that visitors will expect.

Cultural and heritage tourism in Northern Ireland

Northern Ireland is fortunate in that it contains a world-famous site, the Giant's Causeway, which attracts just under 400,000 visitors (recorded) per year. The Causeway is officially designated as an Area of Outstanding Natural Beauty and a World Heritage Site. Northern Ireland, however, has many other lesser-known natural and built attractions which offer diversity and choice for tourists, such as the Marble Arch caves, Derry City's walls and, more recently, the Exploris wildlife centre in Portaferry.

Central government is a major owner and operator of sites within Northern Ireland, accounting for 29% of visitor attractions, while LAs provide an additional 31%. This position has been viewed as '... a quite exceptional asset ...' (Myerscough 1996). NITB, in its *Development strategy 1995–2000*, fully recognized the importance of heritage attractions. The report stated that '... apart from providing a rewarding experience for visitors, attractions often provide the main reason or motivation for visitors to make a day trip ...' (NITB 1995).

The private-sector share of attractions is 29% and the National Trust possesses 10%. These figures disguise the significant growth that has taken place in private-sector attractions in recent years. It is clear, however, that government has a major responsibility for the overall provision of attractions.

On the demand side, it is widely acknowledged that

consumer demands are becoming increasingly sophisticated. Visitors' interests and their reasons for travelling are also becoming more specialized. The rich and colourful customs and culture of Northern Ireland are a valuable resource which have the ability, if suitably developed, to attract special interest visitors. Consequently, the NITB's current strategy is engaged in niche areas to accommodate the shift towards cultural tourism. The rationale for developing this niche is based on the strength of the cultural product, coupled with the changing demographic and social trends, which indicate great potential for growth. A report which examined the cultural sector identified a number of benefits to Northern Ireland based on further development of this area (**Table 48.4**). It is estimated that cultural tourists have added more than £3 billion to the rest of the UK economy per year (*Belfast Telegraph* 1999). In 1992, 98% of visitors to the Republic of Ireland were influenced by the opportunity to visit 'cultural and historic' places.

Increasingly, the importance of cultural tourism is being evidenced both by practitioner and academic interest in the field. Innovative cross-border courses aimed at encouraging cultural tourism have been developed, backed by the EU Peace Fund, Bord Fáilte and the NITB. These programmes utilize further education colleges and other facilities, using professional tutors to provide high-quality training to those involved in arts and culture. Academic institutions are also keen to pursue this niche. Cultural postgraduate and certificate courses are currently operating within the two universities in Northern Ireland, The Queen's University of Belfast and the University of Ulster.

CONCLUSION

Peace and stability within Northern Ireland offer great potential. This will challenge both Northern Ireland and its tourism industry. It is widely recognized that tourists have numerous destinations from which to choose. The prospect of peace means that Northern Ireland will be in a better position to compete with similar destinations such as the Republic and Scotland. The development and planning of tourism within the region will stretch the competencies and imaginations of the major players in government and the private sector alike.

This chapter has outlined the case for a greater role by the private sector — which is central to enabling and facilitating a quality tourism product. Key areas for the private sector include the development of attractions within cultural and heritage tourism. Perhaps the most significant impact on tourism both in Northern Ireland and the Republic is the emergence of an all-island tourist board. Given the relatively small size of the island, one of the main areas for this body is marketing. Finally, the importance of peace to the future of Northern Ireland and its tourism industry cannot be overemphasized —

the past number of years present a sobering picture.

Bibliography

Arts Council for NI *et al.* 1998 *The cultural sector: a development opportunity for tourism in Northern Ireland summary report.* Belfast.
Belfast Telegraph 1999 'Countdown to devolution: people who will decide' (November 30).
Collins, N. and Cradden, T. 1997 *Irish politics today.* Manchester.
Collins, N. 1999 *Political issues in Ireland today.* Manchester.
Myerscough, J. *1996 The arts and the Northern Ireland economy,* Northern Ireland Research Council, Research Monograph 2, prepared for the NITB. Belfast.
NIEC (Northern Ireland Economic Council) 1997 *Rising to the future challenge of tourism in Northern Ireland, Report 121.* Belfast.
NITB (Northern Ireland Tourism Board) 1995 *Northern Ireland Tourism Board development strategy 1995–2000.* Belfast.
NITB (Northern Ireland Tourism Board) 1998 *Annual report (1996/7).* Belfast.

Local Authority Perspectives

BRENDAN KELLEHER

This chapter looks at the historic evolution of legislation relating to heritage, the public interest and popular movements as well as the more recent development of national, international and European actions of relevance to Irish local authorities. Factors that either empower or restrict these authorities and the manner in which they respond are discussed and relevant examples given. The concluding section offers a re-appraisal of what has been achieved to date, and considers the prospects for local authority involvement in the protection of heritage in the future. For the purposes of this essay, the definition of 'heritage' is taken to include the following items: natural heritage, for instance, mountains, rivers, lakes, coastal areas, ecological habitats, flora, fauna, landscapes (including those influenced by man); the built environment, for example, buildings, structures, urban forms, streetscapes, man-made waterways, and cultural heritage, landscape, music, folklore, place-names, local history, genealogical records and works of art or history.

Until the 1960s, local authorities had been relatively immune from legislation impacting on heritage. Prior to the *Local Government (Planning and Development) Act* of 1963, the principal measures influencing local authorities were the *National Monuments Acts* of 1930 and 1954, and these had limited effect. From the introduction of the *Planning Acts* onwards, an escalating pace and number of legislative innovations in relation to both the man-made, natural and cultural heritage took place and are still ongoing, as the recent production of the government's *Planning and Development Act* 1999 indicates. Certain of the act's more important proposals will be considered where relevant in what follows. This body of national law was substantially added to after Ireland joined the EEC in 1973 when, as a member state, the country was obliged to comply with a growing number of Directives and Regulations adopted by the EU. International concern for the global environment

has also in recent times begun to have trickle-down effects in both European, national and local actions by public authorities at all levels, as Sustainable Development becomes the accepted mode of behaviour. Integral to this is reform of the manner in which the process is undertaken. This has in turn stimulated reform of local public administration.

All of this change has not been without pain. Local authorities have had to modify their own systems and ways of doing things. Extra resources, including trained personnel, have had to be applied to meet the requirements imposed by this stream of heritage legislation. Some have coped better than others as the demands have tended to exceed the resources available at any particular time. Notwithstanding this, local authorities have responded with some remarkably innovative actions. This has happened in a context in which public concern for the heritage has evolved from being the prerogative of the few to a concern of the many. While the world is now viewed as a shared global village, at the commencement of a new millennium the need for inspirational thinkers and explorers, albeit better equipped but facing no less intractable problems, is just as pressing as it was at the start of the twentieth century. How our heritage will fare in all of this and in what way local authorities will respond depends as much on the institutional environment as on prevailing public opinion.

NATURAL HERITAGE
The *Local Government (Planning and Development) Acts* and proposed legislative measures (1963–99) incorporate a wide range of provisions relating to 'amenities' and their protection, either by 'listing' in Development Plans or controlling developments which could impact on them. These amenities include the following elements of the natural heritage:

506

- scenic landscapes

- views of scenic importance

- sites of natural scientific interest

- flora and fauna of special interest

- woodlands and trees of special interest or amenity

In practice, most planning authorities rely on the listing system as a means of controlling development by modification or refusal of permission for such development. Another mechanism employed to protect scenic landscapes was to 'zone' or designate them as 'high amenity' areas and implicitly, if not explicitly, as a corollary unsuitable for development. For many years, this led to an unsatisfactory situation, particularly in relation to open space or amenity zoning applied to sensitive landscapes where local authorities could be caught in a compensation trap for such refusals. It was not until the adoption of the so-called 'compensation act' in 1990 that this loophole was closed.

Additional provisions can be used to make special protection orders with greater force, for instance Tree Preservation Orders (TPOs), Special Amenity Area Orders (SAAOs) and Conservation Orders. A major deterrent in the matter of conserving areas of great natural beauty and of recreational or ecological interest has continued to be the cumbersome procedure for first making Special Amenity Area Orders. (In Northern Ireland and the UK, such areas can be designated as Areas of Outstanding Natural Beauty [AONBs] and must be confirmed by the Secretary of State.) This and the consequent requirement of making a management plan and the resource implications associated with both has deterred most planning authorities from making them. The Liffey Valley SAAO is one of only a few to have been created. For landscapes of national importance, excluding lands in public ownership, this can hardly be construed as satisfactory. Furthermore, the concept of sustainability, together with the often emotive debate as to what constitutes heritage landscapes of national importance, may require new approaches as they come under threat from afforestation, intensive farming, wind farming and communications infrastructure. Because nature conservation is considered to be more appropriately addressed under other legislation, the 1976 *Wildlife Act* or EU Habitats Directive, it will not now be an objective of SAAOs, which will be limited to areas of outstanding natural beauty or special recreational value. The power of confirming SAAOs will also be transferred from the Minister for the Environment and Local Government to An Bord Pleanála.

Effective protection of flora or fauna, which under the

Planning and Development Acts required a further Conservation Order, is now more properly a function of the state's National Parks and Wildlife Service, through the EU Directives and the 1976 *Wildlife Act*, which is currently being updated under the 1999 *Wildlife Amendment Bill*. The recently published *Planning and Development Act* 1999 proposes to make a number of significant changes in the planning legislation relating to our natural heritage. These will remove some of the defects in existing planning and amend and extend the remit of what remains.

Tree Preservation Orders constitute one of the most effective means of protecting woodlands of amenity value, a living part of the heritage. For woodlands of national ecological importance, for instance indigenous oak forests, the newly introduced designations under the EU's Habitats Directive offer separate protection by the state itself. In my experience, all the TPOs made by my own authority have been appealed by land owners to An Bord Pleanála — evidence, perhaps, of a fundamental cultural resistance to measures to protect the natural heritage — and fortunately confirmed on appeal. Thus, positive measures to protect the natural heritage under the *Planning and Development Acts* have tended to be used to a very limited extent. This has placed greater reliance on the planning control system, which is basically reactive to development proposals. Inherent in this is the risk of either responding too late or ineffectively to threats to the heritage, and the incentive to would-be depradators to 'shoot first and ask questions later'. The 1999 bill proposed to transfer the power for making TPOs from the executive (manager) to the elected members (reserved function), inserting a right of objection by affected parties directly to the planning authority, while retaining An Bord Pleanála as an appellant authority. Improved post-TPO management arrangements are also suggested. Whether or not this will increase the number of orders remains to be seen.

Another difficulty arises in relation to so-called exempted development, that is development which, as defined in the Local Government (Planning and Development) Regulations, does not require planning permission. Originally, when the 1963 act and associated regulations were introduced, most forms of agricultural development were exempt from planning. As the years have passed, and as agriculture has intensified and concern for the well-being of the natural environment has increased, more and more aspects of agriculture are being made amenable to the planning laws. Unfortunately, this has not prevented destruction of much of Ireland's natural heritage, and particularly those parts not considered to be of major importance, such as local woodlands and wetlands, which nevertheless constitute essential ingredients of the landscape.

Reflecting concerns that have arisen from the failure to

protect these integral elements of much of Ireland's rural landscape, the 1999 bill proposed the introduction of new powers to enable planning authorities to designate Landscape Conservation Areas. The declared purpose of the measure is to allow planning authorities to control the removal of hedges and ditches, the division of commonage, afforestation and land reclamation which are now largely exempt from planning control. However, the measure is both subject to the minister defining the types and extent of development to be controlled and to both the minister and the planning authority first consulting with other state agencies, for example the powerful Department of Agriculture and Food, which is unlikely to be slow in representing the interests of the farming community. This potentially significant provision in turn raises questions as to the capacity of planning authorities to develop an appropriate methodology for assessment and definition of what constitutes landscapes suitable for conservation.

Other non-agricultural developments have also impacted severely on the country's natural heritage and have only recently been reined in by recent de-exemption from planning. A case in point is golf courses. Often gravitating to high-quality scenic or natural landscapes, partly due to the image being sought for the finished product, partly because of the unsuitability of such areas for viable agricultural production, this erstwhile benign use became the subject of passionate debate by proponents and opponents alike. As a consequence of public concerns being voiced and a realization that in certain circumstances golf courses could be environmentally damaging to the natural and scenic landscape, an amendment was inserted into the 1994 Regulations to de-exempt the activity. Interestingly, the Council of Europe, in the 1997 publication *Questions and answers: No. 3 Tourism and the environment*, quotes golf as an activity that can have significant adverse impacts on the natural environment. A further measure was proposed in the 1999 bill which is likely to strengthen controls over land uses such as golf courses with a potential to impact negatively on the natural heritage.

Permission for development is a primary responsibility of local authorities. This power is largely vested in the county/city manager, although there are exceptional instances when the elected council can direct the manager to make a decision to their liking. It is also only at the council's discretion that the manager can contravene the Development Plan. In some cases this has led to interesting contests of will and public opinion insofar as the natural heritage is concerned. One particular instance involved a proposed golf course in a wetland in the Clonakilty estuary in west Cork. Listed in the County Development Plan as a specific conservation objective, the habitat became the focus of competing pressures to either protect or develop it. Requiring a 75%

vote of the council to materially contravene the plan, the motion was passed and the county manager obliged against his better judgement to grant permission. A hotly contested appeal to An Bord Pleanála ensued, which determined that the works were not exempt from planning permission and post-appeal re-commenced works were also the subject of a successful third-party injunction by an environmental non-governmental organisation (NGO) and the state. The conflict eventually resolved itself in favour of state acquisition literally on the steps of the Supreme Court, but not before a protracted journey through the council, Planning Appeals Board and High Court. Complex issues of planning law were raised in the process and the possibility of European law entering the fray was also present.

Disappointed recipients of decisions from An Bord Pleanála and from planning authorities can, in exceptional circumstances, seek a judicial review in the Republic's High Court. Sometimes these cases have raised fundamental points of law requiring at times recourse to the highest court in the land, the Supreme Court. This forum has not been found wanting, and has delivered judgements relating to heritage that have constituted a body of case law which in turn has influenced the legislature in bringing forward amending legislation. A case in point was the proposal by the state, through the Commissioners of Public Works, the body charged with the custody of the national heritage, to build an interpretative centre at Mullaghmore for the purpose of presenting and explaining the unique natural characteristics of the karstic Burren region in county Clare.

Considered until then to be exempt from planning, the courts decided — on a majority decision of the Supreme Court — that the development was *ultra vires* or outside the statutory remit of the Commissioners. Amending planning legislation was introduced by government to rectify this deficiency, which had the effect of introducing a requirement on all public bodies, including local authorities, to go through the planning process in respect of most of their developments. A planning application was as a consequence then lodged by the state. This in turn was appealed successfully by objectors to the proposal, with the result that the partially completed development had to be removed and the ambitions of the state aborted. A cascade effect followed for a number of other similar centres. The unfortunate episode left bitterly divided communities, a humiliated state agency, hitherto noted for its outstanding commitment to the national heritage, and a raging debate as to the most appropriate means of maintaining heritage. It also highlighted the need for effective conflict resolution and public participation mechanisms.

The 1976 *Wildlife Act* (currently in the process of amendment) is the principal measure relating to natural heritage; its provisions constitute the statutory basis for wildlife (flora and fauna) conservation. (The aforementioned 1999 bill expands the scope of these to include the protection of fish and aquatic invertebrates as well as sites of geological and geomorphological value.) The 1976 act acknowledges the conservation role of the planning acts and endeavours to supplement them. These provisions have not always proven to be reliable, however, particularly when the requirement of private ownership consent has not been willingly forthcoming. I have witnessed the widespread destruction of habitat because of the difficulties and limitations inherent in both the *Wildlife* and *Planning and Development Acts*. To an extent, the recent designations under the EU's Habitats and Wildbird Directives, and the draft Natural Heritage Area designations under the *Wildlife Act* — pending its amendment! — have stemmed the on-going haemorrhage of loss.

As a consequence, the number of reserves and refuges established under the 1976 act was minimal. In one notable case in county Cork, the Gearagh, a significant remnant of a once extensive alluvial woodland reputed to be the only one of its type west of the Rhine river and providing a unique habitat for both flora and fauna, it took the combined efforts of the principal landowner, the state's Electricity Supply Board, whose acquisition and development of the area for hydro-electric power generation in the 1950s led to its dramatic reduction in the first instance, together with the National Parks and Wildlife Service, Cork County Council and a keen local conservationist, to arrest its continuing decline.

Cork County Council also actively supported efforts to extend wildbird refuge status for the Douglas estuary, an internationally important wildbird habitat in Cork harbour, in the late 1970s with the support of the Irish Wildbird Conservancy (now Birdwatch Ireland), University College, Cork, concerned residents and the very active involvement of the state's wildlife ranger responsible for the area. In both this and the Gearagh, negotiations with established wildfowling interests had first to be successfully concluded. The downsides have been perhaps best — or more correctly worst — represented by the failure to prevent the almost callous destruction of a nationally important wildbird habitat on the Cork coast at Ballycotton, despite the best efforts of both local and state agencies.

A somewhat different challenge presented itself at Lough Hyne near Baltimore in west Cork, albeit with much happier consequences. Here, a deep-sea lough with unique zoological and geomorphological attributes fills and partially empties tidally through a narrow rapids channel. Its surrounding hilly and highly scenic catchment was threatened by sporadic holiday housing development, which in turn posed a danger to the distinctive biology of the lough through septic tank discharges. Abortive efforts were made under the *Planning and Development Acts* in the early 1970s to afford greater protection to the lough by advocating strict controls on potentially polluting developments, but they did not receive sufficient support at the time from elected members of Cork County Council. In response, however, to concerns expressed by An Taisce and suggestions made by that organization as to appropriate protection mechanisms, the state introduced regulations to control the use of the lough for recreational, exploration and educational purposes. This effectively established Lough Hyne as Ireland's first marine reserve under the 1976 *Wildlife Act*. These measures have since been complemented on the landward side by strict planning controls on development by the local authority, thus protecting the integrity of both the marine and terrestrial natural heritage.

Notwithstanding these successes, in my opinion it was the advent of the EU's Habitats and Wildbird Directives that has provided the best prospect of protecting our natural heritage. The government is obliged to transpose these obligations into Irish law under threat of sanction by the European Commission in the event of its failure to do so. Local authorities, as agents of state policy, have a consequent obligation to take account of the Directives' application to sites within their administrative jurisdiction. These requirements have already affected local authorities both in respect of their own developments and also in relation to projects suggested by other public agencies and private developers. Both proponents of and objectors to development have relied on the Directives to support their side of the argument.

In a landmark case in Spain concerning the Santona Marshes, a habitat of European importance and implicitly protected by the Habitats Directive, the European Court found on an action taken by the Commission that the Spanish authorities had contravened the Directive, even though it had not been transposed into state law as required by the Commission, by permitting or not preventing the intrusion of various developments, including public works, into the marsh (Case C – 44/95). The principle of 'direct effect' thus applied, namely when the European Parliament adopts such Directives (or Regulations) and requires member states to transpose them into state law by a specified date, failure to do so will not be accepted as a basis for transgressing the particular Directive or Regulation by either the state or its organs, including local authorities.

Under the EU Habitats Directive (92/43/EEC), the state has had to identify special areas of conservation — or candidate SACs — which automatically have force of law and have to be respected by public authorities and private developers, through the licensing or permitting of the latters' development proposals. The procedure for designating Special Protection Areas (SPAs) under the EU Birds Directive (79/409/EEC) is simpler, with the member states required to define areas frequented by important bird species and migratory species, including wetlands. Many of the candidate SACs and SPAs relate to coastal areas where ecological biodiversity is significant and often include lands both within a local authority's administrative jurisdiction (usually terminating at high watermark on the coastal foreshore) and 'lands' or tidal areas and seas within the administrative jurisdiction of the state. In certain instances where the remit of a local authority includes tidal reaches or the high seas, both the state, local authorities and other public agencies may be affected by the same designations.

For example, in parts of Cork harbour, the actions of the state, county council and the port authority — albeit now 'privatized' — are subject to these designations and the obligations that flow from them. Efforts to evade these responsibilities, in the interests of facilitating economic development of ports, led to the Lappel Bank court case involving the UK government (case C – 355/90). In this instance, the state contrived to omit part of an area of natural heritage importance that would fall to be protected under an EU Directive, as it was required for port development. The European Court found against the UK government and effectively required it first to designate the entire area prior to seeking a derogation on grounds of over-riding social or economic need, as provided for in the Habitats Directive. A local authority would thus also be constrained by the provisions of the Directive when assessing proposals for development in such areas.

The European Commission has also produced guidelines relating to the protection of wetlands, *Wise use and conservation of wetlands*, as part of the EU's Fifth Environmental Action Programme, *Towards sustainability*. These set down the principles that should be adhered to by member states when considering and permitting (essential) development in such areas. They include the requirement to ensure that alternative, less harmful, options are considered, that appropriate mitigation of harmful effects is undertaken, and that compensatory measures are provided for habitat loss.

In my limited experience of the issue, differences of opinion can easily arise as to the degree of importance of the habitat in question, the significance of the impacts and the adequacy of the compensatory measures, whatever about the necessity for the impacting development. This also appears to be the case elsewhere. It has led to some disquiet as to the methods of measurement used in assessing habitat quality and the scale of impacts on it on the one hand, and the fear that any development could be portrayed as significant on the other. Earlier uncertainty as to the right of planning authorities to refuse, without the risk of compensation,

development likely to impact on sites of natural heritage value have been allayed by provisions introduced in the 1997 European Communities (Natural Habitats) Regulations, and by proposals in the 1999 *Planning and Development Act*. These specify, *inter alia*, the natural heritage sites that can be protected without incurring financial liability.

An earlier European Directive on Environmental Impact Assessment (85/337/EEC) — which was initially transposed into Irish law in 1989 via the European Communities (Environmental Impact Assessment) Regulations — has had a profound influence on the level of consideration since afforded to major developments which can potentially impact adversely on the environment, including the natural heritage. While the purpose of the Directive is to ensure that an appropriate assessment is made of these potential influences, where they do occur mitigation and, in the case of the natural environment, compensation measures are required. Additionally, alternative courses of action or different modes of development to that proposed may also have to be investigated.

In the case of a major road development suggested by a local authority, for example in the construction of the Jack Lynch Tunnel under the River Lee and associated approach roadworks, which entailed adverse impact on designated wildbird areas of Cork harbour, Cork Corporation was required by the Minister for the Environment both to apply mitigation measures and also to provide replacement habitat to compensate for that removed by the roadworks. In another case entailing EU Structural Funds, Blarney, county Cork, gained a major amenity from the routing of the re-aligned Cork-Mallow Road, when fenland acquired as part of the project was retained and enhanced as a public amenity. Provisions of the 1999 *Wildlife (Amendment) Bill* will, when enacted, also require local authorities to consult the state in relation to any proposal by them which is likely to adversely affect protected sites, and to take appropriate steps to avoid damage.

Although the specified types of development to which the Environmental Impact Assessment (EIA) process applies are nominated by the EU, member states have the discretion to set thresholds below which an Environmental Impact Study (EIS) will not be mandatory, unless in the opinion of the relevant planning authority it would still have significant environmental effect. Under the 1989 EIA Regulations, the Irish government based their thresholds on the sole criterion of size. This led to a successful challenge by the European Commission at the European Court of Justice (C–150/97), which concluded that size alone was an insufficient criterion to meet with the fundamental objectives of the 1985 Directive and that the nature, location and cumulative effects of projects had also to be considered. Some categories of development, such as telecommunications masts, which have a potential cumulatively to diminish the character of the landscape, are not subject to the EIA regulations. Others which are subject to them, such as windfarms, only require an EIS for projects or sites of a particular size. The situation has been remedied by new EIA and related planning and development regulations introduced in 1999 arising from the European Commission's updating of the 1985 Directive (97/11/EC). The 1999 *Planning Act* proposing the incorporation of the environmental impact assessment process directly into primary legislation (as opposed to the current use of regulations under the *European Community Act* 1972) also contains provisions to give the Minister for the Environment and Local Government discretion both to specify additional developments to which assessment should apply and to expand the threshold system to include alternative bases for assessment. The European Court revision of the EIA Directive and the proposed planning legislation changes suggest a much more pervasive future application of the process to activities and sites hitherto considered to be exempt. This raises a further question as to whether the EIA process should, or could, be usefully applied to programmes as opposed to projects. The 1999 *Planning and Development Act* suggests it will.

The Cohesion Fund of the EU has also been used directly to intervene in the protection of the natural heritage, notably in relation to the conservation of Irish raised bogs — a form of wetland habitat facing gradual extinction through man-made impacts. A project to conserve 1,000 ha of Clara and Raheenmore bogs in county Offaly and utilize the habitat to develop sustainable tourism has benefited from the fund. The Council of Europe has also made significant advances in relation to the natural heritage by developing a series of strategies and charters relating to various aspects of it, for instance the *Pan-European biological and landscape diversity strategy* of 1995, and through current efforts to draft a European Landscape Convention which protects important landscapes and respects the complex inter-relationship between their natural and cultural components. This latter initiative is being developed through the Congress of Local and Regional Authorities and will, I believe, lead to greater awareness of this aspect of European heritage as well as of the means to conserve it. The Irish government is also proposing, under the 1999 *Wildlife (Amendment) Bill*, to give explicit expression to ministerial responsibilities deriving from Ireland's ratification of the UN Convention on Biodiversity.

The 1995 *Heritage Act* established the Heritage Council, whose functions are to propose policies and priorities for Ireland's national heritage. It can provide advice or assistance, *inter alia*, to local authorities in relation to these functions. The act also contains some interesting extended meanings or definitions of heritage.

In particular, the first definitions of 'landscape' and 'seascape' in Irish legislation, to my knowledge, are given here. The former definition may be regarded as an entree to consideration of the inherited, man-altered, landscape that often distinguishes one society or culture from another and is now regarded widely as being as important a part of the heritage as that derived primarily from natural causes. Current proposals by the Irish government to encourage the development of offshore windfarms will generate interest and debate as to what constitutes a coastal landscape or seascape of significant natural or perhaps cultural heritage value, as evidenced by recent clashes of opinion as to the appropriateness of wind turbines on the Aran Islands. Furthermore, extensive definitions of flora, fauna and geology, as well as the inclusion of 'heritage gardens and parks', make the prospective remit of this act more widely applicable to heritage than some of the other measures referred to.

From my experience, local authorities, faced with a demanding and at times ambiguous set of obligations in respect of the natural heritage, and equipped with extremely limited resources to protect it, have relied largely on the development control mechanism and in a mainly re-active manner. While there are some striking examples of success, in general I feel it would be fair to say that these have been relatively few. Local authorities have had to go through a learning curve, first of all in comprehending natural heritage, secondly in accepting legal obligations to protect it, and thirdly in translating these into effective action. Lack of resources has been a continuous hindrance in attempting to move from a purely re-active mode to a more positive one.

Time pressures and other demands on local authorities have tended to reduce these actions to the prescriptive, with insufficient follow-through. As a consequence of the wider ambit of European Regulations in particular, more and more of these authorities' activities are affected. This has tended to bring in a wider range of county council departments than was originally the case, thus spreading the burden and associated interest in the natural heritage. I can recall a time when, in the case of my own authority, this was seen as the sole responsibility of the Planning Department!

In conclusion, it would be fair to say that the natural environment has been more resistant to influence by local authorities, apart from designation of landscapes and their indirect protection through the control of development and some limited acquisition of certain areas of ecological or scientific interest, with responsibility tending either to pass upwards to the state or otherwise remain with the landowner.

MAN-MADE HERITAGE

The principal enactments relating to man's legacy to Ireland's built heritage are those already referred to, with the exception of the *Wildlife Act*. A number of other acts also impinge on the built heritage, either directly or indirectly. The EIA Regulations again have a bearing on this area similar to that described for natural heritage. The cornerstone 1963 *Planning and Development Act* does not contain the word 'heritage'. It does, however, in its preamble include the terms for 'the preservation and improvement of amenities'. Somewhat disingenuously, the act fails to define 'amenities'. It does list the amenities for which conservation — in the act referred to as either 'preservation' or 'reservation' — objectives can be made in the statutory Development Plans of local authorities. Two key functions in the acts are firstly the definition of these conservation objectives — a mandatory requirement of Development Plans — and secondly the control of development, including that of the authority itself, which could impact on these objectives.

Development Plans have to contain development objectives 'for preserving, improving and extending amenities'. As a consequence of these provisions, local authorities throughout the Republic have designated or 'listed' sites and buildings of historic, archaeological, architectural, scientific and recreational or scenic significance in their development plans with a view to their protection. Any ambiguity about a local authority's discretion in the matter of listing buildings of 'architectural, artistic or historic interest' is removed by a provision of the 1999 *Planning and Development Act*. (Even with the listing system, and the protections afforded by the *National Monuments Acts*, serious incidents continue to occur, for instance the recent removal of most of the earthworks said to be associated with one of the ancient sites of ceremonial Celtic activity, Tailtiu, near Teltown, in county Meath. The alleged lack of knowledge of the status of the monument is poor compensation for damage done, however.)

A similar process is followed in relation to such amenities in the north of Ireland and elsewhere in the UK. However, the introduction of Conservation Area protective designations constituted a significant difference between Irish and British legislation until quite recently. Conservation Area planning, and the financial resources to go with it, have long been a part of the UK and NI system. Up to 40 villages, towns and urban areas have been protected under this legislation in the north since the early 1970s. No similar provision existed in the Republic's planning acts and reliance had instead concentrated on community and tourism initiatives. However, the Irish government has now remedied this deficiency by including a provision in the 1999 *Planning and Development Act* to enable local authorities to designate such areas in their Development Plans. A companion enactment, the 1999 *Architectural Heritage (National Inventory) and Historic Monuments (Miscella-*

neous Provisions) Act, provides for the establishment of a national inventory of the architectural heritage. The inventory will be available for use by local authorities in the performance of their statutory planning and development functions.

A number of landmark decisions in the Republic's courts have confirmed the standing and importance of these designations and the obligations on both the local authorities themselves and on owners and prospective developers. Other important decisions have been made on appeal to An Bord Pleanála in the Republic and to the Secretary of State in the north. In 1983, a proposal by Sligo County Council to site a refuse dump in the environs of one of that county's most important archaeological monuments, Carrowmore megalithic cemetery, provoked a hostile response from local residents. The eventual outcome had to wait until the Supreme Court decided in 1989 that the council's action was in breach of its own Development Plan, which the court decided 'forms an environmental contract between the planning authority and the people'. The judgement confirmed the obligation that the Development Plan process implies, not only for the generality of development but also for that proposed by the authority itself.

A proposal to build a major tourism facility, an historic theme park and souvenir shop, in the environs of one of Ireland's premier historic monuments, the Rock of Cashel, was permitted by the local authority in 1990. Although supported by the local community, the development was successfully appealed by the Arts Council, An Taisce and some residents of the nearby town. The reasons given by the Planning Appeals Board make interesting reading, and in my view encapsulate the conflicts that can so easily arise when local or specific interest needs are given undue precedence over broader national priorities. In this case, notwithstanding the accepted economic benefits that the proposal could bring to the area, the over-riding integrity of an important part of the national heritage was seen as paramount by the Board.

In addition to its own direct actions on heritage property in its ownership, local authorities, in their planning policies and co-operative actions with other owners, can significantly influence the context in which conservation decisions are made, for example, as mentioned earlier, by allowing easements from normal planning requirements in return for beneficial conservation proposals or by tying development permits to conservation investment. Expert conservation advice is sometimes requested of developers of heritage properties or sourced out-house, and more recently in-house, by the local authority itself so as to inform its decision in responding to planning applications. This may entail obtaining the services of architectural historians or industrial archaeologists, depending on the building or site. This process is also helpful in both improving the local authority's capacity to respond to similar situations in future and in educating developers and their consultants.

Archaeological conservation has been one — some would say the only — aspect of our heritage that has received early recognition by the state. Urgently in need of updating, the 1987 *National Monuments (Amendment) Act's* introduction followed a series of crises affecting the national heritage in the intervening years from 1954. Further consolidation followed in the 1994 act. From a local perspective, the acts have a number of important implications for local authorities, namely:

• local authorities can establish a national (now historic) monuments advisory committee, whose functions could include advising the elected council on the expenditure of public monies on monuments;

• local authorities could become owners or guardians of national monuments, conserve them, make bye-laws in relation to them, and remove (to museums) threatened objects. The definition of what constitutes an historic monument has been significantly broadened to allow for post-1700 structures and monuments 'associated with the commercial, cultural, economic, industrial, military, religious or social history of the place or country';

• the introduction of the concept of an 'archaeological area' exclusive of the area of an historic monument;

• the compilation of a register of historic monuments;

• the establishment of records of monuments.

Local authorities such as Cork County Council have long-established National Monuments Committees, which have been instrumental in a variety of roles in relation to its local heritage. In the Cork situation, the Committee, comprised of a mixture of elected councillors and non-elected experts, has undertaken research, produced information booklets, financially assisted voluntary groups and organizations in conserving the built heritage, conserved heritage structures in its ownership or guardianship and 'interpreted' them for the public. For its size and resources, the Committee has achieved much for heritage, and in a variety of ways. Maintenance of such committees is, I believe, essential to that local participative aspect of the Sustainable Development process now being promoted, and should, if possible, be safeguarded in whatever new arrangements are proposed for Ireland's heritage.

Completion by the state of Sites and Monuments Records (SMRs) for urban and rural areas has added enormously to the stock of potential listed sites in the Development Plans of these authorities, notwithstanding

their automatic inclusion in the new Record of Monuments established by the state in the 1994 act. It raises questions as to the appropriate policies that might best be followed in relation to conservation of this heritage, given its scale, and the lack of financial and manpower resources to deal with it. With the completion of the SMRs of antiquities in many of the local authority areas — a record, incidentally, which has dramatically extended the potential number of listed sites in Cork county, for example, to *ca.* 16,000 — the scale of the conservation and protection requirement has been dramatically re-defined. Additionally, the need to maintain and update the SMRs in order to take account of both gains and losses is likely to impose further demands on resources, although the recording of antiquities is a matter in the first instance for the state. As stated earlier, a very small proportion of this will fall to direct conservation action by the local authority itself. The bulk of it will simply require that nothing be done other than ensure its inviolability for future generations. Effective planning control will have a bearing on whether this is to be so.

In the wider countryside, as in the older mediaeval towns and cities, local authorities have become more active in conserving Ireland's archaeological heritage. The cities of Waterford, Cork and Limerick have made notable advances in this regard, the former through archaeological investigation and conservation, the latter two through the combination of conservation with modern construction, although not without attendant controversy. Employment of archaeologists by these boroughs on a temporary basis, which is generously aided by the Office of Public Works under a culturally orientated and EU-assisted employment scheme, provided badly needed expertise. An extension of this to some of the larger county authorities — as is the case with Cork County Council — could, in my view, be justified, because, at present, most local authorities rely on occasional employment of archaeological consultants for specific needs. This consultancy advice is usually orientated to so-called 'rescue' archaeology and to a lesser degree to the policy and control functions of these authorities. This may change in line with the current direction of government policy on the conservation of the built environment as a whole.

Although these measures are of quite recent origin — and to an extent generated by the past neglect of our medieval towns and cities — they have produced consequent benefits through the excavation, recording and conservation of sites and artefacts. Furthermore, they have raised awareness of the archaeological richness of our older cities and towns, and in turn created opportunities of commemorating this in ways which are of economic benefit to these areas. What was once regarded as the debit of antiquity has converted to an increasingly positive credit as towns have exposed their treasures for environmental, economic and tourism purposes.

Aimed at the elimination of land dereliction, the 1990 *Derelict Sites Act* has a number of requirements which can impinge on heritage. The act, in its definition of derelict urban areas, excludes from its provisions sites listed in Development Plans, but this exclusion does not appear to apply to other — by implication rural — areas except for monuments listed under the *National Monuments Acts*. As the local authority has the power to define the measures necessary to be undertaken, either by the owner or by the local authority itself if the owner fails to do so, and includes demolition, a tension can arise between an authority's amenity, safety and conservation objectives. The provisions of the 1999 *Planning and Development Act* will, as passed into law, remove some of this ambiguity as they will oblige local authorities to consider whether a notice (requiring remedial works to be undertaken by the owner) should be issued under this act or under the *Derelict Sites Act*, and it will be a requirement to preserve the structure as far as possible where the local authority undertakes the works itself. If, for whatever reason, demolition of a heritage structure is the only practicable outcome, an accurate survey and photographic record of such structures is required and must be lodged with one of the public archives, local museum or library, or local or national archives, as is currently the case with the planning control system. The Irish Architectural Archive in Dublin maintains a record of threatened or disappearing buildings of note. In the case of potentially dangerous listed buildings, local (sanitary) authorities are now required by the 1999 *Architectural Heritage (National Inventory) and Historic Monuments (Miscellaneous Provisions) Act* to ensure that remedial works also try, as far as possible, to preserve the monument.

Introduced to encourage renewal of run-down urban areas, the tax-driven incentives arising from the designations under the 1986 *Urban Renewal Act* have generated a significant amount of development. However, the incentives have been criticized, *inter alia*, for tending to favour demolition and re-building rather than renewal of properties. In subsequent designations, the government has adjusted the criteria with a view to remedying this imbalance and encouraging retention of buildings that merit it. The process also imposes an obligation on local authorities clearly to identify those elements of the built heritage worthy of protection in advance of designation.

The 1987 *Finance Act* introduced fiscal changes to assist the owners of historic properties to cope with their on-going maintenance. Aimed principally at 'big houses' or historic demesnes, this legislation offers investment write-offs against the tax liability of owners keen to conserve their properties effectively. A *quid pro quo* in the form of a public benefit was that eligible properties were to be open to public access for a specified minimum number of days each year. The provisions of the act have helped to maintain some of the state's great houses and demesnes in relatively pristine condition, and stayed the advent of the otherwise almost inevitable tendency to sell off or develop parts of the demesnes for uses that can often irrevocably alter the original context and setting of the big house. This is a constant headache for planning authorities faced, on the one hand, with a property on a downward cycle of decline, an owner who may not have sufficient capital and income for tax write-off purposes, and, on the other, a property market that can place a much higher value on the holding if granted permission for development. Relying on a wealthy 'white knight' to rescue the situation is usually impractical. Recent *Finance Acts* have further fine-tuned these incentives.

The 1999 *Planning and Development Act* proposes much stronger if not radical measures relating to the protection of the built heritage, including the imposition of a 'duty of care' on owners and occupiers of listed buildings to ensure they do not become endangered and, where likely, to undertake preventative works required by the local authority. Failing that, the local authority can undertake the works and, as a last resort, compulsorily purchase the building if necessary. This measure, now passed into law, will considerably strengthen the corporate hand of local authorities faced with particular property owners who deliberately neglect such properties in anticipation of speculative gain from less encumbered sites. However, it begs the question once more as to the resources available to local authorities for the policing of these provisions, given the 'Cinderella' status of enforcement in many planning departments.

The 1991 Building Regulations purport to ensure that building construction is undertaken with due regard to good practice and in the interests of safety of both occupiers and other user of buildings, and the principal local authorities are charged with these responsibilities. A set of prescriptive standards covering various aspects of a building's construction and layout have to be met if a structure, other than a dwelling, is to obtain a fire certificate from the local authority's fire department. If it fails to do so, it can be closed down. Two modes by which acceptable fire and associated safety standards can be achieved are set out in the Regulations; one is finely detailed and prescriptive as to what is required, the other establishes broad parameters that have to be satisfied. This discretion has relevance to the conservation and use of heritage buildings, many of which were constructed at a time when standards of fire protection and safety of occupants were a lot less demanding.

Works, even by way of extension or modification, on a heritage building (other than a dwelling) or a change of

Fig. 49.1 Ballincollig Gunpowder Mills, county Cork (1794–1903), one of the largest local authority conservation / amenity schemes in Ireland.

use requiring planning permission could render the whole building subject to the Regulations. A prescriptive response by the local authority, more appropriate to a new building, could result in the installation of fire prevention and safety measures unsuited or even damaging to the architectural or historic integrity of the structure. A more suitable response that balances the sensitivity of the building against the equally important need to provide for fire protection and safety is, in my opinion, usually possible. This latter approach has been successfully applied in a number of cases involving the conversion or change of use of heritage buildings in Cork county and elsewhere.

Unlike other member states of the EU, Ireland has perhaps less in terms of built heritage and in experience of dealing with its refurbishment when issues of fire protection and safety arise. Negotiating acceptable solutions, even between the respective functional departments within local authorities, not to mind between developers and the authority, can in such circumstances be difficult. That said, it is a developing science that will inevitably improve as local authorities gain more experience of the process and as the state recognizes the need for clearer guidance for heritage buildings.

Apart from the statutory obligations on local authorities, many have initiated voluntary actions aimed at protecting and enhancing the built heritage in their areas. These discretionary initiatives have taken various forms, but have generally been targeted at the man-made heritage. In Cork county, a notable example has been the establishment of so-called 'planning clinics' by the County Architect's Department in the older urban district towns. While principally of an architectural emphasis, they have helped to raise awareness of the built character of these towns — which in many cases had remained intact since the nineteenth century — and secured its retention. Such studies have not been universally successful in maintaining the awareness of the urban heritage and the measures needed to maintain it, however, as they require the constant application of personnel over a long period to do so. Local authorities often find it difficult to provide this unless dedicated staff are both available and prepared to give the commitment.

Building on the principles of the Tidy Towns movement, Kinsale UDC and Cork County Council, in co-operation with the local community, initiated a series of innovative actions. An architectural study was commissioned for the town and a 'planning clinic' set up to use its findings as a basis for advising property owners and developers. The local authority also commenced a programme of townscape improvement works. A developing core of restaurateurs established a 'good food circle' — soon to become an intrinsic part of Kinsale's revived economy and image. And the state was convinced of its obligations to acquire and conserve one of the town's most dramatic monuments, Charlesfort. Thus a 'virtuous circle' was created in which one beneficial step led to the next. This has, I believe, also contributed in some cases to negative conservation trends not entirely dissimilar to that experienced in Dublin in the 1970s, namely a penchant for pastiche replacement. This is unfortunately being repeated on a national scale at the risk of depriving future generations of a heritage of the twentieth century. But more about this later.

Equally notable have been the critical interventions by local authorities in the conservation of important heritage buildings. The list at this stage is too numerous to mention, but includes an extensive range of vernacular, municipal and industrial buildings throughout the country. From Blennerville Windmill in Kerry, through such buildings as the Kildare market house and Clonakilty grain mill, to early eighteenth-century residential Fenns Quay terrace in Cork city, the variety and diversity of buildings and uses to which they are put is impressive. The costs associated with the public acquisition and management of substantial heritage properties have generally tended to be borne only by the larger authorities in the Dublin region, for example, as in the case of Malahide Castle Demesne, where the property is also used as a major public amenity for a large urban population.

Cork County Council was directly involved in two flagship heritage conservation projects in the Cork area, the restoration of the eighteenth-century Royal Gunpowder Mills at Ballincollig west of Cork city (**Fig. 49.1**) and the conservation of the fifteenth-century Barryscourt castle at Carrigtohill (**Fig. 49.2**) east of the city, both of which obtained EU Structural Funding. Great care was taken in both instances to ensure authenticity in reconstruction, and extensive research preceded the works. Each also required the dedication of staff resources and the recruitment of expert advice on a contract basis. Without EU funding, it is doubtful whether either of these projects would have happened.

Cork Corporation's success in obtaining significant funding under the EU's Programme for the Conservation of European Cities for its Historic Centre Action Plan (Cork Corporation and Urban Initiatives, 1994), which contains a suite of measures to conserve and celebrate the ancient core of the city, is also a case in point. While this innovative and widely commended project re-interprets the medieval city's structure in an integrated set of land use, transport and conservation measures, the failure to achieve a similar level of response for the re-discovered traces of Viking Dublin in earlier decades must now be acknowledged as an opportunity lost, even if one admits that recent redevelopment of the Temple Bar area incorporates vital indicators of the capital's

Fig. 49.2 Restoration of the sixteenth-century Barryscourt Castle, county Cork.

medieval past.

The Conservation Grant section of the Urban and Village Renewal Scheme, part of the Republic's Operational Programme for Urban and Rural Development, has also provided a welcome respite for our architectural heritage. In partnership with the owners, the Kingston Trust, Cork County Council has used this scheme to initiate a much-needed restoration of a unique and still occupied classical range of domestic and ancillary buildings in the formal planned town of Mitchelstown in the north of the county. While these interventions are important, they nevertheless represent only a small fraction of the threatened stock of listed heritage buildings. Other means of protection are urgently required. A government policy supportive of these actions is happily now in train with the first national architectural conservation grants scheme (1999) providing a modest but psychologically important incentive to owners of heritage properties and administered through local authorities' newly appointed conservation officers. Local authorities have also begun to react more positively to voluntary trusts established to undertake conservation work on the built heritage, although difficulties and differences will continue to arise as to priorities and policies. While these are largely a phenomenon of the cities, there are some notable examples of small-town ventures other than Kinsale. Carlingford, county Louth, is a case in point.

Concern for the built environment has also led to the recently declared intention of the Republic's Heritage Service, Dúchas, to establish a National Inventory of Architectural Heritage as a means of comprehensively documenting and evaluating the built heritage of Ireland. The Council of Europe has also been active in promoting interest in collaboration on, and the protection of, the European patrimony, for example through the so-called Grenada Convention of 1985 which set out to protect the European architectural heritage. In turn, these initiatives have both influenced and interacted with actions of both the EU and UN, and directly influenced the actions of member states of the EU, including Ireland, the most recent incidence of which relates to the state's intention to establish the aforementioned National Inventory of Architectural Heritage.

It is obvious from the foregoing that the extent of legal provisions and actions relating to the man-made heritage *vis-à-vis* the natural is substantial. It may also symbolize the relative standing of both, in a national cultural perspective, whatever about the relativity at European or international levels.

CULTURAL HERITAGE

Under the 1991 *Local Government Act*, a local authority can participate in the provision of 'amenities, facilities and services' related to, or actually engage in, *inter alia*, artistic and cultural activities, as well as environmental and heritage protection and improvement. The latter consolidate the powers of local authorities in relation to the built and natural heritage; the former in relation to our cultural heritage. The fourth schedule of the act defines 'artistic and cultural activities' as inclusive of the provision of art galleries, arts centres, concert halls, museums, theatres, opera houses and the holding of artistic and cultural performances, exhibitions and events.

Local authorities frequently participate in the organization of events which can have their roots in our cultural heritage. Commemorations of the two-hundredth anniversary of the 1798 Rising, for example, saw these authorities taking a very active part in recalling this tragic period in Ireland's history. Equally, local authorities have supported the more joyful celebrations of the country's artistic traditions whether music, literature or dance.

Local councils are also obliged by the 1994 *Local Government Act* 'to make arrangements for the proper management, custody, care and conservation of local records and local archives and for the inspection by the public of local archives', and can acquire such material. The material is in a wide range of formats, from printed to electronic, and may include the records of the local authorities themselves. Part of the task of protecting Ireland's cultural heritage is the storage and conservation of important local records in archives and artefacts in local authority museums. There are many good examples of such establishments throughout the country, from the award-winning Monaghan County Museum to the joint Cork City/County Archives located in Christ Church within the mediaeval city. Public libraries also perform a useful function in this regard by providing access to references and sources of local history and by publishing helpful historical guides from time to time.

The role of county and city museums faces a fresh challenge from the 'new wave' of interpretative and visitor centres, raising issues of function, content, durability, educational and research potential, and not least financing. Local authorities have risen to this challenge by improving the presentation and diversity of material exhibited. The appointment of Arts Officers by such authorities is a further positive process, not alone in relation to maintaining the cultural heritage, but also as regards the creation of an artistic heritage for future generations through the encouragement of interest, participation in and support for the arts and by facilitating contemporary artistic development.

One curious but recurring omission in the *Local Government (Planning and Development) Acts*, affecting the cultural or folkloric heritage, is the inability of planning authorities to require developers — particularly of housing estates — to respect the place-names or linguistic or other characteristics of localities. It is a situation which must speak volumes for the contemporary cultural aspirations of the Irish middle classes that inappropriate and frequently misspelt importations from another civilization are used to conjure up some image of well-being, class or whatever. As a consequence, Cork County Council recently established a Place-names Committee with the intention of raising awareness of the rich cultural heritage associated with the legacy of recorded localities. Fortunately, the 1999 *Planning Act* proposes to give planning authorities the power to improve the conditions regarding the naming of developments, and will inevitably lead to some interesting debate about contemporary Irish cultural expression.

REFLECTIONS

The built and natural heritage in Ireland has traditionally been associated with negative property values, except for certain types of heritage properties that can benefit from market demand in particular locations such as the Dublin region and select coastal areas. Similarly, ecologically sensitive parts in the countryside have also, until recently, been treated by the generality of the farming community as a burden or hindrance to the optimization of land use and maximization of income.

In the case of heritage buildings and sites, the often high cost of maintenance, limitations on use or works by state and local authorities, and concerns over public liability — particularly in the case of trespass — make it unattractive to many owners to attempt conservation. Indeed the question that arises is why individual owners should be obliged to carry an unnecessary burden in the national interest? The same question can be applied to areas of natural heritage importance. While farmers have been the traditional custodians of much of this heritage, the philanthropic discretion available to, for example, eighteenth- and nineteenth-century landed estate owners has to all intents and purposes disappeared in the modern Irish Republic. To an extent, I believe this is as much attributable to changing societal values as to membership of the European Union. In the latter regard the impact of the Common Agricultural Policy (CAP) and its component productivity aids and supports have unwittingly contributed more to the degradation of the natural heritage than any other single factor. I have personally come across many examples of well-intentioned 'improvement' of 'useless' land that has resulted in the loss of valuable local habitats. The intensification of agriculture has also transformed the rural landscape of the Republic — as it had already done in the UK — through the removal of hedgerow and natural features. The landscape that had characterized the country for

many generations went through a major and largely unremarked transition in a very short space of time. Fortunately the EU, in its reform of CAP and its application of compensatory measures to support the natural environment, has begun to recognize these contradictions and make provision for their resolution. Whether this will be sufficient to change the development culture of the new Ireland, however, remains to be seen. At least the combined measures have targeted both priority habitat and species (flora and fauna) as well as the wider rural landscape, for instance by encouraging environmentally friendly farming practices and the retention and planting of trees, and the 1999 *Planning Act* also suggests some future intervention by planning authorities in the matter.

My own personal opinion is that there continues to be a societal deficit, namely in community perceptions, as to the value, if any, inherent in the biodiversity of our natural heritage and the goodwill of the public at large to protect it. This sense of community responsibility so evident in, for example, the Tidy Towns movement is curiously lacking in relation to the rural environment. The relative achievements of the country's respective voluntary conservation organizations, namely the National Trust in the north of Ireland and An Taisce in the Republic, perhaps highlights the differences even within the island of Ireland! Without this perceptual value of heritage, I believe that there is a reasonable prospect that environmentally sensitive farming practices will not outlast the life-span of prevailing financial incentives. Other mechanisms or innovations may be needed.

Critical to the value placed on heritage is the state's influence through its policies and supports. Without financial assistance to 'owners' of the heritage assets they will continue to be under severe pressure. State intervention of a financial or fiscal nature in such circumstances has the potential to tip the balance in favour of conservation and against destruction or benign neglect. The premium put by the state, representing the people, on threatened heritage assets has therefore to be carried to some extent by all the people and not just by the individual property owners. Local authorities may also be capable of influencing the value placed on these assets. Listing, *per se*, is generally regarded as negative in the absence of compensatory financial supports. Such subvention is limited by the resources of local authorities, although examples do exist of modest financial assistance to owners of buildings that are considered particularly worthy of it. As this support is now slowly becoming available in government policies for the national architectural heritage, the wheel may finally be about to turn. Local authorities can also resort to reduction or elimination of standard development charges for costly but worthwhile projects that secure the conservation or renewal of heritage buildings or sites.

Exceptional use changes can also be employed to provide a financially rewarding incentive to developers to retain rather than remove a heritage building. 'Planning gain', a term applied to this policy, can, however, be controversial and, unless properly handled, may destroy or damage the monument or context it strives to protect. What tends to be critical is the balance that is achieved between the development and conservation modes. 'Revolving funds' are another possible mechanism that may be employed by local authorities, and by conservation groups as well, in the rehabilitation of threatened heritage buildings. Their value is most in evidence when market forces will not of themselves justify a restoration or renewal project on the basis of financial returns. The principle entails acquisition, refurbishment — often with the use of publicly funded community work training schemes — and subsequent sale on the open market. The proceeds are then invested in another heritage property, and so on. While such schemes tend to be uneconomic on normal property market criteria, they have incidental values such as the employment, re-training and conservation skills benefits, and can also contribute to the initiation of regeneration in run-down areas which the market itself will not necessarily ensure. There is a further argument, based on the sustainability concept, that conservation, as opposed to demolition and re-building, is far less energy intensive when account is taken of the total energy mass demand of both options. Conservation also tends to re-use rather than replace building materials.

Can publicly funded urban heritage conservation and tax-based designations impart a specific local community gain, and, if so, is this measurable in financial terms? In static property market conditions, it is reasonable to surmise that upgrading of key local properties will tend to raise the value of other adjacent buildings. This appears to be borne out by what has happened in areas such as the South Parish in Cork's inner city, a focus of renewal by the corporation, and in Kinsale, now a premier tourism resort in county Cork and more recently in coastal towns such as Clonakilty and Youghal. In such cases, should there be a means of recouping some of this windfall gain, other than by a re-valuation, as a contribution to the very process that creates it? Should these merit some form of local betterment tax that could be used, in the manner of the revolving funds, either to assist other run-down areas or to encourage further investment in conservation of the areas themselves?

Bord Fáilte's 'Heritage Town' designations and the Urban and Village Renewal Schemes under the Operational Programme for Rural and Urban development, in addition to the various schemes for urban and coastal resort renewal, all have the potential to raise property values in the areas targeted. Every fiscal intervention can disrupt the operation of the property market. Unexpected winners and losers may result, as has been evidenced by mid-term review of the Republic's Urban Renewal Schemes, for instance, by favouring 'new build' rather than refurbishment of properties, and investors rather than property owners. The knack — from the state's and local authorities' perspective — is to swing this balance away from relatively painless personal or corporate windfall gain towards a more pervasive community benefit, while at the same time protecting or enhancing the built heritage.

For deprived communities, whether urban or rural, conservation premia have tended to accrue to those who are already reasonably well off. Some form of 'community weighting' of these beneficiaries or their assets might be appropriate. This need not necessarily be purely financial, for instance in scenic rural areas rights-of-way would provide a wider community benefit, and in urban areas some contribution could be considered towards either enhancement of local amenities — such as the provision of local urban space or public sculpture — or the upgrading or provision of street furniture.

Partnership with the private sector is also being spoken of as a means of bridging the financial gap that is resulting from the Republic's gradual weaning off EU funding. This may also result in more imaginative ways of financing conservation of heritage in all its forms. If so, a role for local authorities can be expected.

Local government reform, as currently proposed, will transform local administration procedures in the Irish Republic. Accompanied by the government's National Strategy for Sustainable Development, it heralds a new era in participatory democracy, that is if it works as envisaged. Its principal relevance to heritage will, I believe, lie in the on-going involvement of local communities in determining their own future. So what is different to the present situation, one might ask. As explained earlier, local authorities have to go through an extensive public participation process in that most wide-ranging of exercises affecting heritage, the making of the statutory Development Plan. In future, the drafting of such plans will be influenced to a much greater degree, and at all stages, by the active involvement of local communities, other public agencies and NGOs. Whether this will manifest itself in the form of 'lobbyism' or constructive dialogue, and whether it will substantially influence the form and content of these plans, remains to be seen. I believe it will tend to redress the balance of influence that presently accrues to the development lobby.

One of the greatest challenges posed by this deeper level of local participation will, I feel, be the quality of informed opinion brought to the debate on heritage issues. Given the large number of bodies now charged with some aspect of development in any one area, the need for co-ordination and access to expert opinion is all the more critical. In their absence, there is, I would argue, a real danger of paralysis of action and the generation of 'lowest common denominator' plans. Empowerment of local communities has not yet, I believe, produced the hoped-for benefits it claims to create. There is a limit to the resources and expertise that local communities can themselves bring to bear on their problems. That is not to say that such communities cannot make a valuable contribution, or indeed in certain instances go it alone successfully on certain issues. It may be that a 'community of interest', that is specific interest groups rather than a 'community of place', namely local community groups, will have the resources and staying power to achieve greater benefits for heritage. Furthermore, wider debate and participation may not of themselves be sufficient to resolve fundamental conflicts of opinion. There is an evident need, in my view, for the introduction of skilled negotiators capable of resolving these conflicts through a process of consensus-building. The technique is likely to be increasingly resorted to in cases of a particularly complex nature or involving deep community concerns.

A further difficulty is posed by the squeeze on the traditional main providers of these resources, the local authority itself. This has been exacerbated by the tendency to devolve more responsibilities from central to local government. The contracting out of services, in the absence of the retention of a suitable core of expertise, assumes an efficiency of resource utilization which is questionable in this changed environment. Participation in, and servicing of, an increasingly numerous range of agencies raises questions as to the capacity of the local authority effectively to contribute to the process in the absence of sufficient resources. Relocating or even further distancing these resources in new organizational structures could, in my opinion, only serve to diminish their effectiveness.

At least a partial recognition that extra resources are needed at local authority level is the recent appointment of 'conservation officers' in these authorities in the Republic to protect the built environment. Perhaps the greatest benefit these changes can bring is the learning process on all sides arising from co-operative action on issues of common concern. Will this, however, prevent the future replication of divisive conflicts such as we have seen in the Burren or at Wood Quay? A further step which might usefully be considered, again mirroring the proposed establishment of conservation officers posts in local authorities, would be the appointment of an 'eco-counsellor' or natural heritage officer. Eco-counsellors are largely a child of the Benelux countries and are trained *animateurs* with a professional background whose task is to animate, inspire and assist local communities in best practice measures to protect the natural heritage.

The Heritage Council has recently initiated a pilot scheme of funding the appointment of 'heritage officers' to a limited number of local authorities in the Republic. Their intended remit is to advise on the protection and preservation of heritage in general. A focussing instead on those elements of the local landscape such as hedgerows, woodlands, wetlands and the like, which would supplement European and national reserves by maintaining biodiversity, would avoid duplicating the state service and other areas of heritage currently being handled by local authority conservation specialists. The relatively new academic branch of environmental sciences and studies is currently producing professionals who may need a 'polishing' in the social sciences to equip them better for this role. Perhaps in time, and as a consequence of these changes, it may be possible to envisage a rural equivalent of the Tidy Towns model being developed for the natural environment and supported by the entire community.

CONCLUSION

Having entered the new millennium, it is a good time to review what has happened to Irish heritage in the past thirty years or so and to see whether this will give us confidence and vision to meet future challenges. To summarize, a broad heritage balance sheet might contain the credits and debits listed below:

FACTORS INFLUENCING LOCAL AUTHORITIES' RESPONSE TO HERITAGE

• rapid economic growth has had a largely negative impact on the physical heritage

• popular conservation movements have had some exceptional impacts on both private and public behaviour towards heritage

• these movements have helped to raise public awareness of heritage, but not always of a sympathetic nature, indicating an information/education deficit as much as inadequate processes towards reaching consensus

• politicization of the environment through the green movement has helped to place heritage on the agenda of all the political parties

• national legislation for heritage has tended to take inordinately lengthy periods to be enacted and has, in some cases, been anticipated by landmark decisions of the courts

• European legislation impacting on the heritage has dramatically affected, for the better, both the administrative context and operational incorporation at local authority level, and also generated positive community perception of its importance

• contradictions evident in the EU's conservation and sectoral economic policies impacting on heritage have been transferred into the national context with unfortunate results for heritage; recent change at EU level is remedying some of these contradictions

• local authorities, and the state itself, are now amenable to much the same controls as private developers; this has helped to raise awareness of local sensitivities and encourage dialogue between the authorities, local communities and NGOs

• the move towards sustainability on a global scale, implying more community involvement on a local scale, is likely to have major consequences for the heritage debate; it remains to be seen whether it will produce what it promises

• reform of local government will also impact on heritage; whether administrative change will provide a more effective guarantee for its protection will depend on the resources devoted to it.

Irish heritage has now passed the threshold not only of the much-cliched new millennium but is also, in my view, on the edge of a cultural revolution. A similar dynamism has already electrified the nation in a wide range of contemporary artistic achievements. Can this be extended to our other heritage areas? And, if so, can it be used to create the basis for a heritage of the third millennium? There is a danger that the extant physical heritage will be fossilised, albeit wrapped up in new clothes, as in the form of over-restored 'authentic' historic towns or through being totally 'interpreted' in a new medium that contributes little to conservation *per se*. Heritage, to survive, needs a living role in contemporary society. Heritage is part of our on-going civilization, not just the remaindered past. It is dynamic and requires responses that are not static.

Driven by the EU, belated measures for protection of the natural heritage have also been put in place. Equally, a new role for the extant natural heritage bespeaks innovation in this sphere as well. Perhaps a model already exists in the current proposals by government for the architectural heritage. This could be replicated for natural heritage. Signs in the EU of a move away from prescriptive mechanisms towards locally sustainable action have, in my view, to be looked at with some alarm in the Irish context, particularly because of our recent

record in relation to the natural environment. In the absence of financial compensations for good behaviour, it presupposes a change of heart and mind for which there is little evidence to date. Perhaps this is an unduly negative view which hopefully may be proven wrong!

Local authorities will, in any future context, continue to exercise a critical role in relation to the national heritage. Proximity to the people, representativeness, education and professionalism still have, I believe, the potential to ensure that this should be a force for the better. Whether it will, or rather the degree to which it can, depends as much on the existence of an alert and informed community as on the regulatory environment derived from national or international forces. There continues to be little room for complacency.

Bibliography

Council of Europe 1997 *Questions and answers: No. 3 Tourism and the environment.* Strasbourg.
European Commission 1995 *Wise use and conservation of wetlands. Communication from the European Commission to the Council and European Parliament.* Luxembourg.

Local Authority Advisory Committees

MICHAEL A. MONK AND JOHN CRONIN

The International Council on Monuments and Sites (ICOMOS) Lausanne Charter for the Protection and Management of the Archaeological Heritage of 1990 stresses the need for local involvement in heritage management by stating that: 'Local commitment and participation should be actively sought and encouraged as a means of promoting the maintenance of the archaeological heritage' (ICOMOS 1990, Article 6: Maintenance and Conservation). The primary focus of this chapter is the role that Irish local authorities can have in managing non-artefact archaeological heritage. The present system as established under the *National Monuments Act* 1930 is examined initially, as are the workings of an active local advisory Committee. It will be argued that the precedent set by urban local authorities in appointing City Archaeologists in the 1980s is one that should be applied to all such regionally based agencies. The paper concludes with a discussion of how this service might operate.

LEGAL BACKGROUND

The *National Monuments Act* 1930 and three subsequent amendment acts in 1954, 1987 and 1994 form the legal framework for the protection and management of archaeological heritage in Ireland. When the 1930 act entered the statute books, it largely incorporated much of what had been stated in the Ancient Monument Code while at the same time abolishing the distinction that existed between 'Ancient Monuments' and 'National Monuments'. While the majority of powers under the legislation were vested in the Commissioners of Public Works and the Minister of Finance, under Section 21 of the 1930 act, a National Monuments Advisory Council (NMAC) was to be established. The function of the Council was to advise and assist the Commissioners of Public Works on issues arising from the operation of the provisions of the act or 'any other matter affecting national monuments and the protection and preservation thereof'.

At a sub-national level, it is noteworthy that significant powers were given to local authorities for taking national monuments into their guardianship. Under Section 22 of the principal act, local advisory committees could be set up. While their establishment was not mandatory, where a Committee was constituted its responsibilities were:

(i) to represent the functional area of the local authority that sponsored its foundation;

(ii) to advise the local authority in matters arising from its duties under law in relation to national monuments, and

(iii) to make such representations to the local authority, the Commissioners of Public Works or to the NMAC 'as it may think fit in relation to national monuments in its functional area' (Section 22 [5]).

Membership of these committees was not restricted to elected representatives of the local authority and could include 'persons having practical experience or special knowledge of or interest in architecture, archaeology or some kindred subject'. However, sub-section 2 stated that the Committee was to comprise no fewer than three and not more than five members.

The role of the National Monuments Advisory Council, as set up by the 1930 *National Monuments Act*, was to advise, assist and make representations to the Commissioners of the Office of Public Works 'on any matters arising on or relating to carrying the execution of the Act or any other matter affecting national monuments' (Clause 21, p. 29), and on their protection and preservation. Over the course of time, from 1930 onwards and until the demise of the Advisory Councils, one of their principal functions was to offer advice on development schemes that affected national monuments. However, this role was increasing delegated to officers of the

522

National Monuments section of the Office of Public Works, although in theory it was still necessary to have the decisions of the officers sanctioned by the Council at its intermittent meetings. The ineffectiveness of its working in this respect was instrumental in its demise in the early 1980s, bringing about the loss of an important independent advisory voice in the management of the nation's archaeological heritage.

The *National Monuments (Amendment) Act* 1954 amended many elements of the principal act, such as introducing 'temporary preservation orders', 'listing orders' and creating a new constitution for the NMAC. The NMAC was now to have a part to play in selecting monuments for listing orders. Such monuments were those selected or reported by the National Monuments Advisory Council and considered by the Commissioners of Public Works to be monuments of 'national impor- tance', with others that were thought fit for listing by the Commissioners. The composition of the local committees was affected by the amendment of Section 22 (2) of the principal act in Section 12 of the 1954 act, such that no fewer than three nor more than ten persons were to be appointed.

In the *National Monuments (Amendment) Act* 1987, under Section 4, the Minister for Finance was empowered to establish a 'Historic Monuments Council' (HMC). It was envisaged that this Council would replace the by then defunct National Monuments Advisory Council. The purpose of the new body was to 'advise and assist' the Commissioners in matters arising from the execution of the provisions of the *National Monuments Acts* and 'other matters affecting historic monuments or other archaeological areas or wrecks, and their protection and preservation'. If the operation of the National Monuments Advisory Council had been used as a rule of thumb, this latter qualification of duties would have been dominated by the examination of referred planning applications. Membership of the HMC was to be drawn from those selected by various government departments and representatives of the principal academic institutions in the country. The 1987 act also altered Section 22 (1) of the principal act so that, in accordance with the creation of the Register of Historic Monuments in Section 5, the local committees were now to be known as Historic Monuments Advisory Committees. However, the Historic Monuments Council was never appointed and the powers of the National Monuments Advisory Council were subsumed by the Heritage Council under Section 6 (2) of the *Heritage Act* of 1995 (Myles 1999).

CURRENT SITUATION AND CASE STUDY

From the discussion above, it is clear that the principal function of a Local Advisory Committee is to advise its parent body on matters pertaining to all archaeological

and historical sites and monuments in its functional area, irrespective of whether those sites are in the care of the local authority or not. Since the introduction of the present planning system in 1963, local committees have had a significant role to play in advising on development proposals that affect known archaeological sites. Indeed, with the publication of Sites and Monuments Records for all counties in the 1980s and their integration in planning registers, Local Advisory Committees have had to cope with the referral of even greater numbers of planning applications. In addition, as public awareness of the heritage amenity value of the archaeological sites/monuments has grown, increasing numbers of requests for assistance and advice on the enhancement of the archaeological inheritance are brought before these committees by elected members.

Although there has been confusion over the years surrounding the relationship of Local Authority Advisory Committees with central, national-based agencies, more recently, since the demise of the National Monuments Advisory Council and the ill-fated Historic Monuments Council, active local committees have increased their interaction and co-operation with the National Monuments Service of Dúchas (the state's Heritage Service). For the purpose of this chapter, the remainder of this section details the functions and responsibilities that one such local authority National Monuments Advisory Committee has evolved. The case study is that of Cork County Council.

In 1969, Cork County Council established a National Monuments Advisory Committee. Over the years since then, the Committee's role and responsibilities have expanded in response to both increased threats to archaeological heritage from modern development and the growth of public awareness of the amenity value of the built and archaeological heritage. Currently, the functions of the Committee can best be divided into the following categories.

(i) *SITE MANAGEMENT AND CONSERVATION:*
The management of all national monuments and archaeological sites vested in Cork County Council, especially disused graveyards and all associated monuments situated therein.

(ii) *PROVISION OF TECHNICAL/SPECIALIST ADVICE:*
The Committee has a significant role in advising all departments within the local authority which have cause to manage the built and archaeological heritage — particularly in the area of development advice and devel- opment control planning.

(iii) *COMMUNITY ADVICE:*
Acting as an advisory body to local community initiatives in terms of developments and works involving the built

and archaeological heritage.

Developing policy for the local authority and acting as a conduit of policy from and to central government agencies such as the Heritage Council and Dúchas.

To carry out this work on a regular basis, the Committee receives an annual subvention from the local authority.

Site management and conservation
With respect to site management and conservation, the Committee has been involved in ongoing conservation works at a number of sites (Monk 1996). At Bridgetown Augustinian Priory near Castletownroche in north Cork, works have included remedial conservation, the design and erection of discrete interpretative signs, the publication of an archaeological and architectural survey including a comparative analysis of other Augustinian sites in Ireland (O'Keeffe 1999). Similarly, limited archaeological survey and excavation have been carried out in advance of conservation works at a number of ruined medieval churches in Cork County Council ownership such as at Aghacross, Ballynoe, Courtaparteen, Durrus and Mourneabbey. For Aghacross, a detailed study of the church and graveyard was published in 1995 (Hanley, Weaver and Monk 1995). In all cases, on-site archaeological excavation has been conducted under license from the National Monuments Service of Dúchas, and conservation works have been carried out using traditional materials and in accordance with international conservation standards. In addition, since the coming into effect of Section 12 of the *National Monuments (Amendment) Act* 1994, all such works on known archaeological sites require that two months notice be given to the National Monuments Service.

The Committee has developed the following procedure for selecting sites for conservation and archaeological works. Either in response to a request from a local community group or as an initiative from within the Committee itself, these steps are taken. At the *assessment* stage, an initial reconnaissance report is compiled by one of the specialist members of the Committee on

(i) the historical and archaeological significance of the site/building and

(ii) the main features and physical state of repair of the building(s) and related structures.

This is followed by an *evaluation* where, following approval from the Committee, a detailed archaeological report and structural report are commissioned. These reports indicate the levels of intervention required on-site, the time-scale and costs involved. Following a discussion by the Committee, a budget for the project is determined and the *intervention* stage can commence. Given the nature of local authority funding, such projects require annual review.

The Committee has also part-funded projects for which it has had both indirect and/or minimal responsibility. Examples of this include the restoration, maintenance and presentation of the Royal Gunpowder Mills at Ballincollig and the restoration of Rossleague Martello Tower in Cork Harbour. It has been supportive of the establishment and work of the Barryscourt Castle Trust.

Provision of technical/specialist advice
In this area, the Committee has a particular responsibility arising from the functions of the local authority as a planning body with a duty to undertake development control. This aspect of the work has grown to such an extent that an archaeological officer has been appointed to the county council under the auspices of the Committee and the Planning Department. The post is jointly funded by the county council and Dúchas.

In practice, all planning applications submitted to the Planning Department of Cork County Council are monitored for potential impacts on known archaeological sites. Where development proposals are deemed to have archaeological implications, copies of these applications are forwarded to both the archaeological officer and the National Monuments Service of Dúchas for their observation and advice. Working in close co-operation, these agencies assess the likely impact of development upon any archaeological remains or monuments within or adjacent to the development site. On the basis of this assessment, the Planning Department is offered advice which may in some instances lead to:

(i) a requirement that the applicant commission a detailed appraisal of available information about a site or area before a planning application is submitted or approved — this is usually referred to as a desk-based assessment;

(ii) a requirement that the applicant commission a field evaluation in the form of a survey or excavation to find out more about a site before a planning application is submitted or approved;

(iii) conditions attached to a grant of planning permission requiring the applicant to commission archaeological investigation and recording before or during development — this can variously involve trial excavation or a watching/monitoring brief, or

(iv) a refusal of the submission on the ground that the

archaeological remains are of sufficient importance to warrant preservation.

It is an aspiration of the Committee that all development works carried out by the local authority which are likely to have an impact on archaeological sites be brought to the attention of the Committee at the design stage for its advice and recommendation

Community advice

Under the auspices of the Local Committee, the archaeological officer of the county council is available for pre-planning consultation for any development proposal and for the provision of advice to local community groups. It is planned shortly to issue a series of leaflets and booklets that provide information to the general public on matters relating to heritage.

It is, however, in the care and conservation of grave-yards that the Local Advisory Committee of Cork County Council has greatest involvement with local communities. When one considers that the local authority has approximately 300 graveyards in its own care, and that many of these contain ruined medieval churches and associated ecclesiastical monuments, it is obvious that this topic is of importance. The Committee has recognized that sufficient resources will never exist to maintain and manage these sites to the level that it or local communities would desire. The Committee has also recognized that local communities must be involved in developing conservation plans for these sites as they are, in a sense, the people who will ensure the preservation and protection of these sites.

In response to this situation, the Committee has endeavoured to conduct a base-line survey of the historical/archaeological significance, structural remains and current condition of graveyards in its care and to use this study to establish a priority list of sites that require urgent protection and conservation. The base-line survey is nearing completion. The database and archives of the Cork Archaeological Survey at University College, Cork, have proved invaluable for this work (Ronan 1999).

Policy formulation

The advisory Committee has an important role in developing policy for the local authority and acting as a conduit of policy from and to central government agencies such as the Heritage Council and Dúchas. Under the review of the current County Development Plan, the Committee has been invited to contribute policy documents and make recommendations for the inclusion of sites of archaeological, historical or architectural importance for protection in the County Development Plan.

The Committee has contributed comment to national policy debates on a number of occasions, in particular in 1986 in response to the measure that subsequently became the *National Monuments (Amendment) Bill* of 1987. In more recent times, this has continued and, for example, in response to the proposed National Heritage Plan of the Department of Arts, Heritage, Gaeltacht and the Islands in 1998, the Committee recommended that any such plan should be conceived as only a component of a wider National Land-Use Plan, as it was the Committee's opinion that, wherever possible, heritage conservation should be integrated into national economic and land-use objectives.

Indeed the response to the proposed heritage plan made a strong case for the necessity of close local authority involvement with heritage matters and for this to be recognized by central government. It proposed that it was imperative that an effective two-way communication between central and local authorities be created, and suggested that a devolved, region-based tier of the Heritage Service would be the most appropriate conduit for such communication.

THE FUTURE OF LOCAL AUTHORITY ADVISORY COMMITTEES

It must be stated, from reviewing the situation in county Cork, that there are a number of problems in fulfilling all the responsibilities that can accrue to Local Authority Advisory Committees. These problems, of course, are related to a lack of funding, but, far more importantly, stem from the lack of existing in-house technical skill to support and augment the decisions made by the Committee. This is particularly true with respect to building conservation works and the necessary recording that precedes any maintenance which local committees wish to see being carried out.

In addition, expectations in regard to fulfilling archaeological or conservation standards on jobs such as graveyard maintenance have changed radically in recent years. These are areas which, in the past, have been seen as routine maintenance in the sole charge of area engineers, and a consistent pattern of consultation with archaeological officers now needs to be established. Large-scale engineering works such as road building, which must take into consideration the possibility of below-surface archaeological features, also need to establish a more consistent pattern of consultation via officers responsible to the local authorities' national monuments committees.

Another difficulty is the lack of a formalized inter-action between Local Advisory Committees and central government agencies such as Dúchas and the Heritage Council. Local Authority Committees are well placed to disseminate policy and best practice guidelines to local groups, and similarly to forward suggestions for improvement in management practices affecting the built and archaeological heritage to national bodies. In any area of endeavour, a commitment to subsidiarity and Sustainable Development hinges on informed action operating at a local level. This is most certainly the case with respect to the management and protection of the archaeological and built heritage.

In any proposed changes to the structure of heritage management in Ireland, it will be necessary to ensure that effective organization exists at local, regional and national tiers. Local Authority Advisory Committees are the basis on which effective local action can be orchestrated. To operate this structure successfully, it will be necessary to have more formalized positions within local authorities for archaeological and conservation staff. Such archaeological and conservation officers should not be attached simply to planning departments (as has been the case in Ireland in recent years) but should be in a position to advise the local authority on all matters relating to archaeology and conservation.

In effect, there is a need for a county-based archaeological and conservation officer service which operates on behalf of the council as a whole under the auspices of a Local Monuments Advisory Committee. The Committee's make-up should reflect a balance between the appointed officers of the local authorities, the elected representatives and independent specialist advisors. Heritage officers have recently been appointed in counties Kerry and Galway, but it is not yet clear how these officials will fit into the scheme outlined above.

CONCLUSION

This chapter has stressed the importance of maintaining and expanding local involvement in the management and policy formation of the archaeological and built heritage — as stressed in recent international archaeological heritage policy documents. It is argued that the Local Monuments Advisory Committees set up by the 1930 *National Monuments Act* are ideally placed to provide the basis for a more developed interactive management structure, with officers appointed for archaeological and conservation matters attached to the Committees (which themselves might have a balanced membership between elected public representatives — councillors — and specialist advisors from outside the local authority). The present and developing responsibility of these Committees has been outlined by reference to the Committee which is at present the most active in the country — that of county Cork. The contribution and workings of the latter body have been outlined in order both to provide some basis for the adoption of a more widespread scheme and to raise issues about how the workings of these Committees might be improved. We would argue that for a local scheme of management to work successfully, it needs to interact, when necessary, in all areas of its responsibilities with a regional as well as a national structure. This two-way communication should occur in a non-hierarchical fashion between the centralized state bodies (Dúchas, and the Heritage Council) and those at a regional and local level.

Bibliography

Hanley, K., Weaver, M. and Monk, J. 1995
    *An archaeological survey of St Molagga's
    Church, Aghacross, Mitchelstown, Co. Cork*,
    County Council Archaeological Monographs
    No. 1. Cork.
International Council on Monuments and Sites 1990
    *Charter for the protection and management
    of the archaeological heritage*. Lausanne.
Monk, M. A. 1996 'County Cork's National Monuments
    Committee shows the way', *Archaeology
    Ireland* **10**, 3, p. 5.
Myles, F. 1999 'The HMACs and the protection of the
    archaeological heritage,' MUBC thesis, UCD.
O'Keeffe, T. 1999 *An Anglo-Norman monastery:
    Bridgetown Priory and the architecture of the
    Augustinian Canons Regular in Ireland*.
    Kinsale.
Ronan, S. 1999 *A report on graveyards containing features
    of archaeological importance that are under the
    care of Cork County Council*, submitted to Cork
    County Council NMAC (unpublished). Cork.

The Man-Made Heritage:
The Legislative and Institutional Framework

THE LEGISLATION

The provision for the care of archaeological monuments in Ireland by the state began with the passing of the *Irish Church Act* in 1869. Some limited works before this had been carried out by the old Kilkenny Archaeological Society (later to become the Royal Society of Antiquaries of Ireland). For instance, in 1857, they spent £180 on Jerpoint Church, county Kilkenny, and undertook limited work at the Nun's Church, Clonmacnoise, county Offaly. The main objective of the *Irish Church Act* of 1869 was to disestablish the Church of Ireland. Churches still in use with their graveyards were vested in the Representative Body of the Church of Ireland. Other graveyards were eventually taken over by the county councils. There remained a number of buildings and graveyards not in current use and a category of 'National Monuments' was devised to provide for the care of these. The Commissioners of Public Works were given the job of looking after these newly categorized archaeological sites. The Board of Works was entrusted with the care of these monuments because no other more suitable government organization existed in Ireland. Until the introduction of the *Ancient Monuments Protection Act* of 1882 there was no provision for the care of archaeological monuments by the state. In 1874, when the ecclesiastical remains on the Rock of Cashel were vested it was stated that it was to be preserved as a national monument and not to be used as a place of public worship. The present position following on from this is that any building being habitually used for ecclesiastical purposes cannot be a national monument. For example Holy Cross, county Tipperary, once it was restored and used as a parish church, ceased to have the status of a national monument. This meant in effect that the Commissioners of the Office of Public Works lost control of an important archaeological monument.

In 1875, the first Inspector of National Monuments was appointed and large important ecclesiastical sites such as Glendalough, Monasterboice and Athenry were vested in the Commissioners. The first Inspector was Sir Thomas Deane, who was one of a well-known family of architects, and up until the position of Inspector of National Monuments was done away with by the Commissioners in late 1980s, the works side of monuments care was always under the direction of an architect. In 1896, the Commissioners gave instructions to the Inspector that his operation in relation to ruins was to be limited to what was necessary for preservation, such as the securing of loose stones, preventing infiltration of water, clearing away rubbish, 'where, by doing so, portions of the buildings now hidden may, with advantage, be brought to view but carefully to avoid any attempt at restoration'. Despite these instructions, some restoration work did take place at places like Glendalough, Cormac's Chapel on the Rock of Cashel as well on many of the early monastic sites on the small off-shore islands. Unfortunately, most of these sites were not properly recorded prior to conservation work. Sites that were not vested in the Office of Public Works could also have a guardianship order placed on them. For instance the owner of Trim Castle would not, until quite recently, hand over the monument to the state, so, in order to undertake conservation work, it was necessary to take control of the site. The weak point of the 1882 act was that it only protected a scheduled monument against damage by anyone other than the owner. This completely ignored the fact that the owner was the most likely person to destroy the site, as witnessed by the large-scale destruction of archaeological sites in the 1970s and '80s when land grant schemes were extensively used.

Local authorities until 1930 had no power to strike a rate for the upkeep of monuments and still do not have the staff or expertise to deal with conservation work on archaeological sites. Under the 1898 *Local Government (Ireland) Act,* the county councils were empowered, with

527

the owner's consent, to become guardians of ancient or medieval structures as defined by the *Ancient National Monuments Protection Act* of 1892. Under the *Land Acts* of 1903 and 1923, any monuments of historic, traditional, artistic or archaeological interest which were situated on land purchased by the Land Commission could be vested in the Board of Works.

Robert Cochrane in 1899 became the Inspector of Monuments, and he was responsible for increasing the amount of information published in the Board's Annual Reports. Some of these monument reports were so detailed that they were published as separate guidebooks to a site or a group of sites. Unfortunately, these detailed reports ceased to be published after 1939. When the *National Monuments Act* of 1930 was passed, Harold Leask was appointed the first full-time Inspector of National Monuments. This act is still the principal statute governing the care of monuments in the Irish Republic. One innovation in this act was the introduction of the Preservation Order. Although this order protects an endangered site, it does not empower the National Monuments Section of the Department of Arts, Heritage, Gaeltacht and the Islands (DAHGI), now Dúchas (formerly the Office of Public Works), to carry out conservation or maintenance work on the monument. However, the Department has the power to make Guardianship Orders, as pointed out above. Trim Castle, county Meath, remained in private hands until the owner agreed to sell it to the state in 1992, but had been in guardianship for more than thirty years prior to the agreement of sale. This allowed archaeological excavation and conservation works to take place at the site. Other well-known monuments had Guardianship Orders placed on them mainly because the owners were unwilling to sell or donate them to the state. The passage tomb at Dowth recently transferred from private to state ownership. Famous castles such as Maynooth, Carlow, Limerick and Castleroche as well as monastic sites such as Lusk, Muckross, Kells Priory (county Kilkenny) and the megalithic tombs at Creevykeel had and in some cases still have Guardianship Orders placed on them since they are still in private hands. The 1994 amendment allows the heritage minister to acquire by agreement or compulsorily any monument that is, in her opinion, a national monument or part of a monument as well as any land in the vicinity of such a monument.

The *National Monuments Act* of 1930 also brought in a prohibition on unlicensed archaeological excavations. The National Monuments Section of DAHGI is the body responsible for issuing licences for archaeological excavation, and this has been extended to include metal detecting and large-scale monitoring of soil stripping for motorways or other large-scale ground disturbance. The 1994 *National Monuments Amendment Act* further strengthened state control on archaeological licences by giving the National Museum a vetting role which would help that institution control the treatment and movement of archaeological artefacts. The 1994 amendment also included wrecks by stating that 'the site of a wreck or an archaeological object that is lying on or in or under the sea bed or on land covered by water, and where such wreck or object is in, or in the vicinity of an area' is protected under the legislation.

The *National Monuments Amendment Act* of 1954 introduced the temporary preservation order which allowed the Commissioners (now the minister or her agents) to make an order immediately to restrain any person from damaging in anyway whatsoever a monument or archaeological site for a period of six months. This has the advantage of placing a temporary restraint on developers who might not be willing to fulfil archaeological conditions. When the archaeology of the site or monument has been resolved one way or another, the order can be allowed to expire or a new temporary order issued or if necessary a full preservation order. Another new power under the 1954 act was listing. This gave the Commissioners the power to compel the owner of an endangered site to give two months' notice of intention to carry out any alterations to a monument. This system of giving two months' notice gave the authority time to place a preservation order on a site if they considered that the owner was liable to damage it. Unfortunately, neither listing or preservation orders were ever placed on title deeds so that new owners of properties with protected sites would not necessarily be aware of the status of these archaeological sites.

The 1987 amendment gave a much wider definition to 'monument', briefly which was that it included anything above or below the ground or water, affixed or not. It also included any place comprising the remains or traces of any such building, structure or erection, cave, stone or natural product or any such tomb, grave and so forth. This amendment also strengthened some of the provisions of the original act and later amendments, including the total prohibition of the use of detecting devices in or at a site of archaeological interest, and gave the power to the Commissioners to issue licences for the legitimate use of such devices. It also added to legislation for the protection of wrecks by prohibiting diving, survey or salvage, location or exploration of a wreck or archaeological object. A wreck was defined as anything over 100 years old. It empowered the Commissioners with the right to grant licences for certain types of survey work and the use of detection devices on wrecks. The 1987 amendment also made provision for the setting up of the Historic Monuments Council which was to advise and assist the Commissioners in relation to any matter respecting the carrying into execution the provisions of *National Monuments Acts* 1930–87. However, this Council, which was meant to replace the National

Monument Advisory Council, never came into being. This amendment also established the Register of Historic Monuments which in fact replaced the old listing system. But this register was to contain a list of all known archaeological sites in the state and these sites were to be listed in *Iris Oifigiúil* (Ireland's official journal). The problem with this piece of legislation was that the ownership of each site, to be registered, had to be established. The 1994 amendment introduced legislation which got around this problem by establishing a record of monuments comprised of all the archaeological sites known to Dúchas, the National Monuments Section, from their database, mainly through the Sites and Monuments Records (SMRs) which had been published for all the counties by 1992. The SMRs are the basis for the recorded monuments and are being updated for each county following fieldwork. It is expected that all fieldwork being carried out by the survey, which is then published in inventory form, will be finalised by the year 2005. However, the recorded monuments register was finished by the end of 1997 prior to the conclusion of the initial preliminary field survey. It therefore follows that this register of recorded monuments will have to be continually updated according as new information is added to the database. The advantage of the recorded monuments legislation over that of the registration method of the 1987 amendment is that the onus is on the owner of the archaeological site to consult the list and the accompanying map of the record and to make sure that he/she is complying with the law. The owners do not have to be notified individually of the fact that they have a recorded site on their property. However, it is desirable that a system of notification be set up even though there are in the region of 120,000 archaeological sites in the Republic of Ireland. Having set up such all-embracing legislation for the protection of our heritage, it is quite obvious that some system of policing and enforcement needs to be put in place. A system of county archaeologists and/or district wardens should be initiated to give physical or visible support to the legislation.

PLANNING REGULATIONS AND ARCHAEOLOGY
Under Local Government (Planning and Development) Regulations, the local authorities are obliged to send notice of any planning application which is likely to have an impact on a monument to the DAHGI National Monuments Section, to enable archaeological conditions to be inserted into the planning permission, if it is to be granted, or to give time to offer advice on outright refusal, if so desired. However, the local authorities are not obliged to include the suggested conditions and often insert their own or completely ignore those of Dúchas. Under Section 12 of the *National Monuments (Amendment) Act* 1994 local authorities are required to give two months' notice of any proposed work within or outside a local authority's functional area which might have an impact on an archaeological monument. Should the local authority grant planning permission without taking due notice of archaeological conditions suggested by Dúchas, the Department may if it so wishes appeal the decision to An Bórd Pleanála. This does not, of course, mean that the Board will give its decision in favour of the objectors. Should the appeal fail Dúchas could, if they saw fit, place a preservation order on the archaeological site, effectively stopping the development until such time as its conditions were adhered to.

In March 1997, the European Convention on the Protection of the Archaeological Heritage was ratified by Ireland. The Convention, which is known as the Valletta Convention, is a revised and updated version of the one signed in London 1969 to which Ireland was not a party. The Convention lays down European standards for the protection of the archaeological heritage, and sets out a range of obligations, which signatories undertake to implement. It further states that the archaeological heritage shall include structures, constructions, groups of buildings, developed sites, moveable objects, monuments of other kinds as well as their context, whether situated on land or under water. Under Article 2, each party to the Convention undertakes the maintenance of an inventory of its archaeological heritage and the designation of protected monuments and areas. Other articles cover the procedures for the authorization and supervision of excavation and other archaeological activities and require that these activities are only undertaken in a scientific manner. Under Article 4, each party undertakes to implement measures for the physical protection of the archaeological heritage, and it mentions that public authorities should provide for the conservation and maintenance of the archaeological heritage, preferably *in situ*. Under Article 5, it states that each party undertakes 'to seek to reconcile and combine the respective requirements of archaeology and development plans by ensuring that archaeologists participate' in various areas of the planning process, and, in particular, that 'archaeologists, town and regional planners systematically consult one another in order to permit' various other things to take place, such as making sure there are sufficient time and resources for a scientific study of the archaeological site and for the result of the excavation to be published. Under Article 7, it states that each party should undertake the updating of surveys, inventories and maps of archaeological sites in the area within its jurisdiction.

THE INSTITUTIONAL FRAMEWORK
As pointed out above, Dúchas, the Heritage Division of DAHGI, formerly the National Monuments, Office of Public Works, is the main body responsible for the preservation of the man-made heritage. The legal and

planning framework in relation to the Heritage Division's responsibility has also been outlined above. The heritage section on the archaeological side is divided into three main areas, Archaeological Survey, Archaeological Excavation and Planning. The Archaeological Survey for a long time almost stood as a separate entity, but by 1983, little progress had been made and no publications had resulted from almost 20 years of fieldwork. Up until this point, the Survey was attempting to carry out detailed work and had made little progress. It had been set up initially to record pre-1700 AD archaeological sites so that the Commissioners would be able to put in place a grand plan for the protection for its archaeological heritage. However, since there is something in the region of 120,000 archaeological sites in the Republic of Ireland, a small team of archaeologists (max. seven) would not have completed a detailed survey within the foreseeable future. The government therefore in 1983 made the decision to drop all detailed survey, except for county Louth, which was fairly well advanced at that stage, and to commence rapid reconnaissance work with a view to completing this stage in a reasonable time. Sites and Monuments Records, mainly paper-based archaeological surveys, were to be the first stage of campaign. The SMRs were completed by 1992, and, they form the basis for the recorded monuments as mentioned above, but they also form the main monuments archive in Dúchas. This archive is extensively used by the archaeologists in the Planning section of Dúchas and by individuals in the private sector who are employed to carry out archaeological work by developers. It is also used to a lesser extent by researchers for academic purposes. The archive at this time is still mainly in hard-copy form, but some of the original SMR information and the basic site descriptions are available on computer. A small portion of the field notes but none of the back-up material has also been placed on computer. It is hoped within the next few years, as part of the in-house GIS, that all the available information stored in files will be placed on the computer database. It is feasible that preliminary archaeological fieldwork will be completed by the year 2005, and that the archaeological inventories which have been published for almost half the twenty-six counties will be completed in another ten years. This will provide

Fig. 51.1 Trim Castle, county Meath, aerial view before restoration.

Fig. 51.2 Trim Castle, county Meath, undergoing archaeological excavation.

an invaluable record of our archaeological remains and the basis for the planning of our archaeological heritage as well as for academic studies.

Other archaeological surveys have been undertaken by various county councils and FÁS, including an almost detailed volume of county Donegal, parts of county Kerry and Ikerrin, county Tipperary. Detailed survey takes place on the megalithic structures by archaeologists formerly in the Ordnance Survey Office, and now attached to DAHGI, and most of the tombs of the Republic of Ireland have been published. Other minor surveys of baronies have also taken place, and most of the information from all these surveys has been incorporated into the Dúchas archive with the co-operation of those responsible for the work.

On the planning side, it has been pointed out that the archaeologists working in this section depend on the archive and in particular on the recorded monuments maps and manuals. All planning applications which are likely to have an impact on an archaeological site are referred to the archaeologists dealing with planning, including road schemes and other large-scale projects.

When a licence to excavate or monitor soil stripping is applied for to Dúchas, a method statement has to be attached to the application. This method statement is scrutinized by the archaeologist dealing with that area, to make sure the archaeological conditions set by the planning authority on the advice of Dúchas are adhered to. Frequently the developers of large-scale works, whether roads or buildings, will discuss the archaeological requirements with Dúchas prior to submission for planning permission. In this way, if there is agreement between the developer and Dúchas prior to submission of a planning application, the whole planning process will be much smoother. For instance, local authorities and the National Roads Authority will discuss the archaeological implications of the selection of certain routes, taking into consideration the cost of resolving the archaeology as opposed to moving the line of the roadway. The archaeologists in the Planning section therefore offer advice and help the prospective developers in relation the possible impact of their development and the resolution of any such impact. As well as giving advice and requesting archaeological conditions

Fig. 51.3 Trim Castle, county Meath, after recent restoration work.

to be placed in planning permissions, Dúchas monitors forestry applications to make sure they will have no impact on our archaeological heritage. One major problem exists in the control of the archaeological heritage and that is enforcement. It is all very well placing archaeological conditions in planning permissions and having all of our archaeological sites protected under the 1994 *National Monuments (Amendment) Act*, but there is at present no archaeological back-up in the form of staff who would be free to police the legislation. Therefore, a system of nationwide wardens needs to be put in place to make sure that our archaeological heritage is not being destroyed. It is also imperative that local authorities take their responsibilities seriously in relation to the management of the archaeological patrimony. There is one major area where the Minister for Arts, Heritage, Gaeltacht and the Islands does not appear to be able to exercise control on our archaeological heritage, and that is in the peat milling industry. A small wetland unit with about three full-time archaeologists and part-time field team survey and monitor the peatlands where archaeological material once preserved

in the peat is being exposed and milled away. It should also be noted that anyone intending to carry out an archaeological excavation must hold a licence which is issued by Dúchas. All applicants for a licence must satisfy an interview board that they are qualified academically and have sufficient experience to direct an archaeological excavation. It is also necessary to hold a licence for testing, monitoring and soil stripping. This control of licensing should help the state to make sure that any archaeological excavations are undertaken by fully qualified archaeologists and that the work is of a professional standard. As part of the licensing regulations, the licence-holder is obliged to submit a full stratigraphic report on the results of the excavation to Dúchas as well as to the National Museum.

Under the national monuments legislation, Dúchas is are also responsible for underwater archaeology. A small unit consisting of one director and two archaeologists was contracted to compile an SMR of wrecks so that a database of them could be established to form the basis for the recorded underwater archaeological heritage. No state institution has yet accepted responsibility for our industrial heritage, and the vast bulk of this material lies outside the responsibility of the archaeological survey.

Archaeological excavation was first undertaken by the Office of Public Works in the 1960s on national monuments prior to and in conjunction with conservation work. In the early days of this work, there was only one archaeologist who was the Assistant Inspector of National Monuments. In the early 1970s, three more archaeologists were recruited to the section, and their main work was also excavation as well as doing the preservation and listing orders. While this section is still responsible for excavation prior to conservation, most of the work is contracted out, since the permanent staff do not have the time to undertake large-scale projects such as that recently undertaken at Trim Castle, county Meath. There are six main National Monuments Districts which have their own team of workmen, clerk of works and architects. These district offices are responsible for the upkeep of the national monuments in their area. Archaeologists are also assigned to each district as part of their duties, and are responsible for work in those areas that is likely to have an impact on archaeological remains. In effect, there is in place a team of workmen and professionals for each district. Large-scale projects for national monuments also have project teams put in place which will include the architects in charge of the district, an archaeologist and an administrator.

CASE STUDY

Trim Castle is a fairly typical project where large-scale works took place with a view to presenting the site to the public. The castle was acquired in 1992, and when EU Structural Funds became available, it was decided that large-scale conservation works should take place with a view to making the site safe and accessible to the public. Prior to major conservation works, the building was carefully studied in order to discover how the castle was constructed and in how many phases it was built. During the course of this study, it was discovered that timbers buried in the castle walls were sufficiently well preserved to obtain dendrochronological dates. Fourteen samples were taken from various levels of the keep which gave three definite phases of building. Large-scale excavations took place all around the keep to see if the forebuilding for the first floor entrance could be found, and any associated drawbridge structure, as well as to reveal the full extent of the fosse which encloses the building. As well as excavating for presentation purposes, there was a certain element of research which helped in the interpretation of the castle. For instance, the great hall, which was built in the later thirteenth century, was revealed, even though only its foundations were discovered. These archaeological discoveries tied in well with the architectural interpretation of the building and were used in the presentation of the site to the public. It should be

pointed out that the historical references were not particularly helpful and in fact were misleading in relation to dating of the different phases of building. However, the earlier historical references to the earthwork castle and its burning down shortly after being built in 1174 were confirmed by the excavation of part of the ringwork castle. This project has been a useful exercise in team-work and has demonstrated the necessity of closely studying and recording a building in detail before and during the programme of conservation. It should also be pointed out that the castle was not in state care until 1992, and had a Guardianship Order placed on it which allowed access to the building for basic conservation work prior to the recent major campaign. It should also be noted that were it not for Structural funding, this large-scale project probably would never have taken place. It is therefore imperative that we adopt an integrated approach to the conservation and preservation of our man-made heritage.

Bibliography

Sweetman, P. D. 1992 'The Archaeological Survey of Ireland' in *Inventories of monuments and historic buildings in Europe*, pp. 112–5.

Sweetman, P. D. 1998 'The development of Trim Castle in the light of recent research', *Chateau Gallard* 18.

Wheeler, H. 1985 'The national monuments of Ireland', *Archaeologia Cambrensis* 134.

The Heritage Council/An Chomhairle Oidhreachta

MICHAEL STARRETT

This chapter examines the elements involved in the establishment of a new heritage organization. It touches on the historical context but concentrates primarily on the post-1995 period, when legislation led to the members of the Heritage Council being appointed, and on the steps subsequently taken to translate the vision into reality, to move from theory to practice. Areas covered include the legislation, obstacles to development and, of course, aspects of the philosophy and corporate identity which need to be considered where any new venture is concerned. Financial realities are taken into consideration and the paper concludes by looking to the future, seeing how the Council's work can secure long-term benefits for the national heritage.

BACKGROUND

One has to go back to 1982 to find the first proposed legislation for a Heritage Council in Ireland. The original draft *Heritage Council Bill* 1982 was the focus of attention of a non-statutory National Heritage Council established in 1988 by the then Taoiseach, Charles J. Haughey, T.D. In 1989, work on a new draft bill began, taking account of changes in thinking as regards national heritage, its policy development and management. Much of this thinking was influenced by the National Heritage Council which, through its work and wide range of responsibilities, sought to provide an indication of the breadth and scope of the nation's heritage, and in particular sought to reunite the natural and built aspects of this inheritance. Those responsibilities, whilst non-statutory, came to be reflected in the statutory measure which is the *Heritage Act* 1995. The members of the National Heritage Council must take much credit for the priority accorded to the establishment of a statutory Heritage Council following its first meeting with the then Minister of Arts, Culture and the Gaeltacht, Michael D. Higgins, T.D., in 1993. The Heritage Council was duly established under the 1995 *Heritage Act*. This act, signed

by the then President Mary Robinson in July of that year, created an independent Council with a statutory responsibility to propose policies and priorities for the identification, protection, preservation and enhancement of the national heritage (*http://www.heritagecouncil.ie*). The Council's function, therefore, is primarily as a policy-oriented body.

THE LEGISLATION

There is no doubt that the legislation which led to the establishment of the Heritage Council provides the organization with great strength. For the first time in Ireland, a body existed which has its responsibilities for the national heritage defined in law. Furthermore, through the act and its very wide definition of the national heritage (which includes monuments, archaeological objects, heritage objects, architectural heritage, flora, fauna, wildlife habitats, landscapes, seascapes, wrecks, geology, heritage gardens and parks and inland waterways), the Council was in a position to look at policies and priorities for all aspects of heritage. There has been a tendency in the past to compartmentalize heritage, to look at our built or natural or cultural inheritance in isolation. The *Heritage Act* avoided this trap, and in a truly ecological sense allowed the Council to consider the interdependence of all the elements, and to devise its work and programmes accordingly. The Council's primary responsibility under the act is to to propose policies and priorities for the identification, protection, preservation and enhancement of the national heritage. The Council is, in addition, charged with the following duties:

(i) to promote interest, education, knowledge and pride in, and facilitate the appreciation of the national heritage;

(ii) to co-operate with public authorities, educational

bodies and other organizations and persons in the promotion of the functions of the Council, and

(iii) to promote the co-ordination of all activities relating to the functions of Council.

The opportunity presented by the *Heritage Act*, and the challenge which faced the newly constituted Council, were to translate the above words into actions which would ultimately be of benefit to the national heritage. To do that, the Council needed to develop an organization which would allow it to carry out its functions effectively and efficiently, and which, very importantly, reflected its own culture and philosophy.

THE BEGINNING

The beginning, work-wise, for the Heritage Council occurred with the appointment in July 1995 by the then Minister for Arts, Culture and the Gaeltacht, Michael D. Higgins, of the Council's first Chairperson, the late Freda Rountree, and sixteen Council members. (Ruth Delaney was later appointed chairperson to succeed Freda Rountree.) The skills and expertise of the Chairperson and the Council members mirrored the complex and detailed definition of national heritage referred to earlier.

The act states that 'each member of the Council shall be a person who in the opinion of the Minister has an interest in, or knowledge or experience of, or in relation to, the national heritage'. All aspects of heritage, both natural and built, were represented by the appointments. In addition, those elements of heritage such as family history and the museums sector which are usually more closely associated with our cultural traditions also received due attention. The act required that the Council establish Standing Committees on wildlife, archaeology, architectural heritage and inland waterways. Thus the Council, at its inception, had its own legislation, seventeen Council members, four Standing Committees and a small number of civil servants, seconded from the then Department of Arts, Culture and the Gaeltacht, to provide secretarial support.

Few, if any, of those appointed to the Council were aware of the legacy which they were about to inherit, in the form of grants committed by the previous non-statutory National Heritage Council. The latter, whilst it had been fundamental in advising on the legislation which established the statutory Council, had, through the various government departments to which it had been responsible, committed a very considerable amount of money to be paid in grant form beyond its own lifetime.

THE LEGACY

Council members, its committee members and, of course, its support staff, were under no illusion as

regards the challenge and the opportunity presented by the *Heritage Act*. As a major piece of legislation, it could provide immense benefits for the national heritage. However, as the Council came to terms with the scale of its task, it soon realized that much of its funding was already committed. In the first months of its existence, the new Heritage Council had no clearly identifiable budget. In the financial year 1996 (beginning in January 1996), the Council's budget was £1.9m. As the Council appointed its own contract workers and staff, it soon became apparent that the total inherited grant commitment amounted to £2.2m, the greater part of which was for architectural heritage work. As the Council developed its policies, it found itself paying grant monies for projects which did not fully match its own emerging priorities for the national heritage.

As can be imagined, this led to some fairly lengthy discussions with the minister of the day to point out the difficulties presented. In essence, and despite the difficulties, the Council at an early stage decided to honour the committed grants, even though under the *Heritage Act* the award of grants is a discretionary rather than a mandatory function. As a matter of record, it is worth recording that, by prudent financial management, the inherited 'debt' had been reduced to just under £0.7m by the end of 1997 and to £0.2m by 1998. Clearing the debt had, however, militated against the Council's ability to be immediately proactive in support of its primary function of policy development.

BUILDING AN EFFECTIVE ORGANIZATION

The memorandum to government on the Council's finance identified a staff ceiling for it of fifteen. In February 1996, the Council advertised the post of Chief Executive. This appointment was confirmed in April 1996 and the appointee took up office on 1 August 1996. In the three-month period between appointment and actually taking up the new post, the Chief Executive was fortunate in being able to spend a considerable time at the Council's headquarters (then in Dublin) getting to know the Council and Committee members, attending Council meetings and talking to the support staff. What was most impressive was the enthusiasm and commitment of all those involved, not only with regard to their own areas of expertise but also the development of the role of the new organization. It was widely accepted that the new body required a clear focus for its activities.

This focus was provided following two team-building days held in summer and autumn 1996. All Council members, Committee members and staff in post were invited and the vast majority attended. The outcome of deliberations resulted in an agreed objective for the organization as a whole, namely, to work with all interested agencies and individuals in order to identify, protect, interpret, promote and enhance Ireland's heritage. This objective was a clear statement that the Council saw itself as an entity which would engage with others to achieve its own statutory responsibilities. As a relatively small agency (primarily non-executive in function), such an approach was not only pragmatic but essential to establishing the confidence of the many other agencies with heritage responsibilities. A further outcome of the team-building days was to reinforce the desire throughout the organization that the Council take forward its responsibilities for heritage in a non-compartmentalized manner. It was agreed that all of the Council's work would be carried out within three broad areas of activity:

(i) collecting data on Ireland's heritage: to develop the framework for a definitive database to benefit Ireland's cultural heritage;

(ii) promoting pride in Ireland's heritage: to facilitate and build on the increased understanding, appreciation, enjoyment and conservation of the national heritage, and

(iii) proposing policy and providing advice for Ireland's heritage: to develop an integrated approach to the development and implementation of policy on the national heritage, thus improving the quality and effectiveness of its input into government policy.

From each of these areas, key policies were developed and agreed. Actions necessary to achieve them were prioritized and a structure put in place which would translate policy into action and realize the objectives. The key policies in each area may be summarized as follows:

(i) *Data collection*
• to identify all agencies involved in Ireland's heritage;

• to identify gaps in information;

• to identify all sources of data and information relevant to the functions of the Heritage Council;

• to collate available information in a manner which improves access to it;

• to establish the current levels of interest in and understanding of the national heritage.

(ii) *Promoting pride in Ireland's heritage*
• to give the national heritage a central place in local and community development;

• to produce a communication plan for the Heritage Council;

• to produce practical advice for crafts people working in the heritage area;

• to recognize best practice through the establishment of themed award schemes;

• to grant-aid projects which meet Heritage Council criteria both for their quality of work and benefit to the national heritage;

• to produce practical advice on conservation and enhancement of the natural and built environment;

• to encourage the appreciation of heritage through the school curriculum;

• to develop a programme of seminars and activities based on the national heritage.

(iii) *Proposing policy and providing advice*
• to identify areas where legislation and policy can be improved for the benefit of the national heritage;

• to propose new policies and legislation where appropriate;

• to secure independent audit and assessment of relevant areas of work of the Council;

• to promote the application of the principles of best practice for the benefit of the national heritage;

• to publish advice on heritage practice in association with partner agencies;

• to maintain a detailed awareness of national, European and international influences on our heritage;

• to consult widely with key partners.

A series of actions flowed from these policies. In autumn 1997, the Minister for Arts, Heritage, Gaeltacht and the Islands, Ms Síle de Valera, T.D., formally launched *The Plan 1997–2000*, the Council's strategic document, which highlighted its policy and objectives up to the start of the millennium. The plan was fully costed and ambitious, and put into the public domain the work which Council intended to carry out.

THE STRUCTURE
Having identified its overall objectives, key policies and priority actions, the Council needed to put in place a

Table 52.1 The Heritage Council / An Chomhairle Oidhreachta					
Committees 2000 (to June)					
Standing Committee on Archaeology	Standing Committee on Inland Waterways	Standing Committee on Wildlife	Standing Committee on Architecture	Museums and Archives Committee	Education and Communication Committee
John Waddell *Chairperson*	Ruth Delany *Chairperson*	Micheline Sheehy Skeffington *Chairperson*	Orna Hanly *Chairperson*	Michael Ryan *Chairperson*	Ruth Delaney *Chairperson*
10 members	8 members	10 members	11 members	9 members	6 members

structure which was going to work efficiently in order that the objectives could be achieved. The key elements of the structure, each with agreed responsibilities, and included in *The Plan 1997–2000* and included here in terms of their current status (mid-2000) are:

Council — responsible for all major policy and financial matters, structure development, procedures and performance review.

Committees — (**Table 52.1**) to perform functions delegated by the Council and advise it on policy and action in their functional areas.

Working Groups — to carry out specific time-limited tasks for the Council or Committees.

Staff — (**Table 52.2**) to conduct day-to-day business, to provide expert policy advice and to undertake development and representational work as required.

By the spring of 1997, the major part of the Council's structure was functioning. Two additional Committees were established, covering Museums and Archives and Education and Promotion, twelve of the projected full-time staff were in place and a number of small working groups had been established to carry out particular aspects of policy development which would be proposed to government.

FINANCING THE HERITAGE COUNCIL'S PLAN

The Heritage Council is, of course, a national body with specific statutory responsibilities for the national heritage. Its administrative costs come directly from the national exchequer. This represents 23% of its total budget. The remaining funding is provided by the National Lottery. In 1996, the Council had a budget of £1.9m. In 1997 that increased to £3.0m and in 1998 and 1999 to £4.0m.

The doubling of Council's budget over a twelve-month period would seem reasonable by any modern standards. However, when matched against the costed projections to the year 2000 published by Council in its *Plan*, the shortfall in heritage spending at policy level becomes apparent. The projected figures were ambitious but realistic. Council has matched its proposed expenditure to specific budget areas and in many cases to specific projects. The budget area and the proposed expenditure in each area as they were intended to have been in the late 1990s are shown in **Table 52.3**.

The Council's *Plan 1997–2000* provides details of where and how the money was to have been targeted

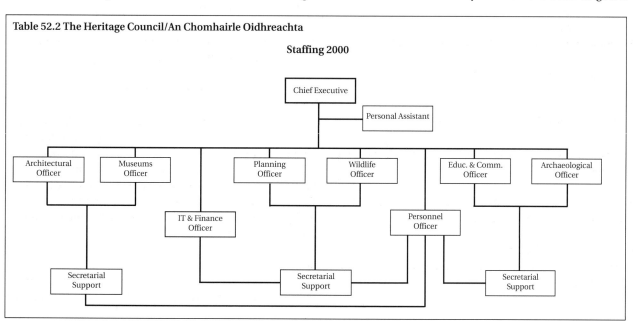

Table 52.2 The Heritage Council/An Chomhairle Oidhreachta

Staffing 2000

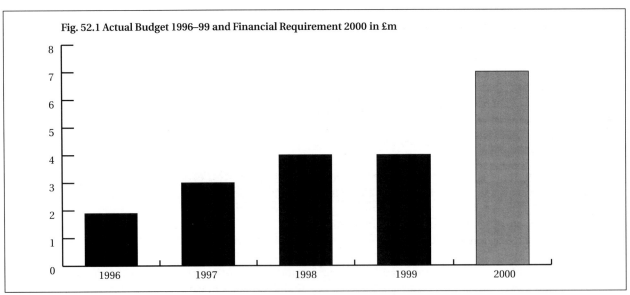

Fig. 52.1 Actual Budget 1996–99 and Financial Requirement 2000 in £m

over each year. **Fig. 52.2** shows the breakdown of areas of expenditure for the year 1997.

The Council recognized at a very early stage that even taking into account the very healthy state of the economy, it was unlikely to secure all its funding needs from central government sources. It could be argued that the *Heritage Act* anticipated this, as it contains sections which provide the Council with a degree of freedom and flexibility to raise funding from other sources. There is a need to secure core funding from the state. It is, however, an entirely modern and acceptable approach to financial management that agencies should seek to attract other sources of funding.

FUNDING STRATEGIES

The Council put in place a number of plans to secure funding for the national heritage. The fundamental basis for all these strategies is that the financing is not for the Heritage Council *per se* but is for heritage projects on the widest front. The Council developed a portfolio of such projects for which funding is required but which it did not initially have the resources to assist. A number of

Table 52.3 Summary of Estimated Expenditure 1997 — Anticipated Financial Requirements 1998–2000

AREA	1997 £	1998 £	1999 £	2000 £
Collection of Data	320,000.00	458,000.00	325,000.00	270,000.00
Promotion of Pride	250,000.00	425,000.00	460,000.00	395,000.00
Proposing Policy	170,000.00	245,000.00	280,000.00	340,000.00
Administration/Staffing	702,000.00	950,000.00	1,200,000.00	1,400,000.00
Heritage Grants	150,000.00	1,000,000.00	1,000,000.00	1,000,000.00
Contingency	150,000.00	200,000.00	250,000.00	300,000.00
Discovery Programme	630,000.00	800,000.00	900,000.00	1,000,000.00
*Grant Commitments	600,000.00	1,500,000.00	250,000.00	
Buildings at Risk		3,000,000.00	5,000,000.00	6,000,000.00
Research and Development	20,000.00	10,000.00	20,000.00	30,000.00
Fundraising Partnerships		30,000.00	40,000.00	50,000.00
Biodiversity		40,000.00	500,000.00	1,000,000.00
**Headquarters		1,000,000.00	100,000.00	
TOTALS	**2,992,000.00**	**9,658,000.00**	**10,325,000.00**	**11,785,000.00**

* Maximum possible sum

** Special allocation for acquisition and fitting out of permanent HQ

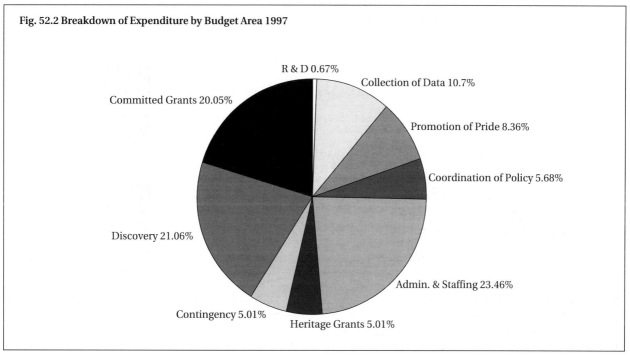

Fig. 52.2 Breakdown of Expenditure by Budget Area 1997

R & D 0.67%
Collection of Data 10.7%
Committed Grants 20.05%
Promotion of Pride 8.36%
Coordination of Policy 5.68%
Discovery 21.06%
Admin. & Staffing 23.46%
Contingency 5.01%
Heritage Grants 5.01%

avenues were explored in association with national and international agencies, all of which expressed interest in becoming involved in supporting heritage projects. Council saw to it that its strategies translated those expressions of interest into the hard cash required to allow our national heritage to develop in a sustainable manner.

PROGRESS TO DATE
The Council reviews implementation of its work programmes on a regular basis. Its review of the *Plan 1997–2000* is ongoing and much has been achieved. Since its establishment, Council fulfilled its primary function of proposing policies and priorities for the national heritage by making recommendations to the minister in the following areas, among others:

• state sector spend on the national heritage;

• impact of forestry on the national heritage;

• impact of existing agricultural schemes on the natural heritage;

• building regulations and the architectural heritage;

• planning and the national heritage.

In addition, the Council awarded grants through a number of specific schemes including a community grant scheme which seeks to promote pride in our heritage at a local community level. Partnership initiatives have been developed with local authorities and in

particular a pilot scheme to appoint Heritage Officers in local authorities is well advanced.

THE FUTURE
Council members are appointed for a five-year period. The period of appointment of the first Heritage Council ended in July 2000. The Council, whilst recognizing that its work is designed to produce benefits in the long run, is obviously keen that tangible benefits to the national heritage will have been identified over the first five years. Those benefits were of both a policy and a practical nature. From a practical point of view, the Council has supported heritage initiatives which meet its own overall objectives. Support was of a financial kind (and the sums required were often very small), but assistance was often given through advice or general guidance. The expertise available to the Council through the structure it has established is substantial, and providing that advice, freely given on many occasions, was encouraged right throughout the organization. The development, and indeed acceptance, of policies which will produce long-term benefits for our heritage is ultimately what the Council intended to achieve. Conducting the necessary research (data collection) and carrying out the appropriate consultation within a five-year time scale was no easy task, particularly when an organization had to be developed from scratch. It was the Council's intention, however, that for each of the areas of national heritage which were identified as priorities in its *Plan 1997–2000*, policies and priorities were proposed to government, or at the very least seemed sufficiently far advanced, in order for the new Council members to take the organization forward in the twenty-first century.

The Arts Council/An Chomhairle Ealaíon

Nessa O' Mahony and Mary Hyland

The Arts Council/An Chomhairle Ealaíon is the development agency for the arts in Ireland and is the primary source of support for the individual creative and interpretative artist. Underpinning its decisions and policies is the principle that everyone is entitled to access to and participation in the arts. As an autonomous state body the Arts Council works in two distinct but obviously linked spheres: as a policy-maker advising government, and as direct support of artists and arts organizations.

POLICY AND STRUCTURE

The first *Arts Plan*, prepared by the Arts Council in 1994 and adopted by government in 1995, was the first national plan for the arts in the history of the state. The plan described the Arts Council's strategies for promoting quality and innovation in all aspects of the practice of the arts, and for encouraging genuine participation in the arts.

Following extensive consultation with the sector throughout 1998, the Arts Council submitted its second plan for the arts, covering the period 1999 to 2001, to the Department of Arts, Heritage, Gaeltacht and the Islands in early May and it was submitted to cabinet in July. The new *Arts Plan* proposes a more developmental approach for the Arts Council. The purpose of this is to create a new environment in which the arts can flourish and be appreciated at home, while gaining greater international recognition abroad.

The core objectives of the plan are the promotion of excellence and innovation, the development of participation in, and audiences for, the arts and the development of the arts sector itself. The Arts Council will conduct extensive research to identify the developmental needs of the sector, will target funding at particular need areas, promote the international dimension for Irish art and artists and work closely with local authorities to promote activities at a local level.

Building on the first *Arts Plan*, the second plan was shaped by reflection, research and by dialogue. It addressed those issues arising out of a series of consultative fora, as well as those analysed in *Succeeding better*, the recent Indecon/PricewaterhouseCoopers report. The Arts Council looks forward to the opportunity of working with arts practitioners to shape the future of arts policy in the new three-year period.

The more popularly recognized face of the Arts Council is in its role as supporter of artists and art organizations. The support takes many forms, including advice, usually in the form of liaison with the relevant arts officer; information, through its freely available publications, and direct financial assistance. It can do this principally because it receives grant-in-aid annually from government as part of the national budget. In 2000, this amounted to £34.5m in revenue and capital funding, which the Council allocated to more than 400 arts organizations and some 500 individual artists. The annual grant-in-aid received by the Council has, since 1986, included money from the National Lottery.

As a publicly accountable body, the Arts Council publishes an annual report and accounts to provide the Oireachtas and the general public with an overview of the year's work. In addition, it produces a number of publications detailing funding opportunities and criteria and the work of the Arts Council. The Council is also committed to developing its accessibility through the use of information technology. It has its own website (*http://www.artscouncil.ie*) and each of its staff has an e-mail address for increased access. Aosdána, the association of creative artists established by the Arts Council, also has a website (*http://www.artscouncil.ie/aosdana*), carrying information on the organization and its activities.

The Arts Council is made up of 16 members and a chairperson, all voluntary, who ae appointed by government for a period of not more than five years. The current Council was appointed in June 1998 and is supported by a 32-member staff which includes a director, four assistant directors and officers in areas such as drama, film, music, visual arts, dance, opera and local development. The Council usually meets in full plenary meetings ten times a year, and there are more frequent meetings of a range of specialist committees made up of Council members.

In all its activities, the Arts Council recognizes that Ireland is a bilingual society and provides equally for artists and audiences who use Irish and English. Furthermore, it has a bilingual policy in relation to its own publications. The highest concentration of artistic activity through the medium of Irish is in literature and drama, but there is a significant Irish-language dimension within a number of other disciplines including music and film. The Council also supports the Irish Traditional Music Archive and several multidisciplinary arts festivals which operate bilingually. In allocating funds to the arts in Irish, the Council does not apply a 'quota-based' approach. Instead, it looks for means of identifying the particular developmental needs of arts practitioners and communities working bilingually or exclusively in Irish and forms appropriate partnerships to address these needs. An example here is the creation and funding of three full-time specialist arts officer posts for Gaeltacht areas, in a joint action with Údarás na Gaeltachta.

The Arts Council is also keen to establish cross-border arts activities and works closely with the Arts Council of Northern Ireland. A tangible example of the co-operation between the two Councils is the evolution of agreed mechanisms for considering applications made to both Councils. All-island resource organizations in music, literature and other practices receive funding from both Councils, and the Arts Council has supported tours by Irish performance companies and visual art exhibitions in Northern venues. Multidisciplinary festivals and community arts provide much scope for cross-border and co-operative exchanges and are funded accordingly. The Tyrone Guthrie Centre in Annaghma-kerrig, an artists' retreat in county Monaghan, is funded jointly by the two Councils.

FINANCIAL PLANNING

The pattern of the Arts Council's work over the year is set by the annual allocation of funds from government and the needs of the applicants for those funds. Each year the Council sets aside a number of days to discuss broad policy issues, and this discussion forms the basis of the Council's budget for the year. In formulating policy the Arts Council is keenly aware of the necessity for consultation with both the arts community and the wider public, as evidenced by the extensive consultation that took place during the preparation of the second *Arts Plan*.

The budget is prepared with reference to the Council's own development priorities and the needs of artists and arts organizations as reflected in the applications received. The budget must also take into account the Council's role in arts research and advocacy, and its own running costs. Policy and demand determine the budget priorities within each arts discipline or arts practice. These vary widely, depending on the level of development of the particular arts discipline and the other systems of support available. The Council may decide on both short- and long-term strategies, shaped by its own informed view, as well as by independent research and consultation with the arts sector.

Within the main budget, there is a partnership budget which represents the Council's expenditure on strategic partnerships in a number of key areas, principally that of local authorities. This is a key aspect of funding in that it supports artistic activity at local level and stimulates and encourages expenditure on local arts from other agencies. To date, of the 33 local authorities in the Republic of Ireland, 32 now employ arts officers. The actual programmes in each county are extremely diverse and include residencies, festivals, exhibitions, performances and so forth. Currently more than 80 festivals are grant-aided by the Council. As well as increasing access to the arts at community level, these festivals can also have a major economic impact in the locality.

The Arts Council also engages in partnership arrangements with other statutory and non-statutory bodies including the National Youth Council of Ireland, Macra na Feirme and the health boards of the Eastern Regional Health Authority. In the Arts and Disability area, the Council has been involved in partnership projects involving Youthreach, FÁS and other agencies, which aim to provide support to people with disabilities to pursue a career in the arts by providing training opportunities in management, administration, facilitation and technical skills.

Direct support to artforms comes through funds which are allocated under separate budget programmes. In 2000, the Arts Council, for the first time, spent money on the basis of cross-disciplinary programmes and sub-programmes rather than according to artform. This was because the cross-discipline approach allowed Council to focus more clearly on what organizations did, and the extent to which their activities met the Council's own strategic priorities. The programmes range from awards to individual artists (Programme 1) to projects and schemes (Programme 2), revenue and minor capital grants to professional, service and representative organizations (Programme 3) and major capital grants (Programme 4).

Each year, the Arts Council allocates a dedicated fund for capital purposes. In 2000, there was a capital provision of over £4m in the Council's budget. This was distributed in three areas: equipment, small buildings and repairs, and major proposals. The Council believes that providing good buildings and facilities for the arts is central to their development. Special priority is given to projects which involve increasing physical access to arts venues for those with special needs. This can involve ramps, audio loop systems, signage, lifts, toilet facilities and the like.

In the recent past applications for capital funds have helped broaden the scope of this funding category. One such innovative programme to receive funding was the Music Instrument Fund for Ireland which was established to create a pool of high-quality musical instruments for loan to talented young musicians from all over the country.

The procedures for applicants seeking funds is clearly laid out. Individual artists should direct their application to the Artists' Support Executive. Traditionally, the Arts Council has provided revenue funding to arts organizations on an annual basis, inviting applications for funding and taking decisions on grant allocations each year. However, from the year 2000 onwards, the Arts Council has begun to move to another basis for funding arts organizations. It has piloted an approach with a number of organizations to fund them on a three-year basis. This will allow groups to extend their capacity to plan, and to allow funding and planning horizons to complement each other. The Arts Council will move to fund a greater number of organizations on a multi-annual basis later in 2000.

In supporting and promoting Irish culture, the Arts Council does not look solely to artistic work carried out on the island of Ireland, but provides both direct and indirect support for the international dimension of the arts. Direct support includes travel awards, exchange programmes and ARTFLIGHT. A variety of resource organizations whose activities have a strong international dimension are also assisted, and these have included Theatre Shop and *Circa* magazine. The international arts experience of many Irish artists and audiences is greatly enhanced by foreign artists and production companies who visit one of the many international festivals throughout the country or who tour around Irish venues. Therefore support is given to major exhibition venues hosting significant international work and to international film, drama, music and literature festivals.

In the EU context the Arts Council has been nominated as Ireland's Cultural Contact Point. It is responsible for providing information about future cultural policy at European level and the dissemination of information and application forms for the current arts-related production companies or building-based organizations. The majority of arts organizations include production companies, publishers and promoters. The Council regards these as the powerhouse of the arts in Ireland in that they bring together creative and interpretative artists, managers, design and production staff and technical specialists of all kinds. They represent a major point of interaction between the public and artists, whether they are playwrights, actors, visual artists, musicians, dancers or writers.

THE INDIVIDUAL ARTIST

The Arts Council's goals are to support individual artists to achieve their full artistic potential, and to improve the viability of the the arts as a career, in Ireland and abroad; to direct funding towards excellence and innovation in the promotion of the arts, and to support artists working through Irish and in indigenous arts (chiefly traditional music and dance) to achieve their full potential and increase audiences.

The Arts Council/An Chomhairle Ealaíon annually makes around 450 awards to individuals throughout all of the artforms. Awards range in value from *ca.* £600–£8,000 (for some two-year bursaries) and are assessed competitively. The Arts Council and Aer Lingus collaborate in operating ARTFLIGHT — a scheme that offers opportunities to almost 1,000 artists and people working in the arts to travel outside Ireland.

The Arts Council and the British Council co-fund the 'Go See' award which enables people working in the arts to travel in Britain and Ireland to develop professional contacts and to explore touring, exchange or co-operative artistic ventures. Bord na Gaeilge also contributes to the fund.

ELIGIBILITY

Awards are open to people born or resident in Ireland and Northern Ireland. Due to the competitive nature of the awards and schemes, and the large number of applicants, it is not possible to make an award to all eligible applicants. Anyone considering applying for funding should obtain a copy of *Awards and opportunities*, a guide to Arts Council awards, bursaries and schemes.

Other support for the individual artist comes through Aosdána, an affiliation of artists which was established by the Arts Council in 1983. It honours those artists whose work has made an outstanding contribution to the arts in Ireland, in order to encourage, and in some cases assist them financially, in devoting their energies fully to their art.

CONCLUSION

In 1999, the government adopted the Arts Council's second *Arts Plan 1999–2001* and committed £100m in funding for that three-year period. The £34.5m committed in 2000 represented a 23% increase on the previous year. Despite these advances, direct public expenditure on the arts and museums in Ireland remains low when compared with other European countries. According to a report published in March 2000 by the International Arts Bureau, out of nine countries surveyed, Ireland's per capita spend on arts and museums was £10.48 in 1997, compared with £14.07 (including Lottery funding) in Northern Ireland, £14.23 in England (Lottery funding included), £17.35 in Scotland (including Lottery funding) and £19.98 in Australia.

The Arts Council would like to see substantial further growth in funding, in order to fully realise the opportunities for development now open to the arts in Ireland. Meanwhile, it is continuing the tasks set out in the second *Arts Plan* to promote artistic excellence and innovation, to develop participation in and audiences for the arts and to build capacity in the arts sector.

Bibliography

Arts Council (Ireland) 1951–98 *Annual report.* Dublin.
Arts Council (Ireland) 1986 *Art matters.* Dublin.
Arts Council (Ireland) 1992 *The guide to exhibition venues in Ireland.* Dublin.
Arts Council (Ireland) 1995 *Views of theatre in Ireland,* Dublin.
Arts Council (Ireland) 1998a *About the Arts Council.* Dublin.
Arts Council (Ireland) 1998b *Arts Council (Ireland) revenue funding.* Dublin.
Arts Council (Ireland) 1998c *Via — your guide to international arts information.* Dublin.
Arts Council (Ireland) 1999a *Local authorities and the arts: a four-year perspective.* Dublin.
Arts Council (Ireland) 1999b *The Arts Plan 1999–2001.* Dublin.
Arts Council (Ireland) 2000 *Awards and opportunities.* Dublin.
Arts Council (Ireland) and Arts Council of Northern Ireland 1999 *Arts and disability handbook.* Dublin.
Clancy, P. *et al.* 1994 *The public and the arts: a survey of behaviour and attitudes in Ireland.* Dublin.
Combat Poverty Agency 1997 *Poverty: access and participation in the arts.* Dublin.
Erika E. King Associates 1998 *Film in Ireland: the role of the Arts Council.* Dublin.
Kennedy, B. 1990 *Dreams and responsibilities: the state and the arts in independent Ireland.* Dublin.
Leatherdale, A. and Todd, V. n.d. *Shall we dance? A report on vocational dance training.* Dublin.

The Role of FÁS

PATRICK CARLETON

FÁS (Foras Áiseanna Saothair), since its inception in 1967 (it was formerly ANCO, the training authority), has contributed in a significant way to the preservation and promotion of Ireland's rich heritage. It currently administers a broad range of community-based programmes within the South West region, for example, which enhance the area's social, economic and cultural development. Such programmes include:

• Community Enterprise Programme (CEP)

• Community Youth Training Programme (CYTP)

• Community Employment (CE)

• Community Response (CR).

The CEP scheme deals with project management, the provision of a business development officer and the general administration of projects. CYTP contributes through the restoration and reconstruction of buildings and sites, CE through the provision of caretakers, catering, tour guide service and security, and CR in the context of research and administration. All FÁS projects are managed by professional, qualified personnel, and they work in close co-operation with the local community.

The types of heritage project sponsored by the organization include genealogical surveys and research, parish indexation, tracing ancestry through to museums, graveyard surveys/restoration, tourism-related ones and the revival of culture through folklore, song, dance and theatre. FÁS has adopted an integrated approach in the development and management of its projects. Such integrated co-operation is evidenced in those listed below:

• *Jeanie Johnston* Project, Tralee, county Kerry

• Sliabh Luachra Heritage Centre, Scartaglen, county Kerry

• Michael J. Quill, Visitors Centre, Kilgarvan, county Kerry

• Bealick Mill Restoration, Macroom, county Cork

• Model Village, Clonakilty, county Cork

• Jameson Heritage Centre, Midleton, county Cork

These projects will be considered in some detail later in the chapter, but first we examine the key FÁS programmes through which assistance is provided and the principles underlying the organization's contribution to social and cultural advancement in Ireland.

COMMUNITY PARTICIPATION AND PROGRAMME EVALUATION

FÁS will consider any project from any group which is non-commercial and which will represent community interest. To ensure the relevance and quality of training for the young persons involved, the organization carefully examines each proposal in terms of its worth as a training vehicle and its long-term benefit to the local community. In this connection, it may be noted that in recent years there has been a marked increase in the number of tourism-related projects such as heritage and interpretative centres. All proposed projects are examined by a local vetting committee, which is comprised of representatives from trade unions, the Construction Industry Federation and FÁS. Each venture is evaluated in the light of the training opportunities it provides, the availability of young unemployed persons and, finally, the benefit to the local community. Once approved at local level, projects are then submitted for final sanction to the National Vetting Committee in

Dublin. This process brings about objectivity in project selection. One of its primary strengths is the strong community involvement in both the implementation and design of the scheme. FÁS adopts a 'bottom up' approach, examining suggestions and advice from local bodies. This ensures that the sponsoring groups are involved from conception onwards to completion.

FÁS, in conjunction with the sponsoring group, recruits the participants locally, pays training allowances for the duration of the project, as well as food and accommodation allowances where required. The organization also pays a grant to the sponsor to facilitate the employment of a supervisor. FÁS supplies administrative backup, office facilities and equipment. Furthermore, a FÁS instructor implements the training programme and maintains liaison with the sponsoring group. The broader objectives of community- and tourism-based projects are:

(i) to provide on-the-job training and experience to local unemployed;

(ii) to facilitate the transfer of skills from skilled crafts persons to first-time job seekers, and

(iii) to increase local awareness of tourism opportunities and potential.

FÁS is fully committed to assisting communities in their efforts to enhance local social and tourist facilities. The concept of building FÁS programmes around community-based activities helps construct an invaluable relationship between the state, local people and the unemployed. Towards this end, various detailed means of assistance are furnished, and these mechanisms are now considered individually in turn.

CEP

The Community Enterprise Programme provides a package of advice, training and financial assistance to community groups who want to become involved in the creation of economically viable jobs to help themselves. It makes resources available to local groups to assist them in developing their own ideas and in tapping into the resources and services of other statutory, commercial or voluntary bodies. The types of product and service provided by community groups are varied, and frequently emerge from the identification of a local resource which is under-utilized. They often involve small manufacturing projects with the potential to fill a market niche. Gaps in locally provided services also represent important opportunities. The programme concentrates its assistance and support on supplementing the skill and expertise of local groups. Its thrust is to assist groups through the development stages of a

business, from the initial idea to trading.

Many groups who are interested in local enterprise as a means of creating employment may often need advice and support in further developing their ideas. As with any commercial venture, not only is technical and commercial expertise vital to success but group-building skills, particularly in the case of communities, are also necessary.

Having committed themselves to the enterprise option, the group is now in a position to generate and investigate possible job-creation ideas. At this stage, through the help of FÁS, the group completes a business development plan. During this process, if necessary, FÁS can provide grant aid for feasibility studies to quantify the market and commercial viability of the idea.

If a number of identified project ideas have passed the initial feasibility stage and show some viable potential, the group may apply to FÁS for grant aid for the recruitment of an Enterprise Worker. The role of this person is to appraise the initial feasibility of the ideas, including market research, assessing initial costs and capital requirements and developing the business idea to the point of start-up. At this start-up stage, the community group can make an application to FÁS for grant aid for recruitment of a project manager and later on worker wage subsidies, depending on the stage of evolution of the project. During the life of the business, FÁS will help the management group with further development, where necessary, to run the project more effectively. At various stages, further grant aid may be made available for diversification and development of products or services. Under the CEP programme, training modules (**Table 54.1**) are provided at various stages in the project's development

During the start-up stages of the business, FÁS will be available to help with advice and expertise when required. Consultation with a Local Enterprise Development Officer is an option to help the group decide how best these training modules can be used to meet their particular training and development needs.

Groups may enter this process at various stages of development. The training provided is flexible and the delivery can be customized to suit the specific needs of the business at hand. Through this staged approach to a project, the group builds up the skills necessary to manage a developing enterprise. Ongoing monitoring of progress is seen as vital in all aspects of the training modules provided. Advice and access to other state supports are also offered. In particular, co-operatives can be helped further by the FÁS Co-operative Development Unit.

At the time of writing (late 1999), a development grant of up to £2,000 toward product investigation and group development may be provided. Up to £17,500 is available towards the employment of an Enterprise Worker for a

Table 54.1

MODULE	NO. OF SESSIONS	OBJECTIVES	DEVELOPMENT OF THE BUSINESS
A	6	To clarify objectives and explore enterprise options.	Enterprise group forms for the first time.
B	11	Strengthen group organization and links to community.	Group is formed, explores possible business ideas.
C	10	Identify a business idea and test market and feasibility.	Group identifies and tests possible business idea.
D	24	Fundamental business management and business plan.	Group prepares for start-up following feasibility test.
E	10	Monitor key business areas.	Group trades for first time. Critical issues and performance monitoring.
F	3	Performance review.	Group is trading.

period of 52 weeks to develop the specific business ideas to the point of start-up. Alternately this grant, *pro rata*, can be used toward consultancy costs for the development of specific business ideas. Furthermore, assistance is forthcoming towards the costs of development and management of the new project by the following means. A commercial aid grant of £14,000 is forthcoming to meet the management and administration cost of the new commercial enterprise for a period of one year. On a minimum salary of £5,000 per worker, a commercial aid grant in the form of wage subsidies is available for commercially viable projects in manufacturing (up to £3,750 per worker) and selected services sectors (up to £2,500 per worker). FÁS will also assist in the delivery of training modules to help the community group investigate, develop and manage the particular enterprise project.

CYTP

The FÁS Community Youth Training Programme provides training for unemployed young people aged between 16–25 years who have registered for employment with FÁS Employment Services Office. The FÁS South West Region operating budget for the programme for 1999 was £1.3 million. Involvement in the programme enhances the trainees' prospects of employment and helps improve confidence and self-reliance.

FÁS will consider projects from any community group which is non-commercial and which represents local interests. Groups having projects providing suitable training for young people and benefiting the community must submit their suggestion to a Community Services Manager, at the local Training Centre, for help in the development and planning stages. To ensure the broadest scope of training for young people, FÁS encourages communities to forward a wide variety of proposals. Many of the projects submitted to date have centred on the renovation, construction and decoration of premises. FÁS also welcomes proposals involving engineering-type skills and suggestions with a social, historical or cultural orientation. Projects are approved only where it can be shown that they could not be carried out in the normal contractual manner.

All proposals are examined by a local project committee. Each project is evaluated in the light of the training opportunities it provides, the availability of young unemployed people and the benefits to the community. Once recommended at local level, projects are submitted for approval to FÁS, the Irish Congress of Trade Unions and the Construction Industry Federation. FÁS pays training allowances to trainees on the CYTP programme. It also provides grants to the sponsor to facilitate the employment of a supervisor. A FÁS instructor implements training, monitors the standard of training on the job and liaises with the sponsor. The responsibilities of the community group (the sponsor) are:

Stage 1: to compile a proposal and submit it to the Manager, Community Services, at the local FÁS Training Centre (advice on the information required in the proposal, for instance training opportunities, advantages to community, funding of purchasing of materials and so forth, is available from the Centre):

Stage 2: to confirm, where relevant, ownership of site or property involved, obtain any authorizations required, such as planning permission, provide all necessary specifications of work required, employ, in consultation with FÁS, a supervisor, provide the required insurance cover, supply materials and equipment/machinery to standards demanded by statutory regulations.

CE

Community Employment is a FÁS programme that benefits both the community and the participants. Over 5,500 participants were employed on over 360 CE projects throughout the South West region with a total investment in excess of £41 million during 1999. The projects included such areas as sport, recreation, heritage, environment, urban and rural renewal, research, arts, community advice, tourism, schools, care for the elderly and many others.

CE provides those who are unemployed with valuable part-time work opportunities and training development options. To qualify for the part-time integration option one must be:

• 21 years of age or over and in receipt of Unemployment Benefit, Unemployment Assistance or Lone Parent's Allowance for one year or longer, or

• be a member of the Travelling Community of any age in receipt of Unemployment Benefit or Unemployment Assistance for any period or on Lone Parent's Allowance for one year or longer, or

• be registered with the National Rehabilitation Board.

To qualify for the Part-Time Job option one must be:

• 35 years of age or over and in receipt of Unemployment Benefit or Unemployment Assistance or Lone Parent's Allowance for one year or longer, or

• a member of the Travelling Community of any age in receipt of Unemployment assistance or Lone Parent's Allowance for one year or longer, or

• 35 years of age or over and registered with the National Rehabilitation Board.

To make up the qualifying requirement, an applicant may combine a period in receipt of the above payments with a period on a recognized training or employment programme.

There is an increased emphasis on the provision of local job-related training/development for participants to support their progression into employment. Improved selection/vetting of projects ensures their linkage to subsequent placement opportunities. The provision of development modules for sponsor groups has been expanded further to support this process. Specific and focussed training is aimed at the Sponsor Management Groups to support them in achieving the maximum outcome for their project. FÁS Community Services continually monitors progression routes taken by Community Employment participants to ascertain information on the levels of advancement shown by them. Participants who are not placed in employment near the end of their period on CE are referred back to FÁS Placement Services for further progression support.

CR

Community Response projects are non-construction programmes subject to the same conditions that apply to CYTP. CR programmes include heritage-based projects of a genealogical and research nature as well as surveys. The aim of genealogical projects, for example, is to transcribe parish records from book format to computer format in order to protect and preserve the valuable church book registers of births, marriages and deaths, and to provide easy access to these sources via information technology (IT) to the public at home and abroad. Projects follow a definite professional code of practice in archival material and research techniques. A given scheme will also carry out research work in local history, for instance archaeological surveys, graveyard surveys and items on local places, people and events of the past. Current genealogical projects in the region featuring Parish Indexation include:

• Cork City Ancestral Project (Diocese of Cork and Ross)

• Mallow Heritage Centre (Cloyne Diocese)

• Killarney Genealogy Project (Kerry Diocese).

During the course of FÁS involvement in projects, in many cases the organization's contribution to the socio-economic benefit to the community becomes the springboard for regeneration. For example, FÁS initially became involved in the Blennerville Windmill Project, Tralee, county Kerry, through the Community Enterprise Programme, leading to CYTP participation and finally the management of the project. However, this involvement has been the catalyst for other ventures in which FÁS are heavily committed, for instance the *Jeanie Johnston* Project, to be discussed shortly. These schemes in themselves have been the motivators for both business and community to develop Tralee's heritage tourism potential.

HERITAGE PROJECTS IN THE SOUTH WEST REGION
Having reviewed the guiding principles and individual means whereby FÁS contributes to community and cultural development, we shall now examine a range of projects in which it had a significant impact. Examples

are given from throughout the South West and reflect a variety of activities. The background to and evolution of each project is summarized and attention is drawn to the specific FÁS programmes which have been in operation in each case.

THE JEANIE JOHNSTON PROJECT

The *Jeanie Johnston* Project is one of the most ambitious maritime heritage ventures undertaken in Ireland in recent years. It involves the construction of a full-size sailing replica of the famous Irish emigrant barque (a nineteenth-century sailing ship) *Jeanie Johnston* (1847–58), which carried Irish emigrants from Tralee to Baltimore, New York and Quebec during the Famine years. Unlike the infamous 'coffin ships' of the period, the *Jeanie Johnston* never lost a passenger or crew member during sixteen months of trans-Atlantic voyages. At the time of writing, the replica ship was being built at Blennerville, near Tralee, by young people from Ireland, north and south, working under the supervision of experienced shipwrights through FÁS. The reborn vessel was being constructed under the CYTP programme with its young workers trained in the skills of shipbuilding by an international team of shipwrights. In June 2000 the *Jeanie Johnston* was to make her Millennium Voyage to North America, visiting over 20 cities and bringing with her the hopes and good wishes of a new and peaceful Ireland. The *Jeanie Johnston* Project binds Ireland, north and south, both unionist and nationalist. It links the country with its extended communities in the United States and Canada, and harnesses the good-will for Ireland that exists in Britain, Continental Europe and North America. It provides job opportunities and skills training for unemployed young people. It safeguards traditional skills which were being lost, focuses attention on Ireland's maritime heritage while also commemorating a defining moment in the history of our island.

The project is being promoted by the broadly based *Jeanie Johnston* Memorial Committee, a not-for-profit group chaired by Dr Henry Lyons of the Institute of Technology in Tralee. The group has a track record of success in completing major undertakings. Previous achievements include the restoration of Blennerville Windmill and Tralee Steam Railway. In January 1999, the *Jeanie Johnston* Committee was awarded the AIB/RTÉ Better Ireland National Award for Community Development. The total cost of the venture is £4.5m. Financial support is being provided by the Irish government, the European Union, the International Fund for Ireland, Shannon Development, FÁS, municipal authorities, state agencies and the friends of Ireland in the United States and Canada. The project continues to attract a high public and international profile. It has featured on the US PBS network, UTV and German ZDF Channel, as well as news reports in the London *Times*, *Irish Times*, *ArMen* (a French sailing periodical) and the German publication *Kieler Nachrichten*.

SLIABH LUACHRA HERITAGE CENTRE

Sliabh Luachra, spanning the Cork/Kerry border, has always been central to Irish cultural history. It was here that certain of the Fianna legends were located, some of the earliest Christian settlements in the country lie within the region and the works of its poets, such as Aoghan Ó Rathaille and Eoghan Rua Ó Súilleabháin, give expression in verse to many parts of Gaelic cultural heritage. Sliabh Luachra has always been famous for its music, and the region acts as both a reservoir and a primary source of authentic musical tradition. The great fiddle player, Pádraig O'Keeffe, came from the area. A monument has been erected in Scartaglin to his memory. Some other famous musicians from the locality include Den Tarrant, Denis Murphy, Julia Clifford, Tom Billy Murphy and Gerry McCarthy. During the traditional music and dance revival of the 1960s and 1970s, Sliabh Luachra's cultural ethos became (and remains) a dominant one, both at home and world-wide.

The village of Scartaglin has for centuries been central to this tradition, and its annual *fleadh cheoil*, now running for over thirty years, has become a mecca for traditional music lovers nationally and internationally who seek the authentic, uncommercialized musical heritage of mountain, valley and glen. The Cultural Heritage Centre at Scartaglin gives a structured and coherent expression to this authentic traditional ethos by providing a resource centre for various activities and a focal point for the Sliabh Luachra region. The Centre incorporates:

• Ceolann, a multi-purpose exhibition area;

• a book and music shop with catering facilities;

• evening entertainment;

• an academic programme;

• a recording capability and an IT facility.

Seven committee members have been involved in the project since its commencement. In late 1999 there were seven CE scheme participants and eight trainees on the CYTP programme.

MICHAEL J. QUILL VISITORS CENTRE

Michael J. Quill Visitors Centre (**Fig. 54.1**) is a cross-community initiative which honours a famous son of Kilgarvan. The idea of commemorating Mike Quill, founder and first President of the powerful Transport

Fig. 54.1 Michael Quill centre, Kilgarvan, county Kerry.

Workers Union of America, in his native place, originated in New York among his contemporaries. Kilgarvan emigrants contacted the Kilgarvan Community Enterprise Committee, which wholeheartedly supported the proposal and began working towards making it a reality. Fundraising commenced on both sides of the Atlantic and $70,000 was realized by supporters in New York.

Following extensive consultation and research, the Kerry Parents and Friends Association were invited to submit a proposition for a fitting memorial to Mike Quill which would also benefit the local community. The Association proposed to establish a resource centre in Kilgarvan named after Quill which would provide training and employment opportunities for adults with a learning disability (mental handicap) living in the Kilgarvan and Kenmare areas. Employment opportunities for non-disabled local people were also part of the proposal. Agreement was reached and the former Church of Ireland church, St Peters, was identified as a suitable location for the Mike Quill Centre. A local committee representative of many community groups was established to oversee and support the project.

The Kerry Parents and Friends Association Successfully applied to FÁS for a CYTP project, and work commenced in 1992. Over the following three years, the building was renovated in its original style with no effort and little expense spared in sourcing and using original materials, for instance slates. Stained-glass windows were expertly restored and weather-glazed and remain a feature of the building.

Extensive site excavation and development were necessary to provide car and coach parking facilities. Stone excavated from the site was used to build traditional stone walls throughout which have attracted favourable comment from locals and visitors. These stone walls were built by young FÁS workers who took enormous pride in their work. The site layout includes walkways and areas for picnics and relaxation overlooking the magnificent Roughty Valley and Ardtully Castle.

The Mike Quill Centre provides three full-time jobs for local people from April to September each year. In addition, six people with a learning disability work five days each week, under the supervision of a qualified craft instructor, making craft items for sale at the Centre. Many of the other items on sale in the Centre have been made locally or in workshops for people with disabilities throughout the country. During the winter months, the Quill Centre is used by the Kerry Parents and Friends Association and local community groups.

Fig. 54.2. Bealick Mill, Macroom, county Cork.

The Michael J. Quill Centre is a truly cross-community initiative which continues to draw on the indigenous resources the Kilgarvan district. It has become a primary tourist focal point and is an accredited Tourist Information Centre and Bureau de Change. The Centre has co-operated with local community groups and business interests in promoting tourism in the Kilgarvan area. It advertizes extensively in the tourist market. FÁS continues to be involved with the Quill Centre through a Kilgarvan Community Council Community Employment Scheme. The gardens are maintained through the CE scheme and in 1998 won the Tidy Towns Southern Region Best Public Building Gardens Award. The Michael J. Quill Visitors Centre is therefore a manifestation of statutory and voluntary local community initiative at its best.

BEALICK MILL RESTORATION PROJECT

In 1989 a group came together with a dream of developing Bealick Mill (**Fig 54.2**) as a centre for the community and a focal point for visitors to the area near its home town of Macroom, county Cork. Research revealed a rich history and archaeological background, underlining the importance of a faithful restoration of the site. Although 10,000 visitors pass through the region

every day during the summer months, Macroom did not have a significant attraction to make them break their journey. A plan was devised to develop Bealick Mill as a resource for visitors and the local community, with displays on the history of corn-milling and of electricity in Cork, while also providing multifunctional public spaces and recreational facilities. Among further plans for the development are the provision of units for producers of quality handcrafts, who will offer training courses over the winter months. A shop front for local produce is planned in the recreational area. Maintaining the historical integrity of the project has always been of paramount importance.

The awesome power of running water was one of our earliest sources of energy. Of the 1,500 or so grain mills in Ireland in the nineteenth century, almost all were powered by water wheels. The Bealick Mill 20-ton water wheel (now restored) was built prior to 1860 by McSwineys of Cork, the only one of three of its type constructed by a Cork foundry still in existence. A diagonal weir, built on a loop of the River Laney, provided an almost year-round supply of water to the mill. After flowing through the wheel pit, the water was discharged via the tail race into the Laney, below the mill buildings. In times of flooding, water was diverted from

Fig. 54.3 Clonakilty Model Village, county Cork.

the main feeder channel through a by-pass channel east of the mill race.

In 1899, the Macroom and District Electric Lighting Syndicate Ltd was established, under the guidance of electrical engineers Thomas Bird and Alan Dewsbury, to supply electric street lighting to Macroom. By 1907, John Looney was their electrical engineer and by 1910, he had become the owner of the Bealick Mill. In the next ten years, he had expanded the activities to include a sawmill and also moved his bicycle repair business there. He remained there until 1940, when he sold the mill to Francis Horgan, following reverses caused by the arrival of the Electricity Supply Board in 1935 and the hardship of the Economic War.

Now restored, the millwheel still powers the homes of the Horgan family, and will supply the needs of the Bealick Mill Centre when restoration is complete. Bealick Mill is a multistorey corn mill, built in the early nineteenth century on the site of an earlier mill. The upper storeys were used to store grain from the fertile grain countryside round about. Until the elevator was installed, corn to be ground was carried in bags to the upper floors. Here it was delivered to up to six millstones and, when ground, it travelled to the ground floor along wooden grain chutes.

The soil in the area was ideal for the growing of oats for oatmeal, which was ground at Bealick Mill. Macroom Oatmeal, recommended by the well-known cookery expert Darina Allen of Ballymaloe House, was produced at the mill. Its national and international renown is due to its distinctive roasted flavour, as the oats were roasted in a kiln drier before milling. Because of the country's damp climate, Irish mills usually had to use a grain drier, and the original kiln survives at Bealick Mill. Corn from the area was shipped by rail directly to the Port of Cork for international export. Milling was an important source of income in the Cork area, and there were 59 corn mills in Cork in 1915.

Along with the goal of restoring an historic building for public usage, a complimentary objective of the project was to provide a vehicle through which unemployed young people of the area might find a route back into the workplace. This aim has been successfully achieved, thanks to a partnership with a FÁS CYTP Programme operating on site. To date, in excess of 40 youths have been placed in full-time employment with local firms and industry around Macroom by virtue of having taken part in this CYTP. In late 1999, ten youths were participating in the extended scheme.

WEST CORK MODEL VILLAGE PROJECT

West Cork, a popular tourist destination, has a model

village — the first of its type in Ireland (**Fig. 54.3**). It shows the architectural highlights of the region's six main towns. The construction of the village at Clonakilty has given work to over 60 school-leavers who would otherwise have had no hope of a job. Many European countries have model villages, like Switzerland with its Swiss miniature site at Melide, just outside Lugano in the south, almost on the frontier with Italy. The country's most famous buildings, including its castles, and also its railways and lake steamers, are replicated in 1/25th scale. The same principle, almost to the same scale — 1/24th — lies behind the West Cork Model Village.

Arising from extensive research in the late 1980s, spearheaded by the West Cork Heritage Group, the Clonakilty Enterprise Board, along with the support of the Clonakilty UDC, the site was secured, planning permission obtained and the Model Village came on stream. The Model Village offers glimpses of west Cork in miniature. The village illustrates and promotes many of the attractive buildings and features of the region in three-dimensional format. An all-weather Visitor's Centre has been constructed on site to the design of the original Clonakilty railway station. The building houses a reception area, a model railway guidance control area, together with audio-visual and mounted displays, fittings and railway artefacts, a waiting room and a restaurant, both styled after the 1940s era. This building is open all year round and presents various cultural, educational and recreational aspects of west Cork life and industry of fifty years ago.

The village project includes miniature replicas of many historical and attractive buildings of six west Cork towns — Clonakilty, Bandon, Bantry, Kinsale, Skibbereen and Dunmanway. Models are completed to the most exacting standards of design, materials and finish details. All were carefully crafted in Clonakilty under the critical super-vision and direction of Cork County Council's Architec-tural Department. Each of the towns is linked by a fully automated working replica of the West Cork Railway and feeder services as they existed in the period from the 1930s to the 1950s. The miniature railway is comple-mented by appropriate railway buildings, sidings, turntables, signalling hardware, platform equipment and furniture. In addition, the park includes miniature replicas of Clonakilty, Bantry Bay and Kinsale harbour.

The old industries of Clonakilty are reproduced. In the nineteenth century, and again in the 1930s, flax growing in the area and linen weaving in the town were important. So too were the old Shannonvale Flour Mills between the town and Bandon, and Deasy's brewery, a Clonakilty landmark for nearly two centuries. Other buildings in the district being depicted include Bantry House and Allmann's Distillery, Bandon. Besides the railway, the Model Village shows the old-style boats that used to ply the harbours of Bantry and Kinsale. Also represented are the sand-lighter boats that once brought coal and industrial products to Clonakilty's harbour and shipped out local produce. Rural electrification, which started in the region in the 1940s, making a huge social impact, is included.

The project cost was £1 million, with labour being provided by FÁS. Three-quarters of the costs were met by European Union Structural Funds, with Cork County Council and Clonakilty Urban District Council between them providing £160,000, the balance coming from within the local community. Some 70,000 visitors now come to see the project annually.

JAMESON HERITAGE CENTRE

In 1975, the Old Distillery at Midleton closed down and a new distillery was opened on an adjacent site. For the next fourteen years the Old Distillery lay unused with all the decay and deterioration one might expect in this situation. In October 1989, a storm blew the roof off the Maltings Building into the playing fields of the adjacent school. Something had to be done. Should the site be allowed to become a total ruin, should the buildings be repaired, or should some alternative use for them be found?

By way of background, Midleton Distillery comprises some eleven and a half acres, with many major buildings. These date back to 1790 when the first building was constructed as a woollen mill by the family of Marcus Lynch. It was to employ over 1,100 men, women and children. It is doubtful whether the woollen mill ever functioned, but certainly in the early 1800s it was used as a military barracks during the Napoleonic Wars. In 1825, the site was purchased by James Murphy of Cork Distil-leries, who commenced whiskey production in 1827. For the next one hundred and fifty years, the Distillery supplied Midleton and Paddy Whiskies and later the spirit for Cork Dry Gin and vodkas.

A study in 1980 indicated that it would be possible to construct the Old Distillery into a Visitor Centre, but there were several barriers:

• the initial cost of the project was uncertain;

• its financial viability was questionable;

• little market information was available;

• the scope of the project was daunting.

It did, however, offer several positive features:

• the site and its buildings are unique, it is one of the finest industrial archaeological sites left intact in Ireland, according to expert opinion;

• it is located on the main Euroroute Cork/Rosslare — one of the busiest tourist routes in Ireland — and is adjacent to the main street in Midleton;

• some of the major equipment such as stills, water wheel and much of the distilling plant were still *in situ*;

• no comparable facility existed in Ireland to promote Irish whiskey. Irish Distillers Group have visitor centres in Dublin and Bushmills, but these are not comparable to the Scotch Whiskey trail in the Scottish Highlands.

Irish Distillers Ltd (IDL) made available the building and materials and FÁS supplied a supervisor and support for the trainees. This was a case of mutual need — FÁS were anxious to establish a project in Midleton because it was an unemployment blackspot, and IDL wished to get essential restoration work done. At this time Bord Fáilte had access to European Regional Development Fund (ERDF) monies. They wanted to support projects in the Cork area that would enhance the tourist market. They were particularly interested in large-scale projects offering unique products and presented in a professional manner. Finally, after obtaining a small amount of money for preliminary design, approval was received from IDL and their parent company, Pernod Ricard, to proceed with the project based on a business plan which showed that it would be self-sustaining after start-up.

In 1990, construction work began and the Centre opened in May 1992. The project cost was in excess of £2m, of which ERDF provided some £750,000. At peak, the project employed about eighty people during the construction phase. Its benefits include:

• an asset for Midleton, where the UDC and local bodies had embarked on a major programme to improve the town — culminating in second place for its category in 1993 in the Tidy Towns Scheme;

• a continuing CYTP Programme with FÁS, which trains up to ten people at a time, with a 65% success rate in placement;

• spin-off benefits to the town in shopping, restaurants and hotel accommodation;

• opportunities for young language graduates to practise their skills;

• the establishments of east Cork as a tourist destination in its own right in conjunction with The Cobh Heritage Centre, Barryscourt Castle, Trabolgan Centre, Fota Island and Ballymaloe House and Cookery School.

There are also the following additional noteworthy features arising from this investment:

• a unique visitor centre based in beautifully restored old buildings which portrays the history and tradition of Irish whiskey;

• an audio-visual display and guided tours in six languages — English, French, German, Italian, Spanish and Japanese;

• high-class weather-independent facilities for visitors, including a restaurant, a bar for product tasting and a shop selling a wide variety of branded merchandise;

• professional displays of the history of the buildings, the industry and displays of artifacts associated with the industry;

• an art gallery to promote Jameson through its association with the arts.

V.I.P. visitors such as the President of Ireland and the President of Portugal, EU Commissioners and ministers have visited the site. In 1998 alone there were 110,000 visitors. Seven full-time and up to 27 permanent seasonal jobs in Midleton arise from it. A further eight jobs in security, catering, cleaning and maintenance are provided.

CONCLUSION

There are over 3,600 FÁS-sponsored community projects currently operating throughout the country, achieving considerable economic and social impact in their respective communities. The South West Region has 380 projects in areas such as heritage, arts, community services, community enterprise and culture, providing 6,500 people with training and employment opportunities. Numerous communities have achieved an excellent degree of social and economic development and have contributed significantly to the 'Celtic Tiger' economy. The Community Initiative Awards were established by FÁS to recognize the contribution made by community groups and participants on FÁS-supported projects throughout Ireland. One of the major achievements of local communities in the past number of years has been the professional way they have developed their resources. FÁS looks forward to a continued successful collaboration with these organizations and thereby to the strengthening of both society and tradition in Ireland.

The National Trust in Northern Ireland

IAN B. MCQUISTON

The National Trust — or to give its full title The National Trust for Places of Historic Interest or Natural Beauty — is one of Europe's leading conservation bodies. It is a registered charity, a not-for-profit organization, which jealously guards its independence from government; its name might suggest that it is run by or has some affiliation with the state, but that is not the case. It pursues its purposes throughout England, Wales and Northern Ireland. The National Trust for Scotland is a separate and independent body with very similar ideals to the National Trust, and there is understandably a close working relationship between the two organizations.

The National Trust is incorporated by act of Parliament, *The National Trust Acts* 1907–71 and *The National Trust Act (Northern Ireland)* 1946, and it carries out its statutory purposes through the ownership and management of property. The core purpose, or what today might be referred to as its mission statement, is set out in the *National Trust Act* 1907 thus:

The National Trust shall be established for the purposes of promoting the permanent preservation for the benefit of the nation of lands and tenements (including buildings) of beauty or historic interest and as regards lands for the preservation (so far as practicable) of their natural aspects, features and animal and plant life.

Today, the Trust is the UK's largest private landowner, with responsibility for over 600,000 acres of land of outstanding natural beauty (some 30,000 acres in Northern Ireland), including the protection of some 575 miles of coastline (58 miles in Northern Ireland). In addition to owning and managing land and buildings, the Trust can offer a wider net of protection by accepting restrictive covenants over properties. A crucial provision afforded to the Trust by statute is its unique power, along with The National Trust for Scotland, to declare its property 'inalienable', and indeed most property held by

the Trust is in fact inalienable. This means that the Trust cannot voluntarily sell or mortgage property and it can, for example, object to compulsory purchase orders of its own land or buildings by invoking a Special Parliamentary Procedure. Through its rich and diverse collection of properties, the Trust is able to demonstrate its commitment to public access and enjoyment, that is 'for the benefit of the nation', to the conservation of landscapes (natural and historic), the promotion of sound environmental practices and the support of local communities.

The National Trust could not achieve its purposes without the generous support of over 2.6 million members (35,000 in Northern Ireland) and the 40 million or so people who visit its cultural, industrial and countryside properties each year. The Trust employs almost 3,300 full-time staff (140 in the north) in a wide variety of professional, technical and administrative positions, augmented by some 4,000 seasonal staff (250 in Northern Ireland) and, most importantly, by over 35,000 volunteers collectively giving the Trust 2 million hours work each year.

THE BEGINNINGS

The National Trust was formally established, and registered under the *Companies Act*, on 12 January 1895. The ceremony took place in Grosvenor House, the Duke of Westminster's London home, following several years of preparatory work by a small group of committed and far-sighted individuals. On 12 January 1995, a celebration lunch on the occasion of the Trust's Centenary was held at the same venue, attended by representatives of the many families, organizations, bodies and supporters who had helped the charity through its first one hundred years.

There were three key people behind the move to establish a National Trust, imaginative individuals who even then in the late nineteenth century detected an increasing threat to the countryside and buildings of England, Wales and Ireland. They were three very different people. Miss Octavia Hill, reputedly the main driving force, was a social worker of vision who had gained an international reputation with her housing schemes for the poor in Marylebone and the East End of London. She was joined by Sir Robert Hunter, a solicitor with a special concern for the open countryside of Surrey and who, as Honorary Solicitor to the Commons Preservation Society, had fought important battles to save common lands and forests from enclosure. The third founder was Canon Hardwicke Rawnsley, vicar of Wray in the Lake District of Cumberland, who had become deeply concerned that the unspoilt beauty of the Lakes would be lost to posterity.

Among the many meetings which must have taken place prior to 1895 was one reported in *The Times* on 17 November 1893 and attended by a number of leading personalities and opinion formers of the day. Illustrating an Irish dimension from the very start was the recorded presence of the Marquess of Dufferin and Ava whose home was at Clandeboye on the edge of Bangor in county Down. The Marquess went on to serve as President of the National Trust from 1900 to 1902.

The first property to come to the newly formed National Trust was the gift of 4.5 acres of coastline at Dinas Oleu in North Wales a matter of weeks after its formation. This was followed by the purchase, for £10, of the fourteenth-century timber-framed clergy house in Alfriston (Sussex). Another £10 secured a much more substantial historic building, the sixteenth-century Barrington Court in Somerset. A further and early connection with Ireland came with the ninth acquisition, a gift, of Kanturk Castle in county Cork. This happened in 1900. There were no further Irish properties acquired until after partition in 1920 and the consequent establishment of Northern Ireland. The title to Kanturk Castle has been transferred from the National Trust to An Taisce (The National Trust of Ireland) as part of the latter organization's fiftieth anniversary celebrations.

In 1935, the offer of two properties in Northern Ireland — Killynether House near Newtownards, county Down and Ballymoyer House and Glen in county Armagh — prompted the National Trust to establish a more organized presence in the province. As a result, a Northern Ireland Committee was formed and it met for the first time on 1 May 1936.

STRUCTURE AND GOVERNANCE

The National Trust, by virtue of its accumulated responsibilities over more than one hundred years, is a complicated and complex organization. Managing its affairs in as open a way as possible while being true to core principles and responsibilities is a continuing challenge.

The National Trust has been governed by a Council since the first 1907 act, with various refinements over the years culminating in the present arrangements prescribed in the 1971 act. This act sets out in considerable detail how the Council is constituted, its powers and duties, the appointment and remuneration of a Chairman, the establishment of an Executive Committee and Regional Committees. The Council consists of fifty-two members; twenty-six are elected on a rolling basis by the membership at annual general meetings and twenty-six are nominated by bodies whose influence the Trust values. These bodies are enumerated by statute and are reviewed by the membership every six years. At present, examples of those bodies and persons authorized to nominate a member of Council include the British Ecological Society, the Linnean Society, the National Federation of Women's Institutes, the National Trust for Scotland, the Royal Horticultural Society, the Schools Curriculum and Assessment Authority, the Secretary of State for Northern Ireland, the Society for the Protection of Ancient Buildings and the Youth Hostels Association. These are illustrative of the wide range of the Trust's work and of the desire of the Trust to engage with others who might have a more tightly focussed ambition or remit, but whose work and experience are relevant to what the Trust seeks to achieve on a broader canvas.

The Council delegates many responsibilities to an Executive Committee made up of all the Regional Chairpersons and some members of Council, not to exceed twenty-five in number but with members of Council being a majority. The Executive Committee is in turn advised by a Properties Committee, responsible for reviewing policy for the management of properties and, importantly, for the consideration of proposed acquisitions, and by a Finance Committee. Various panels have been established, utilizing the voluntary services of acknowledged experts, to give specialist advice to the Properties and Finance Committees and to staff. Regional Committees have been established to advise and supervise the Trust's activities in their areas; there are twelve, including the Committee for Wales and the Committee for Northern Ireland.

Staff are located in three head office locations — at London, Westbury and Cirencester — in the regional offices and on the properties. Among the disciplines to be found at head office and regional offices are historic buildings, marketing and communications, finance, fundraising, enterprises, land agency, volunteering and personnel. These have available to them more specialized advisory services covering a wide range of activities from gardening and forestry to paintings, ceramics and textile conservation. Generally, the Trust has within its family expertise in most areas, which it readily shares, but if support is unavailable, it will source help from the best of what is available outside the organization.

FUNDING

The National Trust is a large and complex organization and its funding is no less complex, bearing in mind that maintaining property to a high standard in perpetuity is very expensive. As new properties, buildings and land are added, the Trust is challenged to ensure that funds are in place to meet the consequent liabilities. The general policy at present is to set up an endowment fund for each property at the time of acquisition, calculated to generate sufficient income to ensure that over a fifty-year time-frame the property will not become an additional burden on what the Trust calls its General Fund. Many past acquisitions have insufficient endowments and will be a continuing drain on the General Fund. Most of the properties in Northern Ireland are run at an operational deficit and benefit from support drawn from the General Fund. This policy can lead to difficult choices when the acquisition of new properties is being considered; if the funds are not there to create a sufficient endowment to support future maintenance, the Trust may have no option but to refuse the acquisition.

The General Fund is the Trust's 'free money', not tied to any specific property, and is therefore the capital pool which supports the Trust's activities. One measure of this reserve is, in the absence of any further income, how long the charity could keep going. Currently, the period of cover is six months. The Trust puts considerable effort into planning, and a cornerstone of the current three-year *National strategic plan* (1998–2001) is that there should be a steadily improving position, creating the financial strength which will allow the Trust to pursue its destiny.

Taking the latest accounts, those for 1998/1999, the Trust generated £182 million in income and expended some £152 million. The breakdown is shown in **Table 55.1**.

These figures show the fundamental importance of the membership base in terms of income and the extent to which the Trust can deploy its resources on the core activities of maintenance in relation to the costs of administration

The Trust in Northern Ireland has been fortunate to receive financial support for projects from the European Regional Development Fund, the Northern Ireland Tourist Board, the International Fund for Ireland, the Department of Education and the Department of the Environment for Northern Ireland. Without this support, often in partnership with the private sector, it would not have been possible to reach the current level of achievement and activity.

ENTERPRISE NEPTUNE

From its first acquisition, the National Trust has been drawn to the coastline. This concern culminated in the launch in May 1965 of the most successful and enduring

Table 55.1

INCOME: £182 MILLION

Membership subscriptions	30%
Legacies	18%
Investment income	14%
Rental income	11%
National Trust Enterprises (shops, tea-rooms, etc.)	7%
Grants	6%
Admission fees	5%
Gifts	4%
Appeals	4%
Sales of leases	2%

EXPENDITURE: £152 MILLION

Routine maintenance and conservation	60%
Capital projects	24%
Membership, publicity and education	10%
Acquisitions	5%
Charity administration	1%

campaign ever undertaken by the National Trust — Enterprise Neptune — with the aim of protecting coastline of outstanding beauty. It has been incredibly successful in raising on average some £1 million each year to assist with the acquisition and management of coastal properties, and continues as the Neptune Coastline Campaign.

The seeds of this remarkable campaign are to be found in Northern Ireland. Up until 1964, the Northern Ireland Committee of the National Trust continued to be financially independent, and by that time it had acquired several important coastal sites — White Park Bay, Cushendun and the Giant's Causeway — all in county Antrim. If further stretches of coastline were to be acquired with funds to be found in Northern Ireland, then a special initiative was required. So it was that the Ulster Coastline Appeal was launched in March 1962, and by June 1994 had raised sufficient funds to complete the North Antrim Cliff Path. Encouraged by the success of this regional venture, the Trust concluded that action on a nationwide scale was needed.

A survey was undertaken in 1963 to assess the 3,000 miles that make up the coastline of England, Wales and Northern Ireland, and to identify the stretches that were of outstanding beauty and therefore worthy of protection. The results showed that one-third was already ruined, one-third was of little interest, but one-third was of outstanding natural beauty and deserved to be preserved. By 1997, 571 miles of coastline had been acquired. Included in this total are some surprises; for example, the 500th mile was the acquisition in 1988 for £1 from British Coal of the coal-blackened beach at

Fig. 55.1 Castle Coole House, county Fermanagh, exterior after restoration.

Easington in county Durham, an area which the survey had described as irrevocably ruined by industrial exploitation and waste. Twenty years later, the collieries were facing closure, the local communities had been wracked by the miners' strike and there were signs that longshore drift would sweep away the coal waste from the beaches. The Trust argued that here was an opportunity to acquire a property and show how it could rehabilitate the landscape and give encouragement to the local community. It is very doubtful if Orford Ness in Suffolk would have passed muster in the 1963 Survey. This five-mile stretch of shingle, bought in 1993, had been an ideal place for twentieth-century military research. Many structures remain as a testament to those activities, adding powerfully to the mournful beauty of the most important shingle spit cuspate foreland in England.

Northern Ireland has continued to benefit from Enterprise Neptune, with many coastal acquisitions including Carrick-a-rede, Murlough Bay, Portstewart Strand and the Bann Estuary, along the north coast, many areas within Strangford Lough and along the Mourne coast in county Down, and most recently the townland of Ballyconagan on Rathlin Island, an acquisition also supported by the Heritage Lottery Fund.

BUILT HERITAGE

It is a continuing perception that the National Trust is an organization that looks after stately homes, and although it does have responsibility for some 200 houses open to the public — 88 large country houses and 43 associated with famous people such as Rudyard Kipling, Beatrix Potter, William Wordsworth, Thomas Hardy, George Bernard Shaw and Sir Winston Churchill — it only possessed two houses of any size until the mid-1930s.

At the National Trust's annual general meeting in 1934, the Marquess of Lothian made an impassioned speech in which he explained that the country houses of Britain were under sentence of death, and that the axe which was destroying them was taxation in the form of death duties. Lord Lothian went on to devise the Country House Scheme which enabled the Trust to accept country houses in lieu of death duties, with the proviso that an endowment in the form of land or money should also be given to provide for maintenance. The required legislation was duly passed and is found in the *National Trust Acts* of 1937 and 1939, and in the *National Trust Act (NI)* 1946. The first house to come to the Trust under the Country House Scheme was Wightwick Manor (inspired by the Arts and Crafts Movement) in Staffordshire, to be followed all too soon by Lord Lothian's own home, the Jacobean jewel of Blickling Hall in Norfolk, following his premature death in 1940. Northern Ireland benefited under the scheme with the acquisition of the idiosyncratic Castle Ward house in 1953. Within Northern Ireland, the National Trust is now responsible for some 330 buildings, of which 220 are buildings listed because of their special architectural merit or historic interest. The list includes not only major mansions but also a wide range of smaller buildings — out-buildings, mills, cottages and vernacular buildings. The Trust is responsible for two small villages of contrasting styles: in county Antrim, the core of the Clough Williams-Ellis designed village of Cushendun, and in county Down, the more informal and vernacular former fishing village of Kearney.

The history of Ireland from the earliest to modern times can be discovered on National Trust properties which include many important archaeological monuments and historic landscapes. In Northern Ireland, there are some 145 recorded archaeological sites on Trust property, of which twelve are scheduled sites. Historic landscape surveys are bringing new information to light, informing the management and conservation work on landscapes and buildings. For example, at Dunseverick Castle on the north Antrim coast, a site of major archaeological significance, the Trust has been conserving the fragile structures by careful consolidation. These precarious remains of the strongly defended MacDonnell castle on an enclosed cliff-top promontory are sited on a much older early Christian eighth- or ninth-century fort, a royal site mentioned in the Irish annals.

Numerous historic landscape features and structures survive in the desmesnes of Ulster's important country houses, many in the care of the National Trust. Extensive archaeological research on the demesne landscapes at Castle Ward (county Down), Downhill (county Londonderry) and Florence Court, Castle Coole and Crom Estate (county Fermanagh), has been undertaken. Industry was never far away from the workings of the country house, many of which were built by industrialists or out of the profits of industrial activity. The surviving legacy of brickworks, quarries, limekilns, sawmills and farms illustrates the level of self-sufficiency attained by many

country estates in providing raw materials and income for the maintenance of the estate. In the provision of domestic services, such estates relied on technology, including pump-houses (Castle Coole and Florence Court where a ram pump still operates), gasworks (Castle Ward, Mount Stewart, and The Argory, where an acetylene plant is intact), sewage works, breweries, laundries (The Argory, Castle Ward and Castle Coole) and ice houses (Florence Court, Castle Coole, Castle Ward, Slieve Donard). The importance of recording and preserving such evidence lies in the fact that these buildings are testimony to the contribution made by domestic staff, servants and tenants in the running of such estates.

Fig. 55.2 Gray's Printing Press.

Industrial remains and artefacts occur on country house estates and in the wider countryside, towns and villages, and the Trust has been active in their preservation, although the philosophy to be adopted in their interpretation and presentation has evolved. From a position of static display, efforts have been made to make the sites operational to give a more evocative feeling of how the processes might have been in their hey-day. This can be seen at Gray's Printing Press (**Fig. 55.2**), associated with John Dunlap, printer of the American Declaration of Independence, where the sanitized museum approach is being altered to reintroduce the smell of ink (even ink stains on the floor!) and the clatter of the presses. The water-powered sawmill at Florence Court now demonstrates its trade with the attendant scream of the saw blade and eruption of sawdust, while the process of turning cereal into flour is demonstrated in the throbbing water-powered mill at Castle Ward. The unbearably noisy business of beetling linen cloth is appreciated by visitors to the delightfully sited mill at Wellbrook west of Cookstown in county Tyrone.

The acquisition of Patterson's Spade Mill, near

Fig. 55.3 School group exploring the middle causeway columns and Giant's Wishing Chair, Giant's Causeway, county Antrim.

Templepatrick in county Antrim, took this philosophy to its ultimate development. Here the Trust was concerned to conserve a craft process rather than the physical structures which contained it. This was a departure from the traditional approach of seeking out the best physical or architectural manifestations of a particular industry. At the last surviving water-powered spade mill in the British Isles the skills inherent in the production of hand-crafted spades are being encouraged, and visitors can not only appreciate the various stages involved in the production of spades but can purchase a spade of their choosing.

NATURAL HERITAGE

From its inception, the National Trust has been concerned with countryside or landscape conservation, reflecting the enthusiasm of the founders and their perception of the value of such areas. Mention has already been made of the critical importance of the coastline and the particular efforts of the Trust to conserve the best of what remains. The importance, or value, of countryside to all sectors of society is well illustrated in the acquisition, in 1902, of the Trust's first property in the Lake District — the woods and parkland at Brandlehow on the west side of Derwentwater — when factory workers in many northern cities responded to the appeal launched by Canon Rawnsley. The concept of the Trust acquiring nature reserves was raised within months of its formation, when a distinguished entomologist suggested that it should save Wicken Fen in Cambridgeshire, the only substantial area of East Anglian fen still undrained; the Trust now owns 600 acres designated as National Nature Reserve at Wicken Fen.

Nationally, the Trust is responsible for 70 nature reserves and 339 Sites of Special Scientific Interest, covering almost every type of habitat and species of plant or animal. In Northern Ireland, the Trust's estate includes eight National Nature Reserves and ten Areas of Special Scientific Interest.

The first Nature Reserve to be established on the island of Ireland was at Murlough immediately north of Newcastle in county Down. Here, some 700 acres were acquired by the National Trust in 1967. The morphology and history of development of the dunes within Murlough National Nature Reserve are unique within the British Isles and are of international significance. There is a range of communities and a rich flora and fauna, including a large number of rare and local species. Other sites of high nature conservation interest include Slieve Donard, Crom Estate, the Bann Estuary and the entire north Antrim coast (including Rathlin Island) of which the Giant's Causeway sector (**Fig. 55.3**) has been designated a UNESCO World Heritage Site.

Perhaps nowhere in the Trust is its commitment to the natural environment better illustrated than on Strangford Lough. This, the largest sea lough in the British Isles, boasts an unrivalled wealth of wildlife, delicately balanced and dependant on tides, the variety of habitats found between seabed and shoreline, and, critically, how it interacts with the demands of society for recreation and commercial return.

The National Trust formed its Strangford Lough Wildlife Scheme in 1966 in response to the growing demands and pressures made by people on the natural resources of the Lough. This was an innovative initiative at that time which has subsequently been underpinned by designation as an Area of Outstanding Natural Beauty, an Area of Special Scientific Interest, a National Nature Reserve, a Marine Nature Reserve and a Special Area of Conservation. Some 2,000 marine animal and plant species have been found within the Lough, which represents 72% of all the species recorded around the Northern Ireland coastline; of these, 28 are exclusive to Strangford Lough. The Lough is one of the most important breeding sites for common seals in Ireland. Each winter, around 70,000 birds (wildfowl, waders, gulls and auks) overwinter on the Lough, the highlight being the arrival of up to 15,000 pale-bellied brent geese after a 3,000 kilometre journey from Arctic Canada. The Trust's commitment to the protection of the Lough is achieved by its active management of 10,000 acres of foreshore and sea bed, 50 islands, woodlands, wetlands, salt-marsh and agricultural fields. Wardens and other staff and volunteers monitor and protect wildlife sites, manage habitats and species, undertake biological surveys, protect the foreshore from encroachments, liaise with farmers and Lough users, provide for public access and provide a comprehensive interpretation and education service for all classes of visitor.

It is not surprising, given the Trust's statutory remit to preserve areas of natural beauty or historic interest, that this should bring forward requests to look after important gardens. The acquisition of gardens in their own right, and not merely as appendages to houses, started with the acquisition of Hidcote in Gloucestershire in 1948, and today the National Trust looks after 130 important gardens which together include the largest collection of cultivated plants in the world. In 1949, Lord Aberconway entrusted some 100 acres of his garden at Bodnant in North Wales to the National Trust, the same year in which Lady Londonderry enquired about the Trust taking over the splendid gardens she had created at Mount Stewart in county Down; Mount Stewart gardens transferred to the Trust in 1955. Many superb landscape gardens passed to the Trust, including Stourhead in Wiltshire, Claremont in Surrey, Studley Royal and Rievaulx Terrace in Yorkshire and Stowe Landscape Gardens in Buckinghamshire, one of the supreme creations of the Georgian era. These gardens, and others, employed variously the talents of Sir John Vanbrugh, Charles Bridgeman, William Kent, Capability Brown and Humphrey Repton. The 1,900 acres of woodland, parkland and wetland at Crom on the shores of Upper Lough Erne in county Fermanagh owe much to the watercolourist and garden designer, William Sawrey Gilpin, a follower of the picturesque movement.

SOCIAL PURPOSE

There is little doubt that the three founders of the National Trust were inspired to bring social change to people: they were providing green lungs for urban poor. The Trust is unable to deliver its obligation to give 'benefit to the nation' without interesting its members at every level. There is some evidence that the Trust had lost sight of its founding social role, but, inspired by its centenary, the Trust is now reaffirmed in its mission at all levels. There are a number of social relationships which characterize the Trust's activities:

(i) the fundamental charge on the Trust, under statute, to promote conservation values and to conserve land and buildings significant to people;

(ii) the need to respect local distinctiveness, involving relationships which emphasize the needs and aspiration of local communities. This is manifested in community involvement, local consultation, public meetings, providing housing for local people, being sensitive to local history and culture and so forth;

(iii) the provision of facilities and opportunities for understanding and the enjoyment of natural beauty and historic interest. These could include trails and guided walks, lectures, visitor centres, footpath creation, information in newspapers, television, regional and local newsletters, space in houses and countryside for community events, volunteering and education. In Northern Ireland, the Trust's commitment to education is seen in the use of its properties, for curriculum-based activities, by some 42,000 pupils and teachers each year. One-third of these pupils come under the Schools Community Relations Programme, when groups from both traditions across the province are introduced to their shared heritage by co-operative work at key sites which have dedicated National Trust Education Officers. The current key sites are Florence Court, The Argory,

Springhill, Mount Stewart, Castle Ward and The Giant's Causeway;

(iv) the importance of lowering the barriers to access and enjoyment and of providing 'access for all'. This means lowering physical barriers (the needs of children or disabled, mentally challenged, elderly visitors and the like), financial barriers (transport arrangements) and cultural barriers (by information, education, breaking down middle-class image, community outreach);

(v) a strategy of benevolent land ownership through which stronger relationships can be developed with tenants and local communities, for instance the provision of playing fields for the Cushendun Gaelic Athletic Association Club in county Antrim;

(vi) the creation of a sense of belonging among staff, volunteers, trainees, members and others associated with the National Trust and through them the creation and development of social networks;

(vii) by developing relationships with other organizations, and to empower and inspire others to pursue similar ideals to those of the National Trust. This includes relationships with voluntary organizations, government and the private sector, but also with disadvantaged communities (for instance Collin Glen in west Belfast) and those wishing to maintain and revive traditional skills;

(viii) by supporting local economies through the employment of local contractors, local staff, facilitating tourist development, providing work experience and training.

Bibliography

Brown, R. 1990 *Strangford Lough: the wildlife of an Irish sea lough*. Belfast.

Evans, D. M., Salway, P. and Thackray, D. (eds) 1996 *The remains of distant times: archaeology and the National Trust*. Suffolk.

Fedden, R. 1974 *The National Trust: past and present*. London.

Gallagher, L. and Rogers, R. 1992 *Castle, coast and cottage: the National Trust in Northern Ireland*. Belfast.

Gaze, J. 1988 *Figures in a landscape: a history of the National Trust*. London.

Jenkins, J. and Patrick, J. 1994 *From acorn to oak tree: the growth of the National Trust 1885–1994*. London.

Newby, H. (ed) 1995 *The National Trust: the next hundred years*. London.

Pye-Smith, C. 1990 *In search of Neptune: a celebration of the National Trust's coastline*. London.

Sandwith, H. and Stainton, S. 1991 *The National Trust manual of housekeeping*. New York.

Waterson, M. 1994 *The National Trust: the first hundred years*. London.

An Taisce

MARY SLEEMAN

An Taisce — the National Trust for Ireland — is recognized nationally and internationally as the leading voluntary and independent environmental organization in Ireland. Its objective is the conservation of the country's heritage, both natural and built, for the common good. This chapter describes its background and areas of activity, and explores some of the issues it faces in the next phase of its existence

HISTORY: FIFTY YEARS A-GROWING

In post-war Ireland, the need for an environmental group was recognized as pressure grew to modernize the country's infrastructure, promote industrialization and improve farming (has anything changed?). The push for a conservation body came from various special-interest groups such as the Royal Irish Academy, the Royal Society of Antiquaries of Ireland, the Dublin Naturalist's Field Club, An Óige, the Geographical Society of Ireland and the Irish Society for the Preservation of Birds. Representatives from these bodies organized a public meeting 'for those interested in the preservation of places of interest and beauty in Ireland', which met on 26 September 1946 at the Mansion House in Dublin. At this it was agreed to form a group which would pursue the following aims:

• the preservation of places of natural interest or beauty and their amenities;

• the preservation of structures having national, architectural, historical or artistic interest and their amenities;

• the preservation of furniture and chattels of historic or artistic importance;

• the promotion of access to and enjoyment of such places and properties;

• the establishment of an association to be called 'An Taisce' (meaning 'to treasure' or 'the treasury') — 'The National Trust for Ireland'.

Many of the founding members came from the academic/professional world, notable amongst them scientists George Mitchell and Lloyd Praeger, and also included prominent members of the Irish aristocracy. In order to broaden the range of membership, people like Seán McBride and Cearbhall Ó Dálaigh were co-opted into the movement. The first meeting of An Taisce was held on 15 July 1948 at 19 Dawson Street, Dublin. The activities of the organization in its early days were mainly confined to nature conservation. Subscription was a modest sum of 10s per year and there was a membership roll of about 250.

The nature of An Taisce changed dramatically in 1963 when it was named as a prescribed body in the *Local Government (Planning and Development) Act* of that year. Furthermore, Statutory Instrument No. 2211 (1964), made under the authority of the 1963 act, requires planning authorities to send An Taisce notice of applications for development in areas which appear to be 'of special amenity', or where the development seems 'unduly close to any cave, site, feature or other object of archaeological, geological or historical interest, or in either case, would obstruct any scheme for improvement of the surroundings of, or any means of access to any such place, object or structure'. However, no funding from either the state or local authorities was provided to assist An Taisce, the only voluntary body nominated to carry out this statutory function.

An Taisce has recently celebrated its fiftieth anniversary. Its membership is open to all who have a genuine concern for the environment; in 1999, for example, it had an enrolment of over 5,000, and the cost of membership is £30 annually (with various concessions available). The age profile of An Taisce members is quite elderly and former President Mary Robinson, at the celebration of its fiftieth anniversary, set a challenge for An Taisce to attract more young members. The body is now a company limited by guarantee under the *Companies Act* as well as a registered charity (No. 4741). Its headquarters, since 1984, is the restored early eighteenth-century Tailors Hall, Back Lane, Dublin 8. It is governed by an elected council which meets several times a year. There are a number of specialist committees and working groups (natural environment, built environment, industry) which discuss various specialist matters, create policy and lobby the relevant authorities regarding these issues. It employs a small number of staff, currently two administrators, one planner and three persons in its Environment/Education Unit, all based in Dublin. An Taisce has assumed an important educational role, including the Green Schools project. This and other projects like the Blue Flag (beaches) and the National Spring Clean Campaign are organized by An Taisce of behalf of various government departments with funding from the European Union. During the 1960s, An Taisce began to form local committees to give a better national spread to the organization. Today there are 'Area Associations' in Carlow, Clare, Cork, West Cork, Donegal NW, Donegal SW, Dublin City, Dublin SW, Dublin South County, Dún Laoghaire, Fingal, Galway, Kerry, Kildare, Kilkenny, Limerick, Louth, Meath, Sligo, Tipperary North, Tipperary South, Waterford and Wexford.

AN TAISCE AT PRESENT

An Taisce deals with a wide range of issues relevant to the management and conservation of the environment. The broad spread of its activities is summarized as follows (as listed in the association's 1996 handbook):

• An Taisce is a body which has the right to receive and the responsibility to comment on certain planning applications referred to it by local authorities. It also comments on draft Development Plans when these are referred to it.

• An Taisce lobbies official agencies whose work impacts on the environment.

• An Taisce puts forward proposals for legislation to remedy existing deficiencies in the law relating to conservation and preservation issues.

• It holds and manages a small number of properties in the interest of their conservation (see Appendix 1).

• It is interested in all aspects of the environment and has specialist committees studying and making recommendations on environmental and planning policy.

• It tries to inform public opinion as an instrument to improve environmental policy.

• It co-operates with other voluntary bodies on common issues.

• An Taisce is a member of the European Environmental Bureau, The World Conservation Union, Europa Nostra, IBI, the Foundation of European Environmental Education and European Partners for the Environment. It has also co-operated with the World Wide Fund For Nature on several projects.

• It encourages the continued use of old buildings and the sensitive restoration of such buildings.

• An Taisce has an Environmental Education Unit which at present runs the following four campaigns:

(i) Blue Flag — a scheme for monitoring clean beaches which it operates and monitors for the Department of the Environment.

(ii) National Spring Clean-up Campaign — this involves coordinating the National Anti-Litter Campaign in April of each year. This is supported by the Department of the Environment. An Taisce has recently been asked to carry out a baseline study of litter, litter awareness and tourism amenities in six pilot sites in county Tipperary on behalf of the Tipperary Rural and Business Development Institute and the Tipperary Tourism Forum.

(iii) The Young Reporter On The Environment competition is also organized by An Taisce. This is supported by the Department of Education and Science and the Irish Energy Centre.

(iv) Green Schools — a European-wide environmental education programme that aims to promote and acknowledge school environmental projects. It is organized by An Taisce in partnership with schools and local authorities.

• An Taisce has long published its own journal, *Living Heritage*. In 1999, it introduced an informative newsletter for circulation to all its members.

• It produces policy reports, for instance *Forestry — policy and practice* (1990), *New partnership for Sustainable Development in the regions* (1994).

It should be emphasized that An Taisce is a voluntary organization without government subvention, and its ability to respond to these objectives varies greatly, depending on the degree of priority, the personnel and expertise available at a particular place and time, as well as other considerations.

AREA ASSOCIATIONS — A CORK PERSPECTIVE

The activities of the associations differ from area to area, ranging from lecture series and outings to practical clean-ups and tree audits. Our experiences in An Taisce, Corcaigh, over the last four years are varied, with a mixed sense of success and failure. Like many associations, the Cork group consists of a small active team and a much larger dormant but supportive membership. Planning-related activities take up much of our time; however, we have managed to get involved in various other projects aimed at the protection of the local environment. Our main activities have been:

• public lectures over the winter months relating to environmental issues;

• summer group outings to local sites of interest;

• organizing a very successful 'Built Environment Conference' at UCC in conjunction with Cork Corporation;

• making observations to the Development Plans for Youghal, Midleton, Kinsale, Macroom, Mallow and Cork City, including in most cases a comprehensive new list of buildings and other heritage features recommended by us for listing in the plans;

• making submissions to various official bodies on rezoning, waste management plans and the like;

• receiving numerous planning applications, responding to as many as possible and taking out an appeal in a small number of cases;

• organizing, in co-operation with East Cork Area Development, a litter campaign in east Cork as part of the National Spring Clean-Up programme.

The planning process is one of the major instruments used to control development and conserve the natural and built heritage. The recent unprecedented economic boom and consequent growth in building activity have resulted in a deluge of planning applications to local authorities. There is huge demand for new building land. This development has put enormous pressure on some of the most vulnerable parts of our environment: green belts, waste and marginal land, woodland and scrub land, derelict or unused buildings and so forth. There has been no equivalent rush to protect these areas. An Taisce, Corcaigh, due to the nature of the organization (scarcity of manpower, resources, time), must deal selec-

tively with planning issues. In 1998 alone, for example, we received over 1,000 letters (to an overworked honorary secretary), mostly containing planning applications being referred to us by the planning authorities. Dealing properly with any one of these can involve visits to the relevant planning office and an on-site inspection. One unfortunate consequence of this is the bad press we sometimes receive: 'the knockers - An Taisce object to everything!'. We often feel trapped between the power and influence of development and the bureaucratic cautiousness of local authorities. It is not unknown for committee members to be contacted at home by developers or their agents. Another vexation is the endemic practice of allowing retrospective planning approval. An Taisce, Corcaigh, has tried to focus its energy on making constructive observations to development plans. Unfortunately, very often our observations are not taken on board and we sometimes get the impression that our submissions receive a low priority rating.

PROTECTION OF THE NATURAL AND BUILT ENVIRONMENT

In this country, buildings dating to the eighteenth and nineteenth centuries are chiefly protected by being listed in local authorities' Development Plans; all buildings which are known to predate 1700 AD, and a selection of later ones, are covered by the various *National Monuments Acts*. The following are a number of critical points relevant to the current operation of the listing system:

• the number of buildings listed is much too small a fraction of the surviving eighteenth- and nineteenth-century building stock;

• there is a bias in the listing towards particular aspects of the built heritage, with an over-emphasis on rare atypical examples;

• the rating system (local, regional, national, international) is misunderstood by local authorities as implying that 'local' and 'regional' examples are somehow less worthy of protection;

• most listings are based on those supplied by the (now disbanded) development agency An Foras Forbartha in the 1970s and early 1980s — little heed was paid by the relevant local authorities to their recommendations;

• recent work in county Cork by the Archaeological Survey of Ireland has revealed that there is a far greater richness to our eighteenth- and nineteenth-century built heritage than was appreciated before;

• the listings are too focussed on 'architectural' buildings, with too few examples of thatched dwellings, bridges, walls, shop fronts, demesne features and street furniture;

• most listing does not automatically mean protection, but rather that the protection of the building will be considered in the planning process;

• most authorities have no information on their listed buildings (apart from the lists themselves) nor do they often know why a particular building was listed.

An Taisce has welcomed the exciting new planning legislation envisaged in the *Local Government Act* 1999. This act recognizes that the current measures for protecting our built heritage are not sufficient, and it provides a new framework to deal with the problem. The buildings for listing are now to be based on a survey by The Architectural Survey of Ireland, part of Dúchas, the Heritage Service. However, the final decision 'to list or not to list' still remains with the local authority. An Taisce is worried that the same thing may happen as did with the architectural surveys of An Foras Forbartha, where the take-up was very erratic and some authorities ignored them completely. Without compulsion, implementing the proposed new system could be very slow. For example, the town of Kinsale, which promotes itself as an 'historic town', took nearly thirty years before it included An Foras Forbartha recommendations in the 1998 Development Plan. Furthermore, only items which An Foras Forbartha suggested were of 'regional' and 'national' importance were included; all those listed as 'local' were ignored.

Until there is an informed and comprehensive inventory of buildings and features in Development Plans, and until this is vigorously enforced, a great part of our built heritage which should be protected is at risk. An Taisce looks forward to the conclusion of the relevant survey by the Architectural Survey of Ireland, whose completion target date is 2010. This initiative, driven by the Granada Charter, should provide an informed and comprehensive protection list. But why wait until that time? What will we do until then? When An Taisce, Corcaigh, receives a planning application to demolish or convert old buildings, we feel that much can be done in the present system with a little co-operation from the local authority. For example, in a number of recent cases involving the proposed demolition or restoration of an old building, we have suggested that a record of the building be made by an expert independent consultant so that an informed decision can be made about its fate. Why can this practice not be used more widely?

Problems relating to the protection of our natural environment appear to be very similar to those effecting the built environment. Membership of the European Union is forcing us to come up with better measures for protecting certain types of landscape (see Appendix 2).

These measures are welcome but are surely inadequate to conserve much of what we feel should be protected. Again, as with the built environment, what is being protected is the rare and exotic at the expense of the more ordinary, for example, the Special Areas of Conservation (SAC), selected on the basis of rarity, danger of extinction or outstanding examples of their type. They make up only 5% of the countryside. The Rural Environment Protection Scheme (REPS) was introduced after the European Union Common Agricultural Policy (CAP) reform in 1992. Its adoption was vigorously encouraged by An Taisce. It has had a positive effect in protecting landscape (and lifestyle) in areas which a SAC-type programme seldom includes (for example, low-intensity farmland). We feel that this type of incentive scheme for sensitive farming should be greatly expanded.

A LANDSCAPE POLICY

Cork County Council's Environmental Forum (which includes a variety of groups, among them An Taisce) is about to publish an exciting and challenging document entitled *The landscape of Cork report — towards integrated and sustainable management of our landscape into the next millennium*. This proposes that the council carry out a comprehensive ecological survey, mapping and evaluation of the entire county. The results would enable the council to allow development and guarantee adequate protection of our natural environment. The government is committed to Local Agenda 21 and Sustainable Development, as outlined in the official publication *Sustainable Development: a strategy for Ireland*. This defines Sustainable Development as something which An Taisce, Corcaigh, does not see as being the reality of development in this city or county.

THE FUTURE

Addressing the 1996 Annual General Meeting of An Taisce, Professor Frank Convery, chairperson, made the following point: 'when the economy is growing rapidly, it is vital that growth, in both content and direction, be fashioned which ensures that it nurtures environmental endowments rather than destroys them'. This is where An Taisce sees its role in the future. Frank Convery made the following suggestions in this respect:

• reform the planning system to ensure that development is consistent with the maintenance and enhancement of natural endowments;

• put in place a workable mechanism for the conservation of our built endowments;

• place an immediate moratorium on tax incentives which are channelling investment into urban centres without adequate consideration of their impact;

• remove any subsidies which may be encouraging environmental damage, and enforce penalties for environmental damage;

• bring in institutional reform whereby every government department has an officer responsible for monitoring the environmental performance of the department;

• develop genuine partnerships at local and regional level focussed on the identification and implementation of sustainable forms of development;

• redirect public investment to support forms of transport, industry, farming, energy and forestry which are in harmony with proper conservation practice.

CONCLUSION

An Taisce, a voluntary organization, has worked in a variety of ways over the last fifty years to conserve the physical heritage of Ireland, both natural and built, for the common good. Sustainable Development, in which there is respect for the environment, is the way forward, but needs much more effort if it is to be achieved. An Taisce must continue to pursue the spirit of Local Agenda 21 — Sustainable Development from national to local level. Robert Lloyd Praeger, first president of the society, set the agenda for the organization fifty years ago: it was to form 'a solid body of public opinion ... to safeguard our treasures, both of the past and the present ... for the benefit of all the people'. Finally, a thanks to all those environmental crusaders who have worked tirelessly over the last fifty years in An Taisce with only Ireland's best interest at heart.

Appendix 1

Although ownership of properties is not a leading priority for An Taisce at present, it has acquired a number of sites in various ways over the years, including the following:

• 13-mile stretch of the Boyne Canal;

• 10 acres of Booterstown marsh;

• Crocnafaarragh, county Donegal — 6,5000 acres of rough mountain countryside;

• Weighbridge House, Gort, county Galway;

• Town garden and bird sanctuary at Wellington Place, Morehampton Road, Dublin 4;

• The Burren, county Clare — 38 acres near Mullaghmore;

• Kanturk Castle, county Cork;

• Mongan Bog, county Offaly;

• Gull Island — a group of small islands off Donegal coast;

• Rough Island (off Mulroy Bay);

• Oweninny Bog, county Mayo — 21 acres of fen.

Source: *An Taisce handbook* (1996).

Appendix 2

ca. 750,000 ha designated in 1998 as Natural Heritage Areas (NHA).

Four hundred areas (*ca.* 650,000 ha) of Special Areas of Conservation (SAC) were selected from the NHA areas to satisfy the EU Habitats Directive (1997).

One hundred and nine sq. miles (*ca.* 230,000 ha) of Special Protected Areas (SPA) were selected from the NHA areas to meet the criteria for EU Bird Directive (1979)

Source: Buckley 1998, 17.

Bibliography

Aalen, F. H. A., Whelan, K. and Stout. M. (eds) 1997 *Atlas of the Irish rural landscape*. Cork.
Anon. 1997 'Celebrating half a century of An Taisce achievements', *Living Heritage* **14**, 1 (Winter).
An Taisce 1996 *Association handbook guidelines and practical information*. Dublin.
Buckley, P. 1998 'Legislation and protected areas for conservation of biological diversity' in M. Deevy (ed) *The Irish heritage and environment directory 1999* (Dublin), pp. 13–20.
Department of Environment 1997 *Sustainable Development: a strategy for Ireland*. Dublin.
Environmental Forum, Cork County Council (forthcoming) *The landscape of Cork report — towards integrated and sustainable management of our landscape into the next millennium*.
Garner, W. 1980 *Kinsale architectural heritage national heritage inventory*. Dublin.

Civic Trusts

Jackie Uí Chionna

One of the most significant developments in the area of Irish heritage over the past twenty years has been the formation of Civic Trusts throughout the thirty-two counties. The Civic Trust movement began in Ireland with the establishment of Trusts in Belfast (in November 1982) and Limerick (in February 1983), but the concept of bodies such as Civic Trusts taking a pro-active role in the protection and promotion of the natural and built heritage had begun much earlier in the United Kingdom. In this chapter, I shall look at the circumstances which prompted the growth of the Civic Trusts movement, the criteria laid down for establishing such bodies and the way in which Trusts are currently addressing heritage and environmental issues in their own communities. How the Trusts themselves are structured and managed, the sources of funding they attract and the type of projects they initiate are further issues to be addressed. Finally, the article evaluates the current status of Civic Trusts, how they are viewed by the public and by the state and what the future holds for the movement in Ireland.

BACKGROUND

The first Civic Trust was established by Lord Douglas Sands in the UK in 1957 and took the form of an independent charity whose basic objective was to encourage high standards of environmental care in places where people live and work rather than in the world of showpiece houses and landscapes. This in itself was a fairly revolutionary concept, and went to the nub of what is now an established notion, namely that, in E. Estyn Evans' opinion, 'the ordinary whole of every day is heritage'. Everything from the vernacular architecture of small country villages to the two-up two-downs of the industrial heartlands was finally given appropriate recognition as the important facets of the patrimony of the United Kingdom which they represent. The Civic Trust movement set out to provide everyone, regardless of social class or position, not only with a role in preserving the national heritage but also to imbue them with a sense of responsibility for preserving it. Civic Trusts presented a way in which the ordinary citizen could make a very real contribution to the conservation and enhancement of the historic environment, thereby turning what may have been an interest in local history into an assumption of responsibility for the preservation of that local history, and this 'hands on' approach was to prove very successful.

The first Civic Trust realized that its efforts at national level needed to be backed up by a network of already established voluntary local groups — such as historical and archaeological societies — with similar aims. With these organizations coming on board as affiliates of the Civic Trust, the movement grew rapidly and began to incorporate a wide range of local groups. The success of local Civic Trusts encouraged the formation of further regionally based amenity societies which took on the Civic Trust structure. There are now over 1,000 such societies affiliated to the Civic Trust in the UK, with a total membership of over 300,000. It is a measure of how successful the Civic Trust concept has been in attaining its objectives that it is now recognized that Trusts have done more than any other non-statutory organization to promote higher environmental standards in the UK.

THE MOVEMENT IN IRELAND

In the early 1980s, the Civic Trust organization extended to Ireland with the establishment of Trusts in Belfast (1982) and Limerick (1983). Since then there was a steady growth throughout Ireland, particularly in the 1990s. At present, there are seventeen Civic Trusts established in the thirty-two counties — at Askeaton, Belfast, Birr, Carlingford Lough, Cork, Dublin, Ennis, Foyle, Galway, Kilkenny, Limerick, Navan, Newry and Mourne, Roscommon, Tralee, Waterford and West Waterford. Their activities are many and varied, but all have as their primary objective the protection, preservation and enhancement of the natural and built environment through positive action. Most Trusts would cite the fact that, with limited manpower and resources at their disposal, state agencies and local authorities cannot be expected to meet all of the demands involved in the conservation and enhancement of the national heritage. Local groups, therefore, wished to take a pro-active role in improving and conserving their own surroundings. The Civic Trust structure has proved to be an ideal way of administering such a role, and also in mustering the manpower and resources to initiate and maintain heritage and environmental projects on the ground.

Although each Civic Trust is an independent body, and there is no national Civic Trust organization, the various Trusts nonetheless maintain contact with each other whenever and wherever appropriate. Despite the independent nature of the individual Trusts, the criteria for qualifying as a Trust are clearly laid down and must be complied with by any organization hoping to attain status. To qualify as a Civic Trust, an organization must be a democratically constituted body which seeks to offer informed, knowledgeable and non-partisan opinion about the local environment and which, through its pro-active approach, undertakes projects to effect an improvement of this environment. Each Trust must have a Constitution or Memorandum and Articles of Association, and most Trusts have adopted the legal structure of companies limited by guarantee, having no share capital. In this way, the majority of Trusts meet the criteria for charitable status which one must apply for through the Charities Section of the Revenue Commissioners.

Charitable status has many important advantages in that it means that an organization is not liable for DIRT, Corporation Tax, Income Tax or Capital Gains Tax. Exemption from Capital Acquisitions Tax, Stamp Duty on transfer of land and Probate Tax can be acquired from the Capital Taxes Division, Dublin Castle, once initial charitable status has been approved. These are very important considerations should the Civic Trust assume the ownership of a building or other property, either through purchase or as a bequest. As the scale and scope of projects undertaken by Civic Trusts continue to expand to incorporate larger and more costly projects, the tax advantages of charitable status for Civic Trusts will become even more significant.

Civic Trusts are closely associated in some cases with the local authority for the area, and receive a degree of financial support from these agencies towards their annual operational costs. Such an association offers obvious advantages to both parties in that the local authority may see environmental/heritage projects completed which would have been outside the scope or budget of their environmental enhancement programme, and the Civic Trusts, on the other hand, can avail of the goodwill of the local authority in providing ancillary support where necessary. The work completed by Ennis Civic Trust on their Waterways Project and that undertaken by Limerick Civic Trust on the city's Potato Market are excellent examples of what can be done when Civic Trusts work in tandem with the local authority. It is also the case that, in some instances, planning application fees are waived by local authorities in respect of environmental/heritage projects undertaken by charities such as Civic Trusts.

A good working relationship with the local authority is therefore highly desirable, and this can be achieved by maintaining regular contact with an authority and continually updating them on present and future projects. One important point with regard to local authorities and Civic Trusts is the fact that, once environmental projects have been completed by the Trust concerned, the ongoing maintenance of the scheme may prove problematic. It is essential, therefore, that one of two things happens — either that the Trust itself continues to maintain the project to a very high standard (which in the interest of its own reputation is obviously highly desirable in any case) or that an agreement is reached with the local authority whereby they take over the ongoing care of the scheme once it has been completed by the Civic Trust. In this latter case, although the local authority has now inherited a long-standing maintenance expense, it has still benefited in that it has been saved the manpower, material and administration costs of managing a project from scratch, so it can be said to be in a win-win situation.

In the main, however, Trusts attract the bulk of their income through annual membership subscriptions, fundraising drives for specific projects or special fundraising events. As with all voluntary bodies, sourcing funds is a constant concern for Civic Trusts. Apart from membership subscriptions and annual subventions from local authorities, money can also be raised for specific projects by means of local sponsorship, grant aid from the Heritage Council, the Department of Arts, Heritage, Gaeltacht and the Islands, Bord Fáilte and from the EU. It is a measure of the high regard in which Civic Trusts are held, due to their responsible attitude to projects and the successful completion of a number of major ventures, that the *Operational Programme 1994–1999 for local urban and rural development* (Sub-Programme 3) specifically identified Civic Trusts, stating that 'support will be provided to civic trusts, conservation groups and local authorities to promote conservation measures in towns throughout the country'.

The object of these grants — which were given on the basis of matching funds from local sources — was to rehabilitate the built environment in city or town centre areas through the conservation and restoration of urban architecture and heritage buildings. A number of Civic Trusts, including those of Limerick, Cork and Dublin, have already benefited significantly from grants allocated through the Programme. In the case of all three Trusts, the restoration of Georgian buildings was undertaken. Galway Civic Trust also benefited when it received funding to restore a fishery watchtower, originally built in 1853 and which is architecturally unique in an Irish context. In undertaking projects on the ground, most Civic Trusts are highly dependant on the support of FÁS, who provide manpower in the form of Community Employment schemes. Here again, the management structure of Civic Trusts makes them very attractive sponsors in the eyes of FÁS, and much excellent work has been done by Trusts under the auspices of such schemes.

Wherever a Trust can afford it, a full-time manager/ director is employed. He/she is responsible for the day-to-day running of the Trust, the identification and administration of projects, fundraising, raising public awareness, servicing the membership and other activities. As a full-time manager myself, I can testify to the fact that having a 'public face' for the Trust, someone whom the public can associate with the Trust and form a relationship with, is an essential element in making a Trust successful.

The efforts of volunteers can only go so far in promoting an organization, but the importance of appointing a professional to oversee the work of the Trust, identify and manage new projects, and, as has already been mentioned, initiate fundraising and membership drives, cannot be overestimated. I think it is fair to say that the most successful Trusts to date have been those which have set themselves the task of appointing a full-time manager/director and, in so doing, have increased both the profile and productivity level of their Trusts. Where resources or the scope of work involved do not justify the appointment of a full-time officer, then the work of the Civic Trust management committee becomes ever more critical, but success is possible if the necessary amount of effort is put in by all the parties involved.

Regardless of size, location, whether a full-time officer is employed or not, the achievement to date of all our Civic Trusts can, in my view, be attributed to one fact — that in every case the work of individual Civic Trusts has been very practical and the results tangible. Civic Trusts are not, and should not, be 'talking shops' — they are task-based organizations which offer their members an opportunity to make a real difference to their environment. The nature of the projects undertaken may vary considerably in terms of their scale and cost — projects have ranged from the restoration of a series of Georgian houses in Limerick by Limerick Civic Trust to the planting of 2,000 daffodil bulbs by Galway Civic Trust

— but in each case the name of the Trust is associated with an undertaking which is showing tangible outcomes on the ground.

Initiating and subsequently completing a project is one thing — as has already been mentioned, ongoing maintenance of that project is another matter and one which Civic Trusts must address on a regular basis. If public goodwill is not to be lost, it is essential that the scheme must be continually maintained once completed. Individual members, who in the main are drawn from the public as well as local businesses, industries, financial institutions and so forth, pay their annual subscriptions so that they — and their company's name — can be associated with good works. If, for example, a beautifully restored riverside garden, proudly displaying its 'Civic Trust Project' plaque, is allowed to deteriorate and again become an eyesore, this reflects badly not only on the Trust itself but on all those who contributed towards the initiation of the project. A disappointed or embarrassed member is a member who will not renew his/her subscription next year, so there is an element of 'customer care' involved in maintaining projects, as well as the obvious moral responsibility which attaches itself to undertaking civic-related work.

Whether they have a full-time manager/director or not, Civic Trusts are generally run by a board of directors who identify projects, secure funding for same and oversee the work to its completion and beyond. The compilation of this Board is usually critical to the success of the Trust since it should contain people who have a specific skill which they can apply to the Trust's successful operation. Galway Civic Trust, for example, numbers amongst its board members an architect, a solicitor, an accountant, a civil engineer, a clergyman, two local councillors, a local historian and a number of successful business people, all of whom contribute their own expertise to the management of the various projects undertaken by it. From practical experience, I can confirm the old adage that 'if you want something done, ask a busy person', since all of the Board Members I have encountered in the years since the Galway Civic Trust was established have given unselfishly of their time in what are extremely busy and productive lives. From a practical point of view, it is also important to have on one's board/committee individuals who are well known and well respected as 'achievers' in either the business or civic spheres. Most Trusts will confirm that they rely on the corporate/business sectors for the bulk of their finances, so having directors/board members who can tap into these areas through personal contacts can make the difference between balancing the books at the end of the year or facing a deficit.

As well as undertaking environmental improvement projects itself, a Civic Trust can also act in an advisory capacity to other local environmental/historical groups, and may work in conjunction with such groups on specific projects. It is also part of the Trusts' remit to encourage greater public participation in the preservation and enhancement of one's own environment, and this has been very successfully achieved through the annual Civic Trusts Ireland Environmental Awards. This awards scheme is organized annually by the seventeen Civic Trusts throughout Ireland, and is specifically designed to acknowledge the improvements to the environment made by small voluntary groups or individuals, achievements which would otherwise go unnoticed or unpublicized. The definition of 'environmental improvement' is extremely broad, but it is based on the objective of enhancing the environment for the common good. Each Trust runs a local competition to identify two projects — one infrastructural, one environmental — which then go on to represent their region in the national final. The awards scheme, which is sponsored by the Gulbenkian Foundation, has been extremely successful in identifying the marvellous work being done at a local level by environmentally concerned citizens. It has also had the effect of strengthening the Civic Trust network, since a different Trust hosts the presentation of the awards each year, and the occasion provides an opportunity for all Civic Trusts to meet up and exchange news and ideas.

CONCLUSION

The significant expansion of the Civic Trust movement in recent years is indicative of the need for such bodies within our society. With the rapid growth and development which Ireland has been experiencing over the past twenty years has come prosperity, but also a threat to our built and natural environment. In the face of such dramatic change, as citizens we cannot afford to abdicate all responsibility for the care of our natural and historic environment to the state or local authorities. A Civic Trust has been found to be an excellent way of allowing local people to participate in the care of their built heritage to the extent that they are able — be it in the form of paying an annual membership contribution (and thereby be continually updated on the Trust's activities) or becoming more actively involved as a director of the Trust. Civic Trusts can operate in a very complimentary way to the work of organizations such as Dúchas, An Taisce, the Department of Arts, Heritage, Gaeltacht and the Islands, local authorities and local historical/archaeological and environmental groups.

Public awareness of the work which the Civic Trusts do is growing all the time, and as more and more projects come on stream, the effectiveness of the Civic Trust structure cannot fail to be recognized at both local and national levels. In addition, with the growth of the Trusts has come an acknowledgement by state and other bodies that there is an important role for the Trusts to play in the whole area of conservation and environmental care. As strong, local, proactive bodies, they can be seen to be playing an important part in the conservation and promotion of national heritage, and to have their finger on the pulse of how local communities wish to see their heritage and environment cared for. Given the trend from national government towards devolving responsibility for aspects of the nation's traditions to local communities, I feel it is inevitable that there will be an increasing support for the role which Civic Trusts play in the community, and that a series of formal supportive measures for Civic Trusts must inevitably be forthcoming from the state.

Private-sector Archaeology

Martin E. Byrne

This chapter summarizes the evolution of the discipline of archaeology in Ireland during recent centuries and introduces the role of the archaeologist operating in the private sector as an integral part of the story. It outlines the concept of the archaeological heritage and legislative protection, and indicates how private-sector archaeologists deal with the requirements of such legislation in their work. Archaeology is a significant and non-renewable component of Irish heritage, both in terms of landscape and culture. Ireland has a rich and diverse archaeological inheritance, one which, according to Condit (1991, 111), 'is becoming more and more recognized as being one of the country's greatest resources'. However, it has also been noted that 'while the intrinsic value of archaeology is readily accepted, archaeological sites are not always afforded an appropriate status when they come into conflict with other factors' (Johnson 1998, 13). The paper explores what these conflicting forces may be, and examines the part archaeologists in the private sector can play in reconciling the needs of archaeology as a discipline with those of a range of other interests.

ORIGINS

Archaeology in this country has a complex background which can be traced, according to Ryan (1991, 14), 'to two traditions: native historical scholarship and the curiosity of the people in the eighteenth-century enlightenment.' A great number of antiquities were noted and identified during Ascendancy times. Interest flowered in the early nineteenth century with the establishment of the Placenames Section of the Ordnance Survey, where Irish scholars such as John O'Donovan and Eugene O'Curry worked with George Petrie. A common philosophy among antiquarians in the early to middle part of the same century was concern for the object rather than the site, and many viewed monuments as potential repositories of artefacts rather than as struc-

tures which deserved study in their own right. Professional enquiry about the antiquity of man in Ireland grew from a broader scientific tradition which swept through the country especially from the mid-nineteenth century onwards. Multidisciplinary organizations such as the Cuvierian Society in Cork, the Belfast Natural History and Philosophical Society and the Royal Irish Academy already exemplified the growing absorption with scientific matters which sparked study and debate regarding, amongst other things, human origins in Ireland and the field monuments dotted across the countryside. The extraordinary vision of the Royal Irish Academy led to the creation of collections of antiquities, and these artefacts formed an essential core of the holdings of the National Museum of Ireland when they passed into its care in 1891. The formulation of historical and archaeological societies and field clubs throughout the country further helped in establishing a consciousness of field monuments and an interest in field archaeology. The establishment of the Royal Society of Antiquarians of Ireland (founded as the Kilkenny Archaeological Society in 1849) provided an important focus for historical and archaeological studies, resulting in pioneering work on the preservation of monuments *in situ*.

Growing public awareness and scholarly enquiry led, perhaps indirectly, to the consolidation of archaeology as an academic pursuit. The early years of the twentieth century witnessed the foundation of university chairs in archaeology. To put this evolution in context, as noted by Woodman (1985, 6), '... there was in 1900 only one Chair of Archaeology [in the British Isles] not necessarily concerned with Greco-Roman Classical Archaeology — the Disney Chair of Archaeology in Cambridge.' Although establishing archaeology as an academic study was an uphill struggle in many European countries, the record in Ireland was much better, '... as by the 1930's, all three Colleges [of the National University of Ireland] had

Chairs of Archaeology, an obvious testament to the richness of our material culture' (*ibid.*). These institutions provided a vehicle for study and research. Indeed, the number of excavation and survey projects undertaken by or through academic centres was matched only by those carried out under the auspices of government agencies, both north and south, with the latter usually initiating excavation works associated with the conservation of monuments and their subsequent presentation to the public.

The practice of archaeology in Ireland up until the early to mid-1980s was generally one that viewed the resource as existing for the purpose of testing hypotheses about general propositions relating to life in the past. This was especially so within the academic framework which was very much to the fore in terms of excavation and survey. Coupled with this were the investigations and excavations undertaken by the Office of Public Works, even though these were usually conducted as part of an overall monument conservation policy. Although many of the excavations undertaken by the National Museum were carried out at sites which had been accidentally discovered, these 'rescue' excavations were generally quite small as regards scale and time. However, a major change subsequently took place in relation to the preservation and investigation of the archaeological heritage. Since the 1960s, the rate of destruction of archaeological sites, both urban and rural, increased dramatically. While some sites were investigated, either by means of excavation or survey, the work was, in the main, undertaken by archaeologists employed by the state institutions. But the resources of these institutions were limited, while there were growing threats to the archaeological heritage by construction development. Furthermore, there was a developing appreciation amongst the general public of the wealth of Ireland's archaeological heritage. The National Museum excavations at Wood Quay in Dublin, for instance, brought the awareness of urban archaeology to centre stage in public perception. Furthermore, the involvement of archaeologists in the Cork — Dublin Gas Pipeline (Cleary *et al.* 1987) indicated the richness and potential of previously unknown archaeological remains that existed in subsurface/low-visibility environments. Coupled with these developments, the Archaeological Survey unit of the Office of Public Works had been established to produce a record and inventory of all known archaeological sites and/or areas of archaeological potential throughout the country. These events, amongst others, led to a greater demand for archaeological involvement in construction projects. While these demands were initially made on larger development schemes such as roads, quarries and pipelines, there was a growing understanding that many other developments might interfere with, destroy or otherwise impact on the

archaeological heritage. Increasingly, development projects required archaeological involvement to satisfy planning conditions, the terms of state and European funding and the like. These requirements led directly to a small number of archaeologists involving themselves in the private sector to accommodate the needs created by such development.

From the mid-1980s onwards, the numbers of archaeologists employed in the private sector grew in tandem with changes in and implementation of legislation. In the mid– to late 1980s, the numbers employed full-time in the sector could be measured in tens, while today there are in excess of five hundred people employed in the private sector. Many are taken on directly by archaeological consultancies and companies which operate throughout the country. There are now upwards of thirty such independent companies and consultancies located all over Ireland serving the needs of archaeology and development. These range from large organizations which specialize in substantial private and local authority projects to individuals who undertake work on behalf of small developments, as well as single projects on behalf of the larger companies and consultancies. The work carried out by archaeologists in the sector is predominantly in response to the requirements of development projects, although in more recent years, the limited manpower resources of Dúchas, the Heritage Service, have also led to this agency contracting private-sector archaeologists to undertake excavations in advance of conservation of national and other monuments, such as the projects completed at Trim and Maynooth Castles.

PRIVATE-SECTOR ARCHAEOLOGY: THE WORK AND ITS CONTEXT

While most people may be familiar with the excavation brief of an archaeologist, they are likely to have less understanding of other forms of archaeological response. These are outlined in what follows, to indicate the primary functions archaeologists in the private sector fulfil. It is also important to realise that such practitioners operate within a clearly defined legislative framework. Much of this framework has already been outlined elsewhere in the present volume. We begin with a brief review of other Irish statutory requirements not previously discussed, and then pay closer attention to important EU measures which impact on the day-to-day operations at issue here.

LEGISLATION

The principal legislation relating to the protection of Ireland's archaeological heritage has been dealt with in other chapters here. Archaeologists working in the private sector in Ireland also have to operate within other legislative provisions. The *Gas Act* 1976 placed a statutory responsibility on An Bord Gáis regarding the protection of the archaeological heritage in the course of pipeline construction. The *Harbours Act* 1996 provides that harbour companies established under the act shall have regard to heritage matters, while the *Fisheries (Amendment) Act* 1997 requires that natural and man-made heritage will be taken into account in aquaculture licensing. The *Turf Development Act* 1998 stipulates that Bord na Móna is to have a responsibility regarding the protection of the archaeological heritage. The European Community's Environmental Impact Assessment (EIA) Regulations 1989, amended 1999 (the EIA Regulations), provide for the implementation in Ireland of the Environmental Impact Assessment Directives. EC Council Directive 85/337/EEC (amended by Directive 97/11/EC) was implemented in this country by means of Statutory Instruments 349 of 1989 and 93 of 1999 respectively. As a result of these regulations, certain classes of development, defined in the regulations, require that an Environmental Impact Statement (EIS) be prepared in relation to the development. This requirement operates both within the guidelines of the planning acts and within the legislative control framework of other measures such as the *Roads Act* and the *Foreshore Act*.

In summary, an EIA must be prepared by, or on behalf of, a developer (state or private) when a proposed development is likely to have significant effects on the environment. The EIA must contain, *inter alia*, a description of the project, a description of the likely effects of the construction and operation of the scheme and the suggested measures to avoid, reduce and, if possible remedy, the adverse effects. The EIA must contain an account of the likely significant effects (if any) and proposed steps to ameliorate these influences on human beings, fauna, flora, soil, water, air, climate, the landscape, the interaction between the above, material assets and cultural heritage. Archaeological, architectural and historical concerns are examined under the 'Cultural Heritage' rubric which can be defined, in terms of an EIA, as being assumed to comprise all humanly created or derived features on the landscape, including portable artefacts, which reflect the prehistoric, historic, architectural, engineering and/or social history of the study area, with a cut-off point based on obsolescence, items having gone out of common use and/or reflective of skills and techniques no longer practised.

ASSESSMENT STUDY

Private-sector archaeologists carry out various tasks within the context of the foregoing legislation when going about their work. The first of these is the Assessment Study. The principal step in any Assessment/Desk-top Study is for the archaeologist to examine the plans of a proposed development, preferably in as full and as detailed a way as possible.

From this, one can determine requirements like earth-moving, foundation and service trench excavations, foundation details and landscaping relevant to the development. In determining the archaeological profile of the proposed project, a number of avenues of research are open to the archaeologist. These include in-depth examination of cartographic, documentary and aerial photographic sources as well as detailed field-walking of the site. Non-destructive geophysical survey techniques might be used in determining the extent of any archaeological sites within the boundaries of the development. Furthermore, one could also undertake some exploratory/test excavations, as described below. Following a consideration of the archaeological study and development plans, a statement on the impacts that the scheme, as proposed, will have on archaeology can be formulated. This statement may include a description of the impacts on the visible archaeological remains, the further investigation of possible sites or ways of mitigating impacts on probable and unpredictable remains which could turn up in the course of construction.

In many cases, it is advisable to seek the services of an archaeologist to undertake such an assessment prior to the finalization of development proposals, in order that any changes can be implemented at the project's design stage. This can help avoid costly delays, costly in terms of both time and money, especially if the project needs to go through the planning process. If a scheme meets the criteria set out in EIS legislation, or if an EIS is required by a planning authority, then an Assessment Study, similar to that outlined above, will be included under the 'Cultural Heritage' heading of the EIS. Any development located within an 'urban zone of archaeological potential' should have an Assessment Study undertaken because of the complexity of subsurface archaeological remains that might exist within such areas. In addition, it is current government policy that linear developments, especially, but not necessarily, those over one kilometre in length, should be subjected to an archaeological assessment (DAHGI 1999b, 26).

TEST EXCAVATION

Test excavation may be used to determine the nature and extent of archaeological deposits, features or structures that might be present at a location in which it is proposed to undertake development works, in order that an assessment can be made of the archaeological impact of the proposed development on such features and deposits. It generally takes the form of the excavation, by hand, machine or a combination of both, of a number of pits or trenches within the boundaries of a development site, especially within the confines of the construction area. Test excavation is a very useful tool when designing the foundations of a building, especially in an urban context, where one seeks to ensure *in situ* preservation of archaeological material. Furthermore, where it is accepted and agreed that a known archaeological site must be removed to allow development to proceed, then test excavation can be used to assist in the planning and costing of full-scale scientific excavation.

MONITORING

This involves an archaeologist being present in the course of the carrying out of development works, especially topsoil stripping in 'greenfield' areas, in order that any unknown subsurface features or deposits can be identified. Such features can then be assessed, especially through test excavation, or protected. Monitoring is usually carried out where development works, such as building projects, road, water and sewerage schemes, are being undertaken '... in the vicinity of known or suspected archaeological sites or monuments but [where] there are only slight grounds for believing that the particular location contains archaeological deposits or features (and especially if the development works are minor in nature)' (DAHGI 1999b, 28).

OTHER

Other works that archaeologists undertake include underwater surveys, especially around the coast. However, an increasing aspect of underwater work is that of the investigation of fords and other river crossings, or where specific development works, such as roads or pipes, cross rivers. Generally, such surveys and investigations are undertaken as a component of an overall Assessment Study. Archaeologists are also involved in topographical surveys, especially when examining the archaeological heritage from a landscape perspective, while the surveying and recording of architectural or other extant archaeological features is usually carried out by an archaeologist with appropriate training.

One further field of work, now almost exclusively the domain of those employed in the private sector, is that of post-excavation services. The latter may include the identification and analysis of pottery, the identification and analysis of such items as animal bones, beetles or seeds from archaeological deposits which aid in the overall interpretation of an archaeological site, as well as helping better to understand past environments and living conditions. Furthermore, the conservation of the many objects recovered through archaeological involvement in development projects is also undertaken by a number of specialists employed in the sector.

MEETING OFFICIAL REQUIREMENTS

As indicated above, much of the work of the archaeologist is conducted as a response to conditions included in grants of planning in respect of certain development types or in response to recommendations from the state

archaeological agencies. The latter recommendations are usually issued in reply to a query either from a local authority or the consulting engineers acting on behalf of a local authority. Many of these enquiries are sent in relation to planned sewerage, water or road improvement schemes which do not reach the EIS threshold. A typical recommendation from the National Monuments and Historic Properties Section of Dúchas, the Heritage Service, in response to a query in relation to such a scheme, is as follows:

> Please note that due to the nature and extent of the proposed scheme, there is a possibility that archaeological material may be encountered during the construction phase of the works. It is therefore recommended that an archaeologist be employed to carry out Archaeological Monitoring of the scheme at construction phase.
>
> The archaeologist should be provided in advance with a set of all available plans, sections, etc. for the proposed scheme. The archaeologist should also be provided in advance with a schedule of works and the archaeologist shall specify when archaeological inspections shall be carried out. It may not be necessary to have an archaeologist in attendance on site on a full time basis for the entire duration of the scheme. Having received detailed plans and the schedule of works, the archaeologist shall outline the required archaeological approach to the scheme. The required archaeological monitoring/site inspections should be carried out under licence to the Department of Arts, Heritage Gaeltacht and the Islands.

Here, the actual requirement is for an Archaeological Assessment to be undertaken in advance of construction works, and the minimum level of response during construction is that monitoring be conducted. However, should the scheme have an impact on a known site or monument, then the archaeologist may suggest some type of mitigation to ensure the protection of such a site. This might take the form of Archaeological Testing in order to determine the extent of the site and the rerouting of the scheme around such a site. This is more usual in the case of schemes that require the laying of pipes which might easily be rerouted. Alternatively, it might be necessary to undertake a full-scale excavation of the site in order to allow the project to proceed. The latter case usually involves the construction of roads, where changes to the route cannot be effected as easily as with pipe schemes.

In many instances, especially in relation to developments requiring consents of planning, the archaeological condition might more clearly specify the level of archaeological response and compliance. As described above, the actual wording of such a condition may have come directly from Dúchas; unfortunately, many local authorities include their own form of wording which can lead to confusion and difficulties for both the applicant and the archaeologist involved. (This point will be expanded upon more fully below.) A typical archaeological condition in relation to a development located close to a known archaeological site, or located within an urban area, is as follows:

The applicant shall employ an archaeologist to carry out an Archaeological Assessment of the proposed development site. The archaeologist shall prepare and submit a report describing the results of the Archaeological Assessment to the National Monuments Service, Dúchas, The Heritage Service, and the Local Authority prior to the commencement of site preparation works and/or construction works.

The Archaeological Assessment shall be based on documentary research and on the excavation of a number of test trenches within the proposed development site. The location of test trenches within the site shall be specified by the archaeologist employed, having examined the plans for the proposed development.

The assessment will involve the preparation of a report on the nature, extent, location and levels of archaeological material within the proposed development site, based on the excavation of these test trenches. Where archaeological material is shown to be present, a detailed Archaeological Impact Statement shall be included in the report. The potential impact of the proposed development on the archaeology within the site shall be described in detail. The impact statement shall give specific information on the extent, levels and location of all proposed foundations, service trenches, access roadway and all other sub-surface works associated with the development.

It is essential that the Archaeological Assessment Report be submitted to the Local Authority and the National Monuments Service, Dúchas, The Heritage Service, prior to the commencement of site preparation and/or construction works. The developer shall be prepared to be advised by the National Monuments Service with regard to the appropriate course of action should archaeological material be discovered. Further archaeological requirements may be identified by the National Monuments Service, Dúchas The Heritage Service, pending the results of the Archaeological Assessment.

This particular condition provides a specific briefing document for the archaeological consultant, requesting that an Archaeological Assessment, including Testing, be undertaken in relation to the proposed development. The form of such an assessment is clearly laid out and there can be no ambiguity as to what is required. Furthermore, the obligation on the applicant with regard to what might happen if archaeological material is uncovered and impacted upon is also introduced, and it is implied that no development works should begin until the results of the assessment are analysed and responded to. In some cases, the wording might include a line such as '... construction works shall not commence on site until written authorisation has been issued by

Dúchas The Heritage Service ...'.

The instances mentioned above indicate the two main spheres of activity in which an archaeologist might be involved as regards development projects, namely proactive and reactive. In the proactive role, the archaeologist participates in the design or pre-planning phase of a development, working as a team member in order that the project is well structured and thought out. The identification of possible impacts that any design proposal might have on any sites and monuments, either known or of archaeological potential, can be addressed almost immediately and the best development model can be designed. This is especially true of large infrastructural schemes such as road design, or in the planning of industrial and housing complexes. The same holds good for small-scale developments, but unfortunately archaeological involvement may only be requested after the development has been finalized and/or planning approval sought. In the reactive role, the archaeologist may be required to assess any given development as a condition of planning or, in terms of local authority schemes, after the construction contracts have been signed. In these cases, unnecessary design changes and costly delays might result from the identification of archaeological sites and monuments, whether high- or low-visibility in form. Furthermore, in some instances, full-scale excavation of a site might be required which could have been undertaken during the lead-in phase to a particular development.

CURRENT CONCERNS

As can be seen from the foregoing, archaeologists operating in the private sector, especially those who work in a consultative/managerial role, are very much involved in 'development-led' projects and act in such a manner as to ensure that design measures are implemented which allow for minimal, if any, impacts on the archaeological heritage (although, unfortunately, this is not always the case). Many function as consultants, working in a proactive role, as well as contractors, operating in a reactive capacity when providing the management and staff required for the implementation of excavation and monitoring projects. As a consequence of both changes to and the implementation of legislation, coupled with unprecedented increases in development projects, this particular sector of the archaeological profession became firmly established in a period of about fifteen years. However, the picture is not altogether rosy. Despite the changes in legislation and the creation of private consultancies and companies, the present immense scale of development is causing problems because of overstretched resources. There are many issues now coming to the surface which, unless properly addressed, will lead to a greater strain on the archaeological resource in terms of both identification and protection, and these will be outlined in what follows. Even though there are a number of areas of conflict between the developments needs of the country as a whole and the protection of the archaeological heritage, nevertheless the overall picture has some positive aspects to it. In the past, many of those involved in the construction industry, including developers, builders and development agencies, viewed archaeology as an unnecessary and costly hindrance which caused delays to the implementation of projects as well as unexpected increases in the overall cost-base of such projects. On the other hand, archaeologists looked on the development and construction industry with suspicion, believing that such groups would leave no stone unturned in attempting to ensure that archaeological issues could be discreetly avoided. However, while a certain amount of conflict still exists, this has begun to be resolved through interaction between the two groups. Furthermore, the involvement of archaeologists at the early design stage, and indeed even prior to site purchase, has meant that issues relating to both time and perceived costs are now factored into the overall design and implementation concepts.

LICENSING

We now turn to a brief overview of some issues causing problems at present. Much of the physical investigative work conducted by archaeologists, by means of test and full-scale excavations, must be undertaken under licence from the Department of Arts, Heritage, Gaeltacht and the Islands. This legal requirement has been in effect since 1930 and is used as a control to secure, amongst other desiderata, best practise and professional standards in the carrying out of excavations. In more recent times, most monitoring work is also required to be undertaken under licence. While the reasons for such licensing are laudable, the implementation of the policy has caused difficulties for Dúchas, for archaeologists in general and also for the completion of development projects. At present, there is no classification or categorization of licences. All are referred to as 'Excavation Licences', and before an archaeologist is granted a first-time licence, he/she must be assessed by an interview panel. In addition, before anyone can apply for the licence, they have to acquire a certain amount of 'hands on' experience. At present, there are fewer that one hundred archaeologists qualified to hold a licence who are working in the private sector. This low figure, coupled with the fact that only a very small number of first-time applicant archaeologists are fulfilling the criteria set out by the licensing authority, means that the available manpower is very much overstretched. One of the reasons for this is that an individual is unable to hold multiple licences, while the licences are both person- and site/project-specific. It is now generally agreed that

this system is antiquated and that a graded licensing system, similar to that operated in the United States, might be more appropriate.

The issuing of licences has also caused problems for the licensing authority which, in many ways, has become a victim of the relative success of legislative protection policies. Currently, only one individual deals with licence applications in Dúchas. In 1990, approximately one hundred and twenty licence applications were dealt with by the licensing authority. By way of contrast, over 1,000 applications were received during 1999. This has lead to delays in both the processing and issuing of licences as well as the overall implementation of policies regarding the licensing of excavations. The shortage in personnel dealing with the licence applications, coupled with similar restrictions in the archaeology and planning area, means that the central agency responsible for the protection of the archaeological patrimony is very much overstretched, bringing the system close to collapse. Indeed, shortages in the archaeology and planning area have led to situations where individual archaeologists have to deal with all archaeological queries, from planning authorities, developers and archaeologists, for a range of counties. Thus one individual deals with all enquiries relating to Wexford, Wicklow, Carlow, Kildare, Laois, Offaly and Kilkenny. This, understandably, has led to huge pressures on the system in the issuing of recommendations to planning authorities. This, in turn, can have a detrimental effect on the protection of the archaeological heritage.

RECOMMENDATIONS AND CONDITIONS

Related to the latter topic is the implementation of Dúchas-based recommendations as to the conditions of planning outlined earlier. In some instances where an assessment, including testing, has been recommended, a planning authority may take it upon itself to put in a monitoring clause. This can have an adverse effect on the overall development project, as archaeological material which is revealed through monitoring will require some form of mitigation following a determination of its nature and extent through testing. This might range from avoidance to a redesign of foundations and site layout or to full excavation. In the latter cases, it might be necessary for construction to be halted while the excavation is undertaken, while redesign of a site layout could require an additional application for planning approval. In some instances, planning authorities may not include any condition pertaining to the archaeological potential of a site, despite a recommendation for such. In this case, the original grant of planning might be appealed to An Bord Pleanála, resulting in delays to the implementation of the project. Furthermore, in some situations, a planning authority may include an archaeological condition in relation to a development without seeking the advice of Dúchas. In this case, the implementation of the development may also be retarded, as there might be delays associated with the issuing a licence by Dúchas until a desk-top type assessment is prepared.

Associated with the problems outlined above is the overall concept of the protection of the archaeological heritage through planning legislation. At present, there is no audit system in place to determine whether archaeological conditions are actually being complied with, as it is up to each planning authority to verify that such conditions are being implemented. (The only way in which Dúchas know whether conditions are being observed is when they receive licence applications from archaeologists or a request to proceed with unlicensed monitoring.) Furthermore, at present, the Department of Arts, Heritage, Gaeltacht and the Islands has it in mind to enter into arrangements with some local authorities with a view to employing local authority archaeologists. This arrangement exists at present in Cork city and county, county Kerry, Limerick city and Dublin city. There seems to be a consensus that such local authority archaeologists would be employed to assess planning applications, inspect developments to determine whether the appropriate archaeological conditions were being implemented, undertake assessments in relation to local authority schemes, as well as becoming involved in the general protection of the archaeological heritage within the relevant authority area. While a move of this kind would be welcome in terms both of archaeology and development, it is clear that such a broad range of duties could not be undertaken by one individual alone, especially in relation to county council areas, and that the concept would only be successful if a significant number of archaeological staff were employed.

QUALIFICATIONS AND TRAINING

The question of education is also to the fore within the private sector. Most people employed in archaeology have obtained primary degrees in Arts, while many have masters degrees in some relevant field of archaeological study. However, there is a need for more vocational training for archaeologists in terms of the overall education and application of skills. In some instances, those with a masters degree may only have spent up to ten days on an archaeological excavation during the entire length of their third-level education. Some attempts have been made to redress this situation, such as via the Masters in Practical Archaeology offered by the Department of Archaeology at UCC. It is very difficult for consultancies and companies to implement long and detailed training programmes within their own resources, given the type of work in which they are involved. Consequently, there is a need for all sectors to identify the changing requirements of the profession as a

whole and to discuss how archaeologists may be educated to a basic practitioner level. In this respect, the national representative body for archaeologists, the Irish Association of Professional Archaeologists (IAPA), has a central role to play. At present there are moves afoot to disband this body and to establish a new organization with institute status. This new entity could aid in the development of the profession at large, especially the private sector, in running workshops and short-term courses as part of its overall corporate identity.

IAPA is currently involved in publishing a range of codes of best practice for its membership, as well as in the preparation of technical papers on various archaeological issues such as human remains (Buckley *et al.* 1999), underwater archaeology and wetland archaeology. It is to be hoped that the establishment of a more formal corporate body in the near future will help standardize the practice of archaeology as well as shaping its role in society as a whole.

CONCLUSION

Archaeology in Ireland has a long and auspicious tradition which, for a considerable time, remained confined within certain sectors, for instance academia. However, changes in attitude among the general public and legislators with regard to the appreciation and protection of the archaeological heritage have led to major transformations within the profession generally. The variety of organizations employing archaeologists to undertake work on their behalf has grown considerably in the last fifteen years. Allied to this are the work opportunities which now exist for individual practitioners within the private sector, although many of these are vulnerable to the economic cycles of expansion and contraction in employment.

One must always bear in mind that the overall justification for professional archaeological practice is the safeguarding of the resource for future generations, as well as the investigation of those sites which cannot be preserved using 'best prevailing standards', although there is considerable doubt as to whether the present overstretched structures, within both the state and private sectors, can cope with the ever-increasing demands on their respective resources, or indeed whether they are appropriately equipped towards this end. The concept of 'developer pays' has led to many improvements in the field, especially with regard to assessment studies. Furthermore, the awareness of archaeological issues, especially in the context of development, among other professions has increased as they come into more formal contact with archaeologists.

However, many other approaches are at risk in light of the present trends in archaeology, foremost of which are concepts central to the interests of academic enquiry, namely the necessity to integrate the results of the numerous archaeological discoveries that have been made and investigated as a result of 'development-led' archaeology. The integration of such investigations into academic study can be of immense use to broader research agendas, which were curtailed in the past due to prohibitive financial considerations. These discoveries are important in expanding the notion of archaeological landscapes as the discovery of many previously unknown low-visibility sites comes to form part of the archaeological record. They also help establish more appropriate and coherent policies for archaeological resource and heritage management. We shall no doubt be judged by future generations on how effectively we shall have aligned practical day-to-day development requirements with such research strategies.

Bibliography

Buckley, L., Murphy, E. and Ó Donnabháin, B. (compliers) 1999 *The treatment of human remains: technical paper for archaeologists.* Dublin.

Cleary, R. M., Hurley, M. F. and Twohig, E. 1987 *Archaeological excavations on the Cork-Dublin gas pipeline (1981–2)*, Cork Archaeological Studies 1. Cork.

Condit, T. 1991 'Archaeology' in K. Bradley, C. Skeehan and G. Walsh (eds) *Environmental Impact Assessment: a technical approach* (Dublin), pp. 111–15.

DAHGI (Department of Arts, Heritage, Gaeltacht and the Islands) 1999a *Policy and guidelines on archaeological excavation.* Dublin.

DAHGI (Department of Arts, Heritage, Gaeltacht and the Islands) 1999b *Framework and principles for the protection of the archaeological heritage.* Dublin.

Johnson, G. 1998 *Archaeology and forestry in Ireland.* Kilkenny.

Ryan, M. (ed) 1991 *The illustrated archaeology of Ireland.* Dublin.

Woodman, P. C. 1985 *Seeing is believing — problems of archaeological visibility.* Inaugural Lecture Series No. 2, UCC. Cork.

FÁS and Ireland's Archaeological Heritage

JOHN SHEEHAN

Since its establishment in 1988, FÁS (Foras Áiseanna Saothair) has been involved in literally hundreds of projects which relate to heritage, arts and the environment. These range widely in nature and type, encompassing, for instance, aspects of history, genealogy, archaeology, folklore, music and theatre. No other state body or organization, with the exception of the Heritage Council, operates within a heritage remit as broad as that which FÁS has developed for itself. Neither does any other body interface directly with local organizations and communities to the same degree as FÁS does. The purpose of this chapter, which is written from the experience of one who worked as a co-ordinator on a FÁS heritage project for some years (the Iveragh Peninsula Archaeological Survey), is to consider and discuss the role of FÁS in the area of heritage studies and development in Ireland —particularly those relating to archaeology.

BACKGROUND

FÁS was established through the amalgamation of AnCO (An Chomhairle Oiliúna), the National Manpower Service and the Youth Employment Agency as part of the state's response to the alarmingly high levels of unemployment that characterized Ireland's economy during much of the 1980s. AnCO was the largest of these three bodies and mainly operated by providing skill-based industrial training schemes from within a network of regional centres. For some years before its amalgamation into FÁS, however, it had begun a process of broadening the range and type of its training activities to include community-based projects. These did not necessarily involve the provision of industrial-type skills, nor were they usually based within its regional training centres. In terms of the training opportunities these projects provided, the emphasis was focussed on transferable, rather than specific, skills. It was during this phase that AnCO first became involved in heritage as a

vehicle for training. Among the most notable of its early heritage projects was the field-survey of archaeological sites and monuments conducted in the barony of Ikerrin, county Tipperary (Stout 1984), which was one of a series of heritage and environment projects administered by AnCO in partnership with the Roscrea Heritage Society.

In purely pragmatic terms, one of the main values of community-based heritage projects to AnCO, and subsequently to FÁS, was that they could be established and run practically anywhere. By their nature they generally did not require the equipment and facilities available in the organization's regional training centres, each of which is located in cities or regional and county towns. Consequently, such projects could be established at town, village or parish level under FÁS External Training programmes (now Community Services). In an era of unprecedented unemployment levels, this presented an opportunity to FÁS to react to the economic situation by expanding the numbers of training projects throughout the country without having to expend large amounts of capital on centralized infrastructure.

During this period, government instructed FÁS several times to expand the numbers both of its trainees and its training programmes. This, in turn, contributed to further increases in the numbers of heritage projects being initiated. A related factor in the rise of the FÁS heritage project, which was equally relevant, was the increasing level of emphasis being placed by many agencies on the role of tourism, particularly cultural tourism, within the overall economy. The fact that jobs in the tourism sector of the economy were cheaper to create than those in its mainstream industrial sector contributed to this increased focus. Inevitably, however, the importance and value of heritage increasingly came to be judged in terms of its economic potential. Given the background of FÁS as an organization involved in training for industry, it is perhaps not surprising that the general equation of heritage with a form of industry appealed to it. In many instances, unfortunately, the corollary was that the academic value of a heritage resource was not considered to be of primary importance in itself and was not included among the primary criteria used in the assessment of potential training projects. In this sense FÁS contributed towards an increased acceptance, particularly at local community level, of the tendency to justify heritage validity in economic terms. It was, of course, not the only government agency responsible for this development.

The assessment process through which proposals for potential FÁS projects are considered, whether these are to be conducted under the CYTP (Community Youth Training Programme), CEP (Community Enterprise Programme) or SES (Social Employment Scheme) programmes, is of interest in this regard. Any organization or group which represents community interests and is non-commercial in nature may submit a proposal for consideration. While it may encourage and facilitate the preparation of such proposals, FÁS does not officially initiate them. The proposals are examined and assessed at regional level by a committee consisting of representatives from FÁS, the CIF (Construction Industry Federation) and the trade unions. The criteria which may be examined include: the availability of unemployed people in the relevant location; the actual training opportunities the project may provide; whether long-term benefits to the local community may arise from the project and, finally, the likelihood of strong community backing for and involvement with it. Occasionally, depending on the nature of the proposal, the regional committee might also consider if its implementation is likely to lead towards an increased level of awareness within the local community of the practical value of a resource. It may be observed that the benefits and value of a potential project and of the resource on which it is based are primarily measured in social or economic, rather than in academic, terms. This is unfortunate, though it is also understandable given the *raison d'être* of FÁS as a training agency. Nevertheless, it may be argued that academic research can sometimes benefit in this process.

The degree to which different numbers of heritage projects have been operated by FÁS in its various regions appears to be influenced by several variables. Primarily, it is related to the amount of demand there is at local community level for such projects. This, in turn, is influenced by many factors, including the differing levels of community activism and organized heritage awareness that exist within each region. Perhaps the single most important factor, however, is the nature of the local economy and the extent to which tourism contributes to it. In an important tourism region such as Cork/Kerry, for instance, the total number of FÁS heritage projects initiated over the past decade or so is greatly in excess of those undertaken, for instance, in Laois/Offaly, a region which is not perceived as remotely comparable in terms of the importance of its tourism industry. Indeed, the scale of several of the FÁS projects in the former region, such as the West Cork Model Railway Village in Clonakilty and the Blennerville Windmill project in Tralee, does not find parallel outside the more established tourism regions.

Due to the broad variety of heritage projects that FÁS has become involved in, it is not possible to discuss all categories of them here. A selection of projects which relate to archaeology is considered, however, in order to illustrate their range and diversity. This is also a means of drawing attention to some of the problems that have been associated with certain types of projects, as well as considering the successes of others.

BUILDING RESTORATION

Throughout the country, numerous buildings, mainly of nineteenth-century date, have been restored to use under different types of FÁS schemes. In architectural or historical terms, some of these buildings are of regional importance including, for example, the spectacular RIC barracks at Cahersiveen, county Kerry, now in use as a heritage centre, and the group of vernacular houses at Cill Rialaig, also in Kerry, which now serves as artists' residences and workshops. Other examples include buildings, such as mills, that form part of the industrial archaeological heritage. The majority, however, comprise buildings of purely local significance, such as redundant school-houses or churches, which are often put to new use as community or social services centres.

It is an unfortunate fact, however, that the quality of many such restoration projects leaves something to be desired. The removal and non-replacement of old renders from walls, the application of strap-pointing to traditional stonework, the replacement of roofing slate with asbestos tiles and the use of inappropriate thatching styles have been characteristic of building restoration projects involving FÁS throughout the country. Objections to the use of such approaches are not just confined to aesthetic considerations. Several of the techniques and practices mentioned above can also result in damage to the actual fabric of buildings in the long term.

The restoration and use of old buildings is important in heritage terms as they can lead to increased recognition and appreciation of their place in the heritage of a locality. It is often the case that, without the use of FÁS training schemes, it would not be financially feasible to undertake such projects. The prevalence of poor standards has itself created a demand for improvement, however. As a result, several architectural conservation and training companies, which sometime work in consultation with FÁS, have been established. The existence of these, in conjunction with recent publications on the subject of conserving and repairing traditional stone walls and buildings (for instance McAfee 1997, 1998), should contribute to an overall improvement in the standards of FÁS building restoration projects.

GRAVEYARD CLEAN-UPS

Few types of FÁS projects have given rise to more negative reaction in the past than the ubiquitous graveyard clearance schemes. These were usually undertaken in association with local community or heritage groups, and frequently it was the older cemeteries, areas of potentially high archaeological sensitivity, that were the focus of attention (A. I. 1990). Sometimes, clearance was carried out in an excessive manner, such as using heavy machinery to remove overgrowth, which could technically amount to illegal excavation under national monuments legislation. On other occasions, chemical weedkillers were used to deal with overgrowth, an approach that can have devastating consequences on the potentially rare plants and insects which sometimes exist in the relatively undisturbed environments of old graveyards. Excessive cleaning of headstones, sometimes involving sand-blasting, resulted in damage to their inscriptions and led to their accelerated erosion. In other cases, ivy was removed from buildings without advance provision being made for necessary conservation works.

It should be noted that FÁS did make efforts to control its graveyard clearance schemes. A series of guidelines, for instance, were produced by the organization in order to mitigate recurring problems (Doran 1986, 1989). Indeed, many graveyards were sensitively and competently dealt with. However, guidelines were not always implemented properly at local level and, in some cases, FÁS personnel did not seem to have been aware of their existence. The situation was complicated by the fact that some graveyard clearances were carried out, without specific sanction from FÁS, as part of wider environmental improvement schemes under its SES programme. In such cases, FÁS was not necessarily aware of the full plans of the well-intentioned but sometimes ill-informed local groups who sponsored these schemes. Despite this, however, it must be acknowledged that responsibility for a considerable amount of irreversible damage to Ireland's graveyard heritage ultimately lies with FÁS, largely because of its failure to implement appropriate standards.

In recent years, as a result of consultations initiated by the National Monuments Service of the Office of Public Works (now Dúchas), it was agreed that FÁS require local groups to commission an archaeologist to prepare a guideline report for each scheme involving an archaeologically sensitive graveyard. Such reports and their recommendations must be approved by Dúchas before the funding of schemes can be sanctioned by FÁS (Kirwin 1992, 6; Bourke et al. 1995, 8). While this development had the potential to lead towards an improvement in standards, this did not universally prove to be the case. The experience of archaeologists involved as advisors on such schemes was that, in many instances, there was a failure by local groups fully to understand the import of their recommendations and to execute them as required. In addition, the important question of the provision of ongoing archaeological supervision during the operation of certain projects was, they felt, 'largely ignored if not discouraged by both FÁS and local community groups' (IAPA 1994). Part of the reason for this arises from the position of FÁS that it is not its responsibility, but that of the local group, to raise the funding necessary to engage archaeological advice. In cases where archaeological supervision is required on a regular basis, local groups often prove unable to provide such funding.

FÁS has been involved in many graveyard clearance and maintenance projects which were carried out in a responsible manner and which resulted in positive outcomes. In overall terms, however, the organization has also been responsible for much damage. The fault for this is largely its own and relates to its failure firmly to establish and follow appropriate regulatory mechanisms for this type of project. If FÁS changed its policy and assumed responsibility for funding the specialist advice and monitoring which is necessary for the proper operation of such projects, rather than delegating this function to local groups, there is little doubt but that the general standards of these would improve significantly.

EXCAVATION

The role played by FÁS in archaeological excavation and post-excavation projects has generally been impressive. In several cases, excavation of important sites, which might not otherwise have been economically feasible, was made possible with the assistance of FÁS. In Waterford, for instance, no less than one-fifth of the area of the Viking Age settlement was excavated using workers recruited under a FÁS scheme during the late 1980s and early 1990s (Hurley et al. 1997). The total area amounted to the largest excavated portion of any historic city in Europe, and the results of the project are of international importance.

Like many other excavation projects involving FÁS, the Waterford campaign was carried out under an SES programme. There are drawbacks, however, to using this type of scheme for archaeological excavation projects. The workers, for instance, were selected and recruited by FÁS without any input from the archaeologists involved in the project. More importantly, as SES schemes operated on a week-on/week-off basis, there was a limit to the level of understanding of the relationships between site contexts that could be achieved by workers operating without continuity. In addition, the regulations and conditions of the SES scheme itself were sometimes frustrating from the point of view of the archaeologists involved. In the example of the Waterford excavations, for instance, there were cases of experienced excavators who could not be taken on the scheme because they had not been unemployed for long enough to satisfy its eligibility criteria, while, on the other hand, workers with a natural aptitude for archaeology had to leave the scheme when their eligibility expired (Forbes 1987, 13). It should be noted, however, that in many similar instances, FÁS showed a willingness to facilitate projects by adopting flexible approaches to such problems.

In the past, FÁS has also facilitated, in conjunction with bodies such as Dúchas and the Heritage Council, the completion of post-excavation projects. For instance, it was involved in work arising from the excavation of important medieval sites at Skiddy's Castle and Christ Church, Cork (Cleary *et al*. 1997). In such cases, the involvement of FÁS has not only helped bring projects to publication stage but has also contributed towards keeping down the overall costs of what is usually an expensive process.

SURVEY

A small number of projects involving the descriptive survey of archaeological sites and monuments have been run by FÁS, usually as part of its Community Response Training Programme. Most of these have been conducted in parts of counties Mayo, Tipperary and Kerry. It is unclear why this type of project has been confined to these areas, though the willingness of local FÁS personnel to support such initiatives is probably an important factor in this regard.

The purpose of these surveys, apart from the obvious one of providing young trainees with opportunities to develop their skills and potential within a work environment, is to publish their results. This has been achieved with only a limited degree of success. For instance, only two of the three FÁS surveys conducted in Kerry and one of the six baronies surveyed in the north Tipperary/south Offaly region have been published (Stout 1984; Toal 1995; O'Sullivan and Sheehan 1996). Part of the reason for this relates to the policy of not funding publications, though it is also clear that some of the local heritage groups which sponsor these surveys fail to achieve their fund-raising targets. The result is that most of the archaeological surveys conducted by FÁS exist only in archive form. Thus, while FÁS may achieve its primary aim of providing training, the full archaeological benefits of some survey projects are not realized.

Normally, there is a high ratio of trainees to qualified archaeologists on FÁS archaeological survey projects.

The fact that the majority of personnel is untrained in archaeology results in obvious disadvantages. For instance, it inevitably takes longer to complete a survey of an area under such schemes than under those which employ only professional archaeologists. However, there can also be considerable advantages to FÁS surveys from the archaeological perspective and the high discovery rates of previously unrecorded monuments on some of them testifies to this.

The Iveragh Peninsula Archaeological Survey, which conducted its fieldwork from 1986 until 1993, made important discoveries within almost all of the monument categories represented in this part of Kerry (O'Sullivan and Sheehan 1996). For instance, when the survey commenced, there were virtually no *fulachta fiadha* on record from the peninsula. Subsequent field investigation, conducted by trainees under the supervision of archaeologists, yielded almost fifty examples. The most dramatic discovery rate, however, was that of prehistoric rock art: in 1973, a total of forty-four individual examples, occurring at seventeen separate locations, was on record from Iveragh and the survey increased these figures to one hundred and nineteen and forty-three respectively. This remarkable result was achieved as a result of intensive fieldwork which was only made possible by the nature of the survey itself. The economic and financial factors relating to manpower costs which constrain certain activities on Dúchas's Archaeological Survey of Ireland do not apply to the same extent on a FÁS survey. In the former, for instance, it would not usually be considered cost-efficient to engage large numbers of personnel in non-specific programmes of fieldwalking exercises. On FÁS surveys, however, this can prove to be a viable and archaeologically rewarding tactic. In Iveragh, for example, teams of trainees, under the supervision of archaeologists, regularly fieldwalked tracts of bog and mountain on which there were no recorded field monuments, and significant numbers of monuments of varying date and type were discovered and recorded. For instance, work on the lower slopes of Mullagharakill Mountain resulted in the discovery of a complex of nineteen examples of rock art in the townland of Kealduff Upper; this site now ranks as the second-greatest concentration of rock art in Ireland. Elsewhere on the peninsula, significant numbers of previously unrecorded megaliths, standing stones and middens were also discovered in this way. It is important to point out that the majority of sites and monuments of this type, owing to their nature and size, would not have been detected using conventional aerial photographic or other non-field-based survey techniques.

Another major advantage in carrying out a programme of archaeological fieldwork under a FÁS programme is that the majority of personnel involved are from the locality. A consequence of this on the Iveragh project was that there was a very good level of rapport between the survey teams and the local landowners. It is felt that this often resulted in the acquisition of important archaeological and topographical information which otherwise might not have been so readily forthcoming. Information from local people frequently led to the discovery of previously unrecorded archaeological monuments.

Finally, a third major advantage — of a long-term nature — of a FÁS archaeological survey again arises from the fact that the majority of the personnel are native to the survey area. On completion of their period of employment on such a project most trainees will have gained some appreciation of the archaeological heritage of their area. This appreciation will inevitably be shared to some extent within their community. Since the Iveragh project was a community-based enterprise, the professional staff was regularly involved in organizing local fieldtrips, while lectures and slide-shows were delivered in schools and other venues for the local public as well as for tourists. Archaeological exhibitions were also regularly mounted in local libraries and at tourist outlets. Although most of these events were held in order to raise funds for those expenses not covered by FÁS (such as publication costs), they also helped inform local communities about their archaeological heritage. These types of events, which could not — understandably — be conducted to the same scale by Dúchas, will almost certainly contribute towards the future preservation of archaeological sites on the peninsula.

FÁS archaeological surveys, when properly established and conducted, have the potential to achieve valuable results in a number of different arenas. That this potential has not always been achieved is unfortunate. This is due in the first instance to FÁS itself, which lays greater stress on the training elements of such projects than on their archaeological benefits and value. This attitude has sometimes resulted in a reluctance by archaeologists to commit themselves to this type of employment. In the second instance, it is due to local sponsoring groups failing to appreciate the difficulties involved in raising sufficient funding to publish the results of these surveys.

CONCLUSION

The contribution that FÁS has made to Irish archaeology is varied both in nature and quality. Many criticisms can and have been made of its involvement. It should be borne in mind, however, that, first and foremost, FÁS exists to perform important social and economic functions. The mistakes it has been responsible for in relation to heritage, while they cannot be condoned, must be seen in this light. By the same token, it should be commended for its successes.

Bibliography

A. I. 1990 'FÁS restoration scheme causes grave concern', *Archaeology Ireland* **4**, 3, p. 5.

Bourke, E. *et al.* 1995 *The care and conservation of graveyards*. Dublin.

Cleary, R. M. *et al.* 1997 *Skiddy's Castle and Christ Church, Cork: excavations 1974–77 by D. D. C. Twohig*. Cork.

Doran, L. 1986 *AnCO guidelines for community heritage projects*. Dublin.

Doran, L. 1989 *FÁS guidelines for graveyard and archaeological survey projects*. Dublin.

Forbes, W. 1987 'Waterford's medieval heritage and job creation', *Decies* **35**, pp. 7–15.

Hurley, M. F. *et al.* 1997 *Late Viking Age and medieval Waterford: excavations 1986–92*. Waterford.

IAPA 1994 'Meeting of archaeologists advising graveyard schemes', *Bulletin of the Irish Association of Professional Archaeologists* **19**, pp. 13–14.

Kirwin, S. 1992 'Guidelines for archaeologists acting as advisors to graveyard clearance schemes', *Bulletin of the Irish Association of Professional Archaeologists* **16**, pp. 6–8.

McAfee, P. 1997 *Irish stone walls: history, building, conservation*. Dublin.

McAfee, P. 1998 *Stone buildings: conservation, repair, building*. Dublin.

O'Sullivan, A. and Sheehan, J. 1996 *The Iveragh Peninsula: an archaeological survey of South Kerry*. Cork.

Stout, G. T. 1984 *Archaeological survey of the Barony of Ikerrin*. Roscrea.

Toal, C. 1996 *North Kerry archaeological survey*. Dingle.

Management's Heritage

DONNCHA KAVANAGH

To understand what heritage management means we should, at the very least, ask 'What is management?' This is the question that the present chapter addresses. It seems to me that a most appropriate way to deal with the issue, especially in a book about heritage, is to focus on management's own history and genesis. Through examining this history we can

(a) develop a deeper understanding of the techniques and concepts that constitute 'management';

(b) assess whether it is appropriate to import the ideology into the domain of heritage;

(c) provide a basis for selecting particular techniques and models of organizing;

(d) anticipate management's negative aspects and the problems it is likely to generate, and

(e) sensitize ourselves to alternative models of organization.

Such an exercise is clearly likely to overly simplify the issues or exclude major dissenting positions, although such problems are, in my view, more than offset by the value that an historical approach, albeit abbreviated, provides.

I begin this chapter by synopsizing the main attributes of what I term 'classical managerialism'. This paradigm or ideology has its origin in disparate philosophical developments of the seventeenth century which took root and spread apace during the eighteenth and nineteenth centuries. I sketch out this development and describe how a coherent paradigm was synthesized in the early decades of the twentieth century. Internal and external critique, prompted particularly by the great Depression of the 1930s, exposed serious problems in

this classical (or naive?) managerialism. I describe these critiques and also allude to how managerialism successfully re-invented itself during the twentieth century, accommodating many, but not all, of the criticisms. Finally, I discuss the implications that this historical sketch has for our understanding of 'management' in the context of heritage.

MANAGERIALISM: GENESIS

Cork Airport's foyer displays two large bronze statues commemorating two of Ireland's sporting legends, Christy Ring and Jack Charlton. Ring is depicted as a graceful yet powerful athlete in the heat of a hurling match, while the former Irish soccer manager is shown calmly enjoying a spot of fishing. Symbolically, the statues are important because they indicate the extent to which the cult of the manager has taken root in the Irish sporting psyche and popular culture. Who, for example, could name the manager of any Cork team that Ring played in during the 1950s, or of any Irish soccer team prior to the 1970s? We can notionally set the mid-1970s, when managers like Kevin Heffernan in Dublin and Mick O'Dwyer in Kerry rose to public prominence, as the approximate birth-date of managerialism, at least in Irish sport. More broadly, managerialism has swept through a range of other domains outside of business, including the arts, religion, government, the public sector, education, the voluntary sector and heritage. This is the context in which the concept of 'heritage management' must be understood.

At the outset, it is worth remembering that 'management' has always occurred in every domain of human endeavour. The relevant questions, however, are about how the managing is done, the kind of management that should be employed and the basis for preferring different ways of managing. Notwithstanding the undoubted heterogeneity in the practice of management, we can still identify a type of

Fig. 60.1 Management Time-line

YEAR	WRITER/EVENT	CONTRIBUTION
1637	Descartes	Egocentrism/Reductionism
1687	Newton	Rationalism/Scientific Method
1700–1800	The Enlightenment	Science/Reason/Progress
1776	Smith	Reductionism/*Laissez-faire*/Voluntarism
1789	French Revolution	Liberty/Equality/Fraternity
1859	Darwin	Evolution/Determinism
1867	Marx	Critique of Capitalism
1908	Ford	Mass Production/Consumerism
1921	Weber	Theory of Bureaucracy
1929	Stock Market Crash	Crisis
1933	Mayo	Humanist Critique of Fordism
1935	Keynes	Policy Critique of *laissez-faire*
1975	Williamson	Hierarchy = Market Failure

management, which I term classical managerialism, which dominates contemporary discourse to the point where it can be considered an ideology. It has seven main dimensions or traits that transcend particular techniques and models: androcentrism, hierarchism, egocentrism, rationalism, reductionism, representationalism, standardization, and in this section we shall discuss the nature and development of each of these. To facilitate the discussion, the accompanying time-line (**Fig. 60.1**) provides a useful summary and road map of some key contributions, even if it risks reducing the paradigm to individual writers or events.

ANDROCENTRISM

Classical managerialism centres the world on the male, and females, where considered at all, are invariably allocated a peripheral role. This is undoubtedly due to the development of management thought in the three spheres of the military, public sector bureaucracies and engineering practice, each of which was dominated by men and by a 'masculine' world-view. This world-view in turn is founded on deeper concepts, such as the Aristotelian division of the universe into the private and public spheres, that go right back to the origins of western civilization. Feminist scholars, and others like the economic philosopher, J. S. Mill, have argued that this dichotomy has been used to confine women to passive ('being') states in the private sphere and men to active ('doing') states in the public sphere. Surprisingly, the management literature is devoid of (and due) a broad and thorough feminist analysis and critique of the

gendering of management theory and practice.

HIERARCHISM

Within classical managerialism, it is axiomatic that organizations have a hierarchical ranking of offices that provide clear lines of command. The basic principle is that an employee should receive orders from only one superior — a process known as unity of command — thus creating a line of authority from superior to subordinate as well as giving a sense that organizations have a 'top' and a 'bottom'. Some feminist scholars have linked this hierarchical view with management's innate androcentrism on the basis that hierarchy is but a variant of patriarchy. Other scholars would say that the received faith in hierarchies is deeply embedded in social custom and religious doctrine as well as being based on the demonstrated success of hierarchies throughout history.

EGOCENTRISM

Egocentrism, or the centring of the world on the individual, is a third important attribute of managerialism. We can trace this philosophy at least as far back as 1637 when Descartes asserted that the thinking, doubting self was the primary and primordial entity, rather than, for example, God. The impact of this was profound insofar as it provided a philosophical justification for human agency or 'voluntarism', in contrast to the alternative 'determinist' view that individuals are but pawns acting out pre-defined roles within prior structures or grand narratives. The cult of the manager, or the belief that a single individual can enact a radical organizational change, is an obvious manifestation of this voluntarist philosophy. This heroic culture is especially dominant in the United States, where it is well articulated by business magazines like *Fortune*. In Europe, it is often tempered by a more acute appreciation that individual actions always take place within and are enabled by social and material structures. Nonetheless, it is probably fair to say that the cult of the manager now dominates both sides of the Atlantic. The payment some time ago of £17m in bonuses over three years to the Chief Executive of Ryanair — which, with only 700 employees, was a relatively small company in international terms — is but one European example of the ideology in practice.

This egocentric philosophy also impacted on the popular understanding of the degree to which the state should intervene in the commercial world. Here, the most important contribution was by Adam Smith who, in 1776, provided a compelling argument against state intervention in the market. Smith's thesis was that if buying was left to individual agents then their (egocentric and rational) desire to get the best value for their money would ensure, through the 'invisible hand' of the market, that producers would be as efficient as possible. The policy implication of this thesis was called *laissez-faire*, which is the principle that governments should not intervene in the market, even when, as happened during the Irish Famine, it seems obvious that they should.

RATIONALISM

If the egocentric character of managerialism is rooted in the mid-seventeenth century, then so too is its commitment to rationalism. Here the key figure is Isaac Newton, whose scientific method provided a major catalyst to Enlightenment thought during the eighteenth century. Central to the scientific method is a commitment to impartiality, objectivity, analysis and measurement, as well as a belief in progress through scientific endeavour. Likewise, managerialism has adopted many of these attributes and through doing so has justified and supported its position as a social practice. So, for example, MBA students are trained routinely to analyse organizational situations in a quasi-scientific fashion in which they, as analysts, take an 'objective' position above and outside the situation, in much the same way as scientists distance themselves from a laboratory experiment. Managerialism also endorses the conventional scientific epistemology which holds that scientific facts have universal application: just as the laws of gravity hold on the moon as much as in Manchester, so too can a theory of management, once 'proven', apply to a large organization in Maine and to a small workshop in Lyon. It is this epistemological commitment to universalism that fuels the search by students of management across the globe for prescrip-

tions that will identify both the causes and effects of business phenomena.

REDUCTIONISM

Descartes' influence on management thought is doubly significant because, as well as developing his egocentric ideas, he also articulated a philosophy of reductionism which probably constitutes the most enduring of managerialism's core tenets. Descartes saw the universe as a giant mechanism, not unlike the innards of a clock, consisting of innumerable elements all fitting and working together. For him, any system could best be understood, and hence managed, by breaking it down into its component parts. His ideas were developed by Adam Smith, who described the increased efficiencies that could be gained by the division of labour at work and the routinization of life generally. The principle that dividing up was essential for successful organization was demonstrated in practice by Eli Whitney in 1801 when he showed how guns could be assembled quickly from stacks of interchangeable parts. This principle of division proved successful, even addictive, and before long the notion of organization was axiomatically understood as involving the delineation and maintenance of boundaries. Soon, hierarchical organizations consisted of a myriad of horizontal divisions between levels and vertical divisions between functions. In addition, managers were distinguished from workers, owners from managers, staff from line personnel, and people inside an organization from those outside it. This technique undoubtedly proved successful, at least on the basis of production efficiency, and it formed the basis for rapid development in industrial technology and organization during the nineteenth century.

REPRESENTATIONALISM

Management has always been about control, and managers quickly realized that one could never become powerful over a large number if one had to engage with each individual in a group. Thus, the successful management of large organizations required that effective techniques of abbreviation and representation be devised whereby those at the top of the organization could control those at the lower levels. Such techniques range from mathematical models to accounting records to management reports.

STANDARDIZATION

The seventh basic attribute of classical managerialism was a belief in standardization or homogenization. This belief grew out of the reductionist philosophy sparked by Descartes' writings in the seventeenth century and further developed by Adam Smith in the eighteenth. By the beginning of the twentieth century, this idea had become virtually an ideology, most famously captured by

Henry Ford's slogan that his customers could have his Model T 'in any colour as long as it's black!' The extreme importance placed on the ability to produce standard products continues to remain a core concern of business and is a main reason why quality standards like ISO 9000 have been implemented so widely over the last decade or more.

Standardization means that not only are all products the same, but so too are component parts and the tasks involved in manufacture and distribution; at the extreme, even individual workers can be 'standardized'. Moreover, since identical products require identical forms of consumption, this homogenization necessarily extends from the productive realm to that of consumption. It took a number of centuries to develop such a model of mass production/consumption, and it is often termed 'Fordism', in recognition of Henry Ford's influence in its development. In the next section, we shall discuss this in more detail.

SYNTHESIS: FORD AND WEBER

The demographic expansion of the eighteenth century provided a fertile environment in which the arts of administration and government could develop. This development proceeded apace during the nineteenth century as the focus of employment shifted from the farm to the factory. In hindsight, classical managerialism probably reached its peak in the early twentieth century, when its key principles and techniques were independently synthesized in two distinct domains by Henry Ford and Max Weber. Ford recognized that it would be possible to manufacture products at a low unit cost if he systematically applied the approach on a much larger scale than had previously been attempted. In applying the principle of reduction to the extreme, he was able to reduce tasks to their most basic elements whereupon he could either use unskilled labour or else replace the human by a machine. In addition, he made a significant innovation in the traditional approach to production by adopting the principle that the worker should remain in a fixed position while the product moved through the factory. His ability to produce the Model T in high volume meant that it sold for less than a tenth of the price of a craft-built car in the United States in 1916. The result of his innovations was that his large production plants supplanted the traditional, craft workshops and he quickly took 50% of the automobile market.

While mass production was central to Ford's success, it was, on its own, insufficient. Ford's key insight was that he would make massive profits if, and only if, there was mass consumption as well as production. Ford's ingenious solution was to pay his workers the then outlandishly high rate of $5 per eight-hour day, which ensured their compliance with the strict code of discipline required on the assembly line — guaranteeing

Ford's ability to produce — and it also provided them with sufficient income and leisure time to consume the mass-produced products. The scheme would only succeed if the workers bought cars and not, for example, alcohol, which meant that Ford had to extend the disciplinary regime of the workplace to the social life of the workers. This extension meant that Fordism was not simply about perfecting an assembly line; in essence, it was an attempt to engineer a whole way of living.

At around the same time as Henry Ford was revolutionizing the structure of industry and society in America, a German sociologist and economist, Max Weber, was producing the definitive texts on the nature of bureaucracy. According to Weber, a bureaucracy

(a) consists of a hierarchical structure of offices bound by rules, with each office having a specific sphere of competence requiring certain technical skills;

(b) is based on the principle that office holders cannot own the means of production associated with the office nor can they appropriate bureaucratic office, and

(c) requires that all administrative acts, decisions and rules are formulated and recorded in writing.

Weber clearly based his theory of bureaucracy on his observations of the routinization and mechanization of industry. He was in no doubt that the needs of mass administration made bureaucracy completely indispensable since

... a bureaucracy is capable of attaining the highest degree of efficiency, and is in this sense formally the most rational known means of exercising authority over human beings. ([1921] 1968, p. 223)

Weber's analysis remains fresh to this day, and bureaucracies, in both the public and private sectors, continue to exhibit most of the characteristics that he first catalogued.

DECONSTRUCTION

Ford's great experiment in social and organizational change in the early part of the century followed over two centuries of relentless scientific and industrial development. At that time, there was a real sense that progress could continue unabated and that there were no limits to human potential. Indeed, these beliefs continue to be strongly held today, notwithstanding the twentieth-century experience of world wars, social inequalities and environmental degradation. In the context of business, many of Ford's beliefs are still regarded as axiomatic to good business practice, even if classical managerialism reached its high watermark by 1920. What happened over the remainder of the last century was that the paradigm was inexorably criticized from both within and without, or, to borrow a term from literary theory, it was repeatedly deconstructed (that is, its inherent paradoxes were exposed). In this section we briefly discuss some of the more important critiques.

First, Fordism proved that the contradictions and instabilities in capitalism, which Marx had first identified, were actually real. Marx had argued out that capitalism is based on the principle that

(a) there has to be a surplus value between the cost of a product's inputs (which include the labour cost) and its value in the market, and

(b) the owner of capital can legitimately appropriate the whole of this surplus.

The difficulty, however, is that this gap means that labour, in aggregate, will have insufficient funds to purchase the commodities, in aggregate, that it produces. This was compounded during Fordism when increased labour efficiency and mechanization reduced the demand for labour, and hence, as night follows day, increased unemployment. Marx predicted that these enigmas would result in a series of crises in which there would be idle production capacity (capital), idle labour (unemployed workers) and a glut of commodities and inventory in the market.

Such conditions prevailed in the Depression of the 1930s, much to the bewilderment of capitalists like Henry Ford. The English economist, John Maynard Keynes, first identified the policy of *laissez-faire* (the non-interference by governments in the market) as the root of the problem. This was a key insight because *laissez-faire* had underpinned economic philosophy for over a century. Keynes argued that, during a depression, the imbalance between production and consumption that Fordism entailed could not be redressed by individual consumers, since they lacked the necessary resources. Instead, he claimed that the only actors in the economy with real power to act were investors and governments. This suggested that, during a depression, either private investment should be enlarged or there should be public substitutes for private investment. The problem, as Keynes saw it, was to stabilize capitalism through an appropriate set of scientific managerial strategies and government interventions in the economy. In this way managerialism survived, albeit regulated and supported by the substantial legislative and material resources of governments.

Second, managers, informed by the work of psychologists like Elton Mayo and Abraham Maslow, came to understand that classical management, taken to the extreme, actually decreased efficiency, because de-skilled workers were less motivated and more likely to strike or disrupt production. To counter any adverse affect to the 'bottom line', managers had to develop and implement techniques that were much more subtle than the sledge-hammer approach of classical management. Today, libraries are well stocked with books describing a multitude of recipes, buzzwords and programmes on how to change, re-engineer, motivate and manage an organization's human resources. However, despite the hyperbole, very few of these prescriptions envisage fundamental change in the managerialist paradigm. For example, I have yet to come across a 'how to' management book that says that managers should be paid less! Neither has the paradigm addressed the central paradox in its libertarian philosophy of human agency. The paradox is that an individual's freedom to act means nothing unless it constrains another individual's freedom. In other words, a theory in which agency is equally distributed among everyone is not viable. Traditionally, managerialism has avoided this enigma, or else it has implicitly accepted its truth and taken the logical step, as Ford did, of shifting all responsibility for the organization of work from the worker to the manager.

In contrast, the third attack on managerialism did raise questions about the paradigm's core tenets. This attack came from an unlikely source: biology. In 1859, Charles Darwin published *The Origin of the Species*, and its impact was so great that it ultimately affected fundamental understandings about organizing and the ontological status of the manager. The key insight that theoreticians and practitioners drew from Darwin's work was that the power of the individual (either human being or organization) was much less than egocentric or voluntarist philosophies like managerialism presumed. Evolutionary theory suggested that the environment selected out the most suitable organisms, leaving the others to die out. Moreover, any individual organism has a very limited ability to adapt to the environment, since its particular situation owes more to a combination of chance and prior evolutionary paths than to any specific actions on its part — either the organism 'fits' or it does not, and if the latter, then *c'est la vie*. Applying this philosophy to social and organizational settings fundamentally undermined the core egocentric tenet of managerialism, because if change was determined by the 'environment', then the individual manager's power to effect change was severely limited, if not absent. And if this was the case, what justification was there for believing managers or for paying them such high salaries? Neither was this just empty speculation, because the available data suggested that change in many industries does follow an evolutionary logic. For example, it could easily be argued that the small craft workshops in the car industry of the early twentieth century simply did not fit an environment more suited to large organizations. And, contrary to the philosophy of managerialism, the managers of these workshops were clearly unable to effect any change in their situation.

Darwin's theory also cast doubt on the value of planning, a basic and precious managerial competence. According to his theory, the future unfolds on the basis of chance, unlikely mutations and particular combinations of circumstances, and at any point in time it is impossible to predict with any certainty. At best, we can say that the future will be similar to the present, but the nature and scope of any change from the present is always beyond us. For managers, the theory says that attempts to map out an organization's long-term future or strategic plan are pointless, since outcomes invariably escape intentions. In recent years, this point has been expressed and developed by Henry Mintzberg, who has long argued that strategic planning, as conventionally understood within management, rarely achieves its explicit objective.

Fourth, managerialism has been attacked by those it has displaced to the margins. Feminists, for example, have argued that the androcentrism in contemporary organizations and society has created a 'glass ceiling' that effectively confines women to the lower offices in business and bureaucracy. Up until relatively recently, the feminist movement had concentrated its effort on basic issues like suffrage, equal pay and conditions, and is only now beginning to engage and critique the managerialist paradigm at a more fundamental level. Marxist scholars have also contributed a large volume of literature critiquing the capitalist system and the relative position of workers and managers. If this critique has lost much of its potency with the collapse of the great experiments in communism, Marx's ideas continue to influence a range of social and organizational theorists. In particular, the Critical Theorists have taken up some of his concepts to mould a powerful argument against the spread of managerialism. There is now a large body of work in this tradition, so I can deal with just one of their hypotheses, and in summary form at that.

Critical Theorists argue that corporations provide meaning around a very narrow set of instrumental values — namely power and money — compared to language-based 'primary institutions' like the family, community, and religion. Much as Fordism showed that businesses ignore wider social issues at their peril, the Critical Theorists argue that these primary institutions provide a fundamental function of system co-ordination through balancing the relatively shallow value-system of managerialism with 'deeper' values based on loyalty, tradition, community, family honour and so forth. In particular, these institutions provide meaning and coherent value systems to those who lose within the managerialist system (and managerialism must, axiomatically, produce losers as well as winners). This thesis suggests that, as life becomes more corporatized, there will be a corresponding increase in the demands placed on families, religions and community.

Ultimately, these institutions become 'overloaded' and, as they are perceived to be unable to fulfil their function, they are supplemented by more bureaucracy and/or co-ordination through the instrumental values of the market. For example, where once we might have turned to friends and relatives for help and support in dealing with the general difficulties of life, we are now more likely to purchase such assistance from counsellors either directly or through the state system. Once this vicious circle gets going, the primary institutions gradually break down as society loses faith in their value. In addition, the Critical Theorists argue that managerialism defiles the sanctity of human beings in two ways. First, it distils the human character down to the ability to reason, compute and decide, which necessarily diminishes other attributes like emotion and romance and activities like play and the carnivalesque. Marx said it well back in 1848 when he wrote that we have 'drowned the most heavenly ecstasies of religious fervour, of chivalrous enthusiasm, of Philistine sentimentalism, in the icy water of egotistic calculation'. Second, managerialism constitutes individuals as mere objects of impartial and neutral managerial decision-making. As well as debasing human identity, this also downplays the moral and ethical issues involved in management decisions and actions. The Critical Theorists argue that the cumulative consequence of these factors is that managerialism ends up narrowing the human character and destroying the social and natural environment. At the very least, the arguments make it clear that we cannot simply represent management as a purely technical-rational-instrumental activity and turn a blind eye to the social relations through which managerial work is accomplished and upon which it ultimately depends.

NEO-MANAGERIALISM: THE MANAGER STRIKES BACK

Paradoxically, the mounting arguments against managerialism have had little impact, and it continued to gain more adherents during the second half of the twentieth century. This was undoubtedly due to critics' inability to go beyond criticism and articulate a viable alternative to both capitalism and communism (since the latter was an even more obvious failure than the former). Furthermore, managerialism proved itself adept at re-invention through reflexive criticism. The fashion for management fads (**Fig. 60.2**) is but one example of this re-invention.

These fashions have been concocted and promulgated by both business academics and management 'gurus' like Rosabeth Moss Kanter, Tom Peters, Peter Drucker, Charles Handy and Michael Porter. While there is a bewildering array of buzzwords and guru-speak, possibly

Fig. 60.2 Business Fads 1965–2000

1965–75	1975–85	1985–2000
T-Group Training	Restructuring	Intrapreneuring
Brainstorming	Portfolio Management	MBWA
Theory X and Y	Theory Z	Culture
Satisfiers and Dissatisfiers	Diversification	Kanban
Decision Trees	Learning Curve	Just-in-Time
Management by Objectives	Value Chain	Knowledge Working
Managerial Grid	Quality Circles	World-Class Manufacturing
	Strategic Business Units	Post-Fordism
	Zero-Base Budgeting	Postmodernism
	Matrix Management	Relationship Marketing
	Focused Factories	De-layering
	TQM	Clusters
	ISO 9000	Core Competencies
		Virtual Factories
		Hypermanagement
		Empowerment
		Business Process Re-engineering

the most important thesis that emerged during the 1980s was that large, bureaucratic organizations were no longer suited to the business environment. This argument was put forward most forcibly by the gurus who typically contrasted 'traditional' and 'emerging' organizational forms in a manner illustrated in **Fig. 60.3**.

Leveraging Darwin, they advised businesses to either 'change or die'. Darwin's theory was important because implicitly it gave ontological priority to the market, the business equivalent of the habitat in which organisms compete for resources. Of course managerialists have always ritually celebrated the market, but they received a considerable fillip in the 1980s when gurus suggested that networks of small organizations were more appropriate than individual large firms. This was because working through this idea in practice meant that more transactions were carried out in the market than within firms. The thesis received further support from economists like Oliver Williamson, who argued that the presence of organizations (firms and bureaucracies) was a sign that the market had 'failed'. In essence, organizations were depicted as deviant phenomena or aberrations from the norm of the market. Most importantly, this rhetoric (there was little empirical evidence supporting the assertions) made no distinction between public and private organizations, merging both under the umbrella term 'hierarchy', the more negative side of the market-hierarchy dichotomy.

This duly provided Conservative governments in the United Kingdom with an intellectual basis for widespread privatization of the public services and the transfer of government assets to the private sector during the 1980s. In addition, the blurring of the categorical

distinctions between public and private sectors meant that the ideology of managerialism quickly colonized those areas that still remained within the public sector. The traditional role of bureaucracy was further diluted by the argument that, while it was accepted that Keynesian macro-regulation of supply and demand had to be provided by the state when the economy was dominated by large, mass-producing firms, this balancing could now be automatically and more efficiently provided by the market when the economy consisted of flexible networks of small firms.

MANAGEMENT IN HERITAGE

The above short history provides a sketch of the discourse out of which the notion of 'heritage management' has emerged. We can, for example, see that the commercialization of heritage is but a logical next step in the spread of managerialism and the apparent demise of bureaucracy and hierarchies. However, this will only be of academic interest unless those in the heritage sector (industry) can learn real lessons from the story and acquire an understanding of likely future developments. It is to these issues that I turn in this final section of the chapter.

The first point to make is that one should be sceptical of dualistic thinking that depicts a dichotomy between, for example, the public and private sectors or between markets and hierarchies (firms and bureaucracies). Such dichotomous thinking underpins the belief that activities which were previously understood as being the remit of the state — heritage is one such example — should be transferred to the private sector. The biggest flaw in such thinking is that it reduces ontologically distinct

Fig. 60.3 Organizational Forms

	TRADITIONAL	EMERGING
UNIT OF ANALYSIS	Firm	Network
ENVIRONMENT	Stable, Competitive, Economies of Scale Permanent, Mechanistic, Centralized	Dynamic, Competitive and Co-operative, Economies of Scope
ORGANIZATION	Hierarchical, Functional Boundaries	Temporary, Organic, De-centralized, Heterarchical, Fluid Boundaries
MANAGER	Analyst, Specialist	Synthesist, Generalist
WORKER	Unskilled, Uneducated	Skilled, Educated
TASK	Linear, Simple, Physical, Focus on Content, Homogeneous	Non-linear, Complex, Intellectual, Focus on Process, Heterogeneous

phenomena to a single discriminating category.

For example, transaction cost economics, which is based on the market-hierarchy dichotomy, uses efficiency as the single criterion for divining a transaction's appropriate location. Ethics, justice and moral values do not enter the equation unless they can be reduced to the same efficiency calculus. This leads us to what I think is the most important argument in defence of bureaucracy. It is simply that bureaucratic institutions are set up to provide and ensure equity, neutrality, probity, permanence and accountability, and this list, it should be noted, does not include efficiency. Thus, arguing that bureaucracies are not as efficient as the market is as daft as saying that cricket is a bad game because there aren't enough goals scored in it. Unfortunately, this fairly basic point has not been made nearly enough, allowing glib claims about how managerialism is 'transforming' the public service to go uncontested. This, of course, does not mean that business practices that have originated and proved successful in the private sector should have no place in public bureaucracies, or that hierarchies are inherently 'better' than the market. The point is that a commensurate measure of performance is not available.

The essence of the argument is that imperfections in bureaucracy are not, of themselves, a sufficient basis for replacing bureaucracy with managerialism. Bad bureaucratic practices can (and usually should) be replaced by good bureaucratic practices rather than by an alternative ideology. Throwing the bureaucratic baby out with the bath-water of poor practice may simply change problems rather than eradicate them. In particular, one can expect that as the ideology of entrepreneurial innovation colonizes the bureaucratic domain, then there will be an increasing incidence of corruption, inequity, fraud and inordinate risk-taking.

A second issue relates to the commercialization of heritage that is part of the general tendency to re-imagine the social as part of the economic. Such commercialization turns 'heritage' into a commodity that is sold — exchanged for money — in the market. Here, Marx's ideas are worth repeating. Central to Marx's thesis was his view that human identity is created through productive and creative activity: in his words, man, by

acting on the external world and changing it . . . at the same time changes his own nature.

He further argued that capitalist markets are characterized by a process through which the products of human labour are reduced to abstract 'exchange values'. Capitalist markets, therefore, are a great circulating web of transubstantiating commodities and money in which workers

appropriate the produce of the labour of others by alienating that of their own labour.

Accordingly, for the market to operate, man — retaining Marx's wording for consistency and convenience — must become detached from the product of his labour and, since humanity is founded on productive activity, this detachment necessarily results in the type of disorientation that he terms 'alienation'. This thesis exposes an important paradox in the idea that heritage should be commercialized. In most cases we axiomatically relate the term 'heritage' to an individual or group identity, which is why the word heritage is usually preceded by possessive pronouns like our, your, my, their. Marx's alienation thesis means that this link is severed; what was previously seen to be 'our' heritage now becomes simply heritage. The positive side of this is that heritage becomes available, through the market, to a wider group; the negative is that it may also become unowned (or disowned).

To finish on an optimistic note, we should remark that Marx's thesis is undermined by the fact that the proletariat revolt, which he saw as the logical outcome of alienation, has not occurred in capitalist markets, suggesting that his thesis must be flawed. Nevertheless, his ideas do suggest that commercialization has the potential ultimately to sterilize heritage. The likelihood of this is increased because the commodification of heritage necessarily involves both abbreviation (packaging) and standardization (because of the need for economies of scale), both of which are liable to diminish the intrinsic nature of heritage. To guard against this situation, it is important that those who are besotted by heritage have confidence in their own skills, abilities and traditions and refuse to be overawed by either managers or management. Indeed UCC's higher *Diploma in Irish Heritage Management* is an admirable manifestation of this principle in practice.

Those involved in heritage management must also have the confidence to be sceptical of existing normative models of administration, because these have primarily emerged in competitive environments dominated by large, functionally and hierarchically organized, American, manufacturing firms. The heritage sector, in contrast, consists of dynamic networks of small organizations co-operating with one another and with the public sector, not unlike the craft networks that Fordism displaced. And while Fordism celebrated standardization, heritage is necessarily about difference. At the very least, heritage managers might desist from the twentieth-century fashion of using the ship as the major metaphor of management. Instead, they could return to the seventeenth century when the word 'economy'— which is derived from the Greek words *oikos*, a house, and *nomos*, a law — referred solely to the administration of a household and when the family provided the primary managerial metaphor. For whereas a ship has to be managed, the family, like our heritage, has to be cared for.

Bibliography

Alvesson, M. and Willmott, H. 1996 *Making sense of management: a critical introduction*. London.

Capra, F. 1982 *The turning point*. London.

Deetz, S. 1992 *Democracy in an age of corporate colonization*. Ithaca, New York.

du Gay, P. 1995 'Organizing identity: entrepreneurial governance and public management' in S. Hall and P. du Gay (eds), *Questions of cultural identity* (London).

Fincham, R. and Rhodes, P. S. 1992 *The individual, work and organization: behaviour studies for business and management*. Oxford.

Harvey, D. 1989 *The condition of postmodernity. An enquiry into the origins of social change*. Oxford.

Kanter, R. M. 1985 *The change masters: corporate entrepreneurs at work*. London.

Lynch, J. J. and Roche, F. W. 1995 *Business management in Ireland*. Dublin.

Mintzberg, H. and Waters, J. 1985 'Of strategies, deliberate and emergent', *Strategic Management Journal* 6 (July/September), pp. 257–72.

Mintzberg, H. 1994 *The rise and fall of strategic planning*. New York.

Morgan, G. 1986 *Images of organization*. Beverly Hills.

Murray, R. 1989 'Fordism and post-Fordism' in S. Hall and M. Jacques (eds) *New times* (London), pp. 38–47.

Osborne, D. and Gaebler, T. 1992 *Reinventing government: how the entrepreneurial spirit is transforming the public sector*. Reading, MA.

Peters, T. and Waterman, R. 1982 *In search of excellence*. New York.

Piore, M. and Sabel, C. 1984 *The second industrial divide: possibility for prosperity*. New York.

Pugh, D. S. (ed) 1990 *Organization theory*. London.

Pugh, D. S. and Hickson, D. J. 1989 *Writers on organizations*. London.

Reed, M. and Hughes, M. (eds) 1992 *Rethinking organization*. London.

Tiernan, S. D., Morley, M. J. and Foley, E. 1996 *Modern management: theory and practice for Irish students*. Dublin.

Weber, M. [1921] 1968 *Economy and society*. Totowa, N.J.

Managing Development and Developing Managers

JAMES FAIRHEAD

The question may legitimately be asked: 'what can educators do to help improve the process by which heritage projects are identified, developed and implemented?' This chapter responds to the enquiry in a number of ways. Firstly, by outlining a conception of managing and organizing that is informed by an 'interpretive' perspective. It describes this approach and suggests it is particularly appropriate for a heritage context, especially as compared with more traditional management research and teaching approaches. Secondly, the article presents a short case study, consisting of a brief episode in the life of a manager working on a heritage development project. It offers a brief analysis of the case, and goes on to suggest how students of heritage (and heritage managers) might themselves approach it and learn about the shortcomings of conventional 'project management' strategies in a heritage context. The chapter proposes that the management aspects of the heritage management task can more suitably be taught through the use of similar cases and open-ended project work. Finally, it suggests that academics and heritage policy-makers might usefully work together to encourage the production of case study material such as this, designed to stimulate what might be termed a philosophical debate about the nature of managing within the heritage context. Ongoing personal development among heritage managers may be brought about by the production of such material and through the setting up of heritage networks and mentoring schemes.

THE NATURE AND SIGNIFICANCE OF 'INTERPRETATION' IN ORGANIZATIONS

In a heritage management context, 'interpretation' is perhaps most naturally thought of as an intellectual endeavour which aims to create understanding and insight into traditions, artefacts and environments. Yet, quite fundamentally, interpretation is also at the heart of the everyday experience of working in an organization and being a manager. For, as numerous work-place studies have shown, in almost any organizational environment there is endemic tension, paradox and complexity. Knowledge about aims, contexts and causal connections is, at best, very partial (Weick 1995). The process which facilitates and guides organizational actions is thus arguably just as accurately described in 'soft' terms as it is in 'hard' terms, and many observers of organizations would nowadays reckon that the ability of managers to 'muddle through' in the face of uncertainty (Lindblom 1959), to tolerate ambiguity (Peters and Waterman 1982), to retrofit problems into pre-determined solutions (Cohen, March and Olsen 1972) and to 'make sense' of ambiguous environmental cues by creating 'workable fictions' (Weick 1995) are all aspects of managerial competence, requiring quite sophisticated interpretive skills that are just as important as the skills necessary for 'information-processing' and 'decision-making'. Indeed, even within the decision-making literature itself (the so-called 'behavioural' approach), there is a substantial body of research which emphasizes the central role that interpretation of context plays in managerial decision-making. Interpretation and sense-making processes are seen as mediating between an uncertain world and decision-making routines, so that 'right decisions' in organizations are effectively constructed through social and political processes rather than being objectively 'discovered' through the application of reason.

Paradoxically, therefore, while an interpretive perspective on organizations is still a minority taste among management academics, it can reasonably be argued that managers, for their part, are implicitly interpretivist, and effective managers perhaps more consciously so (Fairhead 1998). How, then, can we characterise an interpretive view of organizations and management?

Firstly, we might say that the interpretive perspective stresses the importance of 'getting in close' to people in organizations and their interactions, and paying attention to the world as they individually and collectively see it. As it happens, managers themselves may often be likewise intimate and fine-grained in their analyses of organizational life — and this ability is often thought to distinguish between successful and less successful innovators (Kanter 1983; Pinchot 1985). Organizational researchers, on the other hand, have tended to survey organizations from a distance, by means of cross-sectional quantitative analysis, and write about them in 'formalist' terms which de-emphasize the processes and content of interactions. Hence, in both research and teaching, there has historically been an emphasis on 'discovering' and communicating the forms and patterns whereby (it is believed) organizational phenomena can be understood (for instance the 4Ps and the 7Ss; flat versus tall organizations; organic versus mechanistic structures) rather than investigating the interactions through which such conceptions may be continually and significantly re-interpreted.

Secondly, and more specifically, an interpretive view aims to look at how people in organizations *themselves* interpret and see 'patterns' in their interactions, thereby effectively defining the situations they find themselves in and their rationales for action. These interpretations may be in a sense 'wrong' or 'fictional' but, as has been famously observed, if they are defined by people as real, they are real in their consequences (Thomas 1951). Here again we might note that traditional research and teaching approaches will tend to ignore such attributions as being too 'subjective' or difficult to access, even if it is generally acknowledged that such 'sense-making' processes are an important part of strategy making and strategy implementation.

Thirdly, an interpretive approach to organizations pays particular attention to the inferred symbolic dimensions of actions, environments and artefacts, since it is believed that it is through symbols, very largely, that organizations create and sustain meaning (Pondy *et al.* 1983). As has been often pointed out (for example, Linstead and Grafton-Small 1992), organizational theorizing has tended to overemphasize the extent to which the creation and maintenance of symbols within an organization is the prerogative of more senior levels of management, and underestimates the unpredictability of the meaning-creation process as a result.

This implies a fourth, less well-appreciated objective, of any interpretive approach to organizations, which is to develop higher-level or 'outsider' interpretations of the higher-level recipes, rules or programmes which may in a sense be 'generating' behaviour (Geertz 1973). While it has been fashionable for some time now in management studies to emphasize how 'strong cultures' in some sense

constitute such programmes (Peters and Waterman 1982), it has been suggested that the 'rules' of organizational culture may actually be quite un-homogeneous, inherently ambiguous and paradoxical, and consequently much more open to re-negotiation by individuals and groups than the text-book culture metaphor would suggest (Martin 1992).

In summary then, it is suggested that managing in organizations is very significantly an exercise in the symbolic manipulation and interpretation of meaning. Within a heritage context, we shall further argue, it is all the more important for managers to be aware of the symbolic dimensions of the management task — as exemplified by the following short case study episode, which is a judiciously fictionalized version of an actual case history. While it has been fictionalized primarily to preserve confidentiality and to create a suitable teaching vehicle, the wider advantages of using avowedly fictional treatments of otherwise 'factual' phenomena are attracting increasing attention in the social sciences (Latour 1996).

CASE EPISODE: THE REGENERATION OF ARKLE CITY
It had seemed like the dream job. Almost total freedom to do things properly. In charge of an agency that was pretty much independent and had solid political support. Quite a generous budget. A young and enthusiastic hand-picked project management team, which shared Gavin's vision of a regenerated historic and cultural quarter in Arkle City.

But, mused Gavin, there's no such thing as a free lunch. People were baying for blood. The 'forces of darkness' were putting pressure on the planners at City Hall to obstruct the development at every turn and in every little way. As a result, it was difficult to get any sense of action at all. A lot of people's noses had been badly put out of joint by Gavin's proposal winning the day. The city's commercial mafia particularly. But still, the message should have got through to the planners, you would have thought. By all the logic, they should have been on his side. He'd had all their bosses into the project office to hear the audio-visual presentation, and they'd had every opportunity to ask questions or even raise the odd objection. But, still more ridiculous, at almost every turn, Gavin's plans were being criticized by all the groups that should have been the project team's natural constituency: the conservationists, the heritage lobbies, the national Institute of Architects, the residents' association, the local traders, even some of the people who had benefited from the generous development grant provisions. And, of course, trust the media to stir things up! They'd all been nice as pie at the launch party and only too happy to drink all the *Buck's Fizz*, but they totally ignored most of the important and useful information that the team had painstakingly put together for the *press pack*. Typical ...

It was all very well for people to complain about 'haste'. The project had a mandate for only five years and there was no time to hang around going through the niceties. Thank God for the team — they were willing to work all hours to ensure that the vision for the scheme, translated painstakingly into a detailed specification, was implemented to the letter by the squads of professionals, contractors and sub-contractors working on the individual projects. If it weren't for the fact that the team was so close, the pressure would have been unbearable. And it had been good to take a day off last Sunday, the ten-pin bowling had been hilarious and the late night salsa session at Zorba's had been amazing ...

Gavin's reverie was abruptly shattered by the harsh shrilling of one of his two telephones. It was his Taskia, his assistant:

'I'm sorry Gavin, it's the Chairman of the Heritage Committee of the Institute of Architects. He's saying that you're not the only person who's busy. He doesn't see why they should come here again; they're insisting that you go over to the Institute instead. And he's still going on about the repository, saying it never should have been demolished ...'.

With an audible groan, Gavin asked for him to be switched through ...

An interpretive case analysis

An interpretive view of this case would focus initially, as discussed above, on the interactions between the various actors, it would attempt to infer more about the assumptions and definitions that they bring with them to the situation and how these are re-affirmed or modified during the course of events.

Even if such an account can necessarily not be validated as in any sense a 'true' representation, an interpretive perspective would aim for it to be at least a workable enough version of events. For it is argued that in order to act at all in ambiguous and uncertain situations, managers must construct interpretations that need not be accurate or strictly rational, just as long as they are plausible (Starbuck and Milliken 1988; Sutcliffe 1994; Weick 1995). Organizational life requires participants to be able to live with this ambiguity, rather than be paralyzed by it, and it is through making such interpretations, and re-interpreting and revising them as events unfold, that managers are able to manage. Indeed, in the Arkle City case, we might note that some time after this episode, both Gavin's views of the project stakeholders, and theirs of him, were to change quite profoundly. What appears to have caused this re-assessment was actually one of the stakeholders skilfully analyzing project interactions and seeing that a vicious

circle of (symbolic) interaction needed to be broken out of, if the project was to succeed.

Let us turn now, therefore, to our own form of interpretive analysis, in order to show how managers can (and do) make similar such analyses. One approach might be to 'read' organizational interactions to see what assumptions appear to be entailed *with respect to four broad areas* (see Schein 1985 for a similar approach). Firstly, assumptions about the 'boundaries' of legitimate action, involvement and interest. Who, in crude terms, is viewed as being 'in' or 'onside' and who as 'outside'? From what we read, we might infer that Gavin sees the project team boundaries as something difficult and maybe even dangerous to cross. For whatever reason (stress perhaps?), he is apparently avoiding interaction with other would-be stakeholders, only grudgingly accepting their claims on his time. In some cases, he effectively characterizes them as 'beyond the pale'. Interactions, such as they are, appear to be at arm's length — even within the internal team, one gets the sense that roles are clearly prescribed and demarcated, and that there may be little room for overlapping areas of authority and involvement.

Secondly, given these interactions, an interpretive approach might look at what assumptions the actors bring with them about the governance of relationships. Are they seen to be governed necessarily by either dominance or submission? Or is the possibility entertained that there can be a degree of symbiosis and give-and-take, with people able to conceive of working through each other's interests and aspirations, rather than on or against them? In this case, both within his team and beyond it, Gavin appears to see relationships as being characterized as a struggle for hegemony: as leader, he must necessarily dominate — or be dominated, in which event his position as leader is in question.

Thirdly, we might ask what assumptions are made about the nature and range of legitimate bases of knowledge, truth and 'reality'. In other words, 'what are the acceptable ways of knowing and deciding upon appropriate action and behaviour?' Here, we might infer that Gavin sees himself and his team as the pre-eminent source of authority, expertise and legitimacy in the sense that they view themselves as guardians of the 'project plan'. Other potential sources of authority are seen as being in conflict with the achievement of the plan and, in line with our earlier inferences about his relationship style, we might think that he presses into service a range of managerial and rhetorical techniques and artefacts, not only as symbolic bearers of ultimate truth but also as *instruments of domination*. From this account of events, at any rate, it seems that press packs, audio-visual presentations, briefings and even *Buck's Fizz* are lined up and deployed in militaristic fashion. Even Gavin's 'vision' appears armour-plated within a 'specification'.

Finally, note too that the project team's world-view appears to embody particular assumptions about time — the project end-date seems all-important, and progress towards this is seen as necessarily relentless and inexorable, not admitting of random 'niceties'.

Implications for a heritage context

While Gavin may indeed be making such assumptions as we have uncovered, they would in all likelihood be unknown to him and effectively taken for granted. The value of our (necessarily brief) analysis and interpretation is precisely that it allows us to speculate on what is normally not open to question, and to go on from there to ask ourselves whether such assumptions are appropriate for a heritage context.

In sum, the analysis could be taken as suggesting that Gavin's way of seeing the world is conditioned by the traditional 'machine-metaphor' view of organization (Morgan 1986). This is indeed a view that suffuses what might be termed 'project management' situations and has historically been thought entirely natural in such a context. More specifically, we might say that, within projects, there tends to be quite explicit emphasis on the rational and calculable aspects of defining and measuring tasks and objectives, being able to demonstrate measurable (and more or less 'straight-line') progress towards these end-states at any time during a project's life, and on achieving this notional efficiency by means of specialization, focus and codified procedures.

Yet, in the current age of rapid change and innovation, doubts are being raised about the validity of this traditional model of managing. For example, isolated teams of specialists would appear to perform less effectively than teams of more balanced composition (Belbin 1991). Lack of differentiation may increase the likelihood of 'group-think' (Janis 1982). A preoccupation with task at the expense of 'relationship' issues is likely to diminish group performance (Gronhaug and Kauffman 1988). The key performance issue for project teams is not efficient information processing but effective information creation and the elicitating of tacit knowledge (Nonaka 1989). This creativity may be enhanced, not by specialization and order, but by differentiation, role overlap and the dis-ordering of established routines (Weick 1987; Nonaka 1988) — at least in the early stages of a project's life. Because of this, managerial effectiveness may be associated as much with peregrination and procrastination as with planned purposefulness (Fairhead and O'Sullivan 1996).

In a heritage environment, the case for questioning project management orthodoxies may be still stronger. For heritage artefacts are, by their nature, rare, special, apart from the common run, and in a sense thereby 'sacred'. Indeed, nominal project objectives — the estab-lishment of heritage environments and their related artefacts within a given cost and time-frame — may, in an important sense, be subordinate to the creation and maintenance of an appropriate sense of political/social agreement and *communitas* among stakeholders, which may itself constitute an important aspect of sacredness (Belk *et al.* 1989).

Thus we might fear that conventional notions of tightly run efficient project management teams may work to undervalue and exclude community participation and hence undermine sacredness. In such a view, there may be simply 'not enough time' to deal with these ill-specified aspects of the project management role. They may all too easily be defined as a cost to a project, as 'noise in the system' rather than a central part of the heritage management endeavour. And in such cases, the likelihood is (as in this instance) that participants enter into a vicious circle: especially when pressurized by public and visible commitments, and a degree of perceived hostility, project teams may tend to reduce complexity by ignoring less well specified objectives and retreating into much less ambiguous specialist task activities. And of course by doing so, they only exacerbate the situation they face with their stakeholders, and paradoxically worsen the position (Weick 1995).

CONCLUSIONS AND RECOMMENDATIONS

Making sense of such paradoxical situations, where 'doing one's best' is actually the worst thing one can do, is as much a philosophical as a technical endeavour. Attempting to predict, and construct, possible resolutions is doubtless still more so. Objectives, as in this case, may be multiple, diffuse and obscure — as much tacit as explicit. Ways of achieving even clearly agreed objectives are likewise multiplicitous — and quite possibly duplicitous. In short, sense-making about organizational endeavours is every bit as taxing as making sense of more obviously philosophical questions. It is in recognizing and embracing this twin challenge of the technical and the philosophical that perhaps the gifted manager is distinguished from the merely competent.

For all sorts of historical and cultural reasons that we have alluded to, both organizations and courses in management may find this a difficult challenge to meet. While organizations are very competent at developing technical aspects of managerial competence, the development of interpretive and philosophical skills is often left to chance. For their part, traditional courses in management, if they over-emphasize the extent to which theoretical models account totally for organizational realities, may fail to develop either technical or philosophical skills. In cases of such two-fold institutional failure, it is tempting to conclude that 'managers are born, not made'.

Our belief, in contrast, is rather less pessimistic. We would hold that it is desirable, enjoyable and also quite feasible to develop a solid foundation of both technical and interpretive competences among would-be heritage managers. By legitimating and developing the dual intellectual skills of 'soft' interpretation and 'hard' analysis, we can prepare our students for the twin challenge of managing organizations.

But how can this challenge be realised pedagogically? In a variety of ways. Firstly, we would aim to teach very participatively, and encourage a high degree of 'self-organization'. We would hope to achieve a mature balance between traditional lecturing and group discussion.

Secondly, we would hope to maximize the benefits of group discussions by ensuring that our methodologies for dealing with case and class material is very open-ended and only minimally prescriptive. Traditionally, management case studies are lengthy and overflowing with information. The job of the student is to 'reduce' the case through the deployment of theoretical models. This can sometimes turn out to be a rather mechanistic 'information-processing' task. Our case studies, by contrast, informed by a more subjectivist view of organizational life, require students to 'create' information as well as process it. This they do by making assumptions to compensate for incomplete information, by reading between the lines, and by intuitively interpreting organizational situations. While exercising (as managers do) a degree of 'divergent' intelligence, they can also bring to bear more traditional 'convergent' analytical and deductive skills, and benefit from the interplay between these different perspectives.

Thirdly, our project work also demands a similar balance of divergent/convergent skills, and a similar degree of self-organization. From the very first day, we encourage our students to tell us what particular areas of heritage they are interested in, and to give their particular 'take' on this. Facilitated imaginatively, this public airing allows students to align and pool their interests into a 'group project' that investigates some aspect of managing and organizing in the heritage area. The students are, themselves, responsible for choosing their own groups, deciding on a target organization and setting up and negotiating research access. All this, of course, is itself a valuable learning experience. Their brief is very open-ended. Having found a project sponsor, they are first of all required to work with this person to identify a suitable domain for investigation (usually a recently completed activity or an ongoing organizational endeavour, like an annual festival or a regeneration project.) They need to work with the sponsor to identify the actual or potential 'stakeholders' of this project, and then they can begin to research, interpret and analyse in earnest. By using certain open-

ended 'naturalistic' research techniques, the way is open for them to gather (like a detective, investigative journalist or folklorist) rich data that suggests how perceptions, agendas and actions mingle, merge and are 'managed' in their chosen project. In tandem with this, they are encouraged to apply to their emerging data-set a number of theoretical models of organization and management in more traditional analytical fashion. Once again, which models they choose to use is a question that they must answer for themselves.

Eventually, from all this rich assemblage of information, the most tenacious of our students will arrive at a few powerful insights into managerial behaviour, backed up convincingly by comparative analysis of different expert testimonies, and enriched and illustrated by anecdote and verbatim quotations. Even the less-successful projects, in our experience, yield a rich harvest of insight and practical experience. From these projects, little by little, we are able to build up a range of case studies that graphically illustrate some of the complex paradoxes that beset any would-be heritage manager, and which give students the opportunity of 'simulating' their actual responses to the detail of managerial situations — in a classroom environment where it is safe to experiment and, if necessary, fail.

Having said this, there is still a great lack of case study material which deals with this level of actual behavioural detail. And the detail is necessary, because it is on a manager's response to detail that he or she is judged. In order to facilitate the creation of such case studies, and at the same time promote ongoing personal development among heritage managers, we might make one final suggestion. This is that academics, heritage managers and heritage authorities might work together in the same way as has been pioneered successfully by industry and managers in other areas of business. Networking and mentoring schemes such as 'Plato', but ones which incorporate the whole range of potential heritage stakeholders, may have great potential as vehicles for development.

Academics alone cannot pretend to create great managers. Our aim can only be to give would-be managers the confidence and know-how to be able to pitch camp, at will, among the shifting sands of organizational politics and change, and to enact some sort of conceptual map of the terrain. Whether they then successfully navigate the sand-storms is another matter. With the help of practitioners already working in the sector, and other professional stakeholders, we can significantly improve their chances.

Bibliography

Belbin, M. 1991 'Design innovation and the team',
 Design Management Journal (Summer), pp. 38–42.

Belk, R. *et al*. 1989 'The sacred and the profane in
 consumer behaviour: theodicy on the Odyssey,'
 Journal of Consumer Research **16** (June), pp. 1–35.

Cohen, M., March, J. and Olsen, J. 1972 'A garbage can
 model of organizational choice,' *Administrative
 Science Quarterly* **17**, pp. 1–25.

Fairhead, J. 1998 'Paradigm change and leveraged
 learning during the Rover-Honda collaboration',
 Journal of Creativity and Innovation Management
 7, 2 (June), pp. 93–106.

Fairhead. J. and O'Sullivan, D. 1997 'Marriages made in
 heaven: the power of network latency' in G.
 Gemünden, T. Ritter, and A. Walter (eds)
 *Relationships and networks in international
 markets* (Oxford), pp. 305–22.

Gronhaug, K. and Kauffman, G. 1988 *Innovation:
 a cross-disciplinary perspective*. Oslo.

Janis, I. 1982 *Victims of groupthink*. Boston.

Kanter, R. M. 1983 *The change masters*. New York.

Latour, B. 1996 *Aramis or the love of technology*.
 Cambridge, Mass.

Lindblom, C. 1959 'The science of muddling through',
 Public Administration Review **19**, pp. 91–99.

Linstead, S. and Grafton-Small, R. 1992 'On reading
 organizational culture', *Organization Studies* **13**, 3,
 pp. 331–55.

Martin, J. 1992 *Culture in organizations: three
 perspectives*. Oxford.

Morgan, G. 1986 *Images of organization*. London.

Nonaka, I. 1988 'Creating organizational order out of
 chaos: self-renewal in Japanese firms', *California
 Management Review*, pp. 57–73.

Nonaka, I. 1989 *Organizing innovation as a knowledge-
 creation process*, working paper, University of
 California.

Peters, T. and Waterman, R. 1982 *In search of excellence*.
 New York.

Pinchot, G. 1985 *Intrapreneuring*. New York.

Pondy, L., Frost, P., Morgan, G. and Dandridge, T. (eds)
 1983 *Organizational symbolism*. Greenwich, Conn.

Schein, E. 1985 *Organizational culture and leadership*.
 San Francisco.

Starbuck, W. and Milliken, F. 1988 'Executives' perceptual
 filters: what they notice and how they make sense'
 in D. Hambrick (ed) *The executive effect: concept
 and methods for studying top managers*,
 (Greenwich, Conn.), pp. 183–205.

Sutcliffe, K. 1994 'What executives notice: accurate
 perceptions in top management teams', *Academy
 of Management Journal* **37**, pp. 1360–78.

Thomas, W. 1951 *Social behaviour and personality*.
 New York.

Weick, K. 1987 'Substitute for corporate strategy' in D.
 Teece (ed) *The competitive challenge: strategies for
 industrial innovation and renewal* (Cambridge
 Mass.), pp. 220–48.

Weick, K. 1995 *Sense-making in organizations*. Thousand
 Oaks, Cal.

Marketing: Complement or Compromise?

HELEN GUERIN

This chapter will briefly outline the evolution of marketing theory since its emergence as an international field of study. It presents core elements of the marketing concept and explores what marketing has to offer arts, culture and heritage in the new millennium.

Without doubt, many professionals in the areas of arts, culture and heritage would concur, to a greater or lesser extent, with the sentiments expressed by the critic and cultural commentator, Walter Benjamin, in his seminal article entitled 'The work of art in the age of mechanical reproduction' (1936/68). Benjamin believed that art was sacred and that 'churning out prints, film copies and photographs (reproduction) robbed us of the vital aura of art'. He argued that reproduction of the sacred (art) doomed us to a less authentic experience, and would result in life itself becoming less meaningful, eventually leading to utter alienation. Other practitioners might well disagree with this point of view and instead consider reproduction and promotion to be valuable tools in assisting them reach their intended recipients more effectively. Furthermore, recent surveys of audiences in the cultural sector suggest the general public consider that there is now a greater awareness of cultural activity, a factor which can largely be attributed to increased levels of marketing within the sector (Clancy 1994). Whatever one's standpoint, it is accepted that marketing skills in the cultural domain in general are still relatively poor, with few qualified marketers working full-time in this area. Indeed, many artists might also propose that Benjamin's approach would have neglected to consider the implications brought about by the emergence of Pop Art, for example, and that, more recently, his argument has been undermined by the evolution of digital art which actually celebrates the possibilities of reproduction. Such developments beg the question as to whether a figure like Andy Warhol is an artist or a marketing genius or perhaps both. A brief journey through some of the marketing concepts will enable us to explore these diverse and complex issues further.

PERSPECTIVES ON MARKETING

Marketing has been variously seen as residing both in the realm of science (Bartels 1951; Buzzell 1963; Hunt 1976), the realm of humanism (Hutchinson 1952) and that of relativism (Anderson 1983; Peter and Olson 1983), a concept to be discussed again later. It is now generally accepted that our understanding of it emerged out of the scholarly investigation of economics. The dispute is how far marketing has moved away from economics to incorporate other disciplines such as sociology and psychology. A number of contrasting definitions may help convey an appreciation of the marketing discipline in its broadest sense and sketch some of the terms in which this discussion has been conducted over the past half century.

It is widely accepted that the most basic concept underlying marketing is the human need, an idea we shall return to later. A relatively recent account which sparked off debate is the notion that marketing is a pervasive societal activity that is applicable beyond the traditional business arena (Kotler and Levy 1969). Kotler (1972) developed this idea further to propose that 'the core concept of marketing is the transaction. A transaction is the exchange of values between two parties. The things of value need not be limited to goods, services and money; they include other resources such as time, energy and feelings. Transactions occur not only between buyers and sellers, and organizations and clients, but also between any two parties'. Bartels (1988) later rejected this definition as unbounded, and put forward the notion that marketing is firmly rooted in the field of science and business. Peter Drucker (1973) had a more functionalist approach, building on the work of Keith (1960), whose research we shall consider shortly. Drucker holds that 'the aim of marketing is to make selling superfluous. The aim is to know and understand

599

Table 62.1 Classification of Marketing Schools of Thought

	NON-INTERACTIVE PERSPECTIVE	INTERACTIVE PERSPECTIVE
ECONOMIC PERSPECTIVE	1. Commodity	4. Institutional
	2. Functional	5. Functionalist
	3. Regional	6. Managerial
NON-ECONOMIC PERSPECTIVE	7. Buyer behaviour	10. Organizational dynamics
	8. Activist	11. Systems
	9. Macromarketing	12. Social change

Source: *Sheth, Gardner and Garrett 1988*

the customer so well that the product or service fits him so well it sells itself.' According to the American Marketing Association (1985), 'marketing is a process of planning and executing the conception, pricing, promotion and distribution of ideas, goods and services to create exchanges that satisfy individual and organizational objectives' (cited in Kotler and Armstrong 1987). The more modernist attitude as espoused by Baudrillard (1993) is that 'one could view marketing as the symbolic manufacture of consumption and not the satisfaction of needs and wants.' Leiss *et al.* (1990) and McDonagh (1995) accept the latter opinion. This sample of definitions thus illustrates the diverse range of theories which represent current marketing thinking. In fact there are at least a dozen schools of thought actively contributing to the delineation of marketing philosophy (**Table 62.1**).

Probably the most famous and long-standing of the various debates in the field is that of Hunt (1976) versus Anderson (1983) on the issue of whether marketing is science or art. Elizabeth Hirschman (1986) proposes that because marketing is a socially constructed enterprise, research in marketing is in need of input from humanism (**Table 62.2**).

While conflict therefore abounds, there is general consensus that marketing is concerned with exchange of one sort or another between individuals, groups or society as a whole. This allows the concept of marketing to be traced far back to its proper origins in the first marts and markets, when individuals bartered goods and services for other goods and services they needed or wanted, however irrational both the behaviour and context may have been in certain circumstances (Buttimer and Kavanagh 1995, 1996).

Marketing scholarship as we now know it is a relatively recent phenomenon, which emerged during the same period as early management theories around the time of

Table 62.2 Humanistic versus Positivist Research Philosophies in Marketing

THE HUMANIST METAPHYSIC	THE POSITIVIST METAPHYSIC
1. Human beings construct multiple realities.	1. There is a single reality composed of discreet elements.
2. Research and phenomena are mutually interactive.	2. The researchers and the phenomena are independent.
3. Research inquiry is directed towards the development of idiographic knowledge.	3. It is possible and desirable to develop statements of truth that are generalizable across time and context.
4. Phenomenal aspects cannot be segregated into 'causes and effects'.	4. Elements of reality can be segregated into causes and effects.
5. Inquiry is inherently value-laden.	5. It is possible and desirable to discover value-free objective knowledge.

Source: *Hirschman 1986*

the Industrial Revolution. Both management and marketing surfaced as a result of technological changes which affected the economics of the production process, thereby facilitating the evolution of mass production and distribution. Accordingly, there is considerable overlap between management and marketing, management marketing and marketing management. For example, the management theory of the Value Chain, popularized by Porter (1985), has its roots in the Functionalist School of marketing theory in which value emerges from the quality of input from the discrete but interlinked functions of human resources, finance and marketing itself. Indeed, management and marketing complement each other's work and in the cultural sector, marketing is very often the remit of the managing director rather than a separate functional area.

Since the 1960s, Keith's 'three eras' schema of marketing has dominated accounts of the evolution of marketing theory and practice (Brown 1995). Keith's (1960) simple three-part framework, which is still widely used today, explains the heritage of marketing as comprising a production-oriented era, a selling-oriented era and a marketing-oriented era. The first of these lasted from the 1850s until the late 1920s. During this period, producers were obsessed with the manufacturing process and with the launching of new products and by-products to meet the ever-expanding needs of their potential customers. The production concept is based on the philosophy that consumers will favour products that are available and affordable and that management should therefore focus on improving production and distribution efficiency.

This style of marketing can be employed successfully when either demand outstrips supply or when the production process *per se* can be improved to allow cost savings in the creation of the product. The later is commonly associated with Fordism, symbolized by Henry Ford's re-structuring of the manufacturing process for the Model T motor car (1908) to keep production costs down. This made the car affordable, thereby facilitating mass production. Ford complemented this by paying his workers the relatively high wage of $5 per day, thereby giving them the purchasing power necessary to buy his automobiles. Ford is credited with being one of the first to grasp the potential relationship between mass production and mass marketing. The production concept is immortalized in his famous phrase 'they [the customer] can have any colour car so long as it's black'. More recently the electronic goods manufacturer Texas Instruments employed this philosophy to win a large segment of the pocket calculator market. However, unless an organization has other strategic advantages, such as being the market leader or owning key natural resources or intellectual property rights, this can prove to be a difficult marketing strategy in today's extremely competitive global selling environment.

The production concept was closely followed by, and often grouped together with, the product concept. The product concept held that the product was king and that customers would seek out a better item simply because it was intrinsically superior to competing items. This has been a relatively limited marketing strategy employed primarily in the area of luxury goods and services which are in scarce supply. The renowned marketing theorist Theodore Levitt terms this style of marketing 'myopic', arguing that people will not beat a path to a man's door simply because he builds a better mouse-trap. In his seminal article 'Marketing myopia' (1960), he cites the example of the huge financial losses incurred by US railroads due to their focus on the product (railroads) rather than on the business of transportation. This resulted in railroad companies standing still and waiting for business to come to them while aeroplanes, trucks and buses set about serving customer needs with a more marketing-oriented approach.

The second of Keith's above-mentioned three periods was the selling-oriented era, which adopted the philosophy that consumers will not buy enough units of the company's product to return a profit to an organization unless that organization undertakes a large-scale selling and promotions campaign. This style of marketing dominated from the 1930 to the late 1950s. With the emergence of better production methods and more efficient work practices, the general public had an abundance of goods and services to choose from. Naturally, this led to intense competition between manufacturers and eventually to crippling price wars in an attempt to win buyers. Selling-oriented companies usually invested heavily in market analysis and engaged in expensive advertising campaigns to purvey their many and varied products. Hard selling is usually associated with products for which demand is relatively poor and goods or services which need a high degree of personal selling (for instance encyclopaedias). The selling-oriented approach is also commonly used amongst politicians at election time when travelling from door to door trying to win each individual's vote, while customers (constituents) are bombarded with mounds of promotional fliers, newspaper advertisements, interviews in the media and the like. The selling concept is still variously employed today, primarily by large tobacco companies, and can be encapsulated in the hackneyed phrase 'there is a sucker born every minute'.

The third era is that of the marketing-oriented approach, which is said to have emerged in the 1950s. This approach represents the first time organizations focussed on customers' needs and wants and attempted to satisfy them. It is based on the philosophy that achieving organizational goals depends to a large extent on determining the requirements of selected target markets, and delivering the desired satisfactions to these markets more effectively and efficiently than competing companies. Again Levitt gives a good example of how the Hollywood movie studios lost out heavily in the 1950s due to their refusal to embrace television as a new technology with the potential to open up alternative ways of reaching their audiences and thereby increasing potential revenue returns. Needless to say, Hollywood did not wish to be taught a second lesson in the 1990s, and embraced the emerging technologies in film production and software (films and interactive video games), distribution (the Internet, cable television, digital satellite and digital terrestrial) and exhibitions (multiplexes, video stores, DVD and accompanying merchandising). The marketing-oriented philosophy subscribes to the belief that 'the customer is king' and the concept is aptly captured in Regis McKenna's article entitled 'Marketing is everything' (1991).

Although the 'three era' schema was questioned in the late 1980s by the renowned marketing historian Ron Fullerton, who put forward the 'complex flux' model of marketing genealogy in his controversial article 'How modern is marketing ... ?' (1988), it is interesting to note that Fullerton also essentially adopted a period-based approach to the subject, even if he claimed the periods of time to be longer and the degree of overlap to be more pronounced than Keith did. He maintains that the first phase of marketing, the antecedent era, began in the 1500s and extends until 1750. The second period, the era of origins, extends from 1750 to 1870, while that of institutional development emerged in the 1850s and extends up until 1929. According to Fullerton, since 1930 onwards we have been in the era of refinement and formalization.

Since the late 1980s and early 1990s there has been a move towards re-evaluating the role of marketing practice. This has to a large extent been precipitated by the shift in management strategies towards locating manufacturing facilities to low-cost Asian countries. What has emerged as a result of this re-thinking is a more post-modern approach to marketing (Browne 1995), which prophecies the death of the salesman and the re-birth of the customer as the empowered buyer. This is good news for the cultural sector, and will facilitate the development of marketing initiatives specifically targeted at selected groups and individuals. Indeed, it offers the opportunity to build on existing relationships to match those seeking goods and services with those providing such goods and services.

MARKETING HERITAGE: THE REAL AND THE IDEAL

Having looked at the heritage of marketing and the potential conflicts that can arise in relation to conceptualising it, we can consider the potential benefits that may be derived for employing some of the key marketing tools to enhance our cultural experiences. It is fair to say that cultural activities and marketing do not sit comfortably together and that there is still a level of scepticism amongst heritage practitioners as to the usefulness of employing strategic marketing. Indeed, terms such as 'Disneyfication' (Terrell 1991), 'McDonaldization' (Ritzer 1993) and 'Coca Cola-ization' (Nuñez 1989) serve as a reminder of over-zealously embracing all aspects of what was originally developed with a commercial environment in mind. However, we do not want to throw the baby out with the bath-water. What is needed is a more measured understanding, rather than simply to force a commercially-oriented marketing model into the cultural arena.

It is possible to begin one's task of heritage marketing with some simple steps common to all sound business planning and development. The importance of creating a coherent marketing plan and setting achievable goals within a realistic time-frame cannot be overstated. Set out in **Table 62.3** is a framework to guide and inform the development of such a plan to fit the individual organization. One can draw on the marketing plan as a composer would an orchestra, using different instruments to achieve a particular feel or mood or colour, and to develop a unique signature tune for an organization which clients will recognize as its corporate image.

As one advances through the various stages of the marketing plan, it becomes clear how all the pieces fit together and how so many factors can affect the most carefully laid strategies. For example, many museums, heritage sites and concert halls may not have anticipated the recent Y2K problem emerging, in the situational analysis/marketing audit, due to technological changes beyond their control in the environment. Also, cinema owners would not have been able to predict the emergence in their external environment of the technology associated with MPEG 2, 3 and 4, which compress sound and vision so as to allow audio and video streaming over the Internet. Even internal factors, such as market positioning, over which one has a substantial degree of control, can change unexpectedly at short notice due to unforeseen fashions and fads.

Within the marketing plan, the SWOT analysis is a popular tool employed by management to assess an organization's core competencies so as to identify potential opportunities of development as well as draw attention to likely deficiencies within the organization. Many marketing and management gurus maintained from the 1980s onwards and especially throughout the 1990s that, by focusing on what one was good at and 'sticking to the knitting', companies could out-flank any competition (Peters and Waterman 1982; Prahalad and Hamel 1990; Stalk *et al.* 1992). From a more holistic perspective, the SWOT analysis is an excellent tool for assessing progress along a set of objectives. It also allows

Table 62.3 The Marketing Plan

THE MARKETING PLAN

CORPORATE PLAN
•
SITUATION ANALYSIS — MARKETING AUDIT

Internal	*External*	*Environment*
• Market positioning	• Who are your competitors?	• Economic situation
• Profit margin/costs	• Rating re competitors	• Change technology
• Market information	• Product comparisons	• Legal constraints
• Production capacity	• Distribution channel changes	• Social attitudes
• Market share	• Consumer behaviour	• Taxation

•

SWOT ANALYSIS
Strengths/Weaknesses/Opportunities/Threats
•
MARKETING OBJECTIVES AND STRATEGIES
Achievability within resource allocations/Consistent with corporate objectives
•

PRODUCT	PRICE	PROMOTION	PLACE

•

Marketing Budget
Sales Revenues
Cost of Sales
Selling Costs
Advertising and Promotion Costs
Distribution Costs
•
FEEDBACK
Implementation/Action/Monitor/Control
•
MARKET RESEARCH

Source: *Adapted from Brownlie and Saren 1994 and from Brownlie pers. comm.*

one appreciate how the environment can turn a strength into a potential deficiency, and a weakness into a possible opportunity. For example, the fact that we mainly speak English in Ireland proved to be an impediment to the development of indigenous film-making in the early part of the past century. However, as we enter the millennium, our ability to now produce films in English provides Irish film-makers with access to an international market within which the demand for English-language films is currently in excess of 90%. Probably one of the most commonly used tools employed in marketing in general in the cultural arena is the '4 Ps' (product, price, place and promotion). Promotion is very often the cornerstone of most cultural organizations' marketing strategies.

Market research is equally important. This identifies marketing issues, manages and implements the data-collection process, analyses the results and communicates the findings and their implications. Such research can play an important role in assessing the level of awareness of a particular heritage site or event, so as to allow an organization re-position itself in the public eye. For example, the Hollywood majors have being carrying out in-depth market investigations of the cinema-going audience since the 1960s. This has allowed them to segment the market for filmed entertainment and identify the most lucrative sections. Currently, this happens to be the 15–24 year olds, both in terms of frequency of attendance and percentage of income spent on leisure (**Fig 62.4**).

In global terms the cultural sector is considered to be part of the leisure industry. From a marketing perspective, it is worth noting that Irish people spend approximately 17% of their disposable income on leisure

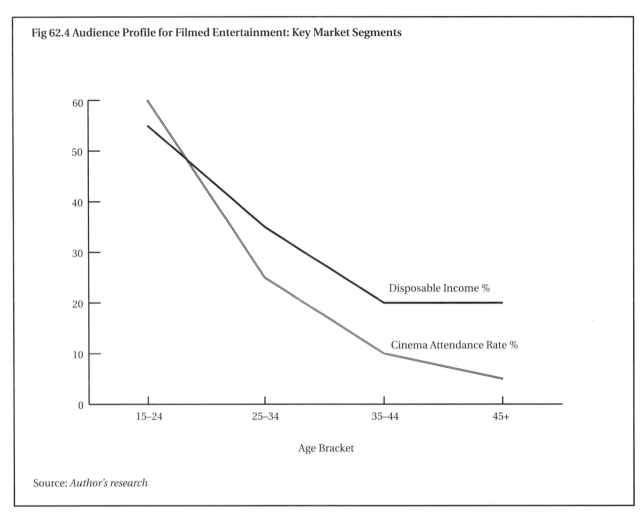

Fig 62.4 Audience Profile for Filmed Entertainment: Key Market Segments

Disposable Income %

Cinema Attendance Rate %

15–24   25–34   35–44   45+

Age Bracket

Source: *Author's research*

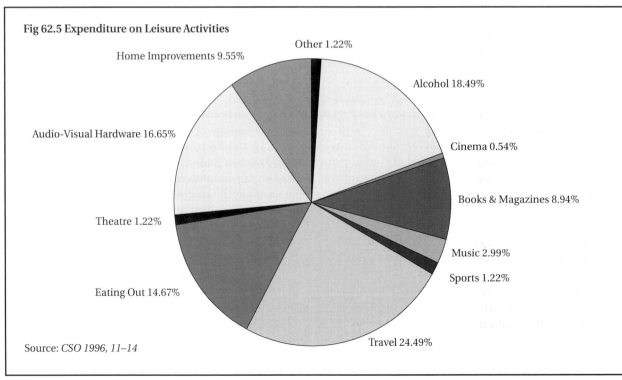

Fig 62.5 Expenditure on Leisure Activities

Other 1.22%

Home Improvements 9.55%

Alcohol 18.49%

Audio-Visual Hardware 16.65%

Cinema 0.54%

Books & Magazines 8.94%

Theatre 1.22%

Music 2.99%

Sports 1.22%

Eating Out 14.67%

Travel 24.49%

Source: *CSO 1996, 11–14*

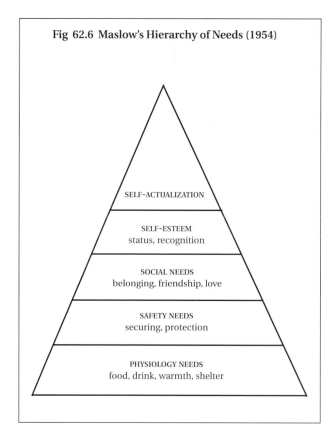

Fig 62.6 Maslow's Hierarchy of Needs (1954)

SELF-ACTUALIZATION

SELF-ESTEEM
status, recognition

SOCIAL NEEDS
belonging, friendship, love

SAFETY NEEDS
securing, protection

PHYSIOLOGY NEEDS
food, drink, warmth, shelter

activities (**Fig 62.5**). Therefore, there is a certain amount of competition for a share of this income.

In addition to the foregoing detailed means of envisaging the interface between marketing and heritage, there are also more general perspectives. The first area we look to is the commonly referred to concept of 'needs'. This notion is borrowed from the field of sociology, from Maslow's 'Hierarchy of Needs' approach (1954), and helps explain why individuals and groups seek to exchange goods and services with each other. A 'need' is defined as a state of felt deprivation. Research shows people respond to different requirements at different times. In the first instance, they are concerned with satisfying basic physiological necessities occasioned by hunger and thirst. Once these have been met, the individual's needs move on to security and protection. From here they progress to social needs, and further to the needs of self-esteem, recognition and status. Finally, once all these have been met, we move on to the self-actualization goals of self-development and self-realization (**Fig. 62.6**). This concept is closely mirrored in the theory of the three segments (Hirschman 1983). According to Hirschman, the key issue in cultural marketing is the motivation behind the creation of the art. The artist is primarily driven by the urge for self-expression (self-actualization). However, the artist also needs to win the respect of his or her peers (self-esteem). Finally, he or she needs to earn a living, however meagre, from their profession (physiological needs). The important point is that the primary motivation is not commercial, as with more entrepreneurial activities. Therefore, it is not useful to impose commercial systems on creative activity. Modification is necessary in order to allow marketing achieve its goal and effectively support the needs of people working in the cultural area.

Certain arguments suggest the field of marketing has been undermined by the *ad hoc* approach of the cultural sector to strategic marketing (Duffy 1994; Clancy *et al.* 1994). According to Duffy, employing consultants on an *ad hoc* basis can lead to over-simplification, or worse, to the bogus history which the industrialization of heritage encourages. Furthermore, consultants can often do more damage than good when asked to formulate a marketing plan for the development of an organization. A case in point would appear to be the ill-fated Celt World in county Waterford, which set out with high hopes and higher expectations but soon found it impossible to meet estimated visitors levels, let alone build on repeat visits. Had the marketing plan been less ambitious and more realistic in terms of what could have been achieved, then the management might have chosen an alternative course of action. There now seems to be a general consensus that any cultural marketing concept should be based on achieving a strategic fit between the products or services being offered so as to maintain the artistic integrity of the creators and satisfy the needs and wants of the audience/spectator/visitor (Guerin 1997).

CONCLUSION

Following the debates from what marketing is to how usefully it may be employed in the heritage context bring us to the conclusion that marketing is a vital aspect of the communication process. It can assist in creating awareness of a particular cultural event. It can inform the general public about the value of a recent archaeological discovery. It stimulates film aficionados to brave the weather and go to a screening of a rare film. Finally, marketing can strategically position an art exhibition so as to encourage potential buyers to actually make the purchase. In fact, it is fair to say that marketing shifts cultural activity beyond the corridors of the elite and pushes it into the mainstream. Facilitating greater access to the creative process has to be good for society as a whole, as it is only through exposure and education that we can adequately appreciate the full value of our heritage. New media technologies are reshaping the ways in which marketing will be perceived in the twenty-first century. The potential of the Internet, web television and digital broadcasting have yet to be fully explored. Hopefully, we shall see the relationship between the cultural sector and marketing expanding, so as to facilitate the development of joint ventures and strategic alliances that will prove mutually beneficial rather than unnecessarily antagonistic.

Bibliography

Anderson, P. F. 1983 'Marketing, scientific progress and scientific method', *Journal of Marketing* **47**, pp. 18–31.

Anderson, P. F. 1986 'On method in consumer research: a critical relativist perspective and scientific method', *Journal of Consumer Research* **13**, pp. 155–73.

Bartels, J. 1988 *The history of marketing thought.* Columbus, Ohio.

Bartels, R. 1951 'Can marketing be a science?', *Journal of Marketing* **16**, pp. 319–28.

Baudrillard, J. 1988 *Jean Baudrillard: selected writings,* ed. M. Poster (Stanford, California), pp. 119-46, 166–84.

Baudrillard, J. 1993 'Hyperreal America', *Economy and Society* **22**, May, pp. 243–52.

Benjamin, W. 1936/68 'The work of art in the age of mechanical reproduction' in *Illuminations,* ed. H. Arendt, trans H. Zohn (New York), pp. 219–53.

Browne, S. 1995 *Postmodern marketing.* London.

Brownlie, D. and Saren, M. 1992 'The 4 Ps of the marketing concept: prescriptive, polemical, permanent and problematical', *European Journal of Marketing* **26**, 4, pp. 34–47.

Buttimer, C. G. and Kavanagh, D. 1995 'Markets and madness' in S. Brown *et al.* (eds) *Proceedings of the marketing eschatology retreat* (Belfast), pp. 60–71.

Buttimer, C. G. and Kavanagh, D. 1996 'Markets, exchange and the extreme' in S. Browne *et al.* (eds) *Marketing apocalypse: eschatology, escapology and the illusion of the end* (London and New York), pp. 145–70.

Buzzell, R. D. 1963 'Is marketing a science?', *Harvard Business Review* **41**, 1, pp. 32–40, 166–70.

CSO (Central Statistics Office) 1996 *National Census (Ireland).* Cork.

Clancy, P. 1994 *Managing the cultural sector.* Dublin.

Clancy, P., Drury, M., Kelly, A., Brannick, T. and Pratschke, S. 1994 *The public and the arts.* Montreal.

Drucker, P. F. 1973 'The theory of business', *Harvard Business Review* **72** (Sept.-Oct.), pp. 95–104.

Drucker, S. 1994 'Las Vegas, theme city', *New York Times,* 13 February, section 5, p. 15.

Duffy, P. 1994 'Conflicts in heritage and tourism' in U. Kochel (ed), *Culture, tourism and development: the case of Ireland* (Liverpool).

Fullerton, R. A. 1988 'How modern is marketing? Marketing's evolution and the myth of the "production era"', *Journal of Marketing* **52** (January), pp. 108–25.

Guerin, H. 1997 'Don't be afraid to fall off the edge of the world', *Cork Review: film* (Cork).

Hirschman, E. 1983 'Aesthetics, ideologies and the limits of the marketing concept', *Journal of Marketing* **47** (Summer), pp. 45–55.

Hirschman, E. 1986 'Humanistic inquiry in market research: philosophy, method and criteria', *Journal of Marketing Research* **23** (August), pp. 237–49.

Hunt, S. D. 1976 'The nature and scope of marketing', *Journal of Marketing* **40** (July), pp. 17–28.

Hutchinson, K. D. 1952 'Marketing as a science: an appraisal', *Journal of Marketing* **16** (January), pp. 286–93.

Keith, P. J. 1960 'The marketing revolution', *Journal of Marketing* **24** (January), pp. 35-8.

Kotler, P. 1972 'A generic concept of marketing', *Journal of Marketing* **36** (April), pp. 46–54.

Kotler, P. and Armstrong, G. 1987 *Marketing: an introduction.* New Jersey.

Kotler, P. and Levy, S. J. 1969 'Broadening the concept of marketing', *Journal of Marketing* **33** (January), pp. 10–15.

Leiss, W., Kline, S. and Jhally, S. 1990 *Social communication in advertising: persons, products and images of well-being.* London.

Levitt, T. 1960 'Marketing myopia', *Harvard Business Review* **38** (July-August), pp. 45–56.

Maslow, A. 1954 *Motivation and personality.* New York.

McDonagh, P. 1995 'Q. Is marketing dying of consumption? A. Yes, and the answer is consumption' in Brown *et al.* 1995, pp. 60–71.

McKenna, R. 1991 'Marketing is everything', *Harvard Business Review* **69** (January-February), pp. 71–9.

Nuñez, T. 1989 'Touristic studies in anthropological perspective' in V. L. Smith (ed) *Hosts and guests: the anthropology of tourism,* 2nd ed. (Philadelphia) pp. 265–74.

Peters, T. and Waterman, R. 1982 *In search of excellence: lessons from America's best-run companies.* New York.

Peter, J. P. and Olson, J. C. 1983 'Is marketing science?', *Journal of Marketing* **47** (Fall), pp. 111–25.

Porter, M. 1985 *Competitive advantage: creating and sustaining superior performance.* New York.

Prahalad, C. W. and Hamel, G. 1990 'The core competence of the corporation', *Harvard Business Review* **68** (May/June), pp. 79–91.

Ritzer, G. 1993 *The McDonaldization of society.* Thousand Oaks, California.

Sheth, J. N., Gardner, D. M. and Garrett, D. E., 1988 *Marketing theory: evolution and evaluation.* New York.

Stalk, G. Evans, P. and Shulman, E. 1992 'Competing on capabilities: the new rules of corporate strategy, *Harvard Business Review* **70** (Mar./Apr.), pp. 57–69.

Terrell, J. 1991 'Disneyland and the future of museum anthropology', *American Anthropologist* **93** (March), pp. 149–53.

Marketing the Ulster History Park

Anthony Candon

It is an almost banal truism that history is a construct and that the past and history are not the same thing. To mediate the past is to create an historical account, because the real past, like the present, is in an inchoate state of becoming that achieves meaning only when a narrative structure is applied. The past is mediated in many forms — as memory recounted, as the written narrative, as visual presentation based on the relic, whether great monument or tiny artefact. We are concerned here with the latter: the narrative in three dimensions. It is a condition of recent decades that the past has become highly commodified. Not, of course, that there is anything new in this: to be utterly simplistic, what was the Renaissance but a repackaging of classical antiquity? Museums, archaeological sites and monuments, heritage attractions — all have succumbed to that late twentieth-century phenomenon, the market. The director of an Irish heritage attraction has, willy-nilly, become, on the one hand, a simple, straight-forward business manager with a product to sell and a bottom line to reach. Yeah, it can be rough out there, but what the hell, it's probably better than selling proprietary brands of soft drink, though the pay is definitely not as good.

On the other hand, while the past may have become commodified, it does not have quite the same cheerful insouciance as a well-known cola. History is complex, nuanced, never settled. It is challenging and subtle. It is wreathed in qualifying footnotes. And, in a divided society, it is also disputed. Yet the vast majority of customers want, and expect to be given, nice gobbits, neatly packaged. The cultural heritage of Ireland is a richly textured tapestry, just as is also that of any other country. The challenge for the manager of a heritage attraction, whether that be a museum, gallery, monument or other historic property, or 'heritage centre', is to be faithful to nuance and texture while at the same time keeping the bottom line in sight and firmly

under control, and presenting the product in an attractive and digestible manner.

The Ulster History Park near Omagh in county Tyrone (*http://www.omagh.gov.uk/historypark.htm*) is best described as an archaeological theme park that presents, on a thirty-five acre (14.5 ha) site, aspects of the settlement history of Ulster from Mesolithic times to the Plantation of Ulster in the early seventeenth century, nearly 10,000 years in an afternoon's stroll. There are fourteen full-scale reconstructions of the homes and other monuments of people in Ireland throughout those ten thousand years, snap-shots in time. The Park has also, of course, a fine reception building that houses an exhibition gallery and audio-visual theatre as well as a cafeteria, a souvenir shop, toilets and offices. The rationale for the History Park is primarily economic: it is there to entice people to the Omagh area to spend money, and to contribute, through tourism, to the development of the District's economy. Any other purpose the Park may have (informational, educational) is subsidiary to that primary function, economic regeneration. The Park is run at a loss but it is, and always has been, recognized that it cannot break even financially: its value lies in the additional spend attracted into the District (the vast bulk of which remains locally) and in the jobs created.

BACKGROUND

The origins of the Ulster History Park go back to a paper written in 1982 by Eric Montgomery, then Chairman of the Ulster American Folk Park (UAFP) and secretary of the Scotch Irish Trust of Ulster which owned the UAFP. In that paper, Mr Montgomery noted that county Tyrone lacked the natural attractions that other counties possessed, such as the lakes of Fermanagh, the Giant's Causeway in Antrim or the Mountains of Mourne in county Down. He referred to the success of Disneyworld in Florida and Aviemore in Scotland. He remarked, 'here

Fig. 63.1 The Ulster History Park, Gortin, county Tyrone.

in Northern Ireland there is the example of our own Ulster American Folk Park which annually attracts more than 65,000 visitors, a quarter of them organized school parties, to its setting in the middle of a remote peat bog in county Tyrone.' To take advantage properly of the tourism potential he perceived to be there, Montgomery stated that it would be necessary to 'create at least one other attraction of a scale similar to the Folk Park as well as developing and publicising other existing features so that the whole area acquires the attractiveness sufficient to pull in the extra visitors.' To that end, he proposed the establishment of another park in the Omagh area which would complement the UAFP Folk Park in its theme, so that together the two parks would act as a 'focal point' to increase the attractiveness of Omagh as a place to visit. The Ulster American Folk Park portrayed life in Ulster in the eighteenth and nineteenth centuries as well as the life emigrants from Ulster made for themselves in North America when they travelled there. Mr Montgomery proposed that the theme of the new Park should be the early settlement of Ireland, from prehistoric times to the seventeenth century.

On foot of the publication of that paper, a Working Party, consisting of representatives of the UAFP, the Northern Ireland Departments of Education, Economic Development, Environment and Agriculture, the Tyrone Industrial Development Group, the Northern Ireland Tourist Board, the Omagh District Council and other bodies, was formed to consider the establishment of the new Park. The Working Party commissioned a feasibility study from architects McCormick Tracey Mullarkey of Derry, and the Working Party report, accompanied by the architects' feasibility study, was published in November 1983. The Working Party endorsed Eric Montgomery's proposal and the feasibility study set out both the proposed content of the new Park and the suggested phasing of construction. The report recommended that what was then tentatively called the Gortin Heritage Park be established. A potential site for the Park was identified (its current location). The Heritage Park would be an archaeological theme park containing a representative selection of monument types from Ireland's earliest prehistory to the Plantation of Ulster in the early seventeenth century. Omagh District Council agreed to be the owner and developer of the new centre.

Construction work commenced in 1985 with labour provided by Enterprise Ulster and funding from the European Regional Development Fund. The nature of the site meant that work proceeded rather slowly, but by late 1987, the District Council felt sufficient progress had been made to advertize for a manager, and the appointee took up his post in April 1988 in the expectation that the Park would open to the public at Easter 1989. For a variety of reasons, however, progress in construction continued to be slow, and it was not until Easter 1990 that the Park, now officially known as The Ulster History Park, opened. At that stage, four exhibits had been completed, with a further two under construction; these were finalized by the late summer of 1990. Staff for the Park were accommodated in a 'portacabin' in the car park. Building work continued in the succeeding years. Additional exhibits were constructed, and a proper reception area containing, in addition to administrative offices and the usual toilet facilities, an exhibition gallery, an audio-visual (AV) theatre, a resource room, souvenir shop and cafeteria, was built. The reception building was officially opened at Easter 1993. By 1995, construction work in the Park had largely been completed and in early July 1996, the final major exhibit, the complex of buildings representing the seventeenth-century Plantation of Ulster, was officially opened. There were now fourteen exhibits on site.

ARCHAEOLOGICAL CONTENT

The history of human settlement in Ireland is more than nine thousand years in duration and therefore any attempt to represent that history must involve a high degree of selectivity. History is selective anyway, and as thirty-five acres can hold only so many reconstructions, so much must be omitted. Great care is thus needed in the choice of structure to be represented. The factors governing the selection of exhibits for the History Park when its design and layout were being worked out were that they should be mainly from Ulster and the northern half of Ireland generally, that they should have strong visual appeal and that, in their forms, they should present contrast and variety. In some instances the reconstructions were based on individual sites, in others the generic form was to be represented. The apparent lack of an overt ideological intent for the Ulster History Park stands in stark contrast to the case of the Navan Centre outside Armagh (an interpretative centre focussed upon the ancient site of Emain Macha and the mediaeval Irish cycle of tales clustered around the epic tale *Táin Bó Cúailnge*), part of whose *raison d'être* was to provide 'an opportunity to explore a common heritage far back beyond the unhappy divisions of more recent history' (Navan Fort Initiative Group 1988; cf. Mallory 1987; Lambkin 1989, 1993, 1994). The list of exhibits in the History Park is as follows:

• *Mount Sandel* huts of the hunter-gatherers of the Mesolithic period

• the *Ballyglass* and *Tankardstown* houses of the farmers of the earlier Neolithic period

• the *Lough Gur* house of the farmers of the later Neolithic period

• the court tomb of the earlier Neolithic period

• the portal tomb of the earlier Neolithic period

• the wedge tomb of the late Neolithic/early Bronze Age

• the stone circle of the Bronze Age

• a standing stone of indeterminate period

• the *fulacht fiadh*, the late Bronze Age cooking place

• an early Christian period field

• the *rath* or ringfort of the early Christian period

• the *crannóg*, the defensive island settlement of the early Christian period

• the monastic enclosure with its church, round tower and other structures of the later early Christian period

• the Norman motte and bailey castle of the mediaeval period

• the manor house, fortified bawn, cottages and mill of the early seventeenth century.

There is, clearly, scope here for a very extensive discussion about what this selection of exhibits means in terms of the view of history it portrays, even leaving aside the question of whether that be a nationalist history or a unionist history (cf. Brady 1994; Walker 1996). Inevitably, there is a degree of linearity here, and history, whatever else it may be, is never linear. Does the selection represent a pre-conceived notion about the headline images of Ireland's past, or does it, perhaps, represent at least in part the then current state of archaeological knowledge? Is visibility in the landscape a factor (cf. Cooney and Grogan 1994, 207–8)? Look at the number of exhibits representing the Neolithic period: what about the Iron Age — where is it represented? Is the Neolithic so prominent because it happens to be one of the best-worked eras of Irish prehistory, while the Iron Age has been relatively neglected? It is a fact that considerably more was known about the Neolithic period than about the Iron Age in the early to mid-1980s, and this remains true today, despite the great increase in our knowledge of the Iron Age since then. What of the Bronze Age, represented only by a stone circle and the *fulacht fiadh*? Why is the period from the twelfth to the early seventeenth centuries represented only by one exhibit, the motte and bailey — what exactly does this say about mediaeval Ulster? More to the point, does it say something about our view of mediaeval Ulster and medieval Ireland? Is there significance in the fact that the two exhibits standing for the last eight hundred years are both also representative of the immigrant, not the native? Is there an 'excluded past' here (Stone and MacKenzie 1990)? These are some of the questions that can be addressed, but this is not the forum for such a discussion. We may, however, note that while there are omissions, most notably from the Iron Age, we adjust for this in the indoor exhibition and in the AV presentation. In fact, the Ulster History Park is more than just the sum of its external displays: it is conceived and executed as an integrated unit, the AV presentation and the exhibition contributing to and underpinning the understanding to be gained from the outdoor exhibits.

THE PRODUCT

It is one thing to describe the History Park and what it contains, even if only briefly. It is another to objectify this as 'product'. Here, the product is that which is sold to the public, and our product is more than just the reconstructions and the interpretations that accompany them. In one short phrase, the product is *A trail through time* .... It is about a vicariously lived experience and the power of the imagination. 'At the Ulster History Park you can enter the homes of people from long ago ...'. You cannot, of course. But you allow yourself the illusion that you can, knowing full-well that time travel is impossible. Where else can you do that? You may see flint being knapped, wool being carded and spun, grain being ground on a saddle quern or a clay pot being made, and you can try your hand at these activities. You take on trust that what you see, what you read, what you are told is the truth, is real. Authenticity is part of the product. You are told that the reconstructions are based on extensive archaeological and historical research; they are works of scholarship, so of course you believe them to be a true and accurate representations of the past. (And here again we come back to what the nature of that past is.) The materials employed in the exhibits are those materials used in the original monuments. Our stone buildings are stone buildings, not concrete-block cores clad with stone.

There are dangers in this approach. We cannot, of course, relive the past. Any encounter with the past, especially remote ages, is a vicarious experience. From the most austere and circumspect scholarship to the crassest, most vulgar 'heritageization', the activity involved is imaginative reconstruction. The reconstruction is not the artefact. It remains a simulacrum. This does not mean that it is not true; if it is honest, it is true (Swiecimski 1989). And objectifying this truth is valid if it is recognized as contingent: knowledge evolves and changes. I am reminded of Croce's famous dictum, 'all history is contemporary history' (quoted, *inter alia*, in Collingwood 1946, 190–204: 202; Marwick 1970, 79;

Danto 1968, 116). As Bennett (1995, 129, 130) has remarked, 'the past, as it is materially embodied in museums and heritage sites, is inescapably a product of the present which organises it. ... the visitor to a museum or historic site is confronted with a set of textually organised meanings whose determinations must be sought in the present.' Or, as Lowenthal more succinctly put it, 'a portrait of any past also reflects the painter's own time' (1985, 410).

Walsh has criticized the Archaeological Resource Centre (ARC) in York in England for providing opportunities for public participation in activities such as flint-knapping, cooking, weaving, spinning and so forth. 'Such presentations are, in fact, quite superficial as they deny any consideration of the contexts within which the activity would have taken place' (1992, 174; for ARC's own self-description see *http://www.jorvik-viking-centre.co.uk/arc.html*). There is an element of truth in this, but only up to a certain point. If you represent to people that they are recreating an activity such as flint-knapping as it *really* was done in the past, then you are involved in falsity, if not fraud. If, on the other hand, you say to people, 'come, try your hand at this: we can't actually reproduce how people in the past would have done it, but by trying it we get some sense of the feel of the materials and the difficulties involved,' you are not misleading them. You are engaging the power of their imagination. Fowler has endorsed using copies of Iron Age tools at Butser Ancient Farm in Britain to engage in the simulation of ancient farming practices; however, it is students in a controlled academic environment who are so engaged (1989, 62–3). So that's all right, then — isn't it?

On occasion, the History Park makes use of historical re-enactment groups to 'live out' 'Planter life in Ulster in the early seventeenth century', or 'noble life on a medieval *crannóg*', or whatever. Both Walsh and Fowler have been very critical of this type of activity. 'Often, the heritage display, with its denial of process, its emphasis on the synchronous spectacle, removes any idea of change through time. ... As the heritage centre or the mock battle offers a representation, which at best provides a manipulated and trivialised snapshot of one element from the past, it removes that event from the wider historical process and context, and thus it serves to promote the distancing of people from places' (Walsh 1992, 137). 'As we all know, the past, or more strictly our perception of it, is both organic and dynamic. In contrast, so-called "living history" re-enactments of it contain a built-in tendency, paradoxically but of their very nature, to perpetuate academically "dead" and often pseudo-historical stereotypes. It seems to me therefore that those who lead people to believe they can experience a chunk of the past by dressing up as medieval knights, or by dirtying their face and climbing

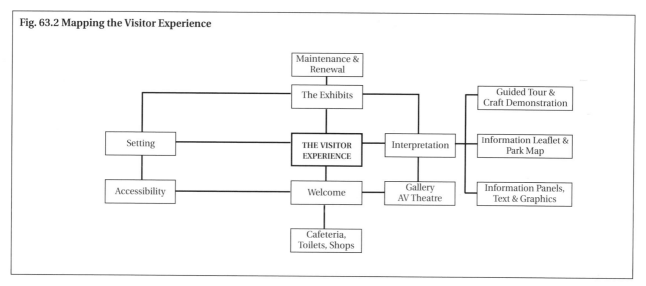

Fig. 63.2 Mapping the Visitor Experience

up a chimney, are being both misleading and cruel' (Fowler 1989, 63).

What both Walsh and Fowler display is a profound and searing contempt for the ordinary person. Certainly, at the Ulster History Park re-enactment is make-believe, fantasy with verisimilitude attached. Visitors know this. Knowing it, however, does not diminish the visitors' enjoyment. They will look at the re-enactors' clothes, at the artefacts they carry, at their other props: it is there that the verisimilitude lies. They will watch whatever drama is unfolding before them, but they will not be deceived into believing that they are witnessing seventeenth- or thirteenth-century life; they will see it for what it is — drama acted out by their contemporaries.

There is one circumstance where illusion can, perhaps, displace reality, and that is when the simulacrum purports to be an exact copy of the original. I still feel uncomfortable about how this happened to me some years ago at Lascaux in the Dordogne in France. The prehistoric cave paintings there had became so popular that visitors were causing damage and they had to be closed to the public. As this was going to mean a loss of tourist revenue to the area, a replica, Lascaux II, was created. The degree of verisimilitude was so real that I forgot, temporarily, that I was looking at a copy, not the original (cf. Boniface and Fowler 1993, 99–100). Most people, most of the time, do not believe literally that they are able to travel through time. To suggest that they can be misled into this is, to say the least, patronising.

We may call our product *A trail through time* … and mean a voyage of the imagination. But in truth when we map the visitor experience, we find that it is both more richly textured and incorrigibly mundane. **Fig. 63.2** provides a graphic representation of this map. What is

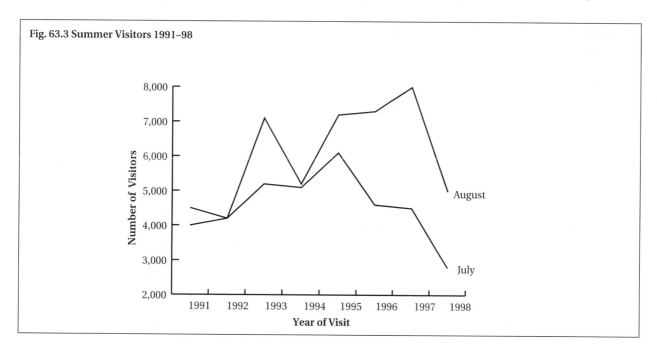

Fig. 63.3 Summer Visitors 1991–98

Table 63.1 Number of Visitors to Selected Northern Ireland Heritage Attractions which charge for Admission						
	1993	1994	1995	1996	1997	1998
Ulster Folk and Transport Museum	181,255	186,656	192,984	198,211	203,501	168,623
Ulster American Folk Park	131,258	117,081	137,440	143,650	118,758	111,250
Dunluce Centre	135,000	118,116	93,274	80,088	75,000	78,000
St Patrick's Trian, Armagh	11,565	60,000	57,027	49,396	48,327	51,115
Navan Centre, Armagh	31,257	60,000	65,500	49,268	40,028	–
Ulster History Park	**41,338**	**41,035**	**51,031**	**46,864**	**41,448**	**35,748**
Tower Museum, Derry	45,000	28,000	32,620	24,368	21,527	18,558

immediately evident is that the visit is a multi-faceted activity that provokes heterogeneous responses. Clean toilets and a nice, hot cup of tea, while not the same as the exhibits (obviously!), still provoke a response in the visitor and have the capacity to determine whether the visit was enjoyable or not. What is the condition of the paths, how steep are they, how easy is it to push a baby buggy or a wheelchair? Are all areas of the Park accessible? Are the exhibits well maintained? Is the Park clean, tidy and well maintained? Is it a pleasant environment? All of these are factors in the visitor experience.

THE BUSINESS ENVIRONMENT

Having developed the product, one has to get out there and market it. In describing the product, we really also define its USP, its unique selling point, and that is its uniqueness, accuracy and credibility, together with its quality. Its uniqueness also gives it its *Wow!* factor.

Northern Ireland does not have a normal tourism environment, for obvious historical reasons. This applies both in the case of inbound tourism from outside the province, and also in the case of the domestic market as well. In these circumstances, the operating climate for the History Park, as for other heritage attractions, is challenging. The market for the Ulster History Park, while potentially very large, is actually rather limited. Effectively, it is confined to Northern Ireland and the border counties of the Republic of Ireland — a population of about two million people. The reason for this is fairly straightforward. Northern Ireland is not seen as an attractive tourism destination because of its unresolved political crisis and, more crucially, because of the perception that it is a violent and dangerous place. Add to this a normal variable such as currency exchange rates, and one can see that things can become difficult. In the last couple of years, the strength of sterling against other European currencies and the US dollar has helped make Northern Ireland an expensive, and therefore a less attractive, destination. Out-of-state visitors do come to the north, but not in anything like the numbers that they

should. (Much of the following discussion related to such numbers is based on data contained in publications of the Northern Ireland Tourist Board. Rather than clutter up the text with individual references, the reader is referred to the bibliography at the end.)

The domestic holiday market is also challenging. There are a variety of factors at play here. These include the political uncertainty, tensions surrounding Orange Order parades (especially, in the last few years, the parade at Drumcree in county Armagh), the weather and cheaper holidays abroad because of the strength of sterling. In addition, the holiday season is exceptionally short in Northern Ireland, really little more than the two months of July and August, the months of the school holidays. Then, when you factor in July ... July used to be a good month for business, but in the last few years, visitor numbers have fallen substantially. **Fig. 63.3** illustrates the situation. Between 1991 and 1995 business during the month of July grew steadily, rising from 4,063 to 6,145 visitors. As can be seen, however, the number of visitors fell back sharply in the following years, falling to only 2,764 in 1998. Visitor numbers in August, however, continued to grow up to 1997 (with the exception of 1994 when they dipped sharply), collapsing in 1998. In fact, 1998 was a disastrous summer. The exchange value of sterling was very high; the weather was appalling; there was a prolonged, tense and violent stand-off between members of the Orange Order and the security forces at Drumcree, linked to which was the murder of the three Quinn children and, on 15 August, the Omagh Bomb which killed 29 people and injured hundreds more — the single worst atrocity in Northern Ireland's bloody recent history.

There is a further issue which needs to be taken into account. That is the huge growth in the number of visitor attractions in Northern Ireland in the last ten years. 'Visitor attraction' is a very broadly defined term, ranging from the Giant's Causeway to the Ulster Museum to Belfast City's Parks. Some of these attractions charge for admission and some are free. There were 88 visitor attractions in 1988; by 1993, the number had risen to 190, and there were 209 in 1998. This is a very positive development in one sense, in that there will be a well-developed infrastructure for visitors when 'normal' tourism eventually gets off the ground; on the other hand, it has made the operating environment much more competitive, even cut-throat in the short term.

The Northern Ireland Tourist Board's annual survey of visitor attractions confirms the grim story of 1998: it recorded a total of 7.7 million visits to attractions in 1998, compared with 8.2 million visits in 1997, a decrease of 6%. While these reports need to be treated with care (to what extent is a lunchtime stroll in Belfast's Botanic Gardens a 'visit'?), the overall trend is clear enough.

The challenge for the Ulster History Park is to get out there into this crowded and abnormal market and make an impact. To a considerable degree, this is what we have succeeded in doing. **Table 63.1** shows that we are in there, mixing it with the best.

What is interesting to note from the Tourist Board's surveys is the performance over time of heritage attractions, both those that charge for admission and those that are free. Now, heritage attraction is a very broad term; here, I have restricted it quite deliberately and excluded the natural heritage. **Table 63.2** lists some of the heritage attractions which charge and their visitor figures between 1993 and 1998. The ranking of the first three has been the same for those six years, despite the year-on-year fluctuations, with the Ulster Folk and Transport Museum well out in front. The Dunluce Centre, however, is not really a heritage attraction, and perhaps should not be included here. Below these is a further group of three whose visitor numbers are generally in the range 40,000–60,000, while quite substantially below these again are the Tower Museum in

Derry and Enniskillen Castle which houses Fermanagh County Museum and the Enniskillings Regimental Museum.

Table 63.2 lists some of the attractions which do not charge for admission. Among these free attractions, the Ulster Museum is way out in front. Then there is Newry Arts Centre, followed by a group of three museums in the range 25,000–60,000, followed by several more arts centres, and lastly Armagh County Museum.

When the visitor numbers for the selected attractions for the six years from 1993 to 1998 are aggregated, some interesting patterns emerge (**Table 63.3**). The busiest single attraction was the Ulster Museum, a free attraction with 1,627 million visitors. It was one of only two locations with more than one million visitors during the period; the other was the Ulster Folk and Transport Museum (UFTM). The next three attractions, in order of their number of visitors, were the UFTM, the UAFP and the Dunluce Centre — all fee-paying. In fifth and sixth positions were two non-fee-paying attractions, Newry Arts Centre and North Down Heritage Centre in Bangor. Seventh was St Patrick's Trian in Armagh, and the Ulster History Park was eighth with 257,464 visitors. Without going into a detailed exposition of the figures in these tables, a number of points emerge. One is the dominant position of the Big Three museums which have now, merged to form a new institution, the National Museums and Galleries of Northern Ireland (Wilson 1995). Secondly, after the Dunluce Centre among the charging attractions and Newry Arts Centre among the free attractions, there is a solid core of attractions that sit in the 40,000–60,000 visitors-per-year range, while below that again at some distance is a small but important group of museums. Thirdly, the emergence of several new heritage centres does not appear to have taken business

Table 63.2 Number of Visitors to Selected Free-of-charge Heritage Attractions in Northern Ireland

	1993	1994	1995	1996	1997	1998
Ulster Museum	246,464	256,020	319,534	240,859	328,823	235,694
Newry Arts Centre	58,057	61,000	65,000	–	75,000	75,500
North Down Heritage Centre, Bangor	54,449	57,596	50,998	45,689	40,889	46,309
Down County Museum, Downpatrick	43,080	34,756	37,083	36,611	33,444	36,140
Irish Linen Centre & Lisburn Museum			21,103*	24,160	25,538	37,938
Cave Hill Heritage Centre	3,000	30,102	66,407	50,000	35,000	36,000
Clotworthy Arts Centre,	–	–	–	–	32,740	31,206
Armagh County Museum	21,817	13,657	18,396	15,205	7,632**	12,547

* The Irish Linen Centre and Lisburn Museum charged for admission in 1995

** Armagh County Museum was closed from July 1997 to March 1998

Table 63.3 Total Visitor Numbers at Selected Attractions, 1993–98

ATTRACTION	CHARGING/NON-CHARGING	TOTALS 93–98	POSITION
Ulster Folk and Transport Museum	C	1,131,230	2
Ulster American Folk Park	C	759,437	3
Dunluce Centre	C	579,478	4
St Patrick's Trian, Armagh	C	277,430	7
Navan Centre, Armagh	C	246,053	9
Ulster History Park	**C**	**257,464**	**8**
Tower Museum, Derry	C	170,073	12
Enniskillen Castle	C	100,413	13
Ulster Museum	NC	1,627,394	1
Newry Arts Centre	NC	334,557	5
North Down Heritage Centre, Bangor	NC	295,930	6
Down County Museum, Downpatrick	NC	221,114	10
Irish Linen Centre & Lisburn Museum	NC	87,636	15
Cave Hill Heritage Centre	NC	220,509	11
Clotworthy Arts Centre, Antrim	NC	63,946	16
Armagh County Museum	NC	89,254	14

away from the longer-established Big Three. Fourthly, while the numbers visiting charging attractions mostly fell in 1998, visitor numbers to the free attractions mostly increased; this can be attributed, at least in part, to the ghastly weather — both the UFTM and the UAFP are open-air centres. The curator of one local museum has attributed the increase in visits to his museum to the poor summer weather in 1998 — his museum was a pleasant, accessible place in which to shelter from the rain, and it was free! One further — and, from my point of view, crucial — factor to emerge from the surveys is that the performance of the Ulster History Park is broadly in line with that of the rest of the sector.

So far, we have looked at both tourism and the domestic visitor market in general terms. There is another segment of the market which is equally important, and that is the schools' one. This sector is important for two reasons. Firstly, its size: in 1998, it accounted for some 46% of all visitors to the Park, while in 1997, school pupils constituted 39% of visitors. Secondly, school children visit the Park throughout most of the school year, thus providing business when otherwise there would be little or none. It has, however, been a market segment that has become much more difficult to do business in lately. As the public purse-strings have tightened in recent years, school budgets have also been squeezed, and many schools are finding it more and more difficult to afford the costs of a trip away. Indeed, the transport element of the school budgets has suffered most. More and more Northern Ireland schools

are telling us that they can no longer afford the cost of hiring a bus to take the children to visit us.

MARKETING

So, how do we go about attracting visitors? In 1999, we did this through a diverse marketing strategy with emphasis on

• new, attractive events;

• greater emphasis on children and families;

• prices retained at 1998 levels;

• new focus on costumed interpreters, and

• new, full colour interpretative panels at each exhibit.

One of our major difficulties has been, and continues to be, our confusion with the Ulster American Folk Park. Last year, we decided to make a virtue of our similarity in name to stress

(a) our existence;

(b) our difference, and

(c) our uniqueness in the northern half of Ireland.

We decided to undertake the following:

- programme of events;

- school tours and workshops;

- distribution of promotional literature;

- carefully targeted advertizing across a range of media;

- shopping centre promotions;

- participation in Northern Irish Tourist Board (NITB)/Visitor Attraction Association of Northern Ireland workshops;

- attendance at teachers' conferences;

- seek 'free' media (especially television) exposure;

- participate in co-operative marketing through NITB, North West Passage, Omagh Tourism;

- joint ticketing with the Ulster American Folk Park;

- survey of visitors during the summer, and

- revamp and make more attractive our website.

Because of the particular difficulties that appeared to be developing in the domestic Northern Ireland schools market, we decided to place special emphasis in 1999 on continuing to grow the schools' market in the Republic of Ireland through

- developing customized product, and

- directly targeting Republic of Ireland schools.

MAINTENANCE AND ARCHAEOLOGICAL INSIGHT
Beyond marketing lies a range of other management activities — personnel management, financial management, maintenance. In the space left to me, I want to look at just one of these — maintenance. A resource like the Ulster History Park, with its extensive grounds, its fourteen exhibits, its large reception building, requires a lot of looking after. The reception building, being a new and modern structure, places relatively light demands on us in this respect. Both the grounds maintenance and the maintenance of the exhibits are, however, onerous. Paths must be kept clear and well-drained, surfaces need periodic renewal, vegetation encroachment has to be managed. Signs and fences have to be painted. There are lawns to be mown — for nearly five months of the year, a full-time job for one man. As new planting comes on there is selective felling of the Norway spruce and, in winter, there is responding to storm damage.

Caring for the exhibits is, of course, a *sine qua non*. Maintaining them includes routine tasks such as lighting fires in the various houses each day and keeping them clean and tidy, as well as controlling weed growth both on and around some of the reconstructions. It also involves repairs to the fabric of the exhibits themselves. From the maintenance point of view, the exhibits fall into two categories: those that are stone-built and those that are made of timber and have thatched roofs. The stone structures do not require quite the same degree of attention as the organic exhibits, though they still need attention. Organic materials, however, such as wood, straw and animal skins, rot, particularly in the damp climate of county Tyrone. This means that there has to be an on-going programme of replacement. For example, the Mesolithic exhibit has to be almost totally renewed periodically. The exhibit consists of two huts, one finished and one left as a framework. The huts are circular in plan and made from long hazel and willow rods driven into the ground at an angle and interwoven to form an igloo-shaped framework. One of these is then covered with deer skins — about ninety in all. We have found through experience that the life-span of the deerskins is no more than three years. Similarly, the timber framework, when exposed to the elements lasts no more than a similar three years. The other exhibits also need care and maintenance, if not quite so radically. At the moment, we are replacing some oak timbers in the walls of one of the Neolithic houses. Roof ridges need ongoing repairs. The light palisade fences on both the *crannóg* and motte and bailey have to be replaced virtually every year, and so on. All of this is both costly and labour intensive.

It has also, however, been instructive. I have just mentioned how we have discovered that the useful life of a deerskin is about three years. Similarly, we have found that split oak planks we used as wall timbers for the Ballyglass and Tankardstown Neolithic houses (Ó Nualláin 1972; Gowen 1988) also have quite a short life — about eight years. The timbers employed were about twenty-five to thirty years old, with average diameters of between 200 mm and 300 mm. These were split length-wise and placed vertically in a shallow foundation trench with packing stones used to help keep them in place. Before putting them into the ground, the ends were treated with a preservative. Nevertheless, that portion of the timber beneath the ground surface, with the exception of the hard core, rotted, though the rest of the plank above ground remained good and solid. This suggests two possibilities: the probable life-span for this type of house may have been relatively short, perhaps no more than eight to twelve years; I should have thought an average life-span of twenty to twenty-five years was probably not unreasonable, a span agreed with by

615

Cooney and Grogan (1994, 48). Alternatively, the timber was not used in quite the same way by the Stone Age farmers as we have employed it: could they have fire-hardened the plank ends before putting them into the ground, and would that have lengthened their useful life? Or, might the timber employed not be the young trees we used, but older trees, the softer, outer wood stripped away, leaving the hard core timber to be used for the planking? These are questions which I have not had the opportunity properly to address as yet.

There are other issues which the practical experience of constructing and maintaining the exhibits has raised. I allude to just one here, and that concerns one of the types of fence described in the early Irish law text, *Bretha Comaithchesa* ('Judgements of neighbourhood'), the *nochtaile* or post and wattle fence (Ó Corráin 1983, 247–51; Kelly 1997, 372–78). When freshly erected, this fence is quite strong and sturdy and is a very effective barrier against animals. However, it rots quickly, so it seems to me that, just as it is relatively quickly erected, it probably originally served to make a temporary enclosure only rather than act as a permanent field boundary. The Ulster History Park is not a controlled archaeological experiment, but nonetheless some useful insights have been gained from its construction and ongoing maintenance.

CONCLUSION

One commentator on heritage has recently suggested that 'History, truly considered, is a verb, not an abstract noun. We history' (Brett 1993, 186). The Ulster History Park is an exercise in 'historying'. We do not pretend to have all the answers or claim to know the past. What we do offer is an opportunity for people to view, picture-postcard like, reconstructions of a selection of monuments done to the best of our ability. The History Park is a series of snap-shots in time, an exercise in historical interpretation. Hewison wrote that 'the past may be beyond recovery, but it is highly susceptible to recuperation' (1997, 135). The past, by definition, is always beyond recovery; it will always ever only be viewed as a reconstruction, whether that be via the academic tome or article in a learned journal, a popular history book or TV documentary, a museum presentation or a trail through time … at the Ulster History Park.

Bibliography

Brady, C. (ed) 1994 *Interpreting Irish history: the debate on historical revisionism*. Dublin.

Brett, D. 1993 'The construction of heritage' in B. O'Connor and M. Cronin (eds) *Tourism in Ireland: a critical analysis* (Cork), pp. 183–202.

Boniface, P. and Fowler, P. 1993 *Heritage and tourism in the global village*. London.

Collingwood, R. G. 1946 *The idea of history*. Oxford.

Cooney, G. and Grogan, E. 1994 *Irish prehistory: a social perspective*. Dublin.

Danto, E. C. 1968 *Analytical philosophy of history*. Cambridge.

Dept of Economic Development 1989 *Tourism in Northern Ireland: a view to the future*. Belfast.

Fowler, P. 1989 'Heritage: a post-modernist perspective' in D. Uzzell (ed) *Heritage interpretation volume 1: the natural and built environment* (London), pp. 57–63.

Gathercole, P. and Lowenthal, D. 1990 *The politics of the past*. London.

Gowen, M. 1988 *Three Irish gas pipelines: new archaeological evidence from Munster*. Dublin.

Hewison, R. 1987 *The heritage industry: Britain in a climate of decline*. London.

Kelly, F. 1997 *Early Irish farming*. Dublin.

Lambkin, B. K. 1989 'Navan Fort and the coming of "Cultural Heritage"', *Emania* **6**, pp. 48–9.

Lambkin, B. K. 1993 'Navan Fort and the arrival of "Cultural Heritage"', *Emania* **11**, pp. 61–4.

Lambkin, B. K. 1994 'The Ulster Cycle, the Navan Centre and the improvement of community relations in Northern Ireland' in J. P. Mallory and G. Stockman (eds), *Ulidia*: Proceedings of the First International Conference on the Ulster Cycle of tales (Belfast), pp. 281–90.

Lowenthal, D. 1985 *The past is a foreign country*. Cambridge.

Mallory, J. P. 1987 'Draft proposal for a Navan Heritage Centre', *Emania* **2**, pp. 32–5.

Marwick, A. 1970 *The nature of history*. London.

Montgomery, E. 1982 *Presenting the past: an outline plan for a YTP project in county Tyrone*. Omagh.

Navan Fort Initiative Group 1988 *Navan at Armagh*. Belfast.

Northern Ireland Tourist Board 1990 *Tourism in Northern Ireland: an indicative plan*. Belfast.

Northern Ireland Tourist Board 1992 *Survey of visitor attractions 1992 report*. Belfast.

Northern Ireland Tourist Board 1994 *Survey of visitor attractions 1993 report*. Belfast.

Northern Ireland Tourist Board 1995a *Survey of visitor attractions 1994 report*. Belfast.

Northern Ireland Tourist Board 1995b *Tourism in Northern Ireland: a development strategy 1995–2000*. Belfast.

Northern Ireland Tourist Board 1996 *Survey of visitor attractions 1995 report*. Belfast.

Northern Ireland Tourist Board 1997 *Survey of visitor attractions 1996 report*. Belfast.

Northern Ireland Tourist Board 1998 *Survey of visitor attractions 1997 report*. Belfast.

Northern Ireland Tourist Board 1999 *Survey of visitor attractions 1998 report*. Belfast.

Northern Ireland Tourist Board and Arts Council of Northern Ireland 1998 *The cultural sector: a development opportunity for tourism in Northern Ireland*. Belfast.

Ó Corráin, D. 1983 'Some legal references to fences and fencing in early Historic Ireland' in T. Reeves-Smith and F. Hamond (eds) *Landscape archaeology in Ireland* (Oxford), pp. 247–51.

Omagh District Council 1992 *Proposal for the development of a visitor/interpretive centre at Gortin History Park, Co. Tyrone, Northern Ireland*. Omagh.

Ó Nualláin, S. 1972 'A Neolithic house at Ballyglass near Ballycastle, Co. Mayo', *Journal of the Royal Society of Antiquities of Ireland* **102**, pp. 49–57.

Scotch Irish Trust of Ulster 1983 *A development plan for the Sperrins: proposal for a Gortin Heritage Centre*. Omagh.

Stone, P. and MacKensie, R., 1990 *The excluded past: archaeology in education*. London.

Swiecimski, J. 1989 'Truths and untruths in museum exhibitions' in D. Uzzell (ed) *Heritage interpretation volume two: the visitor experience* (London), pp. 203–11.

Walker, B. 1996 *Dancing to history's tune: history, myth and politics in Ireland*. Belfast.

Walsh, K. 1992 *The representation of the past: museums and heritage in the post-modern world*. London.

Wilson, A. 1995 *A time for change: a review of major museums in Northern Ireland*. Belfast.

Heritage Marketing on the Internet

DON O'SULLIVAN

People with an interest in Ireland and its heritage, no matter where they are in the world, can access vast amounts of information on the Internet. More than likely, such information seekers will access *ireland.com (http://www.ireland.com/)*, which offers a broad range of information services targeted at Irish people and those interested in Ireland (**Table 64.1**). *Ireland.com* is a portal site for Ireland, published by the Electronic Publishing Division of the *Irish Times*. In the early 1990s the advent of the Internet led to the *Irish Times* redefining its business from being primarily a newspaper company to being an information provider. One of the most significant implications of this redefinition was that in 1994 the *Irish Times* launched one of the first on-line newspapers on the Internet.

Over six years on, the *Irish Times* is one of the most successful on-line newspapers in the world and has the highest traffic (level of usage) of any site in the country. The company also launched a number of related services, which it feels complement the newspaper site. These include *Eurotimes, Sports Extra, Path To Peace* (covering the Northern Ireland peace process), a Saint Patrick's Day site and *Dyoublong* (a James Joyce site centred on Bloomsday). In addition the *Irish Times* has *Irish Ancestors*, a genealogy site accessible from the *Irish Times* home page (*http://scripts.ireland.com/ancestor/*). This site allows users to engage in a genealogical search on-line for a fee of $25.00. The site has been a great commercial success to date and provides an interesting insight to the marketing of Irish heritage in a contemporary context.

In March 1999, all of these sites were located within the *ireland.com* site. *Ireland.com* incorporated all of the existing services plus a new Dublin city guide, business, technology and Irish racing sites. *Ireland.com* is in effect positioned as a 'portal' site for Irish-related information and services. Portals are sites that act as a doorway to areas of the Internet, for certain users. This, in theory, makes it easier for the user to find the specific information required. For the diaspora, issues such as current news, the north, genealogy and St Patrick's Day are amongst the prime areas of interest. Given its brand strength, range of services and unparalleled traffic, by the end of 1999, the *Irish Times* was well equipped to develop itself as a portal for this market. However, as is the case in any dynamic market development, maintenance of this position will require a continuous evolution of the portfolio of services *ireland.com* provides.

THE INTERNET

While the ever-increasing spread of the Internet has impacted on and altered many industries, such as travel and retail, it represents a clear opportunity for the marketing of heritage-related products. The impact of the Internet as a means of promoting and distributing services has been well documented. The Internet offers service providers twenty-four hour global access to markets at significantly reduced costs. In the tourist sector, its use as a means of searching for and purchasing services is well understood. The Internet also offers the potential for selling information directly, particularly specialist or 'niche content' information such as that relating to finance, investment or indeed genealogy.

Although the growth of the Internet is widely reported, it is as well to outline the size of the on-line population prior to discussing the marketing of the *Irish Ancestors* site. By the end of March 2000, the on-line population was estimated to be in the region of 304.36 million adults; these are broken down geographically as in **Table 64.2**.

As can be seen from **Table 64.2** the largest on-line population is in North America followed by Europe. These figures continue to grow, and it is expected that 35% of Europeans will be on-line by 2002.

The existence of an on-line population does not of

Table 64.1 Selection of Services offered by *ireland.com*

SERVICE	DESCRIPTION
Irish Times Newspaper	The daily newspaper with searchable archives, published everyday at 4.00 a.m.
Dyoublong	James Joyce and Bloomsday-related site.
St Patrick's Festival	National holiday-related site.
An Teanga Bheo	A weekly Irish-language section.
Path To Peace	News and discussion related to the Northern Ireland peace process.
Sports Extra	A sports service providing up-to-date results and details of GAA club games throughout the country.
Eurotimes	A European news service looking at news and developments within the EU.
Weather Ireland	Includes a five-day forecast for towns and cities throughout Ireland, satellite images and statistics.
Dublin Live	Information on attractions, eating out, entertainment, travel, accommodation, shopping and traffic.
Technology 2000	Technology-related news and information.
Business	Business news, stock prices etc.

course necessarily imply an on-line market. Indeed many users of the Internet have been reluctant to buy goods and services on-line. This is added to by the 'free' culture that has traditionally dominated on the Internet, with information being provided without charge. Other causes of customer reticence are fears about the security of on-line transactions, concerns about the credibility of on-line companies and difficulties navigating the web. However, as the market has continued to grow, these reservations have begun to abate, most noticeably in the US, where at least 38% of users have purchased on-line. This is in line with trends generally on-line where the North American market had been to the forefront in developments.

The comparatively advanced nature of the on-line marketplace provides clear lessons regarding critical success factors in Internet-based marketing. The more successful companies, either seeking to market products on-line or to generate revenue from on-line advertising, have tended to concentrate on a number of factors as a means of generating traffic. Key amongst these is the provision of quality content or information. Successful sites also tend to be well designed, easy to use and retrieve information from and frequently updated. Speed of download is also important; sparing use of graphics and generally avoiding unnecessary clutter in sites facilitates this. Finally, frequently visited sites are, unsurprisingly, frequently updated. Given these criteria for success, it is easy to see the attractiveness of well-run on-line newspapers. Newspaper organizations have built their success off-line on the provision of quality content frequently updated (daily) which is conveniently laid out. In an on-line world, newspapers are not constrained by the limits of print and can be published throughout the day.

IRELAND.COM

In 1994, the *Irish Times* was the first newspaper in Britain and Ireland, and among the first 30 in the world, to publish on the world-wide web. The *Irish Times* publishes a web edition of the newspaper *(http://www.ireland.com)*, which is the most frequently visited Irish site with, on average 50,000 visitors a day in mid-1998 and this increased to as much as 80,000 during a major news events. The number of regular visitors continued to grow; in January 1998 the site had 1.62 million visits. Traffic to the site, thus expanded, increasing by 40% between October 1997 and March 1998. This increased traffic necessitated a parallel investment in the technology and infrastructure supporting the site. While initially the site bandwith could support 500 users simultaneously accessing the site, by 1998 this had increased to 1,500. As the services offered on the site grew, the web edition of the

Table 64.2 The Global Market: On-line Population

World Total	304,360,000
Africa	2,580,000
Asia/Pacific	68,900,000
Europe	83,350,000
Middle East	1,900,000
Canada & USA	136,860,000
South America	10,740,000
Source: *Nua.ie (end March 2000)*	

619

Table 64.3 Services offered on the *Irish Ancestors* Site

Service	Detail	Cost
What's In A Name	Report on how the surname came into being, variants or related names, published or printed family histories, the distribution of the surname as recorded in 1890 and a graphic of the family coat of arms.	$5.00
Place-names	History of Irish place-names searchable countrywide, by city and by county.	None
Magazine	Link to Roots On-line Magazine updated monthly with articles of interest to people researching their Irish roots.	None
Browse	Provides a general overview of records relevant to Irish family history research, and allows researchers to browse through listings and descriptions of these records.	None
Gen.ie	The *gen.ie* service is a fully comprehensive expert system designed to provide extensive information about all records relevant to a particular Irish ancestor.	$25.00

newspaper became just a part of what was on offer, and this was reflected in the launch of *ireland.com* which in effect houses the various offerings. By the end of May 2000, *ireland.com* was reporting 16.7 million page impressions per month.

As can be seen from the tables shown, the primary audience for *ireland.com* has been North America. In appealing to the nation's diaspora, the site has an advantage in that the primary countries of residence for those of Irish descent (USA, UK and Australia) are all English-speaking. Similar organizations in countries such as Germany and Italy would encounter significant language barriers in attempting to serve fourth- and fifth-generation emigrants.

THE IRISH ANCESTORS SITE

Given the traditionally high levels of emigration from Ireland, there are a large number of people (particularly in the US, UK and Australia) who have Irish roots. This has resulted in a substantial amount of interest in investigating family trees. In 1997, 79,000 of the overseas visitors to Ireland engaged in a genealogical search as part of their trip. The National Library's free genealogical service, which opened in May 1998, was attracting more than 1,000 people a month. It is estimated that, in the process, these tourists spent a total of £30,000,000. This represented a trebling of 'roots tourist' figures over the previous ten years. While this is a substantial number, it reflects a small portion of the overall numbers with Irish

lineage, 70 million globally (an estimated 40 million in the USA alone). However, many people are unwilling to incur the time and cost of visiting Ireland. Even amongst those classifying themselves as 'genealogical enthusiasts', 32% had never visited Ireland.

In 1991, John Grenham, a well-respected Irish genealogist, published *Tracing your Irish ancestors*, a work targeted at those interested in Irish genealogy. In the process of putting the book together, Grenham came to realize that there might be considerable demand for a database containing the information outlined in it. At this point, his thoughts revolved around a CD-ROM or similar format for distributing the information. As a result of this, Grenham spent the subsequent four years compiling and computerizing relevant genealogical information which would ultimately form the backbone of an expert system which Grenham called *Recordfinder*. By 1994–5 he had become convinced of the emerging potential of the Internet as a more appropriate vehicle through which he might market and distribute his service. The nature of the genealogical search as a product and the significance of distance as a cost factor made the Internet an ideal marketing and distribution vehicle.

The difficulty Grenham faced, however, was that there would be significant costs involved in building a site capable of attracting and servicing a high level of traffic. Realizing this, he approached the *Irish Times* Electronic Publishing Division. This culminated in the launch in

April 1998 of the *Irish Ancestors* site. This site offers an extensive guide for exploring Irish genealogy (**Table 64.3**). *Irish Ancestors* lets visitors trace surname roots and get a personalized guide to ancestor records and is the only Internet site to have browse and search facilities. While some of the information on the site is free to access, there is a $25.00 charge for a full genealogical report. This site represented a departure for the *Irish Times* as up to that point information provided on the site had been free to access. The *Irish Ancestors* site was therefore the *Irish Times* first move into paid content.

Prior to being launched, the site was tested thoroughly in-house by staff. This process sought to ensure that the design and navigational features operated effectively and created the desired impression. In the first weeks of April, the site was accessible from the home page, but was not actively promoted. This ensured that traffic to the site was minimized and allowed the site to be altered on foot of initial customer feedback. Since its launch, the site has been a major commercial success, attracting a largely North American readership. It received, on average, 5,000 visits a week, representing 75,000 page impressions a month. The site has also received critical acclaim, being described as the 'perfect site' in the European Interactive Publishing awards of 1998.

The $5.00 and $25.00 charges are paid over the Internet via credit card. The *Irish Times* put in place an electronic commerce facility with secure electronic transaction. Those availing of the site could input their credit card numbers safely as the data were encrypted (coded) prior to being transmitted. This Secure Socket Layer was intended to protect sensitive credit card information while it is being transmitted between customer and retailer and thus allay customer fears.

Gen.ie

Gen.ie is an expert system designed to provide comprehensive information about records relevant to a particular Irish ancestor. Users are asked and encouraged to enter all available information to maximize the effectiveness of the search on their ancestors. This information is used as a basis for the subsequent search based on the extensive information it holds. *Gen.ie* is essentially the Recordfinder system originally developed by Grenham and is still marketed as a stand-alone software product.

DISCUSSION

The *Irish Ancestors* site raises a number of interesting issues regarding the marketing of Irish heritage-related products. It also provides some indication as to how the Internet might impact on the heritage sector and on marketing generally.

As can be seen from the *Irish Ancestors* site, there was a successful coalignment between the market that was being targeted and the vehicle used to access that market. Also, a clear benefit was being offered to customers — a comparatively low-cost speedy genealogical service. *Irish Ancestors* was positioned favourably against the other alternatives available to customers. The do-it-yourself option or employment of a professional genealogist are both significantly more expensive. This price-performance proposition of the *Irish Ancestors* site was a central factor in the success of the service. However, the value proposition did more than ensure market share; by offering a service at $25.00 the site opened up a large segment of the market that would have previously been untapped because of the traditional costs associated with such services. By tapping into this unserved end of the market, *Irish Ancestors* was able to circumvent existing competitors and establish itself as a dominant provider in this end of the market.

From The *Irish Times'* perspective, the organization was in effect attempting to leverage its brand strength by offering additional valued services to its users. By adding services such as *Irish Ancestors*, the company was able to move to the point where it could position itself as a portal site. Their eventual launch of the portal *ireland.com* illustrates the need for organizations to understand their growth in terms of the development of core competencies which can be leveraged into profitable opportunities. In this regard, the *Irish Ancestors* case is a classic example of line and brand extension. While the *Irish Ancestors* site is to some degree an independent service, it benefits greatly from association with the rest of the site. The umbrella brand of the *Irish Times* ensures that the site achieves immediate credibility. Ideally, this credibility is reciprocated by the derivative site. As we can see, considerable time was invested to ensure that the *Irish Ancestors* site was of comparable quality to the parent brand. This illustrates an understanding of the need to reflect the *Irish Times* core brand values in the look and feel of the site. Hence, brand strength is capitalized on via line extension. Of course this in turn, where successful, adds to the overall brand value and further facilitates organizational growth. There is, for example, an obvious synergy between a genealogy site and other heritage-oriented sites such as a St Patrick's Day site and a Bloomsday site. These brand synergies add to the overall competency of the *Irish Times* web presence. As a result, the organization is in a much stronger position now to enter information provision markets on- and off-line than it would have been ten or even five years ago.

The case also provides an interesting example of the need for companies to adopt a flexible understanding of the nature of their business. As can be seen, *Irish Ancestors*, while being in line with the organization's target market and brand values, takes the company into

Table 64.4 Sample of Sources of Information used by *Gen.ie*

- 1851 Index to the townlands and towns, parishes and baronies of Ireland (63,739 place-names).

- Street listings for Dublin, Cork and Belfast (1914 street names).

- 5,455 Irish surnames, related to 14,287 variants.

- Complete listings of Roman Catholic, Church of Ireland Presbyterian, Methodist and other denomination records

  - in the National Archives of Ireland
  - in the National Library of Ireland
  - in local genealogical centres
  - in the Presbyterian Historical Society
  - in the Public Record Office of Northern Ireland
  - in the Family History Library of the Church of Jesus Christ of the Latter-Day Saints
  - in local custody, where relevant
  - published.

- 3,780 parishes/churches/congregations (8,368 record sets).

- Complete listing of all Irish censuses and census substitutes with all transcripts (580 record sources).

- Complete listing of all graveyards in Ireland 1848–1864 with full listing of all transcripts of inscriptions, locations and nature (4,908 graveyards/2,630 transcripts).

- Complete guide to the state records of births, marriages and deaths, with details of all copies and indexes available.

- Complete listing, for 16 counties, of all catalogued estate papers, papers, rent rolls and tenants lists in the National Library and National Archives of Ireland, with details of coverage and locations (250 record sources).

- Extensive listing of estate papers, rent rolls and tenants lists published, and in repositories other than the National Archives and National Library.

- Complete listing of 18th- and 19th-century trade and other directories, including precise details of all towns covered (455 towns, 59 record sources).

- Complete listing of research sources related to specific occupations (58 occupations; 152 record sources).

- Complete listing of published and manuscript passenger lists (56 entries — in progress).

- Complete listing of Genealogical Office manuscripts (621 manuscripts).

- Complete listing of all will abstracts, transcripts and indexes (225 record sources).

- Complete listing of all newspaper indexes and newspaper biographical extracts (50 record sources).

- Complete listing of local history and other relevant periodicals (136 entries).

- Complete listing of record repositories and research service (112 entries).

- Extensive local history bibliography (618 entries).

- Extensive bibliography of published and privately printed family histories (595 entries).

- Surname histories covering 800 of the most common Irish surnames.

- Guide to the Registry of Deeds.

- Outline guides to research sources in the US, Canada and Australia.

- Extensive bibliography of works relating to the Irish abroad (196 works).

- Matheson's *Special report on surnames in Ireland* (1890) detailing the geographical distribution of 2,998 Irish surnames.

- 130 full-colour coats of arms.

Source: *http://scripts.ireland.com/ancestor/database/spec.html*

a fundamentally new area of activity. This type of development provides clear reminders to organizations of both the opportunities and challenges that exist beyond what might, on the face of it, be seen as the company's market boundaries. In the case of the *Irish Times*, the company has made a very conscious decision to embrace the transition from being in the newspaper business to operating as a provider in the broader information industry. The organization's competency is now defined as being 'the ability to deliver news, information and opinion to the highest standard, to create premium advertising vehicles and to provide a higher standard of service to all customers than they received elsewhere'. This type of self-concept, which is inherently market- as opposed to production-oriented, allows the organization to expand their activities over time. The gradual expansion and evolution of the *Irish Times* brand has allowed the organization to maintain a competitive advantage in the markets within which it competes, while at the same time opening up new market opportunities.

Given the penetration of the Internet in the US, Internet-based marketing strategies for Irish heritage enterprises are likely to continue to increase. An interesting facet of this case is that the *Irish Ancestors* site was promoted almost exclusively on-line. On-line promotion is not alone effective, it can also substantially reduce costs traditionally associated with promotion, such as print advertising and mailshots. As the electronic market matures, the potential to promote as well as sell on-line is expected to increase.

Irish Ancestors also illustrates the need to monitor and react to market evolution through product enhancement. Since its launch, a number of augmentations were made. Amongst these is the fact that many surnames were not listed in the current 'What's In A Name' section. This was updated to include a more comprehensive list with greater amounts of information on each name. Other services introduced include a topographical dictionary which gives parish-by-parish information on maps, landscape, land quality, parish notables, churches and so forth, from the early to mid-1800s. This will be partly free with a charge for more detailed information. Information on household distribution provides a county-by-county breakdown on household names. This section is again free but a charge will be levied for detailed breakdowns of household surnames within counties. These changes reflect the careful management not only of the brand but also the product offering.

It remains to be seen how successful *ireland.com* will be. Central to its success will be its ability to regularly attract traffic from the Irish diaspora. In achieving this, the *Irish Ancestors* site obviously has a role to play. Management and marketing of this heritage product to date has been successful largely as a result of the suitability of the product, the technology and the brands involved. As the heritage and electronic markets evolve over time, *Irish Ancestors* will probably have to continue to react and adapt if it is to maintain its position.

Bibliography

Angell, D. 1995 *The Internet business companion: growing your business in the electronic age.* Reading, Mass.

Bishop, B. 1998 *Strategic marketing for the the digital age.* Chicago.

Cronin, M. 1996 *The Internet strategy handbook: lessons from the new frontier of business.* Boston. Mass.

Grenham, J. 1991 *Tracing your Irish ancestors.* Dublin.

Preston, R. 1997 *Electronic marketing and the consumer.* Thousand Oaks, California.

Stroud, D. 1998 *Internet strategies: a corporate guide to exploiting the Internet.* Basingstoke.

Heritage and the Economy of the South-West

EOIN O'LEARY AND TREVOR DONNELLAN

Heritage is more often associated with culture than business. However, the business of providing heritage experiences to tourists, both domestic and foreign, has become increasingly important. This is especially so in Ireland, where the tourist sector has had to differentiate its product from competing sectors in other countries offering 'sun holidays'. The heritage tourism sector was generally regarded as being relatively small, consisting of a small number of heritage attractions which have become increasingly evident around the country. However, the economic effects of heritage tourism may be much more significant than was previously realized, both nationally and regionally.

The aim of this chapter is to estimate the economic impact of heritage tourism on the regional economy of the south-west. This region, which is comprised of the counties of Cork and Kerry, greatly benefitted from the substantial growth in the numbers of tourists visiting Ireland since the late 1980s. It is shown that even though the economic activity of heritage attractions themselves is relatively small, when the additional activity generated in spin-off business is included, the scale of the sector is appreciably more significant. Additionally, the effect of overall spending by overseas tourists to the south-west is shown to have been quite substantial. This impact may be attributed to the presence of heritage attractions, since tourists may visit an area in order to avail of heritage experiences.

The chapter begins by outlining trends in the number of tourist visitors to Ireland during the chosen study period of the mid-1990s, a period which witnessed the significant enhancement of visitor and heritage facilities in Ireland. The south-west is identified as one of Ireland's most important centres for tourism. The heritage sector is defined and trends in visits to heritage attractions are outlined. The scale of spending at heritage attractions in the south-west is then presented. Total overseas holiday visitor spending in the south-west during the period in

question is also estimated. This is followed by a brief description of how the overall impact of the sector may be quantified using a technique known as regional input-output. Finally, the overall impact of the heritage sector in the south-west at the time is presented in terms of the level of additional activity generated in the regional economy through spending in heritage attractions and through overall spending by overseas visitors. The chapter concludes with summary comments on the findings.

TRENDS IN TOURIST NUMBERS

The overall number of overseas visitors to Ireland increased markedly since the late 1980s. **Fig. 65.1** shows that a large proportion of this increase was attributable to overseas tourist or holiday visitors. Between 1987 and 1995, overseas tourist numbers increased by 225%. In 1995, there were 4.256 million overseas visitors to Ireland of which 2.314 million (54%) were holiday visitors.

In addition to foreign tourist business, the scale of Irish domestic tourism was also significant. The percentage of Irish residents who took holidays at home was, at 66%, high by international standards. For example, only 30% of holidays taken by Germans were to destinations within Germany (SOEC 1995). This implies that a significant number of Irish residents holidayed in Ireland each year in the mid-1990s.

The south-west continued to be one of the most important areas for tourism in Ireland. Among overseas holiday visitors to Ireland in 1995, 43% included a visit to the region in their itinerary. Of the other regions, only Dublin (49%) recorded a higher percentage (Bord Fáilte 1997a, 14). The popularity of the south-west was all the more impressive when one considers that the main access points for American and continental visitors to Ireland are located outside the region.

Overseas holiday visitors to Ireland typically visit more than one region during their holiday. Hence, in order to

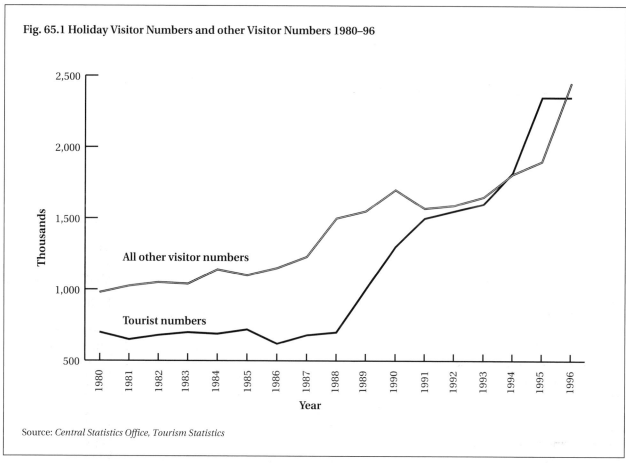

Fig. 65.1 Holiday Visitor Numbers and other Visitor Numbers 1980–96

Source: *Central Statistics Office, Tourism Statistics*

assess the importance of holiday tourism to a region, the relevant measure is the number of overseas holiday visitor bed-nights. The south-west accounted for 23% of all overseas holiday visitor bed-nights in 1995. This percentage was higher than that for the Dublin region (21%) and for all other regions in the country (Bord Fáilte 1997a, 14). This shows the south-west to have been one of the most important tourism areas in the country.

THE NATURE OF HERITAGE TOURISM

Tourism involves foreigners spending leisure time in a country. It results in what economists refer to as 'invisible exports', since the tourist undertakes spending on food, drink and leisure activities while in the country. For this reason, it is difficult to quantify the scale of the tourist sector, since a sizeable portion of revenues earned at tourist attractions, hotels, guesthouses, restaurants and public houses also emanates from spending by Irish people. Moreover, it cannot be assumed that all spending by overseas visitors is tourist expenditure since foreigners also visit the country on business or to visit relatives. Expenditure of Irish people holidaying abroad is referred to as 'invisible imports'. The relatively high tendency among Irish people to holiday at home means that invisible imports are lower than they would be if Irish people had a greater tendency to holiday abroad.

However, all spending by these domestic tourists also creates revenue for the tourist sector.

Part of Ireland's interest as a destination for tourists lies in its its heritage facilities. A report by Tourism Development International (TDI) (1996) contains comprehensive information on Irish visitor attractions. This shows that, during the study period, 60% of domestic and overseas visitors regarded the presence of attractions as an important reason in their decision to visit an area (TDI 1996, 39).

Before we investigate heritage tourism further, it is necessary to define the term 'heritage'. CERT, the state agency responsible for training and employment in the tourism and catering industry, has defined the word as 'Elements of our inherited past that we value' (CERT 1993, 4). These elements may include monuments, parks, wildlife areas, historic houses, gardens, museums, art galleries, festivals and events, as well the more intangible features of heritage like customs, music and writing. Since 1989, Bord Fáilte has targeted the heritage sector as part of its strategy to develop tourism. This involved the development of heritage tourism products that encapsulate the various elements of heritage in a manner deemed to be attractive to the tourist. Considerable resources were subsequently expended in the development of monuments, parks, gardens, wildlife

Table 65.1 Estimated Aggregate Spending at Fee-paying Heritage Attractions in Cork and Kerry, 1995

Category of Spending	Value of Spending £m
Entrance Fees	4.3
Coffees, Teas and Snacks	1.0
Crafts and Souvenirs	1.7
Literature and Posters	0.3
Clothing Items	0.7
Other Items	0.6
Total Spending	**8.7**

Source: *TDI 1996, 57–63 and estimates by the authors*

areas, museums, art galleries, festivals, events and heritage centres.

The various visitor attractions that have resulted have, in official circles, become synonymous with heritage in Ireland. For example, Bord Fáilte use the terms 'visitor attractions' and 'heritage attractions' interchangeably. While it undoubtedly is the case that the vast majority of attractions do attempt to market different aspects of heritage, there are exceptions. For example, Dublin Zoo, which has generally been the second most popular fee-paying attraction in the country, has probably very little to do with Irish heritage. This applies to a lesser extent to Fota Wildlife Park in Cork, since an historic house and arboretum are also present on the site.

Moreover, there are many attractions that are not enumerated as visitor attractions by officialdom. For example, Dunmore Head near the tip of Slea Head on the Dingle peninsula in county Kerry is the most westerly point in mainland Ireland. During peak season, a fee of £5 is charged by the local farmer for a walk out the Head. Also, there are many scenic walks throughout the length and breadth of Ireland for which no fee is charged. Indeed, there is an abundance of heritage experiences to be enjoyed throughout Ireland for no charge whatsoever. To complicate the picture further, there are many events steeped in heritage at which the Irish participate in great numbers with only a sprinkling of tourists present, for example, a visit to Croke Park to see an All-Ireland hurling final or to a *feis cheoil* to hear Irish music.

Unfortunately, information on the numbers of tourists availing of each and every aspect of Irish heritage is very difficult to obtain. Instead, we have to rely on the number and popularity of visitor attractions in the country. As regards fee-paying visitor attractions, there was a substantial increase in the number of these in the country in the recent past. In 1995, there were 259 such attractions in the state. Up to 70% of these were developed since 1984, with 40% being opened after 1989 (TDI 1996, 17). There were also a number of registered

attractions with free admission. In 1994, there were 31 such attractions, most of which were galleries and museums of national significance based in Dublin (Bord Fáilte 1997b, 8).

There was also a significant increase in the number of visits to heritage attractions during the period at issue in this chapter. For fee-paying attractions, a total of 4.1 million visits by both domestic and overseas tourists occurred in 1990. This increased to 8.6 million in 1995, a substantial advance of 110% (TDI 1996, 20). Of this total number of visits, 27% were by Irish citizens, with the remaining 73% being undertaken by overseas tourists. By far the most important category of overseas tourist in terms of visits were those from mainland Europe at 37%, with Britain and Northern Ireland at 17% and North Americans representing a further 14% of this total (TDI 1996, 26). At free attractions, there were 2.4 million visits in 1994. This compares to a slightly higher number in 1993. Nearly 90% of these visits in 1994 were to the non-fee paying attractions located in Dublin (Bord Fáilte 1997b, 8). It should be noted that no data on the numbers of visits to free attractions were published in the Tourist Development International survey for 1995.

When tourists visit an attraction, they may undertake spending in a number of ways. In addition to paying admission fees, where they exist, they may also spend on food in cafes attached to attractions, as well as such items as souvenirs, literature and clothing items where they are available. It has been estimated that the average expenditure per person visiting fee-paying attractions in 1995 was £4.93. This includes admission charges, which averaged £2.31 per visit, and expenditures on other items which made up the remaining £2.62 (TDI 1996, 58–9). Given that the total number of visits to these attractions in the state was 8.6 million, total expenditure in fee-paying attractions therefore amounted to £42.6 million in 1995. This compares very favourably to 1991 where £11.5 million was spent, an increase of 270%. This increase may be explained by a combination of

Table 65.2 Composition of Overseas Visitor Spending in the South-West in 1995

Expenditure Type	£ Million	%
Bed and Board	35.259	23
Other Food and Drink	45.990	30
Sightseeing and Entertaining	12.266	8
Transport	18.396	12
Shopping	27.594	18
Miscellaneous	13.797	9
Total	153.302	100

Source: *Bord Fáilte 1997a, 2 and estimates by the authors*

increasing average spending per visitor and increasing numbers of visits (TDI 1996, 63).

THE HERITAGE SECTOR IN THE SOUTH-WEST

The south-west region had 32 or 12% of the total number of fee-paying attractions located in the state in 1995. Of these, 12 were newly opened in the years 1992–93 (TDI 1996, l6). The attractions ranged from parks like Killarney National Park, to castles like Blarney Castle, to interpretive centres including 'Kerry the Kingdom' based in Tralee and the 'Queenstown Experience' in Cobh, and also to historic houses like Bantry House.

The total number of visits to fee-paying attractions in the south-west increased from over 800,000 in 1990 to 1.6 million in 1995, a sizeable expansion of 100% (TDI 1996, 23). The total of 1.6 million visits (19%) in 1995 was second only to Dublin (23%) in terms of popularity of fee-paying attractions (TDI 1996, 23). Attractions in the region occupied three out of the top ten places for fee-paying visitor attractions in 1995. These were Blarney Castle (4th) with 262,000 visits, Muckross House (9th) with 182,000 and Fota Wildlife Park (10th) with 179,000 (TDI 1996, 24). The region also boasted the top three places for new visitor attractions opened since 1990 (TDI 1996, 24). These were 'Kerry the Kingdom', the Jameson Heritage Centre in Midleton and the Queenstown Experience.

Of the 1.6 million visits to fee-paying attractions in the south-west in 1995, 23% were by Irish people, with the remaining 77% being undertaken by overseas tourists. Once again, the most important category of overseas tourist in terms of visits were from mainland Europe, at 33%, with Britain and Northern Ireland accounting for 18% and North Americans being 17% of this total (TDI 1996, 28).

Out of the 31 free attractions in the state in 1994, only two are deemed to have existed in the region. In 1994, there were a total of only 43,000 visits to these attractions (Bord Fáilte 1997b, 8). This is a very small number, compared to the 1.6 million visits to fee-paying attractions in the area in 1995. However, it should be remembered that a significant number of visitors had heritage experiences without visiting any attractions, whether fee-paying or not.

An estimate of the total spending at fee-paying attractions in the south-west in 1995 is presented in **Table 65.1**. This estimate is derived from the survey results of the expenditure pattern of visitors to fee-paying attractions conducted by Tourist Development International for the year 1995 (TDI 1996, 57–63). Included here is spending by both domestic and foreign visitors. As has already been seen, this is likely to account for the vast majority of spending at heritage attractions, as only two free attractions exist in the region.

At £8.7 million, the spending by visitors to the south-west is slightly higher than the south-west's share of visitors would indicate. This is due to two reasons. First, admission charges were found to be 17% higher in the south-west than the national average (TDI 1996, 18). Second, North American visitors, who on average spent over twice as much as other visitors to these attractions, visited the south-west in greater numbers. North Americans represented 17% of all visitors to fee-paying attractions in the south-west, as opposed to 14% nationally (TDI 1996, 28).

While estimated spending at fee-paying heritage attraction has been presented above, these expenditures do not take place in isolation. Tourists who visit attractions also require accommodation, meals, travel and other forms of entertainment in the course of their holiday. Moreover, tourists who enjoy heritage experiences without visiting attractions also spend on these goods and services in the course of their holiday.

Day-to-day spending of this kind by overseas tourists constitutes invisible exports that may be regarded as additional economic activity due to heritage tourism, since heritage is likely to be a major factor in the attractiveness of Ireland as a holiday destination for these visitors. However, day-to-day spending by domestic tourists does not represent a net addition attributable to this sector, since much of this expenditure would take place anyway. Thus, regardless of whether they are on holiday or not, Irish residents spend a substantial portion of their income on accommodation and food. It would therefore be inappropriate to attribute all day-to-day spending by domestic tourists to the heritage sector.

For this reason, in order to estimate the overall net impact of the heritage sector, it is necessary to examine the extent and breakdown of overall expenditure by overseas holiday visitors during their holiday. It should be noted that this spending includes spending at heritage attractions to the extent to which these tourists visit attractions. However, as already stressed, foreigners do not have to visit attractions in order to have heritage experiences. Spending by overseas tourists on accommodation, food and entertainment, to the exclusion of spending at heritage attractions, may equally be linked to the heritage sector.

In 1995, total overseas holiday visitor spending for the state stood at £1,286 million. In the south-west, total overseas visitor spending amounted to £232.3 million in the same year. This represented 18% of all overseas visitor spending in the state in 1995 (Bord Fáilte 1997, l3).

Of the 1,217 million overseas visitors to the south-west in 1995, it is estimated that 69% were holiday visitors (Bord Fáilte 1997a, 44). Holiday visitors accounted for 5.366 million bed-nights in the region in 1995 (Bord Fáilte 1997a, 43). Total overseas holiday visitor expenditure in the area in 1995 is estimated to have amounted to £53.3 million. **Table 65.2** gives a breakdown of this total estimate into its component parts. This is based on visitor spending profiles for the state (Bord Fáilte 1997a, 12).

Unsurprisingly, accommodation and food and drink account for over half of all expenditure. Shopping represents close to one-fifth, while transport, recreational activities and other items account for the remaining one-third of expenditure.

While this spending, as well as spending at heritage attractions that was presented earlier, was obviously significant, they both refer only to spending directly associated with the heritage sector. They do not take into account the spin-off effects of this spending in the region. The technique of input-output allows such effects to be estimated. The input-output technique and the nature of these spin-offs are now explained.

THE REGIONAL INPUT–OUTPUT MODEL FOR THE SOUTH-WEST

In considering the economic impact of heritage tourism in the south-west, it is essential not only to account for direct impacts, such as the economic activity generated directly in the region, but also to include further impacts in terms of the sectors of the local economy that are linked to the heritage sector. Input-output is an internationally recognized technique for analysing these spin-offs.

The input-output technique has been put into practice by a group including the authors at the Department of Economics, UCC. This has resulted in the development of a regional input-output model for the south-west, the first of its kind in Ireland. Briefly, the input-output model for the region can be described as a detailed table which subdivided the economy into 28 industrial sectors and mapped the extent of linkages between the various industries. A detailed description of the model and of its construction has already been issued (Garhart, Moloney, O'Leary and Donnellan 1997).

Using this model, the overall impact of the heritage sector in the region may be estimated. It should be noted that several studies have already been conducted on the effect of tourism on the national economy (see for example Deane 1987; Deane and Henry 1993 and Henry 1996). This is the first use of the south-west model to estimate the influence of tourism on the regional economy.

Accordingly, the overall impact of spending at fee-paying heritage attractions and total overseas visitor spending may be estimated. The overall impact may be separated into three parts as follows:

(1) DIRECT IMPACTS OF SPENDING BY VISITORS

The direct impact of spending at fee-paying heritage attractions in the south-west is spending by visitors to the region at these attractions. For example, a direct impact is the purchase of a locally published book on the history of the attraction from the attraction's gift shop. The direct impact of overall spending by overseas holiday visitors is spending by these visitors in the region on locally produced goods and services. Spending on accommodation and meals is an example of direct impacts here.

(2) INDIRECT IMPACTS

The indirect impacts are those which occur when local suppliers to businesses in receipt of visitor spending themselves purchase goods and services. When a heritage attraction purchases goods and services in the local economy, a portion of these expenditures is re-spent locally. For example, food products purchased by a restaurant located in a heritage attraction from a local food producer result in that food producer purchasing ingredients, some of which may be from local farmers. Similarly, when an overseas holiday visitor buys an item of clothing from a clothing retailer, this results in the clothing retailer purchasing clothing from a manufacturer in the region. The clothing manufacturer must, in turn, obtain further inputs, some of which may be local,

Table 65.3 Overall Impact of Spending at Fee-paying Heritage Attractions in the South-West, 1995

Impacts	Output £m	Income £m	Employment numbers
Direct	6.95	1.63	230
Overall	9.95	2.23	290

Table 65.4 Overall Impact of Spending by Overseas Holiday Visitors to Cork and Kerry, 1995

Impacts	Output £m	Income £m	Employment numbers
Direct	131.79	31.38	4,460
Total	209.56	46.14	5,960

in order to manufacture these goods. Indirect impacts refer to spin-off activity generated by a sector. Purchases by a business from its suppliers cause the suppliers to make purchases from their own suppliers and so on down the line. The obvious and immediate impact of these acquisitions is on the output of other firms, but there are also impacts on income and employment. Since the input-output table contains measures of wages and salaries per unit of output for each sector, and employment per unit of output for each sector, these impacts may also be estimated.

(3) INDUCED IMPACTS

The induced impacts refer to the additional consumer spending which takes place when the income generated from the direct and indirect impacts is in turn spent. These impacts occur, for example, when persons engaged at a heritage attraction or other business in receipt of tourist spending receive wages and salaries, a portion of which is spent on locally produced goods and services. Also, the indirect impacts described above generate wages and other income for people employed in those businesses, and again a portion of these extra incomes is spent on locally produced goods.

The sum of the direct, indirect and induced impacts, described above, represents the overall impact of spending. These figures are now presented separately for spending at fee-paying visitor attractions and for overall overseas visitor spending.

OVERALL IMPACT OF HERITAGE SECTOR IN THE SOUTH-WEST

It was estimated above that total spending at fee-paying heritage attractions in the south-west was £8.7 million in 1995. While this spending occurred in the region, it

should be noted that not all of it was on items actually produced in the region. As well as buying goods made in the area, tourists will also buy goods produced elsewhere in Ireland or abroad. As a result, adjustment of the above spending estimate is required to remove the portion of spending in the region on items produced outside the region. Thus the direct impact of spending there will be less than the actual spending in the region.

Table 65.3 presents the direct and total impact of this spending of £8.7 million in the south-west. This shows a direct impact of £6.95 million which corresponds to £1.63 million in wages and salaries and 230 jobs. When the indirect and induced impacts are included, this results in an overall impact of £9.95 million of economic activity in the area, corresponding to £2.23 million in wages and salaries and a total of 290 jobs. Thus, the 230 jobs directly attributable to fee-paying heritage attractions were linked to a further 60 jobs in the regional economy.

This presents a narrowly defined estimate of the impact of the heritage sector in the region, since only spending made by tourists while visiting the attraction was included, while spending by tourists on heritage experiences at locations other than at these attractions was excluded. Thus, assuming tourists' visited the south-west in order to avail of a broad range of heritage experiences, then the impact of tourists total spending in the area may be attributed to the heritage sector. Only overseas tourists are included here, since their spending represents the net impact of the heritage sector.

It was estimated above that spending by overseas holiday visitors to the south-west was £153.2 million in 1995. Estimates of the direct and overall impact of this spending on the region are presented in Table 65.4. This shows a direct impact of £132 million which corresponds to £31 million in wages and salaries and 4,460 jobs. When the indirect and induced impacts are included, this results in an overall impact of £210 million of economic activity in the area, corresponding to £46 million in wages and salaries and a total of 5,960 jobs. Thus, the 4,460 jobs directly attributable to spending by overseas visitors were linked to a further 1,500 jobs in the regional economy. This represented a substantial contribution to the economy of the south-west.

CONCLUSION

This chapter has presented estimates of the overall impact of heritage tourism on the regional economy of the south-west. This region benefitted from the substantial growth in the numbers of tourists visiting Ireland since the late 1980s. It has been shown first that, even though the economic activity of fee-paying heritage attractions themselves was relatively small with 230 jobs, when the additional activity generated in spin-off business was included, the overall impact of the sector was increased to 290 jobs. Moreover, when the heritage sector is more broadly defined by assessing the effect of overall spending by foreign tourists to the south-west, it became quite substantial. In total, there were nearly 6,000 jobs linked to the heritage sector defined in this way. This can be attributed to the presence of heritage attractions of all kinds, since many tourists visited the area in order to avail of heritage experiences. It should be noted that these estimates were net impacts, as they only related to spending by overseas tourists. If spending by domestic tourists over and above what they would have spent if they stayed at home is included, then the magnitude of the sector would be even greater.

These results demonstrate that the heritage sector was one with a relatively high degree of linkage with the regional economy. Compared to manufacturing sectors, which are more capital intensive and import a relatively high percentage of their inputs, the heritage sector is labour intensive and uses locally produced inputs. Continued success of this indigenous sector should therefore have considerable additional benefits both in the regional and national economy.

Bibliography

Bord Fáilte 1989 *Tourism in the Irish economy*. Dublin.
Bord Fáilte 1997a *Perspectives on Irish tourism: regions 1991–95*. Dublin.
Bord Fáilte 1997b *Perspectives on Irish tourism: visits to tourist attractions*. Dublin.
Central Statistical Office 1980–86 *Irish statistical bulletin*. Dublin.
Central Statistics Office 1987– *Statistical bulletin*. Dublin.
CERT 1993 *Tourism training ahead: heritage study pack*. Dublin.
Deane, B. 1987 'Tourism in Ireland: an employment growth area', *Administration* **35**, pp. 337–49.
Deane, B. and Henry, E. W. 1993 'The economic impact of tourism', *Irish Banking Review* (Winter), pp. 35–47.
Garhart R., Moloney, R., O'Leary, E. and Donnellan, T. 1997 *An input-output model of south-west Ireland: a preliminary report*, Working Paper No. 1997–3, Department of Economics, UCC. Cork.
Henry, E. W. 1996 *An input-output analysis of new industry in Ireland in 1996*, ESRI General Research Series 107. Dublin.
SOEC (Statistical Office of the European Community) 1995 *Tourism in Europe*. Luxembourg.
TDI (Tourism Development International Ltd) 1996 *1995 Visitor attractions survey: Republic of Ireland*. Dublin.

Investment Decision-Making

FRANK ALLEN AND FINBARR BRADLEY

Decisions about where resources are to be invested and what returns should be expected are not just the preserve of business managers in a commercial environment. Just as individuals decide whether to spend money now or later, or how time should be allocated to one activity or another, people with responsibility for heritage management at any level must also make investment decisions.

Investment managers would be considered negligent if they did not fully assess alternative opportunities, recognize market, credit and other risks associated with proposed projects, and take into account the timing of expected returns. The theory of finance and best market practice are essential tools in deciding whether to invest in a particular project and in projecting returns. Heritage managers may have responsibility for less tangible resources, and the returns are not as easily quantifiable as is the case for investment decision-making based exclusively on market-place criteria. Nonetheless, professionals in heritage management also need to be aware of the principles that underlie exclusively commercial investments, both for use in evaluating their own projects and in influencing market-based decisions. Put another way, those charged with heritage management must be aware of the cost of promoting initiatives that may run counter to satisfying market demands.

The distinction between decisions based solely on market rather than non-market criteria may not always be a useful one, as commercial investments almost always have an impact on the community in which they are located, just as most investments related to supporting or developing a community's heritage should respond in some way to market considerations. Consider, for example:

• What restrictions should a planning authority impose on exploring for minerals in an area of archaeological or ecological significance, and what would be the additional cost of compliance for the mining company?

• How many regular viewers does an Irish-language television station need to attract to justify continued financial support?

• Does the construction of an interpretative centre, attracting more visitors to a location, enhance the heritage value of that location or could it lead to its destruction?

While the main focus of this chapter is on how investment decision-making techniques can be an aid to professional heritage management, the limitations of such techniques should also be recognized. Heritage cannot be measured solely in terms of tourist numbers or potential for commercial development. Most people would acknowledge that a community is poorer if species of fish that swim in its rivers become extinct or if historic place-names for fields and hills are forgotten. However, such a loss is not quantifiable, and financial analysis may, at best, only estimate the cost of preserving such aspects of its heritage.

The following section outlines the basic principles of investment decision-making. We then consider how those principles can be modified to accommodate broader concerns, such as those relating to heritage. The application of financial theory and practice to accommodate the needs of the broader community of stakeholders rather than just maximizing the financial return to shareholders is now reasonably well established, particularly as it relates to environmental issues. We shall present examples of how the same approach can be used to enhance our understanding of the 'value' of natural, man-made and cultural resources that are the responsibility of heritage management. We shall consider how economists regard the role of heritage in development, especially in the area of tourism. While the focus of the chapter is on how professionals in heritage management approach specific investment, both public and private, we shall also suggest directions to improve broader policy-making.

CONCEPT OF VALUE

Finance concerns itself with assigning a monetary value to an asset. In some cases, an asset can be easily valued by reference to a market: the value of shares in AIB can be estimated with reference to stock exchange quotations; quantities of copper or gold are easily valued by reference to the previous day's quote on the London Metals Exchange; or the value of a typical apartment in Dublin today can be reasonably estimated by the price paid recently for a similar property.

Other assets are more difficult to value as the product is not standardized or there is no market to provide a recent quote. It is easy to recognize the importance of sentiment and taste in determining the price for an asset and in explaining why that value can fluctuate so much over time. While these more subjective factors can be important in all asset valuation, their importance increases in estimating the value of items that are not traded. For example, no price might be high enough to tempt a family to sell its heirlooms, although the items may have limited commercial or practical value to others. In a similar sense, it would be hard to imagine any price high enough to compensate the Irish people adequately for the loss of the Book of Kells or the destruction of the Rock of Cashel. Asset valuation almost inevitably requires a combination of objective and subjective valuation in varying measures.

DECISION-MAKING TECHNIQUES

In considering investment decision techniques, it is useful to focus initially on commercial aspects, putting aside for later broader community considerations. In assessing new investment opportunities, financial analysts routinely prepare cash flow projections using different scenarios, and 'discount' these projections in order to obtain today's value. It is important to realize that an investor would prefer to have £1,000 today rather than in a year's time, even if he or she could only put that £1,000 in a bank account and earn interest for the year. Cash flow projections for any investment must therefore be discounted using a factor that takes into account investors' preference for money today rather than in the future, and for the uncertainty associated with projections not being realized. Future returns that are subject to high risk are discounted at a high discount rate, whereas the projected income from a government bond, for example, would be discounted at a low discount rate. In the case of a particular investment, much analysis is devoted to estimating the appropriate discount factor

but, for our purposes, we can use an interest rate that a bank would charge for a loan. Those interested in a comprehensive treatment of basic finance concepts should consult texts such Ross, Westerfield and Jaffe (1995) or Copeland and Weston (1992).

We consider in CASE STUDY 1 a simple example to illustrate a number of different techniques for financial valuation, named net present value (NPV), discounted cash flow (DCF) and internal rate of return (IRR), respectively.

These techniques are very useful in assessing the profitability of proposed investments and in comparing one opportunity with another. However, their limitations are also obvious. The degree of uncertainty associated with cash flow projections is considerable: anticipated profits may not materialize or profitability may exceed initial expectations. Investors recognize these limitations in financial models, but find the discipline of projecting cash flows and comparing one investment opportunity with another in an analytical way very useful in reaching a decision.

More significantly in the context of heritage management, standard finance techniques are useful only in evaluating inflows and outflows that have cash value. Clearly, in the example cited in CASE STUDY 1, the site of the hotel had a value before a developer considered building a hotel there. However, the enjoyment of that resource by walkers, day-trippers and local residents is not easily quantified. It follows, therefore, that the possible loss of that resource if a hotel is built on the site is not included in the investor's cash flow analysis.

While financial models may not be very useful in assessing the value of resources that do not have intrinsic commercial value, they may help in estimating the cost of their protection. Preserving the site of our hotel in its original state would result in the private investors foregoing their net present value or well-being as described above, and perhaps result in the community losing other benefits such as jobs created by the project. Finance helps us to quantify those losses, to some extent, and thus the value the public places on the heritage resource.

PUBLIC PERSPECTIVE

Extending the decision framework on heritage projects to the public realm requires analysts to take society or the community as a whole into account rather than just private goals and profitability. Cost-benefit analysis is used to assess the net social advantage or disadvantage of undertaking a project. Its underlying theory and practice is outlined in Zerbe Jr and Dively (1994). The technique is similar to the NPV and IRR methods outlined in CASE STUDY 1 but social valuations rather than market prices are used. If proper cost-benefit analysis is

CASE STUDY 1. NPV, DCF AND IRR

Suppose an investor is evaluating the desirability of a commercial project, say a new hotel overlooking the source of the Lee at Gougane Barra, Cork. The investor must estimate the initial cost of acquisition, the continuing operating costs, and, with greatest uncertainty, the level of revenues that can reasonably be expected to be earned from guests. Investors estimate these future cash flows by carrying out market analysis, researching the performance of hotels in similar locations and applying their business acumen.

Our investor has prepared cash flow projections and believes that the new hotel can earn revenues of £500,000 in year 1, £1 million in year 2 and so forth as set out in the table below. She has also estimated the operating costs and, after initial losses, while the business is being established, it will offer a steady income of £500,000 a year. These earnings can be projected forward indefinitely, but the investor has decided that once the project has reached a steady level of profitability, she would prefer to sell. She estimates that the hotel could be sold for £20 million at the end of the sixth year. Having considered the return she can earn on investing in other ventures with similar levels of risk, 12% is regarded as an appropriate discount rate. By using a technique called discounted cash flows (DCF), in other words finding the present value equivalent of future money (at a compounded rate of 12% a year), we estimate the present value today of those cash flows to be £11,190,000. If our investor can acquire the hotel for less than that amount, and is confident that the cash flow projections are reasonable, she should invest. If, for example, the hotel can be bought today for £10 million, the net present value (NPV) will be £1,190,000. This is the profit the investor will earn from the hotel project rather than by investing money elsewhere at 12%.

In '000s	Year 1	Year 2	Year 3	Year 4	Year 5	Year 6
Revenues	£500	£1,000	£1,200	£2,000	£2,000	£22,000
Costs	-£700	-£700	-£1,000	-£1,500	-£1,500	-£1,500
	-£200	£300	£200	£500	£500	£20,500
Discount Factor	0.893	0.797	0.712	0.636	0.567	0.507
Present Value of Future Cash Flows	-£179	£239	£142	£318	£284	£10,386

Net Present Value (NPV)   £11,190

Investors often like to think of projects offering a return. It follows from our analysis above that an investment of £11,190,000 would offer a return of 12%. Buying the asset for less than that amount would offer a higher return, so an initial investment of £10 million would offer an internal rate of return (IRR) of a little over 14%. This can be calculated by finding what discount factor should be applied to the projected cash flows to get a present value of the £10 million initial investment. In other words, an IRR of 14% gives an NPV of zero.

performed on a heritage project, a positive result ensures that the project will be socially efficient. In other words, undertaking it and assuming that the outcome matches expectations, it will confer a net benefit on society. Just as accepting only positive net present value projects leads to a company's value or shareholder wealth increasing over time, public sector projects whose benefits outstrip costs should lead to a net improvement in society.

The example in *CASE STUDY 2* illustrates public commitment of resources to a project designed to preserve natural heritage under threat from modern agriculture techniques. Analysis of expenditures on ensuring the continued survival of the corncrake in Ireland can be used to assess resources society is willing to pay to ensure the side-effects of progress are counter-balanced to some extent.

One useful classification in cost-benefit analysis is to make a distinction between projects that are privately beneficial and those that are socially beneficial. In privately beneficial projects, the economic benefits are directly obtainable by individuals, groups or firms and are larger than the associated costs or benefits of alternative uses. In the case of socially beneficial projects, the net benefits to society are large or positive, although no one individual may easily capture these benefits.

Defining precisely the correct decision-making focus, quantifying goals and objectives, examining alternatives and their consequences and the risks associated with all the possible outcomes are critical in public project appraisal work. Extending net present value analysis to take into account social benefits and costs is also essential. Because of the difficulty of such appraisal, comprehensive cost-benefit analysis is not extensively practised in Ireland, except by industrial development agencies such as IDA Ireland and by those evaluating certain projects dealing with the environment and forestry. The publication in June 1999 of the working rules for cost-benefit analysis in relation to EU Community Support Framework proposals was therefore timely (CSF Evaluation Unit 1999). This sets out a series of proposed guidelines for public-sector projects. The Department of Finance has considered their implementation for projects supported by the EU or national government.

In the case of public sector projects, it is not only more difficult to define in operational terms the interests of decision-makers, but also to agree on how to satisfy the often-conflicting objectives of various interested parties. Some argue there may not necessarily be conflict between maximizing shareholder value and satisfying the goals of all relevant parties, or stakeholders. The Shell Company's recent contribution to this debate (1998) is noteworthy in this regard. It argues that there is no evidence of a fundamental conflict between sustainable

CASE STUDY 2. CAN THE CORNCRAKE SURVIVE MODERN AGRICULTURE?

The corncrake, more often heard than seen, has long featured prominently in Irish country life. Stories of corncrakes' warning song from throughout the country attest to the bird's historical presence all over Ireland. However, changing agricultural practices, and especially increased mechanization in mowing, have threatened the survival of the corncrake in Ireland as in other European countries. The 1993 Birdwatch Ireland/Royal Society for the Protection of Birds (RSPB) Corncrake Census recorded 174 singing male corncrakes in Ireland, a decline of over 80% since the previous survey in 1988. The decline continued further in 1994, with just 129 recorded. Following increases in 1995 and 1996, corncrake numbers fell from 184 in 1996 to 148 in 1997. The remaining national population was found to be concentrated in four main areas: the Moy Valley in county Mayo; the Shannon Callows in the midlands; North Donegal and the Erne Catchment area in county Fermanagh. Extinction in face of the inevitable modernization of agricultural practice appeared to be the corncrake's fate.

Conservation measures introduced on a phased basis appear to have reversed the decline in corncrake numbers. A Corncrake Conservation Project and Grant Scheme funded by the Irish government's Heritage Service, Dúchas, and by the RSPB offers an interesting example of how market forces can be influenced to accommodate the needs of heritage management.

The Scheme offers farmers with corncrakes on their land grants of £90 per hectare (Shannon Callows) or £120 per hectare (Mayo and Donegal) to delay mowing their land until 1 August, after corncrake chicks have been hatched. A further £20 per hectare is paid to farmers who opt to mow fields from the centre outwards, to allow young corncrakes to escape under the cover of grass. A tiered Late Cover Grant Scheme is also offered in the Shannon Callows. A number of farmers are offered a grant of £110 per hectare to delay mowing until 15 August or £150 per hectare to delay mowing until 1 September.

The co-operation of farmers, government agencies, NGOs and local media has been critical to the success of the conservation efforts. Participation in this voluntary scheme is high, with over 80% of eligible farmers in the Shannon Callows opting to take part. According to the BirdWatch Ireland Annual Report (1997), for example, the total cost of the Scheme in 1997 was Shannon Callows (£57,560), Mayo/West Connacht (£17,062) and Donegal (£17,356). The position of the corncrake in Ireland remains very fragile, but their numbers have increased since the introduction of the conservation scheme. Strong interest in and support for the scheme have shown that market requirements and heritage considerations can be reconciled at modest cost. Careful planning and consultation with all interested parties succeeded in reaching consensus on the 'value' to the community of protecting the habitat of an endangered species.

value creation and long-term shareholder value creation. For value creation to be sustainable, a company must acknowledge and manage the full range of relevant economic, social and environmental costs associated with its activities. It suggests adding together indicators based on three components of value added, namely,

(i) economic/market,

(ii) environmental and

(iii) social, in order to track a company's total net value added over time.

For the heritage management professional, applying cost-benefit analysis is especially complex because of the need to quantify benefits and costs that often have no market or monetary values. Attributes such as landscape, wildlife and amenity areas must be assessed although their intangible benefits are not traded in any marketplace and private property rights may not exist. The environment, for example, is often treated as a free good, except perhaps where comprehensive environment impact statements are required.

It is useful in cost-benefit analysis to segregate the value of a project into two components, one that uses market prices and the other non-market prices to value resources. The net present value framework can be used to discount cash flows in the former case. Where market prices do not exist, other approaches are necessary. Valuation is especially difficult where existence values are high, reflecting what the public believe something is worth having 'in existence' even if not everybody actually receives direct benefits from it. For example, knowing landscape of special natural characteristics will not be disturbed by development might be valued highly by individuals even if they themselves never intend visiting it in person. In addition, people derive value from the potential availability of a resource at some future stage. By not exploiting some element of the country's physical heritage now, this presents a valuable option which may be exercised later.

From a valuation point of view, heritage shares many characteristics of protected areas such as national parks, scientific reserves, wildlife sanctuaries, natural monuments and landmarks. Dixon and Sherman (1990) provide a comprehensive analysis of methods to assess benefits and costs. They make the distinction between individual preferences which are expressed by market prices and those that may be inferred from experimental methods such as surveys.

A distinction also needs to be made between situations where market prices exist and those where they do not. In the latter case, classified by economists as market imperfections, surrogate or shadow prices may be used.

These are prices paid for a closely associated good or service traded in the marketplace. To the extent that it is difficult to obtain a perfect substitute, adjustments often have to be made. Hedonic pricing techniques attempt to measure how the prices of market goods are influenced by non-market effects. For instance, valuation can be based on the effect of a heritage centre on property prices in the vicinity. Travel-cost methods are based on assessing the expenditures people are willing to commit to reach a heritage area in order to indicate its value to society.

If market or surrogate market prices cannot be obtained, it may be possible to question people directly about how they would react to the possible loss of part of their heritage. Willingness to pay for improvement or willingness to accept compensation for damage to heritage can measure social benefits of some proposed action. Contingent valuation methods are based on asking individuals how much payment would be required to keep them at a certain initial level of satisfaction if the item under analysis were removed. Estimates can also be obtained by means of techniques based on simulated bidding or trade-off games. These types of approach are now sometimes applied by US courts for environmental damage assessment.

In this country, it would have been intriguing if, during the debate surrounding the establishment of TnaG and its continued functioning as TG4 (see *CASE STUDY 3*), such techniques were used to gauge the Irish public's assessment of the value they placed on nurturing the Irish language. For instance, various scenarios linking the number of potential Irish speakers in the future to different levels of expenditures might suggest how serious the public really is about supporting the language as a living medium.

As an alternative to attempting to assess benefits directly, it is sometimes possible to measure the costs that would be imposed if items or areas of heritage were converted to some other, perhaps commercial, use. Rather than attempting to measure the benefits of some action (such as protecting a natural heritage area), opportunity-cost approaches can be used to assess income foregone by protecting it from development. One could attempt to value the benefits of the best alternative use of land (say for housing) rather than trying to capture directly the benefits of a natural heritage area.

POLICY IMPLICATIONS

There are essentially two different philosophical views on how heritage should be valued. One perspective is that heritage has intrinsic worth to a community or society apart from any potential it has to generate commercial revenues. The general view of economists, on the other hand, is that the value of heritage hinges on the benefits generated through its exploitation, say

---

CASE STUDY 3. DOES IRISH-LANGUAGE TELEVISION OFFER VALUE FOR MONEY?

The Irish government's decision to provide resources for the development of an Irish-language television station offers an interesting example of how a decision to invest public money for heritage-related projects can expose differing views as to the value of such investment.

Irish speakers, both in Gaeltacht areas and elsewhere, had long complained about the inadequacy of Irish-language television programming. While RTÉ has broadcast some very high quality Irish-language programmes over the years, their range tended to be limited and hours of broadcasting minimal. Irish speakers argued that as television has adopted an increasingly important role in contemporary life and that, as the choice of programming otherwise available has broadened, there had been little development in Irish-language broadcasting. The government accepted the argument that an Irish-language television station could contribute to the promotion of Irish as a vernacular. It was also thought to respond to the demands of children in Irish-medium education and a wider Irish-speaking community. Financial resources were provided for a new television station and Teilifís na Gaeilge (TnaG) went on air in 1997.

The decision to finance TG4 proved to be controversial before its launch and has remained so since then. This is despite apparent community goodwill towards the Irish language and generally favourable reviews for much of TG4's programming. Does this mean that TG4 has not been a success? It may be that in establishing TG4, the promoters were not sufficiently clear in the objectives and standards set for the station. This makes its performance difficult to measure and may also be the source of some of the controversy.

TG4 has been criticized for its low 'ratings' or numbers of viewers. The declining numbers of people for whom Irish is a vernacular or who can speak Irish fluently both make it inevitable that Irish-language television viewers will be limited in number but also provide the basis for public support. If such programming had mass-market appeal, it could derive greater financial support from associated advertising. On the other hand, if very few people watch TG4, it cannot be thought to achieve its objectives. This argues strongly for the investment to have been justified on the basis of a defined market and quantified targets set for market penetration. The discussion on TG4 in the media was an argument about whether an Irish-language television station would be a white elephant. An alternative approach would have been to debate whether provision of Irish-medium television would respond to the real needs of communities and families who are endeavouring to maintain Irish as a vernacular, and whether the goodwill of the wider community towards Irish is sufficient to make the financial contribution necessary. Such a debate could have established performance standards by which the investment would be measured, and forced people to realize that if heritage has an emotional value to them, it may also require a financial investment for its preservation.

through enhanced tourism and leisure prospects. Accordingly, items of heritage are really only special if they are able to tap into or satisfy consumer demand. The role of heritage in stimulating tourism and thereby contributing to economic growth is used to indicate its net contribution to the welfare of society.

Culture and heritage are cited as major contributory factors stimulating Irish tourism. It is difficult, nevertheless, to grasp exactly what is meant by either term in official tourism reports. There is little doubt but that state tourism policy as it impacts on heritage is largely driven by what might be described as a 'utilitarian' approach. Objectives such as maximizing the profit of firms providing goods and services to tourists or generating an optimal level of direct and indirect tourist expenditures seem to supersede non-commercial considerations. The language used illustrates this way of thinking: heritage, like any tourist 'product', must be branded, marketed or developed to garner as much as possible of tourist expenditures. Markets are prioritized in terms of spending power; those not making an adequate contribution must be abandoned in favour of more lucrative niches.

Economic indicators such as the contribution of tourism to the balance of payments, employment created, value-added and tourist numbers are used to track performance over time. The Republic of Ireland had 6 million overseas visitors in 1999, and they are estimated to have spent £1.8 billion during their stay. It is not sufficient, moreover, to measure direct expenditures by tourists and employment created in the tourist industry to assess economic impact. Various other indirect economic effects result in employment creation in organizations serving the tourism sector and their multiplier effect must be calculated.

Commentators who emphasize heritage's positive value to the quality of life of a community regard the dominant role of economic objectives as flawed since they believe that it not only underestimates the true worth but can lead to actions which result in losses to future generations. Moreover, little research has been conducted on the precise role of motivation in driving heritage tourism. More than half of overseas visitors, for example, are estimated to include a visit to at least one place described as of natural, cultural or historical interest during their stay. According to Bord Fáilte (1992), 60% of all overseas-originating holidays taken in Ireland could be classified as car touring/landscape and culture enjoyment. These tourists are probably motivated by an interest in heritage, running the gamut from none to very enthusiastic. The key challenge in analysing heritage tourism is attempting to link market segments with actual desires or motivations of tourists. A study might throw up some interesting results and policy implications. For instance, shifting policies to attract those with

an educational or specialist cultural motivation might in the long-term prove more attractive. The key policy issue is time perspective and the trade-off between the perceived needs and tastes of present and future generations. Often, decisions are undertaken to satisfy present-day sectional interests which may not prove beneficial when evaluated in hindsight.

Various reports written by Bord Fáilte (for example, 1992 and 1996) exemplify an economics-led or short-term perspective. According to the Bord, its objective is 'to increase the level of economic activity in Ireland through increasing demand within the tourism sector'. Specifically, it sets out to create additional employment, attract foreign earnings, increase the level of value added, generate increased exchequer earnings and contribute to an improved regional distribution of income.

Under the Operational Programme for Tourism (1998), an unprecedented £652 million, 56% of which (£369 million) the EU contributed, was to have been invested in Irish tourism between the years 1994 and 1999. In addition to support given to the product development of heritage projects, a total of £125 million was targeted at natural and cultural tourism in order, as the Programme states, to 'make Ireland's heritage and culture more accessible and attractive to overseas visitors'.

National/Regional Cultural activities (for instance the National Museum) account for £71 million, while £27 million each was designated for National Monuments and Historic Properties (for example Castletown House) and the Natural Environment (for instance Grand and Royal Canal extensions). The Programme leaves little doubt where its priorities lie. Money was to be spent spent for 'further improving our tourist product to fill gaps in the market', and, to achieve this, 'the product will be sold with sophisticated aggression on the world market'.

It is no surprise that non-commercial considerations for supporting heritage or cultural appreciation are often overwhelmed by the Bord's desire to achieve economic objectives. As a result, heritage projects worthy of support, because of their intrinsic significance or community benefit, often find it difficult to receive public funding if they cannot be justified using economic criteria. The reverse also holds true. Areas of special heritage value or historical significance may in the long term prove to have far more attractive benefits if conserved, but may be damaged in the short term because more attractive private gains can be achieved through exploitation. While sustainability is now the catch-phrase in official tourism policy, an enhanced level of public debate is needed on whether narrow economic goals should play such a dominant role without proper assessment of the long-term implications for community life.

CONCLUSION

Investment decisions in heritage management possess all the complexity of purely commercial investment decision-making but with the added dimension of responsibility to protect resources that almost by definition cannot adequately be valued by solely commercial criteria. That responsibility is exercised not only on behalf of a community that should be consulted and educated about the resources' intrinsic worth but is also exercised in trust for past and future communities.

Decision-making techniques and practices that are well established for commercial investment can provide a useful framework for decisions relating to heritage management, albeit accompanied by those caveats we have discussed. The limitations of financial models for dealing with uncertainty and in contexts where markets do not assign a value to an asset are well recognized. It follows that even with greater sophistication in analytical methods, such an approach will always result in a partial, although still useful, analysis.

Decisions relating to heritage management inevitably require policy-makers to make choices regarding what is worth preserving, what objectives are to be achieved, and what benefits people are willing to forego today to preserve a community's heritage for future generations. The challenge for professionals in heritage management is to use analytical tools from a range of disciplines, such as economics, finance and accounting, to improve the sophistication of decision-making in a non-commercial environment. There is a clear necessity for further refinement of financial models for such uses. The need to modify decision-making tools to cater for the special needs of the Irish context is also apparent. The recent publication by The Heritage Council of a series of policy papers on topics such as state-sector expenditure on heritage, agriculture and the national heritage and forestry and the national heritage is most welcome as aids to policy-makers.

The government's decision to develop an integrated national plan for the management of our national heritage offers an ideal opportunity to look again at trade-offs the community needs to make in preserving its heritage. These trade-offs must be made in deciding how much resources should be directed at heritage rather than other areas, as well as the allocation of funds among various heritage categories.

In recent decades, Ireland has received generous EU support to develop heritage-related projects. As the level of financial support available from the EU is substantially reduced in years to come, we are likely to face more debate on the choices we must make as a community. Our hope is that an enhanced degree of sophistication in investment analysis will facilitate this debate.

A key issue is how we, as a society, integrate the democratic process with such analytical techniques in order to make decisions that prove optimal for this and future generations.

Bibliography

BirdWatch Ireland 1998 *Annual report 1997*. Dublin.
BirdWatch Ireland 2000 *Annual report 1999*. Dublin.
Bord Fáilte 1992 *Tourism marketing plan 1993–97*. Dublin.
Bord Fáilte 1998 *The Fáilte business: tourism's role in economic growth*. Dublin.
CSF (Community Support Framework) *Evaluation Unit 1999 Proposed working rules for cost-benefit analysis*. Dublin.
Department of Tourism and Trade 1998 *Tourism 2000: guide to the operational programme for tourism, 1994–99*. Dublin.
Dixon, J. A. and Sherman, P. B. 1990 *Economics of protected areas: a new look at benefits and costs*. London.
Ross, S. A., Westerfield, R. and Jordan, B. D. 1995 *Fundamentals of corporate finance*, third edition. Irwin, Chicago.
Shell Company 1998 *The Shell report — 1998: profits and principles — does there have to be a choice?* Royal Dutch/Shell Group of Companies.
Weston, J. Fred and Copeland, T. E. 1992 *Managerial finance*, ninth edition. Fort Worth.
Zerbe Jr, R. O. and Dively, D. D. 1994 *Benefit-cost analysis in theory and practice*. New York.

Entrepreneurialism

Deirdre Hunt

This chapter takes a two-fold approach to its subject matter. It first presents a case study offering a practical illustration of the blend of heritage, management and entrepreneurship. This case study reports a conversation with Mr Des McWilliams, Managing Director (MD) of McWilliams Sailmakers, based in Crosshaven, county Cork, which took place in September 1999. McWilliams Sailmakers typifies many of the characteristics of craft enterprises. Family-owned and run, the company developed out of a pre-existing hobby and broader sail-making traditions as a means of combining a passion for sailing with the need to generate income. It has survived by constantly redefining product market position and network alliances in a cultural framework which its MD judges to be antipathetic and lacking in understanding of Small Business craft. The second strand of the paper explores in general terms the wider questions which arise from this particular example. It considers how one might conceptualize issues of specific concern to heritage enterprises and also their interaction with the wider economy.

McWILLIAMS SAILMAKERS

Traditionally, the skill in sail-making consisted in working around the cloth, judging how to utilize the wind to blow the sail into the appropriate shape. In the last thirty years, major changes have shifted the skill input. Improvements in the technology of material weaving and finishing, together with the development of new high-tech materials, have removed much of the guess-work. The advent of CAD/CAM production has further oriented the sailmaker's skill towards design. The new technologies have opened up new possibilities for experimentation and networked collaboration, initially by fax and now Internet based. Design has become divided from production, which in theory can be located anywhere there is web access. It is driven ever more by cost, and, in the case of craft, by labour considerations.

Skill today is concentrated on the design, diagnostic service and repair areas. All of this demands long-term involvement, both in the activity of competitive and leisure sailing as well as in the handling of sails and their components. I can look at a sail and see how it sets, see where deformation or wear have occurred, and tell you immediately its history, components and prognosis. That is where craft know-how is at its most focussed. There is also an enormous amount of such know-how tied into appropriate usage, the when/how aspects, and then there are the wider business issues: knowing who the main players are, the competitors, which of them have been down-loading your web page information, the profile of the sub-contractors, suppliers you can collaborate with and under what terms. To survive, you have to understand and be understood by the world of sailing, a world that at the beginning of the twenty-first century is taken up with leisure, which represents one of the major growth sectors in the developed economies.

From this perspective, with the Irish economy now booming, one might expect that sail-making would be enjoying a strong roll in this country. Not so. My only competitor is currently packing up manufacturing, and with him will go all that know-how. Why is he doing so? I shall deal primarily with factors that are within our own control. My views reflect operating over many years in Ireland as well as my experience of working on the Small Business Forum in 1994, which brought senior public-sector officials and owner-managers together for the first time. This experience highlighted for me the profound gap that exists between the public sector and entrepreneurs. It is this divide that leads to the endless creation of public sector demands that are hostile to the development of craft enterprises in Ireland.

Both sides contribute to the mutual bafflement. Public-sector officials, particularly those involved with wealth creation, tend to be macro-economists with little or no Small Business background. Their training has provided them with industry models derived from external, deemed successful, economies, such as the UK and USA, with their large manufacturing corporates run by similar bureaucratic cadres. These are the models of excellence and relationships that the public-sector official brings to his dealings with entrepreneurs. In contrast to officials and those from the corporate sector, entrepreneurs find it almost impossible to cooperate, and they are not good at communicating their perspectives and needs. The lack of common understanding which leads to defective policy-making is clearly seen in approaches to risk. When dealing with public services, the whole concept of risk seems absolutely alien to their nature. And the effect? Well, it means that public policy tends not to build in safety nets. One can see this most clearly in the treatment of company failures. In such cases, the Revenue gets super-preferential treatment in that it has first call on all monies retrieved (*Finance Act* 1986, section 115). For the business, this means that there is no way back. Pay cannot be used as a security to leverage additional finance and allow a new start to be made. There are no second chances here. The same section prevents banks from lending to Small Businesses against their book debts, which are a major source of collateral in the sector. This is especially galling given the previously poor payment record of the same public sector.

The equivalent dominant macro-economic background particularly evident in Finance leads to the perception that what represents a good idea for them will be good for all. They just cannot see that it is really the other way round. What is good for us is good for them. The more we make, the more they make. The decision that all Small Businesses shall pay VAT on invoices instead of on cash receipts was one small example. This gained the Revenue an immediate (but once-off) capital inflow, but at the cost of acute cash flow difficulties for the Small Business population in Ireland. Ironically, the UK removed this requirement in order to assist Small Businesses in the very month that the measure was instituted here.

It seems that, for Finance, all changes must be revenue neutral and must show pay back in twelve months. Yet most craft companies, often family businesses, work with generational perspectives in mind. To these companies such short-termism is illogical and frequently constraining of long-term investments with their long-term pay backs. What such officials cannot deal with are grey processes, yet that is what entrepreneurs mainly do. Employee reward is also a bone of contention. In the current 'Tiger' environment, we are hard pressed to retain and reward good staff. We are conscious of the cyclical nature of the business and have weathered some great storms. We would like to institute profit-sharing without incurring excessive tax bills for our employees.

That is, we would like to reward our staff instead of the government. The only profit-sharing schemes countenanced by government involve share distribution. What use is this to Small Businesses? We are competing for staff. Must the multi-nationals be handed further competitive advantages over us?

To thrive, we need the room to make mistakes to create profit and get on with the job. Much that is amiss here can be seen to centre around the word 'compliance'. Compliance costs are not only high in Ireland but appear often illogical. In my own case, compliance requires me to employ 1.5 people to meet legal requirements. In our sister company in the UK, the figure is 0.5. Take the INTERSTAT and VIES forms which enumerate our imported raw materials. Historically, such work was done by the public sector and paid for by our taxes. Now, this administration has been moved into my office at my cost. I see no consequent tax reduction. But it is not just complying. There is the accompanying feeling that even when we do comply we are not trusted. In terms of PAYE, for example, directors, their spouses and any of their children working part-time, unlike their non-family counterparts, do not qualify for the £1,000 PAYE allowance. One can only surmise that the Revenue has made the judgement that the family Small Business participant is gaining undeclared benefits from the enterprise.

If risk and compliance are dividing points, reward, as mentioned earlier, is a third area. Here, public policy-makers are really into sustaining the *status quo*. From this perspective, all change must be current outcome neutral and pay back in twelve months. This point of view does not provide a basis for rewarding wealth creation, which by its very nature tends to be one-off, rarely recurs in the same way and reflects a unique individual contribution (not length of service and defined organizational position). The cultural norms for reward are set by the public sector overall. This leads to a situation where activities which would make craft business more viable are deemed illegal. Let us look at some examples. In generating an even flow of work in a highly seasonal business, for instance, it would make sense to take deposits. The drawback is that I can only charge VAT on the total invoice and must lend the rest of the VAT to government at zero interest.

Add web-based trading to our current e-mail supported design and this craft company begins to move into the high-tech arena, except that we are not seen as such. Policy needs to evolve to encompass both new start-up high-tech and existing companies as they begin to utilize new transformational technologies. This also means we need greater support to develop and sustain new kinds of trading. McWilliams Sailmakers is now part of a franchised network of sailmakers. The new networked strategy allows us to secure local purchasing and therefore retain revenue locally. This move, critical to our survival, was developed with the advice and financial assistance of FORBAIRT. To them goes the only bouquet! Public policy-makers therefore need to re-envision craft-based Small Business, not as single units but as networked players.

THE BUSINESS CONTEXT

Discussion linking management, heritage and entrepreneurship is a recent occurrence. Ten years ago, the emphasis in the heritage management debate was on the creation, organization and development of large-scale, often hierarchical, centrally driven entities manned by professional cadres, career managers. In this model, which derived from American corporate models, increasing effectiveness in something called the 'heritage sector' was initially equated with managerializing existing public-sector cadres. This was to take place via the development of new hitherto unconsidered concepts such as performance indicators, mission statements and client charters. What was not seen at this point was that the move carried with it part of the logic for what subsequently became known as privatization. Why not, as well as or rather than managerializing the civil service, hand over to professional managers in private-sector corporations many of the services, including heritage, that the state has come to provide for its citizens? Privatization of services continues to be a major characteristic of contemporary developed economies, bringing implications not least for government itself with it. For in a privatized economy, shorn of the direct provision of goods and services, the task of government becomes that of positive environment creation and regulation.

As these later two concepts have been explored and widely applied, so the understanding of what encompasses environment has also markedly widened and deepened. If the creation of a positive environment was initially seen as the provision of supportive legal and fiscal measures, it was gradually held to encompass a far wider range of processes, including access to skill and life-long learning, and the provision of seed and venture capital, information and appropriate physical settings. But if the role of government as provider changed during the 1990s, so the understanding of organizational excellence has also altered. Although the early 1990s still held to a concept of organizational and executive excellence dominated by large and in particular large corporate manufacturing models, this subsequently changed. Four major shifts have characterized the recent past, the demise of large-scale manufacturing systems, the emergence of the knowledge economy and the development of networked delivery systems made up of large numbers of Small Business and micro-enterprise participants clustered *pro tempore* around particular projects, and all of this occurring within an increasingly globalized market.

This is good news for heritage activities which are now more dominated by Small Business and micro-enterprises as well as the sole trader. Growing on heritage means supporting networked small enterprises as they deliver knowledge-based intangible and tangible products, both goods and services, to an increasingly global and remote customer base. With the downturn in large-scale manufacturing has come the realization that entrepreneurs, not managers, are the real economic drivers, and, as such, have a strong legitimate claim to priority government support. And even if the large organization still appears to dominate the heritage landscape, the reality is that, behind that name, what exists on the ground is more and more a small devolved project team with a defined budget which in policy delivery terms needs to be conceived of as a Small Business unit run by entrepreneurs. A major transformation in thinking about heritage development is an awareness that support of heritage means devising more effective assistance for the Small Business population which *inter alia* includes heritage providers.

Recognition of the role of entrepreneurs and Small Business as economic engines in turn demands a radical realignment of existing mind-sets and policy, and in dynamic economies this change is occurring. As is clear from the recent OECD (1998) report, *Fostering entrepreneurship*, currently, all developed economies have put or are putting in place Small Business support legislation. In addition, many governments are attempting to realign existing systems, whether fiscal or economic, to make them more accessible to Small Business participants. As summarized in the OECD report, government policies in relation to Small Business tend to be similar world-wide. These cover increasing labour-market flexibility, that is creating the opportunities which allow potential entrepreneurs, both employed and unemployed, to move into self-employment, reduction in the administrative burden of government, mitigation of the severity of bankruptcy legislation, development of pro-active entrepreneurship programmes accessible both regionally and locally and the instigation of widespread attitude changes utilizing positive role models. The development of flexibility supports has comprised fiscal featherbedding for start-ups, including soft loans, subsidized training with learning credits, access to training systems for the long-term unemployed and mature returnees to the labour market, as well as designated, subsidized physical serviced space. The development of a wide variety of Small Business incubators offering both physical space coupled with a variety of learning, mentoring and marketing services has been widespread in developed economies. Many good examples exist of such measures centered on craft/heritage activities.

Ireland has the beginnings of a good track record here,

having directly involved entrepreneurs in the initial jump-starting of Small Business legislation in the early 1990s which culminated in the Government of Ireland's *Small Business task force report* (1994). This provided an initial agenda for legislation aimed at creating a positive environment for such business. This agenda has been gradually implemented by all subsequent governments. More recently, the effort was pushed further forward by the report *New ways of living and working: teleworking in Ireland* (National Advisory Council on Teleworking 1999, see also *http://www.irglow.ie/enterp/telework*). This importantly developed a code of practice which was agreed by both employers, the social partners and Small Business organizations, setting out for the first time agreed parameters for the development of subcontracted knowledge-based distanced work.

Reduction in the role of government has been variously interpreted, but a consistent theme has been the attempt to lessen the administrative demands made by government on the owner-manager. In Ireland, this has been a recurrent argument of the Small Business Federation, which has regularly listed in the press in excess of 1,000 forms which have to be completed by the Small Business owner in the course of one year to comply with government demands. This impact awareness has come to form part of wider government sensitivities towards the Small Business sector. It is also to be found at European Union level where one of the major responsibilities of the former DG 23, the Directorate for Small Business, was to evaluate and demand change from other proposing Directorates if suggested Directives were seen to impose excessive compliance costs on the Small Business sector. The highlighting of bankruptcy legislation may at first appear curious. But, as drafted in many jurisdictions, the consequences of bankruptcy for individual entrepreneurs can be draconian, and may act as a major deterrent to any subsequent attempt by the entrepreneur to re-enter the market. By way of contrast, the legal consequences of bankruptcy in the USA are relatively light, with the bankruptcy culturally evaluated as a learning experience, thus encouraging the learner to try again. Having succeeded in mainstreaming Small Business legislation, there is now a necessity to localize this to fit it more exactly with the needs of entrepreneurs in the heritage area. We need to ensure that we begin to create support processes that are both Small Business and heritage-orientated. We shall return to this issue in greater detail later in the present chapter.

But perhaps it is the attitudinal approaches to entrepreneurship that have provided the greatest challenge. Or, as it has been put to me, unless you can change the aspirations of the mothers you will not increase the pool of indigenous entrepreneurs. Traditionally, the mothers' aspirations were for sons to become doctors, lawyers and priests. So how can government hope to transform such preferences? The Scottish example may be of some interest here. Contemplating devolution, the Scots identified that they had one of the lowest business start-up rates in Europe (Scottish Enterprise 1993). Through Scottish Enterprise, attempts have been made to reverse this profile. They have tackled the issue in a variety of ways, first isolating the main inhibitors, lack of personal role models and negative cultural images. The long heavy industry background in Scotland, mining, steel-making, ship-building or mass production manufacturing, has meant that few Scots have had any contact with entrepreneurs within their own immediate circles. Scottish entrepreneurs, if they were known of at all, existed as distant male historical figures, many of whom, such as Carnegie, had played out their lives outside Scotland, and there were no women. Culturally, entrepreneurs were constructed as morally suspect, deceitful opportunists benefiting from others' misfortune and at the same time leading over-worked, stressful lives with a high risk of defeat and loss. Not much here to motivate and lead to the abandonment of maternal aspirations. If the Scottish economy was to reposition itself into growth sectors, this demanded a significant increase in the numbers and ability range of those entering self-employment. The approaches taken to achieve this goal were varied, well-funded and sustained over time. Using Scottish media road-shows, national competitions, funding and training support, Scottish Enterprise set about changing the image, identifying and highlighting existing Scottish entrepreneurs. The programme developed was inclusive, with role models being drawn from and identified among women, ethnic minorities, the young and the old. Currently, there appears to be evidence of a positive increase in both the numbers and educational levels of those entering self-employment in Scotland.

In Ireland, the problem, as the Small Business Task Force *Report* (1994) showed, has not been one of start-up; Small Business start-up is on a par with start-ups elsewhere in developed economies. Rather the difficulty is one of closure. Small Businesses in Ireland close faster than elsewhere. One suggestion has been that this reflects the role of Small Business as a panacea for the long-term unemployed, whereas in reality the thrust should be to increase the up-take of self-employment among graduate populations. The profile in this way reflects that of Scotland, with those least likely to possess appropriate skills and resources and hence survive taking up self-employment. As in Scotland, there is a need to change the image and to main-stream entrepreneurship as a main-line life choice. There is some evidence that this is slowly beginning with the emergence of enterprise-focused graduate and undergraduate programmes in the third-level sector in this country. If we compare Ireland to other growth economies, it is clear that the rate of start-up and survival in the Small Business sector needs to continue and to increase, and we need to emphasize that all of this entry and growth can occur within a range of heritage environments.

One way in which this can be demonstrated is by comparing Small Business growth trends in the developed economies. The Small Business population continues to expand within the EU and the USA. Growth has been particularly strong in the areas traditionally seen as the province of heritage management, that is high information content leisure products. Goldfinger (1994) has identified the core characteristics of current high-growth products as being tied to short-term recurrent demand and associated with frivolity/leisure. The heritage product fits such a profile. But there are also organizational characteristics to be borne in mind. The new information economy would appear to be largely sourced and delivered via small networked enterprises. This new economy, as currently constituted, has several defining features: information is the raw material, the market is global, bounded only by virtual access, the organizational norm is temporary and networked and reverse marketing determines what is sought, combined and paid for by the individual customer. From this it follows that possession of the ability to access and recombine information responding to particular demand in contemporary societies forms the major source of added value. Sourcing and reformulating also constitute a central core of heritage activities.

To tie this vision more clearly into our understanding of heritage, one needs to make a distinction between information-supported and information-centred enterprises. All organizations, to exist, depend on the effective use of information. Information-supported enterprises utilize information to support a central tangible product which is the result of information, craft knowledge, market contacts, employment of specific insight as it relates to regulations and operational demands. In contrast to information-centred products, the product itself exists as an intangible reflection of inputted knowledge to be used to extend the information resources of the recipient. But, as Handy (1984) points out, it is not just intangibility that distinguishes the information-centred organization but the fact that the intangible products that it generates can be reproduced *ad infinitum*, without losing any aspect of the original creation. The example cited is that of Mickey Mouse, still going strong after fifty years and not diminished by having been constantly resold every four minutes over that length of time. Successful intangible product enterprises are therefore ones which have yielded product with very short recurrent demand curves. Economies which as a whole have developed such companies will exhibit high growth. Growth in heritage activities would thus seem to be increasingly tied to the development of such intangible, short, recurrent demand products. I am thinking here of on-line heritage material, interactive kiosk-accessed CD-ROM material, visual and aural presentational output.

The definition of heritage has always acknowledged the contribution of craft workers to the heritage sector. I would readily admit that determining what a craft is has been a contentious matter for some time. Within Ireland, craft has been defined as the production of tangible products incorporating an aesthetic element. The dominant tradition has been that of the individual craft worker selling directly to the market. This has considerably benefited from joint marketing approaches, with subsidized access to international fairs. Repeated attempts to develop small communal workshops with shared production and marketing approaches also have a long tradition, if relatively short lives. This perspective appears to exclude many of the activities which in earlier periods were classified as crafts in Ireland. A comparison of current understanding of craft in mainland Europe serves to echo this earlier Irish understanding. In mainland Europe, the term 'craft' is upheld by the descendants of the medieval craft guilds and encompasses a wide range of activities, from glove-making, brick-laying and silver-smithing to electricians. The guild tradition also existed in Ireland and covered many of the undertakings nowadays regarded as guild activities in mainland Europe. But this largely medieval city-state phenomenon in Europe has a far earlier history in Ireland where we can identify a range of ventures tied to the allocation of roles in the late Bronze Age period which we would see as craft activities. Metal-working, leather, sail and cheese-making all formed important craft groups in the society and continued to do so. As new technologies emerged, so new groupings were developed around the relevant skills with access to such skill increasingly restricted and ritualized. Such an evolution is clearly seen in the development of electrical craft guilds in mainland Europe. The latter category is of interest, as it clearly demonstrates that the definition of craft can change as new technologies emerge. This would suggest that, within the Irish context, new types of craft groupings are constantly evolving which could form the basis for heritage support. As the range and sophistication of heritage projects increase, so one can envisage the development of a craft sector devoted to heritage presentation covering both tangible and virtual systems. One could imagine the development of totally on-line globally accessible heritage products emerging from such craft groupings and kite-marked as a form of quality assurance by the craft association. And it is the implications for the management and development of this type of activity that I wish to explore. Where do heritage activities fit within the emerging economy, and how does the development of e-commerce relate to the overall focus of this chapter, the heritage entrepreneur?

If the central activities in heritage are the reconstruction and accessing of past information, the development of the information and communication technology (ICT), economy and heritage activities must be seen as mutually interdependent and transformational. The question is in what ways? The up-take of ICT technologies has a wide range of discernible effects, not only in terms of organizational optimization but also of markets and product viability. According to Freeman (Freeman and Soete 1985), information technologies offer four main types of economic advantage in terms of speed, storage, flexibility and networking. Speed allows access to area-enhanced turn-round and an ability to work with large databases. Storage capacity facilitates the collection and access to large databases hitherto requiring lengthy work at tremendous cost. Accessing dispersed information and reformulating it to meet demand forms a central activity in the heritage spectrum. Flexibility enables customization of through-put and faster response to market demand, whilst networking capacity leads to the evolution of the networked organization. Such developments have not only allowed Small Business to operate at a physical distance from parent companies and/or significant customers, but have created a new range of Small Businesses which, while small in scale, are off-shoots of the technology itself. The world of heritage is therefore increasingly mutually dependent on ICT-related small enterprises, web designers, web masters, CD-ROM producers, video editors and translators on line.

According to Hilt and Bryniolfsson (1997), ICT is associated with a work system that is decentralized, with autonomy incentives that account for decreased observability, increased importance of the knowledge worker and knowledge work, and all of this is consistent across industries. Implicit in this approach is the argument that organizationally this technology has a fragmenting logic which, if examined, can over time only lead to Small Business-dominated economies. The heritage entrepreneur will therefore increasingly work within ever-expanding micro-enterprise communities drawn together through mutually defined interdependencies.

In a framework in Ireland in which, until recently, heritage development was dominated by large public-sector delivery, how might this transformation process occur? Zuboff's (1988) work provides some insights in this regard as she examines the process of introducing information technologies into large organizations, in so doing coining the terms 'automate' and 'informate'. For her, this process follows three stages. During the first, which she called 'automate', the focus and justification for the introduction of the new technology is cost-driven,

the effect is on the bottom line. ICT applications at this point are focussed on reducing the number of employees by automating information flow and handling process, making the information flow in the organization faster and less labour-intensive. The effect of this type of automation is clearly to lead to redundancy, a decline in overtime coupled with a reduction in unskilled and semi-skilled jobs in the areas of paper handling and low-level administration, with a concomitant increase in demand for upskilling and new skills, in particular in the ICT area. In this stage, however, the emphasis is on enhancing the effectiveness of existing systems, that is, tinkering with but not transforming the organization.

Stage Two, the informate stage, involves a development whereby the information provided by the new work tools must be used to get the work done. Here manual work is firmly replaced by computer-based routines, and the possession of these skills becomes a *sine qua non* of employment. At this point the application of ICT systems begins both to enhance existing operational effectiveness as well as to create new information-based opportunities. This new capacity allows access to deepen and extend, in a non-locational specific manner, information closely related to existing operational processes, immediate global market intelligence and supply chain capacity information. But, as well as enhancing existing processes, the development of an ICT-infused organization creates information by-products which can lead to the creation of new business opportunities in their own right. One can think here of control application consultancies, niche market analysis, bureau and web-based employment agencies specializing in heritage-associated projects as all being off-shoots from this stage and certainly leading to an increase in the Small Business population. But it is the third stage, as identified by Zuboff, that is of particular interest to the heritage-as-craft entrepreneurialism discussion. In this stage the organization can be seen as fundamentally transformed. Stage Three involves the development of new ways of working, new management roles and the formation of the networked organization, in other words the networked Small Business economy.

In the new ICT world, the most effective strategy is that which allows decision-making to happen at the point at which information enters an organization. This carries with it a logic of desegregation and the rise of the networked organization. Thus the development of the information economy is one that is supportive of small enterprises, but not isolated small enterprises, rather enterprises that in shifting ways can come together to respond to differing market demand. And this is also changing radically. The growth of ICT opens up global market access. Such access allows for the creation of viable demand for what were hitherto low-demand products. This can easily be seen in the collectibles auction markets where global access has for the first time provided a sufficient volume of trade to create adequate profit to allow for the expansion of this new market, with all that market development requires in terms of sustaining promoters and delivering to customers. The implications for heritage, including craft providers, are very profound. The use of ICT will allow craft/heritage producers to be accessed globally. It enables hitherto scattered demand populations to be consolidated, and makes viable the commercial creation of products having minority appeal with hitherto intermittent and low market demand. But the shift is also to reverse marketing, whereby the individual customer decides on what product they require. The focus on the unique is also good news for the heritage product producer, allowing for a move to more commissioned products. So at both an organizational and market demand level, the logic is towards the establishment of small networked enterprises actively involved in creating and trading product globally. It is in this ICT trading context that the role of the entrepreneur emerges as central. For it is the quality of the individual trader operating as a trading enterprise that may increasingly come to dominate the role of heritage. This requires that we take a look at what it means to be an entrepreneur and trader, and to envisage the most appropriate devices to assist such individuals.

ENTREPRENEURIALISM: DEFINITIONS AND THE DESIGN OF SUPPORT SYSTEMS

The term 'entrepreneur' entered the English language via French. France has always been a tiered society and continues to be so to this day, much given to hierarchical classification of its citizens. It was as part of this classificatory system that entrepreneurs were first identified (Cantillon 1775). The term as it emerged was used to designate economic actors who created profit by functioning as intermediaries. Literally translated, it means 'the taker-in-between'. The word, as with the contemporary French term for entrepreneurs, *auto-didacte*, carries with it implications of being outside the established social order, independent and opportunistic. Entrepreneurs acted as brokers, combining elements in a new way to create new wealth. In a world dominated by inherited wealth and agricultural peasants, both saw the entrepreneur as the main engine of economic change and growth.

The rise of the industrial manufacturing economy witnessed a decline in interest in the entrepreneur, with the focus shifting onto the capitalist managers. The long-term dominance of Marxist analysis served only to reinforce this perspective. For Marx (1850 [1976]), the entrepreneur belonged, if anywhere, to the *petite bourgeoisie*, who might or might not be supportive of social reform but who would inevitably be swept away in the impending revolution which was to lead to the triumph of the proletariat. Little or no analysis therefore occurred of the entrepreneur *per se*, even in neo-classical economics, and one must look to the Austrian school for the re-emergence of this study.

For Krirzner (1973), the entrepreneur is someone who is alert to profitable opportunities for exchange. In this model, the entrepreneur acts as the link between suppliers and customers. Profit comes not, as in the Marxist model, from ownership of tangible goods but from the possession of additional knowledge. Therefore, the skill of the entrepreneur consists of identifying, putting together and seeing the use that can be made of hitherto already existing but fragmented information. The product of the entrepreneur, that with which he trades, is newly minted knowledge. In this model, the entrepreneur comes to possess knowledge which is unique to him and is of sufficient interest to others to have commercial value.

For Brockhouse (1980), the emphasis is on risk-taking. In this approach, entrepreneurs are involved in the offsetting of risk. The entrepreneur is not a gambler *per se* but is able to assess risk and is prepared to take the consequences, whether profit or loss. Clearly, if the entrepreneur only loses, he will not remain in the market long-term but will be wiped out. Entrepreneurs will therefore continue to exist if they are able, using information, better to assess the implied risk than others and, secondly, are knowledgeable about where and under what conditions risk can be offset. Both of these activities depend on effective usage of privileged knowledge, and behind these models it is easy to see strong links to eighteenth-century rationalism.

With Stackler (as discussed in Herbert 1982), there is a shift in emphasis and an acknowledgement of more intuitive skills as forming an essential feature of entrepreneurial behaviour, with a stress on creativity. In this model, the entrepreneur's main comparative advantage is the ability to think laterally. This ability is tied to a wider environment of turbulence and unpredictability. It is Stackler's contention that the entrepreneur's ability to see possibilities amid uncertainty is what leads to his success. In this model, the entrepreneur identifies potential and manages to have committed resources to allow such potential to be realized. Implicit in this theory are communication and persuasive abilities. The model also suggests that the growth of entrepreneurial behaviour is in some way tied to the emergence of economic unpredictability and turbulence. Such periods are characterized by the failure of existing solutions and the need to understand and explore the emerging possibilities and profit from these new challenges.

In these creative ability models, the entrepreneur is combining both creativity and rational thinking to achieve success. In contradistinction to the model of the capitalists, the entrepreneur need own no physical resources. The entrepreneur stands as distinctive due to his ability to put together existing resources, which come in the form of information, in a way that meets an emerging need. He is able, through being open to and aware of new information, to assess the relative risk of particular activities in a more proficient way than other potential competitors, and is therefore capable of making informed choices as to what activity he becomes involved in. The involvement may be on behalf of others also, and it is from this acting on behalf of others that the fee, and therefore profit, arises.

This ability to exact a fee indicates that the entrepreneur is not functioning in a depopulated universe but within a particular market context which consists of economic actors capable of resourcing the entrepreneur, forming connections and able to utilize what he offers. The concept of laying off risk also implies others capable, both in terms of experience, judgement and resources, of accepting the risk offered. In a somewhat less integrated way, certain of the models stress creative thinking, a concept which stretches beyond the narrowly defined rational into other areas of human thought. However described, the essence of creativity as identified for the entrepreneur would appear to consist of the ability to combine a range of sources in a new manner within a rationale which may appear initially to be based on instinct.

All these models have at their base an emphasis on knowledge. Entrepreneurs generate profit not because they control tangible resources but rather because they use intangible resource knowledge creatively. And all of these activities involving a range of distinctive actors have significant implications for the development of support systems for entrepreneurs. At the beginning of this chapter, I argued that the role of government had increasingly become one of environment regulator. Here, one can extend the analysis further and identify the function of assigned regulator, that is a body charged on behalf of government with creating propitious environments for designated populations such as entrepreneurs. The debate in relation to heritage then becomes a discussion of the development and management of effective support systems for entrepreneurs in this sector. Some of this discussion will clearly be generic, relating to all Small Business and all entrepreneurs. In generic terms, all of the entrepreneurial models cited in essence imply that the information comes to one physically static point where the entrepreneur is to be found, and therefore all support should equally be directed towards that one physical location.

Approaching academic models of entrepreneurship, one is struck by their emphasis on the independent individual. The creation and management of support for entrepreneurs in the heritage sector would thus need to start with this premise, with assistance focussed on the one driver, the entrepreneur. This has implications both of scale and style. Here scale means one. Under the umbrella title of 'resource poverty management', discussion in the Small Business literature has centred on the limitations that arise from the restricted number of individuals involved in executive and management activities in the small enterprise. But even if we concede that entrepreneurs may well continue to preside over growing companies, the evidence is that they tend to retain significant personal decision-making in their own hands. One of the many challenges confronting the enterprise support designer is how to deliver aid to one decision-maker in a way that will not overwhelm, in terms of time, cost and complexity. In addition, the literature demonstrates that the frequently highly charged emotional identification of the entrepreneur with his company also means that he will relate to, define and deliver administrative and decision-making tasks in a highly personalized way. This leads to the requirement that a support system needs to mimic this highly personalized mode of operation, thus reflecting the entrepreneur's necessity for on-going emotional ownership of all aspects of the firm. The management of support for this sector thus demands the flexibility to allow for high levels of localization and personal adaptation to sustain the requirement for psychological ownership and acceptability.

If the message from analysis of entrepreneurial models is that profit derives from information manipulation, the support response is clear. It is necessary to allow for proactive interrogation on behalf of the entrepreneur, for information identification, sourcing and reassemblage of knowledge, both of existing and emerging knowledge, in ways that reduce cost and increase profit by freeing up time, increasing accuracy and enhancing capacity. Heritage management support therefore needs to allow the entrepreneur to identify contracts, contact and supply information to clients. Pulling from a readily accessible information base, it must have a facility which will allow information to be searched and categorized in ways that meet particular clients' needs. Search activities, even given the reduction in costs that IT database access implies, are still expensive both *per se* and in terms of opportunity costs. The creation of external support for heritage enterprises has to be able to allow for the establishment, storage of and access to information that is entrepreneur-specific tried and true. The system should ensure ease of contact, access to and replies to inquiries. It must allow for negotiation to enable information requests to be met or decisions to be clarified before other activities, for example purchasing, to occur and the decision to commit resources to products is executed. There are also implications in terms of security and confidentiality that will be of importance to the entrepreneur. Support mechanisms must facilitate access to information in a way that meets the time-scale of the entrepreneur and his clients, both up- and down-stream.

Paralleling the distinction that we have already seen between the rational and the creative, support systems also need to integrate imagining. A recent media distinction is being made in the USA between hard news, classified as major disasters and political events ('Earth-quake strikes Kobe', 'The Euro is launched in Europe'), soft news ('Ten thousand trout die from eating poisoned spiders', CBS morning news 4 June 1998) and rumour. The emergence and use of the Druge website is a well known example of this latter type of increasingly sought-out source of information, a kind of pre-news, unsub-stantiated but referred to and trawled by those involved in soft news and hard news. Any component entrepre-neurial support system would need to provide infor-mation along this complete continuum in order to assist yet another feature of the entrepreneur's existence, which is seen to be based on first mover advantage and rapid adaptation. Such features are often cited as major survival and growth characteristics of the entrepreneur. Far less frequently has this characteristic been associated with the ability to access soft news. It could well be argued that as entrepreneurs begin to surf for soft news, their ability to respond to emerging demand will be further enhanced, and with this their ability to survive and grow.

If the classical economic models provide one type of insight into the provision of managed support for the entrepreneur, psychological models of entrepreneurship furnish yet another. The two psychological approaches which have dominated the field are personality devel-opment and learning theory. The first of these perspec-tives reflects the work of McClelland (1961), with additional points of view developed by De Vries (1980).

In the personality development approach, entrepre-neurs are held to behave in certain ways that distinguish them from the general non-entrepreneurial population due to early development experiences, in particular ones that emphasise the abuse of power, unpredictability, loss of control and individual decision-making. Self-employment here emerges as a need driven by individuals' necessity to position themselves so that they always remain in control of their economic life and are never subject to external domination. This perspective identifies a range of defining traits which in broad terms consist of the requirement for achievement, internal locus of control, high propensity for risk-taking, a need for independence and involvement in innovative behaviour, a determined compulsive creativity, with time perceived as a fast-moving precious commodity.

From a more positive viewpoint, Koa (1989) has argued

that this development perspective, grounded in Freudian /Kleinian assumption about the determinant qualities of early childhood experiences, was not sufficient. Rather he argued that a more Jungian explanation could also be found which laid emphasis on middle-life development, and looked at enterprise creation as part of a reformation of goals, once major life achievements had been met, such as career success and the raising of family. A similar approach, if underdeveloped, is to be seen in Maslow's 'Hierarchy of Needs' approach which, simply stated, argues that the requirement for creativity only emerges after other more central needs such as physical survival and safety ones have been satisfied. Maslow never went on to examine the role that enterprise creation might play in satisfying such requirements, but it is clear that entrepreneurial activity might well provide such a vehicle.

Timmens (1985) contributes yet another distinctive approach to the psychological understanding of entre-preneurship, namely learning theory. He questions what it is in the area of learning that distinguishes a successful entrepreneur from one who fails. Focussing on internal dynamics, he suggests that the way the entrepreneur learns from failure is the critical distinguishing feature. To learn, he notes the entrepreneur must have some means of identifying the steps involved in leading to failure decisions as opposed to successful ones, some common basis for comparing and contrasting and referring.

From a support systems perspective, what could the response be to these main psychological approaches to understanding entrepreneurial behaviour? It is clear that in some instances there is overlap. For example, the need for achievement translated into enterprise support terms could well demand access to a decision database, as could the learning theory approach. Both could be seen to be positively responsive to support which offered the possibility of building in achievement milestones and decision trails. There is also a style issue here. How can the support systems give feedback in a way that does not demotivate the recipient? And, realistically, the news may well be bad as well as terrifying, particularly given the informed gambling style of the entrepreneur.

This may also be a parameter question. For example, certain Small Business advisors will argue that entrepre-neurs need supporting early in their activities and to be guided before they get into serious trouble. But who decides what is serious? Then there are the internal locus of control aspects. The populist image of the entre-preneur as tyrant, controlling everything, appearing everywhere and creating systems that carry out his every whim, suggests that supporting such an individual can be fraught. The psychological trait approach taken by McClelland (1961) endorses this view of the entrepreneur as dictator, controlling in a hierarchical way, insisting that all decision-making and information flow from and return to him. This type of decision-making style and organizational form is seen as distinguishing the entrepreneur from the manager. For the external support strategist there are two challenges, how to mimic the entrepreneur's style of behaviour so that the support system developed becomes acceptable, and how to extend the power and range of the one-person focus system so that the entrepreneur is motivated to learn how to use the support offered, perceiving it as a way of extending his control. As the literature clearly shows, entrepreneurs like risk-taking. But they are not risk takers to the point of destruction. Therefore, the more they can reduce risk by having access to superior sources of information, that is information that is more rapidly accessed and is more relevant than the commentators, then the happier they will be. Translated into support-system delivery, this means a requirement for access to customized information related directly to the interests of the entrepreneur. It may well be that here again the distinction between hard news and rumour also holds good. The entrepreneur will need access both to routine information as well as to emerging trends, both types of information will impact on his decision-making ability and therefore his capacity to sustain risk.

But should we be discussing external provision at all? Entrepreneurs, according to the trait school, having had negative experiences in their youth, abhor dependence. From this it follows that the more a system can allow direct access and control, the better. Shifting information support on-line was a major feature of the USA Small Business Administration strategy in the 1990s. This has helped to match the need for high levels of independence associated with entrepreneurial populations. Such a move received further impetus with the G7 initiative on the global SME (1997–99). Thus working through public-sector Small Business agencies has reconceptualized the delivery of external enterprise support as being primarily on-line. With this shift has emerged the aspiration to create external support systems that appear as far as possible as extensions of the entrepreneur, accessible only to him or his designates, and hostile to all potential invaders. In addition, it offers significant possibilities for localization and individualization.

A further major obstacle to the up-take of enterprise support systems lies in our current ignorance as to how entrepreneurs learn. In terms of external provision of support, the dominant intervention role in use stems from a deficit perspective. From this perspective, entrepreneurs need to catch up with the good practice currently in evidence in big business. Current styles of intervention developed have therefore been task- not process-oriented, with a focus on providing training for those particular skills and tasks defined as being important for the effective running of business, all of

which are seen as generic, and for which read 'large business'. A good example of this approach would be the development of face-to-face and stand-alone and networked applications of support systems such as book-keeping, business planning, liquidity debt control systems and stock inventory. What is now emerging is an understanding that learning, and with it up-take of support, needs to be far more processual and contextually based (Hunt 1994). To understand this more clearly, one could do worse than start from a proposition basis. Proposition entrepreneurs who become task-oriented are more likely to fail. Therefore, systems that only support task functions ill serve the entrepreneur. Research suggests that effective support systems for entrepreneurs need to assist processes within cultural contexts rather than tasks. Proposition entrepreneurs who are process-oriented are more successful. From this it follows that learning rather than tasks should be at the core of any support system for entrepreneurs in the heritage sector.

Approaching a support system, one needs to raise questions such as how far does the system support key issues in the learning and development process? How far are functional facilities linked to learning, via training, tracking and feedback systems? Does the functional approach link to process, in other words, an over-arching understanding which brings together all the functional elements as part of the development of co-ordination skills and judgement, a process approach? Overall, how far does the system provide reflective facilities for the entrepreneur? And having done all that, how do you sell the support system to the entrepreneur, motivating her both to take the initial step and to continue to use the system?

The marketing aspects stemming from the adoption of such on-line entrepreneurial ICT support systems have been little examined, yet there is surely a link. De Vries (1980) argues that entrepreneurs appear most like impresarios, leading and co-ordinating in a very flamboyant manner. It is clear from the literature that entrepreneurs like the image associated with that word and are therefore attracted to activities which reinforce the impresario idea. From a systems support point of view, these cultural features surely translate into marketing features. For example, in terms of persuading the entrepreneur to commit to on-line delivered support and to a particular system, how far does an emphasis on innovation become part of the sales pitch? To what extent does the marketing strategy aim to stress the fit between innovative technology and entrepreneurial cultures with its positive affirmation on innovation? How far does the marketing copy enhance the image of the entrepreneur as an innovator at the leading edge? How far does the system motivate the entrepreneur to learn to use it by offering him new challenges to overcome?

CONCLUSION

The concepts of heritage and entrepreneurship share many core attributes. Both affirm change and the positive nature of enquiry. Each is concerned with communicating new insights to end-users. Both act as brokers linking disparate elements to achieve a new creative synthesis. Both are positive players in their areas of thrills, spills and fun, the area of entertainment spanning both popular and elitist cultures, in the current period of profound technological change. The development of more accessible and powerful ICT is opening up new possibilities to access more effectively and closely defined aspects of heritage involving more globally scattered participants. Possibilities for new types of heritage product, and with that new types of heritage craft, will emerge from this development. It is easy to understand how, in the early days of the Irish state, the need to reformulate heritage was seen as a vital political activity to be defined centrally and supported publically. In a more assured period, as government moves from central provider to regulator, the development and provision of heritage, it may be argued, can be better managed though the creation and regulation of a positive environment for heritage activities. That means that it is the entrepreneur, the flamboyant, creative, resource-finding, risk-taking intermediary of the enterprise models, who becomes the energizing force in heritage. And here both entrepreneur and government come together. Because if, for the entrepreneur, the central processes are creativity and the management of risk, for government the central heritage task is the creation and management of an environment that encourages risk, stimulates resources and preserves and promotes cultural sources.

Bibliography

Brockhouse, R. 1980 'Risk-taking propensities of entrepreneurs', *Academy of Management Journal* **23**, 3, pp. 500–09.

Cantillon, R. 1775 *Essai sur la nature du commerce in générale*, ed. H. Higgs (London).

Freeman, R., Soete, P. 1985 'Information and organisational change in the thinking organisation' in H. P. Simms (ed) *Dynamics of organisational social cognition* (London), pp. 80–95.

G7 1999 *Collected papers: G7 electronic commerce conferences*, Bonn, 7–9 April 1997. Dallas.

Goldfinger, C. 1994 *L'utile et le futile: l'économie de l'immateriel*. Paris.

Government of Ireland 1994 *Task force on small business*. Dublin.

Handy, C. 1984 *Understanding organisations*, 2nd ed. Harmondsworth.

Hebert, R. F. 1982 *The entrepreneur: mainstream views and radical critiques*. New York.

Hilt, L. and Brynjolfsson, E. 1997 'Information technology and international forms of organisation: an exploratory analysis', *Journal of Management Information Systems* **14**, 2, pp. 725–47.

Hunt, D. 1994 *Telematic trading: towards the global SME*. Babson. Boston.

De Vries, M. 1980 *The entrepreneurial personality: organisational paradoxes*. London.

Koa, J. J. 1989 *Entrepreneurship, creativity and organisation*. New York.

Kritzner, I. M. 1973 *Competition and entrepreneurship*. Chicago.

McClelland, D. C. 1961 *The achieving society*. Princeton, New Jersey.

National Advisory Council on Teleworking 1999 *New ways of living and working: teleworking in Ireland*. Dublin.

Marx, K. and Engles, F. [1976] *Collected works*. London.

OECD (Organisation for Economic Cooperation and Development) 1998 *Fostering entrepreneurship*. Paris.

Scottish Enterprise 1993 *Scottish business birth rate: a national enquiry*. Glasgow.

Timmons, J. A. 1985 *New venture creation: a guide to entrepreneurship*, 2nd ed. Irving, Illinois.

Zuboff, S. 1988 *In the age of the smart machine: the future of work and power*. New York.

The Irish Music Industry

PAULA CLANCY

This chapter describes the history, industry structure and performance of Irish popular music and examines the implications for its future as an important element of Ireland's economy. Following a brief description of the evolution of Irish popular music and an analysis of both the structure of the industry which has emerged and the level of success achieved, the paper discusses the sources of this success and analyses the constraints on current and future competitiveness. The study forms part of an extensive research project commissioned by the National Economic and Social Council (Clancy and Twomey 1997). The popular Irish music industry dates back to the late 1960s and early 1970s. It is widely regarded as one of our most important cultural enterprises with internationally successful Irish popular music artists such as U2, Enya, Van Morrison and Sinéad O'Connor chief amongst our biggest exports. The industry is most commonly defined as consisting of a number of smaller sub-sectors, including not only artists and record companies but also publishers, promoters, managers and activities associated with recording, live music and retailing. In this article, the music industry is more narrowly conceived of as comprising the originators of the music product, which in turn is defined as the musical composition, its live performance and the recording made of it. Using this definition, the originators are both the artist and record company. Other components are treated as part of either the industry's supplier or buyer chain.

INDUSTRY HISTORY
GLOBAL CONTEXT
The music industry is 'one integral component of an increasingly global network of inter-connected leisure and entertainment industries' (Negus 1992, 1). Its domination by a few multidimensional large corporations has been one of its characteristic features since the 1920s. Through a series of mergers and acquisitions, the names changed throughout the twentieth century, but the global structure has remained essentially the same (Negus 1992). The recording industry was initially formed in North America and Europe. This is where key manufacturing operations and retail practices evolved and where artistic and commercial policies developed. The activities of transnational corporations have been concentrated within a 'triad' composed of the US, Europe and Japan. The majority of the world production and consumption takes place there. The dominant markets for popular music are also in these regions. Recently, Europe has overtaken the US as the biggest market, while the fastest-growing markets are in Asia (IFPI 1995). The location of hardware manufacturing plants and software recording facilities follows this pattern. The global production and consumption of popular music are now defined by the North Atlantic Anglo-American cultural movements of sounds and images, and European, US and Japanese dominance of finance and music hardware (Negus 1992, 14).

THE IRISH POPULAR MUSIC INDUSTRY
The Irish popular music industry dates back to the late 1960s and early 1970s. Prior to then popular music in Ireland comprised concerts of light classical works and variety shows, Irish traditional music as exemplified by the activities of organizations such as Comhaltas Ceoltóirí Éireann and Gael Linn as well as folk and jazz music — all of these having a very small specialist following. Very little of this activity was of any economic significance. While there was an established local demand for traditional music, particularly in rural areas, even the best-known and most accomplished traditional exponents were unable to earn a living as performers (Richards 1976). Popular dance music was provided by showbands during the 1950s and 1960s, and consisted primarily of cover versions of hit songs from the UK and the US. This latter type was purely domestic in nature but it did enjoy huge popularity. It also provided signif-

icant employment. Industry sources indicate that, during the relevant period, there were over 500 seven-piece bands and over 50 four-piece groups with support staff in the country.

Up to the mid-1970s, recordings made in Ireland concentrated on traditional music and poetry and were confined purely to the domestic market. Those Irish acts with aspirations to international success in rock music, many of which composed their own music, were forced to leave Ireland, both because of the dominance of the showbands and also because of the absence of any infrastructure in Ireland to support their development. Well-known examples include Rory Gallagher, Van Morrison, Thin Lizzy and the Boomtown Rats. There was little outlet for Irish rock music, with very few clubs where rock bands could play. The recording studios were not of sufficient standard to compete internationally and the showbands monopolized radio play. The big international bands were not attracted to play in Ireland and there was no local supporting infrastructure in the form of promoters and agents. Notwithstanding this vacuum, the success abroad of bands and artists such as Thin Lizzy provided embryonic rock bands in Ireland with inspiration and confidence. The actions of two individual bands, Horslips and the Boomtown Rats, both of which launched their careers in Dublin, and in the case of Horslips remained committed to winning international success from a Dublin base, are regarded as being influential in the development of the nascent Irish popular music industry. Each was important in a different way: the Boomtown Rats in demonstrating the capability of Irish acts to compete successfully in the UK and, subsequently, the US, with little prior domestic success, and Horslips in revealing that international success was achievable from an Irish base.

In the late 1970s, there were a series of key and parallel developments: the formation of the Irish rock band U2, who went on to become one of the biggest global successes in popular music; the launch of the music magazine *Hot Press*; the proliferation of pirate radio stations; the Dave Fanning Rock Show on the national radio station, 2FM, and the opening of Windmill Lane Recording Studios.

In the 1980s, U2 dominated the global popular music market, creating a climate of openness to and interest in Irish bands as a promising source of international musical repertoire. There was now a developing domestic infrastructure of the different components of the music industry supporting a growing number of local young bands and artists, although these still had little capacity to compete internationally. By the 1980s, all of the six major record companies (for which see below) were represented by subsidiaries here in Ireland, although their principal function was to develop the small Irish market as an outlet for international reper-

toire. Nevertheless, there was some development of local Irish repertoire, principally for sale in the domestic market.

The rock band U2 is regarded as key to the evolution of some of these elements of the Irish infrastructure to a level capable of competing internationally. For example, top international acts came to record and rehearse in Ireland because of a desire to work in Windmill Lane, the Irish recording studios used by U2. The group also used Irish crews when they toured abroad, thus enabling Irish sound engineers, stage engineers and roadies to gain international experience. Subsequent to U2 a number of Irish rock acts have achieved international success: Sinéad O'Connor, Enya, The Cranberries and more recently Boyzone, The Corrs and Westlife.

In addition to developments in the rock and pop genres, Irish traditional and folk music progressed in parallel, often crossing the boundary between folk and popular music, although not achieving the levels of success of the small number of rock acts. In the 1960s, there was a resurgence of interest in the traditional/folk genre, much of which was due to the work of organizations such as Comhaltas Ceoltóirí Éireann. In this genre artists such as Seán Ó Riada, The Dubliners, Planxty and The Chieftains achieved a degree of international success. Artists currently associated with this genre, Mary Black, Christy Moore, Clannad and others, have been able to build sustainable careers in popular music, relying heavily on the local market but also achieving significant record sales in other markets, principally the UK, the US and Germany.

INDUSTRY STRUCTURE AND PERFORMANCE
STRUCTURE
The indigenous Irish music industry is characterized as a set of primarily small-scale activities operated /controlled by a relatively small number of firms and individuals. **Fig. 68.1** sets out the structure of the industry as this is most commonly conceived in industry reports and discussion. It identifies a chain of activity from the initial point of music creation through to when the music product, either via live performance or recorded music, reaches the end-user. In practice, the business of making music is more complex and varied than this figure represents. For example, while composers and performers can and often are two separate activities, it is now the norm for composers to perform their own music. Similarly, performers may launch a record by forming their own record company and an increasing number of performers retain control of their own publishing. The manager, crucial to the artists' career development, may be recruited subsequent to a band securing a record contract with a company, while the producer, a key figure in the recording process, may be employed by the artist rather

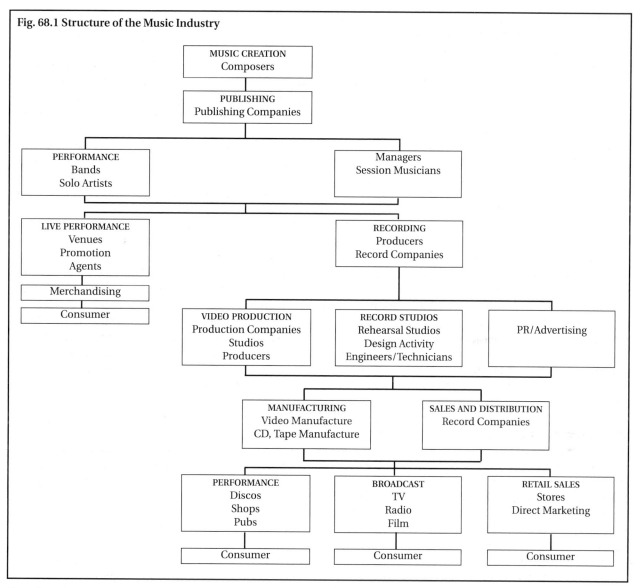

Fig. 68.1 Structure of the Music Industry

than the record company.

The artists — the songwriters and performers of music — are at once both the industry's core inputs and outputs as well as the primary source of value in the Irish context. The musical product is both the starting point of an industrial process as well as its final outcome (Frith 1987). The record company is also key to the industrial process in that it is the main mover in the chain of activity which transforms music into the recorded product.

ARTISTS

Economically viable artists in the Irish industry are commonly divided into three tiers: international artists, including the band U2, Enya, The Cranberries, Boyzone, Van Morrison and Sinéad O'Connor; middle-sector acts, for example, Mary Black, Eleanor McEvoy and Francis Black primarily serving the domestic market but with some export activity, and 'Irish' local music produced for the domestic audience only.

It can be estimated with reasonable certainty that there are fewer than sixty Irish artists signed to one of the labels owned or controlled by the 'big six' international record companies, of which around half are signed to the subsidiaries located here in Ireland. In addition, there are a number of Irish artists who are signed to independent labels. However, while signing a record contract is a necessary first step towards building a reputation either in the domestic or international markets, it is no guarantee of success. In practice the industry world-wide is high risk with a very high failure rate. It is estimated that just one in eight of the artists signed to one of the majors achieves success (Negus 1992, 40) and each year only a handful of new artists, sourced from any nationality, is signed with one of the global record companies. The market saturation with new records, the emphasis on reproducing back catalogues and the global strategy of the majors to create 'the total star' means that opportunities for new artists, including Irish artists, are very poor.

RECORD COMPANIES

The structure of the Irish record company industry is one of domination by six overseas organizations, namely, Bertelsmann Music Group (BMG), EMI Music, Polygram, MCA Music, Sony Music Entertainment Inc. and Warner Music Group, which control 80% of the domestic market, reflecting their position in the global market. There are also a handful of smaller, partially or wholly foreign-owned companies and a large number of small indigenous independent record companies. Each of the six majors is part of a larger corporate structure involved in other related industries. Each is also characterized by enormous financial resources and capital mobility, capable of funding aggressive growth strategies. The combination of capital intensity with market internationalization (the majority of European markets are dominated by international pop and classical music) means that economies of scale are both critical and achievable in manufacturing, distribution and retail. For example, for UK record labels, the revenue from sales to the rest of the world, particularly to North America and Europe, is a more important source of income than domestic sales. Revenue from British sales alone is often not sufficient to cover the overheads and costs involved.

All of the 'big six' major record corporations have subsidiaries in Ireland, established for at least ten years. Many are here considerably longer, for example EMI have had a subsidiary in Ireland since 1960. Initially, these subsidiaries were involved in manufacturing (which ceased about twenty years ago) as well as distribution. Sony, which operated as CBS Records until 1987, has been in Ireland for more than twenty-five years. Until the 1990s, these subsidiaries were little more than distribution depots and marketing wings of the UK company. In addition, there are a small number of wholly or part foreign-owned independent companies.

There is a limited number of smaller foreign-owned companies also with branches located in Ireland and there is a large number of small independent record companies, the great majority of which are cottage industries, employing fewer than five people, with many employing only one person. The principal function of many of these is to launch records on behalf of acts/solo artists who are unable to win a record contract with an established company. Barriers to entry to the industry at this level are low. The failure rate of indigenous record companies is estimated to be high. If an independent company becomes successful, usually because of its success with a single act, it is vulnerable to take-over by a 'major' or by a large foreign-owned independent.

Export activity for the small company is crucial, given the small size of the Irish market. Industry sources indicate that absolute export activity is extremely limited. Smaller companies with limited financial and marketing resources have difficulty in developing export markets fully (IFPI 1993). Traditionally, the export market has been confined to countries with strong Irish affiliations such as the UK, the US and Australia. However, the international market has been extended by traditional artists such as The Chieftains and Clannad. It is suggested that their experimentation with different instruments and other musical disciplines has led to the development of new markets for Irish music in other countries such as Germany and Sweden (IFPI 1993).

INDUSTRY PERFORMANCE

There is evidence to support the contention that Ireland has achieved considerable comparative success in terms of the number of internationally successful artists quite out of proportion to the size of the country's population. However, it is difficult to estimate the economic contribution of these artists to Ireland. While industry informants suggest that most are Irish residents, the majority are signed to international record companies located in either the UK or the US, with the result that most of the financial benefits accrue to these economies. Stripping out the activities of these 'stars', the picture of the Irish music industry is one of more limited development. Given its structure comprising a handful of foreign-owned global record companies and a much larger number of small-scale enterprises, very few indigenous companies are economically viable or can be regarded as competitive. They are hampered by difficulties in relation to capital and access to the necessary export markets.

Industry reports suggest that there is a large pool of talented composers and performers in Ireland (IBEC 1995, 19). However, the very fluid employment profile of the industry makes it difficult to be precise on the numbers employed — popular music bands and solo artists come and go very quickly, a consequence of the relatively low barriers to entry. Indeed, estimates vary widely, due to differences in what is being measured and the ways in which different categories of composers and performers are combined. In addition, regardless of estimates of numbers, few are actually earning an economic wage (Burke 1993, 52). Furthermore, available figures suggest that fewer than 10% of the estimated population of artists have a contract with a record company. Total estimates of employment in all record companies based in Ireland, both domestic and foreign-owned, range between 66 and 250.

The domestic market for recorded music is small in absolute terms, it is dominated by imports and its growth rate, while impressive, lags somewhat behind the global rate and is certainly exceeded by a number of other fast-growing countries and regions. Data on export levels and markets for locally produced recorded music are very sketchy and therefore difficult to draw conclusions from in relation to growth and future prospects. Live performance, exploitation of intellectual property rights and merchandizing are the other major revenue-generating activities of the industry. Again, the picture which emerges is primarily one of potential earning capability, the scale of which is difficult to determine because of the non-availability or unreliability of information.

SOURCES OF SUCCESS AND COMPETITIVE CONSTRAINTS
To the degree that the Irish music industry is successful, taking into account its successful artists, we can identify a small number of sources for this success. There are a number of positive environmental conditions: the fact that we are an English-speaking nation; the development of a 'brand' name for Ireland as an attractive location supported by a range of tax measures and as a source of successful artists, and, a somewhat more contested view, the 'quality' of the Irish environment for music as one conducive to the development of musicians. In addition, the international nature of our domestic market coupled with the extent of the Irish 'diaspora' are argued to be a positive factor.

ENGLISH-SPEAKING
The fact that Ireland is primarily English-speaking is commonly regarded as the most important reason for the comparative international success of Irish artists. The English language is the primary language of global popular music and the first language of the US, the biggest market in the world, which accounts for almost one-third of world record sales. World sales of recordings have always been dominated by those made by both British and North American artists.

However, the continuation of the predominance of English in international repertoire in the future is not certain. There is evidence to suggest that the important future markets will not be primarily English-speaking (MBI 1995; Rutten 1996). This, together with the increasing importance of 'national' musics, is believed to account for a deterioration in the economic performance of the global 'megastar'. It suggests that 'there is a limit to the economic rationale that a global industry should concentrate on providing the same products to as many customers in as many countries as possible' (Rutten 1996, 72).

IRELAND AS BRAND
In many ways 'Ireland Inc.' represents a unique cultural formation and as such has become a brand name, providing benefits to Ireland as a preferred location for international music industry players. The reputation of Ireland also provides access to international markets. Audiences are more receptive to Irish artists and important gatekeepers within the international music industry are more open to them. Ireland's brand name as a location derives from a number of separate but interrelated characteristics. First, the cultural trait of friendliness combined with a respect for privacy creates an attractive environment. Second, there is a perception of Ireland as a fashionable centre for those involved in all aspects of the entertainment industries, including film, music, leisure and fashion design. Third comes Ireland's reputation as a country particularly rich in the arts, historically as well as currently in literature and, more recently, since the advent of U2, in popular music. Fourth, a specific interest in the 'Celtic' influence on music combined with the perceived emphasis on a tradition of live music activity in Ireland (regarded as a major attraction for the tourist industry) is important. Fifth, the sense of Ireland as a non-colonial/imperialist state provides a positive image in some of the important markets, particularly in Europe. Sixth, Ireland's cultural position somewhere between American and English musical culture, provides Irish artists with the advantage of familiarity with the music in these two markets. Seventh, Ireland is currently a tax-friendly environment for composers.

While there is consensus that this 'brand reputation' is a reality, providing actual if intangible benefits to the music industry and beyond that to the tourist industry, its sustainability is somewhat more in doubt. The perception of Ireland as the place to be can easily be destroyed or overtaken by some chance event or fashion trend. Those who argue from this perspective emphasize the need to put in place the necessary infrastructure to support and to underpin the predominantly ephemeral reasons why people chose to locate in Ireland or to be more open to Irish products.

QUALITY OF IRISH POPULAR MUSIC ARTISTS
Notwithstanding the degree of comparative success and indications that Ireland has a higher per capita pool of performers compared to other nations, there is a contested view as to whether Ireland is comparatively richer in the quality of artists. There are those who argue strongly that Ireland possesses an inherited resource in storytelling and in performance which is adapted to provide Irish popular musicians with a natural advantage. However, a number of industry informants insist that the success of U2 is unique, a result of a particular combination of musical talent, management, vision and drive. For those who have achieved international success since U2, such as Sinéad O'Connor, Enya and The Cranberries, a combination of luck and determination is viewed as responsible, although the presence of an indigenous music industry infrastructure and the growing reputation of Ireland as a source of successful acts is deemed to have contributed to their success.

IRISH MARKET DEMAND CONDITIONS

It can be argued that Irish domestic demand conditions, compared to markets other than the dominant UK and US, have a largely positive impact on the competitive advantage of Irish popular music 'stars'. This is because Irish consumer tastes are shaped in large part by international music trends, controlled by global companies based most commonly in the UK and the US. In this sense, the Irish are sophisticated consumers of the dominant genre, the international music repertoire. Because, too, of the international nature of the Irish popular music market, artists can more readily 'cross over' to an international repertoire. The Irish market cannot, however, be regarded as a leader or shaper of demand in other markets, as is reflected in the fact that popular artists still find it necessary to become successful abroad prior to, rather than following, achievement in the local market.

Irish emigrants are more faithful to Irish cultural forms of entertainment than is the case with other nationalities, and thus there is an important audience network in foreign markets, particularly for forms of music associated with traditional and folk genres. In this regard the nearly seventy million people of Irish descent worldwide and the 18% of the US population claiming Irish ancestry suggest that this factor should play a large part in 'pulling' through demand for Irish music. This has important implications as a potentially larger market for the local or national Irish genres which do not 'cross over' to international repertoire, particularly in light of the earlier discussion of the limited opportunities in the Irish market.

COMPETITIVE CONSTRAINTS

The recent and present success of Irish artists, then, is largely attributable to a combination of environmental conditions and to the nature of Irish market demand conditions. However, those conditions which have been shown to be helpful in relation to artist success are an insufficient basis to support the development of the broader indigenous industry and are, indeed, themselves vulnerable to being overtaken by changes in fashion and in consumer tastes for popular music.

FIRM STRATEGY AND STRUCTURE

The artists' primary need is for access to record companies capable of building an international career. This is not present in Ireland because of limited local artist development by the subsidiaries of the majors located here and an absence of domestic companies capable of doing so. The international nature of the popular music industry necessarily drives the competitive strategies of Irish-based record companies, both the subsidiaries of the global companies which dominate the Irish industry and the local independent sector.

Global record companies are increasing their focus on local repertoire in two circumstances. First, they are doing so where there is significant demand in local markets which are of sufficient scale to provide good economic returns. A second reason, and the one which is relevant to Irish conditions, is the development of local artists who have the potential to 'cross over' to other markets (MBI 1995). Nonetheless, development of locally signed artists for the international market by subsidiaries of the 'majors' located in Ireland is extremely limited and, in practice, takes second place to the marketing of acts from Britain and the US.

Local record companies operate in a difficult competitive environment. The predominance of imported international repertoire in the domestic market, combined with the high cost and high risk of investment in artists, particularly in relation to marketing abroad, are only some of the difficulties they face. The small share of the domestic market held by Irish-owned companies is such that access to export markets is crucial and in turn is dependent on resources not at present available to the small indigenous companies, including availability of finance and skills, particularly international marketing. In this regard, co-operative arrangements with firms, especially in other markets, would be helpful, but as yet there is little evidence of significant direct interaction within Ireland, either between independents and the subsidiaries of the majors or between the independents themselves.

WEAKNESS OF SUPPLIER INDUSTRIES

In virtually all cases, successful Irish artists go abroad to sign record contracts. Indeed, the most important factors driving local artists with international potential overseas are the scarcity of strong domestic record companies and the domination of the industry by subsidiaries of the 'majors', whose primary concern is the sale of international repertoire. However, an additional factor is the weakness of important supplier services in Ireland. The categories of supplier services examined comprised publishers, artist management, recording studios, producers, manufacturing/duplication, design/photography, mastering, merchandizing and business and legal services. Some supplier components have a certain degree of international competitiveness. Compared to other countries outside the UK and the US, there is also an impressive rate of growth of the number of entities in supplier industry segments likely to have a depth and level of activity which has contributed to the modest level of success of both local and/or second tier artists and also to some independent companies. However, while most of the important supplier components are present to some degree, the majority of enterprises are small in size, including those industries, for example publishing and manufacturing, where scale is important, and few are commercially viable. The small scale of the Irish market means that indigenous supplier industries require access to export markets for growth, which is at present quite limited. There is also limited use of the available supplier services by the subsidiaries of the 'majors', who, in other circumstances, might have provided indigenous supplier companies with an important and also sophisticated market outlet. Therefore, artists with international potential will still go abroad for access to record and publishing contracts, management and business/legal services. Once these contracts are achieved, other services in these markets are also used, including production and recording as well as marketing and promotion.

Thus, most of the financial benefits from artist success accrue to the economies in which the global record companies, as well as other components, are located. Even to retain the economic benefits which arise as a consequence of artist residency in Ireland depends on a more aggressive promotion of local artist development. The problem which faces the indigenous Irish industry in attempting to translate the presence of successful artists into a sustainable, competitive local music industry rests with the global nature of the industry and the hegemony of the major international music companies which render its strategic direction certainly beyond the control and possibly also the influence of national players and policy intervention.

SIZE AND COMPOSITION OF MARKET DEMAND
In addition to these difficulties, there are a number of other challenges facing the Irish popular music industry. While the international nature of the Irish domestic market for popular music has been identified as having a positive impact on the success of Irish artists, it has the problem of smallness in both absolute and relative terms. It is dominated by imports, such that local artists and local independent record companies are hampered in terms of access to retail and distributions channels as well as the crucially important air play. Its growth rate, while impressive, lags somewhat behind the global rate and is exceeded by a number of other fast-developing countries and regions. Given the global nature of domestic demand, its impact on more 'local' music, that is music which is not likely to 'cross over' to become part of the international repertoire, is less positive. While evidence of increasing diversification of musical tastes may provide significant potential for 'local' music in the future (Rutten 1996), in an industry where scale is a key driving force, the size and potential rate of growth of the Irish market do not of themselves encourage large-scale investment in purely 'local' music. In addition to the problem of small size, the composition of the Irish music market is heavily influenced by international repertoire so that, for the foreseeable future, growth for local artists

and indigenous record companies specializing in 'local' music will continue to depend on export markets, an aspect not, at least as yet, well developed in Ireland. This is notwithstanding the contention that the Irish music industry is facilitated in reaching export audiences through the Irish 'diaspora'.

SKILL SHORTAGES
There are a number of conditions which are important not only to sustain the environment for producing artists of high quality but also for other necessary developments outlined above, and which are absent or poorly developed in Ireland. In addition to the low, albeit increasing, level of investment in the advancement of local artists on the part of the subsidiaries of the 'majors', and the difficulties of access to finance, there is also an underdevelopment of skills in international marketing, other business support services including artist management and specific creative and technical personnel, most importantly producers. Specialized educational facilities appear to be underdeveloped compared with other markets, although a number of industry informants are of the view that many of the skills required in the music industry can be obtained through experience only. Such experience is available only to a limited extent in Ireland because of the small scale of the industry here. Finally, the infrastructure to achieve export market access is important if local artists signed to local record companies are to be successful. As yet, this is still poorly developed in Ireland.

STRATEGIES FOR THE FUTURE?
The argument presented by industry advocacy statements suggests that the solution to the competitive difficulties of the indigenous Irish popular music industry lies in the provision of incentives to encourage local artist development by both subsidiaries of the 'majors' and indigenous companies as well as the fostering of a local infrastructure of supplier industries. For example, the IBEC (1995) report, *Striking the right note*, calls for financial incentives such as allowing double tax deduction of recording costs, the extension of 'Artists' Exemption' to all creative aspects of the music industry and the application of favourable corporate tax rates to more elements of the industry. The report also called for better access for music-related businesses to supports offered by state agencies. Such development would be the means of encouraging continuing local residency of successful Irish artists and in attracting foreign artists and producers to relocate to Ireland. These steps are also important for the 'second tier' of artists, those who remain 'local' in appealing only to the domestic market and to specialized niche export markets, and those who have some 'cross over' appeal internationally. For such artists, the presence of a strong independent sector of

Table 68.1 Components of the Irish Popular Music Industry

	RELATED INDUSTRIES IN IRELAND	
	Tourism	

IMPORTANT IRISH INPUTS		CUSTOMERS IN IRELAND
Publishing Companies		Consumers
Producers/Sound Engineers		Distributors
Public Relations		Retailers
Advertisers	CORE ACTIVITY	Record Stores
Artist Management	Artists	
Promoters/Agents	Record Companies	
Music Event Management		
Manufacturing CDs/Tape		
Duplication		
Studio Design		

	SUPPORTING SERVICES AND ORGANIZATIONS
	State Development Agencies
	Media Marketing Specialists
	Training/Educational Facilities
	Collection Societies
	Trade Associations
	Lobby/Advocacy Groups
	Specialist Music Media

record companies, in addition to the full array of supplier industries, is an important factor in their advancement. Such companies increase the opportunities for aspiring artists and, because of lower initial capital outlay, are also more likely to offer longer lead times to attract consumer interest, a feature which is important for the nurturing of new and innovative music. This second tier of artists also provide the seed bed from which a sustainable, albeit small, number of 'mega' stars will emerge.

As noted from the above discussion, these kinds of development have not as yet taken place on a scale which would give Ireland a competitive advantage. It is possible that this is because Ireland is still at an early stage in the evolution of its music industry. This, indeed, is the implied argument of industry bodies, who point to the expansion of the industry since the 1970s, both in terms of numbers of entities as well as density of activity, to support this view. While it is true that most indigenous record companies and supplier enterprises are struggling as economic entities, their increased activity, combined with the real, if modest, levels of success achieved, has influenced other beneficial developments. These include, for example, the formation of Irish-based trade bodies and advocacy groups and the establishment of an independent national music rights organization. The fact that these are geographically concentrated within the greater Dublin area has facilitated the flow of infor-mation and development of explicit industry strategies for the welfare of the industry. The existence of a limited number of specialized courses and tax incentives and state-supported international marketing is more than likely a result, at least in part, of pressure from trade associations and other advocacy and lobby groups comprising representatives of the different industry segments (see **Table 68.1**).

The brand reputation of Ireland as a centre for popular music is partly an outcome of the international success of a number of Irish stars and is also likely to be a contributing factor in their decision to continue to live in Ireland. Thus, it seems reasonable to suggest that, if Ireland is to maintain its brand reputation as an attractive location and also to reproduce and develop its music industry as an important element of its economic and cultural life, it is important to retain its interna-tionally successful Irish artists as resident in Ireland, accepting that these stars will continue to link into the global music industry. Second, in order to build on the existing image and brand reputation of Ireland, it is important to provide an environment which is conducive to the emergence of a sustainable flow of artists. The presence of a local network of viable local record companies, some supplier industries and a support infrastructure consisting of a combination of tax incentives, educational facilities and market access insti-tutions is likely to be necessary for this, at least at the early stages of an artist's development.

POLICY IMPLICATIONS

Does it then make strategic sense for industrial policy to support the continued development of a music industry in Ireland? The argument for support rests not only on the economic value of the music industry and the need to enhance the conditions under which that economic value is realized, but also on interdependent collective positive externalities, provided through the existence of a robust music industry (Durkan 1994). A strong argument for a policy of continued support to the industry is its contribution, albeit intangible and difficult to quantify, to Ireland's 'brand' reputation as an attractive location. This is of most importance to the tourism industry, but also to those economic sectors dependent on foreign investment and the related capability to attract and retain skilled able people in the economy (Durkan 1994; O'Hagan and Duffy 1987).

What, then, is needed for industry development? Given the international nature of the industry and its domination by global companies, government initiatives are likely to have only a minor influence. Some measures have already been taken to assist the industry, primarily a range of tax incentives intended to promote the continued residence of artists here in Ireland. There are also tax schemes to encourage capital investment in firms and artist development. As it seems likely that these have had a positive influence on industry progress to date, they should be continued. Direct support for local artist development is now provided in other countries and is widely regarded as crucial to the sustainability of the industry.

Provision for a general arts education in primary and second level curricula is widely regarded as inadequate. For music to be rooted in society in such a way as to foster new and innovative talent, a knowledge and appreciation of music in all its forms is important. Similarly, major gaps have been identified in what might be termed the business education of those working in the industry, particularly marketing, finance and law.

Industry informants argue that to facilitate an increase in development of artists locally and to attract industry players of world stature, Ireland needs to bring its supplier and supporting industries to international, if not world-class status. However, direct government support for this strategy must be considered carefully in light of the international nature of the industry and the mobility inherent in many of these industry segments.

Despite the degree of geographic proximity and the small scale of the Irish industry, there is little evidence of the emergence of the kind of direct relationships between independent record companies or between independent record companies and the local subsidiaries of the 'majors' in the domestic market which has been identified as important for artist development. Furthermore, the international nature of the industry creates a requirement for trans-national linkages of all kinds. While there is evidence of a number of such linkages, their development carries heavy resource implications which, at present, act as a constraint on their development. An added difficulty is the lack of clarity in the literature on how, and in what circumstances, intervention to foster cooperation is successful (Staber 1996). These issues suggest that a more proactive but experimental approach to promoting and facilitating various kinds of linkages should be considered.

Bibliography

Burke, A. 1993 *Tune innovation and the supply of composer-entrepreneurs*, IMRO Report No. 2, Services Industries Research Centre, University College, Dublin.

Clancy, P. and Twomey, 1997 *Clusters in Ireland: the Irish popular music industry: an application of Porter's cluster analysis*, NESC Research Series, Paper No. 2. Dublin.

Durkan, J. 1994 *The economics of the arts in Ireland*. Dublin.

Frith, S. 1987 'The industrialisation of popular music' in J. Lull. (ed) *Popular music and communications* (Newbury Park), pp. 53–77.

International Federation of the Phonographic Industry (IFPI) 1994 *The recording industry in Europe*. London.

Irish Business and Employers Confederation (IBEC) 1995 *Striking the right note: a submission to government on the development of the Irish music industry*. Dublin.

Music Business International (MBI) 1995 *MBI world report 1995*. London.

Negus, K. 1992 *Producing pop: culture and conflict in the popular music industry*. London.

O'Hagan, J. W. and Duffy C. T. 1987 *The performing arts and the public purse: an economic analysis*. Dublin.

Richards, J. M. 1976 *Provision for the arts*. Dublin.

Rutten, P. 1996 'Global sounds and local brews: musical developments and music industry in Europe' in European Music Office (EMO) *Music in Europe* (Brussels).

Simpson Xavier Horwath Consulting (SXH) 1994 *A strategic vision for the Irish music industry*. Dublin.

Staber, U. 1996 'Networks and regional development: perspectives and unresolved issues' in U. H. Staber, N. V. Schaefer and B. Sharma (eds) *Business networks for prospects for regional development* (Berlin and New York), pp. 1–22.

Airline Deregulation and Tourism

TONY BARLOW AND MARK O'BOYLE

As a small peripheral island, Ireland's ability to trade with the outside world is heavily dependent on the quality of its air and sea transport links. Inevitably, from the foundation of the state successive governments paid considerable attention to the development of those links. As far as the airline industry was concerned, this was to be done by having a strong state-owned airline which would look after the nation's interest (Share 1986). The late 1980s, however, saw a significant change in Irish civil aviation policy. Important as it was, mere provision would no longer suffice for Ireland's needs. The cost of exporting had to be reduced and this included transport costs.

Nowhere was this more true than in the case of tourism, where the consumer was transported to the 'product' and not vice-versa. Something had to be done to boost this major job-creating industry. The apparent success of US airline deregulation in reducing fares seemed to suggest a way of improving the competitiveness of the Irish tourism product. As a consequence, support for airline liberalization in the European Community (later the European Union) and elsewhere became a linchpin of Irish transport and tourism policy. This chapter will attempt to assess the degree to which it was successful, based on results from a series of simple econometric models. As such the paper provides an illustration of the way in which economic analysis may contribute to the appraisal of tourism policy. The econometric estimates upon which the results are based are reported in Barlow and O'Boyle (1998).

In Section 1, the structure of regulation and deregulation by the Irish government and its rationale for both is reviewed. Section 2 discusses the factors which give rise to the level of airfares. This involves the discussion of the econometric model, with an examination of the variables considered to be appropriate therein. This is followed by an investigation of the results of the study. In Section 3 there is a review of the variables appropriate to the investigation of the level of tourist demand. Section 4 examines the results of the estimates obtained from using the tourism models. This is all part of an attempt to measure the success or otherwise of deregulation of the airline industry for tourists in the Irish case. Section 5 concludes with a discussion of policy implications and an assessment of the outlook for the liberalization of European Union policy.

REGULATION AND DEREGULATION

Given its small size, population and its relative poverty, the development of civil aviation in Ireland was surprisingly rapid. This was aided by its geographical position at the western edge of Europe, making it ideal as a refuelling stop for early transatlantic propeller-driven passenger aircraft. The Irish government saw the development of aviation links with Europe and North America as crucial to the economic advancement of the country itself. As a result, by 1936, only three years after France, Ireland had its own semi-state airline, Aer Lingus. Aer Lingus itself was jointly owned by British European Airways, a nationalized UK airline (itself a precursor to the privatized British Airways). Like most of its European counterparts, Aer Lingus was protected from the full rigours of competition by the Air Navigation Order of 1935. This empowered the relevant minister to prohibit international flights to and from Ireland 'with a view to the limitation or regulation of competition as may be considered necessary in the public interest'.

Over the years, Ireland developed air links with other countries in Europe and elsewhere. In each case, competition was regulated by bi-lateral agreements between the two states involved. These agreements were wide-ranging in their scope: limiting market entry, fixing capacity and restricting price competition. The 1946 Irish-French agreement (Dept of Foreign Affairs 1946) was typical of the agreements that governed air routes to and from Ireland and most countries in Europe. Airlines on the route had to be designated by one or other government. Capacity, or the number of seats offered, was to be fixed by the 'competent aeronautical authorities' and divided equally unless the airlines agreed differently. Fares were to be fixed by the airlines on the advice of the International Air Traffic Association (IATA).

Far from encouraging competition, these arrangements appear to have created a framework for the airlines to formulate their own commercial agreements. According to the European Civil Aviation Conference report (1981), these did not just include the capacity, scheduling and pricing issues mentioned in bi-lateral agreements. They also included arrangements to act as the agents of each other in ticketing and baggage handling. Many also agreed to pool and share their revenues on particular routes. The combined result of the agreements by the airlines and governments of Europe was that the same report found that only 2% of European international routes had more than one airline per state, and between 75% and 85% of tonne-kilometres were operated under revenue-pooling agreements.

The situation was no different on the routes between Ireland and the UK. Indeed, the Anglo-Irish bi-lateral agreement of the time went so far as to specify Aer Lingus, BEA and, later, British Airways *by name*. Despite the fact that since 1966 the latter had sold its remaining stake in Aer Lingus, both maintained revenue-sharing, ticketing and baggage handling arrangements on top of the restrictions on competition imposed by the bi-lateral agreement. As one Aer Lingus representative put it (quoted in Share 1986), 'circumstances made it sensible for the two parties to get together in their mutual interest and to work as closely as possible on common problems'. The post-war bi-lateral agreements between Ireland and most of the countries with which it had air links intended that fares should remain at what the Irish-French agreement (Dept of Foreign Affairs 1946) described as 'reasonable levels, with particular regard to economy of operation, normal profits and the characteristics of the service'. Unfortunately, since it was the government (in effect the shareholders) who decided what was reasonable, little was done to keep fares down. Indeed, even if the governments had wished to control fare levels, it would be difficult to do so, given that the airlines tended not to furnish them with the information required to set such a reasonable fare (Barrett 1990).

To make matters worse, as Douglas and Miller (1972) noted in their study on regulation of the US airline industry, regulation tended to discourage cost cutting by the airlines, leading to higher fares and inefficiency. With most means of competition restricted by either government or commercial agreement, the airlines tended instead to increase expenditure on associated items such as decor, steward uniforms and food. This put pressure on margins and ultimately fares. In the Irish

case, this 'inefficiency' manifested itself in a monopoly transfer in the form of abnormally high wage costs, with Aer Lingus having among the third-highest wage costs of OECD airlines, according to Barrett (1990). This contrasted sharply with the position of the UK airlines which were operated on competitive internal routes.

However, as the demand for foreign holidays among lower-income groups rose in Europe and North America during the 1970s and 1980s, the position of regulation in Ireland became untenable. Scheduled carriers could not hope to meet this demand and maintain their increasingly expensive forms of non-price competition. Inevitably, there were those who found ways to circumvent the regulations. In the UK especially, charter companies (which were only intended to cater for travelling groups) invented bogus 'clubs' in order to supply cheap holidays to the ever eager public (Holloway 1988). In line with theory, moreover, the benefits of breaking the rules of this cartel also proved too tempting for the airlines themselves. They used so-called 'bucket-shops' to offer unfilled seats on off-peak scheduled flights, increasing their load factor and margins, since the bulk of costs associated with a particular flight (labour, airport fees, wear and tear and a large proportion of fuel costs) have to be spent regardless of the number of passengers on board. If an airline can increase the number of seats filled or the load factor on a flight, it can boost its margins on that journey. In some cases tickets were selling at 70-75% of their normal price (Airline Users Committee 1976). Under such conditions, it was becoming increasingly difficult to justify the high fare levels on most routes.

The 1980s also saw the growing acceptance of contestability theory among influential economists and policy makers in the US and later in Europe. Traditional economic theory suggests that because in an industry such as the airlines route network economies favour larger companies in an oligopolistic or monopolistic market, it may be necessary to regulate it in order to prevent abuses. Contestability theory, on the other hand, proposes that oligopolistic or monopolistic markets may not be detrimental to the interests of the consumer, if entry into and exit from that market are perfectly free. In such a market the mere threat of entry by a lower-price or more efficient new entrant will ensure that it is in the interests of the incumbent company to keep its prices at a competitive level. The principal contestability theorists, Baumol Panzer and Willig (1988), put it that an aircraft was 'capital on wings', allowing it to move virtually unhindered from city-pair market to city-pair market in a deregulated environment. The 'city-pair market' is a term used in transport economics to refer to the market for a service in the two cities or towns at the ends of the route served. As a consequence, this should deter monopoly pricing even on routes which have low

Table 69.1 London-Dublin and Major Routes ex-London compared by Passenger Growth 1980–85 (ranked by Passenger Growth)

Destination	Passenger nos 1985 (000s)	Load factor	Fares increase 1980–85 (%)*	Passenger growth (%)
Edinburgh	1,033.9	62.7	31.9	58.3
Manchester	869.1	59.8	45.5	41.9
Glasgow	1,080.8	62.6		40.4
Frankfurt	997.4	70.6	31.9	40.1
Aberdeen	460.3	64.6	43.2	34.5
Belfast	895.3	60.8	29.2	30.7
Average	*980.1*	*65.5*	*43.7*	*29.9*
Amsterdam	1,312.5	70.8	38.5	24.1
Brussels	719	61.7	43.6	20.4
Paris	2,438.3	73.9	63.2	17.1
Dublin	994.3	75.2	72.6	2.8

Source: *Barrett (1990) from Civil Aviation Authority, Paper 87005: Competition on the main domestic trunk routes*

*The increase in the UK Retail Price Index for the same period was 41.5%.

traffic densities and are thus served by virtual monopolies (Bailey 1981; Kahll 1979). As Baumol, Panzar and Willig (1988) stated: 'the intellectual foundations of (US) deregulation of the airlines, trucking and buses, includes the recognition of the power of potential entry'.

During the same period, the shortcomings of airline regulation were also a cause for concern in Ireland's tourist industry with the uncompetitive air fares only exacerbating the situation. Whereas Mediterranean destinations, in particular, benefited from the availability of cheap fares from charter companies' bogus 'clubs' and 'bucket-shop' ticket sales, Ireland with its stringent regulations did not. Even on other northern European routes, where these types of fares were less readily available, charter flights were forcing scheduled carriers to lower prices, whereas fares to Ireland remained uncompetitive. This is clear from **Table 69.I** above, which shows that not only had the London-Dublin route the highest increase in fares but also the worst rate of passenger growth during the period immediately before deregulation. The table, which has been taken from Barrett (1990), has been ordered to highlight the lack of passenger growth on the London-Dublin route. Evidence of inefficiency is also apparent from the fact that load factors on the Dublin route were the highest and should therefore give airlines flying it a cost advantage. A Price Waterhouse (1987) study carried out on behalf of the Irish government also found air fares to Ireland to be uncompetitive. It suggested that greater pricing flexibility and licences for new routes and for new airlines should be granted.

AIR FARES

Economic theory suggests that, with a given state of technology, price is a function of cost and the factors pertaining to the market. In an attempt to capture these factors in a simple model, the cost incurred by the airlines in providing their service and the degree of competition between them were used. Although the determination of both fares and tourism demand from North America, Europe and UK was investigated, this chapter will concentrate on the last market because it represents the furthest extreme of deregulation as carried out in Ireland. The equation consisted of a dependent variable (the air fare on a given route) and a number of independent variables (measuring the degree of competition on a route and the cost incurred in flying it). The relevant variables are discussed in turn.

Although the air fare is the dependent variable in the fares' equation, it is also one of the independent variables that are believed to influence tourism demand. The same raw data were used in both sets of equations. In terms of the tourism equations, few previous studies had used such a variable over time (Artus 1972; Stronge 1983 and Summary 1987). While Artus and Stronge only used transatlantic fares published by the US Department of Commerce, no similar data were published for either the UK or the rest of Europe. Instead, it was decided to follow an approach similar to that followed by Summary (1987) in her study of tourism demand in Kenya. She used an average of fares on a number of routes for European markets, whereas in our study a weighted average of fares to Dublin from Paris, Frankfurt, Amsterdam and Milan was used. Summary employed the fares from London and New York as 'gateway' routes from the UK and US respectively. Where a number of airports serve a single city, it is nevertheless considered as one airport system. Thus, 'London' here refers to all four major airports in operation at the time (Heathrow, Gatwick, Luton and Stansted). Similarly for New York or

Paris. The four fares were weighted in accordance with the proportion of overall European visitors from each country to Ireland during the 1972–1989 period. In this study, the air fares used were the average economy class excursion fare, including all non-apex discounts as quoted in the April edition of the ABC *World airways guide* for each year. Apex fares were excluded because they tend to be incomparable in their terms and conditions and were not quoted for all the routes.

For the UK, the use of London as a 'gateway' airport was justified on the grounds that tourists from London and the south-east of England made up over 43% of the total number of those travelling from the UK on holiday (Bord Fáilte 1990). The inclusion of business travellers, and traffic generated from those visiting friends and relatives (VFRs), would probably increase this proportion. Another area of possible inaccuracy in the fares equation is the use of only one type of fare. For instance, Barrett (1990) found that fares had fallen by between 34% and 66% depending on ticket type. By using only excursion fares, the fares employed in the equations may not take account of the full range of the decline in fares.

THE AIRLINE COSTS VARIABLE

The choice of independent variables for the fares equations is more troublesome, due to the paucity of the data available. Ideally, the cost per passenger on each route should be used here, but no such route-by-route data are available. Aer Lingus does publish standard airline cost data in its annual reports, which would have been a better measure of costs since they take into account the distance flown. Unfortunately, two incompatible measures were used by the company before and after 1979, making the data useless in their original form. This meant that the cost variable used in the air fares' equations is the total cost of transportation activity of Aer Lingus per passenger in Europe. This is used as a proxy for UK costs per passenger.

This measure assumes that costs incurred by the overall Aer Lingus Group outside its airline business have no bearing on its formulation of airfares. It has, however, been suggested that some of the losses incurred in the group's core business may have been subsidized by its non-transportation activities (Dalby 1992).

THE COMPETITION VARIABLES

The most popular variable used by economists to represent the degree of competition in a market is the concentration ratio for that market. In this case, the data would have to be on a 'city-pair market' basis, information which is not available for the entire period studied for the route involved. Instead, a different variable was used, reflecting the diverse conditions in each and the complexity of competition and regulation.

On those few routes where competitors were allowed to enter the market, the number of airlines flying the route, as quoted by the ABC *World airways guide*, was used as the variable. This included the London market, where the 'open-skies' agreement of 1986 had allowed free access to the market by new entrants.

The third variable relating to the nature of competition on a route was the prices of fares in the preceding years. There are two reasons for this. Firstly, theory, notably Sweezy's (1939) kinked demand curve analysis. This is based on his idea of companies facing a demand curve which was kinked at the existing price. Increases in price would not be matched and result in substantial loss in demand. Falls in price would be matched and provide little demand increase. The theory suggests that oligopolistic industries, such as the airline industry, may be slow to change prices for fear of retaliation. As such, fares adjust to entry over a number of years. Secondly, the process of regulation itself would have led to a certain amount of inertia during the early years of the study. On the London-Dublin route, for instance, the high fares of 1973 were maintained until 1976 (see **Fig. 69.1**).

This also suggests that only a part of the impact of competition on fares may have been felt in the first year. This is modelled by means of what is referred to as partial adjustment. With partial adjustment the impact of changes in costs or changes in the number of competitors is assumed to take place over a number of years with declining impact.

AIRFARES RESULTS

The UK airfares equation has a high degree of explanatory power, explaining an estimated 69% of the variation in airfares between the UK and Ireland. The coefficients of the independent variables, meanwhile, all have the expected signs and were all statistically significant. The coefficient of the previous year's fares is positive and significant (at the 5% level). This supports the view that a significant proportion of the adjustment of the fare to changes in the independent variables takes place in the first year. Meanwhile, the cost coefficient indicates that when costs increase, a substantial proportion of the costs come through into an increase in fares.

On the other hand, the results suggest that competition has had a dramatically beneficial effect on airfares on the London-Dublin route. This result is in line with a substantial body of research which finds that fares are markedly higher on routes served by only one airline than they are on routes with an active body of competitors, and tend to decline significantly with the entry of a second and third competitor (Bornstein 1989; Hurdle *et al.* 1989; Abramovitz and Brown 1993).

The results, in stark contrast to those in more regulated markets, suggest that the Irish and British

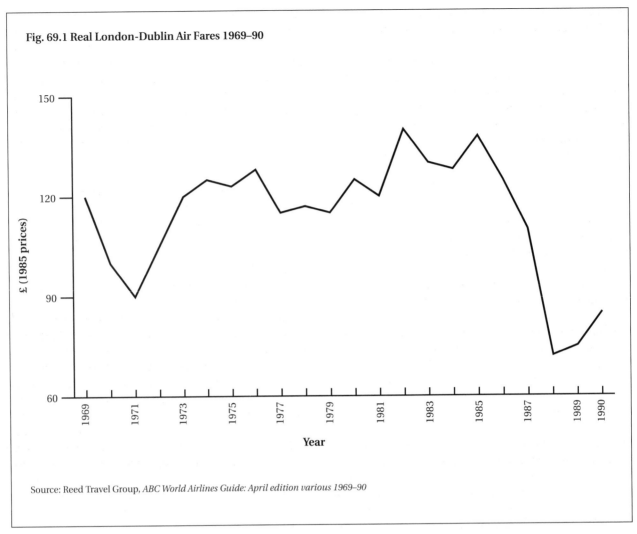

Fig. 69.1 Real London-Dublin Air Fares 1969–90

Source: Reed Travel Group, *ABC World Airlines Guide: April edition various 1969–90*

governments' 'open-skies' policy allowed competition to flourish with significant benefits to the consumer. In relation to the wider debate over EU liberalization, it also gives strong support to the hypothesis that freedom of entry into a city-pair market would benefit consumers. In addition, the absence of restrictions on airline capacity on the route is also likely to influence the strength of this result.

THE TOURISM MODELS

The forces influencing the purchase choice of tourists are broadly similar to those facing the consumer of any good. However, the nature of tourism and tourists is such that the conditions of demand are different from those of other goods (O'Hagan and Harrison 1984a). Perhaps the biggest of these differences is the fact that tourism does not constitute one product but a combination of otherwise unrelated goods and services, many of which are purchased by non-tourists. Indeed, in many ways what distinguishes tourism demand from other forms of demand is not what is demanded but who is demanding it. This process of separating the tourist 'wheat' from the

non-tourist 'chaff' lies at the root of many of the difficulties associated with measuring demand in this industry.

Defining a tourist is not as easy as it seems, since the everyday use of the term 'tourist' is somewhat misleading when dealing with tourism as an economic phenomenon. Hunziker's definition, which was once widely used for research purposes, is a good example. He defined it as 'the sum of phenomena and relationships arising from the travel and stay of non-residents (in a region) in so far as they do not lead to permanent residence or are connected with any earning activity' (quoted in Bukart and Medlik 1988). This, however, does not account for the fact that visits connected with work or business can have the same effect on a destination as visits for leisure or other purposes. Thus, modern definitions use the term 'visitor' rather than 'tourist' and include business people and others whose incomes arise outside the destination. The term 'tourist' is used throughout this chapter in preference to the technical term 'visitor', but with the same meaning unless stated otherwise. The exact definition employed here is that of the United Nations Conference on International Travel and Tourism in 1963. Simply put, visitors are all those who temporarily stay in a country for the purpose of leisure or business. The word 'leisure' is interpreted broadly to include religious, sporting, academic and a host of other activities besides holiday-making.

This definition means that the combination of goods and services purchased by tourists will vary widely according to their motivation for visiting a destination. Goodall (1988) notes three commonly-used categories of tourist:

(i) *Those travelling on business:* This form of tourism has a *derived demand*, with visits undertaken not for their own sake but as a necessary input in the production or sales of other goods. There is a high degree of obligation in the choice of destination and as a result this will imply a lower elasticity of demand. In other words people are likely to be less sensitive to price changes.

(ii) *Those travelling for recreation:* These are the people who are generally described as tourists. Unlike business travel this is a *final demand*, with the tourist deriving satisfaction from the visit itself. As they have a high degree of discretion in their choice of destination, they are likely to be the most price sensitive.

(iii) *Those visiting friends or relations (VFRs):* This third group is only singled out in studies of countries, such as Ireland, where they constitute a significant proportion of tourists. Through travelling for their own satisfaction, they are often considered to be somewhat less 'price sensitive' than those travelling for purely recreational purposes. This is because they are under a higher degree of obligation to visit friends or family. They also incur lower costs of accommodation in their country of destination because they may stay with their friends or relatives.

It should, of course, be noted that these divisions are not clear-cut, as tourists may visit a destination with more than one objective.

THE TOURISM DEMAND VARIABLES

For the purposes of the econometric analysis, two measures of tourism activity were used as dependent variables in two separate tourism demand models. The first and most readily available of these consists of the numbers travelling to Ireland from a given generator market. This is the least dependent on survey data and therefore is least prone to the inaccuracies associated with such data. Indeed, Burkart and Medlik (1989) suggest that this may be the most accurate measure of tourist activity in countries like Ireland that have a limited number of entry points. Walsh (1996), in a

comparable study, also uses this definition. However, although a model employing tourist numbers as the dependent variable may show that liberalization had an effect on Irish tourism, it is of limited use to those in the industry. The primary value which they derive from tourism is the money spent by tourists. As a result many economic studies, including those of Artus (1972), Barry and O'Hagan (1972) and Stronge (1983), use tourism expenditure as a measure of tourism activity. But, changes in airfares may affect the choice of destination or precipitate the substitution of expenditure in the destination for expenditure on travel. Thus, a reduction in fares to Ireland could boost tourism earnings by encouraging more visits to the country or by allowing people to spend more on arrival. Of course, it is quite possible that both effects occurred. In order to investigate the impact of fare changes on spending on arrival, a series of equations using expenditure per visitor was also employed.

Both tourist numbers and expenditure data were taken from Bord Fáilte Éireann *Annual reports* (1970–91), which are based on the company's Survey of Travellers leaving the country. These data were used in preference to those collated by the Central Statistics Office (CSO) for two reasons. First, Bord Fáilte divides the data according to the residence of the tourist, while the CSO measures the numbers travelling by the route taken and therefore includes those travelling via a particular region. Second, Bord Fáilte data are the largest complete data set, since the format of the CSO data has changed over the period of the study. Expenditure data were converted to constant price terms, in this case 1985 values, for the purpose of the study.

THE INCOME VARIABLE

As might be expected, income levels in a generator market are generally considered to be crucial in determining the level of tourism. Growing wealth, improving holiday entitlements and more equitable distribution of wealth in the western world have been vital to the long-term development of the tourist industry (Bull 1991). However, the short-term changes in the wealth of generator markets are of more importance here.

Previous studies are divided on the type of variable to be used to measure the effect of income changes on tourism. The choice is based on the dependent variable used and the assumptions made about the buyer decision process. While many tourism demand studies use an income measure such as *per capita* personal disposable income or Gross National Product (Artus 1972; Blackwell 1970; Stronge 1983 and Summary 1987, among others), *per capita* total foreign tourism expenditure has also been employed. O'Hagan and Harrison (1984a, b) used the latter variable in order to assess the effect on a destination's market share in a generator market, while Barry and O'Hagan (1972) made use of total British tourism expenditure as a possible determinant of British tourism expenditure in Ireland. In both cases, it was assumed that the tourist had the following decision-making process:

(i) the decision to holiday;

(ii) the choice between 'home' and foreign holiday;

(iii) the choice of foreign destination.

The use of foreign expenditure can also be justified if this is accepted as the real process and if it is assumed that there is little substitution between foreign travel and other non-holiday products (Barry and O'Hagan 1972).

Insofar as it can be said of any effort to generalize the mental processes of consumers, this buyer decision process is quite plausible. However, it is flawed in a number of important ways. First, it takes no account of the approach of those travelling on business or visiting friends and relations. The high degree of obligation on these travellers makes the focus on destination choice alone a dubious exercise. This is particularly true of tourists from the UK, the majority of whom travel to Ireland for the latter reasons (Bord Fáilte 1990). It also ignores the crucial decision to travel in the first instance. As a luxury good, economic theory would suggest that tourism is only available to those with discretionary income, that is income remaining after necessities such as food have been purchased. In most, if not all, generator markets studied, consumers have, on the whole, satisfied their demand for basic necessities. Thus, any changes in total income are, to a very large degree, changes in discretionary income (Barry and O'Hagan 1972). Such changes will lead to the tourist choosing between expenditure on travel and on other 'unnecessary' goods. Therefore, it is discretionary income which would be the best variable to use.

In the absence of available data on either discretionary income or disposable income for all the generator markets studied, *per capita* GDP was used. For the sake of consistency, all data for the income variable were taken from OECD data for the UK, North America and the European Community (EC).

THE HOLIDAY PRICE VARIABLE

The fundamental economic laws of supply and demand suggest that holidays should behave like most other products where price is concerned. Therefore, if their price moves in one direction, their demand will move in the other. Similarly, changes in a substitute's prices should have the usual, cross-price effects. Thus, if the price of a holiday in the UK moves in one direction, demand for Irish holidays will move in the same

direction. Given the multi-product nature of tourism, the relative prices of individual components within the total can be just as important as the total price itself. Bull (1991) suggests that these may have a significant effect on the destination decision. He proposes that two of the major components are the cost of carriage and the overall cost of the destination, especially accommodation. In order to get a better insight into the impact of airline liberalization, the cost of carriage was considered separately from the rest of the holiday price.

The use of Consumer Price Indices (CPI) may give rise to a number of problems. First, the goods used in compiling the Consumer Price Index and their individual weightings are unlikely to be the same as that of a 'tourist index', which would be most appropriate. Therefore, the accuracy or otherwise of the variable is unknown. Second, one of the services included in the Irish CPI is air travel. This would make it difficult to distinguish between the impact of a fall in air fares and a fall in the price of other goods with any accuracy. There is, therefore, a possibility of what is technically referred to as multicollinearity in the subsequent regression. However, since air fares constitute such a small part of the index, the effect is likely to be negligible. The third difficulty with using CPIs is that their design and construction may differ in Ireland and its tourism markets, making them incompatible. Yet again, the root cause of this problem is that the types and proportion of goods bought by tourists are unknown. As this is seemingly inevitable, given the nature of tourism, there is little can be done to deal with it.

For consistency, the real exchange rate variables were calculated using data from similar sources to those employed for the income variable. OECD data were used for the CPIs of the UK, North America and the EC, which were all to the base 1985 = 100.

THE PROMOTION VARIABLE

Modern marketing theory, generally, advises that it is easier to tailor a product to the needs of its consumers than vice versa. This is not usually the case with tourism, due to the fact that, as Gray (1970) noted, the type of tourism product a destination can provide is to some extent predetermined by its natural attributes. He also suggests that recreational tourists can be subdivided into those seeking a cultural experience (wanderlust tourists) and those seeking relaxation, perhaps in the sunshine (sunlust tourists), with each attracted to a different kind of destination. Given its climate, Ireland could only be described as a wanderlust destination. As such, Ireland is fortunate to have many features that are attractive to these tourists, including scenic beauty, a reputation for friendliness and a number of sites of historical or cultural interest. Furthermore, the country's long history of emigration provides a ready-made market and creates a heightened awareness of Ireland in North America and the UK (Economist Intelligence Unit 1983).

Besides maintaining Ireland's scenery, its historic sites and providing the supporting infrastructure for tourists, the government, Bord Fáilte and Aer Lingus must promote these positive images and cultivate these long-standing links. The two semi-state bodies are the most important in terms of day-to-day promotion. Therefore, their annual promotional expenditure seemed the most obvious measure to estimate the impact of promotion on tourism demand. However, since it was not possible to ascertain what proportion of the spending of Aer Lingus went on advertising Ireland, its expenditure was excluded. The spending of Bord Fáilte in each region, as quoted in its annual reports, was used in the UK, European and North American equations as the measure of promotion. However, the variable was not used in the expenditure per person equation, since promotion by Bord Fáilte tended to be destination-orientated. Therefore, this spending was irrelevant to the purchasing decisions of tourists who have already arrived in the country.

THE NORTHERN IRELAND VARIABLE

Those in the tourism industry can alter or preserve a destination's natural attributes, change its promotional activity and, as in the case of airline liberalization, attempt to reduce the cost of its product. Nevertheless, their businesses are at the mercy of a whole host of non-economic factors over which they have little or no control. These factors vary both in their nature and impact on tourism. Some, such as the advent of wide-bodied jet aircraft, pre-empt increases in tourist demand and are unlikely to have an impact in the short term (Holloway 1989). Other events have an immediate impact, such as the 1968 student riots in France which Artus (1972) found to have reduced that country's tourism receipts by 7.2%.

In the case of Ireland anecdotal evidence suggests a number of positive and negative factors affecting demand. Thus, while environmental awareness may have benefited the country's image in mainland Europe in the latter part of the 1980s, North American tourist demand was dampened by fears of terrorist attacks during the Gulf War in 1991. However, it is the 'Troubles' in Northern Ireland that have figured most prominently in studies of Irish tourism. A consultancy study on behalf of the Irish Tourism Industry Confederation (1989) noted that there was a widespread perception of Ireland as a dangerous place, arising from media coverage of violence in Northern Ireland. Not surprisingly, this impression was most prevalent in the UK, with both O'Hagan and Harrison (1984) and Clarke and Ó Cinnéide (1981) finding it to be a significantly negative factor in determining tourist demand from that country. For this

reason, and in light of the current prospects for lasting peace, the inclusion of a variable measuring the negative impact of the 'Troubles' was considered worthwhile.

Generally, given their qualitative nature, such factors are usually represented by a dummy variable. For instance, O'Hagan and Harrison (1984 a, b) used a dummy variable with a value of O for the years preceding the 'Troubles' (1964–72) and 1 for subsequent years. The violence associated with the 'Troubles' is generally considered to have begun in August 1969, continuing with varying intensity throughout the period studied here. O'Hagan and Harrison (1984a, b), however, found using a dummy variable from 1972 more successful. Given that the 1969–1991 period is under study in this chapter, the use of such a dummy variable was considered inappropriate. Ideally, some measure of the extent of media coverage of violence in Northern Ireland in each generator market would be most suitable. This was rejected on the grounds that it was impractical for a study covering a twenty-year period. Using a dummy variable for those events which were likely to receive the most attention was also rejected, as it would have been too subjective. The variable eventually used was the numbers killed each year in violence related to the 'Troubles'. Taken from the British Government's publication *Social trends*, these are compiled by the RUC for Northern Ireland. Thus the data exclude fatalities on the British mainland, in the Republic and elsewhere. Nevertheless, it seems reasonable to assume that the number of fatalities measured would have coincided with periods involving the escalation of violence in Northern Ireland itself. Given its controversial nature, other sources, such as the New Ireland Forum or the press, inevitably disagree on how to measure both the extent of the 'Troubles' and their impact. However, all concur on general trends.

UNITED KINGDOM RESULTS FOR TOURIST NUMBERS

The UK equations are the main focus of this study, for three very important reasons. First being that, despite the Northern Ireland 'Troubles', Great Britain remains the largest generator market for Irish tourism, accounting for 55% of all overseas tourists to Ireland and 41% of expenditure in 1994, as research indicates. Secondly, Ireland and the UK have long established social, cultural and economic links, not least of which are to the large Irish community in that country. As such, reasonably priced air travel between the two is in the interest of all Irish people in both countries, not just the tourist industry. Finally, the 'open-skies' agreement between the Irish and UK governments was but a precursor to a similar agreement spanning the whole of the European Union.

If the 'open-skies' policy of the Irish and British governments has indeed benefited the consumer, to what extent, if any, has it resulted in an improvement in Irish tourism? The tourist numbers equation is taken first, as it is perhaps the most obvious measure of performance. Once again, the model had a high degree of explanatory power, accounting for more than 90% of changes in the number of tourists visiting annually. In addition, the coefficients of all but one of the variables were statistically significant. However, the one variable that was not significant at the 5% level was Bord Fáilte promotional expenditure which, in addition, did not have the *a priori* expected sign. The results indicate that after taking account of the influence of the other factors in the model, increases in promotional expenditure were associated with falls in tourism numbers. A similar result was evident in the North American equation. Although these results were not strongly significant, they are in line with anecdotal evidence that Bord Fáilte may have increased its expenditure in 'bad' years in an effort to maintain Ireland's market share. For instance, Bord Fáilte was said to be marketing aggressively in the US to counter the effects of the Chernobyl disaster in 1986 (*Business and Finance* 1986).

As might be expected of a luxury item, the income elasticity of UK tourists, as measured by the income coefficient, is positive and greater than one. This means that tourism is more than proportionately sensitive to fluctuations in consumer incomes. What is more interesting is that the coefficient is lower than that recorded in the corresponding North American and European equations, probably reflecting the higher proportions of those visiting friends or relations. Walsh (1996) also found that income had more influence on North American tourists. Indeed, income was surprisingly not significant in influencing demand from the UK in her study. However, the omission of a fares variable, and the inclusion of the 'Troubles' simply in terms of a zero-one dummy, may account for these differences.

It is no surprise either to find that the Northern Ireland coefficient is likewise significant, suggesting that fluctuations in the level of violence associated with the 'Troubles' did indeed play a part in the decision to visit Ireland. Although this result occurred in all the markets studied, the coefficient is particularly large in this equation, reflecting the obvious political sensitivities involved. The strong growth in tourists from the UK and elsewhere during the 1994–1996 IRA ceasefire lends further credence to this result. The real exchange rate variable and the air fares variable have very similar elasticities. They are both statistically significant, negative and inelastic, suggesting that an increase in either would dampen tourism demand but less than proportionately.

All things being equal, the tourist equation suggests the 30% fall in fare prices between 1986 and 1990 resulted in a 10% to 15% increase in UK tourist numbers

in the first year. The long-run impact was substantially greater.

THE EXPENDITURE PER TOURIST EQUATION

This equation is of the same form as the tourism equation and uses the same variables except for the Northern Ireland violence variable and the promotional expenditure variable. Although there was good reason why these two latter variables might affect the decision to visit Ireland, there is no reason to suppose that they should affect spending once the tourist has arrived.

This equation offers an insight into whether fare prices are important in determining the amount spent on the non-travel elements of a holiday. (The results of the equation are that it is able to explain the data well in terms of R-squared and F-statistic values.) All of the coefficients were significant, and suggest that expenditure per tourist was more than proportionately influenced by changes in UK income. The impact of changes in the real exchange rate are proportional. That is that a 1% rise in the real exchange rate between Britain and Ireland would give rise to a 1% fall in the expenditure per tourist. The positive coefficient on the air fares variable would appear to indicate that higher air fares seem to be associated with an increased expenditure by UK tourists in Ireland. This, however, may partly reflect the high proportions of so-called VFRs in this market and others who may be involved in short-term stays. Such persons who may be low spenders are likely to be discouraged from their trips by high fares, leaving the higher income, high-spending traveller increasing the average expenditure per tourist. In other equations for European and North American tourists, higher fares reduce spending per tourist.

As may be expected, the level of real income per head of population is the main determinant of non-travelling expenditure. As is usual for a luxury item, this result suggests that the income elasticity of tourist expenditure is positive and elastic. In other words, tourist expenditure responds more than proportionately to rises in tourist income. It is worth noting during the 1987–91 period, when fares fell substantially, the amount spent per tourist also fell. However, overall expenditure rose, pushed by the sheer weight of numbers. In this context, the fall in air fares brought on by the Anglo-Irish 'open-skies' policy had a very important positive overall impact on tourist expenditure. It may also be the case that the lower average expenditure of those visiting friends and relatives may be partly compensated for by the higher spending of the friends and relatives themselves!

CONCLUSION

In the mid-1980s, the Irish government radically altered its commercial aviation policy. Until that time, policy had focussed on maintaining air links with the rest of the world through protecting the state-owned national airline from the full rigours of competition. Inspired by the US experience, the government renegotiated its bilateral airline agreement with a like-minded UK, replacing it with Europe's first 'open-skies' agreement. Ireland also became an advocate for airline liberalization across the member states of the then European Community. Though wider social and economic issues played some role in this policy reversal, it was also intended to increase foreign demand for tourism in Ireland, through reduced fares.

In seeking to assess the success or otherwise of the new policy in reducing the cost to passengers flying to Ireland, a simple econometric model of the factors determining air fares was estimated. The results of this analysis strongly suggested that deregulation did indeed have a major effect on reducing fares between London and Dublin. The statistical estimates from the equation were that the impact of another entrant onto the Dublin-London route could have reduced average fares by between 10% and 15% in the first year and substantially more over subsequent years. To test whether this had a knock-on effect on the number of tourists visiting Ireland, another econometric model was employed examining the factors influencing the number of UK tourists visiting Ireland. This study found that UK incomes, air fares, the real exchange rate and the level of violence in Northern Ireland were all significant factors in influencing the numbers of tourists visiting Ireland. It confirmed that the fall in fares had a major impact on the numbers coming to Ireland. Somewhat surprisingly, after allowing for the aforementioned factors, promotional expenditure by Bord Fáilte seemed to vary inversely with tourist numbers. It may be that more expenditure was applied during years when tourist prospects would have otherwise appeared bleak.

A further model was estimated to explain variations in tourist expenditure on arrival in the country. In this model, it was found that in the case of UK tourists the lower air fares reduced the average expenditure per tourist. This was presumably because the additional tourists, who had been attracted by the lower fares, were not any more likely to spend while visiting. If anything, they were likely to spend less. This may well be because they would visit more frequently, so that even though their expenditure per trip was reduced, their overall expenditure per person in Ireland might have risen. This is in line with the overall rise in total tourist expenditure.

The broadly positive impact of deregulation on air fares from London to Dublin and the resulting beneficial effect on tourism have all been part of the move towards deregulation within the airline industry. From 1977 to the present, airline regulation has undergone a dramatic transformation world-wide. Formal restraints on commercial aviation within Europe have been liberalized considerably over the past decade, culminating in the opening of intra-European Union aviation markets to any EU carrier in April 1997.

However, it is still far from clear to what extent the results of this study will be emulated on a broader EU-wide level. The vast variation in scale will obviously make a difference, placing greater emphasis on the crucial ability of new entrants to have access to major 'hub' airports. Kahn (1980) and Shephard (1990), in the US context, both noted a propensity of large incumbent airlines to control entry into their chosen hubs. In this regard, it is worth noting that Ryanair was denied access to London's Heathrow Airport, which is one of Europe's key 'hubs'. Kahn and Shephard also point to the ability of larger airlines, either together or in concert, to take advantage of computerized reservations systems, loyalty schemes and discriminatory pricing to maintain market share. Barrett (1990) also noted the lower baggage handling charges paid by incumbent airlines at Heathrow, putting new entrants at a competitive disadvantage.

With regard to applying the apparent link between airline deregulation and tourism to other countries or air routes, it should be noted that circumstances in the British market are unique from an Irish point of view. In lowering air fares between Ireland and Britain, deregulation tapped a hitherto latent market, the so-called 'Ryanair generation'. They are members of the Irish community who, prior to deregulation, wished to visit 'home' more often but who lacked either time for the cheap but long ferry journey or the money to fly regularly. There is no comparable segment in any of Ireland's other major generator markets. This is not to say that, were EU airline liberalization to be successful, there would be no potential benefits for Irish tourism. On the contrary, there is considerable anecdotal evidence to suggest that Ireland's success in attracting tourists from the UK is not confined to Irish emigrants, and the European numbers equation also suggested that further fare reductions would increase tourism from Continental Europe.

Bibliography

Airline User's Committee 1976 *European airfares: a report bv the A.U.C. to the Civil Aviation Authority.* London.

Artus, J. R. 1972 'An econometric analysis of international travel', *IMF Staff Papers* **19**, pp. 579–613.

Bailey, E. E. and Panzar, J. C. 1981 'The contestability of airline markets during the transition to deregulation', *Journal of Law and Contemporary Problems* **44** (Winter), pp. 125–45.

Barlow, A. C. and O'Boyle, M. 1998 *The impact of airline deregulation on tourism in Ireland, an econometric analysis* [mimeo]. Cork.

Barrett, S. D. 1990 'Deregulating European aviation — a case study', *Transportation* 16, pp. 311–27.

Barry, R. and O'Hagan, J. W. 1972 'An econometric study of British tourist expenditure in Ireland', *Economic and Social Review* 3, pp. 143–61.

Baumol W. J., Panzer J. and Willig, R. D. 1988 *Contestable markets and the theory of industrial structure.* San Diego.

Bord Fáilte Éireann 1970–91 *Annual reports and accounts.* Dublin.

Bord Fáilte Éireann 1990 *Know your market: Britain.* Dublin.

Bull, A. 1991 *The economics of travel and tourism.* Melbourne.

Burkart, A. J. and Medlik, S. 1988 *Tourism: past, present and future.* Oxford.

Business and Finance 1986 'Fear of European flying hits visits to IDA sites', *Business and Finance* 22, 34, p. 3.

Clark, W. and Ó Cinnéide, B. 1981 *Tourism in the Republic of Ireland and Northern Ireland,* Co-operation North Paper 5. Dublin.

Dalby, D. 1992 'On a wing and a prayer', *The Sunday Tribune:* Business Section, 25 October.

Department of Foreign Affairs 1946 *Agreement between the Government of Ireland and the Provisional Government of the French Republic concerning air transport,* Treaty Series, 1946 (3). Dublin.

Department of Foreign Affairs 1988 *Memorandum of understanding between the aeronautical authorities of Ireland and of United Kingdom,* Treaty Series, 1988 (2). Dublin.

Douglas, G. and Miller, J. 1974 *Economic regulation of domestic air transport: theory and policy.* Washington D.C.

Economist Intelligence Unit 1983 'National report No. 86: Ireland', *EIU International Tourism Quarterly* 3, pp. 27–36.

European Civil Aviation Conference 1981 *Report of the Task Force on Competition in Intra-European Air Services.* London.

Goodall, B. 1988 'How tourists choose their holidays', in Goodall, B. and Ashworth, G. (eds), *Marketing in the tourist industry: the promotion of destination regions* (London).

Government of Ireland 1984 *Building on reality: Programme for National Development 1985–87* (Dublin), pp. 47–49.

Gray, H. P. 1970 *International travel-international trade.* Lexington.

Holloway, J. C. 1989 *The business of tourism.* London.

Irish Tourism Industry Confederation 1989 *Doubling Irish tourism: a market-led strategy.* Dublin.

Kahn, A. E. 1979 'Applications of economics to an imperfect world', *American Economic Review* 69, 2, pp. 1–13.

Kahn, A. E. 1988 'Surprises of airline deregulation', *The American Economic Review* 78, 2, pp. 316–21.

O'Hagan, J. W. and Harrison, M. T. 1984a 'Market-share of U.S. tourist expenditure in Europe: an econometric analysis', *Applied Economics* 16, 6, pp. 919–31.

O'Hagan, J. W. and Harrison, M. T 1984b 'U.K. and U.S. visitor expenditure in Ireland: some econometric findings', *Economic and Social Review* 15, 3, pp. 195–207.

Price Waterhouse 1987 *Improving the performance of Irish tourism.* Dublin.

Share, B. 1986 *The flight of the Iolar: the Aer Lingus experience.* Dublin.

Stronge, W. 1983 'The overseas demand for tourism in the United States', *Journal of Regional Studies* 12, 3, pp. 323–43.

Summary, R. 1987 'Estimation of tourism demand by multivariate analysis', *Tourism Management* 8, 4.

Sweezy, P. M. 1939 'Demand under conditions of oligopoly', *Journal of Political Economy* 47 (Aug.), pp. 568–73.

United Nations 1963 *Recommendations on international travel and tourism.* Rome.

Walsh, M. 1996–7 'Demand analysis in Irish tourism', *Journal of the Statistical and Social Inquiry Society of Ireland* 24, 4.

Enterprise Accountability and Accounting

The term 'accountability' refers to the responsibility or expectation to report on performance or behaviour which exists between a person or organization and others. While this concept is as old as the practice of accounting itself, it is only with the development of more democratic societies and a greater understanding of the role of organizations in those societies that the concept has been expanded. As late as 1975, for example, it was necessary for *The corporate report* to declare:

In our view there is an implicit responsibility to report publicly (whether or not required by law or regulation) incumbent on every economic entity whose size or format renders it significant. By economic entity we mean every sort of organisation in modern society, whether a department of central government, a local authority, a co-operative society, an unincorporated firm, a limited company, or a non-profit seeking organisation, such as a trade or professional association, a trade union or a charity.

It should be noted that *The corporate report* considered as important only those organizations which 'have significant economic implications for the community as a whole', although it did admit that a definition of such 'must be a matter of arbitrary and largely subjective judgement'. Obviously, the relative size of communities and of the organizations which inhabit them would have a bearing on this judgement.

However, the concept of accountability should not necessarily be limited to entities whose significance is defined in economic terms. Modern societies aim to preserve and nurture values other than exclusively economic ones, and in those circumstances it is reasonable to expect that organizations formed to foster and develop such values should be accountable also in some way.

Two forms of accountability may, for example, be identified as affecting heritage enterprises:

(1) *Public accountability* might apply where it is assumed that there is a responsibility to the public. This could involve accountability for probity, legality, efficiency or performance at a relatively low level; or accountability for effectiveness or policy on a higher plane. Although accounting, in the narrow sense, is the usual mechanism whereby the former is achieved, the latter is more dependent on disclosure and personal judgement and is better served by a broader form of report which modern accounting provides.

(2) *Managerial accountability* could also be relevant, particularly in hierarchical organizations, either involving the relationship between senior management and subordinates or that between directors and shareholders. Management may also be accountable to other parties such as lenders, employees and so forth. Accounting, again, is the most common mechanism employed in these situations.

Although sometimes referred to as an 'art', accounting, in fact, may more usefully be thought of as assisting management in the following ways:

(a) by collecting, summarizing and recording, in a systematic way, detailed information, usually of a financial nature, about day-to-day transactions. This is commonly referred to as book-keeping;

(b) through the preparation of periodic (annual or, perhaps, half-yearly) reports, incorporating significant measurements, to be presented to outside parties such as promoters, lenders, government and the like, on behalf of management. This is known as financial reporting. These reports typically include the balance sheet, income and expenditure (or profit and loss) account and the cash flow statement, all of which may be prepared on a more frequent basis and used also for internal control purposes;

(c) as an aid to planning and controlling day-to-day activities through the preparation of budgets and other reports and analyses for use within the organization. This is referred to as management accounting.

However, to be effective, any accounting system must be 'tailored' to the nature of the organization concerned if it is to achieve the level of accountability expected or required, and this in turn is determined, to a greater or lesser extent, by the structural, legal and financial characteristics of that organization and also by its size and objectives.

The purpose of this chapter is, therefore, to examine briefly some of the factors which could affect the concept of accountability referred to above and how it might be implemented in heritage enterprises generally.

TO WHOM SHOULD HERITAGE ENTERPRISES BE ACCOUNTABLE?

The corporate report considered the fundamental objective of corporate reports to be to communicate economic measurements of and information about the resources and performance of the reporting entity useful to those having reasonable rights to such information.

This aim allows not only for the satisfaction of the commercial and financial interests of users but also for other interests of a non-financial nature. In the case of heritage enterprises, such interests could include environmental, educational, historical and cultural ones of many kinds which citizens and local inhabitants might consider to be part of their birthright and, consequently, entitling them to some form of accountability from those charged with their maintenance. If funds have been provided, either directly, by subscription or other means, this would add greater force to such expectations.

THE NATURE AND OBJECTIVES OF HERITAGE ENTERPRISES

At the outset, a distinction must be made between a 'heritage object', such as an archaeological site preserved for research purposes, and a 'heritage enterprise' formed (say) to promote an interest in heritage among a wider public and, usually, requiring both finance and investment and formal management structures such as might be needed, for example, for an interpretative centre. Enterprises of this kind are generally classified into broad categories like 'natural', 'man-made', 'cultural', 'performing arts' and so on according to their heritage activities, although there may be considerable variety of undertaking and differences of scale amongst them. Regrettably, no overall register of Irish heritage enterprises appears to exist, and no survey has been undertaken to establish objectives, ownership, funding,

structure, details of governance and the like. Consequently, the specific objectives for which these entities have been established can only be generally inferred. A tentative list might include some of the following:

• to preserve what is worthwhile from the past;

• to facilitate and promote research;

• to educate;

• to encourage visitors to places and regions;

• to promote products and tourism;

• to operate on a profitable or non-profit or subsidized basis;

• to operate on a voluntary or non-voluntary basis;

• to provide competent heritage management.

While it is probably reasonable to assume that most heritage enterprises would seek to meet some of these objectives, the problem remains as to how success in their achievement can be measured. Ideally, the wider concept of accountability might suggest that some form of report be made in which that achievement is addressed or from which it might be deduced. But, although accounting may provide some of the answers to these questions, it must be recognized that it cannot provide them all, particularly those of a qualitative kind. It should, therefore, be the responsibility of management to develop and report measures which address these objectives.

OWNERSHIP AND FUNDING OF HERITAGE ENTERPRISES

The word 'ownership' is used here with reference to the ultimate responsibility for the development and funding of an enterprise. Thus a department of government might be considered to be an 'owner', even if this was not true in a strictly legal sense. As already noted, no research is readily available to establish who, in fact, 'owns' Irish heritage enterprises and, consequently, the general categories of ownership must again be developed from general observation. The following list is suggested as representative of most categories:

• government agencies, for instance the Office of Public Works;

• local authorities;

• museums and art galleries;

• local communities;

• tourist bodies;

• commercial companies;

• trusts;

• individuals.

Ownership and basic funding of enterprises usually go together, and it is primarily for the benefit of owners that most reports on enterprises will normally be prepared in the form of final accounts like the balance sheet. However, much depends upon the importance of the particular enterprise as a component of an owner's overall affairs. For example, a heritage enterprise run by (say) Cork County Council is unlikely to be of other than minor importance in the overall context of that particular local authority's affairs, and therefore public reporting on it may not be considered relevant. Detailed reporting on that particular venture may thus be for internal management consumption only. Furthermore, the form of the report will be dictated by county council practices in that regard. It follows that, because many (possibly most) Irish heritage enterprises are owned by public bodies and consequently are of lesser significance in relation to the overall size of those bodies, only in special circumstances will individual reports be prepared for wide circulation. It also follows that the form of report will be influenced by the traditional form of reporting adopted by those bodies.

Nonetheless, there may be circumstances where it is considered politic for even public bodies to make disclosures concerning such activities, for example to harness local community support or to convey 'good news' of some kind. Accountability to outside parties, such as lenders or fund raisers or 'friends of the enterprise' or local communities, may also be deemed necessary or important or strategically sensible in particular circumstances. In the case of other categories of owners, there may exist contractual relationships, such as loan obligations or grant receipts, which require that regular reports be submitted.

COMPANY STRUCTURE AND ACCOUNTABILITY
The need for an identifiable organizational structure usually becomes apparent at an early stage of a heritage enterprise's development, and the adoption of some form of legal status is therefore normally recommended. This will result in the enterprise being recognized in law as a legal personality distinct from its members, enabling it to sue (and be sued), to contract, acquire property, employ people and so on. An added and very important

advantage is that individual members will not generally be liable for the debts and obligations of the enterprise.

THE LIMITED COMPANY
The most popular form of legal status is undoubtedly the limited company, which may be formed for any (legal) purpose; the word 'limited' used in the name indicates that the liability of the members is limited to the amount of their agreed contribution in the event of insolvency. An alternative form, frequently adopted by co-operative organizations, is that of an industrial and provident society. Such, however, may only be formed 'for carrying on any industries, businesses or trades', and consequently may not be suitable for all heritage enterprises.

COMPANY ACCOUNTABILITY
The degree and form of accountability required of companies are provided for by the *Companies Acts*, although the detailed application of the provisions of those acts is dependent on factors too numerous to be dealt with exhaustively here. Thus the following, though generally required, may be expanded upon or limited in particular circumstances.

Proper books of account
All companies are required to keep proper books of account, on an up-to-date and consistent basis, that:

• record and explain the company's transactions;

• enable the financial position to be determined with reasonable accuracy at any time:

• enable the directors to ensure that the final accounts comply with the *Companies Acts*;

• enable the accounts to be readily and properly audited.

Accounts and returns
Every year, an Annual Return must be made to the Companies Office, giving the address of the registered office, stating where the Register of Members is held and supplying details as to the Directors and Secretary. In addition, audited accounts, in a prescribed form, must be filed together with an Auditor's Report and the Report of the Directors. These latter items must also be presented to the members at the annual general meeting. All companies are classified as either public or private by the acts, but many private companies may qualify to be treated as 'small' companies if they satisfy two of the three following conditions:

• the balance sheet total does not exceed £1,500,000;

• turnover ('sales') does not exceed £3,000,000;

• the average number employed does not exceed 50.

It is expected that most Irish heritage enterprises would qualify as 'small' on this basis and thus could avail of several exemptions from the above requirements as set out below:

	RE MEMBERS' ACCOUNTS	RE FILED ACCOUNTS
Profit and Loss Account (or Income and Expenditure Account)	May commence with 'Gross Profit or Loss' and omit 'Turnover' and 'Cost of Sales'	This account need not be filed at all
Balance Sheet	May present an abridged Balance Sheet	May file an abridged Balance Sheet
Directors' Report	Must be presented	Need not be filed
Auditors' Report	Must be presented	Must be filed
Special Statement by Directors and Special Report by Auditors re Exemptions Claimed	Need not be presented	Must be filed

Lesser exemptions are available to companies which qualify as 'medium'-sized. The point to note, however, is that both 'small' and 'medium' companies can reduce the level of accountability below that legally required of larger organizational units.

THE QUALITY OF REPORTED ACCOUNTING INFORMATION

The *Companies Acts* require that the published financial statements of companies give a 'true and fair view' of financial position and performance, and this is now widely accepted as the standard which should be met by all financial reports. However, the acts do not define the meaning of this phrase, and considerable debate has ensued as to how it should be interpreted and put into effect. At one extreme is the view that compliance with technical accounting criteria is sufficient; at the other, a belief that it is a standard to which accounting can only aspire and that its prescription is not possible without reference to circumstances.

However, the acts themselves do recognize that mere adherence to form, by routine compliance with legislative provisions, may at times inhibit a true and fair view being given, and specifically permit departure from such provisions if this is the case. It is clear, then, that slavish adherence to the minimum accounting require-ments of the acts will not result in a true and fair view being given in all circumstances. David Tweedie, a former Chairman of the Accounting Standards Board, writing in 1983, expressed his own view on 'true and fair' as follows:

While the detailed requirements necessary to show a true and fair view will continually evolve as social attitudes and technical skills change, the basic question … will remain. 'If', they should ask, 'I were on the outside and did not have the detailed knowledge of the company … would I be able to obtain a *clear and unambiguous* picture of that reality from these accounts?' If the picture is poorly painted, or worse, fails to represent reality, then the Directors have failed to meet the paramount principle of financial reporting — to show a true and fair view.

This, of course, begs the question as to whether accounts can ever produce 'a clear and unambiguous picture'. While the basic objective of financial statements is to provide information which is useful to users in making decisions, such information must, at the outset, be so material that its omission or mis-statement could influence those decisions. It should also possess qualities of relevance and reliability, as only relevant information can have any useful bearing upon decisions, and reliable information is needed to give confidence in its use. Unfortunately, a 'trade-off' between these two will almost certainly be necessary in order to achieve the overall objective, and this inevitably introduces an element of judgement to the reporting process on the part of preparers.

However, while there is an onus on preparers to produce financial statements which are readily under-standable, a reasonable knowledge of affairs and of accounting and a willingness to study financial reports with due diligence must also be assumed on the part of users. In the final analysis, the courts may have to decide whether or not a particular report complies with the acts, and it is generally accepted that, in making that determi-nation, they will take into consideration prevailing accounting standards and practices.

ACCOUNTING STANDARDS

Accounting standards are developed by the Accounting Standards Board (ASB), a prescribed standard-setting body under UK legislation, with which, however, the accounting profession in Ireland has close links. The Consultative Committee of Accountancy Bodies, of which the Institute of Chartered Accountants in Ireland is a member, is committed to promoting and supporting compliance with accounting standards by professional accountants, either as preparers or as auditors. Standards developed by the ASB are known as Financial Reporting Standards. Other standards, which were developed by the now defunct Accounting Standards Committee, are known as Statements of Standard Accounting Practice. These have been adopted by the ASB and will continue in force under their former title until rescinded or replaced by new standards.

ORGANIZATIONAL ARRANGEMENTS AND INTERNAL CONTROLS

In the early stages of development of any enterprise, the

owner or manager is in a position to perform or oversee all of its operations. However, as it grows larger, it becomes necessary to delegate; once this occurs, a system of control should be established to cope with increased complexity and to check that employees are carrying out their tasks as intended. Such a system is known as an 'Internal Control System' and, although it should be designed to control all the activities of an enterprise, it is the effect upon the quality of accounting information which is of most concern here.

SAS 300, *Accounting and internal control and risk assessments*, provides the following description of such a system:

It includes all the policies and procedures (internal controls) adopted by the directors and management of an entity to assist in achieving their objective of ensuring, as far as possible, the orderly and efficient conduct of its business, including adherence to internal policies, the safeguarding of assets, the prevention and detection of fraud and error, the accuracy and completeness of the accounting records, and the timely preparation of reliable financial information.

Provided there is a good control environment and specific procedures are followed, the reliability of the accounting data produced and of the financial statements prepared will be greatly enhanced because of the reduced possibility of fraud or material error arising if such a system is in place. It is most important, however, that management reinforce the control environment through their own actions. If top management does not provide a good example in this regard, it is unlikely that controls will be adequately maintained in other parts of the enterprise.

THE BENEFIT OF AN AUDIT

The quality of accounting information is assessed by the audit process and, consequently, significant benefits can be derived from having an audit performed on the financial records of an enterprise. In the case of companies, an audit is required by law, and therefore no limit can be placed on the scope of the audit, which will be determined by the auditor concerned. In other cases, management may wish to define the scope of the audit for themselves in order to focus upon particular aspects of the enterprise's affairs. In either case, an audit can be of considerable benefit by drawing the attention of management to weaknesses in the systems of control and by providing reassurance to those concerned of the propriety with which the affairs of the enterprise have been conducted and reported.

THE STATUTORY AUDIT

By law, all companies must appoint auditors to report on any balance sheet and profit and loss account placed before the members at a general meeting. Effectively this requires an annual audit. Only 'registered auditors' are eligible for appointment as auditors of a company. To be registered, an auditor must (in nearly all circumstances) be a member of a body of accountants recognized by the relevant minister and hold a 'practising certificate' from that body. Although the manner in which company auditors are appointed, removed or resign is prescribed by law, their fees will be negotiated with the company either on a time basis or as a fixed amount.

Company auditors are required to report to the members an opinion as to whether the accounts presented give 'a true and fair view' of the company's affairs and of the profit and loss for the period, whether proper books of account have been kept and whether the accounts are in agreement with those books. Other matters must also be referred to in their report. The meaning of the phrase 'true and fair view' has already been commented upon, and auditors must use their own skill and judgement in determining whether the accounts being examined meet this test. A common misunderstanding, however, is that auditors prepare the accounts and that they are somehow responsible for their presentation. Nothing could be further from the truth. Although in the case of smaller organizations they may draft the accounts, they do this in their capacity as accountants and not as auditors. Responsibility for the preparation and presentation of accounts, therefore, always lies with the directors, whereas it is the responsibility of the auditors to report upon those accounts. For example, although the auditors may advise the directors as to the appropriateness of a particular form of presentation, they have no power to require that it be used, and it is up to the directors to accept their advice or not. If the auditors are of the opinion that the final form of presentation adopted does not convey a 'true and fair view' or does not conform with the acts, then it is their duty to refer to that in their report. In practice, it would be rare for directors to oppose the views of the auditors in this regard.

In order to meet their responsibilities, the law confers considerable powers upon auditors to enable them to carry out necessary investigations and to obtain whatever information and explanations are required by them, and, as already noted, no limit may be placed on the scope of that inquiry. However, this should not be understood to mean that the auditors examine every transaction. In fact, considerable reliance is placed upon the internal control system since this is the first line of defence against fraud and error.

FORM OF REPORT

The purpose of a heritage enterprise's annual report to external parties would normally be to provide timely and regular information to users as to objectives, achievements, transactions and financial position. The content of the report must be left to the preparer's judgement and will probably vary with the particular circumstances. Because these enterprises are so different in character, great care should be taken when interpreting the information provided. For example, one enterprise may operate on a 'profit' basis while another may not. Consequently, comparisons of the surplus/deficit on their respective income and expenditure (or profit and loss) accounts will not be meaningful. It should also be understood that a balance sheet is not necessarily a measure of the value of an enterprise!

While it is recommended that a full report be prepared each year, including a full set of audited accounts, it is recognized that simplified accounts may be prepared for particular purposes, for instance in order to incorporate a summary in some other document. If so, it should be ensured that the summary is a fair one and that it contains both a reference to the full accounts and a statement that the summary accounts are not audited.

CONTENT OF THE ANNUAL REPORT
The Annual Report should refer to all the activities of the enterprise and, in particular, distinguish between those of a commercial and non-commercial nature. The report should normally contain the following kinds of information:

• legal and administrative details, providing background information on the constitution of the enterprise;

• a Directors' (or equivalent) Report describing the operations of the enterprise and commenting on the accounts;

• the accounts, with accompanying notes, and the Auditors' Report.

As the Directors (or equivalent) are responsible for the form and content of the report, it should be formally adopted by them and signed by, at least, two on their behalf.

Legal and administrative details
The legal and administrative details provided should include the following :

• a note on the legal status of the enterprise;

• names of Directors and of senior officers;

• registered address;

• names and addresses of relevant organizations or persons, for example, bankers;

• details of any special restrictions on operations, for instance, prohibition on distribution of any surplus.

The Directors' Report (or equivalent)
This would normally contain:

• the objectives of the enterprise and a description of the policies and of the organization employed to achieve them and of any changes in this regard;

• a review of developments, activities and achievements during the year, enabling the user to assess progress and effectiveness;

• a review of transactions and of the financial position to enable the accounts to be properly interpreted;

• other information deemed relevant in individual circumstances.

The accounts
The accounts are a report on the financial activities and resources of the enterprise, and would normally comprise the following (compliance with the *Companies Acts* being assumed in appropriate circumstances):

• an income and expenditure (or profit and loss) account showing income received and expenses incurred;

• a balance sheet showing assets, liabilities and net funds balance or capital and reserves, as appropriate;

• a cash flow statement;

• a statement of accounting policies;

• other notes which expand upon the information in the above accounts;

• corresponding figures for the previous accounting period.

Accounting policies
In the absence of a contrary disclosure, it is assumed that the accounts will have been prepared in accordance with the basic concepts of accruals, prudence, consistency and 'going concern'. However, a clear, fair and brief explanation of all other material accounting policies should be provided, by way of note, to give a full understanding of the basis on which the accounts are prepared. All policies should be consistently applied and any changes disclosed. Examples of such policies would be :

• basis of valuation, namely historical cost;

- depreciation;

- grants;

- stocks.

Accounting for special funds
Because of the nature of heritage enterprises, donations, endowments, legacies, gifts, grants and the like may be made to them with conditions attached which restrict or govern their use and that of any associated assets, liabilities or income, and consequently appropriate disclosure and presentation should be made.

CONCLUSION

Because of the varied nature and extent of heritage enterprises and of the structural organizations surrounding them, it is not possible to be definitive as to what form of accountability is appropriate in every circumstance. Much will depend upon the ownership of the enterprise and on the awareness of directors and management of their perceived responsibilities in this regard. A lot will also depend upon the demands made by relevant parties for greater openness and information concerning these enterprises and of the calls made for recognition of their legitimate interests and concerns. Just as accounting has changed and adapted in past years, and will continue to do so in the future, in response to changes in the financial environment, so also will change occur in the realm of social accounting for what might be considered to be community interests such as heritage enterprises.

Bibliography

Auditing Practices Board 1995 *Accounting and internal control systems and audit risk assessments.* London.
Accounting Standards Board 1991 *The objective of financial statements and the qualitative characteristics of financial information.* London.
Accounting Standards Board 1993 *Foreword to accounting standards.* London.
Accounting Standards Committee 1998 *Accounting for charities. Statement of recommended practice.* London.
Accounting Standards Steering Committee 1975 *The corporate report.* London.
Batsleer, J., Cornforth, C., and Paton, R. 1991 *Issues in voluntary and non-profit management.* Reading, Mass.
Cousins, M. 1994 *A guide to legal structures for voluntary and community organisations.* London.
Hayes, T. 1996 *Management, control and accountability in non-profit/voluntary organisations.* Avebury.

Perks, R. W. 1993 *Accounting and society.* London.
Porter, B., Simon, S. and Hatherly, D. 1996 *Principles of external auditing.* Chichester, New York.
Tweedie, D. 1983 'True and fair rules', *The Accountant's Magazine.*

Basic Accounting

MICHAEL McADOO

In this chapter we shall look at the practical areas of accounting for heritage management.We examine financial statements, their component parts and the users of same, financial records, ratios, taxes and cash flow. The assessment of capital projects is also briefly explored. It is important to stress that the chapter is only an introduction to the topics which require further detailed learning to understand the area fully. It is recognized that not all persons involved in heritage management will have strong numeracy skills. However, a basic knowledge of the areas of accounting is important to enable the right questions to be asked in the interest of proper administration of the cultural enterprises with which an individual or team are likely to be involved.

BOOKKEEPING, ACCOUNTING AND FINANCIAL MANAGEMENT
The importance of this area cannot be over-emphasized, as without records, the enterprise is like a ship without radar, it can only guess as to where it is going and has a limited knowledge as to its present position. To enable an enterprise to budget, cost, or have any form of financial management structure, record keeping is essential. Very often nowadays, this recording is done by computer. However, to understand the real meaning of the information churned out by the computer, a basic appreciation of the how and why of accounting is important. In this chapter, we look at the basics of bookkeeping and accounting, who is effected by these records and of what use they are to the enterprise. It is important to remember that this is an overview and that an in-depth knowledge can only be obtained from further focussed reading and attending courses and seminars on the subject.

FINANCIAL STATEMENTS
These statements consist of two areas:

(a) The profits or losses made during the last financial period.

(b) A statement which shows the assets or liabilities of the business, together with the amount of money financing it, called the balance sheet. These financial statements could be of use to the following:

(1) Shareholders/investors.

(2) Lenders.

(3) Government.

(4) Financial advisors.

(5) Employees.

(6) Commercial parties.

(1) Shareholders/Investors: These are persons who have invested in the business and would be interested to know how their investment is progressing and being protected.

(2) Lenders: These are interested in the financial statements to verify that their lending plus interest can be repaid.

(3) Government: Businesses have to pay taxes such as income tax, VAT, PAYE/PRSI, so the government needs financial statements to assess such matters.

(4) Financial advisors: To enable them to analyse and advise on cash flow and future earnings, so as to review current performance and predict future prospects.

(5) Employees: To keep this important group motivated and interested, extracts from the financial statements are

published. They could also be used in negotiating wage agreements.

(6) Commercial parties: These are suppliers, customers and business competitors who deal with the business and may need to know its status. They may also be interested in takeovers or the purchase of the business.

Not all the above types of users might be interested in the financial statements at one time, rather at different times and for different reasons. It follows, therefore, from the above that presenting the financial statements in a meaningful way is important, so the use of charts or graphs may be considered. It also follows that for financial statements to be effective, there are accounting concepts and conventions to be complied with. These are generally identified as:

(1) Business entity: that all transactions relate to the business only.

(2) Money measurement: that all transactions are valued in money terms only.

(3) Duality: that each transaction has two effects.

(4) Prudence: profit is only taken as it is earned.

(5) Going concern: that the enterprise will continue for the foreseeable future.

(6) Accruals: that income and expenditure is matched to the period.

(7) Consistency: that transactions are treated the same each time.

All these conventions have now been enshrined in accounting practice through Standard Statements of Accounting Practice (SSAPs) and Financial Reporting Standards (FRS), which lay down the method and presentation of this information.

FINANCIAL RECORDS
Each enterprise will have a different type of system to suit its particular need and, as a result, this section can only give a general overview of books and records. For most enterprises, the following account books will be sufficient:

Cash book: This records money that comes into the enterprise and what is done with this money.

Cheques journal: Records the cheques and other outgoings from the bank. Information is obtained from

the cheque stubs and bank statements. The bank balance per the bank statement is regularly agreed with the books.

Petty cash book: Records payments of a minor nature not paid by cheque. Normally, a fixed sum is allocated to petty cash and is topped up regularly under the 'The Imprest System', that is, the previous period expenses are refunded to petty cash to top up the fixed sum.

Purchases day book: Needed for VAT purposes and is a record of purchases made by the enterprise, both for resale and not for resale. Purchase returns are normally listed in the back and are sometimes linked to a purchases ledger. Invoices should be checked before entry as to accuracy and agreed to suppliers statements on a regular basis before payment.

Sales day book: This records credit sales to customers based on invoices issued. This is linked to a sales (debtors) ledger, which identifies amounts due by customers at any time. Sales returns are recorded in the back of the book.

With these basic records, it is possible for an accountant to prepare financial statements that are the profit and loss account and balance sheet. Let us now look at these areas.

THE PROFIT AND LOSS ACCOUNT

This is split into two areas:

(i) *The trading account*, which gives us the gross profit and

(ii) *The profit and loss account*, which shows the profit or loss made by the business.

(iii) Some enterprises may not need a trading account (because they do not sell goods), and the trading and profit and loss accounts are prepared as an income and expenditure account.

The trading account
This is the difference between the sales and cost of sales, giving the gross profit. There will always be a gross profit because anything else would indicate that goods were sold for less than they were purchased for. Cost of sales is normally identified as opening stock plus purchases less closing stock.

The profit and loss account
This is the difference between the gross profit and the running expenses of the business:

Table 71.1 Typical Trading Account

TRADING ACCOUNT FOR THE YEAR ENDED XX/XX/XX	£	£
Sales		54,000
Less cost of sales		
Opening stock	2,000	
Plus purchases	29,000	
	31,000	
Less closing stock	(5,000)	(26,000)
Gross Profit		28,000

Table 71.2

	£	£
Gross Profit:		28,000
Less Expenses:		
Wages	3,500	
Rent	500	
Advertising	200	
Stationery	300	
Postage	150	
Insurance	250	
Motor expenses	150	
Lighting and heating	300	
Depreciation	340	
Carriage outwards	160	
Bad debts written off	200	
Provision for bad debts	100	(6,150)
Net Profit		21,850

Depreciation

This is the writing down of an asset over its expected useful life and is purely a book transaction. There are two basic types of depreciation, straight line and reducing balance. Residual value is the expected scrap value of the asset at the end of its useful life.

Straight Line Method:

$$\frac{\text{Cost of asset less residual value}}{\text{Expected useful life}} = \text{Depreciation per annum}$$

Reducing Balance Method:

Cost of asset less residual value x agreed % each year is calculated on written down value of the previous year.

THE BALANCE SHEET, A PEN PICTURE OF A BUSINESS AT A PARTICULAR POINT.

The balance sheet consists of four distinct areas:

(1) Fixed assets — solid assets.

(2) Current assets, also known as liquid assets.

(3) Current liabilities, amounts payable within one year.

(4) Financed by long-term loans and capital.

Table 71.3 Sample Balance Sheet Layout

Balance sheet as at xx/xx/xx

Fixed Assets	Cost	Depreciation	NBV
Premises	30,000	8,000	22,000
Fixtures and Fittings	25,000	11,000	14,000
	55,000	19,000	36,000

Current Assets (also known as Liquid Assets)		
Stock	3,500	
Debtors and prepayments	1,000	
Cash, bank, on hands	4,500	9,000

Current Liabilities (short term creditors, payable within 1 year)		
Trade	5,500	
Accruals	500	
(expense creditors)		
Bank overdraft	4,500	7,000

Net Current Assets (working capital)		2,000
Net Assets (asset value of business)		38,000

Financed by:		
Long-term loans	10,000	
Balance from		
last account	21,000	
Add net profit	21,850	
	42,850	
Less Drawings	(14,850)	28,000
		38,000

The balance sheet is based on a basic accounting rule: assets = liabilities and capital.

The balance sheet, as shown in **Table 71.3**, has the same core information as on all balance sheets. However, different types of enterprise may have additional subheadings or layout, for instance, partnerships or limited companies.

Much can be learned about the enterprise from the financial statements, and the use of various ratios can enhance that information. Ratios are useful for comparison purposes and look at sets of numbers or compares different areas of an enterprise. There are five key types of accounting ratios.

(1) Liquidity (how much cash the enterprise has).

(2) Profitability.

(3) Use of assets.

(4) Capital structure.

(5) Returns to investors.

Ratios only indicate trends and must be interpreted in

Table 71.4

AREA	TYPE OF RATIO	CALCULATION	EXPLANATION
LIQUIDITY	Current ratio	Current assets: Current liabilities	Shows the amount of cash available to pay immediate debts.
	Quick ratio/Acid test ratio	Current assets less stock: Current liabilities	Stock can lose its value and, in particular, in a break-up situation. This may give more accurate liquid indication.
PROFITABILITY	Gross profit %	$\frac{\text{Gross Profit} \times 100}{\text{Sales}}$	Fluctuations in gross profit could indicate problems, for example, wrong valuation of stock or excessive discounts. Fluctuations must be examined closely.
	Net profit	$\frac{\text{Net profit} \times 100}{\text{Sales}}$	Fluctuation in expenses can cause this to change.
USE OF ASSETS	Sales to fixed assets	Sales compared to fixed assets	Shows the ratio of sales being generated by fixed assets.
	Stock turnover	Average stock/cost of sales x 365 = days *or* cost of sales/average stock = times	The faster the stock is turned over the better the profit.
	Debtor days	$\frac{\text{Debtors} \times 365}{\text{Credit sales}}$	How long debtors (on average) take to pay their debts.
	Creditor days	$\frac{\text{Creditors} \times 365}{\text{Purchases}}$	How long on average the enterprise is taking to pay its debts.
CAPITAL STRUCTURE	Gearing ratio	Debt to equity	Level of debt to owners' equity, the higher the debt ratio, the greater the exposure for investors.
RETURNS TO INVESTORS	Return on capital employed (ROCE)	$\frac{\text{Profit before interest} \times 100}{\text{Capital employed}}$	Shows the capital return to investors.
	Earnings per share	$\frac{\text{Profit after tax and preference}}{\text{share dividends}}$	Return the ordinary shareholder gets for investing in the number of ordinary shares issued by enterprise.
DIVIDEND YIELD		Ordinary dividend/market price of share x 100 (sometimes calculated at nominal value where no market exists).	The higher the % return the better.

conjunction with similar enterprises and economic trends, making sure you compare like with like.

TAXES

All enterprises will come within the tax net to a lesser or greater degree. Where enterprises employ persons, then they will have to deduct PAYE (Pay As You Earn), and PRSI (Pay Related Social Insurance) from those persons at source and pass them on to the tax authorities. Likewise, VAT (Valued Added Tax) has to be considered on the sales of the enterprise and its scale and type of operation. Again, this is collected at source and passed on to the authorities at regular intervals. Depending on the type of enterprise and its structure, income tax or corporation tax will also be a factor and will effect the cash flow and retained profits of the enterprise. Discussions with advisors and reading various government publications on tax matters will enable you to understand these matters.

CASH FLOW

Up to now, we have been talking about the profit of an enterprise. However, the life blood of an enterprise is cash flow and without adequate cash flow, the enterprise will cease to function. It must be emphasized that cash flow is not profit, rather the ability of the enterprise to meet its day-to-day running expenses on time, so the timing of cash flow to the enterprise is important. For example, if an enterprise sold goods on credit and did not receive the cash thereon for two months and had to pay for the goods in one month, then there is a cash flow timing problem. As a result, either the enterprise would have to raise finance to pay for the goods or collect the cash earlier. So the enterprise should prepare a cash flow projection for at least a year and this cash flow should be monitored against the actual position, so that corrective action (if necessary) can be taken quickly.

CAPITAL APPRAISAL

We conclude this quick overview of bookkeeping, accounting and financial management by looking at appraisal of capital investment programmes. For an enterprise to grow it has to be constantly looking at ways of increasing sales and market share. This, in turn, costs money by way of investments and this is generally in short supply. To assess various investment opportunities will mean making judgements as to what is the best value, considering the initial cost of the investment, the degree of risk involved, the life-cycle of the investment and the financial return. There are four main methods of assessing capital projects:

(1) Pay Back.

(2) Accounting Rate of Return (ARR).

(3) Net Present Value (NPV).

(4) Internal Rate of Return (IRR).

It is beyond the scope of this chapter to go into the area in great detail. However, a short explanation and worked example may help to give an understanding of the methods of project assessment.

It is important to recognize that these methods are only a means of assessing the value of cash flow or the outlay of something of economic value (usually cash), at one point in time, which is expected to give economic benefits to the investor at some future time, that is the outlay precedes the benefits.

Pay Back

Pay Back is a simple method of assessing the number of years it takes to pay back the outlay from the expected cash flow in the future.

Accounting Rate of Return (ARR)

This method takes into account the profit which the project is expected to generate and expresses it as a % of the average investment outlay.

$$ARR = \frac{\text{Average Annual Profit}}{\text{Average Investment Outlay}} \times 100\%$$

Net Present Value (NPV)

This takes into account the future value of cash flows, because a £100 today is worth less in a year's time. To use this method, we have to be aware of the expected return on capital, for instance 5% or 10%. Discounting tables are necessary to calculate this method.

Internal Rate of Return (IRR)

This method is that discount rate which will in effect give an NPV of zero. It is a hit–and–miss method, as you have to find a rate at which there will be a positive net cash flow and a rate which will give a negative net cash flow. Somewhere between these two ratios is the rate at which there will be zero cash flow.

Example to illustrate the above methods

The Diamond Heritage Centre are considering two machines to enable them to perform a task efficiently. Both machines have a life-span of five years, at the end of which they will both have a scrap value. The straight line method of depreciation is used by the Diamond Heritage Centre and the expected return on capital is 14%. **Table 71.5** shows the details of both machines.

However, there are many other considerations which should be brought to bear when considering an investment decision. Any good financial management book will give this detail.

Table 71.5

			Machine I	Machine II
			£	£
Year	0	Outlay	(131,000)	(225,000)
	1	Cash flow	40,000	80,000
	2	Cash flow	40,000	80,000
	3	Cash flow	50,000	60,000
	4	Cash flow	60,000	50,000
	5	Cash flow	10,000	50,000
Scrap value			1,000	5,000

The discounting rates are as follows

	14%	16%	18%
Year 1	.877	.862	.847
Year 2	.769	.743	.718
Year 3	.675	.641	.609
Year 4	.592	.553	.516
Year 5	.497	.476	.437

(1) PAY BACK

				Machine I		Machine II
Year	0	Outlay		(131,000)		(225,000)
	1	Cash flow	40,000		80,000	
	2	Cash flow	80,000		160,000	
	3	Cash flow	50,000		220,000	
	4	Cash flow	1,000	131,000	5,000	225,000
				0		0

that is 3 years + $\frac{1,000}{60,000}$ or 3.02 yrs   that is 3 years + $\frac{5,000}{50,000}$ or 3.10 yrs

Machine I takes a shorter period to pay back .08 of year less.

(2) ARR

Machine I   Average profits

Year	1	2	3	4	5
Cash flow	40,000	40,000	50,000	60,000	10,000
Scrap value					1,000
	40,000	40,000	50,000	60,000	11,000
Less depreciation	(2,600)	(26,000)	(26,000)	(26,000)	(26,000)
Net profit	14,000	14,000	24,000	34,000	(15,000)

Calculation of average net profit   71,000/5 = £14,200

Calculation of depreciation
Cost	131,000
Less scrap	(1,000)
Value	130,000
	130,000/5 = £26,000

Average profits   14,200 = 10.8%
Average outlay   130,000

Machine II   Average profits

Year	1	2	3	4	5
Cash flow	80,000	80,000	60,000	50,000	50,000
Scrap value					5,000
	80,000	80,000	60,000	50,000	55,000
Less depreciation	44,000	44,000	44,000	44,000	44,000
Net profit	36,000	36,000	16,000	6,000	11,000

Table 71.5 cont.

Calculation of average net profits	105,000/5 = £21,000

Calculation of depreciation

Cost	225,000
Less scrap	(5,000)
Value	220,000

220,000/5 = £44,000

Average profits	$\frac{21,000}{225,000}$ = 9.3%
Average outlay	

Machine I has a better return.

(3) <u>NPV</u> (14%)

		Machine I		**Machine II**	
Year	0		(131,000)		(225,000)
	1	40,000 x .817 35,080		80,000 x .877 70,160	
	2	40,000 x .769 30,760		80,000 x .769 61,520	
	3	50,000 x .675 33,750		60,000 x .675 40,500	
	4	60,000 x .592 35,520		50,000 x .592 29,600	
	5	10,000 x .497 4,970		50,000 x .497 24,850	
	5+scrap 1,000 x .497 497	140,057	5,000 x .497 2,485	229,115
	NPV		**+£9,755**		**+£4,115**

Both have a positive cash flow.

Machine I	+ 9,775
Machine II	+ 4,115

As Machine I has the greater positive cash flow, then that is the one to opt for.

(4) <u>IRR</u>

Machine I NPV @ 14%   + 9,577   Machine II NPV @ 14%   +4,115

Trial and error calculate negative NPV

Machine I NPV @ 18%   **Machine II NPV @ 16%**

Year	0		(131,000)		(225,000)
	1	40,000 x .847 33,880		80,000 x .862 68,960	
	2	40,000 x .718 28,120		80,000 x .743 59,440	
	3	50,000 x .609 30,450		60,000 x .641 38,460	
	4	60,000 x .516 30,960		50,000 x .553 27,650	
	5	10,000 x .437 4,370		50,000 x .476 23,800	
	5	1,000 x .437 437	128,817	5,000 x .476 2,380	220,690
NPV			-(2,183)		(4,310)

14% + $\frac{9,577}{9,577 + 2,183}$ x 4 = **17.26**   14 % + $\frac{4,115}{4,115 + 4,310}$ x 2 = **14.98**

Machine I	IRR	17.26%
Machine II	IRR	14.98%

CONCLUSION

As can be seen, the topic of bookkeeping, accounting and financial management is vast and in this chapter, we have only touched on the principles. However, the bibliography lists some texts which will help you to further your knowledge.

Bibliography

Arnold, J. and Turley, S. 1996 *Accounting for management decisions.* London.

Atrill, P. and McLaney, E. 1996 *Management accounting for non-specialists.* New York.

McAdoo, M. 1990 *Bonanza or belly up: financial control for the self-employed.* Cork.

Pike, R. and Neale, B. 1993 *Corporate finance and investment, decisions and strategies.* New York.

Copyright and Cultural Heritage

LIA O'HEGARTY

In Irish tradition, there is a well-known story about copyright. As we are told, St Columcille copied by hand the Latin psalter of St Finnian of Clonard. St Finnian objected and the high-king Diarmaid was called in to resolve the dispute. His eminently reasonable judgment in favour of St Finnian was 'To every cow its calf; to every book its copy'. Nowadays, copyright law applies to a wide range of material other than books and protects expressions of ideas in many forms. It applies to works of art generally as well as to various informational works. In fact, copyright forms part of a larger branch of law known as 'intellectual property' (IP) law. The term 'intellectual property' highlights the fact that the fruits of intellectual labour often take the form of intangible objects. To have copyright in a particular work means to have a set of exclusive rights to do (or to authorize) certain activities in relation to that work — not just copying, but performing, adapting and the like. In most instances, a copyright owner will not simply keep these rights for himself but will allow others to exercise them provided he can thereby reap a profit from his endeavours.

After a brief account of the history of copyright, we outline Irish copyright law insofar as it is relevant to persons creating, preserving, documenting and interpreting the cultural heritage. Some aspects of that law, such as the protection of computer software, are not considered. At the time of writing, Irish copyright law is undergoing radical revision. *The Copyright and Related Rights Act* 2000 has become law, but has not yet come into operation. The Act will introduce many changes, and these are discussed briefly here where relevant. We conclude with a broader consideration of the role of copyright law in the advancement of the cultural heritage.

COPYRIGHT: HISTORY AND RATIONALE

A variety of anthropological evidence suggests that there were analogues of intellectual property rights in ancient societies. Individuals in some primitive societies could arrogate to themselves the benefits of innovation by claiming magical powers. Magic was used to 'explain' new techniques and was then construed as essential to the success of those techniques:

the system of beliefs surrounding magic favours the attribution of eldritch abilities to the intellectually and creatively gifted and, relatedly, to those individuals who achieve extraordinary success in their practical endeavours. (Suchman 1992)

Much later, Renaissance guilds achieved similar effects through the ceremonial elements of initiation and apprenticeship. In Imperial China, by contrast, all knowledge was deemed to have come from the past. One was privileged to be the servant of hallowed tradition by transmitting knowledge, whether by means of original writing or copying (Alford 1997). This world-view is radically different from our own; although it reveals an avid enthusiasm for learning, it does not accommodate notions of individual property rights in ideas. Indeed, China had no copyright legislation until recently when the dictates of international trade finally forced it to follow a western model.

In Elizabethan England, bouncers were hired in Shake-spearian theatres to evict members of the audience who attempted to copy down the words of plays (Boyle 1996)! Traditionally, the sheer time and effort involved in copying books by hand often served to deter copyists. The printing press brought new economies of scale. By Royal Charter of 1557, the Stationers' Company (comprising members of the printing trade) was given exclusive rights to publish particular titles and classes of work. Following the expiry of this licensing regime, a statute was passed in 1710, subtitled *An Act for the Encouragement of Learning*, which heralded the introduction of authors' rights. It was from such beginnings that modern English (and later Irish) copyright legislation grew.

Today, copyright law is expanding in various ways, in Europe and beyond. The scope of relevant rights is being extended to cover not only new economic rights to reap profits from one's work but also 'moral' rights to protect the integrity of the work itself. The duration of copyright has recently been extended; throughout the EU, the basic term for which copyright endures has been increased to the lifetime of the author plus seventy years. The range of beneficiaries is also being extended to include, for example, performers.

The law of copyright involves a balance between encouraging creative activity and providing broad public access to the fruits of such activity. Artistic and intellectual creations — by their very nature — may be the product of much time and effort, but once they are produced, their benefits can be widely distributed at little or no extra cost. In the absence of a copyright system, such works, once revealed or released by their makers, could then be freely used and imitated by others without restriction. This system would be unsatisfactory for both the individual and society. Basic notions of fairness and indeed familiar justifications of private property dictate that creators should be entitled to reap some rewards from the fruits of their labour. (Indeed, in the legal systems of some continental European countries, notably France, the rights of creators over their works are considered to be an inherent aspect of the rights of personhood, because a work is an expression of personality.) Equally, to discourage the communication of ideas and the display of art would impoverish the cultural richness of society as a whole. 'The productions of genius and the means of instruction are common property,' wrote the Abbé Gregoire in reaction to iconoclasm during the French Revolution (Sax 1990).

FRAMEWORK OF IRISH LEGISLATION

At the time of writing, the principal piece of Irish law on the topic is the *Copyright Act* 1963 (hereinafter referred to as 'the 1963 Act'). This Act is due to be repealed and replaced by the *Copyright and Related Rights Act* 2000 (hereinafter referred to as 'the new Act'). The new Act has been passed by the Oireachtas and signed into law by the President, but it will not come into operation until the Minister for Enterprise, Trade and Employment makes a commencement order to that effect. It is expected that this will occur in late 2000. Readers should check for themselves whether, at the time of reading, the commencement order(s) and the various Regulations envisaged by the Act have been made by the minister.

The new Act will prospectively confer new copyright protection not only on works created after its commencement but also on works currently 'in'

copyright where that copyright continues beyond the date of its commencement. In other words, many works which are currently protected under the 1963 Act will be given enhanced protection under the new Act when it comes into effect. At that point the 1963 Act will no longer be in force, but its provisions will still govern various issues such as who owns the copyright in a work created before the commencement of the new Act. The precise determination of which Act will apply to each individual case is not addressed here.

If you are working with the cultural heritage you may encounter copyright law in a variety of ways. Let us suppose you are compiling an audio-visual exhibition at a public museum. Two principal issues arise. You are unsure whether you are entitled to reproduce a particular set of images. Furthermore, you are concerned as to whether you can seek redress if your accompanying commentary is plagiarized. Assuming for the moment that Irish law will apply, the following questions must then be addressed.

(1) Are the images copyrighted? Is the text copyrightable? (see section on *COPYRIGHTABLE WORKS*).

Assuming the answers to (1) are in the affirmative: —

(2) In the case of both the images and the text: What does the copyright consist of? In other words, what acts can be restricted? (see section on *CONTENT OF RIGHTS*).

(3) In the case of both the images and the text: What uses of the material are nevertheless permitted? In other words, are there any relevant exceptions to the rules? (see section on *EXCEPTIONS TO INFRINGEMENT*).

(4) Who owns this particular copyright? (see section on *OWNERSHIP OF RIGHTS*). In the hypothetical scenario, you may wish to ascertain

(a) whether copyright in the text actually belongs to you, and/or

(b) who are the owners of copyright in the images in order that you can secure their permission to copy.

(5) How long does the copyright last? (see section on *DURATION OF RIGHTS*). In the hypothetical scenario, you may, for example, discover that copyright once existed in the images but has since expired, so that they are now in the 'public domain'.

(6) Some very practical questions then arise. How do you secure permission from the copyright-owner to use the images? How do you assert your rights with respect to the text? (see section on *ENFORCEMENT OF RIGHTS*).

(7) Finally, other kinds of rights may be relevant. For example: Can you display the images in any manner you choose? (see section on MORAL RIGHTS). Do you have any rights in respect of your recitation of the text, even where you quote other works? (see section on PERFORMERS' RIGHTS).

COPYRIGHTABLE WORKS
'Category I' Works

First, the 1963 Act accords copyright protection to a range of original works, namely literary, dramatic, musical and artistic works. The requirement of originality has a very broad meaning in this context. It is not a requirement of novelty or quality; it simply means that the work must be the original product of the author and not a mere copy. A 'derivative' work such as a play based on a novel will itself attract copyright protection, provided it results from a modicum of creative endeavour. It is settled law that copyright does not extend to ideas as such but only to their embodiment; the new Act clarifies this and specifically excludes, for example, concepts and methods from the scope of copyright law.

Literary works: This category covers written works generally and 'includes any written table or compilation'. The 1963 Act, as interpreted, requires that the work must be in written or other material form. Thus if a public lecture is given in a museum, a member of the audience could take notes and gain copyright in those notes. (This would not, however, automatically entitle him to publish a version of the lecture, whether verbatim or otherwise.) Artistic value is irrelevant, as is literary merit. What matters is that the text resulted from the exercise of some skill or judgment. Thus, for example, a map-and-guide of archaeological sites is a literary work for this purpose, whereas an alphabetically arranged version of a list already available would not qualify. Again, a poetry anthology would qualify for copyright even though the editors may not possess copyright in the individual poems. An annotated version of a text — and certainly a translation — would qualify, whereas a newly invented word or phrase generally would not.

Dramatic works: According to the 1963 Act, this includes not only plays (and film scripts) but also dance or mime shows if reduced to notation. Thus, an impromptu sketch would not be copyrightable as such. The requirement of notation may be quite limiting in relation to dance. Techniques for transmitting or recording choreography range from good memorizing or teaching to basic outline-notation to more advanced methods such as video or computer graphics. It would seem, then, rather ironically, that someone who constructs a folk-dance along traditional lines may get copyright whereas a person who devises (without taking notes) a wholly new show in contemporary dance, which revolutionizes the art of movement, may not.

Musical works: The 1963 Act does not define 'musical work'. Snatches of melody or harmony may be sufficient, as indeed they should: the very fact that a progression of eight notes forming the ground bass of Pachelbel's *Canon in D* has been 'borrowed' so many times by 'pop' musicians surely testifies to its potential versatility. With regard to originality in music, there is obviously a gradation of more or less creative works. Thus, for example, a song melody, not transposed but simply retitled 'piece for flute', would not be an original work, whereas a harmonized version for choir would be, as would in turn a newly arranged, orchestrated version of the choral piece. Interesting legal questions are bound to arise with modern developments in sound technology, such as electro-acoustic music in which standard acoustic instruments are played together with electronic music. Likewise with new developments in compositional style, such as interactive compositions whereby performers are involved in creating a piece as they play it. Machover's *Brain Opera* is such a piece designed for the Internet which is recreated at regular intervals within an overall context defined by Machover.

The new Act specifies that there can be copyright in literary, dramatic or musical works only insofar as they are recorded, whether in writing or otherwise, by or with the consent of the author. In this scheme of things, it will still be a requirement that works be 'fixed', but there may be far greater flexibility as to the forms of fixation than there is at present. For example, recorded speech and the lyrics of a recorded song would be brought expressly within the protection of copyright law.

Artistic works: These can be further divided into the following sub-categories:

(a) includes *paintings; sculpture* (including any cast or model); *drawings* (including any diagram, map, chart or plan); *engravings* (including any etching, lithograph, woodcut, print and the like); and *photographs.* These works are protected 'irrespective of artistic quality'. The issue of originality may be highly pertinent with regard to some processes such as printing and sculpture. The practice in the graphic printing arts is to produce up to fifty 'original' prints (each of which is copyrightable) and then destroy the basic work done on wood or metal as the case may be. In the case of sculpture, a bronze cast created in a foundry from a wax or clay model may itself attract copyright protection.

(b) consists of *works of architecture* (buildings and models for buildings). 'Building' is defined broadly to include any structure.

(c) consists of works of *artistic craftsmanship* other than those in (a) and (b). This would include craft metalwork, pottery and so forth where there is a strong aesthetic element. It should be noted with regard to all artistic works that there is no copyright in an artist's 'style'.

'Category II' Works

The 1963 Act also protects a range of 'entrepreneurial' or 'exploitative' works. This category includes sound recordings, films and broadcasts. Sound recordings comprise the aggregate of sounds embodied in and reproducible by recording, other than film soundtracks. Apart from music recordings, this would include, for example, recordings of Irish dialects or recordings featuring sounds from the natural world such as birdsong. Also in this category are *published editions*: the typographical edition of a literary, dramatic or musical work will itself attract copyright protection.

The new Act abandons the overt distinction between 'Category I' works and 'Category II' works. It adds cable programmes to the list of protected works.

It should be noted that there may be several copyrights in the different elements of an overall work. In some cases these will be owned by different persons. For example, a calligraphist who produces an ornamental text of a poem may possess copyright in the resulting work of artistic craftsmanship although the poet will retain copyright in the text of the poem. In other cases, one person will own several copyrights simultaneously. An example would be a heritage exhibition incorporating both textual and visual elements. However, an exhibition involving no more than a mere arrangement of artefacts or paintings would not be protected in its own right.

CONTENT OF RIGHTS / INFRINGEMENT OF RIGHTS

Copyright generally involves the exclusive right to do (or to authorize) certain acts in relation to a work. Therefore, subject to certain exceptions, it is an infringement of copyright to carry out those acts in relation to the work, or a substantial part thereof, without authorization. The acts restricted by the copyright in a *literary, dramatic* or *musical* work are, first, adapting the work and, second, in relation to the work or any adaptation thereof, reproducing it in any material form, publishing it, broadcasting or transmitting it or performing it in public. These terms merit further consideration. 'Reproduction' includes reproducing in the form of a record or film. 'Publication' generally means issuing to the public. 'Performance' refers, in general, to any mode of visual or acoustic presentation (including by way of recording, film or broadcast) and includes delivery in the case of lectures and speeches. 'Adaptation' in relation to literary or dramatic works includes translation, representation

by pictorial sequence and conversion into dramatic or non-dramatic form, respectively. In relation to musical works, it includes arrangement or transcription.

The acts restricted by copyright in an *artistic* work are: reproducing it in any material form; publishing it; and broadcasting or transmitting it. 'Reproducing' an artistic work includes converting it from two-dimensional to three-dimensional form or vice versa.

The acts restricted by copyright in a *sound recording, film* or *broadcast* are: recording or copying it (including, in the case of a broadcast, photographing or filming the images or recording the sound aspects); playing it in public (including, in the case of a film or broadcast, playing the sound or visual aspect); and broadcasting or transmitting it (or, in the case of a broadcast, re-broadcasting or re-transmitting it).

Sound recordings may, however, be played in public or broadcast as of right provided royalties are paid to the copyright owner (or directly to a licensing body, as is required by the new Act). Making facsimile copies of the typographical arrangements of *published editions* infringes the publisher's copyright.

The new Act purports to clarify and broaden the rights conferred by the 1963 Act, and thereby also the range of restricted acts. Restricted acts are grouped into three main categories, namely copying, making available to the public and adapting. This terminology applies to all types of copyrightable work although it continues to be the case that different specific acts are restricted in respect of different types of work. It is worth noting that, in relation to artistic works, 'adaptation' is now expressly deemed to include an arrangement such as a 'collage'. More significant are the anticipated legal changes considered necessary to keep pace with advances in technology. Thus the new Act includes the following as restricted acts in relation to a copyrighted work: storing the work in any medium (for example on computer); making transient or incidental copies (except where this is technically required by a lawful user for viewing or listening to the work); and making copies available over the Internet.

EXCEPTIONS TO INFRINGEMENT

There is no general 'fair use' exception in Irish law as there is in US law. However, there are particular provisions identifying uses which do not constitute infringements. Some of these are described in terms of 'fair dealing' (which is not defined in the 1963 Act). Various other exemptions are made either in the public interest or for the sake of convenience. Again these vary according to the category of copyrighted work.

Fair dealing with a *Category I* work (whether literary, dramatic, musical or artistic) for the purposes of (a) research or private study or (b) criticism or review (of that or another work), if accompanied by a sufficient

Fig. 72.1 Original or copy? Artist Tom Molloy explores these notions in this pencil drawing (one of a series entitled Seven Photocopies). *His drawing depicts a photocopy of an image — printed in a book — of a still-life painting by Caravaggio.*

acknowledgment, does not constitute an infringement of copyright in the work. Fair dealing for the purpose of reporting current events is likewise not an infringement where it consists of either incorporating a work (other than a photograph) in a film or broadcast or of incorporating a *literary, dramatic* or *musical* work, accompanied by a sufficient acknowledgment, in a newspaper or other periodical.

Specifically with regard to *literary* or *dramatic* works, the reading or recitation in public or by broadcast of a reasonable extract from such works, if acknowledged, is permitted. Various other acts are permitted in respect of *artistic* works, namely: making (and/or publishing) a painting, drawing, engraving or photograph of, or including in a film or broadcast, works of sculpture or artistic craftsmanship which are permanently situated in a public place; incidentally including an artistic work in a film or broadcast; making a three-dimensional object based on a two-dimensional artwork if it does not appear to be a reproduction of the artwork; and using preparatory sketches, plans or models, on which earlier work was based, for the production of subsequent work,

provided the main design of the earlier work is not repeated. The rationale for this last exception becomes clear if we consider, for example, that an artist who produces a second 'series' of works may have already assigned away his copyright in the first 'series'.

There are also some exceptions to the infringement of *'Category II'* works (for example, copying a broadcast for purely private use or using old newsreel films). It is worth noting that copyright in a *published edition* is not infringed by copying for the purposes of research or private study.

The new Act provides for minor amendments to the scheme of exceptions to infringement. With respect to the 'fair dealing' exceptions, it extends their application in general to all works (including works hitherto in *'Category II'*) which have been lawfully made available to the public. 'Fair dealing' is defined as use for a purpose and to an extent which will not unreasonably prejudice the interests of the copyright owner. The new Act exempts various uses in the context of public administration and expressly permits copying from public records. It expressly permits the use of quotations in such a way as does not prejudice the copyright interests of their author, provided sufficient acknowledgment is given. It provides that the copyright in sound recordings is not infringed where such recordings are played by or for non-profit clubs or societies which are charitable or concerned with the advancement of religion, education or social welfare.

The new Act also sets out in detail two new categories of exemption: one in respect of educational establishments and another in respect of libraries and archives. It provides as follows: The copyright in any work is not infringed where non-reprographic copies are made in the course of instruction or preparation for instruction, subject to certain conditions and provided there is a sufficient acknowledgement. Likewise, performances of literary, dramatic or musical works, or the playing or showing of entrepreneurial works at educational establishments for the purposes of instruction, do not infringe copyright. 'Educational establishments' include schools and any other establishments which the minister may in future designate as such. Reprographic copies of extracts (not more than 5% in any year) from literary, dramatic or musical works or from published editions, or fixations of broadcasts or cable programmes, may be made for the educational purposes of such establishments (except where an approved licensing scheme comes into operation, in which case its terms must be complied with).

It is envisaged that the Minister for Enterprise, Trade and Employment will make Regulations setting out different rules for different categories of libraries and archives and designating certain libraries and archives as 'prescribed'. The new Act provides that a librarian or archivist of a prescribed library or archive may supply, for the purpose of research or private study, one copy of an article from a periodical, or one copy of a reasonable portion of a work (except in the latter case where the work has not been lawfully made available to the public and the librarian or archivist should have known that the copyright owner had prohibited copying). There are also provisions to allow for replacement copies and inter-library supply of copies, as well as provisions to prevent multiple copying.

OWNERSHIP OF RIGHTS

As a general rule, copyright in a *'Category I'* work vests in the 'author'. Although the term 'author' is not defined in the 1963 Act, it usually means the person who first fixes the work in its material form. Here we are reminded that copyright does not exist in ideas as such but rather in their mode of expression. The 'author' of a photograph, however, is the owner of the film. Copyright in sound recordings, broadcasts and films is generally held by the person who made the first recording, broadcast or film as the case may be — that is, the producer. Copyright in

published editions is held by the publisher. Of course in many of these cases, the owner will be a company (such as a recording or broadcasting studio or a publishing house) rather than an individual.

If the work is created for a fee or in the course of employment, a different rule applies. A person who commissions a photograph, portrait or engraving gets copyright in the work. Likewise the proprietor of a newspaper or other periodical will get copyright in a literary, dramatic or artistic work authored by an employee — insofar as that work relates to publication in the periodical (and potentially under new legislation, insofar as concerns publication in any periodical). Indeed, as a general rule, the copyright in a work created in the course of employment or apprenticeship vests in the employer or master. Furthermore, where a work is created under the direction or control of the government, copyright then vests in the government.

Where a work is anonymous or pseudonymous, it is nevertheless protected by copyright law (albeit for a lesser period). Where a work is created by two or more authors (as in the case of a co-written book) and where their individual contributions are not distinguishable, each author is entitled to copyright in the entire work. This is known as a situation of 'joint authorship'. Artists do not often realise that assistants such as foundry technicians and printmakers may be designated 'joint authors' where they were involved in the physical creative process (Kaufman 1997). In other cases of collaboration, typically where different genres of artists are involved (for example, a musician, a poet and a choreographer), each author will simply retain copyright in his contributory work.

The new Act defines 'author' as the person who creates a work. It makes some changes to the designation of authorship. For example, it provides new rules for photographs whereby the photographer is considered to be the author (although persons who commission photographs for domestic purposes are given special rights of privacy in photographs), and it includes as the author of a film the principal director as well as the producer. A provision precipitated by new technology is the designation of the author of a computer-generated work as the person who makes the arrangements necessary for its creation.

Establishing the ownership of rights is merely the first step. The next step is to understand how rights can be assigned and acquired. Suppose a playwright asks a novelist for permission to write a play based on the latter's novel. If the novelist decides to grant this permission, he can give it *gratis* or for payment. In this case, he is *licensing* a particular use of his work. Nowadays, copyright material is used so frequently and in so many ways that neither copyright owners nor copyright users would find it practical to grant/seek copyright permission in every case. Much of this work is done by collecting societies (see section on ENFORCEMENT OF RIGHTS). Thus an author may *assign* his rights (transfer them generally) to an agency which will then become owner of the rights and administer them on his behalf, dealing with requests and queries in relation to the work. It is important to remember that the mere fact that you acquire a copy or even the original of a work does not mean that you thereby acquire copyright in it.

DURATION OF RIGHTS

This aspect of Irish law was altered significantly in 1995 by the European Communities (Term of Protection of Copyright) Regulations which purport to implement a European Directive (Dir. 93/98/EEC). Harmonization of the duration of copyright across the EU was an attempt to remove one of the many barriers to the goal of a 'single market'. The basic rule now is that copyright in *'Category I'* works lasts for the lifetime of the author plus seventy years, irrespective of when the work is published. This considerably extends the copyright protection available hitherto under the 1963 Act (which lasted for the lifetime of the author plus fifty years), at least in respect of published works. An unusual effect of this recent law is that it brings certain older works back into copyright. Thus the copyright which had ceased in Ireland (although not in every EU state) in respect of the works of Joyce and Yeats has been revived. On the other hand, the period of protection for unpublished works is reduced on average. (Under the older law, the copyright in previously unpublished works endured for fifty years from the date of their publication.) This change is partially offset by other new rules. A new 'entrepreneur's right' (equivalent to copyright) of twenty-five years' duration is given to persons who publish, for the first time, work in which copyright has expired.

In cases where the term of protection is not calculated from the date of death of the author (for example, in the case of anonymous or pseudonymous works), the Regulations include a maximum term, again ensuring that copyright cannot be indefinitely postponed by non-publication. Anonymous or pseudonymous works are protected for seventy years following publication, but only provided they are published within seventy years of their creation. The new Act sets out separate rules for government copyright, which is to last for one hundred and twenty-five years from the year the work was created or, if the work is lawfully made available to the public within seventy-five years of its creation, then for fifty years following such publication.

Copyright in a *sound recording* is granted for fifty years after it is made, or, if it is lawfully made available to the public within those fifty years, then for fifty years after its publication. Copyright in a *film* extends for the lifetime of the director, film script author, dialogue author or music composer (whichever is the longest) plus seventy years, or, if it is lawfully made available to the public within that period, then for seventy years after such publication. (The Directive stipulates a lesser period for the rights of film producers, however.) Copyright in a *broadcast* subsists for fifty years after first transmission.

These new rules in many respects increase the privileges granted under law, not only for prospective newcomers to copyright but also for many who already hold or have held copyright. There is a saver in respect of cases where the new rules might unfairly take away previous 'rights' or at least expectations. Thus where a work of exploitation or preparation therefore was substantially underway before 1993, persons who simply bring such works to fruition will not be liable for infringement. Where such work took place between 1993 and 1995, persons will be exempt where they were reasonably unaware of the impending changes. The rule whereby copyright subsists in a *published edition* for twenty-five years remains unchanged.

ENFORCEMENT OF RIGHTS / COLLECTION SOCIETIES

Once a work is created, the author is entitled to copyright. No attendant formalities are necessary in order to assert copyright in Ireland. Where appropriate, the affixing of a date and the © symbol serves as a reminder — indeed as a warning! — to others that the copyright exists. (At a later stage, should problems arise, this may defeat a plea of 'innocent infringement'; it may also assist in enforcing the right abroad.) There are, of course, various methods which help to prove authorship and date of creation, in case copyright is later contested. For example, a composer may send to himself by registered post a tape of his new music. If copyright is infringed, the copyright holder can take an action in court against the infringer. If he is successful, a range of remedies are available, such as a court order to cease or withdraw the infringement, compensatory damages and/or an account of any profits made from the infringement. (Where architectural copyright is infringed, the court will not, however, order the demolition of a building or the cessation of building which is underway.) There will soon be a range of new criminal offences on the statute-book to further bolster the enforcement of copyright.

Practically, it may be very difficult to enforce one's own copyright, as this would involve acting as 'watchdog' for any infringements which might occur at any time or place. The most effective means of realizing copyright is often to assign it to an agency (such as a collecting society) or to authorize an agency to enforce it. (Note that, whereas an assignment of copyright must be in writing, a licence to a particular person to use copyrighted material need not be in writing.) The agency will then collect fees for use of the copyright material.

Collecting societies are a common feature of today's *music* world. The Irish Music Rights Organization (IMRO) administers performing rights on behalf of composers (and publishers to whom such rights have been assigned). Perform*ing* rights are a subset of copyright and are to be distinguished from perform*ers'* rights (see below). Persons who wish to 'perform' music in public — whether by way of performing live music or of playing recorded music — must get an annual IMRO licence and pay appropriate royalties. IMRO issues licences in respect of a huge international repertoire of copyright music by means of worldwide arrangements with similar agencies abroad. Phonographic Performance Ireland Ltd (PPI) administers performing and broadcasting rights in sound recordings. This is a different copyright to the composers' or publishers' copyright. Therefore, when a piece of recorded music is played in public, payments may be due to both IMRO and PPI. Another organization called the Mechanical Copyright Protection Society (MCPS) has been involved in negotiating on behalf of composers and publishers with those (generally larger commercial interests) seeking to exploit their reproduction or recording rights. The Irish Copyright Licensing Agency (ICLA) serves as a clearing-house between authors and publishers of *books* and members of the public. The Agency charges set fees to bodies such as universities which are then licensed to photocopy short extracts (for example, in the case of a book, usually 5% or one chapter).

It is expected that, over the coming years, collecting societies will assume greater importance in relation to all types of copyright-protected work. They will frequently be the first 'port of call' for both creators and users of copyright material inquiring as to their rights. Information about such bodies and the scope of their schemes should be more easily available if and when a (voluntary) national register, as envisaged by the new Act, is set up.

MODERN TRENDS IN COPYRIGHT AND RELATED RIGHTS

The first attempt at international cooperation in the field of copyright came in 1886 with the Berne Convention for the Protection of Literary and Artistic Works. Since Ireland is a member of the Berne Union, it must accord the copyright protection granted by Irish law to works originating in other member states. In most respects, our law is in accord with the Convention, but in one major aspect it is not yet so: namely, with regard to moral rights (see below). There is considerable international cooperation in the field of copyright under the umbrella of the World Intellectual Property Organization (WIPO). In 1996 the WIPO Copyright Treaty, a Protocol to the Berne Convention, was concluded in Geneva. Ireland has signed this Treaty but has yet to ratify it. A New Instrument was also concluded dealing with the rights of

performers and phonogram producers entitled the WIPO Performances and Phonograms Treaty (WPPT). There is further international cooperation under the auspices of GATT in the form of the Trade-Related Aspects of Intellectual Property Rights Agreement (TRIPS).

MORAL RIGHTS

The legal traditions of continental Europe recognize 'moral rights' in works of art generally. The integrity of the artist and of his work is the core value at stake here; the artist expresses himself through his artwork and therefore suffers a wrong if his work is distorted. Several French cases serve to illustrate the concept of moral rights (Merryman 1976). The artist, Bernard Buffet, won his case to prevent the separate sale of a painting on a metal panel which had originally been one of several panels forming a single artwork. The grand-daughter of Henri Rousseau won her case against a Paris department store which was displaying reproductions of his paintings with altered colours and images. The sculptor Sudre was awarded compensation when a city council removed and destroyed a sculpture which had been commissioned from him to decorate a public fountain.

In the 1980s, some US states — New York, California and Massachusetts — introduced moral rights legislation. The Californian statute specifically recognizes the 'public interest in preserving the integrity of cultural and artistic creations', and both the Californian and Massachusetts statutes provide for litigation by public interest organizations to preserve works of recognized quality. In 1990 the *Visual Artists Rights Act* introduced moral rights to the US at a federal level. Moral rights are perpetual in several countries and are generally inalienable — that is, they cannot be assigned away. This reflects the fact that they have a personal rather than an economic basis. However, they are frequently waivable — that is, the author may decline to exercise them.

The Berne Convention grants moral rights in respect of literary and artistic works, and Ireland's recognition of these rights is well overdue. The text of the Convention provides for a right of attribution and a right of respect:

the author shall have the right to claim authorship of the work and to object to any distortion, mutilation or other modification of, or other derogatory action in relation to, the said work, which would be prejudicial to his honour or reputation. (Article 6 *bis*)

The new Act purports to introduce these rights in Ireland, using the terms 'paternity right' and 'integrity right', respectively. These will apply to all works hitherto in *Category I* and to films, and will last as long as copyright in the work subsists. The beneficiary of a paternity right is also granted a corollary 'negative' right, lasting for twenty years after his death, not to have a work falsely attributed to him. (Indeed, this latter right already features in the 1963 Act.) There are some exceptions to the application of moral rights (for example, the rights of paternity and integrity do not apply to works in periodicals or in collective works of reference).

Colourful legal questions are bound to arise when new moral rights are given force in Irish law. Public art is a case in point, in particular 'site-specific art'. A controversial example is Richard Serra's sculpture *Tilted Arc* (a wall of rusted steel plates curving across New York's Federal Plaza), which was removed following public outrage. The treatment of items in display collections may be another case in point, although it is reasonable to surmise that a poor exhibition would not violate the integrity of artwork except in extreme cases. There are also new developments in the field of moral rights for performers (see below).

MISCELLANEOUS ECONOMIC RIGHTS

'Economic' rights relate, not to the granting or withholding of permission to use a work, but only to the receipt of profits from exploitation of the work. An important economic right found in continental European traditions is the *droit de suite*. This, like the moral right, is inalienable. The *droit de suite* is the artist's right to royalties each time the work is sold on. It is particularly appropriate for certain visual artworks embodied in a single unique *objet d'art*. It exists in California as a resale royalty right (the royalty being a percentage of the resale price) — but it does not apply to purely private sales. There is a proposal, not yet adopted, for the introduction throughout the EU of a *droit de suite* in original works.

The EU Directive on Rental and Lending Rights (Dir. 92/100/EC) is due to be implemented in Irish legislation. This gives to various copyright holders (and to performers) the exclusive right to authorize rental and lending of copies of their works (or recordings of their performances respectively). 'Rental' means rental for economic or commercial advantage and 'lending' means non-commercial rental via an establishment open to the public. (These terms do not, however, embrace rental or lending for the purposes of public viewing or listening or for on-the-spot reference use.) Thus far, these rights are simply an expansion of the scope of copyright. However, the new Act provides that even where persons transfer their 'rental rights', they will retain a right to equitable remuneration. This means that where their works are (commercially) rented, they will be guaranteed a fair commission which they cannot waive. This is an example of an economic right. As regards public lending, EU states may derogate from the Directive, provided that at least authors of various kinds of work receive remuneration for such lending. Thus, the European Directive envisages a scheme of 'public lending rights'

such as has long since operated in various countries, notably in Scandinavia. However, although Ireland must recognize this scheme in principle, we cannot expect to see it in operation, at least for the time being (as there is broad discretion to exempt various establishments from it). Other new 'economic' rights are on the way for performers (see below).

PERFORMERS' RIGHTS

Performers do not have copyright in relation to their performances, but in certain countries they are granted rights analogous to copyright. While Irish law does not grant rights directly to performers, it confers a certain level of protection on them. The *Performers' Protection Act* of 1968 prohibits the unauthorized recording, filming or broadcasting of a performance (as well as unauthorized attempts to trade in such records or films). In other words, it is a criminal offence to do any of these acts without the consent of the performer(s). There are various defences (analogous to some of the exemptions under copyright law). It appears that the courts, aware of the need for performers' protection, would allow performers themselves to invoke the Act; however, this does not obviate the need for law reform in this area.

The new Act heralds the introduction of performers' rights into Irish law. It covers all kinds of live performances by actors, singers, musicians, dancers or other persons of literary, dramatic, musical or artistic works or (notably) expressions of works of folklore. A performer is given the following rights in respect of the whole or a substantial part of a performance: the right to authorize or prohibit the recording or live broadcasting of the performance and the recording, other than for private and domestic use, of a live broadcast thereof; the right to authorize or prohibit the making of a copy of a recording of the performance, other than for private and domestic use (the 'Reproduction Right'); the right to authorize or prohibit the making available to the public of a recording of the performance or a copy thereof — including by showing or playing it in public, broadcasting it or relaying it over the Internet (the 'Making Available Right'); and the right to authorize or prohibit, in certain circumstances, the issuing to the public in other countries of a recording of the performance or copies thereof (the 'Distribution Right'). Reference has already been made to performers' Rental and Lending Rights (see above *MISCELLANEOUS ECONOMIC RIGHTS*). The new performers' rights will last for either: (a) fifty years from the year when the performance takes place; or (b) fifty years from the year when a recording of the performance is first lawfully made available to the public provided this occurs within the period specified in (a). The new Act envisages a range of exceptions to infringement of performers' rights, which generally parallel those in respect of copyright (except that there is no general exception for research or private study).

Many of the above-mentioned rights stem from the WPPT of 1996. Whereas the treaty applies only in relation to sound performances/recordings, an 'Audio-visual Protocol' is in preparation which would broaden its effect. An optional provision in the Treaty which has found its way into the new Act provides for a new 'economic right' for performers, specifically, a right to equitable remuneration where a (sound) recording of a performance is publicly played, broadcast or relayed over the Internet. The Treaty, and in turn the new Act, seeks to introduce moral rights for performers, specifically, a right of paternity, a right of integrity and a negative right against false attribution.

DATABASES

We have seen that collections of data are already protected as literary works under Irish law, where skill or judgment has been involved in the collation of information. Whereas the laws of most other European countries require a stronger notion of 'intellectual creation' here, many informational works are already within Irish copyright law by virtue of the sheer labour involved in sifting and selecting the information. Our present law is, however, inadequate to deal with the complexities of would-be literary works stored in electronic or digital form. One obstacle is the requirement that literary works exist in written or other material form.

Recently, there has been legislative initiative at a European and international level with regard to copyright in databases. A Directive of 1996 (Dir. 96/9/EC), which was due to be transposed into Irish law by the end of 1997, grants copyright to the authors of databases. The term 'database' is defined as 'a collection of independent works, data or other materials arranged in a systematic or methodical way and individually accessible by any means' (but excluding computer programs used in making or operating the database). Thus the term would include selections of sound and graphics as well as of text.

The new Act purports to implement the European Directive. In this scheme of things, there are now two tiers of protection for databases. The first is *copyright proper*. All EU states must now grant copyright protection in respect of 'original databases', defined as those which by reason of the selection or arrangement of their contents, constitute the author's own intellectual creation. Indeed such a rule is now also mandated by the TRIPS Agreement made under the auspices of GATT. This copyright will be owned by the individual or group who compiled the database. It will last for the same term as applies in respect of other original works (see above *DURATION OF RIGHTS*). It will apply only to collections of data as such, that is, to the selection and arrangement of

material, and not to the material itself, which may or may not be independently copyright-protected, as the case may be. The new Act sets out a range of acts restricted by copyright in original databases. These include, as in the case of other works, copying, making available to the public and making adaptations such as translations and arrangements. However, restrictions will not apply where these acts necessarily form part of a lawful use of the database. A range of exempted acts will be permitted, for example: fair dealing for the purposes of research or private study (in respect of non-electronic databases only); fair dealing for the purpose of criticism, review or reporting current events; and various uses in the context of educational establishments, libraries, archives and public administration.

The second tier of protection for databases will take the form of a novel 'database right'. This *sui generis* right was hitherto unknown in copyright law and so is termed a 'related right' rather than a copyright as such. It will protect the actual contents of databases (that is, the information as opposed to the compilation *per se*) where there was substantial investment in obtaining, verifying or presenting the contents. It will be owned by the person who took the initiative in starting that process and invested therein. In contrast to copyright, it will last for only fifteen years from completion of the database, but will be renewable if the database is changed so that it constitutes a substantial new investment. The acts restricted by this right include extraction (that is, permanent or temporary transfer to another medium) and/or re-utilization (that is, making available to the public) of the whole or of a substantial part of the contents of the database. There is also a range of exempted acts, namely: fair dealing by way of extraction of an already re-utilized database for the purpose of research or private study; fair dealing by way of extraction for the purpose of instruction at an educational establishment; and various uses in the context of public administration.

There is concern this new 'database right' might enable monopolies over information — even over information properly considered part of the common cultural heritage. This is reminiscent of the copyright controversy over the Dead Sea Scrolls which found its way to the law courts of the US and Israel (Carson 1995). To what extent should a scholar be entitled to restrict access to a facsimile edition of the scrolls which incorporates his work in the form of translation, arrangement of fragments and reconstruction of lost portions of text? In earlier drafts of the European Directive, the 'database right' was modified by a compulsory licensing provision obliging the rightholder to license on fair terms the use of material which could not be independently created, collected or obtained from another source. This was omitted from the final Directive on the basis that concerns about monopolies might be dealt with by competition law rather than copyright law (Scales 1997).

The protection traditionally accorded by Irish law to databases as literary works will become redundant once the new Act comes into effect; the definition of 'literary work' therein excludes 'original databases'.

CONCLUSION: THE POLITICS OF COPYRIGHT

The whole of human development is derivative. We stand on the shoulders of the scientists, artists and craftsmen who preceded us .... When we are asked to remember the Eighth Commandment, 'thou shalt not steal', bear in mind that borrowing and developing have always been acceptable. (Laddie 1996)

The system of copyright as it stands today is not without its critics. In the first place, it presupposes the notion that isolated individuals create works entirely on their own — that is, the notion of exclusive authorship. Some critics from postmodern philosophy and cultural studies denounce the individuality of the artist as a Romantic fiction and proclaim, with Barthes, 'the death of the author' (Barthes 1977). According to this claim, advances in technology do not call for more stringent copyright laws but rather announce their redundancy.

A more tempered strand of criticism argues that we must re-imagine our notion of authorship and introduce group rights and societal rights into the equation. It has been suggested that our creative practices are 'largely derivative, generally collective, and increasingly corporate and collaborative' (Woodmansee and Jaszi 1996). A similar critique has been used by advocates on behalf of developing countries to resist attempts by international lawyers to forge a universal copyright system. Copyright law (and indeed IP law in general) both prevents the transfer of knowledge into developed countries and leaves them powerless against the arrogation of their intellectual property. The following comment on the patent system applies equally to copyright:

While the products of formal knowledge systems have been protected as 'property', those of informal, traditional systems have been tagged the freely available 'cultural heritage of humanity'. (Roht-Arriaza 1996)

Much intellectual property is denied legal protection because it does not originate from a particular individual or does not materialize in a particular form. Examples include folk music and dance, collective artwork, oral literature and traditional patterns. For instance, is it fair that a French pop-group should gain exclusive rights in a 'hit single' produced by sampling Pygmy songs and mixing these with synthesised music (ICIP 1997)? Or, closer to home, is it appropriate to categorize Irish tradi-

tional music as 'public domain' material while allowing collectors and arrangers to assert copyright in their versions (McCann 1999)? These criticisms remind us of the historical and geographical contingency of our contemporary understanding of copyright:

By representing cultures in the image of the undivided possessive individual we obscure people's historical agency and transformations, their internal differences, the productivity of intercultural contact, and the ability of peoples to culturally express their position in a wider world. (Coombe 1993)

The Bellagio Declaration 1993 calls for new rights protecting folkloric works and the cultural heritage. There have been significant developments in international law for the protection of tangible cultural property, but, up to now, less attention has been given to the intangible heritage, although it too be the target of a kind of 'theft'. The Bellagio Conference made a twofold appeal. First, it called for the protection of folklore by extending IP-type rights to communities. How might this be achieved? An Australian project has proposed the following rights for indigenous peoples:

• the equivalent of 'moral rights' to prevent debasement or offensive use of their heritage (for example, the performance of a ceremonial dance 'out of context');

• the right to proper attribution of expressions of their heritage (which may of course involve recognition of collective ownership);

• 'economic rights' to share in royalties;

• the equivalent of copyright such that authorization should be sought for various uses of their heritage (ICIP 1997).

With regard to this latter point, the UNESCO Model Provisions for National Laws on the Protection of Expressions of Folklore (1982) seek to strike a balance whereby specific authorization would be required for commercial use of folklore and so forth, but not for educational or illustrative uses or for the creation of new (derivative) works based on folklore.

The second theme emerging at the Bellagio Conference was that our current IP laws have gone too far in one direction and should be curtailed. A primary concern for the law should be to protect 'a vigorous and diverse public domain, a "commons" of scientific, literary, and artistic raw material'. Only in this context can creative activity be properly stimulated. Too many IP rights may actually result in less innovation, less engagement with the culture heritage and less informed public debate. Boyle (1996) has questioned the easily made assumption that the advance of the Internet signals the need for ever more IP rights. He considers that recent developments in copyright law simply benefit the few (for example corporate investors), whereas the losses are spread over an inchoate group, that is the public at large. Perhaps the equivalent of the 'environmental movement' is required, Boyle suggests, in order to increase awareness of the 'commons' of culture and knowledge which is threatened by an extreme focus on private property rights.

Some countries already have legislation requiring payment of fees for commercial exploitation of 'public domain' works (that is, works never, or no longer, protected by copyright) or providing for sanctions by the state or a public body for prejudicial use of such works. The new Irish Act touches only tangentially on the questions of access to and protection of folkloric works. It provides that neither copyright nor performers' rights of folklore are infringed when a recording of a performance of a such a work is made for the purposes of including it in an archive maintained by a designated non-profit body (provided the performer does not object to this). Furthermore, a copy of such a recording may be furnished to a person for the purposes of private study or research. However, these rules are stated to apply, not to works of folklore generally, but only to 'anonymous works ... not lawfully made available to the public'. There are also provisions to allow for designated bodies to copy certain types of broadcasts for archival purposes.

The complexities of modern copyright law reflect not only the advance of technology but also the complexity of the creative process itself. We should not place a naive faith in copyright as the guardian of creativity. As we have seen, many of the new copyright-related rights developed in the EU are designed precisely to stimulate commercial exploitation of culture. On the other hand, it may be unhelpful simply to oppose the terms 'creation' and 'consumption'. Our interaction as individuals with the cultural heritage takes place on many levels — from composing music to studying manuscripts to visiting a gallery — and in all of these ways we repossess, transform and recreate culture.

Bibliography

Alford, W. 1997 *To steal a book is an elegant offense: Chinese intellectual property law in historical context.* Stanford.

Barthes, R. 1977 *Image, music, text* (trans. Stephen Heath). London.

Berryman, C. A. 1994 'Toward more universal protection of intangible cultural property', *Journal of Intellectual Property Law* **1**, pp. 293–333.

Boyle, J. 1996 *Shamans, software and spleens: law and the construction of the information society.* Cambridge, Massachusetts.

Carson, C. A. 1995 'Raiders of the lost scrolls: the right of scholarly access to the content of historic documents', *Michigan Journal of International Law* **16** , pp. 299–348.

Clark, R. and Smyth, S. 1997 *Intellectual property law in Ireland.* Dublin.

Coombe, R. 1993 Paper delivered at Bellagio Conference, quoted in P. O'Keefe, Conference Report, *International Journal of Cultural Property*, **4**, pp. 388–89.

Goldstein, P. 1994 *Copyright's highway: from Gutenberg to the celestial jukebox.* New York.

ICIP Project 1997 *'Our culture — our future': proposals for the recognition and protection of indigenous cultural and intellectual property. (http://www.icip.lawnet.com.au.)* Australia.

Kaufman, J. F. 1997 'The surprise partner!', *Sculpture* **16**, p. 44.

Laddie, H. 1996 'Copyright: over-strength, over-regulated, over-rated', *European Intellectual Property Review* **18**, p. 253.

McCann, A. 1999 'Addressing the social: Irish traditional music and the copyright debate', Irish World Music Centre website (*www.ul.ie/~imro/*).

Merryman, J. H. 1976 'The refrigerator of Bernard Buffet', *Hastings Law Journal* **27**, pp. 1023–49.

O'Hanlon, N. 1998 'Time is money — the impact of the term "Directive" on Irish copyright law', *The Bar Review* **3**, pp. 451–57.

Roht-Arriaza, N. 1996 'Of seeds and shamans: the appropriation of the scientific and technical knowledge of indigenous and local communities', *Michigan Journal of International Law* **17**, pp. 919–65.

Sax, J. 1990 'Heritage preservation as public duty: the Abbé Gregoire and the origins of an idea', *Michigan Law Review* **88**, pp. 1142–69.

Scales, L. 1997 'The European Database Directive — an example to the rest of the world?', *Irish Intellectual Property Law Review* **2**, pp. 21–27.

Suchman, M. C. 1989 'Invention and ritual: notes on the interrelation of magic and intellectual property in preliterate societies,' *Columbia Law Review* **89**, pp. 1264–94.

The Bellagio Declaration 1993 'Cultural Agency/Cultural Authority: Politics and Poetics of Intellectual Property in the Post-Colonial Era, statement of the Bellagio Conference 11 Mar. (text of Declaration and Discussion reproduced in *International Journal of Cultural Property* **4**, pp. 388–96).

Woodmansee, M. and Jaszi, P. 1996 'The Ethical Reaches of Authorship', *South Atlantic Quarterly* **95**, 4, pp. 947–77.

EDITORS AND CONTRIBUTORS

EDITORS

BUTTIMER, NEIL lectures in the Department of Modern Irish, UCC. His research and publications deal with medieval and pre-Famine Gaelic Ireland, together with contemporary cultural policy. He established UCC's *Diploma in Irish Heritage Management* in 1990. He is Hon. Editor of the *Journal of the Cork Historical and Archaeological Society*. His previous editorial work includes (with P. O'Flanagan) *Cork: history and society* (1993), *Catalogue of Irish manuscripts in the University of Madison-Wisconsin* (1989) and (with J. Doan) *Proceedings of the Harvard Celtic Colloquium* **1** (1981).

RYNNE, COLIN is Director of the Masters in Irish Heritage Management programme at UCC. His research interests are medieval Irish agriculture and the industrial archaeology of Ireland. His publications include *The archaeology of Cork city and harbour* (1993), *'At the Sign of the Cow': the Cork Butter Market 1770–1924* (1998) and *The industrial archaeology of Cork city and its environs* (1999).

GUERIN, HELEN is Director of the Audio-Visual Centre, UCD. She has researched and published on the audio-visual sector in Ireland. She is a former coordinator of UCC's *Diploma in Irish Heritage Management*.

CONTRIBUTORS

ALLEN, FRANK is Head of Infrastructure Finance at KBC Project Finance in the International Financial Services Centre, Dublin. A graduate of UCC and the Massachusetts Institute of Technology, he worked for many years at the World Bank Group.

BARLOW, TONY lectures in the Department of Economics, UCC. He has written on the economics of tourism and on the financing of higher education.

BEGGS, ROSALIND lectures in the School of Leisure and Tourism at the University of Ulster (Magee College). Her main research is in the marketing of tourism on which she has published in various academic marketing journals.

BELL, JONATHAN is Head of the Curatorial Division at the Ulster Folk and Transport Museum. His publications relate to both Irish agricultural history and general museological issues.

BRADLEY, FINBARR a former Professor of Finance at Dublin City University, is currently a director of INTINN, a company which delivers education and consultancy services.

BREEN, COLIN was formerly Director of the Maritime Archaeology Survey within Dúchas and is now Lecturer in Maritime Archaeology at the University of Ulster, Coleraine.

BYRNE, MARTIN is a principal of Byrne, Mullins & Associates, Archaeological Consultants. His research interests include the use of prospecting techniques in archaeology.

BYRNES, EMMET works in University College, Dublin, and is a specialist in Environmental Impact Assessment and Irish landscape archaeology.

CANDON, ANTHONY is manager of the Ulster History Park, Omagh, county Tyrone. An archaeologist and historian, his research interests include archaeological reconstruction, and society and politics in pre-Norman Ireland.

CARLETON, PATRICK is Manager, Community Services, FÁS South West Region.

CHERRY, STELLA is Curator of the Cork Public Museum, and has published on the Maori and native Americans, *fulachta fiadha* and Sheela-na-Gigs.

CLANCY, PAULA is Head of the School of Business & Humanities at Dún Laoghaire Institute of Art, Design & Technology. Her research and publications include the development of appropriate business models for cultural industries, as well as management issues for the arts, media and entertainment sectors.

COLLINS, NEIL is Professor and Head of the Department of Government at UCC. His research interests are in Irish politics and public policy.

CONDIT, TOM, an archaeologist with Dúchas, the state Heritage Service, is an aerial photography specialist and has published widely on Irish landscape archaeology.

COOKE, PAT manages Kilmainham Gaol and the Pearse Museum on behalf of Dúchas, and has written articles on arts and culture management.

COONEY, GABRIEL is a Professor in the Department of Archaeology, University College, Dublin. His published works include *Irish prehistory: a social perspective* (1994, with Eoin Grogan) and *Landscapes of Neolithic Ireland* (2000).

COX, RON is Director of the Centre for Civil Engineering Heritage at TCD. His principal research interests are civil engineering heritage and engineering biography.

CRAIG, DAVID V. is Director of the National Archives. His edition of the Memoranda Roll of the Irish Exchequer for 1309–10 will shortly be published.

CRANITCH, MATT lectures at the Cork Institute of Technology in electronic engineering and music technology. His is an acclaimed traditional musician, and is researching the fiddle music of Sliabh Luachra at the University of Limerick.

CRONIN, JOHN an archaeologist and town planner, is conservation officer with Donegal County Council.

CROWLEY, JOHN lectures in Geography at UCC. His main research areas are in cultural and historical geography, tourism and heritage management.

CULLINANE, JOHN P. lectures in Plant Science at UCC and is an Irish dance historian. He has published six books and over sixty articles on the topic, and is the founder of the Cullinane Archive Collection of some 4,000 Irish dance history items.

DESPLANQUES, MARIE-ANNICK is the Research Coordinator in Folklore and Ethnology/Béaloideas at UCC, where she initiated and manages the Folklore and Ethnology Archive and the Northside Folklore Project. She has published internationally in the areas of urban ethnology, ethnomusicology and folklore and gender.

DONNELLAN, TREVOR is an economist with Teagasc — The Agriculture & Food Development Authority. Previously he worked at the Department of Economics, UCC, where he was involved in research which focussed on the structure and interaction of sectors in the regional economy.

FAIRHEAD, JAMES lectures in the management of innovation at the Department of Management and Marketing, UCC, where he studies innovation in both private and public sector organizations.

FLETCHER, VALERIE C. is the Official Publications and European Documentation Centre Librarian at UCC. Her research interests are in official publications.

HAMOND, FRED is a self-employed industrial archaeologist. He is a founder-member of the Industrial Heritage Association of Ireland and is the author of *Coast & Glens AONB — industrial heritage* (1991).

HARRISON, JOHN is a principal of John Harrison & Associates, Heritage Development. His main interests are in heritage interpretation, with particular reference to Irish folklore.

HERRIES DAVIES, GORDON is former Professor of Geography at TCD, a geologist and historian of science. He has written books ranging from the study of Ireland's geomorphology to the official history of the Geological Survey of Ireland.

HILL, JOHN is Professor of Media Studies at the University of Ulster. He is the author of *Sex, class and realism: British cinema 1956–63* (1986) and *British cinema in the 1980s* (1998) and co-author of *Cinema and Ireland* (1987).

HOLLAND, PATRICK is Curator of Tipperary South Riding County Museum. He has published on the Anglo-Normans in county Galway, as well as on museological and other historical topics.

HOURIHAN, KEVIN lectures in the Department of Geography, UCC. He has published research papers on urban studies in Irish and international journals and, with B. Brunt, has edited *Perspectives on Cork* (1998).

HURLEY, MAURICE F. is City Archaeologist with Cork Corporation and was previously Senior Archaeologist with Waterford Corporation. He has published on archaeological excavations of Cork and Waterford.

HUMPHRIES, TOM is an *Irish Times* journalist.

HUNT, DEIRDRE is Associate Professor of Management and Marketing at UCC. Her research and publications are on enterprise policy and knowledge formulation.

HYLAND, MARY was formerly Film Officer at the Arts Council/An Chomhairle Ealaíon.

IRELAND, AIDEEN M. was appointed Archivist with the Public Record Office of Ireland in 1981, the forerunner of the National Archives to which she is now affiliated. She was elected the first ever Irish chairperson of the Society of Archivists in 1999.

KAVANAGH, DONNCHA lectures in management at UCC's Department of Management and Marketing. His research interests include management and organization theory and time and space in contemporary networks.

KEARNEY, COLBERT is Professor of English at UCC where he teaches and publishes on Anglo-Irish literature.

KELLEHER, BRENDAN is Chief Planning Officer, Cork County Council. His principal research interests are planning systems and natural and man-made heritage.

KIRAKOWSKA, MÁIRE DOMHNAT is Head of Technical Services at the Boole Library, UCC.

LAMMEY, DAVID is Head of Readers Services in the Public Record Office of Northern Ireland. He has published on eighteenth-century Irish politics and society and is contributing to the *New Dictionary of National Biography* (Oxford University Press).

LEE, J. J. is Professor of History at UCC and visiting professor at Glucksman Ireland House, New York University. His publications include *Ireland 1912–85* (1989).

LONG, GERARD is an Assistant Keeper 1 at the National Library of Ireland. He edited *Books beyond the Pale* (1996) for the Rare Books Group of the Library Association of Ireland, and is preparing a history of the NLI.

McADOO, MICHAEL is a company affiliations consultant on small business development with Gordon Lane and Co., registered auditors and accountants, Cork. He has taught accounting at UCC and for the Cork Vocational Education Committee.

McPARLAND, MAIGHREAD was Senior Conservator, National Gallery of Ireland, 1975–99, and is currently coordinator of its Millennium Wing.

McQuiston, Ian B. was appointed first Director of Environmental Protection in the Department of the Environment for Northern Ireland in 1986. He was Director of the National Trust in Northern Ireland from 1990 to 1999.

Meagher, John lectures in UCC's Department of Accounting, Finance and Information Systems. His main research interests are accounting history, accounting for the insurance industry and the accounting and management interface.

Moloney Davis, Helen is an Assistant Librarian at the Boole Library, UCC, with responsibility for Special Collections. She has published on early Egyptian archaeology and her research areas include library history.

Monaghan, Nigel T. is Assistant Keeper in the Natural History Division of the National Museum of Ireland. His research and publications are on the history of the NMI's natural science collections, the fauna of Ice Age Ireland and the history of Irish geology.

Monk, Michael A. lectures in the Department of Archaeology, UCC. He has edited (with J. Sheehan) *Early medieval Munster: archaeology, history and society* (1998).

Moss, Rachel lectures in the Department of History of Art at TCD. Her main area of research is in the field of medieval Irish architecture.

Mullane, Fidelma lectures in Heritage Management at the Department of Geography, UCC, and has been a member of the state's Bord na Gaeilge.

Mulqueen, Mark is Cork City Arts Officer. He has compiled *Cork city arts development plan, 2000–2005* (2000), published by Cork Corporation.

Murray, Kevin lectures in the Department of Early and Medieval Irish, UCC, where he is affiliated to the LOCUS Project. Medieval Irish language and literature, as well as law and place-names, are among his interests.

Murray, Peter is Curator of the Crawford Municipal Art Gallery, Cork. His research and publications deal with the history of Irish art from the 1800s.

Nicholls, Kenneth is retired Lecturer in History at UCC. He is primarily interested in legal and social history of the period 1300–1800, as well as Irish genealogy and place-name study. He is the author of *Gaelic and gaelicised Ireland in the Middle Ages* (1972).

Nolan, William lectures in Geography at UCD. He is the author of *Fassadin* (1979), *Tracing the past* (1982) and is series editor of Geography Publications' *Irish County History and Society* series, of which thirteen volumes have been issued to date.

O'Boyle, Mark has worked for Price Waterhouse and Euromonitor Plc. He is currently a research executive with Tourism Development International, Dublin.

O'Brien, John B. (d. 1999) was Statutory Lecturer in History at UCC. His publications and research were on economic history and Ireland's links with Australia.

Ó Corráin, Donnchadh is Professor of History at UCC. His publications include *Ireland before the Normans* (1972) and over sixty articles. He is the founder-editor of *Peritia* (1982–), an international journal of medieval studies.

Ó Crualaoich, Gearóid is Statutory Lecturer in Folklore and Ethnology/Béaloideas at UCC. His research and publications concentrate on mythological legend, life-cycle ritual and traditional technology.

O'Donovan, Grace lectures in plant ecology at the Department of Environmental Resource Management, UCD. Her publications include over twenty articles and, with J. Feehan, *The magic of Coole* (1993) and *The bogs of Ireland* (1996).

Ó GIOLLÁIN, DIARMUID lectures in Folklore and Ethnology/Béaloideas at UCC. Ethnology and popular cultural studies are among his research interests. His most recent publication is *Locating Irish folklore: tradition, modernity, identity* (2000).

O'HEGARTY, LIA is a barrister-at-law. She is now Parliamentary Legal Adviser at the Houses of the Oireachtas. Her research interests include constitutional law and environmental law.

O'LEARY, EOIN lectures in the Department of Economics at UCC. His research and publications are in the area of regional growth and convergence.

O'MAHONY, NESSA is Head of Public Affairs with the Arts Council/An Chomhairle Ealaíon.

Ó MURCHADHA, DIARMUID is affiliated to the LOCUS Project, Department of Early and Medieval Irish, UCC. His main interests are medieval Irish history and onomastics. His publications include *Liam de Róiste* (1976), *Family names of county Cork* (1985) and *Annals of Tigernach: index of names* (1997).

O'SULLIVAN, DON lectures in UCC's Department of Management and Marketing.

REARDEN, NUALA lectures in social studies at the Cork Institute of Technology, where her research focus is on social policy and public policy.

ROURKE, GRELLAN D. is Senior Conservation Architect with Dúchas, with research interests in stone conservation and early dry-stone construction.

SCROOPE, ANN is principal of Scroope Design. The company has been involved with award-winning heritage-related projects in the private and public sectors.

SHEEHAN, JOHN lectures in the Department of Archaeology, UCC. His research areas include Ireland's Viking Age and early medieval ecclesiastical archaeology. He has co-authored *The Iveragh Peninsula: an archaeological survey of south Kerry* (1996) and edited *Early medieval Munster: archaeology, history and society* (1998, with M. A. Monk).

SLEEMAN, MARY has been Chairperson of An Taisce, Corcaigh, since 1998. She is an archaeologist, and has been attached to the Cork Archaeological Survey since 1982.

STARRETT, MICHAEL is Chief Executive of the Heritage Council.

SWEETMAN, DAVID is the Chief Archaeologist in Dúchas. He is general editor of the County *Archaeological inventory* series and author of *The medieval castles of Ireland* (1999).

TEEHAN, VIRGINIA is University Archivist and Director, Heritage Office, UCC. She co-authored *Standards for the development of archives in Ireland* (1997) and compiled *The provision of genealogical services in Ireland* (2000).

UÍ CHIONNA, JACKIE has been Manager of Galway Civic Trust since 1993, and includes the history of Irish sailing among her research interests.

PICTURE AND MAP CREDITS

We would like to thank the following for allowing us to use their pictures:

Tony Balfe/UCC Library Collection, 93, 94; Commissioners of Irish Lights, 59; Crawford Muncipal Art Gallery, Cork, 237, 238; Tom Curtis, 6; Dúchas, 353, 354, 530–532; FÁS CYTP Project, 549–551; John Feehan, 5; Folklore Project Archive Collection, 184; Lawrence Collection, 306; Northside Folklore Project Archive Collection, 185; Grace O'Donovan, 12; PRONI, 332, 333; Rubicon Gallery, Dublin, 688; The National Trust, 557, 558, 559; Ulster Folk and Transport Museum, 435.

Maps by Michael Murphy, Cartographer/UCC, vi, 84, 86, 87, 89.

and the world wars, 82
Urban Pilot Projects, 44
urban redevelopment, 41
Urban Renewal Act 1986, 514

urban renewal schemes, 43–5, 88, 90, 517, 519
U2's success and Irish music industry, 650, 651, 653

V

Valetta Convention, 18, 529
value creation, sustainable, 632, 634
vandalism, 64
Venice Charter, 364, 365, 367
vernacular architecture, 65–6
    definitions of, 71–2, 73–4
    and folklore, 73–5
    and identity in contemporary Ireland, 75–7
Viking Age settlement, 581
visitor attraction economics, Northern Ireland, 612–14
visitor centres, 376
visitor considerations, 395–6
visitor experience, 610–12
visitor facilities, 391–2
visitor needs and behaviour patterns, 380
visitor numbers forecasts, 371
visitor profile, 388
visitor spending in the south-west 1995, 627
Visual Artists Rights Act (US) 1990, 691
visual arts in Ireland, 233–4
    'Academic Realism,' 236–8, 240
    after 'Academic Realism,' 238–41
    birth of the Arts Council, 238–9
    commercial galleries, 256–7
    current government funding for, 233, 242, 251–7
    current Irish artists living abroad, 247–51
    future of, Arts Council and, 257–8
    installation art, 243
    politics and, 234–6, 242, 243
    and public art, 90, 241–2, 497–8
    and the Royal Hibernian Academy, 239–40
    teaching and, 236
        Cork, 245–7
        Dublin, 244–5
    temporary exhibitions, 255–6
    women and, 237–8
Vocational Education Committees, 493
vocational training, 477, 577
voluntary organizations, 450
volunteer work camps, 13
wakes, 174

W

Waterford archaeological excavations, 43
Webb, David Allardice, 7
West Cork Arts Centre, 400
West Cork Model Village project, 551–2
wetland archaeological sites, 25
wetlands and mires, 6–7
    bogs, 3–4
    callows and fens, 3–4
    lakes and turloughs, 2
    rivers, 2–3
Wexford Opera Festival, 231
Wexford Slobs, 6
White Stag Group, 234, 237
Wicklow National Park, 11
Wildlife Act 1976, 7, 8, 507, 508–9, 512
Wildlife Amendment Bill 1997, 497, 507, 510
Wildlife Trusts, 8
'Wood Quay crisis,' 41–2, 46
woodlands, 4, 10–11
woodlands inventory, 9
World Biosphere Reserve, 6, 11
World Heritage list, 81
World Intellectual Property Organization, 691
wrecks *see* shipwrecks
Wyse Jackson, P., 7

Y

Yeats, W. B., 111, 226